UPGRADING AND REPAIRING PCs

21st Edition

Scott Mueller

800 East 96th Street,
Indianapolis, Indiana 46240

Contents at a Glance

Upgrading and Repairing PCs, 21st Edition

ISBN-13: 978-0-7897-5000-6
ISBN-10: 0-7897-5000-7

Library of Congress Cataloging-in-Publication Data in on file.

Printed in the United States of America

First Printing: March 2013

Trademarks

All terms mentioned in this book that are known to be trademarks or service marks have been appropriately capitalized. Que Publishing cannot attest to the accuracy of this information. Use of a term in this book should not be regarded as affecting the validity of any trademark or service mark.

Warning and Disclaimer

Every effort has been made to make this book as complete and as accurate as possible, but no warranty or fitness is implied. The information provided is on an "as is" basis. The author and the publisher shall have neither liability nor responsibility to any person or entity with respect to any loss or damages arising from the information contained in this book or from the use of the DVD or programs accompanying it.

Bulk Sales

Que Publishing offers excellent discounts on this book when ordered in quantity for bulk purchases or special sales. For more information, please contact

U.S. Corporate and Government Sales
1-800-382-3419
corpsales@pearsontechgroup.com

For sales outside of the U.S., please contact

International Sales
international@pearsoned.com

Editor-in-Chief
Greg Wiegand

Acquisitions Editor
Rick Kughen

Development Editor
Todd Brakke

Managing Editor
Sandra Schroeder

Project Editor
Mandie Frank

Copy Editor
Sheri Cain

Indexer
Erika Millen

Proofreader
Gill Editorial Services

Technical Editor
Chris Crayton

Editorial Assistant
Cindy Teeters

Media Producer
Dan Scherf

Designer
Anne Jones

Compositor
Bronkella Publishing

Contents

11 Optical Storage 525

12 Video Hardware 609

13 Audio Hardware 679

Dedication

In memory of Mark Reddin. His wonderful technical input and insight over the years have made a tremendous impact on this and many other books. You will be missed.

About the Author

Scott Mueller is the president of Mueller Technical Research (MTR), an international research and corporate training firm. Since 1982, MTR has produced the industry's most in-depth, accurate, and effective seminars, books, articles, videos, and FAQs covering PC hardware and data recovery. MTR maintains a client list that includes Fortune 500 companies, the U.S. and foreign governments, major software and hardware corporations, as well as PC enthusiasts and entrepreneurs. Scott's seminars have been presented to several thousands of PC support professionals throughout the world.

Scott personally teaches seminars nationwide covering all aspects of PC hardware (including troubleshooting, maintenance, repair, and upgrade), A+ Certification, and data recovery/forensics. He has a knack for making technical topics not only understandable, but entertaining; his classes are never boring! If you have ten or more people to train, Scott can design and present a custom seminar for your organization.

Although he has taught classes virtually nonstop since 1982, Scott is best known as the author of the longest-running, most popular, and most comprehensive PC hardware book in the world, *Upgrading and Repairing PCs*, which has become the core of an entire series of books, including *Upgrading and Repairing PCs*, *Upgrading and Repairing Laptops*, and *Upgrading and Repairing Windows*.

Scott's premiere work, *Upgrading and Repairing PCs*, has sold more than two million copies, making it by far the most popular and longest-running PC hardware book on the market today. Scott has been featured in *Forbes* magazine and has written several articles for *PC World* magazine, *Maximum PC* magazine, the Scott Mueller Forum, various computer and automotive newsletters, and the Upgrading and Repairing PCs website.

Contact MTR directly if you have a unique book, article, or video project in mind or if you want Scott to conduct a custom PC troubleshooting, repair, maintenance, upgrade, or data-recovery seminar tailored for your organization:

Mueller Technical Research

> Web: www.muellertech.com
> Email: info@muellertech.com
> Forum: www.forum.scottmueller.com

Scott has a forum exclusively for his readers at www.forum.scottmueller.com. Anybody can view the forum, but posting is only available to registered members.

If you have suggestions or comments about the book or new book or article topics you would like to see covered, send them to info@muellertech.com.

Acknowledgments

I must give a *very* special thanks to Rick Kughen at Que. Through the years, Rick is the number-one person responsible for championing this book and the *Upgrading and Repairing* series. I cannot say enough about Rick and what he means to all the *Upgrading and Repairing* books. With all that he's been through on this book, I have a feeling I might be responsible for a few gray hairs. (Sorry!)

I'd also like to thank Todd Brakke for doing the development editing for this edition, which was fairly substantial considering all the rewrites and new material. His excellent tips and suggestions really helped to keep the material concise and up-to-date.

Special thanks also go to Sheri Cain, who helped tremendously with the editing, and to Mandie Frank, for shepherding the manuscripts through a tight publishing schedule. I'd also like to thank the proofreader, illustrator, designer, and indexer, who worked so hard to complete the finished product and get this book out the door! They are a wonderful team that produces clearly the best computer books on the market. I am happy and proud to be closely associated with all the people at Que.

I also want to say thanks to my publisher, Greg Wiegand, who has stood behind all the *Upgrading and Repairing* book and video projects. Greg is a fellow motorcycle enthusiast—someday, hopefully, we can go riding together.

All the people at Que make me feel as if we are on the same team, and they are just as dedicated as I am to producing the best books possible.

I would like to thank both my wife Lynn and my son Emerson for helping to produce the DVD that comes with the book. Emerson did the camera work, and Lynn did all of the editing, rendering, and DVD production using the very machine that you see me build in the video. I hope you enjoy the DVD as much as we enjoyed producing it.

Many readers write me with suggestions and even corrections for the book, for which I am especially grateful. I welcome any and all of your comments and even your criticisms. I take them seriously and apply them to the continuous improvement of this book. Interaction with my readers is the primary force that helps maintain this book as the most up-to-date and relevant work available *anywhere* on the subject of PC hardware.

Finally, I want to thank the thousands of people who have attended my seminars; you have no idea how much I learn from each of you and all of your questions!

Accessing the Media Included with this Book

Don't forget about the free bonus content available online! You'll find a cache of helpful material to go along with this book, including 90 minutes of video. You'll also find complete PDF copies of the 19th and 20th editions, as well as many pages of valuable reference material that's particularly useful for those maintaining legacy equipment.

Register this eBook to unlock the companion files that are included in the Print edition DVD.

Follow the steps below:

1. Go to quepublishing.com/register and log in or create a new account.
2. Enter the ISBN: 9780789750006
3. Enter the following code when prompted: URPCSDVD21E
4. Click on the "Access Bonus Content" link in the Registered Products section of your account page, to be taken to the page where your content is available. The video files will play in your browser. Click the links to the 19th and 20th edition PDFs, and other materials to view them, or right-click and choose to save the file to your computer.

Note

If you would like to download the videos to your computer, simply right-click the video and choose Save As. Note that the video files are large and will download slowly.

We Want to Hear from You!

As the reader of this book, *you* are our most important critic and commentator. We value your opinion and want to know what we're doing right, what we could do better, what areas you'd like to see us publish in, and any other words of wisdom you're willing to pass our way.

We welcome your comments. You can email or write to let us know what you did or didn't like about this book—as well as what we can do to make our books better.

Please note that we cannot help you with technical problems related to the topic of this book.

When you write, please be sure to include this book's title and author as well as your name and email address. We will carefully review your comments and share them with the author and editors who worked on the book.

Email: feedback@quepublishing.com

Mail: Que Publishing
         ATTN: Reader Feedback
         800 East 96th Street
         Indianapolis, IN 46240 USA

Reader Services

Visit our website and register this book at quepublishing.com/register for convenient access to any updates, downloads, or errata that might be available for this book.

Introduction

Welcome to *Upgrading and Repairing PCs,* 21st Edition. Since debuting as the first book of its kind on the market in 1988, no other book on PC hardware has matched the depth and quality of the information found in this tome. This edition continues *Upgrading and Repairing PCs'* role as not only the best-selling book of its type, but also the most comprehensive and complete PC hardware reference available. This book examines PCs in depth, outlines the differences among them, and presents options for configuring each system.

The 21st edition of *Upgrading and Repairing PCs* provides you with the in-depth knowledge you need to work with the most recent systems and components and gives you an unexcelled resource for understanding older systems. As with previous editions, we worked to make this book keep pace with the rapid changes in the PC industry so that it continues to be the most accurate, complete, and in-depth book of its kind on the market today.

I wrote this book for all PC enthusiasts who want to know everything about their PCs: how they originated; how they've evolved; how to upgrade, troubleshoot, and repair them; and everything in between. This book covers the full gamut of PC-compatible systems, from the oldest 8-bit machines to the latest high-end 64-bit multicore processors and systems. If you need to know everything about PC hardware from the original to the latest technology on the market today, this book and the accompanying information-packed disc is definitely for you.

Upgrading and Repairing PCs also doesn't ignore the less glamorous PC components. Every part of your PC plays a critical role in its stability and performance. Over the course of this book, you'll find out exactly why your motherboard's chipset might just be the most important part of your PC and what can go wrong when you settle for a run-of-the-mill power supply that can't get enough juice to that monster graphics card you just bought. You'll also find in-depth coverage of technologies such as new Intel Ivy Bridge and AMD Trinity core processors (including those with integrated graphics (including those with integrated graphics), how your choice of processor affects virtualization support, DDR3 memory, high-performance graphics cards based on AMD and NVIDIA GPUs for the fastest 3D gaming and the latest developments in OpenGL and DirectX 3D APIs, SATA 6Gbps and upcoming SATA Express interfaces, Thunderbolt and USB 3.0 interfaces in the latest motherboards, advances in solid-state drives, the benefits of 80 PLUS power supplies, and more—it's all in here, right down to the guts-level analysis of your mouse and keyboard.

Book Objectives

Upgrading and Repairing PCs focuses on several objectives. The primary objective is to help you learn how to maintain, upgrade, and troubleshoot your PC system. To that end, *Upgrading and Repairing PCs* helps you fully understand the family of computers that has grown from the original IBM PC, including all PC-compatible systems. This book discusses all areas of system improvement, such as motherboards, processors, memory, and even case and power-supply improvements. It covers proper system and component care, specifies the most failure-prone items in various PC systems, and tells you how to locate and identify a failing component. You'll learn about powerful diagnostics hardware and software that help you determine the cause of a problem and know how to repair it.

As always, PCs are moving forward rapidly in power and capabilities. Processor performance increases with every new chip design. *Upgrading and Repairing PCs* helps you gain an understanding of all the processors used in PC-compatible computer systems.

This book covers the important differences between major system architectures, from the original Industry Standard Architecture (ISA) to the latest PCI Express interface standards. *Upgrading and Repairing PCs* covers each of these system architectures and their adapter boards to help you make decisions about which type of system you want to buy in the future and help you upgrade and troubleshoot such systems.

The amount of storage space available to modern PCs is increasing geometrically. *Upgrading and Repairing PCs* covers storage options ranging from larger, faster hard drives to state-of-the-art solid-state storage devices.

When you finish reading this book, you will have the knowledge to upgrade, troubleshoot, and repair almost any system and component.

The 21st Edition DVD-ROM

The 21st edition of *Upgrading and Repairing PCs* includes a DVD that contains valuable content that greatly enhances this book!

There's the all-new DVD video with new segments showing a detailed tour of a high-end Z77 chipset motherboard, a detailed comparison of SSD (solid-state drive) to HDD (hard disk drive) technology, plus information about choosing a case and power supply. There are in-depth segments showing how to build a system using these components from scratch, including motherboard and chassis preparation, component installation, and finally cabling, including the dreaded front-panel connections.

The DVD-ROM content includes my venerable Technical Reference material, a repository of reference information that has appeared in previous editions of *Upgrading and Repairing PCs* but has been moved to the disc to make room for coverage of newer technologies. The DVD-ROM also includes the complete 19th edition of this book, the complete 20th edition of the book, a detailed list of acronyms, and much more available in printable PDF format. There's more PC hardware content and knowledge here than you're likely to find from any other single source.

My Website: upgradingandrepairingpcs.com

Don't forget about Que's dedicated *Upgrading and Repairing PCs* website! Here, you'll find a cache of helpful material to go along with the book you're holding. I've loaded this site with tons of material—mine as well as from other authors—ranging from video clips to book content and technology updates.

If you discover that the video on this book's disc isn't enough, you'll find even more of my previously recorded videos on the website. Not to mention that it is the best place to look for information on all of Que's *Upgrading and Repairing* titles.

I also have a private forum (www.forum.scottmueller.com) designed exclusively to support those who have purchased my recent books and DVDs. I use the forum to answer questions and otherwise help my loyal readers. If you own one of my current books or DVDs, feel free to join in and post questions. I endeavor to answer each question personally, but I also encourage knowledgeable members to respond. Anybody can view the forum without registering, but to post a question of your own you need to join. Even if you don't join in, the forum is a tremendous resource because you can still benefit from all the reader questions I have answered over the years.

Be sure to check the informit.com/upgrading website for more information on all my latest books, videos, articles, FAQs, and more!

A Personal Note

When asked which was his favorite Corvette, Dave McLellan, former manager of the Corvette platform at General Motors, always said, "Next year's model." Now with the new 21st edition, next year's model has just become this year's model, until *next* year that is....

I believe that this book is absolutely the best book of its kind on the market, and that is due in large part to the extensive feedback I have received from both my seminar attendees and book readers. I am so grateful to everyone who has helped me with this book through each edition, as well as all the loyal readers who have been using this book, many of you since the first edition was published. I have had personal contact with many thousands of you in the seminars I have been teaching since 1982, and I enjoy your comments and even your criticisms tremendously. Using this book in a teaching environment has been a major factor in its development. Some of you might be interested to know that I originally began writing this book in early 1985; back then it was self-published and used exclusively in my PC hardware seminars before being professionally published by Que in 1988.

In one way or another, I have been writing and rewriting this book for almost 30 years! In that time, *Upgrading and Repairing PCs* has proven to be not only the first, but also the most comprehensive and yet approachable and easy-to-understand book of its kind. With this new edition, it is even better than ever. Your comments, suggestions, and support have helped this book to become the best PC hardware book on the market. I look forward to hearing your comments after you see this exciting new edition.

—Scott

Development of the PC

Computer History: Before Personal Computers

Many discoveries and inventions have directly and indirectly contributed to the development of the PC and other personal computers as we know them today. Examining a few important developmental landmarks can help bring the entire picture into focus.

Timeline

The following is a timeline of significant events in computer history. It is not meant to be complete; it's just a representation of some of the major landmarks in computer development:

1617 John Napier creates "Napier's Bones," wooden or ivory rods used for calculating.

1642 Blaise Pascal introduces the Pascaline digital adding machine.

1822 Charles Babbage introduces the Difference Engine and later the Analytical Engine, a true general-purpose computing machine.

1906 Lee De Forest patents the vacuum tube triode, used as an electronic switch in the first electronic computers.

1936 Alan Turing publishes "On Computable Numbers," a paper in which he conceives an imaginary computer called the Turing Machine, considered one of the foundations of modern computing. Turing later worked on breaking the German Enigma code.

1936 Konrad Zuse begins work on a series of computers that will culminate in 1941 when he finishes work on the Z3. These are considered the first working electric binary computers, using electromechanical switches and relays.

1937 John V. Atanasoff begins work on the Atanasoff-Berry Computer (ABC), which would later be officially credited as the first electronic computer. Note that an *electronic* computer uses tubes, transistors, or other solid-state switching devices, whereas an *electric* computer uses electric motors, solenoids, or relays (electromechanical switches).

1943 Thomas (Tommy) Flowers develops the Colossus, a secret British code-breaking computer designed to decode teleprinter messages encrypted by the German army.

1945 John von Neumann writes "First Draft of a Report on the EDVAC," in which he outlines the architecture of the modern stored-program computer.

1946 ENIAC is introduced, an electronic computing machine built by John Mauchly and J. Presper Eckert.

1947 On December 23, William Shockley, Walter Brattain, and John Bardeen successfully test the point-contact transistor, setting off the semiconductor revolution.

1949 Maurice Wilkes assembles the EDSAC, the first practical stored-program computer, at Cambridge University.

1950 Engineering Research Associates of Minneapolis builds the ERA 1101, one of the first commercially produced computers.

1952 The UNIVAC I delivered to the U.S. Census Bureau is the first commercial computer to attract widespread public attention.

1953 IBM ships its first electronic computer, the 701.

1954 A silicon-based junction transistor, perfected by Gordon Teal of Texas Instruments, Inc., brings a tremendous reduction in costs.

1954 The IBM 650 magnetic drum calculator establishes itself as the first mass-produced computer, with the company selling 450 in one year.

1955 Bell Laboratories announces the first fully transistorized computer, TRADIC.

1956 MIT researchers build the TX-0, the first general-purpose, programmable computer built with transistors.

1956 The era of magnetic disk storage dawns with IBM's shipment of a 305 RAMAC to Zellerbach Paper in San Francisco.

1958 Jack Kilby creates the first integrated circuit at Texas Instruments to prove that resistors and capacitors can exist on the same piece of semiconductor material.

1959 IBM's 7000 series mainframes are the company's first transistorized computers.

1959 Robert Noyce's practical integrated circuit, invented at Fairchild Camera and Instrument Corp., allows printing of conducting channels directly on the silicon surface.

1960 Bell Labs designs its Dataphone, the first commercial modem, specifically for converting digital computer data to analog signals for transmission across its long-distance network.

1961 According to *Datamation* magazine, IBM has an 81.2% share of the computer market in 1961, the year in which it introduces the 1400 series.

1964 IBM announces System/360, a family of six mutually compatible computers and 40 peripherals that can work together.

1964 Online transaction processing makes its debut in IBM's SABRE reservation system, set up for American Airlines.

1965 Digital Equipment Corp. introduces the PDP-8, the first commercially successful minicomputer.

1969 The root of what is to become the Internet begins when the Department of Defense establishes four nodes on the ARPAnet: two at University of California campuses (one at Santa Barbara and one at Los Angeles) and one each at Stanford Research Institute and the University of Utah.

1971 A team at IBM's San Jose Laboratories invents the 8-inch floppy disk drive.

1971 The first advertisement for a microprocessor, the Intel 4004, appears in *Electronic News*.

1971 The Kenbak-1, one of the first personal computers, is advertised for $750 in *Scientific American*.

1972 Intel's 8008 microprocessor makes its debut.

1973 Robert Metcalfe devises the Ethernet method of network connection at the Xerox Palo Alto Research Center.

1973 The Micral is the earliest commercial, nonkit personal computer based on a microprocessor, the Intel 8008.

1973   The TV Typewriter, designed by Don Lancaster, provides the first display of alphanumeric information on an ordinary television set.

1974   Researchers at the Xerox Palo Alto Research Center design the Alto, the first workstation with a built-in mouse for input.

1974   Scelbi advertises its 8H computer, the first commercially advertised U.S. computer based on a microprocessor, Intel's 8008.

1975   Telenet, the first commercial packet-switching network and civilian equivalent of ARPAnet, is born.

1975   The January edition of *Popular Electronics* features the Altair 8800, which is based on Intel's 8080 microprocessor, on its cover.

1976   Steve Wozniak designs the Apple I, a single-board computer.

1976   The 5 1/4-inch floppy disk drive is introduced by Shugart Associates.

1977   Tandy RadioShack introduces the TRS-80.

1977   Apple Computer introduces the Apple II.

1977   Commodore introduces the PET (Personal Electronic Transactor).

1979   Motorola introduces the 68000 microprocessor.

1980   Seagate Technology creates the first hard disk drive for microcomputers, the ST-506.

1981   Xerox introduces the Star, the first personal computer with a graphical user interface (GUI).

1981   Adam Osborne completes the first portable computer, the Osborne I, which weighs 24 pounds and costs $1,795.

1981   IBM introduces its PC, igniting a fast growth of the personal computer market. The IBM PC is the grandfather of all modern PCs.

1981   Sony introduces and ships the first 3 1/2-inch floppy disk drive.

1981   Philips and Sony introduce the CD-DA (compact disc digital audio) format.

1983   Apple introduces its Lisa, which incorporates a GUI that's similar to the one introduced on the Xerox Star.

1983   Compaq Computer Corp. introduces its first PC clone that uses the same software as the IBM PC.

1984   Apple Computer launches the Macintosh, the first successful mouse-driven computer with a GUI, with a single $1.5 million commercial during the 1984 Super Bowl.

1984   IBM releases the PC-AT (PC Advanced Technology), three times faster than original PCs and based on the Intel 286 chip. The AT introduces the 16-bit ISA bus and is the computer on which all modern PCs are based.

1985   Philips introduces the first CD-ROM drive.

1986   Compaq announces the Deskpro 386, the first computer on the market to use Intel's 32-bit 386 chip.

1987   IBM introduces its PS/2 machines, which make the 3 1/2-inch floppy disk drive and VGA video standard for PCs. The PS/2 also introduces the MicroChannel Architecture (MCA) bus, the first plug-and-play bus for PCs.

1988   Apple cofounder Steve Jobs, who left Apple to form his own company, unveils the NeXT Computer.

1988   Compaq and other PC-clone makers develop Enhanced Industry Standard Architecture (EISA), which unlike MicroChannel retains backward compatibility with the existing ISA bus.

1988   Robert Morris's worm floods the ARPAnet. The 23-year-old Morris, the son of a computer security expert for the National Security Agency, sends a nondestructive worm through the Internet, causing problems for about 6,000 of the 60,000 hosts linked to the network.

1989   Intel releases the 486 (P4) microprocessor, which contains more than one million transistors. Intel also introduces 486 motherboard chipsets.

1990   The World Wide Web (WWW) is born when Tim Berners-Lee, a researcher at CERN—the high-energy physics laboratory in Geneva—develops Hypertext Markup Language (HTML).

1993   Intel releases the Pentium (P5) processor. Intel shifts from numbers to names for its chips after the company learns it's impossible to trademark a number. Intel also releases motherboard chipsets and, for the first time, complete motherboards.

1995   Intel releases the Pentium Pro processor, the first in the P6 processor family.

1995   Microsoft releases Windows 95 in a huge rollout.

1997   Intel releases the Pentium II processor, essentially a Pentium Pro with MMX instructions added.

1997   AMD introduces the K6, which is compatible with the Intel P5 (Pentium).

1998   Microsoft releases Windows 98.

1998   Intel releases the Celeron, a low-cost version of the Pentium II processor. Initial versions have no cache, but within a few months Intel introduces versions with a smaller but faster L2 cache.

1999   Intel releases the Pentium III, essentially a Pentium II with SSE (Streaming SIMD Extensions) added.

1999   AMD introduces the Athlon.

1999   The IEEE officially approves the 5GHz band 802.11a 54Mbps and 2.4GHz band 802.11b 11Mbps wireless networking standards. The Wi-Fi Alliance is formed to certify 802.11b products, ensuring interoperability.

2000   The first 802.11b Wi-Fi-certified products are introduced, and wireless networking rapidly builds momentum.

2000   Microsoft releases Windows Me (Millennium Edition) and Windows 2000.

2000   Both Intel and AMD introduce processors running at 1GHz.

2000   AMD introduces the Duron, a low-cost Athlon with reduced L2 cache.

2000   Intel introduces the Pentium 4, the latest processor in the Intel Architecture 32-bit (IA-32) family.

2001   The industry celebrates the 20th anniversary of the release of the original IBM PC.

2001   Intel introduces the first 2GHz processor, a version of the Pentium 4. It takes the industry 28 1/2 years to go from 108KHz to 1GHz but only 18 months to go from 1GHz to 2GHz.

2001   Microsoft releases Windows XP, the first mainstream 32-bit operating system (OS), merging the consumer and business OS lines under the same code base (NT 5.1).

2001   Atheros introduces the first 802.11a 54Mbps high-speed wireless chips, allowing 802.11a products to finally reach the market.

2002   Intel releases the first 3GHz-class processor, a 3.06GHz version of the Pentium 4. This processor also introduces Intel's Hyper-Threading (HT) technology, appearing as two processors to the OS.

2003   Intel releases the Pentium M, a processor designed specifically for mobile systems, offering extremely low power consumption that results in dramatically increased battery life while still offering relatively high performance.

2003   AMD releases the Athlon 64, the first x86-64 (64-bit) processor for PCs, which also includes integrated memory controllers.

2003   The IEEE officially approves the 802.11g 54Mbps high-speed wireless networking standard.

2004   Intel introduces a version of the Pentium 4 codenamed Prescott, the first PC processor built on 90-nanometer technology.

2004   Intel introduces EM64T (Extended Memory 64 Technology), which is a 64-bit extension to Intel's IA-32 architecture based on (and virtually identical to) the x86-64 (AMD64) technology first released by AMD.

2005   Microsoft releases Windows XP x64 Edition, which supports processors with 64-bit AMD64 and EM64T extensions.

2005   The era of multicore PC processors begins as Intel introduces the Pentium D 8xx and Pentium Extreme Edition 8xx dual-core processors. AMD soon follows with the dual-core Athlon 64 X2.

2006   Apple introduces the first Macintosh systems based on PC architecture, stating they are four times faster than previous non-PC-based Macs.

2006   Intel introduces the Core 2 Extreme, the first quad-core processor for PCs.

2006   Microsoft releases the long-awaited Windows Vista to business users. The PC OEM and consumer market releases would follow in early 2007.

2007   Intel releases the 3x series chipsets with support for DDR3 memory and PCI Express 2.0, which doubles the available bandwidth.

2007   AMD releases the Phenom processors, the first quad-core processors for PCs with all four cores on a single die.

2008   Intel releases the Core i-Series (Nehalem) processors, which are dual- or quad-core chips with optional Hyper-Threading (appearing as four or eight cores to the OS) that include an integrated memory controller.

2008   Intel releases the 4x and 5x series chipsets, the latter of which supports Core i-Series processors with integrated memory controllers.

2009   Microsoft releases Windows 7, a highly anticipated successor to Vista.

2009   AMD releases the Phenom II processors in 2-, 3-, and 4-core versions.

2009   The IEEE officially approves the 802.11n wireless standard, which increases net maximum date rate from 54Mbps to 600Mbps.

2010   Intel releases six-core versions of the Core i-Series processor (Gulftown) and a dual-core version with integrated graphics (Clarkdale). The Gulftown is the first PC processor with more than 1 billion transistors.

2010   AMD releases six-core versions of the Phenom II processor.

2011   Intel releases the second-generation Core i-Series processors (Sandy Bridge) along with new 6-Series motherboard chipsets. The chipsets and motherboards are quickly recalled due to a bug in the SATA host adapter. The recall costs Intel nearly a billion dollars and results in a several month delay in the processors and chipsets reaching the market.

2012   Intel releases the third-generation Core i-Series processors (Ivy Bridge) and complementing Panther Point 7-Series chipsets. Noted advancements include integrated USB 3.0 support, PCI Express 3.0 support, and Tri-Gate transistor technology.

2012   AMD releases socket AM3+ FX-8000, FX-6000, and FX-4000 series eight, six, and four-core processors, as well as the "Trinity" accelerated processing unit.

2012   Microsoft releases Windows 8, featuring touch-screen input, including a version supporting ARM processors, used in mobile phone and tablet/pad devices.

2012   Microsoft releases its Surface tablet, available in an Intel processor-based version with Windows 8 Pro and an ARM processor-based version with Windows RT.

Electronic Computers

A physicist named John V. Atanasoff (with associate Clifford Berry) is officially credited with creating the first true digital electronic computer from 1937 to 1942, while working at Iowa State University. The Atanasoff-Berry Computer (called the ABC) was the first to use modern digital switching techniques and vacuum tubes as switches, and it introduced the concepts of binary arithmetic and logic circuits. This was made legally official on October 19, 1973 when, following a lengthy court trial, U.S. Federal Judge Earl R. Larson voided the ENIAC patent of Eckert and Mauchly and named Atanasoff as the inventor of the first electronic digital computer.

Military needs during World War II caused a great thrust forward in the evolution of computers. In 1943, Tommy Flowers completed a secret British code-breaking computer called Colossus, which was used to decode German secret messages. Unfortunately, that work went largely uncredited because Colossus was kept secret until many years after the war.

Besides code-breaking, systems were needed to calculate weapons trajectory and other military functions. In 1946, John P. Eckert, John W. Mauchly, and their associates at the Moore School of Electrical Engineering at the University of Pennsylvania built the first large-scale electronic computer for the military. This machine became known as ENIAC, the Electrical Numerical Integrator and Calculator. It operated on 10-digit numbers and could multiply two such numbers at the rate of 300 products per second by finding the value of each product from a multiplication table stored in its memory. ENIAC was about 1,000 times faster than the previous generation of electromechanical relay computers.

ENIAC used approximately 18,000 vacuum tubes, occupied 1,800 square feet (167 square meters) of floor space, and consumed around 180,000 watts of electrical power. Punched cards served as the input and output; registers served as adders and as quick-access read/write storage.

The executable instructions composing a given program were created via specified wiring and switches that controlled the flow of computations through the machine. As such, ENIAC had to be rewired and switched for each program to be run.

Although Eckert and Mauchly were originally given a patent for the electronic computer, it was later voided and the patent awarded to John Atanasoff for creating the Atanasoff-Berry Computer.

Earlier in 1945, the mathematician John von Neumann demonstrated that a computer could have a simple, fixed physical structure and yet be capable of executing any kind of computation effectively by means of proper programmed control without changes in hardware. In other words, you could change the program without rewiring the system. The *stored-program technique*, as von Neumann's ideas are known, became fundamental for future generations of high-speed digital computers and has become universally adopted.

The first generation of modern programmed electronic computers to take advantage of these improvements appeared in 1947. This group of machines included EDVAC and UNIVAC, the first commercially available computers. These computers included, for the first time, the use of true random access memory (RAM) for storing parts of the program and the data that is needed quickly. Typically, they were programmed directly in machine language, although by the mid-1950s progress had been made in several aspects of advanced programming. The standout of the era is the UNIVAC (Universal Automatic Computer), which was the first true general-purpose computer designed for both alphabetical and numerical uses. This made the UNIVAC a standard for business, not just science and the military.

Modern Computers

From UNIVAC to the latest desktop PCs, computer evolution has moved rapidly. The first-generation computers were known for using vacuum tubes in their construction. The generation to follow would use the much smaller and more efficient transistor.

From Tubes to Transistors

Any modern digital computer is largely a collection of electronic switches. These switches are used to represent and control the routing of data elements called *binary digits* (or *bits*). Because of the on-or-off nature of the binary information and signal routing the computer uses, an efficient electronic switch was required. The first electronic computers used vacuum tubes as switches, and although the tubes worked, they had many problems.

The type of tube used in early computers was called a *triode* and was invented by Lee De Forest in 1906 (see Figure 1.1). It consists of a cathode and a plate, separated by a control grid, suspended in a glass vacuum tube. The cathode is heated by a red-hot electric filament, which causes it to emit electrons that are attracted to the plate. The control grid in the middle can control this flow of electrons. By making it negative, you cause the electrons to be repelled back to the cathode; by making it positive, you cause them to be attracted toward the plate. Thus, by controlling the grid current, you can control the on/off output of the plate.

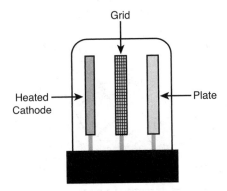

FIGURE 1.1 The three main components of a basic triode vacuum tube.

Unfortunately, the tube was inefficient as a switch. It consumed a great deal of electrical power and gave off enormous heat—a significant problem in the earlier systems. Primarily because of the heat they generated, tubes were notoriously unreliable—in larger systems, one failed every couple of hours or so.

The invention of the transistor was one of the most important developments leading to the personal computer revolution. The transistor was invented in 1947 and announced in 1948 by Bell Laboratory engineers John Bardeen and Walter Brattain. Bell associate William Shockley invented the junction transistor a few months later, and all three jointly shared the Nobel Prize in Physics in 1956 for inventing the transistor. The transistor, which essentially functions as a solid-state electronic switch, replaced the less-suitable vacuum tube. Because the transistor was so much smaller and consumed significantly less power, a computer system built with transistors was also much smaller, faster, and more efficient than a computer system built with vacuum tubes.

The conversion from tubes to transistors began the trend toward miniaturization that continues to this day. Today's small laptop PC (or Ultrabook) and even Tablet PC systems, which run on batteries, have more computing power than many earlier systems that filled rooms and consumed huge amounts of electrical power.

Although there have been many designs for transistors over the years, the transistors used in modern computers are normally Metal Oxide Semiconductor Field Effect Transistors (MOSFETs). MOSFETs are made from layers of materials deposited on a silicon substrate. Some of the layers contain silicon with certain impurities added by a process called *doping* or *ion bombardment*, whereas other layers include silicon dioxide (which acts as an insulator), polysilicon (which acts as an electrode), and metal to act as the wires to connect the transistor to other components. The composition and arrangement of the different types of doped silicon allow them to act both as a conductor or an insulator, which is why silicon is called a *semiconductor*.

MOSFETs can be constructed as either NMOS or PMOS types, based on the arrangement of doped silicon used. Silicon doped with boron is called *P-type* (positive) because it lacks electrons, whereas silicon doped with phosphorus is called *N-type* (negative) because it has an excess of free electrons.

MOSFETs have three connections, called the *source, gate,* and *drain*. An NMOS transistor is made by using N-type silicon for the source and drain, with P-type silicon placed in between (see Figure 1.2). The gate is positioned above the P-type silicon, separating the source and drain, and is separated from the P-type silicon by an insulating layer of silicon dioxide. Normally there is no current flow between N-type and P-type silicon, thus preventing electron flow between the source and drain. When a positive voltage is placed on the gate, the gate electrode creates a field that attracts electrons to the P-type silicon between the source and drain. That in turn changes that area to behave as if it were N-type silicon, creating a path for current to flow and turning the transistor on.

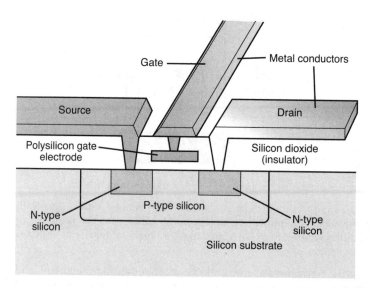

FIGURE 1.2 Cutaway view of an NMOS transistor.

A PMOS transistor works in a similar but opposite fashion. P-type silicon is used for the source and drain, with N-type silicon positioned between them. When a negative voltage is placed on the gate, the gate electrode creates a field that repels electrons from the N-type silicon between the source and drain. That in turn changes that area to behave as if it were P-type silicon, creating a path for current to flow and turning the transistor "on."

When both NMOS and PMOS field-effect transistors are combined in a complementary arrangement, power is used only when the transistors are switching, making dense, low-power circuit designs possible. Because of this, virtually all modern processors are designed using CMOS (Complementary Metal Oxide Semiconductor) technology.

Compared to a tube, a transistor is much more efficient as a switch and can be miniaturized to microscopic scale. Since the transistor was invented, engineers have strived to make it smaller and smaller. In 2003, NEC researchers unveiled a silicon transistor only 5 nanometers (billionths of a meter) in size. Other technologies, such as Graphene and carbon nanotubes, are being explored to produce even smaller transistors, down to the molecular or even atomic scale. In 2008, British researchers unveiled a Graphene-based transistor only 1 atom thick and 10 atoms (1nm) across, and in 2010, IBM researchers created Graphene transistors switching at a rate of 100 gigahertz, thus paving the way for future chips denser and faster than possible with silicon-based designs.

In 2012, Intel introduced its Ivy Bridge processors using a revolutionary new Tri-Gate three-dimensional transistor design, manufactured using a 22nm process. This design was first announced by Intel back in 2002; however, it took 10 years to complete the development and to create the manufacturing processes for production. Tri-Gate transistors differ from conventional two-dimensional planar transistors in that the source is constructed as a raised "fin," with three conducting channels between the source and the drain (see Figure 1.3). This allows much more surface area for conduction than the single flat channel on a planar transistor and improves the total drive current and switching speed with less current leakage. Intel states that this technology also allows for lower voltages, resulting in up to a 50% reduction in power consumption while maintaining or even increasing overall performance.

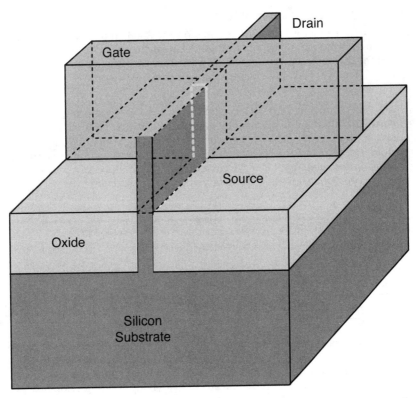

FIGURE 1.3 Intel Tri-Gate transistor using a fin-shaped source/drain for more surface area between the source and gate.

Integrated Circuits

The third generation of modern computers is known for using integrated circuits instead of individual transistors. Jack Kilby at Texas Instruments and Robert Noyce at Fairchild are both credited with having invented the *integrated circuit (IC)* in 1958 and 1959. An IC is a semiconductor circuit that contains multiple components on the same base (or substrate material), which are usually interconnected without wires. The first prototype IC constructed by Kilby at TI in 1958 contained only one transistor, several resistors, and a capacitor on a single slab of germanium, and it featured fine gold "flying wires" to interconnect them. However, because the flying wires had to be individually attached, this type of design was not practical to manufacture. By comparison, Noyce patented the "planar" IC design in 1959, where all the components are diffused in or etched on a silicon base, including a layer of aluminum metal interconnects. In 1960, Fairchild constructed the first planar IC, consisting of a flip-flop circuit with four transistors and five resistors on a circular die only about 20mm² in size. By comparison, the Intel Core i7 quad-core processor based on the 22nm Ivy Bridge microarchitecture incorporates 1.4 billion transistors (and numerous other components) on a single 160mm² die!

History of the PC

The fourth generation of the modern computer includes those that incorporate microprocessors in their designs. Of course, part of this fourth generation of computers is the personal computer, which itself was made possible by the advent of low-cost microprocessors and memory.

Birth of the Personal Computer

In 1973, some of the first microcomputer kits based on the 8008 chip were developed. These kits were little more than demonstration tools and didn't do much except blink lights. In April 1974, Intel introduced the 8080 microprocessor, which was 10 times faster than the earlier 8008 chip and addressed 64KB of memory. This was the breakthrough that the personal computer industry had been waiting for.

A company called MITS introduced the Altair 8800 kit in a cover story in the January 1975 issue of *Popular Electronics*. The Altair kit, considered by many to be the first personal computer, included an 8080 processor, a power supply, a front panel with a large number of lights, and 256 bytes (not kilobytes) of memory. The kit sold for $395 and had to be assembled. Assembly back then meant you got out your soldering iron to actually finish the circuit boards—not like today, where you can assemble a system of premade components with nothing more than a screwdriver.

Note

Micro Instrumentation and Telemetry Systems was the original name of the company founded in 1969 by Ed Roberts and several associates to manufacture and sell instruments and transmitters for model rockets. Ed Roberts became the sole owner in the early 1970s, after which he designed the Altair. By January 1975, when the Altair was introduced, the company was called MITS, Inc., which then stood for nothing more than the name of the company. In 1977, Roberts sold MITS to Pertec, moved to Georgia, went to medical school, and became a practicing physician. Considered by many to be the "father of the personal computer," Roberts passed away in 2010 after a long bout with pneumonia.

The Altair included an open architecture system bus later called the *S-100 bus,* so named because it became an industry standard and had 100 pins per slot. The S-100 bus was widely adopted by other computers that were similar to the Altair, such as the IMSAI 8080, which was featured in the movie *WarGames.* The S-100 bus open architecture meant that anybody could develop boards to fit in these slots and interface to the system, and it ensured a high level of cross-compatibility between different boards and systems. The popularity of 8080 processor–based systems inspired software companies to write programs, including the CP/M (control program for microprocessors) OS and the first version of the Microsoft BASIC (Beginners All-purpose Symbolic Instruction Code) programming language.

IBM introduced what can be called its first personal computer in 1975. The Model 5100 had 16KB of memory, a built-in 16-line-by-64-character display, a built-in BASIC language interpreter, and a built-in DC-300 cartridge tape drive for storage. The system's $8,975 price placed it out of the mainstream personal computer marketplace, which was dominated by experimenters (affectionately referred to as *hackers*) who built low-cost kits ($500 or so) as a hobby. Obviously, the IBM system was not in competition for this low-cost market and did not sell as well by comparison.

The Model 5100 was succeeded by the 5110 and 5120 before IBM introduced what we know as the IBM Personal Computer (Model 5150). Although the 5100 series preceded the IBM PC, the older systems and the 5150 IBM PC had nothing in common. The PC that IBM turned out was more closely related to the IBM System/23 DataMaster, an office computer system introduced in 1980. In fact, many of the engineers who developed the IBM PC had originally worked on the DataMaster.

In 1976, a new company called Apple Computer introduced the Apple I, which originally sold for $666.66. The selling price was an arbitrary number selected by one of Apple's cofounders, Steve Jobs. This system consisted of a main circuit board screwed to a piece of plywood; a case and power supply were not included. Only a few of these computers were made, and they reportedly have sold to collectors for more than $20,000. The Apple II, introduced in 1977, helped set the standard for nearly all the important microcomputers to follow, including the IBM PC.

The microcomputer world was dominated in 1980 by two types of computer systems. One type, the Apple II, claimed a large following of loyal users and a gigantic software base that was growing at a fantastic rate. The other type, CP/M systems, consisted not of a single system but of all the many systems that evolved from the original MITS Altair. These systems were compatible with one another and were distinguished by their use of the CP/M OS and expansion slots, which followed the S-100 standard. All these systems were built by a variety of companies and sold under various names. For the most part, however, these systems used the same software and plug-in hardware. It is interesting to note that none of these systems was PC compatible or Macintosh compatible, the two primary standards in place today.

A new competitor looming on the horizon was able to see that to be successful, a personal computer needed to have an open architecture, slots for expansion, a modular design, and healthy support from both hardware and software companies other than the original manufacturer of the system. This competitor turned out to be IBM, which was quite surprising at the time because IBM was not known for systems with these open-architecture attributes. IBM, in essence, became more like the early Apple, whereas Apple became like everybody expected IBM to be. The open architecture of the forthcoming IBM PC and the closed architecture of the forthcoming Macintosh caused a complete turnaround in the industry.

The IBM Personal Computer

At the end of 1980, IBM decided to truly compete in the rapidly growing low-cost personal computer market. The company established the Entry Systems Division, located in Boca Raton, Florida, to develop the new system. The division was intentionally located far away from IBM's main headquarters in New York, or any other IBM facilities, so that it would be able to operate independently as a separate unit. This small group consisted of 12 engineers and designers under the direction of Don Estridge and was charged with developing IBM's first real PC. (IBM considered the previous 5100 system, developed in 1975, to be an intelligent programmable terminal rather than a genuine computer, even though it truly was a computer.) Nearly all these engineers had come to the new division from the System/23 DataMaster project, which was a small office computer system introduced in 1980 and the direct predecessor of the IBM PC.

Much of the PC's design was influenced by the DataMaster design. In the DataMaster's single-piece design, the display and keyboard were integrated into the unit. Because these features were limiting, they became external units on the PC, although the PC keyboard layout and electrical designs were copied from the DataMaster.

Several other parts of the IBM PC system also were copied from the DataMaster, including the expansion bus (or input/output slots), which included not only the same physical 62-pin connector, but also almost identical pin specifications. This copying of the bus design was possible because the PC used the same interrupt controller as the DataMaster and a similar direct memory access (DMA) controller. Also, expansion cards already designed for the DataMaster could easily be redesigned to function in the PC.

The DataMaster used an Intel 8085 CPU, which had a 64KB address limit and an 8-bit internal and external data bus. This arrangement prompted the PC design team to use the Intel 8088 CPU, which offered a much larger (1MB) memory address limit and an internal 16-bit data bus, but only an 8-bit external data bus. The 8-bit external data bus and similar instruction set enabled the 8088 to be easily interfaced into the earlier DataMaster designs.

IBM brought its system from idea to delivery of functioning systems in one year by using existing designs and purchasing as many components as possible from outside vendors. The Entry Systems Division was granted autonomy from IBM's other divisions and could tap resources outside the company, rather than go through the bureaucratic procedures that required exclusive use of IBM resources. IBM contracted out the PC's languages and OS to a small company named Microsoft. That decision was the major factor in establishing Microsoft as the dominant force in PC software.

Note

IBM had originally contacted Digital Research (the company that created CP/M, then the most popular personal computer OS) to have it develop an OS for the new IBM PC. However, Digital was leery of working with IBM and especially balked at the nondisclosure agreement IBM wanted Digital to sign. Microsoft jumped on the opportunity left open by Digital Research and, consequently, became the largest software company in the world. IBM's use of outside vendors in developing the PC was an open invitation for the after-market to jump in and support the system—and it did.

On August 12, 1981, a new standard was established in the microcomputer industry with the debut of the IBM PC. Since then, hundreds of millions of PC-compatible systems have been sold, as the original PC has grown into an enormous family of computers and peripherals. More software has been written for this computer family than for any other system on the market.

The PC Industry 30 Years Later

In the 30 years since the original IBM PC was introduced, many changes have occurred. The IBM-compatible computer, for example, advanced from a 4.77MHz 8088-based system to 4GHz (4,000MHz) multicore systems that are hundreds of thousands or more times faster than the original IBM PC (in actual processing speed, not just clock speed). The original PC had only one or two single-sided floppy drives that stored 160KB each using DOS 1.0, whereas modern systems can have several terabytes (trillion bytes) or more of hard disk storage.

A rule of thumb in the computer industry (called *Moore's Law*, originally set forth by Intel cofounder Gordon Moore) is that available processor performance and disk-storage capacity doubles every one and a half to two years, give or take.

Since the beginning of the PC industry, this pattern has held steady and, if anything, seems to be accelerating.

Moore's Law

In 1965, Gordon Moore was preparing a speech about the growth trends in computer memory and made an interesting observation. When he began to graph the data, he realized a striking trend existed. Each new chip contained roughly twice as much capacity as its predecessor, and each chip was released within 18–24 months of the previous chip. If this trend continued, he reasoned, computing power would rise exponentially over relatively brief periods.

Moore's observation, now known as Moore's Law, described a trend that has continued to this day and is still remarkably accurate. It was found to not only describe memory chips, but also accurately describe the growth of processor power and disk drive storage capacity. It has become the basis for many industry performance forecasts. As an example, in less than 40 years the number of transistors on a processor chip increased more than half a million fold, from 2,300 transistors in the 4004 processor in 1971 to 1.4 billion transistors in some of the Ivy Bridge quad-core i-Series processors released in 2012.

In addition to performance and storage capacity, another major change since the original IBM PC was introduced is that IBM is not the only manufacturer of PC-compatible systems. IBM originated the PC-compatible standard, of course, but today it no longer sets the standards for the system it originated. More often than not, new standards in the PC industry are developed by companies and organizations other than IBM.

Today, Intel, Microsoft, and AMD are primarily responsible for developing and extending the PC hardware and software standards. Some have even taken to calling PCs "Wintel" systems, owing to the dominance of the first two companies. Although AMD originally produced Intel processors under license and later produced low-cost, pin-compatible counterparts to Intel's 486 and Pentium processors (AMD 486, K5/K6), starting with the Athlon AMD has created completely unique processors that are worthy rivals to Intel's own models.

In more recent years, the introduction of hardware standards such as the universal serial bus (USB), Peripheral Component Interconnect (PCI) bus, Accelerated Graphics Port (AGP) bus, PCI Express bus, ATX motherboard form factor, as well as processor socket and slot interfaces show that Intel is the driving force behind PC hardware design. Intel's ability to design and produce motherboard chipsets as well as complete motherboards has enabled Intel processor–based systems to first adopt newer memory and bus architectures as well as system form factors. Although in the past AMD has on occasion made chipsets for its own processors, the company's acquisition of ATI has allowed it to become more aggressive in the chipset marketplace.

PC-compatible systems have thrived not only because compatible hardware can be assembled easily, but also because the most popular OS was available from a third party (Microsoft) instead of IBM. The core of the system software is the basic input/output system (BIOS); this was also available from third-party companies, such as AMI, Phoenix, and others. This situation enabled other manufacturers to license the OS and BIOS software and sell their own compatible systems. The fact that DOS borrowed the functionality and user interface from both CP/M and UNIX probably had a lot to do with the amount of software that became available. Later, with the success of Windows, even more reasons would exist for software developers to write programs for PC-compatible systems.

One reason Apple's Macintosh systems have never enjoyed the market success of PC systems is that Apple has often used proprietary hardware and software designs that it was unwilling to license to other companies. This proprietary nature has unfortunately relegated Apple to a meager 5 to 7% market share in personal computers.

One fortunate development for Mac enthusiasts was Apple's shift to Intel x86/x64 processors and PC architecture in 2006, resulting in greatly improved performance and standardization as compared to the previous non-PC-compatible Mac systems. Although Apple has failed to adopt many of the industry-standard component form factors used in PCs (rendering major components such as motherboards and power supplies non-interchangeable), the PC-based Macs truly are PCs from a hardware standpoint, using all the same processors, chipsets, memory, buses, and other system architectures that PCs have been using for years. I've had people ask me, "Is there a book like *Upgrading and Repairing PCs* that covers Macs instead?" Well, since 2006, Macs have essentially *become* PCs, meaning that they are now covered in this book by default! The move to a PC-based architecture was without a doubt one of the smartest moves Apple has made—besides reducing component costs, it has allowed Macs to finally perform on par with PCs.

Apple could even become a real contender in the OS arena (taking market share from Microsoft) if the company would only sell its OS in an unlocked version that would run on non-Apple PCs. Unfortunately, for now, even though Apple's OS X operating system is designed to run on PC hardware, it is coded to check for a security chip found only on Apple motherboards. There are ways to work around the check (see OSx86project.org), but Apple does not support them.

Apple's shift to a PC-based architecture is one more indication of just how popular the PC has become. After 30-plus years, the PC continues to thrive and prosper. With far-reaching industry support and an architecture that is continuously evolving, I say it is a safe bet that PC-compatible systems will continue to dominate the personal computer marketplace for the foreseeable future.

PC Components, Features, and System Design

What Is a PC?

When I begin one of my *Upgrading and Repairing PCs* seminars, I like to ask the question, "What exactly is a PC?" Most people immediately answer that PC stands for *personal computer*, which is true. Many continue by defining a personal computer as any small computer system purchased and used by an individual, which is also true. However, although it is true that all PCs are personal computers, not all personal computers are PCs. For example, all of Apple's pre-2006 Motorola/IBM processor–based Macintosh systems, older 8080/Z-80 processor–based CP/M machines, and even my old Apple][+ system are considered personal computers, but most people wouldn't call them PCs, least of all the Mac users! For the true definition of what a PC is, we must look deeper.

Calling something a PC implies that it is something much more specific than just any personal computer. One thing it implies is a familial relation to the original IBM PC from 1981. In fact, I'll go so far as to say that IBM literally *invented* the type of computer we call a PC today; that is, IBM designed and created the first one, and IBM's definition set all the standards that made the PC distinctive from other personal computers. Note that I'm not saying that IBM invented the personal computer; many recognize the historical origins of the personal computer in the MITS Altair, introduced in 1975, even though other small computers were available prior. Clearly, IBM did not invent the personal computer; however, it did invent the type of personal computer that today we call the PC. Some people might take this definition a step further and define a PC as any personal computer that is "IBM compatible." In fact, many years back, PCs were called either *IBM compatibles* or *IBM clones*, paying homage to the origins of the PC at IBM.

Some Personal Computer Trivia

Although the 1975 MITS Altair is often credited as the first personal computer, according to the Blinkenlights Archaeological Institute (www.blinkenlights.com), the first personal computer was the Simon, created by Edmund C. Berkeley and described in his 1949 book, *Giant Brains, or Machines That Think*. The plans for Simon were available for purchase by Berkeley Enterprises as well as published in a series of 13 articles in *Radio Electronics* magazine from 1950 to 1951.

The term *personal computer* may have first appeared in a November 3, 1962 *New York Times* article quoting John W. Mauchly (co-creator of ENIAC). The article was reporting on Mauchly's vision of future computing, and he was quoted as saying, "There is no reason to suppose the average boy or girl cannot be master of a personal computer."

The first machine advertised as a "personal computer" was the Hewlett-Packard 9100A, a 40-pound programmable desktop electronic calculator released in 1968. Advertisements for the $4,900 system called it "the new Hewlett-Packard 9100A personal computer." The end of the ad stated, "If you are still skeptical, or of faint heart, ask for a demonstration. It will affirm, assure (and only slightly delay) your entry into the solid-state of personal computing power." (See www.vintagecalculators.com.)

The reality today is that, although IBM clearly designed and created the PC in 1981 and controlled the development and evolution of the PC standard for several years thereafter, IBM is no longer in control of the PC standard; that is, it does not dictate what makes up a PC today. IBM lost control of the PC standard in 1987 when it introduced its PS/2 line of systems. Up until then, other companies that were producing PCs literally copied IBM's systems right down to the chips, connectors, and even the shapes (form factors) of the boards, cases, and power supplies. After 1987, IBM abandoned many of the standards it created in the first place, and the designation "IBM compatible" started to be considered obsolete.

If a PC is no longer defined as an IBM-compatible system, then what is it? The real question seems to be, "Who is in control of the PC standard today?" That question is best broken down into two parts. First, who is in control of PC software? Second, who is in control of PC hardware?

Why Is This Important?

I'm often asked why it is important to understand the history, development, and evolution of the PC. The simple truth is that doing so makes you a much better technician, troubleshooter, and problem solver! PCs have become complicated devices with a lot of quirks and idiosyncracies, and much of this was caused by one important design parameter; backward compatibility. It is amazing, but one can actually run many 1981 programs on a modern system, and in many cases even connect old hardware as well. Modern PCs may look very different and be far more powerful and capable than the first PCs built in 1981, but internally they have a lot of the same "DNA." Understanding how the design of the PC has evolved into what we use today will help you especially when solving problems as you will have a deeper understanding of why things are done the way they are and what problems can be caused by it. For example, even though many modern systems come with solid-state drives (SSDs), those drives are built to essentially look and act like magnetic hard disk drives, even appearing as if they have internal structures like "tracks" and "sectors." If you had not previously learned about magnetic drives, you wouldn't understand why SSDs are designed the way they are and what problems might occur because of it (such as why in some cases they might appear to slow down dramatically after a period of use). Knowing the history and development of PC architecture will make you much more in-tune with how and why modern systems are designed and especially how they function and potentially fail.

Who Controls PC Software?

Most of the people in my seminars don't hesitate for a split second when I ask this question; they immediately respond, "Microsoft!" I don't think there is any argument with that. Microsoft clearly controls the dominant operating systems (OSs) used on PCs, which have evolved from the original MS-DOS to DOS/Windows 3.x, then to Windows 9x/Me, then to Windows NT/2000/XP, and now to Windows Vista/7/8.

Microsoft has effectively used its control of the PC OSs as leverage to also control other types of PC software, such as drivers, utilities, and applications. For example, many utility programs originally offered by independent companies, such as disk caching, disk compression, disk encryption, file defragmentation, file structure repair, firewalls, and even simple applications such as calculator and notepad programs, are now bundled in Windows. Microsoft bundles more comprehensive applications, such as web browsers, word processors, and media players, ensuring an automatic installed base for these applications—much to the dismay of companies who produce competing versions. Microsoft also leverages its control of the OS to integrate its own networking software and applications suites more seamlessly into the OS than others. That's why it dominates most of the PC software universe—from OSs to networking software to utilities, from word processors to database programs to spreadsheets.

In the early days of the PC, IBM hired Microsoft to provide most of the core software for the PC. IBM developed the hardware, wrote the basic input/output system (BIOS), and hired Microsoft to develop the disk operating system (DOS) as well as several other programs and utilities for the PC. In what was later viewed as perhaps the most costly business mistake in history, IBM failed to secure exclusive rights to the DOS it had contracted from Microsoft, either by purchasing it outright or by an exclusive license agreement. Instead, IBM licensed it nonexclusively, which subsequently allowed Microsoft to sell the same MS-DOS code it developed for IBM to any other company that was interested. Early PC cloners such as Compaq eagerly licensed this OS code, and suddenly consumers could purchase the same basic MS-DOS OS with several different company names on the box. In retrospect, that single contractual error made Microsoft the dominant software company it is today and subsequently caused IBM to lose control of the very PC standard it had created.

As a writer (of words, not software), I can appreciate what an incredible oversight this was. Imagine that a book publisher comes up with a great idea for a popular book and then contracts with an author to write it. Then, by virtue of a poorly written contract, the author discovers that he can legally sell the same book (perhaps with a different title) to all the competitors of the original publisher. Of course, no publisher I know would allow this to happen; yet that is exactly what IBM allowed Microsoft to do back in 1981. By virtue of its deal with Microsoft, IBM lost control of the software it commissioned for its new PC.

In the PC business, software enjoys copyright protection, whereas hardware can be protected only by patents, which are much more difficult, time-consuming, and expensive to obtain. And in the case of U.S. patents, they also expire 20 years after filing. According to the U.S. patent office, "any new and useful process, machine, manufacture, or composition of matter, or any new and useful improvement thereof" can be patented. This definition made it difficult to patent most aspects of the IBM PC because it was designed using previously existing parts that anybody could purchase off the shelf. In fact, most of the important parts for the original PC came from Intel, such as the 8088 processor, 8284 clock generator, 8253/54 timer, 8259 interrupt controller, 8237 DMA (direct memory access) controller, 8255 peripheral interface, and 8288 bus controller. These chips made up the heart and soul of the original PC motherboard.

Because the design of the original PC was not wholly patented and virtually all the parts were readily available, almost anybody could duplicate the hardware of the IBM PC. All one had to do was purchase the same chips from the same manufacturers and suppliers IBM used and design a new motherboard with a similar circuit. IBM made it even easier by publishing complete schematic diagrams of its motherboards and adapter cards in detailed and easily available technical reference manuals. These manuals even included fully commented source code listings for the ROM BIOS code. I have several of these early IBM manuals and still refer to them for specific component-level PC design information. In fact, I highly recommend these original manuals to anybody who wants to delve deeply into PC hardware design. Although they are long out of print, they do turn up in the used book market and online auction sites such as eBay.

The difficult part of copying the IBM PC was the software, which is protected by copyright law. Both Compaq and Phoenix Software (today known as Phoenix Technologies) were among the first to develop a legal way around this problem, which enabled them to functionally duplicate (but not exactly copy) software such as the BIOS. The BIOS is defined as the core set of control software that drives the hardware devices in the system directly. These types of programs are normally called device drivers, so in essence, the BIOS is a collection of all the core device drivers used to operate and control the system hardware. The operating system (such as DOS or Windows) uses the drivers in the BIOS to control and communicate with the various hardware and peripherals in the system.

▶▶   See Chapter 5, "BIOS," **p. 263**.

The method Compaq and Phoenix used to legally duplicate the IBM PC BIOS was an ingenious form of reverse-engineering. They used two groups of software engineers, the second of which were specially screened to consist only of people who had never before seen or studied the IBM BIOS code. The first group studied the IBM BIOS and wrote a detailed description of what it did. The second group read the description written by the first group and set out to write from scratch a new BIOS that did everything the first group had described. The result was a new BIOS written from scratch, and although the resulting code was not identical to IBM's, it had the same functionality.

This is called a "clean room" approach to reverse-engineering software, and if carefully conducted, it can escape any legal attack. Because IBM's original PC BIOS had a limited and yet well-defined set of functions and was only 8,096 bytes long, duplicating it through the clean-room approach was not difficult. As the IBM BIOS evolved, keeping up with any changes IBM made was relatively easy. Discounting the power-on self test (POST) and BIOS Setup (used for configuring the system) portion of the BIOS, most motherboard BIOSs, even today, have only about 32KB to 128KB of active code, and modern OSs ignore most of it anyway by loading code and drivers from disk. In essence, the modern motherboard BIOS serves only to initialize the system and load the OS. Today, although some PC manufacturers still write some of their own BIOS code, most source their BIOS from one of the independent BIOS developers. Phoenix and American Megatrends (AMI) are the leading developers of BIOS software for PC system and motherboard manufacturers. A third major producer of BIOS software, Award Software, is owned by Phoenix Technologies, which continues to sell Award BIOS–based products.

After the motherboard hardware and BIOS of the IBM PC were duplicated, all that was necessary to produce a fully IBM-compatible system was MS-DOS. Reverse-engineering DOS, even with the clean-room approach, seemed to be a daunting task at the time, because DOS is much larger than the BIOS and consists of many more programs and functions. Also, the OS has evolved and changed more often than the BIOS, which by comparison has remained relatively constant. This means that the only way to get DOS on an IBM compatible back in the early 1980s was to license it. This is where Microsoft came in. Because IBM (who hired Microsoft to write DOS in the first place) did not ensure that its license agreement with Microsoft was exclusive, Microsoft was free to sell the same DOS it designed for IBM to anybody else who wanted it. With a licensed copy of MS-DOS, the last piece was in place and the floodgates were open for IBM-compatible systems to be produced whether IBM liked it or not.

Note

MS-DOS was eventually cloned, the first of which was DR-DOS, released by Digital Research (developers of CP/M) in 1988. By all rights, DR-DOS was more than just a clone; it had many features not found in MS-DOS at the time, inspiring Microsoft to add similar features in future MS-DOS versions as well. In 1991, Novell acquired DR-DOS, followed by Caldera in 1996 (who released a version of the source code under an open-source license), followed by Lineo in 1998, and finally by DRDOS (www.drdos.com) in 2002.

Free and open-source DOS versions have been independently produced, upgraded, and maintained by the DR-DOS/OpenDOS Enhancement Project (www.drdosprojects.de) as well as the FreeDOS Project (www.freedos.org).

Note

From 1996 to 1997, an effort was made by the more liberated thinkers at Apple to license its BIOS/OS combination, and several Mac-compatible machines were developed, produced, and sold. Companies such as Sony, Power Computing, Radius, and even Motorola invested millions of dollars in developing these systems, but shortly after these first Mac clones were sold, Apple canceled the licensing! By canceling these licenses, Apple virtually guaranteed that its systems would not be competitive with Windows-based PCs. Along with its smaller market share come much higher system costs, fewer available software applications, and fewer options for hardware repair, replacement, and upgrades as compared to PCs. The proprietary form factors also ensure that major components such as motherboards, power supplies, and cases are available only from Apple at high prices, making out-of-warranty repair, replacement, and upgrades of these components not cost effective.

Now that Apple has converted its Mac systems to PC architecture, the only difference between a Mac and a PC is the OS they run, so a PC running OS X essentially becomes a Mac, whereas a Mac running Windows becomes a PC. This means that the only thing keeping Mac systems unique, beyond its design style, is the ability to run OS X. To this end, Apple includes code in OS X that checks for an Apple-specific security chip, thus preventing OS X from running on non-Apple PCs. Although this does create an incentive to buy Apple-brand PCs, it also overlooks the huge market for selling OS X to non-Apple PC users. For example, if Apple had sold OS X to PC users while Microsoft was delaying the release of Vista, OS X would have taken a large amount of market share from Windows.

Note

Despite Apple's attempts to prevent OS X from running, the OSx86 Project (www.osx86project.org) has information showing how to get OS X installed and running on standard PCs.

Who Controls PC Hardware?

It is clear that Microsoft has always had the majority control over PC software by virtue of its control over the dominant PC OSs, but what about the hardware? It is easy to see that IBM controlled the PC hardware standard up through 1987. After all, IBM invented the core PC motherboard design; the original expansion bus slot architecture (8/16-bit ISA bus); the ROM BIOS interface, serial and parallel port implementations; video card design through VGA and XGA standards; floppy and hard disk interface and controller implementations; power supply designs; keyboard interfaces and designs; the mouse interface; and even the physical shapes (form factors) of everything from the motherboard to the expansion cards, power supplies, and system chassis.

But, to me, the real question is which company has been responsible for creating and inventing newer and more recent PC hardware designs, interfaces, and standards? When I ask people that question, I normally see some hesitation in their responses—some people say Microsoft (but it controls the software, not the hardware), and some say HP or Dell, or they name a few other big-name system manufacturers. Some, however, surmise the correct answer—Intel.

I can see why many people don't immediately realize this; I mean, how many people actually own an Intel-brand PC? No, not just one that says *Intel Inside* on it (which refers only to the system having an Intel processor), but a system that was designed and built by, or even purchased through, Intel. Believe it or not, many people today do have Intel PCs!

Certainly, this does not mean that consumers have purchased their systems from Intel because Intel does not sell complete PCs to end users. You can't currently order a system from Intel, nor can you purchase an Intel-brand system from somebody else. What I am talking about are the major components inside, including especially the motherboard as well as the core of the motherboard—the chipset.

▶▶   See Chapter 4, "Motherboards and Buses," **p. 155**.

▶▶   See Chapter 4's section, "Chipsets," **p. 181**.

How did Intel come to dominate the interior of our PCs? Intel has been the dominant PC processor supplier since IBM chose the Intel 8088 CPU in the original IBM PC in 1981. By controlling the processor, Intel naturally controlled the chips necessary to integrate its processors into system designs. This naturally led Intel into the chipset business. It started its chipset business in 1989 with the 82350 Extended Industry Standard Architecture (EISA) chipset, and by 1993 it had become—along with the debut of the Pentium processor—the largest-volume major motherboard chipset supplier. Now I imagine Intel sitting there, thinking that it makes the processor and all the other chips necessary to produce a motherboard, so why not just eliminate the middleman and make the entire motherboard, too? The answer to this, and a real turning point in the industry, came about in 1994 when Intel became the largest-volume motherboard manufacturer in the world. By 1997, Intel made more motherboards than the next eight largest motherboard manufacturers combined, with sales of more than 30 million boards worth more than $3.6 billion!

After an industry downturn in 2001, Intel concentrated on its core competency of chip making and began using Chinese contract manufacturers such as Foxconn to make Intel-branded motherboards. Since then, contract manufacturers, such as Asus, Foxconn, ECS, MSI, and GIGABYTE, have essentially taken over the market for motherboard manufacturing. Regardless of which company actually manufactures the boards, the main part of any motherboard is the chipset, which contains the majority of the motherboard circuitry. These days, about 80% of PCs on the market use Intel processors, and the majority of those are plugged in to motherboards built using Intel chipsets.

Intel controls the PC hardware standard because it controls the PC motherboard and most of the components on it. It not only makes many of the motherboards being used in systems today, but it also supplies the majority of processors and motherboard chipsets to other motherboard manufacturers.

Intel also has had a primary hand in developing several PC hardware standards, such as the following:

- Universal serial bus (USB) 1.1, 2.0, and 3.0 for connecting peripheral devices.
- Thunderbolt high-speed serial data interface integrating both PCI-Express and DisplayPort over a single cable.
- Peripheral Component Interconnect (PCI) local bus interface.
- Accelerated Graphics Port (AGP) interface for higher-performance video cards than could be implemented via PCI.
- PCI Express (originally known as 3GIO), the interface selected by the PCI Special Interest Group (PCI SIG) to replace both PCI and AGP as the high-performance bus for PCs.
- Industry-standard motherboard form factors such as ATX (including variations such as micro-ATX and FlexATX) and BTX (including variations such as microBTX, nanoBTX, and picoBTX). ATX is still the most popular, and beginning in 1996-1997, it replaced the somewhat long-in-the-tooth IBM-designed Baby-AT form factor, which had been used since the early 1980s.
- Front Panel I/O form factor defining the connectors, cables, and signals used to connect motherboards to the external switches, LEDs, and front ports on industry standard chassis.
- Advanced Host Controller Interface (AHCI) to provide a standard method for controlling Serial ATA (SATA) host adapters.
- HD Audio specification defining the architecture and control of audio controllers on the PCI bus.

- Wireless Display (WiDi) to transmit 1080p HD video and 5.1 surround sound from devices to displays through a wireless connection.
- Desktop Management Interface (DMI) for monitoring system hardware functions.
- Dynamic Power Management Architecture (DPMA), Advanced Power Management (APM), and Advanced Configuration and Power Interface (ACPI) standards for managing power use in the PC.

Intel dominates not only the PC, but the entire worldwide semiconductor industry. According to the sales figures compiled by iSuppli, Intel has nearly twice the sales revenue of the next closest semiconductor company (Samsung) and more than seven times that of competitor AMD (see Table 2.1).

Table 2.1 Top 25 Semiconductor Companies Ranked by 2011 Semiconductor Sales

2011 Rank	Company	2011 Revenue (Millions)	2011 Market Share	2010 Rank	2010 to 2011 Change
1	Intel Corporation[1]	$49,685	15.9%	1	+23.0%
2	Samsung Electronics	$29,242	9.3%	2	+3.0%
3	Texas Instruments[2]	$14,081	4.5%	4	+8.4%
4	Toshiba Semiconductor	$13,362	4.3%	3	+2.7%
5	Renesas Electronics	$11,153	3.6%	5	-6.2%
6	Qualcomm[3]	$10,080	3.2%	9	+39.9%
7	STMicroelectronics	$9,792	3.1%	7	-5.4%
8	Hynix	$8,911	2.8%	6	-14.2%
9	Micron Technology	$7,344	2.3%	8	-17.3%
10	Broadcom	$7,153	2.3%	10	+7.0%
11	Advanced Micro Devices	$6,483	2.1%	12	+2.2%
12	Infineon Technologies	$5,403	1.7%	13	-14.5%
13	Sony	$5,153	1.6%	14	-1.4%
14	Freescale Semiconductor	$4,465	1.4%	16	+2.5%
15	Elpida Memory	$3,854	1.2%	11	-40.2%
16	NXP	$3,838	1.2%	17	-4.7%
17	NVIDIA	$3,672	1.2%	20	+14.9%
18	Marvell Technology Group	$3,448	1.1%	18	-4.4%
19	ON Semiconductor[4]	$3,423	1.1%	26	+49.4%
20	Panasonic Corporation	$3,365	1.1%	15	-32.0%

[1] *Intel Corporation acquired Infineon Technologies wireless division.*
[2] *Texas Instruments acquired National Semiconductor.*
[3] *Qualcomm acquired Atheros Communications.*
[4] *ON Semiconductor acquired Sanyo semiconductor division.*

As you can see by these figures, it is no wonder that a popular industry news website called The Register (www.theregister.com) uses the term "Chipzilla" when referring to the industry giant.

White-Box Systems

Many of the top-selling system manufacturers do design and make their own motherboards, especially for their higher-end systems. According to *Gartner Research*, the top PC manufacturers for the last several years have consistently been names such as Lenovo (formerly IBM), HP, Dell, and Acer. These companies both design and manufacture their own motherboards and purchase existing boards from motherboard manufacturers. In rare cases, they even design their own chips and chipset components for their own boards. Although sales are high for these individual companies, a large segment of the market is what those in the industry call the *white-box systems*.

White-box is the term used by the industry to refer to what would otherwise be called *generic* PCs—that is, PCs assembled from a collection of industry-standard, commercially available components. The white-box designation comes from the fact that historically most of the chassis used by this type of system have been white (or ivory or beige).

The great thing about white-box systems is that they use industry-standard components that are interchangeable. This interchangeability is the key to future upgrades and repairs because it ensures that a plethora of replacement parts will be available to choose from and will be interchangeable. For many years, I have recommended avoiding proprietary systems and recommended more industry-standard white-box systems instead.

Companies selling white-box systems do not usually manufacture the systems; they assemble them. That is, they purchase commercially available motherboards, cases, power supplies, disk drives, peripherals, and so on and assemble and market everything together as complete systems. Some companies such as HP and Dell manufacture some of their own systems as well as assemble some from industry-standard parts. In particular, the HP Pavilion and Dell Dimension lines are composed largely of mainstream systems made with mostly industry-standard parts. PC makers using mostly industry-standard parts also include high-end game system builders such as Alienware (owned by Dell).

Note

There can be exceptions for all these systems; for example, some Dell Dimension XPS systems use proprietary parts such as power supplies. I recommend avoiding such systems, due to future upgrade and repair hassles.

Others using industry-standard components include Acer, CyberPower, Micro Express, and Systemax, but hundreds more could be listed. In overall total volume, this ends up being the largest segment of the PC marketplace today. What is interesting about white-box systems is that, with few exceptions, you and I can purchase the same motherboards and other components that any of the white-box manufacturers can (although we would probably pay more than they do because of the volume discounts they receive). We can assemble a virtually identical white-box system from scratch ourselves, but that is a story for Chapter 19, "Building or Upgrading Systems."

System Types

PCs can be broken down into many categories. I like to break them down in two ways: by the design or width of the processor bus (often called the *front side bus*, [*FSB*]) as well as by the width of the internal registers, which dictates the type of software that can be run.

When a processor reads data, the data moves into the processor via the processor's external data connection. Traditionally, this connection has been a parallel bus; however, in newer chips it is a serialized point-to-point link, transferring fewer bits at a time but at a much higher rate. Older designs often had several components sharing the bus, whereas the newer point-to-point links are exclusively between the processor and the chipset.

▶▶   See Chapter 3's section, "Data I/O Bus," **p. 42**.

Table 2.2 lists all the Intel and AMD x86 and x86-64 processors, their data bus widths, and their internal register sizes.

Table 2.2   Intel and AMD x86 and x86-64 Processors and Their Data Bus/Register Widths

Processor	Data Bus Width	Register Size
8088	8-bit	16-bit
8086	16-bit	16-bit
286	16-bit	16-bit
386SX	16-bit	32-bit
386DX/486/5x86	32-bit	32-bit
Intel/AMD x86 w/FSB	64-bit	32-bit
AMD x86 w/HyperTransport	16-bit	32-bit
AMD x86-64 w/HyperTransport	16-bit	64-bit
Intel x86-64 w/FSB	64-bit	64-bit
Intel x86-64 w/QPI	20-bit	64-bit
Intel x86-64 w/DMI	4-bit	64-bit

FSB = Front Side Bus (parallel bus)
HT = HyperTransport (serial point-to-point)
QPI = QuickPath Interconnect (serial point-to-point)
DMI= Direct Media Interface (serial point-to-point)

A common confusion arises in discussions of processor "widths." Some people take the width to refer to how many bits of data can be read or written at a time, whereas others refer to the size of the internal registers, which control how much data can be operated on at a time. Although many processors have had matching data bus widths and internal register sizes, they are not always the same, which can lead to more confusion. For example, most Pentium processors have 64-bit data bus widths and yet include internal registers that are only 32 bits wide. AMD and Intel processors with x86-64 architecture have 64-bit internal registers and can run in both 32-bit and 64-bit modes. Thus, from a software point of view, there are PC processors capable of running 16-bit, 32-bit, and 64-bit instructions. For backward compatibility, those having 64-bit registers can also run 32-bit and 16-bit instructions, and those with 32-bit registers can run 16-bit instructions. In any case, remember that bus widths and register sizes are completely unrelated. Note that most newer processors use serial buses that are narrow, but also very fast.

▶▶   See Chapter 3's section, "Internal Registers (Internal Data Bus)," **p. 44**.

▶▶   See Chapter 3's section, "Processor Specifications," **p. 35**.

System Components

A modern PC is both simple and complicated. It is simple in the sense that over the years, many of the components used to construct a system have become integrated with other components into fewer and fewer actual parts. It is complicated in the sense that each part in a modern system performs many more functions than did the same types of parts in older systems.

This section briefly examines all the components and peripherals in a modern PC system. Each item is discussed further in later chapters.

The components and peripherals necessary to assemble a basic modern PC system are listed in Table 2.3.

Table 2.3   Basic PC Components

Component	Description
Motherboard	The core of the system. It really is the PC; everything else is connected to it, and it controls everything in the system. Motherboards are covered in Chapter 4.
Processor	Often thought of as the "engine" or "brain" of the computer. It's also called the central processing unit (CPU). Many processors include a graphics processing unit (GPU) as well. Processors are covered in Chapter 3.
Memory (RAM)	The *system memory* is often called *RAM* (random access memory). This is the primary working memory that holds all the programs and data the processor is using at a given time. Memory is discussed in Chapter 6.
Case/chassis	The frame or chassis that houses the motherboard, power supply, disk drives, adapter cards, and any other physical components in the system. The case is covered in Chapter 18.
Power supply	Feeds electrical power to the internal components in the PC. The power supply is covered in detail in Chapter 18.
Hard drive	The primary high-capacity storage media for the system. Hard disk drives are discussed in Chapter 9.
Optical drive	CD (compact disc), DVD (digital versatile disc), and BD (Blu-ray disc) drives are relatively high-capacity, removable-media, optical drives; most newer systems include drives featuring write/rewrite capability. These drives are covered in Chapter 11.
Keyboard	The primary device on a PC that is used by a human to communicate with and control a system. Keyboards are covered in Chapter 15.
Mouse	Although many types of pointing devices are on the market today, the first and most popular device for this purpose is the mouse. The mouse and other pointing devices are discussed in Chapter 15.
Video card*	Contains the GPU (graphics processing unit), which controls the information you see on the monitor. Video cards are covered in Chapter 12.
Monitor	The monitor or display shows information and is controlled by the video card. Monitors are covered in Chapter 12.
Sound card*	Enables the PC to generate complex sounds. Sound cards and speakers are discussed in detail in Chapter 13.
Network*	Most PCs ship with a wired and/or wireless network interface. Network cards are covered in Chapter 17.

Components marked with an asterisk (*) may be integrated into the motherboard or processor on many systems.

Processor Types and Specifications

Microprocessor History

The brain or engine of the PC is the processor—sometimes called *microprocessor* or *central processing unit* (CPU). The CPU performs the system's calculating and processing. The processor is one of the two most expensive components in the system (the other being the video card). In higher-end systems, the processor can cost up to four or more times more than the motherboard it plugs into. Intel is generally credited with creating the first microprocessor in 1971 with the introduction of a chip called the 4004. Today Intel still has control over the processor market, at least for PC systems, although AMD has garnered a respectable market share. For the most part, PC-compatible systems use either Intel processors or Intel-compatible processors from AMD.

Tip

One of the easiest ways to learn about your computer's processor (speed, number of cores, and cache sizes), chipset, and other features is to run the free CPU-Z program. You can download it from www.cpuid.com. Later in this chapter, you will see how CPU-Z works to display system information.

It is interesting to note that the microprocessor had existed for only 10 years prior to the creation of the PC! Intel released the first microprocessor in 1971; IBM created the PC in 1981. Over three decades later, we are still using systems based more or less on the design of that first PC. The processors powering our PCs today are still backward compatible in many ways with the Intel 8088 that IBM selected for the first PC in 1981.

The First Microprocessor

Intel was founded on July 18, 1968 (as N M Electronics) by two ex-Fairchild engineers, Robert Noyce and Gordon Moore. Almost immediately, they changed the company name to Intel and were joined by cofounder Andrew Grove. They had a specific goal: to make semiconductor memory practical and affordable. This was not a given at the time, considering that silicon chip–based memory was at least 100 times more expensive than the magnetic core memory commonly used in those days.

At the time, semiconductor memory was going for about a dollar a bit, whereas core memory was about a penny a bit. Noyce said, "All we had to do was reduce the cost by a factor of a hundred, then we'd have the market; and that's basically what we did."

By 1970, Intel was known as a successful memory chip company, having introduced a 1Kb memory chip, much larger than anything else available at the time. (1Kb equals 1,024 bits, and a byte equals 8 bits. This chip, therefore, stored only 128 bytes—not much by today's standards.) Known as the 1103 dynamic random access memory (DRAM), it became the world's largest-selling semiconductor device by the end of the following year. By this time, Intel had also grown from the core founders and a handful of others to more than 100 employees.

Because of Intel's success in memory chip manufacturing and design, Japanese manufacturer Busicom asked Intel to design a set of chips for a family of high-performance programmable calculators. At the time, all logic chips were custom-designed for each application or product. Because most chips had to be custom-designed specific to a particular application, no one chip could have widespread usage.

Busicom's original design for its calculator called for at least 12 custom chips. Intel engineer Ted Hoff rejected the unwieldy proposal and instead proposed a single-chip, general-purpose logic device that retrieved its application instructions from semiconductor memory. As the core of a four-chip set including read-only memory (ROM), random access memory (RAM), input/output (I/O) and the 4004 processor, a program could control the processor and essentially tailor its function to the task at hand. The chip was generic in nature, meaning it could function in designs other than calculators. Previous chip designs were hard-wired for one purpose, with built-in instructions; this chip would read a variable set of instructions from memory, which would control the function of the chip. The idea was to design, on a single chip, almost an entire computing device that could perform various functions, depending on which instructions it was given.

In April 1970, Intel hired Frederico Faggin to design and create the 4004 logic based on Hoff's proposal. Like the Intel founders, Faggin came from Fairchild Semiconductor, where he had developed the silicon gate technology that would prove essential to good microprocessor design. During the initial logic design and layout process, Faggin had help from Masatoshi Shima, the engineer at Busicom responsible for the calculator design. Shima worked with Faggin until October 1970, after which he returned to Busicom. Faggin received the first finished batch of 4004 chips at closing time one day in January 1971, working alone until early the next morning testing the chip before declaring, "It works!" The 4000 chip family was completed by March 1971 and put into production by June 1971. It is interesting to note that Faggin actually signed the processor die with his initials (F.F.), a tradition that others often carried out in subsequent chip designs.

There was one problem with the new chip: Busicom owned the rights to it. Faggin knew that the product had almost limitless application, bringing intelligence to a host of "dumb" machines. He urged Intel to repurchase the rights to the product. Although Intel founders Gordon Moore and Robert Noyce championed the new chip, others within the company were concerned that the product would distract Intel from its main focus: making memory. They were finally convinced by the fact that every four-chip microcomputer set included two memory chips. As the director of marketing at the time recalled, "Originally, I think we saw it as a way to sell more memories, and we were willing to make the investment on that basis."

Intel offered to return Busicom's $60,000 investment in exchange for the rights to the product. Struggling with financial troubles, the Japanese company agreed. Nobody in the industry at the time, even Intel, realized the significance of this deal, which paved the way for Intel's future in processors.

The result was the November 15, 1971 introduction of the 4-bit Intel 4004 CPU as part of the MCS-4 microcomputer set. The 4004 ran at a maximum clock speed of 740KHz (740,000 cycles per second, or nearly 3/4 of a megahertz), contained 2,300 transistors in an area of only 12 sq. mm (3.5mm×3.5mm), and was built on a 10-micron process, where each transistor was spaced about 10 microns (millionths of a meter) apart. Data was transferred 4 bits at a time, and the maximum addressable memory was only 640 bytes. The chip cost about $200 and delivered about as much computing power as ENIAC, one of the first electronic computers. By comparison, ENIAC relied on 18,000 vacuum tubes packed into 3,000 cubic feet (85 cubic meters) when it was built in 1946.

The 4004 was designed for use in a calculator but proved to be useful for many other functions because of its inherent programmability. For example, the 4004 was used in traffic light controllers, blood analyzers, and even in the NASA Pioneer 10 deep-space probe. You can see more information about the legendary 4004 processor at www.intel4004.com and www.4004.com.

In April 1972, Intel released the 8008 processor, which originally ran at a clock speed of 500KHz (0.5MHz). The 8008 processor contained 3,500 transistors and was built on the same 10-micron process as the previous processor. The big change in the 8008 was that it had an 8-bit data bus, which meant it could move data 8 bits at a time—twice as much as the previous chip. It could also address more memory, up to 16KB. This chip was primarily used in dumb terminals and general-purpose calculators.

The next chip in the lineup was the 8080, introduced in April 1974. The 8080 was conceived by Frederico Faggin and designed by Masatoshi Shima (former Busicom engineer) under Faggin's supervision. Running at a clock rate of 2MHz, the 8080 processor had 10 times the performance of the 8008. The 8080 chip contained 6,000 transistors and was built on a 6-micron process. Similar to the previous chip, the 8080 had an 8-bit data bus, so it could transfer 8 bits of data at a time. The 8080 could address up to 64KB of memory, which was significantly more than the previous chip.

The 8080 helped start the PC revolution because it was the processor chip used in what is generally regarded as the first personal computer, the Altair 8800. The CP/M operating system (OS) was written for the 8080 chip, and the newly founded Microsoft delivered its first product: Microsoft BASIC for the Altair. These initial tools provided the foundation for a revolution in software because thousands of programs were written to run on this platform.

In fact, the 8080 became so popular that it was cloned. Wanting to focus on processors, Frederico Faggin left Intel in 1974 to found Zilog and create a "Super-80" chip, a high-performance, 8080-compatible processor. Masatoshi Shima joined Zilog in April 1975 to help design what became known as the Z80 CPU. The Z80 was released in July 1976 and became one of the most successful processors in history. In fact, it is still being manufactured and sold today.

The Z80 was not pin compatible with the 8080, but combined functions such as the memory interface and RAM refresh circuitry, which enabled cheaper and simpler systems to be designed. The Z80 incorporated a superset of 8080 instructions, meaning it could run all 8080 programs. It also included new instructions and new internal registers; therefore, whereas 8080 software would run on the Z80, software designed for the Z80 would not necessarily run on the older 8080. The Z80 ran initially at 2MHz (later versions ran up to 25MHz), contained 8,500 transistors, and could access 64KB of memory. The Z80 is still used in products such as scientific and graphing calculators and has been developed into faster versions with larger memory addressing space by Zilog and many other vendors. Descendents of the Z80 are currently used in audio processing chips, telecom, and peripheral controllers.

RadioShack selected the Z80 for the TRS-80 Model 1, its first PC. The chip also was the first to be used by many pioneering personal computer systems, including the Osborne and Kaypro machines. Other companies followed, and soon the Z80 was the standard processor for systems running the CP/M OS and the popular software of the day.

Intel released the 8085, its follow-up to the 8080, in March 1976. The 8085 ran at 5MHz and contained 6,500 transistors. It was built on a 3-micron process and incorporated an 8-bit data bus. Even though it predated the Z80 by several months, it never achieved the popularity of the Z80 in personal computer systems. It was, however, used in the IBM System/23 Datamaster, which was the immediate predecessor to the original PC at IBM. The 8085 became most popular as an embedded controller, finding use in scales and other computerized equipment.

Along different architectural lines, MOS Technologies introduced the 6502 in 1976. Several ex-Motorola engineers who had worked on Motorola's first processor, the 6800, designed this chip. The 6502 was an 8-bit processor like the 8080, but it sold for around $25, whereas the 8080 cost about $300 when it was introduced. The price appealed to Steve Wozniak, who placed the chip in his Apple I and Apple II/II+ designs. The chip was also used in systems by Commodore and other system manufacturers. The 6502 and its successors were used in game consoles, including the original Nintendo Entertainment System (NES), among others. Motorola went on to create the 68000 series, which became the basis for the original line of Apple Macintosh computers. The second-generation Macs used the PowerPC chip, also by Motorola and a successor to the 68000 series. Of course, the current Macs have adopted PC architecture, using the same processors, chipsets, and other components as PCs.

In the early 1980s, I had a system containing both a MOS Technologies 6502 and a Zilog Z80. It was a 1MHz (yes, that's one megahertz!) 6502-based Apple II+system with a Microsoft Softcard (Z80 card) plugged into one of the slots. The Softcard contained a 2MHz Z80 processor, which enabled me to run both Apple and CP/M software on the system.

All these previous chips set the stage for the first PC processors. Intel introduced the 8086 in June 1978. The 8086 chip brought with it the original x86 instruction set that is still present in current x86-compatible chips such as the Core i Series and AMD FX. However, it was a reduced-feature version of the 8086, the Intel 8088, that became the processor used by the first IBM PC.

To learn more about the 8086 and 8088, see the section, "P1 (086) Processors."

PC Processor Evolution

Since the first PC came out in 1981, PC processor evolution has concentrated on four main areas:

- Increasing the transistor count and density
- Increasing the clock cycling speeds
- Increasing the size of internal registers (bits)
- Increasing the number of cores in a single chip

Intel introduced the 286 chip in 1982. With 134,000 transistors, it provided about three times the performance of other 16-bit processors of the time. Featuring on-chip memory management, the 286 also offered software compatibility with its predecessors. This revolutionary chip was first used in IBM's benchmark PC-AT, the system upon which all modern PCs are based.

In 1985 came the Intel 386 processor. With a new 32-bit architecture and 275,000 transistors, the chip could perform more than five million instructions per second (MIPS). Compaq's Deskpro 386 was the first PC based on the new microprocessor.

Next out of the gate was the Intel 486 processor in 1989. The 486 had 1.2 million transistors and the first built-in math coprocessor. It was some 50 times faster than the original 4004, equaling the performance of some mainframe computers.

Then, in 1993, Intel introduced the first P5 family (586) processor, called the Pentium, setting new performance standards with several times the performance of the previous 486 processor. The Pentium processor used 3.1 million transistors to perform up to 90 MIPS—now up to about 1,500 times the speed of the original 4004.

Note

Intel's change from using numbers (386/486) to names (Pentium/Pentium Pro) for its processors was based on the fact that it could not secure a registered trademark on a number and therefore could not prevent its competitors from using those same numbers on clone chip designs.

The first processor in the P6 (686) family, called the Pentium Pro processor, was introduced in 1995. With 5.5 million transistors, it was the first to be packaged with a second die containing high-speed L2 memory cache to accelerate performance.

Intel revised the original P6 (686/Pentium Pro) and introduced the Pentium II processor in May 1997. Pentium II processors had 7.5 million transistors packed into a cartridge rather than a conventional chip, allowing the L2 cache chips to be attached directly on the module. The Pentium II family was augmented in April 1998, with both the low-cost Celeron processor for basic PCs and the high-end Pentium II Xeon processor for servers and workstations. Intel followed with the Pentium III in 1999, essentially a Pentium II with Streaming SIMD Extensions (SSE) added.

Around the time the Pentium was establishing its dominance, AMD acquired NexGen, which had been working on its Nx686 processor. AMD incorporated that design along with a Pentium interface into what would be called the AMD K6. The K6 was both hardware and software compatible with the Pentium, meaning it plugged in to the same Socket 7 and could run the same programs. As Intel dropped its Pentium in favor of the more expensive Pentium II and III, AMD continued making faster versions of the K6 and made huge inroads in the low-end PC market.

In 1998, Intel became the first to integrate L2 cache directly on the processor die (running at the full speed of the processor core), dramatically increasing performance. This was first done on the second-generation Celeron processor (based on the Pentium II core), as well as the Pentium IIPE (performance-enhanced) chip used only in laptop systems. The first high-end desktop PC chip with on-die full-core speed L2 cache was the second-generation (Coppermine core) Pentium III introduced in late 1999. After this, all major processor manufacturers began integrating L2 (and even L3) cache on the processor die, a trend that continues today.

AMD introduced the Athlon in 1999 to compete with Intel head to head in the high-end desktop PC market. The Athlon became successful, and it seemed for the first time that Intel had some real competition in the higher-end systems. In hindsight, the success of the Athlon might be easy to see, but at the time it was introduced, its success was anything but assured. Unlike the previous K6 chips, which were both hardware and software compatible with Intel processors, the Athlon was only software compatible and required a motherboard with an Athlon supporting chipset and processor socket.

The year 2000 saw a significant milestone when both Intel and AMD crossed the 1GHz barrier, a speed that many thought could never be accomplished. In 2001, Intel introduced a Pentium 4 version running at 2GHz, the first PC processor to achieve that speed. November 15, 2001 marked the 30th anniversary of the microprocessor, and in those 30 years processor speed had increased more than 18,500 times (from 0.108MHz to 2GHz). AMD also introduced the Athlon XP, based on its newer Palomino core, as well as the Athlon MP, designed for multiprocessor server systems.

In 2002, Intel released a Pentium 4 version running at 3.06GHz, the first PC processor to break the 3GHz barrier, and the first to feature Intel's Hyper-Threading (HT) Technology, which turns the processor into a virtual dual-processor configuration. By running two application threads at the same time, HT-enabled processors can perform tasks at speeds 25—40% faster than non-HT-enabled processors can. This encouraged programmers to write multithreaded applications, which would prepare them for when true multicore processors would be released a few years later.

In 2003, AMD released the first 64-bit PC processor: the Athlon 64 (previously code-named ClawHammer, or K8), which incorporated AMD-defined x86-64 64-bit extensions to the IA-32 architecture typified by the Athlon, Pentium 4, and earlier processors. That year Intel also released the Pentium 4 Extreme Edition, the first consumer-level processor to incorporate L3 cache. The whopping 2MB of cache added greatly to the transistor count as well as performance. In 2004, Intel followed AMD by adding the AMD-defined x86-64 extensions to the Pentium 4.

In 2005, both Intel and AMD released their first dual-core processors, basically integrating two processors into a single chip. Although boards supporting two or more processors had been commonly used in network servers for many years prior, this brought dual-CPU capabilities in an affordable package to standard PCs. Rather than attempting to increase clock rates, as has been done in the past, adding processing power by integrating two or more processors into a single chip enables future processors to perform more work with fewer bottlenecks and with a reduction in both power consumption and heat production.

In 2006, Intel released a new processor family called the Core 2, based on an architecture that came mostly from previous mobile Pentium M/Core duo processors. The Core 2 was released in a dual-core version first, followed by a quad-core version (combining two dual-core die in a single package) later in the year. In 2007, AMD released the Phenom, which was the first quad-core PC processor with all four cores on a single die. In 2008, Intel released the Core i Series (Nehalem) processors, which are single-die quad-core chips with HT (appearing as eight cores to the OS) that include integrated memory and optional video controllers. Intel also introduced its Atom line of processors, which support x86 instructions but require far less power than conventional processors. Atom was first used in netbooks, but has since also become widely used in tablets and smartphones.

AMD also released its Phenom II series of multicore (up to six-core) processors with support for both DDR2 and DDR3 memory in 2008. In 2011, Intel released the "Sandy Bridge" second generation of Core i-series processors, including four-core and six-core processors with HT Technology, supporting up to 12 execution threads. Some models include an on-die video controller that permits dynamic switching of resources between GPU and CPU (TurboBoost 2.0), depending on the type of processing being performed. Intel also introduced a 3D-fabrication process at 22nm for processors: the 3D Tri-Gate transistor. In 2011, AMD introduced its Fusion processors (APUs), which incorporate Radeon graphics, low power consumption, and acceleration for video, photo, and web operations.

In 2012, Intel released the third-generation Core i-Series processors (Ivy Bridge) and complementing Panther Point chipsets. Ivy Bridge uses the aforementioned 3D Tri-Gate transistor technology Intel developed in 2011. Noted advancements also include integrated USB 3.0 support and PCI Express 3.0 support. AMD released its Socket AM3+ FX-8000 (eight-core), FX-6000 (six-core), and FX-4000 (four-core) processors, as well as "Trinity" APUs (improved versions of its original desktop APUs). AMD's chipsets for these new processors also include integrated support for USB 3.0. 2012 also saw the development of a tablet-optimized version of Windows, Windows RT, which uses RISC-based ARM processors. ARM processors are produced under license by many companies and are also used in non-Windows tablets and smartphones.

Note

Intel began to develop mobile versions of its processors in the early 1990s with the development of the 386 processor. Both Intel and AMD have developed mobile versions of almost all of their processors.

Although a mobile processor may have the same code name, a similar model number, and be based on the same general architecture as its desktop counterpart, it might feature lower clock speeds, smaller cache sizes, and different implementations of some features. The processor features for a particular processor family discussed in this chapter apply to desktop processors. For more information about mobile processors in a given processor family, see the Intel or AMD websites.

16-Bit to 64-Bit Architecture Evolution

The first major change in processor architecture was the move from the 16-bit internal architecture of the 286 and earlier processors to the 32-bit internal architecture of the 386 and later chips, which Intel calls IA-32 (Intel Architecture, 32-bit). Intel's 32-bit architecture dates to 1985. It took a full 10 years for both a partial 32-bit mainstream OS (Windows 95) as well as a full 32-bit OS requiring 32-bit drivers (Windows NT) to surface, and it took another 6 years for the mainstream to shift to a fully 32-bit environment for the OS and drivers (Windows XP). That's a total of 16 years from the release of 32-bit computing hardware to the full adoption of 32-bit computing in the mainstream with supporting software. I'm sure you can appreciate that 16 years is a lifetime in technology.

Now we are near the end of another major architectural jump, as Intel, AMD, and Microsoft have almost completely shifted from 32-bit to 64-bit architectures. In 2001, Intel had introduced the IA-64 (Intel Architecture, 64-bit) in the form of the Itanium and Itanium 2 processors, but this standard was something completely new and not an extension of the existing 32-bit technology. IA-64 was announced in 1994 as a CPU development project with Intel and HP (code-named Merced), and the first technical details were made available in October 1997.

The fact that the IA-64 architecture is not an extension of IA-32 but is instead a new and completely different architecture was fine for non-PC environments such as servers (for which IA-64 was designed), but the PC market has always hinged on backward compatibility. Even though emulating IA-32 within IA-64 is possible, such emulation and support is slow.

With the door now open, AMD seized this opportunity to develop 64-bit extensions to IA-32, which it calls AMD64 (originally known as x86-64). Intel eventually released its own set of 64-bit extensions, which it calls EM64T or IA-32e mode. As it turns out, the Intel extensions are almost identical to the AMD extensions, meaning they are software compatible. It seemed for the first time that Intel had unarguably followed AMD's lead in the development of PC architecture.

However, AMD and Intel's 64-bit processor could only run in 32-bit mode on existing operating systems. To make 64-bit computing a reality, 64-bit OSs and 64-bit drivers are also needed. Microsoft began providing trial versions of Windows XP Professional x64 Edition (which supports AMD64 and EM64T) in April 2005, but it wasn't until the release of Windows Vista x64 in 2007 that 64-bit computing would begin to go mainstream. Initially, the lack of 64-bit drivers was a problem, but by the release of Windows 7 x64 in 2009, most device manufacturers were providing both 32-bit and 64-bit drivers for virtually all new devices. Linux is also available in 64-bit versions, making the move to 64-bit computing possible for non-Windows environments as well.

Another important development is the introduction of multicore processors from both Intel and AMD. Current multicore desktop processors from Intel and AMD have up to eight full CPU cores operating off of one CPU package—in essence, enabling a single processor to perform the work of multiple processors. Although multicore processors don't make games that use single execution threads play faster, multicore processors, like multiple single-core processors, split up the workload caused by running multiple applications at the same time. If you've ever tried to scan for malware while simultaneously checking email or running another application, you've probably seen how running multiple applications can bring even the fastest processor to its knees. With multicore processors available from both Intel and AMD, your ability to get more work done in less time by multitasking is greatly enhanced. A growing number of applications are now optimized for multicore processors; these applications are known as *multithreaded applications*. Multicore processors also support 64-bit extensions, enabling you to enjoy both multicore and 64-bit computing's advantages.

PCs have certainly come a long way. The original 8088 processor used in the first PC contained 29,000 transistors and ran at 4.77MHz. Compare that to today's chips: The AMD eight-core FX-8000 has an estimated 1.2 billion transistors and runs at up to 3.6GHz standard speed (4.2GHz in Turbo Core mode), and high-end six-core Intel Core i7 models have around 2.27 billion transistors and run at up to 3.4GHz or faster. As multicore processors with large integrated caches continue to be used in designs, look for transistor counts and real-world performance to continue to increase well beyond a billion transistors. And the progress won't stop there, because according to Moore's Law, processing speed and transistor counts are doubling every 1.5–2 years.

Processor Specifications

Many confusing specifications often are quoted in discussions of processors. The following sections discuss some of these specifications, including the data bus, address bus, and speed. The next section includes a table that lists the specifications of virtually all PC processors.

Processors can be identified by two main parameters: how wide they are and how fast they are. The speed of a processor is a fairly simple concept. Speed is counted in megahertz (MHz) and gigahertz (GHz), which means millions and billions, respectively, of cycles per second—and faster is better! The width of a processor is a little more complicated to discuss because three main specifications in a processor are expressed in width:

- Data (I/O) bus (also called FSB or front side bus)
- Address bus
- Internal registers

Note that the processor data bus is also called the *front side bus* (FSB), *processor side bus* (PSB), or just *CPU bus*. All these terms refer to the bus that is between the CPU and the main chipset component (North Bridge or Memory Controller Hub). Intel uses the FSB or PSB terminology, whereas AMD uses

Table 3.1   Intel Processor Specifications

Processor	Cores	Process (Micron)	Clock	Voltage	Registers	Data Bus	Max. Memory
8088	1	3.0	1x	5V	16-bit	8-bit	1MB
8086	1	3.0	1x	5V	16-bit	16-bit	1MB
286	1	1.5	1x	5V	16-bit	16-bit	16MB
386SX	1	1.5, 1.0	1x	5V	32-bit	16-bit	16MB
386SL	1	1.0	1x	3.3V	32-bit	16-bit	16MB
386DX	1	1.5, 1.0	1x	5V	32-bit	32-bit	4GB
486SX	1	1.0, 0.8	1x	5V	32-bit	32-bit	4GB
486SX2	1	0.8	2x	5V	32-bit	32-bit	4GB
487SX	1	1.0	1x	5V	32-bit	32-bit	4GB
486DX	1	1.0, 0.8	1x	5V	32-bit	32-bit	4GB
486SL[2]	1	0.8	1x	3.3V	32-bit	32-bit	4GB
486DX2	1	0.8	2x	5V	32-bit	32-bit	4GB
486DX4	1	0.6	2x+	3.3V	32-bit	32-bit	4GB
486 Pentium OD	1	0.6	2.5x	5V	32-bit	32-bit	4GB
Pentium 60/66	1	0.8	1x	5V	32-bit	64-bit	4GB
Pentium 75-200	1	0.6, 0.35	1.5x+	3.5V	32-bit	64-bit	4GB
Pentium MMX	1	0.35, 0.25	1.5x+	2.8V	32-bit	64-bit	4GB
Pentium Pro	1	0.35	2x+	3.3V	32-bit	64-bit	64GB
Pentium II (Klamath)	1	0.35	>2x	2.8V	32-bit	64-bit	64GB
Pentium II (Deschutes)	1	0.35	>2x	2.0V	32-bit	64-bit	64GB
Pentium II PE (Dixon)	1	0.25	>2x	1.6V	32-bit	64-bit	64GB
Celeron (Covington)	1	0.25	>2x	2.8V	32-bit	64-bit	64GB
Celeron A (Mendocino)	1	0.25	>2x	2V	32-bit	64-bit	64GB

only FSB. I usually just like to say *CPU bus* in conversation or when speaking during my training seminars, because that is the least confusing of the terms while also being completely accurate.

The number of bits a processor is designated can be confusing. Most modern processors have 64-bit (or wider) data buses; however, that does not mean they are classified as 64-bit processors. Processors from the 386 through the Pentium 4 and Athlon XP are considered 32-bit processors because their internal registers are 32 bits wide, although their data I/O buses are 64 bits wide and their address buses are 36 bits wide (both wider than their predecessors, the Pentium and K6 processors). Processors since the Intel Core 2 series and the AMD Athlon 64 are considered 64-bit processors because their internal registers are 64 bits wide.

First, I present some tables describing the differences in specifications between all the PC processors; then the following sections will explain the specifications in more detail. Refer to these tables as you read about the various processor specifications, and the information in the tables will become clearer.

Tables 3.1 and 3.2 list the most significant processors from Intel and AMD.

L1 Cache	L2 Cache	L3 Cache	L2/L3 Cache Speed	Multimedia Instructions	Transistors	Introduced
—	—	—	—	—	29,000	June 1979
—	—	—	—	—	29,000	June 1978
—	—	—	—	—	134,000	Feb. 1982
—	—	—	Bus	—	275,000	June 1988
0KB[1]	—	—	Bus	—	855,000	Oct. 1990
—	—	—	Bus	—	275,000	Oct. 1985
8KB	—	—	Bus	—	1.185M	Apr. 1991
8KB	—	—	Bus	—	1.185M	Apr. 1994
8KB	—	—	Bus	—	1.2M	Apr. 1991
8KB	—	—	Bus	—	1.2M	Apr. 1989
8KB	—	—	Bus	—	1.4M	Nov. 1992
8KB	—	—	Bus	—	1.2M	Mar. 1992
16KB	—	—	Bus	—	1.6M	Feb. 1994
2x16KB	—	—	Bus	—	3.1M	Jan. 1995
2x8KB	—	—	Bus	—	3.1M	Mar. 1993
2x8KB	—	—	Bus	—	3.3M	Mar. 1994
2x16KB	—	—	Bus	MMX	4.5M	Jan. 1997
2x8KB	256KB, 512KB, 1MB	—	Core	—	5.5M	Nov. 1995
2x16KB	512KB	—	1/2 core	MMX	7.5M	May 1997
2x16KB	512KB	—	1/2 core	MMX	7.5M	May 1997
2x16KB	256KB	—	Core	MMX	27.4M	Jan. 1999
2x16KB	0KB	—	—	MMX	7.5M	Apr. 1998
2x16KB	128KB	—	Core	MMX	19M	Aug. 1998

Table 3.1   Continued

Processor	Cores	Process (Micron)	Clock	Voltage	Registers	Data Bus	Max. Memory
Celeron III (Coppermine)	1	0.18	>2x	1.75V	32-bit	64-bit	64GB
Celeron III (Tualatin)	1	0.13	>2x	1.5V	32-bit	64-bit	64GB
Pentium III (Katmai)	1	0.25	>2x	2V	32-bit	64-bit	64GB
Pentium III (Coppermine)	1	0.18	>2x	1.75V	32-bit	64-bit	64GB
Pentium III (Tualatin)	1	0.13	>2x	1.45V	32-bit	64-bit	64GB
Celeron 4 (Willamette)	1	0.18	>2x	1.75V	32-bit	64-bit	64GB
Pentium 4 (Willamette)	1	0.18	>2x	1.75V	32-bit	64-bit	64GB
Pentium 4A (Northwood)	1	0.13	>2x	1.5V	32-bit	64-bit	64GB
Pentium 4EE (Prestonia)	1	0.13	>2x	1.5V	32-bit	64-bit	64GB
Pentium 4E (Prescott)	1	0.09	>2x	1.4V	32-bit	64-bit	64GB
Celeron D (Prescott)	1	0.09	>2x	1.4V	64-bit	64-bit	1TB
Pentium D (Smithfield)	2	0.09	>2x	1.4V	64-bit	64-bit	1TB
Pentium D (Presler)	2	0.065	>2x	1.4V	64-bit	64-bit	1TB
Pentium M (Banias)	1	0.13	>2x	1.5V	32-bit	64-bit	64GB
Pentium M (Dothan)	1	0.09	>2x	1.3V	32-bit	64-bit	64GB
Core Duo (Yonah)	2	0.09	>2x	1.3V	32-bit	64-bit	64GB
Core 2 Duo (Conroe)	2	0.065	>2x	1.3V	64-bit	64-bit	1TB
Core 2 Quad (Kentsfield)	4	0.065	>2x	1.3V	64-bit	64-bit	1TB
Core 2 Duo (Wolfdale)	2	0.045	>2x	1.3V	64-bit	64-bit	1TB
Core 2 Quad (Yorkfield)	4	0.045	>2x	1.3V	64-bit	64-bit	1TB
Core i7 (Bloomfield)	4	0.045	>2x	1.4V	64-bit	64-bit	24GB
Core i5/i7 (Lynnfield)	4	0.045	>2x	1.4V	64-bit	64-bit	16GB
Core i3/i5 (Clarkdale)	2	0.032	>2x	1.4V	64-bit	64-bit	16GB
Core i7 (Gulftown)	6	0.045	>2x	1.4V	64-bit	64-bit	24GB
Core i7 (Sandy Bridge)	4	0.032	>2x	1.4V	64-bit	64-bit	8–32GB
Core i5 (Sandy Bridge)	4	0.032	>2x	1.4V	64-bit	64-bit	32GB
Core i3/i5 (Sandy Bridge)	2	0.032	>2x	1.4V	64-bit	64-bit	8-32GB
Atom	1	0.045	>2x	0.9V	64-bit	64-bit	2GB
Core i7 (Sandy Bridge-E)	4–6****	0.032	>2x	1.4V	64-bit	64-bit	64GB
Core i7 (Ivy Bridge)	4	0.022	>2x	1.4V	64-bit	64-bit	32GB
Core i5 (Ivy Bridge)	4	0.022	>2x	1.4V	64-bit	64-bit	32GB
Core i3/i5 (Ivy Bridge)	2	0.022	>2x	1.4V	64-bit	64-bit	32GB

* Dual-core and dual-core with HT Technology have lower counts.

** Instruction Cache Data Cache is 24KB.

***10MB (Stepping M1); 12–15MB (Stepping C1-C2, varies by model).

****Six-core (Stepping C1-C2 has 2.27 billion transistors); four-core (Stepping M) has 1.27 billion transistors.

L1 Cache	L2 Cache	L3 Cache	L2/L3 Cache Speed	Multimedia Instructions	Transistors	Introduced
2x16KB	128KB	—	Core	SSE	28.1M	Feb. 2000
2x16KB	256KB	—	Core	SSE	44M	Oct. 2001
2x16KB	512KB	—	1/2 core	SSE	9.5M	Feb. 1999
2x16KB	256KB	—	Core	SSE	28.1M	Oct. 1999
2x16KB	512KB	—	Core	SSE	44M	June 2001
2x16KB	128KB	—	Core	SSE2	42M	May 2002
>16KB	256KB	—	Core	SSE2	42M	Nov. 2000
>16KB	512KB	—	Core	SSE2	55M	Jan. 2002
>16KB	512KB	2MB	Core	SSE2	178M	Nov. 2003
>16KB	1MB	—	Core	SSE3	125M	Feb. 2004
>16KB	256KB	—	Core	SSE3	125M	June 2004
>32KB	1MB per core	—	Core	SSE3	230M	May 2005
>32KB	2MB per core	—	Core	SSE3	376M	Dec. 2005
>32KB	1MB	—	Core	SSE2	77M	Mar. 2003
>32KB	2MB	—	Core	SSE2	144M	May 2004
>64KB	1MB per core	—	Core	SSE3	151M	Jan. 2006
>64KB	2–4MBper core	—	Core	SSSE3	291M	July 2006
>64KB	4MB per core	—	Core	SSSE3	582M	Dec. 2006
>64KB	3–6MB per core	—	Core	SSSE4.1	410M	Jan. 2008
>64KB	2–6MB per core	—	Core	SSSE4.1	820M	Mar. 2008
>64KB	256KB per core	8MB	Core	SSE4.2	731M	Nov. '08
>64KB	256KB per core	8MB	Core	SSE4.2	774M	Sept. '09
>64KB	256KB per core	4MB	Core	SSE4.2	560M	Jan. '10
>64KB	256KB per core	12MB	Core	SSE4.2	1.17T	March '10
>64KB	256KB per core	8MB	Core	SSE4.2, AVX	995M	Jan. '11
>64KB	256KB per core	6MB	Core	SSE4.2, AVX	624M	Jan. '11
>64KB	256KB per core	3MB	Core	SSE4.2, AVX	504M	Jan. '11
32KB**	512KB	N/A	Core	SSE3, SSSE3	47M	June '08
>64KB	256KB per core	10–15MB***	Core	SSE4.2, AVX	****	Jan. '11
>64KB	256KB per core	8MB	Core	SSE4.2, AVX	1.4B	April '12
>64KB	256KB per core	6MB	Core	SSE4.2, AVX	1.4	April '12
>64KB	256KB per core	3MB	Core	SSE4.2, AVX	*****	June '12

*****Not disclosed by Intel.

1 The 386SL contains an integral-cache controller, but the cache memory must be provided outside the chip.

2 Intel later marketed SL Enhanced versions of the SX, DX, and DX2 processors. These processors were available in both 5V and 3.3V versions and included power management capabilities.

Table 3.2   AMD Processor Specifications

Processor	Cores	Process (Micron)	Clock	Voltage	Registers	Data Bus	Max. Memory
AMD K5	1	0.35	1.5x+	3.5V	32-bit	64-bit	4GB
AMD K6	1	0.35	2.5x+	3.2V	32-bit	64-bit	4GB
AMD K6-2	1	0.25	2.5x+	2.4V	32-bit	64-bit	4GB
AMD K6-3	1	0.25	>2x	2.4V	32-bit	64-bit	4GB
AMD Athlon	1	0.25	>2x	1.8V	32-bit	64-bit	4GB
AMD Duron	1	0.18	>2x	1.8V	32-bit	64-bit	4GB
AMD Athlon (Thunderbird)	1	0.18	>2x	1.8V	32-bit	64-bit	4GB
AMD Athlon XP (Palomino)	1	0.18	>2x	1.8V	32-bit	64-bit	4GB
AMD Athlon XP	1	0.13	>2x	1.8V	32-bit	64-bit	4GB
AMD Athlon XP (Barton)	1	0.13	>2x	1.65V	32-bit	64-bit	4GB
Athlon 64 (ClawHammer/Winchester)	1	0.13, 0.09	>2x	1.5V	64-bit	16-bit	1TB
Athlon 64 FX (SledgeHammer)	1	0.13	>2x	1.5V	64-bit	16-bit	1TB
Athlon 64 X2 (Manchester)	2	0.09	>2x	1.4V	64-bit	16-bit	1TB per core
Athlon 64 X2 (Toledo)	2	0.09	>2x	1.4V	64-bit	16-bit	1TB per core
Athlon 64 X2 (Windsor)	2	0.09	>2x	1.4V	64-bit	16-bit	1TB per core
Athlon X2, 64 X2 (Brisbane)	2	0.065	>2x	1.35V	64-bit	16-bit	1TB per core
Phenom X3/X4 (Toliman/Agena)	3/4	0.065	>2x	1.4V	64-bit	16-bit	1TB per core
Athlon X2 (Kuma)	2	0.065	>2x	1.3V	64-bit	16-bit	1TB per core
Phenom II X2/X3/X4 (Callisto/Heka/Deneb)	2/3/4	0.045	>2x	1.4V	64-bit	16-bit	1TB per core
Athlon II X2 (Regor)	2	0.045	>2x	1.4V	64-bit	16-bit	16GB per core
Phenom II X6 (Thuban)	6	0.045	>2x	1.375–1.4V	64-bit	64-bit	1TB

L1 Cache	L2 Cache	L3 Cache	L2/L3 Cache Speed	Multimedia Instructions	Transistors	Introduced
16+8KB	—	—	Bus	—	4.3M	March 1996
2x32KB	—	—	Bus	MMX	8.8M	Apr. 1997
2x32KB	—	—	Bus	3DNow!	9.3M	May 1998
2x32KB	256KB	—	Core	3DNow!	21.3M	Feb. 1999
2x64KB	512KB	—	1/2-1/3 core	Enh. 3DNow!	22M	June 1999
2x64KB	64KB	—	Core^3	Enh. 3DNow!	25M	June 2000
2x64KB	256KB	—	Core	Enh. 3DNow!	37M	June 2000
2x64KB	256KB	—	Core	3DNow! Pro	37.5M	Oct. 2001
2x64KB	256KB	—	Core	3DNow! Pro	37.2M	June 2002 (Thoroughbred)
2x64KB	512KB	—	Core	3DNow! Pro	54.3M	Feb. 2003
2x64KB	1MB	—	Core	3DNow! Pro (SSE3	105.9M for 0.09 process)	Sept. 2003
2x64KB	1MB	—	Core	3DNow! Pro	105.9M	Sept. 2003
2x64KB per core	256KB/512KB	—	Core	SSE3	154M	June 2005
2x64KB per core	512KB/1MB	—	Core	SSE3	233M	June 2005
2x64KB per core	512KB/1MB	—	Core	SSE3	233.2M	May 2005
2x64KB per core	512KB	—	Core	SSE3	154M	Dec. 2006
2x64KB	512KB	2MB per core	Core	SSE4a	450M	Nov. 2007
2x64KB per core	512KB	MB	Core 2	SSE4a	450M	Dec. 2008
2x64KB per core	512KB	6MB	Core	SSE4a	758M	Jan. 2009
2x64KB	1MB per core	—	Core	SSE4a	234M	June 2009
>64KB	512KB per core	6GB	Core	SSE4.2a	904M	April 2010

Table 3.2 **Continued**

CPU	Cores	Proc	Clk	Vlt	Reg	Dbus	MaxRAM	L1
FX "Zambesi"	8/6/4	0.032	>2x	0.825–1.475	64-bit	64-bit	1 TB	32KB I/16K D per core
A "Llano"	4/2	0.032	>2x	0.9125–1.4125	64-bit	64-bit	1 TB	64KB I/ 64KB D per core
FX "Vishera"	8/6/4	0.032	>2x	0.825–1.475	64-bit	64-bit	1 TB	32KB I/16K D per core
A "Trinity"	8/6/4	0.032	>2x	0.825–1.475	64-bit	64-bit	1 TB	128K/I, 64KB/D

Data I/O Bus

Two of the more important features of a processor are the speed and width of its external data bus. These define the rate at which data can be moved into or out of the processor.

Data in a computer is sent as digital information in which certain voltages or voltage transitions occurring within specific time intervals represent data as 1s and 0s. You can increase the amount of data being sent (called *bandwidth*) by increasing either the cycling time or the number of bits being sent at a time, or both. Over the years, processor data buses have gone from 8 bits wide to 64 bits wide. The more wires you have, the more individual bits you can send in the same interval. All modern processors from the original Pentium and Athlon through the latest Core i7, AMD FX 83xx series, and even the Itanium series have a 64-bit (8-byte)-wide data bus. Therefore, they can transfer 64 bits of data at a time to and from the motherboard chipset or system memory.

A good way to understand this flow of information is to consider a highway and the traffic it carries. If a highway has only one lane for each direction of travel, only one car at a time can move in a certain direction. If you want to increase the traffic flow (move more cars in a given time), you can either increase the speed of the cars (shortening the interval between them), add more lanes, or both.

As processors evolved, more lanes were added, up to a point. You can think of an 8-bit chip as being a single-lane highway because 1 byte flows through at a time. (1 byte equals 8 individual bits.) The 16-bit chip, with 2 bytes flowing at a time, resembles a two-lane highway. You might have four lanes in each direction to move a large number of automobiles; this structure corresponds to a 32-bit data bus, which has the capability to move 4 bytes of information at a time. Taking this further, a 64-bit data bus is like having an eight-lane highway moving data in and out of the chip.

After 64-bit-wide buses were reached, chip designers found that they couldn't increase speed further, because it was too hard to synchronize all 64 bits. It was discovered that by going back to fewer lanes, it was possible to increase the speed of the bits (that is, shorten the cycle time) such that even greater bandwidths were possible. Because of this, many newer processors have only 4-bit or 16-bit-wide data buses, yet they have higher bandwidths than the 64-bit buses they replaced.

Another improvement in newer processors is the use of multiple separate buses for different tasks. Traditional processor design had all the data going through a single bus, whereas newer processors have separate physical buses for data to and from the chipset, memory, and graphics card slot(s).

Address Bus

The *address bus* is the set of wires that carry the addressing information used to describe the memory location to which the data is being sent or from which the data is being retrieved. As with the data

L2	L3	Speed	MMX	Trans	Date
2MB per 2-core module	8MB	Core	SSE 4a/4.2	~2B	Oct. 2011
1MB per core	N/A	Core	SSE 4a/4.2, AVX, AES, FMA	1.45B (4vcore) 758M (2 core)	June 2011
1MB per core	8MB (8.6 core) 4MB (4 core)	Core	SSE 4a/4.2	1.2B	Oct. 2012
1MB per core (4,3 core) 512MB per core (2 core)	8MB (4MB on four-core version)	Core	SSE 4a/4.2, AVX, AES, FMA	1.38B	Oct. 2012

bus, each wire in an address bus carries a single bit of information. This single bit is a single digit in the address. The more wires (digits) used in calculating these addresses, the greater the total number of address locations. The size (or width) of the address bus indicates the maximum amount of RAM a chip can address.

The highway analogy in the previous section, "Data I/O Bus," can show how the address bus fits in. If the data bus is the highway and the size of the data bus is equivalent to the number of lanes, the address bus relates to the house number or street address. The size of the address bus is equivalent to the number of digits in the house address number. For example, if you live on a street in which the address is limited to a two-digit (base 10) number, no more than 100 distinct addresses (00–99) can exist for that street (10^2). Add another digit, and the number of available addresses increases to 1,000 (000–999), or 10^3.

Computers use the binary (base 2) numbering system, so a two-digit number provides only four unique addresses (00, 01, 10, and 11), calculated as 2^2. A three-digit number provides only eight addresses (000–111), which is 2^3. For example, the 8086 and 8088 processors use a 20-bit address bus that calculates a maximum of 2^{20}, or 1,048,576 bytes (1MB), of address locations. Table 3.3 describes the memory-addressing capabilities of processors.

Table 3.3 Processor Physical Memory-Addressing Capabilities

Processor Family	Address Bus	Bytes	KiB	MiB	GiB	TiB
8088, 8086	20-bit	1,048,576	1,024	1	—	—
86, 386SX	24-bit	16,777,216	16,384	16	—	—
386DX, 486, Pentium, K6, Athlon	32-bit	4,294,967,296	4,194,304	4,096	4	—
Pentium w/PAE	36-bit	68,719,476,736	67,108,864	65,536	64	—
64-bit AMD/Intel	40-bit	1,099,511,627,776	1,073,741,824	1,048,576	1,024	1

PAE = Physical Address Extension (supported by Server OS only)

KiB = Kibibytes

MiB = Mebibytes

TiB = Tebibytes

See http://physics.nist.gov/cuu/Units/binary.html for more information on prefixes for binary multiples.

The data bus and address bus are independent, and chip designers can use whatever size they want for each. Usually, however, chips with larger data buses have larger address buses. The sizes of the buses can provide important information about a chip's relative power, measured in two important ways. The size of the data bus indicates the chip's information-moving capability, and the size of the address bus tells you how much memory the chip can handle.

Internal Registers (Internal Data Bus)

The size of the internal registers indicates how much information the processor can operate on at one time and how it moves data around internally within the chip. This is sometimes also referred to as the *internal data bus*. A *register* is a holding cell within the processor; for example, the processor can add numbers in two different registers, storing the result in a third register. The register size determines the size of data on which the processor can operate. The register size also describes the type of software or commands and instructions a chip can run. That is, processors with 32-bit internal registers can run 32-bit instructions that are processing 32-bit chunks of data, but processors with 16-bit registers can't. Processors from the 386 to the Pentium 4 use 32-bit internal registers and can run essentially the same 32-bit OSs and software. The Core 2, Athlon 64, and newer processors have both 32-bit and 64-bit internal registers, which can run existing 32-bit OSs and applications as well as newer 64-bit versions.

Processor Modes

All Intel and Intel-compatible processors from the 386 on up can run in several modes. Processor modes refer to the various operating environments and affect the instructions and capabilities of the chip. The processor mode controls how the processor sees and manages the system memory and the tasks that use it.

Table 3.4 summarizes the processor modes and submodes.

Table 3.4 Processor Modes

Mode	Submode	OS Required	Software	Memory Address Size	Default Operand Size	Register Width
Real	—	16-bit	16-bit	24-bit	16-bit	16-bit
IA-32	Protected	32-bit	32-bit	32-bit	32-bit	32/16-bit
	Virtual real	32-bit	16-bit	24-bit	16-bit	16-bit
IA-32e	64-bit	64-bit	64-bit	64-bit	32-bit	64-bit
	compatibility	64-bit	32-bit	32-bit	32-bit	32/16-bit

IA-32e (64-bit extension mode) is also called x64, AMD64, x86-64, or EM64T.

Real Mode

Real mode is sometimes called 8086 mode because it is based on the 8086 and 8088 processors. The original IBM PC included an 8088 processor that could execute 16-bit instructions using 16-bit internal registers and could address only 1MB of memory using 20 address lines. All original PC software was created to work with this chip and was designed around the 16-bit instruction set and 1MB memory model. For example, DOS and all DOS software, Windows 1.x through 3.x, and all Windows 1.x through 3.x applications are written using 16-bit instructions. These 16-bit OSs and applications are designed to run on an original 8088 processor.

◄◄ See the section, "Internal Registers (Internal Data Bus)," **p. 44**.

◄◄ See the section, "Address Bus," **p. 42**.

Later processors such as the 286 could run the same 16-bit instructions as the original 8088, but much faster. In other words, the 286 was fully compatible with the original 8088 and could run all 16-bit software just the same as an 8088, but, of course, that software would run faster. The 16-bit instruction mode of the 8088 and 286 processors has become known as *real mode*. All software running in real mode must use only 16-bit instructions and live within the 20-bit (1MB) memory architecture it supports. Software of this type is usually single-tasking—that is, only one program can run at a time. No built-in protection exists to keep one program from overwriting another program or even the OS in memory. Therefore, if more than one program is running, one of them could bring the entire system to a crashing halt.

IA-32 Mode (32-Bit)

Then came the 386, which was the PC industry's first 32-bit processor. This chip could run an entirely new 32-bit instruction set. To take full advantage of the 32-bit instruction set, a 32-bit OS and a 32-bit application were required. This new 32-bit mode was referred to as *protected mode*, which alludes to the fact that software programs running in that mode are protected from overwriting one another in memory. Such protection makes the system much more crash-proof because an errant program can't easily damage other programs or the OS. In addition, a crashed program can be terminated while the rest of the system continues to run unaffected.

Knowing that new OSs and applications—which take advantage of the 32-bit protected mode—would take some time to develop, Intel wisely built a backward-compatible real mode into the 386. That enabled it to run unmodified 16-bit OSs and applications. It ran them quite well—much more quickly than any previous chip. For most people, that was enough. They did not necessarily want new 32-bit software; they just wanted their existing 16-bit software to run more quickly. Unfortunately, that meant the chip was never running in the 32-bit protected mode, and all the features of that capability were being ignored.

When a 386 or later processor is running DOS (real mode), it acts like a "Turbo 8088," which means the processor has the advantage of speed in running any 16-bit programs; it otherwise can use only the 16-bit instructions and access memory within the same 1MB memory map of the original 8088. Therefore, if you have a system with a current 32-bit or 64-bit processor running Windows 3.x or DOS, you are effectively using only the first megabyte of memory, leaving all the other RAM largely unused!

New OSs and applications that ran in the 32-bit protected mode of the modern processors were needed. Being stubborn, we as users resisted all the initial attempts at being switched over to a 32-bit environment. People are resistant to change and are sometimes more content with running older software more quickly than with adopting new software with new features. I'll be the first one to admit that I was (and still am) one of those stubborn users myself!

Because of this resistance, true 32-bit OSs took quite a while before getting a mainstream share in the PC marketplace. Windows XP was the first true 32-bit OS that became a true mainstream product, and that is primarily because Microsoft coerced us in that direction with Windows 9x/Me (which are mixed 16-bit/32-bit systems). Windows 3.x was the last 16-bit OS, which some did not really consider a complete OS because it ran on top of DOS.

IA-32 Virtual Real Mode

The key to the backward compatibility of the Windows 32-bit environment is the third mode in the processor: virtual real mode. *Virtual real* is essentially a virtual real mode 16-bit environment that runs inside 32-bit protected mode. When you run a DOS prompt window inside Windows, you have created a virtual real mode session. Because protected mode enables true multitasking, you can actually have several real mode sessions running, each with its own software running on a virtual PC. These can all run simultaneously, even while other 32-bit applications are running.

Note that any program running in a virtual real mode window can access up to only 1MB of memory, which that program will believe is the first and only megabyte of memory in the system. In other words, if you run a DOS application in a virtual real window, it will have a 640KB limitation on memory usage. That is because there is only 1MB of total RAM in a 16-bit environment, and the upper 384KB is reserved for system use. The virtual real window fully emulates an 8088 environment, so that aside from speed, the software runs as if it were on an original real mode–only PC. Each virtual machine gets its own 1MB address space, an image of the real hardware basic input/output system (BIOS) routines, and emulation of all other registers and features found in real mode.

Virtual real mode is used when you use a DOS window to run a DOS or Windows 3.x 16-bit program. When you start a DOS application, Windows creates a virtual DOS machine under which it can run.

One interesting thing to note is that all Intel and Intel-compatible (such as AMD and VIA/Cyrix) processors power up in real mode. If you load a 32-bit OS, it automatically switches the processor into 32-bit mode and takes control from there.

It's also important to note that some 16-bit (DOS and Windows 3.x) applications misbehave in a 32-bit environment, which means they do things that even virtual real mode does not support. Diagnostics software is a perfect example of this. Such software does not run properly in a real mode (virtual real) window under Windows. In that case, you can still run your modern system in the original no-frills real mode by booting to a DOS or Windows 9x/Me startup floppy or by using a self-booting CD or DVD that contains the diagnostic software.

Although 16-bit DOS and "standard" DOS applications use real mode, special programs are available that "extend" DOS and allow access to extended memory (over 1MB). These are sometimes called *DOS extenders* and usually are included as part of any DOS or Windows 3.x software that uses them. The protocol that describes how to make DOS work in protected mode is called *DOS protected mode interface* (DPMI).

Windows 3.x used DPMI to access extended memory for use with Windows 3.x applications. It allowed these programs to use more memory even though they were still 16-bit programs. DOS extenders are especially popular in DOS games because they enable them to access much more of the system memory than the standard 1MB that most real mode programs can address. These DOS extenders work by switching the processor in and out of real mode. In the case of those that run under Windows, they use the DPMI interface built into Windows, enabling them to share a portion of the system's extended memory.

Another exception in real mode is that the first 64KB of extended memory is actually accessible to the PC in real mode, despite the fact that it's not supposed to be possible. This is the result of a bug in the original IBM AT with respect to the 21st memory address line, known as *A20* (A0 is the first address line). By manipulating the A20 line, real mode software can gain access to the first 64KB of extended memory—the first 64KB of memory past the first megabyte. This area of memory is called the *high memory area* (HMA).

IA-32e 64-Bit Extension Mode (x64, AMD64, x86-64, EM64T)

64-bit extension mode is an enhancement to the IA-32 architecture originally designed by AMD and later adopted by Intel.

In 2003, AMD introduced the first 64-bit processor for x86-compatible desktop computers—the Athlon 64—followed by its first 64-bit server processor, the Opteron. In 2004, Intel introduced a series of 64-bit-enabled versions of its Pentium 4 desktop processor. The years that followed saw both companies introducing more and more processors with 64-bit capabilities.

Processors with 64-bit extension technology can run in real (8086) mode, IA-32 mode, or IA-32e mode. IA-32 mode enables the processor to run in protected mode and virtual real mode. IA-32e mode allows the processor to run in 64-bit mode and compatibility mode, which means you can run both 64-bit and 32-bit applications simultaneously. IA-32e mode includes two submodes:

■ **64-bit mode**—Enables a 64-bit OS to run 64-bit applications

■ **Compatibility mode**—Enables a 64-bit OS to run most existing 32-bit software

IA-32e 64-bit mode is enabled by loading a 64-bit OS and is used by 64-bit applications. In the 64-bit submode, the following new features are available:

■ 64-bit linear memory addressing

■ Physical memory support beyond 4GB (limited by the specific processor)

■ Eight new general-purpose registers (GPRs)

■ Eight new registers for streaming SIMD extensions (MMX, SSE, SSE2, and SSE3)

■ 64-bit-wide GPRs and instruction pointers

IE-32e compatibility mode enables 32-bit and 16-bit applications to run under a 64-bit OS. Unfortunately, legacy 16-bit programs that run in virtual real mode (that is, DOS programs) are not supported and will not run, which is likely to be the biggest problem for many users, especially those that rely on legacy business applications or like to run very old games. Similar to 64-bit mode, compatibility mode is enabled by the OS on an individual code basis, which means 64-bit applications running in 64-bit mode can operate simultaneously with 32-bit applications running in compatibility mode.

What we need to make all this work is a 64-bit OS and, more importantly, 64-bit drivers for all our hardware to work under that OS. Although Microsoft released a 64-bit version of Windows XP, few companies released 64-bit XP drivers. It wasn't until Windows Vista and especially Windows 7 x64 versions were released that 64-bit drivers became plentiful enough that 64-bit hardware support was considered mainstream.

Note that Microsoft uses the term *x64* to refer to processors that support either AMD64 or EM64T because AMD and Intel's extensions to the standard IA32 architecture are practically identical and can be supported with a single version of Windows.

Note

Early versions of EM64T-equipped processors from Intel lacked support for the LAHF and SAHF instructions used in the AMD64 instruction set. However, Pentium 4 and Xeon DP processors using core steppings G1 and higher completely support these instructions; a BIOS update is also needed. Newer multicore processors with 64-bit support include these instructions as well.

The physical memory limits for Windows XP and later 32-bit and 64-bit editions are shown in Table 3.5.

Table 3.5   Windows Physical Memory Limits

Windows Version	Memory Limit (32-Bit)	Memory Limit (64-Bit)
8 Enterprise/Professional	4GB	512GB
8	4GB	128GB
7 Professional/Ultimate/Enterprise	4GB	192GB
Vista Business/Ultimate/Enterprise	4GB	128GB
Vista/7 Home Premium	4GB	16GB
Vista/7 Home Basic	4GB	8GB
XP Professional	4GB	128GB
XP Home	4GB	N/A

The major difference between 32-bit and 64-bit Windows is memory support—specifically, breaking the 4GB barrier found in 32-bit Windows systems. 32-bit versions of Windows support up to 4GB of physical memory, with up to 2GB of dedicated memory per process. 64-bit versions of Windows support up to 512GB of physical memory, with up to 4GB for each 32-bit process and up to 8TB for each 64-bit process. Support for more memory means applications can preload more data into memory, which the processor can access much more quickly.

Note

Although 32-bit versions of Windows can support up to 4GB of RAM, applications cannot access more than about 3.25GB of RAM. The remainder of the address space is used by video cards, the system ROM, integrated PCI devices, PCI and PCIe cards, and APICs.

64-bit Windows runs 32-bit Windows applications with no problems, but it does not run 16-bit Windows, DOS applications, or any other programs that run in virtual real mode. Drivers are another big problem. 32-bit processes cannot load 64-bit dynamic link libraries (DLLs), and 64-bit processes cannot load 32-bit DLLs. This essentially means that, for all the devices you have connected to your system, you need both 32-bit and 64-bit drivers for them to work. Acquiring 64-bit drivers for older devices or devices that are no longer supported can be difficult or impossible. Before installing a 64-bit version of Windows, be sure to check with the vendors of your internal and add-on hardware for 64-bit drivers.

Tip

If you cannot find 64-bit drivers designed for Windows Vista or Windows 7, look for 64-bit drivers for Windows XP x64 edition. These drivers often work very well with later 64-bit versions of Windows.

Although vendors have ramped up their development of 64-bit software and drivers, you should still keep all the memory size, software, and driver issues in mind when considering the transition from 32-bit to 64-bit technology. The transition from 32-bit hardware to mainstream 32-bit computing took 16 years. The first 64-bit PC processor was released in 2003, and 64-bit computing really didn't become mainstream until the release of Windows 7 in late 2009.

Processor Benchmarks

People love to know how fast (or slow) their computers are. We have always been interested in speed; it is human nature. To help us with this quest, we can use various benchmark test programs to measure aspects of processor and system performance. Although no single numerical measurement can completely describe the performance of a complex device such as a processor or a complete PC, benchmarks can be useful tools for comparing different components and systems.

However, the only truly accurate way to measure your system's performance is to test the system using the actual software applications you use. Although you think you might be testing one component of a system, often other parts of the system can have an effect. It is inaccurate to compare systems with different processors, for example, if they also have different amounts or types of memory, different hard disks, different video cards, and so on. All these things and more skew the test results.

Benchmarks can typically be divided into two types: component or system tests. *Component benchmarks* measure the performance of specific parts of a computer system, such as a processor, hard disk, video card, or optical drive, whereas *system benchmarks* typically measure the performance of the entire computer system running a given application or test suite. These are also often called *synthetic benchmarks* because they don't measure actual work.

Benchmarks are, at most, only one kind of information you can use during the upgrading or purchasing process. You are best served by testing the system using your own set of software OSs and applications and in the configuration you will be running.

I normally recommend using application-based benchmarks such as the BAPCo SYSmark (www.bapco.com) to measure the relative performance difference between different processors or systems.

Comparing Processor Performance

A common misunderstanding about processors is their different speed ratings. This section covers processor speed in general and then provides more specific information about Intel, AMD, and VIA/Cyrix processors.

A computer system's clock speed is measured as a frequency, usually expressed as a number of cycles per second. A crystal oscillator controls clock speeds using a sliver of quartz sometimes housed in what looks like a small tin container. Newer systems include the oscillator circuitry in the motherboard chipset, so it might not be a visible separate component on newer boards. As voltage is applied to the quartz, it begins to vibrate (oscillate) at a harmonic rate dictated by the shape and size of the crystal (sliver). The oscillations emanate from the crystal in the form of a current that alternates at the harmonic rate of the crystal. This alternating current is the clock signal that forms the time base on which the computer operates. A typical computer system runs millions or billions of these cycles per second, so speed is measured in megahertz or gigahertz. (One hertz is equal to one cycle per second.) An alternating current signal is like a sine wave, with the time between the peaks of each wave defining the frequency (see Figure 3.1).

Note

The hertz was named for the German physicist Heinrich Rudolf Hertz. In 1885, Hertz confirmed the *electromagnetic theory*, which states that light is a form of electromagnetic radiation and is propagated as waves.

A single cycle is the smallest element of time for the processor. Every action requires at least one cycle and usually multiple cycles. To transfer data to and from memory, for example, a processor such as the Pentium 4 needs a minimum of three cycles to set up the first memory transfer and then only a single cycle per transfer for the next three to six consecutive transfers. The extra cycles on the first transfer typically are called *wait states*. A wait state is a clock tick in which nothing happens. This ensures that the processor isn't getting ahead of the rest of the computer.

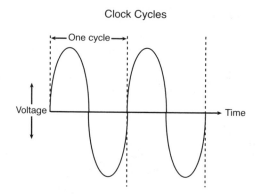

Clock Cycles

FIGURE 3.1 Alternating current signal showing clock cycle timing.

▶▶ See the Chapter 6 section, "Memory Modules," **p. 346**.

The time required to execute instructions also varies:

- **8086 and 8088**—The original 8086 and 8088 processors take an average of 12 cycles to execute a single instruction.

- **286 and 386**—The 286 and 386 processors improve this rate to about 4.5 cycles per instruction.

- **486**—The 486 and most other fourth-generation Intel-compatible processors, such as the AMD 5x86, drop the rate further, to about 2 cycles per instruction.

- **Pentium/K6**—The Pentium architecture and other fifth-generation Intel-compatible processors, such as those from AMD and VIA/Cyrix, include twin instruction pipelines and other improvements that provide for operation at one or two instructions per cycle.

- **P6/P7 and newer**—Sixth-, seventh-, and newer-generation processors can execute as many as three or more instructions per cycle, with multiples of that possible on multicore processors.

Different instruction execution times (in cycles) make comparing systems based purely on clock speed or number of cycles per second difficult. How can two processors that run at the same clock rate perform differently, with one running "faster" than the other? The answer is simple: efficiency.

The main reason the 486 is considered fast relative to the 386 is that it executes twice as many instructions in the same number of cycles. The same thing is true for a Pentium; it executes about twice as many instructions in a given number of cycles as a 486. Therefore, given the same clock speed, a Pentium is twice as fast as a 486, and consequently a 133MHz 486 class processor (such as the AMD 5x86-133) is not even as fast as a 75MHz Pentium! That is because Pentium megahertz are "worth" about double what 486 megahertz are worth in terms of instructions completed per cycle. The Pentium II and III are about 50% faster than an equivalent Pentium at a given clock speed because they can execute about that many more instructions in the same number of cycles.

Unfortunately, after the Pentium III, it becomes much more difficult to compare processors on clock speed alone. This is because the different internal architectures make some processors more efficient than others, but these same efficiency differences result in circuitry that is capable of running at different maximum speeds. The less efficient the circuit, the higher the clock speed it can attain, and vice versa. Another difference is that some of the later processors include varying sizes of L2 and L3 cache.

One of the biggest factors in efficiency is the number of stages in the processor's internal pipeline (see Table 3.6).

Table 3.6   Number of Pipelines per CPU

Processor	Pipeline Depth
Pentium III	10-stage
Pentium M/Core	10-stage
Athlon/XP	10-stage
Athlon 64/Phenom/II/FX	12-stage
Core 2/i3/i5/i7	14-stage
Pentium 4	20-stage
Pentium 4 Prescott	31-stage
Pentium D	31-stage

A deeper pipeline effectively breaks down instructions into smaller microsteps, which allows overall higher clock rates to be achieved using the same silicon technology. However, this also means that overall fewer instructions can be executed in a single cycle as compared to processors with shorter pipelines. This is because, if a branch prediction or speculative execution step fails (which happens fairly frequently inside the processor as it attempts to line up instructions in advance), the entire pipeline has to be flushed and refilled. Thus, if you compared an Intel Core i7 or AMD FX to a Pentium 4 running at the same clock speed, the Core i7 and FX would execute more instructions in the same number of cycles.

Although it is a disadvantage to have a deeper pipeline in terms of instruction efficiency, processors with deeper pipelines can run at higher clock rates on a given manufacturing technology. Thus, even though a deeper pipeline might be less efficient, the higher resulting clock speeds can make up for it. The deeper 20- or 31-stage pipeline in the P4 architecture enabled significantly higher clock speeds to be achieved using the same silicon die process as other chips. As an example, the 0.13-micron process Pentium 4 ran up to 3.4GHz, whereas the Athlon XP topped out at 2.2GHz (3200+ model) in the same introduction timeframe. Even though the Pentium 4 executes fewer instructions in each cycle, the overall higher cycling speeds made up for the loss of efficiency; the higher clock speed versus the more efficient processing effectively cancelled each other out.

Unfortunately, the deep pipeline combined with high clock rates did come with a penalty in power consumption, and therefore heat generation as well. Eventually, it was determined that the power penalty was too great, causing Intel to drop back to a more efficient design in its newer Core microarchitecture processors. Rather than solely increase clock rates, performance was increased by combining multiple processors into a single chip, thus improving the effective instruction efficiency even further. This began the push toward multicore processors.

One thing is clear in all of this confusion: Raw clock speed is not a good way to compare chips, unless they are from the same manufacturer, model, and family.

To fairly compare various CPUs at different clock speeds, Intel originally devised a specific series of benchmarks called the *Intel Comparative Microprocessor Performance* (iCOMP) index. The iCOMP index benchmark was released in original iCOMP, iCOMP 2.0, and iCOMP 3.0 versions.

The iCOMP 2.0 index was derived from several independent benchmarks as an indication of relative processor performance. The benchmarks balance integer with floating-point and multimedia performance.

The iCOMP 2.0 index comparison for Pentium 75 through Pentium II 450 is available in Chapter 3 of *Upgrading and Repairing PCs,* 19ᵗʰ Edition, found in its entirety on the disc packaged with this book.

Until recently, Intel and AMD have rated their latest processors using the commercially available BAPCo SYSmark benchmark suites. SYSmark is an application-based benchmark that runs various scripts to do actual work using popular applications. Many companies use it to test and compare PC systems and components. The SYSmark benchmark is a much more modern and real-world benchmark than the iCOMP benchmark Intel previously used, and because it is available to anybody, the results can be independently verified. You can purchase the SYSmark benchmark software from BAPCo at www.bapco.com or from FutureMark at www.futuremark.com.

The most recent version of the SYSmark benchmark—SYSmark 2012—has become controversial because AMD, NVIDIA, and VIA resigned from BAPco in 2011. These companies withdrew from BAPco because they believe that this version of the SYSmark benchmark is optimized for Intel processors rather than being processor neutral.

AMD's recent processor designs have emphasized the role of the integrated GPU and heterogenous computing (the use of both CPU and GPU for calculations) in its consumer-level designs, while Intel, though its recent processors include integrated GPUs, stresses CPU performance in its designs. Meanwhile, VIA emphasizes ultra-low power consumption and optimization for basic computer tasks. SYSmark 2012's application mix (see Table 3.7) puts little emphasis on AMD and VIA's strengths. As several technology columnists have noted, Intel, AMD, and VIA are no longer pursuing the same goals in processor design, so a common benchmark might no longer make much sense.

Despite the controversy, Anandtech, a leading technology website, has used SYSmark 2012 to rate the latest AMD and Intel processors. You can view the benchmark results for older processors using SYSmark 2007 (the previous benchmark) and many of the most recent processors using SYSmark 2012 at www.anandtech.com/bench/CPU/2.

Until a new benchmark application, one supported by all CPU and GPU manufacturers, is adopted (if ever), here's what I suggest: When you use SYSmark 2012, pay less attention to the overall score, and focus on the scores for specific scenarios that match the work you plan to do with the computers you are responsible for. Table 3.7 lists the scenarios and applications used by SYSmark 2012.

Table 3.7   Scenarios and Software Used by SYSmark 2012

3D Modeling	System Management
Adobe Photoshop CS5 Extended	Mozilla Firefox Installer (several versions)
Autodesk 3ds Max 2011	WinZip Pro 14.5
Autodesk AutoCAD 2011	WinZip Command Line 3.2
Google SketchUp Pro 8	**Web Development**
Data/Financial Analysis	Adobe Photoshop CS5 Extended
Microsoft Excel 2010	Adobe Premiere Pro CS5
Media Creation	Adobe Dreamweaver CS5
Adobe Photoshop CS5 Extended	Mozilla Firefox 3.6.8
Adobe Premiere Pro CS5	Microsoft Internet Explorer 8 (or newer version, if already installed)
Adobe After Effects CS5	

Office Productivity

ABBYY FineReader Pro 10.0	Microsoft Outlook 2010
Adobe Acrobat Pro 9	Microsoft PowerPoint 2010
Adobe Flash Player 10.1	Microsoft Word 2010
Microsoft Excel 2010	WinZip Pro 14.5
Microsoft Internet Explorer 8 (or newer version, if already installed)	Mozilla Firefox 3.6.8

For SYSmark 2004 and SYSmark 2004SE comparisons for processors such as the Core 2 family, Pentium D, Pentium 4 and Pentium Extreme Edition, Celeron D, Pentium III, Athlon 64, Athlon 64 X2, Sempron, and Athlon XP, see Table 3.8 and 3.9 in Chapter 3 of *Upgrading and Repairing PCs*, 19th Edition, which is available in its entirety on the disc packaged with this book.

The SYSmark benchmarks are commercially available application-based benchmarks that are intended to reflect the normal usage of business users employing modern Internet content creation and office applications. However, it is important to note that the scores calculated for a particular processor are produced by complete systems and are affected by things such as the specific version of the processor, the motherboard and chipset used, the amount and type of memory installed, the speed of the hard disk, and other factors. For complete disclosure of the other factors resulting in the given scores, see the reports on the BAPCo website at www.bapco.com.

Cache Memory

As processor core speeds increased, memory speeds could not keep up. How could you run a processor faster than the memory from which you fed it without having performance suffer terribly? The answer was cache. In its simplest terms, *cache memory* is a high-speed memory buffer that temporarily stores data the processor needs, allowing the processor to retrieve that data faster than if it came from main memory. But there is one additional feature of a cache over a simple buffer, and that is intelligence. A cache is a buffer with a brain.

A buffer holds random data, usually on a first-in, first-out basis or a first-in, last-out basis. A cache, on the other hand, holds the data the processor is most likely to need in advance of it actually being needed. This enables the processor to continue working at either full speed or close to it without having to wait for the data to be retrieved from slower main memory. Cache memory is usually made up of static RAM (SRAM) memory integrated into the processor die, although older systems with cache also used chips installed on the motherboard.

▶▶ See the Chapter 6 section, "Cache Memory: SRAM," **p. 329**.

Recent low-cost processor designs typically include two levels of processor/memory cache: Level 1 (L1) and Level 2 (L2). Mid-range and high-end designs also have Level 3 cache. These caches and their functioning are described in the following sections.

Tip

Use the popular CPU-Z utility discussed earlier in this chapter to determine the types and sizes of cache memory in your computer's CPUs.

Internal Level 1 Cache

All modern processors starting with the 486 family include an integrated L1 cache and controller. The integrated L1 cache size varies from processor to processor, starting at 8KB for the original 486DX and now up to 128KB or more in the latest processors.

Note

Multicore processors include separate L1 caches for each processor core. Also, L1 cache is divided into equal amounts for instructions and data.

To understand the importance of cache, you need to know the relative speeds of processors and memory. The problem with this is that processor speed usually is expressed in MHz or GHz (millions or billions of cycles per second), whereas memory speeds are often expressed in nanoseconds (billionths of a second per cycle). Most newer types of memory express the speed in either MHz or in megabyte per second (MBps) bandwidth (throughput).

Both are really time- or frequency-based measurements, and a chart comparing them can be found in Table 6.3 in Chapter 6. In this table, you will note that a 233MHz processor equates to 4.3-nanosecond cycling, which means you would need 4ns memory to keep pace with a 200MHz CPU. Also, note that the motherboard of a 233MHz system typically runs at 66MHz, which corresponds to a speed of 15ns per cycle and requires 15ns memory to keep pace. Finally, note that 60ns main memory (common on many Pentium-class systems) equates to a clock speed of approximately 16MHz. So, a typical Pentium 233 system has a processor running at 233MHz (4.3ns per cycle), a motherboard running at 66MHz (15ns per cycle), and main memory running at 16MHz (60ns per cycle). This might seem like a rather dated example, but in a moment, you will see that the figures listed here make it easy for me to explain how cache memory works.

Because L1 cache is always built into the processor die, it runs at the full-core speed of the processor internally. By full-core speed, I mean this cache runs at the higher clock multiplied internal processor speed rather than the external motherboard speed. This cache basically is an area of fast memory built into the processor that holds some of the current working set of code and data. Cache memory can be accessed with no wait states because it is running at the same speed as the processor core.

Using cache memory reduces a traditional system bottleneck because system RAM is almost always much slower than the CPU; the performance difference between memory and CPU speed has become especially large in recent systems. Using cache memory prevents the processor from having to wait for code and data from much slower main memory, thus improving performance. Without the L1 cache, a processor would frequently be forced to wait until system memory caught up.

Cache is even more important in modern processors because it is often the only memory in the entire system that can truly keep up with the chip. Most modern processors are clock multiplied, which means they are running at a speed that is really a multiple of the motherboard into which they are plugged. The only types of memory matching the full speed of the processor are the L1, L2, and L3 caches built into the processor core.

▶▶ See the Chapter 6 section, "Memory Module Speed," **p. 357**.

If the data that the processor wants is already in L1 cache, the CPU does not have to wait. If the data is not in the cache, the CPU must fetch it from the Level 2 or Level 3 cache or (in less sophisticated system designs) from the system bus—meaning main memory directly.

How Cache Works

To learn how the L1 cache works, consider the following analogy.

This story involves a person (in this case, you) eating food to act as the processor requesting and operating on data from memory. The kitchen where the food is prepared is the main system memory (typically double data rate [DDR], DDR2, or DDR3 dual inline memory module [DIMMs]). The cache controller is the waiter, and the L1 cache is the table where you are seated.

Okay, here's the story. Say you start to eat at a particular restaurant every day at the same time. You come in, sit down, and order a hot dog. To keep this story proportionately accurate, let's say you normally eat at the rate of one bite (byte? <grin>) every four seconds (233MHz = about 4ns cycling). It also takes 60 seconds for the kitchen to produce any given item that you order (60ns main memory).

So, when you arrive, you sit down, order a hot dog, and you have to wait for 60 seconds for the food to be produced before you can begin eating. After the waiter brings the food, you start eating at your normal rate. Pretty quickly you finish the hot dog, so you call the waiter over and order a hamburger. Again, you wait 60 seconds while the hamburger is being produced. When it arrives, you again begin eating at full speed. After you finish the hamburger, you order a plate of fries. Again you wait, and after the fries are delivered 60 seconds later, you eat them at full speed. Finally, you decide to finish the meal and order cheesecake for dessert. After another 60-second wait, you can eat cheesecake at full speed. Your overall eating experience consists of a lot of waiting, followed by short bursts of actual eating at full speed.

After coming into the restaurant for two consecutive nights at exactly 6 p.m. and ordering the same items in the same order each time, on the third night the waiter begins to think, "I know this guy is going to be here at 6 p.m., order a hot dog, a hamburger, fries, and then cheesecake. Why don't I have these items prepared in advance and surprise him? Maybe I'll get a big tip." So you enter the restaurant and order a hot dog, and the waiter immediately puts it on your plate, with no waiting! You then proceed to finish the hot dog and right as you are about to request the hamburger, the waiter deposits one on your plate. The rest of the meal continues in the same fashion, and you eat the entire meal, taking a bite every four seconds, and you never have to wait for the kitchen to prepare the food. Your overall eating experience this time consists of all eating, with no waiting for the food to be prepared, due primarily to the intelligence and thoughtfulness of your waiter.

This analogy describes the function of the L1 cache in the processor. The L1 cache itself is a table that can contain one or more plates of food. Without a waiter, the space on the table is a simple food buffer. When it's stocked, you can eat until the buffer is empty, but nobody seems to be intelligently refilling it. The waiter is the cache controller who takes action and adds the intelligence to decide which dishes are to be placed on the table in advance of your needing them. Like the real cache controller, he uses his skills to literally guess which food you will require next, and if he guesses correctly, you never have to wait.

Let's now say on the fourth night you arrive exactly on time and start with the usual hot dog. The waiter, by now really feeling confident, has the hot dog already prepared when you arrive, so there is no waiting.

Just as you finish the hot dog, and right as he is placing a hamburger on your plate, you say "Gee, I'd really like a bratwurst now; I didn't actually order this hamburger." The waiter guessed wrong, and the consequence is that this time you have to wait the full 60 seconds as the kitchen prepares your brat. This is known as a *cache miss*, in which the cache controller did not correctly fill the cache with the data the processor actually needed next. The result is waiting, or in the case of a sample 233MHz Pentium system, the system essentially throttles back to 16MHz (RAM speed) whenever a cache miss occurs.

According to Intel, the L1 cache in most of its processors has approximately a 90% hit ratio. (Some processors, such as the Pentium 4, are slightly higher.) This means that the cache has the correct data 90% of the time, and consequently the processor runs at full speed (233MHz in this example) 90% of the time. However, 10% of the time the cache controller guesses incorrectly, and the data has to be retrieved out of the significantly slower main memory, meaning the processor has to wait. This essentially throttles the system back to RAM speed, which in this example was 60ns or 16MHz.

In this analogy, the processor was 14 times faster than the main memory. Memory speeds have increased from 16MHz (60ns) to 333MHz (3.0ns) or faster in the latest systems, but processor speeds have also risen to 3GHz and beyond. So even in the latest systems, memory is still 7.5 or more times *slower* than the processor. Cache is what makes up the difference.

The main feature of L1 cache is that it has always been integrated into the processor core, where it runs at the same speed as the core. This, combined with the hit ratio of 90% or greater, makes L1 cache important for system performance.

Level 2 Cache

To mitigate the dramatic slowdown every time an L1 cache miss occurs, a secondary (L2) cache is employed.

Using the restaurant analogy I used to explain L1 cache in the previous section, I'll equate the L2 cache to a cart of additional food items placed strategically in the restaurant such that the waiter can retrieve food from the cart in only 15 seconds (versus 60 seconds from the kitchen). In an actual Pentium class (Socket 7) system, the L2 cache is mounted on the motherboard, which means it runs at motherboard speed (66MHz, or 15ns in this example). Now, if you ask for an item the waiter did not bring in advance to your table, instead of making the long trek back to the kitchen to retrieve the food and bring it back to you 60 seconds later, he can first check the cart where he has placed additional items. If the requested item is there, he will return with it in only 15 seconds. The net effect in the real system is that instead of slowing down from 233MHz to 16MHz waiting for the data to come from the 60ns main memory, the system can instead retrieve the data from the 15ns (66MHz) L2 cache. The effect is that the system slows down from 233MHz to 66MHz.

All modern processors have integrated L2 cache that runs at the same speed as the processor core, which is also the same speed as the L1 cache. For the analogy to describe these newer chips, the waiter would simply place the cart right next to the table you were seated at in the restaurant. Then, if the food you desired wasn't on the table (L1 cache miss), it would merely take a longer reach over to the adjacent L2 cache (the cart, in this analogy) rather than a 15-second walk to the cart as with the older designs.

Figure 3.2 illustrates the cache types and sizes in the AMD A10-5800K processor, as reported by CPU-Z.

Level 3 Cache

Most late-model mid-range and high-performance processors also contain a third level of cache known as *L3 cache*. In the past, relatively few processors had L3 cache, but it is becoming more and more common in newer and faster multicore processors such as the Intel Core i7 and AMD Phenom II and FX processors.

Extending the restaurant analogy I used to explain L1 and L2 caches, I'll equate L3 cache to another cart of additional food items placed in the restaurant next to the cart used to symbolize L2 cache. If the food item needed was not on the table (L1 cache miss) or on the first food cart (L2 cache miss), the waiter could then reach over to the second food cart to retrieve a necessary item.

L3 cache proves especially useful in multicore processors, where the L3 is generally shared among all the cores. Both Intel and AMD use L3 cache in most of their current processors because of the benefits to multicore designs.

Figure 3.3 illustrates the cache types and sizes in the Intel Core i5 2500 Sandy Bridge and the AMD Phenom II X6 1055T as reported by CPU-Z.

CPU

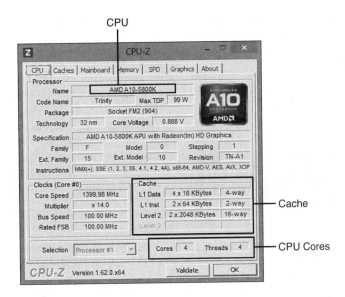

FIGURE 3.2 The AMD A10-5800K processor is a quad-core processor with L1 and L2 cache.

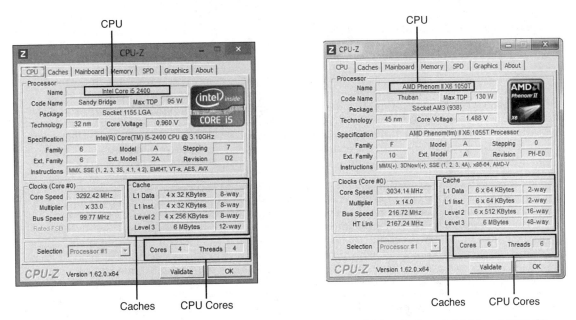

FIGURE 3.3 Two examples of six-core processors with L1, L2, and L3 cache from Intel (a) and AMD (b).

Cache Performance and Design

Just as with the L1 cache, most L2 caches have a hit ratio also in the 90% range; therefore, if you look at the system as a whole, 90% of the time it runs at full speed (233MHz in this example) by retrieving data out of the L1 cache. Ten percent of the time it slows down to retrieve the data from the L2 cache. Ninety percent of the time the processor goes to the L2 cache, the data is in the L2, and 10% of that time it has to go to the slow main memory to get the data because of an L2 cache miss. So, by combining both caches, our sample system runs at full processor speed 90% of the time (233MHz in this case), at motherboard speed 9% (90% of 10%) of the time (66MHz in this case), and at RAM speed about 1% (10% of 10%) of the time (16MHz in this case). You can clearly see the importance of both the L1 and L2 caches; without them the system uses main memory more often, which is significantly slower than the processor.

This brings up other interesting points. If you could spend money doubling the performance of either the main memory (RAM) or the L2 cache, which would you improve? Considering that main memory is used directly only about 1% of the time, if you doubled performance there, you would double the speed of your system only 1% of the time! That doesn't sound like enough of an improvement to justify much expense. On the other hand, if you doubled L2 cache performance, you would be doubling system performance 9% of the time, which is a much greater improvement overall. I'd much rather improve L2 than RAM performance. The same argument holds true for adding and increasing the size of L3 cache, as many recent processors from AMD and Intel have done.

The processor and system designers at Intel and AMD know this and have devised methods of improving the performance of L2 cache. In Pentium (P5) class systems, the L2 cache usually was found on the motherboard and had to run at motherboard speed. Intel made the first dramatic improvement by migrating the L2 cache from the motherboard directly into the processor and initially running it at the same speed as the main processor. The cache chips were made by Intel and mounted next to the main processor die in a single chip housing. This proved too expensive, so with the Pentium II, Intel began using cache chips from third-party suppliers such as Sony, Toshiba, NEC, and Samsung. Because these were supplied as complete packaged chips and not raw die, Intel mounted them on a circuit board alongside the processor. This is why the Pentium II was designed as a cartridge rather than what looked like a chip.

One problem was the speed of the available third-party cache chips. The fastest ones on the market were 3ns or higher, meaning 333MHz or less in speed. Because the processor was being driven in speeds above that, in the Pentium II and initial Pentium III processors, Intel had to run the L2 cache at half the processor speed because that is all the commercially available cache memory could handle. AMD followed suit with the Athlon processor, which had to drop L2 cache speed even further in some models to two-fifths or one-third the main CPU speed to keep the cache memory speed less than the 333MHz commercially available chips.

Then a breakthrough occurred, which first appeared in Celeron processors 300A and above. These had 128KB of L2 cache, but no external chips were used. Instead, the L2 cache had been integrated directly into the processor core just like the L1. Consequently, both the L1 and L2 caches now would run at full processor speed, and more importantly scale up in speed as the processor speeds increased in the future. In the newer Pentium III, as well as all the Xeon and Celeron processors, the L2 cache runs at full processor core speed, which means there is no waiting or slowing down after an L1 cache miss. AMD also achieved full-core speed on-die cache in its later Athlon and Duron chips. Using on-die cache improves performance dramatically because 9% of the time the system uses the L2. It now remains at full speed instead of slowing down to one-half or less the processor speed or, even worse, slowing down to motherboard speed as in Socket 7 designs. Another benefit of on-die L2 cache is cost, which is less because fewer parts are involved. L3 on-die caches offer the same benefits for those times when L1 and L2 cache do not contain the desired data. And, because L3 cache is much larger than L2 cache (6MB in AMD Phenom II and 12MB in Core i7 Extreme Edition), the odds of all three cache levels not containing the information desired are reduced over processors which have only L1 and L2 cache. Let's revisit the restaurant analogy using a 3.6GHz processor. You would now be taking a bite every half second (3.6GHz = 0.28ns cycling). The L1 cache would also be running at that speed, so you could eat anything on your table at that same rate (the table = L1 cache). The real jump in speed comes when you want something that isn't already on the table (L1 cache miss), in which case the waiter reaches over to the cart (which is now directly adjacent to the table) and 9 out of 10 times is able to find the food you want in just over one-quarter second (L2 speed = 3.6GHz or 0.28ns cycling). In this system, you would run at 3.6GHz 99% of the time (L1 and L2 hit ratios combined) and slow down to RAM speed (wait for the kitchen) only 1% of the time, as before. With faster memory running at 800MHz (1.25ns), you would have to wait only 1.25 seconds for the food to come from the kitchen. If only restaurant performance would increase at the same rate processor performance has!

Cache Organization

You know that cache stores copies of data from various main memory addresses. Because the cache cannot hold copies of the data from all the addresses in main memory simultaneously, there has to be a way to know which addresses are currently copied into the cache so that, if we need data from those addresses, it can be read from the cache rather than from the main memory. This function is performed by Tag RAM, which is additional memory in the cache that holds an index of the addresses that are copied into the cache. Each line of cache memory has a corresponding address tag that stores the main memory address of the data currently copied into that particular cache line. If data from a particular main memory address is needed, the cache controller can quickly search the address tags to see whether the requested address is currently being stored in the cache (a hit) or not (a miss). If the data is there, it can be read from the faster cache; if it isn't, it has to be read from the much slower main memory.

Various ways of organizing or mapping the tags affect how cache works. A cache can be mapped as fully associative, direct-mapped, or set associative.

In a *fully associative mapped cache*, when a request is made for data from a specific main memory address, the address is compared against all the address tag entries in the cache tag RAM. If the requested main memory address is found in the tag (a *hit*), the corresponding location in the cache is returned. If the requested address is not found in the address tag entries, a *miss* occurs, and the data must be retrieved from the main memory address instead of the cache.

In a *direct-mapped cache*, specific main memory addresses are preassigned to specific line locations in the cache where they will be stored. Therefore, the tag RAM can use fewer bits because when you know which main memory address you want, only one address tag needs to be checked, and each tag needs to store only the possible addresses a given line can contain. This also results in faster operation because only one tag address needs to be checked for a given memory address.

A *set associative cache* is a modified direct-mapped cache. A direct-mapped cache has only one set of memory associations, meaning a given memory address can be mapped into (or associated with) only a specific given cache line location. A two-way set associative cache has two sets, so that a given memory location can be in one of two locations. A four-way set associative cache can store a given memory address into four different cache line locations (or sets). By increasing the set associativity, the chance of finding a value increases; however, it takes a little longer because more tag addresses must be checked when searching for a specific location in the cache. In essence, each set in an *n*-way set associative cache is a subcache that has associations with each main memory address. As the number of subcaches or sets increases, eventually the cache becomes fully associative—a situation in which any memory address can be stored in any cache line location. In that case, an *n*-way set associative cache is a compromise between a fully associative cache and a direct-mapped cache.

In general, a direct-mapped cache is the fastest at locating and retrieving data from the cache because it has to look at only one specific tag address for a given memory address. However, it also results in more misses overall than the other designs. A fully associative cache offers the highest hit ratio but is the slowest at locating and retrieving the data because it has many more address tags to check through. An *n*-way set associative cache is a compromise between optimizing cache speed and hit ratio, but the more associativity there is, the more hardware (tag bits, comparator circuits, and so on) is required, making the cache more expensive. Obviously, cache design is a series of trade-offs, and what works best in one instance might not work best in another. Multitasking environments such as Windows are good examples of environments in which the processor needs to operate on different areas of memory simultaneously and in which an *n*-way cache can improve performance.

The contents of the cache must always be in sync with the contents of main memory to ensure that the processor is working with current data. For this reason, the internal cache in the 486 family was a *write-through* cache. Write-through means that when the processor writes information to the cache, that information is automatically written through to main memory as well.

By comparison, Pentium and later chips have an internal write-back cache, which means that both reads and writes are cached, further improving performance.

Another feature of improved cache designs is that they are *nonblocking*. This is a technique for reducing or hiding memory delays by exploiting the overlap of processor operations with data accesses. A nonblocking cache enables program execution to proceed concurrently with cache misses as long as certain dependency constraints are observed. In other words, the cache can handle a cache miss much better and enable the processor to continue doing something nondependent on the missing data.

The cache controller built into the processor also is responsible for watching the memory bus when alternative processors, known as *bus masters*, control the system. This process of watching the bus is referred to as *bus snooping*. If a bus master device writes to an area of memory that also is stored in the processor cache currently, the cache contents and memory no longer agree. The cache controller then marks this data as invalid and reloads the cache during the next memory access, preserving the integrity of the system.

All PC processor designs that support cache memory include a feature known as a *translation lookaside buffer* (TLB) to improve recovery from cache misses. The TLB is a table inside the processor that stores information about the location of recently accessed memory addresses. The TLB speeds up the translation of virtual addresses to physical memory addresses.

As clock speeds increase, cycle time decreases. Newer systems no longer use cache on the motherboard because the faster system memory used in modern systems can keep up with the motherboard speed. Modern processors integrate the L2 cache into the processor die just like the L1 cache, and most recent models include on-die L3 as well. This enables the L2/L3 to run at full-core speed because it is now part of the core.

Processor Features

As new processors are introduced, new features are continually added to their architectures to improve everything from performance in specific types of applications to the reliability of the CPU as a whole. The next few sections look at some of these technologies.

System Management Mode (SMM)

Spurred on initially by the need for more robust power management capabilities in mobile computers, Intel and AMD began adding *System Management Mode* (SMM) to its processors during the early 1990s. SMM is a special-purpose operating mode provided for handling low-level system power management and hardware control functions. SMM offers an isolated software environment that is transparent to the OS or applications software and is intended for use by system BIOS or low-level driver code.

SMM was introduced as part of the Intel 386SL mobile processor in October 1990. SMM later appeared as part of the 486SL processor in November 1992, and in the entire 486 line starting in June 1993. SMM was notably absent from the first Pentium processors when they were released in March 1993; however, SMM was included in all 75MHz and faster Pentium processors released on or after October 1994. AMD added SMM to its enhanced Am486 and K5 processors around that time as well. All other Intel and AMD x86-based processors introduced since that time also have incorporated SMM.

SMM is invoked by signaling a special interrupt pin on the processor, which generates a System Management Interrupt (SMI), the highest priority nonmaskable interrupt available. When SMM starts, the context or state of the processor and currently running programs are saved. Then the processor switches to a separate dedicated address space and executes the SMM code, which runs transparently to the interrupted program as well as any other software on the system. Once the SMM task is complete, a resume instruction restores the previously saved context or state of the processor and programs, and the processor resumes running exactly where it left off.

Although initially used mainly for power management, SMM was designed to be used by any low-level system functions that need to function independent of the OS and other software on the system. In modern systems, this includes the following:

- ACPI and APM power management functions
- Universal serial bus (USB) legacy (keyboard and mouse) support
- USB boot (drive emulation)
- Password and security functions
- Thermal monitoring
- Fan speed monitoring
- Reading/writing Complementary Metal Oxide Semiconductor (CMOS) RAM
- BIOS updating
- Logging memory error-correcting code (ECC) errors
- Logging hardware errors besides memory
- Wake and Alert functions such as Wake on LAN (WOL)

One example of SMM in operation occurs when the system tries to access a peripheral device that had been previously powered down to save energy. For example, say that a program requests to read a file on a hard drive, but the drive had previously spun down to save energy. Upon access, the host adapter generates an SMI to invoke SMM. The SMM software then issues commands to spin up the drive and make it ready. Consequently, SMM returns control to the OS, and the file load continues as if the drive had been spinning all along.

Superscalar Execution

The fifth-generation Pentium and newer processors feature multiple internal instruction execution pipelines, which enable them to execute multiple instructions at the same time. The 486 and all preceding chips can perform only a single instruction at a time. Intel calls the capability to execute more than one instruction at a time *superscalar* technology.

Superscalar architecture was initially associated with high-output reduced instruction set computer (RISC) chips. A RISC chip has a less complicated instruction set with fewer and simpler instructions. Although each instruction accomplishes less, the overall clock speed can be higher, which usually increases performance. The Pentium is one of the first complex instruction set computer (CISC) chips to be considered superscalar. A CISC chip uses a richer, fuller-featured instruction set, which has more complicated instructions. As an example, say you wanted to instruct a robot to screw in a light bulb. Using CISC instructions, you would say the following:

1. Pick up the bulb.
2. Insert it into the socket.
3. Rotate clockwise until tight.

Using RISC instructions, you would say something more along the lines of the following:

1. Lower hand.
2. Grasp bulb.
3. Raise hand.
4. Insert bulb into socket.
5. Rotate clockwise one turn.
6. Is bulb tight? If not, repeat step 5.
7. End.

Overall, many more RISC instructions are required to do the job because each instruction is simpler (reduced) and does less. The advantage is that there are fewer overall commands the robot (or processor) has to deal with, and it can execute the individual commands more quickly, and thus in many cases execute the complete task (or program) more quickly as well. The debate goes on whether RISC or CISC is really better, but in reality there is no such thing as a pure RISC or CISC chip—it is all just a matter of definition, and the lines are somewhat arbitrary.

Intel and compatible processors have generally been regarded as CISC chips, although the fifth- and later-generation versions have many RISC attributes and internally break down CISC instructions into RISC versions.

Note

The ARM processor used by Windows RT tablets is a RISC processor. Windows RT uses the same tile-based interface as Windows 8, but x86 software is not compatible with Windows RT.

MMX Technology

MMX technology was originally named for *multimedia extensions*, or *matrix math extensions*, depending on whom you ask. Intel officially states that it is actually not an abbreviation and stands for nothing other than the letters MMX (not being an abbreviation was apparently required so that the letters could be trademarked); however, the internal origins are probably one of the preceding. MMX technology was introduced in the later fifth-generation Pentium processors as a kind of add-on that improves video compression/decompression, image manipulation, encryption, and I/O processing—all of which are used in a variety of today's software.

MMX consists of two main processor architectural improvements. The first is basic: All MMX chips have a larger internal L1 cache than their non-MMX counterparts. This improves the performance of any and all software running on the chip, regardless of whether it actually uses the MMX-specific instructions.

The other part of MMX is that it extends the processor instruction set with 57 new commands or instructions, as well as a new instruction capability called single instruction, multiple data (SIMD).

Modern multimedia and communication applications often use repetitive loops that, while occupying 10% or less of the overall application code, can account for up to 90% of the execution time. SIMD enables one instruction to perform the same function on multiple pieces of data, similar to a teacher telling an entire class to "sit down," rather than addressing each student one at a time. SIMD enables the chip to reduce processor-intensive loops common with video, audio, graphics, and animation.

Intel also added 57 new instructions specifically designed to manipulate and process video, audio, and graphical data more efficiently. These instructions are oriented to the *highly parallel* and often repetitive sequences frequently found in multimedia operations. *Highly parallel* refers to the fact that the same processing is done on many data points, such as when modifying a graphic image. The main drawbacks to MMX were that it worked only on integer values and used the floating-point unit for processing, so time was lost when a shift to floating-point operations was necessary. These drawbacks were corrected in the additions to MMX from Intel and AMD.

Intel licensed the MMX capabilities to competitors such as AMD and Cyrix (later absorbed by VIA), who were then able to upgrade their own Intel-compatible processors with MMX technology.

SSE

In February 1999, Intel introduced the Pentium III processor and included in that processor an update to MMX called *Streaming SIMD Extensions* (SSE). These were also called *Katmai New Instructions* (KNI) up until their debut because they were originally included on the Katmai processor, which was the code name for the Pentium III. The Celeron 533A and faster Celeron processors based on the Pentium III core also support SSE instructions. The earlier Pentium II and Celeron 533 and lower (based on the Pentium II core) do not support SSE.

The Streaming SIMD Extensions consist of 70 new instructions, including SIMD floating point, additional SIMD integer, and cacheability control instructions. Some of the technologies that benefit from the Streaming SIMD Extensions include advanced imaging, 3D video, streaming audio and video (DVD playback), and speech-recognition applications.

The SSE*x* instructions are particularly useful with MPEG2 decoding, which is the standard scheme used on DVD video discs. Therefore, SSE-equipped processors should be more capable of performing MPEG2 decoding in software at full speed without requiring an additional hardware MPEG2 decoder card. SSE-equipped processors are also much better and faster than previous processors when it comes to speech recognition.

One of the main benefits of SSE over plain MMX is that it supports single-precision floating-point SIMD operations, which have posed a bottleneck in the 3D graphics processing. Just as with plain MMX, SIMD enables multiple operations to be performed per processor instruction. Specifically, SSE supports up to four floating-point operations per cycle; that is, a single instruction can operate on four pieces of data simultaneously. SSE floating-point instructions can be mixed with MMX instructions with no performance penalties. SSE also supports data *prefetching*, which is a mechanism for reading data into the cache before it is actually called for.

SSE includes 70 new instructions for graphics and sound processing over what MMX provided. SSE is similar to MMX; in fact, besides being called KNI, SSE was called MMX-2 by some before it was released. In addition to adding more MMX-style instructions, the SSE instructions allow for floating-point calculations and now use a separate unit within the processor instead of sharing the standard floating-point unit as MMX did.

SSE2 was introduced in November 2000, along with the Pentium 4 processor, and adds 144 additional SIMD instructions. SSE2 also includes all the previous MMX and SSE instructions.

SSE3 was introduced in February 2004, along with the Pentium 4 Prescott processor, and adds 13 new SIMD instructions to improve complex math, graphics, video encoding, and thread synchronization. SSE3 also includes all the previous MMX, SSE, and SSE2 instructions.

SSSE3 (Supplemental SSE3) was introduced in June 2006 in the Xeon 5100 series server processors, and in July 2006 in the Core 2 processors. SSSE3 adds 32 new SIMD instructions to SSE3.

SSE4 (also called HD Boost by Intel) was introduced in January 2008 in versions of the Intel Core 2 processors (SSE4.1) and was later updated in November 2008 in the Core i7 processors (SSE4.2). SSE4 consists of 54 total instructions, with a subset of 47 instructions comprising SSE4.1, and the full 54 instructions in SSE4.2.

Advanced vector extensions (AVX) was introduced in January 2011 in the second-general Core i-series "Sandy Bridge" processors and is also supported by AMD's new "Bulldozer" processor family. AVX is a new 256-bit instruction set extension to SSE, comprising 12 new instructions. AVX helps floating-point intensive applications such as image and A/V processing, scientific simulations, financial analytics, and 3D modeling and analysis to perform better. AVX is supported on Windows 7 SP1, Windows Server 2008 R2 SP1, and Linux kernel version 2.6.30 and higher. For AVX support on virtual machines running on Windows Server R2, see http://support.microsoft.com/kb/2517374 for a hotfix.

For more information about AVX, see http://software.intel.com/en-us/avx/. Although AMD has adopted Intel SSE3 and earlier instructions in the past, instead of adopting SSE4, AMD has created a different set of only four instructions it calls SSE4a. Although AMD had planned to develop its own instruction set called SSE5 and release it as part of its new "Bulldozer" processor architecture, it decided to shelve SSE5 and create new instruction sets that use coding compatible with AVX. The new instruction sets include

- **XOP**—Integer vector instructions
- **FMA4**—Floating point instructions
- **CVT16**—Half-precision floating point conversion

3DNow!

3DNow! technology was originally introduced as AMD's alternative to the SSE instructions in the Intel processors. It included three generations: 3D Now!, Enhanced 3D Now!, and Professional 3D Now! (which added full support for SSE). AMD announced in August 2010 that it was dropping support for 3D Now!-specific instructions in upcoming processors.

For more information about 3D Now!, see "3D Now" in Chapter 3 of *Upgrading and Repairing PCs*, 19th Edition, which is supplied on the disc packaged with this book.

Dynamic Execution

First used in the P6 (or sixth-generation) processors, dynamic execution enables the processor to execute more instructions in parallel, so tasks are completed more quickly. This technology innovation is composed of three main elements:

- **Multiple branch prediction**—Predicts the flow of the program through several branches
- **Dataflow analysis**—Schedules instructions to be executed when ready, independent of their order in the original program
- **Speculative execution**—Increases the rate of execution by looking ahead of the program counter and executing instructions that are likely to be necessary

Branch Prediction

Branch prediction is a feature formerly found only in high-end mainframe processors. It enables the processor to keep the instruction pipeline full while running at a high rate of speed. A special fetch/decode unit in the processor uses a highly optimized branch-prediction algorithm to predict the direction and outcome of the instructions being executed through multiple levels of branches, calls, and returns. It is similar to a chess player working out multiple strategies in advance of game play by predicting the opponent's strategy several moves into the future. By predicting the instruction outcome in advance, the instructions can be executed with no waiting.

Dataflow Analysis

Dataflow analysis studies the flow of data through the processor to detect any opportunities for out-of-order instruction execution. A special dispatch/execute unit in the processor monitors many instructions and can execute these instructions in an order that optimizes the use of the multiple superscalar execution units. The resulting out-of-order execution of instructions can keep the execution units busy even when cache misses and other data-dependent instructions might otherwise hold things up.

Speculative Execution

Speculative execution is the processor's capability to execute instructions in advance of the actual program counter. The processor's dispatch/execute unit uses dataflow analysis to execute all available instructions in the instruction pool and store the results in temporary registers. A retirement unit then searches the instruction pool for completed instructions that are no longer data dependent on other instructions to run or which have unresolved branch predictions. If any such completed instructions are found, the retirement unit or the appropriate standard Intel architecture commits the results to memory in the order they were originally issued. They are then retired from the pool.

Dynamic execution essentially removes the constraint and dependency on linear instruction sequencing. By promoting out-of-order instruction execution, it can keep the instruction units working rather than waiting for data from memory. Even though instructions can be predicted and executed out of order, the results are committed in the original order so they don't disrupt or change program flow. This enables the P6 to run existing Intel architecture software exactly as the P5 (Pentium) and previous processors did—just a whole lot more quickly!

Dual Independent Bus Architecture

The Dual Independent Bus (DIB) architecture was first implemented in the sixth-generation processors from Intel and AMD. DIB was created to improve processor bus bandwidth and performance. Having two (dual) independent data I/O buses enables the processor to access data from either of its buses simultaneously and in parallel, rather than in a singular sequential manner (as in a single-bus system). The main (often called *front-side*) processor bus is the interface between the processor and the motherboard or chipset. The second (back-side) bus in a processor with DIB is used for the L2 cache, enabling it to run at much greater speeds than if it were to share the main processor bus.

Two buses make up the DIB architecture: the L2 cache bus and the main CPU bus, often called *FSB (front side bus)*. The P6 class processors, from the Pentium Pro to the Core 2, as well as Athlon 64 processors can use both buses simultaneously, eliminating a bottleneck there. The dual bus architecture enables the L2 cache of the newer processors to run at full speed inside the processor core on an independent bus, leaving the main CPU bus (FSB) to handle normal data flowing in and out of the chip. The two buses run at different speeds. The front-side bus or main CPU bus is coupled to the speed of the motherboard, whereas the back-side or L2 cache bus is coupled to the speed of the processor core. As the frequency of processors increases, so does the speed of the L2 cache.

DIB also enables the system bus to perform multiple simultaneous transactions (instead of singular sequential transactions), accelerating the flow of information within the system and boosting performance. Overall, DIB architecture offers up to three times the bandwidth performance over a single-bus architecture processor.

HT Technology

Intel's HT Technology allows a single processor or processor core to handle two independent sets of instructions at the same time. In essence, HT Technology converts a single physical processor core into two virtual processors.

HT Technology was introduced on Xeon workstation-class processors with a 533MHz system bus in March 2002. It found its way into standard desktop PC processors starting with the Pentium 4

3.06GHz processor in November 2002. HT Technology predates multicore processors, so processors that have multiple physical cores, such as the Core 2 and Core i Series, may or may not support this technology depending on the specific processor version. A quad-core processor that supports HT Technology (like the Core i Series) would appear as an 8-core processor to the OS; Intel's Core i7-3970x has six cores and supports up to 12 threads. Internally, an HT-enabled processor has two sets of general-purpose registers, control registers, and other architecture components for each core, but both logical processors share the same cache, execution units, and buses. During operations, each logical processor handles a single thread (see Figure 3.4).

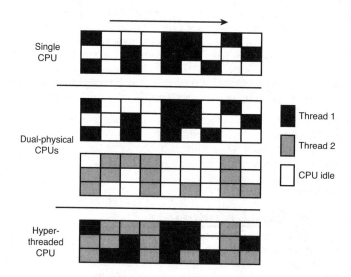

FIGURE 3.4 A processor with HT Technology enabled can fill otherwise-idle time with a second process for each core, improving multitasking and performance of multithreading single applications.

Although the sharing of some processor components means that the overall speed of an HT-enabled system isn't as high as a processor with as many physical cores would be, speed increases of 25% or more are possible when multiple applications or multithreaded applications are being run.

To take advantage of HT Technology, you need the following:

- **Processor supporting HT Technology**—This includes many (but not all) Core i Series, Pentium 4, Xeon, and Atom processors. Check the specific model processor specifications to be sure.
- **Compatible chipset**—Some older chipsets may not support HT Technology.
- **BIOS support to enable/disable HT Technology**—Make sure you enable HT Technology in the BIOS Setup.
- **HT Technology—enabled OS**—Windows XP and later support HT Technology. Linux distributions based on kernel 2.4.18 and higher also support HT Technology. To see if HT Technology is functioning properly, you can check the Device Manager in Windows to see how many processors are recognized. When HT is supported and enabled, the Windows Device Manager shows twice as many processors as there are physical processor cores.

Multicore Technology

HT Technology *simulates* two processors in a single physical core. If multiple simulated processors are good, having two or more *real* processors is a lot better. A multicore processor, as the name implies, actually contains two or more processor cores in a single processor package. From outward appearances, it still looks like a single processor (and is considered as such for Windows licensing purposes), but inside there can be two, three, four, or even more processor cores. A multicore processor provides virtually all the advantages of having multiple separate physical processors, all at a much lower cost.

Both AMD and Intel introduced the first dual-core x86-compatible desktop processors in May 2005. AMD's initial entry was the Athlon 64 X2, whereas Intel's first dual-core processors were the Pentium Extreme Edition 840 and the Pentium D. The Extreme Edition 840 was notable for also supporting HT Technology, allowing it to appear as a quad-core processor to the OS. These processors combined 64-bit instruction capability with dual internal cores—essentially two processors in a single package. These chips were the start of the multicore revolution, which has continued by adding more cores along with additional extensions to the instruction set. Intel introduced the first quad-core processors in November 2006, called the Core 2 Extreme QX and Core 2 Quad. AMD subsequently introduced its first quad-core desktop PC processor in November 2007, called the Phenom.

Note

There has been some confusion about Windows and multicore or hyperthreaded processors. Windows XP and later Home editions support only one physical CPU, whereas Windows Professional, Business, Enterprise, and Ultimate editions support two physical CPUs. Even though the Home editions support only a single physical CPU, if that chip is a multicore processor with HT Technology, all the physical and virtual cores are supported. For example, if you have a system with a quad-core processor supporting HT Technology, Windows Home editions will see it as eight processors, and all of them will be supported. If you had a motherboard with two of these CPUs installed, Windows Home editions would see the eight physical/virtual cores in the first CPU, whereas Professional, Business, Enterprise, and Ultimate editions would see all 16 cores in both CPUs.

Multicore processors are designed for users who run multiple programs at the same time or who use multithreaded applications, which pretty much describes all users these days. A multithreaded application can run different parts of the program, known as *threads,* at the same time in the same address space, sharing code and data. A multithreaded program runs faster on a multicore processor or a processor with HT Technology enabled than on a single-core or non-HT processor.

Figure 3.5 illustrates how a dual-core processor handles multiple applications for faster performance.

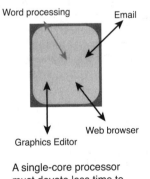

A single-core processor must devote less time to each running application as more applications are launched.

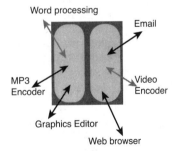

A dual-core processor splits up the workload between the processor cores, enabling it to perform faster with the same workload or handle more applications.

FIGURE 3.5 How a single-core processor (left) and a dual-core processor (right) handle multitasking.

It's important to realize that multicore processors don't improve single-task performance much. If you play non-multithreaded games on your PC, it's likely that you would see little advantage in a multi-core or hyperthreaded CPU. Fortunately, more and more software (including games) is designed to be multithreaded to take advantage of multicore processors. The program is broken into multiple threads, all of which can be divided among the available CPU cores.

Hardware-Assisted Virtualization Support

The ability to run multiple operating systems on a single computer, a technology known as *virtualization*, was originally developed for IBM mainframe computers in 1965. However, it has also been available in PCs for over a decade. By running multiple operating systems and applications on a single computer, a single computer can be used for multiple tasks, can support legacy applications that no longer run on a current operating system, and makes technical support of a wide range of operating systems, utilities, applications, and web browser versions from a single system feasible.

Virtualization can take two forms:

- Hypervisor/client
- Host/guest

With either type of virtualization, a program called a virtual machine manager (VMM) is used to create and manage a virtual machine (VM), which is a section of RAM and hard disk space that is set aside for use by an operating system and its applications. Once a VM is created and started, the user can install an operating system supported by the VMM, install any utilities designed to make the operating system work better inside the VM, and can use the VM as if it is the only operating system running on the hardware. The disk space used by a VM is usually dynamic, expanding from a small size to a pre-set maximum only as needed, and the RAM allocated to a VM is available for other processes when the VM is closed.

In hypervisor/client virtualization, the virtual machine manager (VMM) runs directly on the hardware, enabling VMs to go through fewer layers of emulation for faster performance than with host/guest virtualization. This type of virtualization is sometimes referred to as Type 1 or bare-metal virtualization. This is the type of virtualization performed by Microsoft Hyper-V and most server-class virtualizers.

In host/guest virtualization, a host operating system runs a virtual machine manager (VMM) program. The VMM is used to create and manage operating systems loaded as guests. In this type of virtualization, the connections between hardware and the virtual machine must pass through two layers: the device drivers used by the host operating system and the virtualized drivers used by the VMM. The multilayered nature of host/guest virtualization makes this type of virtualization relatively slow. It is also referred to as *Type 2 virtualization*, and Microsoft Virtual PC and Windows Virtual PC are examples of this type of virtualization.

Most virtualization programs for Windows-based PCs, such as Microsoft Virtual PC 2004 and 2007, use host/guest virtualization. To enable virtualization to run faster and make virtualization more useful, both Intel and AMD have added hardware-assisted virtualization support to their processors. The original edition of Windows Virtual PC for Windows 7 required the use of processors with hardware-assisted virtualization support with the BIOS configured to enable this feature. Although the current version of Windows Virtual PC does not require the use of processors with hardware-assisted virtualization, this feature is highly desirable for any computer that will be used for virtualization.

Note

Windows 8 Pro does not support Windows Virtual PC. Instead, it includes Hyper-V Client. Enable it through the Add/Remove Features from Windows dialog in the Control Panel.

AMD-V

AMD refers to its hardware-assisted virtualization support as AMD-V, although BIOS setup programs might also identify it as VMM or virtualization. Support for AMD-V is almost universal across its processors starting with models supporting Socket AM2 and their mobile counterparts up through current processors for AM3+ and FM2 sockets.

Intel VT-x and VT-D

Intel refers to its hardware-assisted virtualization support as Intel VT-x. Intel supports VT-x on all of its second-generation and third-generation Core i3/i5/i7 processors, and with certain models in older product families. Intel processors with VT-D support also virtualize directed I/O for faster performance of I/O devices in a virtualized environment.

VIA VT

VIA Technologies refers to its hardware-assisted virtualization support as VIA VT. It is present in all Nano-family processors as well as QuadCore and Eden X2 processor families.

Enabling Hardware-Assisted Virtualization Support

To enable hardware-assisted virtualization support on a computer, the following must occur:

- The installed process must support hardware-assisted virtualization
- The BIOS must support hardware-assisted virtualization
- The BIOS settings for hardware-assisted virtualization must be enabled
- A VMM that supports hardware-assisted virtualization must be installed

Note

To determine if a system includes a processor that supports hardware-assisted virtualization, use CPU-Z, and check BIOS settings.

The following sections discuss the major features of these processors and the different approaches Intel and AMD take to bring 64-bit multicore computing to the PC.

Processor Manufacturing

Processors are manufactured primarily from silicon, the second most common element on the planet. (Only the element oxygen is more common.) Silicon is the primary ingredient in beach sand; however, in that form it isn't pure enough to be used in chips.

The process by which silicon is formed into chips is a lengthy one that starts by growing pure silicon crystals via what is called the *Czochralski method* (named after the inventor of the process). In this method, electric arc furnaces transform the raw materials (primarily quartz rock that is mined) into metallurgical-grade silicon. Then to further weed out impurities, the silicon is converted to a liquid, distilled, and then redeposited in the form of semiconductor-grade rods, which are 99.999999% pure. These rods are then mechanically broken into chunks and packed into quartz crucibles, which are loaded into electric crystal pulling ovens. There the silicon chunks are melted at more than 2,500° Fahrenheit. To prevent impurities, the ovens usually are mounted on thick concrete cubes—often on a suspension to prevent vibration, which would damage the crystal as it forms.

After the silicon is melted, a small seed crystal is inserted into the molten silicon and slowly rotated (see Figure 3.6). As the seed is pulled out of the molten silicon, some of the silicon sticks to the seed and hardens in the same crystal structure as the seed. The pulling speed (10–40 millimeters per hour) and temperature (approximately 2,500°F) are carefully controlled, which causes the crystal to grow with a narrow neck that then widens into the full desired diameter. Depending on the chips being made, each ingot is 200mm (approximately 8 inches) or 300mm (12 inches) in diameter and more than 5 feet long, weighing hundreds of pounds.

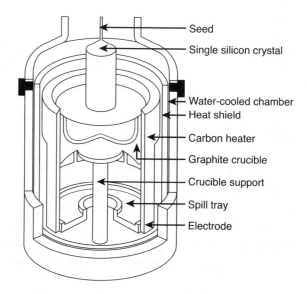

Seed
Single silicon crystal
Water-cooled chamber
Heat shield
Carbon heater
Graphite crucible
Crucible support
Spill tray
Electrode

FIGURE 3.6   Growing a pure silicon ingot in a high-pressure, high-temperature oven.

The ingot is then ground into a perfect 200mm- (8-inch) or 300mm-diameter (12-inch) cylinder, with a small flat or notch cut on one side for handling and positioning. Each ingot is then sliced with a high-precision saw into more than a thousand circular wafers, each less than a millimeter thick. The wafers are then polished to a mirror-smooth surface to make them ready for imprinting. A finished wafer with imprinted chips is shown in Figure 3.6.

Chips are manufactured from the wafers using a process called *photolithography*. Through this photographic process, transistors and circuit and signal pathways are created in semiconductors by depositing different layers of various materials on the chip, one after the other. Where two specific circuits intersect, a transistor or switch can form.

The photolithographic process starts when an insulating layer of silicon dioxide is grown on the wafer through a vapor deposition process. Then a coating of photoresist material is applied, and an image of that layer of the chip is projected through a mask onto the now light-sensitive surface.

Doping is the term that describes chemical impurities added to silicon (which is naturally a nonconductor), creating a material with semiconductor properties. The projector uses a specially created mask, which is essentially a negative of that layer of the chip etched in chrome on a quartz plate. Modern processors have 20 or more layers of material deposited and partially etched away (each requiring a mask) and up to six or more layers of metal interconnects.

As the light passes through a mask, the light is focused on the wafer surface, exposing the photoresist with the image of that layer of the chip. Each individual chip image is called a *die*. A device called a *stepper* then moves the wafer over a little bit, and the same mask imprints another chip die immediately next to the previous one. After the entire wafer is imprinted with a layer of material and photoresist, a caustic solution washes away the areas where the light struck the photoresist, leaving the mask imprints of the individual chip circuit elements and pathways. Then another layer of semiconductor material is deposited on the wafer with more photoresist on top, and the next mask exposes and then etches the next layer of circuitry. Using this method, the layers and components of each chip are built one on top of the other until the chips are completed (see Figure 3.7).

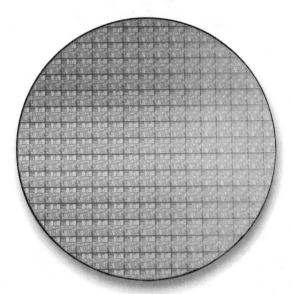

FIGURE 3.7 200mm (8-inch) wafer containing 177 full Pentium 4 Northwood (0.13-micron) processor cores.

Some of the masks add the *metallization* layers, which are the metal interconnects that tie all the individual transistors and other components together. Most older chips use aluminum interconnects, although in 2002 many moved to copper. The first commercial PC processor chip to use copper was the 0.18-micron Athlon made in AMD's Dresden fab, and Intel shifted the Pentium 4 to copper with the 0.13-micron Northwood version. Copper is a better conductor than aluminum and allows smaller interconnects with less resistance, meaning smaller and faster chips can be made. Copper hadn't been used previously because there were difficult corrosion problems to overcome during the manufacturing process that were not as much of a problem with aluminum.

Another technology used in chip manufacturing is called silicon on insulator (SOI). SOI uses a layered silicon-insulator-silicon wafer substrate to reduce parasitic device capacitance, thus reducing current leakage and improving performance. In particular, AMD has used SOI for many of its processors since 2001.

A completed circular wafer has as many chips imprinted on it as can possibly fit. Because each chip usually is square or rectangular, there are some unused portions at the edges of the wafer, but every attempt is made to use every square millimeter of surface.

The industry is going through several transitions in chip manufacturing. The trend in the industry is to use both larger wafers and a smaller manufacturing process. The *process* refers to the size and line spacing of the individual circuits and transistors on the chip, whereas the *wafer size* refers to the diameter of the circular wafers on which the chips are imprinted.

The industry began moving to the 90-nanometer (0.09-micron) process in 2004, the 65-nanometer in 2006, the 45-nanometer process in 2008, the 32-nanometer process in 2010, and the 22-nanometer process in 2012.

In 2002, chip manufacturing began moving from 200mm (8-inch) diameter wafers to larger 300mm (12-inch) wafers. The larger 300mm wafers enable more than double the number of chips to be made compared to the 200mm used previously. In addition, the transitions to smaller and smaller processes enable more transistors to be incorporated into the chip die.

Table 3.8 shows the CPU manufacturing process and silicon wafer size transitions for the first 30 years from when the processor debuted (1971–2001). Table 3.9 shows the continuing evolution of these transitions from 2002 through the present, and all the way to 2022, including several planned future transitions.

With more recent processors, smaller manufacturing processes have also been used to make more space available in each processor die for features such as multiple processor cores, CPU-integrated video, and large L3 caches. Thus, the Nehalem Core i7 six-core processor, although it uses a 45nm process, has a much larger core size than the Pentium 4 Northwood (which was built on a 130nm process): 263 square millimeters for the Nehalem (731 million transistors), versus just 131 square millimeters for Northwood (55 million transistors). As a result, the Nehalem Core i7 processors have a yield of 240 die candidates per wafer, about half of the yield of the Northwood.

These will still be made on 300mm wafers because the next wafer transition isn't expected until 2014, when a transition to 450mm wafers is expected.

Table 3.8   CPU Process/Wafer Size Transitions from 1971 to 2001

Date	1971	1974	1976	1982
Mfg. Process (microns)	10µm	6µm	3µm	1.5µm
Mfg. Process (nanometers)	10,000nm	6,000nm	3,000nm	1,500nm
Wafer Size (millimeters)	50.8mm	76.2mm	100mm	100mm
Wafer Size (inches)	2 in	3 in	4 in	4 in

Intel first used 150mm (6-inch) wafers in 1983 and 200mm (8-inch) wafers in 1993.

Table 3.9   CPU Process/Wafer Size Transitions from 2002 to 2022

Date	2002	2004	2006	2008
Mfg. Process (microns)	0.13µm	0.09µm	0.065µm	0.045µm
Mfg. Process (nanometers)	130nm	90nm	65nm	45nm
Wafer Size (millimeters)	300mm	300mm	300mm	300mm
Wafer Size (inches)	12 in	12 in	12 in	12 in

Intel first used 300mm (12-inch) wafers in 2002.

Note that not all the chips on each wafer will be good, especially as a new production line starts. As the manufacturing process for a given chip or production line is perfected, more and more of the chips will be good. The ratio of good to bad chips on a wafer is called the *yield*. Yields well below 50% are common when a new chip starts production; however, by the end of a given chip's life, the yields are normally in the 90% range. Most chip manufacturers guard their yield figures and are secretive about them because knowledge of yield problems can give their competitors an edge. A low yield causes problems both in the cost per chip and in delivery delays to their customers. If a company has specific knowledge of competitors' improving yields, it can set prices or schedule production to get higher market share at a critical point.

After a wafer is complete, a special fixture tests each of the chips on the wafer and marks the bad ones to be separated later. The chips are then cut from the wafer using either a high-powered laser or a diamond saw.

After being cut from the wafers, the individual dies are retested, packaged, and retested again. The packaging process is also referred to as *bonding* because the die is placed into a chip housing in which a special machine bonds fine gold wires between the die and the pins on the chip. The package is the container for the chip die, which essentially seals it from the environment.

After the chips are bonded and packaged, final testing is done to determine both proper function and rated speed. Different chips in the same batch often run at different speeds. Special test fixtures run each chip at different pressures, temperatures, and speeds, looking for the point at which the chip stops working. At this point, the maximum successful speed is noted and the final chips are sorted into bins with those that tested at a similar speed.

1989	1992	1994	1995	1997	1999	2001
1.0µm	0.8µm	0.6µm	0.35µm	0.25µm	0.18µm	0.13µm
1000nm	800nm	600nm	350nm	250nm	180nm	130nm
150mm	200mm	200mm	200mm	200mm	200mm	200mm
6 in	6 in	8 in	8 in	8 in	8 in	8 in

2010	2012	2014	2016	2018	2020	2022
0.032µm	0.022µm	0.016µm	0.011µm	0.008µm	0.006µm	0.004µm
32nm	22nm	16nm	11nm	8nm	6nm	4nm
300mm	300mm	450mm	450mm	450mm	450mm	450mm
12 in	12 in	18 in	18 in	18 in	18 in	18 in

One interesting thing about this is that as a manufacturer gains more experience and perfects a particular chip assembly line, the yield of the higher-speed versions goes way up. So, of all the chips produced from a single wafer, perhaps more than 75% of them check out at the highest speed, and only 25% or less run at the lower speeds. The paradox is that Intel often sells a lot more of the lower-priced, lower-speed chips, so it just dips into the bin of faster ones, labels them as slower chips, and sells them that way. People began discovering that many of the lower-rated chips actually ran at speeds much higher than they were rated, and the business of overclocking was born. Similarly, some lower-cost multicore processors from AMD have the same physical number of cores as higher-cost ones, but some cores are disabled during manufacturing.

Processor Re-Marking

Processor re-marking, the alterations of chip marking to make a slower chip masquerade as a faster chip, was once a major problem when virtually all processors could be overclocked (run at faster clock speeds than normal). However, with the advent of retail boxed processors, clock multiplier locks in most models, and utility programs such as CPU-Z that can identify processor names and features, processor re-marking is now minimal compared to its heyday over a decade ago.

To make sure your system has the processor you paid for, download and run a copy of CPU-Z (www.cpuid.com/softwares/cpu-z.html). CPU-Z is the *de facto* standard for CPU identification and feature display.

PGA Chip Packaging

Variations on the pin grid array (PGA) chip packaging have been the most commonly used chip packages over the years. They were used starting with the 286 processor in the 1980s and are still used today, although not in all CPU designs. PGA takes its name from the fact that the chip has a grid-like array of pins on the bottom of the package. PGA chips are inserted into sockets, which are often of a zero insertion force (ZIF) design. A ZIF socket has a lever to allow for easy installation and removal of the chip.

Most original Pentium processors use a variation on the regular PGA called staggered pin grid array (SPGA), in which the pins are staggered on the underside of the chip rather than in standard rows and columns. This was done to move the pins closer together and decrease the overall size of the chip when a large number of pins is required. Figure 3.8 shows a Pentium Pro that uses the dual-pattern SPGA (on the right) next to a Pentium 66 that uses the regular PGA. Note that the right half of the Pentium Pro shown here has additional pins staggered among the other rows and columns.

FIGURE 3.8   PGA on Pentium 66 (left) and dual-pattern SPGA on Pentium Pro (right).

Early PGA variations mounted the processor die in a cavity under the substrate, whereas so-called "Flip Chip" versions mount the processor die upside down so that less expensive solder bonding rather than expensive wire bonding can be used to connect the processor die to the chip package.

Unfortunately, there were some problems with attaching the heatsink to an FC-PGA chip. The heatsink sat on the top of the die, which acted as a pedestal. If you pressed down on one side of the heatsink excessively during the installation process (such as when you were attaching the clip), you risked cracking the silicon die and destroying the chip. This was especially a problem as heatsinks became larger and heavier and the force applied by the clip became greater. Intel and AMD now use a metal cap called a *heat spreader* over the top of the CPU to prevent damage when the heatsink is installed. This type of packaging is known as FC-PGA2 and was used by Intel for all Pentium 4 and subsequent chips. AMD began to use it with its Athlon 64 processors and subsequent chips.

Future packaging directions may include what is called *bumpless build-up layer* (BBUL) packaging. This embeds the die completely in the package; in fact, the package layers are built up around and on top of the die, fully encapsulating it within the package. This embeds the chip die and allows for a full flat surface for attaching the heatsink, as well as shorter internal interconnections within the package. BBUL is designed to handle extremely high clock speeds of 20GHz or faster but is not yet necessary.

Single Edge Contact and Single Edge Processor Packaging

Intel and AMD used cartridge- or board-based packaging for some of their processors from 1997 through 2000. This packaging was called *single edge contact cartridge* (SECC) or *single edge processor package* (SEPP) and consisted of the CPU and optional separate L2 cache chips mounted on a circuit board that looked similar to an oversized memory module and that plugged into a slot. In some cases, the boards were covered with a plastic cartridge.

To learn more about SECC and SEPP packaging, see "Single Edge Contact and Single Edge Processor Packaging" in Chapter 3 of *Upgrading and Repairing PCs,* 19th Edition, included in its entirety on the disc packaged with this book.

Processor Socket and Slot Types

Intel and AMD have created a set of socket and slot designs for their processors. Each socket or slot is designed to support a different range of original and upgrade processors. Table 3.10 shows the designations for the various standard processor sockets/slots and lists the chips designed to plug into them.

Sockets 1, 2, 3, and 6 are 486 processor sockets and are shown together in Figure 3.9 so you can see the overall size comparisons and pin arrangements between these sockets. Sockets 4, 5, 7, and 8 are Pentium and Pentium Pro processor sockets and are shown together in Figure 3.10 so you can see the overall size comparisons and pin arrangements between these sockets.

Table 3.10   CPU Socket Specifications

Chip Class	Socket	Pins	Layout	Voltage
486	Socket 1	169	17x17 PGA	5V
	Socket 2	238	19x19 PGA	5V
	Socket 3	237	19x19 PGA	5V/3.3V
	Socket 61	235	19x19 PGA	3.3V
586	Socket 4	273	21x21 PGA	5V
	Socket 5	320	37x37 SPGA	3.3V/3.5V
	Socket 7	321	37x37 SPGA	VRM
686	Socket 8	387	Dual-pattern SPGA	Auto VRM
	Slot 1 (SC242)	242	Slot	Auto VRM
	Socket 370	370	37x37 SPGA	Auto VRM
Intel P4/Core	Socket 423	423	39x39 SPGA	Auto VRM
	Socket 478	478	26x26 mPGA	Auto VRM
	Socket T (LGA775)	775	30x33 LGA	Auto VRM
	LGA1156 (Socket H)	1156	40x40 LGA	Auto VRM
	LGA1366 (Socket B)	1366	41x43 LGA	Auto VRM
	LGA1155 (Socket H2)	1155	40x40 LGA	Auto VRM
	LGA2011	2011	58×43 hexLGA	Auto VRM
AMD K7 class	Slot A	242	Slot	Auto VRM
	Socket A (462)	462	37x37 SPGA	Auto VRM
AMD K8 class	Socket 754	754	29x29 mPGA	Auto VRM
	Socket 939	939	31x31 mPGA	Auto VRM
	Socket 940	940	31x31 mPGA	Auto VRM
	Socket AM2	940	31x31 mPGA	Auto VRM
	Socket AM2+	940	31x31 mPGA	Auto VRM
	Socket AM3	9412	31x31 mPGA	Auto VRM
	Socket AM3+	9412	31x31 mPGA	Auto VRM
	Socket F (1207 FX)	1207	35x35 LGA	Auto VRM
AMD A class	Socket FM1	905	31x31 LGA	Auto VRM
	Socket FM2	904	31x31 LGA	Auto VRM
Server/Workstation	Slot 2 (SC330)	330	Slot	Auto VRM
	Socket 603	603	31×25 mPGA	Auto VRM
	Socket 604	604	31×25 mPGA	Auto VRM
	Socket PAC418	418	38×22 split SPGA	Auto VRM
	Socket PAC611	611	25×28 mPGA	Auto VRM
	LGA771 (Socket J)	771	30×33 LGA	Auto VRM
	Socket M (PGA478MT)	478	26×26 PGA	Auto VRM
	LGA1567	1567	38×43 LGA	Auto VRM
	Socket 940	940	31×31 mPGA	Auto VRM
	Socket F (1207 FX)	1207	35×35 LGA	Auto VRM

1 Socket 6 was never actually implemented in systems.

2 Socket has 941 pins, but CPUs for Socket AM3 have 938 pins.

FC-PGA = Flip-chip pin grid array

PGA2 = FC-PGA with an integrated heat spreader (IHS)

LGA = Land grid array

hexLGA = Land grid array arranged in a hexagonal pattern

OverDrive = Retail upgrade processors

PAC = Pin array cartridge

Supported Processors	Introduced
486 SX/SX2, DX/DX2, DX4 OD	Apr. 1989
486 SX/SX2, DX/DX2, DX4 OD, 486 Pentium OD	Mar. 1992
486 SX/SX2, DX/DX2, DX4, 486 Pentium OD, AMD 5x86	Feb. 1994
486 DX4, 486 Pentium OD	Feb. 1994
Pentium 60/66, OD	Mar. 1993
Pentium 75-133, OD	Mar. 1994
Intel Pentium 75-233+, MMX, OD, AMD K5/K6, Cyrix M1/II	Jan. 1997
Intel Pentium Pro, OD	Nov. 1995
Intel Pentium II/III SECC, Celeron SEPP	May 1997
Intel Celeron/Pentium III PPGA/FC-PGA, VIA/Cyrix III/C3	Nov. 1998
Intel Pentium 4 FC-PGA	Nov. 2000
Intel Pentium 4/Celeron FC-PGA2, Celeron D	Oct. 2001
Intel Pentium 4/Extreme Edition, Pentium D, Celeron D, Pentium dual-core, Core2	June 2004
Intel Pentium, Core i3/i5/i7, Xeon	Sept. 2009
Intel Core i7, Xeon	Nov. 2008
Intel Core i7, i5, i3	Jan. 2011
Intel Core i7	Nov. 2011
AMD Athlon SECC	June 1999
AMD Athlon/Athlon XP/Duron PGA/FC-PGA	June 2000
AMD Athlon 64	Sep. 2003
AMD Athlon 64 v.2	June 2004
AMD Athlon 64 FX, Opteron	Apr.2003
AMD Athlon 64/64FX/64 X2, Sempron, Opteron, Phenom	May 2006
AMD Athlon 64/64 X2, Opteron, Phenom X2/X3/X4, II X4	Nov. 2007
AMD Athlon II, Phenom II, Sempron	Feb. 2009
AMD "Bulldozer" processors	Mid-2011
AMD Athlon 64 FX, Opteron	Aug. 2006
AMD A4, A6, A8, Athlon II, E2, Sempron	Jul. 2011
AMD A4, A6, A8, A10	Sept. 2012
Intel Pentium II/III Xeon	Apr. 1998
Intel Xeon (P4)	May 2001
Intel Xeon (P4)	Oct. 2003
Intel Itanium	May 2001
Itanium 2	July 2002
Intel Xeon	Jun. 2006
Intel Xeon	Jan. 2006
Intel Xeon	April 2011
AMD Athlon 64 FX, Opteron	Apr. 2003
AMD Athlon 64 FX, Opteron	Aug. 2006

PGA = Pin grid array

PPGA = Plastic pin grid array

SECC = Single edge contact cartridge

SEPP = Single edge processor package

SPGA = Staggered pin grid array

mPGA = Micro pin grid array

VRM = Voltage regulator module with variable voltage output determined by module type or manual jumpers

Auto VRM = Voltage regulator module with automatic voltage selection determined by processor voltage ID (VID) pins

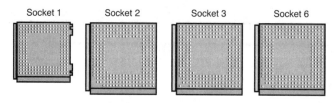

FIGURE 3.9 486 processor sockets.

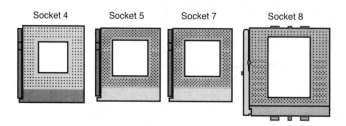

FIGURE 3.10 Pentium and Pentium Pro processor sockets.

When the Socket 1 specification was created, manufacturers realized that if users were going to upgrade processors, they had to make the process easier. The socket manufacturers found that 100 lbs. of insertion force is required to install a chip in a standard 169-pin Socket 1 motherboard. With this much force involved, you easily could damage either the chip or the socket during removal or reinstallation. Because of this, some motherboard manufacturers began using low insertion force (LIF) sockets, which required a smaller 60 lbs. of insertion force for a 169-pin chip. Pressing down on the motherboard with 60–100 lbs. of force can crack the board if it is not supported properly. A special tool is also required to remove a chip from one of these sockets. As you can imagine, even the LIF was relative, and a better solution was needed if the average person was ever going to replace his CPU.

Manufacturers began using ZIF sockets in Socket 1 designs, and all processor sockets from Socket 2 and higher have been of the ZIF design. ZIF is required for all the higher-density sockets because the insertion force would simply be too great otherwise. ZIF sockets almost eliminate the risk involved in installing or removing a processor because no insertion force is necessary to install the chip and no tool is needed to extract one. Most ZIF sockets are handle-actuated: You lift the handle, drop the chip into the socket, and then close the handle. This design makes installing or removing a processor easy.

The following sections take a closer look at those socket designs you are likely to encounter in active PCs.

For more information about Socket 370 (PGA-370), Socket 423, Socket A, and Socket 754, see Chapter 3, "Processor Types and Specifications," of *Upgrading and Repairing PCs*, 19th Edition, found in its entirety on the DVD packaged with this book.

Socket 478

Socket 478 is a ZIF-type socket for the Pentium 4 and Celeron 4 (Celerons based on the Pentium 4 core) introduced in October 2001. It was specially designed to support additional pins for future Pentium 4 processors and speeds over 2GHz. The heatsink mounting is different from the previous Socket 423, allowing larger heatsinks to be attached to the CPU. Figure 3.11 shows Socket 478.

Socket 478 supports a 400MHz, 533MHz, or 800MHz processor bus that connects the processor to the MCH, which is the main part of the motherboard chipset.

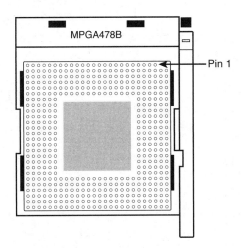

FIGURE 3.11 Socket 478 (Pentium 4) showing pin 1 location.

Socket 478 uses a heatsink attachment method that clips the heatsink directly to the motherboard, and not the CPU socket or chassis (as with Socket 423). Therefore, any standard chassis can be used, and the special standoffs used by Socket 423 boards are not required. This heatsink attachment allows for a much greater clamping load between the heatsink and processor, which aids cooling.

Socket 478 processors use five VID pins to signal the VRM built into the motherboard to deliver the correct voltage for the particular CPU you install. This makes the voltage selection completely automatic and foolproof. A small triangular mark indicates the pin-1 corner for proper orientation of the chip.

Socket LGA775

Socket LGA775 (also called Socket T) is used by the Core 2 Duo/Quad processors, the most recent versions of the Intel Pentium 4 Prescott processor and the Pentium D and Pentium Extreme Edition processors. Some versions of the Celeron and Celeron D also use Socket LGA775. Socket LGA775, unlike earlier Intel processor sockets, uses a land grid array format, so the pins are on the socket, rather than the processor.

LGA uses gold pads (called *lands*) on the bottom of the processor to replace the pins used in PGA packages. It allows for much greater clamping forces via a load plate with a locking lever, with greater stability and improved thermal transfer (better cooling). The first LGA processors were the Pentium II and Celeron processors in 1997; in those processors, an LGA chip was soldered on the Slot-1 cartridge. LGA is a recycled version of what was previously called *leadless chip carrier* (LCC) packaging. This was used way back on the 286 processor in 1984, and it had gold lands around the edge only. (There were far fewer pins back then.) In other ways, LGA is simply a modified version of ball grid array (BGA), with gold lands replacing the solder balls, making it more suitable for socketed (rather than soldered) applications. Socket LGA775 is shown in Figure 3.12.

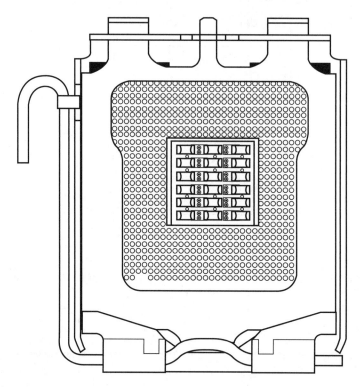

FIGURE 3.12   Socket LGA775 (Socket T). The release lever on the left raises the load plate out of the way to permit the processor to be placed over the contacts.

Socket LGA1156

Socket LGA1156 (also known as *Socket H*) was introduced in September 2009 and was designed to support Intel Core i Series processors featuring an integrated chipset North Bridge, including a dual-channel DDR3 memory controller and optional integrated graphics. Socket LGA1156 uses a land grid array format, so the pins are on the socket, rather than the processor. Socket LGA1156 is shown in Figure 3.13.

Because the processor includes the chipset North Bridge, Socket LGA1156 is designed to interface between a processor and a Platform Controller Hub (PCH), which is the new name used for the South Bridge component in supporting 5x series chipsets. The LGA1156 interface includes the following:

- **PCI Express x16 v2.0**—For connection to either a single PCIe x16 slot, or two PCIe x8 slots supporting video cards.

- **DMI (Direct Media Interface)**—For data transfer between the processor and the PCH. DMI in this case is essentially a modified PCI Express x4 v2.0 connection, with a bandwidth of 2GBps.

- **DDR3 dual-channel**—For direct connection between the memory controller integrated into the processor and DDR3 SDRAM modules in a dual-channel configuration.

- **FDI (Flexible Display Interface)**—For the transfer of digital display data between the (optional) processor integrated graphics and the PCH.

When processors with integrated graphics are used, the Flexible Display Interface carries digital display data from the GPU in the processor to the display interface circuitry in the PCH. Depending on the motherboard, the display interface can support DisplayPort, High Definition Multimedia Interface (HDMI), Digital Visual Interface (DVI), or Video Graphics Array (VGA) connectors.

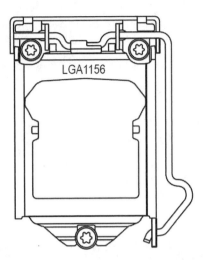

FIGURE 3.13   Socket LGA1156 (Socket H).

Socket LGA1366

Socket LGA1366 (also known as Socket B) was introduced in November 2008 to support high-end Intel Core i Series processors, including an integrated triple-channel DDR3 memory controller, but which also requires an external chipset North Bridge, in this case called an I/O Hub (IOH). Socket LGA1366 uses a land grid array format, so the pins are on the socket, rather than the processor. Socket LGA1366 is shown in Figure 3.14.

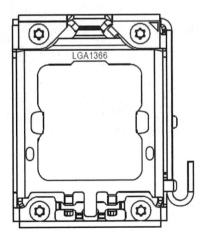

FIGURE 3.14   Socket LGA1366 (Socket B).

Socket LGA1366 is designed to interface between a processor and an IOH, which is the new name used for the North Bridge component in supporting 5x series chipsets. The LGA1366 interface includes the following:

- **QPI (Quick Path Interconnect)**—For data transfer between the processor and the IOH. QPI transfers 2 bytes per cycle at either 4.8 or 6.4GHz, resulting in a bandwidth of 9.6 or 12.8GBps.

- **DDR3 triple-channel**—For direct connection between the memory controller integrated into the processor and DDR3 SDRAM modules in a triple-channel configuration.

LGA1366 is designed for high-end PC, workstation, or server use. It supports configurations with multiple processors.

Socket LGA1155

Socket LGA1155 (also known as *Socket H2*) was introduced in January 2011 to support Intel's Sandy Bridge (second-generation) Core i Series processors, which now include Turbo Boost overclocking. Socket LGA1155 uses a land grid array format, so the pins are on the socket, rather than the processor. Socket LGA1155 uses the same cover plate as Socket 1156, but is not interchangeable with it. Socket LGA1155 is also used by Intel's Ivy Bridge (third-generation) Core i Series processors. LGA1155 supports up to 16 PCIe v3 lanes and 8 PCIe 2.0 lanes.

Socket LGA1155 is shown in Figure 3.15.

FIGURE 3.15   Socket LGA1155 (Socket H2) before installing a processor.

Socket LGA2011

Socket LGA2011 was introduced in November 2011 to support high-performance versions of Intel's Sandy Bridge (second-generation) Core i Series processors (Sandy Bridge-E), which now include Turbo Boost overclocking. LGA2011 supports 40 PCIe 3.0 lanes, quad-channel memory addressing, and fully-unlocked processor multipliers.

Socket LGA2011 uses a land grid array format, so the pins are on the socket, rather than the processor. Socket LGA2011 is shown in Figure 3.16.

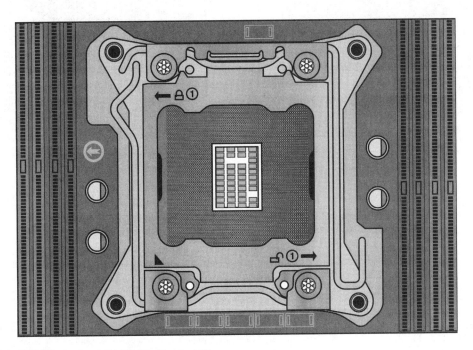

FIGURE 3.16   Socket LGA2011 before installing a processor.

Socket 939 and 940

Socket 939 is used with the Socket 939 versions of the AMD Athlon 64, 64 FX, and 64 X2 (see Figure 3.17). It's also used by some versions of the AMD Opteron processor for workstations and servers. Motherboards using this socket support conventional unbuffered DDR SDRAM modules in either single- or dual-channel mode, rather than the server-oriented (more expensive) registered modules required by Socket 940 motherboards. Sockets 939 and 940 have different pin arrangements and processors for each and are not interchangeable.

Socket 940 is used with the Socket 940 version of the AMD Athlon 64 FX, as well as most AMD Opteron processors (see Figure 3.18). Motherboards using this socket support only registered DDR SDRAM modules in dual-channel mode. Because the pin arrangement is different, Socket 939 processors do not work in Socket 940, and vice versa.

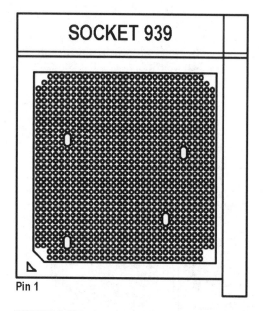

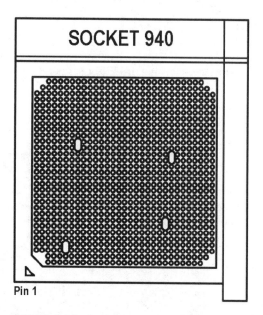

FIGURE 3.17　Socket 939. The cutout corner and triangle at the lower left indicate pin 1.

FIGURE 3.18　Socket 940. The cutout corner and triangle at the lower left indicate pin 1.

Socket AM2/AM2+/AM3/AM3+

In May 2006, AMD introduced processors that use a new socket, called *Socket AM2* (see Figure 3.19). AM2 was the first replacement for the confusing array of Socket 754, Socket 939, and Socket 940 form factors for the Athlon 64, Athlon 64 FX, and Athlon 64 X2 processors.

Although Socket AM2 contains 940 pins—the same number that Socket 940 uses—Socket AM2 is designed to support the integrated dual-channel DDR2 memory controllers that were added to the Athlon 64 and Opteron processor families in 2006. Processors designed for Sockets 754, 939, and 940 include DDR memory controllers and are not pin compatible with Socket AM2. Sockets 939, 940, and AM2 support HyperTransport v2.0, which limits most processors to a 1GHz FSB.

Socket AM2+ is an upgrade to Socket AM2 that was released in November 2007. Although Sockets AM2 and AM2+ are physically the same, Socket AM2+ adds support for split power planes and HyperTransport 3.0, allowing for FSB speeds of up to 2.6GHz. Socket AM2+ chips are backward compatible with Socket AM2 motherboards, but only at reduced HyperTransport 2.0 FSB speeds. Socket AM2 processors can technically work in Socket AM2+ motherboards; however, this also requires BIOS support, which is not present in all motherboards.

Socket AM3 was introduced in February 2009, primarily to support processors with integrated DDR3 memory controllers such as the Phenom II. Besides adding support for DDR3 memory, Socket AM3 has 941 pins in a modified key pin configuration that physically prevents Socket AM2 or AM2+ processors from being inserted (see Figure 3.20).

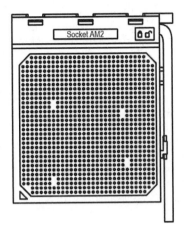

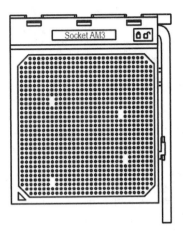

FIGURE 3.19 Socket AM2/AM2+. The arrow (triangle) at the lower left indicates pin 1.

FIGURE 3.20 Socket AM3. The arrow (triangle) at the lower left indicates pin 1.

Socket AM3+ is a modified version of AM3 designed for the new "Bulldozer" processors. It has 938 pins, and also supports processors made for AM3 sockets. Table 3.11 shows the essential differences between Socket AM2, AM2+, AM3, and AM3+.

Table 3.11 Socket AM2, AM2+, AM3, and AM3+ Features

Features	Socket AM2	Socket AM2+	Socket AM3	Socket AM3+
Number of Pins	940	940	938	938
Hyper-Transport (FSB) Support	2.0 (up to 1.4GHz)	3.0 (up to 2.6GHz)	3.0 (up to 2.6GHz)	3.0 (up to 2.6GHz)
Supported Memory	DDR2 (dual-channel)	DDR2 (dual-channel)	DDR3 (dual-channel)	DDR3 (dual-channel)
Supported Processors	Socket AM2, AM2+, or AM3	Socket AM2, AM2+, AM3	Socket AM3	Socket AM3+ or AM3

Here is a summary of the compatibility between AM2, AM2+, AM3, and AM3+ processors and motherboards:

- You cannot install Socket AM2 or AM2+ processors in Socket AM3 motherboards.
- You can install Socket AM2 processors in Socket AM2+ motherboards.
- You can install Socket AM3 or AM2+ processors in Socket AM2 motherboards; however, the BIOS must support the processor, the FSB will run at lower HT 2.0 speeds, and only DDR2 memory is supported.
- You can install Socket AM3 processors in Socket AM2+ motherboards, but the BIOS must support the processor, and only DDR2 memory is supported.
- You can install Socket AM3 processors in Socket AM3+ motherboards, but the BIOS must support the processor.

Although you can physically install newer processors in motherboards with older sockets, and they should theoretically work with reductions in bus speeds and memory support, this also requires BIOS support in the specific motherboard, which may be lacking. In general, you are best off matching the processor to a motherboard with the same type of socket.

Socket F (1207FX)

Socket F (also called *1207FX*) was introduced by AMD in August 2006 for its Opteron line of server processors. Socket F is AMD's first land grid array (LGA) socket, similar to Intel's Socket LGA775. It features 1,207 pins in a 35-by-35 grid, with the pins in the socket instead of on the processor. Socket F normally appears on motherboards in pairs because it is designed to run dual physical processors on a single motherboard. Socket F was utilized by AMD for its Quad FX processors, which are dual-core processors sold in matched pairs, operating as a dual socket dual-core system. Future versions may support quad-core processors, for a total of 8 cores in the system. Due to the high expense of running dual physical processors, only a limited number of nonserver motherboards are available with Socket F.

Socket FM1

Socket FM1 was introduced by AMD in July 2011 for use by accelerated processing units (APUs – CPU plus GPU) and CPUs based on the Llano core. These include the Ax-3xxx series APUs and some Athlon II CPUs, as well as the E2-3200 APU. FM1 has 905 pins in a 31 × 31 grid and uses a PGA socket similar to those used by previous AMD processors. Socket FM1 supports DDR3 memory. It was replaced by Socket FM2.

Socket FM2

Socket FM1 was introduced by AMD in September 2012 for use by its Trinity series of APUs. These include the Ax-5xxx series APUs. FM2 has 904 pins in a 31 × 31 grid and uses a PGA socket similar to those used by previous AMD processors. Socket FM2 supports DDR3 memory. Figure 3.21 illustrates Socket FM2.

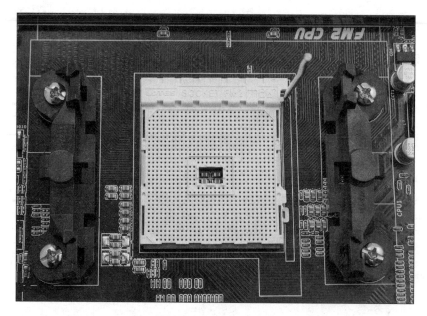

FIGURE 3.21   Socket FM2 before installing a processor.

CPU Operating Voltages

One trend that is clear to anybody who has been following processor design is that the operating voltages keep getting lower. The benefits of lower voltage are threefold. The most obvious is that with lower voltage comes lower overall power consumption. By consuming less power, the system is less expensive to run, but more importantly for portable or mobile systems, it runs much longer on existing battery technology. The emphasis on battery operation has driven many of the advances in lowering processor voltage because this has a great effect on battery life.

The second major benefit is that with less voltage and therefore less power consumption, less heat is produced. Processors that run cooler can be packed into systems more tightly and last longer.

The third major benefit is that a processor running cooler on less power can be made to run faster. Lowering the voltage has been one of the key factors in enabling the clock rates of processors to go higher and higher. This is because the lower the voltage, the shorter the time needed to change a signal from low to high.

Starting with the Pentium Pro, all newer processors automatically determine their voltage settings by controlling the motherboard-based voltage regulator. That's done through built-in VID pins.

For overclocking purposes, many motherboards have override settings that allow for manual voltage adjustment if desired. Many people have found that, when attempting to overclock a processor, increasing the voltage by a tenth of a volt or so often helps. Of course, this increases the heat output of the processor and must be accounted for with adequate cooling.

Note

Although modern processors use VID pins to enable them to select the correct voltage, newer processors that use the same processor socket as older processors might use a voltage setting the motherboard does not support. Before upgrading an existing motherboard with a new processor, make sure the motherboard will support the processor's voltage and other features. You might need to install a BIOS upgrade before upgrading the processor to ensure that the motherboard properly recognizes the processor.

Math Coprocessors (Floating-Point Units)

Older CPUs designed by Intel (and cloned by other companies) used an external math coprocessor chip to perform floating-point operations. However, when Intel introduced the 486DX, it included a built-in math coprocessor, and every processor built by Intel (and AMD and VIA/Cyrix, for that matter) since then includes a math coprocessor. Coprocessors provide hardware for floating-point math, which otherwise would create an excessive drain on the main CPU. Math chips speed your computer's operation only when you are running software designed to take advantage of the coprocessor.

Note

Most applications that formerly used floating-point math now use MMX/SSE instructions instead. These instructions are faster and more accurate than x87 floating-point math.

To learn more about math coprocessors for 8088 through 80386 processors, see "Math Coprocessors (Floating Point Units)" in Chapter 3 of *Upgrading and Repairing PCs*, 19th Edition, included in its entirety on the disc packaged with this book.

Processor Bugs and Steppings

Processor manufacturers use specialized equipment to test their own processors, but you have to settle for a little less. The best processor-testing device to which you have access is a system that you know is functional; you then can use the diagnostics available from various utility software companies or your system manufacturer to test the motherboard and processor functions.

Perhaps the most infamous of these bugs is the floating-point division math bug in the early Pentium processors. This and a few other bugs are discussed in detail later in this chapter.

Because the processor is the brain of a system, most systems don't function with a defective processor. If a system seems to have a dead motherboard, try replacing the processor with one from a functioning motherboard that uses the same CPU chip. You might find that the processor in the original board is the culprit. If the system continues to play dead, however, the problem is elsewhere, most likely in the motherboard, memory, or power supply. See the chapters that cover those parts of the system for more information on troubleshooting those components. I must say that in all my years of troubleshooting and repairing PCs, I have rarely encountered defective processors.

A few system problems are built in at the factory, although these bugs or design defects are rare. By learning to recognize these problems, you can avoid unnecessary repairs or replacements. Each processor section describes several known defects in that generation of processors, such as the infamous floating-point error in the Pentium. For more information on these bugs and defects, see the following sections, and check with the processor manufacturer for updates.

Microcode and the Processor Update Feature

All processors can contain design defects or errors. Many times, you can avoid the effects of any given bug by implementing hardware or software workarounds. Intel documents these bugs and workarounds well for its processors in the processor Specification Update manual that is available from Intel's website. Most of the other processor manufacturers also have bulletins or tips on their websites listing any problems or special fixes or patches for their chips.

Previously, the only way to fix a processor bug was to work around it or replace the chip with one that had the bug fixed. Starting with the Intel P6 and P7 family processors, including the Pentium Pro through Pentium D and Core i7, many bugs in a processor's design can be fixed by altering the microcode in the processor. Microcode is essentially a set of instructions and tables in the processor that control the way the processor operates. These processors incorporate a new feature called reprogrammable microcode, which enables certain types of bugs to be worked around via microcode updates. The microcode updates reside in either the motherboard ROM BIOS or Windows updates and are loaded into the processor by the motherboard BIOS during the POST or by Windows during the boot process. Each time the system is rebooted, the updated microcode is reloaded, ensuring that it will have the bug fix installed anytime the system is operating.

The updated microcode for a given processor is provided by Intel to either the motherboard manufacturers or to Microsoft so the code can be incorporated into the flash ROM BIOS for the board, or directly into Windows via Windows Update. This is one reason it is important to keep Windows up to date, as well as to install the most recent motherboard BIOS for your systems. Because it is easier for most people to update Windows than to update the motherboard BIOS, it seems that more recent microcode updates are being distributed via Microsoft than the motherboard manufacturers.

Processor Code Names

Intel, AMD, and VIA have always used code names when talking about future processors and processor cores. The code names usually are not supposed to become public, but they often do. They can often be found in online and print news and magazine articles talking about future-generation processors.

Sometimes they even appear in motherboard manuals because the manuals are written before the processors are officially introduced.

Intel publishes a fairly complete list of processor, chipset, motherboard, and even Ethernet controller code names on its website (http://ark.intel.com/#codenames). AMD doesn't provide a single document on its site for its code names, but you can use a Google search such as "code name" site:amd.com to find documents on the AMD website that contain code names. You can also find information on other sites by doing a search.

P1 (086) Processors

Intel introduced the 8086 back in June 1978. The 8086 was one of the first 16-bit processor chips on the market; at the time, virtually all other processors were 8-bit designs. The 8086 had 16-bit internal registers and could run a new class of software using 16-bit instructions. It also had a 16-bit external data path, so it could transfer data to memory 16 bits at a time. It contained 29,000 transistors and could run at clock speeds of up to 5MHz.

The address bus was 20 bits wide, which enabled the 8086 to address a full 1MB (2^{20}) of memory. This was in stark contrast to most other chips of that time that had 8-bit internal registers, an 8-bit external data bus, and a 16-bit address bus allowing a maximum of only 64KB of RAM (2^{16}).

Although not directly backward compatible with the 8080, the 8086 instructions and language were similar and enabled older programs to quickly be ported over to run. This later proved important to help jump-start the PC software revolution with recycled CP/M (8080) software.

Unfortunately, most of the personal computer world at the time was using 8-bit processors, which ran 8-bit CP/M (Control Program for Microprocessors) OSs and software. The board and circuit designs at the time were largely 8-bit as well. Building a full 16-bit motherboard, expansion cards, and memory system was costly, pricing such a computer out of the market.

The cost was high because the 8086 needed a 16-bit data bus rather than a less expensive 8-bit bus. Systems available at that time were 8-bit, and slow sales of the 8086 indicated to Intel that people weren't willing to pay for the extra performance of the full 16-bit design. In response, Intel introduced a kind of crippled version of the 8086, called the 8088, in June 1979.

The 8088 processor used the same internal core as the 8086, had the same 16-bit registers, and could address the same 1MB of memory, but the external data bus was reduced to 8 bits. This enabled support chips from the older 8-bit 8085 to be used, and far less expensive boards and systems could be made. However, because it retained the full 16-bit internal registers and the 20-bit address bus, the 8088 ran 16-bit software and was capable of addressing a full 1MB of RAM.

For these reasons, IBM selected the 8-bit 8088 chip (running at 4.77MHz, taking 12 cycles for the average instruction to complete) for the original IBM PC, which was introduced in August of 1981. That event dramatically changed the fate of both Intel and Microsoft, which provided Microsoft Disk Operating System (MS-DOS) version 1.0 for the new computer.

This decision would affect history in several ways. The 8088 was fully software compatible with the 8086, so it could run 16-bit software. Also, because the instruction set was similar to the previous 8085 and 8080, programs written for those older chips could quickly and easily be modified to run. This enabled a large library of programs to be quickly released for the IBM PC, thus helping it become a success. The overwhelming blockbuster success of the IBM PC left in its wake the legacy of requiring backward compatibility with it. To maintain the momentum, Intel has pretty much been forced to maintain backward compatibility with the 8088/8086 in most of the processors it has released since then. Since the fateful decision was made to use an Intel processor in the first PC, subsequent

PC-compatible systems have used a series of Intel or Intel-compatible processors, with each new one capable of running the software of the processor before it.

Years later, IBM was criticized for using the 8-bit 8088 instead of the 16-bit 8086. In retrospect, it was a wise decision. IBM even covered up the physical design in its ads, which at the time indicated its new PC had a "high-speed 16-bit microprocessor." IBM could say that because the 8088 still ran the same powerful 16-bit software the 8086 ran, just a little more slowly. In fact, programmers universally thought of the 8088 as a 16-bit chip because there was virtually no way a program could distinguish an 8088 from an 8086. This enabled IBM to deliver a PC capable of running a new generation of 16-bit software, while retaining a much less expensive 8-bit design for the hardware. Because of this, the IBM PC was actually priced less at its introduction than the most popular PC of the time, the Apple II. For the trivia buffs out there, the IBM PC listed for $1,265 and included only 16KB of RAM, whereas a similarly configured Apple II cost $1,355.

It took over two years between the introduction of the 8088 and the release of the IBM PC. Back then, a significant lag time often occurred between the introduction of a new processor and systems that incorporated it. That is unlike today, when new processors and systems using them often are released on the same day.

Computer users have sometimes wondered why a 640KB conventional-memory barrier exists if the 8088 chip can address 1MB of memory. The conventional-memory barrier exists because IBM reserved 384KB of the upper portion of the 1,024KB (1MB) address space of the 8088 for use by adapter cards and system BIOS. The lower 640KB is the conventional memory in which DOS and software applications execute. Windows and other modern operating systems use memory that is primarily above 1MB.

P2 (286) Processors

In 1982, Intel introduced the Intel 80286 processor, normally abbreviated as 286. The first CPU behind the original IBM PC AT (Advanced Technology), it did not suffer from the compatibility problems that damned the 80186 and 80188. Other computer makers manufactured what came to be known as *IBM clones*, with many of these manufacturers calling their systems AT-compatible or AT-class computers.

When IBM developed the AT, it selected the 286 as the basis for the new system because the chip provided compatibility with the 8088 used in the PC and the XT. Therefore, software written for those chips should run on the 286. The 286 chip is many times faster than the 8088 used in the XT, and at the time it offered a major performance boost to PCs used in businesses. The processing speed, or throughput, of the original AT (which ran at 6MHz) is five times greater than that of the PC running at 4.77MHz. The die for the 286 is shown in Figure 3.22.

The 286 was faster than the 8088 for two reasons: It required only 4.5 cycles to perform the average instruction (versus 12 on the 808x processors), and it handled data in 16-bit chunks. The 286's real mode imitates an 808x processor, and the protected mode can access memory larger than 1MB. The 286 also supports multitasking.

For more about the 286 processor, see Chapter 3 of *Upgrading and Repairing PCs*, 19th Edition, available in its entirety on the disc packaged with this book.

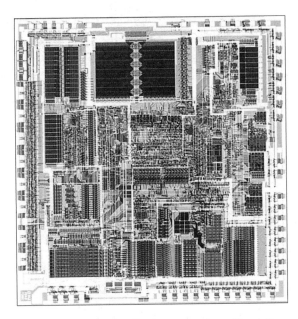

FIGURE 3.22   286 processor die. Photograph used by permission of Intel Corporation.

P3 (386) Processors

The third generation represents perhaps the most significant change in processors since the first PC. The big deal was the migration from processors that handled 16-bit operations to true 32-bit chips. The third-generation processors were so far ahead of their time that it took fully 10 years before 32-bit OSs and software became mainstream, and by that time the third-generation chips had become a memory.

The Intel 80386 (usually abbreviated as 386) caused quite a stir in the PC industry because of the vastly improved performance it brought to the personal computer. Compared to 8088 and 286 systems, the 386 chip offered greater performance in almost all areas of operation.

The 386 is a full 32-bit processor optimized for high-speed operation and multitasking OSs. Intel introduced the chip in 1985, but the 386 appeared in the first systems in late 1986 and early 1987. The Compaq Deskpro 386 and systems made by several other manufacturers introduced the chip; somewhat later, IBM used the chip in its PS/2 Model 80.

The 386 can execute the real-mode instructions of an 8086 or 8088, but in fewer clock cycles. The 386 was as efficient as the 286 in executing instructions—the average instruction took about 4.5 clock cycles. In raw performance, therefore, the 286 and 386 actually seemed to be at almost equal clock rates. The 386 offered greater performance in other ways, mainly because of additional software capability (modes) and a greatly enhanced memory management unit (MMU). The die for the 386 is shown in Figure 3.23.

The 386 can switch to and from protected mode under software control without a system reset—a capability that makes using protected mode more practical. In addition, the 386 includes a new mode, called *virtual real mode*, which enables several real mode sessions to run simultaneously under protected mode.

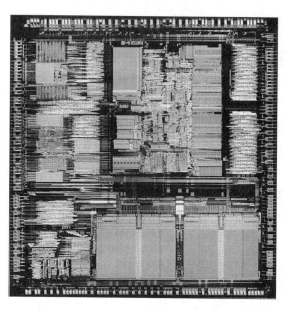

FIGURE 3.23   386 processor die. Photograph used by permission of Intel Corporation.

The protected mode of the 386 is fully compatible with the protected mode of the 286. Intel extended the memory-addressing capabilities of 386 protected mode with a new MMU that provided advanced memory paging and program switching. These features were extensions of the 286 type of MMU, so the 386 remained fully compatible with the 286 at the system-code level.

The 386 chip's virtual real mode was also new. In virtual real mode, the processor could run with hardware memory protection while simulating an 8086's real mode operation. Multiple copies of DOS and other OSs, therefore, could run simultaneously on this processor, each in a protected area of memory. If the programs in one segment crashed, the rest of the system was protected.

Numerous variations of the 386 chip were manufactured, some of which are less powerful and some of which are less power hungry.

To learn more about the members of the 386 chip family, see Chapter 3 of *Upgrading and Repairing PCs*, 19th Edition, available in its entirety on the disc packaged with this book.

P4 (486) Processors

Although fourth-generation processors were more about refinement than redesign, the Intel 80486 (normally abbreviated as 486) was another major leap forward in the race for speed. The additional power available in the 486 fueled tremendous growth in the software industry. Tens of millions of copies of Windows, and millions of copies of OS/2, have been sold largely because the 486 finally made the graphical user interface (GUI) of Windows and OS/2 a realistic option for people who work on their computers every day.

The 486 is a family of processors, consisting of DX, SX, and a number of other variations. Four main features make 486 processors roughly twice as fast as an equivalent MHz 386 chip:

- **Reduced instruction-execution time**—A single instruction in the 486 takes an average of only two clock cycles to complete, compared to an average of more than four cycles on the 386.

- **Internal (Level 1) cache**—The built-in cache has a hit ratio of 90–95%, which describes how often zero-wait-state read operations occur. External caches can improve this ratio further.

- **Burst-mode memory cycles**—A standard 32-bit (4-byte) memory transfer takes two clock cycles. After a standard 32-bit transfer, more data up to the next 12 bytes (or three transfers) can be transferred with only one cycle used for each 32-bit (4-byte) transfer. Thus, up to 16 bytes of contiguous, sequential memory data can be transferred in as little as five cycles instead of eight cycles or more. This effect can be even greater when the transfers are only 8 bits or 16 bits each.

- **Built-in (synchronous) enhanced math coprocessor (some versions)**—The math coprocessor runs synchronously with the main processor and executes math instructions in fewer cycles than previous designs did. On average, the math coprocessor built into the DX-series chips provides two to three times greater math performance than an external 387 math coprocessor chip.

The 486 chip is about twice as fast as the 386 at the same clock rate. You can see why the arrival of the 486 rapidly killed off the 386 in the marketplace. The die for the 486 is shown in Figure 3.24.

FIGURE 3.24   486 processor die. Photograph used by permission of Intel Corporation.

To learn more about the 486 processor family and the 486-based AMD 5x86, see Chapter 3 of *Upgrading and Repairing PCs*, 19th Edition, available in its entirety on the disc packaged with this book.

P5 (586) Processors

After the fourth-generation chips such as the 486, Intel and other chip manufacturers went back to the drawing board to come up with new architectures and features that they would later incorporate into what they called *fifth-generation chips*.

On October 19, 1992, Intel announced that the fifth generation of its compatible microprocessor line (code-named P5) would be named the Pentium processor. The actual Pentium chip shipped on March 22, 1993. Systems that used these chips were only a few months behind.

Note

Pentium, like Celeron and Athlon, has become a brand name in recent years rather than identifying a particular processor type. This section discusses the original Pentium processors for Socket 5 and Socket 7.

The Pentium is fully compatible with previous Intel processors, but it differs from them in many ways. At least one of these differences is revolutionary: The Pentium features twin data pipelines, which enable it to execute two instructions at the same time. The 486 and all preceding chips can perform only a single instruction at a time. Intel calls the capability to execute two instructions at the same time *superscalar technology*. This technology provides additional performance compared to the 486.

With superscalar technology, the Pentium can execute many instructions at a rate of two instructions per cycle. Superscalar architecture usually is associated with high-output RISC chips. The Pentium is one of the first CISC chips to be considered superscalar. The Pentium is almost like having two 486 chips under the hood. Table 3.12 shows the Pentium processor specifications.

Table 3.12   Pentium Processor Specifications

Introduced	March 22, 1993 (First Generation); March 7, 1994 (Second Generation)
Maximum rated speeds	60/66MHz (first generation); 75/90/100/120/133/150/166/200MHz (second generation)
CPU clock multiplier	1x (first generation); 1.5x–3x (second generation)
Register size	32-bit
External data bus	64-bit
Memory address bus	32-bit
Maximum memory	4GB
Integral-cache size	8KB code; 8KB data
Integral-cache type	Two-way set associative; write-back data
Burst-mode transfers	Yes
Number of transistors	3.1 million (first generation); 3.3 million (second generation)
Circuit size	0.8 micron (60/66MHz); 0.6 micron (75MHz-100MHz); 0.35 micron (120MHz and up)
External package	273-pin PGA; 296-pin SPGA; tape carrier
Math coprocessor	Built-in FPU
Power management	SMM; enhanced in second generation
Operating voltage	5V (first generation); 3.465V, 3.3V, 3.1V, 2.9V (second generation)

PGA = Pin grid array
SPGA = Staggered pin grid array

The two instruction pipelines within the chip are called the u- and v-pipes. The *u-pipe*, which is the primary pipe, can execute all integer and floating-point instructions. The *v-pipe* is a secondary pipe that can execute only simple integer instructions and certain floating-point instructions. The process of operating on two instructions simultaneously in the different pipes is called *pairing*. Not all sequentially executing instructions can be paired, and when pairing is not possible, only the u-pipe is used. To optimize the Pentium's efficiency, you can recompile software to enable more instructions to be paired.

The Pentium processor has a branch target buffer (BTB), which employs a technique called *branch prediction*. It minimizes stalls in one or more of the pipes caused by delays in fetching instructions that branch to nonlinear memory locations. The BTB attempts to predict whether a program branch will be taken and then fetches the appropriate instructions. The use of branch prediction enables the Pentium to keep both pipelines operating at full speed. Figure 3.25 shows the internal architecture of the Pentium processor.

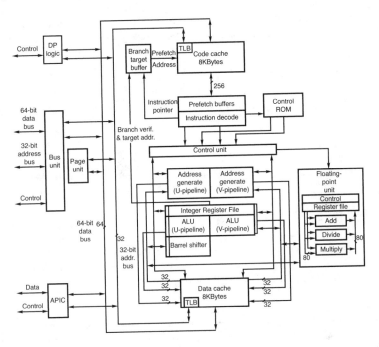

FIGURE 3.25 Pentium processor internal architecture.

The Pentium has a 32-bit address bus width, giving it the same 4GB memory-addressing capabilities as the 386DX and 486 processors. But the Pentium expands the data bus to 64 bits, which means it can move twice as much data into or out of the CPU, compared to a 486 of the same clock speed. The 64-bit data bus requires that system memory be accessed 64 bits wide, so each bank of memory is 64 bits.

Even though the Pentium has a 64-bit data bus that transfers information 64 bits at a time into and out of the processor, the Pentium has only 32-bit internal registers. As instructions are being processed internally, they are broken down into 32-bit instructions and data elements and processed in much the same way as in the 486. Some people thought that Intel was misleading them by calling the Pentium a 64-bit processor, but 64-bit transfers do indeed take place. Internally, however, the Pentium has 32-bit registers that are fully compatible with the 486.

The Pentium, like the 486, contains an internal math coprocessor or FPU. The FPU in the Pentium was rewritten to perform significantly better than the FPU in the 486 yet still be fully compatible with the 486 and 387 math coprocessors. The Pentium FPU is estimated to be two to as much as ten times faster than the FPU in the 486. In addition, the two standard instruction pipelines in the Pentium provide two units to handle standard integer math. (The math coprocessor handles only more complex calculations.) Other processors, such as the 486, have only a single standard execution pipe and one integer math unit.

To learn more about Pentium processors, including the famous floating-point calculation flaw, see Chapter 3 of *Upgrading and Repairing PCs,* 19th Edition, available in its entirety on the disc packaged with this book.

AMD-K5

The AMD-K5 is a Pentium-compatible processor developed by AMD and available as the PR75, PR90, PR100, PR120, PR133, PR166, and PR200. Because it is designed to be physically and functionally compatible, any motherboard that properly supports the Intel Pentium should support the AMD-K5. However, a BIOS upgrade might be required to properly recognize the AMD-K5. The K5 has the following features:

- 16KB instruction cache, 8KB write-back data cache
- Dynamic execution-branch prediction with speculative execution
- Five-stage, RISC-like pipeline with six parallel functional units
- High-performance floating-point unit
- Pin-selectable clock multiples of 1.5x, 1.75x, and 2x

To learn more about the K5 and AMD's P-Rating system for naming these processors, see Chapter 3 of *Upgrading and Repairing PCs,* 19th Edition, available in its entirety on the disc packaged with this book.

Intel P6 (686) Processors

The P6 (686) processors represent a new generation with features not found in the previous generation units. The P6 processor family began when the Pentium Pro was released in November 1995. Since then, Intel has released many other P6 chips, all using the same basic P6 core processor as the Pentium Pro. Table 3.13 shows the variations in the P6 family of processors.

Table 3.13 Intel P6 Processor Variations

Pentium Pro	Original P6 processor, includes 256KB, 512KB, or 1MB of full-core speed L2 cache
Pentium II	P6 with 512KB of half-core speed L2 cache
Pentium II Xeon	P6 with 512KB, 1MB, or 2MB of full-core speed L2 cache
Celeron	P6 with no L2 cache
Celeron-A	P6 with 128KB of on-die full-core speed L2 cache
Pentium III	P6 with SSE (MMX2), 512KB of half-core speed L2 cache
Pentium IIPE	P6 with 256KB of full-core speed L2 cache
Pentium IIIE	P6 with SSE (MMX2) plus 256KB or 512KB of full-core speed L2 cache
Pentium III Xeon	P6 with SSE (MMX2), 512KB, 1MB, or 2MB of full-core speed L2 cache

The main new feature in the fifth-generation Pentium processors was the superscalar architecture, in which two instruction execution units could execute instructions simultaneously in parallel. Later fifth-generation chips also added MMX technology to the mix. So then what did Intel add in the sixth generation to justify calling it a whole new generation of chip? Besides many minor improvements, the real key features of all sixth-generation processors are Dynamic Execution and the DIB architecture, plus a greatly improved superscalar design.

Pentium Pro Processors

Intel's successor to the Pentium is called the Pentium Pro. The Pentium Pro was the first chip in the P6 or sixth-generation processor family. It was introduced in November 1995 and became widely available in 1996. The chip is a 387-pin unit that resides in Socket 8, so it is not pin compatible with earlier Pentiums. The chip is unique among processors because it is constructed in a multichip module (MCM) physical format, which Intel calls a *dual-cavity PGA package*. Inside the 387-pin chip carrier are two dies. One contains the actual Pentium Pro processor, and the other contains a 256KB, 512KB, or 1MB L2 cache. (The Pentium Pro with 256KB cache is shown in Figure 3.26.) The processor die contains 5.5 million transistors, the 256KB cache die contains 15.5 million transistors, and the 512KB cache die(s) have 31 million transistors each—for a potential total of nearly 68 million transistors in a Pentium Pro with 1MB of internal cache! A Pentium Pro with 1MB cache has two 512KB cache die(s) and a standard P6 processor die (see Figure 3.27). The incorporation of L2 cache is one of the most enduring legacies of the Pentium Pro because this feature has been incorporated into virtually every Intel and AMD processor built since, with the notable exception of the original Celeron.

FIGURE 3.26 Pentium Pro processor with 256KB L2 cache. (The cache is on the left side of the processor die.) Photograph used by permission of Intel Corporation.

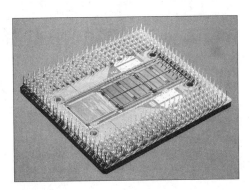

FIGURE 3.27 Pentium Pro processor with 1MB L2 cache. (The cache is in the center and right portions of the die.) Photograph used by permission of Intel Corporation.

For more information about the Pentium Pro, see Chapter 3 of *Upgrading and Repairing PCs*, 19th Edition, available in its entirety on the disc packaged with this book.

Pentium II Processors

Intel revealed the Pentium II in May 1997. Prior to its official unveiling, the Pentium II processor was popularly referred to by its code name, Klamath, and was surrounded by much speculation throughout the industry. The Pentium II is essentially the same sixth-generation processor as the Pentium Pro, with MMX technology added (which included double the L1 cache and 57 new MMX instructions); however, there are a few twists to the design. The Pentium II processor die is shown in Figure 3.28.

From a physical standpoint, it was a big departure from previous processors. Abandoning the chip in a socket approach used by virtually all processors up until this point, the Pentium II chip is characterized by its SEC cartridge (SECC) design. The processor, along with several L2 cache chips, is mounted on a small circuit board (much like an oversized-memory SIMM), as shown in Figure 3.29, and the circuit board is then sealed in a metal and plastic cartridge. The cartridge is then plugged into the motherboard through an edge connector called Slot 1, which looks much like an adapter card slot.

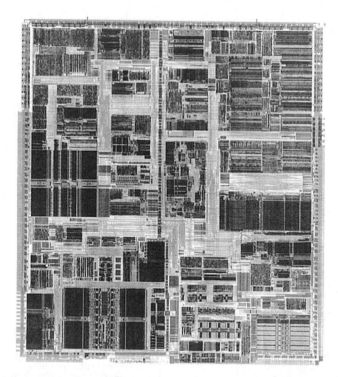

FIGURE 3.28 Pentium II Processor die. Photograph used by permission of Intel Corporation.

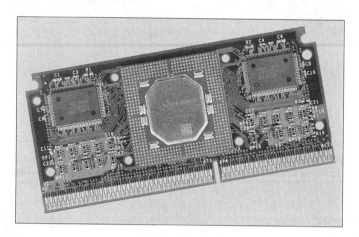

FIGURE 3.29 Pentium II processor board (normally found inside the SEC cartridge). Photograph used by permission of Intel Corporation.

The two variations on these cartridges are called SECC (single edge contact cartridge) and SECC2.

The SECC2 version was cheaper to make because it uses fewer overall parts. It also allowed for a more direct heatsink attachment to the processor for better cooling. Intel transitioned from SECC to SECC2 in the beginning of 1999; all later PII chips, and the Slot 1 PIII chips that followed, use the improved SECC2 design.

By using separate chips mounted on a circuit board, Intel could build the Pentium II much less expensively than the multiple die within a package used in the Pentium Pro. Intel could also use cache chips from other manufacturers and more easily vary the amount of cache in future processors compared to the Pentium Pro design.

Intel offered Pentium II processors with the speeds listed in Table 3.14.

Table 3.14   Speeds for Pentium II Processors and Motherboards

CPU Type/Speed	CPU Clock	Motherboard Speed
Pentium II 233MHz	3.5x	66MHz
Pentium II 266MHz	4x	66MHz
Pentium II 300MHz	4.5x	66MHz
Pentium II 333MHz	5x	66MHz
Pentium II 350MHz	3.5x	100MHz
Pentium II 400MHz	4x	100MHz
Pentium II 450MHz	4.5x	100MHz

Aside from speed, the best way to think of the Pentium II is as a Pentium Pro with MMX technology instructions and a slightly modified cache design. It has the same multiprocessor scalability as the Pentium Pro, as well as the integrated L2 cache. The 57 new multimedia-related instructions carried over from the MMX processors and the capability to process repetitive loop commands more efficiently are included as well. Also included as a part of the MMX upgrade is double the internal L1 cache from the Pentium Pro (from 16KB total to 32KB total in the Pentium II).

For more information about the Pentium II, see Chapter 3 of *Upgrading and Repairing PCs*, 19th Edition, available in its entirety on the disc packaged with this book.

Pentium III

The Pentium III processor, shown in Figure 3.30, was released in February 1999 and introduced several new features to the P6 family. It is essentially the same core as a Pentium II with the addition of SSE instructions and integrated on-die L2 cache in the later versions. SSE consists of 70 new instructions that dramatically enhance the performance and possibilities of advanced imaging, 3D, streaming audio, video, and speech-recognition applications.

Originally based on Intel's advanced 0.25-micron CMOS process technology, the PIII core started out with more than 9.5 million transistors. In late 1999, Intel shifted to a 0.18-micron process die (code-named Coppermine) and added 256KB of on-die L2 cache, which brought the transistor count to 28.1 million. The last version of the Pentium III (code-named Tualatin) uses a 0.13-micron process and has 44 million transistors; motherboards made before the Tualatin-core versions of the Pentium III generally do not support this processor because of logical pinout changes. The Pentium III was manufactured in speeds from 450MHz through 1.4GHz, as well as in server versions with larger or faster cache known as the Pentium Xeon. The Pentium III also incorporates advanced features such as a 32KB L1 cache and either half-core speed 512KB L2 cache or full-core speed on-die 256KB or 512KB L2 with cacheability for up to 4GB of addressable memory space. The PIII also can be used in dual-processing systems with up to 64GB of physical memory. A self-reportable processor serial number gives security, authentication, and system management applications a powerful new tool for identifying individual systems. Because of privacy concerns when the processor was released, you can disable this feature in the system BIOS on most systems that use the Pentium III or Celeron III processors.

FIGURE 3.30   Pentium III processor in SECC2 (Slot 1) and FC-PGA (Socket 370) packages.

Pentium III processors were made available in Intel's SECC2 form factor, which replaced the more expensive older SECC packaging. The SECC2 package covers only one side of the chip and allows for better heatsink attachment and less overall weight. Architectural features of the Pentium III processor include the following:

- **Streaming SIMD extensions (SSE)**—Seventy new instructions for dramatically faster process-ing and improved imaging, 3D streaming audio and video, web access, speech recognition, new user interfaces, and other graphics and sound-rich applications.

- **Intel processor serial number**—Serves as an electronic serial number for the processor and, by extension, its system or user. You can enable or disable this feature as desired in the BIOS Setup. The serial number enables the system/user to be identified by company internal networks and applications. You can use the processor serial number in applications that benefit from stronger forms of system and user identification, such as the following:

  - **Applications using security capabilities**—Managed access to new Internet content and services; electronic document exchange.

  - **Manageability applications**—Asset management; remote system load and configura-tion.

Although the initial release of Pentium III processors was made in the improved SECC2 packaging, Intel later switched to the FC-PGA package, which is even less expensive to produce and enables a more direct attachment of the heatsink to the processor core for better cooling. The FC-PGA version plugs into Socket 370 but can be used in Slot 1 with a slotkey adapter.

All Pentium III processors have either 512KB or 256KB of L2 cache, which runs at either half-core or full-core speed. Pentium III Xeon versions have 512KB, 1MB, or 2MB of L2 cache that runs at full-core speed. The Pentium III Xeon is a more expensive version of the Pentium III designed for servers and workstations. All PIII processor L2 caches can cache up to 4GB of addressable memory space and include ECC capability.

Celeron

The Celeron processor is a chameleon, more of a marketing name than the name of an actual chip. In its first two versions it was originally a P6 with the same processor core as the Pentium II; later it came with the same core as the PIII, then the P4 and Core 2, while more recent versions are based on the Core i3 processor core. The Celeron name represents essentially a version of Intel's current mainstream chip that Intel has repackaged for lower-cost PCs.

In creating the original Celerons, Intel figured that by taking a Pentium II and deleting the separate L2 cache chips mounted inside the processor cartridge (and deleting the cosmetic cover), it could create a "new" processor that was basically just a slower version of the Pentium II. As such, the first 266MHz and 300MHz Celeron models didn't include L2 cache. Unfortunately, this proved to have far too great a crippling effect on performance, so starting with the 300A versions, the Celeron received 128KB of on-die full-speed L2 cache, which was actually faster and more advanced than the 512KB of half-speed cache used in the Pentium II it was based on at the time! In fact, the Celeron was the first PC processor to receive on-die L2 cache. It wasn't until the Coppermine version of the Pentium III appeared that on-die L2 cache migrated to Intel's main processors.

Needless to say, this caused a lot of confusion in the marketplace about the Celeron. Considering that the Celeron started out as a "crippled" Pentium II and then was revised to actually be superior in some ways to the Pentium II on which it was based (all while selling for less), many didn't know just where the Celeron stood in terms of performance. Fortunately, the crippling lack of L2 cache existed only in the earliest Celeron versions; all of those at speeds greater than 300MHz have on-die full-speed L2 cache.

Since then, the Celeron has been released in many different versions, with each newer one based on the then-current mainstream processor. The latest Celerons use the same basic 32nm "Sandy Bridge" core as more expensive Core i-series second-generation processors. The difference is that the Celeron versions are offered in lower processor and bus clock speeds and with smaller caches, to justify a lower price point.

Because Intel has offered Celeron and Celeron D processors in many distinctive variations, it's easy to get confused as to which is which, or which is available at a specific speed. By identifying the spec number of a particular chip and looking up the number on the Intel product information website (http://ark.intel.com/Default.aspx), you can find out the exact specification, including socket type, voltage, stepping, cache size, and other information. If you don't know the spec number, you can still look up the processor by the model number or by the code name (such as Sandy Bridge), or you can use software such as CPU-Z (www.cpuid.com) to find more detailed information about an installed processor.

Intel Pentium 4 Processors

The Pentium 4 was introduced in November 2000 and represented a new generation in processors (see Figure 3.31). If this one had a number instead of a name, it might be called the 786 because it represents a generation beyond the previous 686 class processors. Several variations on the Pentium 4 have been released, based on the processor die and architecture. Several of the processor dies are shown in Figure 3.32.

FIGURE 3.31 Pentium 4 FC-PGA2 processor.

The main technical details for the Pentium 4 include the following:

- Speeds ranging from 1.3GHz to 3.8GHz.
- Software compatible with previous Intel 32-bit processors.
- Some versions supporting EM64T (64-bit extensions) and Execute Disable Bit (buffer overflow protection).
- Processor (front-side) bus that runs at 400MHz, 533MHz, 800MHz, or 1,066MHz.
- Arithmetic logic units (ALUs) that run at twice the processor core frequency.
- Hyper-pipelined (20-stage or 31-stage) technology.
- HT Technology support in all 2.4GHz and faster processors running an 800MHz bus and all 3.06GHz and faster processors running a 533MHz bus.
- Deep out-of-order instruction execution.
- Enhanced branch prediction.
- 8KB or 16KB L1 cache plus 12K micro-op execution trace cache.
- 256KB, 512KB, 1MB, or 2MB of on-die, full-core speed 256-bit-wide L2 cache with eight-way associativity.
- L2 cache that can handle all physical memory and supports ECC.
- 2MB of on-die, full-speed L3 cache (Extreme Edition).
- SSE2-SSE plus 144 new instructions for graphics and sound processing (Willamette and Northwood).
- SSE3-SSE2 plus 13 new instructions for graphics and sound processing (Prescott).
- Enhanced floating-point unit.
- Multiple low-power states.

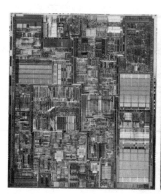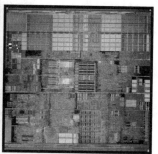

FIGURE 3.32   The CPU dies for the Pentium 4 CPU based on the Willamette, Northwood, and Prescott cores.

Intel abandoned Roman numerals for a standard Arabic numeral 4 designation to identify the Pentium 4. Internally, the Pentium 4 introduces a new architecture that Intel calls *NetBurst microarchitecture*, which is a marketing term and not a technical term. Intel uses NetBurst to describe hyper-pipelined technology, a rapid execution engine, a high-speed (400MHz, 533MHz, 800MHz, or 1,066MHz) system bus, and an execution trace cache. The hyper-pipelined technology doubles or triples the instruction pipeline depth compared to the Pentium III (or Athlon/Athlon 64), meaning more and smaller steps are required to execute instructions. Even though this might seem less efficient, it enables much higher clock speeds to be more easily attained. The rapid execution engine enables the two integer ALUs to run at twice the processor core frequency, which means instructions can execute in half a clock cycle. The 400MHz/533MHz/800MHz/1,066MHz system bus is a quad-pumped bus running off a 100MHz/133MHz/200MHz/266MHz system clock transferring data four times per clock cycle. The execution trace cache is a high-performance Level 1 cache that stores approximately 12K decoded micro-operations. This removes the instruction decoder from the main execution pipeline, increasing performance.

Of these, the high-speed processor bus is most notable. Technically speaking, the processor bus is a 100MHz, 133MHz, 200MHz, or 266MHz quad-pumped bus that transfers four times per cycle (4x), for a 400MHz, 533MHz, 800MHz, or 1,066MHz effective rate. Because the bus is 64 bits (8 bytes) wide, this results in a throughput rate of 3,200MBps, 4,266MBps, 6,400MBps, or 8,533MBps.

In the Pentium 4's 20-stage or 31-stage pipelined internal architecture, individual instructions are broken down into many more substages than with previous processors such as the Pentium III, making this almost like a RISC processor. Unfortunately, this can add to the number of cycles taken to execute instructions if they are not optimized for this processor. Another important architectural advantage is HT Technology, which can be found in all Pentium 4 2.4GHz and faster processors running an 800MHz bus and all 3.06GHz and faster processors running a 533MHz bus. HT enables a single processor to run two threads simultaneously, thereby acting as if it were two processors instead of one. For more information on HT Technology, see the section "HT Technology," earlier in this chapter.

The Pentium 4 initially used Socket 423, which has 423 pins in a 39×39 SPGA arrangement. Later versions used Socket 478; the final versions use Socket T (LGA775), which has additional pins to support new features such as EM64T (64-bit extensions), Execute Disable Bit (protection against buffer overflow attacks), Intel Virtualization Technology, and other advanced features. The Celeron was never designed to work in Socket 423, but Celeron and Celeron D versions are available for Socket 478 and Socket T (LGA775), allowing for lower-cost systems compatible with the Pentium 4. Voltage selection is made via an automatic voltage regulator module installed on the motherboard and wired to the socket.

Table 3.15 includes a guide to Pentium 4 processor features as well as those for the Pentium 4 Extreme Edition, which is discussed in more detail in the next section. For information on the features unique to a specific processor, see the Intel Product Information website at http://ark.intel.com/Default.aspx.

Table 3.15   Pentium 4 Processor Information

Processor Model Number	CPU Speed	Bus Speed	L2-Cache	L3 Cache	CPU Core	Mfg. Process
P4 631-661	3.00–3.60GHz	800MHz	2MB	—	Cedar Mill	65nm
Celeron D 347-365	3.06–3.60GHz	533MHz	512KB	—	Cedar Mill	65nm
P4 620-670	2.80–3.80GHz	800, 1,066MHz	2MB	—	Prescott 2M	90nm
P4 2.26-3.8	2.26–3.80GHz	533, 800MHz	1MB	—	Prescott	90nm
Celeron D 310-355	2.26–3.80GHz	533, 800MHz	1MB	—	Prescott	90nm
P4 EE	3.20–3.46GHz	800, 1,066MHz	512KB	2MB	Gallatin	130nm
P4 1.6-3.4	1.60–3.40GHz	400, 533, 800MHz	512KB	—	Northwood	130nm
Celeron 1.8A-2.8	1.80–2.80GHz	400MHz	128KB	—	Northwood	130nm
P4 1.3-2.0	1.30–2.00GHz	400MHz	256KB	—	Willamette	180nm
Celeron 1.7-1.8	1.70–1.80GHz	400MHz	128KB	—	Willamette	180nm

EE = Extreme Edition
SSE = Streaming SIMD Instructions (MMX)
HT = Hyper-Threading Technology

NX = Execute Disable Bit
EIST = Enhanced Intel SpeedStep Technology
VT = Virtualization Technology

Pentium 4 Extreme Edition

In November 2003, Intel introduced the Extreme Edition of the Pentium 4, which is notable for being the first desktop PC processor to incorporate L3 cache. The Extreme Edition (or Pentium 4EE) is basically a revamped version of the Prestonia core Xeon workstation/server processor, which has used L3 cache since November 2002. The Pentium 4EE has 512KB of L2 cache and 2MB of L3 cache, which increases the transistor count to 178 million transistors and makes the die significantly larger than the standard Pentium 4. Because of the large die based on the 130-nanometer process, this chip was expensive to produce, and the extremely high selling price reflects that. The Extreme Edition was targeted toward the gaming market, where people are willing to spend extra money for additional performance. The additional cache doesn't help standard business applications as well as it helps power-hungry 3D games.

In 2004, revised versions of the Pentium 4 Extreme Edition were introduced. These processors are based on the 90-nanometer (0.09-micron) Pentium 4 Prescott core but with a larger 2MB L2 cache in place of the 512KB L2 cache design used by the standard Prescott-core Pentium 4. Pentium 4 Extreme Edition processors based on the Prescott core do not have L3 cache.

The Pentium 4 Extreme Edition was produced in both Socket 478 and Socket T form factors, with clock speeds ranging from 3.2GHz to 3.4GHz (Socket 478) and from 3.4GHz to 3.73GHz (Socket T).

Pentium 4 Power Supply and Cooling Issues

Compared to older processors, the Pentium 4 requires a lot of electrical power. Because of this, starting in February 2000, Intel changed the ATX motherboard and power supply specifications to support a CPU voltage regulator module powered from 12V instead of 3.3V or 5V, as with previous designs. By using the 12V power, more 3.3V and 5V power is available to run the rest of the system, and the over-

Transistors	Die Size	Max. Power	SSE	HT	64-Bit	NX	EIST	VT	Socket
188M	81mm²	65–86W	SSE3	Yes	Yes	Yes	Some	—	LGA775
188M	81mm²	65–86W	SSE3	—	Yes	Yes	—	—	LGA775
169M	135mm²	84–115W	SSE3	Yes	Yes	Yes	Most	Some	LGA775
125M	112mm²	84–115W	SSE3	Some	Some	Some	—	—	478, LGA775
125M	112mm²	84–115W	SSE3	—	Some	Some	—	—	478, LGA775
178M	237mm²	92.1–110.7W	SSE2	Yes	—	—	—	—	478, LGA775
55M	131mm²	46.8–89W	SSE2	Some	—	—	—	—	478
55M	131mm²	52.8–68.4W	SSE2	—	—	—	—	—	478
42M	217mm²	51.6–71.8W	SSE2	—	—	—	—	—	423, 478
42M	217mm²	63.5–66.1W	SSE2	—	—	—	—	—	478

all current draw is greatly reduced with the higher voltage as a source. PC power supplies normally generate more than enough 12V power, but the previous ATX motherboard and power supply designs originally allotted only one pin for 12V power (each pin is rated for only 6 amps), so additional 12V lines were necessary to carry this power to the motherboard.

The fix appears in the form of a CPU power connector called the ATX12V connector. Any motherboard having the ATX12V connector requires that you supply power to it. If you are using an older ATX power supply that lacks the proper ATX12V connector, several companies sell adapters that convert a standard Molex-type peripheral power connector to the ATX12V connector. Typically, a 300-watt (the minimum recommended) or larger power supply has more than adequate levels of 12V power for both the drives and the ATX12V connector.

If your power supply is less than the 300-watt minimum recommended, you may need to purchase a replacement supply.

▶▶ See the Chapter 18 section, "Motherboard Power Connectors," **p. 870**.

Cooling a high-wattage processor such as the Pentium 4 requires a large active heatsink. These heavy (sometimes more than 1 lb.) heatsinks can damage a CPU or destroy a motherboard when subjected to vibration or shock, especially during shipping. To solve this problem with Pentium 4 motherboards, various methods have been used to secure the heatsink in the system. Intel's specifications for Socket 423 added four standoffs to the ATX chassis design flanking the Socket 423 to support the heatsink retention brackets. These standoffs enabled the chassis to support the weight of the heatsink instead of depending on the motherboard, as with older designs. Vendors also used other means to reinforce the CPU location without requiring a direct chassis attachment. For example, Asus's P4T motherboard was supplied with a metal reinforcing plate to enable off-the-shelf ATX cases to work with the motherboard.

Socket 478 systems do not require special standoffs or reinforcement plates; instead, they use a scheme in which the CPU heatsink attaches directly to the motherboard rather than to the CPU socket or chassis. You can install motherboards with Socket 478 into any ATX chassis; no special standoffs are required.

Socket T (LGA775) systems use a four-side frame-locking mechanism that holds the processor in place. The heatsink is positioned over the processor, and locking pins attach it to the motherboard. Later LGA sockets use a similar design.

Because the Pentium 4 processor family has been manufactured in three socket types with a wide variation in clock speed and power dissipation, make sure that you choose a heatsink made specifically for the processor form factor and speed on a particular system if you need to replace a heatsink.

Intel Pentium D and Pentium Extreme Edition

Intel introduced its first dual-core processors, the Pentium Extreme Edition and Pentium D, in May 2005. Although these processors used the code name Smithfield before their introductions, they are based on the Pentium 4 Prescott core. In fact, to bring dual-core processors to market as quickly as possible, Intel used two Prescott cores in each Pentium D or Pentium Extreme Edition processor. Each core communicates with the other via th MCH (North Bridge) chip on the motherboard (see Figure 3.33).

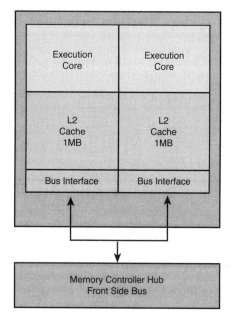

FIGURE 3.33 The Pentium D and Pentium Extreme Edition's processor cores communicate with each other via the chipset's MCH (North Bridge) chip.

Table 3.16   Pentium D and Pentium Extreme Edition Processors

Processor Model	CPU Speed	Bus Speed	L2 Cache	CPU Core	Mfg. Process
Pentium EE 955-965	2	3.46–3.73GHz	1,066MHz	4MB	Presler
Pentium D 915-960	2	2.80–3.60GHz	800MHz	4MB	Presler
Pentium EE 840	2	3.20GHz	800MHz	2MB	Smithfield
Pentium D 805-840	2	2.66–3.20GHz	533, 800MHz	2MB	Smithfield

EE = Extreme Edition   *HT = Hyper-Threading Technology*
SSE = Streaming SIMD Instructions (MMX)   *NX = Execute Disable Bit*

For this reason, you cannot use Intel 915 and 925 chipsets and some third-party chipsets made for the Pentium 4 with the Pentium D or Pentium Extreme Edition. Intel's 945 series, 955X, and 975X desktop chipsets, and the E7230 workstation chipset, are the first Intel chipsets to support these processors. The nForce 4 series from NVIDIA also works with these processors.

▶▶ See the Chapter 4 sections, "Intel 945 Express Family," **p. 203** and "Intel 955X and 975X Family," **p. 204**, for more information on these chipsets.

Following are the major features of the Pentium D:

- Clock speeds of 2.66GHz–3.6GHz
- 533MHz or 800MHz processor bus
- EM64T 64-bit extensions
- Execute Disable Bit support
- 65- or 90-nanometer manufacturing process
- 2MB/4MB L2 cache (1MB/2MB per core)
- Socket T (LGA775)

The 830, 840, and 9xx models also include Enhanced Intel Speed Step Technology, which results in cooler and quieter PC operation by providing a wide range of processor speeds in response to workload and thermal issues.

The Pentium Extreme Edition is a high-end version of the Pentium D, but with the following differences:

- HT Technology is supported, enabling each core to simulate two processor cores for even better performance with multithreaded applications.
- Enhanced Intel Speed Step Technology is not supported.
- It includes unlocked clock multipliers, enabling easy overclocking.

Table 3.16 compares the features of the various Pentium D and Pentium Extreme Edition processors.

Max. Power	SSE	HT	64-Bit	NX	EIST	VT	Socket	
65nm	130W	SSE3	Yes	Yes	Yes	—	Yes	LGA775
65nm	95–130W	SSE3	—	Yes	Yes	Yes	Some	LGA775
90nm	130W	SSE3	Yes	Yes	Yes	—	—	LGA775
90nm	95–130W	SSE3	—	Yes	Yes	Some	—	LGA775

EIST = Enhanced Intel SpeedStep Technology
VT = Virtualization Technology

Intel Core Processors

During production of the Pentium 4, Intel realized that the high power consumption of the NetBurst architecture was becoming a serious problem. As the clock speeds increased, so did the power consumption. At the heart of the problem was the 31-stage deep internal pipeline, which made the processor fast but much less efficient. To continue evolving processors with faster versions featuring multiple cores, a solution was needed to increase efficiency and reduce power consumption dramatically. Fortunately, Intel had the perfect solution in its mobile processors, already regarded as the most efficient PC processors in the world. Starting with the Pentium M, Intel's mobile processors used a completely different internal architecture from its desktop processors such as the Pentium 4. In fact, the Pentium M mobile processor was originally based on the Pentium III! To create a powerful new desktop processor, Intel started with the highly efficient mobile processors and then added several new features and technologies to increase performance. These new processors were designed from the outset to be multicore chips, with two or more cores per physical chip. The result of this development was the Core processor family, which was released on July 27, 2006 as the Core 2.

Intel Core 2 Family

The highly efficient Core microarchitecture design featured in the Core 2 processor family provides 40% better performance and is 40% more energy efficient than the previous generation Pentium D processor. It is also interesting to note that the Core 2 Duo processor is Intel's third-generation dual-core processor; the first generation was the Pentium D processor for desktop PCs, and the second generation was the Core Duo processor for mobile PCs.

The naming of both the Core 2 processor and the Core microarchitecture is somewhat confusing because the Core name was also used on the Core Solo and Core Duo processors, which were the successors to the Pentium M in Intel's mobile processor family. What is strange is that the Core Solo and Duo do *not* incorporate Intel's Core microarchitecture, and although they served as a developmental starting point for the Core 2, the Core Solo and Duo are internally different and not in the same family as the Core 2 processors. Because the Core Solo and Core Duo processors are considered mobile processors only, they are not covered here.

The Core 2 was released as a dual-core processor, but since then quad-core versions have also been released. The dual-core versions of the Core 2 processors have 291 million transistors, whereas the quad-core versions have double that, or 582 million. They include 1MB or 2MB of L2 cache per core, with up to 8MB total L2 in the quad-core versions. Initially, all were built on 300mm wafers using a 65nm process, but since then 45nm versions have been released as well.

The highlights of the Core microarchitecture include the following:

- **Wide dynamic execution**—Internal execution cores that are 33% wider than in previous generations, allowing each core to execute up to four full instructions simultaneously. Further efficiencies are achieved through more accurate branch prediction, deeper instruction buffers for greater execution flexibility, and additional features to reduce execution time.

- **Intelligent power capability**—An advanced power-gating capability that turns on individual processor subsystems only if they are needed.

- **Advanced smart cache**—A multicore optimized cache that increases the probability that each execution core can access data from a shared L2 cache.

■ **Smart memory access**—Includes a capability called memory disambiguation, which increases the efficiency of out-of-order processing by providing the execution cores with the intelligence to speculatively load data for instructions that are about to execute.

■ **Advanced digital media boost**—Improves performance when executing Streaming SIMD Extension (SSE) instructions by enabling 128-bit instructions to be executed at a throughput rate of one per clock cycle. This effectively doubles the speed of execution for these instructions compared to previous generations.

The Core 2 family includes both dual-core and quad-core processors under five different names:

■ **Core 2 Duo**—Standard dual-core processors

■ **Celeron**—Ultra-Low-end single or dual-core processors

■ **Pentium**—Low-end dual-core processors (faster than Celeron with larger cache)

■ **Core 2 Quad**—Standard quad-core processors

■ **Core 2 Extreme**—High-end versions of either dual-core or quad-core processors

Figure 3.34 shows a cutaway view of a Core 2 Duo chip, revealing the single dual-core die underneath the heat spreader.

FIGURE 3.34   Core 2 Duo cutaway view.

All Core 2 family processors support 64-bit extensions, as well as SSSE3 (Supplemental SSE3), which adds 32 new SIMD instructions to SSE3. These processors also support Enhanced Intel Speedstep Technology (EIST), and most provide support for hardware Virtualization Technology.

Table 3.17 details the various processors in the Core 2 family.

Table 3.17   Core 2 Family Processors

Processor Model Number	Cores	CPU Speed	Bus Speed	L2 Cache	CPU Core
Core 2 Duo E8190-E8600	2	2.66–3.33GHz	1,333MHz	6MB	Wolfdale
Core 2 Duo E7200-E7600	2	2.53–3.06GHz	1,066MHz	3MB	Wolfdale-3M
Celeron E3200-E3300	2	2.40–2.50GHz	800MHz	1MB	Wolfdale-3M
Core 2 Extreme X6800	2	2.93GHz	1,066MHz	4MB	Conroe XE
Core 2 Duo E6300-E6850	2	1.86–3.00GHz	1,066, 1,333MHz	2, 4MB	Conroe
Celeron 220-450	1	1.20–2.20GHz	533–800MHz	512KB	Conroe-L
Core 2 Duo E6300-E6400	2	1.86–2.13GHz	1,066MHz	2MB	Conroe
Core 2 Duo E4300-E4700	2	1.80–2.60GHz	800MHz	2MB	Conroe
Celeron E1200-E1600	2	1.60–2.40GHz	800MHz	512KB	Conroe
Core 2 Extreme QX9xxx	4	3.00–3.20GHz	1,333–1,600MHz	12MB	Yorkfield XE
Core 2 Quad Q9xxx	4	2.66–3.00GHz	1,333Hz	12MB	Yorkfield
Core 2 Quad Q9xxx	4	2.50–2.83GHz	1,333Hz	6MB	Yorkfield-6M
Core 2 Quad Q8xxx	4	2.33–2.66GHz	1,333Hz	4MB	Yorkfield-6M
Core 2 Quad Q7xxx	4	2.20–2.90GHz	800MHz	2MB	Yorkfield-6M
Core 2 Extreme QX6xxx	4	2.66–3.00GHz	1,066–1,333MHz	8MB	Kentsfield XE
Core 2 Quad Q6xxx	4	2.13-2.66GHz	1,066MHz	8MB	Kentsfield

SSE = Streaming SIMD Instructions (MMX)
HT = Hyper-Threading Technology
NX = Execute Disable Bit

EIST = Enhanced Intel SpeedStep Technology
VT = Virtualization Technology

Note

With the introduction of the Core series of processors, Intel has used the Pentium name for processors that are more powerful than Celerons but less powerful than the current mainstream processors. For example, the most recent Pentium processors are based on the Ivy Bridge design but feature lower clock speeds, smaller cache sizes, and less powerful integrated graphics than Core i3 or faster Ivy Bridge processors.

Intel (Nehalem) Core i Processors

The Core i processor family replaced the Core 2 and includes two different microarchitectures: The first generation of Core i processors is based on the Nehalem microarchitecture, and the second generation uses Sandy Bridge microarchitecture.

Nehalem Architecture

The Nehalem microarchitecture's key features include the integration of the memory controller into the processor, and in some models, the entire North Bridge including an optional graphics processor in a separate core on the processor die (see Chapter 12, "Video Hardware," for details). The first Core i

Mfg. Process	Max. Power	SSE	64-Bit	NX	EIST	VT	Socket
45nm	65W	SSSE4.1	Yes	Yes	Yes	Most	LGA775
45nm	65W	SSSE4.1	Yes	Yes	Yes	Some	LGA775
45nm	65W	SSSE3	Yes	Yes	Yes	Yes	LGA775
65nm	75W	SSSE3	Yes	Yes	Yes	Yes	LGA775
65nm	65W	SSSE3	Yes	Yes	Yes	Yes	LGA775
65nm	19–35W	SSSE3	Yes	Yes	—	—	LGA775
65nm	65W	SSSE3	Yes	Yes	Yes	Yes	LGA775
65nm	65W	SSSE3	Yes	Yes	Yes	—	LGA775
65nm	65W	SSSE3	Yes	Yes	Yes	—	LGA775
45nm	130–150W	SSSE4.1	Yes	Yes	Yes	Yes	LGA775, LGA771
45nm	65–95W	SSSE4.1	Yes	Yes	Yes	Yes	LGA775
45nm	65–95W	SSSE4.1	Yes	Yes	Yes	Yes	LGA775
45nm	65–95W	SSSE4.1	Yes	Yes	Yes	Some	LGA775
45nm	65–95W	SSSE4.1	Yes	Yes	Yes	—	LGA775
65nm	130W	SSSE3	Yes	Yes	Yes	Yes	LGA775
65nm	95–105W	SSSE3	Yes	Yes	Yes	Yes	LGA775

Series processor was the Core i7 introduced in November 2008. Initially built on a 45nm process, later Core i Series processors were built on an improved 32nm process allowing for smaller die, lower power consumption, and greater performance. All support DDR3 memory and include L3 cache, and some models include support for HT Technology. See Table 3.18 for details.

There are two main variants in the first-generation (Nehalem) Core i Series Family: high-end versions that use Socket LGA1366 and more mainstream models that use Socket LGA1156. The latter main-stream models include a fully integrated North Bridge, including a dual-channel DDR3 memory controller, graphics interface, and even an optional full-blown graphics processor (Larrabee). Because the entire North Bridge functionality is integrated into the processor, Socket LGA1156 chips use a slower 2GBps DMI as the FSB connection to the South Bridge component on the motherboard.

Core i 900 Series processors using Socket LGA1366 include a triple-channel DDR3 memory controller and a high-performance FSB called QPI (Quick Path Interconnect) that connects to the North Bridge component (called an I/O Hub or IOH) on the motherboard (see Figure 3.35). The IOH implements the PCIe graphics interface.

Core i7 and i5 processors also support Turbo Boost (built-in overclocking), which increases the performance in heavily loaded processor cores while reducing performance to cores that are lightly loaded or have no work to perform. Turbo Boost is configured through the system BIOS.

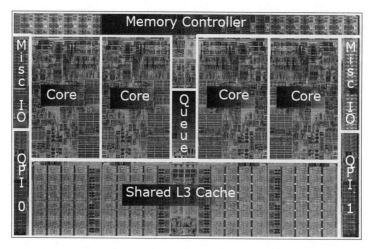

FIGURE 3.35   Core i7 900 series processor die. Photograph courtesy of Intel.

Table 3.18   Core i Series Family Processors Using Nehalem Microarchitecture

Processor Model Number	Number of Cores	CPU Speed	Bus Speed	L2 Cache	L3 Cache
Core i7 9xxX EE	6	3.33–3.46GHz	6.4GHz	1.5MB	12MB
Core i7 9xx EE	4	3.20–3.33GHz	6.4GHz	1MB	8MB
Core i7 970	6	3.2GHz	4.8GHz	1.5MB	12MB
Core i7 9xx	4	2.66–3.20GHz	4.8GHz	1MB	8MB
Core i7 8xx	4	2.66–.3.06GHz	2.5GHz	1MB	8MB
Core i5 7xx	4	2.40–2.80GHz	2.5GHz	1MB	8MB
Core i5 6xx	2	3.2–3.66GHz	2.5GHz	1MB	4MB
Core i3 5xx	2	2.93–3.33GHz	2.5GHz	1MB	4MB

* This CPU core also used by Pentium Processor
G6950-60

EE = Extreme Edition
SSE = Streaming SIMD Instructions (MMX)

Table 3.19   Core i Series Family Processors Using Sandy Bridge Microarchitecture

Processor Model Number	Number of Cores	CPU Speed	Bus Speed	L2 Cache
Core i7 39xx	6	3.2–4.0GHz	5GHz	1MB
Core i7 38xx	4	3.6GHz	5GHz	1MB
Core i7 2xxx	4	2.80–3.40GHz	5GHz	1MB
Core i5 25xx	4	2.3–3.3GHz	5GHz	1MB
Core i5 24xx	4	2.5–3.1GHz	5GHz	1MB
Core i5 2390	2	2.7GHz	5GHz	1MB
Core i5 23xx	4	2.8–2.9GHz	5GHz	1MB
Core i3 21xx	2	2.5–3.1GHz	5GHz	1MB

EE = Extreme Edition
SSE = Streaming SIMD Instructions (MMX)

NX = Execute Disable Bit
VT = Virtualization Technology

The initial members of the Core i Series Family included the Core i5 and i7 processors. These were later joined by the low-end i3 processors. Table 3.18 details the various processors in the first-generation Core i Series family.

Sandy Bridge Architecture

Intel introduced the second generation of Core i-series processors, those based on the Sandy Bridge microarchitecture, in January 2011 (see Table 3.19). The Sandy Bridge microarchitecture includes, as its predecessor did, an integrated memory controller and North Bridge functions.

However, Sandy Bridge has many new features, including an in-core graphics processor on some models (see Chapter 12 for details); the new AVX 256-bit SSE extensions; a new Level 0 instruction cache for holding up to 1,500 decoded micro-ops; a more accurate branch prediction unit; the use of physical registers to store operands; improved power management; Turbo Boost 2.0 for more scaled responses to adjustments in core usage, processor temperature, current, power consumption, and operating system states; and a dedicated video decoding/transcoding/encoding unit known as the multi-format codec (MFX). All Sandy Bridge processors use a 32nm manufacturing process.

CPU Core	Mfg. Process	Max. Power	SSE Version	TB	64-Bit	NX	VT	HTT	Socket
Gulftown	32nm	130W	4.2	Yes	Yes	Yes	Yes	Yes	LGA1366
Bloomfield	45nm	130W	SSE4.2	Yes	Yes	Yes	Yes	Yes	LGA1366
Gulftown	32nm	130W	4.2	Yes	Yes	Yes	Yes	Yes	LGA1366
Bloomfield	45nm	130W	SSE4.2	Yes	Yes	Yes	Yes	Yes	LGA1156
Lynnfield	45nm	82–95W	SSE4.2	Yes	Yes	Yes	Yes	Yes	LGA1156
Lynnfield	45nm	95W	SSE4.2	Yes	Yes	Yes	Yes	—	LGA1156
Clarkdale*	32nm	73–87W	SSE4.2	Yes	Yes	Yes	Yes	Yes	LGA1156
Clarkdale	32nm	73W	SSE4.2	Yes	Yes	Yes	Yes	Yes	LGA1156

NX = Execute Disable Bit
VT = Virtualization Technology
HTT = Hyper-Threading Technology
TB = Turbo Boost

L3 Cache	Max. Power	SSE Version	TB2.0	64-Bit	NX	VT	HTT	Socket
12-15MB	130–150W	4.2, AVX	Yes	Yes	Yes	Yes	Yes	LGA2011
10MB	130W	4.2, AVX	Yes	Yes	Yes	Yes	Yes	LGA2011
8MB	65–95W	4.2, AVX	Yes	Yes	Yes	Yes	Yes	LGA1155
6MB	45–95W	4.2, AVX	Yes	Yes	Yes	Yes	—	LGA1155
6MB	65–95W	4.2 , AVX	Yes	Yes	Yes	Yes	Yes	LGA1155
3MB	35W	4.2, AVX	Yes	Yes	Yes	Yes	Yes	LGA1155
6MB	95W	4.2, AVX	Yes	Yes	Yes	Yes	—	LGA1155
3MB	35–65W	4.2, AVX	No	Yes	Yes	Yes	Yes	LGA1155

HTT = Hyper-Threading Technology
TB2.0 = Turbo Boost 2.0

Sandy Bridge processors using LGA 2011 processor sockets are classified as Sandy Bridge-E.

Sandy Bridge also includes Pentium processors in the 967-997, B940-B980, G620-G645T, and G840-G870 series. These processors feature lower clock speeds, less powerful integrated GPUs, and smaller cache sizes than Core i processors. Celeron processors in the B720, 847E, 787-797, 807-887, B710, B800-B840, G440-G465, and G350-G555 series are also based on Sandy Bridge but feature smaller cache sizes and slower clock speeds than Pentium processors based on Sandy Bridge.

Ivy Bridge Architecture

Intel introduced the third generation of Core i-series processors, those based on the Ivy Bridge microarchitecture, in April 2012 (see Table 3.20). The Ivy Bridge microarchitecture represents an improved version of the Sandy Bridge microarchitecture. Ivy Bridge features support for PCI Express 3.0, a new 3D fabrication process at 22nm, lower power consumption, support for low-voltage DDR3 memory, and support for DirectX 11 graphics with integrated HD Graphics 4000. Existing Sandy Bridge motherboards can use Ivy Bridge CPUs, but a BIOS update might be needed in some cases. Table 3.20 lists Core I series processors using Ivy Bridge microarchitecture.

Table 3.20   Core i Series Family Desktop Processors Using Ivy Bridge Microarchitecture

Processor Model	Number of Cores	CPU Speed	Bus Speed	L2 Cache	Max. L3 Cache
Core i7 3770 series	4	2.50–3.40GHz	5GHz	1MB
Core i5 35xx	4	2.3–3.4GHz	5GHz	1MB
Core i5 34xx*	4	2.9–3.2GHz	5GHz	1MB
Core i5 33xx	4	2.7–3.1GHz	5GHz	1MB
Core i3 32xx	4	2.8–3.4GHz	5GHz	1MB

EE = Extreme Edition
SSE = Streaming SIMD Instructions (MMX)
NX = Execute Disable Bit
VT = Virtualization Technology

HTT = Hyper-Threading Technology
TB = Turbo Boost
* 3470T features two cores with HTT support

AMD K6 Processors

How did AMD begin to design and produce P6-type processors in its own facilities (fabs)? It's an interesting story that began with a company called NexGen and its Pentium rival, the Nx586. After using NexGen technology for its first P6-class processors, AMD later designed and fabricated the Athlon and Duron processors, which were true sixth-generation designs using their own proprietary connections to the system.

NexGen Nx586

NexGen was founded by Thampy Thomas, who hired some of the people formerly involved with the 486 and Pentium processors at Intel. At NexGen, developers created the Nx586, a processor that was functionally the same as the Pentium but not pin compatible. As such, it was always supplied with a motherboard; in fact, it was usually soldered in. NexGen did not manufacture the chips or the motherboards they came in; for that it hired IBM Microelectronics. Later NexGen was bought by AMD, right before it was ready to introduce the Nx686—a greatly improved design by Greg Favor and a true

Processors with power levels below 35W are also available but not listed here. See http://ark.intel.com and search for "Ivy Bridge" to see lower-powered processors in this family.

Pentium processors in the G2100 series also use the Ivy Bridge microarchitecture but feature smaller cache sizes and have only two cores without HTT, compared to Core i3's four cores with HTT.

Intel Atom

Intel introduced its Atom ultra low power processors in 2008 and refreshed the line with new models with integrated graphics (D25xx series) in 2012. Although a few vendors have created very low-end desktop computers using Atom, this processor is designed primarily for netbooks, tablets, home servers, and other specialized uses. It is a 64-bit processor fully compatible with x86 and 64-bit versions of Windows and other operating systems, and some models support HT Technology. However, it supports only SSSE3 instructions, has a 4GB memory limit, and includes only two cores. To learn more about Atom, see http://ark.intel.com.

SSE Power	Version	TB2.0	64-Bit	NX	VT	HTT	Socket	
8MB	45–77W	4.2, AVX	Yes	Yes	Yes	Yes	Yes	LGA1155
6MB	45–77W	4.2, AVX	Yes	Yes	Yes	Yes	–	LGA1155
6MB	35–77W	4.2 , AVX	Yes	Yes	Yes	Yes	–	LGA1155
6MB	65–77W	4.2, AVX	Yes	Yes	Yes	Yes	–	LGA1155
3MB	35–55W	4.2, AVX	No	Yes	Yes	Yes	Yes	LGA1155

competitor for the Pentium. AMD took the Nx686 design and combined it with a Pentium electrical interface to create a drop-in Pentium-compatible chip called the K6, which actually outperformed the original from Intel.

The Nx586 had all the standard fifth-generation processor features, such as superscalar execution with two internal pipelines and a high-performance integral L1 cache with separate code and data caches. One advantage is that the Nx586 includes separate 16KB instruction and 16KB data caches, compared to 8KB each for the Pentium. These caches keep key instructions and data close to the processing engines to increase overall system performance.

The Nx586 also includes branch prediction capabilities, which are one of the hallmarks of a sixth-generation processor. Branch prediction means the processor has internal functions to predict program flow to optimize the instruction execution.

The Nx586 processor also featured a RISC core. A translation unit dynamically translates x86 instructions into RISC86 instructions. These RISC86 instructions were designed specifically with direct support for the x86 architecture while obeying RISC performance principles. They are simpler and easier to execute than the complex x86 instructions. This type of capability is another feature normally found only in P6 class processors.

The Nx586 was discontinued after the merger with AMD, which then took the design for the successor Nx686 and released it as the AMD-K6.

AMD-K6 Series

The AMD-K6 processor is a high-performance sixth-generation processor that is physically installable in a P5 (Pentium) motherboard. It essentially was designed for AMD by NexGen and was first known as the Nx686. The NexGen version never appeared because AMD purchased it before the chip was due to be released. The AMD-K6 delivers performance levels somewhere between the Pentium and Pentium II processor because of its unique hybrid design.

The K6 processor contains an industry-standard, high-performance implementation of the new multimedia instruction set, enabling a high level of multimedia performance for the period. The K6-2 introduced an upgrade to MMX that AMD calls 3DNow!, which adds even more graphics and sound instructions. AMD designed the K6 processor to fit the low-cost, high-volume Socket 7 infrastructure. Initially, it used AMD's 0.35-micron, five-metal layer process technology; later the 0.25-micron process was used to increase production quantities because of reduced die size, as well as to decrease power consumption.

AMD-K6 processor technical features include the following:

- Sixth-generation internal design, fifth-generation external interface
- Internal RISC core, which translates x86 to RISC instructions
- Superscalar parallel execution units (seven)
- Dynamic execution
- Branch prediction
- Speculative execution
- Large 64KB L1 cache (32KB instruction cache plus 32KB write-back dual-ported data cache)
- Built-in floating-point unit
- Industry-standard MMX instruction support
- System Management Mode
- Ceramic pin grid array (CPGA) Socket 7 design
- Manufactured using 0.35-micron and 0.25-micron, five-layer designs

The AMD-K6 processor architecture is fully x86 binary code compatible, which means it runs all Intel software, including MMX instructions. To make up for the lower L2 cache performance of the Socket 7 design, AMD beefed up the internal L1 cache to 64KB, twice the size of the Pentium II or III. This, plus the dynamic execution capability, enabled the K6 to outperform the Pentium and come close to the Pentium II and III in performance for a given clock rate.

There were two subsequent additions to the K6 family, in the form of the K6-2 and K6-3. The K6-2 offered higher clock and bus speeds (up to 100MHz) and support for the 3DNow! instruction set. The K6-3 added 256KB of on-die full-core speed L2 cache. The addition of the full-speed L2 cache in the K6-3 was significant because it enabled the K6 series to fully compete with the Intel Pentium III processor family, although it did cause the processor to run hot, resulting in its discontinuation after a relatively brief period.

The original K6 has 8.8 million transistors and is built on a 0.35-micron, five-layer process. The die is 12.7mm on each side, or about 162 square mm. The K6-3 uses a 0.25-micron process and incorporates 21.3 million transistors on a die only 10.9mm on each side, or about 118 square mm.

AMD K7 Processors

The Athlon, Duron, and Athlon XP are all members of AMD's K7 processor family, which represented a clean break with AMD's previous plug compatibility with Intel processors. Instead, AMD developed its own processor slot and socket design and became a serious rival to Intel in both performance and price.

AMD Athlon

The Athlon is AMD's successor to the K6 series. It was designed as a new chip from the ground up and does not interface via the Socket 7 or Super7 sockets like its previous chips. In the initial Athlon versions, AMD used a cartridge design, called Slot A, almost exactly like that of the Intel Pentium II and III (see Figure 3.36). This was because the original Athlons used 512KB of external L2 cache, which was mounted on the processor cartridge board. The external cache ran at one-half core, two-fifths core, or one-third core, depending on which speed processor you had.

In June 2000, AMD introduced a revised version of the Athlon (code-named Thunderbird) that incorporates 256KB of L2 cache directly on the processor die. This on-die cache runs at full-core speed and eliminates a bottleneck in the original Athlon systems. Along with the change to on-die L2 cache, the Athlon was also introduced in a version for AMD's own Socket A (Socket 462), which replaced the Slot A cartridge version (see Figure 3.37).

FIGURE 3.36 AMD Athlon processor for Slot A (cartridge form factor).

FIGURE 3.37 AMD Athlon XP 0.13-micron processor for Socket A (PGA form factor).

Although the Slot A cartridge looks a lot like the Intel Slot 1, and the Socket A looks like Intel's Socket 370, the pinouts are completely different and the AMD chips do not work in the same motherboards as the Intel chips. This was by design because AMD was looking for ways to improve its chip architecture and distance itself from Intel. Special blocked pins in either socket or slot design prevent accidentally installing the chip in the wrong orientation or wrong slot. Socket A versions of the Athlon closely resemble the Duron.

The Athlon was manufactured in speeds from 500MHz up to 1.4GHz and uses a 200MHz or 266MHz processor (front-side) bus called the EV6 to connect to the motherboard North Bridge chip as well as other processors. Licensed from Digital Equipment, the EV6 bus is the same as that used for the

Alpha 21264 processor, later owned by Compaq. The EV6 bus uses a clock speed of 100MHz or 133MHz but double-clocks the data, transferring data twice per cycle, for a cycling speed of 200MHz or 266MHz. Because the bus is 8 bytes (64 bits) wide, this results in a throughput of 8 bytes times 200MHz/266MHz, which amounts to 1.6GBps or 2.1GBps. This bus is ideal for supporting PC1600 or PC2100 DDR memory, which also runs at those speeds. The AMD bus design eliminates a potential bottleneck between the chipset and processor and enables more efficient transfers compared to other processors. The use of the EV6 bus is one of the primary reasons the Athlon and Duron (covered later) chips perform so well.

The Athlon has a large 128KB of L1 cache on the processor die and one-half, two-fifths, or one-third core speed 512KB L2 cache in the cartridge in the older versions; 256KB of full-core speed cache in Socket A Athlon and most Athlon XP models; and 512KB of full-core speed cache in later Athlon XP models. All PGA Socket A versions have the full-speed cache. The Athlon also supports MMX and the Enhanced 3DNow! instructions.

The initial production of the Athlon used 0.25-micron technology, with newer and faster versions being made on 0.18-micron and 0.13-micron processes. Later versions were built using copper metal technology, a first in the PC processor business.

In most benchmarks, the AMD Athlon is equal, if not superior, to the Intel Pentium III. AMD also beat Intel to the 1GHz mark by introducing its 1GHz Athlon two days before Intel introduced the 1GHz Pentium III.

AMD Duron

The AMD Duron processor (originally code-named Spitfire) was announced in June 2000 and is a derivative of the AMD Athlon processor in the same fashion as the Celeron is a derivative of the Pentium II and III. Basically, the Duron is an Athlon with less L2 cache; all other capabilities are essentially the same. It is designed to be a lower-cost version with less cache but only slightly less performance. In keeping with the low-cost theme, Duron contains 64KB on-die L2 cache and is designed for Socket A, a socket version of the Athlon Slot A. Except for the Duron markings, the Duron is almost identical externally to the Socket A versions of the original Athlon.

Essentially, the Duron was designed to compete against the Intel Celeron in the low-cost PC market, just as the Athlon was designed to compete in the higher-end Pentium III market. The Duron has since been discontinued and replaced by the Sempron.

AMD Athlon XP

As mentioned earlier, the last of the Socket A-based Athlon processors is called the Athlon XP. This is basically an evolution of the previous Athlon, with improvements in the instruction set so it can execute Intel SSE instructions and a new marketing scheme that directly competed with the Pentium 4. Athlon XP also adopted a larger (512KB) full-speed on-die cache.

AMD uses the term *QuantiSpeed* (a marketing term, not a technical term) to refer to the architecture of the Athlon XP. AMD defines this as including the following:

- **A nine-issue superscalar, fully pipelined microarchitecture**—This provides more pathways for instructions to be sent into the execution sections of the CPU and includes three floating-point execution units, three integer units, and three address calculation units.

- **A superscalar, fully pipelined floating-point calculation unit**—This provides faster operations per clock cycle and cures a long-time deficiency of AMD processors versus Intel processors.

- **A hardware data prefetch**—This gathers the data needed from system memory and places it in the processor's Level 1 cache to save time.

■ **Improved translation look-aside buffers (TLBs)**—These enable the storage of data where the processor can access it more quickly without duplication or stalling for lack of fresh information.

These design improvements wring more work out of each clock cycle, enabling a "slower" Athlon XP to beat a "faster" Pentium 4 processor in doing actual work.

The first models of the Athlon XP used the Palomino core, which is also shared by the Athlon 4 mobile (laptop) processor. Later models have used the Thoroughbred core, which was later revised to improve thermal characteristics. The different Thoroughbred cores are sometimes referred to as Thoroughbred-A and Thoroughbred-B. Athlon XP processors use a core with 512KB on-die full-speed L2 cache known as *Barton*. Additional features include the following:

■ 3DNow! Professional multimedia instructions (adding compatibility with the 70 additional SSE instructions in the Pentium III but not the 144 additional SSE2 instructions in the Pentium 4)

■ 266MHz or 333MHz FSB

■ 128KB Level 1 and 256KB or 512KB on-die Level 2 memory caches running at full CPU speed

■ Copper interconnects (instead of aluminum) for more electrical efficiency and less heat

Also new to the Athlon XP is the use of a thinner, lighter organic chip packaging compound similar to that used by Intel Pentium 4 processors. Figure 3.38 shows the Athlon XP processor that uses the Barton core.

FIGURE 3.38 AMD Athlon XP 0.13-micron processor with 512KB of L2 cache for Socket A (PGA form factor). Photo courtesy of Advanced Micro Devices, Inc.

This packaging allows for a more efficient layout of electrical components. The last versions of the Athlon XP were made using a 0.13-micron die process that results in a chip with a smaller die that uses less power, generates less heat, and is capable of running faster than the previous models. The most recent 0.13-micron versions of the Athlon XP run at actual clock speeds exceeding 2GHz.

The Athlon XP was replaced by Socket A versions of the Sempron.

Athlon MP

The Athlon MP was AMD's first processor designed for multiprocessor support, making it suitable for server and workstation usage. The Athlon MP was produced in the following four versions, which are similar to various Athlon and Athlon XP models:

- **Model 6 (1GHz, 1.2GHz)**—This model is similar to the Athlon Model 4.
- **Model 6 OPGA (1500+ through 2100+)**—This model is similar to the Athlon XP Model 6.
- **Model 8 (2000+, 2200+, 2400+, 2600+)**—This model is similar to the Athlon XP Model 8.
- **Model 10 (2500+, 2800+, 3000+)**—This model is similar to the Athlon XP Model 8, but with 512KB of L2 cache.

All Athlon MP processors use the same Socket A interface used by later models of the Athlon and all Duron and Athlon XP processors.

The Athlon MP was replaced by the AMD Opteron. For more details about the Athlon MP, see the AMD website.

AMD K8 Processors

AMD's K8 family of processors includes the first 64-bit desktop processors, which set the standard for 64-bit extensions of the venerable 32-bit x86 architecture. The K8 family is the first x86 processors to integrate the memory controller, and also includes the first truly integrated dual-core processors. Although early versions of the K8 family were plagued by frequent socket changes, recent and current versions of the family offer an easy upgrade path to more advanced designs and DDR2 and DDR3 support.

AMD Athlon 64 and 64 FX

The AMD Athlon 64 and 64 FX, introduced in September 2003, are the first 64-bit processors for desktop (and not server) computers. Originally code-named ClawHammer, the Athlon 64 and 64 FX are the desktop element of AMD's 64-bit processor family, which also includes the Opteron (code-named SledgeHammer) server processor. The first Athlon 64 and 64 FX (shown in Figure 3.39) are essentially Opteron chips designed for single-processor systems. In some cases, they have decreased cache or memory bandwidth capabilities.

FIGURE 3.39   AMD Athlon 64 FX (Socket 939 version). Photo courtesy of AMD.

Besides support for 64-bit instructions, the biggest difference between the Athlon 64 and 64 FX and most other processors is the fact that their memory controller is built in. The memory controller is traditionally normally part of the motherboard chipset North Bridge or Memory Controller Hub (MCH) chip, but the Athlon 64 and 64 FX incorporate the memory controller in the processor. This means that the typical CPU bus architecture is different with these chips. In a conventional design, the processor talks to the chipset North Bridge, which then talks to the memory and all other components in the system. Because the Athlon 64 and 64 FX have integrated memory controllers, they talk to memory directly, but they also talk to the North Bridge for other system communications. Separating the memory traffic from the CPU bus allows for improved performance not only in memory transfers, but also in CPU bus transfers. The main difference in the Athlon 64 and 64 FX is in the configurations of cache sizes and memory bus widths.

Following are the major features of the Athlon 64 design:

- Speeds ranging from 1.0GHz to 3.0GHz.
- Between 68.5 million transistors (512KB L2 cache versions) and 129 million transistors (1MB L2 cache versions).
- 12-stage pipeline.
- DDR memory controller with ECC support integrated into the processor (instead of the North Bridge or MCP, as in other recent chipsets).
- Socket 754 features single-channel memory controller; Socket 940, 939, and AM2 feature dual-channel memory controller.
- 128KB L1 cache.
- 512KB or 1MB of on-die full-speed L2 cache.
- Support for AMD64 (also called IA-32e or x86-64) 64-bit extension technology (extends 32-bit x86 architecture).
- Up to 3.2GBps (Socket 754) or 4GBps (Socket 940, 939, and AM2) Hypertransport link to chipset North Bridge.
- Addressable memory size up to 1TB, greatly exceeding the 4GB or 64GB limit imposed by 32-bit processors.
- SSE2 (SSE plus 144 new instructions for graphics and sound processing).
- Multiple low-power states.
- 130-nanometer (see Figure 3.40), 90nm, or 65nm cores.

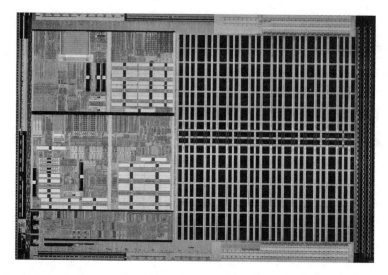

FIGURE 3.40 AMD Athlon 64 die (130-nanometer process, 106 million transistors, 193 sq. mm). Photo courtesy of AMD.

Table 3.21 Athlon 64 and 64 FX Processor Information

Processor Model Number	Cores	CPU Speed	Bus Speed	L2 Cache	CPU Core
Athlon 64 3500+-3800+	1	2.20–2.40GHz	1,000MHz	512KB	Lima
Athlon 64 3000+-3500+	1	1.80–2.20GHz	1,000MHz	512KB	Winchester
Athlon 64 1500+-3400+	1	1.00–2.40GHz	800, 1,000MHz	512KB	Venice
Athlon 64 3500+-4000+, FX-55-57	1	2.20–2.80GHz	1000MHz	512KB, 1MB	San Diego
Athlon 64 3000+-4000+	1	1.80–2.60GHz	1,000MHz	512KB	Orleans
Athlon 64 3200+-3500+	1	2.00–2.20GHz	1,000MHz	512KB	Manchester
Sempron 3000+-3800+	1	1.60–2.20GHz	800MHz	128, 256KB	Manila
Sempron 2500+-3500+	1	1.40–2.00GHz	800, 1,000MHz	128, 256KB	Palermo
Athlon 64 FX-51-53	1	2.20–2.40GHz	800MHz	1MB	SledgeHammer
Athlon 64 2800+-3800+	1	1.80–2.40GHz	800, 1,000MHz	512KB	Newcastle
Athlon 64 2800+-4000+, FX-53-55	1	1.80–2.60GHz	800, 1000MHz	512KB, 1MB	ClawHammer
Sempron 3000+-3100+	1	1.80GHz	800MHz	128, 256KB	Paris

SSE = Streaming SIMD Instructions (MMX)   Cool'n'Quiet = Power-saving technology

NX = Execute Disable Bit   VT = Virtualization Technology

The Athlon 64 FX differs from the standard Athlon 64 in the following ways:

- Supports only Socket 940, 939, or AM2.
- Has dual-channel DDR or DDR2 memory controller with ECC support.
- Socket 940 versions require registered memory.
- Features speeds from 2.2GHz to 2.8GHz.
- 1MB L2 cache (standard).

Although AMD has been criticized by many, including me, for its confusing performance-rating processor names in the Athlon XP series, AMD also uses this naming scheme with the Athlon 64. AMD developed its own chipsets for the Athlon 6 but also encouraged chipset development by third parties, including ATI (which AMD acquired in 2006 for both its chipset and GPU design experience).

The various models and features of the Athlon 64 and 64 FX are summed up in Table 3.21.

Mfg. Process	Max. Power	SSE	64-Bit	NX	Cool'n' Quiet	VT	Socket
65nm	45W	SSE3	Yes	Yes	Yes	Yes	AM2
90nm	67W	SSE2	Yes	Yes	Yes	—	939
90nm	51–89W	SSE3	Yes	Yes	Yes	—	754, 939
90nm	67–104W	SSE3	Yes	Yes	Yes	—	939
90nm	35–62W	SSE3	Yes	Yes	Yes	Yes	AM2
90nm	67W	SSE3	Yes	Yes	Yes	—	939
90nm	35–62W	SSE3	Yes	Yes	Most	—	AM2
90nm	62W	SSE2, SSE3	Most	Yes	Some	—	754, 939
130nm	89W	SSE2	Yes	Yes	—	—	940
130nm	89W	SSE2	Yes	Yes	Yes	—	754, 939
130nm	89–104W	SSE2	Yes	Yes	Yes	—	754, 939
130nm	62W	SSE2	—	Yes	—	—	754

The Athlon 64 and 64 FX were available in four socket versions, the core features of which are detailed in Table 3.22. Note that Socket 940 supports only slower and more expensive registered DIMMs.

Table 3.22   AMD Athlon 64 and 64 FX Socket and Memory Types

Socket	Processor	Channels	Type
754	Athlon 64	Single-channel	DDR
940	Athlon 64 FX	Dual-channel	Registered SDRAM
939	Athlon 64/64 FX	Dual-channel	DDR
AM2	Athlon 64/64 FX	Dual-channel	DDR2

The Athlon 64 essentially comes in three versions: a Socket 754 version that has only a single-channel memory bus, an improved Socket 939 version that has a dual-channel memory bus, and an even better Socket AM2 version that has a dual-channel DDR2 bus. The Athlon 64 FX is also available in three versions: a Socket 940 version that uses expensive (and slower) registered memory, an improved Socket 939 version that uses unbuffered memory, and an updated version that uses dual-channel DDR2. The Socket 939 versions of the Athlon 64 and 64 FX are essentially the same chip, differing only in the amount of L2 cache included. For example, the Athlon 64 3800+ and Athlon 64 FX-53 both run at 2.4GHz and run dual-channel memory. The only difference is that the 3800+ has only 512KB of L2 cache, whereas the FX-53 has 1MB of L2 cache. Because the 64 and 64 FX chips are essentially the same, you need to read the fine print to determine the minor differences in configuration.

The Athlon 64 FX can draw up to 104W or more of power, which is high but still somewhat less than the more power-hungry Pentium 4 processors. As with the Pentium 4, motherboards for the Athlon 64 and 64 FX generally require the ATX12V connector to provide adequate 12V power to run the processor voltage regulator module.

The initial version of the Athlon 64 is built on a 0.13-micron (130-nanometer) process. Subsequent versions use either a 0.09-micron (90nm) or a .065-micron (65nm) process.

AMD Sempron

AMD introduced the Sempron line of processors in 2004 as a replacement for the Duron brand and to provide an economy line of processors designed to compete with the Intel Celeron D. Just as the Intel Celeron name long ago ceased to identify a particular processor and instead is a brand that identifies various types of low-cost, reduced-performance processors, AMD's Sempron brand follows a similar course. Sempron identifies Socket A processors based on the Athlon XP as well as Socket 754, 939, AM2, and AM3 processors based on the Athlon 64 and 64 X2.

The Socket A version of the AMD Sempron is based on the Athlon XP processor, whereas the Socket 754, 939, AM2, and AM3 versions are based on the Athlon 64. Sempron X2 models are dual-core processors based on the Athlon X2. The difference is that the Sempron versions are offered in lower processor and bus clock speeds, with smaller caches and sometimes limited features to justify a lower price point.

Because AMD has offered Sempron processors in many distinctive variations, it's easy to get confused as to which is which and what features are included in a specific model. By looking up the processor on the AMD Desktop Processor Comparison website (http://products.amd.com/en-us/ DesktopCPUResult.aspx), you can find out the exact specification, including socket type, voltage, revision, cache size, and other information about the chip. You can also use software tools, such as CPU-Z (www.cpuid.com), to find more detailed information about a given processor.

AMD Athlon X2, 64 X2, and 64 FX

The 64-bit Athlon 64 processors were designed with multicore updates in mind from the beginning. The desktop Athlon 64 X2 was introduced in May 2005. The Athlon 64 X2 uses several core designs, with different options and features.

The following are major features of the Athlon 64 X2:

- 65nm or 90nm manufacturing process
- Actual clock speeds of 1.9GHz–3.0GHz
- Socket 939, AM2, and 1207FX form factors
- 1GHz HyperTransport interconnect (4GBps bandwidth)

The design of these processors has always included room for the second processor core along with a crossbar memory controller to enable the processor cores to directly communicate with each other without using the North Bridge, as with Intel's initial dual-core processors. Figure 3.41 illustrates the internal design of the Athlon 64 X2.

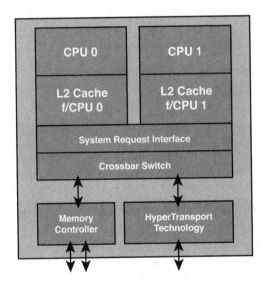

FIGURE 3.41 The Athlon 64 X2 uses the integrated crossbar memory controller present from the beginning of the Athlon 64 processor design to enable the processor cores to communicate with each other.

The result is that most existing systems based on Socket 939 Athlon 64 can be upgraded to a dual-core processor without a motherboard swap. As long as the motherboard supports the processor and a dual-core BIOS upgrade is available from the motherboard or system vendor, the upgrade is possible.

Another benefit of AMD's approach is the lack of a performance or thermal penalty in moving to a dual-core design. Because the Athlon 64 design included provisions for a dual-core upgrade from the beginning, the thermal impact of the second core is minimal, even though the dual-core processors run at the same speeds as their single-core predecessors.

Table 3.23 provides a detailed comparison of the various dual-core Athlon X2, 64 X2, and Athlon 64 FX processors.

Table 3.23 Athlon X2, 64 X2, and 64 FX Processor Information

Processor Model Number	Cores	CPU Speed	Bus Speed	L2 Cache	CPU Core
Athlon X2 4450B-5600B	2	2.3–2.9GHz	1GHz	1MB	Brisbane
Athlon X2 3250e-5050e	2	1.5–2.6GHz	1GHz	1MB	Brisbane
Athlon X2 BE-2xxx	2	1.9–2.3GHz	1GHz	1MB	Brisbane
Sempron X2 2100-2300	2	1.8–2.2GHz	800MHz	512KB	Brisbane
Athlon 64 FX 70-74	2	2.6–3.0GHz	1GHz	2MB	Windsor
Athlon 64 X2 3600+-6000+	2	1.9–3.0GHz	1GHz	512KB–2MB	Windsor
Athlon 64 FX-60	2	2.6GHz	1GHz	2MB	Toledo
Athlon 64 X2 3800+-4800+	2	2.0–2.4GHz	1GHz	1–2MB	Toledo
Athlon 64 X2 3600+-4600+	2	2.0–2.4GHz	1GHz	512KB–1MB	Manchester

SSE = Streaming SIMD Instructions (MMX)   *Cool'n'Quiet = Power-saving technology*
NX = Execute Disable Bit   *VT = Virtualization Technology*

AMD K10 Processors (Phenom, Phenom II, Athlon II, Athlon X2, Sempron)

The K9 was a stillborn project within AMD, resulting in a skip from the K8 to the K10 architecture. The first K10 processors were the Phenom models released in November 2007.

The AMD Phenom family of processors was designed as a flexible family of chips available with 1–6 K10 cores in a single die. These include the Phenom, Phenom II, Athlon II, and some models of the Athlon X2 and Sempron processors. The initial versions used Socket AM2+, which included support for DDR2 memory. Later versions used Sockets AM3 and AM3+, which support DDR3 memory. Figure 3.42 illustrates a Phenom II X6 processor for Socket AM3.

FIGURE 3.42 The Phenom II X6 conceals six cores and memory controllers for both DDR2 and DDR3 memory beneath its protective metal spreader plate.

Mfg. Process	Max. Power	SSE	64-Bit	NX	Cool'n'Quiet	VT	Socket
65nm	45–65W	SSE3	Yes	Yes	Yes	Yes	AM2
65nm	22–45W	SSE3	Yes	Yes	Yes	Yes	AM2
65nm	45W	SSE3	Yes	Yes	Yes	Yes	AM2
65nm	65W	SSE3	Yes	Yes	Yes	—	AM2
90nm	125W	SSE3	Yes	Yes	Yes	Yes	AM2, 1207FX
90nm	65–125W	SSE3	Yes	Yes	Yes	Yes	AM2
90nm	110W	SSE3	Yes	Yes	Yes	—	939
90nm	89–110W	SSE3	Yes	Yes	Yes	—	939
90nm	89–110W	SSE3	Yes	Yes	Yes	—	939

The Phenom X3, X4, and Athlon X2 processors were made on a 65nm process, whereas the Phenon II, Athlon II, and Sempron 1xx processors use a smaller 45nm process, resulting in a smaller die with overall lower power consumption and higher performance. Figure 3.43 illustrates the interior design of the Phenom II X6 processor.

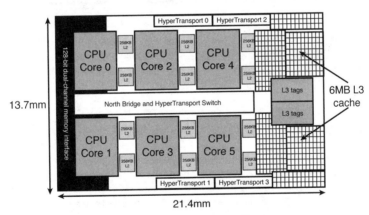

Phenom IIx6 core diagram

FIGURE 3.43 A simplified diagram of the Phenom II X6 core's major components.

The higher-end chips in this family include three, four, or six cores, L3 cache, and higher clock rates and HyperTransport bus speeds (2GHz).

Table 3.24 provides a detailed comparison of the various AMD K10 family processors.

Table 3.24   AMD K10 Family Processor Information

Processor Model Number	Cores	CPU Speed	Bus Speed	Turbo Core	L2 Cache	L3 Cache
Phenom II X6	6	2.6–3.3GHz	2GHz	Yes	3MB	6MB
Phenom II X4	4	2.9–3.5GHz	2GHz	Yes	2MB	6MB
Phenom II X4*	4	2.5–3.7GHz	1.8–2GHz	No	2MB	4–6MB
Athlon II X4	4	2.2–3.8GHz	2GHz	No	2MB	—
Phenom II X3	3	2.4–3.2GHz	2GHz	No	1.5MB	6MB
Athlon II X3	3	2.2–3.4GHz	2GHz	No	1.5MB	—
Phenom II X2	2	2.8–3.5GHz	2GHz	No	1MB	6MB
Phenom II X2	2	3.4GHz	2GHz	No	1MB	6MB
Athlon II X2	2	1.6–3.3GHz	2GHz	No	1–2MB	—
Athlon II 1xxu	1	1.8–2GHz	1.8–2GHz	No	1MB	—
Sempron 1xx	1	2.7–2.9GHz	2GHz	No	1MB	—
Phenom X4	4	1.8–2.6GHz	1.6–2GHz	No	2MB	2MB
Phenom X3	3	1.9–2.5GHz	1.6–1.8GHz	No	1.5MB	2MB
Athlon X2	2	2.3–2.8GHz	1.8GHz	No	1MB	2MB

AM3 processors can also be used in Socket AM2+ motherboards with appropriate BIOS update

SSE = Streaming SIMD Instructions (MMX)

NX = Execute Disable Bit

Cool'n'Quiet = Power-saving technology

VT = Virtualization Technology

*Model 840 has no L3 cache

Zosma = Thuban with two cores disabled

AMD "Bulldozer" and "Piledriver" FX Processors

AMD introduced its follow-up to its K10 architecture, the Bulldozer architecture, in October 2011. Although FX processors in this family use the same Socket AM3+ as late-model K10 processors do, the internal design of Bulldozer processors is very different from its predecessors.

Note

Bulldozer is also known as K11, but Bulldozer is the more common name for this architecture.

Bulldozer processors are modular. Each module contains a single L1 instruction cache, a multi-branched instruction decoder, and a multilayer dispatch controller. The dispatch controller is connected to two integer processing clusters and a single floating point unit. The results are connected

CPU Core	Process	Max. Power	SSE	64-Bit	NX	Cool'n'Quiet	VT	Socket
Thuban	45nm	95–125W	SSE4a	Yes	Yes	Yes	Yes	AM3
Zosma	45nm	95–125W	SSE4a	Yes	Yes	Yes	Yes	AM3
Deneb	45nm	95–140W	SSE4a	Yes	Yes	Yes	Yes	AM3
Propus	45nm	45–95W	SSE4a	Yes	Yes	Yes	Yes	AM3
Heka	45nm	65–95W	SSE4a	Yes	Yes	Yes	Yes	AM3
Rana	45nm	45–95W	SSE4a	Yes	Yes	Yes	Yes	AM3
Callisto	45nm	80W	SSE4a	Yes	Yes	Yes	Yes	AM3
Regor	45nm	80W	SSE4a	Yes	Yes	Yes	Yes	AM3
Regor	45nm	25–65W	SSE4a	Yes	Yes	Yes	Yes	AM3
Sargas	45nm	20W	SSE4a	Yes	Yes	Yes	Yes	AM3
Sargas	45nm	45W	SSE4a	Yes	Yes	Yes	Yes	AM3
Agena	65nm	65–140W	SSE4a	Yes	Yes	Yes	Yes	AM2+
Toliman	65nm	65–95W	SSE4a	Yes	Yes	Yes	Yes	AM2+
Kuma	65nm	95W	SSE4a	Yes	Yes	Yes	Yes	AM2+

Propus = Deneb with no (or disabled) L3 cache
Heka = Deneb with one core disabled
Rana = Propus with one core disabled

Callisto = Deneb with two cores disabled
Toliman = Agena with one core disabled
Kuma = Agena with two cores disabled

to a write coalescing cache, a core interface unit, and up to 2MB of L2 cache. A module is commonly referred to as a dual-core processor, although only the integer clusters are dualed (see Figure 3.44). A Bulldozer CPU includes 8MB of L3 cache memory, and Bulldozer CPUs were manufactured in eight-core, six-core, and four-core versions, known collectively as Zambezi.

Other features in Bulldozer include AMD's Turbo Core (a built-in overclocking feature) and new CPU instructions (AES, AVX, FMA4, and XOP). These instructions support faster encryption, floating point math, rendering, and video transcoding on software optimized for them. Bulldozer uses a 32nm manufacturing process, compared to the 45nm used by most K10-class parts. FX processors based on Bulldozer are completely unlocked for easier overclocking. AMD sells an optional liquid cooler for FX Bulldozer and Piledriver CPUs.

Bulldozer processors are optimized for multithreaded software, but performance benchmarks were disappointing, as most applications were not optimized for Bulldozer's new architecture. Further specifications for Bulldozer processers are listed in Table 3.25.

Table 3.25 lists the processors using Bulldozer microarchitecture.

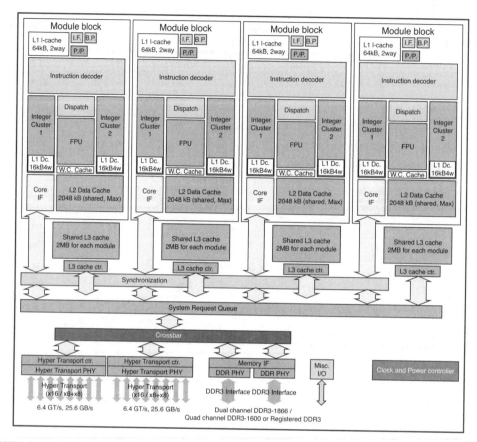

FIGURE 3.44 A block diagram of an eight-core Bulldozer CPU. Source: http://commons.wikimedia.org/wiki/
File:AMD_Bulldozer_block_diagram_(8_core_CPU).PNG.

Table 3.25 AMD FX Processors Using Bulldozer Microarchitecture

Processor	Cores	CPU Speed	Bus Speed	Turbo Core	L2 Cache	L3 Cache	Max. Power	64-bit	NX	Cool 'n' Quiet	VT	Unlocked
FX 81xx	8	3.1–3.6GHz	2.2GHz	Yes	4MB	8MB	125W	Yes	Yes	Yes	Yes	Yes
FX 61xx	6	3.3GHz	2.2GHz	Yes	3MB	8MB	95W	Yes	Yes	Yes	Yes	Yes
FX 41xx	4	3.8GHz	2.0GHz	No	2MB	8MB	125W	Yes	Yes	Yes	Yes	Yes

AMD introduced an improved version of its Bulldozer architecture, Piledriver, in October 2012. Compared to Bulldozer, Piledriver includes these improvements:

- More accurate branch predictor
- Support for the latest integer instructions FMA4 and F16C
- Improved L1 and L2 cache designs
- Faster clock speeds

Table 3.26 lists the FX processors using Piledriver microarchitecture. These processors use the Vishera core.

Table 3.26   AMD FX Processors Using Piledriver Microarchitecture

Processor	Cores	CPU Speed	Bus Speed	Turbo Core	L2 Cache	L3 Cache	Max. Power	64-Bit	NX	Cool'n' Quiet	VT	Unlocked
FX 83xx	8	3.5–4.0GHz	2.2GHz	Yes	4MB	8MB	125W	Yes	Yes	Yes	Yes	Yes
FX 63xx	6	3.5GHz	2.0GHz	Yes	3MB	8MB	95W	Yes	Yes	Yes	Yes	Yes
FX 43xx	4	3.8GHz	2.0GHz	Yes	2MB	8MB	95W	Yes	Yes	Yes	Yes	Yes

AMD Fusion/HSA (Heterogeneous Systems Architecture) APUs

Fusion was the original name for a variety of AMD mobile, desktop, and server processors with in-core graphics, which are now classified under the Heterogeneous Systems Architecture (HSA) designation. AMD refers to these processors as advanced processing units (APUs).

Note

AMD dropped the Fusion name after it was discovered that a Swiss firm, Arctic (originally Arctic Cooling), had been using Fusion for its power supply products since 2006, hence the change to the HSA designation.

AMD has released several lines of APUs, including the C-series (primarily for notebooks) and the E-series (used in notebooks and a few very low-cost desktops). However, the primary product line for desktops is the A-series, which has used two core designs. The initial A-series designs use the Llano core, based on Bulldozer, but with no L3 cache, while the second series uses the Trinity core, based on Piledriver, but again with no L3 cache. The Llano core uses Socket FM1 and includes models with two, three, or four cores and up to 4MB of L2 cache. The Trinity core uses Socket FM2 and provides faster clock speeds, better GPU performance, and better thermal management. It also features two to four cores with up to 4MB of L2 cache. Table 3.27 compares these processors.

Table 3.27   AMD A-Series Processors

Processor	Cores	CPU Speed	Bus Speed	Turbo Core	L2 Cache	GPU
A10-5800K	4	3.8GHz	2.2GHz	Yes	4MB	HD7600D
A10-5700	4	3.4GHz	2.2GHz	Yes	4MB	HD7600D
A8-5600K	4	3.6GHz	2.2GHz	Yes	4MB	HD7560D
A8-5500	4	3.2GHz	2.2GHz	Yes	4MB	HD7560D
A8-3870K	4	3.0GHz	2.2GHz	No	4MB	HD6550D
A8-3850	4	2.9GHz	2.2GHz	No	4MB	HD6550D
A8-3800	4	2.4GHz	2.2GHz	Yes	4MB	HD6550D
A6-5400K	2	3.6GHz	2.2GHz	Yes	1MB	HD7540D
A6-3670K	4	2.7GHz	2.2GHz	No	4MB	HD6530D
A6-3650	4	2.6GHz	2.2GHz	No	4MB	HD6530D
A6-3600	4	2.1GHz	2.2GHz	Yes	4MB	HD6530D
A6-3500	4	2.1GHz	2.2GHz	Yes	3MB	HD6530D
A4-5300	3	3.4GHz	2.2GHz	Yes	1MB	HD7480D
A4-3400	2	2.7GHz	2.2GHz	No	1MB	HD6410D
A4-3300	2	2.5GHz	2.2GHz	No	1MB	HD6410D

To learn more about AMD APUs (Accelerated Processing Units), see the AMD APUs website at www.amd.com/us/products/desktop/apu/Pages/apu.aspx.

Processor Upgrades

Since the 486, processor upgrades have been relatively easy for most systems. With the 486 and later processors, Intel designed in the capability to upgrade by developing standard sockets that would take a variety of processors. This trend has continued to the present, with most motherboards being designed to handle a range of processors in the same family.

To maximize your motherboard, you can almost always upgrade to the fastest processor your particular board will support. Because of the varieties of processor sockets and slots—not to mention voltages, speeds, and other potential areas of incompatibility—you should consult with your motherboard manufacturer to see whether a higher-speed processor will work in your board. Usually, that can be determined by the type of socket or slot on the motherboard, but other things such as the voltage regulator and BIOS can be deciding factors as well.

For example, if your motherboard supports Socket AM2+, you might be able to upgrade from a dual-core Athlon X2 or quad-core processor in the Phenom II family, because they all can use the same socket. Before purchasing a new CPU, you should verify that the motherboard has proper bus speed, voltage settings, and ROM BIOS support for the new chip. Visit the motherboard or system manufacturer's website to obtain the most up-to-date processor compatibility information and to download BIOS updates that might be necessary.

Max. Power	64-Bit	NX	Cool'n'Quiet	VT	Unlocked	Core
100W	Yes	Yes	Yes	Yes	Yes	Trinity
65W	Yes	Yes	Yes	Yes	No	Trinity
100W	Yes	Yes	Yes	Yes	Yes	Trinity
65W	Yes	Yes	Yes	Yes	No	Trinity
100W	Yes	Yes	Yes	Yes	Yes	Llano
100W	Yes	Yes	Yes	Yes	No	Llano
65W	Yes	Yes	Yes	Yes	No	Llano
65W	Yes	Yes	Yes	Yes	Yes	Trinity
100W	Yes	Yes	Yes	Yes	Yes	Llano
100W	Yes	Yes	Yes	Yes	No	Llano
65W	Yes	Yes	Yes	Yes	No	Llano
65W	Yes	Yes	Yes	Yes	No	Llano
65W	Yes	Yes	Yes	Yes	No	Trinity
65W	Yes	Yes	Yes	Yes	No	Llano
65W	Yes	Yes	Yes	Yes	No	Llano

Tip

If you are trying to upgrade the processor in a preassembled or retail store-bought system, you might have few processor upgrade options using the BIOS provided by the system vendor. If you can figure out who made the motherboard (and if it is not a proprietary unit), you might be able to contact the motherboard manufacturer for a more updated BIOS that supports more processors. You can also use the BIOSAgentPlus website (http://biosagentplus.com) to scan your computer, determine if a BIOS update is available, and download it.

Upgrading the processor can, in some cases, double the performance of a system. However, if you already have the fastest processor that will fit a particular socket, you need to consider other alternatives. In that case, you really should look into a complete motherboard change, which would let you upgrade to one of the latest processors at the same time. If your chassis design is not proprietary and your system uses an industry-standard ATX motherboard design, I normally recommend changing the motherboard and processor together rather than trying to find an upgrade processor that will work with your existing board. Keep in mind that new memory might also be necessary.

Overclocking

Another form of processor upgrade is to set the processor speed to run faster than the rating on the chip; this is called overclocking. In many cases, you can get away with a certain amount of overclocking, because Intel, AMD, and others often build safety margins into their ratings. So, a chip rated for, say, 3GHz might in fact run at 3.5GHz or more but instead be down-rated to allow for a greater margin of reliability. By overclocking, you are using this margin and running the chip closer to its true maximum speed. I don't normally recommend overclocking for a novice, but if you are comfortable playing with your system settings, and you can afford and are capable of dealing with potential consequences, overclocking might enable you to get another 10%–20% or more performance from your system.

Overclocking is usually applied to the processor, but it can also be applied to other components in the system, including memory, video cards, bus speeds, and more.

When chips run faster, they run hotter, so cooling upgrades and modifications usually go hand-in-hand with overclocking. Systems that run cool tend to be more stable and more reliable, so even if you don't overclock your system, ensuring that it runs cool is essential for trouble-free operation. Many systems are not properly designed or configured for optimal cooling even at their standard speeds, much less when overclocked.

Overclocking PCs dates all the way back to the original 4.77MHz IBM PC and 6MHz AT systems of the early 1980s. In fact, IBM made overclocking the AT easy because the quartz crystal that controlled the speed of the processor was socketed. You could obtain a faster replacement crystal for about a dollar and easily plug it in. The first several editions of this book covered how to perform this modification in detail, resulting in a system that was up to 1.5 times faster than it started out. Modern systems allow overclocking without replacing any parts by virtue of programmable timer chips and simple and easy-to-change BIOS Setup options. Some processors, such as Intel Extreme Edition and AMD Black Edition processors, are especially suited to overclocking because they feature unlocked core multipliers. However, some overclocking is possible with almost any processor.

Quartz Crystals

To understand overclocking, you need to know how computer system speeds are controlled. The main component controlling speed in a computer is a quartz crystal. Quartz is silicon dioxide (SiO_2) in crystalline form. Oxygen and silicon are the most common elements on earth (sand and rock are mostly silicon dioxide), and computer chips are made mainly from silicon. Quartz is a hard, transparent material with a density of 2649 kg/m³ (1.531 oz/in³) and a melting point of 1750°C (3,182°F). Quartz is brittle but with a little bit of elasticity, which is perhaps its most useful attribute.

In crystalline form, quartz can generate regular and consistent signal pulses to regulate electronic circuits, similar to the way a metronome can regulate music. Quartz crystals are used because they are *piezoelectric*, which is defined as having a property that generates voltage when subjected to mechanical stress. The opposite is also true—that is, quartz generates mechanical stress or movement when subjected to a voltage. Piezoelectricity was discovered by Pierre and Jacques Curie in 1880, and it is the essential feature of quartz that makes it useful in electronic circuits.

Piezoelectricity works two ways, meaning that if a voltage is generated when you bend a crystal or apply voltage to a crystal, it bends (contracts, expands, or twists) in a similar fashion. Although the crystal is mostly brittle in nature, it is still somewhat elastic, such that any deformation tends to snap back and then occur again, resonating or vibrating at a natural frequency as long as the voltage is present. Much like a tuning fork or the pipes in an organ, the natural resonant frequency depends on the size and shape of the crystal. In general, the smaller and thinner it is, the faster it vibrates.

The actual movement is exceedingly small, on the order of 68 nanometers (billionths of a meter) per centimeter, which in a normal crystal is only a few atoms in length. Although the movement is small, it is also quite rapid, which means tremendous forces can be generated. For example, the surface acceleration of a 50MHz crystal can exceed five million times the force of gravity.

Crystal resonators are made from slabs of quartz sawed from raw quartz crystal stock. The raw stock slabs are cut into squares, rounded, and ground into flat discs called *blanks*. The thinner the disc, the higher the resonant frequency; however, there are limits as to how thin the discs can be made before they break. The upper limit for fundamental mode resonators is approximately 50MHz. At that frequency, the discs are paper thin and are generally too fragile to withstand further grinding. Still, higher-frequency crystals can be achieved by using harmonics of the fundamental frequency, resulting in crystals of up to 200MHz or more. Even higher frequencies can be achieved by using frequency synthesizer circuits, which use a base crystal-generated frequency fed to a circuit that then generates multiples of frequency that can extend well into the gigahertz or terahertz range. In fact, crystal-based frequency synthesizer circuits generate the high operating speeds of modern PCs.

The crystal packages, as well as the shape of the actual quartz crystals inside the packages, can vary. The packages are usually a metal can that is either cylindrical or oblong in shape, but they can also have other shapes or be constructed of plastic or other materials (see Figure 3.45).

The sliver of quartz inside the package is normally disc shaped, but it is shaped like a tuning fork in some examples. Figure 3.46 shows a cylindrical crystal package with the cover removed, exposing the tuning fork–shaped sliver of quartz inside.

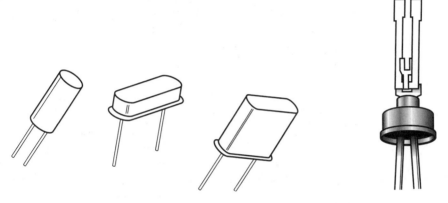

FIGURE 3.45 Crystal packages of varying shapes.

FIGURE 3.46 Crystal interior showing the quartz tuning fork.

Most crystals use a disc-shaped sliver of quartz as a resonator. The disc is contained in a hermetically sealed evacuated enclosure. Figure 3.47 shows the interior view of a typical crystal with a disc-shaped resonator inside. The quartz disc inside has electrodes on each side, allowing voltage to be applied to the disc. The details are shown in Figure 3.48.

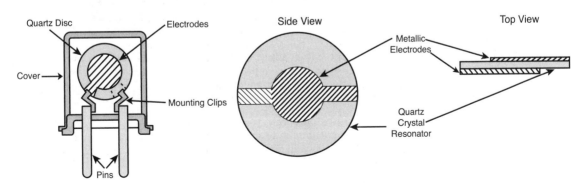

FIGURE 3.47 Figure showing the disc-shaped resonator.

FIGURE 3.48 Disc-shaped quartz resonator details.

Walter G. Cady was the first to use a quartz crystal to control an electronic oscillator circuit in 1921. He published his results in 1922, which led to the development of the first crystal-controlled clock by Warren A. Marrison in 1927. Today, all modern computers have multiple internal oscillators and clocks, some for controlling bus and processor speeds and at least one for a standard time-of-day clock.

Modern PC Clocks

A typical PC has at least two crystals on the motherboard; the main crystal controls the speed of the motherboard and motherboard circuitry, and the other controls the real-time clock (RTC). The main crystal is always 14.31818MHz (it might be abbreviated as 14.318 or just 14.3), and the RTC crystal is always 32.768KHz.

Why 14.31818MHz?

The original 1981 vintage IBM PC ran at 4.77MHz, a speed derived by taking a 14.31818MHz crystal and using a divider circuit to divide the frequency by 3 to get 4.77MHz. Many people were confused as to why IBM chose to run the processor at 4.77MHz; after all, the 8088 processor they used was rated for 5MHz, and all they would have had to do to run it at that speed was change the main crystal from 14.318MHz to 15MHz instead. Well, the truth is that if they did that, they would have had to add more crystals to the design. You see, the same 14.318MHz crystal that was divided by 3 to run the processor was also divided by 4 to get 3.58MHz, which is the *exact* frequency needed for the NTSC color video modulation signal to be compatible with color TV.

But that's not all: Another circuit divided the crystal frequency by 12 to get 1.193182MHz, which was used by an 8253 programmable three-channel 16-bit interval timer/counter chip. Each channel could be used to take an input clock signal and produce an output signal by dividing by an arbitrary 16-bit number. Channel 0 was used to make the time-of-day clock ticks. It was programmed by the BIOS to call INT 08h every 65,536 ticks, which was about 18.2 times per second (or about every 55 milliseconds). The software routines linked to INT 08h caused the time-of-day clock to be updated and could chain to any other activities that needed to be done periodically. Channel 1 was used to tell the DMA to refresh the dynamic RAM every 72 cycles (about 15 microseconds), and channel 2 was used to make an audio signal for the speaker (beeps)—different tones could be made by changing the divisor.

So by carefully choosing a 14.318MHz crystal instead of 15MHz or some other speed, the IBM engineers were able to design a motherboard in which a single crystal could run the processor, video card, time-of-day clock, memory refresh, and even beep tones. The single-crystal design allowed the motherboard to be manufactured with fewer parts and at a lower cost.

As a testament to their foresight, all modern PCs are still controlled by a 14.318MHz crystal! This crystal, in conjunction with a frequency timing generator chip, derives virtually all the frequencies used on a modern motherboard by the CPU, buses, memory, and more.

PCs don't run at 14.318MHz, so how can a crystal of that speed be used? And what happens when you install a different processor? How does the system adjust the bus and other speeds to accommodate the new chip? The answer is that a special chip called a *frequency timing generator* (FTG) or *frequency synthesizer* is used in conjunction with the crystal to derive the actual speeds of the system. Figure 3.49 shows a portion of a motherboard with an FTG chip and a 14.318MHz crystal below it.

The RTC in the original PC was notoriously inaccurate, so starting with the IBM AT in 1984, IBM added a separate 32.768KHz crystal to count time independent from the speed of the system. This crystal is used on all modern motherboards as well. Figure 3.50 shows a 32.768KHz crystal next to a chipset South Bridge or I/O controller hub, which contains the RTC circuitry and CMOS RAM.

FIGURE 3.49 An ICS 9250 frequency timing generator chip with a 14.318MHz crystal.

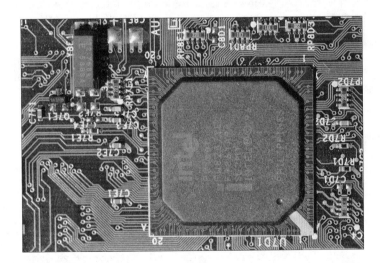

FIGURE 3.50 Chipset South Bridge (I/O controller hub) incorporating an RTC, along with the 32.768KHz clock crystal.

Most frequency synthesizer chips used on PC motherboards are made by a handful of companies, including Integrated Device Technology (www.idt.com; formerly Integrated Circuit Systems) and Cypress Semiconductor (www.cypress.com; formerly International Microcircuits Inc. [IMI]). These chips use phased locked loop (PLL) circuitry to generate synchronized processor, PCI, AGP, and other bus timing signals that are derived from a single 14.318MHz crystal. The crystal and frequency synthesizer chip are usually situated near the processor and main chipset component of the motherboard.

The amazing thing about these chips is that most of them are programmable and adjustable, so they can change their frequency outputs via software, which results in the system running at different speeds. Because all CPUs are based on the speed of the CPU bus, when you change the CPU bus speed generated by the frequency synthesizer chip, you can change the speed of your processor. Because the PCI, AGP, and memory buses are often synchronized with the speed of the processor bus, when you change the processor bus speed by a given percentage, you also change the speed of those other buses by the same percentage. The software to accomplish this is built into the BIOS Setup menus of most modern motherboards.

Overclocking Tips

Most modern motherboards automatically read the CPU and memory components to determine their proper speed, timing, and voltage settings. Originally, these settings were controlled by jumpers and switches, but in most modern boards you can enter the BIOS Setup to change these settings to manual and then use the menu options in the BIOS Setup to alter the speed of the system. Because such alterations can make the system unstable, most systems are designed to boot into the BIOS Setup at a default low speed so you are not locked out from making changes in the future. This makes overclocking as simple as changing a few menu options and then rebooting to test the selections you've made.

The concept for overclocking is simple: You change the settings to increase the speed of the processor, memory, buses, and so on, until the system becomes unstable. Then you can go back in and reduce the settings until the system is stable again. In this manner, you find the maximum sustainable speed for a system. Because each processor is different, even ones with the same ratings can end up allowing different maximum stable speeds.

Why can some chips be clocked faster than others? The reason is in how they are manufactured and marked. As an example, the first Pentium 4 chips based on the Prescott core used die that were 112 square mm on 300mm wafers, resulting in a maximum of 529 full die per wafer. Due to defects, many of those die wouldn't work, but let's say that 423 (about an 80% yield) were good. Intel initially sold the Prescott core processors at speeds from 2.4GHz through 3.4GHz, which meant that all the die on each wafer were designed to potentially run at the highest rated speed. However, out of the good (working) die, testing would show that although some of those would indeed run at the highest 3.4GHz rated speed, others would work reliably only at lower speeds. The finished chips would have been sorted into bins according to their speed test results.

Early in manufacturing a given processor design, the sorted bins of chips at the end of the line would contain more that passed only the lower speed tests, and fewer that ran at the highest speeds. This is why the fastest chips are the most expensive—generally fewer of the chips produced on a given day will pass the testing at that speed. Eventually, however, as the manufacturing processes and chip design are tweaked, more and more of the finished chips end up passing the higher-speed tests. But because lower-speed chips are priced less and sell more, the manufacturer might have to dip into the faster bins and mark those chips at the lower speeds to fill the larger number of orders.

Essentially what I'm saying is that chipmakers such as Intel and AMD make all the chips on a wafer identically and try to make them so they will all run at the highest speeds. If you purchase one of the lesser-rated chips, you really have the same chip (die) as the higher-rated versions; the difference is the higher-rated ones are guaranteed to run at the higher speeds, whereas the lower-rated ones are not. That is where overclockers come in.

Tip

The current speed of a processor might not be its actual rated speed, either because of overclocking or because some recent systems reduce processor speed when the system is not heavily tasked. Both Intel and AMD have developed software tools that can properly identify the rated speed of a processor.

For newer Intel processors, use the Intel Processor Identification Utility; for older chips, use the Intel Processor Frequency ID Utility. Both of these are available from www.intel.com/support/processors/sb/CS-015477.htm.

For AMD processors, use either the AMD CPU Info program or the AMD Clock program. To find these, visit http://support.amd.com, select Drivers and Downloads, All Processors. Then search for *CPU info* and *AMD Clock*.

One drawback of the Intel and AMD programs is that they only work on their respective brands of chips. Another excellent utility that works on both Intel and AMD processors is the CPU-Z program available from www.cpuid.com. I routinely install this program on any systems I build or service because it provides universal processor (and chipset) identification. See example readouts earlier in this chapter.

Users who overclock their systems purchase chips rated at lower speeds and essentially do their own testing to see if they will run at higher speeds. They can also start with the highest-rated chips and see whether they can run them even faster, but success there is much more limited. The most successful overclocking is almost always with the lowest-rated speed of a given design, and those chips are also sold for the lowest price. In other words, statistically you might be able to find many of the lowest-speed grade chips that are capable of running at the highest-speed grade (because they are essentially identical during manufacture); however, if you start with the highest-speed grade, you might be able to increase the speed only a small percentage.

Just remember that a difference exists between the rated speed of a chip and the actual maximum speed at which it runs. Manufacturers such as Intel and AMD have to be conservative when they rate chips, so a chip of a given rating is almost always capable of running at least some margin of speed faster than the rating—the question is, how much faster? Unfortunately, the only way to know that is by trying it out—that is, by testing chips individually.

Unlocking Cores

A variation of overclocking is the unlocking of disabled cores on AMD Phenom II and Athlon II processors for better performance in single-threaded and multithreaded applications and when multitasking. As Table 3.24 indicates, many of AMD's X3 and X2 K10-based processors are based on X4 designs that have one or two cores disabled.

If you unlock these cores using a method such as enabling the Advanced Clock Calibration (ACC) feature in the system BIOS (see www.tomshardware.com/reviews/unlock-phenom-ii,2273-5.html for details), one of the following results can take place:

- The unlocked core may function perfectly. This is the result if a core were disabled strictly to enable the chip to be sold as an X3 rather than an X4.

- Your system boots and runs normally, but the "unlocked" core can't be detected or used. A core disabled because of moderate problems would result in this problem.

- Your system might not boot or might not be able to run Windows until you reset the ACC setting in your system BIOS to its default mode. More serious core stability problems would cause this result.

- You could destroy your processor or motherboard. This would be the result if the core were disabled because it contained a short.

To be able to try unlocking disabled cores, you need a motherboard that has an adjustable ACC setting in the system BIOS (many motherboards using the AMD750 South Bridge [SB] feature this option) and a motherboard BIOS that does not include AMD-provided microcode to prevent unlocking via the ACC adjustment routine.

Although the AMD850 South Bridge used on the latest motherboards does not include an ACC option, motherboard vendors such as ASUS and Gigabyte have added an ACC chip to their motherboards and added core unlocking capabilities to their BIOS setups. MSI also offers unlocking but is using a purely BIOS-based unlock routine for its motherboards with the SB850 processor.

If you do unlock an additional core or two, you might enjoy faster performance and better multi-threaded and multitasking operating for free, or you might find your system to be unstable or unable to start. Before you assume that a system that runs with an unlocked core is truly stable, use some of the tests I recommend in Chapter 20, "PC Diagnostics, Testing, and Maintenance."

Note

The latest four-core and six-core FX processors from AMD cannot have their additional cores unlocked because the leads have been cut during production.

Bus Speeds and Multipliers

Modern processors run at a multiple of the motherboard speed, and the selected multiple is usually locked within the processor; therefore, all you can do to change speeds is change the processor bus speed settings. The processor bus is also called the *CPU bus*, *FSB*, or *processor side bus* (PSB), all of which are interchangeable terms.

For example, I built a system that uses an Intel Pentium 4 3.2E processor, which typically runs at 3,200MHz on an 800MHz CPU bus. Thus, the processor is locked to run at four times the speed of the CPU bus. I was able to increase the CPU bus speed from 800MHz to 832MHz, which meant the processor speed increased from 3,200MHz to 3,328MHz, which is 128MHz faster than the rating. This took all of about 60 seconds to reboot, enter the BIOS Setup, make the changes in the menu, save, and reboot again. This was only a 4% increase in overall speed, but it didn't cost a penny, and testing proved that the system was just as stable as it was before.

Many motherboards allow changes in speed of up to 50% or more, but a processor rarely sustains speeds that far above its rating without locking up or crashing. Also note that, by increasing the speed of the processor bus, you may be increasing the speed of the memory bus, PCI bus, or PCI Express (or AGP) bus by the same percentage. Therefore, if your memory is unstable at the higher speed, the system will still crash, even though the processor might have been capable of sustaining it. The lowest common denominator prevails, which means your system will run faster only if all the components are up to the challenge.

Overclocking Pitfalls

If you are intent on overclocking, there are several issues to consider. One is that most processors sold since 1998 are multiplier-locked before they are shipped out. Processors that are locked ignore any changes to the multiplier setting on the motherboard. Although originally done to prevent re-markers from fraudulently relabeling processors (creating "counterfeit" chips), multiplier locking has impacted the computing performance enthusiast, leaving tweaking the motherboard bus speed as the only easy way (or in some cases, the only way possible) to achieve a clock speed higher than standard.

Tip

Intel's K-series Core i7 and i5 processors have unlocked clock multipliers, as do AMD's Black Edition FX, Phenom II Phenom, and Athlon X2 processors, as well as AMD's A-series K-class processors. Choose these processors along with a motherboard that offers adjustable clock settings in its BIOS for easy overclocking.

You can run into problems increasing motherboard bus speed as well. Most older Intel motherboards, for example, simply don't support clock speeds other than the standard settings. Some newer enthusiast-oriented Intel boards have "burn-in" or "override" features that allow you to increase the default processor bus speed (and the speed of the processor core), voltages, and multiplier (for unlocked CPUs). Most other brands of motherboards also allow changing the bus speeds. Note that small incremental changes in clock multiplier speeds, rather than large jumps, are the best way to coax a bit more performance out of a particular processor. This is because a given chip is generally overclockable by a certain percentage. The smaller the steps you can take when increasing speed, the more likely that you'll be able to come close to the actual maximum speed of the chip without going over that amount and causing system instability.

For example, say you have a Socket 775 motherboard running a 2.4GHz Core 2 Quad processor at a CPU FSB speed of 1,066MHz. The motherboard permits 1MHz adjustments of the CPU bus clock speed (which is multiplied by 4 to obtain the FSB) to enable you to fine-tune your processor speed. The base clock frequency is 266MHz and is multiplied by 4 to obtain the motherboard bus (FSB) speed, which is then further increased by the CPU multiplier:

$$800MHz \times 3.5 = 2,800MHz, \text{ or } 2.8GHz$$

By adjusting the CPU clock frequency, you can change the FSB and CPU core clock speeds as shown in Table 3.28.

Table 3.28   Core Clock, FSB, and CPU Speed Relationships

Base Clock Frequency	Bus Multiplier (Fixed)	Resulting FSB Speed	CPU Core Multiplier (Locked)	Resulting Processor Speed
266MHz	4X	1,066MHz	9X	2.400GHz
268MHz	4X	1,072MHz	9X	2.412GHz
270MHz	4X	1,080MHz	9X	2.430GHz
272MHz	4X	1,088MHz	9X	2.448GHz
274MHz	4X	1,096MHz	9X	2.466GHz
276MHz	4X	1,104MHz	9X	2.484GHz
278MHz	4X	1,112MHz	9X	2.502GHz
280MHz	4X	1,120MHz	9X	2.520GHz
282MHz	4X	1,128MHz	9X	2.538GHz
284MHz	4X	1,136MHz	9X	2.556GHz
286MHz	4X	1,144MHz	9X	2.574GHz
288MHz	4X	1,152MHz	9X	2.592GHz
290MHz	4X	1,160MHz	9X	2.610GHz
292MHz	4X	1,168MHz	9X	2.628GHz
294MHz	4X	1,176MHz	9X	2.646GHz
296MHz	4X	1,184MHz	9X	2.664GHz
298MHz	4X	1,192MHz	9X	2.682GHz
300MHz	4X	1,200MHz	9X	2.700GHz

As you can see in this example, by increasing the base clock from 266MHz to 300MHz, you increase the FSB from 1,066MHz to 1,200MHz and the CPU core speed from 2.4GHz to 2.7GHz, nearly a 13% increase. Typically, increases on the order of 10–20% are successful. You might be able to achieve more if your system offers excellent cooling and you can also adjust CPU multiplier, voltage, and other settings.

Overclocking Sandy Bridge and Ivy Bridge Processors

The Sandy Bridge and Ivy Bridge Core i-series processors from Intel have made drastic changes in how overclocking works. The clock generator is incorporated into the 6-series chipsets that support Sandy Bridge processors and in the 7-series chipsets for Ivy Bridge processors, so that you can no longer independently adjust the speeds of buses such as PCI Express or DMI. The BCLK frequency is also locked at 100MHz (it was 133MHz with adjustments up or down in the Nehalem Core i-series processors).

If you want to have maximum overclock potential for a Core i-series Sandy Bridge or Ivy Bridge processor, look for model numbers ending in K (for example, Core i7-2600K or Core i7-3770K) and choose a motherboard with a chipset designed for overclocking, such as the P67 or Z68 (Sandy Bridge) or the Z77 or Z75 (Ivy Bridge). Core i7 and i5 Sandy Bridge and Ivy Bridge processors without the K suffix allow limited overclocking ("limited unlocking") up to four speed ranges (bins) above the normal turbo frequency (maximum clock speed). For example, a processor with a turbo frequency of 3.7GHz could be overclocked to 4.1GHz with one core running, 4.0GHz with two cores running, and so on. Again, you need an overclock-friendly chipset to make this happen.

Core i3 Sandy Bridge and Ivy Bridge chips don't include Turbo Boost and thus don't support overclocking. Consequently, if you want to overclock Sandy Bridge or Ivy Bridge processors, your choice of processor and chipset is more important than ever before.

CPU Voltage Settings

Another trick overclockers use is playing with the voltage settings for the CPU. All modern CPU sockets and slots have automatic voltage detection. With this detection, the system determines and sets the correct voltage by reading certain pins on the processor. Some motherboards do not allow manual changes to these settings. Other motherboards allow you to tweak the voltage settings up or down by fractions of a volt. Some experimenters have found that by either increasing or decreasing voltage slightly from the standard, a higher speed of overclock can be achieved with the system remaining stable. Some motherboards allow adjusting the voltage settings for the FSB, chipset, and memory components, allowing for even more control in overclocking situations.

My recommendation is to be careful when playing with voltages because you can damage the processor or other components in this manner. Even without changing voltage, overclocking with an adjustable bus speed motherboard is easy and fairly rewarding. I do recommend you make sure you are using a high-quality board, good memory, and especially a good system chassis with additional cooling fans and a heavy-duty power supply. See Chapter 18, "Power Supplies," for more information on upgrading power supplies and chassis. Especially when you are overclocking, it is essential that the system components and the CPU remain properly cooled. Going a little bit overboard on the processor heatsink and adding extra cooling fans to the case never hurts and in many cases helps a great deal when hotrodding a system in this manner.

Processor Cooling

Heat can be a problem in any high-performance system. The higher-speed processors consume more power and therefore generate more heat. The processor is usually the single most power-hungry chip in a system, and in most situations, the fan inside your computer case is incapable of handling the load without some help.

Heatsinks

At one time, a *heatsink* (a special attachment for a chip that draws heat away from the chip) was needed only in systems in which processor heat was a problem. However, starting with the faster Pentium processors in the early 1990s, heatsinks have been a necessity for every processor since.

A heatsink works like the radiator in your car, pulling heat away from the engine. In a similar fashion, the heatsink conducts heat away from the processor so it can be vented out of the system. It does this by using a thermal conductor (usually metal) to carry heat away from the processor into fins that expose a high amount of surface area to moving air. This enables the air to be heated, thus cooling the heatsink and the processor. Just like the radiator in your car, the heatsink depends on airflow. With no moving air, a heatsink is incapable of radiating the heat away. To keep the engine in your car from overheating when the car is not moving, auto engineers incorporate a fan. Likewise, a fan is incorporated somewhere inside your PC to move air across the heatsink and vent it out of the system. In some systems, the fan included in the power supply is enough when combined with a special heatsink design; in most cases, though, an additional fan must be attached directly over the processor heatsink to provide the necessary levels of cooling. Case fans are also typical in recent systems to assist in moving the hot air out of the system and replacing it with cooler air from the outside.

The heatsink is normally attached with clips or snap-in retainers. A variety of heatsinks and attachment methods exist. According to data from Intel, heatsink clips are the number-two destroyer of motherboards (screwdrivers are number one), which is one reason the company moved away from metal clips to plastic fasteners for its latest designs. When installing or removing a heatsink that is clipped on, be sure you don't scrape the surface of the motherboard.

Heatsinks are rated for their cooling performances. Typically, the ratings are expressed as a resistance to heat transfer in degrees centigrade per watt (°C/W), where lower is better. Note that the resistance varies according to the airflow across the heatsink.

Active Heatsinks

To ensure a constant flow of air and more consistent performance, most heatsinks incorporate fans so they don't have to rely on the airflow within the system. Heatsinks with fans are referred to as *active* heatsinks (see Figure 3.51). Active heatsinks have a power connection. Older ones often used a spare disk drive power connector, but most recent heatsinks plug into dedicated heatsink power connections common to most motherboards. The Socket 478 design uses two cams to engage the heatsink clips and place the system under tension. The force generated is 75 lbs., which produces a noticeable bow in the motherboard underneath the processor. This bow is normal, and the motherboard is designed to accommodate it. The high degree of force is necessary to prevent the heavier heatsinks from pulling up on the processor during movement or shipment of the system, and it ensures a good bond for the thermal interface material (thermal grease).

Figure 3.52 shows the design used on most Socket AM3+, AM3, AM2+, AM2, FM1, FM2, 940, 939, and 754 processors, featuring a cam and clip assembly on one side. Similar to the Socket 478 double-cam assembly, this design puts 75 lbs. of force between the heatsink and the processor. Bowing of the motherboard is prevented in this design by the use of a special stiffening plate (also called a *backing plate*) underneath the motherboard. The heatsink retention frame actually attaches to this plate through the board. The stiffening plate and retention frame normally come with the motherboard, but the heatsink with fan and the clip and cam assembly come with the processor.

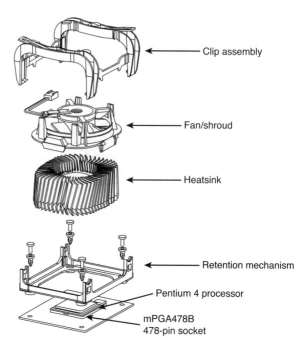

Clip assembly

Fan/shroud

Heatsink

Retention mechanism

Pentium 4 processor

mPGA478B
478-pin socket

FIGURE 3.51 Active heatsink suitable for a Pentium 4 processor using Socket 478.

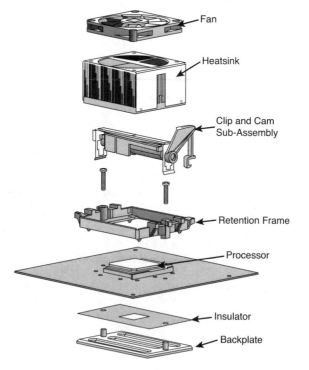

Fan

Heatsink

Clip and Cam
Sub-Assembly

Retention Frame

Processor

Insulator

Backplate

FIGURE 3.52 Active heatsink and cam retention mechanism used on Socket AM3+, AM3, AM2+, AM2, FM2, FM1, 940, 939, and 754 processors.

Tip

One of the best reasons to use the motherboard-based power connectors for the fan is that most system BIOS setup programs can display the fan performance and report it to a system monitoring program. Because some processors—particularly older Athlon processors—can be destroyed in a few moments by a malfunctioning processor heatsink fan, this feature can help prevent a disaster inside your system.

If you need to purchase an active heatsink, be aware that some on the market are of poor quality. The bad ones have fan motors that use sleeve bearings, which freeze up after a short life. I recommend only fans with ball-bearing motors, which last about 10 times longer than the sleeve-bearing types. Of course, they cost more—but only about twice as much, so you'll save money in the long run.

Newer fans include four-wire power connectors, which feature the standard power, ground, and tach wires found in three-wire fans, but they also add a fourth wire for fan-speed control. These are known as PWM (Pulse Width Modulation) fans because they use pulse width modulation signals from the motherboard to control their speed more precisely and with more variations in speed. Standard three-wire fans have internal thermal resistors (thermistors) that control fan speed, and these normally offer only two-speed operation. With the PWM setup, the motherboard can monitor system and processor temperatures and variably control the fan speed to maintain the desired temperatures.

Heatsinks designed for LGA775, LGA1156, LGA1366, LGA1155, or LGA2011 sockets usually include plastic retainer clips that snap into holes in the motherboard. To install this type of heatsink, you merely align the tops of the clips such that the arrows are rotated all the way to the left (opposite the direction of the arrow) and then press the tops down until the bottom parts click and lock into the holes in the motherboard. To remove the heatsink, you insert a flat blade screwdriver into the slot under the arrows and then rotate the tops in the direction of the arrows. As you rotate each clip, it will pop out of the motherboard. Figure 3.53 shows an active heatsink for Socket LGA1155 processors, featuring these snap-in retainers.

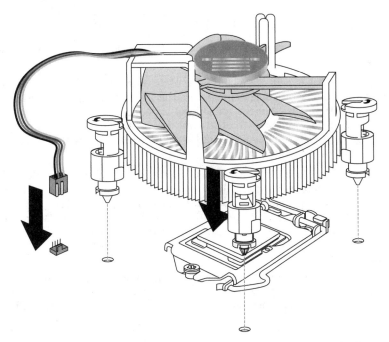

FIGURE 3.53 LGA1155 boxed processor heatsink showing snap-in retainers and a four-wire PWM fan.

Purchasing a Heatsink

With the variety of processor designs on the market today, you also need to match the thermal output of the processor to the thermal-handling capability of the heatsink you plan to use. The heatsink performance required by a given processor depends on two main figures: the maximum allowable case temperature as well as the maximum power output. Refer to the upcoming section, "Heatsink Ratings and Calculations," to see how you can calculate the maximum thermal resistance you need. You can always install a heatsink with a lower thermal resistance, which will only improve the cooling, but you should never install a heatsink that has a higher thermal resistance than your processor requires.

Processors sold as boxed or retail versions from Intel and AMD include high-quality active heatsinks designed to work under the worst possible ambient conditions. One of the main reasons I recommend purchasing boxed processors is that you are guaranteed to get a high-quality heatsink with the processor, one that is designed to cool the processor under the worst conditions and that should last the life of the system.

If you purchase an OEM processor that comes without a heatsink, you can expect to pay anywhere from $25 to $60 for a high-quality active fan heatsink, with some of the boutique models costing even more. You'll invariably pay more for the most efficient, best-cooling active heatsinks, and those overclockers who swear by these devices usually also believe that the extra expense is worthwhile.

Note

Passive heatsinks are basically aluminum-finned radiators that are more difficult to integrate because they rely on airflow from an external source, usually provided by a chassis-mounted fan that sometimes features a duct to direct airflow directly through the fins on the heatsink. Passive heatsinks are seldom used on current processors, although they have been popular in the past on name-brand systems. Passive heatsinks connected to heatpipes are currently popular for chipset cooling.

"Boutique" Heatsinks

A large market exists for high-end "boutique" heatsink products, many of which have shapes and designs that would qualify them more as industrial art than an internal computer component. These fancy heatsinks are popular with overclockers as well as those who like to modify their systems in general.

Although I certainly appreciate a good-looking piece of hardware as much as anybody, as an engineer I am more concerned about performance than appearance. Most of the boutique designs do in fact have outstanding thermal performance, but the actual level of performance is rarely documented (making comparisons difficult) and may come with other costs besides a high price. These drawbacks include awkward sizes, excessive weight that could damage the processor or motherboard, and attachment hardware that can be difficult to use.

Perhaps my main beef is the lack of technical documentation. The primary specification for the thermal performance of a heatsink is the thermal resistance, specified in degrees Celsius per watt. The lower this figure, the better the performance. Unfortunately, most of the boutique heatsinks on the market don't include this figure in their specifications. Without knowing the thermal resistance, you have no easy way to compare the performance of one heatsink to another.

Heatsink Ratings and Calculations

When cooling a processor, the heatsink transfers heat from the processor to the air. This capability is expressed in a figure known as *thermal resistance*, which is measured in degrees Celsius per watt (C/W). The lower the figure, the lower the thermal resistance and the more heat the heatsink can remove from the CPU.

To calculate the heatsink your processor requires, you can use the following formula:

$$R_{total} = T_{case} - T_{inlet}/P_{power}$$

T_{case} is the maximum allowable CPU case temperature, T_{inlet} is the maximum allowable inlet temperature to the CPU heatsink, and P_{power} is the maximum power dissipation of the processor. For example, the Intel Core i7-3960X Processor Extreme Edition is rated for a maximum case temperature of 68°C and has a thermal design power of 130 watts. Intel recommends a maximum heatsink inlet temperature of 43.4°C, which means the heatsink required to properly cool this chip needs to be rated 0.18°C/W, or (68°C − 43.4°C) / 130W. Chips with lower TDP need less powerful cooling, which explains why chips with higher TDPs use larger heatsinks, and why overclocking enthusiasts sometimes use liquid cooling with the fastest processors.

Another useful formula can describe processor power:

$$P_{power} = C \times V^2 \times F$$

P_{power} is the maximum power output of the processor, C is the capacitance, V^2 is the voltage squared, and F is the frequency. From this you can see that if you double the frequency of a processor, it consumes twice as much power, and if you double the voltage, it consumes four times as much power. Consequently, if you lower the voltage by half, it consumes only one-fourth the power. These relationships are important to consider if you are overclocking your processor because a small increase in voltage has a much more dramatic effect than a similar increase in speed.

In general, increasing the speed of a processor by 5% increases the power consumption by only the same amount. Using the previous heatsink calculation, if the processor speed was increased by 5%, the 103W processor would now draw 108.15W and the required heatsink rating would go from 0.34°C/W to 0.32°C/W, a proportional change. In most cases, unless you are overclocking to the extreme, the existing heatsink should work. As a compromise, you can try setting the voltage on manual and dropping it a small amount to compensate, thereby reducing the power consumption. Of course, when you drop the voltage, the CPU might become unstable, so you need to test it. As you can see, changing all these settings in the interest of overclocking can take a lot of time when you consider all the testing required to ensure everything is working properly. You have to decide whether the rewards are worth the time and energy spent on setting it up and verifying the functionality.

Note that most professional heatsink manufacturers publish their °C/W ratings, whereas many of what I call the "boutique" heatsink vendors do not. In many cases the manufacturers of the more extreme heatsinks don't do the testing that the professional manufacturers do and are more interested in the looks than the actual performance.

Installing a Heatsink

To accomplish the best possible transfer of heat from the processor to the heatsink, most heatsink manufacturers specify some type of thermal interface material to be placed between the processor and heatsink. This typically consists of a ceramic, alumina, or silver-based grease but can also be in the form of a special pad or even a type of double-stick tape. Some are called *phase-change* material because they change viscosity (become thinner) above certain temperatures, enabling them to better flow into minute gaps between the chip and heatsink. In general, thermal greases offer higher performance than phase-change materials, but because they always have a lower viscosity, they flow more easily, can be messy to apply, and (if too much is used) can spill from the sides onto the socket and motherboard. Figure 3.54 illustrates preapplied thermal material on typical AMD and Intel heatsinks packaged with processors.

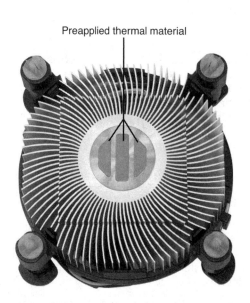

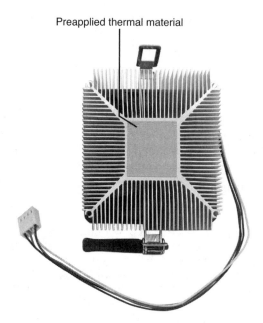

FIGURE 3.54 Preapplied thermal material on an Intel heatsink for a Core i5-2500 processor (a) and an AMD heatsink for an A10-5800K processor (b).

No matter what type you use, a thermal interface aid such as thermal grease or phase-change material can improve heatsink performance dramatically compared to installing the heatsink dry. Thermal interface materials are rated by thermal conductance (in which case higher is better) or thermal resistance (in which case lower is better). Unfortunately, several industry-standard rating scales measure performance, often making product comparisons difficult. Some measure the thermal conductivity; others measure the thermal resistance; and the scales used can vary greatly. The most commonly reported specification is thermal resistance in degrees centigrade per watt (°C/W) for an interface layer 0.001-inch thick and 1 square inch in size. For a given material, the thinner the interface layer or the larger the area, the lower the resistance. In addition, due to other variables such as surface roughness and pressure, it is often impossible to directly compare different materials even if they appear to use the same ratings scale.

I've seen actual tests of multiple brands of thermal greases, and in most cases the differences in temperature readings between different brands are insignificant. For that reason, I generally don't get too excited about different brands of thermal grease; most of the premium products on the market have surprisingly similar performance.

Liquid Cooling

One of the more extreme methods for cooling a PC is to use some form of liquid cooling. Liquids have a much greater thermal carrying capacity than air, and as processors run hotter and hotter, it can be advantageous or even necessary to use a form of liquid cooling to dissipate the extreme levels of heat generated, especially in smaller or more confined spaces.

Several forms of liquid cooling are available, including the following:

- Heat pipes
- Water cooling
- Refrigeration

Each of these uses a liquid or vapor to absorb the heat of the processor or other components and take that heat to a heat exchanger where it must eventually be dispersed to the air. So, all liquid cooling involves air cooling as well; it just removes the exchange of heat to the air to a remote place. Also, the heat exchanger (radiator) used can be much larger than what would fit directly on the processor or other chips, which is another reason liquid cooling offers much greater cooling capacity.

Of all the types of liquid cooling available, heat pipes are the only type that is practical and cost-effective in production-level PCs. Water cooling and especially refrigeration are limited to those who are pursuing extreme overclocking and are willing to pay the high prices and put up with all the drawbacks and disadvantages that come with these two options.

Note

Intel released its own liquid-cooling solution for processors in late 2011: the RTS2011LC. Manufactured by Asetek for Intel, this cooling system costs less than $90. However, its performance is little better than air cooling, and its design (compatible with all four sockets made for Core i-series processors) makes installation extremely difficult. AMD also teamed up with Asetek in late 2011 to launch a similar product for its FX processors, but it no longer offers a liquid-cooling solution.

Thermally Advantaged Chassis

PC power supplies have always contained a fan. For many years, that single fan in the power supply bore the responsibility of cooling not only the supply, but also the entire system and even the processor. In fact, PCs prior to the 486 didn't even use heatsinks on the processor because they generated only a couple of watts of heat. Passive heatsinks first became a standard fixture on processors with the 486DX2 in 1992, which used up to 5.7W of power. Active heatsinks first appeared on the retail Pentium processors from Intel (called Overdrive processors) and became a standard fixture on boxed or retail Pentium II and III and AMD Athlon models in 1997 and later. Most chassis up until that time did not incorporate a cooling fan, except for what was in the power supply.

Chassis fans first became popular in OEM systems in the mid-1990s because they usually used less expensive passive heatsinks on the processor. It was more efficient to use a single chassis fan to cool both the chassis and the processor and save money by using a passive heatsink (without a fan) on the processor. By 2000, with the Pentium 4, many systems began using both an active processor heatsink (with a fan) and a chassis fan. Most modern systems include three fans—one in the power supply, one in the active heatsink on the processor, and one for the rear of the chassis. Some systems have additional fans (a second rear fan and a front-mounted fan for cooling hard disk drives are popular add-ons), but three is the most common and most cost-effective design.

Unfortunately, with high-performance processors reaching and even exceeding the 100W power level, it has become impossible for a standard chassis design to cool the system without resorting to adding more fans or using more exotic (and expensive) liquid cooling setups. A minor breakthrough in chassis design has occurred that can allow even processors consuming more than 100W to be adequately cooled in a three-fan system, without employing exotic solutions or even adding fans.

As you know from the formula earlier in this chapter, processor power consumption is proportional to speed and is proportional to the square of the voltage it consumes. Even though processor voltages have been decreasing, speeds have been increasing at a much more rapid pace, such that power consumption is reaching all-time high levels beyond 120W. To combat this heat, heatsink manufacturers have increased the efficiency of processor heatsinks significantly over the past 10–15 years. Heatsinks are available today with thermal resistances on the order of 0.33°C/W or less. Unfortunately, conventional air-cooled heatsinks are fast approaching the limits of the technology.

Improving Thermal Performance

One cost-effective method of improving heatsink performance is to reduce the ambient temperature around the processor, which means lowering the temperature of air entering the heatsink. To ensure proper cooling for their boxed (retail) processors, Intel and AMD specify maximum temperature limits for the air that enters the heatsink fan assembly. If the air temperature entering the heatsink goes over that amount, the heatsink cannot adequately cool the processor. Because they must account for extreme circumstances, all modern systems and heatsinks are designed to operate properly if the external environmental ambient temperature in the room is 35°C (95°F). This means that, in general, PCs are designed to work in environments of up to that temperature. To operate in environments with higher temperatures than that, PCs require more specialized designs. Table 3.29 shows the maximum heatsink air inlet temperatures allowed for various processors with factory-installed heatsinks.

Table 3.29   Maximum Heatsink Inlet Temperatures for Various Processors

Environmental Temp.	Max. Heatsink Inlet Temp.	Processor Type
35°C (95°F)	45°C (113°F)	Older AMD and Intel processors
35°C (95°F)	42°C (107.6°F)	AMD Athlon and newer processors
35°C (95°F)	40°C (104°F)	Intel Pentium 4 and newer processors
35°C (95°F)	38°C (100.4°F)	Some high-end or "extreme" processors

As you can see, for a long time new processors continually made more demands on system cooling. With the recent trend on the part of Intel and AMD to increase speed through chip design rather than pure clock speed increases, this trend has plateaued to an extent. The most demanding processors today require that the internal chassis temperature remain at or below 40°C (104°F), even if the system is running in a room temperature of 35°C (95°F). The internal temperature rise, or preheating of air inside the system, is typically caused by heat from components such as motherboard chipsets, graphics cards, memory, voltage regulators, disk drives, and other heat-generating components (including the processor). Even with all these devices producing heat, the specifications for many newer processors require that the air temperature inside the chassis at the heatsink rise only to 3°C (5.4°F) over ambient. This places extreme demands on the chassis cooling.

Conventional chassis are incapable of maintaining that low of a differential between the chassis interior and ambient temperatures. The only way to achieve that has been by adding an excessive number of fans to the system, which unfortunately adds cost and significantly adds to the noise level. Many systems with multiple fans on the front, rear, and sides are still incapable of maintaining only 3°C (5.4°F) over ambient at the processor heatsink.

Both Intel and AMD have been releasing documents describing the thermal attributes of their processors and guides showing ideas for cooling systems and chassis designs that can adequately cool the system. Chassis that have been specifically designed to improve cooling for the processor by maintaining a temperature of 40°C or less at the processor heatsink inlet are often referred to as *thermally advantaged chassis*. Using a thermally advantaged chassis allows the processor to remain cool, even under extreme environmental conditions, and it reduces noise. Most modern processors and chassis incorporate cooling systems that can adjust the speeds of the fans. If the temperatures remain below specific limits, the fans run at lower speeds, thus reducing the noise level. If temperatures rise, so do fan speeds and noise. In general, thermally advantaged chassis enable fan speeds to remain lower, resulting in quieter operation.

The original specification for a thermally advantaged chassis was known as the Chassis Air Guide design guide (CAG), originally published in May 2002 and revised in September 2003. The CAG provided specifications for a processor duct and for an additional vent in the side cover for adapter cards such as graphics boards. The CAG was developed at a time when the dominant processors in the marketplace, the Intel Pentium 4 family, had thermal design power specifications as high as 140W.

Since the replacement of the Pentium 4 by cooler-running Core 2 and Core i-series processors and the development of Bulldozer and Piledriver processors from AMD, most of which have thermal design power specifications of 125W or less, the requirements for a thermally advantaged chassis have changed. The CAG design guide has now been replaced by the Thermally Advantaged Chassis (TAC) design guide (numbered version 2.0 to reflect its origin as an update of the CAG).

Note

If you are building a small form factor PC, such as for a home theater or server, see the Thermally Advantaged Small Chassis (TASC) Design Guide, version 1.0, available at the Formfactors.org website.

To meet the TAC Design Guide version 2.0 requirements (available from the System Design section of www.formfactors.org), the following specifications are recommended:

- Accepts an industry-standard ATX, MicroATX, or FlexATX motherboard
- Accepts an industry-standard ATX, SFX, or TFX power supply with integral exhaust fan
- Uses a processor with an active heat sink designed for the processor
- Uses a side cover with an optimized side vent of 100mm wide by 150mm tall. The recommended open area should be at least 60%.
- Provides a primary chassis rear exhaust fan of 92mm or larger.

Note

One of the major recommendations of the original Chassis Air Guide (CAG) Design Guide was the use of a processor duct to deliver air directly to the processor heatsink. Although this was an effective solution to processor cooling, a motherboard upgrade with a different location for the processor than on the original motherboard would cause the processor duct to be unable to provide effective processor cooling. For this reason, the Thermally Advantaged Chassis (TAC) Design Guide, which replaces the CAG, no longer includes this recommendation.

To learn more about using and making a processor duct, see "Processor Duct" and "Adding a Processor Duct" in Chapter 3 of *Upgrading and Repairing PCs*, 19th Edition, available in its entirety on the disc packaged with this book.

Because a thermally advantaged chassis is much better at cooling for little extra cost, I highly recommend that you look for these features on the next system you buy or build.

Processor Troubleshooting Techniques

Processors are normally reliable. Most PC problems are with other devices, but if you suspect the processor, you can take some steps to troubleshoot it. The easiest thing to do is to replace the microprocessor with a known-good spare. If the problem goes away, the original processor is defective. If the problem persists, the problem is likely elsewhere.

Table 3.30 provides a general troubleshooting checklist for processor-related PC problems.

Table 3.30   Troubleshooting Processor-Related Problems

Problem Identification	Possible Cause	Resolution
System is dead, no cursor, no beeps, no fan.	Power cord failure.	Plug in or replace power cord. Power cords can fail even though they look fine.
	Power supply failure.	Replace the power supply. Use a known-good spare for testing.
	Motherboard failure.	Replace motherboard. Use a known-good spare for testing.
	Memory failure.	Remove all memory except one bank and retest. If the system still won't boot, replace bank 1.
System is dead, no beeps, or locks up before POST begins.	All components either not installed or incorrectly installed.	Check all peripherals, especially memory and graphics adapter. Reseat all boards and socketed components.
System beeps on startup, fan is running, no cursor onscreen.	Improperly seated or failing graphics adapter.	Reseat or replace graphics adapter. Use known-good spare for testing.
	Display not configured to use display cable in use	Select correct display cable type.
System powers up, fan is running, no beep or cursor.	Processor not properly installed.	Reseat or remove/reinstall processor and heatsink.
Locks up during or shortly after POST.	Poor heat dissipation.	Check CPU heatsink fan; replace if necessary with one of higher capacity.
	Improper voltage settings.	Set motherboard for proper core processor voltage.
	Wrong motherboard bus speed.	Set motherboard for proper speed.
	Wrong CPU clock multiplier.	Set motherboard for proper clock multiplier.
	Unlocked failed core.	Relock unlocked processor core.
Improper CPU identification during POST.	Old BIOS.	Update BIOS from manufacturer.
	Board not configured properly.	Check manual and set board accordingly to proper bus and multiplier settings.
System won't start after new processor is installed.	Processor not properly installed.	Reseat or remove/reinstall processor and heatsink.
	BIOS doesn't support new processor.	Update BIOS from system or motherboard manufacturer.
	Motherboard can't use new processor.	Verify motherboard support.
	Unlocked processor core failed.	Reset motherboard to use only working cores.

Problem Identification	Possible Cause	Resolution
OS will not boot.	Poor heat dissipation.	Check CPU fan (replace if necessary); it might need a higher-capacity heatsink or heatsink/fan on the North Bridge chip.
	Improper voltage settings.	Reset motherboard for proper core voltage.
	Wrong motherboard bus speed.	Reset proper speed.
	Wrong CPU clock multiplier.	Reset clock proper clock multiplier.
	Applications will not install or run.	Improper drivers or incompatible hardware; update drivers and check for compatibility issues.
System appears to work, but no video is displayed.	Monitor turned off or failed.	Check monitor and power to monitor. Replace with known-good spare for testing.
	Monitor configured to use a different signal input type.	Select correct signal input type (VGA, HDMI, DVI, DisplayPort). Check cable connection between monitor and computer.

If during the POST the processor is not identified correctly, your motherboard settings might be incorrect or your BIOS might need to be updated. Check that the motherboard is configured correctly for your processor, and make sure you have the latest BIOS for your motherboard.

If the system seems to run erratically after it warms up, try setting the processor to a lower speed setting. If the problem goes away, the processor might be defective or overclocked.

Many hardware problems are really software problems in disguise. Be sure you have the latest BIOS for your motherboard, as well as the latest drivers for all your peripherals. Also, it helps to use the latest version of your given OS because there usually will be fewer problems.

Motherboards and Buses

Motherboard Form Factors

Without a doubt, the most important component in a PC system is the main board or motherboard. Virtually every internal component in a PC connects to the motherboard, and its features largely determine what your computer is capable of, not to mention its overall performance. Although I prefer the term *motherboard*, other terms such as *main board*, *system board*, and *planar* are interchangeable. This chapter examines the various types of motherboards available and those components typically contained on the motherboard and motherboard interface connectors.

Several common form factors are used for PC motherboards. The *form factor* refers to the physical dimensions (size and shape) as well as certain connector, screw hole, and other positions that dictate into which type of case the board will fit. Some are true standards (meaning that all boards with that form factor are interchangeable), whereas others are not standardized enough to allow for interchangeability. Unfortunately, these nonstandard form factors preclude any easy upgrade or inexpensive replacement, which generally means that you should avoid them. The more commonly known PC motherboard form factors include the following:

Obsolete Form Factors

- Baby-AT (PC and XT)
- Full-size AT
- LPX (semiproprietary)
- NLX
- WTX
- BTX, microBTX, picoBTX

Modern Form Factors

- ATX and variants; microATX, FlexATX, DTX/Mini-DTX, and ITX/Mini-ITX

PC motherboard form factors have evolved over the years from the Baby-AT form factor boards based on the original IBM PC and XT to the current ATX form factor (and variants) used in most desktop and tower systems. ATX has a growing number of variants, mostly in smaller sizes designed to fit different market segments and applications. The short-lived BTX form factors relocated major components to improve system cooling and incorporate a thermal module but failed to receive widespread adoption.

Anything that does not fit into one of the industry-standard form factors should be considered proprietary. Unless there are special circumstances, I do not recommend purchasing systems based on proprietary board designs. They are difficult to upgrade and expensive to repair because components such as the motherboard, case, and power supply are not interchangeable with other systems. I often call proprietary form factor systems "disposable" PCs because that's what you must normally do with them when they are too slow or need repair out of warranty.

Obsolete Form Factors

The following sections examine industry-standard motherboard form factors no longer in use but which can be found on older systems.

PC and XT

The first popular PC motherboard was, of course, the original IBM PC released in August 1981. Figure 4.1 shows how this board looked. IBM followed the PC with the XT motherboard in March 1983, which had the same size and shape as the PC board but had eight slots instead of five. Both the IBM PC and XT motherboards were 9 inch ×13 inch. Also, the slots were spaced 0.8 inches apart in the XT instead of 1 inch apart as in the PC (see Figure 4.2). The XT also eliminated the little-used cassette port in the back, which was supposed to be used to save BASIC programs on cassette tape instead of the much more expensive (at the time) floppy drive.

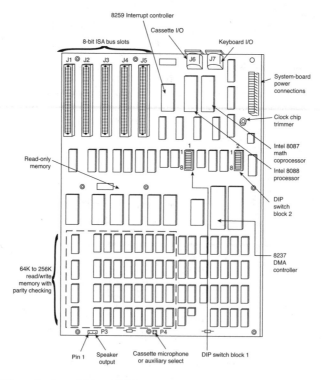

FIGURE 4.1   IBM PC motherboard (circa 1981).

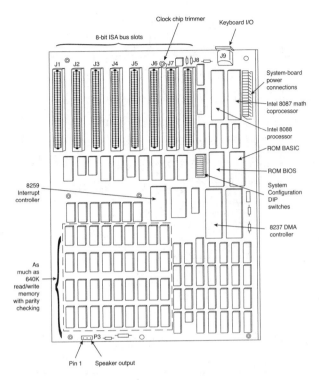

FIGURE 4.2 IBM PC-XT motherboard (circa 1983).

Note

The Technical Reference section of the disc accompanying this book contains detailed information on the PC (5150) and XT (5160). All the information there is printable.

The minor differences in the slot positions and the deleted cassette connector on the back required a minor redesign of the case. In essence, the XT was a mildly enhanced PC, with a motherboard that was the same overall size and shape, used the same processor, and came in a case that was identical except for slot bracketry and the lack of a hole for the cassette port. Eventually, the XT motherboard design became popular, and many other PC motherboard manufacturers of the day copied IBM's XT design and produced similar boards.

Full-Size AT

The full-size AT motherboard form factor matches the original IBM AT motherboard design. This allows for a large board of up to 12 inches wide by 13.8 inches deep. The full-size AT board first debuted in August 1984, when IBM introduced the Personal Computer AT (advanced technology). To accommodate the 16-bit 286 processor and all the necessary support components at the time, IBM needed more room than the original PC/XT-sized boards could provide. So for the AT, IBM increased the size of the motherboard but retained the same screw hole and connector positions of the XT design. To accomplish this, IBM essentially started with a PC/XT-sized board and extended it in two directions (see Figure 4.3).

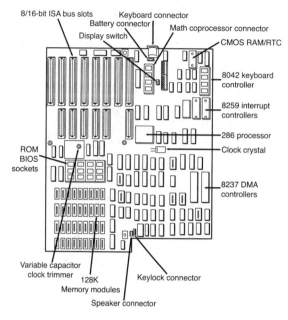

8/16-bit ISA bus slots · Keyboard connector
Battery connector | Math coprocessor connector
Display switch
CMOS RAM/RTC
8042 keyboard controller
8259 interrupt controllers
286 processor
ROM BIOS sockets
Clock crystal
8237 DMA controllers
Variable capacitor clock trimmer
128K Memory modules
Keylock connector
Speaker connector

FIGURE 4.3 IBM AT motherboard (circa 1984).

Note

The Technical Reference section of the disc enclosed with this book contains detailed coverage of the AT and the XT Model 286.

A little more than a year after being introduced, the appearance of chipsets and other circuit consolidation allowed the same motherboard functionality to be built using fewer chips, so the board was redesigned to make it slightly smaller. Then, it was redesigned again as IBM shrank the board down to XT-size in a system it called the XT-286 (introduced in September 1986). The XT-286 board was virtually identical in size and shape to the original XT, a form factor which would later be known as *Baby-AT*.

The keyboard connector and slot connectors in the full-size AT boards still conformed to the same specific placement requirements to fit the holes in the XT cases already in use, but a larger case was still required to fit the larger board. Because of the larger size of the board, a full-size AT motherboard only fits into full-size AT desktop or tower cases. Because these motherboards do not fit into the smaller Baby-AT or mini-tower cases, and because of advances in component miniaturization, they are no longer being produced by most motherboard manufacturers—except in some cases for dual processor server applications.

The important thing to note about the full-size AT systems is that you can always replace a full-size AT motherboard with a Baby-AT (or XT-size) board, but the opposite is not true unless the case is large enough to accommodate the full-size AT design.

Baby-AT

After IBM released the AT in August 1984, component consolidation allowed subsequent systems to be designed using far fewer chips and requiring much less in the way of motherboard real estate.

Therefore, all the additional circuits on the 16-bit AT motherboard could fit into boards using the smaller XT form factor.

The Baby-AT form factor is essentially the same form factor as the original IBM XT motherboard. The only difference is a slight modification in one of the screw hole positions to fit into an AT-style case. These motherboards also have specific placement of the keyboard and slot connectors to match the holes in the case. Note that virtually all full-size AT and Baby-AT motherboards use the standard 5-pin DIN type connector for the keyboard. Baby-AT motherboards can replace full-size AT motherboards and fit into several case designs. Because of its flexibility, from 1983 into early 1996, the Baby-AT form factor was the most popular motherboard type. Starting in mid-1996, Baby-AT was replaced by the superior ATX motherboard design, which is not directly interchangeable. Figure 4.4 shows the onboard features and layout of a late-model Baby-AT motherboard.

The easiest way to identify a Baby-AT form factor system without opening it is to look at the rear of the case. In a Baby-AT motherboard, the cards plug directly into the board at a 90° angle; in other words, the slots in the case for the cards are perpendicular to the motherboard. Also, the Baby-AT motherboard has only one visible connector directly attached to the board, which is the keyboard connector. Typically, this connector is the full-size 5-pin DIN type connector, although some Baby-AT systems use the smaller 6-pin mini-DIN connector (sometimes called a *PS/2-type connector*) and might even have a mouse connector. All other connectors are mounted on the case or on card edge brackets and are attached to the motherboard via cables. The keyboard connector is visible through an appropriately placed hole in the case.

▶▶ See the Chapter 15 section, "Keyboard/Mouse Interface Connectors," **p. 751**.

All Baby-AT boards conform to specific widths and screw hole, slot, and keyboard connector locations, but one thing that can vary is the length of the board. Versions have been built that are smaller than the full 9 inches × 13 inches; these are often called *mini-AT*, *micro-AT*, or even things such as *2/3-Baby* or *1/2-Baby*. Even though they might not be the full size, they still bolt directly into the same case as a standard Baby-AT board and can be used as a direct replacement for one.

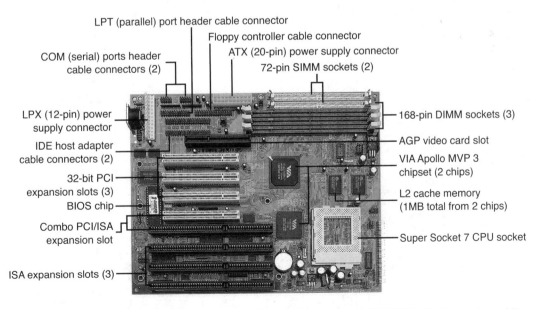

FIGURE 4.4 A late-model Baby-AT motherboard, the Tyan Trinity 100AT (S1590). Photo courtesy of Tyan Computer Corporation.

LPX

The LPX and mini-LPX form factor boards were a semiproprietary design that Western Digital originally developed in 1987 for some of its motherboards. The *LP* in LPX stands for Low Profile, which is so named because these boards incorporate slots that are parallel to the main board, enabling the expansion cards to install sideways. This allows for a slim or low-profile case design and overall a smaller system than the Baby-AT.

Although Western Digital no longer produces PC motherboards, the form factor lived on, and many other motherboard manufacturers duplicated the general design. Unfortunately, because the specifications were never laid out in exact detail—especially with regard to the bus riser card portion of the design—these boards are termed *semiproprietary* and are not interchangeable between manufacturers. Some vendors, such as IBM and HP, have built LPX systems that use a T-shaped riser card that allows expansion cards to be mounted at the normal 90° angle to the motherboard but still above the motherboard. This lack of standardization means that if you have a system with an LPX board, in most cases you can't replace the motherboard with a different LPX board later. You essentially have a system you can't upgrade or repair by replacing the motherboard with something better. In other words, you have what I call a "disposable PC," something I would not normally recommend that anybody purchase.

Most people were not aware of the semiproprietary nature of the design of these boards, and they were extremely popular in what I call "retail store" PCs from the late 1980s through the late 1990s. This would include primarily Compaq and Packard Bell systems, as well as many others who used this form factor in their lower-cost systems. These boards were most often used in low-profile or Slimline case systems, but they were found in tower cases, too. These were often lower-cost systems such as those sold at retail electronics superstores. LPX is considered obsolete today.

LPX boards are characterized by several distinctive features (see Figure 4.5). The most noticeable is that the expansion slots are mounted on a bus riser card that plugs into the motherboard. In most designs, expansion cards plug sideways into the riser card. This sideways placement allows for the low-profile case design. Slots are located on one or both sides of the riser card depending on the system and case design. Vendors who use LPX-type motherboards in tower cases sometimes use a T-shaped riser card instead, which puts the expansion slots at the normal right angle to the motherboard but on a raised shelf above the motherboard.

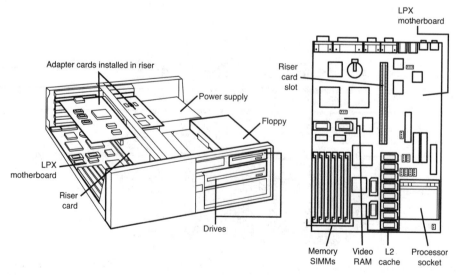

FIGURE 4.5   Typical LPX system chassis and motherboard.

Another distinguishing feature of the LPX design is the standard placement of connectors on the back of the board. An LPX board has a row of connectors for video (VGA 15-pin), parallel (25-pin), two serial ports (9-pin each), and mini-DIN PS/2-style mouse and keyboard connectors. All these connectors are mounted across the rear of the motherboard and protrude through a slot in the case. Some LPX motherboards might have additional connectors for other internal ports, such as network or small computer systems interface (SCSI) adapters. Because LPX systems use a high degree of motherboard port integration, many vendors of LPX motherboards, cases, and systems refer to LPX products as having an "all-in-one" design.

The standard form factor used for LPX and mini-LPX motherboards in many typical low-cost systems is shown in Figure 4.6.

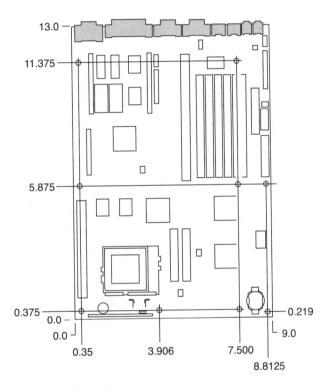

FIGURE 4.6 LPX motherboard dimensions.

Figure 4.7 shows two typical examples of the connectors on the back of LPX boards. Note that not all LPX boards have the built-in audio, so those connectors might be missing. Other ports (such as universal serial bus, or USB) might be missing from what is shown in these diagrams, depending on exactly which options are included on a specific board; however, the general layout will be the same.

The connectors along the rear of the board would interfere with locating bus slots directly on the motherboard, which accounts for why riser cards are used for adding expansion boards.

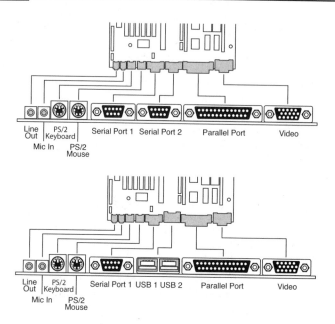

FIGURE 4.7 LPX motherboard back panel connectors.

NLX

NLX is a low-profile form factor designed to replace the nonstandard LPX design used in previous low-profile systems. Introduced in November 1996 by Intel, NLX was a popular form factor in the late 1990s for Slimline corporate desktop systems from vendors such as Compaq, HP, and Toshiba. Since 2000, many Slimline systems have used variations on the FlexATX motherboard instead.

NLX is similar in initial appearance to LPX, but with numerous improvements designed to enable full integration of the latest technologies. NLX is basically an improved version of the proprietary LPX design, but, unlike LPX, NLX is fully standardized, which means you should be able to replace one NLX board with another from a different manufacturer—something that was not possible with LPX.

The main characteristic of an NLX system is that the motherboard plugs into the riser, unlike LPX where the riser plugs into the motherboard. Therefore, the motherboard can be removed from the system without disturbing the riser or any of the expansion cards plugged into it. In addition, the motherboard in a typical NLX system literally has no internal cables or connectors attached to it! All devices that normally plug into the motherboard—such as drive cables, the power supply, the front panel light, switch connectors, and so on—plug into the riser instead (see Figure 4.8). By using the riser card as a connector concentration point, you can remove the lid on an NLX system and literally slide the motherboard out the left side of the system without unplugging a single cable or connector on the inside. This allows for unbelievably quick motherboard changes; in fact, I have swapped motherboards in less than 30 seconds on NLX systems!

Such a design was a boon for the corporate market, where ease and swiftness of servicing is a major feature.

As with most of the form factors, you can identify NLX via the unique input/output (I/O) shield or connector area at the back of the board (see Figure 4.9). You only need a quick look at the rear of any given system to determine which type of board is contained within. Figure 4.9 shows the unique stepped design of the NLX I/O connector area. This allows for a row of connectors all along the bottom and has room for double-stacked connectors on one side.

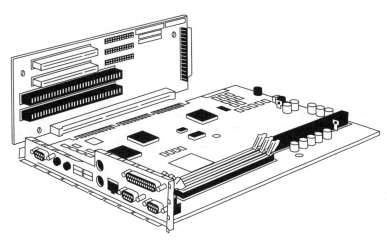

FIGURE 4.8 NLX motherboard and riser combination.

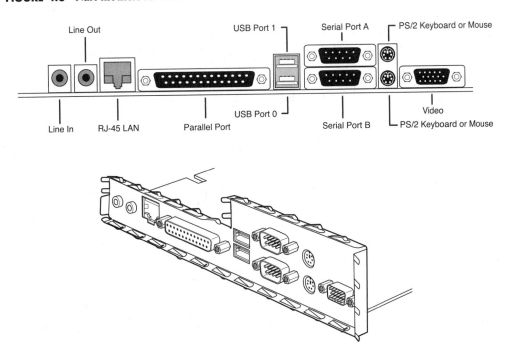

FIGURE 4.9 Typical NLX motherboard rear connector layout.

Although NLX is a standard form factor—just as the ATX family is—most NLX products were sold as part of complete systems aimed at the corporate market. Few aftermarket motherboards have been developed in this form factor. The microATX and FlexATX form factors have superseded NLX in the markets formerly dominated by LPX.

WTX

WTX was a board and system form factor developed for the mid-range workstation market; however, most vendors making workstations and servers have used the ATX form factor. WTX went beyond ATX and defined the size and shape of the board and the interface between the board and chassis, as well as required chassis features.

WTX was released in September 1998 (1.0) and updated in February 1999 (1.1). Since then, however, WTX has been officially discontinued, and there will be no further updates.

BTX

Balanced Technology Extended (BTX) is a motherboard form factor specification that Intel released in September 2003, with 1.0a and 1.0b updates released in February 2004 and July 2005, respectively. BTX was designed to address the ever-increasing component power and cooling requirements, as well as enabling improved circuit routing and more flexible chassis designs. However, the recent trend toward more power efficient dual-core processor designs has slowed the need for the benefits inherent in the BTX standard, which has in turn slowed the adoption of BTX, causing Intel to announce in late 2006 that it was abandoning future BTX development. BTX was popular in many mass-produced retail-branded PCs sold between 2005 and 2007, such as those by Dell, Gateway, and others. Since then the BTX form factor has largely been abandoned.

BTX is not backward-compatible with ATX or other designs. A full-size BTX board is 17% larger than ATX, allowing room for more integrated components onboard. The I/O connectors, slots, and mounting holes are in different locations than with ATX, requiring new chassis designs. However, the power supply interface connectors are the same as in the latest ATX12V specifications, and newer ATX, TFX, SFX, CFX, and LFX power supplies can be used. The latter two power supply form factors were specifically created to support compact and low-profile BTX systems.

The primary advantages to BTX include optimized inline component layout and routing, optimized airflow path, a support and retention module (SRM) for heavy heatsinks, scalable board dimensions, low-profile options, and flexible power supply designs with connector types that are compatible with ATX designs.

BTX includes three definitions of motherboard size, as shown in Table 4.1.

Table 4.1   BTX Motherboard Form Factors

Form Factor	Max. Width	Depth	Max. Area	Size Versus BTX
BTX	12.8 in. (325mm)	10.5 in. (267mm)	134 sq. in. (867 sq. cm)	—
microBTX	10.4 in. (264mm)	10.5 in. (267mm)	109 sq. in. (705 sq. cm)	19% smaller
PicoBTX	8.0 in. (203mm)	10.5 in. (267mm)	84 sq. in. (542 sq. cm)	37% smaller

Each board has the same basic screw hole and connector placement requirements. So, if you have a case that fits a full-size BTX board, you can also mount a microBTX or picoBTX board in that same case (see Figure 4.10). Obviously, if you have a smaller case designed for MicroBTX or picoBTX, you won't be able to put the larger microBTX or BTX boards there.

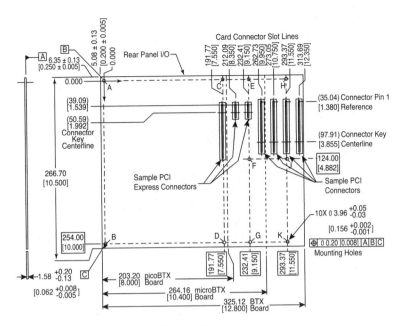

FIGURE 4.10 BTX specification 1.0a motherboard dimensions.

BTX requires up to 10 mounting holes and supports up to seven slots, depending on the size, as shown in Table 4.2.

Table 4.2 BTX Motherboard Mounting Holes

Board Size	Mounting Holes	Max. Slots
BTX	A, B, C, D, E, F, G, H, J, K	7
microBTX	A, B, C, D, E, F, G	4
picoBTX	A, B, C, D	1

BTX also clearly specifies volumetric zones around the motherboard to prevent interference from the chassis or internal components such as drives, which allows for maximum interchangeability without physical interference or fit problems.

With processors exceeding 100W in thermal output, as well as voltage regulators, motherboard chipsets, and video cards adding to the thermal load in a system, BTX was designed to allow all the high-heat-producing core components to be mounted inline from front to back, so that a single high-efficiency thermal module (heatsink) can cool the system. This eliminates the need for an excessive number of fans. The thermal module includes a heatsink for the processor, a high-efficiency fan, and a duct to direct airflow through the system. Extra support for the thermal module is provided under the board via an SRM, which provides structural support for heatsinks that are much heavier than allowed in ATX designs (see Figure 4.11).

BTX uses the same power connectors as in the latest power supply form factor specifications, including a 24-pin main connector for the board and a 4-pin ATX12V connector for the CPU voltage regulator module. The particular power supply form factor used depends mostly on the chassis selected.

A typical tower system has components arranged as shown in Figure 4.12.

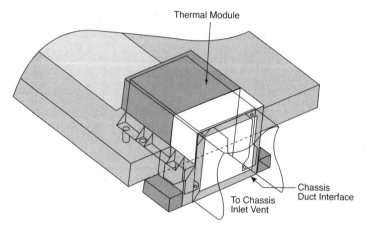

FIGURE 4.11 BTX thermal module containing a processor heatsink and fan.

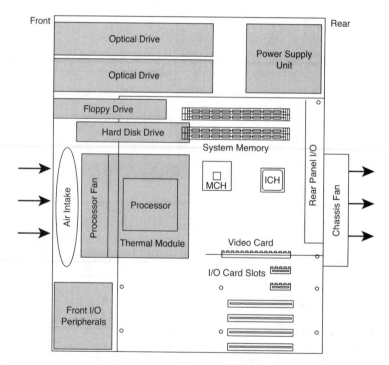

FIGURE 4.12 BTX tower chassis layout.

From Figure 4.12, you can see that the main heat-producing core components are centrally located inline from front to rear, allowing the most efficient thermal design. Air flows from front to rear through the center, cooling the processor, motherboard chipset, memory, and video card.

To support the heavy processor heatsink and thermal module assembly, an SRM is mounted under the board. The SRM is essentially a metal plate affixed to the chassis under the board, and the thermal module is bolted directly to the SRM instead of to the motherboard. This helps carry the weight of the module and prevents excessive loads from being applied to the processor and motherboard, especially during the shipping and handling of the system.

The BTX I/O connector area is similar to ATX, except that it is at the opposite side of the rear of the board. The size of the area is slightly shorter but wider than ATX, allowing a large number of interfaces and connectors to be built into the motherboard.

Systems using BTX were produced primarily from 2005 through 2007 by companies such as Dell and Gateway. After that, a lack of new BTX motherboards and cases forced most system manufacturers and builders to abandon BTX and revert to the more popular ATX-based form factors. Other large manufacturers such as HP never jumped on the BTX bandwagon, instead staying with ATX-based systems. Because of the lack of BTX component popularity and other problems, I recommend avoiding BTX systems and components such as motherboards and chassis because they will be difficult to upgrade or replace in the future. ATX remains by far the most popular and recommended form factor for system builders and upgraders.

ATX and Other Modern Form Factors

The following sections cover the industry-standard form factors, including ATX, that are popular on modern systems.

ATX

The ATX form factor was the first of a dramatic evolution in motherboard form factors. ATX is a combination of the best features of the Baby-AT and LPX motherboard designs, with many new enhancements and features thrown in. The ATX form factor is essentially a Baby-AT motherboard turned sideways in the chassis, along with a modified power supply location and connector. The most important thing to know initially about the ATX form factor is that it is physically incompatible with either the previous Baby-AT or the LPX design. In other words, a different case and power supply are required to match the ATX motherboard. These case and power supply designs have become common and are found in most new systems.

Intel initially released the official ATX specification in July 1995. It was written as an open specification for the industry. ATX boards didn't hit the market in force until mid-1996, when they rapidly began replacing Baby-AT boards in new systems. The ATX specification was updated to version 2.01 in February 1997, 2.03 in May 2000, 2.1 in June 2002, and 2.2 in February 2004. Intel publishes these detailed specifications so other manufacturers can use the interchangeable ATX design in their systems. The current specifications for ATX and other current motherboard types are available online from the Desktop Form Factors site: www.formfactors.org. ATX is the most popular motherboard form factor for new systems and will continue to be popular in the future. An ATX system will be upgradeable for many years to come, exactly like Baby-AT was in the past.

ATX improved on the Baby-AT and LPX motherboard designs in several major areas:

- **Built-in double high external I/O connector panel**—The rear portion of the motherboard includes a stacked I/O connector area that is 6 1/4 inches wide by 1 3/4 inches tall. This enables external I/O connectors to be located directly on the board and minimizes the need for cables running from internal connectors to the back of the case as with Baby-AT designs.

- **Single main keyed internal power supply connector**—The ATX specification includes a keyed and shrouded main power connector that is easy to plug in and install. This connector also features pins for supplying 3.3V to the motherboard, helping to minimize the use of built-in voltage regulators that are susceptible to failure.

▶▶   See the Chapter 18 section, "Motherboard Power Connectors," **p. 870**.

- **Relocated CPU and memory**—The CPU and memory modules are relocated so they can't interfere with bus expansion cards and can easily be accessed for upgrade without removing any of the installed bus adapters.

- **Relocated internal I/O connectors**—The internal I/O connectors for the floppy and hard disk drives are relocated to be near the drive bays and out from under the expansion board slot and drive bay areas.

- **Improved cooling**—The CPU and main memory are designed and positioned to improve overall system cooling compared to Baby-AT and older designs.

- **Lower cost to manufacture**—The ATX specification eliminates the need for the rat's nest of cables to external I/O port connectors found on Baby-AT motherboards.

Figure 4.13 shows the typical ATX system layout and chassis features, as you would see them looking in with the lid off on a desktop, or sideways in a tower with the side panel removed. Notice how virtually the entire motherboard is clear of the drive bays and how the devices such as CPU, memory, and internal drive connectors are easy to access and do not interfere with the bus slots.

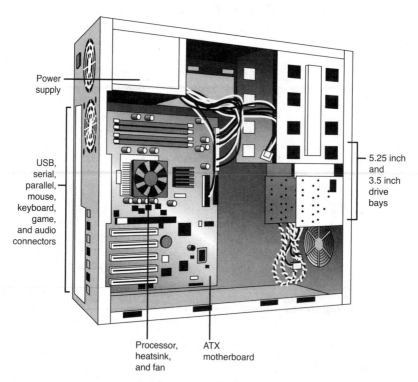

FIGURE 4.13   Typical ATX system layout.

Note

Although most ATX systems mount the power supply near the processor (on top in most tower arrangements), this is not a requirement of the standard. Some systems mount the power supply in other locations (such as on the bottom).

The ATX motherboard shape is basically a Baby-AT design rotated sideways 90°. The expansion slots are now parallel to the shorter side dimension and do not interfere with the CPU, memory, or I/O connector sockets (see Figure 4.14). In addition to a full-size ATX layout, Intel originally specified a Mini-ATX design, which is a fully compatible subset of ATX that fits into the same case:

■ A full-size ATX board is 12 inches wide×9.6 inches deep (305mm×244mm).

■ The Mini-ATX board is 11.2 inches×8.2 inches (284mm×208mm).

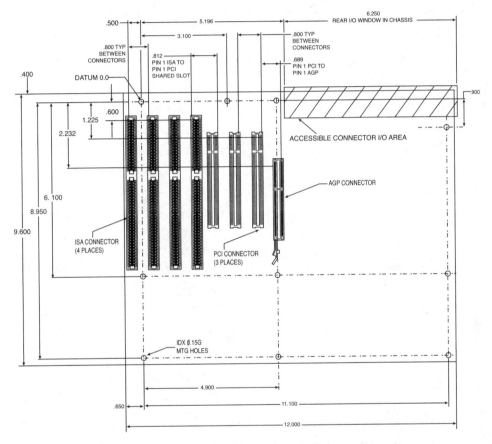

FIGURE 4.14 ATX specification 2.2 motherboard dimensions. Modern ATX systems no longer include ISA expansion slots.

Mini-ATX is not an official standard; instead, it is simply referenced as a slightly smaller version of ATX. In fact, all references to Mini-ATX were removed from the ATX 2.1 and later specifications. Two smaller official versions of ATX exist, called microATX and FlexATX. They are discussed in the following sections.

Although the case holes are similar to the Baby-AT case, cases for Baby-AT and ATX are generally incompatible. The ATX power supply design is identical in physical size to the standard Slimline power supply used with Baby-AT systems; however, they also use different connectors and supply different voltages.

The best way to tell whether your system has an ATX-family motherboard design without removing the lid is to look at the back of the system. Two distinguishing features identify ATX. One is that the expansion boards plug directly into the motherboard. There is usually no riser card as with LPX and NLX (except for certain Slimline systems, such as rack-mounted servers), so the slots are usually perpendicular to the plane of the motherboard. Also, ATX boards have a unique double-high connector area for all the built-in connectors on the motherboard (see Figure 4.15 and Table 4.3). This is found just to the side of the bus slot area and can be used to easily identify an ATX board. Note that the colors listed in Table 4.3 might vary on some systems.

Table 4.3 Built-In Ports Usually Found on ATX Motherboards

Port Description	Connector Type	Connector Color
PS/2 mouse port	6-pin Mini-DIN	Green
PS/2 keyboard port	6-pin Mini-DIN	Purple
USB 2.0 ports	Dual Stack USB	Black
USB 3.0 ports	Dual Stack USB	Blue
Parallel port	25-pin D-Submini	Burgundy
Serial port	9-pin D-Submini	Teal
VGA analog video port	15-pin HD D-Submini	Dark blue
MIDI/Game port	15-pin D-Submini	Gold
Audio ports: L/R in, front L/R out, rear L/R out, center/LFE out, Microphone L/R in	1/8 in. (3.5mm) Mini-Phone	Light blue, lime green, black, orange, pink
S-Video TV out (not shown)	4-pin Mini-DIN	Black
IEEE 1394/FireWire port	6-pin IEEE 1394	Gray
10/100/1000 Ethernet LAN	8-pin RJ-45	Black
Optical S/PDIF audio out	TOSLINK	Black
DVI digital video out	DDWG-DVI	White
Digital S/PDIF audio out	RCA Jack	Orange
SCSI (not shown)	50/68-pin HD	Black
Dial-up modem Modem (not shown)	4-pin RJ-11	Black
Composite video out (not shown)	RCA Jack	Yellow
eSATA port	eSATA	Black

DIN = Deutsches Institut für Normung e.V.
USB = Universal serial bus
VGA = Video graphics array
HD = High density
MIDI = Musical Instrument Digital Interface
L/R = Left and right channel
LFE = Low frequency effects (subwoofer)
S-Video = Super Video
IEEE = Institute of Electrical and Electronics Engineers
LAN = Local area network

RJ = Registered jack
S/PDIF = Sony/Philips Digital Interface
TOSLINK = Toshiba optical link
DVI = Digital visual interface
DDWG = Digital Display Working Group
RCA = Radio Corporation of America
SCSI = Small computer systems interface
HDMI = High definition multimedia interface
A/V = audio/video
eSATA = external SATA

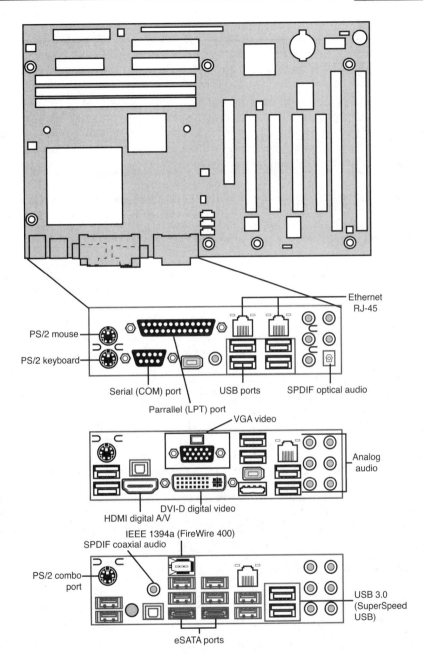

FIGURE 4.15   ATX motherboard and rear panel connections from legacy and modern systems.

Note

Most ATX motherboards feature connectors with industry-standardized color codes (shown in the previous table). This makes plugging in devices much easier and more foolproof: You merely match up the colors. For example, most PS/2 keyboards have a cable with a purple plug, whereas most PS/2 mice have a cable with a green plug. Even though the keyboard and mouse connectors on the motherboard appear the same (both are 6-pin Mini-DIN types), their color-coding matches the plugs on the respective devices. Therefore, to plug them in properly, you merely insert the purple plug into the purple connector and the green plug into the green connector. This saves you from having to bend down to try to decipher small labels on the connectors to ensure you get them right. Some systems have a single PS/2 port (sometimes marked in both green and purple) that can be used for either device.

The specifications and related information covering the ATX and related form factors are available from the Form Factors website at www.formfactors.org. The Form Factors site provides form factor specifications and design guides, as well as design considerations for new technologies, information on initiative supporters, vendor products, and a form factor discussion forum.

Note

Some sdmotherboards, especially those used in server systems, come in nonstandard ATX variations collectively called *extended ATX*. This is a term applied to boards that are compatible with ATX but that are deeper. Standard ATX is 12 inches × 9.6 inches (305mm × 244mm), whereas extended ATX boards are up to 12 inches × 13 inches (305mm × 330mm). Because technically no official "extended ATX" standard exists, compatibility problems can exist with boards and chassis claiming to support extended ATX. When purchasing an extended ATX board, be sure it will fit in the chassis you intend to use. Dual Xeon processors fit in a standard ATX-size board, so choose a standard ATX-size board for maximum compatibility with the existing ATX chassis.

microATX

microATX is a motherboard form factor Intel introduced in December 1997 as an evolution of the ATX form factor for smaller and lower-cost systems. The reduced size compared to standard ATX allows for a smaller chassis, motherboard, and power supply, thereby reducing the cost of the entire system. The microATX form factor is also backward-compatible with the ATX form factor and can be used in full-size ATX cases. Of course, a microATX case doesn't take a full-size ATX board. This form factor has become popular in the low-cost PC market. Currently, mini-tower chassis systems dominate the low-cost PC market, although their small sizes and cramped interiors severely limit future upgradeability.

The main differences between microATX and standard or Mini-ATX are as follows:

- Reduced width motherboard (9.6 inches [244mm] instead of 12 inches [305mm] or 11.2 inches [284mm])
- Fewer I/O bus expansion slots (four maximum, although most boards feature only three)
- Smaller power supply optional (SFX/TFX form factors)

The microATX motherboard maximum size is only 9.6 inches × 9.6 inches (244mm × 244mm) as compared to the full-size ATX size of 12 inches × 9.6 inches (305mm × 244mm) or the Mini-ATX size of 11.2 inches × 8.2 inches (284mm × 208mm). Even smaller boards can be designed as long as they conform to the location of the mounting holes, connector positions, and so on, as defined by the standard. Fewer slots aren't a problem for typical home or small-business PC users because more components such as sound and video are usually integrated on the motherboard and therefore don't require separate slots. This higher integration reduces motherboard and system costs. External buses, such as USB, 10/100/1000 Ethernet, and optionally 1394 (FireWire), can provide additional expansion out of the box. The specifications for microATX motherboard dimensions are shown in Figure 4.16.

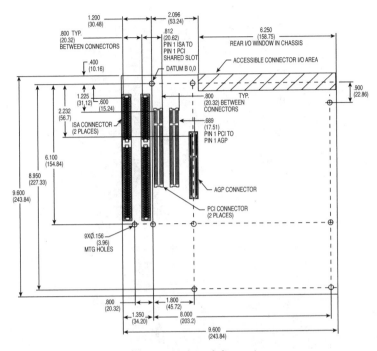

FIGURE 4.16 microATX specification 1.2 motherboard dimensions.

Smaller form factor (called SFX or TFX) power supplies have been defined for optional use with micro-ATX systems, although the standard ATX supply also works fine because the connectors are the same. The smaller size SFX/TFX power supplies encourage flexibility in choosing mounting locations within the chassis and allow for smaller systems that consume less power overall. However, SFX/TFX power supplies may lack sufficient power output for faster or more fully configured systems. Because of the high power demands of most modern systems, most third-party microATX chassis are designed to accept standard ATX power supplies, although microATX systems sold by vendors such as Compaq, HP, and eMachines typically use some type of SFX or TFX power supply to reduce costs.

▶▶ See the Chapter 18 section, "Power Supply Form Factors," **p. 849**.

The microATX form factor is similar to ATX for compatibility. The similarities include the following:

- Standard ATX power connectors
- Standard ATX I/O panel
- Mounting holes and dimensions are a subset of ATX

These similarities ensure that a microATX motherboard can easily work in a standard ATX chassis with a standard ATX power supply, as well as the smaller microATX chassis and SFX/TFX power supply.

The overall system size for a microATX is small. A typical case is only 12–14 inches tall, about 7 inches wide, and 12 inches deep. This results in a kind of micro-tower or desktop size. A typical microATX motherboard is shown in Figure 4.17.

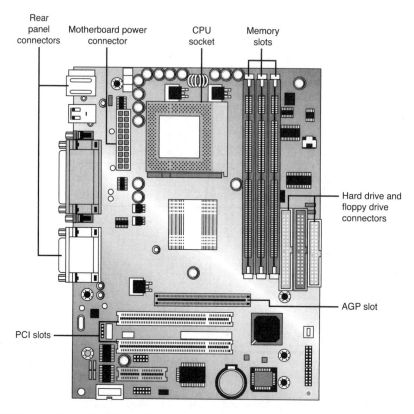

FIGURE 4.17 A typical microATX motherboard's dimensions are 9.6 inches × 9.6 inches.

As with ATX, Intel released microATX to the public domain to facilitate adoption as a de facto standard. The specification and related information on microATX are available through the Desktop Form Factors site (www.formfactors.org).

FlexATX

In March 1999, Intel released the FlexATX addendum to the microATX specification. This added a new and even smaller variation of the ATX form factor to the motherboard scene. FlexATX's smaller design is intended to allow a variety of new PC designs, especially extremely inexpensive, smaller, consumer-oriented, appliance-type systems. Some of these designs might not even have expansion slots, allowing expansion only through USB or IEEE 1394/FireWire ports.

FlexATX defines a board that is up to 9 inches × 7.5 inches (229mm × 191mm), which is the smallest of the ATX family boards. In all other ways, FlexATX is the same as ATX and microATX, making FlexATX fully backward compatible with ATX or microATX by using a subset of the mounting holes and the same I/O and power supply connector specifications (see Figure 4.18).

Most FlexATX systems use SFX/TFX (small or thin form factor) type power supplies (introduced in the microATX specification), although if the chassis allows it, a standard ATX power supply can be used.

The addition of FlexATX gave the family of ATX boards four definitions of size (three are the official standards), as shown in Table 4.4.

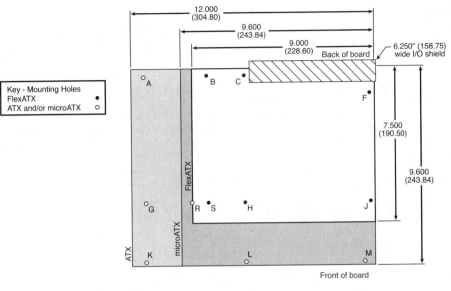

Form Factor	Mounting Hole Locations	Notes
• FlexATX	B, C, F, H, J, S	
• microATX	B, C, F, H, J, L, M, R, S	Holes R and S were added for microATX form factor. Hole B was defined in full-AT format.
• ATX	A, C, F, G, H, J, K, L, M	Hole F must be implemented in all ATX 2.03–compliant chassis assemblies. The hole was optional in the ATX 1.1 specification.

FIGURE 4.18 Size and mounting hole comparison between ATX, microATX, and FlexATX motherboards.

Table 4.4 ATX Motherboard Form Factors

Form Factor	Max. Width	Max. Depth	Max. Area	Size Comparison
ATX	12.0 in. (305mm)	9.6 in. (244mm)	115 sq. in. (743 sq. cm)	—
Mini-ATX	11.2 in. (284mm)	8.2 in. (208mm)	92 sq. in. (593 sq. cm)	20% smaller
microATX	9.6 in. (244mm)	9.6 in. (244mm)	92 sq. in. (595 sq. cm)	20%
FlexATX	9.0 in. (229mm)	7.5 in. (191mm)	68 sq. in. (435 sq. cm)	41% smaller

Note that these dimensions are the maximums allowed. Making a board smaller in any given dimension is always possible as long as it conforms to the mounting hole and connector placement requirements detailed in the respective specifications. Each board has the same basic screw hole and connector placement requirements, so if you have a case that fits a full-size ATX board, you could also mount a microATX or FlexATX board in that same case. Obviously, if you have a smaller case designed for microATX or FlexATX, you can't put the larger Mini-ATX or full-size ATX boards in that case.

DTX and Mini-DTX

The DTX (and Mini-DTX) specification was released in February 2007 by AMD as smaller variations of the microATX and FlexATX specifications, respectively. DTX boards are up to 8 inches × 9.6 inches, whereas Mini-DTX boards are a shorter version at only 8 inches × 6.7 inches. Mini-DTX boards incorporate only four mounting holes (C, F, H, and J), whereas DTX boards add two more for a total of six (C, F, H, J, L, and M). Refer to Figure 4.19 for the respective hole locations. The size of the DTX and Mini-DTX boards as they relate to FlexATX are shown in Table 4.5. The narrow 8-inch width for both DTX and Mini-DTX boards allows for only two expansion slots. Although AMD is no longer supporting DTX and Mini-DTX, vendors are producing Intel Atom-based systems based on the Mini-DTX standard. Motherboards produced in these form factors can be installed in microATX, FlexATX cases, or Mini-ITX cases.

ITX and Mini-ITX

FlexATX defines a board that is up to 9 inches × 7.5 inches. A FlexATX board can be smaller than that, but how much smaller? By analyzing the FlexATX specification—and, in particular, studying the required mounting screw locations—you can see that a FlexATX board could be made small enough to use only four mounting holes (C, F, H, and J). Refer to Figure 4.16 for the respective hole locations.

According to the FlexATX standard, the distance between holes H and J is 6.2 inches, and the distance between hole J and the right edge of the board is 0.25 inches. By leaving the same margin from hole H to the left edge, you could make a board with a minimum width of 6.7 inches (0.25 inches + 6.2 inches + 0.25 inches) that would conform to the FlexATX specification. Similarly, the distance between holes C and H is 6.1 inches, and the distance between hole C and the back edge of the board is 0.4 inches. By leaving a minimum 0.2-inch margin from hole H to the front edge, you could make a board with a minimum depth of 6.7 inches (0.4 inches + 6.1 inches + 0.2 inches) that would conform to the FlexATX specification. By combining the minimum width and depth, you can see that the minimum board size that would conform to the FlexATX specification is 6.7 inches × 6.7 inches (170mm × 170mm).

VIA Technologies Platform Solutions Division wanted to create a motherboard as small as possible, yet not define a completely new and incompatible form factor. To accomplish this, in March 2001 VIA created a board that was slightly narrower in width (8.5 inches instead of 9 inches) but still the same depth as FlexATX, resulting in a board that was 6% smaller and yet still conformed to the FlexATX specification. VIA called this ITX but then realized that the size savings were simply too small to justify developing it further, so it was discontinued before any products were released.

In April 2002, VIA created an even smaller board that featured the absolute minimum width and depth dimensions allowed by FlexATX. The company called it Mini-ITX. In essence, all Mini-ITX boards are simply FlexATX boards that are limited to the minimum allowable dimensions. All other aspects, including the I/O aperture size and location, screw hole locations, and power supply connections, are pure FlexATX. A Mini-ITX board fits in any chassis that accepts a FlexATX board; however, larger boards will not fit into a Mini-ITX chassis.

The Mini-ITX form factor was designed by VIA especially to support VIA's low-power embedded Eden ESP and C3 E-Series processors. However, third-party vendors have also adopted this form factor for use with low-power netbook-class chips such as Intel's Atom and AMD's E- and C-series, as well as with more powerful processors such as Intel's Core i3 or Core i5, and AMD's Phenom, Athlon 64 X2, Athlon 64, Athlon II, Phenom II, or Sempron 100. Mini-ITX systems that use these processors can be used as multimedia servers and small form factor PCs as well as for set-top boxes and computing appliances.

The size of the DTX and ITX families of motherboards as they relate to FlexATX is shown in Table 4.5.

Table 4.5   Comparing FlexATX to DTX and ITX Motherboard Families Form Factors

Form Factor	Max. Width	Max. Depth	Max. Area	Size Comparison to FlexATX
DTX	8.0 in. (203mm)	9.6 in. (244mm)	77 sq. in. (495 sq. cm)	14% larger
FlexATX	9.0 in. (229mm)	7.5 in. (191mm)	68 sq. in. (435 sq. cm)	—
ITX	8.5 in. (215mm)	7.5 in. (191mm)	64 sq. in. (411 sq. cm)	6% smaller
Mini-DTX	8.0 in. (203mm)	6.7 in. (170mm)	54 sq. in. (346 sq. cm)	21% smaller
Mini-ITX	6.7 in. (170mm)	6.7 in. (170mm)	45 sq. in. (290 sq. cm)	34% smaller
Nano-ITX	4.7 in. (120mm)	4.7 in. (120mm)	22 sq. in. (144 sq. cm)	67% smaller
Pico-ITX	3.9 in. (100mm)	2.8 in. (72mm)	11 sq. in. (72 sq. cm)	83% smaller

Whereas the still-born ITX format was virtually the same as FlexATX in size (which is probably why it was discontinued before any were sold), the Mini, Nano, and Pico-ITX form factors are considerably smaller than FlexATX, as is the mini-DTX.

To take advantage of the smaller Mini-ITX format, several chassis makers have produced small chassis to fit these boards. Most are the shape of a small cube, with one floppy and one optical drive bay visible from the front. The layout of a typical Mini-ITX motherboard, the ASRock M67M-ITX, is shown in Figure 4.19. Nano-ITX and Pico-ITX can fit into slimline (half-U) cases that can be used horizontally or vertically.

Mini-ITX motherboards can offer a full range of input-output ports. And, while designs that use VIA processors typically feature soldered-in place processors and lack PCIe expansion slots, designs that use Intel or AMD processors support a wide range of processors and feature a PCIe slot. However, Mini-ITX and smaller motherboards in the family are not suitable when you need a highly expandable system (most feature only one expansion slot) or when you plan to use processors with more than 100W thermal design power (TDP).

The smaller Nano-ITX and Pico-ITX motherboards use soldered-in-place low-power netbook/embedded-class processors from VIA, Intel, or AMD.

Note

The official site for ITX information is www.via.com.tw/en/products/embedded/. The site www.mini-itx.com is often mistaken for an official site, but it is actually a vendor that specializes in ITX systems and component sales.

Proprietary Designs

Motherboards that are *not* one of the industry standard form factors, such as any of the ATX, DTX, or ITX formats, are deemed *proprietary* or *semiproprietary*. Most people purchasing PCs should avoid proprietary designs because they do not allow for a future motherboard, power supply, or case upgrade, which limits future use and serviceability of the system. Proprietary systems are disposable PCs because you can neither upgrade them nor easily repair them. The problem is that the proprietary parts often come only from the original system manufacturer, and they usually cost much more than industry standard parts. Therefore, after your proprietary system goes out of warranty, it is essentially no longer worth upgrading or repairing. If the motherboard or any component on it goes bad, you will be better off purchasing a completely new standard system than paying many times the normal price for a new proprietary motherboard. In addition, a new industry standard motherboard would be newer and faster than the one you would be replacing. In a proprietary system, the replacement board would not only cost way too much, but it would be the same as the one that failed.

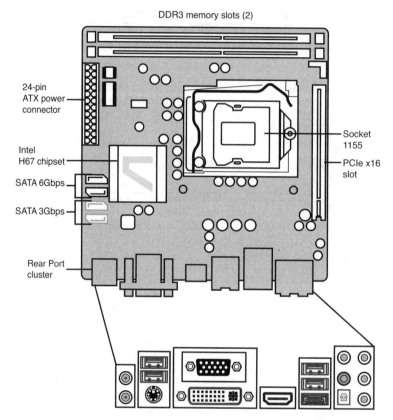

FIGURE 4.19   Top and rear views of the ASRock H67M-ITX motherboard, a third-party Mini-ITX motherboard with support for interchangeable processors and PCIe video.

Processor Sockets/Slots

The CPU is installed in either a socket or a slot, depending on the type of chip.

Starting with the 486 processors, Intel designed the processor to be a user-installable and replaceable part and developed standards for CPU sockets and slots that would allow different models of the same basic processor to plug in. One key innovation was to use a zero insertion force (ZIF) socket design, which meant that you could easily install or remove the processor with no tools. ZIF sockets use a lever to engage or release the grip on the chip, and with the lever released, the chip can be easily inserted or removed. The ZIF sockets were given a designation that was usually imprinted or embossed on the socket indicating what type it was. Different socket types accepted different families of processors. If you know the type of socket or slot on your motherboard, you essentially know which types of processors are designed to plug in.

◀◀   See the Chapter 3 section, "Processor Socket and Slot Types," **p. 75**.

Table 4.6 shows the designations for the various industry-standard processor sockets/slots and lists the chips designed to plug into them.

Table 4.6   CPU Socket Specifications

System Class	Socket	Pins	Layout	Voltage	Supported Processors
Intel 486	Socket 1	169	17x17 PGA	5V	Intel 486 SX/SX2, DX/DX2, DX4 OverDrive
	Socket 2	238	19x19 PGA	5V	Intel 486 SX/SX2, DX/DX2, DX4, DX4 OverDrive, 486 Pentium OverDrive
	Socket 3	237	19x19 PGA	5V/3.3V	Intel 486 SX/SX2, DX/DX2, DX4, DX4 OverDrive, 486 Pentium OverDrive, AMD Am486, Am5x86
	Socket 6*	235	19x19 PGA	3.3V	Intel 486 DX4, 486 Pentium OverDrive
Intel 586	Socket 4	273	21x21 PGA	5V	Intel Pentium 60/66, OverDrive
(Pentium)	Socket 5	320	37x37 SPGA	3.3V/3.5V	Intel Pentium 75-133, OverDrive
	Socket 7	321	37x37 SPGA	VRM	Intel Pentium 75-233+, MMX, OverDrive, AMD K5/K6, Cyrix 6x86/M1/MII
Intel 686 (Pentium II/III)	Socket 8	387	Dual-pattern SPGA	Auto VRM	Intel Pentium Pro, Pentium II OverDrive
	Slot 1 (SC242)	242	242-pin slot	Auto VRM	Intel Pentium II/III SECC, Celeron SEPP, VIA/Cyrix III/C3
	Socket 370	370	37x37 SPGA	Auto VRM	Intel Celeron/Pentium III PPGA/FC-PGA, VIA/Cyrix III/C3
Intel Pentium 4/Core	Socket 423	423	39x39 SPGA	Auto VRM	Intel Pentium 4 FC-PGA
	Socket 478	478	26x26 mPGA	Auto VRM	Intel Pentium 4/Celeron FC-PGA2, Celeron D
	LGA775 (Socket T)	775	30x33 LGA	Auto VRM	Intel Pentium 4/Extreme Edition, Pentium D, Celeron D, Pentium Dual-Core, Core 2 Duo/Extreme/Quad, Xeon
	LGA1155 (Socket H2)	1155	40x40 LGA	Auto VRM	2nd gen. Intel Pentium, Core i Series, Xeon
	LGA1156 (Socket H)	1156	40x40 LGA	Auto VRM	1st gen. Intel Pentium, Core i Series, Xeon
	LGA1366 (Socket B)	1366	41x43 LGA	Auto VRM	1ST gen. Intel Core i Series, Xeon
	LGA1356 (Socket B)	1356	41x43 LGA	Auto VRM	2nd/3rd gen. Intel Core i Series, Xeon
	LGA2011 (Socket R)	2011	58x43 LGA	Auto VRM	2nd/3rd gen. Intel Core i7-E Series, Xeon
AMD K7	Slot A	242	242-pin slot	Auto VRM	AMD Athlon SECC
	Socket A (462)	462	37x37 SPGA	Auto VRM	AMD Athlon, Athlon XP/MP, Duron, Sempron, Geode NX
AMD K8	Socket 754	754	29x29 mPGA	Auto VRM	AMD Athlon 64, Sempron

Table 4.6   Continued

System Class	Socket	Pins	Layout	Voltage	Supported Processors
	Socket 939	939	31x31 mPGA	Auto VRM	AMD Athlon 64/64 FX/64 X2, Sempron, Opteron
	Socket 940	940	31x31 mPGA	Auto VRM	AMD Athlon 64 FX, Opteron
	Socket AM2	940	31x31 mPGA	Auto VRM	AMD Athlon 64/64 FX/64 X2, Sempron, Opteron, Phenom
	Socket AM2+	940	31x31 mPGA	Auto VRM	AMD Athlon 64/64 X2, Opteron, Phenom X2/X3/X4/II X4
	Socket AM3	941	31x31 mPGA	Auto VRM	AMD Athlon II, Phenom II, Sempron
	Socket AM3+	942	31x31 mPGA	Auto VRM	AMD "Bulldozer" core processors
	Socket F (1207 FX)	1207	35x35 x2 LGA	Auto VRM	AMD Athlon 64 FX, Opteron
	Socket FM1	905	31x31 mPGA	Auto VRM	AMD "Llano" Fusion core processors
	Socket FM2	904	31x31 mPGA	Auto VRM	AMD "Trinity" Fusion core processors
Server and Workstation	Slot 2 (SC330)	330	330-pin slot	Auto VRM	Intel Pentium II/III Xeon
	Socket PAC418	418	38x22 split SPGA	Auto VRM	Intel Itanium
	Socket PAC611	611	25x28 mPGA	Auto VRM	Itanium 2
	Socket 603	603	31x25 mPGA	Auto VRM	Intel Xeon
	Socket 604	604	31x25 mPGA	Auto VRM	Intel Xeon
	LGA 771 (Socket J)	771	30x33 LGA	Auto VRM	Intel Core 2 Extreme, Xeon
	Socket 940	940	31x31 mPGA	Auto VRM	AMD Athlon 64FX
	Socket F (1207 FX)	1207	35x35 x2 LGA	Auto VRM	AMD Athlon 64 FX, Opteron
	Socket G34	1974	oLGA	Auto VRM	AMD Opteron "Magny-Cours MCM," "Interlagos"
	Socket C32	1207	oLGA	Auto VRM	AMD Opteron "Lisbon," "Valencia"

* Socket 6 was never actually implemented in systems.

FC-PGA = Flip-chip pin grid array

FC-PGA2 = FC-PGA with an integrated heat spreader (IHS)

OverDrive = Retail upgrade processors

PAC = Pin array cartridge

PGA = Pin grid array

PPGA = Plastic pin grid array

SECC = Single edge contact cartridge

SEPP = Single edge processor package

SPGA = Staggered pin grid array

mPGA = Micro pin grid array

VRM = Voltage regulator module with variable voltage output determined by module type or manual jumpers

Auto VRM = Voltage regulator module with automatic voltage selection determined by processor voltage ID (VID) pins

oLGA = organic LGA

Core i-series 2nd Gen. = "Sandy Bridge"

Core i-series 3rd Gen. = "Ivy Bridge"

Originally, all processors were mounted in sockets (or soldered directly to the motherboard). However, both Intel and AMD temporarily shifted to a slot-based approach for their processors in the late 1990s because the processors began incorporating built-in L2 cache, purchased as separate chips from third-party Static RAM (SRAM) memory chip manufacturers. Therefore, the processor then consisted not of one but of several chips, all mounted on a daughterboard that was then plugged into a slot in the motherboard. This worked well, but there were additional expenses in the extra cache chips, the daughterboard itself, the slot, optional casings or packaging, and the support mechanisms and physical stands and latches for the processor and heatsink. All in all, slot-based processors were expensive to produce compared to the previous socketed versions. With the advent of the second-generation Celeron, Intel began integrating the L2 cache directly into the processor die, meaning no extra chips were required. The second-generation (code-named Coppermine) Pentium III also received on-die L2 cache, as did the second-generation Athlon (code-named Thunderbird) processor from AMD. With on-die L2 cache, the processor was back to being a single chip again, which also meant that mounting it on a separate board plugged into a slot was unnecessary. All modern processors now have integrated L2 cache (and most high-end processors from Intel and AMD also have large integrated L3 cache) and use the socket form. As a bonus, on-die cache runs at full processor speed, instead of the one-half or one-third speed of the cache in slot-based processors.

Chipsets

We can't talk about modern motherboards without discussing chipsets. The *chipset* is the motherboard; therefore, any two boards with the same chipsets offer essentially the same level of performance and features.

Depending on the model, the chipset may contain the processor bus interface (called front side bus, or FSB), memory controllers, bus controllers, I/O controllers, and more. All the primary circuits of the motherboard are contained within the chipset. If the processor in your PC is like the engine in your car, the chipset represents the drivetrain and chassis. It is the framework in which the engine rests and is its connection to the outside world. The chipset is the frame, suspension, steering, wheels and tires, transmission, drive shaft, differential, and brakes. The chassis in your car is what gets the power to the ground, allowing the vehicle to start, stop, and corner. In the PC, the chipset represents the connection between the processor and everything else. The processor can't talk to the adapter boards, devices, memory (in some models), and so on without going through the chipset. If you think of the processor as the brain, the chipset is the spine and central nervous system.

Because the chipset controls the interface or connections between the processor and just about everything else, the chipset ends up dictating which type of processor you have; how fast the buses run; and in some cases what speed, type, and amount of memory you can use. In fact, the chipset might be the single most important component in your system—possibly even more important than the processor. I've seen systems with a slower processor but a better chipset outperform systems with a faster processor, much like how a car with less power might win a race through better cornering and braking. When deciding on a system, I often start by choosing the chipset, because the chipset decision dictates the processor, I/O, and expansion capabilities.

Chipset Evolution

When IBM created the first PC motherboards, it used several discrete (separate) chips to complete the design. Besides the processor and optional math coprocessor, many other components were required to complete the system. These other components included items such as the clock generator, bus controller, system timer, interrupt and DMA controllers, CMOS RAM and clock, and keyboard controller. Additionally, many other simple logic chips were used to complete the entire motherboard circuit, plus, of course, things such as the actual processor, math coprocessor (floating-point unit), memory, and other parts. Table 4.7 lists all the primary chip components used on the original PC/XT and AT motherboards.

Table 4.7 Primary Chip Components on PC/XT and AT Motherboards

Chip Function	PC/XT Version	AT Version
Processor	8088	80286
Math coprocessor (floating-point unit)	8087	80287
Clock generator	8284	82284
Bus controller	8288	82288
System timer	8253	8254
Low-order interrupt controller	8259	8259
High-order interrupt controller	—	8259
Low-order DMA controller	8237	8237
High-order DMA controller	—	8237
CMOS RAM/real-time clock	—	MC146818
Keyboard controller	8255	8042

In addition to the processor/coprocessor, a six-chip set was used to implement the primary motherboard circuit in the original PC and XT systems. IBM later upgraded this to a nine-chip design in the AT and later systems, mainly by adding more interrupt and DMA controller chips and the nonvolatile Complementary Metal Oxide Semiconductor (CMOS) RAM/real-time clock chip. All these motherboard chip components came from Intel or an Intel-licensed manufacturer, except the CMOS/clock chip, which came from Motorola. Building a clone or copy of one of these IBM systems required all these chips plus many smaller discrete logic chips to glue the design together, totaling 100 or more individual chips. This kept the price of a motherboard high and left little room on the board to integrate other functions.

In 1986, a company called Chips and Technologies introduced a revolutionary component called the 82C206—the main part of the first PC motherboard chipset. This was a single chip that integrated all the functions of the main motherboard chips in an AT-compatible system. This chip included the functions of the 82284 clock generator, 82288 bus controller, 8254 system timer, dual 8259 interrupt controllers, dual 8237 DMA controllers, and even MC146818 CMOS/clock chip. Besides the processor, virtually all the major chip components on a PC motherboard could now be replaced by a single chip. Four other chips augmented the 82C206 acting as buffers and memory controllers, thus completing virtually the entire motherboard circuit with five total chips. This first chipset was called the CS8220 chipset by Chips and Technologies. Needless to say, this was a revolutionary concept in PC motherboard manufacturing. Not only did it greatly reduce the cost of building a PC motherboard, but it made designing a motherboard much easier. The reduced component count meant the boards had more room for integrating other items formerly found on expansion cards. Later, the four chips augmenting the 82C206 were replaced by a new set of only three chips, and the entire set was called the New Enhanced AT (NEAT) CS8221 chipset. This was later followed by the 82C836 Single Chip AT (SCAT) chipset, which finally condensed all the chips in the set to a single chip.

Other chip manufacturers rapidly copied the chipset idea. Companies such as Acer, Erso, Opti, Suntac, Symphony, UMC, and VLSI each gained an important share of this market. Unfortunately for many of them, the chipset market has been a volatile one, and many of them have long since gone out of business. In 1993, VLSI had become the dominant force in the chipset market and had the majority of the market share; by the next year, VLSI (which later was merged into Philips Semiconductors), along with virtually everybody else in the chipset market, was fighting to stay alive. This is because a new chipset manufacturer had come on the scene, and within a year or so of getting serious, it was totally dominating the chipset market. That company was Intel, and after 1994, it had a virtual lock on the chipset market. If you have a motherboard built since 1994 that uses or accepts an Intel processor, chances are good that it has an Intel chipset on it as well.

Although ATI (prior to its merger with AMD), NVIDIA, VIA Technologies, and Silicon Integrated Systems (SiS) provided a wide variety of alternatives to Intel chipsets during the first decade of the twenty-first century, Intel is once again the sole maker of chipsets for its current processors.

What happened to Intel's former rivals? AMD has focused its former ATI chipset business squarely on making chipsets for its own processors, whereas VIA Technologies is primarily an embedded CPU/ motherboard builder and SiS now focuses on HDTV and streaming media. The last rival to Intel, NVIDIA, was unable to reach agreement with Intel over support for the new Core i-series processors and stopped developing chipsets for Intel in late 2009.

If you use current models of AMD processors, you can choose from motherboards that use either AMD or NVIDIA chipsets.

It is interesting to note that the original PC chipset maker, Chips and Technologies, survived by changing course to design and manufacture video chips and found a niche in that market specifically for laptop and notebook video chipsets. Chips and Technologies was subsequently purchased by Intel in 1998 as part of Intel's video strategy.

Intel Chipsets

You can't talk about chipsets today without discussing Intel because it currently owns the majority of the chipset market. It is interesting to note that we probably have Compaq to thank for forcing Intel into the chipset business in the first place!

The thing that started it all was the introduction of the Enhanced Industry Standard Architecture (EISA) bus designed by Compaq in 1989. At that time, Compaq had shared the bus with other manufacturers in an attempt to make it a market standard. However, Compaq refused to share its EISA bus chipset—a set of custom chips necessary to implement this bus on a motherboard.

Enter Intel, who decided to fill the chipset void for the rest of the PC manufacturers wanting to build EISA bus motherboards. As is well known today, the EISA bus failed to become a market success, except for a short-term niche server business, but Intel now had a taste of the chipset business—and this it apparently wouldn't forget. With the introduction of the 286 and 386 processors, Intel became impatient with how long it took the other chipset companies to create chipsets around its new processor designs; this delayed the introduction of motherboards that supported the new processors. For example, it took more than two years after the 286 processor was introduced for the first 286 motherboards to appear and just over a year for the first 386 motherboards to appear after the 386 had been introduced. Intel couldn't sell its processors in volume until other manufacturers made motherboards that would support them, so it thought that by developing motherboard chipsets for a new processor in parallel with the new processor, it could jumpstart the motherboard business by providing readymade chipsets for the motherboard manufacturers to use.

Intel tested this by introducing the 420 series chipsets along with its 486 processor in April 1989. This enabled the motherboard companies to get busy right away, and in only a few months the first 486 motherboards appeared. Of course, the other chipset manufacturers weren't happy; now they had Intel as a competitor, and Intel would always have chipsets for new processors on the market first!

Intel then realized that it made both processors *and* chipsets, which were 90% of the components on a typical motherboard. What better way to ensure that motherboards were available for its Pentium processor when it was introduced than by making its own motherboards as well and having these boards ready on the new processor's introduction date? When the first Pentium processor debuted in 1993, Intel also debuted the 430LX chipset as well as a fully finished motherboard. Now, besides the chipset companies being upset, the motherboard companies weren't too happy, either. Not only was Intel the major supplier of parts needed to build finished boards (processors and chipsets), but it was now building and selling the finished boards as well. By 1994, Intel dominated the processor and chipset markets and had cornered the motherboard market as well.

Since then, as Intel develops new processors, it develops chipsets and motherboards simultaneously, which means they can be announced and shipped in unison. This eliminates the delay between introducing new processors and waiting for motherboards and systems capable of using them, which was common in the industry's early days. For the consumer, this means no waiting for new systems. Since the original Pentium processor in 1993, we have been able to purchase ready-made systems on the same day a new processor is released.

Intel Chipset Model Numbers

Starting with the 486 in 1989, Intel began a pattern of numbering its chipsets as shown in Table 4.8.

Table 4.8   Intel Chipset Model Numbers

Chipset Series	Supported Processors and Other Features
420xx	P4 (486)
430xx	P5 (Pentium), EDO memory
440xx	P6 (Pentium Pro/PII/PIII), AGP, SDRAM memory
450xx	P6 workstation (Pentium Pro/PII/PIII Xeon), SDRAM memory
8xx	PII/PIII/P4, AGP, DDR memory
9xx	Pentium 4/D, Core 2, PCI Express, DDR2 memory
3x	Core 2, PCI Express, DDR2/DDR3 memory
4x	Core 2, PCI Express 2.x, DDR2/DDR3 memory
5x	Original Core i Series, PCI Express 2.x
6x	2nd gen. Core i Series, PCI Express 2.x
7x	3rd gen. Core I Series, PCI Express 3.x

The chipset numbers listed here are abbreviations of the actual chipset numbers stamped on the individual chips. For example, one of the popular Pentium II/III chipsets was the Intel 440BX chipset, which consisted of two components: the 82443BX North Bridge and the 82371EB South Bridge. Likewise, the 865G chipset supports the Pentium 4 and consists of two main parts: the 82865G graphics memory controller hub (GMCH; replaces the North Bridge and includes integrated video) and an 82801EB or 82801EBR I/O controller hub (ICH5 or ICH5R; replaces the South Bridge). Finally, the Z68 chipset supports Socket LGA1155 versions of the second-generation Core i7 and i5 Series processors. The Z68 uses the 82Z68 chip; like other 6-series chipsets, it is a single-chip chipset.

Intel has used three distinct chipset architectures:

- North/South Bridge (used by 400-series chipsets)
- Hub (used by 800-series, 900-series, 3x, 4x, and 5x chipsets)
- Single-chip (used by 6x, 7x series chipsets)

Tip

On older systems, you might be able to identify the chipset by reading the logo (Intel or others) as well as the part number and letter combinations on the larger chips on your motherboard. However, on all recent motherboards, the North Bridge/ GMCH/MCH/IOH chip on recent motherboards is covered up with a passive or active heatsink, and virtually all recent motherboards use a heatsink on the South Bridge or ICH chip. To determine the chipset used in these systems, I recommend software such as the Intel Chipset Identification Utility (http://downloadmirror.intel.com/18498/eng/ChipUtil.exe) or CPU-Z (http://cpuid.com).

Intel Integrated Graphics Architecture

Intel began producing motherboard chipsets with integrated video starting with the 810 chipset in April 1999. Intel took this a step further in January 2010 when it introduced the first processors with integrated video, the Clarkdale Core i-Series processors. By building the graphics directly into the motherboard chipset or processor, no other graphics chip or video memory was required, meaning that video could be essentially included in a PC for "free." Many of the processors and chipsets including integrated graphics also support slots for graphics cards, meaning that the integrated graphics could easily be upgraded by adding one or more discrete graphics cards.

See Table 12.2 in Chapter 12, "Video Hardware," for the types and features for the integrated graphics available in Intel motherboard chipsets and processors over the years.

AMD Integrated Graphics Architecture

Before its takeover by AMD, ATI offered a number of chipsets with integrated graphics, and AMD has continued to do so. AMD's Fusion series of accelerated processing units (APUs), which combine the CPU with video, was first released in early 2011 for use in notebook and netbook products, and by mid-2011 for desktop computers. Although AMD's Fusion family has come to market later than Intel's CPU-integrated products, AMD Fusion is built on its former ATI division's long experience with all levels of graphic processing.

Note

Traditionally, integrated video has never been fast enough for serious gamers or other users requiring high-speed displays. Instead, integrated video can offer reasonable graphics performance for virtually no cost. However, the new generation of CPUs incorporating graphics now rival mid-range graphics cards.

I often recommend using processors or motherboards that feature integrated graphics as well as a slot for adding a video card later; that way you can start off by saving money using the integrated graphics and later upgrade to a higher performance video solution by merely adding a card.

▶▶ See the Chapter 12 sections, "Integrated Video/Motherboard Chipsets," **p. 611** and "CPUs with Integrated Video," **p. 616**.

Traditional North/South Bridge Architecture

Most of Intel's earlier chipsets as well as earlier non-Intel chipsets use a multitiered architecture incorporating what are referred to as North and South Bridge components, as well as a Super I/O chip:

- **North Bridge**—So named because it is the connection between the high-speed processor bus and the slower AGP and Peripheral Component Interconnect (PCI) buses. The North Bridge is what the chipset is named after, meaning that, for example, what we call the 440BX chipset is derived from the fact that the actual North Bridge chip part number for that set is 82443BX.

- **South Bridge**—So named because it is the bridge between the PCI bus (66/33MHz) and the even slower ISA bus (8MHz).

- **Super I/O chip**—It's a separate chip attached to the ISA bus that is not really considered part of the chipset and often came from a third party, such as National Semiconductor or Standard MicroSystems Corp. (SMSC). The Super I/O chip included commonly used peripheral items combined into a single chip. Note that more recent South Bridge chips include Super I/O functions (such chips are known as Super-South Bridge chips), so that the most recent motherboards based on a North/South Bridge architecture no longer include a separate Super I/O chip.

▶▶ See "Super I/O Chips," **p. 228**.

Figure 4.20 shows a typical AMD Socket A motherboard using North/South Bridge architecture with the locations of all chips and components.

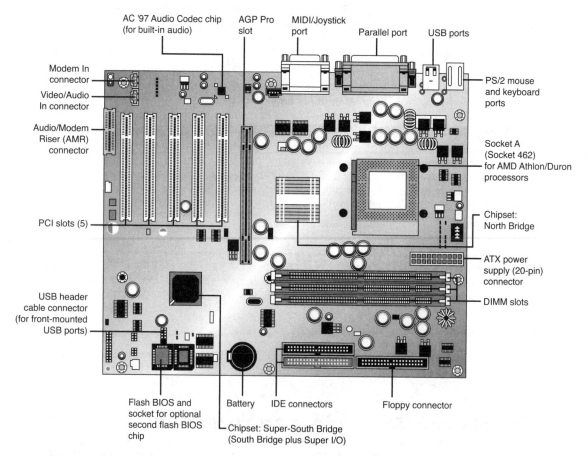

FIGURE 4.20 A typical Socket A (AMD Athlon/Duron) motherboard showing component locations.

The North Bridge is sometimes referred to as the PAC (PCI/AGP Controller). It is essentially the main component of the motherboard and is the only motherboard circuit besides the processor that normally runs at full motherboard (processor bus) speed. Most modern chipsets use a single-chip North

Bridge; however, some of the older ones actually consisted of up to three individual chips to make up the complete North Bridge circuit.

The South Bridge is the lower-speed component in the chipset and has always been a single chip. The South Bridge is a somewhat interchangeable component in that different chipsets (North Bridge chips) often are designed to use the same South Bridge component. This modular design of the chipset allows for lower cost and greater flexibility for motherboard manufacturers. Similarly, many vendors produce several versions of pin-compatible South Bridge chips with different features to enable more flexible and lower-cost manufacturing and design.

The South Bridge connects to the 33MHz PCI bus and contains the interface or bridge to the 8MHz ISA bus (if present). It also typically contains dual ATA/IDE hard disk controller interfaces, one or more USB interfaces, and in later designs even the CMOS RAM and real-time clock functions. In older designs, the South Bridge contained all the components that make up the ISA bus, including the interrupt and DMA controllers.

The third motherboard component, the Super I/O chip, is connected to the 8MHz ISA bus or the low pin count (LPC) bus and contains all the standard peripherals that are built into a motherboard. For example, most Super I/O chips contain the serial ports, parallel port, floppy controller, and keyboard/mouse interface. Optionally, they might contain the CMOS RAM/clock, IDE controllers, and game port interface as well. Systems that integrate IEEE 1394 and SCSI ports use separate chips for these port types.

Most recent motherboards that use North/South Bridge chipset designs incorporate a Super-South Bridge, which incorporates the South Bridge and Super I/O functions into a single chip.

Hub Architecture

Beginning in 1999, chipsets from Intel began using hub architectures in which the former North Bridge chip is now called a Memory Controller Hub (MCH) or an I/O Hub (IOH) and the former South Bridge is called an I/O Controller Hub (ICH). Systems that include integrated graphics use a Graphics Memory Controller Hub (GMCH) in place of the standard MCH. Rather than being connected through the PCI bus as in a standard North/South Bridge design, they are connected via a dedicated hub interface that is at least twice as fast as PCI. The hub design offers several advantages over the conventional North/South Bridge design:

- **It's faster**—The Accelerated Hub Architecture (AHA) interface that the 8xx series uses has twice the throughput of PCI. The 9xx and newer series chipsets use an even faster version called DMI (Direct Media Interface), which is 7.5 to 14 times faster than PCI.

- **Reduced PCI loading**—The hub interface is independent of PCI and doesn't share or steal PCI bus bandwidth for chipset or Super I/O traffic. This improves performance of all other PCI bus–connected devices because the PCI bus is not involved in these transactions.

- **Reduced board wiring**—The AHA interface is 8 bits wide and requires 15 signals to be routed on the motherboard, whereas DMI is 4 bits wide and requires 8 differential pairs of signals. By comparison, PCI requires that no fewer than 64 signals are routed on the board, causing increased electromagnetic interference (EMI) generation, greater susceptibility to signal degradation and noise, and increased board manufacturing costs.

This hub interface design allows for a much greater throughput for PCI devices because there is no South Bridge chip (also carrying traffic from the Super I/O chip) hogging the PCI bus. Due to bypassing PCI, the hub interface also enables greater throughput for devices directly connected to the I/O controller hub (formerly the South Bridge), such as the higher-speed ATA-100/133, Serial ATA 3Gbps, and USB interfaces.

There are two main variations on the hub interface:

- **AHA (Accelerated Hub Architecture)**—Used by the 8xx series of chipsets. AHA is a 4X (quad-clocked) 66MHz 8-bit (4 × 66MHz × 1 byte = 266MBps) interface, which has twice the throughput of PCI (33MHz × 32 bits = 133MBps).

- **DMI (Direct Media Interface)**—Used by the 9xx and later series chipsets. DMI is basically a dedicated four-lane (4-bit-wide) PCI Express connection allowing for 1GBps (250GHz × 4 bits) in each direction simultaneously, which is 7.5 to 14 times faster than PCI. DMI 2.0 was introduced in 2011, and runs at 2GBps in each direction simultaneously.

These hub interface designs are also economical, being only 4 or 8 bits wide. Although this seems too narrow to be useful, there is a reason for the design. The lower pin count for the AHA and DMI hub connections means that less circuit routing exists on the board, less signal noise and jitter occur, and the chips have many fewer pins, making them smaller and more economical to produce. So, by virtue of a narrow—but fast—design, the hub interface achieves high performance with less cost and more signal integrity than with the previous North/South Bridge design.

The ICH also includes a new LPC bus, consisting basically of a stripped 4-bit-wide version of PCI designed primarily to support the motherboard ROM BIOS and Super I/O chips. Because the same four signals for data, address, and command functions are used, only 9 other signals are necessary to implement the bus, for a total of 13 signals. This dramatically reduces the number of traces connecting the ROM BIOS chip and Super I/O chips in a system as compared to the 98 ISA bus signals necessary for older North/South Bridge chipsets that used ISA as the interface to those devices. The LPC bus has a maximum bandwidth of 16.67MBps, which is much faster than ISA and more than enough to support devices such as ROM BIOS and Super I/O chips.

Figure 4.21 shows a typical Intel chipset–based motherboard that uses hub architecture.

HyperTransport and Other Processor/Chipset Interconnects

Intel is not alone in replacing the slow PCI bus connection between North and South Bridge–type chips with faster architectures that bypass the PCI bus. Currently, AMD uses the HyperTransport bus for chipset interconnects to support its Socket AM3+ and earlier standard CPUs, but it also uses its proprietary Unified Media Interface (UMI) for its A-series chipsets for APUs. Before NVIDIA exited the chipset business in 2010, it also used HyperTransport. HyperTransport, introduced in 2001 by the HyperTransport Technology Consortium (www.hypertransport.org), transmits packets using a DDR connection (sending on the rising and falling edges of the clock signal) between the CPU, memory, and the chipset. 64-bit AMD desktop and most chipset implementations use a single 16-bit link, whereas 64-bit AMD server processors such as the Opteron support up to three 16-bit links. HyperTransport is used both with dual-chip chipsets and with single-chip chipsets developed by AMD and NVIDIA.

Table 4.9 lists HyperTransport versions and speeds.

Table 4.9   HyperTransport Versions

Version Number	Maximum Bandwidth (32-Bit Links)	When Introduced	Example Product
1.x	12.8Gbps	2001	AMD Socket 754 processors
2.0	22.4Gbps	2004	AMD Socket 939 processors
3.0	41.6Gbps	2006	AMD Socket AM2+, AM3 processors
3.1	51.2Gbps	2008	AMD Socket AM3+ processors

AMD processors and chipsets supporting HyperTransport use 16-bit links, so actual throughput is lower than shown.

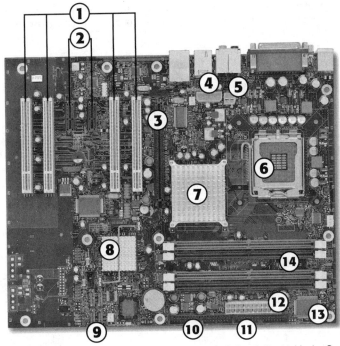

1. PCI expansion slots (4)
2. PCI Express x1 slots (2)
3. PCI Express x16 slot
4. Alternate power connector
5. ATX12V power supply connector
6. Socket LGA775
7. MCH (Memory Controller Hub) aka North Bridge

8. ICH (I/O Controller Hub) aka South Bridge
9. SATA/RAID host adapter connectors
10. ATA/IDE host adapter connector
11. Floppy controller connector
12. 24-pin ATX power supply connector
13. Super I/O chip
14. DDR2 DIMM sockets

FIGURE 4.21 Typical PCIe-based motherboard showing chipset and other component locations. Illustration courtesy of Intel Corporation.

Other companies that have introduced high-speed chipset interconnects include the following:

- **VIA**—VIA created the V-Link architecture to connect its North and South Bridge chips at speeds matching or exceeding Intel hub architecture. V-Link uses a dedicated 8-bit data bus in three versions: 4x V-Link, 8x V-Link, and Ultra V-Link. 4x V-Link transfers data at 266MBps (4 × 66MHz), which is twice the speed of PCI and matches the speed of Intel's AHA and HI 1.5 hub architectures. 8x V-Link transfers data at 533MBps (4 × 133MHz), which is twice the speed of Intel's AHA interface. Ultra V-Link transfers data at 1GBps.

- **SiS**—SiS's MuTIOL architecture (also called HyperStreaming) provided performance comparable to VIA's 4x V-Link; the second-generation MuTIOL 1G used in more recent SiS's chipsets provides performance comparable to VIA's Ultra V-Link and Intel's DMI architectures. Chipsets that support MuTIOL use separate address, DMA, input data, and output data buses for each I/O bus master. MuTIOL buffers and manages multiple upstream and downstream data transfers over a bidirectional 16-bit data bus.

- **ATI**—ATI (now owned by AMD) used a high-speed interconnect called A-Link in its 9100-series IGP integrated chipsets. A-Link runs at 266MBps, matching Intel's AHA interface as well as first-generation V-Link and MuTIOL designs.

In the following sections, let's examine the popular chipsets used from the 486 to the present.

Intel's Early 386/486 Chipsets

Intel's first real PC motherboard chipset was the 82350 chipset for the 386DX and 486 processors. This chipset was not successful, mainly because the EISA bus was not popular and many other manufacturers were making standard 386 and 486 motherboard chipsets at the time. The market changed quickly, and Intel dropped the EISA bus support and introduced follow-up 486 chipsets that were much more successful.

Table 4.10 shows the Intel 486 chipsets.

Table 4.10   Intel 486 Motherboard Chipsets

Chipset	420TX	420EX	420ZX
Code name	Saturn	Aries	Saturn II
Date introduced	Nov. 1992	March 1994	March 1994
Processor	5V 486	5V/3.3V 486	5V/3.3V 486
Bus speed	Up to 33MHz	Up to 50MHz	Up to 33MHz
SMP (dual CPUs)	No	No	No
Memory types	FPM	FPM	FPM
Parity/ECC	Parity	Parity	Parity
Max. memory	128MB	128MB	160MB
L2 cache type	Async	Async	Async
PCI support	2.0	2.0	2.1
AGP support	No	No	No

AGP = Accelerated graphics port
FPM = Fast page mode
PCI = Peripheral component interconnect
SMP = Symmetric multiprocessing (dual processors)
Note: PCI 2.1 supports concurrent PCI operations.

The 420 series chipsets were the first to introduce the North/South Bridge design.

Fifth-Generation (P5 Pentium Class) Chipsets

With the advent of the Pentium processor in March 1993, Intel introduced its first Pentium chipset: the 430LX chipset (code-named Mercury). This was the first Pentium chipset on the market and set the stage as Intel captured this lead and ran with it. Other manufacturers took months to a year or more to get their Pentium chipsets out the door. Since the debut of its Pentium chipsets, Intel has dominated the chipset market for Intel processors. Table 4.11 shows the Intel Pentium motherboard chipsets. Note that none of these chipsets supports AGP; Intel first added support for AGP in its chipsets for the Pentium II/Celeron processors.

Table 4.11   Intel Pentium Motherboard Chipsets (North Bridge)

Chipset	430LX	430NX	430FX	430MX	430HX	430VX	430TX
Code Name	Mercury	Neptune	Triton	Mobile Triton	Triton II	Triton III	n/a
Date Introduced	March 1993	March 1994	Jan. 1995	Oct. 1995	Feb. 1996	Feb. 1996	Feb. 1997
CPU Bus Speed	66MHz	66MHz	66MHz	66MHz	66MHz	66MHz	66MHz
CPUs Supported	P60/66	P75+	P75+	P75+	P75+	P75+	P75+
SMP (Dual CPUs)	No	Yes	No	No	Yes	No	No
Memory Types	FPM	FPM	FPM/EDO	FPM/EDO	FPM/EDO	FPM/EDO/ SDRAM	FPM/EDO/ SDRAM
Parity/ECC	Parity	Parity	Neither	Neither	Both	Neither	Neither
Max. Memory	192MB	512MB	128MB	128MB	512MB	128MB	256MB
Max. Cacheable	192MB	512MB	64MB	64MB	512MB	64MB	64MB
L2 Cache Type	Async	Async	Async/ Pburst	Async/ Pburst	Async/ Pburst	Async/ Pburst	Async/ Pburst
PCI Support	2.0	2.0	2.0	2.0	2.1	2.1	2.1
AGP Support	No	No	No	No	No	No	No
South Bridge	SIO	SIO	PIIX	MPIIX	PIIX3	PIIX3	PIIX4

EDO = Extended data out
FPM = Fast page mode
PIIX = PCI ISA IDE Xcelerator
SDRAM = Synchronous dynamic RAM
SIO = System I/O
SMP = Symmetric multiprocessing (dual processors)

Note

PCI 2.1 and later supports concurrent PCI operations, enabling multiple PCI cards to perform transactions at the same time for greater speed.

Sixth-Generation (P6 Pentium Pro/II/III Class) Chipsets

Because the Pentium Pro, Celeron, and Pentium II/III were essentially the same processor with different cache designs and minor internal revisions, the same chipsets could be used for Socket 8 (Pentium Pro), Socket 370 (Celeron/Pentium III), and Slot 1 (Celeron/Pentium II/III) designs.

Table 4.12 shows the chipsets used on Pentium Pro motherboards.

Note

PCI 2.1 supports concurrent PCI operations.

Table 4.12   Pentium Pro Motherboard Chipsets (North Bridge)

Chipset	450KX	450GX	440FX
Code Name	Orion	Orion Server	Natoma
Workstation Date Introduced	Nov. 1995	Nov. 1995	May 1996
Bus Speed	66MHz	66MHz	66MHz
SMP (Dual CPUs)	Yes	Yes (up to 4)	Yes
Memory Types	FPM	FPM	FPM/EDO/BEDO
Parity/ECC	Both	Both	Both
Maximum Memory	1GB	4GB	1GB
L2 Cache Type	In CPU	In CPU	In CPU
Maximum Cacheable	1GB	4GB	1GB
PCI Support	2.0	2.0	2.1
AGP Support	No	No	No
AGP Speed	n/a	n/a	n/a
South Bridge	Various	Various	PIIX3

AGP = Accelerated graphics port
BEDO = Burst EDO
EDO = Extended data out
FPM = Fast page mode
Pburst = Pipeline burst (synchronous)
PCI = Peripheral Component Interconnect
PIIX = PCI ISA IDE Xcelerator
SDRAM = Synchronous dynamic RAM
SIO = System I/O
SMP = Symmetric multiprocessing (dual processors)

For the Celeron and Pentium II/III motherboards, Intel offered the chipsets in Table 4.13. 4xx series chipsets incorporate a North/South Bridge architecture, whereas 8xx series chipsets support the newer and faster hub architecture. P6/P7 (Pentium III/Celeron, Pentium 4, and Xeon) processor chipsets using hub architecture are shown in Table 4.14.

Table 4.13   P6 Processor Chipsets Using North/South Bridge Architecture

Chipset	440FX	440LX	440EX	440BX	440GX	450NX	440ZX
Code Name	Natoma	None	None	None	None	None	None
Date Introduced	May 1996	Aug. 1997	April 1998	April 1998	June 1998	June 1998	Nov. 1998
Part Numbers	82441FX, 82442FX	82443LX	82443EX	82443BX	82443GX	82451NX, 82452NX	82453NX, 82454NX
Bus Speed	66MHz	66MHz	66MHz	66/100MHz	100MHz	100MHz	66/100MHz
Supported Processors	Pentium II	Pentium II	Celeron	Pentium II/III, Celeron	Pentium II/III, Xeonpro	Pentium II/III, Xeon	Celeron, Pentium II/III
SMP (Dual CPUs)	Yes	Yes	No	Yes	Yes	Yes, up to four	No
Memory Types	FPM/EDO/BEDO	FPM/EDO/SDRAM	EDO/SDRAM	SDRAM	SDRAM	FPM/EDO	SDRAM
Parity/ECC	Both	Both	Neither	Both	Both	Both	Neither
Maximum Memory	1GB	1GB EDO/512MB SDRAM	256MB	1GB	2GB	8GB	256MB
Memory Banks	4	4	2	4	4	4	2
PCI Support	2.1	2.1	2.1	2.1	2.1	2.1	2.1
AGP Support	No	AGP 2x	AGP 2x	AGP 2x	AGP 2x	No	AGP 2x
South Bridge	82371SB (PIIX3)	82371AB (PIIX4)	82371EB (PIIX4E)	82371EB (PIIX4E)	82371EB (PIIX4E)	82371EB (PIIX4E)	82371EB (PIIX4E)

Table 4.14   P6 (Pentium III/Celeron) Processor Chipsets Using Hub Architecture

Chipset	810	810E	815[3]	815E[3]	815EP
Code Name	Whitney	Whitney	Solano	Solano	Solano
Date Introduced	April 1999	Sept. 1999	June 2000	June 2000	Nov. 2000
Part Number	82810	82810E	82815	82815	82815EP
Bus Speed	66/100MHz	66/100/133MHz	66/100/133MHz	66/100/133MHz	66/100/133MHz
Supported Processors	Celeron, Pentium II/III	Celeron, Pentium II/III	Celeron, Pentium II/III	Celeron, Pentium II/III	Celeron, Pentium II/III
SMP(dual CPUs)	No	No	No	No	No
Memory Types	EDO SDRAM	SDRAM	SDRAM	SDRAM	SDRAM
Memory Speeds	PC100	PC100	PC133	PC133	PC133
Parity/ECC	Neither	Neither	Neither	Neither	Neither
Maximum Memory	512MB	512MB	512MB	512MB	512MB
AGP Slot	No	No	AGP 4x	AGP 4x	AGP 4x
Integrated Video	AGP 2x	AGP 2x	AGP 2x	AGP 2x	No
South Bridge (ICH)	82801AA/ AB (ICH/ICH0)	82801AA (ICH)	82801AA (ICH)	82801BA (ICH2)	82801BA (ICH2)

AGP= Accelerated graphics port
BEDO = Burst EDO
EDO = Extended data out
FPM = Fast page mode
ICH = I/O controller hub
Pburst = Pipeline burst (synchronous)

PCI = Peripheral Component Interconnect
PIIX = PCI ISA IDE Xcelerator
SDRAM = Synchronous dynamic RAM
SIO = System I/O
SMP = Symmetric multiprocessing (dual processors)

Note

Pentium Pro, Celeron, and Pentium II/III CPUs have their secondary caches integrated into the CPU package. Therefore, cache characteristics for these machines are not dependent on the chipset but are quite dependent on the processor.

Up until the release of the single-chip 6x series, most Intel chipsets were designed as a two-part system, using a North Bridge (MCH or GMCH in hub-based designs) and a South Bridge (ICH in hub-based designs) component. Often the same South Bridge or ICH component can be used with several different North Bridge (MCH or GMCH) chipsets.

To learn more about the South Bridge chips used in Intel 386 and early 486 chipsets, see Chapter 3 of *Upgrading and Repairing PCs*, 19th Edition, supplied in its entirety on the DVD packaged with this book.

820	820E	840	815P	815EG	815G
Camino	Camino	Carmel	Solano	Solano	Solano
Nov. 1999	June 2000	Oct. 1999	March 2001	Sept. 2001	Sept. 2001
82820	82820	82840	82815EP	82815G	82815G
66/100/133MHz	66/100/133MHz	66/100/133MHz	66/100/133MHz	66/100/133MHz	66/100/133MHz
Pentium II/III, Celeron	Pentium II/III, Celeron	Pentium III, Xeon	Celeron, Pentium III	Celeron, Pentium III	Celeron, Pentium III
Yes	Yes	Yes	No	No	No
RDRAM	RDRAM	RDRAM	SDRAM	SDRAM	SDRAM
PC800	PC800	PC800 dual-channel	PC100, PC133	PC66, PC100	PC133
Both	Both	Both	Neither	Neither	Neither
1GB	1GB	4GB	512MB	512MB	512MB
AGP 4x	AGP 4x	AGP 4x	AGP 4x	No	No
No	No	No	No	AGP 2x	AGP 2x
82801AA (ICH)	82801BA (ICH2)	82801AA (ICH)	82801AA/ AB (ICH/ICH0)	82801BA (ICH2)	82801AA/ AB (ICH/ICH0)

Several third-party companies also produced chipsets designed to support P6-class processors, including ALi Corporation (formerly known as Acer Laboratories), VIA Technologies, and SiS. ALi (Acer Labs, Inc.) spun off its chipset division in 2003 as ULi Electronics; then ULi was acquired by NVIDIA in 2006. ALi manufactured a variety of chipsets for the P6-class processors. Most of these were similar in form and function to the Intel offerings.

Seventh/Eighth-Generation (Pentium 4/D, Core 2, and Core i) Chipsets

The Pentium 4 and Celeron processors using Socket 423 and those made for Socket 478 are essentially the same processors with different cache designs and minor internal revisions, so the same chipset can be used for both processors. The Pentium 4 processor in Socket 775 is different from its predecessors; consequently, most 9xx-series chipsets support only the Socket 775 version of the Pentium 4, as well as the newer Core 2 series of processors.

Tables 4.15 and 4.16 show the 8xx-series chipsets Intel made for Pentium 4 and Celeron 4 processors. These chipsets use Intel's hub architecture, providing an interconnect speed of 266MBps between the MCH/GMCH and the ICH chips.

Table 4.15   Pentium 4 8xx-Series Chipsets from Intel Introduced 2000–2002

Chipset	850	850E	845	845E
Code Name	Tehama	Tehama-E	Brookdale	Brookdale-E
Date Introduced	Nov. 2000	May 2002	Sept. 2001 (SDRAM); Jan. 2002 (DDR)	May 2002
Part Number	82850	82850E	82845	82845E
Bus Speeds	400MHz	400/533MHz	400MHz	400/533MHz
Supported Processors	Pentium 4, Celeron	Pentium 4, Celeron	Pentium 4, Celeron	Pentium 4, Celeron
SMP (Dual CPUs)	No	No	No	No
Memory Types	RDRAM (PC800) dual-channel	RDRAM (PC800, 1066 dual-channel)	PC133 SDRAM, SDRAM	DDR 200/266 SDRAM
Parity/ECC	Both	Both	ECC	ECC
Maximum Memory	2GB	2GB (PC800); 1.5GB (PC1066)	2GB (PC2100 DDR); 3GB (PC133 SDRAM)	2GB
Memory Banks	2	2	2 (PC2100); 3 (PC133)	2
PCI Support	2.2	2.2	2.2	2.2
PCI Speed/Width	33MHz/32-bit	33MHz/32-bit	33MHz/32-bit	33MHz/32-bit
AGP Slot	AGP 4x (1.5V)	AGP 4x (1.5V)	AGP 4x (1.5V)	AGP 4x (1.5V)
Integrated Video	No	No	No	No
South Bridge (Hub)	ICH2	ICH2	ICH2	ICH4

Table 4.16   Intel 8xx-Series Chipsets Introduced in 2003 for Pentium 4

Chipset	848P	865P	865PE
Code Name	Breeds Hill	Springdale-P	Springdale-PE
Date Introduced	Feb. 2004	May 2003	May 2003
Part Number	82848P	82865P	82865PE
Bus Speeds	800/533/400MHz	533/400MHz	800/533/400MHz
Supported Processors	Pentium 4, Celeron, Celeron D	Pentium 4, Celeron, Celeron D	Pentium 4, Celeron, Celeron D
SMP (Dual CPUs)	No	No	No
Memory Types	DDR266/333/400 single-channel	DDR266/333 dual-channel	DDR333/400 dual-channel
Parity/ECC	Neither	Neither	Neither
Maximum Memory	2GB	4GB	4GB
Memory Banks	2	2	2
PCI Support	2.3	2.3	2.3

845GL	845G	845GE	845GV	845PE
Brookdale-GL	Brookdale-G	Brookdale-GE	Brookdale-GV	Brookdale-PE
July 2002	July 2002	Oct. 2002	Oct. 2002	Oct. 2002
82845GL	82845G	82845GE	82845GV	82845PE
400MHz	400/533MHz	400/533MHz	400/533MHz	400/533MHz
Pentium 4, Celeron	Pentium 4, Celeron	Pentium 4, Celeron	Pentium 4, Celeron	Pentium 4, Celeron
No	No	No	No	No
DDR 200/266 SDRAM	PC133 SDRAM, DDR 200/266 SDRAM	PC133 SDRAM, DDR 200/266 SDRAM	DDR 333/ 266 SDRAM	DDR 200/266 SDRAM
Neither	ECC	Neither	Neither	Neither
2GB	2GB	2GB	2GB	2GB
2	2	2	2	2
2.2	2.2	2.2	2.2	2.2
33MHz/32-bit	33MHz/32-bit	33MHz/32-bit	33MHz/32-bit	33MHz/32-bit
None	AGP 4x (1.5V)	AGP 4x (1.5V)	None	AGP 4x (1.5V)
Intel Extreme Graphics 200MHz	Intel Extreme Graphics 200MHz	Intel Extreme Graphics 266MHz	Intel Extreme Graphics 200MHz	No
ICH4	ICH4	ICH4	ICH4	ICH4

865G	865GV	875
Springdale-G	Springdale-GV	Canterwood
May 2003	May 2003	April 2003
82865G	82865GV	82875
800/533/400MHz	800/533/400MHz	800/533MHz
Pentium 4, Celeron, Celeron D	Pentium 4, Celeron, Celeron	Pentium 4, Celeron, Celeron D
No	No	No
DDR333/400 dual-channel	DDR333/400 dual-channel	DDR333/400 dual-channel
Neither	Neither	ECC
4GB	4GB	4GB
2	2	2
2.3	2.3	2.3

Table 4.16 Continued

Chipset	848P	865P	865PE
PCI Speed/Width	33MHz/32-bit	33MHz/32-bit	33MHz/32-bit
Video	AGP 8x	AGP 8x	AGP 8x
Integrated Video	No	No	No Graphics 2
Gigabit (GbE) Ethernet Support*	No	Yes	Yes
South Bridge (Hub)	ICH5/ICH5R	ICH5/ICH5R	ICH5/ICH5R

GbE connects directly to the MCH/GMCH chip, bypassing the PCI bus. It is implemented by the optional Intel_82547E1 Gigabit Connection chip.

Table 4.17 lists the ICH chips used by 8xx-series Pentium 4/Celeron 4 chipsets made by Intel.

Table 4.17 I/O Controller Hub Chips for Pentium 4 8xx-Series Chipsets

Chip Name	ICH0	ICH	ICH2
Part Number	82801AB	82801AA	82801BA
ATA Support	UDMA-33	UDMA-66	UDMA-100
SATA Support	No	No	No
SATA RAID	No	No	No
USB Support	1C/2P	1C/2P	2C/4P
USB 2.0	No	No	No
CMOS/Clock	Yes	Yes	Yes
PCI Support	2.2	2.2	2.2
LPC Support	Yes	Yes	Yes
Power Management	SMM/ACPI 1.0	SMM/ACPI 1.0	SMM/ACPI 1.0
10/100 Ethernet	No	No	No

ICH = I/O controller hub
SATA = Serial ATA
USB = Universal serial bus
xC/xP = Number of controller/number of ports
ATA = AT attachment (IDE)

UDMA = Ultra-DMA ATA
LPC = Low-pin-count bus
SMM = System management mode
ACPI = Advanced configuration and power interface

865G	865GV	875
33MHz/32-bit	33MHz/32-bit	33MHz/32-bit
AGP 8x	—	AGP 8x
Intel Extreme Graphics 2	Intel Extreme	No
Yes	Yes	Yes
ICH5/ICH5R	ICH5/ICH5R	ICH5/ICH5R

ICH4	ICH5	ICH5R
82801DB	82801EB	82801ER
UDMA-100	UDMA-100	UDMA-100
No	SATA-150	SATA-150
No	No	RAID 0, RAID 1
3C/6P	4C/8P	4C/8P
Yes	Yes	Yes
Yes	Yes	Yes
2.2	2.3	2.3
Yes	Yes	Yes
SMM/ACPI 2.0	SMM/ACPI 2.0	SMM/ACPI 2.0
Yes	Yes	Yes

In mid-2004, Intel introduced the 915/925 series of chipset for the Pentium 4 and Celeron 4. These chipsets, code-named Grantsdale and Alderwood before their introduction, were the first Intel chipsets to support several Socket 775 processors, DDR2 memory, and PCI Express for both video and other high-speed I/O uses (such as Gigabit Ethernet).

In 2005, Intel introduced its first dual-core chip for desktop processors (the Pentium D) as well as a processor designed for maximum single-core performance (the Pentium Extreme Edition). To support these new processors as well as Socket 775 Pentium 4 processors with HT Technology, Intel released the 945, 955, and 975 chipsets.

Because of the greater performance needed to support these high-speed technologies, the 9xx-series chipsets used a faster hub architecture than what was used by the 8xx-series chipsets. This interconnect design, known as DMI, runs at 1GBps in each direction. Table 4.18 lists the 9xx-series chipsets for the Pentium 4; Table 4.19 lists the 9xx-series chipsets for the Core 2, Pentium D, and Pentium Extreme Edition (they also support the Pentium 4); and Table 4.20 lists the ICH6 and ICH7 families of I/O controller hub chips used with 9xx-series chipsets.

Table 4.18   Intel 9xx-Series Chipsets for Pentium 4

Chipset	910GL	915P	915PL	915G
Code Name	Grantsdale-GL	Grantsdale-P	Grantsdale-PL	Grantsdale-G
Date Introduced	Sept. 2004	June 2004	March 2005	June 2004
Part Number	82910GL	828915P	828915GPL	828915G
Bus Speeds	533MHz	800/533MHz	800/533MHz	800/533MHz
Supported Processors	Pentium 4, Celeron, Celeron D	Pentium 4, Celeron, Celeron D	Pentium 4, Celeron D	Pentium 4, Celeron, Celeron D
Memory Types	DDR333/400 dual-channel	DDR333/400 dual-channel, DDR2	DDR333/400	DDR333/400 dual-channel DDR2
Parity/ECC	Neither	Neither	Neither	Neither
Maximum Memory	2GB	4GB	2GB	4GB
PCI Support	PCIe x1, PCI 2.3	PCIe x1, x16, PCI 2.2	PCIe x1, x16, PCI 2.3	PCIe x1, x16, PCI 2.3
PCI Express x16 Video	No	Yes	Yes	Yes
Integrated Video	Intel GMA 900	No	No	Extreme Graphics 3
South Bridge (hub)	ICH6 family	ICH6 family	ICH6 family	ICH6 family

*B-2 stepping and above are required for ECC support.
915GL does not support HT Technology.
GMA 900 = Graphics Media Accelerator 900.

Table 4.19   Intel 9xx-Series Chipsets for Core 2, Pentium D, Pentium Extreme Edition, and Pentium 4

Chipset	975X	955X
Code Name	Glenwood	Glenwood
Date Introduced	Nov. 2005	April 2005
Part Number	82975X	82955X
Bus Speeds	1066/800MHz	1066/800MHz
Supported Processors	Pentium Extreme Edition, Pentium D, Pentium 4 with HT Tech (Socket 775)	Pentium Extreme Edition, Pentium D, Pentium 4 with HT Tech (Socket 775)
Memory Types	DDR2 667/533MHz dual-channel	DDR2 667/533MHz dual-channel
Parity/ECC	ECC	ECC
Maximum Memory	8GB	8GB
PCI Support	PCIe x1, x16, PCI 2.3	PCIe x1, x16, PCI 2.3
PCIe x16 Video	Yes, dual slots	Yes
Integrated Video	No	No
South Bridge (Hub)	ICH7 family	ICH7 family

915GV	915GL	925X	925XE
Grantsdale-GV	Grantsdale-GL	Alderwood	Alderwood-E
June 2004	March 2005	June 2004	Nov. 2004
828915GV	828915GL	82925X	82925XE
800/533MHz	533MHz	800/533MHz	1066/800MHz
Pentium 4, Celeron, Celeron D	Pentium 4, Celeron, Celeron D	Pentium 4, Celeron, Celeron D	Pentium 4 (90nm)
DDR333/ 400 dual-channel DDR2	DDR333/ 400 dual-channel	DDR2	DDR2 533/ 400 dual channel
Neither	Neither	ECC*	Neither
4GB	4GB	4GB	4GB
PCIe x1, PCI 2.2 PCI 2.2	PCIe x1, PCI 2.2	PCIe x1, x16, PCI 2.3	PCIe x1, x16, PCI 2.3
No	No	Yes	Yes
Extreme Graphics 3	Extreme Graphics 3	No	No
ICH6 family	ICH6 family	ICH6 family	ICH6 family

945G	945P	945PL
Lakeport-G	Lakeport-P	Lakeport-PL
May 2005	May 2005	March 2006
82945G	82945P	82945PL
1066/800/533MHz	1066/800/533MHz	800/533MHz
Pentium D, Pentium 4 with HT Tech (Socket 775)	Pentium D, Pentium 4 with HT Tech (Socket 775)	Pentium D, Pentium 4 with HT Tech (Socket 775)
DDR2 667/533/400MHz, dual-channel	DDR2 667/533/400MHz dual-channel	DDR2 533/400MHz dual-channel
Neither	Neither	Neither
4GB	4GB	4GB
PCIe x1, x16, PCI 2.3	PCIe x1, x16, PCI 2.3	PCIe x1, x16, PCI 2.3
Yes	Yes	Yes
Intel GMA 900	No	No
ICH7 family	ICH7 family	ICH7 family

Table 4.20   Intel 9xx Chipset I/O Controller Hub (ICH) Specifications (aka South Bridge)

Features	ICH6	ICH6R	ICH7	ICH7R	ICH8	ICH8R
PATA Support*	UDMA-100	UDMA-100	UDMA-100	UDMA-100	No	No
SATA Support	1.5Gbps, 4 drives	1.5Gbps, 4 drives	3Gbps, 4 drives	3Gbps, 4 drives	3Gbps, 4 drives	3Gbps, 6 drives
SATA RAID	No	0, 1, 10	No	0, 1, 10, 5	No	0, 1, 10, 5
USB 2.0 Support	6 ports	6 ports	8 ports	8 ports	10 ports	10 ports
CMOS/Clock	Yes	Yes	Yes	Yes	Yes	Yes
PCI Support	PCI 2.3, PCIe 1.0a	PCI 2.3, PCIe 1.0a	PCI 2.3, PCIe 1.0a	PCI 2.3, PCIe 1.0a	PCI 2.3, PCIe 1.1	PCI 2.3, PCIe 1.1
Number of PCI Express Lanes	4	4	4	6	6	6
LPC Support	Yes	Yes	Yes	Yes	Yes	Yes
Power Management	SMM/ACPI 1.0	SMM/ACPI 1.0	SMM/ACPI 3.0	SMM/ACPI 3.0	SMM/ACPI 3.0	SMM/ACPI 3.0
Ethernet	10/100	10/100	10/100	10/100	10/100/1000	10/100/1000
Audio Support	HD Audio, AC '97	HD Audio, AC '97	HD Audio	HD Audio	HD Audio	HD Audio

ICH = I/O controller hub

USB = Universal serial bus

xC/xP = Number of USB controllers/number of ports

PATA = Parallel AT attachment (IDE)

UDMA = Ultra-DMA ATA

LPC = Low-pin-count bus

SMM = System management mode

ACPI = Advanced configuration and power interface

HT Tech = Hyperthreading

*One ATA port supporting two ATA/IDE drives

Intel 915 Family

The Intel 915 chipset family, code-named Grantsdale during its development, was introduced in 2004. The Grantsdale family comprises six members (910GL, 915PL, 915P, 915G, 915GV, and 915GL), all of which support the 90nm Pentium 4 Prescott core. These chipsets are the first to support the Socket 775 processor interface outlined in Chapter 3, "Processor, Types and Specifications." These chipsets replaced the 865 Springdale family of chipsets.

The 915P, 915G, 915GV, 915GL, and 915PL models are designed to support the HT Technology feature built into most recent Pentium 4 processors and to support bus speeds up to 800MHz. All five chipsets support dual-channel DDR memory up to 400MHz and PCI Express x1 as well as PCI version 2.3 expansion slots. The 915P, 915G, and 915GV chipsets also support the then-new DDR2 memory standard at speeds up to 533MHz.

The 915P and 915PL used a PCI Express x16 slot for high-speed graphics, whereas the 915G had a PCI Express x16 slot as well as integrated Intel Graphics Media Accelerator 900 (originally known as Extreme Graphics 3). The 915GV, 915GL, and 910GL use Intel Graphics Media Accelerator 900 but do not include a PCI Express x16 slot. Graphics Media Accelerator 900 is a partial implementation of DirectX 9, but it lacks the vertex shaders found on fully compatible DirectX 9 GPUs from ATI and NVIDIA.

The 910GL is the low-end member of the family, lacking support for DDR2 RAM, 800MHz bus speeds, and PCI Express x16 video. The 910GL was designed to be matched with Intel Celeron or the Celeron D processors to produce a low-cost system.

All 915-series MCH/GMCH chips used the ICH6 family of South Bridge (I/O Controller Hub or ICH) replacements detailed in Table 4.20.

Intel 925X Family

The Intel 925 chipset family includes two members: the 925X and the 925XE. The Intel 925X chipset, code-named Alderwood, was released in 2004. It was designed to replace the 875P Canterwood chipset. Unlike the 915 series of chipsets, which continued to support older DDR memory, the 925X supported only DDR2 memory. The 925X also supported ECC memory, providing a fast and accurate platform for mission-critical applications. To further improve performance, it used an optimized memory controller design.

The 925X supported the Pentium 4 Extreme Edition and the Pentium 4 in Socket 775 form factors. It also includes PCI Express x1, PCI Express x16 (video), and PCI version 2.3 expansion slots. The I/O controller hub used the ICH6 family of South Bridge replacements detailed in Table 4.20.

The 925XE was an updated version of the 925X, adding support for 1,066MHz FSB speeds; however, it dropped support for the Pentium 4 Extreme Edition processor and for ECC memory.

Intel 945 Express Family

The Intel 945 Express chipset family (code-named Lakeport) was released in 2005 and included three members: 945G, 945P, and 945PL. These chipsets, along with the 955X and 975X, were the first to support Intel's new dual-core Pentium D processors, but they also support Pentium 4 HT Technology processors using Socket 775.

The 945G and 945P were aimed at what Intel refers to as the "performance PC" market segment. They offered FSB speeds up to 1,066MHz and up to 4GB of dual-channel DDR2 memory (two pairs) running at up to 667MHz. Both featured PCI Express x16 support, but the 945G also incorporates Intel Graphics Media Accelerator 950 integrated graphics.

The 945PL—aimed at what Intel refers to as the "mainstream PC" segment—supported only two memory modules (one pair of dual-channel modules) running at up to 533MHz and a maximum memory size of 2GB. It also supported PCI Express x16.

All members of the 945 family supported the ICH7 family of I/O controller hub chips listed in Table 4.20. The ICH7 family differs from ICH6 in the following ways:

- It has support for 300MBps Serial ATA.
- It has support for SATA RAID 5 and Matrix RAID (ICH7R only).
- It has support for two additional PCI Express x1 ports (ICH7R only).

Figure 4.22 compares the features of the 945G and 915G chipsets.

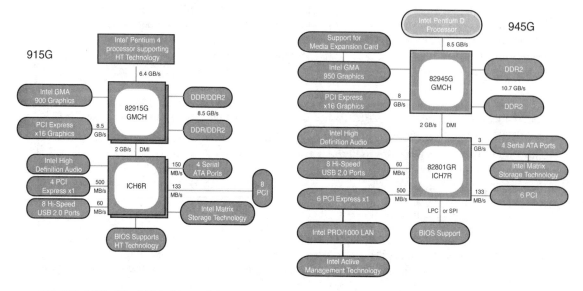

FIGURE 4.22 The 915G chipset (left) was the first Intel chipset to support both PCI Express x16 and integrated graphics. The 945G chipset (right) offers similar features but supports faster integrated graphics, faster SATA hard disks, and more PCI Express x1 slots than the 915G.

Intel 955X and 975X Family

The Intel Glenwood chipset family was released in 2005 and includes two members: the 955X and 975X. These chipsets, along with the 945 family, were the first to support Intel's new dual-core Pentium D processors, but they also supported the high-performance single-core Pentium Extreme Edition processors and existing Pentium 4 HT Technology processors using Socket 775. Intel categorized these chipsets as entry-level workstation and performance PC chipsets.

Although these chipsets were numbered in different series, most of their features are identical. Both supported FSB speeds of 800MHz and 1,066MHz and supported up to four DDR2 667/533MHz memory modules (two pairs of dual-channel modules) for a maximum 8GB of system memory. Both supported ECC memory—a must for workstation operation—and both used the ICH7 family of I/O controller hub chips listed in Table 4.20.

The 955X and 975X differed from each other in their video support. The 955X supported a single PCI Express x16 video card, whereas the 975X supported two PCI Express video cards in CrossFire dual-slot operation.

Intel 96x Series

The 96x series (code-named Broadwater) was introduced in June 2006 and was designed to support the Core 2 processors, including dual- and quad-core versions. There were several models in the series, each with slightly different features. The Q963 and Q965 were the most basic versions. Both featured integrated GMA 3000 video; however, the Q965 included support for a PCIe x16 slot (allowing for a video card upgrade). It also supported faster 800MHz DDR2 memory. The P965 deleted the integrated video for those only wanting to use PCIe x16 cards. Finally, the G965 included all the features of the other chipsets while adding even better integrated GMA X3000 video, along with support for a PCIe x16 upgrade slot. Table 4.21 shows the major features of these chipsets.

Table 4.21   Intel 96x Chipsets for Core 2

Chipset	Q963	Q965	P965	G965
Code Name	Broadwater	Broadwater	Broadwater	Broadwater
Date Introduced	June 2006	June 2006	June 2006	June 2006
Part Number	82Q963 GMCH	82Q965 GMCH	82P965 MCH	82Q965 GMCH
Supported Processors	Core 2, Pentium D, Pentium 4	Core 2, Pentium D, Pentium 4	Core 2, Pentium D, Pentium 4	Core 2, Pentium D, Pentium 4
CPU FSB	1066/800/533MHz	1066/800/533MHz	1066/800/533MHz	1066/800/533MHz
Max Memory	8GB	8GB	8GB	8GB
Memory Type	Dual-Channel DDR2	Dual-Channel DDR2	Dual-Channel DDR2	Dual-Channel DDR2
Memory Speed	667/533MHz	800/667/533MHz	800/677/533MHz	800/667/533MHz
Integrated Graphics	GMA 3000	GMA 3000	No	GMA X3000
External Graphics	No	1 PCIe x16	1 PCIe x16	1 PCIe x16
I/O Controller Hub	ICH8 family	ICH8 family	ICH8 family	ICH8 family

Intel 3x and 4x Series Chipsets

Introduced in June 2007, the 3x series chipset family (code-named Bearlake) was designed to support the Core 2 processors in both dual- and quad-core versions. The 4x series followed in March 2008 and basically added DDR3 memory support, plus faster PCIe 2.x slots and improved integrated graphics.

Some of the 3x and 4x series chipsets also included integrated GMA (Graphics Memory Accelerator) graphics, and some of those include Clear Video Technology, which can enhance video playback and support High Definition Media Interface (HDMI).

The 3x and 4x series are available in a number of versions, including some with integrated video, support for faster CPU and memory speeds, as well as more memory and slots. Tables 4.22 and 4.23 show the different 3x and 4x series chipsets.

Table 4.22   Intel 3x Chipset Specifications

Chipset	P31	G31	Q33	G33
Code Name	Bearlake	Bearlake	Bearlake	Bearlake
Date Introduced	Aug. 2007	Aug. 2007	June 2007	June 2007
Supported CPUs	Core 2 Duo/Quad, Pentium Dual-Core	Core 2 Duo/Quad, Pentium Dual-Core	Core 2 Duo/Quad, Pentium Dual-Core	Core 2 Duo/Quad, Pentium Dual-Core
CPU FSB	800/1066MHz	800/1066/1333MHz	800/1066/1333MHz	800/1066/1333MHz
Max. Memory	4GB	4GB	8GB	8GB
Memory Channels	Dual-Channel	Dual-Channel	Dual-Channel	Dual-Channel
Memory Type and Speed	DDR2 667/800	DDR2 667/800	DDR2 667/800	DDR2 667/800
Integrated Graphics	No	GMA 3100	GMA 3100	GMA 3100, Clear Video Technology
External Graphics	1 PCIe x16, 1 PCIe x4	1 PCIe x16	1 PCIe x16	1 PCIe x16
I/O Controller Hub	ICH7 family	ICH7 family	ICH9 family	ICH9 family

Table 4.23   Intel 4x Chipset Specifications

Chipset	G41	Q43	B43	G43
Code Name	Eaglelake	Eaglelake	Eaglelake	Eaglelake
Date Introduced	Sep. 2008	Sep. 2008	Dec. 2008	June 2008
Supported CPUs	Core 2 Duo/Quad, Pentium Dual-Core	Core 2 Duo/Quad, Pentium Dual-Core	Core 2 Duo/Quad, Pentium Dual-Core	Core 2 Duo/Quad, Pentium Dual-Core
CPU FSB	800/1066/1333MHz	800/1066/1333MHz	800/1066/1333 MHz	800/1066/1333MHz
Max. Memory	8GB	16GB	16GB	16GB
Memory Channels	Dual-Channel	Dual-Channel	Dual-Channel	Dual-Channel
Memory Type and Speed	DDR3 800/1066, DDR2 667/800	DDR3 800/1066, DDR2 667/800	DDR3 800/1066/1333, DDR2 667/	DDR3 800/1066, DDR2 667/800
Integrated Graphics	GMA X4500	GMA X4500	GMA X4500	GMA X4500
External Graphics	1 PCIe x16	1 PCIe x16 2.0	1 PCIe x16 2.0	1 PCIe x16 2.0
I/O Controller Hub	ICH7 family	ICH10 family	ICH10 family	ICH10 family

Q35	G35	P35	X38
Bearlake	Bearlake	Bearlake	Bearlake
June 2007	Aug. 2007	June 2007	Sep. 2007
Core 2 Duo/Quad, Pentium Dual-Core	Core 2 Duo/Quad, Pentium Dual-Core	Core 2 Duo/Quad, Pentium Dual-Core	Core 2 Duo/Quad/Extreme
800/1066/1333MHz	800/1066/1333MHz	800/1066/1333MHz	800/1066/1333MHz
8GB	8GB	8GB	8GB
Dual-Channel	Dual-Channel	Dual-Channel	Dual-Channel
DDR2 667/800	DDR2 667/800	DDR3 800/1066/1333, DDR2 667/800/1066	DDR3 800/1066/1333, DDR2 667/800/1066
GMA 3100	GMA X3500, Clear Video Technology	No	No
1 PCIe x16	1 PCIe x16	1 PCIe x16, 1 PCIe x4	2 PCIe x16 2.0
ICH9 family	ICH8 family	ICH9 family	ICH9 family

P43	Q45	G45	P45	X48
Eaglelake	Eaglelake	Eaglelake	Eaglelake	Bearlake
June 2008	Sep. 2008	June 2008	June 2008	March 2008
Core 2 Duo/Quad, Pentium Dual-Core	Core 2 Duo/Quad, Pentium Dual-Core	Core 2 Duo/Quad, Pentium Dual-Core	Core 2 Duo/Quad, Pentium Dual-Core	Core 2 Duo/Quad/ Extreme, Pentium Dual-Core
800/1066/1333MHz	800/1066/1333MHz	800/1066/1333MHz	800/1066/1333MHz	1066/1333/1600MHz
16GB	16GB	16GB	16GB	8GB
Dual-Channel	Dual-Channel	Dual-Channel	Dual-Channel	Dual-Channel
DDR3 800/1066, DDR2 667/800	DDR3 800/1066, DDR2 667/800	DDR3 800/1066, DDR2 667/800	DDR3 800/1066/1333, DDR2 667/800/1066	DDR3 1066/1333/1600, DDR2 800/1066 533/667/800/1066
No	GMA X4500	GMA X4500HD	No	No
1 PCIe x16 2.0	1 PCIe x16 2.0	1 PCIe x16 2.0	1 PCIe x16 2.0, 2 PCIe x8 2.0	2 PCIe x16 2.0
ICH10 family	ICH10 family	ICH10 family	ICH10 family	ICH9 family

The 3x and 4x series chipsets are designed as a two-chip set solution and must be combined with a corresponding ICH chip. The ICH contains interfaces for the SATA ports (some with RAID capability), non-video PCIe slots, USB ports, and integrated HD audio and LAN connections. Table 4.24 shows the specific ICH chips that are used with 3x and 4x series chipsets.

Table 4.24   Intel 3x/4x/5x Chipset I/O Controller Hub (ICH) Specifications (aka South Bridge)

Features	ICH7	ICH7R	ICH8
PATA Support	UDMA-100	UDMA-100	No
SATA Support	3Gbps, 4 drives	3Gbps, 4 drives	3Gbps, 4 drives
SATA RAID	No	0, 1, 10, 5	No
USB 2.0 Support	8 ports	8 ports	10 ports
CMOS/Clock	Yes	Yes	Yes
PCI Support	PCI 2.3, PCIe 1.0a	PCI 2.3, PCIe 1.0a	PCI 2.3, PCIe 1.1
Number of PCI Express Lanes	4	6	6
LPC Support	Yes	Yes	Yes
Power Management	SMM/ACPI 3.0	SMM/ACPI 3.0	SMM/ACPI 3.0
Ethernet	10/100	10/100	10/100/1000
Audio Support	HD Audio	HD Audio	HD Audio

Intel 5x Series Chipsets

The Intel 5x series of chipsets is designed to support the original Core i Series processors. These processors and chipsets have a distinctly different design from previous Intel chipsets and represent a new level of system integration. In fact, the 5x series actually has two completely different subseries, with the first two examples being the X58 IOH (I/O Hub) introduced in November 2008, and the P55 PCH (Platform Controller Hub) introduced in September 2009. Perhaps the biggest difference between the 5x series chipsets and its predecessors is that the memory controller is no longer part of the chipset, having been moved directly into the Core i Series processors instead. Placing the memory controller in the processor means that the memory modules are directly connected to the processor instead of the North Bridge chipset component, allowing for a dedicated connection between the processor and memory. Although this sounds like (and is) a good idea, it's not a new one. This is something that AMD introduced in the Athlon 64 as far back as 2003.

With the memory controller integrated into the processor, the only function left for the North Bridge is to act as an interface to the PCIe video card slots. Because the North Bridge no longer controls memory, Intel changed the name from MCH to IOH in the 5x series chipsets that support socket LGA1366 processors. Figure 4.23 shows the block diagram of a system with a socket LGA1366 Core i Series processor on a motherboard with an X58 Express chipset. In the diagram, you can also see the use of the traditional ICH (I/O Controller Hub), which supports interfacing to SATA, USB, and other components in the system.

ICH8R	ICH9	ICH9R	ICH10	ICH10R
No	No	No	No	No
3Gbps, 6 drives	3Gbps, 6 drives	3Gbps, 6 drives	3Gbps, 6 drives	3Gbps, 6 drives
0, 1, 10, 5	No	0, 1, 10, 5	No	0, 1, 10, 5
10 ports	12 ports	12 ports	12 ports	12 ports
Yes	Yes	Yes	Yes	Yes
PCI 2.3, PCIe 1.1	PCI 2.3, PCIe 1.1	PCI 2.3, PCIe 1.1	PCI 2.3, PCIe 1.1	PCI 2.3, PCIe 1.1
6	6	6	6	6
Yes	Yes	Yes	Yes	Yes
SMM/ACPI 3.0	SMM/ACPI 3.0b	SMM/ACPI 3.0b	SMM/ACPI 3.0b	SMM/ACPI 3.0b
10/100/1000	10/100/1000	10/100/1000	10/100/1000	10/100/1000
HD Audio	HD Audio	HD Audio	HD Audio	HD Audio

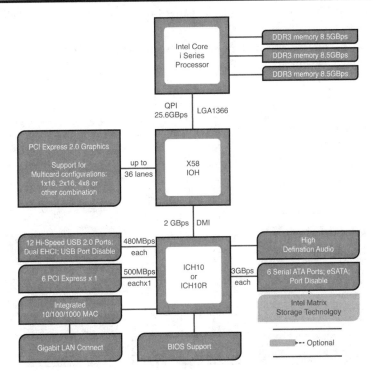

FIGURE 4.23 Block diagram of a system with a socket LGA1366 Core i Series processor and an X58 Express chipset.

Currently, the only 5x series chipset for socket LGA1366 processors is the X58 Express, for which Table 4.25 lists the features.

Table 4.25   Intel 5x Chipset for Socket LGA1366 Processors

Chipset	X58 Express
Code Name	Tylersburg
Date Introduced	Nov. 2008
Part Number	82X58 (IOH)
Supported CPUs	Core i Series w/socket LGA1366
CPU FSB	6.4GTps QPI (25.6GBps)
Integrated Graphics	No
External Graphics	2 PCIe 2.0 x16
I/O Controller Hub	ICH10 family

In systems using socket LGA1156 Core i Series processors, Intel has taken this component consolidation even further by incorporating not only the memory controller, but also the PCI Express video interface directly into the processor. In effect, this means that Intel has built the entire North Bridge part of the chipset right into the processor, reducing the motherboard chipset from two chips down to one. The remaining South Bridge chip has the same functions as what Intel previously called the ICH, but to differentiate it from previous designs, it changed the designation to PCH (Platform Controller Hub) instead.

Figure 4.24 shows the block diagram of a system with a socket LGA1156 Core i Series processor on a motherboard with a P55 chipset. In the diagram you can see that the functionality of the North Bridge is now part of the CPU, reducing the chipset to a single South Bridge (now called PCH) component.

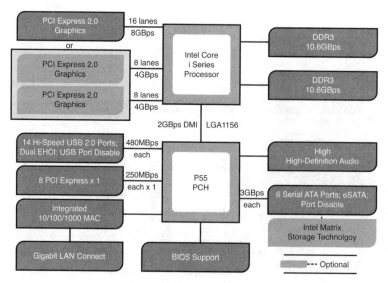

FIGURE 4.24   Block diagram of a system with a socket LGA1156 Core i Series processor and a P55 chipset.

By building the external video interface directly into the processor, Intel is also able to produce processors with integrated graphics processing. Several of the 5x series chipsets (such as the H55, H57, and Q57) support the FDI (Flexible Display Interface), which requires a Core i Series processor with integrated graphics. Using FDI, video signals are sent from the GPU in the processor to the PCH, which then implements the physical interface to the display (that is, DisplayPort, HDMI, DVI, or VGA). Table 4.26 shows the 5x series chipsets for socket LGA1156 Core i Series processors.

Table 4.26 Intel 5x Chipsets for Socket LGA1156 Core i Series Processors

Chipset	H55	P55	H57	Q57	P57
Code Name	Ibex Peak	Ibex Peak	Ibex Peak	Ibex Peak	Ibex Peak
Date Introduced	Dec. 2009	Sep. 2009	Dec. 2009	Dec. 2009	Dec. 2009
Part Number	BD82H55 (PCH)	BD82P55 (PCH)	BD82H57 (PCH)	BD82Q57 (PCH)	BD82P57 (PCH)
Supported CPUs	Core i Series w/ socket LGA1156	Core i Series w/ socket LGA1156	Core i Series w/ socket LGA1156	Core i Series w/ socket LGA1156	Core i Series w/ socket LGA1156
CPU FSB	2.5GTps DMI (2GBps)	2.5GTps DMI (2GBps)	2.5GTps DMI (2GBps)	2.5GTps DMI (2GBps)	2.5GTps DMI (2GBps)
Flexible Display Interface	Yes	No	Yes	Yes	No
PCI Express Lanes	6 PCIe 2.0	8 PCIe 2.0	8 PCIe 2.0	8 PCIe 2.0	8 PCIe 2.0
SATA Support	3.0Gbps, 6 drives	3.0Gbps, 6 drives	3.0Gbps, 6 drives	3.0Gbps, 6 drives	3.0Gbps, 6 drives
USB 2.0 Support	12 ports	14 ports	14 ports	14 Ports	14 ports

Intel 6x Series Chipsets

The Intel 6x series of chipsets is designed to support the 2nd generation Core i Series processors (code-named Sandy Bridge). These chipsets are similar to the 5x series, with the main differences being faster transfer rates on several of the interfaces and support for newer processors. The first chipsets in the 6x series were introduced in January 2011.

Like the 5x series chipsets, the 6x series consists of only a South Bridge component called the PCH (Platform Controller Hub), since the circuitry normally associated with the North Bridge (that is, memory controller, optional graphics) has been integrated into the processor.

Figure 4.25 shows the block diagram of a system with a socket LGA1155 2nd generation Core i Series processor on a motherboard with a P67 chipset. In the diagram, you can see that the functionality of the North Bridge is now part of the CPU, reducing the chipset to a single South Bridge (now called PCH) component.

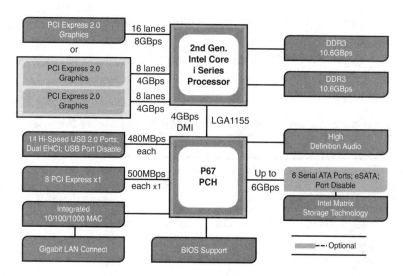

FIGURE 4.25   Block diagram of a system with a socket LGA1155 2nd gen. Core i Series processor and a P67 chipset.

By building the external video interface directly into the processor, Intel is also able to produce processors with integrated graphics processing. Most of the 6x series chipsets support the FDI (Flexible Display Interface), which requires a Core i Series processor with integrated graphics. Using FDI, video signals are sent from the GPU in the processor to the PCH, which then implements the physical interface to the display (that is, DisplayPort, HDMI, DVI, or VGA). Table 4.27 shows the 6x series chipsets for socket LGA1155 2nd generation Core i Series processors.

Table 4.27   Intel 6x Chipsets for Socket LGA1155 2nd Generation Core i Series Processors

Chipset	H67	P67	Q67	Q65	B65	H61
Code Name	Cougar Point	Cougar Point	Cougar Point	Cougar Point	Cougar Point	Cougar Point
Date Introduced	Jan. 2011	Jan. 2011	Jan. 2011	Jan. 2011	Jan. 2011	Jan. 2011
Supported CPUs	2nd gen. Core i Series w/socket LGA1155	2nd gen. Core i Series w/socket LGA1155	2nd gen. Core i Series w/socket LGA1155	2nd gen. Core i Series w/socket LGA1155	2nd gen. Core i Series w/socket LGA1155	2nd gen. Core i Series w/socket LGA1155
CPU FSB	5GTps DMI (4GBps)	5GTps DMI (4GBps)	5GTps DMI (4GBps)	5GTps DMI (4GBps)	5GTps DMI (4GBps)	5GTps DMI (4GBps)
Flexible Display Interface	Yes	No	Yes	Yes	Yes	Yes
PCI Express Lanes	8 PCIe 2.0	8 PCIe 2.0	8 PCIe 2.0	8 PCIe 2.0	8 PCIe 2.0	6 PCIe 2.0
6.0Gbps SATA Support	2 drives	2 drives	2 drives	1 drive	1 drive	None
3.0Gbps SATA Support	4 drives	4 drives	4 drives	5 drives	5 drives	4 drives
USB 2.0 Support	14 ports	14 ports	14 ports	14 ports	12 ports	10 ports

Just a few weeks after the 6x chipsets were released, there was a minor problem found with the 3Gbps SATA ports in the B2 and earlier steppings. Due to a voltage and internal current leakage problem, the ports could degrade over time, eventually causing read errors. This problem did not affect the 6Gbps SATA ports, so one workaround was to only connect drives to those ports. Intel quickly issued a recall, as did all motherboard and system manufacturers that had sold motherboards with the affected B2 step chips. Intel began shipping fixed B3 stepping chipsets to motherboard manufacturers in February 2011, and new motherboards with the fixed chipsets were on the market by April 2011. Any motherboards or systems sold after that date should be unaffected by this problem.

Intel 7x Series Chipsets

The Intel 7x series of chipsets is designed to support the 3rd generation Core i Series processors (code-named Ivy Bridge). These chipsets are similar to the 6x series, with the main difference being integrated USB 3.0 ports. Most of these chipsets also support Sandy Bridge processors, but a BIOS upgrade might be necessary on some motherboards.

Figure 4.26 shows the block diagram of a system with a socket LGA1155 3rd generation Core i Series processor on a motherboard with a Z77 chipset.

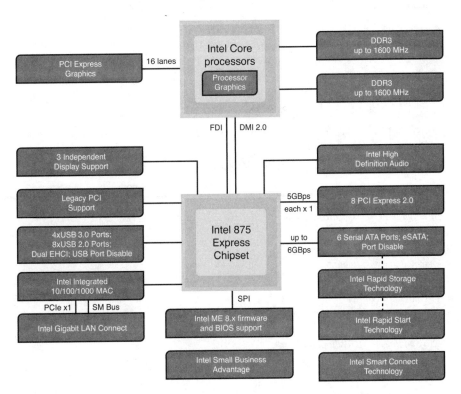

FIGURE 4.26 Intel Core i-series 3rd-generation processor and Z77 chipset block diagram.

Table 4.28 shows the 7x series chipsets for socket LGA1155 3rd generation Core i Series processors.

Table 4.28   Intel 7x Chipsets for Socket LGA1155 3rd Generation Core i Series Processors

Chipset	Z77	Z75	Q77	Q75	H77	B75
Code Name	Panther Point	Panther Point	Panther Point	Panther Point	Panther Point	Panther Point
Date Introduced	2 Q 2012	2 Q 2012	2 Q 2012	2 Q 2012	2 Q 2012	2 Q 2012
Supported CPUs	3rd. Core i Series w/socket LGA1155	3rd gen. Core i Series w/socket LGA1155	3rd gen. Core i Series w/socket LGA1155	3rd gen. Core i Series w/socket LGA1155	3rd gen. Core i Series w/socket LGA1155	3rd gen. Core Series w/socket LGA1155
CPU FSB	5GTps DMI (4GBps)	5GTps DMI (4GBps)	5GTps DMI (4GBps)	5GTps DMI (4GBps)	5GTps DMI (4GBps)	5GTps DMI (4GBps)
Flexible Display Interface	Yes	Yes	Yes	Yes	Yes	Yes
PCI Express Lanes	8 PCIe 2.0	8 PCIe 2.0	8 PCIe 2.0	8 PCIe 2.0	8 PCIe 2.0	6 PCIe 2.0
6.0Gbps SATA Support	2 drives	2 drives	2 drives	2 drives	1 drive	1 drive
3.0Gbps SATA Support	4 drives	4 drives	4 drives	5 drives	5 drives	5 drives
3.0Gbps eSATA Support	Yes	Yes	Yes	Yes	Yes	Yes
PCI Support	No	No	Yes	Yes	No	Yes
10/100/1000 Ethernet	Yes	Yes	Yes	Yes	Yes	Yes
HD Audio	Yes	Yes	Yes	Yes	Yes	Yes
Additional Features*	1, 2, 3, 5, 7, 8, 9, 10	1, 2, 3, 5, 7, 8, 9	1, 2, 3, 4, 5, 6, 7, 8	1, 2, 3, 5	1, 2, 3, 4, 5	2, 3, 4, 5
USB 2.0 Support	10 ports	10 ports	10 ports	10 ports	10 ports	8 ports
USB 3.0 Support	4 ports	4 ports	4 ports	4 ports	4 ports	4 ports

Some features optional; see specifications for specific motherboard using this chipset for details.

1 = Intel Rapid Storage Technology
2 = Intel Rapid Start Technology
3 = Intel Smart Connect Technology
4 = Intel Small Business Advantage
5 = Intel Anti-Theft Technology
6 = Intel Virtualization Technology for Directed I/O (VT-D)
7 = Intel Trusted Execution Technology
8 = Intel Active Management Technology
9 = Intel Extreme Tuning Support
10 = Intel Smart Response Technology

Table 4.29 provides more information about the advanced and optional features noted in Table 4.28.

Table 4.29   Advanced and Optional Features in Intel 7x Chipsets

Feature	Benefit
Intel Rapid Storage Technology	Enhanced version of Intel Matrix Storage Technology, supports SATA RAID 1, 5, and 10 and eSATA up to 3Gbps
Intel Rapid Start Technology	Faster system startup on computers with SSDs; works with Smart Response Technology
Intel Smart Connect Technology	Automatic updates of cloud-based information (social networks, email, news) from the S3 standby state
Intel Small Business Advantage	Network and system management features for small business networks
Intel Anti-Theft Technology (Intel AT)	Protects data on laptops and ultrabooks by disabling access
Intel Virtualization Technology for Directed I/O (VT-D)	Enhances virtualized connections to hardware
Intel Trusted Execution Technology	Hardware-based malware protection
Intel Active Management Technology (Intel AMT)	Features for better management and protection of systems over corporate networks
Intel Extreme Tuning Support	Support for maintaining standard clock rates to other system components even when processor is overclocked
Intel Smart Response Technology	Intelligent caching of application and data blocks to the system's SSD to improve system responsiveness; works with Smart Response Technology

Third-Party Chipsets for Intel Processors

Over the years, SiS, ULi (now part of NVIDIA), ATI (now part of AMD), and VIA have produced chipsets for Intel processors. The following sections discuss some of the more popular versions of these chipsets by vendor.

SiS Chipsets

SiS offered several chipsets for Intel processors, including integrated chipsets, chipsets for use with discrete video accelerator cards, and some that support Rambus RDRAM. SiS chipsets for the Pentium 4 and Pentium D use one of several high-speed South Bridge equivalents (SiS 96x series Media I/O chips) instead of integrating North and South Bridge functions into a single chip. SiS North and South Bridge chips for the Pentium 4 and Pentium D use a high-speed 16-bit connection known as MuTIOL (Multi-Threaded I/O Link) instead of the slow PCI bus as with older chipsets.

For more information about SiS chipsets made for the Pentium 4 and Pentium D, see "SiS Chipsets," in Chapter 4, "Motherboards and Buses," of *Upgrading and Repairing PCs,* 19th Edition, found in its entirety on the DVD packaged with this book.

ULi Electronics Chipsets

ULi Electronics (formerly known as ALi Corporation and Acer Laboratories, and later acquired by NVIDIA) has produced several chipsets for the Pentium 4 and Celeron 4 processors, such as the Aladdin P4 and the M168x series. ULi also produced several South Bridge chips in the M15xx series for the Pentium 4 as well as AMD Athlon XP and Athlon 64 processors.

For more information about ULi (ALi) chipsets made for the Pentium 4, see "ULi Electronics Chipsets," in Chapter 4, "Motherboards and Buses," of *Upgrading and Repairing PCs*, 19th Edition, found in its entirety on the DVD packaged with this book.

ATI Chipsets

ATI's original line of chipsets for the Pentium 4 integrated Radeon VE-level 3D graphics, DVD play-back, and dual-display features with high-performance North Bridge and South Bridge designs. ATI used its high-speed A-Link bus to connect its North and South Bridge chips. These included the ATI IGP 330/340/350/360 series. The Radeon 9x00 IGP family was ATI's second generation of chipsets for the Pentium 4. The 9x00 IGP North Bridge chips featured Radeon 9200-level graphics with DirectX 8.1 hardware support and support for multiple monitors. On the other hand, the companion IXP 300 South Bridge supported Serial ATA and USB 2.0 as well as six-channel audio. The Radeon 9x00 IGP family included the 9100 IGP, 9100 Pro IGP, and 9000 Pro IGP.

ATI's line of Pentium 4/Core2–compatible chipsets included the RC410 (integrates Radeon X300 3D graphics) and the RS400 (integrates Radeon X300 3D graphics and includes support for PCI Express x16 video). Both were sold under the Radeon Xpress 200 brand name. Although ATI had made South Bridge chips in the past, its Radeon Xpress 200 North Bridge chips could be paired with either ATI's own IXP 450 or ULi's M157x South Bridge chips. ATI's South Bridge chips included the IXP 150, 200, 250, 300, 400, and 450.

For a comparison chart of ATI chipsets for the Pentium 4, see "ATI Chipsets," in Chapter 4, "Motherboards and Buses," of *Upgrading and Repairing PCs*, 19th Edition, found in its entirety on the DVD packaged with this book.

VIA Chipsets

VIA Technologies produced a number of chipsets for Pentium 4 processors in its P4X, P4M, PT8 and PM8 series, as well as South Bridge chips (VT series). The PT8 and PM series also supported Intel's Core 2 processors. Although VIA Technologies still lists a wide range of chipsets on its website (www.via.com.tw), the website states: "*Note: VIA no longer sells some or all of these chipsets."

For a comparison of VIA Technologies' chipsets for Pentium 4, see "VIA Chipsets," in Chapter 4, "Motherboards and Buses," of *Upgrading and Repairing PCs*, 19th Edition, found in its entirety on the DVD packaged with this book.

NVIDIA Chipsets for Intel Processors

Although NVIDIA is not licensed to produce chipsets for the Intel i-series Core processors, it offered a wide variety of chipsets for Intel processors from the Pentium 4 through the Core 2 Extreme series until withdrawing from the business in 2010. The final offerings included the nForce 600 and nForce 700i series, and the GeForce 7 and GeForce 9000 series with integrated video.

The 600i series included support for Gigabit Ethernet, DDR2 memory, PCIe 1.x, SATA and PATA drives with RAID support, and HD audio. Some models also included support for two-way SLI.

The 700i series included support for Gigabit Ethernet, two or three-way SLI, SATA and PATA drives with RAID support, and PCIe version 2.0. DDR2 or DDR3 memory was supported, depending upon the specific chipset in use.

The GeForce 9000 series included support for DDR2 or DDR3 memory, Gigabit Ethernet, SATA 3Gbps, HD Audio, and DirectX 10 graphics.

The GeForce 7 series was based on the nForce 600 series and supports DDR2 memory, DirectX 9.0 Shader model 3 graphics, PCIe x16 and x1, HD Audio, and RAID. Most models supported Gigabit Ethernet.

Chipsets for AMD Processors

AMD took a gamble with its Athlon family of processors. With these processors, AMD decided for the first time to create a chip that was Intel compatible with regard to software but not directly hardware or pin compatible. Whereas the K6 series would plug into the same Socket 7 that Intel designed for the Pentium processor line, the AMD Athlon and Duron would not be pin compatible with the Pentium II/III and Celeron chips. This also meant that AMD could not take advantage of the previously existing chipsets and motherboards when the Athlon and Duron were introduced; instead, AMD would have to either create its own chipsets and motherboards or find other companies that would.

The gamble has paid off. AMD bootstrapped the market by introducing its own chipset, referred to as the AMD-750 chipset (code-named Irongate). The AMD 750 chipset consists of the 751 system controller (North Bridge) and the 756 peripheral bus controller (South Bridge). AMD followed with the AMD-760 chipset for the Athlon/Duron processors, which was the first major chipset on the market supporting DDR SDRAM for memory. It consisted of two chips—the AMD-761 system bus controller (North Bridge) and the AMD-766 peripheral bus controller (South Bridge). Similarly, AMD established a new standard chipset architecture for its line of 64-bit processors—the Athlon 64 and Opteron—by developing the AMD-8000 chipset. AMD's pioneering efforts inspired other companies, such as VIA Technologies, NVIDIA, SiS, and ATI (now part of AMD) to develop chipsets specifically designed to interface with AMD processors. In 2006, AMD purchased ATI, essentially bringing both motherboard chipsets and video processors in-house. This put AMD on a level more equal to Intel because it gave the company the capability to produce most of the chips necessary to build a system around its processors. Since then, AMD and NVIDIA have produced the majority of chipsets for AMD-based systems, and, since the withdrawal of NVIDIA from the chipset business in 2010, AMD is now the only vendor of chipsets for its processors.

AMD Athlon Chipsets

The original AMD Athlon was a Slot A processor chip, but subsequent versions used Socket A—as do the Athlon XP, Duron, and some versions of the Sempron. Although similar in some ways to the Pentium III and Celeron, the AMD chips use a different interface and require different chipsets. AMD was originally the only supplier for Athlon chipsets, but VIA Technology, ULi Electronics, SiS, and NVIDIA produced a large number of chipsets with a range of features.

AMD produced several chipsets for Athlon and Duron processors: the AMD-750 and AMD-760/MP/MPX. The major features of these chipsets are compared in Table 4.30 and described in greater detail in the following sections.

Table 4.30   AMD Athlon/Duron Processor Chipsets Using North/South Bridge Architecture

Chipset	AMD-750	AMD-760
Code Name	Irongate	None
Date Introduced	Aug. 1999	Oct. 2000
Part Number	AMD-751	AMD-761
Bus Speed	200MHz	200/266MHz

Table 4.30 Continued

Chipset	AMD-750	AMD-760
Supported Processors	Athlon/Duron	Athlon/Duron
SMP (Dual CPUs)	No	Yes
Memory Type	SDRAM	DDR SDRAM
Memory Speed	PC100	PC1600/PC2100
Parity/ECC	Both	Both
Maximum Memory	768MB	2GB buffered, 4GB registered
PCI Support	2.2	2.2
AGP Support	AGP 2x	AGP 4x
South Bridge	AMD-756	AMD-766
ATA/IDE Support	ATA-66	ATA-100
USB Support	1C/4P	1C/4P
CMOS/Clock	Yes	Yes
ISA Support	Yes	No
LPC Support	No	Yes
Power Management	SMM/ACPI	SMM/ACPI

AGP = Accelerated graphics port
ATA = AT attachment (IDE) interface
DDR-SDRAM = Double data rate SDRAM
ECC = Error-correcting code
ISA = Industry Standard Architecture
LPC = Low-pin-count bus
PCI = Peripheral Component Interconnect
SDRAM = Synchronous dynamic RAM
SMP = Symmetric multiprocessing (dual processors)
USB = Universal serial bus

AMD Athlon 64 Chipsets

The Athlon 64 processor required a new generation of chipsets, both to support its 64-bit processor architecture and to allow for integration of the memory controller into the processor. (The memory controller has traditionally been located in the North Bridge chip or equivalent.) As a consequence, some vendors do not use the term *North Bridge* to refer to the chipset component that connects the processor to AGP video.

AMD 8000 (8151) Chipset

The AMD 8000 was AMD's first chipset designed for the Athlon 64 and Opteron families. Its architecture was substantially different from the North Bridge/South Bridge or hub-based architectures we are familiar with from the chipsets designed to support Pentium II/III/4/Celeron and AMD Athlon/Athlon XP/Duron processors.

The AMD-8000 chipset was often referred to as the *AMD-8151* because the AMD-8151 provided the connection between the Athlon 64 or Opteron processor and the AGP video slot—the task usually performed by the North Bridge or MCH hub in other chipsets. The name of the North Bridge or MCH hub chip is usually applied to the chipset. However, AMD referred to the AMD-8151 chip as the AGP Graphics Tunnel chip because its only task was to provide a high-speed connection to the AGP slot on the motherboard. The other components of the AMD-8000 chipset included the AMD-8111 HyperTransport I/O hub (South Bridge) and the AMD-8131 PCI-X Tunnel chip.

Due to delays in the development of the AMD-8151 AGP Graphics Tunnel chip, most vendors through late 2003 used the AMD-8111 HyperTransport I/O hub alone or along with the AMD-8131 PCI-X Tunnel chip to provide a mixture of PCI and PCI-X slots on motherboards optimized as servers. Newer systems have incorporated the AMD-8151 chip to provide AGP video, but the AMD-8000 chipset was used primarily as a workstation/server chipset instead of as a desktop chipset.

The AMD-8151 AGP Graphics tunnel has the following major features:

- Supports AGP 2.0/3.0 (AGP 1x–8x) graphics cards
- 16-bit up/down HyperTransport connection to the processor
- 8-bit up/down HyperTransport connection to downstream chips

Following are the AMD-8111 HyperTransport I/O hub (South Bridge) chip's major features:

- PCI 2.2-compliant PCI bus (32-bit, 33MHz) for up to eight devices
- AC'97 2.2 audio (six-channel)
- Six USB 1.1/2.0 ports (three controllers)
- Two ATA/IDE host adapters supporting up to ATA-133 speeds
- Real-time clock (RTC)
- LPC bus
- Integrated 10/100 Ethernet
- Eight-bit up/down HyperTransport connection to upstream chips

The AMD-8131 HyperTransport PCI-X tunnel chip's major features include these:

- Two PCI-X bridges (A and B) supporting up to five PCI bus masters each
- PCI-X transfer rates up to 133MHz
- PCI 2.2 33MHz and 66MHz transfer rates
- Independent operational modes and transfer rates for each bridge
- Eight-bit up/down HyperTransport connection to upstream and downstream chips

Figure 4.27 shows the architecture of the AMD-8151 chipset for Athlon 64.

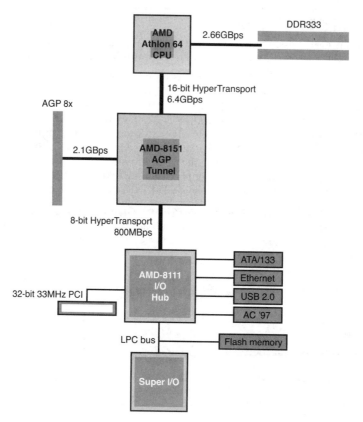

FIGURE 4.27 Block diagram of the AMD 8000 chipset for Athlon 64.

AMD (Formerly ATI) Chipsets for Athlon 64, Sempron, Phenom

One of the expectations of AMD's acquisition of ATI in 2006 was the release of AMD/ATI chipsets for AMD processors. Since then, AMD has released several to support the Athlon 64, Sempron, and Phenom processors. Tables 4.26 through 4.29 summarize the major features of these chipsets, and Table 4.30 covers the corresponding South Bridge components.

While Intel chipsets are closely tailored to particular Intel processor families, AMD North Bridge and South Bridge components can be mixed and matched. Thus, you may find motherboards based on the same North Bridge component to have different features depending upon the South Bridge component used.

AMD (ATI) 480X and 500-Series Chipsets

The 480X, 570X (aka 550X), and 580X chipsets were the last chipsets developed by ATI before the AMD takeover. All three could be used with the ATI-developed SB600, although the 480X could also be paired with the ULi M1575 South Bridge. All chipsets in this family included some level of support for ATI (now AMD) CrossFire dual-GPU rendering, but only the 580X supported both PCIe x16 slots running in x16 mode. See Table 4.31 for details.

When paired with the SB600, these chipsets included 7.1 High-Definition Audio, 10 USB 2.0 ports, one PATA/133 port, and four SATA 3Gbps ports. The SATA ports could be operated in RAID 0, 1, 0+1, and RAID 10 modes. See Table 4.30 for a comparison of AMD (ATI) South Bridge chips.

AMD 690 Series

AMD's 690 series of chipsets included the 690V and 690G. Both supported integrated video, but the 690G offered faster integrated video with support for HDMI, dual-link DVI-D output, and support for HDCP encryption for Blu-ray and HDTV playback. The 690V supported only VGA output. These chipsets also used the SB600 South Bridge. See Table 4.31 for details.

Table 4.31 AMD/ATI 400, 500, and 600 Series Chipsets for Phenom, Athlon 64, and Sempron Processors

Features	480X, CrossFire Xpress 1600	570X, 550X, CrossFire Xpress 3100	580X, CrossFire Xpress 3200	690V	690G
Code Name	RD480	RD570	RD580	RS690C	RS690
Date Introduced	Oct. 2006	June 2007	Oct. 2006	Feb. 2007	Feb. 2007
Supported CPUs	Athlon 64, Sempron	Phenom, Athlon 64, Sempron	Phenom, Athlon 64, Sempron	Athlon 64, Sempron	Phenom, Athlon 64, Sempron
CPU FSB	1GTps (2GBps)	1GTps (2GBps)	1GTps (2GBps)	1GTps (2GBps)	1GTps (2GBps)
CrossFire Enabled	Yes, x8+x8	Yes, x16+x8	Yes, x16+x16	No	No
PCIe Version	1.0a	1.0a	1.0a	1.0a	1.0a
Total Number of PCIe Lanes	20	26	36	20	20
Integrated Video	No	No	No	Yes	Yes
South Bridge	SB600; ULi M1575	SB600	SB600	SB600	SB600

AMD 700 Series Chipsets

The AMD 700 series of chipsets were in the process of development by ATI when ATI was absorbed into AMD in late 2006, although the first models in the series were not released until late 2007. See Table 4.32 to compare the features of these chipsets.

The 740 and 740G are the last AMD (ATI) chipsets to support PCIe version 1.0a; all others in the series support PCIe version 2, which doubles the throughput of PCIe 1.x. The 740 and 740G are also the last cards with 1GTps FSB; the remainder of the series features 2.6GTps FSB.

The 760G and 780G are the first chipsets to support CrossFire Hybrid, a variation of CrossFire that enables integrated video to work in conjunction with a PCIe x16 video card for faster 3D rendering and gaming; the 785G, the last chipset in the series, also supports CrossFire Hybrid. The 790GX supports both CrossFire Hybrid and CrossFire X for faster 3D rendering and gaming. The 770 and higher models introduced AMD OverDrive, which enables the user to perform overclocking, memory tuning, and system monitoring tasks from the Windows desktop without restarting the computer.

The high-performance 790FX is the first AMD chipset to support quad CrossFire X (up to four PCIe video cards in x8 mode) as well as dual x16 operation.

While some members of the series can use the SB600 South Bridge, AMD introduced a new series of South Bridge chips in the 700 series for use with the 700 series North Bridge chips. The SB700 series includes support for SATA 3Gbps devices, eSATA support, RAID support (0, 1, 10 modes), up to 12 USB 2.0 ports, and two USB 1.1 ports. Some also include integrated Super I/O and RAID 5 support.

Table 4.32 AMD/ATI 700 Series Chipsets for Phenom, Athlon 64, and Sempron Processors

Features	740	740G	760G	770
Code Name	RX740	RS740	RS780L	RX780
Date Introduced	2008	2008	2009	Nov. 2007
Supported CPUs	Phenom, Athlon 64, Sempron	Phenom, Athlon 64, Sempron	Phenom, Athlon 64, Sempron	Phenom, Athlon 64, Sempron
CPU FSB	1GTps (2GBps)	1GTps (2GBps)	2.6GTps (5.2GBps)	2.6GTps (5.2GBps)
CrossFire Enabled	No	No	Hybrid	No
OverDrive Enabled	No	No	No	Yes
PCIe Version	1.0a	1.0a	2.0	2.0
Total Number of PCIe Lanes	20	20	20	22
Integrated Video	No	Yes	Yes	No
South Bridge	SB600, SB700, SB750	SB600, SB700, SB710, SB750	SB600, SB700, SB710, SB750	SB700, SB710, SB750

AMD 800 Series Chipsets

AMD's 800 series chipsets are designed for use with Socket AM3 processors such as the Phenom II, Athlon II, and some models of the Sempron. In addition to supporting newer processors, the 800 series also includes models with support for CrossFire Hybrid (880G and 890GX), two card CrossFire X (890GX and 890FX), and up to four card CrossFire X (890FX). All chipsets in the 800 series include PCIe 2.0 and a 2.6GTps FSB. See Table 4.33 for details.

The 800 series also includes two new South Bridge chips: the SB810 and SB850. These chipsets are the first AMD South Bridge chips to eliminate support for the venerable PATA interface but include support for up to six SATA ports with RAID support, include Gigabit SATA, and HD audio. The 800 series also includes two PCIe 2.0 lanes (2 x1 or 1 x2).

Table 4.33 AMD/ATI800 Series Chipsets for Phenom II, Athlon II, and Sempron Processors

Features	870	880G	890GX	890FX
Code Name	RX880	RS880	RS880D	RD890
Date Introduced	2009	2009	2009	2009
Supported CPUs	Phenom II, Athlon II, Sempron	Phenom II, Athlon II, Sempron	Phenom II, Athlon II, Sempron	Phenom II, Athlon II, Sempron
CPU FSB	2.6GTps (5.2GBps)	2.6GTps (5.2GBps)	2.6GTps (5.2GBps)	2.6GTps (5.2GBps)
CrossFire Enabled	No	Hybrid	Yes, x8+x8 or Hybrid	Yes, x8+x8+8x+8x or x16+x16
PCIe Version	2.0	2.0	2.0	2.0
Total Number of PCIe Lanes (NB)	22	22	22	38
Integrated Video	No	Yes	Yes	No
South Bridge	SB600, SB700, SB750	SB600, SB750	SB710, SB750, SB810, SB850	SB710, SB750, SB810, SB850

780G	780V	790GX	790X	790FX	785G
RS780	RS780C	RS780D	RD780	RD790	RS880
2008	2008	2008	Nov. 2007	Nov. 2007	2009
Phenom, Athlon 64, Sempron	Phenom, Athlon 64, Sempron	Phenom, Athlon 64, Sempron	Phenom, Athlon 64, Sempron	Phenom, Athlon 64, Sempron	Phenom, Athlon 64, Sempron
2.6GTps (5.2GBps)	2.6GTps (5.2GBps)	2.6GTps (5.2GBps)	2.6GTps (5.2GBps)	2.6GTps (5.2GBps)	4GTps (8GBps)
Hybrid	No	Yes, x8+x8	and Hybrid Yes, x8+x8	Yes, x8+x8+x8+x8 or x16+x16	Hybrid
Yes	Yes	Yes	Yes	Yes	Yes
2.0	2.0	2.0	2.0	2.0	2.0
22	22	22	22	38	22
Yes	Yes	Yes	No	No	Yes
SB750	SB750	SB600, SB700, SB750	SB600, SB750	SB710, SB750, SB810, SB850	SB710, SB750, SB810, SB850

AMD 900 Series Chipsets

AMD's 900 series chipsets are designed to support FX "Bulldozer" and "Piledriver" processors that use the AM3+ processor socket. These chipsets can also support Socket AM3 processors when a suitable BIOS is installed.

All 900-series chipsets use the latest HyperTransport version 3.1 interconnect to achieve an FSB speed of 3.2GTps, and the first three chipsets in the series support various levels of ATI CrossFire X and NVIDIA SLI for multi-GPU 3D gaming and rendering. See Table 4.34 for details.

The SB920 and SB950 South Bridge chips include support for up to six SATA 6Gbps devices, RAID, HD Audio, and four PCIe x1 slots. See Table 4.35 for details.

Figure 4.28 illustrates the 990FX chipset's block diagram.

Table 4.34 AMD 900 Series Chipsets for FX, Phenom II, Athlon II, and Sempron Processors

Features	970	980G	990X	990FX
Code Name	RD970	RD980	RD990	RD990
Date Introduced	2011	2011	2011	2011
Supported CPUs	FX ("Bulldozer," "Piledriver,") Phenom, Phenom II, Athlon II, Athlon	FX ("Bulldozer," "Piledriver,") Phenom, Phenom II, Athlon II, Athlon	FX ("Bulldozer," "Piledriver,") Phenom, Phenom II, Athlon II, Athlon	FX ("Bulldozer," "Piledriver,") Phenom, Phenom II, Athlon II, Athlon
CPU FSB	3.2GTps (6.4GBps)	3.2GTps (6.4GBps)	3.2GTps (6.4GBps)	3.2GTps (6.4GBps)
CrossFire Enabled	No*	No*	Yes, x8+x8	Yes, x8+x8+8x+8x or x16+x16

Table 4.34   Continued

Features	970	980G	990X	990FX
PCIe Version	2.0	2.0	2.0	2.0
Total Number of PCIe Lanes (NB)	22	22	22	42
Integrated Video	No	Yes	No	No
South Bridge	SB920, SB950	SB920, SB950	SB920, SB950	SB920, SB950

Some motherboard makers configure systems with two PCIe slots running in x8 mode for CrossFire X and SLI support.

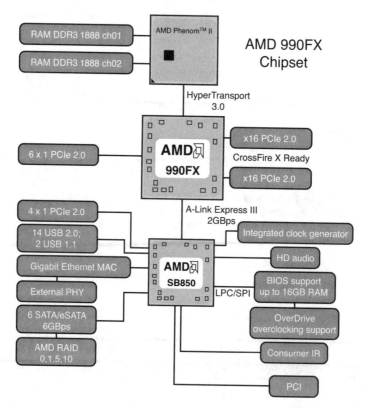

FIGURE 4.28 Block diagram of the AMD 990FX chipset for Socket AM3+ processors.

Table 4.35   AMD/ATI Chipset South Bridge Components

Features	SB600	SB700	SB710	SB750	SB810	SB850	SB920	SB950
Date Introduced	2006	2007	2008	2008	2010	2010	2011	2011
SATA Ports	4 drives, 3Gbps	6 drives, 3Gbps	6 drives, 3Gbps	6 drives, 3Gbps	6 drives, 3Gbps	6 drives, 6Gbps	6 drives, 6Gbps	6 drives, 6Gbps

Features	SB600	SB700	SB710	SB750	SB810	SB850	SB920	SB950
USB 2.0 Ports	10	12	12	12	14	14	14	14
USB 1.1 Ports	—	2	2	2	2	2	2	2
Audio Support	HD Audio	HD Audio	HD Audio	HD Audio	HD Audio	HD Audio	HD Audio	HD Audio
PATA Support	2 drives, 133MBps	2 drives, 133MBps	2 drives, 133MBps	2 drives, 133MBps	2 drives, 133MBps	2 drives, 133MBps	—	—
Integrated Super I/O	No	Yes	Yes	Yes	Yes	Yes	Yes	Yes
PCIe 2.0 interface	No	No	No	No	Yes (2 x1 or 1 x2)	Yes (2 x1 or 1 x2)	Yes (4 x1)	Yes (4 x1)
Integrated Ethernet	No	No	No	No	Gigabit	Gigabit	Gigabit	Gigabit
RAID Support	RAID 0, 1, 0+1	RAID 0, 1, 0+1	RAID 0, 1, 0+1	RAID 0, 1, 0+1, 5	RAID 0, 1, 10	RAID 0, 1, 10, 5	RAID 0, 1, 10	RAID 0, 1, 10, 5

AMD A-Series Chipsets

AMD's A series chipsets are designed to support AMD desktop APUs (CPUs with integrated graphics) that use the FM1 or FM2 processor sockets. These chipsets are also referred to as Fusion Controller Hubs (FCH) and are single-chip chipsets.

All A-series chipsets use the Unified Media Interface (UMI) interconnect between the APU and the FCH. UMI uses four PCIe 2.0 lanes for a bandwidth of 2GBps, and all include four-channel HD audio and SATA 3Gbps support See Table 4.36 for specific features of each chipset.

Figure 4.29 illustrates the A85 chipset's block diagram.

Table 4.36 AMD A-series Chipsets for AMD Desktop APUs

Features	A45	A55	A75	A85
Code Name	Hudson-D1	Hudson-D2	Hudson-D3	Hudson-D4
Date Introduced	2011	2011	2011	2012
Supported CPUs	"Brazos" FM1 E-series, A-series	"Lynx" FM1 E2-series, A-series	"Lynx" FM1 E2-series, A-series	"Virgo" FM2 A4, A6, A8, A10 5xxx
USB 1.1 ports	2	2	2	2
USB 2.0 ports	14	14	10	10
USB 3.0 ports	0	0	4	4
SATA 3Gbps	6 ports	6 ports	N/A	N/A
SATA 6Gbps	N/A	N/A	6 ports	8 ports

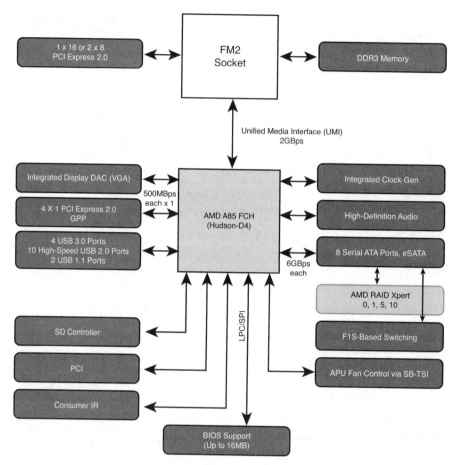

FIGURE 4.29 A block diagram of the A85 chipset for AMD A-series APUs.

Third-Party Chipsets for AMD Processors

Thanks to AMD's encouragement of third-party chipset development for its Athlon and later processor series, a number of chipset vendors developed chipsets for AMD processors, most notably VIA, SiS, and NVIDIA.

VIA Chipsets

Until recently, VIA Technologies, Inc., was the largest chipset and processor supplier outside of Intel and AMD. Originally founded in 1987, VIA is based in Taipei, Taiwan, and is the largest integrated circuit design firm on the island. VIA is a fabless company, which means it farms out the manufacturing to other companies with chip foundry capability.

To learn more about VIA's chipsets for AMD processors, see "VIA Chipsets for AMD" and "VIA Chipsets for Athlon 64" in Chapter 4, "Motherboards and Buses," of *Upgrading and Repairing PCs*, 19th Edition, included in its entirety on the DVD packaged with this book.

SiS Chipsets

SiS has produced a variety of chipsets for the Athlon, Duron, Athlon XP, and Athlon 64 processors, some of which use a single-chip design and others of which use a high-speed two-chip design similar to other vendors' chipsets.

For more information, see "SiS Chipsets for AMD" and "SiS Chipsets for Athlon 64" in Chapter 4, "Motherboards and Buses," of *Upgrading and Repairing PCs*, 19th Edition, included in its entirety on the DVD packaged with this book.

NVIDIA Chipsets

NVIDIA, although best known for its popular GeForce line of graphics chipsets, also became a popular vendor of chipsets for the AMD Athlon/Duron/Athlon XP processor family thanks to its nForce product families. The original nForce was a descendant of the custom chipset NVIDIA created for the Microsoft Xbox console game system. For more information about nForce and nForce 2, see "NVIDIA nForce Chipsets for AMD." For more information about nForce 3 and nForce 4 chipsets, see "NVIDIA Chipsets for Athlon 64." Both are found in Chapter 4, "Motherboards and Buses," of *Upgrading and Repairing PCs*, 19th Edition, included in its entirety on the DVD packaged with this book.

Although NVIDIA is no longer developing chipsets for AMD processors, its final lineup of nForce chipsets for AMD 64-bit processors included the following families: nForce 500, nForce 600, nForce 700, and nForce 900; the GeForce chipsets with integrated graphics for AMD 64-bit processors are in the GeForce 6 series, GeForce 7 series, and GeForce 8 series.

The nForce 500 series supported AMD processors using the AM2 socket such as the Athlon 64 X2, Athlon 64, and Sempron models based on the Athlon 64. Models labeled SLI support two-way or three-way SLI, and all models include support for PATA and SATA hard disks (most support 3Gbps), RAID, and integrated audio (AC97 or HD audio, depending upon the individual model). Fast or Gigabit Ethernet support varies with chipset model. For details, see www.nvidia.com/page/nforce5_amd.html.

The nForce 600 series for AMD included one chipset, the 680a, which supports Athlon 64 FX processors in Socket L1/1207. The 680a includes dual PCIe x16 slots, a PCIe x8 slot, and up to eight PCIe x1 slots. It supports 12 SATA 3Gbps devices and four PATA devices, and RAID. It includes HD audio, 20 USB ports, and four Gigabit Ethernet ports. For details, see www.nvidia.com/page/nforce_600a.html.

The nForce 700 series for AMD included six chipsets: the 720D, 720a, 730a, 740a SLI, 750a SLI, and the 780a SLI. These chipsets included support for PCIe 2.0, SATA, and PATA drives including RAID, 12 USB 2.0 ports, and Gigabit Ethernet. For more information about processors supported, PCIe slots, and RAID configurations, see www.nvidia.com/docs/IO/35382/LC_motherboard_AMD_Nov08_web.pdf.

The nForce 900 series for AMD included one chipset, the 980a SLI, supporting processors in Sockets AM2, AM2+, and AM3, including Phenom, Phenom II, Athlon X2, and Athlon. It supports PCIe version 2, has 35 PCIe lanes, and can support three-way SLI. For more information, see www.nvidia.com/object/product_nforce_980a_sli_us.html.

NVIDIA also supported SLI on AMD's 900-series chipsets.

Super I/O Chips

A third major chip once seen on many PC motherboards is called the Super I/O chip. This is a chip that integrates devices formerly found on separate expansion cards in older systems. Newer motherboards lacking legacy ports have little need for Super I/O chips, and features they once included such as the CMOS RAM are usually integrated into the South Bridge chipset component.

In most late-model chipsets, the South Bridge chip now includes the functionality of Super I/O chips as well as providing support for the ports that have replaced the legacy ports incorporated into Super I/O chips, such as USB, SATA, and IEEE-1394.

For more information about Super I/O chips, see "Super I/O Chips" in Chapter 4, "Motherboards and Buses," of *Upgrading and Repairing PCs*, 19th Edition, included in its entirety on the DVD packaged with this book.

Motherboard Connectors

A modern motherboard contains a variety of connectors. Figure 4.30 shows the connector locations on a typical motherboard. Several of these connectors, such as power supply connectors, serial and parallel ports, and keyboard/mouse connectors, are covered in other chapters.

This section has figures and tables showing the configurations and pinouts of most of the other interface and I/O connectors you will find.

▶▶ See the Chapter 18 section, "AT/LPX Power Supply Connectors," **p. 870**.

▶▶ See the Chapter 14 section, "Serial Ports," **p. 730**, and "Parallel Ports," **p. 734**.

▶▶ See the Chapter 15 section, "Keyboard/Mouse Interface Connectors," **p. 751**.

▶▶ See the Chapter 14 section, "Universal Serial Bus (USB)," **p. 704**.

▶▶ See the Chapter 7 section, "An Overview of the IDE Interface," **p. 377**.

One of the biggest problems many people overlook when building and upgrading systems is the front panel connections. Connectors that don't match between the motherboard and chassis are one of the small but frustrating things that can be problematic in an otherwise smooth upgrade or system build. Having dependable standards for these connections would help, but unfortunately no official standard for the front panel connectors existed until October 2000, when Intel published the "Front Panel I/O Connectivity Design Guide." You can find the latest version of this guide, along with the motherboard form factor specifications, at www.formfactors.org.

Before this standard was published, no official standard existed, and anarchy ruled. In addition, even though most chassis gave you individual tiny connectors for each function, some of the bigger system builders (for example, Dell, Gateway, and others) began using specialized inline or dual-row header connectors so they could build systems more quickly and efficiently. Coincidentally, most of those vendors used Intel boards, hence Intel's development of a standard.

The front panel guide details a 10-pin keyed header connector for the main front panel switch/LED functions, as well as a 10-pin keyed USB header, a 10-pin keyed IEEE 1394 (FireWire/i.LINK) header, a 10-pin keyed audio header, and a 6-pin keyed IR header. The pinouts and configurations of these and other motherboard-based connectors are shown in the following figures and tables. Figure 4.31 details the front panel switch/LED header connector.

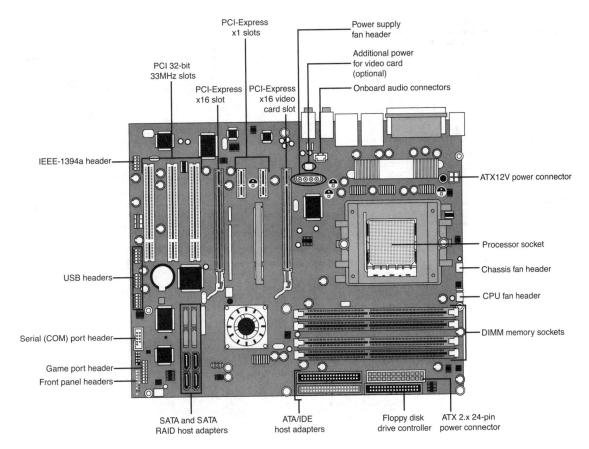

FIGURE 4.30 Typical motherboard connectors.

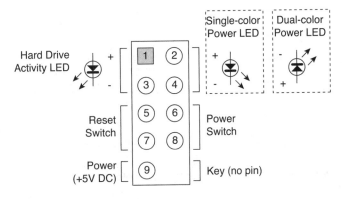

FIGURE 4.31 Front panel switch/LED header connector.

The pinout of the standard front panel switch/LED connector is shown in Table 4.37.

Table 4.37 Front Panel Switch/LED Connector Pinout

Signal	Description	Pin	Pin	Signal	Description
Hard Disk Activity LED				*Power/Sleep/Message LED*	
HD_LED+	Hard disk LED+	1	2	PWR_LED GRN+	Single-color LED+
HD_LED-	Hard disk LED–	3	4	PWR_LED_YEL+	Dual-color LED+
Reset Button				*Power On/Off Button*	
GND	Ground	5	6	FP_PWR	Power switch
FP_RESET	Reset switch	7	8	GND	Ground
Power				*Not Connected*	
+5V	Power	9	10	N/C	Not connected

Some chassis provide a single 10-pin header connector for the front panel switch/LED connections, but most provide individual 2-pin connectors for the various functions. If 2-pin connectors are used, they are connected as shown in Figure 4.32. Note that you can easily replace the multiple 2-pin connectors with a single 10-pin connector; some chassis even include an adapter for this purpose.

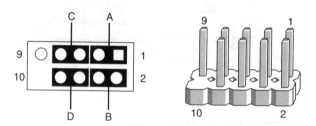

FIGURE 4.32 Standard front panel switch/LED connections using 2-pin connectors.

The 2-pin connections to a standard 10-pin front panel switch/LED connector are shown in Table 4.38.

Table 4.38 Front Panel Switch/LED Connections Using Multiple Connectors

Connector	Pins	Description
A	1 and 3	Hard disk activity LED
B	2 and 4	Power LED
C	5 and 7	Reset switch
D	6 and 8	Power switch

A chassis can use either a single-color or dual-color LED for the Power LED function. A dual-color LED can provide more information about the various power and message states the system might be in, including power on/off, sleep, and message-waiting indications. Table 4.39 shows the possible states and meanings for both single- and dual-color power LEDs.

Table 4.39 Power LED Indications

LED Type	LED State	Description	ACPI State
Single-color	Off	Power off or sleeping	S1, S3, S5
	Steady green	Running	S0
	Blinking green	Running, message waiting	S0
Dual-color	Off	Power off	S5
	Steady green	Running	S0
	Blinking green	Running, message waiting	S0
	Steady yellow	Sleeping	S1, S3
	Blinking yellow	Sleeping, message waiting	S1, S3

Many motherboards do not follow the industry-standard guidelines for front panel switch/LED connections, and many use alternative designs, one of which is shown in Figure 4.33.

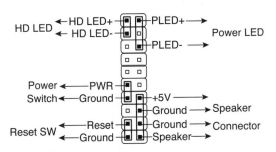

FIGURE 4.33 Alternative front panel switch/LED connector configuration.

Some of Intel's older motherboards, as well as those made by other motherboard manufacturers, used a single-row pin header connector for the front panel connections, as shown in Figure 4.34.

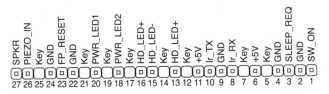

FIGURE 4.34 Alternative single-row front panel connector configuration.

Table 4.40 shows the designations for the front panel motherboard connectors used on some motherboards.

Table 4.40 Alternative Single-Row Front Panel Connector Pinout

Connector	Pin	Signal Name
Speaker	27	SPKR
	26	PIEZO_IN
	25	Key (no pin)
	24	GND

Table 4.40   Continued

Connector	Pin	Signal Name
Reset	23	FP_RESET
	22	GND
None	21	Key (no pin)
Sleep/Power LED	20	PWR_LED1 (green)
	19	Key (no pin)
	18	PWR_LED2 (yellow)
None	17	Key (no pin)
Hard Drive LED	16	HD_LED+
	15	HD_LED-
	14	Key (no pin)
	13	HD_LED+
None	12	Key (no pin)
IrDA	11	+5V
	10	Ir_TX
	9	GND
	8	Ir_RX
	7	Key (no pin)
	6	+5V
None	5	Key (no pin)
Sleep/Resume	4	GND
	3	SLEEP_REQ
Power On	2	GND
	1	SW_ON

To adapt the connectors in your chassis to those on your motherboard, in some cases you need to change the connector ends by removing the terminals and reinserting them into different positions. For example, I had a chassis that used a 3-pin power LED connection, whereas the motherboard had only a 2-pin connection. I had to remove one of the terminals, reinsert it into the middle position on the 3-pin connector, and then plug the connector into the motherboard so that two pins were mated and the third empty position was hanging off the end of the connector. Fortunately, the terminals are easy to remove merely by lifting a latch on the side of the connector and then sliding the terminal and wire back out. When the terminal is inserted, the latch automatically grabs the terminal and locks it into position.

Most motherboards include USB connectors (also called USB headers), which are designed to be connected to front-mounted or rear bracket USB connectors in the chassis. There are two standards: one for USB 1.1/2.0 ports, and another for USB 3.0 ports. USB 1.1/2.0 headers use a single 10-pin keyed connector to provide two USB 1.1 or 2.0 connections. The pinout of a standard dual USB 1.1/2.0 motherboard header connector is shown in Figure 4.35 and Table 4.41.

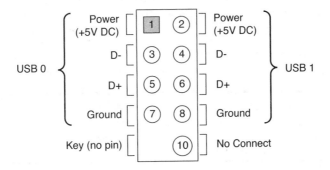

FIGURE 4.35 Dual-USB 1.1/2.0 header connector configuration.

Table 4.41   USB 1.1/2.0 Header Connector Pinout

Description	Signal Names	Pin	Pin	Signal Names	Description
Port 0 +5V	USB0_PWR	1	2	USB1_PWR	Port 1 +5V
Port 0 Data-	USB_D0-	3	4	USB_D1-	Port 1 Data-
Port 0 Data+	USB_D0+	5	6	USB_D1+	Port 1 Data+
Port 0 Ground	GND	7	8	GND	Port 1 Ground
No pin	Key	9	10	NC/Shield	No Connect/Shield

Many chassis include multiple inline connectors for the dual USB–to–front panel or rear bracket connection, instead of a single keyed connector. An example of this is shown in Figure 4.36.

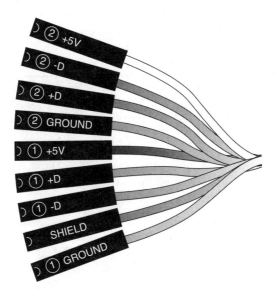

FIGURE 4.36 Front panel USB cable using multiple individual nonkeyed connectors.

Using the multiple individual connectors shown in the previous figure, you would have to plug each connector into the proper pin. Some internal chassis USB cables use two 5-pin inline connectors, in which case you just need to ensure that you don't put them on backward. Consult your motherboard and chassis manual for more information if you are unsure about your particular connections.

Caution

If your chassis uses multiple individual nonkeyed connections for USB 1.1/2.0 header cables, you must be sure to connect them properly to the connector on the motherboard. If you connect them improperly, you can cause a short circuit to occur that can damage the motherboard or any USB peripherals you plug into the front panel connectors. Higher-quality motherboards usually have self-healing fuses on the power signals, which can prevent damage if such a situation occurs.

USB 3.0 motherboard headers use a two-row design with 19 pins (the 20th pin is missing). Figure 4.37 shows a typical USB 3.0 motherboard header.

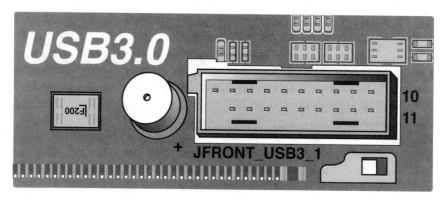

FIGURE 4.37   A typical USB 3.0 motherboard header uses a 19-pin connector.

Table 4.42 lists the pinout for a standard USB 3.0 motherboard header.

Table 4.42   USB 3.0 Header Connector Pinout

Description	Signal Name	Pin	Pin	Signal Name	Description
N/A	N/A	(No pin)	1	Vbus	Power
Power	Vbus	19	2	IntA_P1_SSRX–	USB3 ICC Port1 SuperSpeed Rx–
USB3 ICC Port2 SuperSpeed Rx–	IntA_P2_SSRX–	18	3	IntA_P1_SSRX+	USB3 ICC Port1 SuperSpeed Rx+
USB3 ICC Port2 SuperSpeed Rx+	IntA_P2_SSRX+	17	4	GND	Ground
Ground	GND	16	5	IntA_P1_SSTX–	USB3 ICC Port1 SuperSpeed Tx–
USB3 ICC Port2 SuperSpeed Tx–	IntA_P2_SSTX–	15	6	IntA_P1_SSTX+	USB3 ICC Port1 SuperSpeed Tx+

Description	Signal Name	Pin	Pin	Signal Name	Description
USB3 ICC Port2 SuperSpeed Tx+	IntA_P2_SSTX+	14	7	GND	Ground
Over Current Protection	ID	13	8	IntA_P1_D–	USB3 ICC Port1 D– (USB2 Signal D–)
USB3 ICC Port1 D+ (USB2 Signal D+)	IntA_P1_D+	12	9	IntA_P1_D+	USB3 ICC Port1 D+ (USB2 Signal D+)
USB3 ICC Port1 D– (USB2 Signal D–)	IntA_P1_D–	11	10	ID	Over Current Protection

On motherboards and systems with both USB 2.0 and USB 3.0 ports, use USB 3.0 ports for hard drives and other devices that support USB 3.0, and use USB 2.0 ports for lower-speed devices that support either USB 2.0 or USB 1.1.Although IEEE 1394 (FireWire/i.LINK) is not present on all motherboards, many mid-range and high-end boards do incorporate this feature or offer it as an option. You can also add FireWire via an expansion card, and many of the cards have header connectors for front panel or rear bracket connections similar to that found on a motherboard. Figure 4.38 and Table 4.43 show the pinout of the industry-standard FireWire header connector.

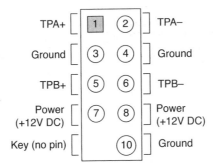

FIGURE 4.38   IEEE 1394 (FireWire/i.LINK) header connector configuration.

Table 4.43 IEEE 1394 (FireWire/i.LINK) Connector Pinout

Pin	Signal Name	Pin	Signal Name
TPA+	1	2	TPA–
Ground	3	4	Ground
TPB+	5	6	TPB–
+12V (Fused)	7	8	+12V (Fused)
Key (no pin)	9	10	Ground

Note that the FireWire header connector has the same physical configuration and keying as a USB connector. This is unfortunate because it enables a USB front panel cable to be plugged into a FireWire connector, and vice versa. Either situation could cause a short circuit.

Caution

You must not plug a USB cable into a FireWire header connector or a FireWire cable into a USB header connector. Doing so causes a short circuit that can damage the motherboard, as well as any peripherals you plug into the front panel connectors. Higher-quality motherboards usually have self-healing fuses on the power signals, which can prevent damage if such a situation occurs.

Motherboards that have integrated audio hardware usually feature a front panel audio header connector. The pinout of the industry-standard front panel audio header connector is shown in Figure 4.39 and Table 4.44.

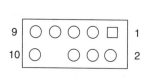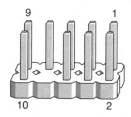

FIGURE 4.39   Front panel audio header connector configuration.

Table 4.44   Front Panel Audio Connector Pinout

Description	Signal Name	Pin	Pin	Signal Name	Description
Microphone input	AUD_MIC	1	2	AUD_GND	Analog audio ground
Microphone power	AUD_MIC_BIAS	3	4	AUD_VCC	Filtered +5V for analog audio
Right channel audio	AUD_FPOUT_R	5	6	AUD_RET_R	Right channel return
Ground or headphone	GND/HP_ON	7	8	KEY	No pin amplifier control
Left channel audio	AUD_FPOUT_L	9	10	AUD_RET_L	Left channel return

Some motherboards include an infrared data connector that connects to an infrared optical transceiver on the chassis front panel. This enables communication via infrared with cell phones, PDAs, laptops, printers, or other IrDA devices. The industry-standard pinout for IrDA connections on a motherboard is shown in Figure 4.40 and Table 4.44.

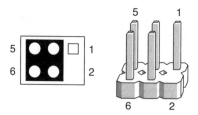

FIGURE 4.40   Infrared data front panel header connector configuration.

Table 4.45   Infrared Data Front Panel Connector Pinout

Description	Signal	Pin	Pin	Signal	Description
No connect	NC	1	2	Key	No pin
IR_power	+5V	3	4	GND	Ground
IrDA serial output	IR_TX	5	6	IR_RX	IrDA serial input

Other miscellaneous connectors might appear on motherboards; several are shown in Tables 4.45–4.54.

Table 4.46   Battery Connector

Pin	Signal	Pin	Signal
1	Gnd	3	KEY
2	Unused	4	+4 to 6V

Table 4.47   LED and Keylock Connector

Pin	Signal	Pin	Signal
1	LED Power (+5V)	4	Keyboard Inhibit
2	KEY	5	Gnd
3	Gnd		

Table 4.48   Speaker Connector

Pin	Signal	Pin	Signal
1	Ground	3	Board-Mounted Speaker
2	KEY	4	Speaker Output

Table 4.49   Chassis Intrusion (Security) Pin-Header

Pin	Signal Name
1	Ground
2	CHS_SEC

Table 4.50 Wake on LAN Pin-Header

Pin	Signal Name
1	+5 VSB
2	Ground
3	WOL

Table 4.51 Wake on Ring Pin-Header

Pin	Signal Name
1	Ground
2	RINGA

Table 4.52 CD Audio Connector

Pin	Signal Name	Pin	Signal Name
1	CD_IN-Left	3	Ground
2	Ground	4	CD_IN-Right

Table 4.53 Telephony Connector

Pin	Signal Name	Pin	Signal Name
1	Audio Out (monaural)	3	Ground
2	Ground	4	Audio In (monaural)

Table 4.54 ATAPI-Style Line In Connector

Pin	Signal Name	Pin	Signal Name
1	Left Line In	3	Ground
2	Ground	4	Right Line In (monaural)

Note

Some boards have a board-mounted piezo speaker. It is enabled by placing a jumper over pins 3 and 4, routing the speaker output to the board-mounted speaker. Removing the jumper enables a conventional speaker to be plugged in.

Most modern motherboards have three or four fan connectors for use with the processor fan, rear chassis fan, front chassis fan, and voltage regulator (power) fan (see Table 4.55). They generally use the same 3-pin connector, with the third pin providing a tachometer signal for optional speed monitoring. If the motherboard is capable of monitoring the fan speed, it can sound an alarm when the fans begin to slow down due to bearing failure or wear. The alarm sound can vary, but it normally comes from the internal speaker and might be an ambulance siren–type sound.

Table 4.55   Fan Power Connectors

Pin	Signal Name
1	Ground
2	+12V
3	Sense tachometer

Caution

Do not place a jumper on this connector; serious board damage will result if the 12V is shorted to ground.

System Bus Types, Functions, and Features

The heart of any motherboard is the various buses that carry signals between the components. A *bus* is a common pathway across which data can travel within a computer. This pathway is used for communication and can be established between two or more computer elements.

The PC has a hierarchy of different buses. Most modern PCs have at least three buses; some have four or more. They are hierarchical because each slower bus is connected to the faster one above it. Each device in the system is connected to one of the buses, and some devices (primarily the chipset) act as bridges between the various buses.

The main buses in a modern system are as follows:

- **Processor bus**—Also called the FSB, this is the highest-speed bus in the system and is at the core of the chipset and motherboard. This bus is used primarily by the processor to pass information to and from cache or main memory and the North Bridge of the chipset. This is generally the fastest bus in the system, and the speed and width depend on the specific processor and chipset combination.

- **PCI Express**—The PCI Express (PCIe) bus is a third-generation development of the PCI bus that began to appear in mid-2004. PCI Express is a differential signaling bus that can be generated by either the North Bridge or the South Bridge. The speed of PCI Express is described in terms of lanes. Each bidirectional dual-simplex lane provides a 2.5Gbps (PCIe version 1), 5Gbps (PCIe version 2), or 10Gbps (PCIe version 3) transfer rate in each direction (250MBps, 500MBps, or 1GBps effective speed). PCI Express video cards generally use the x16 slot, which provides 4,000MBps, 8,000MBps, or 16,000MBps in each direction. Most chipsets released after 2008 include PCIe version 2.0, and PCIe version 3.0 is now supported by some of the latest processors (which now perform the former North Bridge functionality of controlling high-speed expansion slots).

- **PCI bus**—This is a 33MHz 32-bit bus found in virtually all systems since the days of the Intel 486 CPU. Some newer systems include an optional 66MHz 64-bit version (mostly workstations or server-class systems). This bus is generated by either the chipset North Bridge in North/South Bridge chipsets or the I/O Controller Hub in chipsets using hub architecture. This bus is manifested in the system as a collection of 32-bit slots, normally white in color and numbering from one to three on most motherboards. Peripherals, such as SCSI adapters, network cards, video cards, and more, can be plugged into PCI bus slots. PCI Express is a faster development of the PCI bus.

Some older motherboards feature a special connector called an *Audio Modem Riser (AMR)* or a *Communications and Networking Riser (CNR)*. These are dedicated connectors for cards that are specific to the motherboard design to offer communications and networking options. They are *not* designed to be general-purpose bus interfaces, and few cards for these connectors are offered on the open market. Usually, they're offered only as an option with a given motherboard. They are designed such that a motherboard manufacturer can easily offer its boards in versions with and without communications options, without having to reserve space on the board for optional chips. Normal network and modem options offered publicly, for the most part, are still PCI based because the AMR/CNR connection is somewhat motherboard specific. Figure 4.41 compares these connectors. Current motherboards have abandoned AMR and CNR slots.

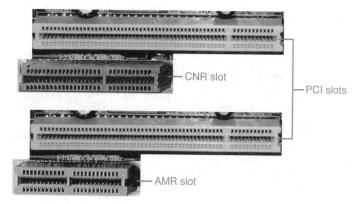

FIGURE 4.41 The AMR slot and CNR slot compared to PCI slots. When the AMR slot is used, the PCI slot paired with it cannot be used.

Several hidden buses exist on modern motherboards—buses that don't manifest themselves in visible slots or connectors. I'm talking about buses designed to interface chipset components, such as the Direct Media Interface (DMI), the HyperTransport interface, and the LPC bus. DMI is basically a dedicated four-lane (4-bit-wide) PCI Express connection allowing for 1GBps (version 1.0) or 2GBps (version 2.0) each direction simultaneously.

The most recent chipsets from major third-party vendors also bypass the PCI bus with direct high-speed connections, the most common of which is HyperTransport, between chipset components.

▶▶ See "Traditional North/South Bridge Architecture," **p. 185**.

In a similar fashion, the LPC bus is a 4-bit bus that has a maximum bandwidth of 16.67MBps; it was designed as an economical onboard replacement for the ISA bus. In systems that use LPC, it typically connects Super I/O chip or motherboard ROM BIOS components to the main chipset. LPC is faster than ISA yet uses far fewer pins and enables ISA to be eliminated from the board entirely.

The system chipset is the conductor that controls the orchestra of system components, enabling each to have its turn on its respective buses. Table 4.56 shows the widths, speeds, data cycles, and overall bandwidth of virtually all PC buses in use today.

For performance information about the performance of older bus types such as ISA, EISA, VL-BUS, and MCA, see Table 4.71 in Chapter 4, "Motherboards and Buses," in *Upgrading and Repairing PCs*, 19th Edition, available in its entirety on the DVD packaged with this book.

Table 4.56 Bandwidth (in MBps) and Detailed Comparison of Most PC Buses and Interfaces

Bus Type	Bus Width (Bits)	Bus Speed (MHz)	Data Cycles per Clock	Bandwidth (MBps)
PC-Card (PCMCIA)	16	10	1	20
CardBus	32	33	1	133
PCI	32	33	1	133
PCI 66MHz	32	66	1	266
PCI 64-bit	64	33	1	266
PCI 66MHz/64-bit	64	66	1	533
PCI-X 66	64	66	1	533
PCI-X 133	64	133	1	1,066
PCI-X 266	64	266	1	2,133
PCI-X 533	64	533	1	4,266
PCI Express 1.x	1	2,500	0.8	250
PCI Express 1.x	16	2,500	0.8	4,000
PCI Express 1.x	32	2,500	0.8	8,000
PCI Express 2.x	1	5,000	0.8	500
PCI Express 2.x	16	5,000	0.8	8,000
PCI Express 2.x	32	5,000	0.8	16,000
PCI Express 3.x	1	8,000	~0.98	1,000
PCI Express 3.x	16	8,000	~0.98	16,000
PCI Express 3.x	32	8,000	~0.98	32,000
Intel Hub Interface 8-bit	8	66	4	266
Intel Hub Interface 16-bit	16	66	4	533
AMD HyperTransport 2x2	2	200	2	100
AMD HyperTransport 4x2	4	200	2	200
AMD HyperTransport 8x2	8	200	2	400
AMD HyperTransport 16x2	16	200	2	800
AMD HyperTransport 32x2	32	200	2	1,600
AMD HyperTransport 2x4	2	400	2	200
AMD HyperTransport 4x4	4	400	2	400
AMD HyperTransport 8x4	8	400	2	800
AMD HyperTransport 16x4	16	400	2	1,600
AMD HyperTransport 32x4	32	400	2	3,200
AMD HyperTransport 2x8	2	800	2	400
AMD HyperTransport 4x8	4	800	2	800
AMD HyperTransport 8x8	8	800	2	1,600

Table 4.56   Continued

Bus Type	Bus Width (Bits)	Bus Speed (MHz)	Data Cycles per Clock	Bandwidth (MBps)
AMD HyperTransport 16x8	16	800	2	3,200
AMD HyperTransport 32x8	32	800	2	6,400
ATI A-Link	16	66	2	266
SiS MuTIOL	16	133	2	533
SiS MuTIOL 1G	16	266	2	1,066
VIA V-Link 4x	8	66	4	266
VIA V-Link 8x	8	66	8	533
AGP	32	66	1	266
AGP 2X	32	66	2	533
AGP 4X	32	66	4	1,066
AGP 8X	32	66	8	2,133
RS-232 Serial	1	0.1152	1/10	0.01152
RS-232 Serial HS	1	0.2304	1/10	0.02304
IEEE 1284 Parallel	8	8.33	1/6	1.38
IEEE 1284 EPP/ECP	8	8.33	1/3	2.77
USB 1.1/2.0 Low-Speed	1	1.5	1	0.1875
USB 1.1/2.0 Full-Speed	1	12	1	1.5
USB 2.0 High-Speed	1	480	1	60
USB 3.0 SuperSpeed	1	5000	2	500
IEEE 1394a S100	1	100	1	12.5
IEEE 1394a S200	1	200	1	25
IEEE 1394a S400	1	400	1	50
IEEE 1394b S800	1	800	1	100
IEEE 1394b S1600	1	1,600	1	200
ATA PIO-4	16	8.33	1	16.67
ATA-UDMA/33	16	8.33	2	33
ATA-UDMA/66	16	16.67	2	66
ATA-UDMA/100	16	25	2	100
ATA-UDMA/133	16	33	2	133
SATA-150	1	750	2	150
SATA-300	1	1,500	2	300
SATA-600	1	3,000	2	600
SCSI	8	5	1	5
SCSI Wide	16	5	1	10

Bus Type	Bus Width (Bits)	Bus Speed (MHz)	Data Cycles per Clock	Bandwidth (MBps)
SCSI Fast	8	10	1	10
SCSI Fast/Wide	16	10	1	20
SCSI Ultra	8	20	1	20
SCSI Ultra/Wide	16	20	1	40
SCSI Ultra2	8	40	1	40
SCSI Ultra2/Wide	16	40	1	80
SCSI Ultra3 (Ultra160)	16	40	2	160
SCSI Ultra4 (Ultra320)	16	80	2	320
FPM DRAM	64	22	1	177
EDO DRAM	64	33	1	266
PC66 SDRAM DIMM	64	66	1	533
PC100 SDRAM DIMM	64	100	1	800
PC133 SDRAM DIMM	64	133	1	1,066
PC1600 DDR DIMM (DDR200)	64	100	2	1,600
PC2100 DDR DIMM (DDR266)	64	133	2	2,133
PC2700 DDR DIMM (DDR333)	64	167	2	2,666
PC3200 DDR DIMM (DDR400)	64	200	2	3,200
PC3500 DDR (DDR433)	64	216	2	3,466
PC3700 DDR (DDR466)	64	233	2	3,733
PC2-3200 DDR2 (DDR2-400)	64	200	2	3,200
PC2-4300 DDR2 (DDR2-533)	64	267	2	4,266
PC2-5400 DDR2 (DDR2-667)	64	333	2	5,333
PC2-6400 DDR2 (DDR2-800)	64	400	2	6,400
PC3-8500 (DDR3-1066)	64	533	2	8.500
PC3-10600 (DDR3-1333)	64	667	2	1,333
PC3-12800 (DDR3-1600)	64	800	2	1,600
PC3-14900 (DDR3-1866)	64	933	2	1,866
PC3-16000 (DDR3-2000)	64	1,000	2	2,000
RIMM1200 RDRAM (PC600)	16	300	2	1,200
RIMM1400 RDRAM (PC700)	16	350	2	1,400
RIMM1600 RDRAM (PC800)	16	400	2	1,600
RIMM2100 RDRAM (PC1066)	16	533	2	2,133
RIMM2400 RDRAM (PC1200)	16	600	2	2,400
RIMM3200 RDRAM (PC800)	32	400	2	3,200
RIMM4200 RDRAM (PC1066)	32	533	2	4,266

Table 4.56   Continued

Bus Type	Bus Width (Bits)	Bus Speed (MHz)	Data Cycles per Clock	Bandwidth (MBps)
RIMM4800 RDRAM (PC1200)	32	600	2	4,800
33MHz 486 FSB	32	33	1	133
66MHz Pentium I/II/III FSB	64	66	1	533
100MHz Pentium I/II/III FSB	64	100	1	800
133MHz Pentium I/II/III FSB	64	133	1	1,066
200MHz Athlon FSB	64	100	2	1,600
266MHz Athlon FSB	64	133	2	2,133
333MHz Athlon FSB	64	167	2	2,666
400MHz Athlon FSB	64	200	2	3,200
533MHz Athlon FSB	64	267	2	4,266
400MHz Pentium 4 FSB	64	100	4	3,200
533MHz Pentium 4 FSB	64	133	4	4,266
800MHz Pentium 4 FSB	64	200	4	6,400
1066MHz Pentium 4 FSB	64	267	4	8,533
266MHz Itanium FSB	64	133	2	2,133
400MHz Itanium 2 FSB	128	100	4	6,400

Note: ISA, EISA, VL-Bus, and MCA are no longer used in current motherboard designs.

MBps = Megabytes per second

ISA = Industry Standard Architecture, also known as the PC/XT (8-bit) or AT-Bus (16-bit)

LPC = Low-pin-count bus

DD Floppy = Double Density (360/720KB) Floppy

HD Floppy = High Density (1.2/1.44MB) Floppy

ED Floppy = Extra-High Density (2.88MB) Floppy

EISA = Extended Industry Standard Architecture (32-bit ISA)

VL-Bus = VESA (Video Electronics Standards Association) Local Bus (ISA extension)

MCA = MicroChannel Architecture (IBM PS/2 systems)

PC-Card = 16-bit PCMCIA (Personal Computer Memory Card International Association) interface

CardBus = 32-bit PC-Card

Hub Interface = Intel 8xx chipset bus

HyperTransport = AMD chipset bus

V-Link = VIA Technologies chipset bus

MuTIOL = Silicon Integrated System chipset bus

PCI = Peripheral Component Interconnect

AGP = Accelerated Graphics Port

RS-232 = Standard Serial port, 115.2Kbps

RS-232 HS = High Speed Serial port, 230.4Kbps

IEEE 1284 Parallel = Standard Bidirectional Parallel Port

IEEE 1284 EPP/ECP = Enhanced Parallel Port/Extended Capabilities Port

USB = Universal serial bus

IEEE 1394 = FireWire, also called i.LINK

ATA PIO = AT Attachment (also known as IDE) Programmed I/O

ATA-UDMA = AT Attachment Ultra DMA

SCSI = Small computer systems interface

FPM = Fast Page Mode, based on X-3-3-3 (1/3 max) burst mode timing on a 66MHz bus

EDO = Extended Data Out, based on X-2-2-2 (1/2 max) burst mode timing on a 66MHz bus

SDRAM = Synchronous dynamic RAM

RDRAM = Rambus dynamic RAM

DDR = Double data rate SDRAM

DDR2 = Double data rate two SDRAM

DDR3 = Double data rate three SDRAM

DDR4 = Double data rate four SDRAM

CPU FSB = Processor front side bus

Note that many of the buses use multiple data cycles (transfers) per clock cycle to achieve greater performance. Therefore, the data transfer rate is higher than it would seem for a given clock rate, which allows for an easy way to take an existing bus and make it go faster in a backward-compatible way.

The Processor Bus (FSB)

The *processor bus* (also called the FSB) is the communication pathway between the CPU and motherboard chipset—more specifically the North Bridge or Memory Controller Hub. Over time, the FSB has run at faster speeds to support faster processor, memory, and motherboard speeds. But as the previous table indicates, there are many other buses running at different speeds in typical systems. The Socket 7 architecture used by Intel's Pentium processors in the mid-1990s, the Socket 478 architecture used by Intel processors in the early 21st century, and the Socket 939 architecture used by AMD processors in the middle of the last decade represent significant milestones in processor bus designs. Socket 939's pioneering use of an integrated memory controller in the processor is now followed by both AMD and Intel processors.

For an in-depth comparison of the processor and other buses found in systems on Socket 7 (Intel and AMD), Socket 478 (Intel), and Socket 939 (AMD) processors, see "The Processor Bus (Front Side Bus)" in Chapter 4, "Motherboards and Buses," in *Upgrading and Repairing PCs*, 19th Edition, available in its entirety on the DVD packaged with this book.

Types of I/O Buses

Since the introduction of the first PC, many I/O buses have surfaced. The reason is simple: Faster I/O speeds are necessary for better system performance. This need for higher performance involves three main areas:

- Faster CPUs
- Increasing software demands
- Greater multimedia requirements

Each of these areas requires the I/O bus to be as fast as possible.

One of the primary reasons new I/O bus structures have been slow in coming is compatibility—that old catch-22 that anchors much of the PC industry to the past. One of the hallmarks of the PC's success is its standardization. This standardization spawned thousands of third-party I/O cards, each originally built for the early bus specifications of the PC. If a new high-performance bus system was introduced, it often had to be compatible with the older bus systems so the older I/O cards would not be obsolete. Therefore, bus technologies seem to evolve rather than make quantum leaps forward.

You can identify different types of I/O buses by their architectures. The main types of I/O buses are detailed earlier in this chapter.

The main differences among buses consist primarily of the amounts of data they can transfer at one time and the speeds at which they can do it. The following sections describe the various types of PC buses.

The ISA Bus

Industry Standard Architecture (ISA) is the bus architecture that was introduced as an 8-bit bus with the original IBM PC in 1981; it was later expanded to 16 bits with the IBM PC/AT in 1984. ISA is the basis of the modern personal computer and was the primary architecture used in the majority of PC systems until the late 1990s.

To learn more about the ISA Bus, including diagrams of 8-bit and 16-bit ISA slots and pinouts, see "The ISA Bus" in Chapter 4 in *Upgrading and Repairing PCs,* 19th Edition, available in its entirety on the DVD packaged with this book.

The Micro Channel Bus

The introduction of 32-bit chips meant that the ISA bus could not handle the power of another new generation of CPUs. The chips could transfer 32 bits of data at a time, but the ISA bus can handle a maximum of only 16 bits. Rather than extend the ISA bus again, IBM decided to build a new bus; the result was the MCA bus. MCA (an abbreviation for *MicroChannel Architecture*) was completely different from the ISA bus and was technically superior in every way. However, because IBM was the only vendor to use it, MCA never became a common standard, and was phased out in 1996.

The EISA Bus

The EISA standard was announced in September 1988 as a response to IBM's introduction of the MCA bus—more specifically, to the way IBM wanted to handle licensing of the MCA bus. Vendors did not feel obligated to pay retroactive royalties on the ISA bus, so they turned their backs on IBM and created their own buses.

Compaq was the primary developer of the EISA standard, which was intended to be the company's way of taking over future development of the PC bus from IBM. Compaq knew that nobody would clone its bus if it was the only company that had it, so it essentially gave the design to other leading manufacturers. Compaq formed the EISA committee, a nonprofit organization designed specifically to control development of the EISA bus. Few EISA adapters were developed. Those that were developed centered mainly on disk array controllers and server-type network cards.

The EISA bus was essentially a 32-bit version of ISA. Unlike the MCA bus from IBM, you could still use older 8-bit or 16-bit ISA cards in 32-bit EISA slots, providing for full backward compatibility. As with MCA, EISA also allowed for automatic configuration of EISA cards via software.

To learn more about the EISA Bus, including pinouts of the EISA slot, see "The EISA Bus" in Chapter 4 in *Upgrading and Repairing PCs,* 19th Edition, available in its entirety on the DVD packaged with this book.

Local Buses (VESA, PCI, PCI Express, AGP)

The I/O buses discussed so far (ISA, MCA, and EISA) have one thing in common: relatively slow speed. The next three bus types that are discussed in the following few sections use the *local bus* concept explained in this section to address the speed issue. The main local buses found in PC systems are

- VL-Bus (VESA local bus)
- PCI
- PCI Express
- AGP

The speed limitation of ISA, MCA, and EISA is a carryover from the days of the original PC when the I/O bus operated at the same speed as the processor bus. As the speed of the processor bus increased, the I/O bus realized only nominal speed improvements, primarily from an increase in the bandwidth of the bus. The I/O bus had to remain at a slower speed because the huge installed base of adapter cards could operate only at slower speeds.

A *local bus* is any bus designed to interact more closely with the processor, or closer to processor throughput. It is interesting to note that the first 8-bit and 16-bit ISA buses were a form of local bus architecture. These systems had the processor bus as the main bus, and everything ran at full processor speeds. When ISA systems ran faster than 8MHz, the main ISA bus had to be decoupled from the processor bus because expansion cards, memory, and so on could not keep up. In 1992, an extension to the ISA bus called the *VESA local bus* (VL-Bus) started showing up on PC systems, indicating a return to local bus architecture. The PCI local bus, developed at about the same time as VL-Bus, supplanted it as the most common high-speed connection until the PCI Express (PCIe) bus became widespread in the 2009 and beyond time frame. Since then, PCI slots have become fewer in number while PCIe slots have increased.

Depending upon the requirements of the devices connected via expansion slots, it has been common to have two or more bus designs represented in expansion slots on typical desktop PCs. For example, a typical system built in 1993–1994 would feature one or two PCI or VL-Bus slots along with ISA slots. In a typical system built in 1999–2000, you might find a single ISA/PCI combo slot, an AGP slot for video, with the rest of the slots using PCI. Typical systems in the 2006 and later timeframe typically have PCIe and PCI slots. Some of the most recent chipsets from Intel no longer support PCI slots, so in a few years they will no longer be found in systems.

VESA Local Bus

The Video Electronics Standards Association (VESA) 32-bit local bus (VL-Bus) was the most popular local bus design from its debut in August 1992 through 1994. It was used for video and PATA hard disk interfacing. Although the VL-Bus could be adapted to other processors—including the 386 or even the Pentium—it was designed for the 486 and worked best as a 486 solution only. Despite the low cost, after a new bus called PCI became popular, VL-Bus fell into disfavor quickly. It never did catch on with Pentium systems, and there was little or no further development of the VL-Bus in the PC industry.

To learn more about the VL-Bus, see "The VESA Local Bus" in Chapter 4, "Motherboards and Buses," in *Upgrading and Repairing PCs*, 19th Edition, available in its entirety on the DVD packaged with this book.

The PCI Bus

In early 1992, Intel spearheaded the creation of another industry group. It was formed with the same goals as the VESA group in relation to the PC bus. Recognizing the need to overcome weaknesses in the ISA and EISA buses, the PCI Special Interest Group was formed.

The PCI bus specification was released in June 1992 as version 1.0 and since then has undergone several upgrades. Table 4.57 shows the various releases of PCI.

Table 4.57   PCI Specifications

PCI Specification	Released	Major Change
PCI 1.0	June 1992	Original 32/64-bit specification
PCI 2.0	April 1993	Defined connectors and expansion boards
PCI 2.1	June 1995	66MHz operation, transaction ordering, latency changes
PCI 2.2	Jan. 1999	Power management, mechanical clarifications
PCI-X 1.0	Sept. 1999	133MHz operation, addendum to 2.2
Mini-PCI	Nov. 1999	Small form-factor boards, addendum to 2.2
PCI 2.3	March 2002	3.3V signaling, low-profile add-in cards

Table 4.57   Continued

PCI Specification	Released	Major Change
PCI-X 2.0	July 2002	266MHz and 533MHz operation, supports subdivision of 64-bit data bus into 32-bit or 16-bit segments for use by multiple devices, 3.3V/1.5V signaling
PCI Express 1.0	July 2002	2.5GTps per lane per direction, using 0.8V signaling and 8b/10b encoding, resulting in 250MBps per lane
PCIe Express Mini	July 2003	Small form-factor boards, addendum to PCIe 1.0
PCI Express 2.0	Jan. 2007	5GTps per lane per direction, using 0.8V signaling and 8b/10b encoding, resulting in 500MBps per lane
PCI Express 3.0	2010	8GTps per lane per direction, using 0.8V signaling and 128b/130b encoding, resulting in 1GBps per lane.

PCI redesigned the traditional PC bus by inserting another bus between the CPU and the native I/O bus by means of bridges. Rather than tap directly into the processor bus, with its delicate electrical timing (as was done in the VL-Bus), a new set of controller chips was developed to extend the bus, as shown in Figure 4.42.

The PCI bus often is called a *mezzanine bus* because it adds another layer to the traditional bus configuration. PCI bypasses the standard I/O bus; it uses the system bus to increase the bus clock speed and take full advantage of the CPU's data path. Systems that integrate the PCI bus became available in mid-1993 and have since become a mainstay in the PC.

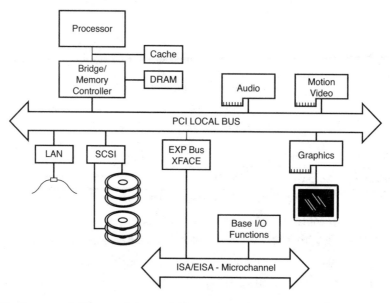

FIGURE 4.42   Conceptual diagram of the PCI bus.

Information typically is transferred across the PCI bus at 33MHz and 32 bits at a time. The bandwidth is 133MBps, as the following formula shows:

33.33MHz × 4 bytes (32 bits) = 133MBps

Until recently, 32-bit 33MHz PCI was the standard found in most PCs. However, most recent PCs now feature PCI Express (PCIe) x1 and PCI Express x16 slots, and some late-model PCs have as few as one PCI slot or have none; not surprisingly, as many recent chipsets no longer support PCI. Table 4.58 compares the specifications for PCI, PCI-X, and PCIe bus types.

Table 4.58   PCI Bus Types

PCI Bus Type	Bus Width (Bits)	Bus Speed (MHz)	Data Cycles per Clock	Bandwidth (MBps)
PCI	32	33	1	133
PCI 66MHz	32	66	1	266
PCI 64-bit	64	33	1	266
PCI 66MHz/64-bit	64	66	1	533
PCI-X 64	64	66	1	533
PCI-X 133	64	133	1	1,066
PCI-X 266	64	133	2	2,132
PCI-X 533	64	133	4	4,266
PCI Express 1.x	1	2,500	0.8	250
PCI Express 1.x	16	2,500	0.8	4,000
PCI Express 1.x	32	2,500	0.8	8,000
PCI Express 2.x	1	5,000	0.8	500
PCI Express 2.x	16	5,000	0.8	8,000
PCI Express 2.x	32	5,000	0.8	16,000
PCI Express 3.x	1	8,000	~0.98	1,000
PCI Express 3.x	16	8,000	~0.98	16,000
PCI Express 3.x	32	8,000	~0.98	32,000

PCI Express 1.x and 2.x use 8b/10b encoding, which transfers 8 bits of data for every 10 bits sent.

PCI Express 3.x uses 128b/130b encoding, which transfers 128 bits of data for every 130 bits sent.

64-bit PCI, 66MHz PCI, and PCI-X slots are found only on server- or workstation-type boards and systems. Aiding performance is the fact that the PCI bus can operate concurrently with the processor bus; it does not supplant it. The CPU can be processing data in an external cache while the PCI bus is busy transferring information between other parts of the system—a major design benefit of the PCI bus.

A PCI adapter card uses its own unique connector. This connector can be identified within a computer system because it typically is offset from the normal ISA, MCA, or EISA connectors found in older motherboards (see Figure 4.43). The size of a PCI card can be the same as that of the cards used in the system's normal I/O bus.

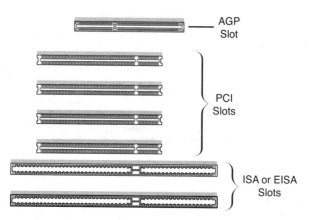

FIGURE 4.43   Typical configuration of 32-bit 33MHz PCI slots in relation to ISA or EISA and AGP slots.

The PCI specification identifies three board configurations, each designed for a specific type of system with specific power requirements; each specification has a 32-bit version and a longer 64-bit version. The 5V specification is for stationary computer systems (using PCI 2.2 or earlier versions), the 3.3V specification is for portable systems (also supported by PCI 2.3), and the universal specification is for motherboards and cards that work in either type of system. 64-bit versions of the 5V and universal PCI slots are found primarily on server motherboards. The PCI-X 2.0 specifications for 266 and 533 versions support 3.3V and 1.5V signaling; this corresponds to PCI version 2.3, which supports 3.3V signaling.

Note

You can find pinouts for the 5V, 3.3V, and universal PCI slots on the disc in the Technical Reference section.

Figure 4.44 compares the 32-bit and 64-bit versions of the standard 5V PCI slot to a 64-bit universal PCI slot. Figure 4.45 shows how the connector on a 64-bit universal PCI card compares to the 64-bit universal PCI slot.

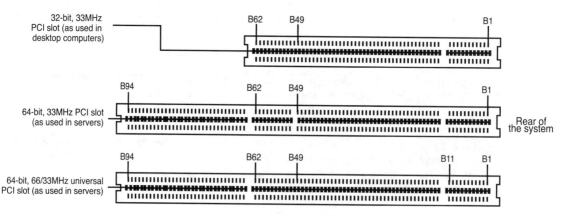

FIGURE 4.44   A 32-bit 33MHz PCI slot (top) compared to a 64-bit 33MHz PCI slot (center) and a 64-bit universal PCI slot that runs at 66MHz (bottom).

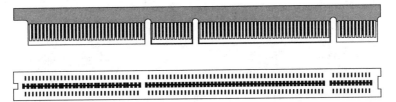

FIGURE 4.45   A 64-bit universal PCI card (top) compared to the 64-bit universal PCI slot (bottom).

Notice that the universal PCI board specifications effectively combine the 5V and 3.3V specifications. For pins for which the voltage is different, the universal specification labels the pin V I/O. This type of pin represents a special power pin for defining and driving the PCI signaling rail.

Another important feature of PCI is the fact that it was the model for the Intel PnP specification. Therefore, PCI cards do not have jumpers and switches and are instead configured through software. True PnP systems are capable of automatically configuring the adapters, whereas non-PnP systems with ISA slots must configure the adapters through a program that is usually a part of the system CMOS configuration. Starting in late 1995, most PC-compatible systems have included a PnP BIOS that allows the automatic PnP configuration.

PCI Express

During 2001, a group of companies called the Arapahoe Work Group (led primarily by Intel) developed a draft of a new high-speed bus specification code-named 3GIO (third-generation I/O). In August 2001, the PCI Special Interest Group (PCI-SIG) agreed to take over, manage, and promote the 3GIO architecture specification as the future generation of PCI. In April 2002, the 3GIO draft version 1.0 was completed, transferred to the PCI-SIG, and renamed PCI Express. Finally in July 2002, the PCI Express 1.0 specification was approved. The specification was updated to 1.1 in April 2005, to 2.0 in January 2007, and to version 3.0 in November 2010. PCI Express 4.0 was announced in late November 2011, but final specifications are not expected until sometime in either 2014 or 2015.

The original 3GIO code name was derived from the fact that this new bus specification was designed to initially augment and eventually replace the previously existing ISA/AT-Bus (first-generation) and PCI (second-generation) bus architectures in PCs. Each of the first two generations of PC bus architectures was designed to have a 10-to-15-year useful life in PCs. In being adopted and approved by the PCI-SIG, PCI Express is now destined to be the dominant PC bus architecture designed to support the increasing bandwidth needs in PCs over the next 10–15 years.

The key features of PCI Express are as follows:

- Compatibility with existing PCI enumeration and software device drivers.
- Physical connection over copper, optical, or other physical media to allow for future encoding schemes.
- Maximum bandwidth per pin allowing for small form factors, reduced cost, simpler board designs and routing, and reduced signal integrity issues.
- Embedded clocking scheme that enables easy frequency (speed) changes compared to synchronous clocking.
- Bandwidth (throughput) that increases easily with frequency and width (lane) increases.
- Low latency suitable for applications requiring isochronous (time-sensitive) data delivery, such as streaming video.

- Hot-plugging and hot-swapping capabilities.
- Power management capabilities.

PCI Express is another example of how the PC has moved from parallel to serial interfaces. Earlier generation bus architectures in the PC have been of a parallel design, in which multiple bits are sent simultaneously over several pins in parallel. The more bits sent at a time, the faster the bus throughput is. The timing of all the parallel signals must be the same, which becomes more and more difficult to do over faster and longer connections. Even though 32 bits can be transmitted simultaneously over a bus such as PCI or AGP, propagation delays and other problems cause them to arrive slightly skewed at the other end, resulting in a time difference between when the first and last of all the bits arrive.

A serial bus design is much simpler, sending 1 bit at a time over a single wire, at much higher rates of speed than a parallel bus would allow. By sending the bits serially, the timing of individual bits or the length of the bus becomes much less of a factor. By combining multiple serial data paths, even faster throughputs can be realized that dramatically exceed the capabilities of traditional parallel buses.

PCI Express is a fast serial bus design that is backward compatible with current PCI parallel bus software drivers and controls. In PCI Express, data is sent full duplex (simultaneously operating one-way paths) over two pairs of differentially signaled wires called a *lane*. Each lane allows for about 250MBps throughput in each direction initially, and the design allows for scaling from 1 to 2, 4, 8, 16, or 32 lanes. For example, a high-bandwidth configuration with 16 lanes allowing 16 bits to be sent in each direction simultaneously would allow up to 4,000MBps bandwidth each way. PCIe 2.0 increases the transfer rate to 500MBps per lane, or 8,000MBps for an x16 connector. This compares to PCI, which has only 133MBps bandwidth (one way at a time). Figure 4.46 compares the PCI Express x1–x16 connectors. Note that the PCI Express x4 and x8 connectors shown in this figure are intended primarily for use in workstations and servers.

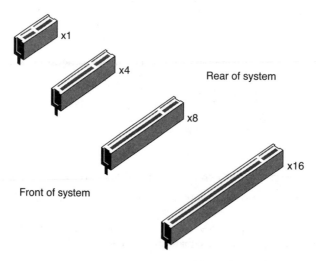

FIGURE 4.46   PCI Express x1, x4, x8, and x16 slots.

PCI Express versions 1 and 2 use an IBM-designed 8-bit-to-10-bit encoding scheme, which allows for self-clocked signals that will easily allow future increases in frequency. The starting frequency is 2.5GHz, and the specification allows increasing up to 10GHz in the future, which is about the limit of copper connections. By combining frequency increases with the capability to use up to 32 lanes,

PCI Express is capable of supporting future bandwidths up to 32GBps. PCI Express version 3 uses 128b/130b encoding for further speed improvements over its predecessors.

PCI Express was designed to augment and replace many of the buses currently used in PCs. It is not only designed to be a supplement to (and the replacement for) PCI slots it can also be used to replace the existing Intel hub architecture, HyperTransport, and similar high-speed interfaces between motherboard chipset components. Additionally, it replaces video interfaces such as AGP and acts as a mezzanine bus to attach other interfaces, such as Serial ATA, USB 2.0. USB 3.0, 1394b (FireWire or i.LINK), Gigabit Ethernet, and more.

Because PCI Express can be implemented over cables as well as onboard, it can be used to create systems constructed with remote "bricks" containing the bulk of the computing power. Imagine the motherboard, processor, and RAM in one small box hidden under a table, with the video, disk drives, and I/O ports in another box sitting on a table within easy reach. This will enable a variety of flexible PC form factors to be developed in the future without compromising performance.

Although PCI Express has not yet replaced PCI or other interfaces, over time, PCI Express has become the preferred general-purpose I/O interconnect. Some of the newest Intel chipsets for the third-generation Core i-series processors no longer support PCI, and even on motherboards that still include PCI slots, there are typically only one or two, with the remainder being PCIe.

The PCIe mini slot found in most late-model laptops is the mobile version of PCIe.

Most recent desktop motherboard designs feature a mix of PCI, PCI Express x1, and x16 slots; workstation and server motherboards have also added PCI Express slots to their typical PCI-X and PCI slots.

For more information on PCI Express, I recommend consulting the PCI-SIG website (www.pcisig.org).

Accelerated Graphics Port

In the mid 1990s, Intel created AGP as a new bus specifically designed for high-performance graphics and video support. AGP is based on PCI, but it contains several additions and enhancements and is physically, electrically, and logically independent of PCI. For example, the AGP connector is similar to PCI, although it has additional signals and is positioned differently in the system. Unlike PCI, which is a true bus with multiple connectors (slots), AGP is more of a point-to-point high-performance connection designed specifically for a video card in a system because only one AGP slot is allowed for a single video card. Intel originally released the AGP specification 1.0 in July 1996 and defined a 66MHz clock rate with 1x or 2x signaling using 3.3V. AGP version 2.0 was released in May 1998 and added 4x signaling as well as a lower 1.5V operating capability.

The final revision for the AGP specification for PCs is AGP 8x, also called AGP 3.0. AGP 8x defines a transfer speed of 2,133MBps, which is twice that of AGP 4x. The AGP 8x specification was publicly announced in November 2000.

Although AGP 8x (2,133MBps) is 16 times faster than 32-bit 33MHz PCI (133MBps), AGP 8x is only about half as fast as PCI Express x16 (4,000MBps). Starting in mid-2004, motherboard and system vendors began to replace AGP 8x with PCI Express x16 expansion slots in high-performance systems. By early 2006, most motherboards featured PCI Express x16 slots in place of AGP.

To learn more about AGP, see "Accelerated Graphics Port" in Chapter 4, "Motherboards and Buses," in *Upgrading and Repairing PCs*, 19th Edition, available in its entirety on the DVD packaged with this book.

System Resources

System resources are the communications channels, addresses, and other signals that hardware devices use to communicate on the bus. At their lowest level, these resources typically include the following:

- Memory addresses
- IRQ (interrupt request) channels
- DMA (direct memory access) channels
- I/O port addresses

These resources are required and used by many components of your system. Adapter cards need these resources to communicate with your system and accomplish their purposes. Not all adapter cards have the same resource requirements. A serial communications port, for example, needs an IRQ channel and I/O port address, whereas a sound card needs these resources and at least one DMA channel.

As systems increased in complexity from the late 1980s on, the chance for resource conflicts also increased. The configuration problem came to a head in the early 1990s, when manual configuration was the norm. Starting around that time, Microsoft and Intel developed PnP, which allowed for automatic detection, management, and configuration of hardware, usually without user involvement. Windows 95 was the first PnP-aware PC operating system (OS), and by the time it was released, most hardware began supporting the PnP standard. Plug and Play was later superseded by Advanced Configuration and Power Interface (ACPI), which combined device configuration and power management into a single specification.

Modern systems with ACPI and modern buses such as PCI and PCI Express rarely have problems configuring these resources. In virtually all cases, the configuration will be automatic and trouble free.

Interrupts

Interrupt request channels, or hardware interrupts, are used by various hardware devices to signal the motherboard that a request must be fulfilled. This procedure is the same as a student raising his hand to indicate that he needs attention.

These interrupt channels are represented by wires on the motherboard and in the slot connectors. When a particular interrupt is invoked, a special routine takes over the system, which first saves all the CPU register contents in a stack and then directs the system to the interrupt vector table. This vector table contains a list of memory addresses that correspond to the interrupt channels. Depending on which interrupt was invoked, the program corresponding to that channel is run.

The pointers in the vector table point to the address of whatever software driver services the card that generated the interrupt. For a network card, for example, the vector might point to the address of the network drivers that have been loaded to operate the card; for a hard disk controller, the vector might point to the BIOS code that operates the controller.

After the particular software routine performs whatever function the card needed, the interrupt-control software returns the stack contents to the CPU registers, and the system resumes whatever it was doing before the interrupt occurred.

Through the use of interrupts, your system can respond to external events in a timely fashion. Each time a serial port presents a byte to your system, an interrupt is generated to ensure that the system reads that byte before another comes in. Keep in mind that in some cases a port device—in particular, a modem with a 16550 or higher UART chip—incorporates a byte buffer that allows multiple characters to be stored before an interrupt is generated.

Hardware interrupts are generally prioritized by their numbers; with some exceptions, the highest-priority interrupts have the lowest numbers. Higher-priority interrupts take precedence over lower-priority interrupts by interrupting them. As a result, several interrupts can occur in your system concurrently, with each interrupt nesting within another.

The ISA bus uses *edge-triggered* interrupt sensing, in which an interrupt is sensed by a changing signal sent on a particular wire located in the slot connector. A different wire corresponds to each possible hardware interrupt. Because the motherboard can't recognize which slot contains the card that used an interrupt line and therefore generated the interrupt, confusion results if more than one card is set to use a particular interrupt. Each interrupt, therefore, is usually designated for a single hardware device. Most of the time, interrupts can't be shared.

Originally, IBM developed ways to share interrupts on the ISA bus, but few devices followed the necessary rules to make this a reality. The PCI bus inherently allows interrupt sharing; in fact, virtually all PCI cards are set to PCI interrupt A and share that interrupt on the PCI bus. The real problem is that there are technically two sets of hardware interrupts in the system: PCI interrupts and ISA interrupts. For PCI cards to work in a PC, the PCI interrupts are first mapped to ISA interrupts, which are then configured as nonshareable. Therefore, on older systems, you must assign a nonconflicting interrupt for each card, even PCI cards. The conflict between assigning ISA IRQs for PCI interrupts caused many configuration problems for early users of PCI motherboards and continued to cause problems even after the development of Windows 95 and its PnP technology.

The solution to the interrupt sharing problem for PCI cards was something called *PCI IRQ Steering*, which has been supported in OSs (starting with Windows 95 OSR 2.x) and BIOSs for more than 15 years. PCI IRQ Steering allows a plug-and-play operating system such as Windows to dynamically map or "steer" PCI cards (which almost all use PCI INTA#) to standard PC interrupts and allows several PCI cards to be mapped to the same interrupt. More information on PCI IRQ Steering is found in the section "PCI Interrupts," later in this chapter.

Hardware interrupts are sometimes referred to as *maskable interrupts*, which means you can mask or turn off the interrupts for a short time while the CPU is used for other critical operations. It is up to the system BIOS and programs to manage interrupts properly and efficiently for the best system performance.

The following sections discuss the IRQs that any standard devices use, as well as what might be free in your system.

8-Bit ISA Bus Interrupts

The PC and XT (the systems based on the 8-bit 8086 CPU) provide for eight different external hardware interrupts. Table 4.59 shows the typical uses for these interrupts, which are numbered 0–7.

Table 4.59 8-Bit ISA Bus Default Interrupt Assignments

IRQ	Function	Bus Slot
0	System Timer	No
1	Keyboard Controller	No
2	Available	Yes (8-bit)
3	Serial Port 2 (COM2:)	Yes (8-bit)
4	Serial Port 1 (COM1:)	Yes (8-bit)
5	Hard Disk Controller	Yes (8-bit)
6	Floppy Disk Controller	Yes (8-bit)
7	Parallel Port 1 (LPT1:)	Yes (8-bit)

If you have a system that has one of the original 8-bit ISA buses, the IRQ resources that the system provides present a severe limitation. Installing several devices that need the services of system IRQs in a PC/XT-type system can be a study in frustration because the only way to resolve the interrupt-shortage problem is to remove the adapter board that you need the least.

16-Bit ISA, EISA, and MCA Bus Interrupts

The introduction of the AT, based on the 286 processor, was accompanied by an increase in the number of external hardware interrupts the bus would support. The number of interrupts was doubled to 16 by using two Intel 8259 interrupt controllers, piping the interrupts generated by the second one through the unused IRQ2 in the first controller. This arrangement effectively makes only 15 IRQ assignments available, and IRQ2 effectively became inaccessible.

By routing all the interrupts from the second IRQ controller through IRQ2 on the first, all these new interrupts are assigned a nested priority level between IRQ1 and IRQ3. Thus, IRQ15 ends up having a higher priority than IRQ3. Figure 4.47 shows how the two 8259 chips were wired to create the cascade through IRQ2 on the first chip.

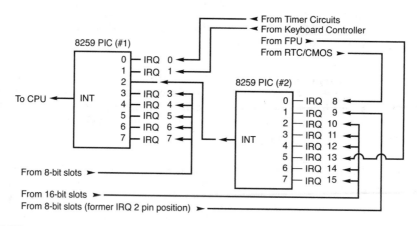

FIGURE 4.47 Interrupt controller cascade wiring.

To prevent problems with boards set to use IRQ2, the AT system designers routed one of the new interrupts (IRQ9) to fill the slot position left open after removing IRQ2. This means that any card you install in a more recent system that claims to use IRQ2 is really using IRQ9 instead.

Table 4.60 shows the typical uses for interrupts in the 16-bit ISA and 32-bit PCI/AGP buses and lists them in priority order from highest to lowest. The obsolete EISA and MCA buses used a similar IRQ map.

Table 4.60 16/32-Bit ISA/PCI/AGP Default Interrupt Assignments

IRQ	Standard Function	Bus Slot	Card Type	Recommended Use
0	System Timer	No	—	—
1	Keyboard Controller	No	—	—
2	2nd IRQ Controller Cascade	No	—	—
8	Real-Time Clock	No	—	—

IRQ	Standard Function	Bus Slot	Card Type	Recommended Use
9	Available (as IRQ2 or IRQ9)	Yes	8/16-bit	Network Card
10	Available	Yes	16-bit	USB
11	Available	Yes	16-bit	SCSI Host Adapter
12	Mouse Port/Available	Yes	16-bit	Mouse Port
13	Math Coprocessor	No	—	—
14	Primary IDE	Yes	16-bit	Primary IDE (hard disks)
15	Secondary IDE	Yes	16-bit	2nd IDE (CD-ROM/Tape)
3	Serial 2 (COM2:)	Yes	8/16-bit	COM2:/Internal Modem
4	Serial 1 (COM1:)	Yes	8/16-bit	COM1:
5	Sound/Parallel 2 (LPT2:)	Yes	8/16-bit	Sound Card
6	Floppy Controller	Yes	8/16-bit	Floppy Controller
7	Parallel 1 (LPT1:)	Yes	8/16-bit	LPT1:

Notice that interrupts 0, 1, 2, 8, and 13 are not on the bus connectors and are not accessible to adapter cards. Interrupts 8, 10, 11, 12, 13, 14, and 15 are from the second interrupt controller and are accessible only by boards that use the 16-bit extension connector because this is where these wires are located. IRQ9 is rewired to the 8-bit slot connector in place of IRQ2, so IRQ9 replaces IRQ2 and, therefore, is available to 8-bit cards, which treat it as though it were IRQ2.

Note

Although the 16-bit ISA bus has twice as many interrupts as systems that have the 8-bit ISA bus, you still might run out of available interrupts because only 16-bit adapters can use most of the newly available interrupts. Any 32-bit PCI adapter can be mapped to any ISA IRQs.

The extra IRQ lines in a 16-bit ISA system are of little help unless the adapter boards you plan to use enable you to configure them for one of the unused IRQs. Some devices are hard-wired so they can use only a particular IRQ, and some of the early 16-bit ISA adapters weren't designed to use 16-bit IRQs (9–15). If you have a device that already uses that IRQ, you must resolve the conflict before installing the second adapter. If neither adapter enables you to reconfigure its IRQ use, chances are that you can't use the two devices in the same system.

PCI Interrupts

The PCI bus supports IRQs that PCI devices can use to signal to the bus that they need attention. The four PCI interrupts are called INTA#, INTB#, INTC#, and INTD#. These INTx# interrupts are *level sensitive*, which means that the electrical signaling enables them to be shared among PCI cards. In fact, all single-device or single-function PCI chips or cards that use only one interrupt must use INTA#. This is one of the rules in the PCI specification. If additional devices are within a chip or onboard a card, the additional devices can use INTB# through INTD#. Because there are few multifunction PCI chips or boards, practically all the devices on a given PCI bus share INTA#.

For the PCI bus to function in a PC, the PCI interrupts must be mapped to ISA interrupts. Because ISA interrupts can't be shared, in most cases each PCI card using INTA# on the PCI bus must be mapped to a different nonshareable ISA interrupt. For example, you could have a system with four PCI slots and four PCI cards installed, each using PCI interrupt INTA#. In most cases, each of these cards would be mapped to a different available ISA interrupt request, such as IRQ9, IRQ10, IRQ11, or IRQ5.

Finding unique IRQs for each device on both the ISA and PCI buses has always been a problem; there simply aren't enough free ones to go around. Setting two ISA devices to the same IRQ has never been possible (the so-called *IRQ sharing* of IRQ4 by COM1/3 and IRQ3 by COM2/4 didn't allow both COM ports to work at the same time), but on most newer systems sharing IRQs between multiple PCI devices might be possible. Newer system BIOSs as well as plug-and-play OSs support a function known as *PCI IRQ Steering*. For this to work, both your system BIOS and OS must support IRQ Steering. Older system BIOSs and Windows 95 or 95A and earlier do not have support for PCI IRQ Steering.

Advanced Programmable Interrupt Controller

As a replacement for the traditional pair of 8259 interrupt controllers, Intel developed the Advanced Programmable Interrupt Controller (APIC) in the mid-1990s. Although all processors since the original Pentium contain an APIC, an APIC must also be present in the motherboard's chipset, and the BIOS and OS must support APIC. APIC support is present on most recent motherboards and has been supported in all Windows releases since Windows 2000. In some systems you can enable or disable APIC support in the system BIOS, but in most it is permanently enabled.

APIC provides support for multiple processors, but it is also used on single-processor computers. The major benefit of APIC for a single processor is support for virtual PCI IRQs above 15. Most APIC implementations support virtual IRQs up to at least 24, and some new systems can go higher, and might even assign IRQs to negative numbers (see Figure 4.48). Although Windows 2000 tends to place PCI IRQs into the traditional ISA range of 0–15, even when APIC is enabled, Windows XP and later make full use of APIC services when installed on a system with APIC enabled. With Windows XP and later, APIC limits IRQ sharing to enable devices to perform better with fewer conflicts. The traditional ISA IRQs 0–15 on the system shown in Figure 4.48 are used only for ISA devices, thus preventing ISA-PCI IRQ conflicts.

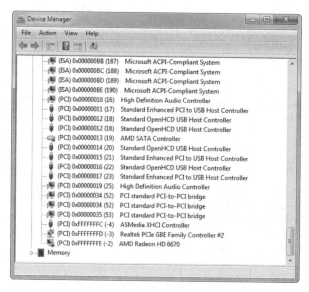

FIGURE 4.48   This system uses PCI IRQs from –2 to –4, from 16 to 25, and from 53 to 54.

Note

APIC must be enabled in the system BIOS before you can install x64 editions of Windows.

IRQ Conflicts

If you manage systems that use ISA slots, you might have the potential for conflicts between the IRQ requirements of add-on cards and the requirements for built-in devices. To learn how to deal with common sources of IRQ conflicts and to free up the maximum number of IRQs, see the section "IRQ Conflicts" in Chapter 4 in *Upgrading and Repairing PCs*, 19th Edition, available in its entirety on the DVD packaged with this book.

DMA Channels

Communications devices that must send and receive information at high speeds use direct memory access (DMA) channels. Conflicts between devices needing to use the same DMA channel were common on systems using ISA slots but are no longer an issue on modern systems.

To learn more about DMA channels and possible conflicts on older systems, see "DMA Channels" in Chapter 4 in *Upgrading and Repairing PCs*, 19th Edition, available in its entirety on the DVD packaged with this book.

I/O Port Addresses

Your computer's I/O ports enable communications between devices and software in your system. They are equivalent to two-way radio channels. If you want to talk to your serial port, you need to know on which I/O port (radio channel) it is listening. Similarly, if you want to receive data from the serial port, you need to listen on the same channel on which it is transmitting.

Unlike IRQs and DMA channels, our systems have an abundance of I/O ports. There are exactly 65,536 ports—numbered from 0000h to FFFFh—which is a feature of the Intel x86 processor design. Even though most devices use up to eight ports for themselves, with that many to spare, you won't run out anytime soon. The biggest problem you have to worry about is setting two devices to use the same port.

Most modern plug-and-play systems resolve port conflicts and select alternative ports for one of the conflicting devices.

One confusing issue is that I/O ports are designated by hexadecimal addresses similar to memory addresses. They are not memory; they are ports. The difference is that when you send data to memory address 1000h, it is stored in your system's DIMM memory. If you send data to I/O port address 1000h, it is sent out on the bus on that "channel," and anybody listening in could then "hear" it. If nobody is listening to that port address, the data reaches the end of the bus and is absorbed by the bus terminating resistors.

Driver programs are primarily what interact with devices at the various port addresses. The driver must know which ports the device is using to work with it, and vice versa. That is not usually a problem because the driver and device come from the same company.

Motherboard and chipset devices usually are set to use I/O port addresses 0h–FFh, and all other devices use 100h–FFFFh. Table 4.61 shows the commonly used motherboard and chipset-based I/O port usage.

Table 4.61 Motherboard and Chipset-Based Device Port Addresses

Address (Hex)	Size	Description
0000–000F	16 bytes	Chipset – 8237 DMA 1
0020–0021	2 bytes	Chipset – 8259 interrupt controller 1
002E–002F	2 bytes	Super I/O controller configuration registers
0040–0043	4 bytes	Chipset – Counter/Timer 1
0048–004B	4 bytes	Chipset – Counter/Timer 2
0060	1 byte	Keyboard/Mouse controller byte – reset IRQ
0061	1 byte	Chipset – NMI, speaker control
0064	1 byte	Keyboard/Mouse controller, CMD/STAT byte
0070, bit 7	1 bit	Chipset – Enable NMI
0070, bits 6:0	7 bits	MC146818 – Real-time clock, address
0071	1 byte	MC146818 – Real-time clock, data
0078	1 byte	Reserved – Board configuration
0079	1 byte	Reserved – Board configuration
0080–008F	16 bytes	Chipset – DMA page registers
00A0–00A1	2 bytes	Chipset – 8259 interrupt controller 2
00B2	1 byte	APM control port
00B3	1 byte	APM status port
00C0–00DE	31 bytes	Chipset – 8237 DMA 2
00F0	1 byte	Math Coprocessor Reset Numeric Error

To find out exactly which port addresses are being used on your motherboard, consult the board documentation or look up these settings in the Windows Device Manager.

Because of the use of PCI and PCIe-based devices (designed from the start for Plug-and-Play configuration), the chances of device conflicts today are almost nil, especially on systems with no legacy hardware. If you need to solve a device conflict with older hardware, see the section "Resolving Resource Conflicts" in Chapter 4 of *Upgrading and Repairing PCs*, (20th Edition), on the DVD packaged with this book.

Motherboard Selection Criteria (Knowing What to Look For)

I am often asked to make recommendations for purchases. Without guidance, many individuals have no rhyme or reason for their selections and instead base their choices solely on magazine reviews or, even worse, on some personal bias. To help eliminate this haphazard selection process, I have developed a simple motherboard selection checklist.

It helps to think like an engineer when you make your selection. Consider every aspect and detail of the motherboards in question. For instance, you should consider present usage as well as future uses and upgrades. Technical support at a professional (as opposed to a user) level is extremely important. Check for manual and driver downloads: Are they easy to find and up to date? The following list includes some of the most important criteria to consider when selecting a motherboard:

■ **Motherboard chipset**—The motherboard chipset is the backbone of a system and is perhaps the single most important part of the motherboard. Compare the features of the available chipsets to ensure that the board will do what you want. For example, some chipsets include support for faster memory, PCIe 2.x or 3.x cards, SATA 6Gbps drives, and optional RAID capabilities. I spend the most time deciding on my next chipset because it affects and influences virtually every other component in the system. I recommend using chipsets that support the latest and fastest Intel or AMD multi-core processors per your preference, such as Intel 7x or AMD AM3+ or FM2 chipsets.

■ **Processor socket**—The processor socket on a motherboard dictates the specific processor makes and models you will be able to install. In most cases you will have a given processor in mind, so choose a motherboard with a socket that supports the processor you want to use. The main sockets in use today on new systems include Socket AM3+, FM1 and FM2 for AMD processors, and Sockets LGA1155 and LGA 2011 for Intel processors. See Table 4.6 (which lists CPU socket specifications) to see what types of processors are supported by each socket. Also check the motherboard specifications for what specific processors are supported by a given motherboard.

■ **Memory**—The type and amount of memory compatible with a system depends on the motherboard you choose. Most motherboards today support DDR3 memory, in single-, dual-, triple-, or quad-channel operation. The number of memory sockets, supported speeds, and other variables also depend on the motherboard, so check the board specifications to see exactly what is supported. DDR4 SDRAM, a faster version of DDR memory, will not be in systems until 2013–2014.

■ **Form factor**—The form factor indicates the size and shape of the board and must be compatible with the chassis or case and power supply. For maximum flexibility, performance, reliability, and ease of use, I recommend motherboards based on the ATX and microATX form factors. Larger form factors such as ATX offer more slots and room for additional integrated components and features. Smaller variations on ATX are also available, but in the end you need to be sure that the motherboard is compatible with the case and power supply you have chosen. I recommend mini-ITX or smaller versions for home theater or similar dedicated or embedded system requirements.

■ **Bus slots**—Current systems offer one to five or more PCI and PCI Express slots (depending on the form factor). Some boards have more than one PCIe x16 (video card) slot, which you may want if you are running multiple video cards in an SLI or CrossfireX arrangement. Make sure the board you choose has the number and types of slots you require. Keep in mind that PCI is disappearing on some motherboards, so if you want to use existing PCI cards, make sure you choose a motherboard that has enough PCI slots or has integrated ports that replace the functionality of your PCI cards.

■ **Onboard ATA interfaces**—All motherboards on the market have included onboard Serial ATA interfaces for some time now, but not all are equal. Look for boards that include at least four to six SATA connectors, with support for 6Gbps operation, at least one eSATA port (if you have eSATA drives or enclosures), as well as optional RAID functionality (if desired). Note that most late model systems include only one Parallel ATA port (for up to two drives) or frequently no Parallel ATA support at all. With the low cost of Serial ATA optical drives, it's probably better to replace existing Parallel ATA with Serial ATA optical drives in your next system build so you can select a motherboard that has the maximum number of Serial ATA ports.

- **Other built-in interfaces**—Ideally, a motherboard should contain as many built-in standard controllers and interfaces as possible. Most boards feature integrated USB, sound, and LAN (look for those offering gigabit Ethernet), whereas others also have integrated video, FireWire, eSATA, dual LAN adapters, and more. Motherboards with the latest generation of USB (USB 3.0) and SATA (6Gbps) are likely to cost more than boards using USB 2.0 and SATA 3Gbps, but by the time you add expansion cards to gain these features, the total cost of upgrading a board lacking these features added to the original motherboard cost usually makes the board with faster ports a better buy.

- **BIOS features**—If you want to overclock your system, you need a BIOS that provides access to CPU clock multiplier settings and voltages as well as memory timings and voltages. If you want to use virtualization, make sure the BIOS supports Intel VT-x or AMD-V settings for hardware-assisted virtualization. To use 3TB or larger hard disks, make sure you use UEFI BIOS (these typically have a graphical UI that can be controlled with either a mouse or the keyboard).

- **Documentation**—Good technical documentation is important. Documents should be easy to download from the manufacturer's site and should include information on any and all jumpers and switches found on the board, connector pinouts for all connectors, specifications for other plug-in components, and any other applicable technical information. Most vendors provide this information in electronic form (using the Adobe Reader PDF format) on their websites, so you can preview the information available for a given motherboard before you buy.

- **Technical support**—Good online technical support goes beyond documentation. It includes easily downloadable driver and BIOS updates, FAQs, updated tables of processor and memory compatibility, and utility programs to help you monitor the condition of your system. In addition to these online support features, make sure the vendor can be contacted through email and by phone.

Most of the time I recommend purchasing boards from better-known motherboard manufacturers such as GIGABYTE, Foxconn, and Intel. These boards might cost a little more, but there is some safety in the more well-known brands. That is, the more boards they sell, the more likely that any problems will have been discovered by others and solved long before you get yours. Also, if service or support is necessary, the larger vendors are more likely to be around in the long run.

Chipset Documentation

As mentioned, documentation is an important factor to consider when you're planning to purchase a motherboard. Most motherboard manufacturers design their boards around a particular chipset, which actually counts as the bulk of the motherboard circuitry. I recommend downloading the chipset datasheets or other technical documentation directly from the chipset manufacturer.

For example, one of the more common questions I hear about a system relates to the BIOS Setup program. People want to know what the "Advanced Chipset Setup" features mean and what the effects of changing them will be. Often they go to the BIOS manufacturer thinking that the BIOS documentation will offer help. Usually, however, people find that there is no real coverage of what the chipset setup features are in the BIOS documentation. You will find this information in the data book provided by the chipset manufacturer. Although these books are meant to be read by the engineers who design the boards, they contain all the detailed information about the chipset's features, especially those that might be adjustable. With the chipset data book, you will have an explanation of all the controls in the Advanced Chipset Setup section of the BIOS Setup program.

Besides the main chipset datasheets, I recommend collecting any data books on the other major chips in the system. This includes Super I/O chips, SATA controllers, and of course the main processor. You will find an incredible amount of information on these components in the datasheets.

BIOS

BIOS Basics

It is often difficult for people to understand the difference between hardware and software in a PC system. The differences can be difficult to understand because both are very much intertwined in the system design, construction, and operation. However, understanding these differences is essential to understanding the role of the BIOS in the system.

BIOS stands for *basic input/output system*, which consists of low-level software that controls the system hardware and acts as an interface between the operating system (OS) and the hardware. Most people know the term BIOS by another name—*device drivers*, or just *drivers*. In other words, the BIOS *is* drivers, meaning all of them. It's essentially the link between hardware and software in a system. More recently the BIOS has been augmented by a specification called the Unified Extensible Firmware Interface (EUFI), which specifies a different software interface for boot and runtime services but still relies on the traditional BIOS for system configuration, power-on self test (POST), and Setup.

The BIOS consists of software that interfaces the hardware to the OS. The BIOS is unique compared to normal software in that some of it is preloaded into read-only memory (or ROM), and some is loaded into RAM from disk.

The BIOS in a running PC is loaded during the system startup from three possible sources:

- Motherboard ROM
- Adapter card ROMs (such as that found on a video card)
- Loaded into RAM from disk (device drivers)

When the PC was introduced, the BIOS software containing all the device drivers for the entire system was collectively burned into one or more nonvolatile read-only memory (ROM) chips (*nonvolatile* means they retain their data even when the power is turned off) and placed on the motherboard. In essence, the drivers were self-contained, preloaded into memory, and accessible any time the PC was powered on.

This ROM chip also contained a power-on self test (POST) program and a bootstrap loader. The bootstrap program was designed to initiate the loading of an OS by checking for and loading the boot sector from a floppy disk or, if one was not present, a hard disk. After the OS was loaded, it could call on the low-level routines (device drivers) in the BIOS to interact with the system hardware. In the early days, all the necessary device drivers were in the BIOS stored in the motherboard ROM. This included drivers for the keyboard, MDA/CGA video adapters, serial/parallel ports, floppy controller, hard disk controller, joystick, and clock.

When the OS loaded, you didn't have to load a driver to interact with those pieces of hardware because the drivers were already preloaded in the ROM. That worked great as long as you didn't add new hardware for which there wasn't a driver in ROM. If you did, you then had two choices. If the hardware you were adding was an adapter card, that card could include a ROM onboard containing the necessary device drivers. The motherboard ROM was programmed to scan a predetermined area of memory looking for any adapter card ROMs, and if any were found, their code was executed, essentially adding their functionality to the existing BIOS. In essence, the motherboard ROM "assimilated" any adapter card ROMs, adding to the "collective" functionality.

This method of adding drivers was required for items such as video cards, which needed to be functional immediately when the PC was powered on. The BIOS code in the motherboard ROM had drivers only for the IBM monochrome display adapter (MDA) and color graphics adapter (CGA) video cards. If you added a video card other than those, the drivers in the motherboard ROM would not support it. That wouldn't be a problem if the new video card had its own drivers in an onboard ROM that would be linked into the BIOS immediately upon throwing the power switch.

If the device did not have an on-board ROM connected to the main system bus, there had to be another way to add the necessary driver to the BIOS collective. A scheme was devised whereby, during the early stages of loading, the MS-DOS startup file (IO.SYS) checked for a configuration file (called CONFIG.SYS) that specified any additional drivers to load to support new hardware. The CONFIG. SYS file, along with any drivers named within, would be placed on the boot drive. When booting, the IO.SYS program would load the specified drivers into memory and link them into the rest of the BIOS, again adding their functionality to the collective whole. In essence, these drivers were loaded from disk into RAM and linked into the BIOS so they could be called on when necessary.

At this point, the BIOS had grown from being entirely contained in the motherboard ROM, to having additional drivers linked in from adapter card ROMs, to having even more drivers linked in after being loaded into RAM during the early stages of the boot process. The BIOS was now constructed of programs located in three physical locations in the system, yet it functioned as a single entity because all the programs were linked via the BIOS subroutine calling system-of-software interrupts. The OS or an application program needing to talk to a specific piece of hardware (for example, to read from the CD-ROM drive) would make a call to a specific software interrupt, and the interrupt vector table would then route the call to the specific part of the BIOS (meaning the specific driver) for the device being called. It did not matter whether that driver was in the motherboard ROM, adapter ROM, or RAM. As far as the system was concerned, memory is memory, and as long as the routine existed at a known memory address, it could be called.

The combination of the motherboard ROM, adapter card ROM, and device drivers loaded from disk into RAM contributed to the BIOS as a whole. The portion of the BIOS contained in ROM chips, both on the motherboard and in some adapter cards, is sometimes called *firmware*, which is a name given to software stored in ROM chips rather than on disk. Of course, after you turned off the system, the drivers in nonvolatile ROM would remain intact, but those in volatile RAM would instantly vanish. That was not a problem, however, because the next time the system was turned back on, it went through the boot process and loaded the necessary drivers from disk all over again.

As the PC has evolved, more and more accessories and new hardware have been devised to add to the system. This means that more and more drivers have to be loaded to support this hardware. Adding new drivers to the motherboard ROM is difficult because ROM chips are relatively fixed (difficult to change), and limited space is available. The PC architecture allows only 256KB of total ROM space.

128KB is for the motherboard ROM, and most of that was already used by the existing drivers, POST, BIOS Setup program, and, of course, the bootstrap loader. Also, only 128KB is allocated for adapter card ROMs, and putting drivers on adapter card ROMs is expensive, not to mention the fact that the video card/GPU ROM takes 32KB of that space. So, most companies developing new hardware for the PC simply wrote drivers designed to be loaded into RAM during the boot process.

As time went on, more and more drivers were being loaded from disk—including drivers that were replacing those in the motherboard. When modern 32-bit and 64-bit versions of Windows are run, corresponding 32-bit and 64-bit drivers are loaded from disk to replace *all* the drivers in the motherboard ROM. Modern OSs cannot use any of the 16-bit drivers found in either the motherboard ROMs or any adapter card ROMs and must use only 32-bit or 64-bit drivers, depending on the version. The 16-bit code in the motherboard ROM is used only to get the system functioning long enough to get the drivers and OS loaded, at which point they take over. In other words, once Windows is loaded, the BIOS (meaning all the drivers) essentially resides entirely in RAM. The motherboard ROM exists only to get the system started, to initialize specific hardware, to offer security in the way of power-on passwords and such, and to perform some basic initial configuration. After the OS is loaded, a whole new set of drivers takes over.

A PC system can be described as a series of layers—some hardware and some software—that interface with each other. In the most basic sense, you can break a PC down into four primary layers, each of which can be broken down further into subsets. Figure 5.1 shows the four layers in a typical PC.

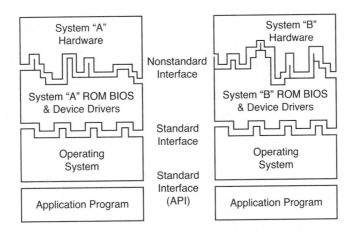

FIGURE 5.1 PC system layers.

The purpose of the layered design is to enable a given OS and applications to run on different hardware. Figure 5.1 shows how two machines with dissimilar hardware can use different sets of drivers (BIOS) to interface the unique hardware to a common OS and applications. Thus, two machines with different processors, storage media, video display units, and so on can run the same OS and applications.

In this layered architecture, the application software programs talk to the OS via what is called an *application programming interface (API)*. The API varies according to the OS you are using and consists of the various commands and functions the OS can perform for an application. For example, an application can call on the OS to load or save a file. This prevents the application itself from having to know how to read the disk, send data to a printer, or perform any other of the many functions the OS can provide. Because the application is completely insulated from the hardware, you can essentially run the same applications on different machines; the application is designed to talk to the OS rather than the hardware.

The OS then interfaces with or talks to the BIOS or driver layer. The BIOS consists of all the individual driver programs that operate between the OS and the actual hardware. As such, the OS never talks to the hardware directly; instead, it must always go through the appropriate drivers. This provides a consistent way to talk to the hardware. It is usually the responsibility of the hardware manufacturer to provide drivers for its hardware. Because the drivers must act between both the hardware and the OS, the drivers typically are OS specific. Thus, the hardware manufacturer must offer different drivers for different OSs. Because many OSs use the same internal interfaces, some drivers can work under multiple OSs. For example, drivers that work under 32/64-bit versions of Windows 7 and 8 usually work under the corresponding versions of Vista; drivers that work under Windows XP usually work under Windows 2000 and NT. This is because Windows 7/8 and Vista are essentially variations on the same core OS, as are Windows XP, Windows 2000, and NT. Although Windows 7/8 and Vista were based on Windows NT, the driver model has changed enough that they generally can't use the same drivers as XP and earlier NT-based OSs.

Because the BIOS layer looks the same to the OS no matter what hardware is above it (or underneath, depending on your point of view), the same OS can run on a variety of systems. For example, you can run Windows on two systems with different processors, hard disks, video adapters, and so on, yet Windows will look and feel pretty much the same to the users on both of them. This is because the drivers provide the same basic functions no matter which specific hardware is used.

As you can see from Figure 5.1, the application and OS's layers can be identical from system to system, but the hardware can differ radically. Because the BIOS consists of drivers that act to interface the hardware to the software, the BIOS layer adapts to the unique hardware on one end but looks consistently the same to the OS at the other end.

The hardware layer is where most differences lie between the various systems. It is up to the BIOS to mask the differences between unique hardware so that the given OS (and subsequently the application) can be run. This chapter focuses on the BIOS layer of the PC.

BIOS and CMOS RAM

Some people confuse BIOS with the CMOS RAM in a system. This confusion is aided by the fact that the Setup program in the BIOS is used to set and store the configuration settings in the CMOS RAM. The BIOS and CMOS RAM are two separate components.

The BIOS on the motherboard is stored in a ROM chip. Also on the motherboard is a chip called the *RTC/NVRAM chip*, which stands for real-time clock/nonvolatile memory. This is where the settings in the BIOS Setup are stored, and it is actually a clock chip with a few extra bytes of memory thrown in. It is usually called the *CMOS chip* because it happens to be made using CMOS (complementary metal-oxide semiconductor) technology.

The first example of this ever used in a PC was the Motorola MC146818 chip, which had 64 bytes of storage, of which 14 bytes were dedicated to the clock function, leaving 50 bytes to store BIOS Setup settings. Although it is called nonvolatile, the chip is actually volatile, meaning that without power, the time/date settings and the data in the RAM portion will in fact be erased. Many consider this chip nonvolatile because it is designed using CMOS technology, which results in a chip that requires little power compared to other chips. A small battery can provide that power when the system is unplugged. This battery-powered clock/memory chip is commonly referred to as "the" CMOS RAM chip; although that is somewhat misleading (almost all modern chips use a form of CMOS technology), the term has stuck. Most RTC/NVRAM chips run on as little as 1 micro amp (millionth of an amp), so they use little battery power to run. Most lithium coin cell batteries can provide power to one of these chips for five years or more before they die and the information stored (including the date and time) is lost.

When you enter the BIOS Setup, configure settings, and save them, the settings are written to the storage area in the RTC/NVRAM chip (otherwise called the *CMOS RAM chip*). Every time your system boots up, software in the BIOS reads the parameters stored in the CMOS RAM chip to determine how to configure the system. A relationship exists between the BIOS and CMOS RAM, but they are two distinct parts of the system.

Some systems used special versions of these chips made by Dallas Semiconductor, Benchmarq, or Odin (such as the DS12885 and DS12887) that include both the RTC/NVRAM chip and the battery in a single component. However, those are uncommon in modern systems today. Although the so-called CMOS RAM chip started out as a discrete chip on the motherboard, in modern systems it is no longer a separate chip, but instead included as one of the functions in the South Bridge, I/O Controller Hub, or Platform Controller Hub component of the motherboard chipset.

Motherboard ROM BIOS

All motherboards have a special chip containing software called the *ROM BIOS*. This ROM chip contains the startup programs and drivers that get the system running and act as the interface to the basic hardware in the system. When you turn on a system, the POST in the BIOS also tests the major components in the system. Additionally, you can run a setup program to store system configuration data in the CMOS memory, which is powered by a battery on the motherboard. This CMOS RAM is often called *NVRAM (nonvolatile RAM)* because it runs on about 1 millionth of an amp of electrical current and can store data for years when powered by a tiny lithium battery.

The motherboard ROM contains a collection of programs embedded in one or more chips, depending on the design of your computer. That collection of programs is the first thing loaded when you start your computer, even before the OS. Simply put, the BIOS in most PCs has four main functions:

- **POST**—POST tests your computer's processor, memory, chipset, video adapter, disk controllers, disk drives, keyboard, and other crucial components.

- **Setup**—The system configuration and setup program is usually a menu-driven program activated by pressing a special key during the POST. It enables you to configure the motherboard and chipset settings along with the date and time, passwords, disk drives, and other basic system settings. You also can control the power-management settings and boot-drive sequence from the BIOS Setup, and on some systems, you can configure CPU timing and clock-multiplier settings. Also, some systems offer a Windows-based application to access BIOS Setup settings.

- **Bootstrap loader**—A routine that reads the first physical sector of various disk drives looking for a valid master boot record (MBR). If one meeting certain minimum criteria (ending in the signature bytes 55AAh) is found, the code within is executed. The MBR program code then continues the boot process by reading the first physical sector of the bootable volume, which is the start of the volume boot record (VBR). The VBR then loads the first OS startup file, which is usually ntldr (Windows XP/2000/NT) or bootmgr (Windows 8/7/Vista). The OS is then in control and continues the boot process.

- **BIOS**—The code that acts as a basic interface between the OS and your hardware when the system is booted and running.

ROM Hardware

Read-only memory (ROM) is a type of memory that can permanently or semi-permanently hold data. It is called *read-only* because it is either impossible or difficult to write to. ROM is also often called *nonvolatile memory* because any data stored in ROM remains even if the power is turned off. As such, ROM is an ideal place to put the PC's startup instructions—that is, the software that boots the system (the BIOS).

Note that ROM and RAM are not opposites, as some people seem to believe. In fact, ROM is technically a subset of the system's RAM. In other words, a portion of the system's random access memory address space is mapped into one or more ROM chips. This is necessary to contain the software that enables the PC to boot up; otherwise, the processor would have no program in memory to execute when it is powered on.

For example, when a PC is turned on, the processor automatically jumps to address FFFF0h, expecting to find instructions to tell the processor what to do. This location is exactly 16 bytes from the end of the first megabyte of RAM space, as well as the end of the ROM. If this location were mapped into regular RAM chips, any data stored there would have disappeared when the power was previously turned off, and the processor would subsequently find no instructions to run the next time the power was turned on. By placing a ROM chip at this address, a system startup program can be permanently loaded into the ROM and will be available every time the system is turned on.

▶▶   For more information about dynamic RAM, see Chapter 6's section, "DRAM," **p. 327**.

Normally, the system ROM starts at address E0000h or F0000h, which is 128KB or 64KB prior to the end of the first megabyte. Because the ROM chip usually is up to 128KB in size, the ROM programs are allowed to occupy the entire last 128KB of the first megabyte, including the critical FFFF0h startup instruction address, which is located 16 bytes from the end of the BIOS space. Some motherboard ROM chips are larger, up to 256KB or 512KB in size. The additional code in these is configured to act as a video card ROM (addresses C0000h–C7FFFh) on motherboards with built-in video and might even contain additional ROM drivers configured anywhere from C8000h to DFFFFh to support additional onboard devices, such as RAID or network adapters.

Figure 5.2 shows a map of the first megabyte of memory in a PC; notice the upper memory areas reserved for adapter card and motherboard ROM BIOS at the end of the first megabyte.

Some think it is strange that the PC would start executing BIOS instructions 16 bytes from the end of the ROM, but this design is intentionally built in to Intel's x86 processors. All the ROM programmer has to do is place a JMP (jump) instruction at that address that instructs the processor to jump to the actual beginning of the ROM—in most cases, close to F0000h—which is about 64KB earlier in the memory map. It's like deciding to read every book starting 16 pages from the end and then having all book publishers agree to place an instruction there to jump back the necessary number of pages to get to page 1. By setting the processor startup location in this way, Intel enabled the ROM to grow to be any size, all the while keeping it at the upper end of addresses in the first megabyte of the memory address space.

Adapter card ROMs are automatically scanned and read by the motherboard ROM during the early part of the boot process—during the POST. The motherboard ROM scans a special area of RAM reserved for adapter ROMs (addresses C0000–DFFFFh) looking for 55AAh signature bytes. This area indicates the start of a ROM.

All adapter ROMs must start with 55AAh; otherwise, the motherboard won't recognize them. The third byte indicates the size of the ROM in 512-byte units called *paragraphs*, and the fourth byte is the actual start of the driver programs. The motherboard ROM uses the size byte for testing purposes. The motherboard ROM adds all the bytes in the ROM and divides the sum by the number of bytes. The result should produce a remainder of 100h. Thus, when creating a ROM for an adapter, the programmer typically uses a "fill" byte at the end to get the checksum to come out right. Using this checksum, the motherboard tests each adapter ROM during the POST and flags any that appear to have been corrupted.

The motherboard ROM automatically runs the programs in any adapter ROMs it finds during the scan. You see this in most systems when you turn them on, and during the POST you see the video card BIOS initialize and announce its presence.

```
                  . = RAM
                  G = Graphics Mode Video RAM
                  M = Monochrome Text Mode Video RAM
                  C = Color Text Mode Video RAM
                  V = Video adapter ROM BIOS
                  a = Reserved for other adapter board ROM
                  r = Additional Motherboard ROM BIOS in some systems
                  R = Motherboard ROM BIOS

                  Conventional (Base) Memory

                       : 0---1---2---3---4---5---6---7---8---9---A---B---C---D---E---F---
                  000000: ................................................................
                  010000: ................................................................
                  020000: ................................................................
                  030000: ................................................................
                  040000: ................................................................
                  050000: ................................................................
                  060000: ................................................................
                  070000: ................................................................
                  080000: ................................................................
                  090000: ................................................................

                  Upper Memory Area (UMA)

                       : 0---1---2---3---4---5---6---7---8---9---A---B---C---D---E---F---
                  0A0000: GGGGGGGGGGGGGGGGGGGGGGGGGGGGGGGGGGGGGGGGGGGGGGGGGGGGGGGGGGGGGGGG
                  0B0000: MMMMMMMMMMMMMMMMMMMMMMMMMMMMMMMCCCCCCCCCCCCCCCCCCCCCCCCCCCCCCCCC
                       : 0---1---2---3---4---5---6---7---8---9---A---B---C---D---E---F---
                  0C0000: VVVVVVVVVVVVVVVVVVVVVVVVVVVVVVVVVaaaaaaaaaaaaaaaaaaaaaaaaaaaaaaa
                  0D0000: aaaaaaaaaaaaaaaaaaaaaaaaaaaaaaaaaaaaaaaaaaaaaaaaaaaaaaaaaaaaaaaa
                       : 0---1---2---3---4---5---6---7---8---9---A---B---C---D---E---F---
                  0E0000: rrrrrrrrrrrrrrrrrrrrrrrrrrrrrrrrrrrrrrrrrrrrrrrrrrrrrrrrrrrrrrrr
                  0F0000: RRRRRRRRRRRRRRRRRRRRRRRRRRRRRRRRRRRRRRRRRRRRRRRRRRRRRRRRRRRRRRRR
```

FIGURE 5.2 PC memory map showing ROM BIOS.

ROM Shadowing

ROM chips by nature are slow, with access times of 100ns (nanoseconds, or billionths of a second) or more, compared to dynamic RAM (DRAM) access times of well under 10ns on most systems. Because of this, in virtually all systems the ROMs are *shadowed*, which means they are copied into RAM at startup to allow faster access during normal operation. The shadowing procedure copies the ROM into RAM and then assigns that RAM the same address as the ROM originally used, disabling the actual ROM in the process. This makes the system seem as though it has ROM running at the same speed as RAM.

ROM Chip Types

The four main types of ROM chips that have been used in PCs are as follows:

- **ROM**—Read-only memory
- **PROM**—Programmable ROM
- **EPROM**—Erasable PROM
- **EEPROM**—Electrically erasable PROM, also sometimes called a flash ROM

No matter which type of ROM your system uses, the data stored in a ROM chip is nonvolatile and remains indefinitely unless intentionally erased or overwritten (in those cases where that is possible).

ROM (True or Mask ROM)

Originally, most ROMs were manufactured with the binary data (0s and 1s) already "cast in" or integrated into the die. The die represents the actual silicon chip. These are called *mask ROMs* because the data is formed into the mask from which the ROM die is photo-lithographically produced. This type of manufacturing method is economical if you are making hundreds of thousands of ROMs with the same information. If you must change a single bit, however, you must remake the mask, which is an expensive proposition. Because of costs and inflexibility, nobody uses mask ROMs anymore.

PROM

PROMs are a type of ROM that is blank when new and must be programmed with whatever data you want. The PROM was invented in the late 1970s by Texas Instruments and has been available in sizes from 1KB (8Kb) to 2MB (16Mb) or more. PROMs can be identified by their part numbers, which usually are 27nnnn—where the 27 indicates the TI type PROM and the nnnn indicates the size of the chip in kilobits (not bytes). For example, most PCs that used PROMs came with 27512 or 271000 chips, which indicate 512Kb (64KB) or 1Mb (128KB), respectively.

Note

Since 1981, all cars sold in the United States have used onboard computers with some form of ROM containing the control software. For example, the 1989 Pontiac Turbo Trans Am I had came with an onboard computer containing a 2732 PROM, which was a 32Kb (4KB) chip in the ECM (electronic control module or vehicle computer) under the dash. This chip contained the vehicle operating software as well as all the data tables describing spark advance, fuel delivery, and other engine and vehicle operating parameters. Many devices with integrated computers use PROMs to store their operating programs.

Although we say these chips are blank when new, they are technically preloaded with binary 1s. In other words, a 1Mb ROM chip used in a PC would come with 1 million (actually 1,048,576) bit locations, each containing a binary 1. A blank PROM can then be programmed, which is the act of writing to it. This usually requires a special machine called a device programmer, ROM programmer, or ROM burner.

Programming the ROM is sometimes referred to as *burning* it because that is technically an apt description of the process. You can think of each binary 1 bit as a fuse, which is intact. Most chips run on 5 volts, but when a PROM is programmed, a higher voltage (normally 12 volts) is placed at the various addresses within the chip. This higher voltage actually blows or burns the fuses at the desired locations, thus turning any given 1 into a 0. Although you can turn a 1 into a 0, you should note that the process is irreversible; that is, you can't turn a 0 back into a 1.

The device programmer examines the program you want to write into the chip and then selectively changes only the 1s to 0s where necessary in the chip.

PROM chips are often referred to as *one-time programmable (OTP)* chips for this reason. They can be programmed once and never erased. Most PROMs are inexpensive (about $3 for a typical PC motherboard PROM), so if you want to change the program in a PROM, you discard it and program a fresh one with the new data.

The act of programming a PROM takes anywhere from a few seconds to a few minutes, depending on the size of the chip and the algorithm the programming device uses. A typical PROM programmer has multiple sockets. This is called a *gang programmer,* and it can program several chips at once, saving time if you have several chips to write with the same data. Less expensive programmers are available with only one socket, which is fine for most individual use.

I use and recommend a programmer from a company called Andromeda Research Labs (www.arlabs. com).

Custom Programming of PROM Chips

I even used a PROM programmer to reprogram the chip in an 1989 Turbo Trans Am, changing the factory preset speed and rpm limiters, turbocharger boost, torque converter lockup points, spark advance, fuel delivery, idle speed, and much more! I also incorporated a switch box under the dash that enables me to switch from among four different chips, even while the vehicle is running. One chip I created I called a "valet chip," which, when engaged, cuts off the fuel injectors at 36 miles per hour and restarts them when the vehicle coasts down to 35 mph. Another chip I created cuts off fuel to the engine altogether, which I engage for security purposes when the vehicle is parked. If you are interested in such a chip-switching device or custom chips for your Turbo Trans Am or Buick Grand National, I recommend you contact Casper's Electronics (www.casperselectronics.com).

EPROM

A once-popular variation of the PROM is the EPROM. An EPROM is a PROM that is erasable. An EPROM chip can be easily recognized by the clear quartz crystal window set in the chip package directly over the die (see Figure 5.3). You can actually see the die through the window! EPROMs have the same 27xxxx part-numbering scheme as the standard PROM, and they are functionally and physically identical except for the clear quartz window above the die.

FIGURE 5.3 An EPROM showing the quartz window for ultraviolet erasing.

The purpose of the window is to allow ultraviolet light to reach the chip die because the EPROM is erased by exposure to intense UV light. The window is quartz crystal because regular glass blocks UV light. You can't get a suntan through a glass window!

Note

The quartz window makes the EPROMs more expensive than the OTP PROMs. This extra expense is needless if erasability is not important.

The UV light erases the chip by causing a chemical reaction, which essentially melts the fuses back together. Thus, any binary 0s in the chip become 1s, and the chip is restored to a new condition with binary 1s in all locations. To work, the UV exposure must be at a specific wavelength (2,537 angstroms), at a fairly high intensity (12,000 uw/cm²), in close proximity (2cm–3cm, or about 1 inch), and last for between 5 and 15 minutes. An EPROM eraser is a device that contains a UV light source (usually a sunlamp-type bulb) above a sealed compartment drawer in which you place the chip or chips.

A professional-type EPROM eraser can handle up to 50 chips at a time. I use a much smaller and less expensive one that erases up to four chips at a time and is both economical and portable. An inexpensive EPROM eraser is available from Andromeda Research Labs (www.arlabs.com).

The quartz crystal window on an EPROM typically is covered by tape, which prevents accidental exposure to UV light. UV light is present in sunlight, of course, and even in standard room lighting, so that over time a chip exposed to the light can begin to degrade. For this reason, after a chip is programmed, you should put a sticker over the window to protect it.

EEPROM/Flash ROM

A more advanced type of ROM is the EEPROM, which stands for *electrically erasable PROM*. These chips are also called *flash ROMs* and are characterized by their capability to be erased and reprogrammed directly in the circuit board they are installed in, with no special equipment required. By using an EEPROM, or flash ROM, you can erase and reprogram the motherboard ROM in a PC without removing the chip from the system or even opening the system chassis.

With a flash ROM or EEPROM, you don't need a UV eraser or device programmer to program or erase chips. Virtually all PC motherboards built since 1994 use flash ROMs or EEPROMs, as do most other computer devices with firmware..

The EEPROM or flash ROM can be identified by a 28xxxx or 29xxxx part number, as well as by the absence of a window on the chip. Having an EEPROM or a flash ROM in your PC motherboard means you can easily upgrade the motherboard ROM without having to swap chips. In most cases, you download the updated ROM from the motherboard manufacturer's website and then run a special program it provides to update the ROM. This procedure is described in more detail later in this chapter.

I recommend that you periodically check with your motherboard manufacturer to see whether an updated BIOS is available for your system. An updated BIOS might contain bug fixes or enable new features or device support not originally found in your system.

▶▶   For more information on updating your PC motherboard flash ROMs, see the section in this chapter, "Upgrading the BIOS," **p. 274**.

Non-PC ROM Upgrades

For the auto enthusiasts out there, you might want to do the same for your car; that is, check to see whether ROM upgrades are available for your vehicle's computer. Now that updates are so easy and inexpensive, vehicle manufacturers are releasing bug-fix ROM upgrades that correct operational problems or improve vehicle performance. In most cases, you must check with your dealer to see whether any new vehicle ROMs are available. If you have a GM car, GM has a website where you can get information about the BIOS revisions available for your car, which it calls Vehicle Calibrations. The GM Vehicle Calibration Information site address is http://calid.gm.com.

Besides updates from the vehicle manufacturer, some aftermarket companies produce ROM upgrades for vehicles. If you are interested in having a custom program installed in your flash ROM–equipped vehicle, I recommend Fastchip (www.fastchip.com), Hypertech (www.hypertech.com), and Superchips (www.superchips.com). If you want to develop your own vehicle calibrations, see www.diy-efi.org for more information.

Flash ROM updates can also be used to add new capabilities to existing peripherals or devices—for example, updating an HD video camera to support higher capacity SDXC flash storage or updating optical rewritable drives to support new media.

These days, many objects with embedded computers controlling them are using flash ROMs; for example, I have updated the flash ROM code (often called *firmware*) in hard drives, solid-state drives (SSDs), optical drives, network routers, wireless access points, network attached storage drives, Blu-ray players, digital cameras, and more. Installing flash ROM or firmware upgrades is as easy as downloading a file from the device manufacturer website and running the update program included in the file. Who knows, one day, you might find yourself downloading flash ROM upgrades for your toaster!

ROM BIOS Manufacturers

Several popular BIOS manufacturers on the market today supply the majority of motherboard and system manufacturers with the code for their ROMs. This section discusses the various available versions.

Several companies have specialized in the development of a compatible ROM BIOS product. The three major companies that come to mind in discussing ROM BIOS software are American Megatrends, Inc. (AMI), Phoenix Technologies, and Award Software (now owned by Phoenix Technologies). Each company licenses its ROM BIOS to motherboard manufacturers so those manufacturers can worry about the hardware rather than the software. To obtain one of these ROMs for a motherboard, the original equipment manufacturer (OEM) must answer many questions about the design of the system so that the proper BIOS can be either developed or selected from those already designed. Combining a ROM BIOS and a motherboard is not a haphazard task. No single, generic, compatible ROM exists, either. AMI, Award, and Phoenix ship many variations of their BIOS code to different board manufacturers, each one custom-tailored to that specific motherboard.

Over the years, some major changes have occurred in the BIOS industry. Intel, perhaps the largest BIOS customer, has switched between Phoenix and AMI for most of its motherboards. Intel originally used a Phoenix BIOS core in its motherboards up through 1995, when it changed to an AMI core. It then used AMI until 1997, when it switched back to Phoenix. In 1999 Intel switched again, this time back to AMI. In each case note that while Intel gets the core BIOS from Phoenix or AMI, they are highly customized for the individual motherboards in which they are installed.

Another major development occurred in late 1998, when Phoenix bought Award. Since then Phoenix has sold both the Phoenix and Award BIOS as different products. The Award BIOS is sold as its standard product, whereas the Phoenix BIOS is sold as a more feature-rich BIOS for high-end systems. Currently, the BIOS market is mostly divided between AMI and Phoenix; however, Phoenix not only develops the BIOS for many systems, but also is the primary BIOS developer responsible for new BIOS development and new BIOS standards.

Another development in recent years has been the creation of separate BIOS products for 32-bit and 64-bit desktop systems, mobile systems, 32-bit and 64-bit servers, and embedded devices. Although all BIOS chips must perform some of the same tasks, a BIOS product optimized for a mobile computer often needs additional support for features such as docking modules, advanced battery power management, as well as bootable USB and removable flash memory devices, whereas a BIOS optimized for a server needs support for features such as advanced hardware monitoring and ECC (error correcting code) memory. By creating customized BIOS versions for different platforms, BIOS vendors provide support for the features needed by a particular computing platform and provide better performance and stability.

Modern BIOS incorporate the Unified Extensible Firmware Interface (UEFI), which, most importantly, allows support for loading modern operating systems from hard drive partitions larger than 2TB, as well as other advanced functionality. Both Phoenix and AMI have core BIOS products supporting the latest UEFI specifications, which most motherboard manufacturers have incorporated in the motherboards they make.

BIOS Hardware/Software

Some important drivers must be active during boot time. For example, how can you boot from a hard disk if the drivers necessary to make the disk interface work must be loaded from that disk? Obviously, at least a minimum level of hard disk drivers must be preloaded into ROM either on the motherboard or on an adapter card for the system to be able to boot.

As another example, how can you see anything onscreen prior to booting if your video card or GPU (graphics processing unit) doesn't have a set of drivers in a ROM? The solution to this could be to provide a motherboard ROM with the appropriate video drivers built in; however, this is impractical because of the variety of video cards/GPUs, each needing its own unique drivers. Instead, when IBM designed the original PC, it designed the PC's motherboard ROM to scan the slots, looking for adapter cards with ROMs on them. If a card was found with a ROM on it, the ROM was executed during the initial system startup phase, before the system began loading the OS from the hard disk.

A few cards (adapter boards) almost always have a ROM onboard, including the following:

- **Video cards/GPUs**—All have an onboard BIOS.

- **RAID (Redundant Array of Independent Disks)** cards enable you to attach multiple drives and array them in different ways to improve reliability, redundancy, and performance. These cards require an onboard BIOS to enable the array to be bootable.

- **Network cards** that support booting directly from a file server have what is usually called a boot ROM or IPL (initial program load) ROM onboard. This enables PCs to be configured on a local area network (LAN) as diskless workstations—also called Net PCs, NCs (network computers), thin clients, or even smart terminals. Intel developed a standard for network booting that it calls the PXE (Preboot eXecution Environment).

- **ATA/Serial ATA (SATA) upgrade boards**—Boards that enable you to attach more or different types of drives than what is typically supported by the motherboard alone. In some cases these cards require an onboard BIOS to enable these drives to be bootable.

Upgrading the BIOS

Motherboard manufacturers tailor the BIOS code to the specific hardware on each board. This is what makes upgrading a BIOS somewhat problematic; the BIOS usually resides in one or more ROM chips on the motherboard and contains code specific to that motherboard model or revision. In other words, you must get your BIOS upgrades from your motherboard manufacturer or from a BIOS upgrade company that supports the motherboard you have, rather than directly from the original core BIOS developer.

Although most BIOS upgrades are done to fix bugs or problems, you must often upgrade the BIOS to take advantage of some other upgrade. For example, a BIOS upgrade often adds support for newer processors, and may add other features like UEFI (Unified Extensible Firmware Interface), larger internal hard drives, bootable optical and USB drives, faster booting, and more.

If you install newer hardware or software and follow all the instructions properly but you can't get it to work, specific problems might exist with the BIOS that an upgrade can fix. This is especially true for newer OSs. Many older systems need to have a BIOS update to properly work with newer technologies and features. Because these problems vary from board to board, it pays to periodically check the board manufacturer's website to see whether updates are posted and what problems they fix. Because new hardware and software that are not compatible with your system could cause it to fail, I recommend you check the BIOS upgrades available for your system before you install new hardware or software—particularly processors and OSs.

Where to Get Your BIOS Update

You must download most BIOS upgrades from the system or motherboard manufacturer's website. The BIOS manufacturers do not offer BIOS upgrades because the BIOS in your motherboard did not come directly from them. In other words, although you may think you have a Phoenix, AMI, or Award BIOS, you really don't! Instead, you have a *custom* version of one of these BIOSs, which was licensed by your motherboard manufacturer and uniquely customized for your particular motherboard. As such, you must get any BIOS upgrades from the motherboard or system manufacturer because they must be customized for your board or system as well.

Determining Your BIOS Version

When seeking a BIOS upgrade for a particular motherboard (or system), you need to know the following information:

- Make and model of the motherboard (or system)
- Version of the existing BIOS

You usually can identify the BIOS you have by watching the screen when the system is first powered up. It helps to turn on the monitor first because some take a few seconds to warm up or become active, and the BIOS information is often displayed for only a few seconds. You may be able to press the Pause key on the keyboard when the BIOS ID information is being displayed, which freezes it so you can record the information. Pressing any other key allows the system startup to resume. If the BIOS version information is not displayed automatically, then you may need to enter the BIOS Setup program in order to see it.

Note

Many PCs do not display the typical POST screen. Instead, they show a logo for the motherboard or PC manufacturer, which is usually referred to as a *splash screen*. To enter BIOS Setup, you must press a key or keys (specific to the BIOS manufacturer). See the section, "Running or Accessing the BIOS Setup Program," for more information. You might hear some in the industry refer to displaying a manufacturer's logo instead of the default POST screen as a *quiet boot*. Often, you can change these BIOS splash screens to your own liking, even including your own company logo or graphic of choice. Intel has free BIOS customization software called the Intel Integrator Toolkit (http://intel.com/go/itk) that enables you to change or restore the splash screen on Intel motherboards, as well as customize many other BIOS settings. Other motherboard manufacturers also offer logo or splash screen customizers; for example, GIGABYTE has a logo utility called Face-Wizard (www.gigabyte.com/MicroSite/121/tech_facewizard.htm) for its motherboards.

Tip

In addition to checking the splash screen or BIOS Setup, you can use a program like CPU-Z or SIV (System Information Viewer) to report the BIOS version, date, and other information. CPU-Z is available free from www.cpuid.com, and SIV is available free from www.rh-software.com.

Checking the BIOS Date

One method of determining the relative age and capabilities of your motherboard ROM is to check the date. The BIOS date is stored in virtually all PCs as an 8-byte text string at memory address FFFF5h.

The date generally indicates when the BIOS code was last updated or compiled by the motherboard manufacturer. Knowing the date of a particular BIOS might give you some clue as to which features might or might not be present. If you are running a 32-bit version of Windows you can use the DEBUG command-line utility to view these addresses. DEBUG presents a prompt of its own, to which you can enter various commands. For example, the ? command displays help information. To find the BIOS date, open a command prompt and execute the DEBUG command. Then at the DEBUG - prompt, enter D FFFF:5 L 8, which instructs DEBUG to display memory at FFFF5 for a length of 8 bytes. DEBUG then displays both the hexadecimal and ASCII codes found at those addresses. When the - prompt returns, you can enter Q to quit DEBUG and return to the command prompt. Figure 5.4 shows how this looked when I ran it on one of my systems.

FIGURE 5.4 Using DEBUG to display the motherboard ROM BIOS date.

In this example, the system shows a motherboard ROM BIOS date of 03/22/05. Note that DEBUG does not work under (and therefore is not included with) 64-bit versions of Windows. In that case you can use free programs like CPU-Z (www.cpuid.com) or SIV (www.rh-software.com) to check the BIOS version and date.

Backing Up Your BIOS

Before updating a BIOS, it is generally a good idea to have a copy of the current BIOS, just in case there are problems with the upgrade. Normally, you would not want to downgrade a BIOS, but there have been situations over the years where some deal-breaking bug in a new release caused problems that required going back to the previous version.

Rather than actually making a backup, it is easiest to see if the currently running (older) version can still be downloaded from the motherboard manufacturer. Many, if not most, motherboard manufacturers maintain an archive of older BIOS versions that can be downloaded and installed as necessary.

If you cannot download the currently running (older) version, then see if it is possible to save a backup copy of the existing BIOS. To make the backup, run the BIOS upgrade program for your board as if you were going to upgrade to the latest version, and check to see if there is an option to save the existing BIOS to a file.

If no older versions can be downloaded and there is no menu option to back up, there may be other ways to make a copy of the BIOS, such as by using the DOS command–based BIOS upgrade software usually found on the BIOS upgrade floppy or CD for the motherboard. For example, if your motherboard has a Phoenix or Award BIOS, you can create a backup using the awdflash.exe program found on the BIOS upgrade disc for your motherboard with the /sy (Save Yes) and /pn (Program No) parameters, as follows:

```
awdflash /sy /pn
```

When the program runs, you are prompted to enter the backup file's name (for example, backup.bin). Press Enter to save the file.

Backing Up Your BIOS Setup (CMOS RAM) Settings

A motherboard BIOS upgrade often wipes out the BIOS Setup settings in the CMOS RAM, resetting everything to defaults. Some BIOS Setup programs offer the ability to save and restore CMOS settings, but unfortunately this capability is not universal. In some cases the new BIOS offers new settings or changes the positions of the stored data in the CMOS RAM, which means a backup and restore won't work.

Although it sounds like a simple concept, actually saving the BIOS Setup settings is somewhat difficult technically because the amount, type, and even location of information stored in the NVRAM (nonvolatile RAM) can vary considerably from one motherboard to another. That being said, there are some possibilities, but they generally won't work with all types of systems.

For example, Lenovo provides both Windows and DOS-based BIOS Settings Capture/Playback Utilities, but these work only on newer ThinkPad laptops. For other systems there are more generic solutions that might work, such as the following:

- **CmosPwd**—www.cgsecurity.org
- **CMOSsave/CMOSrest**—www.mindprod.com

Unfortunately, these don't work on all systems, but they are free to try and use.

In many cases, you are better off manually recording your BIOS Setup parameters. One easy way to do this is to use a digital camera to take pictures of each screen or menu. If you have a parallel printer connected, which is admittedly unlikely, you also might be able to print the screens using the PrtScr (or PrtScn) key on the keyboard. Turn on the printer, start your computer normally, and restart it without turning off the system to initialize the printer. Note that this won't work for printers connected via USB because only parallel printers are directly supported via the BIOS. When recording any changes you made from default settings, pay special attention to any hard drive settings, especially SATA modes (IDE/AHCI/RAID), drive geometry (cylinder/head/sectors per track), or translation (LBA, Large, CHS). These are important because, if you fail to reset them as they were, you might not be able to boot from or access the drives.

Tip

If you use a digital camera to take a picture of each BIOS setup screen, be sure to set the camera to its close-up mode. Also, unless the camera is an SLR (Single Lens Reflex) type, use the camera's LCD screen rather than the optical viewfinder to ensure you get the entire BIOS screen in the photo.

Keyboard Controller Chips

In addition to the main system ROM, some systems have a keyboard-controller microprocessor with its own built-in ROM. The original keyboard controller was an Intel 8042 microcontroller, which incorporates a microprocessor, RAM, ROM, and I/O ports. This was a 40-pin chip that often had a copyright notice identifying the BIOS code programmed into the chip. Modern motherboards have this function integrated into the chipset, specifically the Super I/O or South Bridge chips.

The keyboard controller controls the reset and A20 lines and deciphers the keyboard scan codes. The A20 line is used in extended memory and other protected-mode operations.

Upgrading a Flash BIOS

Virtually all PCs built since 1996 use a flash ROM to store the BIOS. A flash ROM is a type of EEPROM chip you can erase and reprogram directly in the system without special equipment. Older EPROMs required a special ultraviolet light source and an EPROM programmer device to erase and reprogram them, whereas flash ROMs can be erased and rewritten without you even removing them from the system. On some systems, the flash ROM is not a separate chip but may instead be incorporated into the South Bridge chip.

Using flash ROM enables you to load the upgrade into the flash ROM chip on the motherboard without removing and replacing the chip. Normally, these upgrades are downloaded from the manufacturer's website. Depending on the design, some update programs require that you place the software on a bootable floppy or optical disc, whereas others configure the program to run on the next startup (before Windows loads), and still others actually run in Windows as a Windows application.

Some systems allow the flash ROM in a system to be locked (write-protected). In that case, you must disable the protection before performing an update—usually by means of a jumper or switch. Without the lock, any program that knows the correct instructions can rewrite the ROM in your system—not a comforting thought. Without the write-protection, virus programs could be written that overwrite or damage the ROM BIOS code in your system. The CIH virus (also called the Chernobyl virus) was one example that could overwrite the BIOS code on certain motherboards. Instead of a physical write-protect lock, some flash ROM BIOSs have a security algorithm that prevents unauthorized updates. This is the technique Intel uses on its motherboards, eliminating the need for a lock jumper or switch.

Note that motherboard manufacturers do not normally notify you when they upgrade the BIOS for a particular board. You must periodically log on to their websites to check for updates, which you can then download and install at no charge.

Before proceeding with a BIOS upgrade, you must locate and download the updated BIOS from your motherboard manufacturer. Log on to its website, and follow the menus to the BIOS updates page; then select and download the new BIOS for your motherboard.

Note

If a flash BIOS upgrade is identified as being for only certain board revisions of a particular model, be sure you determine that it will work with your motherboard before you install it. You might need to open your system and look for a revision number on the motherboard or for a particular component. Check the vendor's website for details.

Motherboard manufacturers may offer several ways to update the BIOS on a given motherboard, some may run directly from within Windows, and others may need to be run from bootable removable media such as optical, USB, or floppy. You only need to use one of them, so if you have choices, in most cases you should choose the one that is the easiest to perform. Which one you choose may depend on the current state of the system. For example, if the BIOS is corrupt, you may have no other choice but to use the emergency recovery procedures shown in the next section. If the system you are updating is one you are building for the first time and does not yet have a working copy of Windows installed on the hard drive, you may want to use a method that works with other bootable media such as an optical drive, USB flash drive, or floppy drive. If the update files and programs are too large to fit on a floppy, you should run the update from either an optical drive or a USB flash drive.

Most downloadable flash ROM upgrades fit into five main types:

- Windows executable upgrades
- BIOS Setup executable upgrades
- Automated images of bootable media
- User-created bootable media
- Emergency recovery media

The following sections examine each of these in detail.

Windows Executable Upgrade

The Windows executable method is generally the easiest and most popular. It might not be available for older motherboards, but most new boards offer this type of procedure. Performing the actual upgrade couldn't be much easier because basically all you have to do is download the executable upgrade program and run it. The program either runs directly in Windows, or it runs an install routine that temporarily installs the flash upgrade software so it automatically runs on the next startup and then automatically reboots the system and begins the upgrade. In either case, once the upgrade is finished, the system reboots again, and the upgrade is complete. The only drawback to this procedure is that it requires that Windows be installed on the system, so it might not be appropriate for new system builds where the OS isn't installed yet or if you are running an alternative OS, such as Linux.

One potential problem with the Windows executable upgrade method is that if the program runs directly in Windows and the OS is unstable, corrupted, or infected with malware, the BIOS upgrade may be interrupted, potentially requiring a BIOS recovery procedure. Such an event could even destroy the motherboard. Using one of the other methods (such as upgrading from a bootable floppy, CD, or USB flash drive) is preferred if you think the host OS may be unstable.

BIOS Setup Executable Upgrade

Some motherboards now include a flash BIOS upgrade utility in the BIOS. This allows for a BIOS upgrade to be performed in a stable environment outside of Windows, yet without the hassle of having to create DOS-bootable USB flash, optical, or floppy media or entering complicated commands.

This feature is called the *F7 BIOS Flash Update* on Intel motherboards and *M-Flash* on MSI motherboards, and it makes the BIOS upgrade procedure simple. To perform the BIOS upgrade, all you need is a FAT- or FAT32-formatted USB flash drive onto which you have downloaded the BIOS image file from the motherboard manufacturer. Unlike previous upgrades via USB flash drives, the drive only needs to contain the BIOS image file and does not need to be bootable or require any other programs to be installed.

To perform the USB flash-based upgrade on a system using an Intel motherboard, first download the proper BIOS image file for the motherboard and copy it to the root folder of a FAT- or FAT32-formatted USB flash drive. Then restart the system, enter the BIOS Setup and navigate to the Advanced, Boot Configuration menu. Make sure the setting Display F7 to Update BIOS is enabled and that it has been saved. Insert the flash drive into a USB port, restart the system, and follow these steps to complete the process:

1. When prompted during the restart, press F7 to enter the BIOS Flash Update tool.
2. Select the USB flash drive and press Enter.
3. Select the .BIO (BIOS image) file and press Enter. Confirm that you want to update the BIOS by pressing Enter a second time.
4. Wait 2–5 minutes for the update to complete; then, when prompted, remove the USB flash drive and restart the system.

To perform the upgrade on a system using an MSI motherboard, first insert the flash drive, restart the system, and then follow these steps to complete the process:

1. When prompted during the restart, press the Delete key to enter the BIOS Setup.
2. Select the M-Flash menu and change the M-Flash function to BIOS Update.
3. Select the USB flash drive as the source and point to the BIOS image file on the flash drive.

4. Select Flash BIOS and press Enter.

5. Once the upgrade is finished, the system restarts automatically, after which you can remove the flash drive.

As you can see from these examples, updating a modern motherboard via a BIOS Setup–based utility is almost as easy as using a Windows-based utility, yet it has the advantage of working outside of a Windows environment. In fact, it works even with no OS loaded on the system (and without the hassle of creating DOS bootable media), which makes it much easier to update the BIOS on a new motherboard or new system build before you install the OS.

Automated Bootable Media Images

Using automated bootable images is the next easiest method and works with any (or no) OS installed on the system. This is ideal for non-Windows systems or new systems in which the OS hasn't yet been installed. Being able to use this procedure depends on your motherboard manufacturer supplying bootable floppy or optical disc images containing the necessary upgrade files, which you would then use to create the actual upgrade media.

In the case of a floppy, you download the floppy image creation program from the motherboard manufacturer. When you run it, the program prompts you to insert a blank floppy disk into the drive, after which it overwrites the disk with a bootable image containing the bootable OS (most likely DOS or a DOS variant) plus all the files necessary to perform the upgrade. To perform the upgrade, you first ensure that the floppy drive is set in the boot sequence, and then you restart the system with the upgrade floppy disk in the drive. The system should then boot from the floppy, and the upgrade procedure should start and run automatically. Follow any onscreen prompts to complete the upgrade; then when the upgrade is complete, remove the floppy and reboot the system.

Because floppy drives are no longer installed in most systems and the BIOS images for modern motherboards are often too large to fit on a floppy anyway, many motherboard manufacturers offer downloadable images of bootable CDs for BIOS upgrades. These are normally in the form of an *.ISO file, which is an optical disc image file containing a sector-by-sector copy of a disc. To perform the upgrade, you need to write the ISO bootable image file to a blank disc. Unfortunately, Windows versions prior to Windows 7 don't include optical disc burning software that can read or write ISO images, which means that you need a third-party program to accomplish this. Commercial optical disc burning programs are sometimes included with new systems or optical drives, so you might already have the necessary software on your system. If you don't already have such a program, I recommend ImgBurn (www.imgburn.com), which is an excellent free optical disc burning application.

Use your burning program to generate the disc image by copying the ISO file to a blank disc. To perform the upgrade, first ensure that the optical drive is set in the boot sequence; then, restart the system with the upgrade disc in the drive. The system should boot from the disc, and the upgrade procedure should start and run automatically. Follow the prompts to complete the upgrade and then, once the upgrade is complete, remove the disc and reboot the system.

User-Created Bootable Media

Many motherboard manufacturers also offer BIOS upgrades in the form of a raw DOS-based flash utility combined with a BIOS image file, which you can run manually from any DOS-bootable media. Using this technique, you can perform the upgrade from a bootable floppy, optical disc, or even a USB flash drive, regardless of whether the system hard drive is running Windows or Linux or even if it has no OS. The necessary files are normally contained in an archive that you can download from the motherboard manufacturer. Unfortunately, this type of procedure is much more labor intensive than the others because several steps are involved. One particularly difficult part is the manual creation of the bootable media to which you will copy the files. Although it is fairly straightforward and simple to create a bootable floppy, the procedure for creating bootable optical discs or USB flash drives is more involved.

Fortunately, some free utilities are helpful. For creating a bootable CD for BIOS upgrades, I recommend the Clean Boot CD package, which you can download for free from www.nu2.nu/bootcd/#clean. Download the self-extracting executable package into a new folder and run it, which extracts the additional files and folders within. Then follow the directions to copy the flash utility and image files for your motherboard into the proper folder. After the files are in place, you can run the "build-clean" command, which automatically builds and creates an ISO image of a bootable CD, complete with an OS and your files included. You can then use a third-party CD/DVD-burning program such as ImgBurn (www.imgburn.com) to copy the ISO image to an optical disc.

After you have burned the disc, you can boot from it, navigate to the folder where your flash utility and image files are located, and enter the appropriate command to execute the upgrade. For Intel motherboards that use the IFLASH.EXE utility and image files with an *.BIO extension, the proper command would be IFLASH /PF XXX.BIO, where you would replace XXX.BIO with the actual name of the BIO file you have.

You can accomplish the same procedure with a bootable USB flash drive, but just as with the creation of a bootable optical disc, creating a bootable USB flash drive can be somewhat involved. Fortunately, a Windows-based USB format utility (HPUSBDisk.exe) is available for free from HP (http://tinyurl.com/yfz8rdl). To make the flash drive bootable, this program requires a set of DOS system files (command.com, io.sys, and msdos.sys) to write to the flash drive during the format. You can use several versions of DOS, but in most cases I recommend using the system files from DOS 6.22. If you don't have a copy, you can download the DOS 6.22 system files in the form of a bootable floppy image from www.bootdisk.com. Look for the "Non-Windows Based Image Files," and then download the 622c.zip file. Use a program like 7-Zip (www.7-Zip.org) to first extract the .IMG file from the zip file, and then use it again to extract the DOS files from the .IMG file.

To create the bootable flash drive, run the HPUSBDisk.exe program and select the flash device and file system (FAT). Then, check Create a DOS Startup Disk Using System Files Located At and point to the location where you have extracted the necessary DOS files. After that, perform the format.

Note

BIOS and motherboard manufacturers began adding USB boot support during 2001, so if your system dates from around that time or earlier, it might not be able to boot from a USB drive.

When setting up a system to boot from a USB flash drive, the flash drive must be plugged in prior to restarting the system and entering the BIOS setup. In the BIOS setup startup sequence (boot order), the USB flash drive might appear as either a "generic" storage device hard disk or as a type of removable drive, which you should set as the first device in the boot order. In most systems, when the USB flash drive is unplugged, it is automatically removed from the boot order on the next restart.

After the USB flash drive is formatted as a bootable drive, you can add the BIOS flash utility and image file for the motherboard. Plug the bootable USB flash drive into the system you want to upgrade, and then restart the system, run the BIOS setup, and set the USB flash drive to be first in the boot sequence. After you save and exit, the system should boot to DOS from the USB flash drive. At the DOS command prompt, you can then run the proper command to reflash your BIOS.

Conducting a Safe BIOS Upgrade

Because a failure or hang during the flash BIOS update procedure can result in "bricking" the system, when updating a BIOS you want the system to be as stable as possible. With that in mind, when using a Windows or bootable CD-based upgrade I recommend undoing any overclocking and resetting the BIOS Setup settings to Fail-Safe defaults before performing the upgrade.

If you are updating the BIOS using the BIOS Setup–based procedure, you don't need to undo any overclocking settings. That is because when running the BIOS Setup program a system is always running under Fail-Safe settings, which is designed to allow you to reverse any overly aggressive overclocking settings that would cause the system to crash during startup. Most modern motherboards have a feature in the BIOS Setup allowing you to update the BIOS directly from a standard non-bootable USB flash drive, with no other software, discs, and so on necessary. Because the system is always running in fail-safe mode when in the BIOS Setup, you can safely update the BIOS using the BIOS Setup based procedure without having to change or undo overclocking settings.

On some systems, leaving additional external drives connected prevents a BIOS upgrade from working properly. Before you start the flash BIOS upgrade process, disconnect all USB and IEEE 1394 (FireWire) devices except for your keyboard and mouse. If you are booting from a USB flash drive to perform the upgrade, make sure all other USB drives are disconnected.

If you have Byte Merge enabled in the BIOS Setup on an Award BIOS-based system, disable this feature as a precaution before you perform the BIOS upgrade. This is recommended because on some older systems, leaving Byte Merge enabled during a BIOS upgrade can cause the upgrade to fail, corrupting the BIOS in the process. You can reenable this feature after you complete the upgrade. Some BIOS upgrades contain fixes for this problem so it can't happen in the future.

Emergency Flash BIOS Recovery

When you perform a flash BIOS upgrade, you should normally see a warning message onscreen similar to the following:

```
The BIOS is currently being updated. DO NOT REBOOT OR POWER DOWN until the
update is completed (typically within three minutes)...
```

If you fail to heed this warning or something interrupts the update procedure, you can be left with a system that has a corrupted BIOS. This means you will not be able to restart the system and redo the procedure, at least not easily. Depending on the motherboard, you might have to replace the flash ROM chip with one that was preprogrammed by the motherboard manufacturer. This is an unfortunate necessity because a motherboard is nonfunctional until a valid ROM is present. This is one reason I still keep my trusty ROM burner around; it is useful for motherboards with socketed flash ROM chips. In minutes, I can use the ROM burner to reprogram the chip and reinstall it in the board. If "you need a ROM programmer, I recommend the EPROM+ from Andromeda Research Labs (www.arlabs.com).

In most systems, however, the flash ROM is soldered into the motherboard so it can't be easily replaced, rendering the external reprogramming idea moot. However, this doesn't mean the only way out is a complete motherboard replacement. Some motherboards have two ROM chips, with the ability to switch to the second one if the first is corrupted. Other motherboards with soldered-in flash ROMs have a special BIOS Recovery procedure that can be performed, which restores the contents of the chip. This hinges on a special protected part of the flash ROM that is reserved for this purpose, called the *boot block*. The boot block holds a recovery routine that you can use to restore the main BIOS code.

Note

Because of the small amount of code in the boot block area, onscreen prompts are not usually available to direct the procedure. This means that during the procedure the screen remains dark—as if nothing is happening. The procedure can instead be monitored by listening to the internal speaker or looking at the access LED on the drive containing the upgrade media. Normally the procedure causes the system to beep once when it begins and several more times when it ends. During the procedure, you should be able to observe drive activity, indicating that the BIOS image is being read from the drive and written into the flash device.

Different motherboards and BIOS versions may have different recovery techniques. Most motherboards (including those from Intel) that support BIOS recovery incorporate a BIOS configuration jumper, which can set several modes, including a built-in recovery mode. Figure 5.5 shows this jumper on a typical motherboard.

In addition to moving the jumper, the recovery requires that a USB flash drive, optical drive, or floppy drive containing media with the BIOS image file is attached to the system and properly configured.

Before beginning the recovery procedure, you need to download the proper BIOS image file for the motherboard you are recovering. Obviously, you need to do this using another system if the system to be recovered is nonfunctional. The BIOS image file can be downloadable separately, or it can be part of an archive with other files, such as flash programming tools and documentation. In this case you only need the actual image file; none of the other programs or files will be used.

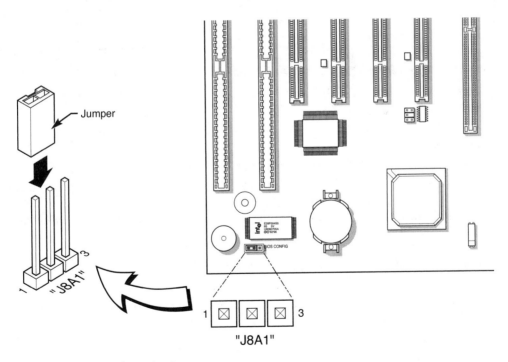

FIGURE 5.5 BIOS configuration jumper.

You can use the optical or USB flash drive methods on motherboards that do not have a built-in floppy controller or for which the recovery file won't fit on a 1.44MB floppy. Although the drive can be virtually any type of CD or DVD optical drive, the actual disc you use should be a CD-R or RW that is burned with the BIOS image file in the root folder and finalized (closed). You can write the recovery file to disc using the built-in CD-burning software found in Windows (XP or later), or you can use third-party software such as the free ImgBurn application (www.imgburn.com). If you are using the USB flash drive method, note that the drive must be formatted using the FAT-32 file system, other file systems such as NTFS won't be readable by the motherboard in recovery mode. To recover the BIOS using the optical drive method, perform the following steps:

1. Burn and finalize a disc (preferably a CD) with a copy of the BIOS image file in the root folder.
2. Place the disc in the primary optical drive of the system to be recovered.
3. Power off the system and remove the BIOS configuration jumper to enable BIOS Recovery mode (refer to Figure 5.5).
4. Power on the system; the recovery should begin automatically.
5. The recovery should complete in 2 to 5 minutes, after which the system will remain running, turn off automatically, or prompt you to turn it off manually.
6. With the system powered off, restore the BIOS configuration jumper to enable normal operation.

Note

A BIOS recovery may corrupt the BIOS Setup information stored in the CMOS RAM. If the error message CMOS/GPNV Checksum Bad...Press F1 to Run SETUP appears during the first boot after the update, press F1 to go into the BIOS Setup Utility, press F9 to load setup defaults, and then press F10 to save and exit to correct the problem.

To recover the BIOS using the USB flash drive method, perform the following steps:

1. Copy the BIOS image file to the root folder of a FAT-32 formatted USB flash drive.
2. Plug the flash drive into a USB port of the system to be recovered.
3. Power off the system and remove the BIOS configuration jumper to enable BIOS Recovery mode (refer to Figure 5.5).
4. Power on the system; the recovery should begin automatically.
5. The recovery should complete in 2 to 5 minutes, after which the system will remain running, turn off automatically, or prompt you to turn it off manually.
6. With the system powered off, restore the BIOS configuration jumper to enable normal operation.

To recover the BIOS using the floppy recovery method, perform the following steps:

1. Copy the BIOS image file to a blank formatted floppy disk.
2. Place the disk in the primary floppy drive attached to the system to be recovered.
3. Power off the system and remove the BIOS configuration jumper to enable BIOS Recovery mode (refer to Figure 5.5).
4. Power on the system; the recovery should begin automatically. You should hear a beep at the start and see activity on the floppy drive during the procedure.
5. The recovery should complete in 2 to 5 minutes, after which the system will remain running, power off automatically, or prompt you to turn it off manually.
6. With the system powered off, remove the floppy disk, and restore the BIOS configuration jumper to enable normal operation.

Because the procedure can vary for different motherboards, I recommend consulting the motherboard manual as well as the BIOS update instructions to see if there is a flash recovery option, and exactly how to use it.

With any of these procedures, wait at least several minutes after all disk and beeping activity stops before restarting the system. When you power the system back on, the new BIOS should be installed and functional. If nothing at all happens, the recovery may have failed, or the board may not feature a separate boot-block section (which contains the recovery code).

Note

The BIOS recovery procedure is often the fastest way to update a large number of machines, especially if you are performing other upgrades at the same time, or the machines are new and do not have a bootable OS installed. For example, this is how updates are sometimes done in a system assembly or production environment.

Motherboard CMOS RAM Addresses

In the original IBM AT system, a Motorola 146818 chip was used as the real-time clock (RTC) and CMOS RAM chip. This special chip had a simple digital clock that used 14 bytes of RAM and an additional 50 more bytes of leftover RAM in which you could store anything you wanted. The designers of the IBM AT used these extra 50 bytes to store the system configuration.

Modern PC systems don't use the Motorola chip; instead, they incorporate the functions of this chip into the motherboard chipset (South Bridge) or Super I/O chip, or they use a special battery and NVRAM module from companies such as Dallas Semiconductor or Benchmarq.

Table 5.1 shows the standard format of the information stored in the 64-byte standard CMOS RAM module. This information controls the configuration of the system and is read and written by the system setup program.

Table 5.1   CMOS RAM Addresses

Offset (Hex)	Offset (Dec)	Field Size	Function
00h	0	1 byte	Current second in BCD[1] (00–59)
01h	1	1 byte	Alarm second in BCD
02h	2	1 byte	Current minute in BCD (00–59)
03h	3	1 byte	Alarm minute in BCD
04h	4	1 byte	Current hour in BCD (00–23)
05h	5	1 byte	Alarm hour in BCD
06h	6	1 byte	Current day of week in BCD (00–06)
07h	7	1 byte	Current day of month in BCD (00–31)
08h	8	1 byte	Current month in BCD (00–12)
09h	9	1 byte	Current year in BCD (00–99)
0Ah	10	1 byte	Status register A
0Bh	11	1 byte	Status register B
0Ch	12	1 byte	Status register C

Table 5.1 Continued

Offset (Hex)	Offset (Dec)	Field Size	Function
0Dh	13	1 byte	Status register D
0Eh	14	1 byte	Diagnostic status
0Fh	15	1 byte	Shutdown code
10h	16	1 byte	Floppy drive types
11h	17	1 byte	Advanced BIOS Setup options
12h	18	1 byte	Hard disk 0/1 types (0–15)
13h	19	1 byte	Keyboard typematic rate and delay
14h	20	1 byte	Installed equipment
15h	21	1 byte	Base memory in 1K multiples, LSB[2]
16h	22	1 byte	Base memory in 1K multiples, MSB[3]
17h	23	1 byte	Extended memory in 1K multiples, LSB
18h	24	1 byte	Extended memory in 1K multiples, MSB
19h	25	1 byte	Hard Disk 0 Extended Type (0–255)
1Ah	26	1 byte	Hard Disk 1 Extended Type (0–255)
1Bh	27	9 bytes	Hard Disk 0 user-defined type information
24h	36	9 bytes	Hard Disk 1 user-defined type information
2Dh	45	1 byte	Advanced BIOS Setup options
2Eh	46	1 byte	CMOS checksum MSB
2Fh	47	1 byte	CMOS checksum LSB
30h	48	1 byte	POST[4] reported extended memory LSB
31h	49	1 byte	POST reported extended memory MSB
32h	50	1 byte	Date century in BCD (00–99)
33h	51	1 byte	POST information flag
34h	52	2 bytes	Advanced BIOS Setup options
36h	54	1 byte	Chipset-specific BIOS Setup options
37h	55	7 bytes	Power-On Password (usually encrypted)
3Eh	62	1 byte	Extended CMOS checksum MSB

1 BCD = Binary-coded decimal
2 LSB = Least significant byte
3 MSB = Most significant byte
4 POST = Power-on self test

Many newer systems have extended CMOS RAM with 2KB, 4KB, or more. The extra room stores the Plug and Play information detailing the configuration of adapter cards and other options in the system. As such, no 100%-compatible standard exists for the way CMOS information is stored in all systems. You should consult the BIOS manufacturer for more information if you want the full details of how CMOS is stored because the CMOS configuration and setup programs typically are part of the BIOS. This is another example of how close the relationship is between the BIOS and the motherboard hardware.

Backup programs and utilities are available in the public domain for CMOS RAM information, which can be useful for saving and later restoring a configuration. Unfortunately, these programs are BIOS specific and function only on the BIOS for which they are designed. As such, I don't usually rely on these programs because they are too motherboard and BIOS specific and do not work on all my systems seamlessly.

Table 5.2 shows the values that might be stored by your system BIOS in a special CMOS byte called the *diagnostic status byte*. By examining this location with a diagnostics program, you can determine whether your system has set trouble codes, which indicate that a problem previously has occurred.

Table 5.2   CMOS RAM Diagnostic Status Byte Codes

7	6	5	4	3	2	1	0	Hex	Function
\multicolumn{8}{l}{Bit Number}									
1	■	■	■	■	■	■	■	80	Real-time clock (RTC) chip lost power.
■	1	■	■	■	■	■	■	40	CMOS RAM checksum is bad.
■	■	1	■	■	■	■	■	20	Invalid configuration information found at POST.
■	■	■	1	■	■	■	■	10	Memory size compare error at POST.
■	■	■	■	1	■	■	■	08	Fixed disk or adapter failed initialization.
■	■	■	■	■	1	■	■	04	Real-time clock (RTC) time found invalid.
■	■	■	■	■	■	1	■	02	Adapters do not match configuration.
■	■	■	■	■	■	■	1	01	Timeout reading an adapter ID.

If the diagnostic status byte is any value other than 0, you typically get a CMOS configuration error on bootup. You can clear these types of errors by rerunning the setup program.

Preboot Environment

Some systems use the Phoenix BIOS preboot environment, which has a graphical user interface (GUI) that allows a user to access the BIOS Setup, extended diagnostics, a backup/restore application, or a full recovery of the original system contents (product restoration to factory-delivered contents). All these applications (except the BIOS Setup) are stored in the *HPA (Host Protected Area)*, a hidden area of the hard drive literally situated past the reported end of the drive. The number and type of applications accessible via the preboot environment depend on which options the OEM selected when designing the system. Figure 5.6 shows the IBM/Lenovo implementation of the Phoenix BIOS preboot environment. This environment is activated by pressing the Enter key on the keyboard during the POST.

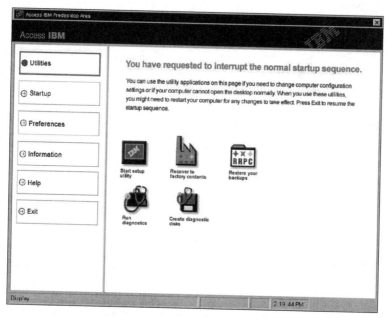

FIGURE 5.6 IBM/Lenovo implementation of the Phoenix BIOS preboot environment.

A graphical preboot environment is especially useful for product recovery. For example, most of the larger system OEMs do a lot more than just install Windows on a system before they deliver it. After installing Windows, they install all the service packs and updates available at the time, as well as all the updated drivers unique to their systems. Then they add customizations, such as special wallpapers or interface customizations, support contact information, online system documentation, and custom utilities designed to make their systems easier to use. Finally, they install applications such as DVD players, Office applications or other productivity software, and more.

This OEM customization represents a lot of work if a user were to have to duplicate this from scratch, so most manufacturers like to include the ability to easily recover the system to the factory-delivered contents, including the OS, drivers, applications, and custom configuration. This was originally provided via several CDs or DVDs, which could be lost or damaged by the user, were sometimes problematic to use, and cost money to produce and deliver with the system. By using a BIOS with a preboot environment, an OEM can instead deliver the contents of the recovery CDs directly on the hard disk and make it accessible via the preboot menu in the BIOS.

Originally, this was done using a hidden partition, which unfortunately could easily be damaged or overwritten by partitioning software or other utilities. In many newer systems, the contents of the recovery disks are instead preinstalled in the HPA, which is accessible via Protected Area Run Time Interface Extension Services (PARTIES), a standard supported on all ATA-4 or newer drives. HPA/PARTIES works by using the ATA SET MAX ADDRESS command to essentially make the drive appear to the system as a slightly smaller drive. Most manufacturers use the last 3GB of the drive for the HPA. Anything from the new max address (the newly reported end of the drive) to the true end of the drive is considered the HPA and is accessible only using PARTIES commands. Figure 5.7 shows the contents of the HPA and the relationship between the HPA and the rest of the drive.

The HPA is more secure than a hidden partition because any data past the end of the drive simply cannot be seen by a normal application, or even a partitioning utility such as Partition Magic or Partition

Commander. This makes it far more secure and immune to damage. Still, if you wanted to remove the HPA, there is a way to reset the max address, thus exposing the HPA. Then, you could run something like Partition Magic or Partition Commander to resize the main partition to include the extra space that was formerly hidden and unavailable. The only consequence is that you would lose access to the product recovery, diagnostics, and backup applications preloaded by the OEM. For some people, this might be desirable because future product recoveries could still be done via the recovery discs (not usually shipped with the system anymore, but still available separately either for free or for a minimal charge), and true hardware diagnostics can still be run via bootable floppies or optical discs. Also, if you are replacing the hard disk, you can temporarily unhide the HPA on the original drive, allowing it to be copied to a new drive. Alternatively, you can use the OEM-supplied recovery discs to install the HPA on the new drive.

Most new systems using Phoenix BIOS come with their recovery software and diagnostics in the HPA because this is part of the newer Phoenix BIOS cores used by a large number of OEMs on desktop and laptop systems built in 2003 or later.

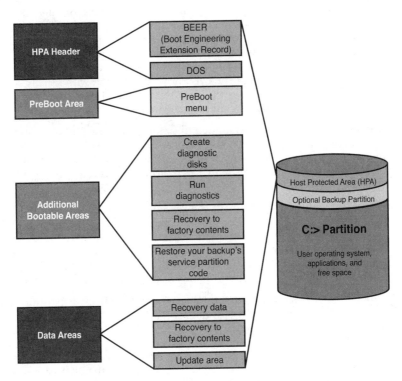

FIGURE 5.7 The Host Protected Area (HPA).

Unified Extensible Firmware Interface (UEFI)

Unified Extensible Firmware Interface (UEFI) defines an interface between an OS and computer hardware and firmware. The interface consists of tables containing system-specific information as well as boot and runtime services that are available to the OS loader and to the OS after it is loaded. These tables and services provide an industry-standard environment for running preboot applications, booting an OS, and providing drivers for devices that need to be active during boot. Because UEFI is based on the EFI specification originated by Intel, it is common to use the terms EFI and UEFI interchangeably.

UEFI was initially created by Intel as just EFI, and the EFI 1.01 specification was originally released in 2000. EFI was an outgrowth of the Intel Boot Initiative (IBI) program that began in 1998. You can see the original Intel EFI specifications at www.intel.com/technology/efi. Intel updated the EFI specification through 2003, and in 2005 it contributed the specification to the Unified EFI (UEFI) Forum, a nonprofit organization formed to promote and manage the UEFI standard. The UEFI Forum is led by representatives from 11 major companies including AMD, AMI, Apple, Dell, HP, IBM, Insyde, Intel, Lenovo, Microsoft, and Phoenix Technologies. You can download the latest version of the UEFI specification from the Unified EFI Forum at www.uefi.org.

Starting in 2011 virtually all Intel and AMD-based motherboards included a BIOS with UEFI support. Operating systems with UEFI support include the 64-bit versions of Windows Vista SP1 and later, including Windows 7 and 8.

UEFI and BIOS Limitations

The original PC BIOS was released in 1981 as part of the first IBM PC. The BIOS at that time consisted of only 8KiB of 16-bit code running in what is known as the "real mode" of Intel x86 (or compatible) processors, which limits memory addressability to just 1 mebibyte (MiB). Since then the BIOS has grown somewhat in size, but it still must run as 16-bit x86 code and fit into a meager 128-kibibyte (KiB) window of memory. In addition, add-on cards that need to be functional at boot time (such as video and RAID cards) must contain a ROM of limited size with 16-bit x86 code. This is why the POST, BIOS Setup, RAID Setup, and other preboot code you normally interact with usually runs in text mode and must be navigated using only the keyboard. All of this looks and feels crude in comparison to the high-res graphical mouse-driven interfaces found in modern OSs.

Another issue is that because the BIOS is so limited in size and functionality (it exists mainly to test/initialize the hardware, and then find and load an OS), a PC without an OS installed (or with one that has been corrupted) has little or no functionality besides entering the BIOS Setup. In other words, you cannot run extensive diagnostics, go online with a web browser, send or receive email, or read or write files.

But perhaps the most important limitation with the PC BIOS is that it was only designed to boot from MBR-formatted disks. Because the MBR can only define up to four primary partitions on a disk of just under 2.2TB in maximum size, BIOS-based systems cannot boot from a drive that is 2.2TB or greater in capacity. That started to be a problem a few years ago for drive arrays as it became possible to combine multiple drives in an array potentially larger than that. But the 2.2-terabyte (TB) limitation started to become an even bigger problem in 2010 when the first 3TB drives were released to the market.

The solution to the limitations caused by the MBR format is a more flexible partitioning scheme called the GUID (globally unique identifier) Partition Table (GPT). The GPT is a newer boot sector and format design that supports up to 128 partitions on a disk of up to 9.4 zettabytes (ZB, where 1 zettabyte = 1 billion terabytes or 1 sextillion bytes). While the GPT breaks the 2.2TB barrier, GPT-formatted drives can only be used as data drives because the PC BIOS supports only MBR and cannot boot from a GPT drive. The solution to the GPT boot problem is UEFI, which replaces the BIOS boot loader with a UEFI loader that supports both MBR and GPT-formatted drives, thus breaking the 2.2TB limitation.

UEFI does not completely replace the BIOS, at least not yet. At a minimum, it runs on top of the BIOS as a replacement for the boot loader and runtime services (see Figure 5.8). UEFI does not specifically define POST or BIOS Setup functionality, but it does allow enhanced versions of those preboot functions to be created along with additional preboot applications. Because of this, a motherboard with UEFI firmware may look exactly like a standard BIOS Setup from the user's perspective, with the only difference being a UEFI Boot option somewhere in the BIOS Setup. Enabling this option allows the UEFI boot loader to replace the BIOS boot loader, thus enabling the ability to boot from a drive 2.2TB or greater in capacity.

FIGURE 5.8 MSI ClickBIOS II UEFI BIOS Main Screen.

Although some UEFI firmware implementations will look like a standard BIOS, most will be notable by their enhanced mouse-driven graphical interfaces combined with additional features not found in older PC BIOS (see Figure 5.8). You may find the following features in the UEFI firmware of motherboards:

- **Diagnostics**—Tests that are much more comprehensive than the standard POST, including tests for memory and hard disks.

- **Live Update**—A tool that can check the motherboard manufacturer website to see if a firmware/BIOS update is available and then automatically download and install the proper update.

- **HDD Backup**—A tool that backs up or clones a hard disk drive (HDD) from outside the OS. This allows for complete backups and easy HDD upgrades.

- **Overclocking**—Enhanced intelligent overclocking utilities that virtually automate the process and can easily undo the settings if they fail.

- **Boot Logo**—The ability to easily update or change the graphical boot logo seen when you turn the system on.

UEFI firmware may also include applications for web browsing, email, and other useful capabilities that can almost make a PC with no OS useful all by itself.

UEFI Support

Even though EFI has been around since 2000, full support in the PC environment was virtually non-existent until 2008, and it wasn't really widespread until 2011. Intel began shipping some of the first motherboards with UEFI boot capability in 2006; however, OS support for UEFI wasn't available until Vista SP1 x64 was released in 2008. MSI shipped a few specific motherboards in 2008 that had optional/experimental UEFI firmware (called *Click BIOS*), but few people really used it because such support really wasn't necessary unless you had a boot drive equal to or greater than 2.2TB in capacity, and drives bigger than that didn't come along until late 2010.

Coinciding with the introduction of the Intel 6x Series chipsets in 2011, many motherboards began including UEFI firmware as a standard feature. This was just in time to support the new 3TB drives that were beginning to appear on the market, as well as the growing move to 64-bit OSs such as Windows 7/8 x64.

If you want to boot from a GPT-formatted disk (2.2TB and larger disks must be formatted as GPT), you need two things: a motherboard with UEFI firmware (at a minimum a UEFI Boot option that is enabled) and an OS with UEFI support. Windows UEFI support is provided only in the 64-bit versions of Vista SP1 and later (including Windows 7/8), whereas most newer 32-bit and 64-bit Linux versions support UEFI as well. Neither Windows XP nor 32-bit versions of Vista or later support UEFI, which means they cannot boot from 2.2TB or larger (or GPT-formatted) drives.

Note that although Windows XP and 32-bit versions of 8/7/Vista cannot boot from GPT disks, they can use GPT-formatted drives as data disks. This support is provided natively in XP x64 and 8/7/Vista x64, but with XP x86 (32-bit) you need a third-party utility such as the Paragon GPT Loader (www.paragon-software.com) or the ASUS Disk Unlocker (www.asus.com) to enable GPT support.

BIOS Setup

You must run the BIOS Setup to configure the CMOS RAM with information about your system's drives and user-selected options before you can use your computer. The Setup program provided with your system is used to select the options you want to use to start your computer.

Running or Accessing the BIOS Setup Program

If you want to run the BIOS Setup program, you usually have to reboot and press a particular key or key combination during the POST. Normally, the correct key to press is displayed onscreen momentarily during the POST. If it flashes past too quickly to read, try pressing the Pause key on the keyboard when it appears. This key freezes the system, allowing you to read the display. Pressing any other key (such as the spacebar) unpauses the system and allows the POST to continue. The major vendors have standardized the following keystrokes to enter the BIOS Setup in recent systems:

- **AMI BIOS**—Press F1 or Del (Delete) during POST.
- **Phoenix BIOS**—Press F1 or F2 during POST.
- **Award BIOS**—Press Del (Delete or Ctrl+Alt+Esc during POST.
- **Microid Research (MR) BIOS**—Press Esc during POST.

If your system does not respond to one of these common keystroke settings, you might have to contact the manufacturer or read the system documentation to find the correct keystrokes.

Some unique ones are as follows:

- **Toshiba notebook/laptop**—Press Esc while powering on the system; then press F1 when prompted.
- **Older Phoenix BIOS**—Boot to a safe-mode DOS command prompt, and then press Ctrl+Alt+Esc or Ctrl+Alt+S.
- **Compaq**—Press F10 during POST.

After you are at the BIOS Setup main screen, you'll usually find a main menu allowing access to other menus and menus of different sections or screens. In the following sections, I go through the menus and submenus found on most Intel motherboards. Although not all motherboards have all of these settings, and other brands may use slightly different settings and terminology, most will be similar in content.

BIOS Setup Menus

Most modern BIOSs offer a menu bar at the top of the screen when you're in the BIOS Setup that controls navigation through the various primary menus. A typical menu bar offers the choices shown in Table 5.3.

Note

The settings covered here help you get a general idea of the type of settings to expect and how the BIOS Setup settings affect your computer. Note, however, that the specific settings you see, their locations, and even the menu titles can vary by the specific motherboard make, model, and BIOS revision.

Table 5.3   BIOS Setup Menus

Setup Menu	Description
Maintenance	Clears passwords and displays processor information. The maintenance menu is displayed only when the BIOS Configuration jumper is set to configure mode.
Main	Configures processor and time/date.
Advanced	Configures advanced chipset and hardware features.
Security	Sets passwords and security features.
Power	Configures power management features and power supply controls.
Boot	Selects boot options.
Exit	Saves or discards changes to Setup program options.

Choosing each of these selections takes you to another menu with more choices.

Maintenance Menu

The Maintenance menu is a special menu for setting the processor speed and clearing the setup passwords. Older motherboards used jumpers to configure the processor bus speed (motherboard speed) and processor multiplier. Most newer boards from Intel and others now offer this control via the BIOS Setup rather than moving jumpers. In the case of Intel, one jumper still remains on the board, called the *configuration jumper*, and it must be set to Configure mode for the Maintenance menu to be available.

Setup displays this menu only if the system is set in Configure mode. To set Configure mode, power off the system and move the configuration jumper on the motherboard from Normal to Configure (refer to Figure 5.7). Because this is the only jumper on a modern Intel board, it is pretty easy to find. When the system is powered back on, the BIOS Setup automatically runs, and you can select the Maintenance menu shown in Table 5.4. After making changes and saving, power off the system and reset the jumper to Normal mode for normal operation.

Table 5.4   Maintenance Menu Settings

Setting	Options	Description
Board ID	—	Value that uniquely identifies the board.
C1E	Enabled Disabled	Allows the system to reduce processor voltage when no work is being done.
Clear All Passwords	OK Cancel	Clears both user and supervisor passwords.
Clear Trusted Platform Module	OK Cancel	Used to clear the Trusted Platform Module (TPM) if you are transferring ownership of the system to a new user.

Table 5.4 Continued

Setting	Options	Description
CPU Frequency Multiplier	User Defined	Sets the ratio between CPU Core Clock and the front side bus (FSB). This setting is present only when Default Frequency Ratio is disabled.
CPU Microcode Update Revision	—	Displays processor's Microcode Update Revision.
CPU Stepping Signature	—	Displays processor's Stepping Signature.
Default Frequency Ratio	Enabled Disabled	Enabled uses processor default frequency ratio. Disabled allows programming of frequency ratio.
Failsafe Watchdog	Enabled Disabled	When enabled, uses a watchdog timer (WDT) to detect boot lockups and reset the system with default settings.
Fixed Disk Boot Sector	Enable Disable	MBR virus protection. Enable: Master boot.
Microcode Revision	—	Displays the processor microcode revision.
Processor Stepping	—	Displays the processor stepping.
Ratio Actual Value	—	Displays the processor core/bus ratio.
Reset Intel AMT to default	—	Resets Intel Active Management Technology (AMT) to the default factory settings.
Use Maximum Multiplier	Automatic Disabled	Works only on multiplier-unlocked processors. Sets CPU speed to default or maximum rated multiplier.

Note that most processors are designed to allow operation only at their default multiplier or frequency ratio (a feature called *speed locking*), whereas some allow higher-than-rated ratios to be selected.

If a user forgets his password, all he has to do is set the configuration jumper, enter the Maintenance menu in BIOS Setup, and use the option provided to clear the password. This function doesn't tell the user what the password was; it simply clears it, allowing a new one to be set if desired. This means the security is only as good as the lock on the system case because anybody who can get to the configuration jumper can clear the password and access the system. This is why some computer cases (chassis) come equipped with locks and chassis intrusion switches that connect to the motherboard, setting a flag in the BIOS Setup indicating that the system has been opened.

Main Menu

The standard BIOS Setup menu dates back to the 286 days, when the complete BIOS Setup consisted of only one menu. In the standard menu, you can set the system clock and record hard disk and floppy drive parameters and the basic video type. Newer BIOSs have more complicated setups with more menus and submenus, so the main menu often is fairly sparse compared to older systems.

The main menu in a modern system reports system information such as the BIOS version, the processor type and speed, the amount of memory, and whether the memory or cache is configured for ECC functionality. The main menu also can set the system date and time.

Table 5.5 shows a typical main menu.

Table 5.5 Main Menu Settings

Setting	Options	Description
Additional System Information	—	Displays system information, motherboard information, chassis information, and so on.
BIOS Version	—	Displays the version of the BIOS currently installed.
Core Multiplexing Technology	Enabled Disabled	When disabled, this setting turns off all but one processor core. You may need to set this for legacy OSs that do not support multiple cores. Depending on the particular processor, the remaining core may have access to more cache, resulting in better performance under certain applications.
Front Side Bus (FSB) Frequency	—	Displays the FSB frequency.
Hyper-Threading Technology	Enabled Disabled	Enables or disables Hyper-Threading Technology (HTT).
L2 Cache RAM Language	— English French	Displays the size of L2 cache. Selects the language the BIOS uses.
Processor Speed	—	Displays the processor speed.
Processor Type	—	Displays the processor type.
System Bus Speed	—	Displays the system bus speed.
System Date	Month/day/year	Sets the current date.
System Memory Speed	—	Displays the system memory speed.
System Time	Hour:minute:second	Sets the current time.
Total Memory	—	Displays the total amount of RAM.

Most older BIOSs report memory as base and extended memory instead of as a single value. Base memory is typically 640KB and sometimes is called *conventional memory*. *Extended memory* is that which is beyond the first megabyte in the system.

You can't change values in the memory fields; they are only for your information because the system counts them automatically. If the memory count doesn't match what you have installed, a problem has likely occurred with some of the memory: It is defective, is not fully seated or properly installed, or is a type that is incompatible with your system.

Advanced Menus

The Advanced menus are used for setting advanced features that the motherboard chipset typically controls. This part of your BIOS setup is somewhat specific to the particular chipset the motherboard uses. Many chipsets are available on the market today, and each has unique features. The chipset setup is designed to enable the user to customize these features and control some of the chipset settings. Table 5.6 shows the typical Advanced menus available.

Table 5.6 Advanced BIOS Menus

Advanced Menu	Description
PCI Configuration	Configures the IRQ priority of individual PCI slots
PCI Express Configuration	Configures PCI express slots
Memory Configuration	Configures memory controller and modules
Boot Configuration	Configures Plug and Play and the NumLock key
Chipset Configuration	Configures advanced chipset features
Peripheral Configuration	Configures peripheral ports and devices
Drive Configuration	Configures ATA devices
Floppy Configuration	Configures the floppy drive
Event Log Configuration	Configures event logging
Video Configuration	Configures video features
USB Configuration	Configures USB support
Fan Control Configuration	Configures fan operation
Hardware Monitoring	Displays voltage, temperature, and fan speeds

Advanced PCI Configuration

The PCI Configuration menu is used to select the IRQ priority of add-on cards plugged into the PCI slots. Auto (the default) should be used to allow the BIOS and OS to assign IRQs to each slot unless specific PCI cards require unique IRQs. See Table 5.7 for a typical example.

Table 5.7 Advanced PCI Configuration Menu Settings

Feature	Options	Description
PCI Slot 1 IRQ Priority	Auto (default), 3, 5, 9, 10, 11	Allows selection of the IRQ priority for PCI bus connector 1
PCI Slot 2 IRQ Priority	Auto (default), 3, 5, 9, 10, 11	Allows selection of the IRQ priority for PCI bus connector 2
PCI Slot 3 IRQ Priority	Auto (default), 3, 5, 9, 10, 11	Allows selection of the IRQ priority for PCI bus connector 3
PCI Slot 4 IRQ Priority	Auto (default), 3, 5, 9, 10, 11	Allows selection of the IRQ priority for PCI bus connector 4

Additional IRQs might be available if onboard devices such as the serial and parallel ports are disabled.

Advanced PCI Express Configuration

The PCI Express Configuration menu is used to configure settings related to the PCI Express bus and slots. See Table 5.8 for a typical example.

Table 5.8 Advanced PCI Express Configuration Menu Settings

Setting	Options	Description
Compliance Test Pattern	Enabled Disabled	Used to verify whether a PCI Express slot remains functional and enabled per PCI Express specification for compliance test card testing.
Link Stability Algorithm	Enabled Disabled	Used for verifying that x16 PCIe Link is up and running for x16 graphics cards.
PCI Express 1.1 Compliance Mode	Enabled Disabled	Used to force the maximum speed of PCI Express 2.x cards to PCIe 1.1 mode.
PCIE x16 Link Retrain GFX Card	Disabled Enabled	Used to adjust the configuration for devices that may need accomodations to function properly when link training. Some PCI Express cards may not be detected properly. Link retraining allows the system to keep trying to train or detect and configure the card. This setting increases the boot time.
PEG Negotiated Width	—	Displays the link train width (x1, x4, x8, x16) of the PCIe device connected in the x16 PCIe slot. This information is provided for determining performance issues with x4, x8, and x16 PCIe cards in an x16 PCIe slot while the Intel Integrated video (PCIe graphics) is enabled and the "PEG Allow > 1" option is disabled on the Advanced Chipset menu.

Advanced Memory Configuration

The options in Table 5.9 set the system's memory configuration. You can possibly change some of these settings to overclock the memory; however, if you run into system instability or other problems, it is recommended that you reset all settings to their default values.

Table 5.9 Advanced Memory Configuration Menu Settings

Setting	Options	Description
CPC Override	Auto Enabled Disabled	Controls Command Per Clock/1n rule mode. When enabled, this setting allows the DRAM controller to attempt Chip Select assertions in two consecutive common clocks.
Memory Frequency	Options vary	Allows you to manually set the memory speed.
Memory Correction	Non-ECC ECC	Allows you to turn error reporting on or off if the system and all the memory installed supports ECC (Error Correction Code).
Memory Mode	—	Displays single or dual channel operation.
SDRAM CAS# Latency	2.0 2.5 3.0	Selects the number of clock cycles required to address a column in memory. Corresponds to CL.
SDRAM Frequency	Auto 266MHz 333MHz 400MHz	Allows override of detected memory frequency value.
SDRAM RAS Act. To Pre.	8 7 6 5	Selects length of time from read to prechange. Corresponds to tRAS, min.

Table 5.9   Continued

Setting	Options	Description
SDRAM RAS# Precharge	4 3 2	Selects the length of time required before accessing a new row.
SDRAM RAS# to CAS# delay	4 3 2	Selects the number of clock cycles between addressing a row and addressing a column. Corresponds to tRCD.
SDRAM Timing Control	Auto Manual— Aggressive Manual— User Defined	Auto sets memory timings according to the memory detected. Manual—Aggressive selects the most aggressive user-defined timings. Manual—User Defined allows manual override of detected settings.
Total Memory	—	Displays the total amount of RAM.

ECC stands for *error correcting code*, which involves the use of extra bits on the memory modules to detect and even correct memory errors on the fly. For ECC to be enabled, the motherboard and chipset must support ECC, and the more expensive ECC DIMMs would have to be installed.

▶▶   See the Chapter 6 section, "ECC," **p. 360**.

Advanced Boot Configuration

The options in Table 5.10 set the system's boot-time options, including plug-and-play (PnP) and keyboard configuration.

Table 5.10   Advanced Boot Configuration Menu Settings

Setting	Options	Description
ASF Support	Enabled Disabled	Disables or enables Alert Standard Format (ASF) support.
Display Setup Prompt	On Off	Displays the F2 to Enter BIOS Setup message during boot.
Limit CPUID MaxVal	Enabled Disabled	Enables/allows some legacy OSs to boot on processors with extended CPUID functions.
Numlock	Off On	Specifies the power-on state of the Numlock feature on the numeric keypad of the keyboard.
Plug & Play O/S	No Yes	Specifies if manual configuration is desired. No lets the BIOS configure all devices in the system. Yes lets the OS configure PnP devices.

Advanced Chipset Configuration Menu

Chipset configuration allows access to settings that control the core of the system. Because of the wide variations in different chipset, motherboard, and BIOS designs, the options you see here may vary greatly from board to board.

Many motherboards include features designed to overclock the system, which enables you to set the system to run the CPU bus (and therefore the CPU itself) and possibly other buses at higher-than-normal rated speeds. These settings are especially useful for stress-testing a system after initial assembly, which is often called a *burn-in test.*

You can use these settings to speed up the processor and interconnected buses such as PCI and AGP. For specifically testing AGP video or PCI adapter cards, some motherboards allow the AGP/PCI bus speed to be set independently of the CPU bus. If you intend to use these settings to speed up a system, be aware that—depending on the specific hardware and software you have—running faster than the default clock speed can reduce system stability and shorten the useful life of the processor, and it might not be covered under warranty. You also might need to invest in better system cooling to offset the extra heat generated by overclocking your system. In general, if you don't know what a particular setting is designed for, it is best to leave it at the default or automatic setting. If problems occur, start by returning all frequency and timing settings to their default values.

Table 5.11 lists settings used by a typical motherboard's Advanced Chipset Configuration menu.

Table 5.11 Advanced Chipset Configuration Menu

Setting	Options	Description
AGP/PCI Burn-In Mode	Default 63.88/31.94 MHz 68.05/34.02 MHz 69.44/34.72 MHz 70.83/35.41 MHz 72.22/36.11 MHz 73.60/36.80 MHz	Enables under- or overclocking the AGP/PCI bus at specific frequencies. The host clock (system bus speed) is not changed. If this option is set to anything other than Default (66.66/33.33MHz), the Host and I/O Burn-In Mode is automatically set to Default.
CSA Device	Auto Disable	Enables or disables the Communication Streaming Architecture (CSA) interface. CSA bypasses the PCI bus to provide a fast dedicated connection for onboard gigabit Ethernet adapters. Auto leaves the CSA device enabled if a device is found on the bus; otherwise, the device is disabled.
DDR2 Voltage	Automatic 1.8 1.9	Automatic: Memory voltage will be adjusted according to the memory detected. Memory voltage can also be manually set for testing or overclocking purposes.
Extended Burn-In Mode	Enabled Disabled	Enabling this option allows the user to select additional values for system overclocking.
Extended Configuration	Default User Defined	Chooses the default or user-defined settings for the extended configuration options.
Host Burn-In Mode	<percentage>	Alters host and I/O clock frequencies to under- or overclock the system. Percentage options are dependent on the board and processor models; may be set up to 30%.
Host Burn-In Mode Type	Positive Negative	Reads the percentage set in Host Burn-In Mode Percentage as either a positive number (increases speed) or a negative number (decreases speed).
Host Spread Spectrum	Down Center	Adjusts the mean frequencies for core system clocks to help prevent electromagnetic interference. Requires additional POST time.

Table 5.11   Continued

Setting	Options	Description
HPET	Enabled Disabled	Enables or disables HPET (High Precision Event Timer) support.
IOAPIC Enable	Enabled Disabled	Enables or disables the I/O Programmable Interrupt Controller.
ISA Enable Bit	Enabled Disabled	When this setting is enabled, a PCI-to-PCI bridge recognizes only 16-bit I/O addresses that are not aliases of 10-bit ISA addresses (within the bridge's assigned I/O range). This helps prevent resource conflicts with ISA devices that might be present in the system (such as serial or parallel ports) and allows VGA-compatible address range mapping for ISA devices. Some older expansion devices require this to be enabled.
MCH Voltage Override	Default 1.525V 1.600V 1.625V 1.725	Allows you to set the Memory Controller Hub (MCH or North Bridge) voltage for testing or overclocking purposes.
PCI Burn-In Mode	Default 36.36MHz 40.00MHz	Enables the selection of specific PCI clock frequencies for testing or overclocking purposes. Default is 33.33MHz.
PCI Express Burn-In Mode	Default 101.32MHz 102.64MHz 103.96MHz 105.28MHz 106.6MHz 107.92MHz 109.24MHz	Enables the selection of specific PCI Express clock frequencies for testing or overclocking purposes. Default is 100.00MHz.
PCI Latency Timer	32 64 96 128 160 192 224 248	Allows you to control the time (in PCI bus clock cycles) that an agent on the PC bus can hold the bus when another agent has requested the bus.
PEG Allow > x1	Enabled Disabled	Enabled allows the system to link train PCI Express devices of widths x4, x8, and x16 in the GMCH x16 slot while leaving the Intel Integrated Graphics (PCIe graphics) enabled. Disabled means that all devices plugged into the GMCH x16 slot will link train as x1 PCIe devices if the Intel Integrated Graphics (PCIe graphics) controller is enabled.
Watchdog Timer	Enabled Disabled	Enabled monitors the system for timeouts and takes corrective action if they occur.

Advanced Peripheral Configuration

The Peripheral Configuration menu is used to configure the devices built in to the motherboard, such as serial ports, parallel ports, and built-in audio and USB ports.

Table 5.12 shows a typical Peripheral Configuration menu and its choices.

Table 5.12   Peripheral Configuration Menu Settings

Setting	Options	Description
Auxiliary Power	Enabled Disabled	Enables or disables on the onboard auxiliary power connector.
Base I/O Address (for the Parallel Port)	378 278	Specifies the base I/O address for the parallel port, if enabled.
Base I/O Address (for the Serial Port)	3F8 2F8 3E8 2E8	Specifies the base I/O address for serial port A, if enabled.
ECP Mode Use DMA	—	DMA Channel 3 is used by default.
Front Panel 1394 Port 1	1394A 1394B	Sets the IEEE 1394 (FireWire) mode for the front-panel 1394 port.
Front Panel 1394 Port 2	1394A 1394B	Sets the IEEE 1394 (FireWire) mode for the second front-panel 1394 port.
Interrupt (for the Parallel Port)	IRQ 5 IRQ 7	Specifies the interrupt for the parallel port, if enabled.
Interrupt (for the Serial Port)	IRQ 3 IRQ 4	Specifies the interrupt for the serial port, if enabled.
Legacy Front Panel Audio	Enabled Disabled	When this setting is enabled, the system assumes that a High Definition audio connector is not present in the system (Legacy audio is present). When this setting is disabled, the system assumes that a High Definition audio connector is present in the system.
Parallel Port Mode	Output Only Bidirectional EPP ECP	Output Only operates in AT-compatible mode. Bidirectional operates in PS/2-compatible mode. EPP is Enhanced Parallel Port mode, a high-speed bidirectional mode for nonprinter peripherals. ECP is Enhanced Capability Port mode, a high-speed bidirectional mode for printers and scanners.
Onboard 1394	Enabled Disabled	Enables or disables the onboard IEEE 1394.
Onboard Audio	Enabled Disabled	Enables or disables the onboard audio.
Onboard LAN Boot ROM	Enabled Disabled	Enables or disables booting from the network.
Onboard LAN	Enabled Disabled	Enables or disables the onboard LAN.

Table 5.12   Continued

Setting	Options	Description
Parallel Port	Disabled Enabled Auto	Auto assigns LPT1 the address 378h and the interrupt IRQ7. An asterisk displayed next to an address indicates a conflict with another device.
Secondary SATA Controller	Enabled Disabled	Enables or disables the secondary SATA controller.
Serial Port	Disabled Enabled Auto	Auto assigns COM1 the address 3F8h and the interrupt IRQ4. An asterisk displayed next to an address indicates a conflict with another device.
Trusted Platform Module	Enabled Disabled	Disables or enables the Trusted Platform Module (TPM) security chip.

I usually recommend disabling the serial and parallel ports if they are not being used because this frees up those resources for other devices and potentially speeds up boot time.

Advanced Drive Configuration

Of all the BIOS Setup menus, the hard-disk settings are some of the most important.

As with many BIOS Setup settings, the default or automatic values are generally recommended. With Auto settings, the BIOS sends a special Identify Drive command to the drive, which responds with information about the correct settings. From this, the BIOS can automatically detect the specifications and optimal operating mode of almost all ATA and SATA hard drives. When you select Auto for a hard drive, the BIOS redetects the drive specifications during POST, every time the system boots. You could swap drives with the power off, and the system would automatically detect the new drive the next time it was turned on.

In addition to the Auto setting, most older BIOSs offered a standard table of up to 47 drive types with specifically prerecorded parameters. Each defined drive type had a specified number of cylinders, number of heads, write precompensation factor, landing zone, and number of sectors. This was used often many years ago, but it is not used today because no current drives conform to the older type parameters.

Note that systems dating from 1997 and earlier usually are limited to a maximum drive size of 8.4GB unless they have a BIOS upgrade. Systems from 1998 and later usually support drives up to 137GB; systems dating from 2002 and beyond usually support drives beyond 137GB (48-bit LBA support), although a BIOS upgrade might be necessary for some systems.

Table 5.13 shows the Drive Configuration menu and options for a typical modern motherboard.

Table 5.13   Advanced Drive Configuration Menu Settings

Setting	Options	Description
Access Mode	CHS LBA Large Auto	Allows you to select the sector translation and addressing mode for drives under 137GB. CHS (cylinder, head, sector) mode supports up to 528MB hard disks. LBA (logical block addressing) mode supports hard disks up to 137GB in size. Large mode supports hard disks above 528MB in size, but it does not support LBA mode.

Setting	Options	Description
ATA/IDE Configuration	Disabled Legacy Enhanced	Specifies the integrated ATA controller. Disabled disables the integrated ATA controller. Legacy enables up to two PATA channels for an OS requiring legacy IDE operation. Enhanced (or Native) enables all SATA and PATA resources.
Cable Detected	—	Displays the type of cable connected to the IDE interface: 40-conductor, 80-conductor, or Serial ATA.
Configure SATA as...	IDE AHCI RAID	IDE allows for backward compatibility with non-SATA-aware OSs or drivers. AHCI enables the Advanced Host Controller Interface, which supports features such as Native Command Queuing (NCQ), hot-plugging, and so on. RAID enables both AHCI and RAID capability. RAID must be configured using the RAID Configuration Utility.
DMA Mode	Auto SWDMA 0 SWDMA 1 SWDMA 2 MWDMA 0 MWDMA 1 MWDMA 2 UDMA 0 UDMA 1 UDMA 2 UDMA 3 UDMA 4 UDMA 5	Specifies the DMA mode for the drive
Drive Installed	—	Displays the type of drive installed.
Hard Disk Pre-Delay	Disabled 3 Seconds 6 Seconds 9 Seconds 12 Seconds 15 Seconds 21 Seconds 30 Seconds	Causes the BIOS to insert a delay before attempting to detect IDE drives in the system. Designed to give time for slower drives to spin up.
Intel RAID Technology	Enabled Disabled	Enables or disables Intel Matrix Storage RAID technology.
Legacy IDE Channels	PATA Pri only PATA Sec only PATA Pri and Sec SATA P0/P1 only SATA P0/P1, PATA Sec SATA P0/P1, PATA Pri	Configures PATA and SATA resources for an OS requiring legacy IDE operation. P0 = SATA connector 0; P1 = SATA connector 1.
Maximum Capacity	—	Displays the capacity of the drive.
Onboard Chip SATA	IDE Controller SATA Disabled	With IDE Controller, both IDE and SATA channels are detected. With SATA Disabled, SATA channels are not detected.

Table 5.13 Continued

Setting	Options	Description
PCI IDE Bus Master	Disabled Enabled	Allows a PCI ATA device to initiate a transaction as a master.
PIO Mode	Auto 0 1 2 3 4	Specifies the ATA PIO mode.
Primary IDE Master	[drive]	Displays the drive installed on this IDE channel. Shows [None] if no drive is installed.
Primary IDE Slave	[drive]	Displays the drive installed on this IDE channel. Shows [None] if no drive is installed.
Secondary IDE Master	[drive]	Displays the drive installed on this IDE channel. Shows [None] if no drive is installed.
Secondary IDE Slave	[drive]	Displays the drive installed on this IDE channel. Shows [None] if no drive is installed.
S.M.A.R.T.	Auto Disable Enable	Enables or disables support for the hard disk's S.M.A.R.T. Self-Monitoring, Analysis, and Reporting Technology) (capability. S.M.A.R.T. allows the early prediction and warning of impending hard disk failures.
First SATA Master	[drive]	Displays the drive installed on this SATA channel. Shows [None] if no drive is installed.
Second SATA Master	[drive]	Displays the drive installed on this SATA channel. Shows [None] if no drive is installed.
Third SATA Master	[drive]	Displays the drive installed on this SATA channel. Shows [None] if no drive is installed.
Fourth SATA Master	[drive]	Displays the drive installed on this SATA channel. Shows [None] if no drive is installed.
Fifth SATA Master	[drive]	Displays the drive installed on this SATA channel. Shows [None] if no drive is installed.
Sixth SATA Master Type	[drive] Auto User	Displays the drive installed on this SATA channel. Shows [None] if no drive is installed. Specifies the IDE configuration mode for IDE devices. Auto fills-in capabilities from the ATA/ATAPI device. User allows capabilities to be changed.
Use Automatic Mode	Enabled Disabled	Allows you to manually set the bootable devices configuration for legacy OSs. Legacy OSs may only allow four devices, which means you must choose to use the IDE controller as one of your four devices.

The SATA controller mode setting is of particular importance. This setting controls how SATA hard drives function and appear to the system and can have a major effect on OS installation and driver issues.

One of the requirements of SATA is that it be capable of fully emulating ATA. This means that a SATA drive should be able to be supported by the same drivers and software as Parallel ATA drives. Although this is true, adherence to this would mean that additional capabilities such as native command queuing could never be supported. To support features beyond standard ATA, SATA has a more powerful "native" mode interface called AHCI (Advanced Host Controller Interface).

The SATA controller on most motherboards has three modes of operation:

- **IDE mode**—Provides legacy ATA emulation with no AHCI or RAID support
- **AHCI mode**—Provides support for native SATA functionality without RAID
- **RAID mode**—Provides both RAID and AHCI support

Any OS or software that supports standard ATA drives also supports SATA drives if the host adapter is set to IDE mode. This means that, for example, you can install Windows on a SATA drive without having to press the F6 key to specify and load additional drivers. However, if you choose AHCI or RAID/AHCI modes, the standard ATA drivers will not work, and you will need AHCI/RAID drivers instead. So if you are installing Windows on a system with a SATA host adapter set to AHCI or RAID mode and Windows does not recognize the drive, you need to press the F6 key and install the AHCI/RAID drivers. Windows XP and earlier only support loading these drivers from a floppy disk, whereas Windows Vista and later support optical drives as well as USB drives (including flash drives). Note that Windows Vista and later include AHCI/RAID drivers for many SATA host adapters on the installation DVD; it is also possible to integrate these drivers into Windows XP install discs. See www.driverpacks.net for mass storage (and other) driverpacks that can easily be slipstreamed into Windows XP install discs, eliminating the need to load them manually during the installation process.

Switching SATA modes in the BIOS setup *after* the OS is installed can cause problems if a SATA drive is the boot drive, and you have not loaded the proper drivers in advance. For example, if you switch modes from IDE to AHCI or RAID on a system running Windows XP or later (including Vista/7/8), on the next boot you will most likely have an immediate blue screen error, as follows:

```
STOP: 0x0000007B (parameter1, parameter2, parameter3, parameter4)

INACCESSIBLE_BOOT_DEVICE
```

In this case, changing the host adapter back to IDE mode should allow the system to boot again.

The hard disk predelay function is to delay accessing drives that are slow to spin up. Some drives aren't ready when the system begins to look for them during boot time, causing the system to display `Fixed Disk Failure` messages and fail to boot. Setting this delay allows time for the drive to become ready before continuing the boot process. Of course, this slows down the boot process, so if your drives don't need this delay, disable this function.

Advanced Floppy Configuration

The Floppy Configuration menu is for configuring the floppy drive and interface. Table 5.14 shows the options in a typical BIOS Setup.

Table 5.14   Advanced Floppy Configuration Menu

Setting	Options	Description
Diskette Controller	Enabled Disabled	Configures the integrated floppy controller.
Diskette Write Protect	Enabled Disabled	Disables or enables diskette drive write protection.
Floppy A	Disabled 360KB 5 1/4 inch 1.2MB 5 1/4 inch 720KB 3 1/2 inch 1.44MB 3 1/2 inch 2.88MB 3 1/2 inch	Selects the floppy drive type.

By enabling the write-protect feature, you can disallow writing to floppy disks. This can help prevent the theft of data as well as help to prevent infecting disks with viruses should they be on the system.

Advanced Event Log Configuration

The Event Logging menu is for configuring the System Management (SMBIOS) and AMT (Active Management Technology) event-logging features. SMBIOS is a DMI-compliant method for managing computers on a managed network. DMI stands for *Desktop Management Interface*, a special protocol that software can use to communicate with the motherboard. AMT allows for powerful remote access and troubleshooting capabilities, including hardware and software inventory, proactive altering, and remote troubleshooting and recovery.

Using SMBIOS and AMT, a system administrator can remotely obtain information about a system. System management applications run by network administrators can use SMBIOS and AMT to report the following DMI information:

- BIOS data, such as the BIOS revision level
- System data, such as installed peripherals, serial numbers, and asset tags
- Resource data, such as memory size, cache size, and processor speed
- Dynamic data such as event detection, including event detection and error logging

Table 5.15 shows a typical Event Logging menu in BIOS Setup.

Table 5.15   Advanced Event Log Configuration Menu

Setting	Options	Description
Clear All DMI Event Log	Yes No	Yes means the DMI Event Log will be cleared at the next POST; then this option automatically resets to No.
DMI Event Log	Enabled Disabled	Enables or disables the storing of POST error messages to the DMI Event Log.
ECC Event Logging	Enabled Disabled	Enables or disables event logging of ECC events.
Event Log Capacity	—	Indicates if there is space available in the Event Log.

Setting	Options	Description
Event Log Validity	—	Indicates if the Event Log information is valid.
Mark DMI Events As Read	[Enter]	Marks all DMI events in the Event Log as read.
View Event Log	[Enter]	Press Enter to show all DMI Event Logs.

Some motherboards with ECC memory also support logging ECC events. I find event logging particularly useful for tracking errors such as ECC errors. Using the View Log feature, you can see whether the system has detected (and corrected) any errors.

Advanced Video Configuration

The Video Configuration menu is for configuring video features. Table 5.16 shows the functions of this menu in a typical modern motherboard BIOS.

Table 5.16   Advanced Video Configuration Menu

Setting	Options	Description
Aperture Size	4MB 8MB 16MB 32MB 128MB 256MB	Establishes the maximum amount of system memory that the OS can use for video memory. This is primarily used for buffering textures for the AGP video device.
DVMT Mode	DVMT Fixed Both	Dynamic Video Memory Technology (DVMT) dynamically allocates video memory based on memory requests made by applications; memory is released once the requesting application has been terminated. With the Fixed option, video memory is allocated during driver initialization to provide a static amount of memory. The Both option allows the combination of both Fixed- and DVMT-type driver allocation methods; used to guarantee a minimum amount of video memory but gives the flexibility of DVMT for enhanced performance.
Frame Buffer Size	1MB 8MB 16MB	Sets the frame buffer size. Frame buffer size is the total amount of system memory locked by the BIOS for video. A larger frame buffer size should result in higher video performance.
Onboard Video Memory Size	32MB 64MB 128MB 256MB	Amount of system memory available for direct access by the graphics device.
PCI/VGA Palette Snoop	Enabled Disabled	Some special VGA cards and high-end hardware MPEG decoders need to be able to look at the video card's VGA palette to determine what colors are currently in use. Enabling this feature turns on this palette "snoop." This option is only rarely needed and should be left disabled unless a video device specifically requires the setting enabled upon installation.

Table 5.16   Continued

Setting	Options	Description
Primary Video Adapter	AGP PCI PCIe Onboard Auto	Allows selecting a specific video controller as the display device that will be active when the system boots.
Secondary Video Adapter	AGP PCI PCIe Onboard Auto	Allows selecting a specific video controller as the secondary display device.

The most common use of this menu is to change the primary video device. This is useful for dual-monitor configurations. Using this feature, you can set the PCI Express, AGP, or PCI video card to be the primary boot device.

Advanced USB Configuration Menu

The USB Configuration menu is used for configuring the USB ports on the system. Table 5.17 shows the functions of this menu in a typical modern motherboard BIOS.

Table 5.17   Advanced USB Configuration Menu

Setting	Options	Description
USB 2.0	Enabled, Disabled	Disabled turns off all USB functionality. This feature can be used for security purposes.
USB 2.0 Legacy Support	Full-Speed Hi-Speed	Configures the USB 2.0 legacy support to Full-Speed (12Mbps) or (480Mbps).
USB EHCI Controller	Enabled, Disabled	Enables or disables high-speed USB transfers (USB 2.0).
USB 3.0 Controller	Enabled, Disabled	Enables or disables the USB 3.0 controller and all USB 3.0 ports.
USB 3.0 Hub Presence	Enabled, Disabled	If disabled, three out of the four internal USB 3.0 ports will be inaccessible.
USB Function	Enabled, Disabled	Enables or disables USB functionality. If Disabled is set, the Advanced USB Configuration menu does not include change-able options. The menu appears blank. This setting is present only when the BIOS configuration jumper is set to Maintenance mode.
USB Legacy	Enabled, Disabled	USB Legacy support allows the BIOS to interact with a USB keyboard and, in limited cases, a USB mouse.
USB Ports	Enabled, Disabled	Enables or disables all USB ports.
USB ZIP Emulation Type	Floppy, Hard Disk	Allows you to set the emulation type for USB zip drives.

Legacy USB support means support for USB keyboards and mice independent of the OS or drivers. If you are using USB keyboards and mice with this option disabled, you will find that the keyboard and mouse are not functional until a USB-aware OS is loaded. This can be a problem when running diagnostics software, older OSs, or other applications that run outside of USB-aware OSs or environments.

Note that even with legacy support disabled, the system still recognizes a USB keyboard and enables it to work during the POST and BIOS Setup. If USB legacy support is disabled (the default on some systems), the system operates as follows:

1. When you power up the computer, USB legacy support is disabled.

2. POST begins.

3. The BIOS temporarily enables USB legacy support. This allows you to use a USB keyboard to enter the setup program or Maintenance mode.

4. POST completes and disables USB legacy support (unless it was set to Enabled while in Setup).

5. The OS loads. While the OS is loading, USB keyboards and mice are not recognized. After the OS loads the USB drivers, the USB devices are recognized.

To install an OS that supports USB when using a USB keyboard or mouse, enable USB legacy support in BIOS Setup and follow the OS's installation instructions. After the OS is installed and the USB drivers are configured, USB legacy support is no longer used and the OS USB drivers take over. However, I recommend that you leave legacy support enabled so the USB keyboard and mouse function while running self-booting or DOS-based diagnostics or when running other non-USB-aware OSs.

USB legacy support is for keyboards and mice only; it doesn't work for USB hubs or other USB devices. For devices other than keyboards or mice to work, you need a USB-aware OS with the appropriate USB drivers.

Advanced Fan Control Configuration Menu

Most systems have one or more chassis fans to help cool the system. Table 5.18 shows the function of the Fan Control Configuration menu on a typical high-performance PC.

Table 5.18   Advanced Fan Control Configuration Menu

Setting	Options	Description
Automatic Fan Detection	Next Boot, Disable, Always	Next Boot detects fans added to the motherboard upon next boot only. Disabled does not detect fans added to the motherboard; new fans may perform erratically. Always detects fans added to the motherboard; may cause a slight delay and increased noise during startup.
Lowest System Fan Speed	Slow, Off	This option defines the system fan speed at the lowest system temperature. Slow allows the fans to continue to run at a reduced speed at low system temperatures. Off turns off the system fans at low system temperatures.
Processor Zone Response	Aggressive, Normal, Slow	Adjusts acoustics for fan heatsink solutions. For less efficient fan heatsink solutions, set CPU Zone Response to Aggressive. For more efficient fan heatsink solutions, set the CPU Zone Response to Slow.
Unlock Intel(R) QST	No, Yes	Unlocking Quiet System Technology (QST) allows the fan control settings to be changed using software.
CPU Fan Control	Enabled, Disabled	Allows the CPU fan to be controlled to optimize acoustics. If this setting is disabled, the CPU fan runs at 100%.
System Fan Control	Enabled, Disabled	Allows the system fans to be controlled to optimize acoustics. If this setting is disabled, system fans run at 100%.

Many newer boards have built-in monitor chips that can read temperature, voltage, and fan speeds. Those that do often include a screen in the BIOS Setup that allows you to view the readings from the monitor chip (see Table 5.19). Usually such boards also include a hardware monitor program that runs under Windows for more convenient monitoring while the system is in use. For example, MSI includes a program called the MSI Control Center for monitoring and controlling its motherboards (see Figure 5.9).

FIGURE 5.9   The MSI Control Center.

Table 5.19   Advanced Hardware Monitoring Display

Feature	Description
+1.5V in	Displays the +1.5V input level
+12V in	Displays the +12V input level
+3.3V in	Displays the +3.3V input level
+5V in	Displays the +5V input level
Ambient Air Temperature	Displays the remote thermal diode temperature
Aux Fan	Displays the aux fan speed
Chassis Inlet Fan	Displays the front chassis fan speed
Chassis Outlet Fan	Displays the rear chassis fan speed
CPU Cooling Fan	Displays the speed of the CPU fan
CPU Temperature	Displays the processor temperature
ICH Temperature	Displays the I/O Controller Hub (ICH) South Bridge temperature
MCH Temperature	Displays the Memory Controller Hub (MCH) North Bridge temperature
VCORE Voltage	Displays the CPU core operating voltage

Security Menu

Most BIOSs include two passwords for security, called the *supervisor* and *user passwords*. These passwords help control who is allowed to access the BIOS Setup program and who is allowed to boot the computer. The supervisor password is also called a *setup password* because it controls access to the setup program. The user password is also called a *system password* because it controls access to the entire system.

If a supervisor password is set, a password prompt is displayed when an attempt is made to enter the BIOS Setup menus. When entered correctly, the supervisor password gives unrestricted access to view and change all the Setup options in the Setup program. If the supervisor password is not entered or is entered incorrectly, access to view and change Setup options in the Setup program is restricted.

If the user password is set, the password prompt is displayed before the computer boots up. The password must be entered correctly before the system is allowed to boot. Note that if only the supervisor password is set, the computer boots without asking for a password because the supervisor password controls access only to the BIOS Setup menus. If both passwords are set, the password prompt is displayed at boot time, and either the user or the supervisor password can be entered to boot the computer. In most systems, the password can be up to seven or eight characters long.

If you forget the password, most systems have a jumper on the board that allows all passwords to be cleared. This means that for most systems, the password security also requires that the system case be locked to prevent users from opening the cover and accessing the password-clear jumper. This jumper is often not labeled on the board for security reasons, but you can find it in the motherboard or system documentation.

Provided you know the password and can get into the BIOS Setup, a password can also be cleared by entering the BIOS Setup and selecting the Clear Password function. If no Clear function is available, you can still clear the password by selecting the Set Password function and pressing Enter (for no password) at the prompts.

Table 5.20 shows the security functions in a typical BIOS Setup.

Table 5.20   Security Settings Menu

Setting	Options	Description
Chassis Intrusion	Enabled, Disabled	Enables or disables the chassis intrusion feature.
Clear User Password	Yes, No	Clears the user password.
Security Option	Setup System	If you set a supervisor or user setting selects setting selects whether the password is required every time the system boots or only when you enter Setup.
Set Supervisor Password	—	Specifies the supervisor password, which can be up to seven alphanumeric characters.
Set User Password	—	Specifies the user password, which can be up to seven alphanumeric characters.
Supervisor Password	—	Reports if a supervisor password is set.
User access Level	Limited No Access View Only Full	Sets BIOS Setup Utility access rights for the user level. This BIOS setting is present only if both a user password and a supervisor password have been set.

Table 5.20   Continued

Setting	Options	Description
User Password	—	Reports if there is a user password set.
VT Technology	Enabled, Disabled	Enables or disables Virtualization Technology.
XD Technology	Enabled, Disabled	Enables or disables Execute Disable memory protection, which can prevent buffer overflow attacks.

To clear passwords if the password is forgotten, most motherboards have a password-clear jumper or switch. Intel motherboards require that you set the configuration jumper, enter the Maintenance menu in BIOS Setup, and select the Clear Password feature. If you can't find the documentation for your board and aren't sure how to clear the passwords, you can try removing the battery for 15 minutes or so—it clears the CMOS RAM. It can take that long for the CMOS RAM to clear on some systems because they have capacitors in the circuit that retain a charge. Note that this also erases other BIOS settings, including the hard disk settings, so you should record them beforehand.

Power Menu

Power management is defined as the capability of the system to automatically enter power-conserving modes during periods of inactivity. Two main classes of power management exist; the original standard was called Advanced Power Management (APM) and was supported by most systems since the 386 and 486 processors. More recently, a new type of power management called Advanced Configuration and Power Interface (ACPI) has been developed and began appearing in systems during 1998. Most systems sold in 1998 or later support the more advanced ACPI type of power management. In APM, the BIOS does the actual power management, and the OS or other software has little control. With ACPI, the power management is done by the OS and BIOS together. This makes the control more centralized and easier to access, and it enables applications to work with the power management. Instead of using the BIOS Setup options, you merely ensure that ACPI is enabled in the BIOS Setup and then manage all the power settings through the Power configuration settings in Windows 98 and later.

Table 5.21 shows the typical power settings found in a managed system.

Table 5.21   Power Settings Menu

Setting	Options	Description
ACPI Suspend Mode (or ACPI Suspend State)	S1 State S3 State	Specifies the ACPI sleep state. S1 = POS (Power On Suspend). Everything remains fully powered. S3 = STR (Suspend To RAM). Only RAM has power. S3 is the recommended setting for maximum power savings.
After Power Failure	Stay Off Last State Power On	Determines the mode of operation once power is restored after a power loss occurs. Stay Off keeps the power off until the power button is pressed. Last State restores the previous power state before power loss occurs. Power On restores power to the computer.
APM	Enabled Disabled	Disables or enables APM (advanced power management).
EIST	Enabled Disabled	Enables or disables Enhanced Intel Speedstep Technology (EIST), advanced CPU power management that includes adjustable frequency and voltage.

Setting	Options	Description
Energy Lake	Enabled Disabled	Disables or enables Energy Lake power management technology. Energy Lake technology introduces two main end-user features: Consumer Electronics (CE)–style power behavior and the ability to maintain system state and data integrity during power loss events.
Hard Drive	Enabled, Disabled	Enables power management for hard disks during APM standby mode.
Inactivity Timer	Off 1 Minute 5 Minutes 10 Minutes 20 Minutes 30 Minutes 60 Minutes 120 Minutes	Specifies the amount of time before the computer enters APM standby mode.
Intel Quick Resume Technology	Enabled Disabled	Enables or disables Intel Quick Resume Technology (QRT), a component of Intel Viiv Technology.
Keyboard Select	Disable Keyboard	Select Keyboard to allow a PS/2 keyboard to wake the system from the S5 state.
Video Repost	Enabled Disabled	Allows the video BIOS to be initialized coming out of the S3 state. Some video controllers require this option to be enabled. This BIOS setting is present only when ACPI Suspend State is set to S3.
Wake on LAN from S5	Stay Off Power-On	Determines how the system responds to a LAN wakeup event when the system is in the ACPI soft-off mode. This BIOS setting is present only on Intel Desktop Boards that include onboard LAN.
Wake on Modem Ring	Stay Off Power-On	Specifies how the computer responds to an incoming call on an installed modem when the power is off.
Wake on PCI PME	Stay Off Power-On	Determines how the system responds to a PCI PME wakeup event.
Wake on PS/2 Mouse from S3	Stay Off Power-On	Determines how the system responds to a PS/2 mouse wakeup event.

When in Standby mode, the BIOS reduces power consumption by spinning down hard drives and reducing power to or turning off monitors that comply with Video Electronics Standards Organization (VESA) and Display Power Management Signaling (DPMS). While in Standby mode, the system can still respond to external interrupts, such as those from keyboards, mice, fax/modems, or network adapters. For example, any keyboard or mouse activity brings the system out of Standby mode and immediately restores power to the monitor.

In most systems, the OS takes over most of the power management settings; in some cases, it can even override the BIOS settings. This is definitely true if the OS and motherboard both support ACPI.

Boot Menu (Boot Sequence, Order)

The Boot menu is used for setting the boot features and the boot sequence (through menus). If you are installing an OS from an optical drive or USB flash drive, you'll want to ensure that the optical or USB drive comes before the hard drive in the boot sequence. Table 5.22 shows the functions and settings available on a typical motherboard.

Table 5.22   Boot Menu Settings

Setting	Options	Description
1st ATAPI CD-ROM Drive	Dependent on installed drives	Specifies the boot sequence from the available optical drives. This list displays up to four ATAPI drives.
1st Hard Disk Drive	Dependent on installed drives	Specifies the boot sequence from the available hard disk drives. This list displays up to 12 hard disk drives.
1st Removable Device	Dependent on installed devices	Specifies the boot sequence from the available removable devices. This list displays up to four removable devices.
1st Boot Device	Removable Device Hard Drive ATAPI CD-ROM Network Disabled	Specifies the boot sequence from the available devices.
2nd Boot Device	Removable Device Hard Drive ATAPI CD-ROM Network Disabled	Specifies the boot sequence from the available devices.
3rd Boot Device	Removable Device Hard Drive ATAPI CD-ROM Network Disabled	Specifies the boot sequence from the available devices.
4th Boot Device	Removable Device Hard Drive ATAPI CD-ROM Network Disabled	Specifies the boot sequence from the available devices.
AddOn ROM Display Mode	Enabled, Disabled	With Enabled, adapter card ROM messages are visible. With Disabled, adapter card ROM messages are hidden.
Boot to Network	Enabled, Disabled	Disables or enables booting from the network.
Boot to Optical Devices	Enabled, Disabled	Disables or enables booting from optical devices (CD/DVD).
Boot to Removable Devices	Enabled, Disabled	Disables or enables booting from removable devices (floppy/USB).
Halt On	All Errors No Errors All, But Keyboard	Used to configure what types of POST errors halt the system boot.
Intel Rapid BIOS Boot	Enabled, Disabled	Allows BIOS to skip certain tests while booting.

Setting	Options	Description
PXE Boot to LAN	Enabled, Disabled	Disables or enables Preboot eXecution Environment boot to LAN.
Scan User Flash Area	Enabled, Disabled	Enables the BIOS to scan the flash ROM for user binary files that are executed at boot time.
Silent Boot	Enabled, Disabled	Disabled displays normal POST messages. Enabled displays OEM logo instead of POST messages.
USB Boot	Enabled, Disabled	Disables or enables booting from USB boot devices.
USB Mass Storage Emulation Type	Auto All Removable, All Fixed Disc Size	Allows you to set the emulation type for USB drives. Auto relies on USB device design and media format to set emulation type. All Removable sets USB mass devices to emulate removable drives. (Master Boot Record format required for USB storage devices.) All Fixed Disc Size sets USB mass devices to emulate fixed discs. Size sets emulation type based on media size.
ZIP Emulation Type	Floppy, Hard Disk	Allows you to set the emulation type for USB Zip drives.
UEFI Boot	Enable, Disable	Enable UEFI (Unified Extended Firmware Interface) Boot to boot from a 2.2TB or larger drive.

Using this menu, you can configure which devices your system boots from and in which order the devices are sequenced. From this menu, you also can access Hard Drive and Removable Devices menus, which enable you to configure the ordering of these devices in the boot sequence. For example, you can set hard drives to be the first boot choice, and then in the hard drive menu, decide to boot from the secondary drive first and the primary drive second. Normally, the default with two drives is the other way around.

The Boot Menu lists up to 12 hard disks and four removable devices, enabling you to choose the preferred boot device; older systems usually list only primary and secondary master and slave (four) drives. This BIOS option enables you to install more than one bootable hard disk in your computer and select which one you want to boot from at a BIOS level, rather than by using a boot manager program. If you need to work with multiple OSs, this menu can be useful.

Most recent systems also enable you to boot from external USB drives, including flash or thumb drives.

If you are booting from a hard drive that is 2.2TB or larger in capacity, you must enable UEFI (Unified Extended Firmware Interface) Boot in the BIOS Setup and install an OS that supports UEFI. Also, you must format the drive using the GUID (Globally Unique Identifier) Partition Table (GPT) format.

Exit Menu

The Exit menu is for exiting the Setup program, saving changes, and loading and saving defaults. Table 5.23 shows the typical selections found in most motherboard BIOSs.

Table 5.23   Exit Menu Settings

Feature	Description
Exit Saving Changes	Exits and saves the changes in CMOS RAM.
Exit Discarding Changes	Exits without saving any changes made in the BIOS Setup.
Load Optimal Defaults	Loads the factory (optimal) default values for all the Setup options.
Load Custom Defaults	Loads the custom defaults for Setup options.
Save Custom Defaults	Saves the current values as custom defaults in CMOS RAM. Normally, the BIOS reads the saved Setup values from CMOS RAM. If this memory is corrupted, the BIOS reads the custom defaults. If no custom defaults are set, the BIOS reads the factory defaults from the flash ROM.
Discard Changes	Discards changes without exiting Setup. The option values present when the computer was turned on are used.

After you select an optimum set of BIOS Setup settings, you can save them using the Save Custom Defaults option. This enables you to quickly restore your settings if they are corrupted or lost. All BIOS settings are stored in the CMOS RAM memory, which is powered by a battery attached to the motherboard.

Additional BIOS Setup Features

Some systems have additional features in their BIOS Setup screens, which might not be found in all BIOSs. Some of the more common features you might see are listed in Table 5.24.

Table 5.24   Additional BIOS Setup Features

Feature	Description
Virus Warning	When this feature is enabled, you receive a warning message if a program attempts to write to the boot sector or the partition table of the hard disk drive. If you get this warning during normal operation, you should run an antivirus or anti-rootkit program to see whether an infection has occurred. This feature protects only the master boot sector, not the entire hard drive. Note that partitioning programs that write to the master boot sector can trigger the virus warning message.
CPU Internal Cache/ External Cache	This allows you to disable the L1 (internal) and L2 (external) CPU caches. This is often used when testing memory, in which case you don't want the cache functioning. For normal operation, both caches should be enabled.
Quick Power-On Self Test	When enabled, this feature reduces the time required to run the POST. A quick POST skips certain steps, such as the memory test.
Swap Floppy Drive	This field is functional only in systems with two floppy drives. Selecting Enabled assigns physical drive B: to logical drive A: and physical drive A: to logical drive B:.
Boot Up Floppy Seek	When this feature is enabled, the BIOS tests (seeks) floppy drives to determine whether they have 40 or 80 tracks. Only 360KB floppy drives have 40 tracks; drives with 720KB, 1.2MB, and 1.44MB capacity all have 80 tracks. Because few modern PCs have 40-track floppy drives, you can disable this function to save time.

Feature	Description
Boot Up System Speed	Select High to boot at the default CPU speed; select Low to boot at a simulated 8MHz speed. The 8MHz option often was used in the past with certain copy-protected programs, which would fail the protection scheme if booted at full speed. This option is not used today.
Gate A20 Option	Gate A20 refers to the way the system addresses memory above 1MB (extended memory). When this feature is set to Fast, the system chipset controls Gate A20. When this feature is set to Normal, a pin in the keyboard controller controls Gate A20. Setting Gate A20 to Fast improves system speed, particularly with protected- mode OSs such as Windows.
Typematic Rate Setting	When this feature is disabled, the following two items (Typematic Rate and Typematic Delay) are irrelevant. Keystrokes repeat at a rate determined by the keyboard controller in your system. When this feature is enabled, you can select a typematic rate and typematic delay.
Typematic Rate	When the Typematic Rate setting is enabled, you can select a typematic rate—the rate (chars/sec) at which characters repeat when you hold down a key—of 6, 8, 10, 12, 15, 20, 24, or 30 characters per second.
Typematic Delay (Msec)	When the Typematic Rate setting is enabled, you can select a typematic delay (the delay before keystrokes begin to repeat) of 250, 500, 750, or 1,000 milliseconds.

PnP BIOS

Originally, installing and configuring devices in PCs was difficult. During installation, the user was faced with the task of configuring the new card by selecting the IRQ, I/O ports, and DMA channel. In the past, users were required to move jumpers or set switches on the add-in cards to control these settings. They needed to know exactly which resources were already in use so they could find a set of resources that did not conflict with the devices already in the system. If a conflict existed, the system might not boot, and the device might fail or cause the conflicting hardware to fail.

PnP is technology designed to prevent configuration problems and provide users with the capability to easily expand a PC. With PnP, the user simply plugs in the new card, and the system configures it automatically for proper operation.

PnP is composed of three principal components:

- PnP BIOS
- Extended System Configuration Data (ESCD)
- PnP OS

The PnP BIOS initiates the configuration of the PnP cards during the bootup process. If the cards previously were installed, the BIOS reads the information from ESCD, initializes the cards, and boots the system. During the installation of new PnP cards, the BIOS consults the ESCD to determine which system resources are available and needed for the add-in cards. If the BIOS is capable of finding sufficient available resources, it configures the cards. However, if the BIOS is incapable of locating sufficient available resources, the PnP routines in the OS complete the configuration process. During the configuration process, the configuration registers (in flash BIOS) on the cards and the ESCD are updated with the new configuration data.

PnP Device IDs

All PnP devices must contain a PnP device ID to enable the OS to uniquely recognize the device so it can load the appropriate driver software. Each device manufacturer is responsible for assigning the PnP ID for each product and storing it in the hardware.

Each manufacturer of PnP devices must be assigned an industry-unique, three-character vendor ID. Then the device manufacturer is responsible for assigning a unique product ID to each product model. After an ID is assigned to a product model, it must not be assigned to any other product model manufactured by the same company (that is, one that uses the same vendor ID).

Note

For a comprehensive list of PnP device IDs, see the Microsoft Plug and Play ID page at http://microsoft.com/whdc/system/pnppwr/pnp/pnpid.mspx.

ACPI

ACPI stands for Advanced Configuration and Power Interface, which defines a standard method for integrating power management as well as system-configuration features throughout a PC, including the hardware, OS, and application software. ACPI goes far beyond the previous standard, called *Advanced Power Management (APM)*, which consists mainly of processor, hard disk, and display control. ACPI controls not only power, but also all the PnP hardware configuration throughout the system. With ACPI, system configuration (PnP) as well as power management configuration are no longer controlled via the BIOS Setup; instead, they are controlled entirely within the OS.

The ACPI specification was created by Intel, Microsoft, and Toshiba; version 1.0 was released in 1996. ACPI became one of the major requirements for Microsoft's PC'97 logo certification program, causing motherboard and BIOS manufacturers to work on integrating ACPI into systems during that time. Intel integrated ACPI support in chipsets starting in April 1998 with the PIIX4E southbridge, and Microsoft added ACPI support in Windows starting with the release of Windows 98 (June 25, 1998) as part of what Microsoft called "OnNow" design. By the time Windows 2000 was released (February 17, 2000), ACPI had universally replaced APM as the primary power management and control interface on new systems.

ACPI enables the system to automatically turn on and off peripherals (such as optical drives, network cards, hard disk drives, and printers), as well as external devices connected to the PC (such as DVRs, televisions, telephones, and stereos). ACPI technology also enables peripherals to turn on or activate the PC. For example, a DVR can turn on the PC, which could then activate a large-screen television and high-fidelity sound system.

ACPI enables system designers to implement a range of power management features with various hardware designs while using the same OS driver. ACPI also uses the PnP BIOS data structures and takes control over the PnP interface, providing an OS-independent interface for configuration and control. Microsoft has included support for ACPI in Windows since Windows 98.

During the system setup and boot process, Windows versions supporting ACPI perform a series of checks and tests to see whether the system hardware and BIOS support ACPI. If support for ACPI is either not detected or found to be faulty, the system typically reverts to standard Advanced Power Management control, but problems can also cause a lockup with either a red or blue screen with an ACPI error code.

Red screens indicate that the problem is probably related to hardware or the BIOS. Blue screens, on the other hand, indicate that the problem is probably related to software or is an obscure problem. The ACPI error codes are described in Table 5.25.

Table 5.25 ACPI Error Codes

Error Code	Description
1xxx -	Indicates an error during the initialization phase of the ACPI driver and usually means the driver can't read one or more of the ACPI tables
2xxx -	Indicates an ACPI machine language (AML) interpreter error
3xxx -	Indicates an error within the ACPI driver event handler
4xxx -	Indicates thermal management errors

Virtually all these errors are the result of partial or incomplete ACPI implementations or incompatibilities in either the BIOS or device drivers. If you encounter any of these errors, contact your motherboard manufacturer for an updated BIOS or the device manufacturers for updated drivers.

BIOS/MBR Error Messages

When a PC system is first powered on, the system runs a POST. If errors are encountered during the POST, you usually see a text error message displayed onscreen. Errors that occur early in the POST might happen before the video card is initialized. These types of errors can't be displayed, so the system uses two other alternatives for communicating the error message. One is beeping—the system beeps the speaker in a specific pattern that indicates which error has occurred.

▶▶ For detailed lists of the BIOS POST beep codes, see Chapter 20, "PC Diagnostics, Testing, and Maintenance,". **p. 975**.

The alternative is to send a hexadecimal error code to I/O port address 80h, which can be read by a special card in one of the bus slots. When the ROM BIOS is performing the POST, in most systems the results of these tests are continuously sent to I/O port 80h so special diagnostics cards called *POST cards* can monitor them (see Figure 5.10). These tests sometimes are called *manufacturing tests* because they were designed into the system for testing it on the assembly line without a video display attached.

FIGURE 5.10 A two-digit hexadecimal code display (left) and a POST card in operation (right).

The POST cards have a two-digit hexadecimal display used to report the number of the currently executing test routine. Before each test is executed, a hexadecimal numeric code is sent to the port, and then the test is run. If the test fails and locks up the machine, the hexadecimal code of the last test being executed remains on the card's display.

Many tests are executed in a system before the video display card is enabled, especially if the display is EGA or VGA. Therefore, many errors can occur that would lock up the system before the system could possibly display an error code through the video system. Because not all these errors generate beep codes, to most normal troubleshooting procedures, a system with this type of problem (such as a memory failure in Bank 0) would appear completely "dead." By using one of the commercially available POST cards, however, you can often diagnose the problem.

These codes are completely BIOS dependent because the card does nothing but display the codes sent to it. Some BIOSs have more detailed POST procedures and therefore send more informative codes. POST cards can be purchased from JDR Microdevices or other sources and are available in both ISA and PCI bus versions.

For simple but otherwise fatal errors that can't be displayed onscreen, most of the BIOS versions also send audio codes that can be used to diagnose such problems. The audio codes are similar to POST codes, but they are "read" by listening to the speaker beep rather than by using a special card.

▶▶ The following section details the text error codes for all the popular BIOS versions. For detailed lists of the BIOS POST beep codes, see Figure 20.1, Chapter 20, **p. 978**.

BIOS Boot Error Messages

During the boot process, the bootstrap loader routine in the motherboard ROM BIOS reads the first physical sector of each of the bootable drives or devices, which is cylinder 0, head 0, sector 1 in CHS mode or logical block address 0 in LBA mode. The code from the first sector is loaded into RAM, and the last two bytes are checked to see whether they match a signature value of 55AAh. If the signature bytes match, that tells the ROM that the first sector contains a valid MBR and that the ROM can continue by transferring control to the MBR code.

If the last 2 bytes of the first physical sector do not match 55AAh, the ROM continues by checking the first physical sector of the next bootable device in the boot sequence until it either finds one with a valid MBR or runs out of devices to check. If, after all the drives or devices in the boot sequence are checked, none are found to have the proper signature bytes indicating a valid MBR, the ROM invokes an interrupt (18h) that calls a subroutine displaying an error message. The specific text or wording of the message varies according to the ROM manufacturer and version. The messages are detailed in the following sections.

IBM BIOS Messages

With no valid MBR or bootable device found, systems with an old IBM BIOS display the infamous ROM BASIC interpreter, which looks like this:

```
The IBM Personal Computer Basic

Version C1.10 Copyright IBM Corp 1981

62940 Bytes free

Ok
```

IBM ROM BASIC

The ROMs of most PCs are similar to the original IBM systems with which they are compatible—with the exception of the ROM BASIC interpreter (also called Cassette BASIC). It might come as a surprise to some PC users, but the original IBM PC actually had a jack on the rear of the system for connecting a cassette tape recorder. This was to be used for loading programs and data to or from a cassette tape. IBM included the cassette port because cassette tapes were used by several early personal computers (including the Apple). Floppy drives were expensive, and hard disks were not even an option yet. However, floppy drives came down in price quickly right at the time the PC was first released, and the cassette port never appeared on subsequent IBM systems. The cassette port also never appeared on PC-compatible systems because floppy drives were cheap by the time they came out.

The reason for having BASIC in ROM was so the original PC could come standard with only 16KB of memory and no floppy drives in the base configuration. Many computer users at the time either wrote their own programs in the BASIC language or ran BASIC programs written by others. The BASIC language interpreter built into the ROM BIOS of these early IBM systems was designed to access the cassette port on the back of the system; by having the interpreter in ROM, all 16 kilobytes of RAM could be used to store a program.

Even after the cassette port was eliminated, IBM left the BASIC code in the motherboard ROM until the early 1990s! I liken this to humans having an appendix. The ROM BASIC in those IBM systems is sort of like a vestigial organ—a leftover that had some use in prehistoric evolutionary ancestors but has no function today.

You can catch a glimpse of this ROM BASIC on older IBM systems that have it by disabling all the disk drives in the system. In that case, with nothing to boot from, those systems unceremoniously dump you into the strange (vintage 1981) ROM BASIC screen.

People used to dread seeing this because it usually meant that the floppy disk or hard disk they were trying to boot from had become corrupted or had failed. Because no compatible systems ever had the BASIC interpreter in ROM, they came up with different messages to display for the same situations in which an IBM system would invoke this BASIC. The most confusing of these was the message from AMI BIOS, which simply said `NO ROM BASIC - SYSTEM HALTED`, which really meant that the system was incapable of booting.

With no valid MBR or bootable device found, some IBM systems display a screen using text graphic characters that look similar to Figure 5.11.

The meaning here is, "Insert a bootable floppy disk into the A: drive and press the F1 key."

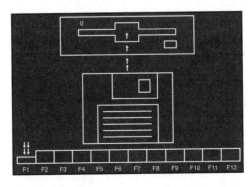

FIGURE 5.11   IBM ROM BIOS display indicating an invalid master boot record.

AMI BIOS Messages

With no valid MBR or bootable device found, systems with an AMI BIOS display the following message:

```
NO ROM BASIC - SYSTEM HALTED
```

This message is confusing to some because it seems to point to a problem with ROM BASIC, which of course is not what it really means! The AMI ROM does not include a BASIC interpreter in the ROM (neither does any other ROMs except those found in old IBM machines), so instead of jumping into BASIC or displaying a useful message indicating there are no bootable devices, it displays this confusing message. The real meaning is the same as for all these messages, which is to say that none of the bootable devices in the boot sequence were found to contain signature bytes indicating a valid MBR in their first physical sectors.

Compaq BIOS Messages

With no valid MBR or bootable device found, systems with a Compaq BIOS display the following message:

```
Non-System disk or disk error

replace and strike any key when ready
```

This is another confusing message because this same (or similar) error message is contained in the DOS/Windows 9X/Me VBR and normally is displayed if the system files are missing or corrupted. So, if you see this message on a Compaq system, you can't be sure whether the problem is in the MBR, VBR, or the system files, which makes tracking down and solving the problem more difficult.

Award BIOS Messages

With no valid MBR or bootable device found, systems with an Award BIOS display the following message:

```
DISK BOOT FAILURE, INSERT SYSTEM DISK AND PRESS ENTER
```

So far, this appears to be the least confusing of these messages. You don't need a secret decoder ring to figure out what it is really trying to say.

Phoenix BIOS Messages

With no valid MBR or bootable device found, systems with a Phoenix BIOS display either the message

```
No boot device available -

strike F1 to retry boot, F2 for setup utility
```

or this one:

```
No boot sector on fixed disk -

strike F1 to retry boot, F2 for setup utility
```

Which of these two messages you see depends on whether no boot devices were found or readable, or a boot sector could be read but was found not to have the proper signature bytes.

MBR Boot Error Messages

If the BIOS has successfully loaded the MBR and checked the signature, and if the signature bytes are correct, the BIOS then passes control to the MBR by running the MBR code. The program code in the

MBR performs a test of the partition table (also contained in the MBR) by checking the Boot Indicator bytes in each of the four partition table entries. These bytes are at offsets 446 (1BEh), 462 (1CEh), 478 (1DEh), and 494 (1EEh) in the MBR. These bytes indicate which of the four possible primary partition table entries contains an active (bootable) partition. A value of 80h at any of these byte locations indicates that particular table entry contains the active partition. Only one of the four Boot Indicator bytes at a time is allowed to indicate an active partition (containing a value of 80h), meaning that if one of them is 80h, the other three must all contain 00h. Going by the rules initially set forth by IBM and Microsoft, only two possible conditions are allowed with respect to all four Boot Indicator bytes:

- All four Boot Indicator bytes are 00h, indicating no Active (bootable) partitions.

- One Boot Indicator byte is 80h and the other three are 00h, indicating one Active (bootable) partition.

If all four Boot Indicator bytes are 00h—which indicates that no active (bootable) partitions exist—then the MBR returns control to the motherboard ROM, which will then normally display one of the error messages listed earlier. This would be an expected result if you were to remove the existing partitions from a drive but had not created new partitions on the drive, or if you had failed to make one of the partitions Active (bootable) when partitioning or repartitioning the drive. For example, when creating multiple partitions on a drive, it is possible to forget to set one of them as Active. If you do this by accident and render your hard drive nonbootable, you can easily correct the problem by booting from a floppy or CD with partitioning software such as FDISK or DISKPART and setting the partition where your OS is installed as Active.

If only one of the Boot Indicator bytes is 80h and the rest are 00h (required for a properly booting system), the system continues the standard boot process by loading the volume boot record (VBR) from the active partition.

Invalid Partition Table

Any other Boot Indicator byte conditions are not allowed and, if present, indicate that the partition table is corrupt, causing the MBR code to generate an error message and stop. For example, if two or more of the Boot Indicator bytes are 80h (indicating multiple Active partitions, which is not allowed) or if any one of the Boot Indicator bytes is any value other than 00h or 80h, the partition table is considered corrupt; the MBR code displays the following error message and halts the system:

```
Invalid partition table
```

If you see this message, you can try rebooting from alternate media or a different drive and then see if you can access the data on the problem drive. Depending on how much of the partition table, MBR, or other sectors on the drive are corrupted, it may be easiest to simply start over by removing and re-creating all the partitions (which will lose any and all data they contain), or investigate data recovery options if you don't have backups and need the data back.

Error Loading Operating System

Once the MBR code makes it past the Boot Indicator byte check, and one of the partitions is marked active (bootable), the MBR code continues by looking at the rest of the information in the active partition table entry to determine the starting sector location for the active partition. The starting sector location is a sector address indicated by both CHS (cylinder/head/sector) and LBA (logical block address) values. The CHS value is used for drives 8.4GB or smaller in capacity, whereas the LBA value is used for drives larger than 8.4GB (pretty much all drives today). The first sector of a partition contains the volume boot record (VBR), which is also known as the *operating system boot record* because it is installed on the drive during the OS partition format process. Once the VBR address of the active partition has been determined, the MBR code reads that sector from the drive.

If the VBR of the active partition can't be read successfully due to a read error (physical problem with the disk), a series of five retries occurs. If after all the retries the VBR still cannot be read, the following message is displayed and the system stops:

```
Error loading operating system
```

This is a bad message to see because it generally indicates physical problems with the drive. However, this message can also appear if the drive parameters are incorrectly entered in the BIOS Setup, or if the VBR sector location as listed in the MBR partition table is invalid. For example, if the MBR contains an invalid VBR address that points to a sector beyond the physical end of the drive, this message results.

If you see this message unexpectedly, first check the BIOS Setup settings for the drive to be sure they are correct, then check the partition table entries, and finally run a diagnostic test of the drive itself. If the drive is bad or going bad and you need the data back, you may require the services of a professional data-recovery outfit.

Missing Operating System

If the MBR code has successfully loaded the VBR with no read errors, the MBR code checks the last two bytes of the VBR for the 55AAh signature. If the signature is not present, the MBR displays the following error message and halts the system:

```
Missing operating system
```

This would be an expected occurrence if, for example, you had just created the partition and had not yet done a high-level format, meaning that the partition has not yet been formatted by the OS, or no OS is yet installed.

Chapter

6

Memory

Memory Basics

This chapter discusses memory from both a physical and a logical point of view. First, we'll examine what memory is, where it fits into the PC architecture, and how it works. Then, we'll look at the various types of memory, speeds, and packaging of the chips and memory modules you can buy and install.

This chapter also covers the logical layout of memory, defining the various areas of memory and their uses from the system's point of view. Because the logical layout and uses are within the "mind" of the processor, memory mapping and logical layout remain perhaps the most difficult subjects to grasp in the PC universe. This chapter contains useful information that removes the mysteries associated with memory and enables you to get the most out of your system.

Memory is the workspace for the processor. It is a temporary storage area where the programs and data being operated on by the processor must reside. Memory storage is considered temporary because the data and programs remain there only as long as the computer has electrical power or is not reset. Before the computer is shut down or reset, any data that has been changed in memory should be saved to a more permanent storage device (usually a hard disk) so it can be reloaded into memory in the future.

Main memory is normally called RAM (random access memory), because you can randomly (as opposed to sequentially) access any location. This designation is somewhat misleading and often misinterpreted. Read-only memory (ROM), for example, is also randomly accessible, yet it is usually differentiated from the system RAM because it maintains data without power and can't normally be written to. Although a hard disk can be used as virtual random access memory, we don't consider that RAM either.

Over the years, the definition of RAM has changed from a simple acronym to become something that means the primary memory workspace the processor uses to run programs, which usually is constructed out of a type of chip called dynamic RAM (DRAM). One of the characteristics of DRAM chips (and therefore most types of RAM in general) is that they store data dynamically, which really has two meanings. One meaning is that the information can be written to RAM repeatedly at any time. The other has to do with the fact that DRAM requires the data to be refreshed (essentially rewritten) every few milliseconds or so; faster RAM requires refreshing more often than slower RAM. A type of RAM called static RAM (SRAM) does not require the periodic refreshing. An important characteristic of RAM in general is that data is stored only as long as the memory has electrical power.

Note

Both DRAM and SRAM memory maintain their contents only as long as power is present. However, a different type of memory known as *flash memory* can retain its contents without power, and it is most commonly used today in solid-state drives (SSDs), digital camera and player media, and USB flash drives. As far as the PC is concerned, a flash memory device emulates a disk drive (not RAM) and is accessed by a drive letter, just as with any other disk or optical drive.

When we talk about a computer's memory, we usually mean the RAM or physical memory in the system, which are the memory chips or modules the processor uses to store primary active programs and data. This often is confused with the term *storage*, which should be used when referring to things such as disk drives (although they can be used as a form of RAM called virtual memory).

RAM can refer to both the physical chips that make up the memory in the system and the logical mapping and layout of that memory. *Logical mapping* and *layout* refer to how the memory addresses are mapped to actual chips and what address locations contain which types of system information.

People new to computers often confuse main memory (RAM) with disk storage because both have capacities that are expressed in similar megabyte or gigabyte terms. The best analogy I've found to explain the relationship between memory and disk storage is to think of an office with a desk and a file cabinet.

In this popular analogy, the file cabinet represents the system's hard disk, where both programs and data are stored for long-term safekeeping. The desk represents the system's main memory, which allows the person working at the desk (acting as the processor) direct access to any files placed on it. Files represent the programs and documents you can "load" into the memory. To work on a particular file, you first must retrieve it from the cabinet and place it on the desk. If the desk is large enough, you might be able to have several files open on it at one time; likewise, if your system has more memory, you can run more or larger programs and work on more or larger documents.

Adding hard disk space to a system is similar to putting a bigger file cabinet in the office—more files can be permanently stored. And adding more memory to a system is like getting a bigger desk—you can work on more programs and data at the same time.

One difference between this analogy and the way things really work in a computer is that when a file is loaded into memory, it is a copy of the file that is actually loaded; the original still resides on the hard disk. Because of the temporary nature of memory, any files that have been changed after being loaded into memory must then be saved back to the hard disk before the system is powered off (which erases the memory). If the changed file in memory is not saved, the original copy of the file on the hard disk remains unaltered. This is like saying that any changes made to files left on the desktop are discarded when the office is closed, although the original files are still preserved in the cabinet.

Memory temporarily stores programs when they are running, along with the data being used by those programs. RAM chips are sometimes termed *volatile storage* because when you turn off your computer or an electrical outage occurs, whatever is stored in RAM is lost unless you saved it to your hard drive. Because of the volatile nature of RAM, many computer users make it a habit to save their work frequently—a habit I recommend. Many software applications perform periodic saves automatically to minimize the potential for data loss.

Physically, the *main memory* in a system is a collection of chips or modules containing chips that are usually plugged into the motherboard. These chips or modules vary in their electrical and physical designs and must be compatible with the system into which they are being installed to function properly. This chapter discusses the various types of chips and modules that can be installed in different systems.

To better understand physical memory in a system, you should understand what types of memory are found in a typical PC and what the role of each type is. Three main types of physical memory are used in modern PCs. (Remember, I'm talking about the type of memory chip, not the type of module that memory is stored on.)

- **ROM**—Read-only memory
- **DRAM**—Dynamic random access memory
- **SRAM**—Static RAM

The only type of memory you normally need to purchase and install in a system is DRAM. The other types are built in to the motherboard (ROM), processor (SRAM), and other components such as the video card, hard drives, and so on.

ROM

Read-only memory, or ROM, is a type of memory that can permanently or semi-permanently store data. It is called read-only because it is either impossible or difficult to write to. ROM also is often referred to as nonvolatile memory because any data stored in ROM remains there, even if the power is turned off. As such, ROM is an ideal place to put the PC's startup instructions—that is, the software that boots the system.

Note that ROM and RAM are not opposites, as some people seem to believe. Both are simply types of memory. In fact, ROM technically could be classified as a subset of the system's RAM. In other words, a portion of the system's random access memory address space is mapped into one or more ROM chips. This is necessary to contain the software that enables the PC to boot; otherwise, the processor would have no program in memory to execute when it was powered on.

The main ROM BIOS is contained in a ROM chip on the motherboard, but there are also adapter cards with ROMs on them. ROMs on adapter cards contain auxiliary BIOS routines and drivers needed by the particular card, especially for those cards that must be active early in the boot process, such as video cards. Cards that don't need drivers active at boot time typically don't have a ROM because those drivers can be loaded from the hard disk later in the boot process.

Most systems today use a type of ROM called *electrically erasable programmable ROM (EEPROM)*, which is a form of flash memory. Flash is a truly nonvolatile memory that is rewritable, enabling users to easily update the ROM or firmware in their motherboards or any other components (video cards, SCSI cards, peripherals, and so on).

◄◄ For more information on BIOS upgrades, see the Chapter 5 section, "Upgrading the BIOS," **p. 274**.

DRAM

Dynamic RAM (DRAM) is the type of memory chip used for most of the main memory in a modern PC. The main advantages of DRAM are that it is dense, meaning you can pack a lot of bits into a small chip, and it is inexpensive, which makes purchasing large amounts of memory affordable.

The memory cells in a DRAM chip are tiny capacitors that retain a charge to indicate a bit. The problem with DRAM is that it is dynamic—that is, its contents can be changed. With every keystroke or every mouse swipe, the contents of RAM change. And the entire contents of RAM can be wiped out by a system crash. Also, because of the design, it must be constantly refreshed; otherwise, the electrical charges in the individual memory capacitors drain and the data is lost. Refresh occurs when the system memory controller takes a tiny break and accesses all the rows of data in the memory chips. The standard refresh time is 15ms (milliseconds), which means that every 15ms, all the rows in the memory are automatically read to refresh the data.

◄◄ See the Chapter 4 section, "Chipsets," **p. 181**.

Unfortunately, refreshing the memory takes processor time away from other tasks because each refresh cycle takes several CPU cycles to complete. In older systems, the refresh cycling could take up to 10% or more of the total CPU time, but with modern systems running in the multigigahertz range, refresh overhead is now on the order of a fraction of a percent or less of the total CPU time. Some systems allow you to alter the refresh timing parameters via the CMOS Setup. The time between refresh cycles is known as *tREF* and is expressed not in milliseconds, but in clock cycles (see Figure 6.1).

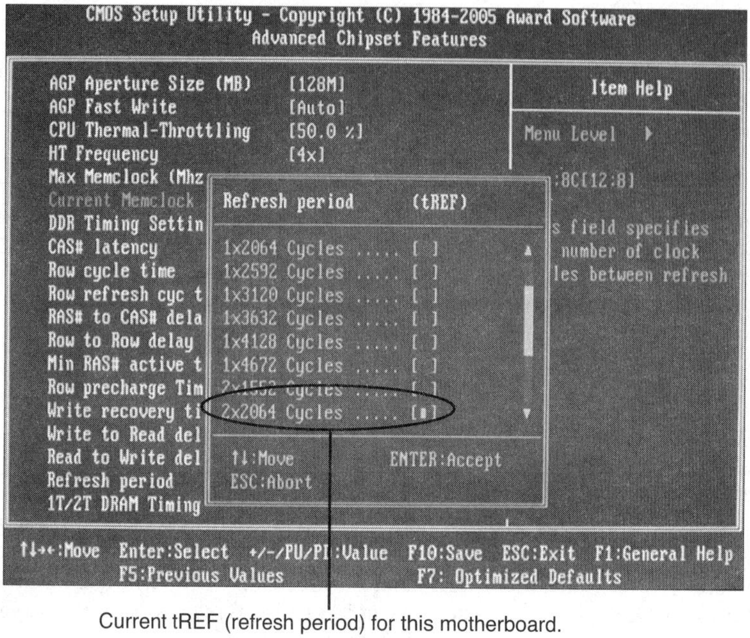

Current tREF (refresh period) for this motherboard.

FIGURE 6.1   The refresh period dialog box and other advanced memory timings can be adjusted manually through the BIOS Setup program.

It's important to be aware that increasing the time between refresh cycles (tREF) to speed up your system can allow some of the memory cells to begin draining prematurely, which can cause random soft memory errors to appear.

A *soft error* is a data error that is not caused by a defective chip. To avoid soft errors, it is usually safer to stick with the recommended or default refresh timing. Because refresh consumes less than 1% of modern system overall bandwidth, altering the refresh rate has little effect on performance. It is almost always best to use default or automatic settings for any memory timings in the BIOS Setup. Many modern systems don't allow changes to memory timings and are permanently set to automatic settings. On an automatic setting, the motherboard reads the timing parameters out of the serial presence detect (SPD) ROM found on the memory module and sets the cycling speeds to match.

DRAMs use only one transistor and capacitor pair per bit, which makes them dense, offering more memory capacity per chip than other types of memory. Currently, DRAM chips are being prepared for production with densities up to 4Gb (512MB) per chip, which at one transistor per bit requires at least 4 billion transistors. The transistor count in memory chips is much higher than in processors because in a memory chip the transistors and capacitors are all consistently arranged in a (normally square) grid of simple repetitive structures, unlike processors, which are much more complex circuits of different structures and elements interconnected in a highly irregular fashion.

The transistor for each DRAM bit cell reads the charge state of the adjacent capacitor. If the capacitor is charged, the cell is read to contain a 1; no charge indicates a 0. The charge in the tiny capacitors is constantly draining, which is why the memory must be refreshed constantly. Even a momentary power interruption, or anything that interferes with the refresh cycles, can cause a DRAM memory cell to lose the charge and thus the data. If this happens in a running system, it can lead to blue screens, global protection faults, corrupted files, and any number of system crashes.

DRAM is used in PC systems because it is inexpensive and the chips can be densely packed, so a lot of memory capacity can fit in a small space. Unfortunately, DRAM is also relatively slow—typically much slower than the processor. For this reason, many types of DRAM architectures have been developed to improve performance. These architectures are covered later in the chapter.

Cache Memory: SRAM

Another distinctly different type of memory exists that is significantly faster than most types of DRAM. SRAM stands for static RAM, which is so named because it does not need the periodic refresh rates like DRAM. Because of the way SRAMs are designed, not only are refresh rates unnecessary, but SRAM is much faster than DRAM and much more capable of keeping pace with modern processors.

SRAM memory is available in access times of 0.25ns or less, so it can keep pace with processors running 4GHz or faster. This is because of the SRAM design, which calls for a cluster of six transistors for each bit of storage. The use of transistors but no capacitors means that refresh rates are not necessary because there are no capacitors to lose their charges over time. As long as there is power, SRAM remembers what is stored. With these attributes, why don't we use SRAM for all system memory? The answers are simple.

Compared to DRAM, SRAM is much faster but also much lower in density and much more expensive (see Table 6.1). The lower density means that SRAM chips are physically larger and store fewer bits overall. The high number of transistors and the clustered design mean that SRAM chips are both physically larger and much more expensive to produce than DRAM chips. For example, a high-density DRAM chip might store up to 4Gb (512MB) of RAM, whereas similar-sized SRAM chips can only store up to 72Mb (9MB). The high cost and physical constraints have prevented SRAM from being used as the main memory for PC systems.

Table 6.1   Comparing DRAM and SRAM

Type	Speed	Density	Cost
DRAM	Slow	High	Low
SRAM	Fast	Low	High

Even though SRAM is impractical for PC use as main memory, PC designers have found a way to use SRAM to dramatically improve PC performance. Rather than spend the money for all RAM to be SRAM memory, they design in a small amount of high-speed SRAM memory, used as cache memory, which is much more cost effective. The SRAM cache runs at speeds close to or even equal to the processor and is the memory from which the processor usually directly reads from and writes to. During read operations, the data in the high-speed cache memory is resupplied from the lower-speed main memory or DRAM in advance. To convert access time in nanoseconds to MHz, use the following formula:

1 / nanoseconds × 1000 = MHz

Likewise, to convert from MHz to nanoseconds, use the following inverse formula:

1 / MHz × 1000 = nanoseconds

Today, we have memory that runs faster than 1GHz (1 nanosecond), but up until the late 1990s, DRAM was limited to about 60ns (16MHz) in speed. Up until processors were running at speeds of 16MHz, the available DRAM could fully keep pace with the processor and motherboard, meaning that there was no need for cache. However, as soon as processors crossed the 16MHz barrier, the available DRAM could no longer keep pace, and SRAM cache began to enter PC system designs. This occurred way back in 1986 and 1987 with the debut of systems with the 386 processor running at speeds of 16MHz to 20MHz or faster. These were among the first PC systems to employ what's called *cache memory*, a high-speed buffer made up of SRAM that directly feeds the processor. Because the cache can run at the speed of the processor, it acts as a buffer between the processor and the slower DRAM in the system. The cache controller anticipates the processor memory needs and preloads the high-speed cache memory with data. Then, as the processor calls for a memory address, the data can be retrieved from the high-speed cache rather than the much lower-speed main memory.

Cache effectiveness can be expressed by a hit ratio. This is the ratio of cache hits to total memory accesses. A *hit* occurs when the data the processor needs has been preloaded into the cache from the main memory, meaning the processor can read it from the cache. A cache *miss* is when the cache controller did not anticipate the need for a specific address and the desired data was not preloaded into the cache. In that case the processor must retrieve the data from the slower main memory, instead of the faster cache. Any time the processor reads data from main memory, the processor must wait longer because the main memory cycles at a much slower rate than the processor. As an example, if the processor with integral on-die cache is running at 3.6GHz (3,600MHz) on a 1,333MHz bus, both the processor and the integral cache would be cycling at 0.28ns, whereas the main memory would most likely be cycling almost five times more slowly at 1,333MHz (0.75ns). So, every time the 3.6GHz processor reads from main memory, it would effectively slow down to only 1,333MHz. The slowdown is accomplished by having the processor execute what are called *wait states*, which are cycles in which nothing is done; the processor essentially cools its heels while waiting for the slower main memory to return the desired data. Obviously, you don't want your processors slowing down, so cache function and design become more important as system speeds increase.

To minimize the processor being forced to read data from the slow main memory, two or three stages of cache usually exist in a modern system, called Level 1 (L1), Level 2 (L2), and Level 3 (L3). The L1 cache is also called *integral* or *internal cache* because it has always been built directly into the processor as part of the processor die (the raw chip). Because of this, L1 cache always runs at the full speed of the processor core and is the fastest cache in any system. All 486 and higher processors incorporate integral L1 cache, making them significantly faster than their predecessors. L2 cache was originally called *external cache* because it was external to the processor chip when it first appeared. Originally, this meant it was installed on the motherboard, as was the case with all 386, 486, and first-generation Pentium systems. In those systems, the L2 cache runs at motherboard and CPU bus speed because it is installed on the motherboard and is connected to the CPU bus. You typically find the L2 cache physically adjacent to the processor socket in Pentium and earlier systems.

◀◀   See the Chapter 3 section, "Cache Memory," **p. 53**.

In the interest of improved performance, later processor designs from Intel and AMD included the L2 cache as part of the processor. In all processors since late 1999 (and some earlier models), the L2 cache is directly incorporated as part of the processor die, just like the L1 cache. In chips with on-die L2, the cache runs at the full core speed of the processor and is much more efficient. By contrast, most processors from 1999 and earlier with integrated L2 had the L2 cache in separate chips that were external to the main processor core. The L2 cache in many of these older processors ran at only half or one-third the processor core speed. Cache speed is important, so systems having L2 cache on the motherboard were the slowest. Including L2 inside the processor made it faster, and including it directly on the processor die (rather than as chips external to the die) made it faster yet.

A third-level or L3 cache has been present in some processors since 2001. The first desktop PC processor with L3 cache was the Pentium 4 Extreme Edition, a high-end chip introduced in late 2003 with 2MB of on-die L3 cache. Although it seemed at the time that this would be a forerunner of widespread L3 cache in desktop processors, later versions of the Pentium 4 Extreme Edition (as well as its successor, the Pentium Extreme Edition) dropped the L3 cache, instead using larger L2 cache sizes to improve performance. L3 cache made a return to PC processors in 2007 with the AMD Phenom and in 2008 with the Intel Core i7, both of which have four cores on a single die. L3 is especially suited to processors with multiple cores because it provides an on-die cache that all the cores can share. Since 2009, L3 cache has become a staple in most processors with two or more cores. Figure 6.2 shows the L1/L2/L3 cache configuration as reported by CPU-Z (www.cpuid.com) for an Intel Core i5-3570K processor.

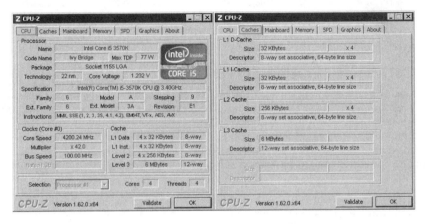

FIGURE 6.2   CPU-Z screenshots showing the CPU/Cache information for an Intel Core i5-3570K processor.

The key to understanding both cache and main memory is to see where they fit in the overall system architecture. See Chapter 4 for diagrams showing recent systems with different types of cache memory.

Memory Standards

For memory to be as inexpensive and interchangeable as possible, industry-standard specifications for both chips and modules have been developed. The Joint Electron Device Engineering Council (JEDEC) Solid State Technology Association creates most industry-standard memory chip and module designs.

JEDEC

JEDEC is the semiconductor engineering standardization body of the Electronic Industries Alliance (EIA), a trade association that represents all areas of the electronics industry. JEDEC, which was created in 1960, governs the standardization of all types of semiconductor devices, integrated circuits, and modules. JEDEC has about 300 member companies, including memory, chipset, and processor manufacturers and practically any company involved in manufacturing computer equipment using industry-standard components.

The idea behind JEDEC is simple: If one company were to create a proprietary memory technology, for example, then other companies that wanted to manufacture components compliant with that memory would have to pay license fees, assuming the company that owned it was interested in licensing at all! Parts would be more proprietary in nature, causing problems with interchangeability or sourcing reasonably priced replacements. In addition, those companies licensing the technology would have no control over future changes the owner company made.

JEDEC helps to prevent that type of scenario for items such as memory by getting all the memory manufacturers to work together creating shared industry standards covering memory chips and modules. JEDEC-approved standards for memory could then be freely shared by all the member companies, and no one single company would have control over a given standard or any of the companies producing compliant components. FPM, SDRAM, DDR, DDR2, DDR3, and DDR4 SDRAM are examples of JEDEC memory standards used in PCs, whereas EDO and RDRAM are proprietary examples. You can find out more about JEDEC standards for memory and other semiconductor technology at www.jedec.org.

Because of variations on speeds (timing), voltage, and other issues, purchasing memory matching the correct industry-standard type doesn't guarantee that it will work in a given system. Always be sure the memory you purchase works with your system or that you can get a refund or replacement if it doesn't. Even though industry standards do exist, allowing modules from many sources to fit a given system, I normally recommend that you look for memory modules that the system or memory manufacturer has approved for the system. Often you can find a list of approved modules or suppliers in the system documentation or on the system or memory module manufacturer's website.

Speed and Performance

The speed and performance issues with memory are confusing to some people because of all the different ways to express the speeds of memory and processors. Memory speed was originally expressed in nanoseconds (ns), whereas the speeds of newer forms of memory are usually expressed in megahertz (MHz) and megabytes per second (MBps) instead. Processor speed was originally expressed in megahertz (MHz), whereas most current processor speeds are expressed in gigahertz (GHz). Although all these different speed units might seem confusing, it is relatively simple to translate from one to the other.

A *nanosecond* is defined as one billionth of a second—a short piece of time indeed. To put some perspective on just how small a nanosecond really is, consider that the speed of light is 186,282 miles (299,792 kilometers) per second in a vacuum. In one billionth of a second (one nanosecond), a beam of light travels a mere 11.80 inches or 29.98 centimeters—slightly less than the length of a typical ruler!

Memory speeds have often been expressed in terms of their cycle times (or how long it takes for one cycle), whereas processor speeds have almost always been expressed in terms of their cycle speeds (number of cycles per second). Cycle time and cycle speed are actually just different ways of saying the same thing; that is, you can quote chip speeds in cycles per second, or seconds per cycle, and mean the same thing.

As an analogy, you could express the speed of a vehicle using the same relative terms. In the United States vehicle speeds are normally expressed in miles per hour. If you were driving a car at 60 miles per hour (mph), it would take 1 minute per mile (mpm). At a faster speed of 120mph, it would take only 0.5mpm, and at a slower 30mph speed it would take 2.0mpm. In other words, you could give the speeds as either mph or mpm values, and they would mean exactly the same thing.

Because it is confusing to speak in these different terms for chip speeds, I thought it would be interesting to see exactly how they compare. Table 6.2 shows the relationship between commonly used clock speeds (MHz) and the nanosecond (ns) cycle times they represent.

Table 6.2 Relationship Between Megahertz (MHz) and Cycle Times in Nanoseconds (ns)

Clock Speed	Cycle Time	Clock Speed	Cycle Time	Clock Speed	Cycle Time	Clock Speed	Cycle Time
4.77MHz	210ns	250MHz	4.0ns	850MHz	1.18ns	2,700MHz	0.37ns
6MHz	167ns	266MHz	3.8ns	866MHz	1.15ns	2,800MHz	0.36ns
8MHz	125ns	300MHz	3.3ns	900MHz	1.11ns	2,900MHz	0.34ns
10MHz	100ns	333MHz	3.0ns	933MHz	1.07ns	3,000MHz	0.333ns
12MHz	83ns	350MHz	2.9ns	950MHz	1.05ns	3,100MHz	0.323ns
16MHz	63ns	366MHz	2.7ns	966MHz	1.04ns	3,200MHz	0.313ns
20MHz	50ns	400MHz	2.5ns	1,000MHz	1.00ns	3,300MHz	0.303ns
25MHz	40ns	433MHz	2.3ns	1,100MHz	0.91ns	3,400MHz	0.294ns
33MHz	30ns	450MHz	2.2ns	1,133MHz	0.88ns	3,500MHz	0.286ns
40MHz	25ns	466MHz	2.1ns	1,200MHz	0.83ns	3,600MHz	0.278ns
50MHz	20ns	500MHz	2.0ns	1,300MHz	0.77ns	3,700MHz	0.270ns
60MHz	17ns	533MHz	1.88ns	1,400MHz	0.71ns	3,800MHz	0.263ns
66MHz	15ns	550MHz	1.82ns	1,500MHz	0.67ns	3,900MHz	0.256ns
75MHz	13ns	566MHz	1.77ns	1,600MHz	0.63ns	4,000MHz	0.250ns
80MHz	13ns	600MHz	1.67ns	1,700MHz	0.59ns	4,100MHz	0.244ns
100MHz	10ns	633MHz	1.58ns	1,800MHz	0.56ns	4,200MHz	0.238ns
120MHz	8.3ns	650MHz	1.54ns	1,900MHz	0.53ns	4,300MHz	0.233ns
133MHz	7.5ns	666MHz	1.50ns	2,000MHz	0.50ns	4,400MHz	0.227ns
150MHz	6.7ns	700MHz	1.43ns	2,100MHz	0.48ns	4,500MHz	0.222ns
166MHz	6.0ns	733MHz	1.36ns	2,200MHz	0.45ns	4,600MHz	0.217ns
180MHz	5.6ns	750MHz	1.33ns	2,300MHz	0.43ns	4,700MHz	0.213ns
200MHz	5.0ns	766MHz	1.31ns	2,400MHz	0.42ns	4,800MHz	0.208ns
225MHz	4.4ns	800MHz	1.25ns	2,500MHz	0.40ns	4,900MHz	0.204ns
233MHz	4.3ns	833MHz	1.20ns	2,600MHz	0.38ns	5,000MHz	0.200ns

As you can see from Table 6.2, as clock speed increases, cycle time decreases proportionately, and vice versa.

Over the evolutionary life of the PC, main memory (what we call RAM) has had a difficult time keeping up with the processor, requiring several levels of high-speed cache memory to intercept processor requests for the slower main memory. More recently, however, systems using DDR, DDR2, and DDR3 SDRAM have memory bus transfer rates (bandwidth) capable of equaling that of the external processor bus. When the speed of the memory bus equals the speed of the processor bus (or some even multiple thereof), main memory performance is closest to optimum for that system.

For example, using the information in Table 6.2, you can see that the 60ns DRAM memory used in the original Pentium and Pentium II PCs up until 1998 works out to be an extremely slow 16.7MHz! This slow 16.7MHz memory was installed in systems running processors up to 300MHz or faster with external processor bus speeds of up to 66MHz, resulting in a large mismatch between processor bus and main memory performance. To alleviate this performance gap, starting in 1998 the industry shifted to faster SDRAM memory, which could match the 66MHz and 100MHz processor bus speeds in use at that time. From that point forward, memory and especially memory bus performance has largely evolved in step with the processor bus, coming out with newer and faster types to match any increases in processor bus speeds.

By the year 2000, the dominant processor bus and memory speeds had increased to 100MHz and even 133MHz, called PC100 and PC133 SDRAM, respectively. Starting in early 2001, double data rate (DDR) SDRAM memory of 200MHz and 266MHz became popular. In 2002, DDR memory increased to 333MHz, and in 2003, the speeds increased further to 400MHz. In 2004, we saw the introduction of DDR2, first at 400MHz and then at 533MHz. DDR2 memory continued to match processor bus speed increases in PCs from 2005 to 2006, rising to 667MHz and 800MHz during that time. By 2007, DDR2 memory was available at speeds of up to 1066MHz. By late 2007, DDR3 came on the market at speeds of 1066MHz, with 1333MHz and 1600MHz appearing in 2008. In 2009, DDR3 memory became the most popular memory type in new systems, and faster speed grades of 1866MHz and 2133MHz were added. When DDR4 is released in 2013, it will start at a speed of 1600MHz, with future speeds of up to twice as much. DDR4 should become popular in new systems in 2015. Table 6.3 lists the primary types and performance levels of PC memory.

Table 6.3   PC Memory Types and Performance Levels

Memory Type	Years Popular	Desktop Module Type	Laptop Module Type	Voltage	Max. Clock Speed	Max. Throughput Single-Channel	Max. Throughput Dual-Channel	Max. Throughput Triple-Channel
Fast Page Mode (FPM) DRAM	1987–1995	30/72-pin SIMM	72/144-pin SODIMM	5V	22MHz	177MBps	N/A	N/A
Extended Data Out (EDO) DRAM	1995–1998	72-pin SIMM	72/144-pin SODIMM	5V	33MHz	266MBps	N/A	N/A
Single Data Rate (SDR) SDRAM	1998–2002	168-pin DIMM	144-pin SODIMM	3.3V	133MHz	1,066MBps	N/A	N/A
Double Data Rate (DDR) SDRAM	2002–2005	184-pin DIMM	200-pin SODIMM	2.5V	400MTps	3,200MBps	6,400MBps	N/A
DDR2 SDRAM	2005–2009	240-pin DDR2 DIMM	200-pin SODIMM	1.8V	1,066MTps	8,533MBps	17,066MBps	N/A
DDR3 SDRAM	2009–2015	240-pin DDR3 DIMM	204-pin SODIMM	1.5V	2,133MTps	17,066MBps	34,133MBps	51,200MBps
DDR4 SDRAM	2015+	284-pin DDR4 DIMM	256-pin SODIMM	1.2V	4,266MTps	34,133MBps	68,266MBps	102,400MBps

MHz = Million cycles per second

MTps = Million transfers per second

MBps = Million bytes per second

DIMM = Dual inline memory module

SODIMM = Small outline DIMM

SIMM = Single inline memory module

Another specification to consider that is related to speed is the *CAS (column address strobe) latency*, which is often abbreviated as *CL*. This is also sometimes called *read latency*, and it's the number of clock cycles occurring between the registration of the CAS signal and the resultant output data, with lower numbers of cycles indicating faster (better) performance. If possible, choose modules with a lower CL figure because the motherboard chipset reads that specification out of the SPD (serial presence detect) ROM on the module and takes advantage of the lower latency through improved memory controller timings. Figure 6.3 shows the memory timing and SPD information as reported by CPU-Z (www.cpuid.com) for a system with DDR3-1600 SDRAM.

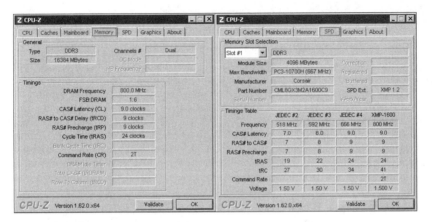

FIGURE 6.3 CPU-Z screenshots showing the Memory/SPD information for a system with DDR3-1600 SDRAM.

The following sections look at these memory types in more detail.

Fast Page Mode DRAM

Standard DRAM is accessed through a technique called *paging*. Normal memory access requires that a row and column address be selected, which takes time. Paging enables faster access to all the data within a given row of memory by keeping the row address the same and changing only the column. Memory that uses this technique is called *Page Mode* or *Fast Page Mode memory*. Other variations on Page Mode were called Static Column or Nibble Mode memory.

Paged memory is a simple scheme for improving memory performance that divides memory into pages ranging from 512 bytes to a few kilobytes long. The paging circuitry then enables memory locations in a page to be accessed with fewer wait states. If the desired memory location is outside the current page, one or more wait states are added while the system selects the new page.

To improve further on memory access speeds, systems have evolved to enable faster access to DRAM. One important change was the implementation of burst mode access in the 486 and later processors. Burst mode cycling takes advantage of the consecutive nature of most memory accesses. After setting up the row and column addresses for a given access, using burst mode, you can then access the next three adjacent addresses with no additional latency or wait states. A burst access usually is limited to four total accesses. To describe this, we often refer to the timing in the number of cycles for each access. A typical burst mode access of standard DRAM is expressed as x-y-y-y; x is the time for the first access (latency plus cycle time), and y represents the number of cycles required for each consecutive access.

Standard 60ns-rated DRAM normally runs 5-3-3-3 burst mode timing. This means the first access takes a total of five cycles (on a 66MHz system bus, this is about 75ns total, or 5 × 15ns cycles), and the consecutive cycles take three cycles each (3 × 15ns = 45ns). As you can see, the actual system timing is somewhat less than the memory is technically rated for. Without the bursting technique, memory access would be 5-5-5-5 because the full latency is necessary for each memory transfer. The 45ns cycle time during burst transfers equals about a 22.2MHz effective clock rate; on a system with a 64-bit (8-byte) wide memory bus, this would result in a maximum throughput of 177MBps (22.2MHz × 8 bytes = 177MBps).

DRAM memory that supports paging and this bursting technique is called *Fast Page Mode* (FPM) memory. This term refers to the ability to access data on the same memory page faster than data on other memory pages.

Most 386, 486, and Pentium systems from 1987 through 1995 used FPM memory, which came in either 30-pin or 72-pin SIMM form.

Another technique for speeding up FPM memory is called *interleaving*. In this design, two separate banks of memory are used together, alternating access from one to the other as even and odd bytes. While one is being accessed, the other is being precharged, when the row and column addresses are being selected. Then, by the time the first bank in the pair is finished returning data, the second bank in the pair is finished with the latency part of the cycle and is now ready to return data. While the second bank is returning data, the first bank is being precharged, selecting the row and column address of the next access. This overlapping of accesses in two banks reduces the effect of the latency or precharge cycles and allows for faster overall data retrieval. The only problem is that to use interleaving, you must install identical pairs of banks together, doubling the number of modules required.

Extended Data Out RAM

In 1995, a newer type of DRAM called extended data out (EDO) RAM became available for Pentium systems. EDO, a modified form of FPM memory, is sometimes referred to as Hyper Page mode. EDO was invented and patented by Micron Technology, although Micron licensed production to many other memory manufacturers.

EDO memory consists of specially manufactured chips that allow a timing overlap between successive accesses. The name *extended data out* refers specifically to the fact that, unlike FPM, the data output drivers on the chip are not turned off when the memory controller removes the column address to begin the next cycle. This enables the next cycle to overlap the previous one, saving approximately 10ns per cycle.

The effect of EDO is that cycle times are improved by enabling the memory controller to begin a new column address instruction while it is reading data at the current address. This is almost identical to what was achieved in older systems by interleaving banks of memory, but unlike interleaving, with EDO you didn't need to install two identical banks of memory in the system at a time.

EDO RAM allows for burst mode cycling of 5-2-2-2, compared to the 5-3-3-3 of standard fast page mode memory. To do four memory transfers, then, EDO would require 11 total system cycles, compared to 14 total cycles for FPM. This is a 22% improvement in overall cycling time. The resulting two-cycle (30ns) cycle time during burst transfers equals a 33.3MHz effective clock rate, compared to 45ns/22MHz for FPM. On a system with a 64-bit (8-byte) wide memory bus, this would result in a maximum throughput of 266MBps (33.3MHz × 8 bytes = 266MBps). Due to the processor cache, EDO typically increased overall system benchmark speed by only 5% or less. Even though the overall system improvement was small, the important thing about EDO was that it used the same basic DRAM chip design as FPM, meaning that there was practically no additional cost over FPM. In fact, in its heyday EDO cost less than FPM yet offered higher performance.

EDO RAM generally came in 72-pin SIMM form. Figure 6.4 (later in this chapter) shows the physical characteristics of these SIMMs.

To actually use EDO memory, your motherboard chipset had to support it. Most motherboard chipsets introduced on the market from 1995 (Intel 430FX) through 1997 (Intel 430TX) offered support for EDO, making EDO the most popular form of memory in PCs from 1995 through 1998. Because EDO memory chips cost the same to manufacture as standard chips, combined with Intel's support of EDO in motherboard chipsets, the PC market jumped on the EDO bandwagon full force.

◀◀ See the Chapter 4 sections, "Fifth-Generation (P5 Pentium Class) Chipsets," **p. 190** and "Sixth-Generation (P6 Pentium Pro/II/III Class) Chipsets," **p. 192**.

EDO RAM was used in systems with CPU bus speeds of up to 66MHz, which fit perfectly with the PC market up through 1998. However, starting in 1998, with the advent of 100MHz and faster system bus speeds, the market for EDO rapidly declined, and faster SDRAM architecture became the standard.

One variation of EDO that never caught on was called *burst EDO* (BEDO). BEDO added burst capabilities for even speedier data transfers than standard EDO. Unfortunately, the technology was owned by Micron and not a free industry standard, so only one chipset (Intel 440FX Natoma) ever supported it. BEDO was quickly overshadowed by industry-standard SDRAM, which came into favor among PC system chipset and system designers over proprietary designs. As such, BEDO never really saw the light of production, and to my knowledge no systems ever used it.

SDRAM

SDRAM is short for synchronous DRAM, a JEDEC standard for a type of DRAM that runs in synchronization with the memory bus. SDRAM delivers information in very high-speed bursts using a high-speed clocked interface. SDRAM removes most of the latency involved in asynchronous DRAM because the signals are already in synchronization with the motherboard clock.

As with any newly introduced type of memory on the market, motherboard chipset support is required before it can be usable in systems. Starting in 1996 with the 430VX and 430TX, most of Intel's chipsets began to support industry-standard SDRAM, and in 1998 the introduction of the 440BX chipset caused SDRAM to eclipse EDO as the most popular type on the market.

SDRAM performance is dramatically improved over that of FPM or EDO RAM. However, because SDRAM is still a type of DRAM, the initial latency is the same, but burst mode cycle times are much faster than with FPM or EDO. SDRAM timing for a burst access would be 5-1-1-1, meaning that four memory reads would complete in only eight system bus cycles, compared to 11 cycles for EDO and 14 cycles for FPM. This makes SDRAM almost 20% faster than EDO.

Besides being capable of working in fewer cycles, SDRAM is capable of supporting up to 133MHz (7.5ns) system bus cycling. Most PC systems sold from 1998 through 2002 included SDRAM memory.

SDRAM is sold in DIMM form and is normally rated by clock speed (MHz) rather than cycling time (ns), which was confusing during the initial change from FPM and EDO DRAM. Figure 6.5 (later in this chapter) shows the physical characteristics of DIMMs.

To meet the stringent timing demands of its chipsets, Intel created specifications for SDRAM called PC66, PC100, and PC133. For example, you would think 10ns would be considered the proper rating for 100MHz operation, but the PC100 specification promoted by Intel called for faster 8ns memory to ensure all timing parameters could be met with sufficient margin for error.

In May 1999, JEDEC created a specification called PC133. It achieved this 33MHz speed increase by taking the PC100 specification and tightening up the timing and capacitance parameters. The faster PC133 quickly caught on for any systems running a 133MHz processor bus. The original chips used in PC133 modules were rated for exactly 7.5ns or 133MHz; later ones were rated at 7.0ns, which is technically 143MHz. These faster chips were still used on PC133 modules, but they allowed for improvements in column address strobe latency (abbreviated as CAS or CL), which somewhat improves overall memory cycling time.

SDRAM normally came in 168-pin DIMMs, running at several speeds. Table 6.4 shows the standard single data rate SDRAM module speeds and resulting throughputs.

Table 6.4   JEDEC Standard SDRAM Module (168-Pin DIMM) Speeds and Transfer Rates

Module Type	Chip Type	Clock Speed	Cycles per Clock	Bus Speed	Bus Width	Transfer Rate
PC66	15ns 10ns	66MHz	1	66MTps	8 bytes	533MBps
PC100	8ns	100MHz	1	100MTps	8 bytes	800MBps
PC133	7.5ns 7ns	133MHz	1	133MTps	8 bytes	1,066MBps

MHz = Million cycles per second

MTps = Million transfers per second

MBps = Million bytes per second

ns = Nanoseconds (billionths of a second)

◀◀ See "Memory Modules," **p. 346**.

Some module manufacturers sold modules they claimed were "PC150" or "PC166," even though those speeds did not exist as official JEDEC or Intel standards, and no chipsets or processors officially supported those speeds. These modules actually used hand-picked 133MHz-rated chips that could run overclocked at 150MHz or 166MHz speeds. In essence, PC150 or PC166 memory was PC133 memory that was tested to run at overclocked speeds not supported by the original chip manufacturer. This overclockable memory was sold at a premium to enthusiasts who wanted to overclock their motherboard chipsets, thereby increasing the speed of the processor and memory bus.

Caution

In general, PC133 memory is considered to be backward compatible with PC100 memory. However, some chipsets or motherboards had more specific requirements for specific types of 100MHz or 133MHz chips and module designs. If you need to upgrade an older system that requires PC100 memory, you should not purchase PC133 memory unless the memory is specifically identified by the memory vendor as being compatible with the system. You can use the online memory-configuration tools provided by most major memory vendors to ensure that you get the right memory for your system.

Typically, you find SDRAM modules rated CL 2 or CL 3.

DDR SDRAM

DDR SDRAM memory is a JEDEC standard that is an evolutionary upgrade in which data transfers twice as quickly as standard SDRAM. Instead of doubling the actual clock rate, DDR memory achieves the doubling in performance by transferring twice per transfer cycle: once at the leading (falling) edge and once at the trailing (rising) edge of the cycle (see Figure 6.4). This effectively doubles the transfer rate, even though the same overall clock and timing signals are used. To eliminate confusion with DDR, regular SDRAM is often called *single data rate* (SDR).

SDR

1 transfer per clock cycle

Clock Freq = 100MHz
Data Freq = 100MHz

DDR

2 transfers per clock cycle

Clock Freq = 100MHz
Data Freq = 200MHz

FIGURE 6.4   SDR versus DDR cycling.

DDR SDRAM first came to market in the year 2000 and was initially used on high-end graphics cards because there were no motherboard chipsets to support it at the time. DDR finally became popular in 2002 with the advent of mainstream supporting motherboards and chipsets. From 2002 through 2005, DDR was the most popular type of memory in mainstream PCs. DDR SDRAM uses a DIMM module design with 184 pins. Figure 6.6 (later in this chapter) shows the 184-pin DDR DIMM.

DDR DIMMs come in a variety of speed or throughput ratings and normally run on 2.5 volts. Table 6.5 compares the types of industry-standard DDR SDRAM modules. As you can see, the raw chips are designated by their speed in megatransfers per second, whereas the modules are designated by their approximate throughput in megabytes per second.

Table 6.5   JEDEC Standard DDR Module (184-Pin DIMM) Speeds and Transfer Rates

Module Type	Chip Type	Base Clock Speed	Cycle Time	Cycles per Clock	Bus Speed	Bus Width	Module Transfer Rate	Dual-Channel Transfer Rate
PC1600	DDR200	100MHz	10.0ns	2	200MTps	8 bytes	1,600MBps	3,200MBps
PC2100	DDR266	133MHz	7.5ns	2	266MTps	8 bytes	2,133MBps	4,266MBps
PC2700	DDR333	166MHz	6.0ns	2	333MTps	8 bytes	2,667MBps	5,333MBps
PC3200	DDR400	200MHz	5.0ns	2	400MTps	8 bytes	3,200MBps	6,400MBps

DDR = Double data rate
MHz = Million cycles per second
MTps = Million transfers per second
MBps = Million bytes per second
ns = Nanoseconds (billionths of a second)

The major memory chip and module manufacturers normally produce parts that conform to the official JEDEC standard speed ratings. However, to support overclocking, several memory module manufacturers purchase unmarked and untested chips from the memory chip manufacturers and then independently test and sort them by how fast they run. These are then packaged into modules with unofficial designations and performance figures that exceed the standard ratings. Table 6.6 shows the popular unofficial speed ratings I've seen on the market. Note that because the speeds of these modules are beyond the standard default motherboard and chipset speeds, you won't see an advantage to using them unless you are overclocking your system to match.

Table 6.6 Overclocked (Non-JEDEC) DDR Module (184-Pin DIMM) Speeds and Transfer Rates

Module Standard	Chip Type	Clock Speed (MHz)	Cycles per Clock	Bus Speed (MTps)	Bus Width (Bytes)	Transfer Rate (MBps)	Dual-Channel Transfer Rate (MBps)
PC3500	DDR433	216	2	433	8	3,466	6,933
PC3700	DDR466	233	2	466	8	3,733	7,466
PC4000	DDR500	250	2	500	8	4,000	8,000
PC4200	DDR533	266	2	533	8	4,266	8,533
PC4400	DDR550	275	2	550	8	4,400	8,800
PC4800	DDR600	300	2	600	8	4,800	9,600

DDR = Double data rate

MHz = Million cycles per second

MTps = Million transfers per second

MBps = Million bytes per second

ns = Nanoseconds (billionths of a second)

Most chipsets that support DDR also support dual-channel operation—a technique in which two matching DIMMs are installed to function as a single bank, with double the bandwidth of a single module. For example, if a chipset supports standard PC3200 modules, the bandwidth for a single module would be 3,200MBps. However, in dual-channel mode, the total bandwidth would double to 6,400MBps. Dual-channel operation optimizes PC design by ensuring that the CPU bus and memory bus both run at the same speeds (meaning throughput, not MHz) so that data can move synchronously between the buses without delays.

The cycle time in nanoseconds (billionths of a second) matches the base clock speed, but DDR modules transfer twice per cycle, so the bus speed frequency is always equal to double the clock frequency. The throughput or bandwidth is simply the bus frequency times the width, which gives the rate at which data can be read from or written to the module.

Typically, you can find DDR modules rated CL 2, 2.5, or 3.

With DDR, it is generally okay to install a module that is faster than the system requires, but you should not install a slower module than the motherboard requires. For example, you can usually install PC2700 memory even if the system requires only PC2100 or even PC1600, but if the system requires PC2700, you should not install the slower PC2100 or PC1600 modules.

DDR2 SDRAM

DDR2 is a faster version of DDR memory. It achieves higher throughput by using differential pairs of signal wires to allow faster signaling without noise and interference problems. DDR2 is still double data rate just as with DDR, but the modified signaling method enables you to achieve higher clock speeds with more immunity to noise and crosstalk between the signals. The additional signals required for differential pairs add to the pin count—DDR2 DIMMs have 240 pins, which is more than the 184 pins of DDR. The original DDR specification officially topped out at 400MHz (although faster unofficial overclocked modules were produced), whereas DDR2 starts at 400MHz and goes up to an official maximum of 1,066MHz.

JEDEC began working on the DDR2 specification in April 1998 and published the standard in September 2003. DDR2 chip and module production actually began in mid-2003 (mainly samples and prototypes), and the first chipsets, motherboards, and systems supporting DDR2 appeared for Intel processor–based systems in mid-2004. At that time, variations of DDR2 such as G-DDR2 (Graphics DDR2) began appearing in graphics cards as well. Mainstream motherboard chipset support for DDR2 on Intel processor–based systems appeared in 2005. Notable for its lack of DDR2 support through 2005 was AMD, whose Athlon 64 and Opteron processor families included integrated DDR memory controllers. AMD processor–based systems first supported DDR2 in mid-2006, with the release of socket AM2 motherboards and processors to match. (AMD's Socket F, otherwise known as 1207 FX, also supports DDR2 memory.)

Note that AMD was almost two years behind Intel in the transition from DDR to DDR2. This is because AMD included the memory controller in its Athlon 64 and all subsequent processors, rather than incorporating the memory controller in the chipset North Bridge, as with the more traditional Intel designs. Although there are advantages to integrating the memory controller in the CPU, one disadvantage is the inability to quickly adopt new memory architectures because doing so requires that both the processor and processor socket be redesigned. However, with the release of the Core i-Series processors in 2008, Intel also moved the memory controller from the chipset into the processor, thus putting Intel and AMD in the same situation in terms of memory architecture.

In addition to providing greater speeds and bandwidth, DDR2 has other advantages. It uses lower voltage than conventional DDR (1.8V versus 2.5V), so power consumption and heat generation are reduced. Because of the greater number of pins required on DDR2 chips, the chips typically use fine-pitch ball grid array (FBGA) packaging rather than the thin small outline package (TSOP) chip packaging used by most DDR and conventional SDRAM chips. FPGA chips connect to the substrate (meaning the memory module in most cases) via tightly spaced solder balls on the base of the chip.

Table 6.7 shows the various official JEDEC-approved DDR2 module types and bandwidth specifications.

Table 6.7   JEDEC Standard DDR2 Module (240-Pin DIMM) Speeds and Transfer Rates

Module Type	Chip Type	Base Clock Speed	Cycle Time	Cycles per Clock	Bus Speed	Bus Width	Module Transfer Rate	Dual-Channel Transfer Rate
PC2-3200	DDR2-400	200MHz	5.00ns	2	400MTps	8 bytes	3,200MBps	6,400MBps
PC2-4200	DDR2-533	266MHz	3.75ns	2	533MTps	8 bytes	4,266MBps	8,533MBps
PC2-5300	DDR2-667	333MHz	3.00ns	2	667MTps	8 bytes	5,333MBps	10,667MBps
PC2-6400	DDR2-800	400MHz	2.50ns	2	800MTps	8 bytes	6,400MBps	12,800MBps
PC2-8500	DDR2-1066	533MHz	1.88ns	2	1,066MTps	8 bytes	8,533MBps	17,066MBps

DDR = Double data rate

MHz = Million cycles per second

MTps = Million transfers per second

MBps = Million bytes per second

ns = Nanoseconds (billionths of a second)

The fastest official JEDEC-approved standard is DDR2-1066, which is composed of chips that run at an effective speed of 1,066MHz (really megatransfers per second), resulting in modules designated PC2-8500 having a bandwidth of 8,533MBps. However, just as with DDR, many of the module manufacturers produce even faster modules designed for overclocked systems. These are sold as modules with unofficial designations and performance figures that exceed the standard ratings. Table 6.8 shows the popular unofficial speed ratings I've seen on the market. Note that because the speeds of these modules are beyond the standard default motherboard and chipset speeds, you won't see an advantage to using these unless you are overclocking your system to match.

Table 6.8   Overclocked (Non-JEDEC) DDR2 Module (240-Pin DIMM) Speeds and Transfer Rates

Module Standard	Chip Type	Clock Speed (MHz)	Cycles per Clock	Bus Speed (MTps)	Bus Width (Bytes)	Transfer Rate (MBps)	Dual Channel- Transfer Rate (MBps)
PC2-6000	DDR2-750	375	2	750	8	6,000	12,000
PC2-7200	DDR2-900	450	2	900	8	7,200	14,400
PC2-8000	DDR2-1000	500	2	1000	8	8,000	16,000
PC2-8800	DDR2-1100	550	2	1100	8	8,800	17,600
PC2-8888	DDR2-1111	556	2	1111	8	8,888	17,777
PC2-9136	DDR2-1142	571	2	1142	8	9,136	18,272
PC2-9200	DDR2-1150	575	2	1150	8	9,200	18,400
PC2-9600	DDR2-1200	600	2	1200	8	9,600	19,200
PC2-10000	DDR2-1250	625	2	1250	8	10,000	20,000

DDR = Double data rate

MHz = Million cycles per second

MTps = Million transfers per second

MBps = Million bytes per second

ns = Nanoseconds (billionths of a second)

Typically, you can find DDR2 modules rated between CL 3 and 6.

DDR3 SDRAM

DDR3 enables higher levels of performance along with lower power consumption and higher reliability than DDR2. JEDEC began working on the DDR3 specification in June 2002, and the first DDR3 memory modules and supporting chipsets (versions of the Intel 3x series) were released for Intel-based systems in mid-2007. Due to initial high cost and limited support, DDR3 didn't start to become popular until late 2008 when Intel released the Core i7 processor, which included an integrated tri-channel DDR3 memory controller. In early 2009, popularity increased when AMD released Socket AM3 versions of the Phenom II, the first from AMD to support DDR3. In 2009, with full support from both Intel and AMD, DDR3 finally began to achieve price parity with DDR2, causing DDR3 to begin to eclipse DDR2 in sales.

DDR3 modules use advanced signaling techniques, including self-driver calibration and data synchronization, along with an optional onboard thermal sensor. DDR3 memory runs on only 1.5V, which is nearly 20% less than the 1.8V that DDR2 memory uses. The lower voltage combined with higher efficiency reduces overall power consumption by up to 30% compared to DDR2.

The 240-pin DDR3 modules are similar in pin count, size, and shape to the DDR2 modules; however, the DDR3 modules are incompatible with the DDR2 circuits and are designed with different keying to make them physically noninterchangeable.

DDR3 modules are available in speeds of 800MHz (effective) and higher. Just as with DDR and DDR2, the true clock speed is half the effective rate, which is technically expressed in million transfers per second (MTps). Table 6.9 shows the JEDEC-approved DDR3 module types and bandwidth specifications.

Table 6.9   JEDEC Standard DDR3 Module (240-Pin DIMM) Speeds and Transfer Rates

Module Type	Chip Type	Base Clock Speed	Cycle Time	Cycles per Clock	Bus Speed	Bus Width	Module Transfer Rate	Dual-Channel Transfer Rate	Tri-Channel Transfer Rate
PC3-6400	DDR3-800	400MHz	2.50ns	2	800MTps	8 bytes	6,400MBps	12,800MBps	19,200MBps
PC3-8500	DDR3-1066	533MHz	1.88ns	2	1,066MTps	8 bytes	8,533MBps	17,066MBps	25,600MBps
PC3-10600	DDR3-1333	667MHz	1.50ns	2	1,333MTps	8 bytes	10,667MBps	21,333MBps	32,000MBps
PC3-12800	DDR3-1600	800MHz	1.25ns	2	1,600MTps	8 bytes	12,800MBps	25,600MBps	38,400MBps
PC3-14900	DDR3-1866	933MHz	1.07ns	2	1,866MTps	8 bytes	14,933MBps	29,866MBps	44,800MBps
PC3-17000	DDR3-2133	1066MHz	0.94ns	2	2,133MTps	8 bytes	17,066MBps	34,133MBps	51,200MBps

DDR = Double data rate

MHz = Million cycles per second

MTps = Million transfers per second

MBps = Million bytes per second

ns = Nanoseconds (billionths of a second)

The fastest official JEDEC-approved standard is DDR3-2133, which is composed of chips that run at an effective speed of 2,133MHz (really megatransfers per second), resulting in modules designated PC3-17000 and having a bandwidth of 17,066MBps. However, just as with DDR and DDR2, many manufacturers produce nonstandard modules designed for overclocked systems. These are sold as modules with unofficial designations, clock speeds, and performance figures that exceed the standard ratings.

Table 6.10 shows the popular unofficial DDR3 speed ratings I've seen on the market. Note that because the speeds of these modules don't conform to the standard default motherboard and chipset speeds, you won't see an advantage to using them unless you are overclocking your system and your motherboard supports the corresponding overclocked processor and memory settings that these modules require. In addition, because these modules use standard-speed chips that are running overclocked, they almost always require custom voltage settings that are higher than the 1.5V that standard DDR3 memory uses. For system stability, I generally don't recommend using overclocked (higher voltage) memory, instead preferring to use only that which runs on the DDR3 standard 1.5V.

Table 6.10 Overclocked (Non-JEDEC) DDR3 Module (240-Pin DIMM) Speeds and Transfer Rates

Module Standard	Chip Type	Clock Speed (MHz)	Cycles per Clock	Bus Speed (MTps)	Bus Width (Bytes)	Transfer Rate (MBps)	Dual-Channel Transfer Rate (MBps)	Tri-Channel Transfer (MBps)
PC3-11000	DDR3-1375	688	2	1375	8	11,000	22,000	33,000
PC3-13000	DDR3-1625	813	2	1625	8	13,000	26,000	39,000
PC3-14400	DDR3-1800	900	2	1800	8	14,400	28,800	43,200
PC3-14900	DDR3-1866	933	2	1866	8	14,933	29,866	44,800
PC3-15000	DDR3-1866	933	2	1866	8	14,933	29,866	44,800
PC3-16000	DDR3-2000	1000	2	2000	8	16,000	32,000	48,000

DDR = Double data rate

MHz = Million cycles per second

MTps = Million transfers per second

MBps = Million bytes per second

ns = Nanoseconds (billionths of a second)

Typically, you can find DDR3 modules rated CL 5 through 10.

DDR4 SDRAM

DDR4 is the latest JEDEC memory standard. It enables higher levels of performance along with lower power consumption and higher reliability than DDR3. JEDEC began working on the DDR4 specification in 2005, with the final specification published in September 2012. Samsung produced the first prototype DDR4 modules in late 2010 and released the first sample 16GB DDR4 module in July 2012. With support expected to be arriving in processors and chipsets in 2014, DDR4 will eventually succeed DDR3 in becoming the most popular type of memory in new systems.

DDR4 modules use a Pseudo Open Drain (POD) interface (previously used in high-performance graphic DRAM) and run on a lower 1.2V voltage (compared to 1.5V for DDR3). This enables DDR4 modules to consume about 40% less power overall than previous DDR3 modules, thus saving energy while also producing less heat. DDR4 also supports write Cyclic Redundancy Check (CRC) to improve system reliability.

284-pin DDR4 modules are 1mm longer and 1mm taller than 240-pin DDR3/DDR2 modules. This was accomplished by making the individual pins only 0.85mm wide, versus the 1mm wide pins used on previous modules. Because of the different size and signaling used, DDR4 modules are both physically and electrically incompatible with previous memory module and socket designs (see Figure 6.5).

DDR4 modules are available in speeds of 1,600MHz (effective) and higher, with speeds of up to 3,200MHz (effective) expected in the future. Just as with DDR, DDR2, and DDR3 the true clock speed is half the effective rate, which is technically expressed in million transfers per second (MTps). Table 6.11 shows the official JEDEC-approved DDR4 module types and bandwidth specifications.

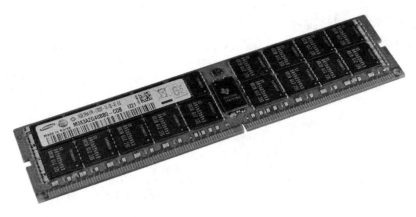

FIGURE 6.5 The industry's first 16GB DDR4 module by Samsung.

Table 6.11 JEDEC Standard DDR4 Module (284-Pin DIMM) Speeds and Transfer Rates

Module Type	Chip Type	Base Clock Speed	Cycle Time	Cycles per Clock	Bus Speed	Bus Width	Module Transfer Rate	Dual-Channel Transfer Rate
PC4-12800	DDR4-1600	800MHz	1.25ns	2	1,600MTps	8 bytes	12,800MBps	25,600MBps
PC4-14900	DDR4-1866	933MHz	1.07ns	2	1,866MTps	8 bytes	14,933MBps	29,866MBps
PC4-17000	DDR4-2133	1066MHz	0.94ns	2	2,133MTps	8 bytes	17,066MBps	34,133MBps
PC4-19200	DDR4-2400	1,200MHz	0.83ns	2	2,400MTps	8 bytes	19,200MBps	38,400MBps
PC4-21300	DDR4-2666	1,333MHz	0.75ns	2	2,666MTps	8 bytes	21,333MBps	42,666MBps
PC4-25600	DDR4-3200	1,600MHz	0.63ns	2	3,200MTps	8 bytes	25,600MBps	51,200MBps

DDR = Double data rate
MHz = Million cycles per second
MTps = Million transfers per second
MBps = Million bytes per second
ns = Nanoseconds (billionths of a second)

The topology of DDR4 is technically not a bus as was used in the DDR3 and earlier memory standards. DDR4 uses a point-to-point connection instead, where each channel in the memory controller is connected to a single module.

RDRAM

Rambus DRAM (RDRAM) was a proprietary (non-JEDEC) memory technology found mainly in certain Intel-based Pentium III and 4 systems from 2000 through 2002. Very few of these systems are still in use today.

For more information about RDRAM and RIMM modules, see Chapter 6, "Memory," in *Upgrading and Repairing PCs*, 19th Edition.

Memory Modules

Originally, PCs had memory installed via individual chips. They are often referred to as *dual inline package* (DIP) chips because of their physical designs. The original IBM XT and AT systems had 36 sockets on the motherboard for these individual chips—and more sockets could often be found on memory cards plugged into the bus slots. I remember spending hours populating boards with these chips, which was a tedious job.

Besides being a time-consuming and labor-intensive way to deal with memory, DIP chips had one notorious problem—they crept out of their sockets over time as the system went through thermal cycles. Every day, when you powered the system on and off, the system heated and cooled, and the chips gradually walked their way out of the sockets—a phenomenon called *chip creep*. Eventually, good contact was lost and memory errors resulted. Fortunately, reseating all the chips back in their sockets usually rectified the problem, but that method was labor intensive if you had many systems to support.

The alternative to this at the time was to have the memory soldered into either the motherboard or an expansion card. This prevented the chips from creeping and made the connections more permanent, but it caused another problem. If a chip did go bad, you had to attempt desoldering the old one and resoldering a new one or resort to scrapping the motherboard or memory card on which the chip was installed. This was expensive and made memory troubleshooting difficult.

A chip was needed that was both soldered and removable, which was made possible by using memory modules instead of individual chips. Early modules had one row of electrical contacts and were called SIMMs (single inline memory modules), whereas later modules had two rows and were called DIMMs (dual inline memory modules) or RIMMs (Rambus inline memory modules). These small boards plug into special connectors on a motherboard or memory card. The individual memory chips are soldered to the module, so removing and replacing them is impossible. Instead, you must replace the entire module if any part of it fails. The module is treated as though it were one large memory chip.

Several types of SIMMs, DIMMs, and RIMMs have been commonly used in desktop systems. The various types are often described by their pin count, memory row width, or memory type.

SIMMs, for example, are available in two main physical types—30-pin (8 bits plus an option for 1 additional parity bit) and 72-pin (32 bits plus an option for 4 additional parity bits)—with various capacities and other specifications. The 30-pin SIMMs are physically smaller than the 72-pin versions, and either version can have chips on one or both sides. SIMMs were widely used from the late 1980s to the late 1990s but have become obsolete.

DIMMs are available in four main types. SDR (single data rate) DIMMs have 168 pins, one notch on either side, and two notches along the contact area. DDR DIMMs, on the other hand, have 184 pins, two notches on each side, and only one offset notch along the contact area. DDR2 and DDR3 DIMMs have 240 pins, two notches on each side, and one near the center of the contact area. All DIMMs are either 64 bits (non-ECC/parity) or 72 bits (data plus parity or error-correcting code [ECC]) wide. The main physical difference between SIMMs and DIMMs is that DIMMs have different signal pins on each side of the module, resulting in two rows of electrical contacts. That is why they are called dual inline memory modules, and why with only 1 inch of additional length, they have many more pins than a SIMM.

Note

There is confusion among users and even in the industry regarding the terms *single-sided* and *double-sided* with respect to memory modules. In truth, the single- or double-sided designation actually has nothing to do with whether chips are physically located on one or both sides of the module, and it has nothing to do with whether the module is a SIMM or DIMM (meaning whether the connection pins are single- or double-inline). Instead, the terms single-sided and double-sided indicate whether the module has one or two internal banks (called *ranks*) of memory chips installed.

A dual-rank DIMM module has two complete 64-bit wide banks of chips logically stacked so that the module is twice as deep (has twice as many 64-bit rows). In most (but not all) cases, this requires chips to be on both sides of the module; therefore, the term *double-sided* often indicates that a module has two ranks, even though the term is technically incorrect.

Single-rank modules (incorrectly referred to as single-sided) can also have chips physically mounted on both sides of the module, and dual-rank modules can have chips physically mounted on only one side. I recommend using the terms *single rank* or *dual rank* instead, because they are much more accurate and easily understood.

Figures 6.6 through 6.12 show a typical 30-pin (8-bit) SIMM, 72-pin (32-bit) SIMM, 168-pin SDRAM DIMM, 184-pin DDR SDRAM (64-bit) DIMM, 240-pin DDR2 DIMM, 240-pin DDR3 DIMM, and 184-pin RIMM, respectively. The pins are numbered from left to right and are connected to both sides of the module on the SIMMs. The pins on the DIMM are different on each side, but on a SIMM, each side is the same as the other and the connections carry through. Note that all dimensions are in both inches and millimeters (in parentheses), and modules are generally available in ECC versions with 1 extra ECC (or parity) bit for every 8 data bits (multiples of 9 in data width) or versions that do not include ECC support (multiples of 8 in data width).

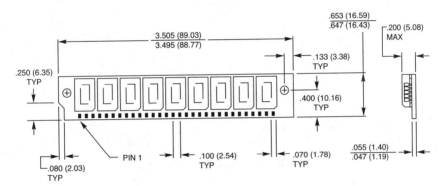

FIGURE 6.6   A typical 30-pin SIMM.

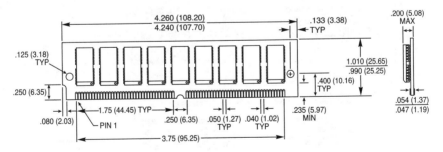

FIGURE 6.7   A typical 72-pin SIMM.

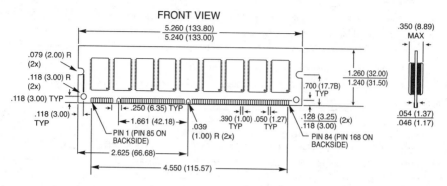

FIGURE 6.8 A typical 168-pin SDRAM DIMM.

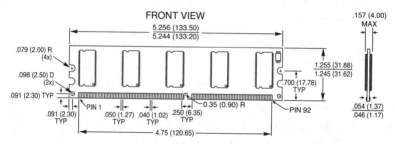

FIGURE 6.9 A typical 184-pin DDR DIMM.

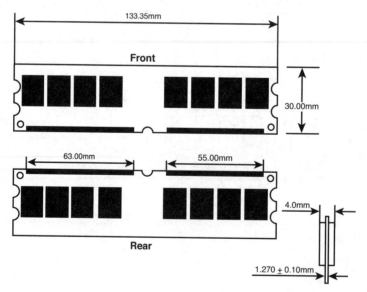

FIGURE 6.10 A typical 240-pin DDR2 DIMM.

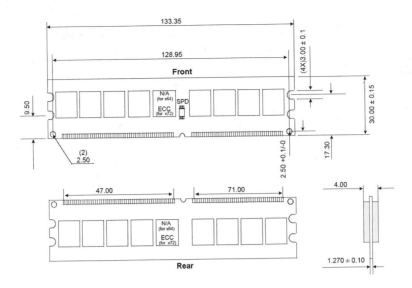

FIGURE 6.11 A typical 240-pin DDR3 DIMM.

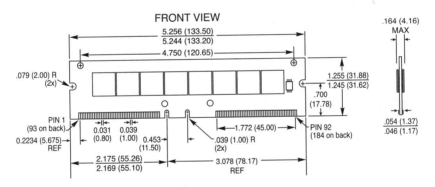

FIGURE 6.12 A typical 184-pin RIMM (RIMM modules use RDRAM).

All these memory modules are fairly compact considering the amount of memory they hold and are available in several capacities and speeds. Table 6.12 lists the various capacities available for SIMMs, DIMMs, and RIMMs.

Table 6.12   SIMM, DIMM, and RIMM Capacities

Capacity	Standard Depth×Width	Parity/ECC Depth×Width
30-Pin SIMM		
256KB	256K× 8	256K×9
1MB	1M×8	1M×9
4MB	4M×8	4M×9
16MB	16M×8	16M×9

Table 6.12 Continued

Capacity	Standard Depth×Width	Parity/ECC Depth×Width
72-Pin SIMM		
1MB	256K×32	256K×36
2MB	512K×32	512K×36
4MB	1M×32	1M×36
8MB	2M×32	2M×36
16MB	4M×32	4M×36
32MB	8M×32	8M×36
64MB	16M×32	16M×36
128MB	32M×32	32M×36
168/184-Pin DIMM/DDR DIMM		
8MB	1M×64	1M×72
16MB	2M×64	2M×72
32MB	4M×64	4M×72
64MB	8M×64	8M×72
128MB	16M×64	16M×72
256MB	32M×64	32M×72
512MB	64M×64	64M×72
1,024MB	128M×64	128M×72
2,048MB	256M×64	256M×72
240-Pin DDR2/DDR3 DIMM		
256MB	32M×64	32M×72
512MB	64M×64	64M×72
1,024MB	128M×64	128M×72
2,048MB	256M×64	256M×72
4,096MB	512M×64	512M×72
184-Pin RIMM		
64MB	32M×16	32M×18
128MB	64M×16	64M×18
256MB	128M×16	128M×18
512MB	256M×16	256M×18
1,024MB	512M×16	512M×18

Memory modules of each type and capacity are available in various speed ratings. Consult your motherboard documentation for the correct memory speed and type for your system. If a system requires a specific speed memory module, you can almost always substitute faster speeds if the one specified is not available. Generally, no problems occur in mixing module speeds, as long as you use modules equal to or faster than what the system requires. Because there's little price difference between the various speed versions, I often buy faster modules than are necessary for a particular application, especially if they are the same price as slower modules. This might make them more usable in a future system that could require the faster speed.

Because SDRAM and newer modules have an onboard SPD ROM that reports their speed and timing parameters to the system, most systems run the memory controller and memory bus at the speed matching the slowest module installed.

Note

A bank is the smallest amount of memory needed to form a single row of memory addressable by the processor. It is the minimum amount of physical memory that the processor reads or writes at one time and usually corresponds to the data bus width of the processor. If a processor has a 64-bit data bus, a bank of memory also is 64 bits wide. If the memory runs dual- or tri-channel, a virtual bank is formed that is two or three times the absolute data bus width of the processor.

You can't always replace a module with a higher-capacity unit and expect it to work. Systems might have specific design limitations for the maximum capacity of module they can take. A larger-capacity module works only if the motherboard is designed to accept it in the first place. Consult your system documentation to determine the correct capacity and speed to use.

Registered Modules

SDRAM through DDR3 modules are available in unbuffered and registered versions. Most PC motherboards are designed to use unbuffered modules, which allow the memory controller signals to pass directly to the memory chips on the module with no interference. This is not only the cheapest design, but also the fastest and most efficient. The only drawback is that the motherboard designer must place limits on how many modules (meaning module sockets) can be installed on the board, and it could limit how many chips can be on a module. So-called double-sided modules that really have multiple banks of chips onboard might be restricted on some systems in certain combinations.

Systems designed to accept extremely large amounts of RAM (such as servers) often require registered modules. A registered module uses an architecture that has register chips on the module that act as an interface between the actual RAM chips and the chipset. The registers temporarily hold data passing to and from the memory chips and enable many more RAM chips to be driven or otherwise placed on the module than the chipset could normally support. This allows for motherboard designs that can support many modules and enables each module to have a larger number of chips. In general, registered modules are required by server or workstation motherboards designed to support more than four sockets. One anomaly is the initial version of the AMD Athlon 64 FX processor, which also uses registered memory because its Socket 940 design was based on the AMD Opteron workstation and server processor. Subsequent Socket 939, AM2, and Socket F versions of the Athlon FX no longer require registered memory.

To provide the space needed for the buffer chips, a registered DIMM is often taller than a standard DIMM. Figure 6.13 compares a typical registered DIMM to a typical unbuffered DIMM.

Tip

If you are installing registered DIMMs in a slimline case, clearance between the top of the DIMM and the case might be a problem. Some vendors sell low-profile registered DIMMs that are about the same height as unbuffered DIMMs. Use this type of DIMM if your system does not have enough head room for standard registered DIMMs. Some vendors sell only this type of DIMM for particular systems.

Registered DIMM

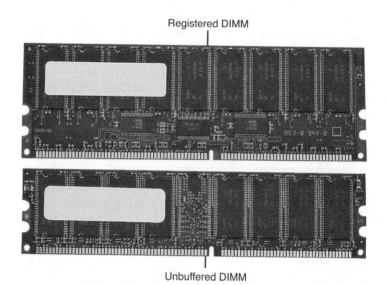

Unbuffered DIMM

FIGURE 6.13   A typical registered DIMM is taller than a typical unbuffered DIMM to provide room for buffer chips.

The important thing to note is that you can use only the type of module your motherboard (or chipset) is designed to support. For most, that is standard unbuffered modules or, in some cases, registered modules.

SDR DIMM Details

SDR DIMMs use a completely different type of presence detect than SIMMs, called *serial presence detect* (SPD). It consists of a small EEPROM or flash memory chip on the DIMM that contains specially formatted data indicating the DIMM's features. This serial data can be read via the serial data pins on the DIMM, and it enables the motherboard to autoconfigure to the exact type of DIMM installed.

DIMMs can come in several varieties, including unbuffered and buffered as well as 3.3V and 5V. Buffered DIMMs have additional buffer chips on them to interface to the motherboard. Unfortunately, these buffer chips slow down the DIMM and are not effective at higher speeds. For this reason, most PC systems (those that do not use registered DIMMs) use unbuffered DIMMs. The voltage is simple—DIMM designs for PCs are almost universally 3.3V. If you install a 5V DIMM in a 3.3V socket, it would be damaged, but keying in the socket and on the DIMM prevents that.

Modern PC systems use only unbuffered 3.3V DIMMs. Apple and other non-PC systems can use the buffered 5V versions. Fortunately, the key notches along the connector edge of a DIMM are spaced differently for buffered/unbuffered and 3.3V/5V DIMMs, as shown in Figure 6.14. This prevents inserting a DIMM of the wrong type into a given socket.

DDR DIMM Details

The 184-pin DDR DIMMs use a single key notch to indicate voltage, as shown in Figure 6.15.

DDR DIMMs also use two notches on each side to enable compatibility with both low- and high-profile latched sockets. Note that the key position is offset with respect to the center of the DIMM to prevent inserting it backward in the socket. The key notch is positioned to the left, centered, or to the right of the area between pins 52 and 53. This indicates the I/O voltage for the DDR DIMM and prevents installing the wrong type into a socket that might damage the DIMM.

DDR2 DIMM Details

The 240-pin DDR2 DIMMs use two notches on each side to enable compatibility with both low- and high-profile latched sockets. The connector key is offset with respect to the center of the DIMM to prevent inserting it backward in the socket. The key notch is positioned in the center of the area between pins 64 and 65 on the front (184/185 on the back), and there is no voltage keying because all DDR2 DIMMs run on 1.8V.

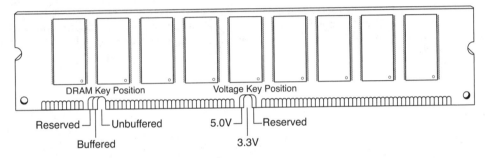

FIGURE 6.14 The 168-pin DRAM DIMM notch key definitions.

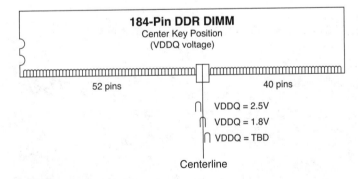

FIGURE 6.15 The 184-pin DDR SDRAM DIMM keying.

DDR3 DIMM Details

The 240-pin DDR3 DIMMs use two notches on each side to enable compatibility with both low- and high-profile latched sockets. The connector key is offset with respect to the center of the DIMM to prevent inserting it backward in the socket. The key notch is positioned in the center of the area between pins 48 and 49 on the front (168/169 on the back), and there is no voltage keying because all DDR3 DIMMs run on 1.5V.

Determining a Memory Module's Size and Features

Most memory modules are labeled with a sticker indicating the module's type, speed rating, and manufacturer. If you are attempting to determine whether existing memory can be used in a new computer, or if you need to replace memory in an existing computer, this information can be essential. Figure 6.16 compares the markings on a 512MB DDR2 module from Crucial Technology and a 2GB DDR2 module from Kingston Technology.

However, if you have memory modules that are not labeled, you can still determine the module type, speed, and capacity if the memory chips on the module are clearly labeled. For example, assume you have a memory module with chips labeled as follows:

MT46V64M8TG-75

By using an Internet search engine such as Google and entering the number from one of the memory chips, you can usually find the data sheet for the memory chips. Consider the following example: Say you have a registered memory module and want to look up the part number for the memory chips (usually eight or more chips) rather than the buffer chips on the module (usually from one to three, depending on the module design). In this example, the part number turns out to be a Micron memory chip that decodes like this:

MT = Micron Technologies (the memory chip maker)

46 = DDR SDRAM

V = 2.5V DC

64M8 = 8 million rows × 8 (equals 64) × 8 banks (often written as 64 Meg × 8)

TG = 66-pin TSOP chip package

–75 = 7.5ns @ CL2 latency (DDR 266)

FIGURE 6.16 Markings on a 512MB DDR2 module (top) from Crucial Technology compared to markings on a 2GB (bottom) DDR2 memory module from Kingston Technology.

The full datasheet for this example is located at http://download.micron.com/pdf/datasheets/dram/ddr/512MBDDRx4x8x16.pdf.

From this information, you can determine that the module has the following characteristics:

- The module runs at DDR266 speeds using standard 2.5V DC voltage.
- The module has a latency of CL2, so you can use it on any system that requires CL2 or slower latency (such as CL2.5 or CL3).
- Each chip has a capacity of 512Mb ($64 \times 8 = 512$).
- Each chip contains 8 bits. Because it takes 8 bits to make 1 byte, you can calculate the capacity of the module by grouping the memory chips on the module into groups of eight. If each chip contains 512Mb, a group of eight means that the module has a size of 512MB ($512Mb \times 8 = 512MB$). A dual-bank module has two groups of eight chips for a capacity of 1GB ($512Mb \times 8 = 1024MB$, or 1GB).

If the module has nine instead of eight memory chips (or 18 instead of 16), the additional chips are used for parity checking and support ECC error correction on servers with this feature.

To determine the size of the module in megabytes or gigabytes and to determine whether the module supports ECC, count the memory chips on the module and compare them to Table 6.13. Note that the size of each memory chip in megabits is the same as the size in megabytes if the memory chips use an 8-bit design.

Table 6.13   Module Capacity Using 512Mb (64Mbit × 8) Chips

Number of Chips	Number of Bits in Each Bank	Module Size	Supports ECC?	Single or Dual Bank
8	64	512MB	No	Single
9	72	512MB	Yes	Single
16	64	1GB	No	Dual
18	72	1GB	Yes	Dual

The additional chip that each group of eight chips uses provides parity checking, which the ECC function employs on most server motherboards to correct single-bit errors.

A registered module contains 9 or 18 memory chips for ECC plus additional memory buffer chips. These chips are usually smaller in size and located near the center of the module, as shown previously in Figure 6.10.

Note

Some modules use 16-bit wide memory chips. In such cases, only four chips are needed for single-bank memory (five with parity/ECC support), and eight are needed for double-bank memory (10 with parity/ECC support). These memory chips use a design listed as capacity times 16, like this: 256Mb × 16.

You can also see this information if you look up the manufacturer and the memory type in a search engine. For example, a web search for *Micron Unbuffered DIMM Design* locates a table showing various DIMM organization, SDRAM density, and other information for listed modules.

As you can see, with a little detective work, you can determine the size, speed, and type of a memory module—even if the module isn't marked, as long as the markings on the memory chips themselves are legible.

Tip

If you are unable to decipher a chip part number, you can use a program, such as CPU-Z (www.cpuid.com) or HWiNFO (www.hwinfo.com) to identify your memory module, as well as many other facts about your computer, including chipset, processor, empty memory sockets, and much more.

Memory Banks

Memory chips (DIPs, SIMMs, SIPPs, and DIMMs) are organized in banks on motherboards and memory cards. You should know the memory bank layout and position on the motherboard and memory cards.

You need to know the bank layout when adding memory to the system. In addition, memory diagnostics report error locations by byte and bit addresses, and you must use these numbers to locate which bank in your system contains the problem.

The banks usually correspond to the data bus capacity of the system's microprocessor. Table 6.14 shows the widths of individual banks based on the type of PC.

Table 6.14   Memory Bank Widths on Various Systems

Processor	Data Bus	Memory Bank Width	Memory Bank Width (Parity/ECC)	30-Pin SIMMs per Bank	72-Pin SIMMs per Bank	DIMMs per Bank
8088	8-bit	8 bits	9 bits	1	—	—
8086	16-bit	16 bits	18 bits	2	—	—
286	16-bit	16 bits	18 bits	2	—	—
386SX, SL, SLC	16-bit	16 bits	18 bits	2	—	—
486SLC, SLC2	16-bit	16 bits	18 bits	2	—	—
386DX	32-bit	32 bits	36 bits	4	1	—
486SX, DX, DX2, DX4, 5x86	32-bit	32 bits	36 bits	4	1	—
x86 and x86-64 running single-channel mode	64-bit	64 bits	72 bits	—	—	1
x86 and x86-64 running dual-channel mode	64-bit	128 bits	144 bits	—	—	2
x86 and x86-64 running tri-channel mode	64-bit	192 bits	216 bits	—	—	3

DIMMs are ideal for Pentium (and higher) systems because the 64-bit width of the DIMM exactly matches the 64-bit width of the Pentium processor data bus. Therefore, each DIMM represents an individual bank, and these can be added or removed one at a time. Many recent systems have been designed to use matched pairs or triples of memory modules for faster performance. So-called "dual-channel" and "tri-channel" designs treat two or three matched modules as a single bank of memory.

The physical orientation and numbering of the SIMMs or DIMMs used on a motherboard are arbitrary and determined by the board's designers, so documentation covering your system or card comes in handy. You can determine the layout of a motherboard or an adapter card through testing, but that takes time and might be difficult, particularly after you have a problem with a system.

Caution

If your system supports dual- or tri-channel memory, be sure you use the correct memory sockets to enable multichannel operation. Check the documentation to ensure that you use the correct sockets. Most multichannel systems still run in single-channel mode if the memory is not installed in a way that permits full multichannel operation, but performance is lower than if the memory were installed properly. Some systems provide dual-channel support if an odd number of modules is installed, as long as the total capacity of two modules installed in one channel equals the size of the single module in the other channel and all modules are the same speed and latency. Again, check your documentation for details.

Memory Module Speed

When you replace a failed memory module or install a new module as an upgrade, you typically must install a module of the same type and speed as the others in the system. You can substitute a module with a different (faster) speed, but only if the replacement module's speed is equal to or faster than that of the other modules in the system.

Some people have had problems when "mixing" modules of different speeds. With the variety of motherboards, chipsets, and memory types, few ironclad rules exist. When in doubt as to which speed module to install in your system, consult the motherboard documentation for more information.

Substituting faster memory of the same type doesn't result in improved performance if the system still operates the memory at the same speed. Systems that use DIMMs or RIMMs can read the speed and timing features of the module from a special SPD ROM installed on the module and then set chipset (memory controller) timing accordingly. In these systems, you might see an increase in performance by installing faster modules, to the limit of what the chipset supports.

To place more emphasis on timing and reliability, there are Intel and JEDEC standards governing memory types that require certain levels of performance. These standards certify that memory modules perform within Intel's timing and performance guidelines.

The same common symptoms result when the system memory has failed or is simply not fast enough for the system's timing. The usual symptoms are frequent parity check errors or a system that does not operate. The POST might report errors, too. If you're unsure of which chips to buy for your system, contact the system manufacturer or a reputable chip supplier.

◄◄ See "Parity Checking," **p. 359**.

Parity and ECC

Part of the nature of memory is that it inevitably fails. These failures are usually classified as two basic types: hard fails and soft errors.

The best understood are hard fails, in which the chip is working and then, because of some flaw, physical damage, or other event, becomes damaged and experiences a permanent failure. Fixing this type of failure normally requires replacing some part of the memory hardware, such as the chip, SIMM, or DIMM. Hard error rates are known as HERs.

The other, more insidious type of failure is the soft error, which is a nonpermanent failure that might never recur or could occur only at infrequent intervals. Soft error rates are known as SERs.

In the late 1970s, Intel made a discovery about soft errors that shook the memory industry. It found that alpha particles were causing an unacceptably high rate of soft errors or single event upsets (SEUs, as they are sometimes called) in the 16KB DRAMs that were available at the time. Because alpha particles are low-energy particles that can be stopped by something as thin and light as a sheet of paper, it became clear that for alpha particles to cause a DRAM soft error, they would have to be coming from within the semiconductor material. Testing showed trace elements of thorium and uranium in the plastic and ceramic chip packaging materials used at the time. This discovery forced all the memory manufacturers to evaluate their manufacturing processes to produce materials free from contamination.

Today, memory manufacturers have all but totally eliminated the alpha-particle source of soft errors, and more recent discoveries prove that alpha particles are now only a small fraction of the cause of DRAM soft errors.

As it turns out, the biggest cause of soft errors today is cosmic rays. IBM researchers began investigating the potential of terrestrial cosmic rays in causing soft errors similar to alpha particles. The difference is that cosmic rays are high-energy particles and can't be stopped by sheets of paper or other more powerful types of shielding. The leader in this line of investigation was Dr. J.F. Ziegler of the IBM Watson Research Center in Yorktown Heights, New York. He has produced landmark research into understanding cosmic rays and their influence on soft errors in memory. One interesting set of experiments found that cosmic ray–induced soft errors were eliminated when the DRAMs were moved to an underground vault shielded by more than 50 feet of rock.

Cosmic ray–induced errors are even more of a problem in SRAMs than DRAMS because the amount of charge required to flip a bit in an SRAM cell is less than is required to flip a DRAM cell capacitor. Cosmic rays are also more of a problem for higher-density memory. As chip density increases, it becomes easier for a stray particle to flip a bit. It has been predicted by some that the soft error rate of a 64MB DRAM is double that of a 16MB chip, and a 256MB DRAM has a rate four times higher. As memory sizes continue to increase, it's likely that soft error rates will also increase.

Unfortunately, the PC industry has largely failed to recognize this cause of memory errors. Electrostatic discharge, power surges, and unstable software can much more easily explain away the random and intermittent nature of a soft error, especially right after a new release of an operating system (OS) or major application.

Although cosmic rays and other radiation events are perhaps the biggest cause of soft errors, soft errors can also be caused by the following:

- **Power glitches or noise on the line**—This can be caused by a defective power supply in the system or by defective power at the outlet.

- **Incorrect type or speed rating**—The memory must be the correct type for the chipset and match the system access speed.

- **RF (radio frequency) interference**—Caused by radio transmitters in close proximity to the system, which can generate electrical signals in system wiring and circuits. Keep in mind that the increased use of wireless networks, keyboards, and mouse devices can lead to a greater risk of RF interference.

- **Static discharges**—These discharges cause momentary power spikes, which alter data.

- **Timing glitches**—Data doesn't arrive at the proper place at the proper time, causing errors. Often caused by improper settings in the BIOS Setup, by memory that is rated slower than the system requires, or by overclocked processors and other system components.

- **Heat buildup**—High-speed memory modules run hotter than older modules. RDRAM RIMM modules were the first memory to include integrated heat spreaders, and many high-performance DDR, DDR2, and DDR3 memory modules now include heat spreaders to help fight heat buildup.

Most of these problems don't cause chips to permanently fail (although bad power or static can damage chips permanently), but they can cause momentary problems with data.

How can you deal with these errors? The best way to deal with this problem is to increase the system's fault tolerance. This means implementing ways of detecting and possibly correcting errors in PC systems. Three basic levels and techniques are used for fault tolerance in modern PCs:

Nonparity

Parity

ECC

Nonparity systems have no fault tolerance. The only reason they are used is because they have the lowest inherent cost. No additional memory is necessary, as is the case with parity or ECC techniques. Because a parity-type data byte has 9 bits versus 8 for nonparity, memory cost is approximately 12.5% higher. Also, the nonparity memory controller is simplified because it does not need the logic gates to calculate parity or ECC check bits. Portable systems that place a premium on minimizing power might benefit from the reduction in memory power resulting from fewer DRAM chips. Finally, the memory system data bus is narrower, which reduces the number of data buffers. The statistical probability of memory failures in a modern office desktop computer is now estimated at about one error every few months. Errors will be more or less frequent depending on how much memory you have.

This error rate might be tolerable for low-end systems that are not used for mission-critical applications. In this case, the extreme market sensitivity to price probably can't justify the extra cost of parity or ECC memory, and such errors then must be tolerated.

Parity Checking

One standard IBM set for the industry is that the memory chips in a bank of nine each handle 1 bit of data: 8 bits per character plus 1 extra bit called the *parity bit*. The parity bit enables memory-control circuitry to keep tabs on the other 8 bits—a built-in cross-check for the integrity of each byte in the system.

Originally, all PC systems used parity-checked memory to ensure accuracy. Starting in 1994, most vendors began shipping systems without parity checking or any other means of detecting or correcting errors on the fly. These systems used cheaper nonparity memory modules, which saved about 10%–15% on memory costs for a system.

Parity memory results in increased initial system cost, primarily because of the additional memory bits involved. Parity can't correct system errors, but because parity can detect errors, it can make the user aware of memory errors when they happen.

Since then, Intel, AMD, and other manufacturers have put support for ECC memory primarily in server chipsets and processors. Chipsets and processors for standard desktop or laptop systems typically lack support for either parity or ECC.

How Parity Checking Works

IBM originally established the odd parity standard for error checking. The following explanation might help you understand what is meant by odd parity. As the 8 individual bits in a byte are stored in memory, a parity generator/checker, which is either part of the CPU or located in a special chip on the motherboard, evaluates the data bits by adding up the number of 1s in the byte. If an even number of 1s is found, the parity generator/checker creates a 1 and stores it as the ninth bit (parity bit) in the parity memory chip. That makes the sum for all 9 bits (including the parity bit) an odd number. If the original sum of the 8 data bits is an odd number, the parity bit created would be a 0, keeping the sum for all 9 bits an odd number. The basic rule is that the value of the parity bit is always chosen so that the sum of all 9 bits (8 data bits plus 1 parity bit) is stored as an odd number. If the system used even parity, the example would be the same except the parity bit would be created to ensure an even sum. It doesn't matter whether even or odd parity is used; the system uses one or the other, and it is completely transparent to the memory chips involved. Remember that the 8 data bits in a byte are numbered 0 1 2 3 4 5 6 7. The following examples might make it easier to understand:

```
Data bit number:      0  1  2  3  4  5  6  7      Parity bit

Data bit value:       1  0  1  1  0  0  1  1        0
```

In this example, because the total number of data bits with a value of 1 is an odd number (5), the parity bit must have a value of 0 to ensure an odd sum for all 9 bits.

Here is another example:

```
Data bit number:      0  1  2  3  4  5  6  7      Parity bit

Data bit value:       1  1  1  1  0  0  1  1        1
```

In this example, because the total number of data bits with a value of 1 is an even number (6), the parity bit must have a value of 1 to create an odd sum for all 9 bits.

When the system reads memory back from storage, it checks the parity information. If a (9-bit) byte has an even number of bits, that byte must have an error. The system can't tell which bit has changed or whether only a single bit has changed. If 3 bits changed, for example, the byte still flags a parity-check error; if 2 bits changed, however, the bad byte could pass unnoticed. Because multiple bit errors (in a single byte) are rare, this scheme gives you a reasonable and inexpensive ongoing indication that memory is good or bad.

ECC

ECC goes a big step beyond simple parity-error detection. Instead of just detecting an error, ECC allows a single bit error to be corrected, which means the system can continue without interruption and without corrupting data. ECC, as implemented in most PCs, can only detect, not correct, double-bit errors. Because studies have indicated that approximately 98% of memory errors are the single-bit variety, the most commonly used type of ECC is one in which the attendant memory controller detects and corrects single-bit errors in an accessed data word. (Double-bit errors can be detected but not corrected.) This type of ECC is known as *single-bit error-correction double-bit error detection* (SEC-DED) and requires an additional 7 check bits over 32 bits in a 4-byte system and an additional 8 check bits over 64 bits in an 8-byte system. If the system uses SIMMs, two 36-bit (parity) SIMMs are added for each bank (for a total of 72 bits), and ECC is done at the bank level. If the system uses DIMMs, a single parity/ECC 72-bit DIMM is used as a bank and provides the additional bits. RIMMs are installed in singles or pairs, depending on the chipset and motherboard. They must be 18-bit versions if parity/ECC is desired.

ECC entails the memory controller calculating the check bits on a memory-write operation, performing a compare between the read and calculated check bits on a read operation, and, if necessary, correcting bad bits. The additional ECC logic in the memory controller is not very significant in this age of inexpensive, high-performance VLSI logic, but ECC actually affects memory performance on writes. This is because the operation must be timed to wait for the calculation of check bits and, when the system waits for corrected data, reads. On a partial-word write, the entire word must first be read, the affected byte(s) rewritten, and then new check bits calculated. This turns partial-word write operations into slower read-modify writes. Fortunately, this performance hit is small, on the order of a few percent at maximum, so the trade-off for increased reliability is a good one.

Most memory errors are of a single-bit nature, which ECC can correct. Incorporating this fault-tolerant technique provides high system reliability and attendant availability. An ECC-based system is a good choice for servers, workstations, or mission-critical applications in which the cost of a potential memory error outweighs the additional memory and system cost to correct it, along with ensuring that it does not detract from system reliability.

Unfortunately, most standard desktop and laptop PC processors, motherboards (chipsets), and memory modules don't support ECC. If you want a system that supports ECC, make sure all the components involved support ECC. This usually means purchasing more expensive processors, motherboards, and RAM designed for server or high-end workstation applications.

RAM Upgrades

Adding memory to a system is one of the most useful upgrades you can perform and also one of the least expensive—especially when you consider the increased performance of Windows, Linux, and their applications when you give them access to more memory. In some cases, doubling the memory can practically double the speed of a computer. But it doesn't always pay to go overboard because adding memory that you don't really need will cost money and power, and you will gain little or nothing in speed. The best philosophy to take when adding RAM to a computer is that "more is better, up to a point."

The maximum physical memory capacity of a system is dictated by several factors. The first is the amount addressable by the processor itself, which is based on the number of physical address lines in the chip. The original PC processors (8086/8088) had 20 address lines, which resulted in those chips being able to recognize up to 1MB (2^{20} bytes) of RAM. The 286/386SX increased memory addressing capability to 24 lines, making them capable of addressing 16MB (2^{24} bytes). Modern x86 processors have from 32 to 36 address lines, resulting in from 4GB to 64GB of addressable RAM. Modern x86-64 (64-bit) processors have 40 address lines, resulting in a maximum of 1TB (1 terabyte) of supported physical RAM.

◄◄   See the Chapter 3 section, "Processor Specifications," **p. 35**.

The operating mode of the processor may place further limits on memory addressability. For example, when the processor is operating in backward-compatible real mode, only 1MB of memory is supported.

◄◄   See the Chapter 3 section, "Processor Modes," **p. 44**.

Note that even though modern 64-bit processors can technically address up to 1TB, modern motherboards or chipsets generally limit the maximum amount of RAM to 8GB, 16GB, or 24GB. The type of software also has an effect. The 32-bit versions of Windows (XP and newer) limit memory support to 4GB (with only about 3.5GB usable by programs), whereas the 64-bit versions limit support to 8GB, 16GB, or 192GB, depending on the edition.

◄◄   See the Chapter 4 section, "Chipsets," **p. 181** for the memory limits on motherboard chipsets.

If you run Windows XP, you should specify a *minimum* of 256MB, and preferably 512MB to 1GB or more depending on the applications you intend to run. If you run 32-bit Windows 7 or Vista, the *absolute minimum* should be 512MB according to Microsoft, but I recommend a minimum of 1GB, with 2GB to 3GB preferred. 64-bit versions of Windows 7 and Windows 8 have a 2GB minimum, but perform better with 4GB or more of memory.

Beyond having the minimum to run the OS you choose, the way you use your system, especially the applications you run, can be the major determining factor as to just how much memory is best. For example, if you are a power user with four or more displays simultaneously connected to your system, each with multiple open applications, or you run memory-intensive applications such as photo- and video-editing programs, or if you use a virtual machine manager (VMM) like Virtual PC or VMware to run multiple OSs simultaneously (each of those with open applications), you might want as much memory as you can possibly install. Many older laptops won't accept as much memory as you might want (or need) to install, so if you upgrade an older system that uses an obsolete (and expensive) type of memory, the best tip might be to consider moving up to a newer system that can accept more memory of a mainstream type that is less expensive.

When purchasing a new system, try to get it with all the memory you need right away. Some motherboards are more limited in the number of memory sockets they contain, and some of those will already be filled when the system is delivered. This means you might need to remove some of the existing memory to add more, which makes future upgrades more expensive. The only caveat here is that I often find that I can purchase memory much more inexpensively from third-party vendors than from the system manufacturer. When purchasing a new system, check on how much the manufacturer charges for the amount of memory you want, as opposed to taking the system with the default minimum and immediately adding the desired memory yourself, purchased from a third-party memory vendor.

The following sections discuss adding memory, including selecting memory chips, installing memory chips, and testing the installation.

Upgrade Options and Strategies

Adding memory can be an inexpensive solution; the cost of mainstream memory is extremely low relative to other system components, and adding more memory can give your computer's performance a big boost.

How do you add memory to your PC? You have two options, listed in order of convenience and cost:

- Adding memory in vacant slots on your motherboard
- Replacing your current motherboard's memory with higher-capacity memory

If you decide to upgrade to a more powerful computer system or motherboard, you usually can't salvage the memory from your previous system. Most of the time it is best to plan on equipping a new board with the optimum type of memory that it supports.

Be sure to carefully weigh your future needs for computing speed and a multitasking OS against the amount of money you spend to upgrade current equipment.

How can you tell if you have enough memory or not? The best way is to run your most demanding applications (all that would be open at the same time and with your largest datasets) and then check the memory usage using the Windows Task Manager (taskmgr.exe). With Task Manager running, click on the Performance tab to see the amount of Physical Memory being used vs. the total available. Under Windows 7/8 and Vista the memory usage is shown both as a percentage of the total as well as an amount. Figure 6.17 shows the Task Manager running on a Windows 7 system reporting 18% or 2.85GB of memory being used on a system with 16GB installed. Figure 6.18 shows the Task Manager running on a Windows XP system reporting 1.63GB being used (under the misnomer "PF Usage") on a system with about 3.5GB of RAM available (4GB minus about 0.5GB reserved by the hardware), which is about 47% of the total. If you see the amount of physical memory being used is higher than around 80% of the total then you might consider adding more memory. In both of these examples the amount of memory installed is more than enough to run the applications that were open at the time; in fact, the system with 16GB installed would have been fine with 8GB or less.

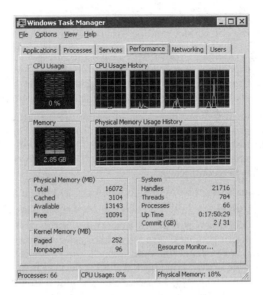

FIGURE 6.17 Windows 7 Task Manager showing 18% or 2.85GB Physical Memory use on a system with 16GB installed.

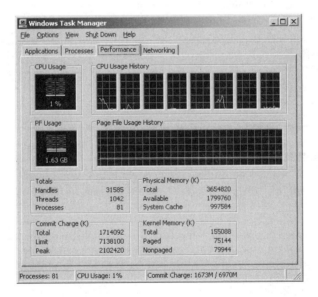

FIGURE 6.18 Windows XP Task Manager showing 47% or 1.63GB Physical Memory use on a system with about 3.5GB available (out of 4GB installed).

Before you add RAM to a system (or replace defective RAM chips), you must determine the memory modules required for your system. Your system documentation has this information.

If you need to replace a defective memory module or add more memory to your system, you have several methods for determining the correct module for your system:

- Inspect the modules installed in your system. Each module has markings that indicate its capacity and speed. RAM capacity and speed were discussed in detail earlier in this chapter. You can write down the markings on the memory module and use them to determine the type of memory you need. Check with a local store or an online memory vendor for help.

- Look up your system using the online memory-configuration utility provided by your preferred memory vendor. Originally, these configuration utilities were primarily for users of name-brand systems. However, most vendors have now added major motherboard brands and models to their databases. Therefore, if you know your system or motherboard brand and model, you can find the memory that is recommended.

- Download and run analysis software that the memory module maker or a third party provides. CPU-Z and similar programs use the SPD chip on each module to determine this information.

- Consult your system documentation. I list this option last for a reason. If you have installed BIOS upgrades, you might be able to use larger and faster memory than your documentation lists as supported by your system. You should check the latest tech notes and documentation available online for your system and check the BIOS version installed in your system to determine which memory-related features it has. A BIOS upgrade might enable your system to use faster memory.

Adding the wrong modules to a system can make it as unreliable as leaving a defective module installed and trying to use the system in that condition.

Note

Before upgrading an older Pentium (P5 class) system beyond 64MB of RAM, be sure your chipset supports caching more than 64MB. Adding RAM beyond the amount supported by your L2 cache controller slows performance rather than increases it. Pentium II and later processors, including the AMD Athlon, Duron, and Sempron families, have the L2 cache controller integrated in the processor (not the chipset), which supports caching up to 4GB and beyond on most newer models.

Purchasing Memory

When purchasing memory, you need to consider certain issues. Some are related to the manufacturing and distribution of memory, whereas others depend on the type of memory you are purchasing.

Suppliers

Many companies sell memory, but only a few companies actually make memory. Additionally, only a few companies make memory chips, but many more companies make memory modules. Most of the companies that make the actual RAM chips also make modules containing their own chips. Other companies, however, strictly make modules; these companies purchase memory chips from several chip makers and then produce modules with these chips. Finally, some companies don't make either the chips or the modules. Instead, they purchase modules made by other companies and relabel them.

I refer to memory modules made by the chip manufacturers as first-party modules, whereas those made by module (but not chip) manufacturers I call *second-party modules*. Finally, those that are simply relabeled first- or second-party modules under a different name are called *third-party modules*. I always prefer to purchase first- or second-party modules if I can because they are better documented. In essence, they have a better pedigree, and their quality is generally more assured. Not to mention that purchasing from the first or second party eliminates one or more middlemen in the distribution process as well.

First-party manufacturers (where the same company makes the chips and the modules) include Micron (www.crucial.com), Infineon (formerly Siemens), Samsung, Mitsubishi, Toshiba, NEC, and others. Second-party companies that make the modules (but not the chips) include Kingston, Viking, PNY, Simple Tech, Smart, Mushkin, and OCZ Technologies. At the third-party level, you are not purchasing from a manufacturer but from a reseller or remarketer instead.

Most of the large manufacturers don't sell small quantities of memory to individuals, but some have set up factory outlet stores where individuals can purchase as little as a single module. One of the largest memory manufacturers in the world, Micron, sells direct to the consumer at www.crucial.com. Because you are buying direct, the pricing at these outlets is often competitive with second- and third-party suppliers.

Considerations in Purchasing DIMMs

When you are purchasing DIMMs, here are the main things to consider:

- Do you need SDR, DDR, DDR2, or DDR3 versions?
- Do you need ECC or non-ECC?
- Do you need standard (unbuffered) or registered versions?
- Do you need a specific voltage?
- What speed grade do you need?
- Do you need a specific CAS latency?

Currently, DIMMs come in SDR (SDRAM), DDR, DDR2, and DDR3 versions. They are not interchangeable because they use completely different signaling and have different notches to prevent a mismatch. High-reliability systems such as servers can use ECC versions, although most desktop systems use the less-expensive non-ECC types. Most systems use standard unbuffered DIMMs, but file server or workstation motherboards designed to support large amounts of memory might require registered DIMMs (which also include ECC support). Registered DIMMs contain their own memory registers, enabling the module to hold more memory than a standard DIMM. DIMMs come in a variety of speeds, with the rule that you can always substitute a faster one for a slower one, but not vice versa.

Some memory modules are designed to run on non-standard voltages, which may be useful when overclocking them. Unfortunately this can also cause problems for systems where stock (non-overclocked) memory settings are used. Standard voltages for DDR, DDR2, and DDR3 modules are 2.5V, 1.8V, and 1.5V, respectively. If you buy a DDR3 module rated at a higher voltage (1.6V or higher) it may not perform reliably when run on the standard 1.5V setting. I've seen systems with constant lockup and crashing problems due to improperly configured memory like this. My recommendation is to only purchase memory rated to run on the standard voltage for that type, which is 1.5V in the case of DDR3.

Another speed-related issue is the CAS latency. Sometimes this specification is abbreviated CAS or CL and is expressed in a number of cycles, with lower numbers indicating higher speeds (fewer cycles). The lower CAS latency shaves a cycle off a burst mode read, which marginally improves memory performance. Single data rate DIMMs are available in CL3 or CL2 versions. DDR DIMMs are available in CL2.5 or CL2 versions. DDR2 DIMMs are available in CL 3, 4, or 5. DDR3 DIMMs are available in CL 5, 6, 7, 8, and 9. With all memory types, the lowest CL number is the fastest (and usually the most expensive) memory type. You can mix DIMMs with different CAS latency ratings, but the system usually defaults to cycling at the slower speeds of the lowest common denominator.

Considerations in Purchasing Obsolete Memory

Many people are surprised to find that obsolete memory types cost much more than those that current systems use. This is because of simple supply and demand; what is least popular generally costs the most. This can make adding memory to older systems cost prohibitive.

Most Pentium systems after 1995 used EDO SIMMs that were non-ECC and rated for 60ns access time. If your system is older than that, you might need FPM memory instead of EDO. The FPM and EDO types are interchangeable in many systems, but some older systems do not accept the EDO type. Some Pentium 4 systems use RIMMs, which are available in 184-pin and 232-pin versions. Although they appear to be the same size, they are not interchangeable. If the system supports ECC, you might need (or want) ECC versions. You can mix ECC and non-ECC modules, but in that case the system defaults to non-ECC mode.

Tip

Instead of buying "new" obsolete memory for older systems, check with computer repair shops, Craigslist, websites specializing in surplus memory, or other users who might have a collection of old parts.

High-reliability systems might want or need ECC versions, which have extra ECC bits. As with other memory types, you can mix ECC and non-ECC types, but systems can't use the ECC capability.

Replacing Modules with Higher-Capacity Versions

If all the memory module slots on your motherboard are occupied, your best option is to remove an existing bank of memory and replace it with higher-capacity modules.

However, just because higher-capacity modules are available to plug into your motherboard, don't automatically assume the higher-capacity memory will work. Your system's chipset, BIOS, and OS set limits on the capacity of the memory you can use. Check your system or motherboard documentation to see which size modules work with it before purchasing the new RAM. You should make sure you have the latest BIOS for your motherboard when installing new memory.

If your system supports dual- or triple-channel memory, you must use modules in matched pairs or triples (depending on which type your system supports) and install them in the correct location on the motherboard. Consult your motherboard manual for details.

Installing Memory Modules

When you install or remove memory, you are most likely to encounter the following problems:

- Electrostatic discharge
- Improperly seated modules
- Incorrect memory configuration settings in the BIOS Setup

To prevent electrostatic discharge (ESD) when you install sensitive memory chips or boards, you shouldn't wear synthetic-fiber clothing or leather-soled shoes because these promote the generation of static charges. Remove any static charge you are carrying by touching the system chassis before you begin, or better yet, wear a good commercial grounding strap on your wrist. You can order one from any electronics parts store. A grounding strap consists of a conductive wristband grounded at the other end through a 1-meg ohm resistor by a wire clipped to the system chassis. Be sure the system you are working on is unplugged.

Caution

Be sure to use a properly designed commercial grounding strap; do not make one yourself. Commercial units have a 1-meg ohm resistor that serves as protection if you accidentally touch live power. The resistor ensures that you do not become the path of least resistance to the ground and therefore become electrocuted. An improperly designed strap can cause the power to conduct through you to the ground, possibly killing you.

Follow this procedure to install memory on a typical desktop PC:

1. Shut down the system and unplug it. As an alternative to unplugging it, you can turn off the power supply using the on/off switch on the rear of some power supplies. Wait about 10 seconds for any remaining current to drain from the motherboard.

2. Open the system. See the system or case instructions for details.

3. Connect a static guard wrist strap to your wrist and then to a metal portion of the system chassis, such as the frame. Make sure the metal plate on the inside of the wrist strap is tight against the skin of your wrist.

4. Some motherboards feature an LED that glows as long as the motherboard is receiving power. Wait until the LED dims before removing or installing memory.

5. Move obstructions inside the case, such as cables or wires, out of the way of the memory modules and empty sockets. If you must remove a cable or wire, note its location and orientation so you can replace it later.

6. If you need to remove an existing module, flip down the ejector tab at each end of the module and lift the module straight up out of the socket. Note the keying on the module.

7. Note the specific locations needed if you are inserting modules to operate in dual-channel mode. The sockets for dual-channel memory might use a different-colored plastic to distinguish them from other sockets, but ultimately you should consult the documentation for your motherboard or system to determine the proper orientation.

8. To insert a module into a socket, ensure that the ejector tabs are flipped down on the socket you plan to use. DIMMs are keyed by one or more notches along the bottom connector edges that are offset from the center so they can be inserted in only one direction, as shown in Figure 6.19.

9. Push down on the module until the ejector tabs lock into place in the notch on the side of the module. It's important that you not force the module into the socket. If the module does not slip easily into the slot and then snap into place, it is probably not oriented or aligned correctly. Forcing the module could break it or the socket. Refer to Figure 6.14 for details.

10. Replace any cables or wires you disconnected.

11. Close the system, reconnect the power cable, and turn on the PC.

After installing the memory and putting the system back together, you might have to run the BIOS Setup and resave with the new amount of memory being reported. Most systems automatically detect the new amount of memory and reconfigure the BIOS Setup settings for you. Most systems also don't require setting any jumpers or switches on the motherboard to configure them for your new memory.

After configuring your system to work properly with the additional memory, you might want to run a memory-diagnostics program to ensure that the new memory works properly.

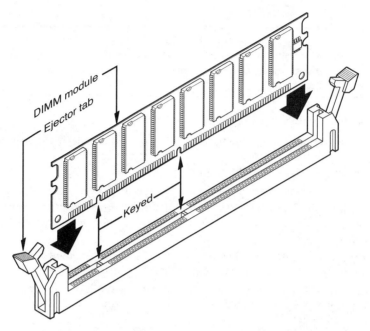

FIGURE 6.19 DIMM key(s) should match the protrusion(s) in the DIMM sockets.

Troubleshooting Memory

Memory problems can be difficult to troubleshoot. For one thing, computer memory is still mysterious to people because it is a kind of "virtual" thing that can be hard to grasp. The other difficulty is that memory problems can be intermittent and often look like problems with other areas of the system, even software. This section shows simple troubleshooting steps you can perform if you suspect you are having a memory problem.

To troubleshoot memory, you first need some memory-diagnostics testing programs. You already have several and might not know it. Every motherboard BIOS has a memory diagnostic in the POST that runs when you first turn on the system. In most cases, you also receive a memory diagnostic on a utility disk that came with your system. Many commercial diagnostics programs are on the market, and almost all of them include memory tests.

When the POST runs, it not only tests memory, but it also counts it. The count is compared to the amount counted the last time BIOS Setup was run; if it is different, an error message is issued. As the POST runs, it writes a pattern of data to all the memory locations in the system and reads that pattern back to verify that the memory works. If any failure is detected, you see or hear a message. Audio messages (beeping) are used for critical or "fatal" errors that occur in areas important for the system's operation. If the system can access enough memory to at least allow video to function, you see error messages instead of hearing beep codes.

See Chapter 20, "PC Diagnostics, Testing, and Maintenance," for detailed listings of the BIOS beep and other error codes, which are specific to the type of BIOS you have.

If your system makes it through the POST with no memory error indications, there might not be a hardware memory problem, or the POST might not be able to detect the problem. Intermittent memory errors are often not detected during the POST, and other subtle hardware defects can be hard for the POST to catch. The POST is designed to run quickly, so the testing is not nearly as thorough as it could be. That is why you often have to boot from standalone diagnostic media (normally an optical disc or a bootable flash drive) and run a true hardware diagnostic to do more extensive memory testing. You can run these types of tests continuously and leave them running for days if necessary to hunt down an elusive intermittent defect.

Fortunately, several excellent memory test programs are available for free download. Here are some I recommend:

- **Microsoft Windows Memory Diagnostic**—included with Vista and later
- **Memtest86**—www.memtest86.com
- **Ultimate Boot CD**—www.ultimatebootcd.com

Not only are these free, but they are available in a bootable format, which means you don't have to install software on the system you are testing. The bootable format is actually required in a way because Windows and other OSs prevent the direct access to memory and other hardware required for testing. These programs use algorithms that write different types of patterns to all the memory in the system, testing every bit to ensure it reads and writes properly. They also turn off the processor cache to ensure direct testing of the modules and not the cache. Some, such as Windows Memory Diagnostic, even indicate the module that is failing should you encounter an error. Note that a version of the Windows Memory Diagnostic is also included with Windows 7/8 and Vista. It can be found as part of the Administrative Tools (mdsched.exe), as well as on the bootable install DVDs under the Repair option.

The Ultimate Boot CD includes Memtest86 and several other memory diagnostic programs. Both the Ultimate Boot CD and the Windows Vista and later install DVDs (containing the Windows Memory Diagnostic) can also be installed on a bootable USB flash drive, which makes them much more convenient to use. To create a bootable flash drive with the Ultimate Boot CD you would use the ubcd2usb command as described in the "Customizing UBCD" page on the www.ultimatebootcd.com website. To create a bootable flash drive version of a Windows 7/8 or Vista installation DVD you can use the Windows 7 USB/DVD download tool provided by Microsoft (http://tinyurl.com/4qfdm4x). Note that although the tool has "Windows 7" in the name, it works on Windows 8 and Vista discs as well. If you want to test the memory on a system that already has Windows 7/8 or Vista installed, merely run the mdsched.exe command or open the Control Panel, Administrative Tools and select the Windows Memory Diagnostic, which will allow you to restart the system and run the test immediately or set the system to run the test automatically on the next restart.

One problem with software-based memory diagnostics is that they do only pass/fail type testing; that is, all they can do is write patterns to memory and read them back. They can't determine how close the memory is to failing—only whether it worked. For the highest level of testing, the best thing to have is a dedicated memory test machine, usually called a *module tester*. These devices enable you to insert a module and test it thoroughly at a variety of speeds, voltages, and timings to let you know for certain whether the memory is good or bad. Versions of these testers are available to handle all types of memory modules. I have defective modules, for example, that work in some systems (slower ones) but not others. What I mean is that the same memory test program fails the module in one machine but passes it in another. In the module tester, it is always identified as bad right down to the individual bit, and it even tells me the actual speed of the device, not just its rating. Companies that offer memory module testers include Tanisys (www.tanisys.com), CST (www.simmtester.com), and Innoventions (www.memorytest.com). They can be expensive, but for a high volume system builder or repair shop, using one of these module testers can save time and money in the long run.

After your OS is running, memory errors can still occur, typically identified by error messages you might receive. Here are the most common:

- **Parity errors**—The parity-checking circuitry on the motherboard has detected a change in memory since the data was originally stored. (See the "How Parity Checking Works" section earlier in this chapter.)

- **General or global protection faults**—A general-purpose error indicating that a program has been corrupted in memory, usually resulting in immediate termination of the application. This can also be caused by buggy or faulty programs.

- **Fatal exception errors**—Error codes returned by a program when an illegal instruction has been encountered, invalid data or code has been accessed, or the privilege level of an operation is invalid.

- **Divide error**—A general-purpose error indicating that a division by 0 was attempted or the result of an operation does not fit in the destination register.

If you are encountering these errors, they could be caused by defective or improperly configured memory, but they can also be caused by software bugs (especially drivers), bad power supplies, static discharges, close proximity radio transmitters, timing problems, and more.

If you suspect the problems are caused by memory, there are ways to test the memory to determine whether that is the problem. Most of this testing involves running one or more memory test programs.

Another problem with software-based diagnostics is running memory tests with the system caches enabled. This effectively invalidates memory testing because most systems have what is called a *write-back cache*. This means that data written to main memory is first written to the cache. Because a memory test program first writes data and then immediately reads it back, the data is read back from the cache, not the main memory. It makes the memory test program run quickly, but all you tested was the cache. The bottom line is that if you test memory with the cache enabled, you aren't really writing to the modules, but only to the cache. Before you run any memory test programs, be sure your processor/memory caches are disabled. Many older systems have options in the BIOS Setup to turn off the caches. Current software-based memory test software such as the Windows Memory Diagnostic and Memtest86 automatically turn off the caches on newer systems.

The following steps enable you to effectively test and troubleshoot your system RAM. Figure 6.20 provides a boiled-down procedure to help you step through the process quickly.

First, let's cover the memory-testing and troubleshooting procedures:

1. Power up the system and observe the POST. If the POST completes with no errors, basic memory functionality has been tested. If errors are encountered, go to the defect isolation procedures.

2. Restart the system and then enter your BIOS (or CMOS) Setup. In most systems, this is done by pressing the Del, F1, or F2 key during the POST but before the boot process begins (see your system or motherboard documentation for details). Once in BIOS Setup, verify that the memory count is equal to the amount that has been installed. If the count does not match what has been installed, go to the defect isolation procedures.

3. Find the BIOS Setup options for cache and then set all cache options to disabled if your system supports this option. Figure 6.21 shows a typical Advanced BIOS Features menu with the cache options highlighted. Save the settings and reboot to bootable media containing the memory diagnostics program.

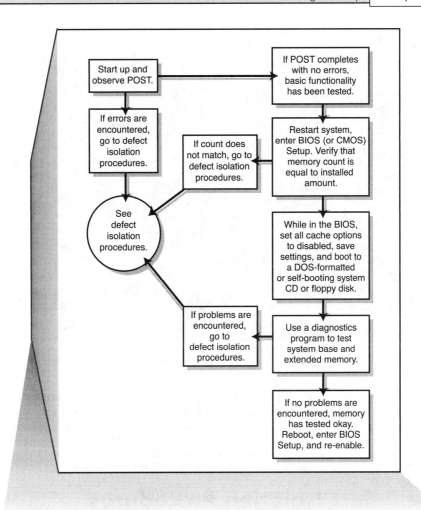

FIGURE 6.20 Testing and troubleshooting memory.

Tip

Most systems do not permit you to disable cache in BIOS setup. In such cases, I recommend using Windows Memory Diagnostic and use its advanced options to disable cache before testing memory.

4. Follow the instructions that came with your diagnostic program to have it test the system base and extended memory. Most programs have a mode that enables them to loop the test—that is, to run it continuously, which is great for finding intermittent problems. If the program encounters a memory error, proceed to the defect isolation procedures.

5. If no errors are encountered in the POST or in the more comprehensive memory diagnostic, your memory has tested okay in hardware. Be sure at this point to reboot the system, enter the BIOS Setup, and re-enable the cache. The system will run very slowly until the cache is turned back on.

Cache options to disable in BIOS

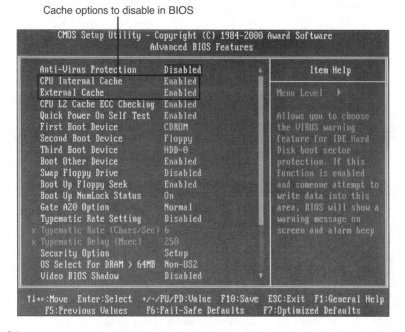

```
          CMOS Setup Utility - Copyright (C) 1984-2000 Award Software
                            Advanced BIOS Features

      Anti-Virus Protection      Disabled                    Item Help
      CPU Internal Cache         Enabled
      External Cache             Enabled        Menu Level   ▶
      CPU L2 Cache ECC Checking  Enabled
      Quick Power On Self Test   Enabled        Allows you to choose
      First Boot Device          CDROM          the VIRUS warning
      Second Boot Device         Floppy         feature for IDE Hard
      Third Boot Device          HDD-0          Disk boot sector
      Boot Other Device          Enabled        protection. If this
      Swap Floppy Drive          Disabled       function is enabled
      Boot Up Floppy Seek        Enabled        and someone attempt to
      Boot Up NumLock Status     On             write data into this
      Gate A20 Option            Normal         area, BIOS will show a
      Typematic Rate Setting     Disabled       warning message on
    x Typematic Rate (Chars/Sec) 6              screen and alarm beep
    x Typematic Delay (Msec)     250
      Security Option            Setup
      OS Select For DRAM > 64MB  Non-OS2
      Video BIOS Shadow          Disabled

   ↑↓→←:Move  Enter:Select  +/-/PU/PD:Value  F10:Save  ESC:Exit  F1:General Help
        F5:Previous Values   F6:Fail-Safe Defaults   F7:Optimized Defaults
```

FIGURE 6.21 For accurate results, before testing memory the CPU Internal (L1) and External (L2) caches should be disabled in the system BIOS Setup on systems having this option.

6. If you are having memory problems yet the memory still tests okay, you might have a problem undetectable by simple pass/fail testing, or your problems could be caused by software or one of many other defects or problems in your system. You might want to bring the memory to a module tester for a more accurate analysis. Some larger PC repair shops have such a tester. I would also check the software (especially drivers, which might need updating), power supply, and system environment for problems such as static, radio transmitters, and so forth.

Memory Defect Isolation Procedures

To use these steps, I am assuming you have identified an actual memory problem that the POST or disk-based memory diagnostics have reported. If this is the case, see the following steps and Figure 6.22 for instructions to identify or isolate which module is causing the problem.

1. Restart the system and enter the BIOS Setup. Under a menu usually called Advanced or Chipset Setup might be memory timing parameters. Select BIOS or Setup defaults, which are usually the slowest settings. If the memory timings have been manually set, as shown in Figure 6.20, reset the memory configuration to By SPD.

2. Save the settings, reboot, and retest using the testing and troubleshooting procedures listed earlier. If the problem has been solved, improper BIOS settings were the problem. If the problem remains, you likely do have defective memory, so continue to the next step.

3. Open the system for physical access to the modules on the motherboard. Identify the bank arrangement in the system. Using the manual or the legend silk-screened on the motherboard, identify which modules correspond to which banks. Remember that if you are testing a multi-channel system, you must be sure you remove all the modules in the same channel.

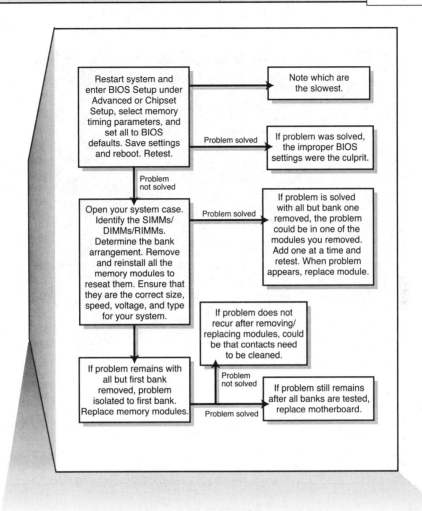

FIGURE 6.22 Follow these steps if you are still encountering memory errors after completing the steps in Figure 6.20.

4. Remove all the memory except the first bank, and then retest using the troubleshooting and testing procedures listed earlier (see Figure 6.23). If the problem remains with all but the first bank removed, the problem has been isolated to the first bank, which you must replace.

5. Replace the memory in the first bank (preferably with known good spare modules, but you can also swap in others that you have removed) and then retest. If the problem still remains after testing all the memory banks (and finding them all to be working properly), it is likely the motherboard is bad (probably one of the memory sockets). Replace the motherboard and retest.

6. At this point, the first (or previous) bank has tested to be good, so the problem must be in the remaining modules that have been temporarily removed. Install the next bank of memory and retest. If the problem resurfaces now, the memory in that bank is defective. Continue testing each bank until you find the defective module.

Change this setting to SPD to revert to the module's default memory timings.

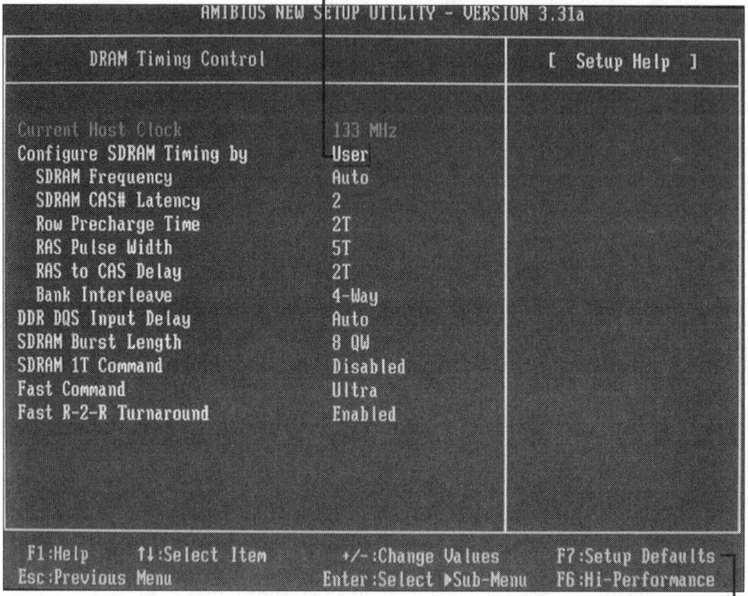

```
          AMIBIOS NEW SETUP UTILITY - VERSION 3.31a
   ┌──────────────────────────────────┬───────────────────┐
   │   DRAM Timing Control             │  [ Setup Help ]   │
   │                                   │                   │
   │ Current Host Clock        133 MHz │                   │
   │ Configure SDRAM Timing by   User  │                   │
   │   SDRAM Frequency           Auto  │                   │
   │   SDRAM CAS# Latency        2     │                   │
   │   Row Precharge Time        2T    │                   │
   │   RAS Pulse Width           5T    │                   │
   │   RAS to CAS Delay          2T    │                   │
   │   Bank Interleave           4-Way │                   │
   │ DDR DQS Input Delay         Auto  │                   │
   │ SDRAM Burst Length          8 QW  │                   │
   │ SDRAM 1T Command            Disabled                  │
   │ Fast Command                Ultra │                   │
   │ Fast R-2-R Turnaround       Enabled                   │
   │                                   │                   │
   │                                   │                   │
   │ F1:Help      ↑↓:Select Item   +/-:Change Values   F7:Setup Defaults
   │ Esc:Previous Menu             Enter:Select ▶Sub-Menu  F6:Hi-Performance
   └───────────────────────────────────────────────────────┘
```

Press F7 to use Setup Defaults for memory and other system timings.

FIGURE 6.23 This system is using user-defined memory timings, which could cause the memory to be unstable.

7. Repeat the preceding step until all remaining banks of memory are installed and have been tested. If the problem has not resurfaced after you have removed and reinstalled all the memory, the problem was likely intermittent or caused by poor conduction on the memory contacts. Often simply removing and replacing memory can resolve problems because of the self-cleaning action between the module and the socket during removal and reinstallation.

The System Logical Memory Layout

The original PC had a total of 1MB of addressable memory, and the top 384KB of that was reserved for use by the system. Placing this reserved space at the top (between 640KB and 1,024KB, instead of at the bottom, between 0KB and 640KB) led to what is often called the *conventional memory barrier*. The constant pressures on system and peripheral manufacturers to maintain compatibility by never breaking from the original memory scheme of the first PC has resulted in a system memory structure that is (to put it kindly) a mess. Almost two decades after the first PC was introduced, even the newest systems are limited in many important ways by the memory map of the first PCs.

The original PC used an Intel 8088 processor that could run only 16-bit instructions or code, which ran in what was called the *real mode* of the processor. These early processors had only enough address lines to access up to 1MB of memory, and the last 384KB of that was reserved for use by the video card as video RAM, other adapters (for on-card ROM BIOS or RAM buffers), and finally the motherboard ROM BIOS.

The 286 processor brought more address lines, enough to allow up to 16MB of RAM to be used, and a new mode called protected mode that you had to be in to use. One area of confusion was that RAM was now noncontiguous; that is, the OS could use the first 640KB and the last 15MB, but not the 384KB of system reserved area that sat in between.

When Intel released the first 32-bit processor in 1985 (the 386DX), the memory architecture of the system changed dramatically. There were now enough address lines for the processor to use 4GB of memory, but this was accessible only in 32-bit protected mode, in which only 32-bit instructions or code could run. Unfortunately, it took 10 years for the industry to transition from 16-bit to 32-bit OSs and applications. From a software instruction perspective, all the 32-bit processors since the 386 are really just faster versions of the same.

When AMD released the first x86-64 processor in 2003 (Intel followed suit in 2004), the 64-bit era was born. In addition to 16-bit and 32-bit modes, these chips have a 64-bit mode (commonly referred to as x64). 64-bit processors have three distinctly different modes, with unique memory architectures in each. For backward compatibility, 64-bit processors can run in 64-bit, 32-bit, or 16-bit modes, and 32-bit processors can run in 32-bit or 16-bit modes, each with different memory limitations. For example, a 64-bit processor running in 32-bit mode can only address 4GB of RAM, and a 64-bit or 32-bit processor running in 16-bit mode can only address 1MB of RAM. All Intel-compatible PC processors begin operation in 16-bit real mode when they are powered on. When a 32-bit or 64-bit OS loads, it is that OS code that instructs the processor to switch into 32-bit or 64-bit protected mode.

When a 32-bit OS such as Windows is loaded, the processor is switched into 32-bit protected mode early in the loading sequence. Then, 32-bit drivers for all the hardware can be loaded, and the rest of the OS can load. In 32-bit protected mode, the OSs and applications can access all the memory in the system up to 4GB. Similarly, on a 64-bit OS, the system switches into 64-bit protected mode early in the boot process and loads 64-bit drivers, followed by the remainder of the OS.

The 32-bit editions of Windows support 4GB of physical memory (RAM). What many don't realize is that the PC system hardware uses some or all of the fourth gigabyte for the BIOS, motherboard resources, memory mapped I/O, PCI configuration space, device memory (graphics aperture), VGA memory, and so on. This means that if you install 4GB (or more) RAM, none of it past 4GB will be seen at all, and most or all of the fourth gigabyte (that is, the RAM between 3GB and 4GB) will be disabled because it is already occupied by other system hardware. This is called the *3GB limit*, which is analogous to the 640K memory limit we had on 16-bit systems in the 1980s. The 16-bit addressing supported 1MB, but the upper 384K was already in use by the system hardware (BIOS, video, adapter ROM, and so on).

Figure 6.24 shows the memory map for system using an Intel G45 chipset, which supports a maximum of 16GB of RAM. For a 32-bit OS, the line labeled "Top of usable DRAM (32-bit OS)" is at 4,096MB. Note that the PCI memory range, FLASH, APIC (Advanced Programmable Interrupt Controller), and Reserved areas take up a total of 770MB of the memory below 4GB. You can also see the 384K (0.375MB) of memory below 1MB that is used by the system. This means that if you are running a 32-bit OS, even if you have 4GB of RAM installed, the amount usable by the OS would be 4,096MB – 770MB – 0.375MB, which is 3,325.625MB (or about 3.24GB, rounded down).

Can any of that unused memory between 3GB and 4GB be reclaimed? For those running a 32-bit OS, the answer is no. However, if you are running a 64-bit OS on a system that supports memory remapping (primarily a function of the motherboard chipset and BIOS), the answer is yes. Most modern motherboard chipsets have a feature that can remap the otherwise disabled RAM in the fourth gigabyte to the fifth (or higher) gigabyte, where it will be both visible to and usable by a 64-bit OS. Note, however, that if the motherboard doesn't support remapping, even when a 64-bit OS is being run, the memory will be lost.

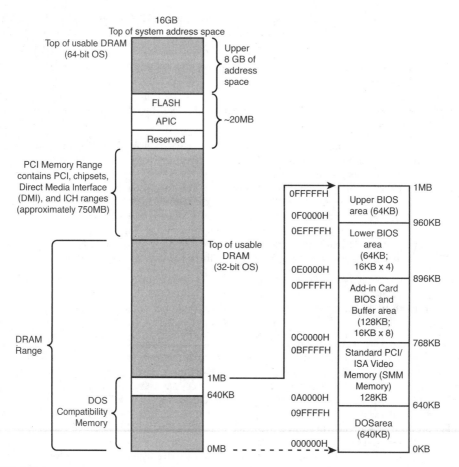

FIGURE 6.24 Memory map for a system using an Intel G45 chipset.

Note that the 3GB limit is not as strictly defined as it was with the 640K limit. This means that if you do install 4GB, you might get to use as much as 3.5GB of it, or possibly as little as 2.5GB or less. It depends largely on the types of buses in the system as well as the type and number of video cards installed. With a single low-end video card, you may have access to 3.5GiB. However, on a newer system with two or more PCIe x16 slots, and especially with two or more high-end PCI Express video cards installed, you may drop the usable limit to something close to 2GiB.

When running 32-bit editions of Windows, I used to recommend installing a maximum of 3GB RAM, because most if not all of the fourth GB is unusable. However, on systems that support dual-channel memory, it is usually cheaper to install two 2GB modules to get 4GB than it is to install two 1GB modules and two 512MB to get 3GB. On desktop systems that support dual-channel memory, you would not want to install three 1GB modules because in that case not all the memory would run in dual-channel mode.

Chapter

7

The ATA/IDE Interface

An Overview of the IDE Interface

The interface used to connect disk drives to a PC is typically called IDE (Integrated Drive Electronics); however, the official name of this interface is ATA (AT Attachment). The ATA designation refers to the fact that this interface was originally designed to connect a combined drive and controller directly to the 16-bit bus found in the 1984 vintage IBM PC-AT (Advanced Technology) and compatible computers. The AT bus is otherwise known as the ISA (Industry Standard Architecture) bus. Although ATA is the official name of the interface, IDE is a marketing term originated by some of the drive manufacturers to describe the drive/controller combination used in drives with the ATA interface. Integrated Drive Electronics refers to the fact that the interface electronics or controller is built into the drive and is not a separate board, as it was with earlier drive interfaces. Although the correct name for the particular IDE interface we most commonly use is technically ATA, many persist in using the IDE designation today. If you are being picky, you could say that IDE refers generically to any drive interface in which the controller is built into the drive, whereas ATA refers to the specific implementation of IDE that is used in most PCs.

ATA was originally a 16-bit parallel interface, meaning that 16 bits are transmitted simultaneously down the interface cable. A newer interface called Serial ATA (SATA) was officially introduced in late 2000 and was adopted in desktop systems starting in 2003 and in laptops starting in late 2005. SATA sends one bit down the cable at a time, enabling thinner and smaller cables to be used, as well as providing higher performance due to the higher cycling speeds it enables. Although SATA is a completely different physical interface design, it is backward compatible on the software level with Parallel ATA (PATA). Throughout this book, *ATA* refers to both the parallel and serial versions. *PATA* refers specifically to the parallel version, and *SATA* refers specifically to the serial version.

Precursors to IDE

Several types of hard disk interfaces have been used for PC hard disks over the years, as shown in Table 7.1. As time has passed, the number of choices has increased; however, many of the older interface standards are obsolete and no longer viable in newer systems.

Table 7.1 PC Drive Interfaces

Interface	When Used
ST-506/412	1978–1989 (obsolete)
ESDI	1983–1991 (obsolete)
Non-ATA IDE	1987–1993 (obsolete)
SCSI	1986–present
PATA (IDE)	1986–present
SATA	2003–present

ST = Seagate Technology
ESDI = Enhanced Small Device Interface
IDE = Integrated Drive Electronics
SCSI = Small Computer Systems Interface
ATA = AT (Advanced Technology) Attachment

Of these interfaces, only ST-506/412 and ESDI are what you could call true disk-controller-to-drive interfaces, and they are obsolete. Non-ATA versions of IDE were used primarily in the IBM PS/2 systems and are also obsolete. Current SCSI, ATA, and SATA are system-level interfaces that usually internally incorporate a chipset-based controller interface. For example, many SCSI, PATA, and SATA drives incorporate the same basic controller circuitry inside the actual drive. The SCSI interface then adds another layer that connects between the drive controller and the PCI (or ISA) bus, whereas PATA and SATA have a more direct connection from the controller to the AT bus attachment interface. Despite their differences, we call a SCSI, PATA, or SATA card a host interface adapter instead of a controller card because the actual controllers are inside the drives. Virtually all modern disk drives use SATA or PATA interfaces to connect to a system.

IDE Origins

Any drive with an integrated controller could be called an IDE drive, although normally when we say IDE, we really mean the specific version of IDE called ATA. No matter what you call it, combining the drive and controller greatly simplifies installation because no separate power or signal cables run from the controller to the drive. Also, when the controller and drive are assembled as a unit, the number of total components is reduced, signal paths are shorter, and the electrical connections are more noise-resistant. This results in a more reliable and less expensive design than is possible when a separate controller, connected to the drive by cables, is used.

Placing the controller, including the digital-to-analog encoder/decoder (endec), on the drive offers an inherent reliability advantage over interfaces with separate controllers such as ST506 and ESDI. Reliability is increased because the data encoding, from digital to analog, is performed directly on the drive in a tight noise-free environment. The timing-sensitive analog information does not have to travel along crude ribbon cables that are likely to pick up noise and insert propagation delays into the signals. The integrated configuration enables increases in the clock rate of the encoder and the storage density of the drive.

The earliest IDE drives were called hardcards and were nothing more than hard disks and controller cards bolted directly together and plugged into a slot as a single unit. Companies such as the Plus Development Division of Quantum took small 3 1/2-inch drives (either ST-506/412 or ESDI) and attached them directly to a standard controller card. The drive/controller assembly then was plugged into an ISA bus slot as though it were a normal disk controller card. Unfortunately, the mounting of a heavy, vibrating hard disk in an expansion slot with nothing but a single screw to hold it in place left a lot to be desired—not to mention the physical interference with adjacent cards, because many of these units were much thicker than a controller card alone.

Several companies got the idea to redesign the controller to replace the logic board assembly on a standard hard disk and then mount it in a standard drive bay just like any other drive. Because the built-in controller in these drives still needed to plug directly into the expansion bus just like any other controller, a cable was run between the drive and one of the slots. This was the origin of IDE.

Origins of ATA

Control Data Corporation (CDC; its disk drive division was later called Imprimis), Western Digital, and Compaq actually created what could be called the first ATA IDE interface drive and were the first to establish the 40-pin ATA connector pinout. The first ATA IDE drive was a 5 1/4-inch half-height CDC Wren II 40MB drive with an integrated WD controller and was initially used in the first Compaq 386 systems in 1986. I remember seeing this drive for the first time in 1986 at the fall COMDEX show. Besides the (at the time) unique 40-pin ribbon cable, I remember being surprised by the green activity LED on the front bezel. (Most drives up until then used red LEDs.)

Compaq was the first to incorporate a special bus adapter in its system to adapt the 98-pin AT-bus (also known as ISA) edge connector on the motherboard to a smaller 40-pin, header-style connector into which the drive would plug. The 40-pin connector was all that was necessary because it was known that a disk controller never would need more than 40 of the ISA bus lines. Smaller 2 1/2-inch ATA drives found in laptop computers use a superset 44-pin or 50-pin connection, which includes additional pins for power and configuration. The pins from the original ISA bus used in ATA are the only signal pins required by a standard-type AT hard disk controller. For example, because a primary AT-style disk controller uses only interrupt request (IRQ) line 14, the primary motherboard ATA connector supplies only that IRQ line; no other IRQ lines are necessary. Even if your ATA interface is integrated within the motherboard chipset South Bridge or I/O Controller Hub chip (as it would be in newer systems) and runs at higher bus speeds, the pinout and functions of the pins are still the same as the original design taken right off the ISA bus.

◀◀ See the Chapter 4 section, "Motherboard Connectors," **p. 228**.

◀◀ See the Chapter 4 section, "The ISA Bus," **p. 245**.

Note

Many people who use systems with ATA connectors on the motherboard believe that a hard disk controller is built into their motherboards, but in a technical sense the controller is actually in the drive. Although the integrated ATA ports on a motherboard often are referred to as controllers, they are more accurately called *host adapters* (although you'll rarely hear this term). You can think of a host adapter as a device that connects a controller to a bus.

Eventually, the 40-pin ATA connector and drive interface design was placed before one of the ANSI standards committees that, in conjunction with drive manufacturers, ironed out some deficiencies, tied up some loose ends, and then published what was known as the CAM ATA (Common Access Method AT Attachment) interface. The CAM ATA Committee was formed in October 1988, and the first working document of the ATA interface was introduced in March 1989. Before the CAM ATA standard, many companies, such as Conner Peripherals (which later merged with Seagate Technology), made proprietary changes to the original interface as designed by CDC. As a result, many older ATA drives from the late 1980s are difficult to integrate into a dual-drive setup because minor differences in the interfaces can cause compatibility problems among the drives. By the early 1990s, most drive manufacturers brought their drives into full compliance with the official standard, which eliminated many of these compatibility problems.

Some areas of the ATA standard have been left open for vendor-specific commands and functions. These vendor-specific commands and functions are the reason it is important to use the OEM-specific programs for testing ATA drives. To work to full capability, the diagnostic program you are using typically must know the specific vendor-unique commands for remapping defects. Unfortunately, these and other specific drive commands differ from OEM to OEM, thus clouding the standard somewhat. Most ATA drive manufacturers publish their drive-formatting/initialization software on their websites.

As I noted at the start of this chapter, PATA is a 16-bit parallel interface that has been largely phased out in favor of the serial interface of SATA. SATA's thinner and smaller cables provide higher performance due to the higher cycling speeds allowed and are considerably easier to work with than the wide PATA ribbon cables. Figure 7.1 shows how the power and data cables SATA uses compare in size to those PATA uses.

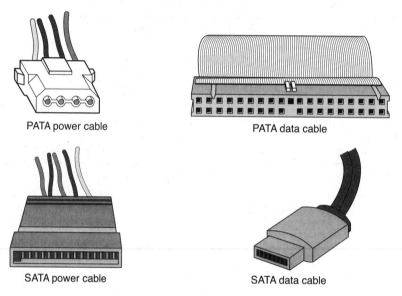

PATA power cable

PATA data cable

SATA power cable

SATA data cable

FIGURE 7.1 SATA data cables are much smaller than those used by PATA, whereas the power cables are similar in size.

ATA Standards

Today, the ATA interface is controlled by an independent group of representatives from major PC, drive, and component manufacturers. This group is called Technical Committee T13 (www.t13.org) and is responsible for all standards relating to the Parallel and Serial ATA storage interfaces. T13 is a part of the International Committee on Information Technology Standards (INCITS), which operates under rules approved by the American National Standards Institute (ANSI), a governing body that sets rules that control nonproprietary standards in the computer industry as well as many other industries. A second group called the Serial ATA International Organization (www.serialata.org) was formed to initially create the SATA standards, which are then passed on to the T13 Committee for refinement and official publication under ANSI. The ATA-7 and ATA-8 standards incorporate both parallel and serial interfaces.

The rules these committees operate under are designed to ensure that voluntary industry standards are developed by the consensus of people and organizations in the affected industry. INCITS specifically develops information processing system standards, whereas ANSI approves the process under which these standards are developed and then publishes them. Because T13 is essentially a public organization, all the working drafts, discussions, and meetings of T13 are open for all to see.

Copies of any of the published standards can be purchased from ANSI (www.ansi.org) or the IHS Standards Store (formerly Global Engineering Documents, http://global.ihs.com). Draft versions of the standards can be downloaded from the T13 Committee or Serial ATA International Organization (SATA-IO) website.

Each newer version of ATA is backward compatible with the previous versions. In other words, older ATA-1 and ATA-2 devices work fine on ATA-7 and ATA-8 interfaces. ATA-7 and ATA-8 include both PATA and SATA. Newer versions of ATA are normally built on older versions, and with few exceptions can be thought of as extensions of the previous versions. This means that ATA-8, for example, is generally considered equal to ATA-7 with the addition of some features.

Table 7.2 breaks down the various ATA standards. The following sections describe recent ATA versions in more detail.

Table 7.2 ATA Standards

Standard	Pro-posed	Pub-lished	With-drawn	PIO Modes	DMA Modes	UDMA Modes	Parallel Speed (MBps)	Serial Speed (MBps)	Features
ATA-1	1988	1994	1999	0–2	0	—	8.33	—	Drives support up to 136.9GB; BIOS issues not addressed.
ATA-2	1993	1996	2001	0–4	0–2	—	16.67	—	Faster PIO modes; CHS/LBA BIOS translation defined up to 8.4GB; PC-Card.
ATA-3	1995	1997	2002	0–4	0–2	—	16.67	—	S.M.A.R.T.; improved signal integrity; LBA support mandatory; eliminated single-word DMA modes.
ATA-4	1996	1998	2012	0–4	0–2	0–2	33.33	—	Ultra-DMA modes; ATAPI Packet Interface; BIOS support up to 136.9GB.
ATA-5	1998	2000	—	0–4	0–2	0-4	66.67	—	Faster UDMA modes; 80-pin cable with auto-detection.
ATA-6	2000	2002	—	0–4	0–2	0-5	100	—	100MBps UDMA mode; extended drive and BIOS support up to 144PB.
ATA-7	2001	2004	—	0–4	0–2	0-6	133	150	133MBps UDMA mode; SATA.
ATA-8	2004	—	—	0–4	0–2	0-6	133	600	Minor revisions for PATA, includes SATA 2.x and 3.x.

S.M.A.R.T. = Self-Monitoring, Analysis, and Reporting Technology
ATAPI = AT Attachment Packet Interface
MB = Megabyte; million bytes
GB = Gigabyte; billion bytes
PB = Petabyte; quadrillion bytes

CHS = Cylinder, Head, Sector
LBA = Logical block address
PIO = Programmed I/O
DMA = direct memory access
UDMA = Ultra DMA (direct memory access)

ATA-1 (ATA Interface for Disk Drives)

ATA-1 defined the original ATA interface, which was an integrated bus interface between disk drives and host systems based on the ISA (AT) bus. These major features were introduced and documented in the ATA-1 specification:

- 40/44-pin connectors and cabling
- Master/slave or cable select drive configuration options
- Signal timing for basic Programmed I/O (PIO) and direct memory access (DMA) modes
- Cylinder, head, sector (CHS) and logical block address (LBA) drive parameter translations supporting drive capacities up to 2^{28}–2^{20} (267,386,880) sectors, or 136.9GB

Although ATA-1 had been in use since 1986, work on turning it into an official standard began in 1988 under the Common Access Method (CAM) committee. The ATA-1 standard was finished and officially published in 1994 as "ANSI X3.221-1994, AT Attachment Interface for Disk Drives." ATA-1 was officially withdrawn as a standard on August 6, 1999.

Although ATA-1 supported theoretical drive capacities up to 136.9GB (2^{28}–2^{20} = 267,386,880 sectors), it did not address BIOS limitations that stopped at 528MB (1024 × 16 × 63 = 1,032,192 sectors). The BIOS limitations would be addressed in subsequent ATA versions because, at the time, no drives larger than 528MB existed.

ATA-2 (ATA Interface with Extensions-2)

ATA-2 was a major upgrade to the original ATA standard. Perhaps the biggest change was almost a philosophical one. ATA-2 was updated to define an interface between host systems and storage devices in general and not only disk drives. The major features added to ATA-2 compared to the original ATA standard include the following:

- Faster PIO and DMA transfer modes
- Support for power management
- Support for removable devices
- PCMCIA (PC Card) device support
- `Identify Drive` command that reports more information
- Defined standard CHS/LBA translation methods for drives up to 8.4GB in capacity

The most important additions in ATA-2 were the support for faster PIO and DMA modes, as well as methods to enable BIOS support up to 8.4GB. The BIOS support was necessary because although ATA-1 was designed to support drives of up to 136.9GB in capacity, the PC BIOS could originally handle drives of up to 528MB. Adding parameter-translation capability now allowed the BIOS to handle drives up to 8.4GB. This is discussed in more detail later in this chapter.

ATA-2 also featured improvements in the `Identify Drive` command that enabled a drive to tell the software exactly what its characteristics are; this is essential for both Plug and Play (PnP) and compatibility with future revisions of the standard.

ATA-2 was also known by unofficial marketing terms, such as Fast-ATA or Fast-ATA-2 (Seagate/ Quantum) and EIDE (Enhanced IDE, Western Digital).

Although work on ATA-2 began in 1993, the standard was not officially published until 1996 as "ANSI X3.279-1996 AT Attachment Interface with Extensions." ATA-2 was officially withdrawn in 2001.

ATA-3 (ATA Interface-3)

ATA-3 was a comparatively minor revision to the ATA-2 standard that preceded it. It consisted of a general cleanup of the specification and had mostly minor clarifications and revisions. The most major changes included the following:

- Eliminated single-word (8-bit) DMA transfer protocols
- Added S.M.A.R.T. (Self-Monitoring, Analysis, and Reporting Technology) support for prediction of device performance degradation
- Made LBA mode support mandatory (previously, it had been optional)
- Added ATA Security mode, allowing password protection for device access
- Provided recommendations for source and receiver bus termination to solve noise issues at higher transfer speeds

ATA-3 built on ATA-2, adding improved reliability, especially of the faster PIO mode 4 transfers; however, ATA-3 did not define faster modes. ATA-3 did add a simple password-based security scheme, more sophisticated power management, and S.M.A.R.T. This enables a drive to keep track of problems that might result in a failure and thus avoid data loss. S.M.A.R.T. is a reliability prediction technology that IBM initially developed.

Work on ATA-3 began in 1995, and the standard was finished and officially published in 1997 as "ANSI X3.298-1997, AT Attachment 3 Interface." ATA-3 was officially withdrawn in 2002.

ATA/ATAPI-4 (ATA with Packet Interface Extension-4)

ATA-4 included several important additions to the standard. It included the Packet Command feature known as the *AT Attachment Packet Interface* (ATAPI), which allowed devices such as CD-ROM and CD-RW drives, LS-120 SuperDisk floppy drives, Zip drives, tape drives, and other types of storage devices to be attached through a common interface. Until ATA-4 came out, ATAPI was a separately published standard. ATA-4 also added the 33MB per second (MBps) transfer mode known as Ultra-DMA or Ultra-ATA. ATA-4 is backward compatible with ATA-3 and earlier definitions of the ATAPI.

Work on ATA-4 began in 1996, and the standard was finished and officially published in 1998 as "ANSI NCITS 317-1998, AT Attachment - 4 with Packet Interface Extension." ATA-4 was officially withdrawn in 2012.

The major revisions added in ATA-4 were as follows:

- Ultra-DMA (UDMA)or Ultra-ATA/33) transfer modes up to Mode 2, which is 33MBps (called UDMA/33 or Ultra-ATA/33)
- Integral ATAPI support
- Advanced power management support
- An optional 80-conductor, 40-pin cable defined for improved noise resistance
- Host protected area (HPA) support
- Compact Flash Adapter (CFA) support
- Enhanced BIOS support for drives over 9.4ZB (zettabytes or trillion gigabytes) in size (even though ATA was still limited to 136.9GB)

The speed and level of ATA support in your system is mainly dictated by your motherboard chipset. Most motherboard chipsets come with a component called either a South Bridge or an I/O Controller

Hub that provides the ATA interface (as well as other functions) in the system. Check the specifications for your motherboard or chipset to see whether yours supports the faster ATA/33, ATA/66, ATA/100, or ATA/133 mode. One indication is to enter the BIOS Setup, put the hard disk on manual parameter settings (user defined), and see which (if any) Ultra-DMA modes are listed. Most boards built in 1998 support ATA/33. In 2000 they began to support ATA/66, and by late 2000 most started supporting ATA/100. ATA/133 support became widespread in mid-2002.

◀◀ See the Chapter 4 section, "Chipsets," **p. 181**.

ATA-4 made ATAPI support a full part of the ATA standard; therefore, ATAPI was no longer an auxiliary interface to ATA but merged completely within it. Thus, ATA-4 promoted ATA for use as an interface for many other types of devices. ATA-4 also added support for new Ultra-DMA modes (also called Ultra-ATA) for even faster data transfer. The highest-performance mode, called UDMA/33, had 33MBps bandwidth—twice that of the fastest programmed I/O mode or DMA mode previously supported. In addition to the higher transfer rate, because UDMA modes relieve the load on the processor, further performance gains were realized.

An optional 80-conductor cable (with cable select) is defined for UDMA/33 transfers. Although this cable was originally defined as optional, it would later be required for the faster ATA/66, ATA/100, and ATA/133 modes in ATA-5 and later.

Support for a reserved area on the drive called the HPA was added via an optional SET MAX ADDRESS command. This enables an area of the drive to be reserved for recovery software.

Also included was support for queuing commands, similar to those provided in SCSI-2. This enabled better multitasking as multiple programs request ATA transfers.

Another standard approved by the T13 committee in 1998 was "ANSI NCITS 316-1998 1394 to AT Attachment - Tailgate," which is a bridge protocol between the IEEE 1394 (i.LINK/FireWire) bus and ATA that enables ATA drives to be adapted to FireWire. A tailgate is an adapter device (basically a small circuit board) that converts IEEE 1394 (i.LINK or FireWire) to ATA, essentially allowing ATA drives to be plugged into a FireWire bus. This enabled vendors to quickly develop IEEE 1394 (FireWire) external drives for backup and high-capacity removable data storage. Inside almost any external FireWire drive enclosure you will find the tailgate device and a standard ATA drive.

▶▶ See the Chapter 14 section, "IEEE 1394 (FireWire or i.LINK)," **p. 718**.

ATA/ATAPI-5 (ATA with Packet Interface-5)

ATA-5 was built on the previous ATA-4 interface. ATA-5 includes Ultra-ATA/66 (also called *Ultra-DMA* or *UDMA/66*), which doubles the Ultra-ATA burst transfer rate by reducing setup times and increasing the clock rate. The faster clock rate increases interference, which causes problems with the standard 40-pin cable used by ATA and Ultra-ATA. To eliminate noise and interference, the newer 40-pin, 80-conductor cable was made mandatory for drives running in UDMA/66 or faster modes. This cable adds 40 additional ground lines between each of the original 40 ground and signal lines, which helps shield the signals from interference. Note that this cable works with older, non-Ultra-ATA devices as well because it still has the same 40-pin connectors.

Work on ATA-5 began in 1998, and the standard was finished and officially published in 2000 as "ANSI NCITS 340-2000, AT Attachment - 5 with Packet Interface."

The major additions in the ATA-5 standard include the following:

■ Ultra-DMA (UDMA) transfer modes up to Mode 4, which is 66MBps (called UDMA/66 or Ultra-ATA/66).

■ The 80-conductor cable now mandatory for UDMA/66 operation.

- Automatic detection of 40- or 80-conductor cables.
- UDMA modes faster than UDMA/33 enabled only if an 80-conductor cable is detected.

The 40-pin, 80-conductor cables support the cable select feature and have color-coded connectors. The blue (end) connector should be connected to the ATA host interface (usually the motherboard). The black (opposite end) connector is known as the *master position*, which is where the primary drive plugs in. The gray (middle) connector is for slave devices.

To use either the UDMA/33 or the UDMA/66 mode, your ATA interface, drive, BIOS, and cable must be capable of supporting the mode you want to use. The operating system also must be capable of handling direct memory access. Windows 95 OSR2 and later versions are ready out of the box, but older versions of Windows 95 and NT (prior to Service Pack 3) require additional or updated drivers to fully exploit these faster modes. Contact the motherboard or system vendor for the latest drivers.

For reliability, Ultra-DMA modes incorporate an error-detection mechanism known as *cyclical redundancy checking* (CRC). CRC is an algorithm that calculates a checksum used to detect errors in a stream of data. Both the host (controller) and the drive calculate a CRC value for each Ultra-DMA transfer. After the data is sent, the drive calculates a CRC value, and this is compared to the original host CRC value. If a difference is reported, the host might be required to select a slower transfer mode and retry the original request for data.

ATA/ATAPI-6 (ATA with Packet Interface-6)

ATA-6 includes Ultra-ATA/100 (also called Ultra-DMA or UDMA/100), which increases the Ultra-ATA burst transfer rate by reducing setup times and increasing the clock rate. As with ATA-5, the faster modes require the improved 80-conductor cable. Using the ATA/100 mode requires both a drive and motherboard interface that supports that mode.

Work on ATA-6 began in 2000, and the standard was finished and officially published in 2002 as "ANSI NCITS 361-2002, AT Attachment - 6 with Packet Interface."

The major changes or additions in the standard include the following:

- Ultra-DMA (UDMA) Mode 5 added, which allows 100MBps (called UDMA/100, Ultra-ATA/100, or just ATA/100) transfers.
- Sector count per command increased from 8 bits (256 sectors, or 131KB) to 16 bits (65,536 sectors, or 33.5MB), allowing larger files to be transferred more efficiently.
- LBA addressing extended from 228 to 248 (281,474,976,710,656) sectors, supporting drives up to 144.12PB (petabytes = quadrillion bytes). This feature is often referred to as 48-bit LBA or greater than 137GB support by vendors; Maxtor referred to this feature as Big Drive.
- CHS addressing was made obsolete; drives must use 28-bit or 48-bit LBA addressing only.

Besides adding the 100MBps UDMA Mode 5 transfer rate, ATA-6 extended drive capacity greatly, and just in time. ATA-5 and earlier standards supported drives of up to only 137GB in capacity, which became a limitation as larger drives were becoming available. Commercially available 3 1/2-inch drives exceeding 137GB were introduced in 2001, but they were originally available only in SCSI versions because SCSI doesn't have the same limitations as ATA. With ATA-6, the sector addressing limit has been extended from 2^{28} sectors to 2^{48} sectors. What this means is that LBA addressing previously could use only 28-bit numbers, but with ATA-6, LBA addressing can use larger 48-bit numbers if necessary. With 512 bytes per sector, this raises the maximum supported drive capacity to 144.12PB. That is equal to more than 144.12 quadrillion bytes! Note that the 48-bit addressing is optional and necessary only for drives larger than 137GB. Drives 137GB or smaller can use either 28-bit or 48-bit addressing.

ATA/ATAPI-7 (ATA with Packet Interface-7)

Work on ATA-7, which began late in 2001, was completed and officially published in 2004. As with the previous ATA standards, ATA-7 is built on the standard that preceded it (ATA-6), with some additions.

The primary additions to ATA-7 include the following:

- Ultra-DMA (UDMA) Mode 6 was added. This allows for 133MBps transfers (called UDMA/133, Ultra-ATA/133, or just ATA/133). As with UDMA Mode 5 (100MBps) and UDMA Mode 4 (66MBps), the use of an 80-conductor cable is required.

- Added support for long physical sectors. This allows a device to be formatted so that there are multiple logical sectors per physical sector. Each physical sector stores an ECC field, so long physical sectors allow increased format efficiency with fewer ECC bytes used overall.

- Added support for long logical sectors. This enables additional data bytes to be used per sector (520 or 528 bytes instead of 512 bytes) for server applications. Devices using long logical sectors are not backward compatible with devices or applications that use 512-byte sectors, such as standard desktop and laptop systems.

- SATA 1.0 incorporated as part of the ATA-7 standard. This includes the SATA physical interconnection as well as the related features and commands.

- The ATA-7 document split into three volumes. Volume 1 covers the command set and logical registers, which apply to both Serial and Parallel ATA. Volume 2 covers the parallel transport protocols and interconnects (PATA), and Volume 3 covers the serial transport protocols and interconnects (SATA).

The ATA/133 transfer mode was originally proposed by Maxtor, and only a few other drive and chipset manufacturers adopted it. Among the chipset manufacturers, VIA, ALi, and SiS added ATA/133 support to their chipsets, prior to moving on to SATA, but Intel decided from the outset to skip ATA/133 in its chipsets in lieu of adding SATA (150MBps or 300MBps). This means the majority of systems that utilize PATA do not support ATA/133; however, all ATA/133 drives do work in ATA/100 mode.

ATA/ATAPI-8

Work on ATA-8 began in 2004, and some initial parts of the standard were published in 2006 and 2008. Other parts are still in progress and continue to be revised as of 2013. As with the previous ATA standards, ATA-8 is built on the standard that preceded it, with some additions. As with the previous version, ATA-8 includes SATA but adds the newer 2.x and 3.x versions of the SATA specification.

The primary features added to ATA-8 include the following:

- The inclusion of SATA 2.x and 3.x for serial transport (physical) and command set functions

- The replacement of read long/write long functions

- Improved HPA management via additional HPA-related commands

- Defined IDENTIFY DEVICE word 217 to report drive rotational speed (rpm), where a value of 1 indicates nonrotating media (solid-state drive)

- Addition of the TRIM command for flash-based solid-state drives (SSDs). This allows the system to inform an SSD which blocks are no longer in use so they can be erased in preparation for future writes

As the development of ATA progresses, it is expected that newer features designed by the SATA-IO committee will be incorporated.

PATA

Parallel ATA was the most widely used drive interface for many years; however, currently it has been almost completely replaced by SATA for new systems. Even so, some new motherboards and drives are still available with PATA support, and many older systems, motherboards, and drives still in service use PATA as well. PATA has unique specifications and requirements regarding the physical interface, cabling, and connectors compared to SATA. The following sections detail the unique features of PATA.

PATA I/O Connector

The PATA interface connector is normally a 40-pin header-type connector with pins spaced 0.1 inch (2.54mm) apart. Generally, it is keyed to prevent the possibility of installing it upside down (see Figures 7.2 and 7.3). To create a keyed connector, the manufacturer usually removes pin 20 from the male connector and blocks pin 20 on the female cable connector, which prevents the user from installing the cable backward. Some cables also incorporate a protrusion on the top of the female cable connector that fits into a notch in the shroud surrounding the mating male connector on the device. The use of keyed connectors and cables is highly recommended. Plugging an ATA cable in backward normally doesn't cause permanent damage; however, it can lock up the system and prevent it from running.

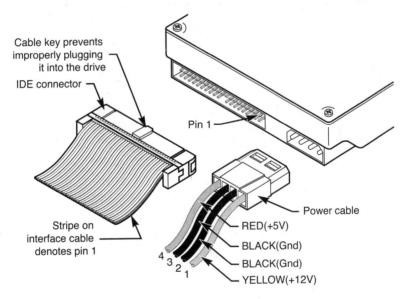

FIGURE 7.2 Typical PATA (IDE) hard drive connectors.

Table 7.3 shows the standard 40-pin PATA (IDE) interface connector pinout.

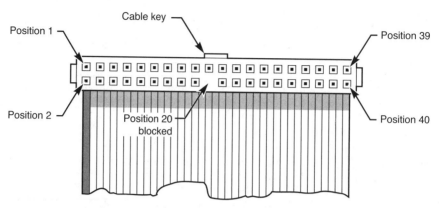

FIGURE 7.3   PATA (IDE) 40-pin interface connector detail.

Table 7.3   Pinout for the 40-Pin PATA Connector

Signal Name	Pin	Pin	Signal Name
-RESET	1	2	GROUND
Data Bit 7	3	4	Data Bit 8
Data Bit 6	5	6	Data Bit 9
Data Bit 5	7	8	Data Bit 10
Data Bit 4	9	10	Data Bit 11
Data Bit 3	11	12	Data Bit 12
Data Bit 2	13	14	Data Bit 13
Data Bit 1	15	16	Data Bit 14
Data Bit 0	17	18	Data Bit 15
GROUND	19	20	KEY (pin missing)
DRQ 3	21	22	GROUND
-IOW	23	24	GROUND
-IOR	25	26	GROUND
I/O CH RDY	27	28	CSEL:SPSYNC[1]
-DACK 3	29	30	GROUND
IRQ 14	31	32	Reserved[2]
Address Bit 1	33	34	-PDIAG
Address Bit 0	35	36	Address Bit 2
-CS1FX	37	38	-CS3FX
-DA/SP	39	40	GROUND

1 Pin 28 is usually cable select, but some older drives could use it for spindle synchronization between multiple drives.
2 Pin 32 was defined as -IOCS16 in ATA-2 but is no longer used.
Note that - preceding a signal name (such as -RESET) indicates the signal is "active low."

The 2 1/2-inch drives found in notebook/laptop-size computers typically use a smaller unitized 50-pin header connector with pins spaced only 2.0mm (0.079 inches) apart. The main 40-pin part of the connector is the same as the standard PATA connector (except for the physical pin spacing), but there are added pins for power and jumpering. The cable that plugs into this connector typically has 44 pins, carrying power as well as the standard ATA signals. The jumper pins usually have a jumper on them (the jumper position controls cable select, master, or slave settings). Figure 7.4 shows the unitized 50-pin connector used on the 2 1/2-inch PATA drives in laptop or notebook computers.

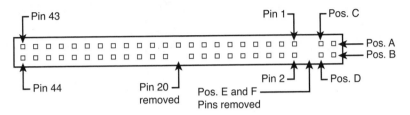

FIGURE 7.4   The 50-pin unitized PATA connector detail (used on 2 1/2-inch notebook/laptop PATA drives with a 44-pin cable).

Note the jumper pins at positions A–D; also notice that the pins at positions E and F are removed. A jumper usually is placed between positions B and D to set the drive for cable select operation. On this connector, pin 41 provides +5V power to the drive logic (circuit board), pin 42 provides +5V power to the motor (2 1/2-inch drives use 5V motors, unlike larger drives that typically use 12V motors), and pin 43 provides a power ground. The last pin (44) is reserved and not used.

Table 7.4 shows the 50-pin unitized PATA interface connector pinout as used on most 2 1/2-inch (laptop or notebook computer) drives.

Table 7.4   The 50-Pin Unitized PATA 2 1/2-Inch (Notebook/Laptop Drive) Connector Pinout

Signal Name	Pin	Pin	Signal Name
Jumper pin	A	B	Jumper pin
Jumper pin	C	D	Jumper pin
KEY (pin missing)	E	F	KEY (pin missing)
-RESET	1	2	GROUND
Data Bit 7	3	4	Data Bit 8
Data Bit 6	5	6	Data Bit 9
Data Bit 5	7	8	Data Bit 10
Data Bit 4	9	10	Data Bit 11
Data Bit 3	11	12	Data Bit 12
Data Bit 2	13	14	Data Bit 13
Data Bit 1	15	16	Data Bit 14
Data Bit 0	17	18	Data Bit 15
GROUND	19	20	KEY (pin missing)

Table 7.4   Continued

Signal Name	Pin	Pin	Signal Name
DRQ 3	21	22	GROUND
-IOW	23	24	GROUND
-IOR	25	26	GROUND
I/O CH RDY	27	28	CSEL
-DACK 3	29	30	GROUND
IRQ 14	31	32	Reserved
Address Bit 1	33	34	-PDIAG
Address Bit 0	35	36	Address Bit 2
-CS1FX	37	38	-CS3FX
-DA/SP	39	40	GROUND
+5V (Logic)	41	42	+5V (Motor)
GROUND	43	44	Reserved

Note

Many lower-cost board and cable manufacturers leave out the keying. Cheaper motherboards often don't have pin 20 removed on their ATA connectors; consequently, they don't supply a cable with pin 20 blocked. If they don't use a shrouded connector with a notch and a corresponding protrusion on the cable connector, no keying exists and the cables can be inserted backward. Fortunately, the only consequence of this in most cases is that the device won't work until the cable is attached with the correct orientation.

Note that some systems do not display video until the ATA drives respond to a spin-up command, which they can't receive if the cable is connected backward. So, if you connect an unkeyed ATA drive to your computer, turn on the computer, and it seems as if the system is locked up (you don't see anything on the screen), check the ATA cable. (See Figure 7.6 for examples of unkeyed and keyed ATA cables.)

In rare situations in which you are mixing and matching items, you might encounter a cable with pin 20 blocked (as it should be) and a board with pin 20 still present. In that case, you can break off pin 20 from the board—or for the more squeamish, remove the block from the cable or replace the cable with one without the blocked pin. Some cables have the block permanently installed as part of the connector housing, in which case you must break off pin 20 on the board or device end or use a different cable.

The simple rule of thumb is that pin 1 should be oriented toward the power connector on the device, which normally corresponds to the stripe on the cable.

PATA I/O Cable

A 40-conductor ribbon cable is specified to carry signals between the bus adapter circuits and the drive (controller). To maximize signal integrity and eliminate potential timing and noise problems, the cable should not be longer than 18 inches (0.46 meters), although testing shows that you can reliably use 80-conductor cables up to 27 inches (0.69 meters) in length.

Note that ATA drives supporting the higher-speed transfer modes, such as PIO Mode 4 or any of the Ultra-DMA (UDMA) modes, are especially susceptible to cable integrity problems. If the cable is too long, you can experience data corruption and other errors that can be maddening. This is manifested in problems reading from or writing to the drive. In addition, any drive using UDMA Mode 5 (66MBps transfer rate), Mode 6 (100MBps transfer rate), or Mode 7 (133MBps transfer rate) must use a special, higher-quality 80-conductor cable. I also recommend this type of cable if your drive is running at UDMA Mode 2 (33MBps) or slower because it can't hurt and can only help. I always keep a high-quality 80-conductor ATA cable in my toolbox for testing drives where I suspect cable integrity or cable length problems. Figure 7.5 shows the typical ATA cable layout and dimensions.

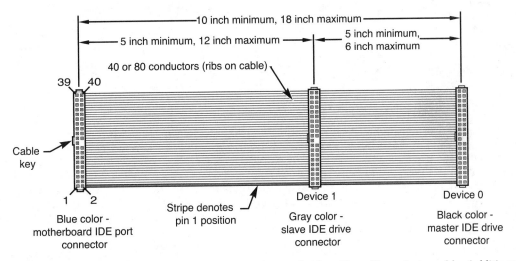

FIGURE 7.5 PATA (IDE) cable, with 40-pin connectors and either 40- or 80-conductor cables (additional wires are grounded in 80-conductor versions).

Note

Most 40-conductor cables do not have color-coded connectors, whereas all 80-conductor cables have color-coded connectors.

The two primary variations of PATA cables in use today—one with 40 conductors and the other with 80 conductors—are shown in Figure 7.6. As you can see, both use 40-pin connectors, and the additional wires in the 80-conductor version are simply wired to ground. The additional conductors are designed to reduce noise and interference and are required when setting the interface to run at 66MBps (ATA/66) or faster. The drive and host adapter are designed to disable the higher-speed ATA/66, ATA/100, and ATA/133 modes if an 80-conductor cable is not detected. In such cases, you might see a warning message when you start your computer if an ATA/66 or faster drive is connected to a 40-conductor cable. You can also use the 80-conductor cable at lower speeds to improve signal integrity. Therefore, it is the recommended version no matter which drive you use.

I once had a student ask me how to tell an 80-conductor cable from a 40-conductor cable. The simple answer is to count the ridges (conductors) in the cable. If you count only 40, it must be a 40-conductor cable, and if you count to 80...well, you get the idea! If you observe them side by side, the difference is clear: The 80-conductor cable has an obviously smoother, less ridged appearance than the 40-conductor cable.

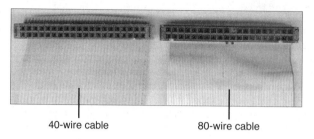

40-wire cable   80-wire cable

FIGURE 7.6   A 40-conductor PATA cable (left) and a 80-conductor PATA cable (right).

Note the keying on the 80-conductor cable that is designed to prevent backward installation. Note also that the poorly constructed 40-conductor cable shown in Figure 7.6 lacks keying. Most good 40-conductor cables include the keying; however, because it is optional, many cheaply constructed versions do not include it. Keying was made mandatory for all 80-conductor cables as part of the standard.

Longer or Rounded Cables

The official PATA standard limits cable length to 18 inches (0.46 meters); however, many of the cables sold are longer, up to 36 inches (0.91 meters) or more in length. I've had many readers write me questioning the length, asking, "Why would people sell cables longer than 18 inches if the standard doesn't allow it?" Well, just because something is for sale doesn't mean it conforms to the standards and will work properly! I see improperly designed, poorly manufactured, and nonconforming items for sale all the time. Many people have used the longer cables and their systems seem to work fine, but I've also documented numerous cases where using longer cables has caused problems, so I decided to investigate this issue more thoroughly.

What I discovered is that you can use longer 80-conductor cables reliably up to 27 inches (0.69 meters) in length, but 40-conductor cables should remain limited to 18 inches, just as the standard indicates.

In fact, an attempt was made to change the PATA standard to allow 27-inch cables. If you read www.t13.org/Documents/UploadedDocuments/technical/e00151r0.pdf, you'll see data from a proposal that shows "negligible differences in Ultra DMA Mode 5 signal integrity between a 27-inch, 80-conductor cable and an 18-inch, 80-conductor cable." This extended cable design was actually proposed back in October 2000, but it was never incorporated into the standard. Even though it was never officially approved, I take the information presented in this proposal as empirical evidence for allowing the use of 80-conductor cables up to 27 inches in length without problems.

To that, I would add another recommendation, which is that in general I do not recommend "rounded" ATA cables. A rounded design has not been approved in the ATA standard, and there is some evidence that it can cause problems with crosstalk and noise. The design of 80-conductor cables is such that a ground wire is interspersed between each data wire in the ribbon, and rounding the cable causes some of the data lines to run parallel or adjacent to each other at random, thereby causing crosstalk and noise and resulting in signal errors.

Of course, many people use rounded cables with success, but my knowledge of electrical engineering as well as the ATA standard has always made me somewhat uncomfortable with their use.

PATA Signals

This section describes in more detail some of the most important PATA signals having to do with drive configuration and installation. This information can help you understand how the cable select feature works, for example.

Pin 20 is used as a key pin for cable orientation and is not connected to the interface. This pin should be missing from any ATA connectors, and the cable should have the pin-20 hole in the connector plugged off to prevent the cable from being plugged in backward.

Pin 39 carries the drive active/slave present (DASP) signal, which is a dual-purpose, time-multiplexed signal. During power-on initialization, this signal indicates whether a slave drive is present on the interface. After that, each drive asserts the signal to indicate that it is active. Early drives could not multiplex these functions and required special jumper settings to work with other drives. Standardizing this function to allow for compatible dual-drive installations is one of the features of the ATA standard. This is why some drives require a slave present (SP) jumper, whereas others do not.

Pin 28 carries the cable select signal (CSEL). In some older drives, it could also carry a spindle synchronization signal (SPSYNC), but that is not commonly found on newer drives. The CSEL function is the most widely used and is designed to control the designation of a drive as master (drive 0) or slave (drive 1) without requiring jumper settings on the drives. If a drive sees the CSEL as being grounded, the drive is a master; if CSEL is open, the drive is a slave.

You can install special cabling to ground CSEL selectively. This installation usually is accomplished through a cable that has pin 28 missing from the middle connector but present in the connectors on each end. In that arrangement, with one end plugged into the motherboard and two drives set to cable select, the drive plugged into the end connector is automatically configured as master, whereas the drive attached to the middle connector is configured as slave. Note that although this is the most common arrangement, it is also possible to make cables where the middle connector is master (and the end is slave), or even to use a Y-cable arrangement, with the motherboard ATA bus connector in the middle, and each drive at opposite ends of the cable. In this arrangement, one leg of the Y would have the CSEL line connected through (master), and the other leg would have the CSEL line open (conductor interrupted or removed), making the drive at that end the slave.

PATA Dual-Drive Configurations

Dual-drive PATA installations can be problematic because each drive has its own controller, and both controllers must function while being connected to the same bus. There has to be a way to ensure that only one of the two controllers responds to a command at a time.

The ATA standard provides the option of operating on the AT bus with two drives in a daisy-chained configuration. The primary drive (drive 0) is called the *master*, and the secondary drive (drive 1) is called the *slave*. You designate a drive as being master or slave by setting a jumper or switch on the drive or by using a special line in the interface called the *cable select (CS) pin* and setting the CS jumper on the drive.

When only one drive is installed, the controller responds to all commands from the system. When two drives (and, therefore, two controllers) are installed, both controllers receive all commands from the system. Each controller then must be set up to respond only to commands for itself. In this situation, one controller must be designated as the master and the other as the slave. When the system sends a command for a specific drive, the controller on the other drive must remain silent while the selected controller and drive are functioning. Setting the jumper to master or slave enables discrimination between the two controllers by setting a special bit (the DRV bit) in the drive/head register of a command block.

Configuring ATA drives can be simple, as is the case with most single-drive installations. Or it can be troublesome, especially when it comes to mixing two older drives from different manufacturers on a single cable.

You can configure most ATA drives with four possible settings:

- Master (single drive)
- Master (dual drive)
- Slave (dual drive)
- Cable select

Most drives simplify this to three settings: master, slave, and cable select. Because each ATA drive has its own controller, you must specifically tell one drive to be the master and the other to be the slave. No functional difference exists between the two, except that the drive that's specified as the slave asserts a signal called DASP after a system reset informs the master that a slave drive is present in the system. The master drive then pays attention to the drive select line, which it otherwise ignores. Telling a drive that it's the slave also usually causes it to delay its spin-up for several seconds to allow the master to get going and thus to lessen the load on the system's power supply.

Until the ATA specification, no common implementation for drive configuration was in use. Some drive companies even used different master/slave methods for different models of drives. Because of these incompatibilities, some drives work together only in a specific master/slave or slave/master order. This situation mostly affects older IDE drives introduced before the ATA specification.

Most drives that fully follow the ATA specification now need only one jumper (master/slave) for configuration. A few also need a slave present jumper. Table 7.5 shows the jumper settings that most ATA drives require.

Table 7.5 Jumper Settings for Most ATA-Compatible Drives on Standard (Non–Cable Select) Cables

Jumper Name	Single-Drive	Dual-Drive Master	Dual-Drive Slave
Master (M/S)	On	On	Off
Slave Present (SP)	Off	On	Off
Cable Select (CS)	Off	Off	Off

Note

If a cable select cable is used, the CS jumper should be set to On and all others should be set to Off. The cable connector then determines which drive will be master or slave.

Figure 7.7 shows the jumpers on a typical ATA drive.

The master jumper indicates that the drive is a master or a slave. Some drives also require a slave present jumper, which is used only in a dual-drive setup and then installed only on the master drive, which is somewhat confusing. This jumper tells the master that a slave drive is attached. With many PATA drives, the master jumper is optional and can be left off. Installing this jumper doesn't hurt in these cases and can eliminate confusion; I recommend that you install the jumpers listed here.

Note

Some drives have these jumpers on the drive circuit board on the bottom of the drive, and as such they might not be visible on the rear.

To eliminate confusion over master/slave settings, most newer systems now use the cable select option. This involves two things. The first is having a special PATA cable that has all the wires except pin 28 running from the motherboard connector to both drive connectors. Pin 28 is used for cable select and is connected to one of the drive connectors (labeled master) and not to the other (labeled slave). Both drives are then configured in cable select mode via the CS jumper on each drive.

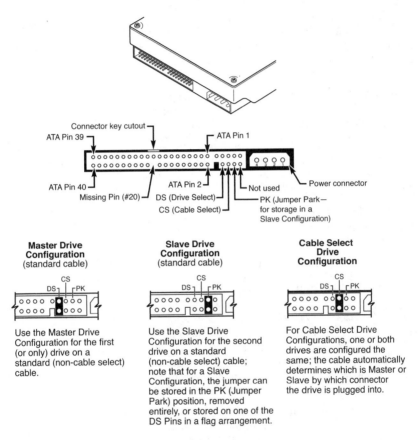

FIGURE 7.7   PATA (IDE) drive jumpers for most drives.

With cable select, the drive that receives signals on pin 28 automatically becomes the master, and the other becomes the slave. Most cables implement this by removing the metal insulation displacement bit from the pin-28 hole, which can be difficult to see at a glance. Other cables have a section of pin 28 visibly cut from the cable somewhere along the ribbon. Because this is such a minor modification to the cable and can be difficult to see, cable select cables typically have the connectors labeled master, slave, and system, indicating that the cable controls these options rather than the drive. All 80-conductor Ultra-ATA cables are designed to use cable select.

With cable select, you simply set the CS jumper on all drives and then plug the drive you want to be the master into the connector labeled master on the cable and the drive you want to be the slave into the connector labeled slave.

The only downside I see to using cable select is that it can restrict how the cable is routed or where you mount the drive that is to be master versus slave because they must be plugged into specific cable connector positions.

PATA PIO Transfer Modes

ATA-2 and ATA-3 defined the first of several higher-performance modes for transferring data over the PATA interface, to and from the drive. These faster modes were the main part of the newer specifications and were the main reason they were initially developed. The following section discusses these modes.

The PIO (programmed I/O) mode determines how fast data is transferred to and from the drive using PIO transfers. In the slowest possible mode—PIO Mode 0—the data cycle time can't exceed 600 nanoseconds (ns). In a single cycle, 16 bits are transferred into or out of the drive, making the theoretical transfer rate of PIO Mode 0 (600ns cycle time) 3.3MBps, whereas PIO Mode 4 (120ns cycle time) achieves a 16.6MBps transfer rate.

Most motherboards with ATA-2 or greater support have dual ATA connectors on the motherboard. Most of the motherboard chipsets include the ATA interface in their South Bridge components, which in most systems is tied into the PCI bus.

Older 486 and some early Pentium boards have only the primary connector running through the system's PCI local bus. The secondary connector on those boards usually runs through the ISA bus and therefore supports up to Mode 2 operation only.

When interrogated with an `Identify Drive` command, a hard disk returns, among other things, information about the PIO and DMA modes it is capable of using. Most BIOSs automatically set the correct mode to match the capabilities of the drive. If you set a mode faster than the drive can handle, data corruption results.

ATA-2 and newer drives also perform Block Mode PIO, which means they use the Read/Write Multiple commands that greatly reduce the number of interrupts sent to the host processor. This lowers the overhead, and the resulting transfers are even faster.

PATA DMA Transfer Modes

ATA drives support two types of transfers: programmed input/output (PIO), and direct memory access (DMA) transfers. DMA means that the data is transferred directly between drive and memory without using the CPU as an intermediary, as opposed to PIO. This offloads much of the work of transferring data from the processor, in effect allowing the processor to do other things while the transfer is taking place. DMA transfers are much faster than PIO transfers and are supported by all modern ATA devices.

There are two distinct types of direct memory access: singleword (8-bit) and multiword (16-bit). Singleword DMA modes were removed from the ATA-3 and later specifications and are obsolete. DMA modes are also sometimes called *busmaster* ATA modes because they use a host adapter that supports busmastering. Ordinary DMA relies on the legacy DMA controller on the motherboard to perform the complex task of arbitration, grabbing the system bus and transferring the data. In the case of busmastering DMA, all this is done by a higher-speed logic chip in the host adapter interface (which is also on the motherboard).

Systems using the Intel PIIX (PCI IDE ISA eXcelerator) and later South Bridge chips (or equivalent) can support busmaster ATA. The singleword and multiword busmaster ATA modes and transfer rates are shown in Tables 7.6 and 7.7, respectively.

Table 7.6   Singleword (8-Bit) DMA Modes and Transfer Rates

8-Bit DMA Mode	Bus Width (Bits)	Cycle Speed (ns)	Bus Speed (MHz)	Cycles per Clock	Transfer Rate (MBps)	ATA Specification
0	16	960	1.04	1	2.08	ATA-1*
1	16	480	2.08	1	4.17	ATA-1*
2	16	240	4.17	1	8.33	ATA-1*

Singleword (8-bit) DMA modes were removed from the ATA-3 and later specifications.

Table 7.7   Multiword (16-Bit) DMA Modes and Transfer Rates

16-Bit DMA Mode	Bus Width (Bits)	Cycle Speed (ns)	Bus Speed (MHz)	Cycles per Clock	Transfer Rate (MBps)	ATA Specification
0	16	480	2.08	1	4.17	ATA-1
1	16	150	6.67	1	13.33	ATA-2*
2	16	120	8.33	1	16.67	ATA-2*

ATA-2 was also referred to as EIDE (Enhanced IDE) or Fast-ATA.

Note that multiword DMA modes are also called *busmaster DMA modes* by some manufacturers. Unfortunately, even the fastest multiword DMA Mode 2 results in the same 16.67MBps transfer speed as PIO Mode 4. However, even though the transfer speed is the same as PIO, because DMA offloads much of the work from the processor, overall system performance is higher. Even so, multiword DMA modes were never very popular and have been superseded by the newer Ultra-DMA modes supported in devices that are compatible with ATA-4 through ATA-7.

Table 7.8 shows the Ultra-DMA modes now supported in the ATA-4 through ATA-7 specifications. Note that you need to install the correct drivers for your host adapter and version of Windows to use this feature.

Table 7.8   Ultra-DMA Support in ATA-4 Through ATA-7

Ultra DMA Mode	Bus Width (Bits)	Cycle Speed (ns)	Bus Speed (MHz)	Cycles per Clock	Transfer Rate (MBps)	ATA Specification
0	16	240	4.17	2	16.67	ATA-4
1	16	160	6.25	2	25.00	ATA-4
2	16	120	8.33	2	33.33	ATA-4
3	16	90	11.11	2	44.44	ATA-5
4	16	60	16.67	2	66.67	ATA-5
5	16	40	25.00	2	100.00	ATA-6
6	16	30	33.00	2	133.00	ATA-7

ATA-4 UDMA Mode 2 is sometimes called Ultra-ATA/33 or ATA-33.
ATA-5 UDMA Mode 4 is sometimes called Ultra-ATA/66 or ATA-66.
ATA-6 UDMA Mode 5 is sometimes called Ultra-ATA/100 or ATA-100.
ATA-7 UDMA Mode 6 is sometimes called Ultra-ATA/133 or ATA-133.

SATA

The development of ATA-8 marked the beginning of the end for the PATA standard that has been in use since 1986. Sending data at rates faster than 133MBps down a parallel ribbon cable originally designed for only 8.3Mbps is fraught with all kinds of problems because of signal timing, electromagnetic interference (EMI), and other integrity problems. The solution, Serial ATA, is an evolutionary replacement for the venerable PATA physical storage interface. When set in non-AHCI/RAID modes (in other words, IDE or legacy mode), SATA is software-compatible with PATA, which means it emulates all the commands, registers, and controls so existing software can run without changes. In other words, the existing BIOSs, operating systems, and utilities that work on PATA also work with SATA.

Of course, they do differ physically—that is, you can't plug PATA drives into SATA host adapters, and vice versa, although signal converters do make that possible. The physical changes are all for the better because SATA uses much smaller and thinner cables with only seven conductors that are easier to route inside the PC and easier to plug in with smaller, redesigned cable connectors. The interface chip designs also are improved, with far fewer pins and lower voltages. All these improvements are designed to eliminate the design problems inherent in PATA.

Figure 7.8 shows the official Serial ATA International Organization working group logo that identifies most SATA devices.

FIGURE 7.8   Serial ATA official logo, which identifies SATA devices.

Although SATA didn't immediately replace PATA, most systems sold following SATA's standardization included SATA interfaces alongside PATA interfaces. Over time, SATA has predominantly replaced PATA as the de facto standard internal storage device interface found in PCs, and most current systems lack PATA support. However, some motherboards and devices with PATA support are still available, and where repairs are considered they will likely remain available at a minimum level for some time.

SATA Standards and Performance

Development for SATA started when the Serial ATA Working Group effort was announced at the Intel Developer Forum in February 2000. The initial members of the Serial ATA Working Group included APT Technologies, Dell, IBM, Intel, Maxtor, Quantum, and Seagate. The original group later became known as the Serial ATA II Working Group, and finally in July 2004, it became the Serial ATA International Organization. These groups have released the following SATA specifications:

- The first SATA 1.0 draft specification was released in November 2000 and was officially published as a final specification in August 2001.

- The first SATA II Working Group extensions to this specification, which made SATA suitable for network storage, were released in October 2002.

- SATA Revision 2 was released in April 2004. It added the 3Gbps (300MBps) signaling speed.

- SATA Revision 2.5 was released in August 2005. It added Native Command Queuing (NCQ), staggered spin-up, hot plug, port multiplier, and eSATA support.

- SATA Revision 2.6 was released in March 2007. It added new internal Slimline and Micro cables and connectors as well as modifications to NCQ.

- SATA Revision 3.0 was released in 2009. It added the 6Gbps (600MBps) signaling speed.

- SATA Revision 3.1 was released in 2011. It added improvements in power management, hardware control, and a Queued Trim Command for improving SSD performance.

- SATA Revision 3.2 was released in 2013. It adds a new interface called SATA Express, which uses SATA commands over a PCIe hardware interface for transfer speeds up to 16Gbps.

You can download the specifications from the Serial ATA International Organization website at www.serialata.org. Since forming, the group has grown to include more than 200 contributor and adopter companies from all areas of industry.

Systems using SATA were released in late 2002 using discrete PCI interface boards and chips. SATA was integrated directly into motherboard chipsets in April 2003 with the introduction of the Intel ICH5 chipset component. Since then, virtually all new motherboard chipsets have included SATA.

The performance of SATA is impressive, although current hard drive designs can't fully take advantage of its bandwidth. Solid State Drives (SSDs), on the other hand, can and do take advantage of all of the bandwidth that SATA has to offer and are the driving force for the introduction of even higher bandwidth standards. Three main variations of the original standard use the same cables and connectors; they differ only in transfer rate performance. SATA Express, in contrast, uses new cables and connectors for dramatically increased throughput. Table 7.9 shows the bandwidth specifications; devices supporting the second-generation 300MBps (3Gbps) version became available in 2005, and devices supporting the third-generation 600MBps (6Gbps) versions became available in 2011. SATA Express devices are expected to be available in 2014.

Table 7.9 SATA Transfer Modes

SATA Type	Signal Rate (Gbps)	Bus Width (Bits)	Bus Speed (MHz)	Data Cycles per Clock	Throughput
SATA-150	1.5	1	1,500	1	150
SATA-300	3.0	1	3,000	1	300
SATA-600	6.0	1	6,000	1	600
SATA Express	8.0	2	16,000	1	1,969*

*Note SATA Express uses 128b/130b encoding, which is 98.5% efficient vs. the 80% efficient 8b/10b encoding used by SATA.

SATA Express

The advent of high-performance SSD (solid-state drive) storage has pushed the need for greater and greater interface bandwidth. SATA 3.0 offers up to 600MBps throughput, which by 2011 many SSDs could deliver. Since then the development of faster and faster drives has been mostly limited by the interface bandwith, and that SATA had become the bottleneck. To eliminate this bottleneck, the Serial ATA International Organization (SATA-IO) first studied doubling the SATA 6Gbps rate to 12Gbps;

however, they found that doing so required extensive (and expensive) changes in cabling and signaling, not to mention that development would take some time. Instead, they decided to take a much easier way out by using the existing PCI Express interface. SATA-IO first announced in 2011 that it was developing a faster version of SATA called SATA Express, which was finally completed and published in 2013 as part of the SATA 3.2 specification.

SATA Express combines PCI Express signaling with the SATA software protocol (command set), plus a new set of cables and connectors that are backward compatible with SATA. When using PCIe 3.0 signaling, SATA Express offers up to 16Gbps in raw data throughput, which translates to nearly 2 gigabytes per second of actual data bandwidth. That is nearly 3.3 times faster than conventional SATA at 600MBps.

Not only is the SATA Express signaling speed much faster, but it is also more efficient, resulting in even higher bandwiths than the raw signaling rate would imply. Conventional SATA uses 8b/10b encoding, which is 80% efficient. That means that 8 out of every 10 bits (or 80%) in the raw data stream are actual data; the other 2 bits (or 20%) are overhead. SATA Express uses the more advanced 128b/130b encoding scheme found in PCI Express 3.0, which is an incredible 98.5% efficient, with only 1.5% overhead. This is achieved by scrambling the raw data to be sent using a known binary polynomial and then unscrambling it at the other end using the inverse polynomial. Because SATA Express uses two PCIe lanes with up to 8Gbps per lane, combined with the more efficient encoding, the end result is a whopping 1,969MBps maximum throughput as compared to 600MBps for conventional SATA.

SATA Express uses a wider cable with 18 conductors vs. the 7 conductors in a standard SATA cable. SATA Express motherboard connectors are backward compatible with SATA, meaning you can plug one or two standard SATA cables into a single SATA Express connector (see Figure 7.9). Connecting conventional SATA drives to a SATA Express port causes the port to shift down to conventional SATA mode.

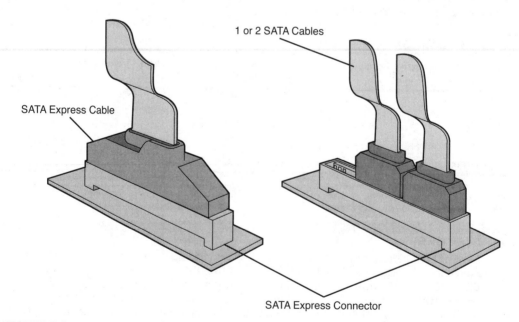

1 or 2 SATA Cables

SATA Express Cable

SATA Express Connector

FIGURE 7.9   SATA Express motherboard and cable connectors, showing backward compatibility with conventional SATA.

With SATA Express offering more than three times the throughput of conventional SATA, high-performance storage devices like SSDs will become even faster in the future.

SATA Cables and Connectors

From Table 7.9, you can see that conventional SATA sends data only a single bit at a time, while SATA Express sends 2 bits. The cable used for SATA has only seven wires (four signal and three ground) and is a thin design, with keyed connectors only 14mm (0.55 inches) wide on each end. This eliminates problems with airflow compared to the wider PATA ribbon cables. Each cable has connectors only at each end, and each cable connects the device directly to the host adapter (typically on the motherboard). There are no master/slave settings because each cable supports only a single device. The cable ends are interchangeable; the connector on the motherboard is the same as on the device, and both cable ends are identical. Maximum SATA cable length is 1 meter (39.37 inches), which is considerably longer than the 18-inch maximum for PATA.

Although SATA-600 uses the same cables and connectors as the previous (slower) versions, it does place higher demands for quality, so some manufacturers will mark higher quality cables with a rating like "SATA 6Gbps." One issue that becomes more of a problem is bending cables. Data moving at the higher 3Gbps and 6Gbps rates can be corrupted when encountering a severe right-angle bend, so it is recommended that when routing SATA cables you do not crimp or bend them sharply with a pliers; use more gradual curves or bends instead. Note that this does not apply to cables with right-angle connectors; the wires in the connectors have multiple bends or curve instead.

SATA uses a special encoding scheme called 8b/10b to encode and decode data sent along the cable. IBM initially developed (and patented) the 8b/10b transmission code in the early 1980s for use in high-speed data communications. Many high-speed data transmission standards, including Gigabit Ethernet, Fibre Channel, FireWire, and others, use this encoding scheme. The main purpose of the 8b/10b encoding scheme is to guarantee that never more than four 0s (or 1s) are transmitted consecutively. This is a form of Run Length Limited (RLL) encoding called RLL 0,4, in which the 0 represents the minimum and the 4 represents the maximum number of consecutive 0s or 1s in each encoded character.

The 8b/10b encoding also ensures that there are never more than six or fewer than four 0s (or 1s) in a single encoded 10-bit character. Because 1s and 0s are sent as voltage changes on a wire, this ensures that the spacing between the voltage transitions sent by the transmitter is fairly balanced, with a more regular and steady stream of pulses. This presents a steadier load on the circuits, increasing reliability. The conversion from 8-bit data to 10-bit encoded characters for transmission leaves several 10-bit patterns unused. Many of these additional patterns provide flow control, delimit packets of data, perform error checking, or perform other special functions.

The physical transmission scheme for SATA uses *differential NRZ* (Non Return to Zero). This uses a balanced pair of wires, each carrying +0.25V (one-quarter volt). The signals are sent differentially: If one wire in the pair carries +0.25V, the other wire carries –0.25V, where the differential voltage between the two wires is always 0.5V (one-half volt). So, for a given voltage waveform, the opposite voltage waveform is sent along the adjacent wire. Differential transmission minimizes electromagnetic radiation and makes the signals easier to read on the receiving end.

A 15-pin power cable and power connector is optional with SATA, providing 3.3V power in addition to the 5V and 12V provided via the industry-standard 4-pin device power connectors. Although it has 15 pins, this new power connector design is only 24mm (0.945 inches). With 3 pins designated for each of the 3.3V, 5V, and 12V power levels, enough capacity exists for up to 4.5 amps of current at each voltage, which is plenty for even the most power-hungry drives. For compatibility with existing power supplies, SATA drives can be made with the original, standard 4-pin device power connector or the new 15-pin SATA power connector (or both). If the drive doesn't have the type of connector you need, adapters are available to convert from one type to the other.

Figure 7.10 shows what the SATA signal and power connectors look like, and Figure 7.11 shows SATA and PATA host adapters on a typical motherboard.

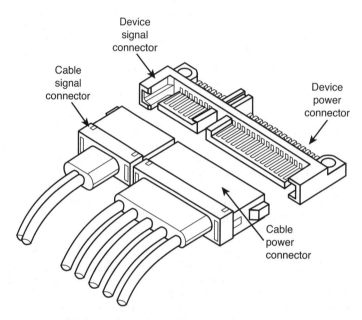

FIGURE 7.10   SATA signal and power connectors on a typical SATA hard drive.

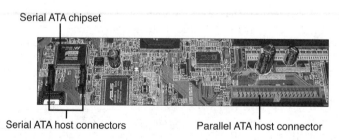

FIGURE 7.11   A motherboard with SATA and PATA host adapters.

The pinouts for the SATA data and optional power connectors are shown in Tables 7.10 and 7.11, respectively.

Table 7.10   SATA Data Connector Pinout

Signal Pin	Signal	Description
S1	Gnd	First mate
S2	A+	Host Transmit +
S3	A-	Host Transmit −

Signal Pin	Signal	Description
S4	Gnd	First mate
S5	B–	Host Receive –
S6	B+	Host Receive +
S7	Gnd	First mate

All pins are in a single row spaced 1.27mm (.050 inches) apart.
All ground pins are longer so they will make contact before the signal/power pins to allow hot-plugging.

Table 7.11 SATA Optional Power Connector Pinout

Signal Pin	Signal	Description
P1	+3.3V	3.3V power
P2	+3.3V	3.3V power
P3	+3.3V	3.3V power
P4	Gnd	First mate
P5	Gnd	First mate
P6	Gnd	First mate
P7	+5V	5V power
P8	+5V	5V power
P9	+5V	5V power
P10	Gnd	First mate
P11	Gnd	First mate
P12	Gnd	First mate
P13	+12V	12V power
P14	+12V	12V power
P15	+12V	12V power

All pins are in a single row spaced 1.27mm (.050 inches) apart.
All ground pins are longer, so they make contact before the signal/power pins to allow hot-plugging.
Three power pins carry 4.5 amps, a maximum current for each voltage.

Mini-SATA (mSATA)

Mini-SATA (mSATA) is a form factor specification developed by Intel for very small solid-state drives (SSDs), primarily in laptop or tablet systems. The mSATA form factor is virtually identical to Mini-PCI Express, which is the form factor used for mobile WLAN (wireless local area network or WiFi) and WWAN (wireless wide-area network) adapters. By using the same card size and shape but with a slightly modified connector design, a Mini-PCIe socket can function in both Mini-PCIe and mSATA modes.

mSATA drives are significantly smaller than the standard 2.5-inch drives used in most laptops (see Figure 7.12).

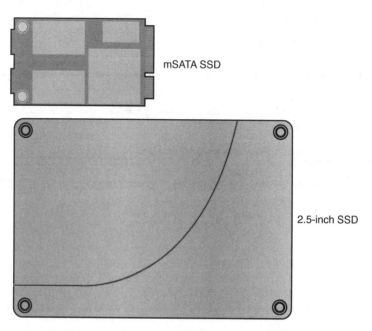

mSATA SSD

2.5-inch SSD

FIGURE 7.12 An mSATA drive compared to a standard 2.5-inch drive.

Tablet devices typically have a dedicated mSATA connector internally, which is designed solely for mSATA SSDs. Many laptops, however, have an internal combination mSATA/WWAN connector, which can accept either an mSATA SSD or a WWAN interface card. Depending on which type of device is installed, the port will automatically switch to the proper mode.

mSATA SSDs are not available in nearly as high capacities as 2.5-inch SSDs, but they are also physically smaller and less expensive. Laptops with mSATA/WWAN ports can have a high-performance mSATA SSD installed as the boot drive, and then use a much cheaper and higher capacity conventional HDD as a data storage drive.

eSATA

When SATA was first released, the ability to run longer cables of up to 1 meter (3.3 ft.) made people think about running cables out of the system to external drives. Some companies jumped on this demand, creating a market for proprietary cable and connector designs allowing SATA drives to be run in external enclosures. Unfortunately, the designs were proprietary, and since SATA cables lacked the shielding and other design criteria to allow external operation, some of the designs were unreliable. Realizing that there was a market for external SATA, the Serial ATA International Organization (SATA-IO) released the official standard for external SATA called eSATA in 2004.

eSATA is a variation on SATA specifically designed for external connections. The main differences between SATA and eSATA are in the cables. eSATA allows for longer cables of up to 2 meters (6.6 ft.), and the cables have extra shielding. The connectors are different both electrically and mechanically as well. They have deeper contacts, metal springs for shielding and mechanical retention, and are designed for up to 5,000 mating cycles vs. only 50 for internal cables. The eSATA cable and port connectors are shown in Figure 7.13.

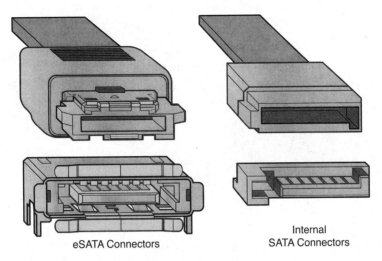

eSATA Connectors

Internal
SATA Connectors

FIGURE 7.13 eSATA (left) and standard internal SATA (right) cable and port connectors compared.

eSATA supports all SATA transfer speeds up to 6Gbps rate (600MBps); however, some are limited to 3Gbps (300MBps) or less. Even at 300MBps, eSATA is significantly faster than other popular external interfaces such as 1394a/FireWire 400 (50MBps) and USB 2.0 (60MBps). In fact, with 300MBps or 600MBps of bandwidth, eSATA is three to six times faster than 1394b/FireWire 800 (100MBps), and even the 3Gbps (300MBps) mode of eSATA is faster than USB 3.0 (5Gbps or 500MBps). How can 300MBps eSATA be faster than 500GBps USB 3.0? One reason is that there is a large amount of overhead in the USB specification to allow for even longer cable lengths (5 meters or 16 ft.), which drops the actual data throughput to well under 400MBps, but the other reality is that any external drive connected via USB 3.0 consists of a SATA drive plus circuitry converting the data from SATA to USB 3.0 inside the enclosure, thereby reducing efficiency even more. When using eSATA, there is no signal conversion inside the external enclosure (eSATA is SATA, after all) making the interface much more efficient. In short, eSATA is just about the ideal connection for external drives, allowing them to work just as if they were internal to the system.

If your system doesn't have an eSATA port built in, you can easily add one using a very inexpensive cable and bracket assembly. The cable will plug into one of your motherboard-based SATA ports, and the other end of the cable will be an eSATA connector mounted in an expansion card bracket (see Figure 7.14). Brackets are available with one or two ports as necessary.

Power Over eSATA (eSATAp)

One drawback to eSATA over USB is that eSATA does not provide power. To rectify this, several manufacturers got together and informally created the eSATA USB Hybrid Port (EUHP) that combines USB and eSATA ports into a single physical connector. The SATA International Organization (SATA-IO) is working to make this an official standard called the Power Over eSATA (eSATAp) specification.

An eSATAp port is basically both a USB port and an eSATA port combined in one single connector (see Figure 7.15). These ports will normally be identified with an "eSATA + USB" notation. They accept standard USB or eSATA cables, and when attached, the proper connections will be made for the desired interface to function. A third option is to plug in an eSATAp cable, which will combine the eSATA and USB signals with +5V or +12V power, allowing the connection of USB, SATA, or eSATAp devices with no separate power adapter necessary. eSATAp ports have become very popular in laptops for connecting high-speed external drives, and you can get bracket adapters to add them to desktop systems (see Figure 7.16).

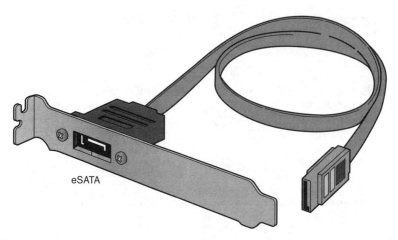

FIGURE 7.14   SATA to eSATA bracket assembly for adding eSATA ports to a system.

FIGURE 7.15   An eSATAP (Power Over eSATA) combination eSATA and USB connector.

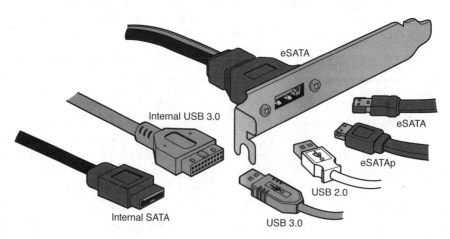

FIGURE 7.16   An eSATAp (Power Over eSATA) bracket showing optional USB 3.0/2.0, eSATAp, and eSATA connections.

There are several variations on eSATAp ports. The USB part of eSATAp can be either USB 2.0 or 3.0, depending on the specific implementation. Just as with standard USB only ports, if the eSATAp port is blue in color, that indicates USB 3.0 capability. Another variation is the eSATA speed. Some supply the full 6Gbps (600MBps) rate of SATA 3.0, while others allow only 3Gbps (300MBps) mode. Finally, another variation is in the power. In most laptop systems, an eSATAp port will only supply +5V power, which is fine for powering external 2.5-inch drives. Desktop versions of eSATAp can supply both +5V and +12V power, allowing external 3.5-inch drives to be powered as well.

Besides allowing faster data transfer than even USB 3.0, connecting external drives using eSATA or eSATAp has another major advantage over USB, and that is bootability. Windows does not allow booting from USB drives; however, drives connected via eSATA or eSATAp do not have that restriction. Windows will treat them the same as if they were internally connected. Using eSATA or eSATAp, one can use and easily swap external bootable drives, a feature especially useful for diagnostics and testing purposes.

SATA Configuration

Configuration of SATA devices is also much simpler because the master/slave or cable select jumper settings used with PATA are no longer necessary.

BIOS setup for SATA drives is also quite simple. Because SATA is based on ATA, autodetection of drive settings on systems with SATA connectors is performed in the same way as on PATA systems. Depending on the system, SATA interfaces will support legacy (usually called "IDE"), AHCI (Advanced Host Controller Interface) or RAID (redundant array of independent disks) modes. In most cases you will want to set AHCI mode for the SATA host adapter to run in its native, most fully featured mode. RAID mode is a superset of AHCI and allows multiple drives to be configured in an array to act as a single drive. (See Chapter 5, "BIOS," for details.)

If you want to use SATA drives but don't want to install a new motherboard with SATA host adapters already included, you can install a separate SATA host adapter into a PCI or PCIe expansion slot (see Figure 7.17). Many of these adapters include RAID capability as well.

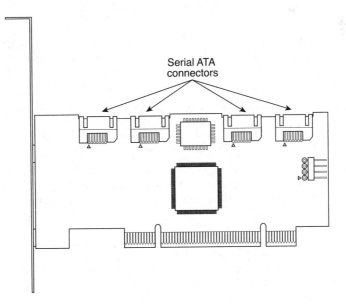

FIGURE 7.17 Typical 4-port SATA RAID host adapter.

Advanced Host Controller Interface (AHCI)

SATA was designed not only as a replacement for PATA, but as an interface that would evolve into something with many more capabilities and features than its predecessor. Initially, compatibility with PATA was one of the most important features of SATA because it enabled a smooth and easy transition from one to the other. This compatibility extends to the driver level, allowing SATA devices to use the same BIOS-level drivers and software as legacy PATA devices.

Although the intent of SATA was to allow an easy transition from PATA, it was also designed to allow future growth and expansion of capabilities. To accomplish this, an enhanced software interface called the *Advanced Host Controller Interface* (AHCI) was initially developed by the AHCI Contributor Group, a group chaired by Intel and originally consisting of AMD, Dell, Marvell, Maxtor, Microsoft, Red Hat, Seagate, and StorageGear. The AHCI Contributor Group released a preliminary version of AHCI v0.95 in May 2003 and released the 1.0 version of the specification in April 2004. You can download the latest version (1.3, released in 2008) from Intel at www.intel.com/technology/serialata/ahci.htm.

AHCI provides an industry-standard, high-performance interface to system driver/OS software for discovering and implementing such advanced SATA features as command queuing, hot-plugging, and power management. AHCI was integrated into SATA-supporting chipsets in 2004 and is supported by AHCI drivers for Windows. The main idea behind AHCI is to have a single driver-level interface supported by all advanced SATA host adapters. This greatly simplifies the installation of operating systems, eliminating the need for custom SATA drivers for each manufacturer's SATA host adapter. For example, Windows Vista and later include AHCI drivers and automatically support any advanced SATA host adapters that are AHCI compatible.

Unfortunately, AHCI drivers are not included by default on the Windows XP and earlier installation CDs, because AHCI was developed long after XP was released. This means, for example, that if you install Windows XP on a system with an integrated SATA host adapter set to AHCI mode, you will probably need to press the F6 key at the beginning of the installation and provide a floppy disk with the AHCI drivers; otherwise, Windows XP will not be able to recognize the drives. The implication here is that the system must include a floppy drive, and you must have copied the drivers to a floppy disk in advance. But what if your system doesn't even include a floppy drive? Fortunately, several solutions are available.

One option is to keep a spare floppy drive in your toolkit and temporarily connect it during the installation. Just open the case, plug in a floppy cable from the floppy drive connector (FDC) on the motherboard to the drive, and connect power to the drive. There is no need to actually mount the drive in the chassis because you will only need to read the disk once at the beginning of the installation.

Another option is to set the SATA host adapter to ATA/IDE compatibility mode (disable AHCI/RAID) in the BIOS Setup, after which you can boot from a standard Windows XP CD and install Windows without requiring special drivers. You could leave the adapter in compatibility mode, but you might be missing out on the performance offered by the advanced capabilities your hard drives support.

Although the first two options can work in most situations, I think the best overall solution is to simply create a custom Windows XP installation disc that already has the SATA AHCI (and even RAID) drivers preinstalled. This can be accomplished via a somewhat tedious manual integration process for each set of drivers, but to make things really easy you can use the menu-driven BTS DriverPacks from www.driverpacks.net to integrate virtually all the popular mass storage drivers directly into your Windows XP install disc. The DriverPacks allow you to easily add all kinds of drivers to your Windows XP installation discs. For example, in addition to the mass storage drivers, I like to integrate the various processor, chipset, and network (both wired and wireless) drivers because all of these still fit on a CD. If you are willing to move to a DVD instead of a CD, you can fit Windows XP and all of the available XP DriverPacks on a single DVD.

Non-Volatile Memory Express (NVMe)

The Advanced Host Controller Interface (AHCI) has long been the preferred software interface for SATA devices. AHCI can be used with conventional SATA as well as SATA Express devices, allowing both to use the same software interface and therefore the same drivers. While using AHCI mode with SATA Express allows for maximum compatibility, it does not allow for maximum performance when interfacing with low-latency devices like solid-state drives (SSDs), which internally behave more like RAM than a spinning disk. To improve the performance of SSDs connected via high-speed PCI Express–based interfaces like SATA Express, a new software interface called the Non-Volatile Memory Host Controller Interface (NVMHCI) was first defined in 2007 by the NVMHCI Workgroup (www.nvmexpress.org), a group including more than 75 major companies from the computing and storage industries. Owing to its intention on being used in combination with PCIe and SATA Express devices, the NVMHCI specification was subsequently named NVM Express (NVMe), and the NVMe specification 1.0 was published in 2011.

Like AHCI before it, NVMe is a software interface specification that defines the commands and functions for communicating with PCIe or SATA Express devices. SSDs are by nature very low latency devices, a characteristic that NVMe is designed to fully exploit. NVMe is also designed to more fully utilize the parallelism built in to modern systems such as multicore hyper-threaded processors, multi-lane buses, and multi-tasking operating systems. The biggest technical difference between AHCI and NVMe is that AHCI supports a single command queue with up to 32 commands, while NVMe supports up to 64K queues with up to 64K commands per queue. Having many more and much deeper queues allows for commands to be far more rapidly delivered to SSDs, where due to their low-latency characteristics they can be processed much more rapidly than drives with spinning disks.

SATA Express host adapters support both AHCI and NVMe modes. Using AHCI mode will allow for backward compatibility with existing AHCI drivers, while choosing NVMe mode will require new NVMe drivers. Since NVMe drivers were not included by default with Windows 8 and earlier versions, NVMe drivers will need to be supplied during the OS installation procedure for Windows to recognize any devices connected to SATA Express host adapters in NVMe mode. Using AHCI mode instead, you can install Windows Vista and later on SATA Express drives right out of the box, with no additional drivers necessary; however, there will be some loss in performance.

SATA Transfer Modes

SATA transfers data in a completely different manner from PATA. As indicated previously, the transfer rates are 1.5Gbps (150MBps), 3Gbps (300MBps), and 6Gbps (600MBps), with most drives today supporting the 3Gbps or 6Gbps rates. Note that speeds are backward compatible—for example, drives supporting the 6Gbps rate also work at 3Gbps or 1.5Gbps. Note that because SATA is designed to be backward compatible with PATA, some confusion can result because the BIOS and drives can report speeds and modes that emulate PATA settings for backward compatibility.

For example, many motherboards detect and report a SATA drive as supporting Ultra DMA Mode 5 (ATA/100), which is a PATA mode operating at 100MBps. This is obviously incorrect because even the slowest SATA mode (1.5Gbps) is 150MBps, and Ultra DMA modes simply do not apply to SATA drives.

PATA and SATA are completely different electrical and physical specifications, but SATA does *emulate* PATA in a way that makes it completely software transparent. In fact, the PATA emulation in SATA specifically conforms to the ATA-5 specification.

This is especially apparent in the `IDENTIFY DEVICE` command that the autodetect routines use in the BIOS to read the drive parameters. The SATA specification indicates that many of the items returned by `IDENTIFY DEVICE` are to be "set as indicated in ATA/ATAPI-5," including available UDMA modes and settings.

The SATA 1 specification also says,

> Emulation of parallel ATA device behavior, as perceived by the host BIOS or software driver, is a cooperative effort between the device and the SATA host adapter hardware. The behavior of Command and Control Block registers, PIO and DMA data transfers, resets, and interrupts are emulated. The host adapter contains a set of registers that shadow the contents of the traditional device registers, referred to as the Shadow Register Block. All SATA devices behave like Device 0 devices. Devices shall ignore the DEV bit in the Device/Head field of received Register FISs, and it is the responsibility of the host adapter to gate transmission of Register FISs to devices, as appropriate, based on the value of the DEV bit.

This means the shadow register blocks are "fake" PATA registers, allowing all ATA commands, modes, and so on to be emulated. SATA was designed to be fully software compatible with ATA/ATAPI-5, which is why a SATA drive can report in some ways as if it were PATA or running in PATA modes, even though it isn't.

ATA Features

The ATA standards have gone a long way toward eliminating incompatibilities and problems with interfacing SATA and PATA drives to systems. The ATA specifications define the signals on the cables and connectors, the functions and timings of these signals, the cable specifications, the supported commands, the features, and so on. The following section lists some of the elements and functions the ATA specifications define.

ATA Commands

One of the best features of the ATA interface is the enhanced command set. The ATA command interface was modeled after the WD1003 controller IBM used in the original AT system. All ATA drives must support the original WD command set (eight commands) with no exceptions, which is why ATA drives are so easy to install in systems today. All IBM-compatible systems have built-in ROM BIOS support for the WD1003, so they essentially support ATA as well.

In addition to supporting all the WD1003 commands, the ATA specification added numerous other commands to enhance performance and capabilities. These commands are an optional part of the ATA interface, but several of them are used in most drives available today and are important to the performance and use of ATA drives in general.

Perhaps the most important is the IDENTIFY DEVICE command. This command causes the drive to transmit a 512-byte block of data that provides all details about the drive. Through this command, any program (including the system BIOS) can find out exactly which type of drive is connected, including the drive manufacturer, model number, operating parameters, and even serial number of the drive. Many modern BIOSs use this information to automatically receive and enter the drive's parameters into Complementary Metal Oxide Semiconductor (CMOS) memory, eliminating the need for the user to enter these parameters manually during system configuration. This arrangement helps prevent mistakes that can later lead to data loss when the user no longer remembers what parameters he used during setup.

The Identify Device data can tell you many things about your drive, including the following:

- Whether the drive has rotating media (and if so, how fast), or whether it is a solid-state drive (SSD) instead
- Whether the TRIM command is supported (or not) on SSDs
- Number of logical block addresses available using LBA mode

- Number of physical cylinders, heads, and sectors available in P-CHS mode
- Number of logical cylinders, heads, and sectors in the current translation L-CHS mode
- Transfer modes (and speeds) supported
- Manufacturer and model number
- Internal firmware revision
- Serial number
- Buffer type/size, indicating sector buffering or caching capabilities
- What security functions are available, and much, much more

Several freely available programs such as HWiNFO (www.hwinfo.com) or CrystalDiskInfo (www.crystalmark.info) can execute this command, then translate and report the information onscreen.

Many other enhanced commands are available, including room for a given drive manufacturer to implement what are called *vendor-unique* commands. Certain vendors often use these commands for features unique to that vendor. Often, vendor-unique commands control features such as low-level formatting and defect management. This is why low-level format or initialization programs can be so specific to a particular manufacturer's ATA drives and why many manufacturers make their own LLF programs available.

ATA Security Mode

Support for drive passwords (called *ATA Security Mode*) was added to the ATA-3 specification in 1995. The proposal adopted in the ATA specification was originally from IBM, which had developed this capability and had already begun incorporating it into ThinkPad systems and IBM 2.5-inch drives. Because it was then incorporated into the official ATA-3 standard (finally published in 1997), most other drive and system manufacturers have also adopted this, especially for laptop systems and 2.5-inch and smaller drives. Note that these passwords are *very* secure. If you lose or forget them, they usually cannot be recovered, and you will never be able to access the data on the drive.

More recently, ATA security has been augmented by drives that support internal encryption/decryption using the Advanced Encryption Standard (AES). Drives supporting AES automatically encrypt all data that is written and automatically decrypt the data when it is read. When combined with a password set via ATA Security mode commands, the data on the drive will be unrecoverable even if the HDD password is bypassed or the media (that is, platters or flash memory chips) are removed from the drive and read directly. When AES encryption is employed on a drive with a strong HDD password, without knowing the HDD password there is essentially no way to recover the data. This type of security is recommended for laptops that can easily be lost or stolen.

Drive security passwords are set via the BIOS Setup, but not all systems support this feature. Most laptops support drive security, but many desktops do not. If supported, two types of drive passwords can be set, called *user* and *master*. The user password locks and unlocks the drive, whereas the master password is used only to unlock. You can set a user password only, or you can set user+master, but you cannot set a master password alone.

When a user password is set (with no master), or when both user+master passwords are set, access to the drive is prevented (even if the drive is moved to a different system), unless the user (or master) password is entered upon system startup.

The master password is designed to be an alternative or backup password for system administrators as a master unlock. With both master and user passwords set, the user is told the user password but not the master password. Subsequently, the user can change the user password as desired; however, a system administrator can still gain access by using the master password.

If a user or user+master password is set, the disk must be unlocked at boot time via a BIOS-generated password prompt. The appearance of the prompt varies from system to system. For example, in ThinkPad systems, an icon consisting of a cylinder with a number above it (indicating the drive number) next to a padlock appears onscreen. If the drive password prompt appears, you must enter it; otherwise, you will be denied access to the drive, and the system will not boot.

As with many security features, a workaround might be possible if you forget your password. In this case, at least one company can either restore the drive to operation (with all the data lost) or restore the drive and the data. That company is Nortek. (See www.nortek.on.ca for more information.) The password-removal procedure is relatively expensive (more than the cost of a new drive in most cases), and you must provide proof of ownership when you send in the drive. As you can see, password restoring is worthwhile only if you absolutely need the data back. Note that even this will not work if the drive employs internal AES encryption. In that case, without the password, the data simply cannot be recovered.

Passwords are not preset on a new drive, but they might be preset if you are buying a used drive or if the people or company you purchased the drive or system from entered them. This is a common ploy when selling drives or systems (especially laptops) on eBay—for example, the seller might set supervisor or drive passwords and hold them until payment is received. Or he might be selling a used (possibly stolen) product "as is," for which he doesn't have the passwords, which renders them useless to the purchaser. Be sure that you do not purchase a used laptop or drive unless you are certain that no supervisor or drive passwords are set.

Most systems also support other power-on or supervisor passwords in the BIOS Setup. In most systems, when you set a supervisor password, it automatically sets the drive password to the same value. In most cases, if a supervisor password is set and it matches the drive user or master password, when you enter the supervisor password, the BIOS automatically enters the drive password at the same time. This means that even though a drive password is set, you might not even know it because the drive password is entered automatically at the same time that you enter the supervisor password; therefore, you won't see a separate prompt for the drive password. However, if the drive is later separated from the system, it will not work on another system or be readable until you enter the correct drive password. Without the services of a company such as Nortek, you can remove a drive password only if you know the password to begin with.

Host Protected Area

Most PCs sold on the market today include some form of automated product recovery or restoration feature that allows a user to easily restore the operating system and other software on the system to the state it was in when the system was new. Originally, this was accomplished via one or more product-recovery discs containing automated scripts that reinstalled all the software that came preinstalled on the system when it was new.

Unfortunately, the discs could be lost or damaged, they were often problematic to use, and including them by default cost manufacturers a lot of money. This prompted PC manufacturers to move the recovery software to a hidden partition of the boot hard drive. However, this does waste some space on the drive—usually several gigabytes. With 60GB or larger drives, this amounts to 5% or less of the total space. Still, even the hidden partition was less than satisfactory because the partition could easily be damaged or overwritten by partitioning software or other utilities, so there was no way to make it secure.

In 1996, Gateway proposed a change to the ATA-4 standard under development that would allow the HPA to be reserved on a drive. This change was ratified, and the HPA feature set was incorporated into the ATA-4 specification that was finally published in 1998. A separate BIOS firmware interface specification called Protected Area Run Time Interface Extension Services (PARTIES) was initiated in

1999 that defined services an operating system could use to access the HPA. The PARTIES standard was completed and published in 2001 as "NCITS 346-2001, Protected Area Run Time Interface Extension Services."

The HPA works by using the optional ATA SET MAX ADDRESS command to make the drive appear to the system as slightly smaller. Anything from the new max address (the newly reported end of the drive) to the true end of the drive is considered the HPA and is accessible only using PARTIES commands. This is more secure than a hidden partition because any data past the end of the drive simply cannot be seen by a normal application or even a partitioning utility. Still, if you want to remove the HPA, you can use some options in the BIOS Setup or separate commands to reset the max address, thus exposing the HPA. At that point, you can run something such as Parted Magic or Partition Commander to resize the adjacent partition to include the extra space that was formerly hidden and unavailable.

Starting in 2003, some systems using Phoenix BIOS have included recovery software and diagnostics in the HPA. Most if not all current drives support the HPA command set; however, because of the complexity in dealing with the hidden area, I have seen most manufacturers back away from using the HPA and revert to a more standard (and easier to deal with) hidden partition instead.

◄◄ For more information on the HPA and what might be stored there, see the Chapter 5 section, "Preboot Environment," **p. 287**.

ATAPI

ATAPI is a standard designed to provide the commands necessary for devices such as optical drives, removable media drives such as SuperDisk and Zip, and tape drives that plug into an ordinary SATA or PATA (IDE) connector. Although ATAPI optical drives use the hard disk interface, they don't necessarily look like ordinary hard disks. To the contrary, from a software point of view, they are a completely different kind of animal. They most closely resemble a SCSI device. All modern ATA optical drives support the ATAPI protocols, and generally the terms are synonymous. In other words, an ATAPI optical drive is an ATA optical drive, and vice versa.

Caution

Most systems starting in 1998 began supporting the Phoenix El Torito specification, which enables booting from ATAPI CD or DVD drives. Systems without El Torito support in the BIOS can't boot from an ATAPI CD or DVD drive. Even with ATAPI support in the BIOS, you still must load a driver to use ATAPI under DOS or Windows. Windows 95 and later (including 98 and Me) and Windows NT (including Windows 2000 forward) have native ATAPI support. Some versions of the Windows 98 and Me CD-ROMs are bootable, whereas all Windows NT, 2000, and newer discs are directly bootable on those systems, thus greatly easing installation.

ATA Drive Capacity Limitations

ATA interface versions up through ATA-5 suffered from a drive capacity limitation of about 137GB (billion bytes). Depending on the BIOS used, you can further reduce this limitation to 8.4GB, or even as low as 528MB (million bytes). This is due to limitations in both the BIOS and the ATA interface, which when combined create even further limitations. To understand these limits, you have to look at the BIOS (software) and ATA (hardware) interfaces together.

Note

In addition to the BIOS/ATA limitations discussed in this section, various operating system limitations exist. These are described later in this chapter.

The limitations when dealing with ATA drives are those of the ATA interface as well as the BIOS interface used to talk to the drive. A summary of the limitations is shown in Table 7.12.

Table 7.12   ATA/IDE Capacity Limitations for Various Sector Addressing Methods

Sector Addressing Method	Total Sectors Calculation	Maximum Total Sectors	Maximum Capacity (Bytes)	Capacity (Decimal)	Capacity (Binary)
CHS: BIOS w/o TL	1024 × 16 × 63	1,032,192	528,482,304	528.48MB	504.00MiB
CHS: BIOS w/ bit-shift TL	1024 × 240 × 63	15,482,880	7,927,234,560	7.93GB	7.38GiB
CHS: BIOS w/ LBA-assist TL	1024 × 255 × 63	16,450,560	8,422,686,720	8.42GB	7.84GiB
CHS: BIOS INT13h	1024 × 256 × 63	16,515,072	8,455,716,864	8.46GB	7.88GiB
CHS: ATA-1/ ATA-5	65536 × 16 × 255	267,386,880	136,902,082,560	136.90GB	127.50GiB
LBA: ATA-1/ ATA-5	2^{28}	268,435,456	137,438,953,472	137.44GB	128.00GiB
LBA: ATA-6+	2^{48}	281,474,976,710,655	144,115,188,075,855,872	144.12PB	128.00PiB
LBA: EDD BIOS	2^{64}	18,446,744,073, 709,551,616	9,444,732,965,739, 290,427,392	9.44ZB	8.00ZiB

BIOS = Basic input/output system
ATA = AT Attachment (IDE)
CHS = Cylinder head sector
LBA = Logical block (sector) address
w/ = with
w/o = without
TL = Translation
INT13h = Interrupt 13 hex
EDD = Enhanced Disk Drive specification (Phoenix/ATA)

MB = megabyte (million bytes)
MiB = mebibyte
GB = gigabyte (billion bytes)
GiB = gibibyte
PB = petabyte (quadrillion bytes)
PiB = pebibyte
ZB = zettabyte (sextillion bytes)
ZiB = zebibyte

This section details the differences between the various sector-addressing methods and the limitations incurred by using them.

Prefixes for Decimal and Binary Multiples

Many readers are unfamiliar with the MiB (mebibyte), GiB (gibibyte), and so on designations I am using in this section and throughout the book. These are part of a standard designed to eliminate confusion between decimal- and binary-based multiples, especially in computer systems. Standard SI (system international or metric system) units are based on multiples of 10. This worked well for most things, but not for computers, which operate in a binary world where most numbers are based on powers of 2. This has resulted in different meanings being assigned to the same prefix—for example, 1KB (kilobyte) could mean either 1,000 (10^3) bytes or 1,024 (2^{10}) bytes. To eliminate confusion, in December 1998 the International Electrotechnical Commission (IEC) approved as an international standard the prefix names and symbols for binary multiples used in data processing and transmission. Some of these prefixes are shown in Table 7.13.

Table 7.13 Standard Prefix Names and Symbols for Decimal and Binary Multiples

Binary Prefixes:				Binary Prefixes:				
Factor	**Symbol**	**Name**	**Value**	**Factor**	**Symbol**	**Name**	**Derivation**	**Value**
10^3	k	Kilo	1,000	2^{10}	Ki	Kibi	Kilobinary	1,024
10^6	M	Mega	1,000,000	2^{20}	Mi	Mebi	Megabinary	1,048,576
10^9	G	Giga	1,000,000,000	2^{30}	Gi	Gibi	Gigabinary	1,073,741,824
10^{12}	T	Tera	1,000,000,000,000	2^{40}	Ti	Tebi	Terabinary	1,099,511,627,776
10^{15}	P	Peta	1,000,000,000,000,000	2^{50}	Pi	Pebi	Petabinary	1,125,899,906,842,624
10^{18}	E	Exa	1,000,000,000,000,000,000	2^{60}	Ei	Exbi	Exabinary	1,152,921,504,606,846,976
10^{21}	Z	Zetta	1,000,000,000,000,000,000,000	2^{70}	Zi	Zebi	Zettabinary	1,180,591,620,717,411,303,424

The symbol for kilo (k) is in lowercase (which is technically correct according to the SI standard), whereas all other decimal prefixes are uppercase.

Under this standard terminology, a megabyte would be 1,000,000 bytes, whereas a mebibyte would be 1,048,576 bytes.

Note

For more information on these industry-standard decimal and binary prefixes, check out the National Institute for Standards and Technology (NIST) website at http://physics.nist.gov/cuu/Units/prefixes.html.

BIOS Limitations

Motherboard ROM BIOSs have been updated throughout the years to support larger and larger drives. Table 7.14 shows the most important relative dates when drive capacity limits were changed.

Table 7.14 Dates of Changes to Drive Capacity Limitations in the ROM BIOS

BIOS Date	Capacity Limit
August 1994	528MB
January 1998	8.4GB
September 2002	137GB
January 2011	2.2TB*

*Note: A UEFI BIOS or enabled UEFI Boot option is required to boot from 2.2TB or larger drives. Some BIOS, had this capability as early as 2006, but it wasn't widespread until 2011.

These dates are when the limits were broken, such that BIOSs older than August 1994 are generally limited to drives of up to 528MB, whereas BIOSs older than January 1998 are generally limited to 8.4GB. Most BIOSs dated 1998 or newer support drives up to 137GB, and those dated September 2002 or newer should support drives larger than 137GB. These are only general guidelines, though; to accurately determine this for a specific system, you should check with your motherboard manufacturer. You can also use the System Information for Windows (SIW) utility from http://gtopala.com/, which tells you the BIOS date from your system and specifically whether your system supports the Enhanced Disk Drive specification (which means drives over 8.4GB).

If your BIOS does not support EDD (drives over 8.4GB), the three possible solutions are as follows:

- Upgrade your motherboard BIOS to a 1998 or newer version that supports >8.4GB.
- Install a BIOS upgrade card, such as the UltraATA cards from www.siig.com.
- Install a software patch to add >8.4GB support.

Of these, the first one is the most desirable because it is usually free. Visit your motherboard manufacturer's website to see whether it has newer BIOSs available for your motherboard that support large drives. If it doesn't, the next best thing is to use a card such as one of the UltraATA cards from SIIG (www.siig.com). I almost never recommend the software-only solution because it merely installs a software patch in the boot sector area of the hard drive, which can result in numerous problems when booting from different drives, installing new drives, or recovering data.

The most recent 2.2TB barrier is not a true BIOS barrier in the same way that the previous barriers were. The issue here is not that the BIOS can't recognize drives 2.2TB or larger; the problem is that it can't normally *boot* from them. Booting from a 2.2TB or larger drive requires a UEFI (Unified Extensible Firmware Interface) BIOS, or at a minimum one with an enabled UEFI Boot option. Drives larger than 2.2TB can be used as data drives even without a UEFI BIOS. Finally, note that both booting from and recognizing a 2.2TB or larger drive as a data drive also requires that the drive be formatted using a GPT (GUID Partition Table). The operating system must have GPT support as well.

CHS Versus LBA

There are two primary methods to address (or number) sectors on an ATA drive. The first method is called *CHS* (cylinder head sector) after the three respective coordinate numbers used to address each sector of the drive. The second method is called *LBA* (logical block address) and uses a single number to address each sector on a drive. CHS was derived from the physical way drives were constructed (and is how they work internally), whereas LBA evolved as a simpler and more logical way to number the sectors regardless of the internal physical construction.

▶▶ For more information on cylinders, heads, and sectors as they are used internally within the drive, see the Chapter 9 section, "HDD Operation," **p. 466**.

The process of reading a drive sequentially in CHS mode starts with cylinder 0, head 0, and sector 1 (which is the first sector on the disk). Next, all the remaining sectors on that first track are read; then the next head is selected; and then all the sectors on that track are read. This goes on until all the heads on the first cylinder are read. Then the next cylinder is selected, and the sequence starts again. Think of CHS as an odometer of sorts: The sector numbers must roll over before the head number can change, and the head numbers must roll over before the cylinder can change.

The process of reading a drive sequentially in LBA mode starts with sector 0, then 1, then 2, and so on. The first sector on the drive in CHS mode would be 0,0,1, and the same sector in LBA mode would be 0.

As an example, imagine a drive with one platter, two heads (both sides of the platter are used), two tracks on each platter (cylinders), and two sectors on each track. We would say the drive has two cylinders (tracks per side), two heads (sides), and two sectors per track. This would result in a total capacity of eight ($2 \times 2 \times 2$) sectors. Noting that cylinders and heads begin numbering from 0—whereas physical sectors on a track number from 1. Using CHS addressing, we would say the first sector on the drive is cylinder 0, head 0, sector 1 (0,0,1); the second sector is 0,0,2; the third sector is 0,1,1; the fourth sector is 0,1,2; and so on until we get to the last sector, which would be 1,1,2.

Now imagine that we could take the eight sectors and—rather than refer directly to the physical cylinder, head, and sector—number the sectors in order from 0 to 7. Thus, if we wanted to address the fourth sector on the drive, we could reference it as sector 0,1,2 in CHS mode or as sector 3 in LBA mode. Table 7.15 shows the correspondence between CHS and LBA sector numbers for this eight-sector imaginary drive.

Table 7.15   CHS and LBA Sector Numbers for an Imaginary Drive with Two Cylinders, Two Heads, and Two Sectors per Track (Eight Sectors Total)

Mode	Equivalent Sector Numbers							
CHS:	0,0,1	0,0,2	0,1,1	0,1,2	1,0,1	1,0,2	1,1,1	1,1,2
LBA:	0	1	2	3	4	5	6	7

As you can see from this example, using LBA numbers is simpler and generally easier to handle; however, when the PC was first developed, all BIOS and ATA drive-level addressing was done using CHS addressing.

CHS/LBA and LBA/CHS Conversions

You can address the same sectors in either CHS or LBA mode. The conversion from CHS to LBA is always consistent in that for a given drive, a particular CHS address always converts to a given LBA address, and vice versa. The ATA-1 document specifies a simple formula that can be used to convert CHS parameters to LBA:

$$LBA = (((C \times HPC) + H) \times SPT) + S - 1$$

By reversing this formula, you can convert the other way—that is, from LBA back to CHS:

$$C = int\ (LBA\ /\ SPT\ /\ HPC)$$
$$H = int\ ((LBA\ /\ SPT)\ mod\ HPC)$$
$$S = (LBA\ mod\ SPT) + 1$$

For these formulas, the abbreviations are defined as follows:

LBA = Logical block address

C = Cylinder

H = Head

S = Sector

HPC = Heads per cylinder (total number of heads)

SPT = Sectors per track

int X = Integer portion of X

X mod Y = Modulus (remainder) of X/Y

Using these formulas, you can calculate the LBA for any given CHS address, and vice versa. Given a drive of 16,383 cylinders, 16 heads, and 63 sectors per track, Table 7.16 shows the equivalent CHS and LBA addresses.

Table 7.16   Equivalent CHS and LBA Sector Numbers for a Drive with 16,383 Cylinders, 16 Heads, and 63 Sectors per Track (16,514,064 Sectors Total)

Cylinder	Head	Sector	LBA
0	0	1	0
0	0	63	62
0	1	0	63
999	15	63	1,007,999
1,000	0	1	1,008,000
9,999	15	63	10,079,999
10,000	0	1	10,080,000
16,382	15	63	16,514,063

BIOS Commands Versus ATA Commands

In addition to the two methods of sector addressing (CHS or LBA), there are two levels of interface where sector addressing occurs. One interface is where the operating system talks to the BIOS (using driver commands); the other is where the BIOS talks to the drive (using ATA commands). The specific commands at these levels are different, but both support CHS and LBA modes. Figure 7.18 illustrates the two interface levels.

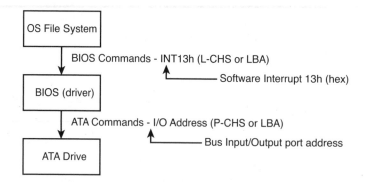

FIGURE 7.18   The relationship between BIOS and physical sector addressing. (In this figure, L-CHS stands for Logical CHS, and P-CHS stands for Physical CHS.)

When the operating system talks to the BIOS to read or write sectors, it issues commands via software interrupt (not the same as an IRQ) INT13h, which is how the BIOS subroutines for disk access are called. Various INT13h subfunctions allow sectors to be read or written using either CHS or LBA addressing. The BIOS routines then convert the BIOS commands into ATA hardware-level commands, which are sent over the bus I/O ports to the drive controller. Commands at the ATA hardware level can also use either CHS or LBA addressing, although the limitations are different. Whether your BIOS and drive use CHS or LBA addressing depends on the drive capacity, age of the BIOS and drive, BIOS Setup settings used, and operating system used.

CHS Limitations (the 528MB Barrier)

The original BIOS-based driver for hard disks is accessed via software interrupt 13h (13 hex) and offers functions for reading and writing drives at the sector level. Standard INT13h functions require that a particular sector be addressed by its cylinder, head, and sector location—otherwise known as *CHS addressing*. This interface is used by the operating system and low-level disk utilities to access the drive. IBM originally wrote the INT13h interface for the BIOS on the PC XT hard disk controller in 1983, and in 1984 the company incorporated it into the AT motherboard BIOS. This interface used numbers to define the particular cylinder, head, and sector being addressed. Table 7.17, which shows the standard INT13h BIOS CHS parameter limits, includes the maximum values for these numbers.

Table 7.17 INT13h BIOS CHS Parameter Limits

Field	Field Size	Maximum Value	Range	Total Usable
Cylinder	10 bits	1,024	0–1023	1,024
Head	8 bits	256	0–255	256
Sector	6 bits	64	1–63	63

The concept of a maximum value given a number of digits is simple: If you had, for example, a hotel with two-digit decimal room numbers, you could have only 100 (10^2) rooms, numbered 0–99. The CHS numbers used by the standard BIOS INT13h interface are binary, and with a 10-bit number being used to count cylinders, you can have only 1,024 (2^{10}) maximum, numbered 0–1,023. Because the head is identified by an 8-bit number, the maximum number of heads is 256 (2^8), numbered 0–255. Finally, with sectors per track there is a minor difference. Sectors on a track are identified by a 6-bit number, which would normally allow a maximum of 64 (2^6) sectors; however, because sectors are numbered starting with 1 (instead of 0), the range is limited to 1–63, which means a total of 63 sectors per track is the maximum the BIOS can handle.

These BIOS limitations are true for all BIOS versions or programs that rely on CHS addressing. Using the maximum numbers possible for CHS at the BIOS level, you can address a drive with 1,024 cylinders, 256 heads, and 63 sectors per track. Because each sector is 512 bytes, the math works out as follows:

```
                   Max. Values
        -------------------------
        Cylinders        1,024
           Heads           256
   Sectors/Track            63
        =========================
   Total Sectors    16,515,072
        -------------------------
   Total Bytes   8,455,716,864
   Megabytes (MB)        8,456
   Mebibytes (MiB)       8,064
   Gigabytes (GB)          8.4
   Gibibytes (GiB)         7.8
```

From these calculations, you can see that the maximum capacity drive addressable via the standard BIOS INT13h interface is about 8.4GB (where GB equals roughly 1 billion bytes), or 7.8GiB (where GiB means *gigabinarybytes*).

Unfortunately, the BIOS INT13h limits are not the only limitations that apply. Limits also exist in the ATA interface. The ATA CHS limits are shown in Table 7.18.

Table 7.18   Standard ATA CHS Parameter Limitations

Field	Field Size	Maximum Value	Range	Total Usable
Cylinder	16 bits	65,536	0–65,535	65,536
Head	4 bits	16	0–15	16
Sector	8 bits	256	1–255	255

As you can see, the ATA interface uses different-sized fields to store CHS values. Note that the ATA limits are higher than the BIOS limits for cylinders and sectors but lower than the BIOS limit for heads. The CHS limits for capacity according to the ATA-1 through ATA-5 specification are as follows:

```
                   Max. Values
----------------------------
      Cylinders         65,536
          Heads             16
Sectors/Track             255
============================
Total Sectors    267,386,880
----------------------------
Total Bytes   136,902,082,560
Megabytes (MB)        136,902
Mebibytes (MiB)       130,560
Gigabytes (GB)          136.9
Gibibytes (GiB)         127.5
```

When you combine the limitations of the BIOS and ATA CHS parameters, you end up with the situation shown in Table 7.19.

Table 7.19   Combined BIOS and ATA CHS Parameter Limits

	BIOS CHS Parameter Limits	ATA CHS Parameter Limits	Combined CHS Parameter Field Limits
Cylinder	1,024	65,536	1,024
Head	256	16	16
Sector	63	255	63
Total sectors	16,515,072	267,386,880	1,032,192
Maximum capacity	8.4GB	136.9GB	528MB

As you can see, the lowest common denominator of the combined CHS limits results in maximum usable parameters of 1,024 cylinders, 16 heads, and 63 sectors, which results in a maximum drive capacity of 528MB. This became known as the 528MB barrier (also called the 504MiB barrier), and it affects virtually all PCs built in 1993 or earlier.

CHS Translation (Breaking the 528MB Barrier)

Having a barrier limiting drive capacity to 528MB or less wasn't a problem when the largest drives available were smaller than that. But by 1994, drive technology had developed such that making drives larger than what the combined BIOS and ATA limitations could address was possible. Clearly a fix for the problem was needed.

Starting in 1993, the BIOS developer Phoenix Technologies began working on BIOS extensions to work around the combined CHS limits. In January of 1994, the company released the "BIOS Enhanced Disk Drive (EDD) Specification," which was later republished by the T13 committee (also responsible for ATA) as "BIOS Enhanced Disk Drive Services (EDD)." The EDD documents detail several methods for circumventing the limitations of older BIOSs without causing compatibility problems with existing software. These include the following:

- BIOS INT13h extensions supporting 64-bit LBA
- Bit-shift geometric CHS translation
- LBA-assist geometric CHS translation

The method for dealing with the CHS problem was called *translation* because it enabled additional subroutines in the BIOS to translate CHS parameters from ATA maximums to BIOS maximums (and vice versa). In an effort to make its methods standard among the entire PC industry, Phoenix released the EDD document publicly and allowed the technology to be used free of charge, even among its competitors such as AMI and Award. The T-13 committee in charge of ATA subsequently adopted the EDD standard and incorporated it into official ATA documents.

Starting in 1994, most BIOSs began implementing the Phoenix-designed CHS translation methods, which enabled drives up to the BIOS limit of 8.4GB to be supported. The fix involved what is termed *parameter translation* at the BIOS level, which adapted or translated the cylinder, head, and sector numbers to fit within the allowable BIOS parameters. There are two types of translation: One works via a technique called *CHS bit-shift* (usually called "Large" or "Extended CHS" in the BIOS Setup), and the other uses a technique called *LBA-assist* (usually called "LBA" in the BIOS Setup). These refer to the different mathematical methods of doing essentially the same thing: converting one set of CHS numbers to another.

CHS bit-shift translation manipulates the cylinder and head numbers but does not change the sector number. It begins with the physical (drive reported) cylinders and heads and, using some simple division and multiplication, comes up with altered numbers for the cylinders and heads. The sectors-per-track value is not translated and is passed unaltered. The term *bit-shift* is used because the division and multiplication math is actually done in the BIOS software by shifting bits in the CHS address.

With CHS bit-shift translation, the drive reported (physical) parameters are referred to as *P-CHS*, and the BIOS-altered logical parameters are referred to as *L-CHS*. After the settings are made in the BIOS Setup, L-CHS addresses are automatically translated to P-CHS at the BIOS level. This enables the operating system to send commands to the BIOS using L-CHS parameters, which the BIOS automatically converts to P-CHS when it talks to the drive using ATA commands. Table 7.20 shows the rules for calculating CHS bit-shift translation.

CHS bit-shift translation is based on dividing the physical cylinder count by a power of 2 to bring it under the 1,024 cylinder BIOS INT13h limit and then multiplying the heads by the same power of 2, leaving the sector count unchanged. The power of 2 used depends on the cylinder count, as indicated in Table 7.20.

Table 7.20   CHS Bit-Shift Translation Rules

Physical (Drive Reported) Cylinders	Physical Heads	Logical Cylinders	Logical Heads	Maximum Capacity
1 < C <= 1,024	1 < H <= 16	C = C	H = H	528MB
1,024 < C <= 2,048	1 < H <= 16	C = C/2	H = H × 2	1GB
2,048 < C <= 4,096	1 < H <= 16	C = C/4	H = H × 4	2.1GB
4,096 < C <= 8,192	1 < H <= 16	C = C/8	H = H × 8	4.2GB
8,192 < C <= 16,384	1 < H <= 16	C = C/16	H = H × 16	8.4GB

The drive reported sector count is not translated.

The logical heads value can't exceed 255 with some operating systems, such as DOS/Win9x/Me.

Here is an example of CHS bit-shift translation:

```
                                        Bit-shift
                         P-CHS            L-CHS
                       Parameters        Parameters
        -------------------------------------------------
          Cylinders       8,000            1,000
              Heads          16              128
      Sectors/Track          63               63
        =================================================
       Total Sectors    8,064,000        8,064,000
        -------------------------------------------------
       Total Bytes  4,128,768,000    4,128,768,000
      Megabytes (MB)       4,129            4,129
      Mebibytes (MiB)      3,938            3,938
      Gigabytes (GB)        4.13             4.13
      Gibibytes (GiB)       3.85             3.85
```

This example shows a drive with 8,000 cylinders and 16 heads. The physical cylinder count is way above the BIOS limit of 1,024, so if CHS bit-shift translation is selected in the BIOS Setup, the BIOS then divides the cylinder count by 2, 4, 8, or 16 to bring it below 1,024. In this case, it would divide by 8, which results in a new logical cylinder count of 1,000—which is below the 1,024 maximum. Because the cylinder count is divided by 8, the head count is then multiplied by the same number, resulting in 128 logical heads, which is also below the limit the BIOS can handle.

So, although the drive reports having 8,000 cylinders and 16 heads, the BIOS and all software (including the operating system) instead see the drive as having 1,000 cylinders and 128 heads. Note that the 63 sectors/track figure is simply carried over without change. The result is that by using the logical parameters, the BIOS can see the entire 4.13GB drive and won't be limited to just the first 528MB.

When you install a drive, you don't have to perform the translation math to convert the cylinders and heads; the BIOS does that for you automatically. All you have to do is allow the BIOS to autodetect the P-CHS parameters and then enable the translation in the BIOS Setup. Selecting Large or ECHS translation in the BIOS Setup enables the CHS bit-shift. The BIOS does the rest of the work for you.

CHS bit-shift is a simple and fast (code-wise) scheme that can work with all drives, but unfortunately it can't properly translate all theoretically possible drive geometries for drives under 8.4GB. To solve this, an addendum was added to the ATA-2 specification to specifically require drives to report certain ranges of geometries to allow bit-shift translation to work. Thus, all drives that conform to the ATA-2 specification (or higher) can be translated using this method.

The 2.1GB and 4.2GB Barriers

Some BIOSs incorrectly allocated only 12 bits for the P-CHS cylinder field, thereby allowing a maximum of 4,096 cylinders. Combined with the standard 16-head and 63-sector limits, this resulted in the inability to support any drives over 2.1GB in capacity. Fortunately, this BIOS defect affected only a limited number of systems with BIOS dates prior to about mid-1996.

Even so, some problems still existed with bit-shift translation. Because of the way DOS and Windows 9x/Me were written, they could not properly handle a drive with 256 heads. This was a problem for drives larger than 4.2GB because the CHS bit-shift translation rules typically resulted in 256 heads as a logical value, as seen in the following example:

	P-CHS Parameters	Bit-shift L-CHS Parameters
Cylinders	12,000	750
Heads	16	256
Sectors/Track	63	63
Total Sectors	12,096,000	12,096,000
Total Bytes	6,193,152,000	6,193,152,000
Megabytes (MB)	6,193	6,193
Mebibytes (MiB)	5,906	5,906
Gigabytes (GB)	6.19	6.19
Gibibytes (GiB)	5.77	5.77

This scheme failed when you tried to install Windows 9x/Me (or DOS) on a drive larger than 4.2GB because the L-CHS parameters included 256 heads. Any BIOS that implemented this scheme essentially had a 4.2GB barrier, so installing a drive larger than that and selecting CHS bit-shift translation caused the drive to fail. Note that this was not a problem for Windows NT or later.

Note

The BIOS is not actually at fault here; the problem instead lies with the DOS/Win9x/Me file system code, which stores the sector-per-track number as an 8-bit value. The number 256 causes a problem because 256 equals 100000000b, which takes 9 bits to store. The value 255 (which equals 11111111b) is the largest value that can fit in an 8-bit binary register and is therefore the maximum number of heads those operating systems can support.

To solve this problem, CHS bit-shift translation was revised by adding a rule such that if the drive reported 16 heads and more than 8,192 cylinders (which would result in a 256-head translation), the P-CHS head value would be assumed to be 15 (instead of 16) and the P-CHS cylinder value would be multiplied by 16/15 to compensate. These adjusted cylinder and head values would then be translated. The following example shows the results:

	P-CHS Parameters	Bit-shift L-CHS Parameters	Revised Bit-shift L-CHS Parameters
Cylinders	12,000	750	800
Heads	16	256	240
Sectors/Track	63	63	63
Total Sectors	12,096,000	12,096,000	12,096,000
Total Bytes	6,193,152,000	6,193,152,000	6,193,152,000
Megabytes (MB)	6,193	6,193	6,193
Mebibytes (MiB)	5,906	5,906	5,906
Gigabytes (GB)	6.19	6.19	6.19
Gibibytes (GiB)	5.77	5.77	5.77

As you can see from this example, a drive with 12,000 cylinders and 16 heads translates to 750 cylinders and 256 heads using the standard CHS bit-shift scheme. The revised CHS bit-shift scheme rule does a double translation in this case, first changing the 16 heads to 15 and then multiplying the 12,000 cylinders by 16/15, resulting in 12,800 cylinders. Then, the new cylinder value is CHS bit-shift-translated (it is divided by 16), resulting in 800 logical cylinders. Likewise, the 15 heads are multiplied by 16, resulting in 240 logical heads. If the logical cylinder count calculates to more than 1,024, it is truncated to 1,024. In this case, what started out as 12,000 cylinders and 16 heads P-CHS becomes 800 cylinders and 240 heads (instead of 750 cylinders and 256 heads) L-CHS, which works around the bug in the DOS/Win9x/Me operating systems.

So far, all my examples have been clean—that is, the L-CHS parameters have calculated to the same capacity as the P-CHS parameters. Unfortunately, it doesn't always work out that way. The following shows a more typical example in the real world. Several 8.4GB drives from Maxtor, Quantum, Seagate, and others report 16,383 cylinders and 16 heads P-CHS. For those drives, the translations would work out as follows:

	P-CHS Parameters	Bit-shift L-CHS Parameters	Revised Bit-shift L-CHS Parameters
Cylinders	16,383	1,023	1,024
Heads	16	256	240
Sectors/Track	63	63	63
Total Sectors	16,514,064	16,498,944	15,482,880
Total Bytes	8,455,200,768	8,447,459,328	7,927,234,560
Megabytes (MB)	8,455	8,447	7,927
Mebibytes (MiB)	8,064	8,056	7,560
Gigabytes (GB)	8.46	8.45	7.93
Gibibytes (GiB)	7.87	7.87	7.38

Note that the revised CHS bit-shift translation rules result in supporting only 7.93GB of the 8.46GB total on the drive. In fact, the parameters shown (with 240 heads) are the absolute maximum that revised CHS bit-shift supports. Fortunately, another translation mode is available that improves this situation.

LBA-Assist Translation

The LBA-assist translation method places no artificial limits on the reported drive geometries, but it works only on drives that support LBA addressing at the ATA interface level. Fortunately, though, virtually all ATA drives larger than 2GB support LBA. LBA-assist translation takes the CHS parameters the drive reports, multiplies them together to get a calculated LBA maximum value (total number of sectors), and then uses this calculated LBA number to derive the translated CHS parameters. Table 7.21 shows the rules for LBA-assist translation.

Table 7.21   LBA-Assist Translation Rules

	Logical Cylinders	Logical Heads	Logical Sectors
1 < T <= 1,032,192	T/1,008	16	63
1,032,192 < T <= 2,064,384	T/2,016	32	63
2,064,384 < T <= 4,128,768	T/4,032	64	63
4,128,768 < T <= 8,257,536	T/8,064	128	63
8,257,536 < T <= 16,450,560	T/16,065	255	63

T = Total sectors, calculated by multiplying the drive-reported P-CHS parameters (C × H × S)

LBA-assist translation fixes the sectors at 63 no matter what and divides and multiplies the cylinders and heads by predetermined values depending on the total number of sectors. This results in a set of L-CHS parameters the operating system uses to communicate with the BIOS. The L-CHS numbers are then translated to LBA numbers at the ATA interface level. Because LBA mode is more flexible at translating, you should use it in most cases instead of CHS bit-shift.

Normally, both the CHS bit-shift and LBA-assist translations generate the same L-CHS geometry for a given drive. This should always be true if the drive reports 63 sectors per track and 4, 8, or 16 heads. In the following example, both translation schemes result in identical L-CHS values:

```
                                    Revised bit-      LBA-assist
                         P-CHS       shift L-CHS        L-CHS
                       Parameters    Parameters       Parameters
          --------------------------------------------------------
          Cylinders       8,192          1,024           1,024
             Heads           16            128             128
      Sectors/Track           63             63              63
          ========================================================
      Total Sectors    8,257,536      8,257,536       8,257,536
          --------------------------------------------------------
        Total Bytes  4,227,858,432  4,227,858,432   4,227,858,432
      Megabytes (MB)       4,228          4,228           4,228
      Mebibytes (MiB)      4,032          4,032           4,032
      Gigabytes (GB)        4.23           4.23            4.23
      Gibibytes (GiB)       3.94           3.94            3.94
```

However, if the drive reports a value other than 63 sectors per track or has other than 4, 8, or 16 heads, LBA-assist translation does not result in the same parameters as CHS bit-shift translation. In the following example, different translations result:

	P-CHS Parameters	Revised bit-shift L-CHS Parameters	LBA-assist L-CHS Parameters
Cylinders	16,383	1,024	1,024
Heads	16	240	255
Sectors/Track	63	63	63
Total Sectors	16,514,064	15,482,880	16,450,560
Total Bytes	8,455,200,768	7,927,234,560	8,422,686,720
Megabytes (MB)	8,455	7,927	8,423
Mebibytes (MiB)	8,064	7,560	8,033
Gigabytes (GB)	8.46	7.93	8.42
Gibibytes (GiB)	7.87	7.38	7.84

The LBA-assist translation supports 8.42GB, which is nearly 500MB more than the revised CHS bit-shift translation. More importantly, these translations are different, which can result in problems if you change translation modes with data on the drive. If you were to set up and format a drive using CHS bit-shift translation and then change to LBA-assist translation, the interpreted geometry could change and the drive could then become unreadable until it is repartitioned and reformatted (which would destroy all the data). Bottom line: After you select a translation method, don't plan on changing it unless you have your data securely backed up.

Virtually all PC BIOSs since 1994 have translation capability in the BIOS Setup, and virtually all offer both translation modes as well as an option to disable translation entirely. If both CHS bit-shift and LBA-assist translation modes are offered, you should probably choose the LBA method of translation because it is the more efficient and flexible of the two. LBA-assist translation also gets around the 4.2GB operating system bug because it is designed to allow a maximum of 255 logical heads no matter what.

You usually can tell whether your BIOS supports translation by the capability to specify more than 1,024 cylinders in the BIOS Setup, although this can be misleading. The best clue is to look for the translation setting parameters in the ATA/IDE drive setup page in the BIOS Setup. See Chapter 5 for more information on how to enter the BIOS Setup on your system. If you see drive-related settings, such as LBA or ECHS (sometimes called Large or Extended), these are telltale signs of a BIOS with translation support. Most BIOSs with a date of 1994 or later include this capability, although some AMI BIOS versions from the mid-1990s locate the LBA setting on a screen different from the hard drive configuration screen. If your system currently does not support parameter translation, you might be able to get an upgrade from your motherboard manufacturer or install a BIOS upgrade card with this capability, such as the LBA Pro card from eSupport.com.

Table 7.22 summarizes the four ways today's BIOSs can handle addressing sectors on the drive: Standard CHS (no translation), Extended CHS translation, LBA translation, and pure LBA addressing.

Table 7.22 Drive Sector Addressing Methods

BIOS Mode	OS to BIOS	BIOS to Drive
Standard (Normal), no translation	P-CHS	P-CHS
CHS bit-shift (ECHS) translation	L-CHS	P-CHS
LBA-assist (LBA) translation	L-CHS	LBA
Pure LBA (EDD BIOS)	LBA	LBA

Standard CHS has only one possible translation step internal to the drive. The drive's actual physical geometry is completely invisible from the outside with all zoned recorded ATA drives today. The cylinders, heads, and sectors printed on the label for use in the BIOS Setup are purely logical geometry and do not represent the actual physical parameters. Standard CHS addressing is limited to 16 heads and 1,024 cylinders, which provides a limit of 504MiB (528MB).

This is often called "Normal" in the BIOS Setup and causes the BIOS to behave like an old-fashioned one without translation. Use this setting if your drive has fewer than 1,024 cylinders or if you want to use the drive with an operating system that doesn't require translation.

ECHS, or "Large" in the BIOS Setup, is CHS bit-shift, and most BIOSs from 1997 and later use the revised method (240 logical heads maximum).

LBA, as selected in the BIOS Setup, indicates LBA-assist translation, not pure LBA mode. This enables software to operate using L-CHS parameters while the BIOS talks to the drive in LBA mode.

The only way to select a pure LBA mode, from the OS to the BIOS as well as from the BIOS to the drive, is with a drive that is over 8.4GB. All drives over 137GB must be addressed via LBA at both the BIOS and drive levels, and most PC BIOSs automatically address any drive over 8.4GB in that manner, as well. In that case, no special BIOS Setup settings are necessary, other than setting the type to auto or autodetect.

Caution

A word of warning with these BIOS translation settings: If you have a drive 8.4GB or less in capacity and switch between Standard CHS, ECHS, or LBA, the BIOS can change the (translated) geometry. The same thing can happen if you transfer a disk that has been formatted on an old, non-LBA computer to a new one that uses LBA. This causes the logical CHS geometry seen by the operating system to change and the data to appear in the wrong location from where it actually is! This can cause you to lose access to your data if you are not careful. I always recommend recording the CMOS Setup screens associated with the hard disk configuration so that you can properly match the setup of a drive to the settings to which it was originally set. This does not affect drives over 8.4GB because in those cases pure LBA is automatically selected.

The 8.4GB Barrier

Although CHS translation breaks the 528MB barrier, it runs into another barrier at 8.4GB. Supporting drives larger than 8.4GB requires leaving CHS behind and changing from CHS to LBA addressing at the BIOS level. The ATA interface had always supported LBA addressing, even in the original ATA-1 specification. One problem was that LBA support at the ATA level originally was optional, but the main problem was that there was no LBA support at the BIOS interface level. You could set LBA-assist translation in the BIOS Setup, but all that did was convert the drive LBA numbers to CHS numbers at the BIOS interface level.

Phoenix Technologies recognized that the BIOS interface needed to move from CHS to LBA early on and, beginning in 1994, published the "BIOS Enhanced Disk Drive Specification (EDD)," which addressed this problem with new extended INT13h BIOS services that worked with LBA rather than CHS addresses.

To ensure industry-wide support and compatibility for these new BIOS functions, in 1996 Phoenix turned this document over to the International Committee on Information Technology Standards (INCITS) T13 technical committee for further enhancement and certification as a standard called the "BIOS Enhanced Disk Drive Specification (EDD)." Starting in 1998, most of the other BIOS manufacturers began installing EDD support in their BIOS, enabling BIOS-level LBA mode support for ATA drives larger than 8.4GB. Coincidentally (or not), this support arrived just in time because ATA drives of that size and larger became available that same year.

The EDD document describes new extended INT13h BIOS commands that allow LBA addressing up to 2^{64} sectors, which results in a theoretical maximum capacity of more than 9.44ZB (zettabytes, or quadrillion bytes). That is the same as saying 9.44 trillion GB, which is 9.44×10^{21} bytes or, to be more precise, 9,444,732,965,739,290,427,392 bytes! I say theoretical capacity because even though by 1998 the BIOS could handle up to 2^{64} sectors, ATA drives were still using only 28-bit addressing (2^{28} sectors) at the ATA interface level. This limited an ATA drive to 268,435,456 sectors, which was a capacity of 137,438,953,472 bytes, or 137.44GB. Thus, the 8.4GB barrier had been broken, but another barrier remained at 137GB because of the 28-bit LBA addressing used in the ATA interface. The numbers work out as follows:

```
                        Max. Values
--------------------------------
Total Sectors           268,435,456
--------------------------------
Total Bytes         137,438,953,472
Megabytes  (MB)             137,439
Mebibytes  (MiB)            131,072
Gigabytes  (GB)              137.44
Gibibytes  (GiB)             128.00
```

By using the new extended INT13h 64-bit LBA mode commands at the BIOS level, as well as the existing 28-bit LBA mode commands at the ATA level, no translation would be required and the LBA numbers would be passed unchanged. The combination of LBA at the BIOS and the ATA interface levels meant that the clumsy CHS addressing could finally die. This also means that when you install an ATA drive larger than 8.4GB in a PC that has an EDD-capable BIOS (1998 or newer), both the BIOS and the drive are automatically set to use LBA mode.

An interesting quirk is that to allow backward compatibility when you boot an older operating system that doesn't support LBA mode addressing (DOS or the original release of Windows 95, for example), most drives larger than 8.4GB report 16,383 cylinders, 16 heads, and 63 sectors per track, which is 8.4GB. For example, this enables a 120GB drive to be seen as an 8.4GB drive by older BIOSs or operating systems. That sounds strange, but I guess having a 120GB drive being recognized as an 8.4GB is better than not having it work at all. If you did want to install a drive larger than 8.4GB into a system dated before 1998, the recommended solution is either a motherboard BIOS upgrade or an add-on BIOS card with EDD support.

The 137GB Barrier and Beyond

By 2001, the 137GB barrier had become a problem because 3 1/2-inch hard drives were poised to breach that capacity level. The solution came in the form of ATA-6, which was being developed during that year. To enable the addressing of drives of greater capacity, ATA-6 upgraded the LBA functions from using 28-bit numbers to using larger 48-bit numbers.

The ATA-6 specification extends the LBA interface such that it can use 48-bit sector addressing. This means that the maximum capacity is increased to 248 (281,474,976,710,656) total sectors. Because each sector stores 512 bytes, this results in the maximum drive capacity shown here:

```
                         Max. Values
------------------------------------
Total Sectors       281,474,976,710,656
------------------------------------
Total Bytes     144,115,188,075,855,872
Megabytes  (MB)         144,115,188,076
Mebibytes  (MiB)        137,438,953,472
Gigabytes  (GB)             144,115,188
Gibibytes  (GiB)            134,217,728
Terabytes  (TB)                 144,115
Tebibytes  (TiB)                131,072
Petabytes  (PB)                  144.12
Pebibytes  (PiB)                 128.00
```

As you can see, the 48-bit LBA in ATA-6 allows a capacity of just over 144PB (petabytes = quadrillion bytes)!

Because the EDD BIOS functions use a 64-bit LBA number, they have a much larger limit:

```
                             Max. Values
-------------------------------------------
Total Sectors       18,446,744,073,709,551,616
-------------------------------------------
Total Bytes     9,444,732,965,739,290,427,392
Megabytes  (MB)        9,444,732,965,739,290
Mebibytes  (MiB)       9,007,199,254,740,992
Gigabytes  (GB)            9,444,732,965,739
Gibibytes  (GiB)           8,796,093,022,208
Terabytes  (TB)                9,444,732,966
Tebibytes  (TiB)               8,589,934,592
Petabytes  (PB)                    9,444,733
Pebibytes  (PiB)                   8,388,608
Exabytes   (EB)                        9,445
Exbibytes  (EiB)                       8,192
Zettabytes (ZB)                         9.44
Zebibytes  (ZiB)                        8.00
```

Although the BIOS services use 64-bit LBA (allowing up to 2^{64} sectors) for even greater capacity, the 144 petabyte ATA-6 limitation is the lowest common denominator that would apply. Still, that should hold us for some time to come.

Because hard disk drives have been doubling in capacity every 1.5 to 2 years (a corollary of Moore's Law), I estimate that it will take us until sometime between the years 2031 and 2041 before we reach the 144PB barrier (assuming hard disk technology hasn't been completely replaced by then). Similarly, I estimate that the 9.44ZB EDD BIOS barrier won't be reached until between the years 2055 and 2073! Phoenix originally claimed that the EDD specification would hold us until 2020, but it seems they were being quite conservative.

The 137GB barrier proved a bit more complicated than previous barriers because, in addition to BIOS issues, operating system issues also had to be considered.

Internal ATA drives larger than 137GB require 48-bit LBA (logical block address) support. This support absolutely needs to be provided in the OS, but it can also be provided in the BIOS. It is best if both the OS and BIOS provide this support, but it can be made to work if only the OS has the support.

Having 48-bit LBA support in the OS requires one of the following:

- Windows XP with Service Pack 1 (SP1) or later.
- Windows 2000 with Service Pack 4 (SP4) or later.
- Windows 98/98SE/Me or NT 4.0 with the Intel Application Accelerator (IAA) loaded and a motherboard with an IAA-supported chipset. See http://downloadcenter.intel.com and search for IAA.

Having 48-bit LBA support in the BIOS requires either of the following:

- A motherboard BIOS with 48-bit LBA support (most of those dated September 2002 or later)
- An ATA host adapter card with onboard BIOS that includes 48-bit LBA support

If your motherboard BIOS does not have the support and an update is not available from your motherboard manufacturer, you may be able to use a card. Promise Technology (www.promise.com) makes several PCI cards with 3Gbps SATA/eSATA interfaces as well as an onboard BIOS that adds 48-bit LBA support.

Note that if you have both BIOS and OS support, you can simply install and use the drive like any other. If you have no BIOS support, but you do have OS support, portions of the drive past 137GB are not recognized or accessible until the OS is loaded. If you are installing the OS to a blank hard drive and booting from an original XP (pre-SP1) CD or earlier, you will only be able to partition up to the first 137GB of the drive at installation time. After installing the OS and then the SP1 (or SP2/SP3) update, you can either partition the remainder of the drive as a second partition in Windows or use a free third-party partitioning program such as Parted Magic to expand the 137GB partition to use the full drive. If you are booting from an XP CD with SP1 or later integrated, Windows will recognize the entire drive during the OS installation and allow partitioning of the entire drive as a single partition greater than 137GB.

Operating System and Other Software Limitations

Note that if you use older software, including utilities, applications, or even operating systems that rely exclusively on CHS parameters, these items will see all drives over 8.4GB as 8.4GB only. You will need not only a newer BIOS, but also newer software designed to handle the direct LBA addressing to work with drives over 8.4GB.

Operating system limitations with respect to drives over 8.4GB are shown in Table 7.23.

Table 7.23 Operating System Limitations

Operating System	Limitations for Hard Drive Size
DOS/Windows 3x	DOS 6.22 or lower can't support drives greater than 8.4GB. DOS 7.0 or higher (included with Windows 95 or later) is required to recognize a drive over 8.4GB.
Windows 9x/Me	Windows 95a (original version) does support the INT13h extensions, which means it does support drives over 8.4GB; however, due to limitations of the FAT16 file system, the maximum individual partition size is limited to 2GB. Windows 95B/OSR2 and later (including Windows 98/Me) support the INT13h extensions, which allow drives over 8.4GB, and they also support FAT32, which allows partition sizes up to the maximum capacity of the drive. However, Windows 95 doesn't support hard drives larger than 32GB because of limitations in its design. Windows 98 requires an update to FDISK to partition drives larger than 64GB.
Windows NT	Windows NT 3.5x does not support drives greater than 8.4GB. Windows NT 4.0 does support drivers greater than 8.4GB; however, when a drive larger than 8.4GB is being used as the primary bootable device, Windows NT will not recognize more than 8.4GB. Microsoft has released Service Pack 4, which corrects this problem.
Windows 2000 and later	All Windows 2000 SP3+, Windows XP SP1+, Windows Vista, Windows 7/8, and later systems support MBR-formatted drives up to 2.19TB by default. 64-bit versions of Windows Vista SP1+ and Windows 7/8 and later support GPT-formatted drives of 2.2TB or larger, up to a maximum of 281TB (256TiB).
Linux	Most versions support MBR-formatted drives up to 2.19TB by default, whereas most current versions support GPT formatted drives of 2.2TB or larger, up to 16TiB or 1EiB depending on the file system.
OS/2 Warp	Some versions of OS/2 are limited to a boot partition size of 3.1GB or 4.3GB. IBM has a Device Driver Pack upgrade that enables the boot partition to be as large as 8.4GB. The HPFS file system in OS/2 supports drives up to 64GB.
Novell	NetWare 5.0 and later support drives greater than 8.4GB.

In the case of operating systems that support drives over 8.4GB, the maximum drive size limitations depend on the BIOS and hard drive interface standard, not the OS. Instead, other limitations come into play for the volumes (partitions) and files that can be created and managed by the various operating systems. These limitations depend on not only the operating system involved, but also the file system that is used for the volume. Table 7.24 shows the minimum and maximum volume (partition) size and file size limitations of the various Windows operating systems. As noted in the previous section, the original version of XP, as well as Windows 2000/NT or Windows 95/98/Me, does not currently provide native support for ATA hard drives that are larger than 137GB. You need to use Windows 7/8, Vista, or XP with Service Pack 1 or later installed to use an ATA drive over 137GB. This does not affect drives attached via USB, FireWire, SCSI, or other interfaces.

Table 7.24 Operating System Volume/File Size Limitations by File System

OS Limitations by File System	FAT16	FAT32	NTFS
Min. volume size (9x/Me)	2.092MB	33.554MB	—
Max. volume size (95)	2.147GB	33.554MB	—
Max. volume size (98)	2.147GB	136.902GB	—

Table 7.24   Continued

OS Limitations by File System	FAT16	FAT32	NTFS
Max. volume size (Me)	2.147GB	8.796TB	—
Min. volume size (NT+)	2.092MB	33.554MB	1.000MB
Max. volume size (NT+)	4.294GB	8.796GB	281.475TB
Max. file size (all)	4.294GB	4.294GB	16.384TB

— = not applicable

NT+ = Windows NT, 2000, XP, Vista, and Windows 7/8

MB = megabyte = 1,000,000 bytes

GB = gigabyte = 1,000,000,000 bytes

TB = terabyte = 1,000,000,000,000 bytes

GPT and the 2.2TB Barrier

Although most of the previous barriers in disk capacity have been hardware related, the 2.2TB barrier is more of a software than a hardware problem. Even more specifically, it is a disk formatting and OS problem, and it's a BIOS problem if you consider boot drives versus data drives.

This problem stems from the way hard disks have been formatted since DOS 2.0 and the first PC hard drives appeared in 1983. Back then IBM and Microsoft came up with a scheme for partitioning drives called the *MBR* (Master Boot Record). The MBR is the first sector on a disk, and it is internally defined with the ability to control four primary partitions. Each partition is described by a 16-byte table entry, with 4-byte (32-bit) fields that define the LBA (Logical Block Address) for both where the partition starts and how big it is.

The largest number that can be written using 32 binary digits is 2^{32}, which is equal to 4,294,967,296. Because each sector is normally limited to 512 bytes, this means that the maximum amount of a drive that can be recognized is 2.2TB. Combine the MBR limitation with the fact that most PC BIOSs can only boot from MBR-formatted drives, and most older operating systems only support MBR-formatted drives for both boot drives and data drives, and you can see that the 2.2TB limitation can be a problem.

Several changes are necessary to break this barrier. The first is to develop a new partitioning scheme without the limitations the MBR imposes. This replacement is called GPT, which stands for GUID (globally unique identifier) Partition Table. Intel initially developed the GPT as part of its EFI (Extensible Firmware Interface) specification in 2000; since then Microsoft and other OS vendors have been incorporating it into operating systems. The GPT uses 64-bit LBA numbers, meaning disks of up to 9.4ZB (8ZiB) can be managed. That's equal to 9.4 *billion* terabytes, a limit that won't be reached any time soon.

Figure 7.19 illustrates the differences between MBR and GPT partitions.

Although GPT breaks the 2.2TB barrier from a drive formatting perspective, other elements must be in place for GPT to be usable in a PC. To format or recognize a GPT-formatted disk, you need an OS that supports GPT. That alone allows you to use GPT-formatted disks as secondary (data) disks, but to boot from a GPT-formatted drive, you also need a motherboard with a UEFI BIOS or UEFI Boot option. Table 7.25 summarizes the requirements to break the 2.2TB barrier.

MBR and GPT Disk Structure Comparison

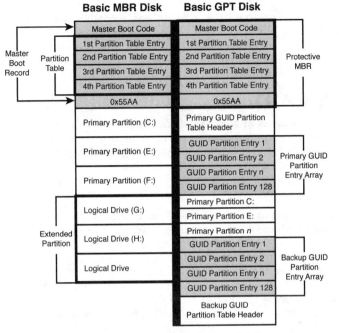

Note: diagram assumes (D:) assigned to optical drive

FIGURE 7.19 GPT includes a backup for partition entries and the partition table header.

Table 7.25 Operating System GPT Boot/Data Disk Support

Operating System	GPT Boot Disk	GPT Data Disk
Windows XP (x86)	No	No[1]
Windows XP (x64)	No	Yes
Windows Vista SP1+ (x86)	No	Yes
Windows Vista SP1+ (x64)	Yes[2]	Yes
Windows 7/8 (x86)	No	Yes
Windows 7/8 (x64)	Yes[2]	Yes
Linux UBUNTU 8.04+/SUSE (x86, x64)	Yes	Yes

Note: x86 = 32-bit, x64 = 64-bit

1 Yes with third-party software such as the Paragon GPT Loader

2 Only on systems with a UEFI BIOS or an enabled UEFI Boot option

Drives 2.2TB or larger can also be supported externally via USB without having to resort to GPT partitioning. This is accomplished within the USB Bridge chipset firmware, which can be designed to present 2.2TB or larger drives using 4K sectors instead of the normal 512-byte sectors. USB enclosures or drive docks with this feature can use standard MBR formatting to allow the drive to be supported in Windows XP with no special software required.

In summary, to use a 2.2TB or larger drive as an internal secondary/data drive, you need to format it using GPT, and you need to run a GPT-aware OS (Vista SP1 or later). Booting from such a drive also requires a UEFI BIOS or an enabled UEFI Boot option. You can use GPT-formatted secondary/data drives with Windows XP by installing third-party GPT support software such as the Paragon GPT Loader (www.Paragon-Software.com).

PATA/SATA RAID

RAID is an acronym for redundant array of independent (or inexpensive) disks and was designed to improve the fault tolerance and performance of computer storage systems. RAID was developed at the University of California at Berkeley in 1987 and was designed so that a group of smaller, less expensive drives could be interconnected with special hardware and software to make them appear as a single larger drive to the system. By using multiple drives to act as one drive, increases in fault tolerance and performance could be realized.

Initially, RAID was conceived to simply enable all the individual drives in the array to work together as a single, larger drive with the combined storage space of all the individual drives, which is called a *JBOD* (Just a Bunch of Disks) configuration. Unfortunately, if you had four drives connected in a JBOD array acting as one drive, you would be four times more likely to experience a drive failure than if you used just a single larger drive. And because JBOD does not use striping, performance would be no better than a single drive either. To improve both reliability and performance, the Berkeley scientists proposed six levels (corresponding to different methods) of RAID. These levels provide varying emphasis on fault tolerance (reliability), storage capacity, performance, or a combination of the three.

Although it no longer exists, an organization called the RAID Advisory Board (RAB) was formed in July 1992 to standardize, classify, and educate on the subject of RAID. The RAB developed specifications for RAID, a conformance program for the various RAID levels, and a classification program for RAID hardware.

The RAID Advisory Board defined seven standard RAID levels, called RAID 0–6. Most RAID controllers also implement a RAID 0+1 combination, which is usually called RAID 10. The levels are as follows:

- **RAID Level 0**—Striping-File data is written simultaneously to multiple drives in the array, which act as a single larger drive. This offers high read/write performance but low reliability. Requires a minimum of two drives to implement.

- **RAID Level 1**—Mirroring-Data written to one drive is duplicated on another, providing excellent fault tolerance (if one drive fails, the other is used and no is data lost) but no real increase in performance as compared to a single drive. Requires a minimum of two drives to implement (same capacity as one drive).

- **RAID Level 2**—Bit-level ECC-Data is split one bit at a time across multiple drives, and error correction codes (ECCs) are written to other drives. This is intended for storage devices that do not incorporate ECC internally. (All SCSI and ATA drives have internal ECC.) It's a standard that theoretically provides high data rates with good fault tolerance, but seven or more drives are required for greater than 50% efficiency, and no commercial RAID 2 controllers or drives without ECC are available.

- **RAID Level 3**—Striped with parity-Combines RAID Level 0 striping with an additional drive used for parity information. This RAID level is really an adaptation of RAID Level 0 that sacrifices some capacity, for the same number of drives. However, it also achieves a high level of data integrity or fault tolerance because data usually can be rebuilt if one drive fails. Requires a minimum of three drives to implement (two or more for data and one for parity).

- **RAID Level 4**—Blocked data with parity—Similar to RAID 3 except data is written in larger blocks to the independent drives, offering faster read performance with larger files. Requires a minimum of three drives to implement (two or more for data and one for parity).

- **RAID Level 5**—Blocked data with distributed parity—Similar to RAID 4 but offers improved performance by distributing the parity stripes over a series of hard drives. Requires a minimum of three drives to implement (two or more for data and one for parity).

- **RAID Level 6**—Blocked data with double distributed parity—Similar to RAID 5 except parity information is written twice using two parity schemes to provide even better fault tolerance in case of multiple drive failures. Requires a minimum of four drives to implement (two or more for data and two for parity).

There are also *nested* RAID levels created by combining several forms of RAID. The most common are as follows:

- **RAID Level 01: Mirrored stripes**—Drives are first combined in striped RAID 0 sets; then the RAID 0 sets are mirrored in a RAID 1 configuration. A minimum of four drives is required, and the total number of drives must be an even number. Most PC implementations allow four drives only. The total usable storage capacity is equal to half of the number of drives in the array times the size of the lowest capacity drive. RAID 01 arrays can tolerate a single drive failure and some (but not all) combinations of multiple drive failures. This is not generally recommended because RAID 10 offers more redundancy and performance.

- **RAID Level 10: Striped mirrors**—Drives are first combined in mirrored RAID 1 sets; then the RAID 1 sets are striped in a RAID 0 configuration. A minimum of four drives is required, and the total number of drives must be an even number. Most PC implementations allow four drives only. The total usable storage capacity is equal to half of the number of drives in the array times the size of the lowest capacity drive. RAID 10 arrays can tolerate a single drive failure and many (but not all) combinations of multiple drive failures. This is similar to RAID 01, except with somewhat increased reliability because more combinations of multiple drive failures can be tolerated, and rebuilding an array after a failed drive is replaced is much faster and more efficient.

Additional custom or proprietary RAID levels exist that were not originally supported by the RAID Advisory Board. For example, from 1993 through 2004, "RAID 7" was a trademarked marketing term used to describe a proprietary RAID implementation released by the (now defunct) Storage Computer Corp.

When set up for maximum performance, arrays typically run RAID Level 0, which incorporates data striping. Unfortunately, RAID 0 also sacrifices reliability such that if any one drive fails, all data in the array is lost. The advantage is in extreme performance. With RAID 0, performance generally scales up with the number of drives you add in the array. For example, with four drives you won't necessarily have four times the performance of a single drive, but many controllers can come close to that for sustained transfers. Some overhead is still involved in the controller performing the striping, and issues still exist with latency—that is, how long it takes to find the data—but performance will be higher than any single drive can normally achieve.

When set up for reliability, arrays generally run RAID Level 1, which is simple drive mirroring. All data written to one drive is written to the other. If one drive fails, the system can continue to work on the other drive. Unfortunately, this does not increase performance, and it also means you get to use only half of the available drive capacity. In other words, you must install two drives, but you get to use only one. (The other is the mirror.) However, in an era of high capacities and low drive prices, this is not a significant issue.

Combining performance with fault tolerance requires using one of the other RAID levels, such as RAID 5 or 10. For example, virtually all professional RAID controllers used in network file servers are designed to use RAID Level 5. Controllers that implement RAID Level 5 used to be very expensive, and RAID 5 requires at least three drives to be connected, whereas RAID 10 requires four drives.

With four 500GB drives in a RAID 5 configuration, you would have 1.5TB of total storage, and you could withstand the failure of any single drive. After a drive failure, data could still be read from and written to the array. However, read/write performance would be exceptionally slow, and it would remain so until the drive was replaced and the array was rebuilt. The rebuild process could take a relatively long time, so if another drive failed before the rebuild completed, all data would be lost.

With four drives in a RAID 10 configuration, you would have only 1TB of total storage. However, you could withstand many cases of multiple drive failures. In addition, after a drive failure, data could still be read from and written to the array at full speed, with no noticeable loss in performance. In addition, once the failed drive is replaced, the rebuild process would go relatively quickly as compared to rebuilding a RAID 5 array. Because of the advantages of RAID 10, many are recommending it as an alternative to RAID 5 where maximum redundancy and performance are required.

Many motherboards include SATA RAID capability as a built-in feature. For those that don't, or where a higher performance or more capable SATA RAID solution is desired, you can install a SATA RAID host adapter in a PCIe slot in the system. A typical PCIe SATA RAID controller enables up to four, six, or eight drives to be attached, and you can run them in RAID Level 0, 1, 5, or 10 mode. Most PCIe SATA RAID cards use a separate SATA data channel (cable) for each drive, allowing maximum performance. Motherboard-based RAID controllers almost exclusively use SATA drives.

If you are considering a SATA RAID controller (or a motherboard with an integrated SATA RAID controller), here are some things to look for:

- RAID levels supported. (Most support 0, 1, 5, and 10. A lack of RAID 5/6 or RAID 10 support indicates a very low-end product.)
- Support for four, six, or eight drives.
- Support for 6Gbps SATA transfer rates.
- PCIe card with onboard controller (provides best performance and future compatibility; note that low-cost PCIe cards are host-based and rely on the CPU).

Software RAID

Some operating systems include software-based RAID capability; in fact, limited RAID 0, 1, and even RAID 5 functionality has been built in to some versions of Windows since Windows 2000. When Microsoft released Windows Home Server in 2007 it greatly enhanced this capability with a feature called Drive Extender, which allowed for the creation and arbitrary expansion of an array using virtually any type of drive (SATA, PATA, USB, FireWire, etc.) in any capacity. Drive Extender creates a virtual drive that is a combination of the assigned physical drives. There is limited redundancy in that by default each file saved on a Drive Extender volume is automatically stored on two different drives such that if one drive fails it can theoretically be replaced without losing any data. If more than one drive fails, then data will be lost. Unfortunately, problems with Drive Extender caused Microsoft to remove the feature from Windows Home Server 2011.

Microsoft has included a newer and better replacement for Drive Extender in Windows 8, which is now called Storage Spaces. Just like Drive Extender, it allows you to build a virtual drive using an array of drives of just about any type or capacity. One area where Storage Spaces differs from Drive Extender is in the redundancy options. In addition to two-way redundancy where data is saved on two drives, Storage Spaces allows for three-way redundancy, meaning that data will be saved on three drives. This also means that up to two drives can fail in the array without losing data. While the redundancy and reliability has been improved, just as with most software-based RAID, performance falls dramatically as compared to either a physical drive or hardware-based RAID, especially in write performance.

While the Storage Spaces feature in Windows 8 looks like an excellent option for a home server with multiple data drives, just like any other RAID array, it doesn't replace the need for backup, meaning you would need somewhere else to back up all of the data on the Storage Spaces virtual drive.

Normally, if you want both performance and reliability, you should look for hardware-based SATA RAID controllers that support RAID Level 5 or 10, or an external storage device with built-in RAID capability. You can install a PCIe-based RAID controller; however, many motherboards have RAID capability built in via the motherboard chipset. Another option is external storage devices like the Drobo (www.drobo.com), which can create and manage virtual drives using the various physical drives mounted in the enclosure. Because they rely on dedicated management hardware, they can offer better performance and reliability than even some hardware-based RAID setups.

Magnetic Storage Principles

Magnetic Storage

Most permanent or semipermanent computer data is stored magnetically, meaning a stream of binary computer data bits (0s and 1s) is stored by magnetizing tiny pieces of metal embedded on the surface of a disk or tape in a pattern that represents the data. Later, this magnetic pattern can be read and converted back into the same original stream of bits. This is the principle of magnetic storage and the subject of this chapter.

History of Magnetic Storage

Before magnetic storage, the primary computer storage medium was punch cards (paper cards with holes punched in them to indicate character or binary data), originally invented by Herman Hollerith for use in the 1890 Census.

The history of magnetic storage dates back to June 1949, when a group of IBM engineers and scientists began working on a new storage device. What they were working on was the first magnetic storage device for computers, and it revolutionized the industry. On May 21, 1952, IBM announced the IBM 726 Tape Unit with the IBM701 Defense Calculator, marking the transition from punched-card calculators to electronic computers.

Four years later, on September 13, 1956, a small team of IBM engineers in San Jose, California, introduced the first computer disk storage system as part of the 305 RAMAC (Random Access Method of Accounting and Control) computer.

The 305 RAMAC drive could store 5 million characters (that's right, only 5MB!) of data on 50 disks, each a whopping 24 inches in diameter. Individual bits were stored at a density of only 2Kb/ sq. inch. Unlike tape drives, RAMAC's recording heads could go directly to any location on a disk surface without reading all the information in between. This random accessibility had a profound effect on computer performance at the time, enabling data to be stored and retrieved significantly faster than if it were on tape.

From these beginnings, in just over 60 years the magnetic storage industry has progressed such that today you can store 4TB (4,000GB) or more on tiny 3 1/2-inch drives that fit into a single computer drive bay.

How Magnetic Fields Are Used to Store Data

All magnetic storage devices read and write data by using electromagnetism. This basic principle of physics states that as an electric current flows through a conductor (wire), a magnetic field is generated around the conductor (see Figure 8.1). Note that electrons actually flow from negative to positive, as shown in the figure, although we normally think of current flowing in the other direction.

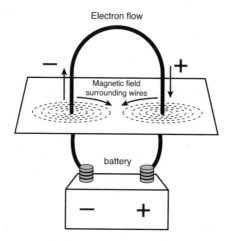

FIGURE 8.1   A magnetic field is generated around a wire when current is passed through it.

Electromagnetism was discovered in 1819 by Danish physicist Hans Christian Oersted, when he found that a compass needle would deflect away from pointing north when brought near a wire conducting an electric current. When the current was shut off, the compass needle resumed its alignment with the Earth's magnetic field and again pointed north.

The magnetic field generated by a wire conductor can exert an influence on magnetic material in the field. When the direction of the flow of electric current or polarity is reversed, the magnetic field's polarity also is reversed. For example, an electric motor uses electromagnetism to exert pushing and pulling forces on magnets attached to a rotating shaft.

Another effect of electromagnetism was discovered by Michael Faraday in 1831. He found that if a conductor is passed through a moving magnetic field, an electrical current is generated. As the polarity of the magnetic field changes, so does the direction of the electric current's flow (see Figure 8.2).

For example, an alternator, which is a type of electrical generator used in automobiles, operates by rotating electromagnets on a shaft past coils of stationary wire conductors, which consequently generates large amounts of electrical current in those conductors. Because electromagnetism works two ways, a motor can become a generator, and vice versa. When applied to magnetic storage devices, this two-way operation of electromagnetism makes it possible to record data on a disk and read that data back later. When recording, the head changes electrical impulses to magnetic fields, and when reading, the head changes magnetic fields back into electrical impulses.

The read/write heads in a magnetic storage device are U-shaped pieces of conductive material, with the ends of the U situated directly above (or next to) the surface of the actual data storage medium. The U-shaped head is wrapped with coils or windings of conductive wire, through which an electric current can flow (see Figure 8.3). When the drive logic passes a current through these coils, it generates a magnetic field in the drive head. Reversing the polarity of the electric current also causes the polarity of the generated field to change. In essence, the heads are electromagnets whose voltage can be switched in polarity quickly.

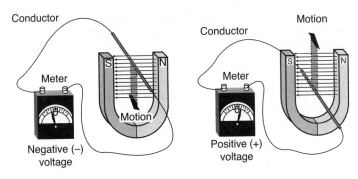

FIGURE 8.2 Current is induced in a wire when passed through a magnetic field.

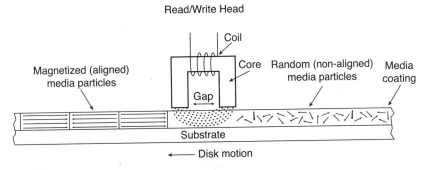

FIGURE 8.3 A magnetic read/write head.

The disk or tape that constitutes the actual storage medium consists of some form of substrate material (such as Mylar for floppy disks, or aluminum or glass for hard disks) on which a layer of magnetizable material has been deposited. This material usually is a form of iron oxide with various other elements added. Each of the individual magnetic particles on the storage medium has its own magnetic field. When the medium is blank, the polarities of those magnetic fields are normally in a state of random disarray. Because the fields of the individual particles point in random directions, each tiny magnetic field is canceled out by one that points in the opposite direction; the cumulative effect of this is a surface with no observable field polarity. With many randomly oriented fields, the net effect is no observable unified field or polarity.

When a drive's read/write head generates a magnetic field (as when writing to a disk), the field jumps the gap between the ends of the U shape. Because a magnetic field passes through a conductor much more easily than through the air, the field bends outward from the gap in the head and actually uses the adjacent storage medium as the path of least resistance to the other side of the gap. As the field passes through the medium directly under the gap, it polarizes the magnetic particles it passes through so they are aligned with the field. The field's polarity or direction—and, therefore, the polarity or direction of the field induced in the magnetic medium—is based on the direction of the flow of electric current through the coils. A change in the direction of the current flow produces a change in the direction of the magnetic field. During the development of magnetic storage, the distance between the read/write head and the media has decreased dramatically. This enables the gap to be smaller and makes the size of the recorded magnetic domain smaller. The smaller the recorded magnetic domain, the higher the density of data that can be stored on the drive.

When the magnetic field passes through the medium, the particles in the area below the head gap are aligned in the same direction as the field emanating from the gap. When the individual magnetic domains of the particles are in alignment, they no longer cancel one another out, and an observable magnetic field exists in that region of the medium. This local field is generated by the many magnetic particles that now are operating as a team to produce a detectable cumulative field with a unified direction.

The term *flux* describes a magnetic field that has a specific direction or polarity. As the surface of the medium moves under the drive head, the head can generate what is called a *magnetic flux* of a given polarity over a specific region of the medium. When the flow of electric current through the coils in the head is reversed, so is the magnetic field polarity or flux in the head gap. This flux reversal in the head causes the polarity of the magnetized particles on the disk medium to reverse.

The flux reversal (or flux transition) is a change in the polarity of the aligned magnetic particles on the surface of the storage medium. A drive head creates flux reversals on the medium to record data. For each data bit (or bits) that a drive writes, it creates a pattern of positive-to-negative and negative-to-positive flux reversals on the medium in specific areas known as *bit cells* or *transition cells*. A bit cell or transition cell is a specific area of the medium—controlled by the time and speed at which the medium travels—in which the drive head creates flux reversals. The particular pattern of flux reversals within the transition cells used to store a given data bit (or bits) is called the *encoding method*. The drive logic or controller takes the data to be stored and encodes it as a series of flux reversals over a period of time, according to the pattern dictated by the encoding method it uses.

Note

The two most popular encoding methods for magnetic media are Modified Frequency Modulation (MFM) and Run Length Limited (RLL). All floppy disk drives and some older hard disk drives use the MFM scheme. Today's hard disk drives use one of several variations on the RLL encoding method. These encoding methods are described in more detail in the section "Data-Encoding Schemes."

During the write process, voltage is applied to the head. As the polarity of this voltage changes, the polarity of the magnetic field being recorded also changes. The flux transitions are written precisely at the points where the recording polarity changes. Strange as it might seem, during the read process, a head does not generate exactly the same signal that was written. Instead, the head generates a voltage pulse or spike only when it crosses a flux transition. When the transition changes from positive to negative, the pulse that the head detects is a negative voltage. When the transition changes from negative to positive, the pulse is a positive voltage spike. This effect occurs because current is generated in a conductor only when passing through lines of magnetic force at an angle. Because the head moves parallel to the magnetic fields it created on the media, the only time the head generates voltage when reading is when passing through a polarity or flux transition (flux reversal).

In essence, while reading from the medium, the head becomes a flux transition detector, emitting voltage pulses whenever it crosses a transition. Areas of no transition generate no pulse. Figure 8.4 shows the relationship between the read and write waveforms and the flux transitions recorded on a storage medium.

You can think of the write pattern as being a square waveform that is at a positive or negative voltage level. When the voltage is positive, a field is generated in the head, which polarizes the magnetic media in one direction. When the voltage changes to negative, the magnetic field induced in the media also changes direction. Where the waveform actually transitions from positive to negative voltage, or vice versa, the magnetic flux on the disk also changes polarity. During a read, the head senses these flux transitions and generates a pulsed positive or negative waveform, rather than the continuously positive or negative waveform used during the original recording. In other words, the signal when reading is 0 volts unless the head detects a magnetic flux transition, in which case it generates a positive or negative pulse accordingly. Pulses appear only when the head is passing over flux transitions on the medium. By knowing the clock timing the drive uses, the controller circuitry can determine whether a pulse (and therefore a flux transition) falls within a given transition cell time period.

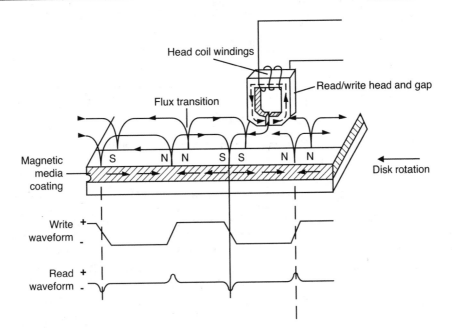

FIGURE 8.4 Magnetic write and read processes.

The electrical pulse currents generated in the head while it is passing over the storage medium in read mode are weak and can contain significant noise. Sensitive electronics in the drive and controller assembly amplify the signal above the noise level and decode the train of weak pulse currents back into binary data that is (theoretically) identical to the data originally recorded.

As you can see, hard disk drives and other storage devices read and write data by means of basic electromagnetic principles. A drive writes data by passing electrical currents through an electromagnet (the drive head), generating a magnetic field that is stored on the medium. The drive reads data by passing the head back over the surface of the medium. As the head encounters changes in the stored magnetic field, it generates a weak electrical current that indicates the presence or absence of flux transitions in the signal as it was originally written.

Read/Write Head Designs

As disk drive technology has evolved, so has the design of the read/write head. The earliest heads were simple iron cores with coil windings (electromagnets). By today's standards, the original head designs were enormous in physical size and operated at low recording densities. Over the years, head designs have evolved from the first simple ferrite core designs into the several types and technologies available today. This section discusses the various types of heads found in PC hard disk drives, including the applications and relative strengths and weaknesses of each.

Several types of heads have been used in hard disk drives over the years:

- Ferrite
- Metal-In-Gap (MIG)
- Thin-film (TF)
- Magneto-resistive (MR)

- Giant magneto-resistive (GMR)
- Perpendicular magnetic recording (PMR)

Note

By the end of 2005, hard drives based on PMR were being used in devices such as portable music players and laptop PCs. Desktop PC hard drives based on the technology became available in 2006.

PMR is covered in more detail at the end of this chapter.

Ferrite

Ferrite heads, the traditional type of magnetic-head design, evolved from the original IBM 30-30 Winchester drive. These heads have an iron-oxide core wrapped with electromagnetic coils. The drive produces a magnetic field by energizing the coils or passing a magnetic field near them. This gives the heads full read/write capability. Ferrite heads are larger and heavier than thin-film heads and therefore require a larger floating height to prevent contact with the disk while it is spinning.

Manufacturers have made many refinements to the original (monolithic) ferrite head design. One type of ferrite head, called a *composite ferrite head*, has a smaller ferrite core bonded with glass in a ceramic housing. This design permits a smaller head gap, which enables higher track densities. These heads are less susceptible to stray magnetic fields than the older monolithic design heads.

During the 1980s, composite ferrite heads were popular in many low-end drives, such as the Seagate ST-225. As density demands grew, the competing MIG and thin-film head designs came to be used in place of ferrite heads, which are virtually obsolete today. Ferrite heads can't write to the higher coercivity media necessary for high-density disk designs and have poor frequency response with higher noise levels. The main advantage of ferrite heads is that they are the cheapest type available.

Metal-In-Gap

MIG heads are a specially enhanced version of the composite ferrite design. In MIG heads, a metal substance is applied to the head's recording gap. Two versions of MIG heads are available: single sided and double sided. Single-sided MIG heads are designed with a layer of magnetic alloy placed along the trailing edge of the gap. Double-sided MIG designs apply the layer to both sides of the gap. The metal alloy is applied through a vacuum-deposition process called *sputtering*.

This magnetic alloy has twice the magnetization capability of raw ferrite and enables the head to write to the higher coercivity thin-film media needed at higher densities. MIG heads also produce a sharper gradient in the magnetic field for a better-defined magnetic pulse. Double-sided MIG heads offer even higher coercivity capability than the single-sided designs.

Because of these increases in capabilities through improved designs, MIG heads were for a time the most popular head design and were used in many hard disk drives in the late 1980s and early 1990s, and most recently in LS-120 (SuperDisk) drives.

Thin-Film

Thin-film heads are manufactured much the same way as a semiconductor chip—through a photo-lithographic process. This process creates many thousands of heads on a single circular wafer and produces a small, high-quality product.

TF heads have an extremely narrow and controlled head gap that is created by sputtering a hard aluminum material. Because this material completely encloses the gap, the area is well protected, minimizing the chance of damage from contact with the spinning disk. The core is a combination of iron and nickel alloy that has two to four times more magnetic power than a ferrite head core.

TF heads produce a sharply defined magnetic pulse that enables them to write at extremely high densities. Because they do not have a conventional coil, TF heads are more immune to variations in coil impedance. These small, lightweight heads can float at a much lower height than the ferrite and MIG heads; in some designs, the floating height is 2 micro-inches or less. Because the reduced height enables the heads to pick up and transmit a much stronger signal from the platters, the signal-to-noise ratio increases and improves accuracy. At the high track and linear densities of some drives, a standard ferrite head would not be capable of picking out the data signal from the background noise. Another advantage of TF heads is that their small size enables the platters to be stacked closer together, enabling more platters to fit into the same space.

Many of the drives in the 100MB–2GB range used TF heads, especially in the smaller form factors. TF heads displaced MIG heads as the most popular head design, but they have now themselves been displaced by newer magneto-resistive heads.

Magneto-Resistive Heads

Magneto-resistive heads, sometimes also referred to as the anisotropic magneto-resistant (AMR) heads, are capable of increasing density four times or greater as compared to the previous inductive-only heads. IBM introduced the first commercially available drive with MR heads in 1991, in a 1GB 3 1/2-inch model, and other manufacturers quickly followed suit.

All heads are detectors; that is, they are designed to detect the flux transitions in the media and convert them back to electrical signals that can be interpreted as data. One problem with magnetic recording is the ever-increasing desire for more and more density, which is putting more information (flux transitions) in a smaller and smaller space. As the magnetic domains on the disk get smaller, the signal from the heads during reading operations becomes weaker; distinguishing the true signal from the random noise or stray fields present becomes difficult. A more efficient read head, which is a more efficient way to detect these transitions on the disk, is therefore necessary.

Another magnetic effect that is well known today is being used in modern drives. When a wire is passed through a magnetic field, not only does the wire generate a small current, but the resistance of the wire also changes. Standard read heads use the head as a tiny generator, relying on the fact that the heads generate a pulsed current when passed over magnetic flux transitions. A newer type of head design pioneered by IBM instead relies on the fact that the resistance in the head wires also changes.

Rather than use the head to generate tiny currents, which must then be filtered, amplified, and decoded, an MR head uses the head as a resistor. A circuit passes a voltage through the head and watches for the voltage to change, which occurs when the resistance of the head changes as it passes through the flux reversals on the media. This mechanism for using the head results in a much stronger and clearer signal of what was on the media and enables the density to be increased.

MR heads rely on the fact that the resistance of a conductor changes slightly when an external magnetic field is present. Rather than put out a voltage by passing through a magnetic-field flux reversal—as a normal head would—the MR head senses the flux reversal and changes resistance. A small current flows through the heads, and this sense current measures the change in resistance. This design provides an output that is three or more times more powerful than a TF head during a read. In effect, MR heads are power-read heads, acting more like sensors than generators.

MR heads were more costly and complex to manufacture than older TF heads because of the additional components and manufacturing steps required:

■ Additional wires must be run to and from the head to carry the sense current.

■ Four to six more masking steps are required.

■ Because MR heads are so sensitive, they are susceptible to stray magnetic fields and require additional shielding.

Because the MR principle can only read data and is not used for writing, MR heads are really two heads in one. The assembly includes a standard inductive TF head for writing data and an MR head for reading. Because two separate heads are built in to one assembly, each head can be optimized for its task. Ferrite, MIG, and TF heads are known as single-gap heads because the same gap is used for both reading and writing, whereas the MR head uses a separate gap for each operation.

The problem with single-gap heads is that the gap length is always a compromise between what is best for reading and what is best for writing. The read function needs a thinner gap for higher resolution; the write function needs a thicker gap for deeper flux penetration to switch the medium. In a dual-gap MR head, the read and write gaps can be optimized for both functions independently. The write (TF) gap writes a wider track than the read (MR) gap reads. Thus, the read head is less likely to pick up stray magnetic information from adjacent tracks.

A typical IBM-designed MR head is shown in Figure 8.5. This figure first shows the complete MR head-and-slider assembly on the end of an actuator arm. This is the part you would see if you opened up a drive. The slider is the block device on the end of the triangular-shaped arm that carries the head. The actual head is the tiny piece shown magnified at the end of the slider, and then the MR read sensor in the head is shown further magnified.

The read element, which is the actual magneto-resistive sensor, consists of a nickel-ferrite (NiFe) film separated by a spacer from a magnetically soft layer. The NiFe film layer changes resistance in the presence of a magnetic field. Layers of shielding protect the MR sensor read element from being corrupted by adjacent or stray magnetic fields. In many designs, the second shield also functions as one pole of the write element, resulting in what is called a merged MR head. The write element is not of MR design but is instead a traditional TF inductive head.

IBM's MR head design employs a Soft Adjacent Layer (SAL) structure, consisting of the MR NiFe film, as well as a magnetically soft alloy layer separated by a film with high electrical resistance. In this design, a resistance change occurs in the NiFe layer as the MR sensor passes through a magnetic field.

As areal densities have increased, heads have been designed with narrower and thinner MR elements. More recent designs have reduced the film width between the side contacts to as little as half a micron or less.

Giant Magneto-Resistive Heads

In the quest for even greater density, IBM introduced a new type of MR head in 1997. Called *giant magneto-resistive (GMR) heads*, they are smaller than standard MR heads but are so named for the GMR effect on which they are based. The design is similar; however, additional layers replace the single NiFe layer in a conventional MR design. In MR heads, a single NiFe film changes resistance in response to a flux reversal on the disk. In GMR heads, two films (separated by a very thin copper conducting layer) perform this function.

The GMR effect was discovered in 1988 in crystal samples that were exposed to high-powered magnetic fields (1,000 times the fields used in hard disk drives). Scientists Peter Gruenberg of Julich, Germany, and Albert Fert of Paris discovered that large resistance changes were occurring in materials composed of alternating thin layers of various metallic elements. The key structure in GMR materials is a spacer layer of a nonmagnetic metal between two layers of magnetic metals. One of the magnetic layers is *pinned*, which means it has a forced magnetic orientation. The other magnetic layer is *free*, which means it is free to change orientation or alignment. Magnetic materials tend to align themselves in the same direction. So if the spacer layer is thin enough, the free layer takes on the same orientation as the pinned layer. What was discovered was that the magnetic alignment of the free magnetic layer would periodically swing back and forth from being aligned in the same magnetic direction as the pinned layer to being aligned in the opposite magnetic direction. The overall resistance is relatively low when the layers are in the same alignment and relatively high when in opposite magnetic alignment.

Figure 8.6 shows a GMR read element.

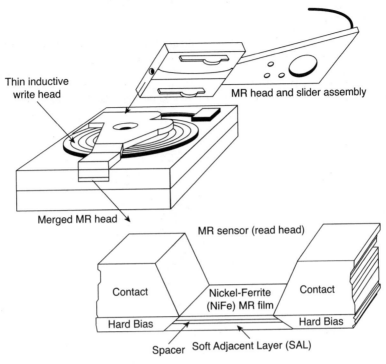

Thin inductive
write head

MR head and slider assembly

Merged MR head

MR sensor (read head)

Contact

Nickel-Ferrite
(NiFe) MR film

Contact

Hard Bias

Hard Bias

Spacer Soft Adjacent Layer (SAL)

FIGURE 8.5 Cross-section of an MR head.

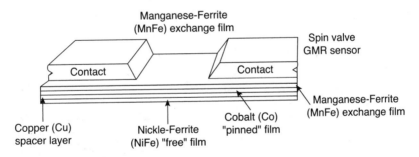

Manganese-Ferrite
(MnFe) exchange film

Spin valve
GMR sensor

Contact

Contact

Manganese-Ferrite
(MnFe) exchange film

Copper (Cu)
spacer layer

Nickle-Ferrite
(NiFe) "free" film

Cobalt (Co)
"pinned" film

FIGURE 8.6 Cross-section of a GMR head.

When a weak magnetic field, such as that from a bit on a hard disk, passes beneath a GMR head, the magnetic orientation of the free magnetic layer rotates relative to that of the other and generates a significant change in electrical resistance due to the GMR effect. Because the physical nature of the resistance change was determined to be caused by the relative spin of the electrons in the different layers, GMR heads are often referred to as spin-valve heads.

IBM announced the first commercially available drive using GMR heads (a 16.8GB 3 1/2-inch drive) in December 1997. Since then, GMR heads have become standard in most 3.5-inch and 2.5-inch drives.

In 2007 Hitachi developed a giant magneto-resistive head using perpendicular current that supports areal densities of up to 1Tbits/sq. inch or more. These are called current perpendicular-to-the-plane giant magneto-resistive heads or CPP-GMR for short, and began appearing in drives starting in 2011.

Head Sliders

The term *slider* describes the body of material that supports the actual drive head. The slider is what actually floats or slides over the surface of the disk, carrying the head at the correct distance from the medium for reading and writing. Older sliders resemble a trimaran, with two outboard pods that float along the surface of the disk media and a central "hull" portion that actually carries the head and read/write gap. Figure 8.7 shows a typical mini slider. Note that the actual head, with the read/write gap, is on the trailing end of the slider.

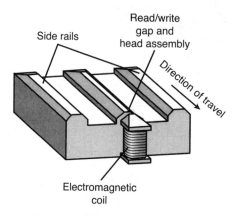

FIGURE 8.7 The underside of a typical head mini slider.

The trend toward smaller and smaller form factor drives has forced sliders to become smaller as well. The typical Mini-Winchester slider design was about 4mm×3.2mm×0.86mm in size. Most head manufacturers have since shifted to smaller Micro, Nano, Pico, or Femto sliders. The Femto sliders in use today are extremely small—about the size of the ball in the tip of a ballpoint pen. Pico and Femto sliders are assembled by using flex interconnect cable (FIC) and chip on ceramic (COC) technologies that enable the process to be completely automated.

Table 8.1 shows the characteristics of the various types of sliders used in hard disk drives.

Table 8.1   Hard Disk Drive Slider Types

			Dimensions			
Slider	**Year Introduced**	**Relative Size**	**L (mm)**	**W (mm)**	**H (mm)**	**Mass Type(mg)**
Mini	1980	100%	4.00	3.20	0.86	55.0
Micro	1986	70%	2.80	2.24	0.60	16.2
Nano (+ Pressure)	1991	62%	2.50	1.70	0.43	7.8
Nano (- Pressure)	1994	50%	2.00	1.60	0.43	5.9
Pico	1997	30%	1.25	1.00	0.30	1.6
Femto	2003	20%	0.85	0.70	0.23	0.6

Smaller sliders reduce the mass carried at the end of the head actuator arms, which provides increased acceleration and deceleration, thus leading to faster seek times. The smaller sliders also require less surface area, allowing the head to track closer to the outer and inner diameters, thus increasing the usable area of the disk platters. Further, the smaller slider contact area reduces the slight wear on the platter surface that occurs during normal startup and spindown of the drive platters. Figure 8.8 shows a magnified photo of a Femto slider mounted on the head gimbal assembly, which is on the end of the head actuator arm.

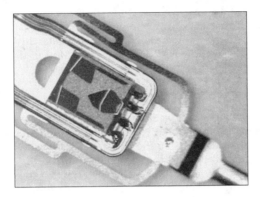

FIGURE 8.8 Magnified head gimbal assembly featuring a Femto slider. (Photo courtesy of Hitachi Global Storage Technologies.)

The newer slider designs also have specially modified surface patterns that are designed to maintain the same floating height above the disk surface, whether the slider is positioned above the inner or outer cylinders. Conventional sliders would increase or decrease their floating heights considerably according to the velocity of the disk surface traveling beneath them. Above the outer cylinders, the velocity and floating height would be higher. This arrangement is undesirable in newer drives that use zoned bit recording, in which the bit density is the same on all the cylinders. When the bit density is uniform throughout the drive, the head floating height should also be relatively constant for maximum performance. Special textured surface patterns and manufacturing techniques enable the sliders to float at a much more consistent height, making them ideal for zoned bit recording drives. For more information on zoned recording, see the section "Disk Formatting" in Chapter 9, "Hard Disk Storage."

A typical Femto air-bearing slider surface design is shown in Figure 8.9.

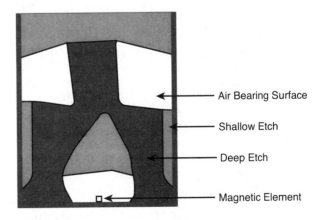

FIGURE 8.9 Femto air-bearing slider surface design.

A Femto slider has three distinct areas with complex shapes designed to achieve a consistent head-to-disk floating height across the disk as well as minimal height loss under high-altitude (low-pressure) conditions. The shallow etch area creates a stepped air inlet allowing airflow to create a positive pressure under the air-bearing surface that lifts the slider away from the disk. The deep etch area creates an opposite negative pressure pocket that simultaneously pulls the slider closer to the disk surface. The combination of positive and negative pressures is designed to balance the force of the suspension arm pushing the slider toward the disk, while keeping the slider at the desired floating height away from the disk surface. The balance of positive and negative pressures stabilizes and reduces the floating height variations commonly found in older slider designs. The first drive using the Femto slider design was the Hitachi 7K60 2 1/2-inch drive released in May 2003. Most of the higher-capacity drives on the market today use this design.

Data-Encoding Schemes

Magnetic storage is essentially an analog medium. The data a PC stores on it, however, is digital information—that is, 1s and 0s. When the drive sends digital information to a magnetic recording head, the head creates magnetic domains on the storage medium with specific polarities corresponding to the positive and negative voltages the drive applies to the head. The flux reversals form the boundaries between the areas of positive and negative polarity that the drive controller uses to encode the digital data onto the analog medium. During a read operation, each flux reversal the drive detects generates a positive or negative pulse that the device uses to reconstruct the original binary data.

To optimize the placement of flux transitions during magnetic storage, the drive passes the raw digital input data through a device called an encoder/decoder (endec), which converts the raw binary information to a waveform designed to optimally place the flux transitions (pulses) on the media. During a read operation, the endec reverses the process and decodes the pulse train back into the original binary data. Over the years, several schemes for encoding data in this manner have been developed; some are better or more efficient than others, which you see later in this section.

Other descriptions of the data-encoding process might be much simpler, but they omit the facts that make some of the issues related to hard drive reliability so critical—namely, timing. Engineers and designers are constantly pushing the envelope to stuff more and more bits of information into the limited quantity of magnetic flux reversals per inch. What they've come up with, essentially, is a design in which the bits of information are decoded not only from the presence or absence of flux reversals, but from the timing between them. The more accurately they can time the reversals, the more information that can be encoded (and subsequently decoded) from that timing information.

In any form of binary signaling, the use of timing is significant. When a read or write waveform is interpreted, the timing of each voltage transition event is critical. Timing is what defines a particular bit or transition cell—that is, the time window within which the drive is either writing or reading a transition. If the timing is off, a given voltage transition might be recognized at the wrong time as being in a different cell, which would throw the conversion or encoding off, resulting in bits being missed, added, or misinterpreted. To ensure that the timing is precise, the transmitting and receiving devices must be in perfect synchronization. For example, if recording a 0 is done by placing no transition on the disk for a given time period or cell, imagine recording ten 0 bits in a row—you would have a long period of time (ten cells) with no activity, no transitions at all.

Imagine now that the clock on the encoder was slightly off time while reading data as compared to when it was originally written. If it were fast, the encoder might think that during this long stretch of 10 cells with no transitions, only nine cells had actually elapsed. Or if it were slow, it might think that 11 cells had elapsed instead. In either case, this would result in a read error, meaning the bits that were originally written would not be read as being the same. To prevent timing errors in drive encoding/decoding, perfect synchronization is necessary between the reading and writing processes. This synchronization often is accomplished by adding a separate timing signal, called a clock signal, to the transmission between the two devices. The clock and data signals also can be combined and transmitted as a single signal. Most magnetic data-encoding schemes use this type of combination of clock and data signals.

Adding a clock signal to the data ensures that the communicating devices can accurately interpret the individual bit cells. Each bit cell is bounded by two other cells containing the clock transitions. Because clock information is sent along with the data, the clocks remain in sync, even if the medium contains a long string of identical 0 bits. Unfortunately, the transition cells used solely for timing take up space on the medium that could otherwise be used for data.

Because the number of flux transitions a drive can record in a given space on a particular medium is limited by the physical nature or density of the medium and the head technology, drive engineers have developed various ways of encoding the data by using a minimum number of flux reversals (taking into consideration the fact that some flux reversals used solely for clocking are required). Signal encoding enables the system to make the maximum use of a given drive hardware technology.

Although various encoding schemes have been tried, only a few are popular today. Over the years, these three basic types have been the most popular:

- Frequency Modulation
- Modified Frequency Modulation
- Run Length Limited

The following sections examine these codes, how they work, where they are used, and any advantages or disadvantages that apply to them. It will help to refer to Figure 8.10 (later in this chapter) as you read the descriptions of these encoding schemes because this figure depicts how each of them would store an "X" on the same media.

Frequency Modulation Encoding

One of the earliest techniques for encoding data for magnetic storage is called Frequency Modulation encoding. This encoding scheme—sometimes called Single-Density encoding—was used in the earliest floppy disk drives installed in PC systems. The original Osborne portable computer, for example, used these single-density floppy disk drives, which stored about 80KB of data on a single disk. Although it was popular until the late 1970s, FM encoding is no longer used.

Modified FM Encoding

Modified Frequency Modulation encoding was devised to reduce the number of flux reversals used in the original FM encoding scheme and, thus, to pack more data onto the disk. MFM encoding minimizes the use of clock transitions, leaving more room for the data. It records clock transitions only when a stored 0 bit is preceded by another 0 bit; in all other cases, a clock transition is not required. Because MFM minimizes the use of clock transitions, it can double the clock frequency used by FM encoding, which enables it to store twice as many data bits in the same number of flux transitions.

Because MFM encoding writes twice as many data bits by using the same number of flux reversals as FM, the clock speed of the data is doubled and the drive actually sees the same number of total flux reversals as with FM. This means a drive using MFM encoding reads and writes data at twice the speed of FM, even though the drive sees the flux reversals arriving at the same frequency as in FM.

Because it is twice as efficient as FM encoding, MFM encoding also has been called double-density recording. MFM is used in virtually all PC floppy disk drives today and was used in nearly all PC hard disks for a number of years. Today, virtually all hard disks use variations of RLL encoding, which provides even greater efficiency than MFM.

Table 8.2 shows the data bit-to-flux reversal translation in MFM encoding.

Table 8.2 MFM Data-to-Flux Transition Encoding

Data Bit Value	Flux Encoding
1	NT
0 preceded by 0	TN
0 preceded by 1	NN

T = Flux transition
N = No flux transition

Run Length Limited Encoding

Today's most popular encoding scheme for hard disks, called *Run Length Limited*, packs up to twice the information on a given disk than MFM does and three times as much information as FM. In RLL encoding, the drive combines groups of bits into a unit to generate specific patterns of flux reversals. Because the clock and data signals are combined in these patterns, the clock rate can be further increased while maintaining the same basic distance between the flux transitions on the storage medium.

IBM invented RLL encoding and first used the method in many of its mainframe disk drives. During the late 1980s, the PC hard disk industry began using RLL encoding schemes to increase the storage capabilities of PC hard disks. Today, virtually every drive on the market uses some form of RLL encoding.

Instead of encoding a single bit, RLL typically encodes a group of data bits at a time. The term *Run Length Limited* is derived from the two primary specifications of these codes, which are the minimum number (the run length) and maximum number (the run limit) of transition cells allowed between two actual flux transitions. Several variations of the scheme are achieved by changing the length and limit parameters, but only two have achieved real popularity: RLL 2,7 and RLL 1,7.

You can even express FM and MFM encoding as a form of RLL. FM can be called RLL 0,1 because as few as zero and as many as one transition cells separate two flux transitions. MFM can be called RLL 1,3 because as few as one and as many as three transition cells separate two flux transitions. (Although these codes can be expressed as variations of RLL form, it is not common to do so.)

RLL 2,7 was initially the most popular RLL variation because it offers a high-density ratio with a transition detection window that is the same relative size as that in MFM. This method provides high storage density and fairly good reliability. In high-capacity drives, however, RLL 2,7 did not prove to be reliable enough. Most of today's highest capacity drives use RLL 1,7 encoding, which offers a density ratio 1.27 times that of MFM and a larger transition detection window relative to MFM. Because of the larger relative timing window or cell size within which a transition can be detected, RLL 1,7 is a more forgiving and more reliable code, which is important when media and head technology are being pushed to their limits.

Another little-used RLL variation called RLL 3,9—sometimes also called Advanced RLL (ARLL)—allows an even higher density ratio than RLL 2,7. Unfortunately, reliability suffered too greatly under the RLL 3,9 scheme; the method was used by only a few now-obsolete controllers and has all but disappeared.

Understanding how RLL codes work is difficult without looking at an example. Within a given RLL variation (such as RLL 2,7 or 1,7), you can construct many flux transition encoding tables to demonstrate how particular groups of bits are encoded into flux transitions.

In the conversion table shown in Table 8.3, specific groups of data that are 2, 3, and 4 bits long are translated into strings of flux transitions 4, 6, and 8 transition cells long, respectively. The selected transitions for a particular bit sequence are designed to ensure that flux transitions do not occur too closely together or too far apart.

Table 8.3 RLL 2,7 Data-to-Flux Transition Encoding

Data Bit Values	Flux Encoding
10	NTNN
11	TNNN
000	NNNTNN
010	TNNTNN
011	NNTNNN
0010	NNTNNTNN
0011	NNNNTNNN

T = Flux transition

N = No flux transition

Limiting how close two flux transitions can be is necessary because of the fixed resolution capabilities of the head and storage medium. Limiting how far apart two flux transitions can be ensures that the clocks in the devices remain in sync.

In studying Table 8.3, you might think that encoding a byte value such as 00000001b would be impossible because no combinations of data bit groups fit this byte. Encoding this type of byte is not a problem, however, because the controller does not transmit individual bytes; instead, the controller sends whole sectors, making encoding such a byte possible by including some of the bits in the following byte. The only real problem occurs in the last byte of a sector if additional bits are necessary to complete the final group sequence. In these cases, the endec in the controller adds excess bits to the end of the last byte. These excess bits are then truncated during any reads so the controller always decodes the last byte correctly.

Encoding Scheme Comparisons

Figure 8.10 shows an example of the waveform written to store the ASCII character X on a hard disk drive by using three encoding schemes.

In each of these encoding scheme examples, the top line shows the individual data bits (01011000b, for example) in their bit cells separated in time by the clock signal, which is shown as a period (.). Below that line is the actual write waveform, showing the positive and negative voltages as well as head voltage transitions that result in the recording of flux transitions. The bottom line shows the transition cells, with T representing a transition cell that contains a flux transition and N representing a transition cell that is empty.

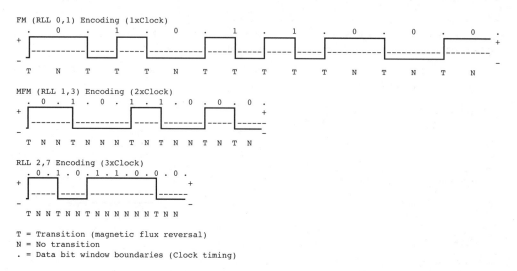

FM (RLL 0,1) Encoding (1xClock)

MFM (RLL 1,3) Encoding (2xClock)

RLL 2,7 Encoding (3xClock)

T = Transition (magnetic flux reversal)
N = No transition
. = Data bit window boundaries (Clock timing)

FIGURE 8.10 ASCII character X write waveforms using FM, MFM, and RLL 2,7 encoding.

The FM encoding example shown in Figure 8.10 is easy to explain. Each bit cell has two transition cells: one for the clock information and one for the data. All the clock transition cells contain flux transitions, and the data transition cells contain a flux transition only if the data is a 1 bit. No transition is present when the data is a 0 bit. Starting from the left, the first data bit is 0, which decodes as a flux transition pattern of TN. The next bit is a 1, which decodes as TT. The next bit is 0, which decodes as TN, and so on.

The MFM encoding scheme also has clock and data transition cells for each data bit to be recorded. As you can see, however, the clock transition cells carry a flux transition only when a 0 bit is stored after another 0 bit. Starting from the left, the first bit is a 0, and the preceding bit is unknown (assume 0), so the flux transition pattern is TN for that bit. The next bit is a 1, which always decodes to a transition-cell pattern of NT. The next bit is 0, which was preceded by 1, so the pattern stored is NN. By using Table 8.2 (shown earlier), you easily can trace the MFM encoding pattern to the end of the byte. You can see that the minimum and maximum numbers of transition cells between any two flux transitions are one and three, respectively, which explains why MFM encoding can also be called RLL 1,3.

The RLL 2,7 pattern is more difficult to see because it encodes groups of bits rather than individual bits. Starting from the left, the first group that matches the groups listed in Table 8.3 is the first three bits, 010. These bits are translated into a flux transition pattern of TNNTNN. The next two bits, 11, are translated as a group to TNNN; and the final group, 000 bits, is translated to NNNTNN to complete the byte. As you can see in this example, no additional bits are needed to finish the last group.

Notice that the minimum and maximum numbers of empty transition cells between any two flux transitions in this example are two and six, although a different example could show a maximum of seven empty transition cells. This is where the RLL 2,7 designation comes from. Because even fewer transitions are recorded than in MFM, the clock rate can be increased to three times that of FM or 1.5 times that of MFM, thus storing more data in the same space. Notice, however, that the resulting write waveform itself looks exactly like a typical FM or MFM waveform in terms of the number and separation of the flux transitions for a given physical portion of the disk. In other words, the physical minimum and maximum distances between any two flux transitions remain the same in all three of these encoding scheme examples.

Partial-Response, Maximum-Likelihood Decoders

Another feature often used in modern hard disk drives involves the disk read circuitry. Read channel circuits using Partial-Response, Maximum-Likelihood (PRML) technology enable disk drive manufacturers to increase the amount of data stored on a disk platter by up to 40%. PRML replaces the standard "detect one peak at a time" approach of traditional analog peak-detect, read/write channels with digital signal processing.

As the data density of hard drives increases, the drive must necessarily record the flux reversals closer together on the medium. This makes reading the data on the disk more difficult because the adjacent magnetic peaks can begin to interfere with each other. PRML modifies the way the drive reads the data from the disk. The controller analyzes the analog data stream it receives from the heads by using digital signal sampling, processing, and detection algorithms (this is the partial response element) and predicts the sequence of bits the data stream is most likely to represent (the maximum likelihood element). PRML technology can take an analog waveform, which might be filled with noise and stray signals, and produce an accurate reading from it.

This might not sound like a precise method of reading data that must be bit-perfect to be usable, but the aggregate effect of the digital signal processing filters out the noise efficiently enough to enable the drive to place the flux change pulses much more closely together on the platter, thus achieving greater densities. Most drives with capacities of 2GB or above use PRML technology in their endec circuits.

Capacity Measurements

In December 1998, the International Electrotechnical Commission (IEC)—the leading international organization for worldwide standardization in electrotechnology—approved as an IEC International Standard the names and symbols for prefixes for binary multiples for use in the fields of data processing and data transmission. Prior to this, a lot of confusion had existed as to whether a megabyte stood for 1 million bytes (106) or 1,048,576 bytes (220). Even so, these new prefixes have yet to be widely adopted, and confusion still reigns. The industry-standard abbreviations for the units used to measure the capacity of magnetic (and other) drives are shown in Table 8.4.

Table 8.4 Standard Abbreviations and Meanings

Abbreviation	Description	Power	Value
K	Kilo	10^3	1,000
Ki	Kibi	2^{10}	1,024
M	Mega	10^6	1,000,000
Mi	Mebi	2^{20}	1,048,576
G	Giga	10^9	1,000,000,000
Gi	Gibi	2^{30}	1,073,741,824
T	Tera	10^{12}	1,000,000,000,000
Ti	Tebi	2^{40}	1,099,511,627,776
P	Peta	10^{15}	1,000,000,000,000,000
Pi	Pebi	2^{50}	1,125,899,906,842,624

According to this prefix standard, 1 mebibyte (1 MiB = 2^{20} B = 1,048,576 B) and 1 megabyte (1MB = 10^6 B = 1,000,000 B) are not equal. Because these prefixes are not in widespread use (and they might never be), M in most cases can indicate both decimal millions of *bytes* and binary *megabytes*. Similarly, G is often used to refer to decimal *billions of bytes* and binary *gigabytes*. In general, memory values are expressed by using the binary values, although disk capacities can go either way. This often leads to confusion in reporting disk capacities because many manufacturers tend to use whichever value makes their products look better. For example, drive capacities are often rated in decimal billions (G - Giga), whereas most BIOS chips and operating system utilities, such as the Windows FDISK, rate the same drive in binary gigabytes (Gi - Gibi). Note also that when bits and bytes are used as part of some other measurement, the difference between bits and bytes is often distinguished by the use of a lower- or uppercase *B*. For example, megabits are typically abbreviated with a lowercase *b*, resulting in the abbreviation *Mbps* for megabits per second, whereas MBps indicates megabytes per second.

Areal Density

Areal density is often used as a technology growth-rate indicator for the hard disk drive industry. *Areal density* is defined as the product of the linear bits per inch (BPI), measured along the length of the tracks around the disk, multiplied by the number of tracks per inch (TPI), measured radially on the disk (see Figure 8.11). The results are expressed in units of megabits or gigabits per square inch (Mb/sq. inch or Gb/sq. inch) and are used as a measure of efficiency in drive recording technology. Current high-capacity drives record at areal densities exceeding 600Gb/sq. inch.

Drives record data in tracks, which are circular bands of data on the disk. Each track is divided into sectors. Figure 8.12 shows an actual floppy disk sprayed with magnetic developer (powdered iron) such that an image of the actual tracks and sectors can be clearly seen. The disk shown is a 5 1/4-inch 360KB floppy, which has 40 tracks per side, with each track divided into nine sectors. Note that each sector is delineated by gaps in the recording, which precede and follow the track and sector headers (where ID and address information resides). You can clearly see the triple gap preceding the first sector, which includes the track and sector headers. Then, following in a counterclockwise direction, you see each subsequent sector, preceded by gaps delineating the header for that sector. The area between the headers is where the sector data is written.

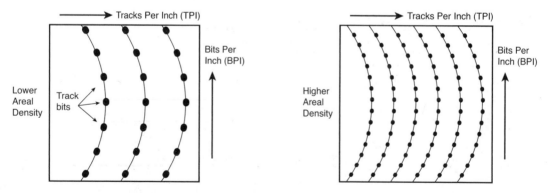

FIGURE 8.11 Areal density, combining tracks per inch and bits per inch.

Notice that sector 9 is longer than the others; this is to enable rotational speed differences between drives, so that all the data can be written before running into the start of the track. Also notice that a good portion of the disk surface isn't used because it is simply impractical to have the heads travel in and out that far, and the difference in length between the sectors on the inner and outer tracks becomes more of a problem.

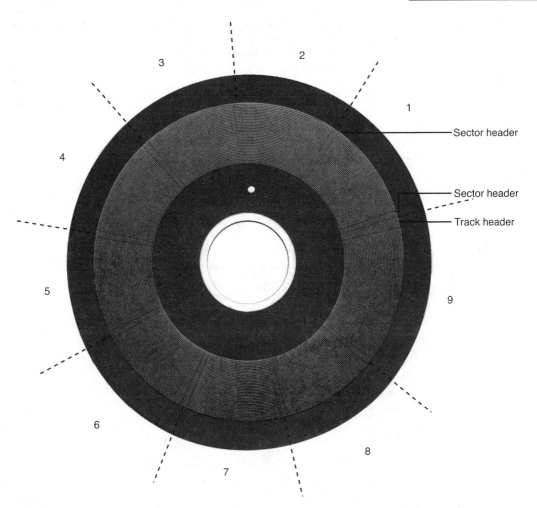

Sector header

Sector header

Track header

FIGURE 8.12 360KB floppy disk media sprayed with magnetic developer (powdered iron) showing the actual track and sector images.

Areal density has been rising steadily since the first magnetic storage drive (the IBM RAMAC, featuring an areal density of 2Kb/sq. inch) was introduced in 1956. Density initially grew at a rate of about 25% per year (doubling every four years); then in the early 1990s the rate accelerated to a growth rate of about 60% per year (doubling every year and a half). The development and introduction of MR heads in 1991, GMR heads in 1997, and AFC pixie dust media in 2001 (see the next section) subsequently drove a further increase in the areal density growth rate to 100% annually. The result of all this growth in density is amazing. In just slightly more than 50 years since the RAMAC drive was introduced, the areal density of magnetic storage has increased more than 200 million fold, from 2Kb/sq. inch in the 1956 RAMAC (5MB of storage on 50 24-inch platters) to beyond 500Gb/sq. inch in 3TB drives in 2010.

Current drives have used perpendicular recording techniques to go well past what was previously considered the point at which the superparamagnetic effect takes place. This is an effect in which the magnetic domains become so small that they are intrinsically unstable at room temperature. Techniques such as perpendicular recording combined with extremely high coercivity media are being employed to enable future magnetic storage densities of up to 1000Gb/sq. inch or more, but beyond that, scientists and engineers might have to look toward other technologies. One such technology being considered for the future is patterned media, in which a disk is preformatted with magnetic domains that can be more tightly packed without interfering with each other. Another possible future technology is holographic storage, in which a laser writes data three-dimensionally in a crystal plate or cube.

Figure 8.13 shows how areal density has increased by a factor of more than 200 million times from when magnetic storage was developed (1956 RAMAC) to the present.

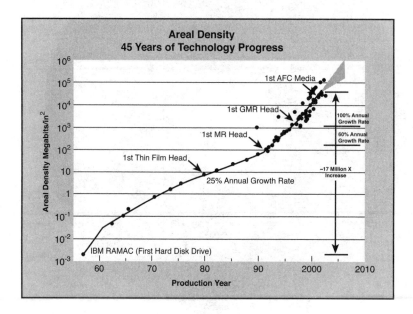

FIGURE 8.13   Evolution of areal density in magnetic disk storage.

To increase areal density while maintaining the same external drive form factors, drive manufacturers have developed media and head technologies to support these higher areal densities, such as ceramic/glass platters, GMR heads, pseudo-contact recording, and PRML electronics, as discussed earlier in this chapter. The primary challenge in achieving higher densities is manufacturing drive heads and disks to operate at closer tolerances. Improvements in tolerances and the use of more platters in a given form factor continue to fuel improvements in drive capacity, but drive makers continue to seek even greater capacity increases, both by improving current technologies and by developing new ones.

To fit more data on a platter of a given size, you must place the tracks more closely together, and the heads must be capable of achieving greater precision in their placements over the tracks. This also means that, as hard disk capacities increase, heads must float ever closer to the disk surface during operation. The gap between the head and disk is as close as 10 nanometers (0.01 microns) in some drives, which is approximately the thickness of a cell membrane. By comparison, a human hair is typically 80 microns in diameter, which is 8,000 times thicker than the gap between the head and disk in some drives. The prospect of actual contact or near contact recording is being considered for future drives to further increase density.

Perpendicular Magnetic Recording

Originally all hard drives and other types of magnetic media recorded data using longitudinal recording, which stores magnetic bits horizontally across the surface of the media. Today, however, perpendicular recording, which aligns magnetic signals vertically on the media surface, is being incorporated in modern drives to achieve higher data densities. This process works because vertically oriented magnetic bits use less space than longitudinally stored bits (see Figure 8.14). Virtually all the major drive vendors are working with perpendicular recording as a way to achieve signal density surpassing what is achievable even with AFC pixie dust media.

Conventional magnetic recording places magnetic domains longitudinally, meaning the domains lie end to end on the disk. This not only limits the density of the domains, but also helps to enable the superparamagnetic effect. Long ago it was realized that if one could place the domains perpendicular to the media (also called a *vertical recording*), the density could be increased, as could the resistance of the domains to the superparamagnetic effect. Although the concept was easy to understand, actually implementing it has been difficult.

Unlike GMR heads and AFC media—both of which can be added relatively easily to existing drive technologies—perpendicular recording requires entirely new read/write head designs. Figure 8.14 shows the difference between perpendicular and longitudinal recording. You can get at least twice the number of magnetic domains in the same space with perpendicular recording.

Using perpendicular recording, the heads are designed to write deep into the media, using a thicker soft magnetic underlayer as a return path for the magnetic field. This enables the domains to be vertically aligned, and thus placed much more closely together without unwanted interaction problems.

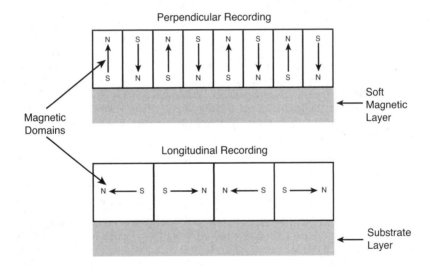

FIGURE 8.14 Perpendicular versus longitudinal recording.

Perpendicular recording was first demonstrated in the late nineteenth century by Danish scientist Valdemar Poulsen, who was also the first person to demonstrate that sound could be recorded magnetically. There weren't many advances in perpendicular recording until 1976 when Dr. Shun-ichi Iwasaki (president of the Tohoku Institute of Technology in Japan) verified the distinct density advantages in perpendicular recording. Then in 1978, Dr. T. Fujiwara began an intensive research and development program at the Toshiba Corporation that eventually resulted in the perfection of floppy disk media optimized for perpendicular recording and the first commercially available magnetic storage devices using the technique.

The first use of perpendicular recording in PCs was with the 3 1/2-inch, 2.88MB ED (extra-high density) floppy format developed by Toshiba and officially announced in 1987, with the ED drives and disks finally reaching production in 1989. IBM officially adopted these drives in its PS/2 systems in

1991, and a number of manufacturers began making them for IBM and other PC manufacturers, including Toshiba, Mitsubishi, Sony, and Panasonic. Because a 2.88MB ED drive can fully read and write 1.44MB HD disks (due to BIOS manufacturers fully integrating 2.88MB floppy support in the BIOS) and because DOS 5.0 and later included support for the 2.88MB format, the change to 2.88MB was an easy one. Unfortunately, due to high media costs and a relatively low increase in data capacity at a time when floppy disks were being replaced by writable CDs, these drives never caught on.

Despite the 2.88MB ED floppy's failure in the marketplace, Toshiba and other companies continued developing perpendicular magnetic recording for other media, especially hard disk drives. Unfortunately, they would find that perpendicular recording technology was too far ahead of its time when it came to hard drives, where the existing technology was well entrenched, and where density evolution was already progressing at rates almost too fast for the industry to assimilate. It would take almost 20 more years before the existing longitudinal recording would begin to run out of steam as it reached 100Gb/sq. inch, and the looming superparamagnetic limit would cause drive engineers to finally find justification for switching to perpendicular recording.

In April 2002, Read-Rite Corporation, a major maker of read/write heads, reached areal densities of 130Gb/sq. inch in a prototype drive using media provided by Maxtor subsidiary MMC Technology. In November 2002, Seagate Technology announced it had achieved areal densities of more than 100Gb/sq. inch in a prototype drive using this technology as well. According to two independent studies published in 2000, perpendicular recording was projected to enable densities of up to 1,000Gb (1 terabit) per square inch in the future, a prediction that is well on its way to becoming true.

Perpendicular recording finally became commercially available in hard disk drives on August 16, 2005, when Toshiba's Storage Device Division announced shipment of the world's first hard disk using PMR technology. These were 1.8-inch drives used primarily in portable consumer electronics devices—most notably the Apple iPod media players, but also found in some of the smallest laptop PCs, such as the Toshiba Libretto series. The first 1.8-inch drives using PMR were the 40GB and 80GB models, which store 40GB on a single platter and are available in single-platter 40GB and dual-platter 80GB versions. These drives featured the highest areal density of any drives then on the market at 133Gb/sq. inch (206Mb/sq. mm). Although not normally used in PCs, these drives can be found in some of the extremely small and lightweight laptop systems such as the Toshiba Libretto.

In June 2006, Toshiba introduced a 200GB 2.5-inch PMR drive only 9.5mm thick and weighing only 98 grams. This became the highest capacity 2.5-inch drive available at the time, and it featured the world's highest areal density (178.8Gb/sq. inch or 277Mb/sq. mm) in a production drive. In October 2006, Toshiba announced it had produced more than one million drives using PMR technology.

Seagate introduced the world's first 2.5-inch PMR-based hard disk with the Momentus 5400.3 160, a 160GB 2.5-inch drive designed primarily for laptops. Although Seagate announced the drive in June 2005, it wasn't actually available for purchase until January 2006. In April 2006, Seagate introduced the Barracuda 7200.10 drive, which was both the first 750GB drive on the market as well as the first 3.5-inch drive to use perpendicular recording.

Other manufacturers have also developed PMR drives; in fact, virtually all hard drive manufacturers have shifted the bulk of their product to PMR-based drives to continue the incredible capacity growth trends in magnetic storage. In January 2007, Hitachi introduced the Deskstar 7K1000, which used perpendicular recording to achieve the milestone of being the world's first 1TB (terabyte) drive. At the introduction, Hitachi noted that it took the storage industry 35 years to move drive capacity from 5MB to 1GB (1956 to 1991), 14 more years to get to 500GB (1991 to 2005), and only two more years (2005 to 2007) to hit 1TB. This clearly shows Moore's Law in effect for magnetic storage. Later, in June 2007, Hitachi introduced the 5K250, a 250GB 2.5-inch drive storing data at 205Gb/sq. inch areal density. Western Digital introduced the first 2TB drive in early 2009, and in 2010 both Seagate and Western Digital introduced the first 3TB drives (external and internal, respectively). In late 2011, Seagate was the first to ship a 4TB external drive, followed by Hitachi with the first 4TB internal drive. These new high-capacity drives store data at areal densities of 600Gb/sq. inch or higher.

Hard Disk Storage

Definition of a Hard Disk

The hard disk drive (HDD) is one of the most important and yet mysterious parts of a computer system. HDDs are sealed units used for nonvolatile data storage. *Nonvolatile*, or semipermanent, storage means that the storage device retains the data even when no power is supplied. Because HDDs store crucial programming and data, the consequences of failures are usually serious. To build, maintain, service, or upgrade a PC system properly, it is important to know how hard disks function.

HDDs contain rigid, circular platters, usually constructed of aluminum or glass (see Figure 9.1). These platters can't bend or flex—hence the term *hard disk*. In most drives you can't remove the platters, which is why they are sometimes called *fixed* disk drives.

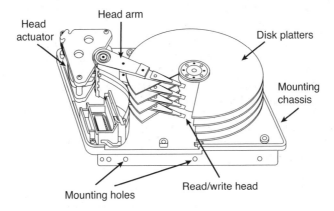

FIGURE 9.1 Hard disk heads and platters.

Note

HDDs are sometimes referred to as *Winchester drives*. This term dates back to 1973, when IBM introduced the model 3340 drive, which had 30MB of fixed platter and 30MB of removable platter storage on separate spindles. The drive was code-named Winchester by project leader Ken Haughton because the original capacity designation (30-30) sounded like the popular .30-30 (caliber-grains of charge) cartridge used by the Winchester 94 rifle introduced in 1895. The original 3340 "Winchester" drive was the first to use a sealed head/disk assembly, and the name has since been applied to subsequent drives using similar technology.

Hard Drive Advancements

The first hard drive appeared in 1956. One year later in 1957, Cyril Northcote Parkinson published his famous compilation of essays titled *Parkinson's Law*, which begins with the statement, "Work expands so as to fill the time available for its completion." A corollary of Parkinson's most famous "law" can be applied to hard drives: "Data expands so as to fill the space available for its storage." This, of course, means that no matter how big a drive you get, you *will* find a way to fill it. I know that I have lived by that dictum since purchasing my first HDD nearly 30 years ago.

Even though I am well aware of the exponential growth of everything associated with computers, I am still amazed at how large and fast modern drives have become. The first hard drive I purchased in 1983 was a 10MB (that's megabyte, not gigabyte) Miniscribe model 2012, which was a 5 1/4-inch (platter) drive that was 203.2mm×146mm×82.6mm or 8 inches×5.75 inches×3.25 inches in overall size and weighed 2.5kg (5.5 lb., which is heavier than many laptop computers)! By comparison, a modern 4TB 3 1/2-inch drive is about 5 3/4 inches×4 inches×1 inch (146mm×102mm×25mm) in overall size, weighs only 1.54 lb. (0.70kg), offering 400,000 times more storage in a package that is about one-sixth the size and one-fourth the weight of my old Miniscribe.

Obviously, the large storage capacities found on modern drives are useless unless you can also quickly transfer the data to and from the disk. The hard disk as found in the original IBM XT in 1983 had a constant data transfer rate from the media of about 100KBps. Today, hard disk drives feature average transfer rates of up to 150MBps or more, while solid-state drives have even faster transfer rates of 550MBps or more. That's from 1,000 to 5,500 times faster!

Much like the increases in drive capacity and performance, the speed of the interface has come a long way since the ST-506/412 interface used in the original IBM-PC and XT, which had a transfer rate of only 5Mbps. Modern interfaces offer data transfer rates of up to 133MBps for Parallel AT Attachment (ATA), up to 600MBps for Serial ATA (SATA) and Serial Attached SCSI (SAS), and up to nearly 2,000MBps for SATA Express. Up until the advent of high-performance Solid-State Drives (SSDs), these interfaces were typically much faster than the individual drives they supported, meaning that the true transfer rate you will see was almost entirely limited by the drive and not the interface you choose. SSDs have changed that game and have been pushing the industry to develop faster interfaces. The modern interfaces have bandwidth to spare for future developments and advances in hard disk technology.

Note

The book *Parkinson's Law* (ISBN: 1-56849-015-1) is still in print and is, in fact, considered one of the essential tomes of business and management study even today.

In 2006, the HDD celebrated its 50th anniversary, a milestone in computing technology. By the time PCs arrived on the scene in 1981, hard drives of 5MB in capacity were available. To give you an idea of how far hard drives have come in the 30+ years they have been used in PCs, I outlined some of the more profound changes in PC-based hard disk storage:

- Maximum storage capacities have increased from the 5MB 5 1/4-inch full-height drives available in 1981 to 4TB in 2012 for 3 1/2-inch half-height drives, 1.5TB for laptop 2 1/2-inch drives, and 250GB for 1.8-inch drives. Hard drives smaller than 200GB are rare in new desktop or even laptop systems.

- Data transfer rates to and from the media (sustained transfer rates) have increased from about 100KBps for the original IBM XT in 1983 to an average of over 150MBps for some of the fastest drives today.

- Average seek times (how long it takes to move the heads to a particular cylinder) have decreased from more than 85ms (milliseconds) for the 10MB drives IBM used in the 1983 vintage PC-XT to as low as 3.3ms for 15,000 rpm drives today.

- My first 10MB hard drive/controller cost $1,695 for the drive and $695 for the controller in 1983. That's equal to more than $5,514 today! Currently you can get 2TB drives (with integrated controller) for around $100 (or less), which means that the price of a typical hard drive today costs well over 200 times less than what it did nearly 30 years ago. HDDs used to be an expensive high-end component; now they are a cheap, almost disposable commodity.

Note

IBM left the hard disk business when it sold its Hard Disk Drive operations division to Hitachi on January 6, 2003. Hitachi Global Storage Technologies (www.hgst.com), which was formed to manufacture, sell, and support both Hitachi and former IBM disk drive products such as Travelstar, Microdrive, Ultrastar, and Deskstar product lines, was then acquired by Western Digital in 2012, making Western Digital the largest HDD manufacturer.

Form Factors

The cornerstone of the PC industry has always been standardization. With disk drives, this is evident in the physical and electrical form factors that comprise modern drives. By using industry-standard form factors, you can purchase a system or chassis from one manufacturer and yet physically and electrically install a drive from a different manufacturer. Form factor standards ensure that available drives will fit in the bay, the screw holes will line up, and the standard cables and connections will plug in. Without these industry standards, there would be no compatibility between different chassis, motherboards, cables, and drives.

You might wonder how these form factors are established. In some cases, it is simply that one manufacturer makes a popular product of a particular shape and connection protocol, and others copy or clone those parameters, making other products that are physically or electrically compatible. In other cases, various committees or groups have been formed to dictate certain industry standards. Then, it is up to the companies that make applicable products to create them to conform to these standards.

Over the years, disk drives have been introduced in several industry-standard form factors, usually identified by the approximate size of the platters contained inside the drive. Table 9.1 lists the various disk drive form factors that have been used in PCs and portables.

Table 9.1   Hard Disk Form Factors

Height	Width	Depth	Volume
5 1/4-Inch Drives			
3.25 in. (82.6mm)	5.75 in. (146.0mm)	8 in. (203.2mm)	149.5 ci (2449.9 cc)
5 1/4-Inch Half-Height Drives			
1.63 in. (41.3mm)	5.75 in. (146.0mm)	8.00 in. (203.2mm)	74.8 ci (1224.9 cc)
3 1/2-Inch Half-Height Drives			
1.63 in. (41.3mm)	4 in. (101.6mm)	5.75 in. (146.0mm)	37.4 ci (612.5 cc)
3 1/2-Inch 1/3-Height Drives			
1.00 in. (25.4mm)	4 in. (101.6mm)	5.75 in. (146.0mm)	23.0 ci (376.9 cc)
2 1/2-Inch Drives			
19.0mm (0.75 in.) 17.0mm (0.67 in.) 12.7mm (0.50 in.) 12.5mm (0.49 in.) 9.5mm (0.37 in.) 8.5mm (0.33 in.) 7mm (0.28 in.)	70.0mm (2.76 in.)	100.0mm (3.94 in.)	133.0 cc (8.1 ci) 119.0 cc (7.3 ci) 88.9 cc (5.4 ci) 87.5 cc (5.3 ci) 66.5 cc (4.1 ci) 59.5 cc (3.6 ci) 49.0 cc (3.0 ci)
1.8-Inch Drives			
9.5mm (0.37 in.) 7.0mm (0.28 in.)	70.0mm (2.76 in.)	60.0mm (2.36 in.)	39.9 cc (2.4 ci) 29.4 cc (1.8 ci)
1.8-Inch PC Card Drives			
8.0mm (0.31 in.) 5.0mm (0.20 in.)	54.0mm (2.13 in.)	78.5mm (3.09 in.)	33.9 cc (2.1 ci) 21.2 cc (1.3 ci)
1-Inch Microdrives			
5.0mm (0.20 in.)	42.8mm (1.69 in.)	36.4mm (1.43 in.)	7.8 cc (0.5 ci)

The first figure listed for each dimension is the dimension on which the standard is based; the second one is derived through a conversion. Some standards are based on SAE (English) measurements, whereas others are based on SI (metric) measurements.

Currently, 3 1/2-inch drives are the most popular for desktops, whereas 2 1/2-inch and smaller drives are popular in laptops and other portable devices. Parallel ATA (PATA) drives have been replaced by SATA drives in new systems. PATA drives will still be available for upgrading older systems, although the choices are becoming more limited.

5 1/4-Inch Drive

Shugart Associates introduced the 5 1/4-inch form factor along with the first 5 1/4-inch floppy drive in 1976. The story goes that founder Al Shugart then left that company and founded Seagate Technologies, which introduced the first 5 1/4-inch (Model ST-506, 5MB capacity) hard disk in 1980, predating the IBM PC. IBM later used the Seagate ST-412 (10MB) drive in some of its PC-XT models, which were among the first PCs to be sold with hard drives built in. The physical format of the 5 1/4-inch hard disk back then was the same as the 5 1/4-inch full-height floppy drive, so both fit the same size bay in a chassis. For example, the original IBM PC and XT models had two 5 1/4-inch full-height bays that could accept these drives. The first portable systems (such as the original Compaq Portable) used these drives as well. Later, the 5 1/4-inch form factor was reduced in height by one-half when the appropriately named 5 1/4-inch half-height floppy drives and hard drives were introduced. This allowed two drives to fit in a bay originally designed for one. The 5 1/4-inch half-height form factor is still used as the form factor for optical drives and is the standard form factor for larger drive bays in all modern desktop PC chassis.

3 1/2-Inch Drive

Sony introduced the first 3 1/2-inch floppy drive in 1981, which used a smaller width and depth but the same height as the half-height 5 1/4-inch form factor. These were called *3 1/2-inch half-height drives*, even though there was no such thing as a "full-height" 3 1/2-inch drive. Rodime followed with the first 3 1/2-inch half-height hard disk in 1983. Later 3 1/2-inch floppy and hard drives would be reduced in height to only 1 inch, which was just under one-third of the original 5 1/4-inch full-height form factor. (These were sometimes called *1/3-height drives*.) Today, the 1-inch high version has become the modern industry-standard 3 1/2-inch form factor.

2 1/2-Inch Drive

PrairieTek introduced the 2 1/2-inch form factor in 1988, which proved to be ideal for laptop and notebook computers. As laptop sales grew, so did sales of the 2 1/2-inch drives. Although PrairieTek was the first with that form factor, other drive manufacturers quickly capitalized on the market by also introducing 2 1/2-inch drives. Finally, in 1994 Conner Peripherals, Inc., paid $18 million for PrairieTek's 2 1/2-inch disk drive technology, and PrairieTek went out of business. Since the 2 1/2-inch drives first appeared, virtually all laptop and notebook systems have used them. Although 2 1/2-inch drives can also be used in desktop systems, the 3 1/2-inch drive continues to dominate the desktop market due to greater capacity and speed and lower cost.

The 2 1/2-inch drives have been manufactured in various thicknesses (or heights), and many notebook and laptop systems are restricted as to how thick a drive they can support. Here are the common thicknesses that have been available:

- 7mm
- 8.5mm
- 9.5mm
- 12.5mm
- 12.7mm
- 17.0mm
- 19.0mm

The most popular sizes over the years have been the 9.5mm and 12.5mm thick versions; however, most current systems use the 9.5mm or 7mm form factors. A thinner drive can almost always be installed in place of a thicker one; however, most systems do not have the room to accept a thicker drive than they were originally designed to use.

The 2.5-inch form factor is also commonly used for SSDs and for hybrid drives (hard disk drives that also include flash memory).

▶▶ To learn more about SSDs, see "SSD (Solid-State Drive)" in Chapter 10, "Flash and Removable Storage."

1.8-Inch Drive

The 1.8-inch drive was introduced by Integral Peripherals in 1991 and has had problems gaining acceptance in the marketplace ever since. This size was initially created because it fit perfectly in the PC Card (PCMCIA) form factor, making it ideal as add-on removable storage for laptop and notebook systems. Unfortunately, the 1.8-inch drive market was slow to take shape, and in 1998 an investment group called Mobile Storage bought Integral Peripherals' 1.8-inch drive technology and Integral Peripherals then went out of business. Several other companies have introduced 1.8-inch drives over the years—most notably HP, Calluna, Toshiba, and Hitachi. HP exited the disk drive market completely in 1996, and Calluna finally ceased operation in 2001. Toshiba introduced its 1.8-inch drives (available in the physical format of a Type II PC Card) in 2000, and Hitachi entered the 1.8-inch drive market in 2003. Toshiba introduced its last 1.8-inch drives in capacities of up to 320GB in 2009. There are no 1.8-inch HDDs currently being manufactured; however, they are still available in the marketplace for repair, and several manufacturers are making SSDs in the 1.8-inch form factor.

The 1.8-inch form factor is also being used by SSD manufacturers such as AMP, Intel, Kingston, KingSpec, and OCZ.

▶▶ To learn more about SSDs, see the Chapter 10 section, "SSD (Solid-State Drive)," **p. 511**.

1-Inch Drives

In 1998, IBM introduced a 1-inch drive called the Microdrive, incorporating a single platter about the size of a quarter! Seagate released similar drives in 2004. Microdrive capacities varied from 170MB to 12GB over the life of these products. These drives were available with several interfaces, but the most popular was that of a Type II Compact Flash (CF) card. This meant the drives could be used in almost any device that took CF cards, including digital cameras, personal digital assistants (PDAs), and MP3 players such as the Apple iPod Mini. IBM's disk drive division was sold to Hitachi in 2003 and combined with Hitachi's storage technology business as Hitachi Global Storage Technologies. Hitachi and Seagate phased out Microdrive production after 2008 since by then flash-based CF cards had surpassed the Microdrives in capacity, performance, and price.

Note

HP introduced a 20MB 1.3-inch disk drive called the KittyHawk in 1992, originally intended for the handheld computer market. In 1994, HP followed with a 40MB model. These small drives were expensive and proved to be too far ahead of their time, as were the handheld computers they were intended for. After two years of low sales, HP discontinued the KittyHawk family.

In 2004, Toshiba introduced the smallest drive to date: the 0.85-inch drive, which is about the size of a postage stamp and stores up to 4GB. This drive was designed for use in cell phones, digital audio players, PDAs, digital still cameras, camcorders, and more. As with the Microdrive, these were eventually discontinued due to the advances in flash memory.

HDD Operation

The basic physical construction of an HDD consists of spinning disks with heads that move over the disks and store data in tracks and sectors. The heads read and write data in concentric rings called *tracks*. These are divided into segments called *sectors*, which typically store 512 or 4,096 bytes each (see Figure 9.2).

HDDs usually have multiple disks, called *platters*, that are stacked on top of each other and spin in unison, each with two sides on which the drive stores data. Most drives have two or three platters, resulting in four or six sides, but some PC hard disks have had up to 12 platters and 24 sides with 24 heads to read them (Seagate Barracuda 180). The identically aligned tracks on each side of every platter together make up a cylinder (see Figure 9.3). An HDD usually has one head per platter side, with all the heads mounted on a common carrier device or rack. The heads move radially across the disk in unison; they can't move independently because they are mounted on the same carrier or rack, called an *actuator*.

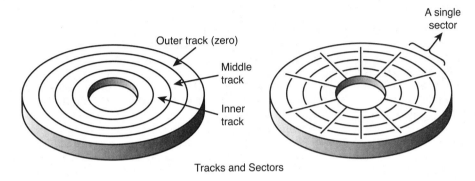

Tracks and Sectors

FIGURE 9.2 The tracks and sectors on a disk.

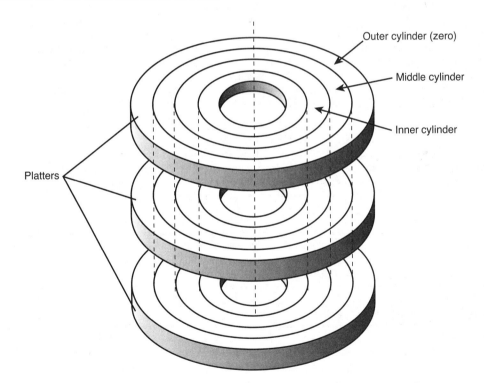

FIGURE 9.3 Hard disk cylinders.

Originally, most hard disks spun at 3,600 rpm—approximately 10 times faster than a floppy disk drive. For many years, 3,600 rpm was pretty much a constant among hard drives. Now, however, most drives spin much faster. Although speeds can vary, modern drives typically spin the platters at either

4,200 rpm, 5,400 rpm, 7,200 rpm, 10,000 rpm, or 15,000 rpm. Most standard-issue drives found in PCs today spin at 7,200 rpm, with high-performance models spinning at 10,000 rpm, although many less-expensive drives still spin at 5,400 rpm. Some of the small 2 1/2-inch notebook drives run at only 4,200 rpm to conserve power, and 15,000 rpm drives are usually found only in high-performance workstations or servers, where their higher prices, heat generation, and noise can be more easily dealt with. High rotational speeds combined with a fast head-positioning mechanism and more sectors per track are what make one hard disk faster overall than another.

The heads in most HDDs do not (and should not!) touch the platters during normal operation. However, on most drives, the heads do rest on the platters when the drive is powered off. In most drives, when the drive is powered off, the heads move to the innermost cylinder, where they land on the platter surface. This is referred to as *contact start stop* (CSS) design. When the drive is powered on, the heads slide on the platter surface as they spin up, until a thin cushion of air builds up between the heads and platter surface, causing the heads to lift off and remain suspended a short distance above or below the platter. If the air cushion is disturbed by a particle of dust or a shock, the head can come into contact with the platter while it is spinning at full speed. When contact with the spinning platters is forceful enough to do damage, the event is called a *head crash*. The result of a head crash can be anything from a few lost bytes of data to a completely ruined drive. Most drives have special lubricants on the platters and hardened surfaces that can withstand the daily "takeoffs and landings" as well as more severe abuse.

Many newer drives do not use CSS design and instead use a load/unload mechanism that does not allow the heads to contact the platters, even when the drive is powered off. First used in the 2 1/2-inch form factor notebook or laptop drives where resistance to mechanical shock is more important, load/unload mechanisms use a ramp positioned just off the outer part of the platter surface, whereas some newer designs position the ramp near the spindle. When the drive is powered off or in a power-saving mode, the heads ride up on the ramp. When the drive is powered on, the platters are allowed to come up to full speed before the heads are released down the ramp, allowing the airflow (air bearing) to prevent head/platter contact.

Because the platter assemblies are sealed and nonremovable, the track densities on the disk can be high. Hard drives today have up to 270,000 or more tracks per inch (TPI) recorded on the media. Head disk assemblies (HDAs), which contain the platters, are assembled and sealed in clean rooms under absolutely sanitary conditions. Because few companies repair HDAs, repair or replacement of the parts inside a sealed HDA can be expensive. Every hard disk ever made eventually fails. The only questions are when the failure will occur and whether your data is backed up.

Caution

It is strongly recommended that you do not even attempt to open an HDD's HDA unless you have the equipment and expertise to make repairs inside. Most manufacturers deliberately make the HDA difficult to open to discourage the intrepid do-it-yourselfer. Opening the HDA voids the drive's warranty.

Note

Although you should never open a disk drive to attempt to repair it, disk drives can operate without a cover. In some of my PC Hardware and Troubleshooting or Data Recovery seminars, I have even removed and installed the covers while the drives were operating! Those drives continue to store data perfectly to this day with their lids either on or off. Keep in mind, of course, that these drives don't contain any valuable information.

If you want to see what hard disks look like on the inside without opening them up, I suggest checking out the Red Hill Hardware Guide's "old gold" hard drive history page at www.redhill.net.au/d/i.php.

The Ultimate HDD Analogy

There is an old analogy that compares the interaction of the heads and the medium in a typical HDD as being similar in scale to a 747 Jumbo Jet flying a few feet off the ground at cruising speed (500+ mph). I have heard this analogy used repeatedly for years, and in the past I even used it myself without checking to see whether the analogy was technically accurate with respect to modern hard drives. It isn't.

Perhaps the most inaccurate aspect of the 747 analogy is the use of an airplane of any type to describe the head-and-platter interaction. This analogy implies that the heads fly low over the surface of the disk, but technically, this is not true. The heads do not fly at all in the traditional aerodynamic sense; instead, they float or ski on a cushion of air that the platters drag around.

A much better analogy would use a hovercraft instead of an airplane; the action of a hovercraft much more closely emulates the action of the heads in an HDD. Like a hovercraft, the drive heads rely somewhat on the shape of the bottom of the head to capture and control the cushion of air that keeps them floating over the disk. By nature, the cushion of air on which the heads float forms only in close proximity to the platter and is often called an *air bearing* by those in the disk drive industry.

I thought it was time to come up with a new analogy that more correctly describes the dimensions and speeds at which an HDD operates today. I looked up the specifications on a specific HDD and then magnified and rescaled all the dimensions involved by a factor of more than 300,000. For my example, I use an IBM Deskstar 75GXP drive, which is a 75GB (formatted capacity), 3 1/2-inch ATA drive. The head sliders (called *pico* sliders) in this drive are about 0.049 inches long, 0.039 inches wide, and 0.012 inches high. They float on a cushion of air about 15 nanometers (nm or billionths of a meter) over the surface of the disk while traveling at an average true speed of 53.55 miles per hour (figuring an average track diameter of about 2 1/2 inches). These heads read and write individual bits spaced only 2.56 micro-inches (millionths of an inch) apart, along tracks separated by only 35.27 micro-inches. The heads can move from one track to another in 8.5 milliseconds during an average seek.

To create my analogy, I magnified the scale to make the head floating height equal to 5 millimeters (about 0.2 inches). Because 5 millimeters is about 333,333 times greater than 15 nanometers (nm), I scaled up everything else by the same amount.

Magnified to such a scale, the heads in this typical hard disk would be about 1,361 feet long, 1,083 feet wide, and 333 feet high. (The length and height would be about equal to the Sears Tower if it were tipped over sideways.) These skyscraper-sized heads would float on a cushion of air that to scale would be only 5mm thick (about 0.2 inches) while traveling at a speed of 17.8 million miles per hour (4,958 miles per second), all while reading data bits spaced a mere 0.85 inches apart on tracks separated by only 0.98 feet!

The proportionate forward speed of this imaginary head is difficult to comprehend, so I'll elaborate. The diameter of the earth at the equator is 7,926 miles, which means a circumference of about 24,900 miles. At 4,958 miles per second, this imaginary skyscraper-sized head would circle the earth once every 5 seconds (at only two-tenths of an inch over the surface)! It would also read 231.33MB in one lap around this equatorial track.

There is also sideways velocity to consider. Because the average seek time of 8.5 milliseconds is defined as the time it takes to move the heads over one-third of the total tracks (about 9,241 tracks in this example), the heads could move sideways within a scale distance of 1.71 miles in that short time. This results in a scale-seek velocity of more than 726,321 mph, or 202 miles per second!

This analogy should give you a new appreciation of the technological marvel that the modern HDD actually represents. It makes the old Jumbo Jet analogy look rather pathetic (not to mention grossly inaccurate), doesn't it?

Tracks and Sectors

A *track* is a single ring of data on one side of a disk. A disk track is too large to manage data effectively as a single storage unit. Individual disk tracks can store more than a megabyte of data, which would be inefficient for storing small files. For that reason, tracks are divided into several numbered divisions known as *sectors*. These sectors represent arc-shaped pieces of the track.

Various types of disk drives split their disk tracks into different numbers of sectors, depending on the density of the tracks. For example, floppy disk formats use 8–36 sectors per track, although hard disks usually store data at a higher density and today can have up to 2,000 or more physical sectors per track.

The sectors on a track are numbered starting with 1, unlike the heads or cylinders that are numbered starting with 0. For example, a 1.44MB floppy disk contains 80 cylinders numbered 0–79 and two heads numbered 0 and 1, whereas each track on each cylinder has 18 sectors numbered 1–18.

Each physical sector stores 512 or 4,096 bytes of data; however, additional bytes of storage are used in sector headers and trailers to manage the tracks and sectors. You might find it helpful to think of each disk sector as being like a page in a book. Each page contains text (data), but the entire page is not filled with text; rather, each page has margins. Information such as chapter titles and page numbers are placed in the margins, and the margins provide "gaps" between text that allow you to visually separate pages of text. These "margins" (headers and trailers) are created during the low-level formatting process, which for modern drives can only be done at the factory.

Each physical sector contains 512 or 4,096 bytes of data. The low-level (and sometimes the high-level) formatting process fills the sector data fields with some specific value or values, such as F6h (hex), 00h, or some repeating test pattern used by the drive manufacturer. Certain bit patterns are more difficult for the electronics on the drive to encode/decode, so these patterns are sometimes used when the manufacturer is testing the drive during initial formatting. A special test pattern might cause errors to surface that a normal data pattern would not show. This way, the manufacturer can more accurately identify marginal sectors during testing.

Each physical sector consists of a number of fields, including the following:

- **Gap**—A break or slack space in the recording that separates sectors allowing for timing and rotational speed variations
- **ID**—Information identifying the physical sector location address and status
- **Sync**—A timing mark for providing disk controller to drive timing alignment
- **Address Mark**—A mark indicating where the data field actually begins
- **Data**—The actual 512 or 4,096 bytes of user data being stored
- **ECC**—Error correction code, a number calculated via a complex polynomial that can detect and possibly even correct errors in the data being read

Additional space for each track is normally used for embedded servo (head guidance) information as well as track index marks and additional gaps for timing purposes. The gaps are like spacings in the recording and serve basically the same function as having gaps of no sound between the songs recorded on a CD or tape, helping the player to identify where one song ends and another begins.

The sector headers and trailers along with additional overhead such as servo (head guidance) information are all created during the low-level format process, which for ATA drives can only be performed at the factory. This overhead accounts for the lost space between the unformatted capacity of a disk and the formatted capacity. For example, a 2MB (unformatted) 3 1/2-inch floppy disk has a formatted capacity of 1.44MB, and an older 38MB unformatted capacity (for instance, a Seagate ST-4038) hard disk has a capacity of only 32MB when it is formatted. Because the hard drives you purchase today can only be low-level formatted at the factory, the manufacturers now advertise only the formatted capacity.

In the quest to create higher and higher capacity drives, drive manufacturers have tried to make the formatting more efficient by minimizing the amount of overhead so that as much of each sector as possible can be used for storing user data. The ratio of the user data in a sector to the total number of bytes physically used by the sector on the disk denotes the sector efficiency. The way tracks and sectors have been formatted over the years has allowed efficiency to improve, but only up to a point.

The sector format on a given drive is dictated by the controller, which was originally a separate entity from the drive. One of the first hard disk controllers used in PCs was the Xebec 1210, the HDD controller used in the vintage 1983–1987 IBM XT. Table 9.2 shows the sector format created by the Xebec 1210/1220 controllers. (The 1220 had an integrated floppy controller.)

Table 9.2   Xebec 1210/1220 (IBM XT) 512-Byte Sector Format

Name	Bytes	Description
Header	89	Gap, ID, Sync, Address Mark
Data	512	User data
Trailer	4	Error Correction Code (ECC)
	605	Total bytes per sector (84.6% efficient)

As you can see from Table 9.2, drives formatted using those controllers had sectors that stored 512 bytes of user data yet consumed 605 total bytes on the disk, for a sector efficiency of 84.6%. Later controllers were able to increase format efficiency by reducing the size of the gap and other information in the header. For example, Table 9.3 shows the sector format created by the Western Digital WD1003 and WD1006 controllers used in the vintage 1984–1987 IBM AT.

Table 9.3   Western Digital WD1003/WD1006 (IBM AT) 512-Byte Sector Format

Name	Bytes	Description
Header	71	Gap, ID, Sync, Address Mark
Data	512	User data
Trailer	4	Error Correction Code (ECC)
	587	Total bytes per sector (87.2% efficient)

These controllers created 512-byte sectors that consumed 587 total bytes on the disk, for an improved sector efficiency of 87.2%. After 1987, the AT disk controller became part of the drive, which is what we call the ATA interface, often also referred to as IDE (Integrated Drive Electronics). Integrated controllers allowed much tighter signal timing and speed, allowing for more sectors to be stored on each track and for additional improvements in sector efficiency.

To further reduce sector overhead, IBM pioneered an innovation called the No-ID sector format, which was first seen in IBM's DSAA family drives in the early 1990s. Using this technology, the ID information was removed from the sector header and instead was determined via other means. To determine sector IDs without the ID information in the header, cylinder information was placed in the embedded servo data already on the disk, which was combined with stricter timing controls and a defect map loaded from the drive into the disk controller RAM on startup. Using the No-ID format, the drive was able to determine sector IDs without having the ID explicitly written in the sector header, resulting in a dramatic improvement in sector efficiency.

Table 9.4 shows the format of a 512-byte sector on a modern drive.

Table 9.4 512-Byte Sector Format in a Modern Drive

Name	Bytes	Description
Header	15	Gap, Sync, Address Mark
Data	512	User data
Trailer	50	Error Correction Code (ECC)
	577	Total bytes per sector (88.7% efficient)

In a modern 512-byte sector format, you can see that the header has been reduced to only 15 bytes, a dramatic reduction from the first PC hard drives where it consumed 89 bytes. But even with that dramatic reduction in the size of the header, the sector on a modern drive still takes up 577 bytes on the disk, resulting in a sector efficiency of 88.7%. Note that although this is typical for a modern drive, the actual specific number of additional bytes required for the sector header and trailer (and therefore the overall efficiency) can vary somewhat from these figures depending on the drive/media type and format.

What is surprising is that while the header has been significantly reduced in size, the trailer containing the ECC information has expanded dramatically such that the overall sector efficiency has only improved by about 1.5% since 1984! This is obviously due to the increase in the size of the ECC information.

ECC

The number of ECC bytes stored (and therefore the size of the sector trailer) has always been a compromise. More ECC bytes means the ability to correct more errors, but it also consumes more space on the disk. The 4 ECC bytes used by the earliest controllers was sufficient to ensure an unrecoverable read error rate of less than 1 in 10^{12} (1 trillion) bits, which is equal to 125GB worth of data. An unrecoverable error is one where the drive cannot read the data properly, even after applying the ECC information to correct it. Recoverable errors are those in which the data is read incorrectly, but the drive uses the ECC information to correct the errors before passing the data on to the system. An unrecoverable error rate of 1 in 10^{12} bits basically means that one would expect to see about one read error for every 125GB worth of data read from the disk. That was more than acceptable when drive capacities were only 5MB to 100MB. You would have to read a 100MB drive front to back 1,250 times before a read error might occur.

However, as drive capacities rose, the need for lower read error rates became necessary. The original read error rate of 1 in 10^{12} bits (one error every 125GB) would be unacceptable today, because it would mean that reading a 1TB drive front to back just *once* would probably result in at least eight unrecoverable errors! Fortunately, newer drives have lower error rates. Since the first PC hard drives came out in the early 1980s, drives/controllers have been produced with primarily four sets of unrecoverable error rates. Table 9.5 shows the number of bits and terabytes read per unrecoverable error for typical drives over the years.

Table 9.5 Bits/Terabytes Read per Error (Unrecoverable Read Error Rates) for Typical Drives

Bits Read per Error	TBs Read per Error	Where/When Utilized
10^{12}	0.125	5MB–100MB Drives (1980s)
10^{13}	1.25	100MB–100GB Drives (1980s–1990s)
10^{14}	12.5	1GB–3TB+ Drives (1990s–Present)
10^{15}	125	RAID/Enterprise Class Drives (1990s–Present)

As you can see from the table, disk drive read error rates fell by a factor of 1,000 times in the first 5MB drives in the early 1980s through the first 1GB drives of the early 1990s, which is understandable because drive capacities increased by a similar factor during that time. However, since the early 1990s, read error rates have remained relatively stagnant, whereas drive capacity has continued to increase by a factor of more than another 1,000 times. In other words, since the 1990s, the reduction in error rate per bits read has not kept pace with the increases in drive capacity.

Most current consumer class drives advertise a 1 in 10^{14} bits error rate, which means one error should be expected for about every 12.5TB of data read. This is alarming when you consider that if you were to read a 3TB drive front to back only five times, you are virtually guaranteed to have a read error. Note that Enterprise/RAID class drives normally advertise a 1 in 10^{15} bits error rate, which is 10 times better than most consumer class drives, but still not what I would expect it to be given the increases in drive capacity since that level was first reached.

Error rate reductions have not kept pace with capacity increases because of efficiency. To reduce the read error rate, you must store more ECC bytes. In addition, as the areal density on the drive media increases, small physical flaws or errors on the disk surface affect more and more bits, requiring more ECC bytes and more complex calculations just to *maintain* a given error rate. A 12-byte ECC was enough to achieve a 1 in 1014 error rate back in 1990; however, this grew to 24 bytes by 1999 and 40 bytes by 2004 just to maintain the same error rate. In other words, even without decreasing the error rate further, the number of ECC bytes has grown from 12 bytes to 50 bytes, creating a significant amount of storage overhead. By 2010, it was found that additional increases in ECC capability for 512-byte sectors would require the number of ECC bytes to increase to the point that it would negate any further increases in density. In other words, a stalemate of sorts has been reached between density and ECC capability.

Fortunately, you can realize a much greater improvement in ECC and sector efficiency by going to larger sectors—that is, increasing the size of the data area, thereby reducing the total number of gaps, headers, and trailers overall. This allows for a larger ECC to be used, while still resulting in greater sector efficiency overall.

Advanced Format (4K Sectors)

When the first PC was introduced in 1981 and for the next 28 years that followed, all the disk drives used in PCs stored exactly 512 bytes of data in each physical sector. This de facto standard began to change in 2009 when the first hard drives storing data in 4,096-byte physical sectors were released. Drives that store 4,096 bytes per sector are called *4K sector* or *Advanced Format* drives. The move to 4K sectors was made necessary due to density increases demanding more powerful ECC (error correction code) calculations, which were taking up an increasing amount of space in each sector.

The transition to 4K sector drives can be traced as far back as 1998 when IBM released a paper identifying the 512-byte sector format as a bottleneck to increased drive capacity and performance. In 2000, the International Disk Drive Equipment and Materials Association (IDEMA, www.idema.org) formed the 4K Block Committee to study and promote the transition to 4K sectors. IDEMA is a trade organization founded in 1986 and consisting of drive manufacturers, component suppliers, and even software companies—basically anybody producing drives or related products. Seagate began shipping 4K sector drives in May 2009 inside USB-attached external hard drives such as the FreeAgent series, whereas Western Digital released the first bare 4K sector drive in December 2009. These products were the first wave in a major change in disk drive designs, as the drive industry as a whole agreed that all new drive platforms introduced after 2011 would be Advanced Format (4K sector) drives. Table 9.6 shows the format of a 4,096-byte sector on a modern 4K sector (Advanced Format) drive.

Table 9.6   Typical 4K-Byte Sector Format

Name	Bytes	Description
Header	15	Gaps, sync, address mark
Data	4,096	User data
Trailer	100	Error-correcting code (ECC)
	4,211	Total bytes per sector (97.3% efficient)

As you can see, the 4K sector (aka Advanced Format) layout uses the same number of bytes for the sector header as modern 512-byte sectored drives, but it increases the size of the ECC field to 100 bytes. Even with the larger ECC required to maintain the standard error rate, this yields a sector format efficiency of 97.3%—almost a 10% improvement. Because of the eight times larger data field, this will also allow further increases in ECC without dramatically reducing the overall efficiency. Figure 9.4 shows the format efficiency improvement from 512-byte sectors to 4K sectors.

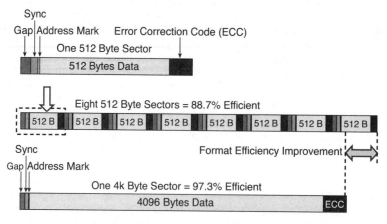

FIGURE 9.4   Format efficiency improvement from 512-byte sectors to 4K sectors.

Although 4K sectors may sound like a simple solution, this transition has many issues. The main problem is that the 512-byte sector format has been so ingrained into PC operating systems (OSs) and other software that changing it causes tremendous compatibility problems. The interim solution to this problem was to have 4K sector drives use internal emulation to act at the interface level as if they are 512-byte sector drives, a format that is called 512e (for 512 emulation) in the industry. But, even with emulation, there can be problems.

Consider what happens when a program writes a single sector to a disk. If the drive is a standard 512-byte sector drive, the one sector is written quickly and efficiently. However, if the drive is a 4K sector drive that is *emulating* a 512-byte sector drive (512e), the drive must read a full 4K sector into controller RAM, update 1/8 of the RAM-based data (512 bytes worth), and then write the full 4K sector back to the disk. This results in a read-modify-write operation that takes much longer than just writing the data to a 512-byte sector drive.

Fortunately, single sector writes rarely happen in the real world, because most file systems (including Windows NT File System, or NTFS) write to disks in 4K clusters, or multiples of 4K. But even if the file system cluster size matches the drive sector size (or is a multiple thereof), there can still be problems with the file system or partition alignment (as discussed in the next section).

Partition Alignment

In 1993, sector addressing was done by cylinder head sector (CHS), and drive manufacturers standardized on an emulated track size of 63 sectors per track. Internally, drives actually used a zoned recording, where the number of sectors per track varied by zone. DOS and Windows disk partitioning software placed the master boot record (MBR) in the first sector of the first track, which was at Cylinder 0, Head 0, sector 1. The volume boot sector (VBR) for the first partition was then placed in the first sector of the second track, which was Cylinder 0 Head 1, sector 1. With the sectors per track standardized at 63, this meant that the first partition started in the 64th sector on the disk, which in logical block address (LBA) terminology would be LBA 63. Note that LBA sector numbering starts with 0.

Because of this, Windows XP and earlier versions will start the first partition on a disk in sector LBA 63. This means that the first sector of the partition (LBA 63) will also be the first sector in NTFS cluster 0, and because cluster 0 is 4K (eight 512-byte sectors) long, it will occupy sectors LBA 63 through 70. The problem with this is that on a 4K-sector drive, this means that NTFS cluster 0 will be part of physical sectors 7 and 8. Likewise, NTFS cluster 1 straddles physical sectors 8 and 9. This means that every time Windows writes to one cluster, the hard drive has to perform two read-modify-write operations, which significantly reduces performance. Figure 9.5 shows how the 4K NTFS clusters, 512-byte logical (emulated) sectors, and 4K physical sectors line up if the drive is partitioned under Windows XP and earlier.

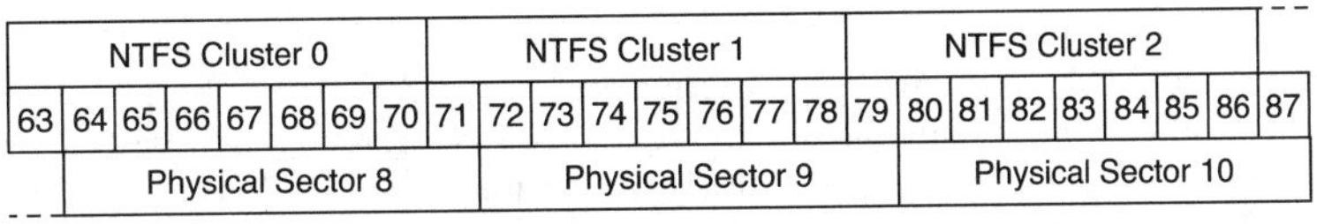

FIGURE 9.5   Default 4K sector drive partition alignment on Windows XP and earlier versions.

Starting with Vista, Windows was designed with an awareness of 4K sector drives, solid-state drives (SSDs), and RAID arrays, all of which deal with data in blocks of 4K or larger. To accommodate alignment for all these types of storage devices, Windows Vista and later automatically creates partitions on 2,048-sector (1MiB) boundaries, which are an even multiple of the larger sectors or storage units used by virtually any storage device. Figure 9.6 shows how the 4K NTFS clusters, 512-byte logical (emulated) sectors, and 4K physical sectors would line up if the drive were partitioned under these operating systems.

NTFS Cluster 0								NTFS Cluster 1								NTFS Cluster 2							
2048	2049	2050	2051	2052	2053	2054	2055	2056	2057	2058	2059	2060	2061	2062	2063	2064	2065	2066	2067	2068	2069	2070	2071	2072
Physical Sector 256								Physical Sector 257								Physical Sector 258							

FIGURE 9.6 Default 4K sector drive partition alignment on Windows Vista and later.

As you can see, Windows Vista and later versions automatically start the first partition at sector LBA 2048, which results in a perfect alignment between the 4K NTFS clusters and the 4K physical sectors. In this case, NTFS cluster 0 would perfectly align with physical sector 256, and so on. Each time one cluster is written, the drive will do a normal write of the matching physical sector, instead of a multiple sector read-modify-write operation as would be the case with a misaligned partition.

Operating systems have used 4K cluster–based file systems (such as NTFS) for many years now. These OSs will naturally work with 4K sector drives, as long as the start of each partition is properly aligned. Table 9.7 shows which OSs automatically create partitions properly aligned for 4K sector drives (including SSDs).

Table 9.7 Typical 4K-Byte Sector Format

Operating System	Automatic 4K Sector/SSD Alignment
Windows XP	No
Windows Vista	Yes
Windows 7/8	Yes
OS X 10.4+	Yes
Linux Ubuntu 8.04+	Yes
SUSE Linux kernel 2.6.34+	Yes
Windows Home Server	No
Windows Home Server 2011	Yes
Server 2003	No
Server 2008	Yes
Server 2012	Yes

Although these OSs automatically create 4K aligned partitions, you can manually create aligned partitions for OSs that don't automatically create them, such as Windows XP. There's an easy way to do this; use an OS that does create aligned partitions to first partition the drive, and then install the older OS into the already existing aligned partition. For example, when installing XP onto a new 4K sector HDD or solid-state drive (SSD), first attach the drive to a system running Vista or later and create and format a single partition, which will be automatically aligned. Then simply install XP into the existing (aligned) partition.

Note

For more information about using large sector drives with Windows (including updates needed for some versions of Windows), see the Microsoft Knowledge Base article number 2510009, "Information about Microsoft support policy for large sector drives in Windows," at http://support.microsoft.com.

You can use at least two methods to check the alignment of a partition under Windows. One is to open a command prompt and enter the following command:

```
wmic partition get Name, StartingOffset
```

The command result shows the starting offset of all the partitions on all the drives connected to the system. For example, here is the output after running the command on a system with two drives installed, each with a single primary partition:

```
Name                    StartingOffset

Disk #0, Partition #0   32256

Disk #1, Partition #0   1048576
```

Another method is to run the msinfo32.exe program at a command prompt or via the Start menu under All Programs, Accessories, System Tools, System Information. Once the program is running, in the left pane select Components, Storage, Disks. Then, in the right pane find the Partition and Partition Starting Offset figures for each of the drives/partitions in the system.

In this example, the first drive has a starting offset of 32,256 bytes. To see if this would be aligned on a 4K sector drive (or SSD), divide that number by 4,096. The result is 7.875, which is not an even number, indicating that this partition is *not* aligned. This is in fact the standard offset created by a non-4K aware OS such as Windows XP, and it is equal to 63×512 bytes, indicating that the partition starts at LBA 63.

To check the alignment for the partition on the second drive, divide the starting offset of 1,048,576 by 4,096. The result is an even 256, which is an even number, indicating that this partition is properly aligned. This in fact is equal to 2,048×512 bytes, indicating that the partition starts at LBA 2,048.

If you have misaligned partitions, you can use a third-party partitioning program like Parted Magic (www.partedmagic.com) to both create aligned partitions as well as move existing partitions into alignment. In addition, most if not all the drive manufacturers that sell 4K sector drives (including SSDs) offer partition alignment utilities that can create new aligned partitions or take existing partitions and align them. Check with your drive manufacturer to see if such a utility is available. Of course, you should back up any existing data on any drive before performing partition alignment or creation.

Disk Formatting

There are two types of disk formats:

- Physical, or low-level formatting
- Logical, or high-level formatting

The FORMAT command on a hard disk performs only the high-level format. The low-level formatting is done at the factory on all modern drives. In addition, partitioning is required before a volume can be high-level formatted, because a hard disk is designed to be used with more than one OS or file system and may have more than one partition or volume. Using multiple operating or file systems on one hard drive is possible by partitioning, which creates multiple volumes on the drive. A *volume* or *logical drive* is any section of the disk to which the OS assigns a drive letter or name.

Consequently, preparing an HDD for data storage involves three steps:

1. Low-level formatting (LLF; done at the factory)
2. Partitioning
3. High-level formatting (HLF)

Low-Level Formatting

During a low-level format, the tracks are divided into a specific number of sectors, creating the inter-sector and intertrack gaps and recording the sector header and trailer information. The sector's data areas are filled with a dummy byte value or a pattern of test values. For hard disks, the number of sectors per track depends on the drive and the controller interface.

The original ST-506/412 MFM controllers always placed 17 sectors per track on a disk, ST-506/412 controllers with RLL encoding increased the number of sectors to 25 or 26 per track, and ESDI drives had 32 or more sectors per track. The ATA drives found in PCs today can have anywhere from 17 to 2,500 or more physical sectors per track, and the number of sectors can vary among different tracks.

Virtually all ATA drives use a technique called *zoned-bit recording* (ZBR), sometimes shortened to *zoned recording*, which writes a variable number of sectors per track. Without zoned recording, the number of sectors (and therefore bits) on each track is a constant. This means the actual number of bits per inch will vary. More bits per inch will exist on the inner tracks, and fewer will exist on the outer. The data rate and rotational speed will remain constant, as will the number of bits per track. Figure 9.7 shows a drive recorded with the same number of sectors per track.

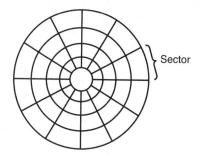

FIGURE 9.7 Standard recording, where the same number of sectors comprises every track.

A standard recording wastes capacity on the outer tracks because it is longer yet holds the same amount of data (more loosely spaced) as the inner tracks. One way to increase the capacity of a hard drive during the low-level format is to create more sectors on the disks' outer cylinders than on the inner ones. Because they have a larger circumference, the outer cylinders can hold more data. Drives without zoned recording store the same amount of data on every cylinder, even though the tracks of the outer cylinders might be twice as long as those of the inner cylinders. The result is wasted storage capacity because the disk medium must be capable of storing data reliably at the same density as on the inner cylinders. When the number of sectors per track is fixed, as in older controllers, the drive capacity is limited by the density of the innermost (shortest) track.

Drives that use zoned recording split the cylinders into groups called *zones*, with each successive zone having more sectors per track as you move outward from the center of the disk. All the cylinders in a particular zone have the same number of sectors per track. The number of zones varies with specific drives, but most drives have between 16 and 32 zones.

Figure 9.8 shows a drive with zoned-bit recording.

Another effect of zoned recording is that transfer speeds vary depending on which zone the heads are in. A drive with zoned recording still spins at a constant speed. Because more sectors exist per track in the outer zones, however, data transfer is fastest there. Consequently, data transfer is slowest when reading or writing to the inner zones. That is why virtually all drives today report minimum and maximum sustained transfer rates, which depend on where on the drive you are reading from or writing to.

As an example, see Table 9.8, which shows the zones defined for a Hitachi Travelstar 5K500.B 2 1/2-inch laptop drive, the sectors per track for each zone, and the resulting data transfer rate.

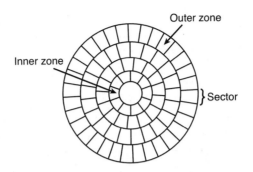

FIGURE 9.8 Zoned recording, where the number of sectors per track increases within each zone, moving out from the center.

Table 9.8   Zoned Recording Information for a Hitachi Travelstar 5K500.B 2 1/2-inch HDD

Zone	Sectors per Track	Transfer Rate (MBps)
0	1,920	117.96
1	1,840	113.05
2	1,800	110.59
3	1,760	108.13
4	1,720	105.68
5	1,680	103.22
6	1,632	100.27
7	1,600	98.30
8	1,560	95.85
9	1,520	93.39
10	1,480	90.93
11	1,440	88.47
12	1,360	83.56
13	1,320	81.10
14	1,296	79.63
15	1,280	78.64
16	1,240	76.19
17	1,200	73.73
18	1,140	70.04
19	1,104	67.83
20	1,080	66.36
21	1,020	62.67
22	960	58.98
23	912	56.03

This drive has a total of 172,676 cylinders, which are divided into 24 zones averaging 7,195 cylinders each. Zone 0 consists of the outermost cylinders, which are the longest and contain the most sectors (1,920 for each track), whereas the inner zone has only 912 sectors per track.

With zoned recording, this drive averages 1,302 sectors per track. Without zoned recording, the number of sectors per track would be limited to 912 for all tracks. The use of zoned recording, therefore, provides nearly a 43% increase in the storage capacity of this particular drive.

Also notice the difference in the data transfer rates for each of the zones. Because the drive spins at 5,400 rpm, it completes a single revolution every 1/90 of a second, or every 11.1 milliseconds. Therefore, the data transfer speed varies depending on which zone you are reading and writing. In the outer zone, the data transfer rate is nearly 118MBps, whereas in the inner zone it is only 56MBps. The average transfer rate for this drive is around 80MBps. This is one reason you might notice huge discrepancies in the results produced by disk drive benchmark programs. A test that reads or writes files on the outer tracks of the disk naturally yields far better results than one conducted on the inner tracks. It might appear as though your drive is running more slowly when the problem is actually that the test results you are comparing stem from disk activity on different zones.

Another thing to note is that this drive conforms to the SATA 3Gbps specification and is capable of an interface transfer speed of 300MBps. As you can see, that is entirely theoretical because the true media transfer speed of this drive varies between about 56MBps and 118MBps, averaging about 80MBps overall. The interface transfer rate is just that: what the interface is capable of. It has little bearing on the actual capabilities of the drive.

The use of zoned recording enables drive manufacturers to increase the capacity of their hard drives by 20%–50% or more compared to a fixed-sector-per-track arrangement. All modern drives use zoned recording.

Partitioning

Creating a partition on an HDD enables it to support separate file systems, each in its own partition.

Each file system can then use its own method to allocate file space in logical units called *clusters* or *allocation units*. Every HDD must have at least one partition on it and can have up to four primary partitions, each of which can support the same or different type file systems. Four common file systems are used by PC OSs today:

- **FAT (file allocation table)**—The standard file system supported by DOS and Windows 9x/Me. FAT is also the default file system used by Windows 2000 and later on flash or other removable drives. FAT partitions support filenames of 11 characters maximum (8 characters + a 3-character extension) under DOS, and 255 characters under Windows 9x (or later). The standard FAT file system uses 12- or 16-bit numbers to identify clusters, resulting in a maximum volume size of 2GiB.

- **FAT32 (FAT, 32-bit)**—An optional file system supported by Windows 95 OSR2 (OEM Service Release 2) and later.

  FAT32 uses 32-bit numbers to identify clusters, resulting in a maximum single volume size of 2TiB (32GiB recommended) and a maximum file size of only 4GiB.

- **exFAT (aka FAT64)**—An optional file system supported by Windows XP (http://support.microsoft.com/kb/955704) and by Vista SP1 and later.

  exFAT uses 64-bit numbers to identify clusters, resulting in a maximum recommended volume (and file) size of 512TiB.

- **NTFS**—The native file system for Windows NT and later that supports filenames up to 256 characters long and volumes (and files) up to (a theoretical) 16EiB. NTFS also provides extended attributes and file system security features that do not exist in the FAT file systems.

Because NTFS is native to Windows 2000 and later (and required for Vista or later boot volumes), NTFS is by far the most common file system in use on nonremovable drives. NTFS, however, is not very compatible with non-Windows systems, has a high amount of overhead, and in general is not designed for removable drives where a "surprise removal" may be common. Because of this the FAT file system is the standard for removable (that is, flash) drives and is accessible by nearly every OS, which makes it the most compatible format for external drives in a mixed OS environment. When formatting removable drives, Windows XP and later will default to FAT for drives that are less than or equal to 2GiB, FAT32 for drives that are greater than 2GiB but less than or equal to 32GiB, and NTFS or exFAT (FAT64) for drives that are larger than 32GiB.

Partitioning normally is accomplished by running the disk partitioning program that comes with your OS. The name and exact operation of the disk partitioning program varies with the OS. For example, Windows 2000 and later use either the Disk Management snap-in component of the Computer Management service (see Figure 9.9) or the DISKPART command, whereas Windows 9x/Me and earlier used the FDISK program. The disk-partitioning tools enable you to select the amount of space on the drive to use for a partition, from a single megabyte (or 1%) of the drive up to the entire capacity of the drive or as much as the particular file system will allow. Normally for simplicity's sake, I recommend using as few partitions as possible per drive. Note that the Disk Management snap-in as well as the DISKPART command included with Windows Vista and later automatically create 4K sector (including SSD) aligned partitions, so I recommend using those versions even if you are creating partitions for use under XP and earlier OSs.

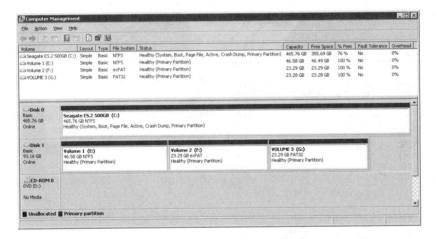

FIGURE 9.9 The Disk Management component of Computer Management in Windows 7, showing drives with NTFS, exFAT, and FAT32 volumes.

Caution

The disk-partitioning tools included in most OSs normally can't be used to change the size of a partition; with a few exceptions, all they can do is remove or create partitions. Unfortunately, the act of removing or creating a partition destroys and loses access to data that was contained in the partition or that was on that part of the disk. To easily resize or otherwise manipulate partitions without destroying data, I recommend free third-party utilities, such as Parted Magic (www. partedmagic.com). Parted Magic is also useful for creating 4K sector aligned partitions as well as moving existing partitions into alignment.

After a drive is partitioned, each partition must then be high-level formatted by the OS that will use it.

High-Level Formatting

During the high-level format, the OS writes the file system structures necessary for managing files and data on the disk. These data structures enable the OS to manage the space on the disk, keep track of files, and even manage defective areas so they do not cause problems.

High-level formatting is not really a physical formatting of the drive (except with floppy disks in some cases), but rather the creation of a table of contents for the disk. True low-level formats of modern hard drives are performed by the manufacturer and technically cannot be performed by the end user. Most hard drive manufacturers make initialization and test programs available, which are the modern substitute for low-level format programs. Although the initialization programs do not technically re-create the sector header or trailer marks, they do rewrite the data portion of all sectors as well as manage defects, including the ability to reassign spare sectors to replace defective sectors. Normally, the only time you run an initialization program is when you are attempting to repair a format that has become damaged (parts of the disk become unreadable) or in some cases when you want to wipe away all data on the drive.

Caution

In Windows XP and earlier, a high-level format does not overwrite the data area of the disk. Instead, it only rewrites the table of contents, leaving the data area sectors intact. This is true whether you use the "quick" or full-format options. As such, unerase utilities such as Recuva (www.piriform.com/recuva) can recover files from a formatted drive because the data sectors are not actually overwritten. However, this behavior was changed for Windows Vista and later, such that the standard full format does overwrite all the sector data with zeros, thereby making the recovery of any previous files or data impossible. You can prevent the overwriting of all data sectors in Vista and later by using the "quick" format option. See the Microsoft KB941961 article at http://support.microsoft.com for more information.

Basic HDD Components

Many types of HDDs are on the market, but nearly all share the same basic physical components. Some differences might exist in the implementation of these components (and in the quality of the materials used to make them), but the operational characteristics of most drives are similar. The basic components of a typical HDD are as follows (see Figure 9.10):

- Disk platters
- Read/write heads
- Head actuator mechanism
- Spindle motor (inside platter hub)
- Logic board (controller or Printed Circuit Board)
- Cables and connectors
- Configuration items (such as jumpers or switches)

The platters, spindle motor, heads, and head actuator mechanisms usually are contained in a sealed chamber called the *head disk assembly* (HDA). The HDA is usually treated as a single component; it is rarely opened. Other parts external to the drive's HDA, such as the logic boards, bezel, and other configuration or mounting hardware, can be disassembled from the drive.

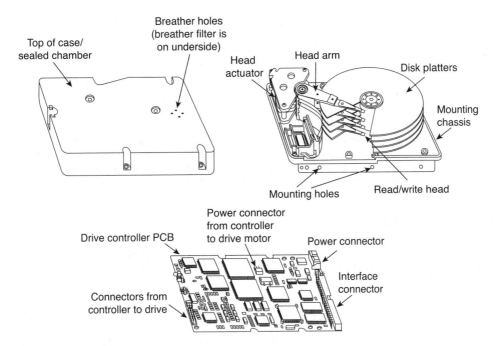

FIGURE 9.10 Typical HDD components.

Hard Disk Platters (Disks)

An HDD has one or more platters, or disks. Hard disks for PC systems have been available in several form factors over the years. Normally, the physical size of a drive is expressed as the size of the platters. Table 9.9 lists the platter sizes that have been associated with PC HDDs.

Table 9.9 Hard Disk Form Factors Versus Actual Platter Sizes

Hard Disk Form Factor	Actual Platter Diameter (mm)	Actual Platter Diameter (in.)	Year Introduced
5.25 in.	130	5.12	1980
3.5 in.	95	3.74	1983
2.5 in.	65	2.56	1988
1.8 in.	48	1.89	1991
1 in.	34	1.33	1999
0.85 in.	21.5	0.85	2004

Larger HDDs that have 8-inch, 14-inch, or even larger platters are available, but these drives are not used with PC systems. Currently, the 3 1/2-inch drives are the most popular for desktop and some portable systems, whereas the 2 1/2-inch and smaller drives are popular in portable and notebook systems.

Most HDDs have two or more platters, although some of the smaller drives used in portable systems and some entry-level drives for desktop computers have only one. The number of platters a drive can have is limited by the drive's vertical physical size. The maximum number of platters I have seen in any 3 1/2-inch drive is 12; however, most drives have six or fewer.

Platters were originally made from an aluminum/magnesium alloy, which provides both strength and light weight. However, manufacturers' desire for higher and higher densities and smaller drives has led to the use of platters made of glass (or, more technically, a glass-ceramic composite). One such material, produced by the Dow Corning Corporation, is called MemCor. MemCor is composed of glass with ceramic implants, enabling it to resist cracking better than pure glass. Glass platters offer greater rigidity than metal (because metal can be bent and glass can't) and can therefore be machined to one-half the thickness of conventional aluminum disks—sometimes less. Glass platters are also much more thermally stable than aluminum platters, which means they do not expand or contract much with changes in temperature. Virtually all modern drives use glass or glass-ceramic platters.

Recording Media

No matter which substrate is used, the platters are covered with a thin layer of a magnetically retentive substance, called the *medium*, on which magnetic information is stored. Three popular types of magnetic media have been used on hard disk platters:

- Oxide media (obsolete)
- Thin-film media
- AFC (antiferromagnetically coupled) media

Oxide Media

The oxide medium is made of various compounds, containing iron oxide as the active ingredient. The magnetic layer is created on the disk by coating the aluminum platter with a syrup containing iron-oxide particles. This syrup is spread across the disk by spinning the platters at high speed; centrifugal force causes the material to flow from the center of the platter to the outside, creating an even coating of the material on the platter. The surface is then cured and polished. Finally, a layer of material that protects and lubricates the surface is added and burnished smooth. The oxide coating is usually about 30 millionths of an inch thick. If you could peer into a drive with oxide-coated platters, you would see that the platters are brownish or amber.

As drive density increases, the magnetic medium needs to be thinner and more perfectly formed. The capabilities of oxide coatings have been exceeded by most higher-capacity drives. Because the oxide medium is soft, disks that use it are subject to head-crash damage if the drive is jolted during operation. Most older drives, especially those sold as low-end models, use oxide media on the drive platters. Oxide media, which have been used since 1955, remained popular because of their relatively low cost and ease of application. Today, however, few if any drives use oxide media.

Thin-Film Media

Thin-film medium is aptly named. The coating is much thinner than can be achieved by the oxide-coating method, but is much stronger. In fact, modern thin-film media are virtually uncrashable. If you could open a drive to peek at the platters, you would see that platters coated with the thin-film medium look like mirrors. Thin-film media are also known as *plated* or *sputtered media* because of the various processes that deposit the thin film on the platters.

Thin-film plated media are manufactured by depositing the magnetic medium on the disk with an electroplating mechanism, in much the same way that chrome plating is deposited on the bumper of a car. The aluminum/magnesium or glass platter is immersed in a series of chemical baths that coat the platter with several layers of metallic film. The magnetic medium layer itself is a cobalt alloy about 1 μ-inch thick.

Thin-film sputtered media are created by first coating the aluminum platters with a layer of nickel phosphorus and then applying the cobalt-alloy magnetic material in a continuous vacuum-deposition process called *sputtering*. This process deposits magnetic layers as thin as 1 μ-inch or less on the disk, in a fashion similar to the way that silicon wafers are coated with metallic films in the semiconductor industry. The same sputtering technique is again used to lay down an extremely hard, 1 μ-inch protective carbon coating. The need for a near-perfect vacuum makes sputtering the most expensive of the processes described here.

The surface of a sputtered platter contains magnetic layers as thin as 1 μ-inch. Because this surface also is smooth, the head can float more closely to the disk surface than was previously possible. Floating heights as small as 10nm (nanometers, or about 0.4 μ-inch) above the surface are possible. When the head is closer to the platter, the density of the magnetic flux transitions can be increased to provide greater storage capacity. Additionally, the increased intensity of the magnetic field during a closer-proximity read provides the higher signal amplitudes necessary for good signal-to-noise performance.

AFC Media

The latest advancement in drive media is called AFC media and is designed to allow densities to be pushed beyond previous limits. Any time density is increased, the magnetic layer on the platters must be made thinner. Areal density (tracks per inch times bits per inch) has increased in hard drives to the point where the grains in the magnetic layer used to store data are becoming so small that they become unstable over time, causing data storage to become unreliable. This is referred to as the *superparamagnetic limit*, and it was originally determined to be between 30Gb/sq. in. and 50Gb/sq. in. However, as technology has advanced, this so-called limit has been pushed further and further back, and commercially produced drives have achieved nearly 500Gb/sq. in., with densities of up to 1,000Gb/sq. in. or more expected in the future.

AFC media consists of two magnetic layers separated by a thin, 3-atom (6 angstrom) film layer of the element ruthenium. IBM has coined the term *pixie dust* to refer to this ultra-thin ruthenium layer. This sandwich produces an AFC of the top and bottom magnetic layers, which causes the apparent magnetic thickness of the entire structure to be the difference between the top and bottom magnetic layers. This allows the use of physically thicker magnetic layers with more stable larger grains, so they can function as if they were really a single layer that was much thinner overall.

IBM introduced AFC media starting with the 2 1/2-inch Travelstar 30GN series of notebook drives introduced in 2001; they were the first drives on the market to use AFC media. IBM then introduced AFC media in desktop 3 1/2-inch drives starting with the Deskstar 120 GXP. AFC media is now used by Hitachi Global Storage Technologies, which owns the former IBM hard drive division, as well as virtually all other hard drive manufacturers. The use of AFC media allowed areal densities to be extended to 100Gb/sq. in. and beyond, and when combined with perpendicular magnetic recording (PMR), densities can grow to more than twice that.

◄◄ For more information about AFC media and other advanced storage technologies, see Chapter 8, "Magnetic Storage Principles," **p. 439**.

Read/Write Heads

An HDD usually has one read/write head for each platter surface (meaning that each platter has two sets of read/write heads—one for the top side and one for the bottom side). These heads are connected, or *ganged*, on a single movement mechanism. The heads, therefore, move across the platters in unison.

Mechanically, read/write heads are simple. Each head is on an actuator arm that is spring-loaded to force the head into contact with a platter. Few people realize that each platter actually is "squeezed" by the heads above and below it. If you could open a drive safely and lift the top head with your finger, the head would snap back down into the platter when you released it. If you could pull down on one of the heads below a platter, the spring tension would cause it to snap back up into the platter when you released it.

Figure 9.11 shows a typical hard disk head-actuator assembly from a voice coil drive.

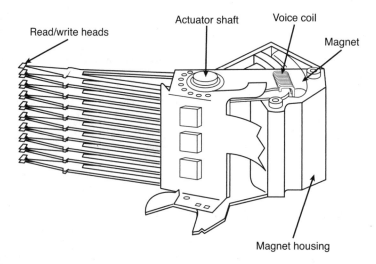

Read/write heads   Actuator shaft   Voice coil   Magnet   Magnet housing

FIGURE 9.11   Read/write heads and rotary voice coil actuator assembly.

When the drive is at rest, the heads are forced into direct contact with the platters by spring tension, but when the drive is spinning at full speed, air pressure develops below the heads and lifts them off the surface of the platter. On a drive spinning at full speed, the distance between the heads and the platter can be anywhere from 0.5 μ-inches to 5 μ-inches or more in a modern drive.

In the early 1960s, HDD recording heads operated at floating heights as large as 200 μ-inches to 300 μ-inches; today's drive heads are designed to float as low as 10nm (nanometers) or 0.4μμ-inches above the surface of the disk. To support higher densities in future drives, the physical separation between the head and disk is expected to drop even further, such that on some drives there will even be contact with the platter surface. New media and head designs will be required to make full or partial contact recording possible.

Caution

The small size of the gap between the platters and the heads is why you should never open the disk drive's HDA except in a clean-room environment. Any particle of dust or dirt that gets into this mechanism could cause the heads to read improperly or possibly even to strike the platters while the drive is running at full speed. The latter event could scratch the platter or the head, causing permanent damage.

To ensure the cleanliness of the interior of the drive, the HDA is assembled in a class-100 or better clean room. This specification means that a cubic foot of air can't contain more than 100 particles that measure up to 0.5 microns (19.7 μ-inches). A single person breathing while standing motionless spews out 500 such particles in a single minute! These rooms contain special air-filtration systems that continuously evacuate and refresh the air. A drive's HDA should not be opened unless it is inside such a room.

Although maintaining a clean-room environment might seem to be expensive, many companies manufacture tabletop or bench-size clean rooms that sell for only a few thousand dollars. Some of these devices operate like a glove box; the operator first inserts the drive and any tools required, closes the box, and then turns on the filtration system. Inside the box, a clean-room environment is maintained, and a technician can use the built-in gloves to work on the drive.

In other clean-room variations, the operator stands at a bench where a forced-air curtain maintains a clean environment on the bench top. The technician can walk in and out of the clean-room field by walking through the air curtain. This air curtain is similar to the curtain of air used in some stores and warehouses to prevent heat from escaping in the winter while leaving a passage wide open.

Because the clean environment is expensive to produce, few companies except those that manufacture the drives are properly equipped to service HDDs.

Read/Write Head Designs

As disk drive technology has evolved, so has the design of the read/write head. The earliest heads were simple iron cores with coil windings (electromagnets). By today's standards, the original head designs were physically enormous and operated at low recording densities. Over the years, head designs have evolved from the first simple ferrite core designs into the magneto-resistive and giant magneto-resistive types available today.

For more information on the various head designs, see Chapter 8.

Head Actuator Mechanisms

Possibly more important than the heads themselves is the mechanical system that moves them: the head actuator. This mechanism moves the heads across the disk and positions them accurately above the desired cylinder. Many variations on head actuator mechanisms are in use, but all fall into one of two basic categories:

- Stepper motor actuators
- Voice coil actuators

The use of one or the other type of actuator has profound effects on a drive's performance and reliability. The effects are not limited to speed; they also include accuracy, sensitivity to temperature, position, vibration, and overall reliability. The head actuator is the single most important specification in the drive, and the type of head actuator mechanism in a drive tells you a great deal about the drive's performance and reliability characteristics.

Stepper Motor Actuators

A stepper motor is an electrical motor that can "step," or move, from position to position, with mechanical detents or click-stop positions. Stepper motors can't position themselves between step positions; they can stop only at the predetermined detent positions. The motors are small (between 1 inch and 3 inches) and can be square, cylindrical, or flat. Stepper motors are outside the sealed HDA, although the spindle of the motor penetrates the HDA through a sealed hole.

Stepper motor mechanisms are affected by a variety of problems, but the greatest one is temperature. As the drive platters heat and cool, they expand and contract, and the tracks on the platters move in relation to a predetermined track position. The stepper mechanism can't move in increments of less than a single track to correct for these temperature-induced errors.

Floppy disk drives position their heads by using a stepper motor actuator. Stepper motor actuators were commonly used on hard drives made during the 1980s and early 1990s with capacities of 100MB or less. All HDDs being manufactured today use voice coil actuators because stepper motors can't achieve the degree of accuracy necessary.

Voice Coil Actuators

The voice coil actuators used in virtually all HDDs made today—unlike stepper motor actuators—use a feedback signal from the drive to accurately determine the head positions and adjust them, if necessary. This arrangement provides significantly greater performance, accuracy, and reliability than traditional stepper motor actuator designs.

A voice coil actuator works by pure electromagnetic force. The construction of the mechanism is similar to that of a typical audio speaker, from which the term *voice coil* is derived. An audio speaker uses a stationary magnet surrounded by a voice coil, which is connected to the speaker's paper cone. Energizing the coil causes it to move relative to the stationary magnet, which produces sound from the cone. In a typical HDD's voice coil system, the electromagnetic coil is attached to the end of the head rack and placed near a stationary magnet. No physical contact occurs between the coil and the magnet; instead, the coil moves by pure magnetic force. As the electromagnetic coils are energized, they attract or repulse the stationary magnet and move the head rack. Systems like these are extremely quick, efficient, and usually much quieter than systems driven by stepper motors.

Unlike a stepper motor, a voice coil actuator has no click-stops or detent positions; rather, a special guidance system stops the head rack above a particular cylinder. Because it has no detents, the voice coil actuator can slide the heads in and out smoothly to any position desired. Voice coil actuators use a guidance mechanism called a *servo* to tell the actuator where the heads are in relation to the cylinders and to place the heads accurately at the desired positions. This positioning system often is called a *closed loop feedback mechanism*. It works by sending the index (or servo) signal to the positioning electronics, which return a feedback signal that positions the heads accurately. The system also is called *servo controlled*, which refers to the index or servo information that accuracy dictates or controls head-positioning.

A voice coil actuator with servo control is not affected by temperature changes as a stepper motor is. When temperature changes cause the disk platters to expand or contract, the voice coil system compensates automatically because it never positions the heads in predetermined track positions. Rather, the voice coil system searches for the specific track, guided by the prewritten servo information, and then positions the head rack precisely above the desired track, wherever it happens to be. Because of the continuous feedback of servo information, the heads adjust to the current position of the track at all times. For example, as a drive warms up and the platters expand, the servo information enables the heads to "follow" the track. As a result, a voice coil actuator is sometimes called a track-following system.

The two main types of voice-coil positioner mechanisms are

- Linear voice-coil actuators
- Rotary voice-coil actuators

The two types differ only in the physical arrangement of the magnets and coils.

A linear actuator moves the heads in and out over the platters in a straight line (see Figure 9.12). The coil moves in and out on a track surrounded by the stationary magnets. The primary advantage of the linear design is that it eliminates the head azimuth variations that occur with rotary positioning systems. (*Azimuth* refers to the angular measurement of the head position relative to the tangent of a given cylinder.) A linear actuator does not rotate the head as it moves from one cylinder to another, thus eliminating this problem.

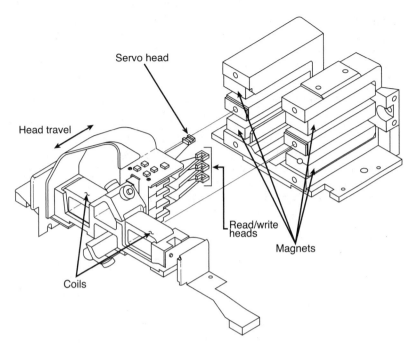

FIGURE 9.12 A linear voice coil actuator.

Although the linear actuator seems to be a good design, it has one fatal flaw: The devices are much too heavy. As drive performance has increased, the desire for lightweight actuator mechanisms has become important.

Rotary actuators also use stationary magnets and a movable coil, but the coil is attached to the end of an actuator arm. As the coil moves relative to the stationary magnet, it swings the head arms in and out over the surface of the disk. The primary advantage of this mechanism is its light weight, which means the heads can accelerate and decelerate quickly, resulting in fast average seek times. (Refer to Figure 9.10, which shows a rotary voice coil actuator.)

The disadvantage of a rotary system is that as the heads move from the outer to the inner cylinders, they rotate slightly with respect to the tangent of the cylinders. This rotation results in an azimuth error and is one reason the area of the platter in which the cylinders are located is somewhat limited. By limiting the total motion of the actuator, the azimuth error is contained to within reasonable specifications. Virtually all voice coil drives today use rotary actuator systems.

Servo Mechanisms

Three servo mechanism designs have been used to control voice coil positioners over the years:

- Wedge servo
- Embedded servo
- Dedicated servo

The three designs are slightly different, but they accomplish the same basic task: They enable the head positioner to adjust continuously so it is precisely positioned above a given cylinder on the disk. The main difference between these servo designs is where the gray code information is actually written on the drive.

All servo mechanisms rely on special information that is written to the disk when it is manufactured. This information is usually in the form of a special code called a *gray code*—a special binary notational system in which any two adjacent numbers are represented by a code that differs in only one bit place or column position. This system enables the head to easily read the information and quickly determine its precise position.

At the time of manufacture, a special machine called a *servowriter* writes the servo gray code on the disk. The servowriter is basically a jig that mechanically moves the heads to a given reference position and then writes the servo information at that position. Many servowriters are themselves guided by a laser-beam reference that determines its own position by calculating distances in wavelengths of light. Because the servowriter must be capable of moving the heads mechanically, the process requires either that the lid of the drive be removed or that access be available through special access ports in the HDA. After the servowriting is complete, these ports are usually covered with sealing tape. You often see these tape-covered holes on the HDA, usually accompanied by warnings that you will void the warranty if you remove the tape. Because servowriting exposes the interior of the HDA, it requires a clean-room environment.

A servowriter is an expensive piece of machinery, costing thousands of dollars, and often must be custom-made for a particular make or model of drive. Some drive-repair companies have servowriting capability, which means they can rewrite the servo information on a drive if it becomes damaged. If a servowriter is not available, a drive with servo code damage must be sent back to the drive manufacturer for the servo information to be rewritten.

Fortunately, damaging the servo information through the disk read and write processes is impossible. Drives are designed so the heads can't overwrite the servo information, even during a low-level format. One myth that has been circulating (especially with respect to ATA drives) is that you can damage the servo information by improper low-level formatting. This is not true. An improper low-level format can compromise the performance of the drive, but the servo information is protected and can't be overwritten. Even so, the servo information on some drives can be damaged by a strong adjacent magnetic field or by jarring the drive while it is writing, which causes the heads to move off track.

The track-following capabilities of a servo-controlled voice coil actuator eliminate the positioning errors that occur over time with stepper motor drives. Voice coil drives are not affected by conditions such as thermal expansion and contraction of the platters. In fact, many voice coil drives today perform a special thermal-recalibration procedure at predetermined intervals while they run. This procedure usually involves seeking the heads from cylinder 0 to some other cylinder one time for every head on the drive. As this sequence occurs, the control circuitry in the drive monitors how much the track positions have moved since the last time the sequence was performed, and a thermal-recalibration adjustment is calculated and stored in the drive's memory. This information is then used every time the drive positions the heads to ensure the most accurate positioning possible.

At one time, most drives had to perform the thermal-recalibration sequence every 5 minutes for the first 30 minutes that the drive was powered on and then once every 25 minutes after that. With some drives, this thermal-recalibration sequence was noticeable because the drive essentially stopped what it was doing, and you heard rapid ticking for a second or so. This was often misinterpreted as the drive having a problem reading data and having to reread it, but this was not true.

As multimedia applications grew in popularity, thermal recalibration became a problem with some manufacturers' drives. The thermal-recalibration sequence sometimes interrupted the transfer of a large data file, such as an audio or a video file, which resulted in audio or video playback jitter. Consequently, some companies released special A/V (audio/visual) drives to hide the thermal-recalibration sequences so they never interrupt a file transfer. Virtually all of today's ATA drives are A/V capable, which means the thermal-recalibration sequences do not interrupt a data transfer.

A/V-capable ATA drives are also used in set-top boxes that are utilized for digital recording, such as the popular TiVo device.

While we are on the subject of automatic drive functions, most of the drives that perform thermal-recalibration sequences also automatically perform a function called a *disk sweep*. Also called *wear leveling* by some manufacturers, this procedure is an automatic head seek that occurs after the drive has been idle for a period of time. The disk-sweep function moves the heads to a cylinder in the outer portion of the platters, which is where the head float-height is highest (because the head-to-platter velocity is highest). Then, if the drive continues to remain idle for another period, the heads move to another cylinder in this area, and the process continues indefinitely as long as the drive is powered on.

The disk-sweep function is designed to prevent the head from remaining stationary above one cylinder in the drive for too long, where friction between the head and platter eventually would dig a trench in the medium. Although the heads are not in direct contact with the medium, they are so close that the constant air pressure from the head floating above a single cylinder could cause friction and excessive wear. Figure 9.13 shows both a wedge and an embedded servo.

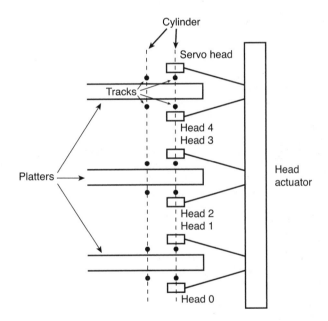

FIGURE 9.13   A wedge and an embedded servo.

Wedge Servo

Early servo-controlled drives used a technique called a *wedge servo*. In these drives, the gray-code guidance information is contained in a "wedge" slice of the drive in each cylinder immediately preceding the index mark. The index mark indicates the beginning of each track, so the wedge-servo information was written in the PRE-INDEX GAP, which is at the end of each track. This area is provided for speed tolerance and normally is not used by the controller.

Some controllers had to be notified that the drive was using a wedge servo so they could shorten the sector timing to allow for the wedge-servo area. If they were not correctly configured, these controllers would not work properly with the drive.

Another problem was that the servo information appears only one time every revolution, which means that the drive often needed several revolutions before it could accurately determine and adjust the head position. Because of these problems, the wedge servo never was a popular design; it no longer is used in drives.

Embedded Servo

An embedded servo is an enhancement of the wedge servo. Instead of placing the servo code before the beginning of each cylinder, an embedded servo design writes the servo information before the start of each sector. This arrangement enables the positioner circuits to receive feedback many times in a single revolution, making the head positioning much faster and more precise. Another advantage is that every track on the drive has its own positioning information, so each head can quickly and efficiently adjust position to compensate for any changes in the platter or head dimensions, especially for changes due to thermal expansion or physical stress.

Most drives today use an embedded servo to control the positioning system. As in the wedge servo design, the embedded servo information is protected by the drive circuits, and any write operations are blocked whenever the heads are above the servo information. Thus, it is impossible to overwrite the servo information with a low-level format, as some people incorrectly believe.

Dedicated Servo

A dedicated servo is a design in which the servo information is written continuously throughout the entire track, rather than just once per track or at the beginning of each sector. Unfortunately, if this procedure were used on the entire drive, no room would be left for data. For this reason, a *dedicated servo* uses one side of one of the platters exclusively for the servo-positioning information. The term *dedicated* comes from the fact that this platter side is completely dedicated to the servo information and can't contain data.

When building a dedicated servo drive, the manufacturer deducts one side of one platter from normal read/write usage and records a special set of gray-code data there that indicates the proper track positions. Because the head that rests above this surface can't be used for normal reading and writing, the gray code can never be erased and the servo information is protected—as in the other servo designs. No low-level format or other procedure can possibly overwrite the servo information. Figure 9.14 shows a dedicated servo mechanism. Typically, the head on top or one in the center is dedicated for servo use.

When the drive moves the heads to a specific cylinder, the internal drive electronics use the signals received by the servo head to determine the position of the read/write heads. As the heads move, the track counters are read from the dedicated servo surface. When the servo head detects the requested track, the actuator stops. The servo electronics then fine-tune the position so the heads are precisely above the desired cylinder before any writing is permitted. Although only one head is used for servo tracking, the other heads are attached to the same rack so that if one head is above the desired cylinder, all the others are as well.

One way of telling whether a drive uses a dedicated servo platter is if it has an odd number of heads. For example, the Toshiba MK-538FB 1.2GB drive that I used to have in one of my systems had 8 platters, but only 15 read/write heads. That drive uses a dedicated servo positioning system, and the 16th head is the servo head. The advantage of the dedicated servo concept is that the servo information is continuously available to the drive, making the head positioning process faster and more precise.

The drawback to a dedicated servo is that dedicating an entire platter surface for servo information is wasteful. Virtually all drives today use a variation on the embedded servo technique instead. Some drives combined a dedicated servo with an embedded servo, but this type of hybrid design is rare. Regardless of whether the servo mechanism is dedicated or embedded, it is far more accurate than the stepper motor mechanisms of the past.

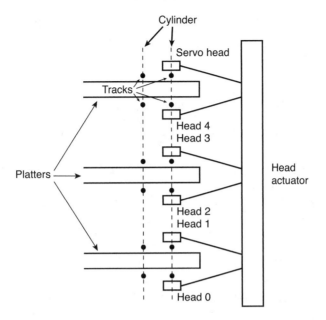

FIGURE 9.14 A dedicated servo, showing one entire head/side used for servo reading.

Of course, as mentioned earlier, today's ATA drives have head, track, and sector-per-track parameters that are translated from the actual physical numbers. Therefore, you usually can't tell from the published numbers exactly how many heads or platters are contained within a drive.

Automatic Head Parking

When you power off an HDD using the CSS design, the spring tension in each head arm pulls the heads into contact with the platters. The drive is designed to sustain thousands of takeoffs and landings, but it is wise to ensure that the landing occurs at a spot on the platter that contains no data. Older drives from the 1980s and early 1990s required manual head parking; you had to run a program that positioned the drive heads to a landing zone—usually the innermost cylinder—before turning off the system. Modern drives automatically park the heads, so park programs are no longer necessary.

Some amount of abrasion occurs during the landing and takeoff process, removing just a "micro puff" from the magnetic medium, but if the drive is jarred during the landing or takeoff process, real damage can occur. Newer drives that use load/unload designs incorporate a ramp positioned outside the outer surface of the platters to prevent contact between the heads and platters, even if the drive is powered off. Load/unload drives automatically park the heads on the ramp when the drive is powered off.

One benefit of using a voice coil actuator is automatic head parking. In a drive that has a voice coil actuator, the heads are positioned and held by magnetic force. When the power to the drive is removed, the magnetic field that holds the heads stationary over a particular cylinder dissipates, enabling the head rack to skitter across the drive surface and potentially cause damage. In the voice coil design, the head rack is attached to a weak spring at one end and a head stop at the other end. When the system is powered on, the spring is overcome by the magnetic force of the positioner. When the drive is powered off, however, the spring gently drags the head rack to a park-and-lock position before the drive slows down and the heads land. On some drives, you could actually hear the "ting... ting...ting...ting" sound as the heads literally bounce-parked themselves, driven by this spring.

On a drive with a voice coil actuator, you activate the parking mechanism by turning off the computer; you do not need to run a program to park or retract the heads, as was necessary with early hard disk designs. In the event of a power outage, the heads park themselves automatically. (The drives unpark automatically when the system is powered on.)

Air Filters

Nearly all HDDs have two air filters. One is called the recirculating filter, and the other is called either a barometric or breather filter. These filters are permanently sealed inside the drive and are designed never to be changed for the life of the drive, unlike many older mainframe hard disks that had changeable filters.

A hard disk on a PC system does not circulate air from inside to outside the HDA or vice versa. The recirculating filter permanently installed inside the HDA is designed to filter only the small particles scraped off the platters during head takeoffs and landings (and possibly any other small particles dislodged inside the drive). Because PC HDDs are permanently sealed and do not circulate outside air, they can run in extremely dirty environments (see Figure 9.15).

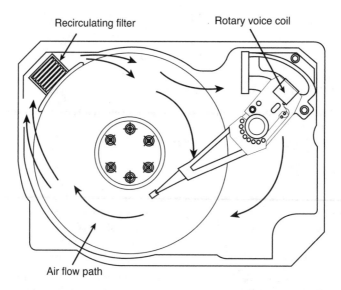

FIGURE 9.15 Air circulation in a hard disk.

The HDA in an HDD is sealed but not airtight. The HDA is vented through a barometric or breather filter element that enables pressure equalization (breathing) between the inside and the outside of the drive. For this reason, most hard drives are rated by the drive's manufacturer to run in a specific range of altitudes, usually from 1,000 feet below to 10,000 feet above sea level. In fact, some hard drives are not rated to exceed 7,000 feet while operating because the air pressure would be too low inside the drive to float the heads properly. As the environmental air pressure changes, air bleeds into or out of the drive so internal and external pressures are identical. Although air does bleed through a vent, contamination usually is not a concern because the barometric filter on this vent is designed to filter out all particles larger than 0.3 microns (about 12 μ-inches) to meet the specifications for cleanliness inside the drive. You can see the vent holes on most drives, which are covered internally by this breather filter. Some drives use even finer grade filter elements to keep out even smaller particles.

I conducted a seminar in Hawaii several years ago, and several of the students were from one of the astronomical observatories atop Mauna Kea. They indicated that virtually all the HDDs they had tried to use at the observatory site had failed quickly, if they worked at all. This was no surprise because the observatories are at the 13,796-foot peak of the mountain, and at that altitude, even people don't function well! At the time, they had to resort to SSDs, tape drives, or even floppy disk drives as their primary storage medium. Some manufacturers produce drives that are hermetically sealed (airtight), although they do still have air inside the HDA. Because they carry their own internal air under pressure, these drives can operate at any altitude and can withstand extremes of shock and temperature. The drives are designed for military and industrial applications, such as systems used aboard aircraft and in extremely harsh environments. They are, of course, more expensive than typical hard drives that operate under ambient pressures.

Hard Disk Temperature Acclimation

Because most hard drives have a filtered port to bleed air into or out of the HDA, moisture can enter the drive, and after some period, it must be assumed that the humidity inside any hard disk is similar to that outside the drive. Humidity can become a serious problem if it is allowed to condense—and especially if you power up the drive while this condensation is present. Most hard disk manufacturers have specified procedures for acclimating a hard drive to a new environment with different temperature and humidity ranges, and especially for bringing a drive into a warmer environment in which condensation can form. This situation should be of special concern to users of laptop or portable systems. If you leave a portable system in an automobile trunk during the winter, for example, it could be catastrophic to bring the machine inside and power it up without allowing it to acclimate to the temperature indoors.

The following text and Table 9.10 are taken from the factory packaging that Control Data Corporation (later Imprimis and eventually Seagate) used to ship with its hard drives:

> If you have just received or removed this unit from a climate with temperatures at or below 50°F (10°C) do not open this container until the following conditions are met, otherwise condensation could occur and damage to the device and/or media may result. Place this package in the operating environment for the time duration according to the temperature chart.

Table 9.10   HDD Environmental Acclimation Table

Previous Climate Temperature	Acclimation Time	Previous Climate Temperature	Acclimation Time
+40°F (+4°C)	13 hours	−10°F (−23°C)	20 hours
+30°F (−1°C)	15 hours	−20°F (−29°C)	22 hours
+20°F (−7°C)	16 hours	−30°F (−34°C) or less	27 hours
+10°F (−12°C)	17 hours		
0°F (−18°C)	18 hours		

As you can see from this table, you must place an HDD that has been stored in a colder-than-normal environment into its normal operating environment for a specified amount of time to allow it to acclimate before you power it on.

Spindle Motors

The motor that spins the platters is called the *spindle motor* because it is connected to the spindle around which the platters revolve. Spindle motors in HDDs are always connected directly; no belts or gears are involved. The motor must be free of noise and vibration; otherwise, it can transmit a rumble to the platters, which can disrupt reading and writing operations.

The spindle motor also must be precisely controlled for speed. The platters in HDDs revolve at speeds ranging from 3,600 rpm to 15,000 rpm (60–250 revolutions per second) or more, and the motor has a control circuit with a feedback loop to monitor and control this speed precisely. Because the speed control must be automatic, hard drives do not have a motor-speed adjustment. Some diagnostics programs claim to measure hard drive rotation speed, but all these programs do is estimate the rotational speed by the timing at which sectors pass under the heads.

There is actually no way for a program to measure the HDD's rotational speed; this measurement can be made only with sophisticated test equipment. Don't be alarmed if some diagnostics program tells you that your drive is spinning at an incorrect speed; most likely, the program is wrong, not the drive. Platter rotation and timing information is not provided through the hard disk controller interface. In the past, software could give approximate rotational speed estimates by performing multiple sector read requests and timing them, but this was valid only when all drives had the same number of sectors per track and spun at the same speed. Zoned-bit recording—combined with the many various rotational speeds used by modern drives, not to mention built-in buffers and caches—means that these calculation estimates can't be performed accurately by software.

On most drives, the spindle motor is on the bottom of the drive, just below the sealed HDA. Many drives today, however, have the spindle motor built directly into the platter hub inside the HDA. By using an internal hub spindle motor, the manufacturer can stack more platters in the drive because the spindle motor takes up no vertical space.

Note

Spindle motors, particularly on the larger form-factor drives, can consume a great deal of 12-volt power. Most drives require two to three times the normal operating power when the motor first spins the platters. This heavy draw lasts only a few seconds or until the drive platters reach operating speed. If you have more than one drive, you should try to sequence the start of the spindle motors so the power supply does not have to provide such a large load to all the drives at the same time. Most SCSI, SAS, and some ATA drives have a delayed spindle-motor start feature.

Traditionally, spindle motors have used ball bearings in their design, but limitations in their performance have now caused drive manufacturers to look for alternatives. The main problem with ball bearings is that they have approximately 0.1 micro-inch (millionths of an inch) of runout, which is lateral side-to-side play in the bearings. Even though that might seem small, with the ever-increasing density of modern drives, it has become a problem. This runout allows the platters to move randomly that distance from side to side, which causes the tracks to wobble under the heads. Additionally, the runout plus the metal-to-metal contact nature of ball bearings allows an excessive amount of mechanical noise and vibration to be generated, and that is becoming a problem for drives that spin at higher speeds.

The solution is a new type of bearing called a *fluid dynamic bearing*, which uses a highly viscous lubricating fluid between the spindle and sleeve in the motor. This fluid serves to dampen vibrations and movement, allowing runout to be reduced to 0.01 micro-inches or less. Fluid dynamic bearings also allow for better shock resistance, improved speed control, and reduced noise generation. The first drives on the market to use fluid dynamic bearings were advanced drives designed for high spindle speeds, high areal densities, or low noise. Over the past few years, fluid dynamic bearings have become standard issue in most hard drives.

Logic Boards

All HDDs have one or more logic boards mounted on them. The logic boards contain the electronics that control the drive's spindle and head actuator systems and present data to the controller in some agreed-upon form. On ATA drives, the boards include the controller itself, whereas SCSI drives include the controller and the SCSI bus adapter circuit.

Many disk drive failures occur in the logic board, not in the mechanical assembly. (This statement does not seem logical, but it is true.) Therefore, you sometimes can repair a failed drive by replacing the logic board rather than the entire drive. Replacing the logic board, moreover, enables you to regain access to the data on the drive—something that replacing the entire drive does not provide. Unfortunately, none of the drive manufacturers sell logic boards separately. The only way to obtain a replacement logic board for a given drive is to purchase a functioning identical drive and then cannibalize it for parts. Of course, it doesn't make sense to purchase an entire new drive just to repair an existing one except in cases in which data recovery from the old drive is necessary. Cannibalizing new drives to repair old drives is a common practice among companies that offer data recovery services. They stock a large number of popular drives they can use for parts to allow data recovery from defective customer drives they receive.

Most of the time, the boards are fairly easy to change with nothing more than a screwdriver. Merely removing and reinstalling a few screws as well as unplugging and reconnecting a cable or two are all that is required to remove and replace a typical logic board.

Cables and Connectors

HDDs typically have several connectors for interfacing to the computer, receiving power, and sometimes grounding to the system chassis. Most drives have at least these three types of connectors:

- Interface connector(s)
- Power connector
- Optional ground connector (tab)

Of these, the interface connectors are the most important because they carry the data and command signals between the system and the drive. In most cases, the drive interface cables can be connected in a daisy-chain or bus-type configuration. Most interfaces support at least two devices. Older interfaces, such as ST-506/412 or ESDI (Enhanced Small Device Interface), used separate cables for data and control signals, but both Parallel and Serial ATA (AT Attachment) drives have a single data connector on each drive.

◄◄ See the Chapter 7 section, "PATA I/O Connector," **p. 387**.

The power is supplied via either a 15-pin SATA power connector or a 4-pin peripheral power connector, both of which can be found on most PC power supplies. Most 3.5-inch and larger HDDs use both 5- and 12-volt power, while most 2.5-inch and smaller drives use only 5-volt power. In drives that use both 5V and 12V power, the 12-volt power runs the spindle motor and head actuator, while the 5-volt power runs the circuitry. Make sure your power supply can supply adequate power for the HDDs installed in your system.

The power consumption of a drive usually varies with the physical size and rotational speed of the unit. The larger and faster the drive is, the more power it requires. More platters add rotational mass that takes more power as well. For example, most of the 3 1/2-inch drives on the market today use roughly one-half to one-fourth the power (in watts) of the older 5 1/4-inch drives. Some of the small (2 1/2-inch) hard disks barely sip electrical power and actually use 1 watt or less!

Configuration Items

To configure a PATA HDD for installation in a system, you may have to set several jumpers properly. SATA drives generally don't need any configuration; however, in some rare cases a jumper may need to be placed to force a SATA drive to use a lower interface transfer rate. This is a rare problem that happens only with some drives and older SATA host adapter chipsets.

◄◄ See Chapter 7, "The ATA/IDE Interface," **p. 377**.

Hard Disk Features

To make the best decision in purchasing a hard disk for your system or to understand what distinguishes one brand of hard disk from another, you must consider many features. This section examines some of the issues you must consider when you evaluate drives:

- Capacity
- Performance
- Reliability
- Cost

Capacity

As stated earlier, a corollary of Parkinson's famous "law" can be applied to hard drives: "Data expands so as to fill the space available for its storage." This, of course, means that no matter how big a drive you get, you *will* find a way to fill it.

If you've exhausted the space on your current hard disk, you might be wondering, "How much storage space is enough?" Because you are more likely to run out of space than have too much, you should aim high and get the largest drive that will fit within your budget. Modern systems are used to store many space-hungry file types, including digital photos, music, video, newer OSs, applications, and games. Photo, audio, and especially video files can take up huge amounts of storage, easily running into hundreds of gigabytes or even terabytes of storage. Although most drives today can hold hundreds of gigabytes, many people are storing several times that.

Running out of space causes numerous problems in a modern system, mainly because Windows, as well as many newer applications, uses a large amount of drive space for temporary files and virtual memory. When Windows runs out of room, system instability, crashes, and data loss are inevitable.

Capacity Limitations

How big a hard drive you can use depends on many factors, including the interface, drivers, OS, and file system you choose.

When the ATA interface was created in 1986, it had a maximum capacity limitation of 137GB (65,536×16×255 sectors). BIOS issues further limited capacity to 8.4GB in systems produced earlier than 1998, and as low as 528MB in systems earlier than 1994. Even after the BIOS issues were resolved, however, the initial 137GB limit of ATA remained. Fortunately, this was broken in the ATA-6 specification drafted in 2001. ATA-6 augmented the addressing scheme used by ATA to allow drive capacity to grow to 144PB (petabytes, or quadrillion bytes), which is 2^48 sectors. This has opened the door allowing PATA and SATA drives over 137GB to be released.

BIOS Limitations

Many older (pre-1998) BIOSs can't handle drives above the 8.4GB limit, and other BIOSs (pre-2002) have other limits, such as 137GB. Some drives ship with a setup or installation disc containing a software BIOS substitute, such as Ontrack's Disk Manager, Phoenix Technologies' EZ-Drive (Phoenix purchased EZ-Drive creator StorageSoft in January 2002), and their OEM offshoots (Drive Guide, MAXBlast, Data Lifeguard, and others). However, I don't recommend using these because they can cause problems if you need to boot from floppy or CD media or if you need to repair the nonstandard MBR these products use.

Internal ATA drives larger than 137GB require 48-bit LBA support. This support *must* be provided in the OS; it can also be provided in the BIOS, or both. It is best if both the OS and the BIOS support it, but it can be made to work if only the OS has the support.

One of the following is required for 48-bit LBA support in the OS:

- Windows 8/7/Vista.
- Windows XP with Service Pack 1 (SP1) or later.
- Windows 2000 with Service Pack 4 (SP4) or later.
- Windows 98/98SE/Me or NT 4.0 with the Intel Application Accelerator (IAA) loaded. This solution works only if your motherboard has an IAA-supported chipset. See http://downloadcenter.intel.com and search for IAA for more information.

And either of the following is required for 48-bit LBA support in the BIOS:

- A motherboard BIOS with 48-bit LBA support (usually dated September 2002 or later)
- An adapter card with onboard BIOS that includes 48-bit LBA support

If you have both OS and BIOS support for 48-bit LBA, you can simply install and use the drive like any other internal drive. On the other hand, if you do not have 48-bit LBA support in the BIOS, but you do have it in the OS, portions of the drive past 137GB are not recognized or accessible until the OS is loaded. This means that if you are installing the OS to a blank hard drive and booting from an original XP (pre-SP1) CD or earlier, you need to partition up to the first 137GB of the drive at installation time. After the OS is fully installed and the service packs added, the remainder of the drive beyond 137GB is recognized. At that point, you can then either partition the remainder of the drive beyond 137GB using the XP Disk Management tools or use a third-party partitioning program such as Parted Magic (www.partedmagic.com) to resize the first partition to use the full drive.

If you are booting from an XP SP1 or later CD (meaning a CD with Service Pack 1 already applied), you can recognize and access the entire drive during the OS installation and partition the entire drive as a single partition greater than 137GB if you like.

Booting from 2.2TB or larger drives requires a newer type of BIOS called UEFI (Unified Extensible Firmware Interface), which supports booting from a new type of partition format called GUID (globally unique identifier) Partition Table (GPT). This is because the traditional MBR disk format only supports drives up to 2.199TB, and legacy (non-UEFI) BIOS can only boot from MBR-formatted drives.

If you need more or faster SATA interface connections, you can use add-on cards from companies such as Promise Technology (www.promise.com). These cards support drives up to and beyond the 137GB limit imposed by the ATA-5 and older standards.

Note that external USB and FireWire drives don't have these capacity issues because they don't rely on the ROM BIOS for support and use OS-managed drivers instead.

Operating System Limitations

More recent OSs, such as Windows Vista and Windows 7/8, don't have problems with larger drives. However, older OSs might have limitations when it comes to using large drives.

Windows XP and earlier versions are limited in capacity to supporting drives less than 2.2TB per physical or logical (that is, RAID) drive, including all partitions. This is due to reliance on the MBR partitioning scheme, which uses 32-bit sector numbering, limiting a physical or logical drive to a maximum of 2^{32} (4,294,967,296) total sectors. Windows 7/8 and Vista SP1+ support a newer partitioning scheme called GPT, which defines sectors using 64-bit numbers, supporting 2^{64}

(18,446,744,073,709,551,616) sectors, for a maximum capacity of 9.44ZB (zettabytes or billion tera-bytes). In practical terms, this means that if you are running XP, you can't normally utilize more than 2TB of a single drive or a RAID array of multiple drives. However, Windows XP can use GPT format-ted drives of 2.2TB or greater in capacity if a third-party GPT utility tool like the Paragon GPT Loader (www.paragon-software.com) is used.

Performance

When you select an HDD, one of the important features you should consider is the performance (speed) of the drive. Hard drives can have a range of performance capabilities. As is true of many things, one of the best indicators of a drive's relative performance is its price. An old saying from the automobile-racing industry is appropriate here: "Speed costs money. How fast do you want to go?"

The speed of a disk drive is typically measured in two ways:

- Transfer rate
- Average access time

Transfer Rate

The transfer rate is probably more important to overall system performance than any other statistic, but it is also one of the most misunderstood specifications. The problem stems from the fact that sev-eral transfer rates can be specified for a given drive; however, the most important of these is usually overlooked.

Don't be fooled by interface transfer rate hype, especially around ATA-133 or SATA-150/300/600. A far more important gauge of a drive's performance is the average media transfer rate, which for a hard disk is significantly lower than the interface rate of 133, 150, 300, or 600MBps. Solid-state drives (SSDs), on the other hand, are often limited by the interface transfer rate, and for maximum performance cur-rent SSDs require the full 600MBps that SATA revision 3 6Gbps ports can provide. On a hard disk the media transfer rate represents the average speed at which the drive can actually read or write data. By comparison, the interface transfer rate merely indicates how quickly data can move between the moth-erboard and the buffer on the drive. The rotational speed of the drive has perhaps the biggest effect on the drive's true transfer speed; in general, drives that spin at 10,000 rpm transfer data faster than 7,200 rpm drives, and 7,200 rpm drives transfer data faster than those that spin at 5,400 rpm. Note, however, that rotational speed is not the only thing to consider—the track linear density plays a huge part in performance as well. For example, the 5,400 rpm 500GB drive in one of my laptops has a maximum transfer rate of 118MBps, whereas the 7,200 rpm 60GB drive in an older laptop has a maximum trans-fer rate of only 44MBps. That means my newer 5400 rpm drive is actually more than 2.6 times faster in actual transfer rate performance, even though it spins over 33% more slowly. If you are looking for performance, be sure to check the true *media* transfer rates of any drives you are comparing.

The confusion results from the fact that drive manufacturers can report up to seven different transfer rates for a given drive. Perhaps the least important (but one that people seem to focus on the most) is the raw interface transfer rate, which for SATA drives is up to 600MBps, and up to 100MBps or 133MBps for older PATA drives. Unfortunately, the drives actually read and write data much more slowly than that; you must use a high-performance SSD instead of a traditional hard disk if you want to fully exploit SATA transfer rates. The more important transfer rate specifications are the media transfer rates, which express how fast a drive can actually read or write data. Media transfer rates can be expressed as a raw maximum, a raw minimum, a formatted maximum, a formatted minimum, or averages of either. Few report the averages, but they can be easily calculated.

The media transfer rate is far more important than the interface transfer rate because the media transfer rate is the true rate at which data can be read from (or written to) the disk. In other words, it tells how fast data can be moved to and from the drive platters (media). It is the rate that any sustained transfer can hope to achieve. This rate is usually reported as a minimum and maximum figure, although many drive manufacturers report the maximum only.

Media transfer rates have minimum and maximum figures because drives today use zoned recording with fewer sectors per track on the inner cylinders than the outer cylinders. Typically, a drive is divided into 16 or more zones, with the inner zone having about half the sectors per track (and therefore about half the transfer rate) of the outer zone. Because the drive spins at a constant rate, data can be read twice as fast from the outer cylinders than from the inner cylinders.

Another issue is the raw transfer rate versus the formatted transfer rate. The *raw* rate refers to how fast bits can be read off the media. Because not all bits represent data (some are intersector, servo, ECC, or ID bits), and because some time is lost when the heads have to move from track to track (latency), the *formatted* transfer rate represents the true rate at which user data can be read from or written to the drive.

Note that some manufacturers report only raw internal media transfer rates, but the formatted transfer rates are about three-fourths of the raw rates. This is because the user data on each track is only about three-fourths of the actual bits stored due to servo, ECC, ID, and other overhead that is stored. Likewise, some manufacturers report only maximum transfer rates (raw, formatted, or both); in that case, you generally can assume that the minimum transfer rate is one-half of the maximum and that the average transfer rate is three-fourths of the maximum.

Finally, one more issue affecting drive performance is size, with physically larger drives having an advantage. For example, assuming equal areal density and rotational speed, 3.5-inch drives offer transfer rates that are about 46% faster than 2.5-inch drives. This is due to the relative difference in track length (circumference) between the two drives. 3.5-inch drives have platters that are 3.74 inches in diameter, while 2.5-inch drives have platters that are 2.56 inches in diameter. This means that each track on a 3.5-inch drive is about 46% longer than those on 2.5-inch drives, and when spinning at the same speed each drive reads a track in the same amount of time.

Let's look at some specific drives as an example. Table 9.11 shows the performance specifications and formatted media transfer rates for several modern 3.5-inch form factor SATA drives.

Table 9.11   Drive Performance Specifications

Make/Model	Capacity	Rotational Speed	Interface Rate	Max. Media Rate	Min. Media Rate	Avg. Media Rate
Seagate Barracuda 7200.14	3TB	7,200rpm	600MBps	210MBps	105MBps	156MBps
Western Digital VelociRaptor*	1TB	10,000rpm	600MBps	200MBps	100MBps	150MBps
Seagate Constellation ES.2	3TB	7,200rpm	600MBps	155MBps	78MBps	116MBps
Western Digital Caviar Black	2TB	7,200rpm	600MBps	138MBps	69MBps	104MBps

The VelociRaptor is actually a 2.5-inch drive in a 3.5-inch form factor carrier.

As you can see, the *true* transfer rates for these drives are much lower than the 600MBps SATA interface transfer rate. Although all these support the 6Gbps (600MBps) SATA transfer rate specification, they have media transfer rates of up to 210MBps maximum, with individual drives averaging between about 104MBps and 156MBps. Note that the fastest performing drive is not the fastest rotating drive because physical size and density has as much or more to do with actual performance as rotational speed does.

Two primary factors contribute to transfer rate performance between drives with equal sized platters: rotational speed and the linear recording density or sector-per-track figures. When you're comparing two drives with the same number of sectors per track, the drive that spins more quickly transfers data more quickly. Likewise, when you're comparing two drives with identical rotational speeds, the drive with the higher recording density (more sectors per track) is faster. A higher-density drive can be faster than one that spins faster—both factors have to be taken into account.

As you can see from these examples, the interface transfer speed is almost meaningless. So, if you were thinking about getting a new motherboard or maybe a separate host adapter card offering a faster interface rate for the sole purpose of increasing drive performance, save your money. To be fair, there will be a slight benefit to higher interface transfer speeds in that data from the buffer on the drive controller can be transferred to the motherboard at interface speed, rather than media speed. These buffers are usually 32MB or less and help only with repetitive transfers of small amounts of data. However, if you perform repetitive transfers frequently, drives with larger buffers can improve performance with applications that perform repetitive transfers. More recently, drives with large Flash memory buffers, called *hybrid* drives, are being manufactured to improve performance for startup and commonly read files. These drives offer near SSD read performance while costing only a little bit more than standard drives.

All other things being equal, a drive that spins faster transfers data faster, regardless of the interface transfer rate. Unfortunately, it is rare that all other things are exactly equal, so you should consult the drive specifications listed in the data sheet or manual for the drive to be sure.

To find the transfer specifications for a given drive, look in the data sheet or preferably the documentation or manual for the drive. These can usually be downloaded from the drive manufacturer's website.

Average Seek Time

Average seek time, usually measured in milliseconds (ms), is the average amount of time it takes to move the heads from one cylinder to another a random distance away. One way to measure this specification is to run many random track-seek operations and then divide the timed results by the number of seeks performed. This method provides an average time for a single seek.

The standard method used by many drive manufacturers when reporting average seek times is to measure the time it takes the heads to move across one-third of the total cylinders. Average seek time depends only on the drive itself; the type of interface or controller has little effect on this specification. The average seek rating is primarily a gauge of the capabilities of the head actuator mechanism.

Note

Be wary of benchmarks that claim to measure drive seek performance. Most ATA drives use a scheme called sector translation, so any commands the drive receives to move the heads to a specific cylinder might not actually result in the intended physical movement. This situation renders some benchmarks meaningless for those types of drives. SCSI drives also require an additional step because the commands first must be sent to the drive over the SCSI bus. These drives might seem to have the fastest access times because most benchmarks don't factor in the command overhead. However, when this overhead is factored in by benchmark programs, these drives receive poor performance figures.

Latency

Latency is the average time (in milliseconds) it takes for a sector to be available after the heads have reached a track. On average, this figure is half the time it takes for the disk to rotate once. A drive that spins twice as fast would have half the latency.

Latency is a factor in disk read and write performance. Decreasing the latency increases the speed of access to data or files and is accomplished only by spinning the drive platters more quickly. Latency figures for most popular drive rotational speeds are shown in Table 9.12.

Table 9.12   Hard Disk Rotation Speeds and Their Latencies

Revs/Minute	Revs/Second	Latency (ms)
3,600	60	8.33
4,200	70	7.14
5,400	90	5.56
7,200	120	4.17
10,000	167	3.00
15,000	250	2.00

Many drives today spin at 7,200 rpm, resulting in a latency time of only 4.17ms, whereas others spin at 10,000 rpm or even 15,000 rpm, resulting in incredible 3.00ms or 2.00ms latency figures. In addition to increasing performance where real-world access to data is concerned, spinning the platters more quickly also increases the data-transfer rate after the heads arrive at the desired sectors.

Average Access Time

A measurement of a drive's average access time is the sum of its average seek time plus latency. The average access time is usually expressed in milliseconds.

A measurement of a drive's average access time (average seek time plus latency) provides the average total amount of time required for the drive to access a randomly requested sector.

Cache Programs and Caching Controllers

At the software level, disk cache programs such as SMARTDRV (DOS) and VCACHE (Windows) can have a major effect on disk drive performance. These cache programs hook into the BIOS hard drive interrupt and intercept the read and write calls to the disk BIOS from application programs and device drivers.

When an application program wants to read data from a hard drive, the cache program intercepts the read request, passes the read request to the hard drive controller in the usual way, saves the data read from the disk in its cache memory buffer, and then passes the data back to the application program. Depending on the size of the cache buffer, data from numerous sectors can be read into and saved in the buffer.

When the application wants to read more data, the cache program again intercepts the request and examines its buffers to see whether the requested data is still in the cache. If so, the program passes the data back from the cache to the application immediately, without another hard drive operation. Because the cached data is stored in memory, this method speeds access tremendously and can greatly affect disk drive performance measurements.

Virtually all drives have varying amounts of cache memory built directly into the drive's onboard controller. I remember the days when 1MB or 2MB of RAM was a lot of memory for an entire system. Today, low-end drives might feature 2–8MB, with mid-range and high-performance drives typically include 16–64MB of cache.

Although software and hardware caches can make a drive faster for routine or repetitive data transfer operations, a cache will not affect the true maximum transfer rate the drive can sustain.

Interleave Selection

In a discussion of disk performance, the issue of interleave was once a common concern. Although traditionally this was more a controller performance issue than a drive issue, modern ATA HDDs with built-in controllers are fully capable of processing the data as fast as the drive can send it. In other words, all modern ATA drives are formatted with no interleave (sometimes expressed as a 1:1 interleave ratio). On older hard drive types, such as MFM and ESDI, you could modify the interleave during a low-level format to optimize the drive's performance. Today, drives are low-level formatted at the factory, and interleave adjustments are a moot topic.

Reliability

When you shop for a drive, you might notice a statistic called the mean time between failures (MTBF) described in the drive specifications. MTBF figures usually range from 300,000 to 1,000,000 hours or more. I usually ignore these figures because they are derived theoretically.

In understanding the MTBF claims, you must understand how the manufacturers arrive at them and what they mean. Most manufacturers have a long history of building drives, and their drives have seen millions of hours of cumulative use. They can look at the failure rate for previous drive models with the same components and calculate a failure rate for a new drive based on the components used to build the drive assembly. For the electronic circuit board, they also can use industry-standard techniques for predicting the failure of the integrated electronics. This enables them to calculate the predicted failure rate for the entire drive unit.

To understand what these numbers mean, you must know that the MTBF claims apply to a population of drives, not an individual drive. This means that if a drive claims to have an MTBF of 500,000 hours, you can expect a failure in that population of drives in 500,000 hours of total running time. If 1,000,000 drives of this model are in service and all 1,000,000 are running simultaneously, you can expect one failure out of this entire population every half-hour. MTBF statistics are not useful for predicting the failure of an individual drive or a small sample of drives.

You also need to understand the meaning of the word *failure*. In this sense, a failure is a fault that requires the drive to be returned to the manufacturer for repair, not an occasional failure to read or write a file correctly.

Finally, as some drive manufacturers point out, this measure of MTBF should really be called mean time to first failure. "Between failures" implies that the drive fails, is returned for repair, and then at some point fails again. The interval between repair and the second failure here would be the MTBF. In most cases, a failed hard drive that would need manufacturer repair is replaced rather than repaired, so the whole MTBF concept is misnamed.

The bottom line is that I do not really place much emphasis on MTBF figures. For an individual drive, they are not accurate predictors of reliability. However, if you are an information systems manager considering the purchase of thousands of PCs or drives per year or a system vendor building and supporting thousands of systems, it might be worth your while to examine these numbers and study the methods used to calculate them by each vendor. Most hard drive manufacturers designate their premium drives as Enterprise class drives, meaning they are designed for use in environments requiring full-time usage and high reliability and carry the highest MTBF ratings. If you can understand the vendor's calculations and compare the actual reliability of a large sample of drives, you can purchase more reliable drives and save time and money in service and support.

S.M.A.R.T.

Self-Monitoring, Analysis, and Reporting Technology (S.M.A.R.T.) is an industry standard providing failure prediction for disk drives. When S.M.A.R.T. is enabled for a given drive, the drive monitors predetermined attributes that are susceptible to or indicative of drive degradation. Based on changes in the monitored attributes, a failure prediction can be made. If a failure is deemed likely to occur, S.M.A.R.T. makes a status report available so the system BIOS or driver software can notify the user of the impending problems, perhaps enabling the user to back up the data on the drive before any real problems occur.

Predictable failures are the types of failures S.M.A.R.T. attempts to detect. These failures result from the gradual degradation of the drive's performance. According to Seagate, 60% of drive failures are mechanical, which is exactly the type of failures S.M.A.R.T. is designed to predict.

Of course, not all failures are predictable, and S.M.A.R.T. can't help with unpredictable failures that occur without advance warning. These can be caused by static electricity, improper handling or sudden shock, or circuit failure (such as thermal-related solder problems or component failure).

S.M.A.R.T. was originally created by IBM in 1992. That year IBM began shipping 3 1/2-inch HDDs equipped with Predictive Failure Analysis (PFA), an IBM-developed technology that periodically measures selected drive attributes and sends a warning message when a predefined threshold is exceeded. IBM turned this technology over to the American National Standards Institute (ANSI) organization, and it subsequently became the ANSI-standard S.M.A.R.T. protocol for SCSI drives, as defined in the ANSI-SCSI Informational Exception Control (IEC) document X3T10/94-190.

Interest in extending this technology to ATA drives led to the creation of the S.M.A.R.T. Working Group in 1995. Besides IBM, other companies represented in the original group were Seagate Technology, Conner Peripherals (now a part of Seagate), Fujitsu, Hewlett-Packard, Maxtor (now a part of Seagate), Quantum (later merged with Maxtor), and Western Digital. The S.M.A.R.T. specification produced by this group and placed in the public domain covers both ATA and SCSI HDDs and can be found in most of the more recently produced drives on the market.

The S.M.A.R.T. design of attributes and thresholds is similar in ATA and SCSI environments, but the reporting of information differs.

In an ATA environment, driver software on the system interprets the alarm signal from the drive generated by the S.M.A.R.T. `report status` command. The driver polls the drive on a regular basis to check the status of this command and, if it signals imminent failure, sends an alarm to the OS where it is passed on via an error message to the end user. This structure also enables future enhancements, which might allow reporting of information other than drive failure conditions. The system can read and evaluate the attributes and alarms reported in addition to the basic `report status` command.

SCSI drives with S.M.A.R.T. communicate a reliability condition only as good or failing. In a SCSI environment, the failure decision occurs at the disk drive and the host notifies the user for action. The SCSI specification provides for a sense bit to be flagged if the drive determines that a reliability issue exists. The system then alerts the end user via a message.

Note that traditional disk diagnostics such as Scandisk work only on the data sectors of the disk surface and do not monitor all the drive functions that are monitored by S.M.A.R.T. Most modern disk drives keep spare sectors available to use as substitutes for sectors that have errors. When one of these spares is reallocated, the drive reports the activity to the S.M.A.R.T. counter but still looks completely defect-free to a surface analysis utility, such as Scandisk.

Drives with S.M.A.R.T. monitor a variety of attributes that vary from one manufacturer to another. Attributes are selected by the device manufacturer based on their capability to contribute to the prediction of degrading or fault conditions for that particular drive. Most drive manufacturers consider the specific set of attributes being used and the identity of those attributes as vendor specific and proprietary.

Some drives monitor the floating height of the head above the magnetic media. If this height changes from a nominal figure, the drive could fail. Other drives can monitor different attributes, such as ECC circuitry that indicates whether soft errors are occurring when reading or writing data. Some of the attributes monitored on various drives include the following:

- Head floating height
- Data throughput performance
- Spin-up time
- Reallocated (spared) sector count
- Seek error rate
- Seek time performance
- Drive spin-up retry count
- Drive calibration retry count

Each attribute has a threshold limit that determines the existence of a degrading or fault condition. These thresholds are set by the drive manufacturer, can vary among manufacturers and models, and can't be changed.

The basic requirements for S.M.A.R.T. to function in a system are simple: You just need a S.M.A.R.T.-capable HDD and a S.M.A.R.T.-aware BIOS or hard disk driver for your particular OS. If your BIOS does not support S.M.A.R.T., utility programs are available that can support it on a given system. Some of these include Norton Utilities from Symantec, DiskCheckup from PassMark Software, and Acronis Drive Monitor.

When sufficient changes occur in the monitored attributes to trigger a S.M.A.R.T. alert, the drive sends an alert message via an IDE/ATA or a SCSI command (depending on the type of HDD you have) to the hard disk driver in the system BIOS, which usually reports the problem during the POST the next time the system boots.

If you want more immediate reporting, you can run a utility that queries the S.M.A.R.T. status of the drive, such as the programs listed earlier. The first thing to do if you receive a S.M.A.R.T. warning is to back up all the data on the drive. I recommend you back up to new media and do not overwrite previous backups you might have, just in case the drive fails before the new backup is complete.

After backing up your data, what should you do? S.M.A.R.T. warnings can be caused by an external source and might not actually indicate that the drive is going to fail. For example, environmental changes such as high or low ambient temperatures can trigger a S.M.A.R.T. alert, as can excessive vibration in the drive caused by an external source. Additionally, electrical interference from motors or other devices on the same circuit as your PC can induce these alerts.

If the alert was not caused by an external source, a drive replacement might be indicated. If the drive is under warranty, contact the vendor and ask whether the company will replace it. The drive vendor may ask you to test the drive with diagnostic software supplied with the drive or downloadable from the vendor's website. If no further alerts occur or if the test does not locate any problems, the problem might have been an anomaly, and you might not need to replace the drive. If you receive further alerts, replacing the drive is recommended. If you can connect both the new and existing (failing) drive to the same system, you might be able to copy the entire contents of the existing drive to the new one, saving you from having to install or reload all the applications and data from your backup. Because standard copy commands and drag-and-drop methods don't copy system files, hidden files, and files that are open, to copy an entire drive successfully and have the destination copy remain bootable, you need a special application such as Symantec Norton Ghost or Acronis True Image.

Note

Special editions of Acronis True Image are available at no charge from Western Digital (Acronis True Image WD Edition for WD drives) and Seagate (DiscWizard for Seagate and Maxtor drives; MaxBlast 5 for Maxtor drives).

Flash and Removable Storage

Alternative Storage Devices

Since the mid-1980s, the primary storage device used by computers has been the hard disk drive. More recently, however, flash-based storage including SSDs (solid-state drives) are increasingly being used as hard drive replacements. Although SSDs can physically replace a hard disk drive (HDD), they operate using a completely different set of principles that may require a treatment unlike that used for conventional HDDs. For data backup, data transport between computers, and temporary storage, secondary removable storage devices such as flash memory devices/drives, optical drives, magnetic tape drives, removable media hard drives, and even floppy drives have been useful supplements to primary storage. Cloud storage, too, now plays a major role in data transfer, storage, and backup. Optical storage, such as CD, DVD, and BD (Blu-ray Disc), is covered in Chapter 11, "Optical Storage."

Flash Memory Devices

Flash memory is a special type of solid-state memory chip that requires no power to maintain its contents. Flash memory cards can easily be moved from digital cameras to laptop or desktop computers and can even be inserted into photo printers or self-contained photo display devices. Flash memory can store any type of computer data, but its original primary application was digital photography. However, more and more digital music players have removable flash memory cards, and so-called *thumb* or *keychain* flash memory devices that plug directly into a USB port have helped make flash memory a mainstream storage medium and a popular replacement for some types of magnetic removable-media storage, particularly floppy disks, Zip drives, and SuperDisk drives. Flash memory in the form of SSDs is rapidly increasing in market share as a high-speed alternative to conventional magnetic hard disk storage.

Flash memory was invented by Fujio Masuoka at Toshiba in the early 1980s, with the original patents filed in late 1981. At the time Toshiba unfortunately didn't know how important this invention was, and by 1988 Intel had introduced competitive versions and quickly took the lead in flash memory development and production.

Flash memory is a type of nonvolatile memory that can be electrically programmed and erased. It was originally used in PC motherboards as EEPROM (electrically erasable programmable read-only memory) chips for storing the motherboard basic input/output system (BIOS). Flash ROMs replaced the EPROM, which could only be programmed or erased by special equipment outside of the motherboard.

Flash memory can be considered sort of a cross between random access memory (RAM) and read-only memory (ROM). Just like RAM, flash memory can be written directly in the system, yet just like ROM it is completely nonvolatile, meaning that it retains data after the power has been turned off (and without a battery like the Complementary Metal Oxide Semiconductor [CMOS] RAM). Besides being nonvolatile, there is one other big difference between flash memory and conventional RAM: The system cannot rewrite Flash memory; it must always erase it first.

When erased, flash memory cells are in a low-voltage state that carries a logical 1 value. The act of writing to (or programming) flash places a charge in the transistor's floating gate, which changes the 1 to a 0. Once a flash cell is programmed (that is, changed to a 0), the only way it can be changed back to a 1 is by erasing it. The problem with this is that, although you can program individual cells or pages, you can only erase cells or pages on a block basis, and a block usually consists of thousands of cells (512KB in most cases). The actual programming and erasing process coaxes electrons into and out of the transistor's floating gate by a process known as Fowler-Nordheim tunneling.

The two major types of flash memory technology are called NOR (Not OR) and NAND (Not AND). Both use the same basic transistor (cell) design, but they differ in how the cells are interconnected. NOR flash works more like dynamic RAM (DRAM), providing high-speed random-access capabilities with the ability to read or write data in single byte quantities. NOR flash is the type of memory used for flash ROMs, such as those found in motherboards, cell phones, and most devices that have updatable firmware.

On the other hand, NAND flash works more like a storage device, reading and writing data in pages or blocks instead of individual bytes. NAND flash is used in devices that store file-oriented data, such as SSDs, USB key or thumb drives, digital cameras and digital film media, music players, and more. NAND flash is denser than NOR flash, storing more data in a given amount of die space and costing less overall for a given amount of storage.

The speed, low power requirements, and compact size of recent flash memory and SSD devices have made flash memory a perfect counterpart for portable devices such as laptop computers and digital cameras, which often refer to flash memory devices as so-called "digital film." Unlike real film, digital film can be erased and reshot. Ultra-compact, USB flash memory drives have all but replaced traditional floppy drives, Zip/SuperDisk drives, and even optical discs for transporting data between systems.

Several types of flash memory devices have been popular, including the following:

- CompactFlash (CF)
- SmartMedia (SM)
- MultiMediaCard (MMC)
- SecureDigital (SD)
- Memory Stick
- ATA Flash
- xD-Picture Card
- Solid-state drive (SSD)
- USB flash devices

Some of these are available in different sizes (Type I/Type II). Table 10.1 shows the various types of solid-state storage used in digital cameras and other devices, listed in order of introduction.

Table 10.1   Different Flash Memory Devices and Physical Sizes

Type	L (mm)	W (mm)	H (mm)	Volume (cc)	Date Introduced
ATA Flash Type II	54.00	85.60	5.00	23.11	Nov. 1992
ATA Flash Type I	54.00	85.60	3.30	15.25	Nov. 1992
CompactFlash (CF) Type I	42.80	36.40	3.30	5.14	Oct. 1995
SmartMedia (SM)	37.00	45.00	0.76	1.27	Apr. 1996
MultiMediaCard (MMC)	24.00	32.00	1.40	1.08	Nov. 1997
CompactFlash (CF) Type II	42.80	36.40	5.00	7.79	Mar. 1998
Memory Stick	21.45	50.00	2.80	3.00	Jul. 1998
Secure Digital (SD)	24.00	32.00	2.10	1.61	Aug. 1999
xD-Picture Card (xD)	20.00	25.00	1.70	0.85	Jul. 2002
Memory Stick Duo	20.00	31.00	1.6	0.99	Jul. 2002
Reduced Size MMC (RS-MMC)	24.00	18.00	1.40	0.60	Nov. 2002
MiniSD	20.00	21.5	1.4	0.59	Mar. 2003
MicroSD	15.00	11.00	1.0	0.165	Jul. 2005
Memory Stick Micro	15.00	12.5	1.2	0.225	Sep. 2005

SSDs and USB flash drives are not listed because they do not have a single standardized form factor. SSDs, normally used as hard disk drive (HDD) replacements, come in different form factors, including the same form factor as 1.8-inch, 2.5-inch, and 3.5-inch HDDs as well as adapter card–based versions that plug into a slot in the motherboard.

CompactFlash

CompactFlash was developed by SanDisk Corporation in 1994 and uses the ATA (AT Attachment) architecture to emulate a disk drive; a CompactFlash device attached to a computer has a disk drive letter just like your other drives. When CompactFlash was first being standardized, even full-sized hard disks were rarely larger than 4GB, so the limitations of the ATA standard were considered acceptable. However, CF cards manufactured after the original Revision 1.0 specification are available in capacities up to 128GiB. While the current revision 6.0 works in [P]ATA mode, future revisions are expected to implement SATA mode.

The original size was Type I (3.3mm thick); a newer Type II size (5mm thick) accommodates higher-capacity devices. Both CompactFlash cards are 1.433-inch wide by 1.685-inch long, and adapters allow them to be inserted into laptop computer PC Card slots. The CompactFlash Association (www.compactflash.org) oversees development of the standard.

SmartMedia

Ironically, SmartMedia (originally known as SSFDC for *solid state floppy disk card*) is the simplest of any flash memory device; SmartMedia cards contain only flash memory on a card without control circuits.

This simplicity means that compatibility with different generations of SmartMedia cards can require manufacturer upgrades of SmartMedia-using devices. Now defunct, the Solid State Floppy Disk Forum originally oversaw development of the SmartMedia standard.

Tip

If you use a SmartMedia-based Olympus digital camera that has the panorama feature, be sure to use Olympus-brand SmartMedia because other brands lack support for the panorama feature.

MultiMediaCard

The MultiMediaCard (MMC) was codeveloped by SanDisk and Infineon Technologies AG (formerly Siemens AG) in November 1997 for use with smart phones, MP3 players, digital cameras, and camcorders. The MMC uses a simple 7-pin serial interface to devices and contains low-voltage flash memory. The MultiMediaCard Association (www.mmca.org) was founded in 1998 to promote the MMC standard and aid development of new products. In November 2002, MMCA announced the development of the Reduced Size MultiMediaCard (RS-MMC), which reduces the size of the standard MMC by about 40% and can be adapted for use with standard MMC devices. The first flash memory cards in this form factor were introduced in early 2004 to support compact smartphones. In 2008, the MMCA merged with JEDEC (www.jedec.org), which is the global leader in developing open standards for the microelectronics industry.

SecureDigital

A SecureDigital (SD) storage device is about the same size as an MMC (many devices can use both types of flash memory), but it's a more sophisticated product. SD, which was codeveloped by Toshiba, Matsushita Electric (Panasonic), and SanDisk in 1999, gets its name from two special features. The first is encrypted storage of data for additional security, meeting current and future Secure Digital Music Initiative (SDMI) standards for portable devices. The second is a mechanical write-protection switch. The SD slot can also be used for adding memory to Palm PDAs. The SDIO standard was created in January 2002 to enable SD slots to be used for small digital cameras and other types of expansion with various brands of PDAs and other devices. The SD Card Association (www.sdcard.org) was established in 2000 to promote the SD standard and aid the development of new products. Note that some laptop computers have built-in SD slots.

Reduced-size versions of SD include MiniSD (introduced in 2003) and MicroSD (introduced in 2005). MiniSD and MicroSD are popular choices for smartphones and can be adapted to a standard SD slot. MicroSD is compatible with the TransFlash standard for mobile phones.

The original SD standard allowed for memory card capacities of up to 2GB. To support higher capacities the SDHC (High Capacity) standard was created in 2006. SDHC supports cards from 4GB to 32GB in capacity. To increase capacity beyond 32GB, the SDXC (eXtended Capacity) format was released in 2009. SDXC supports capacities of up to 2TB. Note that devices are backward compatible, meaning that a device that supports SDXC also supports SDHC and standard SD cards. A device that supports SDHC also accepts standard SD cards, but such a device does not support SDXC cards. Devices that support only standard SD do not support either SDHC or SDXC cards.

Sony Memory Stick

Sony, which is heavily involved in both laptop computers and a variety of digital cameras and camcorder products, has its own proprietary version of flash memory known as the Sony Memory Stick. This device features an erase-protection switch, which prevents accidental erasure of your photographs. Sony has also licensed Memory Stick technology to other companies, such as Lexar Media and SanDisk.

Lexar introduced the enhanced Memory Stick Pro in 2003. Memory Stick Pro includes MagicGate encryption technology, which enables digital rights management, and Lexar's proprietary high-speed memory controller. Memory Stick Pro is sometimes referred to as *MagicGate Memory Stick*.

The Memory Stick Pro Duo is a reduced-size, reduced-weight version of the standard Memory Stick Pro. It can be adapted to devices designed for the Memory Stick Pro.

Sony later released "Mark 2" certified versions of the Memory Stick Pro in 2008. This certification indicated that the cards were suitable for use with AVCHD (Advanced Video Coding High Definition) recording devices. Sony also released a smaller Memory Stick Micro (also called M2) format in 2006, which was designed to compete with microSD. In 2009 Sony announced the Memory Stick XC (eXtended Capacity) format in order to compete with SDXC.

Because the Memory Stick formats are proprietary and only used in Sony devices, I recommend avoiding them wherever possible. In order to avoid using expensive and hard to find proprietary memory, make sure any device you purchase accepts industry standard memory such as SD. Fortunately, Sony's newer devices are including support for industry standard SD memory formats in response to the negative backlash against its proprietary Memory Stick.

ATA Flash PC Card

Although the PC Card (PCMCIA) form factor has been used for everything from game adapters to modems, SCSI (Small Computer Systems Interface) cards, network cards, and more, its original use was computer memory, as the old PCMCIA (Personal Computer Memory Card International Association) acronym indicated.

Unlike normal RAM modules, PC Card memory acts like a disk drive, using the PCMCIA ATA (AT Attachment) standard. PC Cards come in three thicknesses (Type I is 3.3mm, Type II is 5mm, and Type III is 10.5mm), but all are 3.3-inch long by 2.13-inch wide. Type I and Type II cards are used for ATA-compliant flash memory and the newest ATA-compliant hard disks. Type III cards are used for older ATA-compliant hard disks; a Type III slot also can be used as two Type II slots.

xD-Picture Card

In July 2002, Olympus and Fujifilm, the major supporters of the SmartMedia flash memory standard for digital cameras, announced the xD-Picture Card as a much smaller, more durable replacement for SmartMedia. In addition to being about one-third the size of SmartMedia—making it the smallest flash memory format yet—xD-Picture Card media has a faster controller to enable faster image capture.

Both 16MB and 32MB cards (commonly packaged with cameras) record data at speeds of 1.3MBps, whereas 64MB and larger cards record data at 3MBps. The read speed for all sizes is 5MBps. The media is manufactured for Olympus and Fujifilm by Toshiba, and because xD-Picture media is optimized for the differences in the cameras (Olympus's media supports the panorama mode found in some Olympus xD-Picture cameras, for example), you should buy media that's the same brand as your digital camera.

Just as with the proprietary Sony Memory Stick formats, I also recommend avoiding the proprietary xD-Picture card format wherever possible. Instead, I only recommend purchasing devices that use industry standard memory card formats such as SD. Because of the backlash against proprietary formats, Olympus and Fujifilm abandoned xD-Picture card in 2010.

SSD (Solid-State Drive)

In general, a *solid-state drive (SSD)* is any drive using solid-state electronics (that is, no mechanical parts or vacuum tubes). Many people believe that SSDs are a recent advancement in computer technology, but in actuality they have been around in one form or another since the 1950s, well before PCs even existed.

Today, solid-state drives are used for many of the tasks magnetic and optical drives have traditionally performed, including system drives, primary and secondary data storage, and removable-media storage.

Virtual SSD (RAMdisk)

Although most people think of a physical drive when they discuss SSDs, these drives are available in both physical and virtual form. A virtual SSD is traditionally called a RAMdisk because it uses a portion of system RAM to act as a disk drive. The benefits are incredible read/write performance (it is RAM, after all), whereas the drawbacks are the fact that all data is lost when the system powers down or reboots, and that the RAM used for the RAMdisk is unavailable for the operating system (OS) and applications.

RAMdisk software has been available for PCs since right after the PC debuted in late 1981. IBM included the source code to a RAMdisk program (later called VDISK.SYS) in the March 1983 PC DOS 2.0 manual, as part of a tutorial for writing device drivers. (Device driver support was first implemented in DOS 2.0.) IBM later released VDISK.SYS as part of PC DOS 3.0 in August 1984. Microsoft first included a RAMdisk program (called RAMDRIVE.SYS) with MS-DOS 3.2 (released in 1986). Versions of RAMDRIVE.SYS were included in DOS and Windows versions up to Windows 3.1, and a renamed version called RAMDISK.SYS has been included with Windows XP and Windows 7/Vista. However, they are not automatically installed, and they are not well documented. These DOS- or Windows-based RAMdisk programs are useful for creating high-speed SSDs using existing RAM. As an alternative to using RAMDRIVE.SYS, you can use a variety of commercial and freeware utilities available for Windows and for Linux. (See http://en.wikipedia.org/wiki/List_of_RAM_drive_software for links to some of these utilities.)

Flash-Based SSDs

Shortly after the release of the IBM PC in 1981, several companies developed and released physical solid-state drives that could function as direct hard drive replacements. Many of these used conventional dynamic or static RAM, with an optional battery for backup power, whereas others used more exotic forms of nonvolatile memory, thus requiring no power to retain data. For example, Intel had released "bubble" memory in the late 1970s, which was used in several SSD products. Bubble memory was even included in the Grid Compass in 1982, one of the first laptops ever released. Although SSDs can use any type of memory technology, when people think of modern SSDs, they think of those using flash memory. Flash-based SSDs more recently started appearing in commercially available laptop PCs from Dell, Asus, Lenovo, and others in 2007–2008. Since then, many other laptop and desktop PC manufacturers have introduced systems with flash-based SSDs.

Ever since SSDs first became available for PCs in the early 1980s, many have thought that they would universally replace hard drives. Well, it has been nearly 30 years since I first heard that prediction, and it is just now becoming partially true. Until recently, the principle barriers preventing SSDs from overtaking hard disks has been cost per GB and performance. Early SSDs were slower than HDDs, especially when writing data, and performance would often fall dramatically as the drive filled up. The development of controller hardware and operating systems optimized for SSDs have enabled recent SSDs to surpass conventional hard disk drives in performance. Although SSDs are still more expensive per GB than traditional hard disk drives, SSDs are now widely used for applications where cost is not as important as performance and durability: Tablets, smartphones, netbooks, and Ultrabooks use SSDs.

Many systems now strike a balance between the higher performance of SSDs and the greater capacity of conventional hard disk drives by using both technologies. Many Ultrabooks use a small SSD (32GB is a typical size) for the operating system and a conventional or hybrid SATA hard disk for applications and system storage. Many high-performance desktop systems also use an SSD from 128GB to 512GB as a system drive, and a traditional hard disk for additional storage.

Note

A hybrid SATA hard disk includes a small amount of flash memory used to cache most-frequently-used information. To learn more, see Chapter 9.

Virtually all modern SSDs use the SATA (Serial ATA) interface to connect to the PC and appear just like a standard hard disk to the system. Both 2.5-inch and 1.8-inch SSDs are shown in Figure 10.1. Some high-performance SSDs come in a card-based form factor, usually designed for PCI Express slots.

FIGURE 10.1   2.5-inch and 1.8-inch solid-state drives (SSDs).

SLC Versus MLC

As previously mentioned, SSDs use NAND flash technology. Two subtypes of this technology are used in commercially available SSDs: SLC (single-level cell) and MLC (multilevel cell). SLC flash stores 1 bit in a single cell, whereas MLC stores 2 or more bits in a single cell. MLC doubles (or more) the density, and consequently lowers the cost, but this comes at a penalty in performance and usable life. SSDs are available using either technology, with SLC versions offering higher performance, lower capacity, and higher cost. Most mainstream SSDs use MLC technology, whereas more specialized high-end products (mostly for server or workstation systems) use SLC.

One major problem with flash memory is that it wears out. SLC flash cells are normally rated for 100,000 Write/Erase (W/E) cycles, whereas MLC flash cells are normally rated for only 10,000 W/E cycles. When used to replace a standard hard drive, this becomes a problem because certain areas of a hard drive are written to frequently, whereas other areas may be written to only a few times over the life of the drive. To mitigate this wear, SSDs incorporate sophisticated wear-leveling algorithms that essentially vary or rotate the usage of cells so that no single cell or group of cells is used more than another. In addition, spare cells are provided to replace those that do wear out, thus extending the life of the drive. Considering the usage patterns of various types of users, SSD drives are generally designed to last at least 10 years under the most demanding use, and most last much longer than that. As SSD capacity increases, so does the ability of the wear-leveling algorithm to spread out data among available cells.

Note that, because of the way SSDs work internally, the concept of file fragmentation is immaterial, and running a defragmenting program on an SSD does nothing except cause it to wear out sooner. Unlike magnetic drives, which must move the heads to access data written to different physical areas of the disk, an SSD can read data from different areas of memory without delay. The concept of the location of a file becomes moot with wear leveling, in that even files that are presented as contiguous to the file system are actually scattered randomly among the memory chips and cells in the SSD. Because of this, SSDs should *not* be defragmented like traditional magnetic drives.

Note

Windows 7 and 8 are *SSD aware*, which means they can tell an SSD from a standard magnetic drive. These versions of Windows determine this information by querying the drive's rotational speed via the `ATA IDENTIFY DEVICE` command. (SSDs are designed to report 1rpm.) When Windows detects that an SSD is attached, it automatically turns off the background Disk Defragmenter function, thus preserving drive endurance. When using SSDs with Windows Vista and earlier versions, you should manually disable or otherwise prevent any form of defragmentation program or operation from running on SSDs. For maximum performance with any Windows version, install Tweak-SSD, available from www.totalidea.com.

TRIM Command

Another technique to improve SSD endurance and performance is an extension to the ATA interface called the `TRIM` command. This allows an SSD-aware OS (such as Windows 7 or later) to intelligently inform the SSD which data blocks are no longer in use, thus allowing the drive's internal wear leveling and garbage collection routines much more space to work with, which allows the drive to maintain a high level of performance especially after all blocks have been written to at least once. For this to work, both the drive and the OS must support the `TRIM` command. Windows 7 and Server 2008 R2 and later are SSD aware and support the `TRIM` command, whereas earlier versions of Windows do not. SSDs released in 2009 or later generally support the `TRIM` command, whereas those that do not may be able to add support via a firmware upgrade. When you are upgrading the firmware on an SSD, it is highly recommended to have a full backup because in some cases a firmware upgrade reinitializes the drive, wiping all data in an instant.

When an OS deletes a file or otherwise erases data from a drive, it doesn't actually erase data. Instead, the OS simply marks the file allocation or master file tables to indicate that those blocks are available, while leaving the data in them untouched. This works fine on a normal HDD because overwriting is the same as writing, but it greatly hinders a flash drive since a flash drive cannot overwrite data directly. On a flash drive, any overwriting causes the drive to first write any previously existing data to a new block, then erase the block, and finally write the new data. Over time, this results in the SSD filling up and slowing down, even though from the OS point of view there is a lot of empty space.

When `TRIM` is used, whenever a file is deleted, copied, or moved or the drive is reformatted, the drive is immediately informed of all the blocks that are no longer in use. This allows the drive controller to erase the unused blocks in the background, ensuring that there is always a sufficient supply of erased blocks available to keep write performance at near like-new levels.

To further improve SSD performance, Windows 7 and later disable features such as Superfetch and ReadyBoost as well as prefetching on SSDs with random read, write, and flush performance above a certain threshold.

When running a non-TRIM aware OS (Vista, XP, and earlier), you may still be able to take advantage of TRIM by installing a TRIM-aware application. For example, Intel provides a program called the Intel SSD Optimizer (part of the Intel SSD Toolbox) that you can periodically run to report to the drive which files have been deleted. Other SSD manufacturers provide similar tools (often called wiper.exe) as well. If you are running a non-TRIM aware OS with an SSD, check with the SSD manufacturer to see if it has an optimization tool available.

Partition Alignment

Another issue with SSDs is that they are normally designed to read and write 4K pages and to erase data in 512K blocks. Windows XP and earlier OSs normally start partitions 63 sectors into a disk, which means that the OS file system components and clusters overlap pages and blocks, resulting in more pages being read or written, and more blocks being erased than necessary, which can cause a noticeable performance hit.

SSDs perform at their best when partitions are created with the SSD's alignment needs in mind. All the partition-creating tools in Windows 8/7/Vista place newly created partitions with the appropriate alignment, with the first partition starting an even 2048 sectors into the disk. Because this is evenly divisible by both 4K (8 sectors) and 512K (1024 sectors), there is no overlap between OS file system cluster and SSD page/block operations.

Even if you are using Windows 8/7/Vista or another OS that normally creates aligned partitions, you may still have misaligned partitions if the OS was installed into an existing partition or as an upgrade. Many of the drive manufacturers have free partition alignment tools available that can check and even correct the alignment of partitions on the fly. When creating new partitions on an SSD, you can optionally use the DISKPART command to manually set the offset to the start of the first partition such that all partitions on the drive will be properly aligned. With manual intervention, you can ensure that even Windows XP and earlier will create partitions that are properly aligned for maximum performance.

SSD Applications

SSDs are ideal for laptops because they are more rugged (no moving parts), weigh less, and consume less power. The weight savings is fairly minor because the difference between an SSD and a conventional drive of the same (or even greater) capacity is generally only a few grams. The power savings is more real—SSDs only draw about a tenth of a watt compared to about 1 watt for an HDD (average). But even that may be overstated. Although drawing one-tenth the power sounds like a considerable savings, compared to other components such as the CPU, GPU, and display, each of which draw 30 watts or more, the overall power savings in going from a standard HDD to an SSD is relatively low in comparison to the total power consumed.

SSDs are ideal as the boot drive for desktop systems because of their performance. Using an SSD can drop boot or resume from hibernation times dramatically. SSDs are less ideal for storing large amounts of data because capacities are less than what is available for conventional HDDs.

Will your next computer contain an SSD? If you buy a tablet, a netbook, or an Ultrabook, the answer is "very likely." SSDs are big enough to contain the operating system and applications and are rapidly dropping in price per GB compared to magnetic storage. Netbooks, Ultrabooks, and other PCs can use external hard disk drives or cloud-based storage for data storage, and some Ultrabooks include both a small SSD for use by Windows and a larger hybrid hard disk (magnetic storage with a small amount of flash memory) for application and data storage. Tablets can use flash memory slots, cloud-based storage, or both to supplement the capacity of an SSD.

USB Flash Drives

As an alternative to floppy and Zip/SuperDisk-class removable-media drives, USB-based flash memory devices have rapidly become the preferred way to move data between non-networked systems. The first successful drive of this type—Trek's ThumbDrive—was introduced in 2000, and since then hundreds of others have been introduced.

Note

Some USB flash memory drives are even built into watches, pens, bottle openers, and knives (such as the Victorinox SwissMemory Swiss Army Knife).

Unlike other types of flash memory, USB flash drives don't require a separate card reader; they can be plugged into any USB port or hub. Any system running Windows XP or later can immediately recognize, read from, and write to a USB flash drive. As with other types of flash memory, USB flash drives are assigned a drive letter when connected to the computer. Most have capacities ranging from 2GB to 64GB, but can be as large as 256GB with even larger capacities planned for the near future. Typical read/write performance of USB 1.1-compatible drives is about 1MBps. Hi-Speed USB 2.0 flash drives are much faster, providing read speeds ranging from 5MBps to 15MBps and write speeds ranging from 5MBps to 13MBps. SuperSpeed USB (USB 3.0) flash memory drives are now available for USB 3.0 ports common on most modern desktops and laptops. Although some USB 3.0 flash memory drives support read/write performance up to 150MBps, the actual interface is designed to support up to 625MBps (5Gbps). As controllers improve, future USB 3.0 flash memory drives are likely to provide performance closer to the maximum speed of the interface. Because Hi-Speed and SuperSpeed USB USB flash drives vary in performance, be sure to check the specific read/write speeds for the drives you are considering before you purchase one.

USB 3.0 FAQ

Q. Does my computer support USB 3.0? How can I tell?

A. USB 3.0 ports use blue connectors and are typically marked with an SS next to the USB fork icon. In Windows Device Manager, look for an eXtensible Host Controller Interface (XHCI) controller entry in the Universal Serial Bus category.

Q. Will my new 32GB SupersSpeed USB thumbdrive run at SuperSpeed or HighSpeed if I use 2.0 ports?

A. A USB 3.0 drive must be connected to a USB 3.0 port to run at SuperSpeed (5Gbps). If a USB 3.0 drive is connected to a USB 2.0 port, it runs at USB 2.0 speeds (HighSpeed 480Mbps).

Tip

If you have a card reader or scanner plugged into a USB hub or port on your computer, you might need to disconnect it before you can attach a USB flash drive. This is sometimes necessary because of conflicts between the drivers used by some devices. If you suspect this type of problem, use the Windows Safely Remove Hardware icon in the system tray to stop the card reader before you insert the USB flash drive. After the system has recognized the USB flash drive, you should be able to reattach the card reader.

For additional protection of your data, some USB flash drives have a mechanical write-protect switch. Others include or support password-protected data encryption as an option, and most are capable of being a bootable device (if supported in the BIOS). Some drives feature *biometric security*—your fingerprint is the key to using the contents of the drive—whereas others include more traditional security software.

Some companies have produced bare USB flash drives that act as readers for MMC, SD, xD-Picture Card, Compact Flash, and Memory Stick flash memory cards. These USB flash readers are essentially USB flash drives without flash memory storage onboard. You can use them as a card reader or as a USB drive with removable storage.

Comparing Flash Memory Devices

As with any storage issue, you must compare each product's features to your needs. You should check the following issues before purchasing flash memory-based devices:

- Which flash memory products does your camera or other device support? Although adapters allow some interchange of the various types of flash memory devices, for best results, you should stick with the flash memory type your device was designed to use.

- Which capacities does your device support? Flash memory devices are available in ever-increasing capacities, but not every device can handle the higher-capacity devices. Check the device and flash memory card's websites for compatibility information. In some cases, firmware updates can improve a device's compatibility with larger or faster flash memory card standards.

- Are some flash memory devices better than others? Some manufacturers have added improvements to the basic requirements for the flash memory device, such as faster write speeds and embedded security. Note that these features usually are designed for use with particular digital cameras only. Don't spend the additional money on enhanced features if your camera or other device can't use those features.

Only ATA Flash cards can be attached directly to an older laptop computer's PC Card slot. All other devices need their own socket or some type of adapter to transfer data. Figure 10.2 shows how the most common types of flash memory cards compare in size to each other and to a penny.

Table 10.2 provides an overview of the major types of flash memory devices and their currently available maximum capacities.

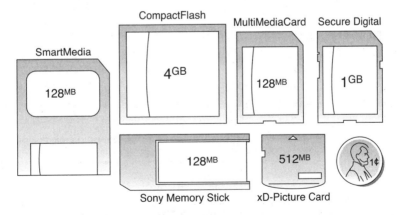

FIGURE 10.2 SmartMedia, CompactFlash, MultiMediaCard, Secure Digital, xD-Picture Card, and Sony Memory Stick flash memory devices. Shown in relative scale to a U.S. penny (lower right).

Table 10.2 Flash Memory Card Capacities

Device	Minimum Capacity	Maximum Capacity	Notes
Compact Flash (CF +)	16MB	128GB	Highest capacity; most flexible format; supported by most digital SLR cameras. Lexar Media and SanDisk also make faster versions of CF+ media; Lexar Media also makes LockTight secured access media.
SmartMedia	16MB	512MB	Popular choice for older Fujifilm and Olympus digital cameras.
MultiMediaCard (MMC)	16MB	4GB	MMC cards can work in most SD slots.
RS-MMC	128MB	2GB	Use adapter to plug in to MMC slots.
Secure Digital (SD)	16MB	2TB	SD cards do not work in MMC slots. Used by most brands of consumer-level digital cameras. SD High Capacity (SDHC) cards have capacities of 4GB up to 32GB Devices that are compatible with SDHC can also use SD cards, but not vice versa. SDXC cards have capacities from 32GB up to a theoretical maximum of 2TB. Devices that are compatible with SDXC cards can also use SDHC and SD cards, but not vice versa.
MiniSD	128MB	4GB	Use adapter to plug in to SD slots.
MicroSD	128MB	16GB	Use adapter to plug in to SD slots.
Memory Stick	16MB	128MB	Developed by Sony and licensed to other vendors. Proprietary—not recommended.
Memory Stick PRO	256MB	4GB	The enhanced high-speed version of Memory Stick Memory Stick with digital rights management support. Proprietary—not recommended.
Memory Stick Pro Duo	256MB	16GB	Reduced-size version of Memory Stick Pro. Proprietary—not recommended.
ATA Flash	16MB	2GB	Plugs directly into a PC Card (PCMCIA) slot without an adapter.
xD-Picture Card	16MB	2GB	Use the same brand as your digital camera for the best results. Proprietary—not recommended.
USB flash drive	16MB	256GB	Some include password-protection and write-protect features.

I normally recommend only devices (cameras, PDAs, and so on) that use Secure Digital (SD, including SD variants like MiniSD or MicroSD), CompactFlash (CF), or USB flash memory. Any of the others I generally do not recommend due to proprietary designs and higher costs as well as limitations in capacity and performance.

Secure Digital has become the most popular format in modern devices. It is reasonably fast and is available in capacities approaching those of CF, and in smaller MiniSD and MicroSD formats, which are physically compatible with the full-sized SD using adapters. SD sockets also take MMC cards, which are basically thinner versions of SD. Note that the opposite is not true—MMC sockets do not accept SD cards.

CF is the most widely used format in professional devices. It offers the highest capacity, in a wide range of speeds in a reasonably small size.

SD Cards Speed Class and UHS Speed Class Markings

SDHC cards, and some SD and most SDXC cards, are marked with a stylized C icon containing a number (see Figure 10.3). This is the speed-class marking. Speed class markings include 2, 4, 6, and 10, with 2, 4, and 10 being the most common. Class 2 cards provide sustained read/write speeds of 2MBps or faster, class 4 cards provide sustained read/write speeds of 4MBps or faster, and so on.

The higher the speed class number, the faster the card can transfer data.

Class 10   Class 4

FIGURE 10.3 Speed Class markings on typical SDHC cards.

Table 10.3 lists the speed-class recommendations for different types of still photo and video recording tasks.

Table 10.3 Recommended Speed Classes for Photo and Video Uses

Speed Class	Single-Shot Still Photography	Continuous Shooting Still Photography (JPEG)	Continuous Shooting Still Photography (RAW)	SD Video	HD Video	Full-HD Video
2	Yes	No	No	Yes	No	No
4	Yes	Yes	No	Yes	Yes	Yes
6	Yes	Yes	Yes	Yes	Yes	Yes
10*	Yes	Yes	Yes	Yes	Yes	Yes

SD Video: Up to 480p (DVD quality)

HD Video: 720p

Full HD Video: 1080p

*Requires high-speed bus interface in supported devices; also supports HD still consecutive recording.

As you can see from Table 10.3, speed-class ratings are a useful guide to selecting suitable cards for use with video recording. However, continuous shooting in still photography is more heavily influenced by maximum card and bus speed. Thus, many vendors of SDHC cards also provide their own maximum speed ratings.

Note

For more information about vendor speed ratings, such as 133X, and how they correspond to speed-class ratings, see this Lexar white paper (PDF format) on "Understanding SD Association Speed Ratings" (available from http://www.lexar.com/ files/product/datasheet/White_Paper_SD_Class_xRating_updatedUHS_Final_1.pdf).

SDHC and SDXC cards might also be labeled with a different marking, the Ultra High Speed (UHS) Class marking. This mark resembles a stylized U with a number inside. U1 indicates a card has a maximum speed of 104MBps. All cards with a UHS class 1 marking are also Class 10 compliant.

File Systems Used by Flash Memory

USB flash memory drives typically use the FAT32 file system, which supports up to 2TB of capacity.

Flash memory cards up to 2GB in size use the FAT16 file system, while SDHC and Compact Flash memory cards with capacities above 2GB use FAT32. SDXC cards have capacities larger than 32GB and use the Microsoft-developed exFAT file system.

To learn more about FAT16 and FAT32, see Chapter 9.

SDXC cards typically use the exFAT (FAT64) file system. exFAT uses a 64-bit address table to support capacities of up to 512TB (recommended) and 64ZB (maximum size). FAT64 is designed specifically for use with flash memory, is optimized for movie recording, and supports universal time coordinate (UTC) time stamps.

Windows Vista SP1, Windows 7 SP1, and newer include built-in support for SDXC. To add support for SDXC to older versions of Windows, see http://support.microsoft.com/kb/955704 and see the service pack requirements.

Note, however, that Windows Vista and 7 may have problems determining the correct size of an SDXC card with a capacity over 32GB. To correct this, downloadable updates for Windows 7 are available at http://support.microsoft.com/kb/976422. The corresponding update for Windows Vista is available at http://support.microsoft.com/kb/975823.

Flash Card Readers

You can purchase several types of devices to enable the data on flash memory cards to be read in a PC. Although it is possible to connect most digital cameras to a PC via USB, in many cases, you must use custom cables.

Card Readers

The major companies that produce flash card products sell card readers that can be used to transfer data from flash memory cards to PCs. These card readers typically plug in to the computer's USB ports for fast access to the data on the card.

In addition to providing fast data transfer, card readers save camera battery power because the camera is not needed to transfer information. Because computer and electronics device users might have devices that use two or more types of flash memory, many vendors now offer multiformat flash memory card readers, such as the SanDisk 12-in-1 Card Reader/Writer shown in Figure 10.4.

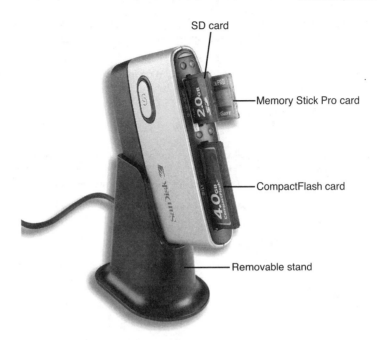

SD card

Memory Stick Pro card

CompactFlash card

Removable stand

FIGURE 10.4 The SanDisk 12-in-1 Card Reader/Writer plugs into a Hi-Speed USB (USB 2.0) port and features a removable stand. (Photo courtesy of SanDisk.)

Card readers are also available as internal bay-mounted devices that plug in to the internal front panel USB port connectors found on most modern motherboards. Other than the mounting location, internal bay mounted card readers are functionally identical to external readers. One problem with internally mounted readers is that you usually have to open the PC to disconnect them. Disconnection is normally required when installing an OS to prevent issues with improper drive letter assignments.

Before you purchase an external card reader, check your PC and your photo printer, either of which may already have a built-in reader. The built-in readers in photo printers are especially convenient because you can often print photos directly from the flash card without having to transfer the files to your PC. Many laptops include a single-slot card reader that supports SD, Memory Stick, and xD-Picture Card media. If you use CompactFlash, you still need to use an external card reader.

Note

USB 3.0 card readers are now available and provide transfer rates that are much faster than USB 2.0 card readers. If you use systems with USB 3.0 ports, consider upgrading to a USB 3.0 card reader for faster file copying performance.

ReadyBoost Support

Microsoft Windows Vista and newer all include support for using high-speed flash memory cards and USB drives as a disk cache known as ReadyBoost.

When you configure flash memory as ReadyBoost, it is used to hold information about application files and libraries that has been loaded into memory by SuperFetch. SuperFetch helps improve system performance by providing information from RAM rather than directly from disk.

Using ReadyBoost to hold SuperFetch information can help improve your computer's performance if it has a slow hard disk (4.0 or lower score on the Windows Experience Index [WEI]) or if you have limited system RAM (4GB or less).

A flash memory device must have at least 256MB of free space to be usable with ReadyBoost. Maximum size of the ReadyBoost cache varies by the file system used by the device:

- 4GB on a device using FAT32
- 32GB on a device using NTFS

Windows automatically tests an eligible flash memory device for ReadyBoost-compatibility when you plug it in. When a device is tested by Windows to determine if it is ReadyBoost-compatible, the random read/write speed of the media must meet the following minimums:

- 2.5MBps throughput for random 4KB reads
- 1.75MBps throughput for random 1MB writes

ReadyBoost is used only for non-sequential disk reads. To help determine the performance improvement that ReadyBoost provides on a specific system, use the Performance Monitor tool in the Computer Management console and enable the ReadyBoost Cache counters (cache read bytes/sec, cache reads/sec, skipped read bytes/sec, and skipped reads/sec). Note that Windows 7 supports multiple ReadyBoost cache devices.

Note

Conventional USB 2.0-based card readers are usually not fast enough for use with ReadyBoost, but laptop internal card readers or USB card readers designed for use by high-performance Compact Flash (CF) media are typically fast enough.

To learn more about ReadyBoost, see http://technet.microsoft.com/en-us/magazine/ff356869.aspx. To learn more about setting up Performance Monitor to display ReadyBoost Cache counters, see http://www.techrepublic.com/blog/window-on-windows/keep-tabs-on-readyboost-with-windows-7s-performance-monitor/2257.

Note

For the purposes of data storage, USB flash memory drives that are too slow to support ReadyBoost are still compatible with Windows. To enable ReadyBoost on a USB flash drive or flash memory card, open the card's properties sheet and click the ReadyBoost tab. Windows will test the device's performance and advise you whether the drive or card is fast enough to support ReadyBoost. Click Use this device (Windows will select the recommended size of the ReadyBoost cache on the drive). Click Apply, and then OK to begin using the drive or card for ReadyBoost.

To disable ReadyBoost, select Do not use this device.

Cloud-Based Storage

Cloud-based storage (remote storage that is accessed by the Internet) has become a popular alternative to flash-based or optical storage for data storage, exchange, and backup.

Although some earlier cloud-based storage services used proprietary interfaces, the trend is increasingly in the direction of making cloud-based storage, sync, or backup look and act like another drive folder.

Although cloud-based storage services mimic a local folder, they use powerful encryption technologies to protect data from unauthorized users. The performance of cloud-based storage depends primarily upon the speed of your Internet connection and the priority level of the service running on your computer. Typically, automatic cloud-based backup services run at a low priority to avoid slowing down users' normal experience of using their devices. However, the trade-off is that restoration of lost data can take several days or longer.

Before choosing a cloud-based storage, sync, or backup service, look at capacity, prices, and performance. Typically, lower-cost or free services have limits on capacity and run more slowly than paid versions. If you are looking at cloud-based storage for a group of workers or family members, be sure to compare the costs and features of a shared plan over multiple individual plans.

Floppy Disk Drives

Alan Shugart is generally credited with inventing the floppy disk drive in 1967 while working for IBM. One of Shugart's senior engineers, David Noble, actually proposed the flexible medium (then 8 inches in diameter) and the protective jacket with the fabric lining. Shugart left IBM in 1969, and in 1976 his company, Shugart Associates, introduced the minifloppy (5 1/4-inch) disk drive. It, of course, became the standard eventually used by personal computers, rapidly replacing the 8-inch drives. Shugart also helped create the Shugart Associates System Interface (SASI), which was later renamed *small computer system interface (SCSI)* when approved as an American National Standards Institute (ANSI) standard.

Sony introduced the first 3 1/2-inch microfloppy drives and disks in 1981. The first significant company to adopt the 3 1/2-inch floppy for general use was Hewlett-Packard in 1984 with its partially PC-compatible HP-150 system. The adoption of the 3 1/2-inch drive in the PC was solidified when IBM started using the drive in 1986 in some systems and finally switched its entire PC product line to 3 1/2-inch drives in 1987.

In 2002, many companies started selling systems without floppy drives. This started with laptop computers, where internal floppy drives were first eliminated and replaced with external (normally USB) drives. By 2003, virtually all systems sold, be it desktop or laptop, no longer included a floppy drive, although sometimes you can purchase an external USB model as an option. An optional USB floppy drive can be used as a bootable drive if the BIOS permits it, as is the case with most recent systems.

Note

To learn more about floppy drives, see the section "Floppy Disk Drives" in Chapter 10, "Flash and Removable Storage" of the previous edition of *Upgrading and Repairing PCs*, 20th Edition, included on the DVD packaged with this book.

Tape Drives

Tape drives and media were once a somewhat popular form of magnetic storage for backup use. Although the drives were expensive, the tape media was cheap, allowing multiple backup sets to be inexpensively created. As hard drive capacities increased, however, the capacity of tape media could not keep pace, and using multiple tapes to back up a single drive meant time-consuming and error-prone media swaps. The performance of tape drives also suffered in relation to hard disks, greatly increasing the time it took for a backup to complete. Hard drives also become much less expensive, such that it was cheaper and easier to simply purchase more hard drives for backups. Over time, all these factors have caused tape backup drives and media to no longer be suitable for standard desktop or laptop PC backups. Currently, tape drives and media are only used for high-end server backups.

The most common types of tape backups in use today include LTO Ultrium 5 (with a native/compressed capacity of 1.5/3.0TB), LTO Ultrium 4 (800GB/1.6TB), LTO Ultrium 3 (400/800GB), and SDLT (160/320GB).

Optical Storage

Optical Technology

There are basically three types of disk storage for computers: magnetic, *flash memory*, and optical. In *magnetic* storage, data is recorded magnetically on rotating disks. *Flash memory*, such as SSDs and flash memory cards, store information in special memory cells that can be written, erased, and rewritten but retain information when power is turned off. *Optical* disc storage is similar to magnetic disk storage in basic operation, but it reads and writes using light (optically) instead of magnetism. Although most magnetic disk storage is fully read and write capable many times over, many optical storage media are either read-only or write-once. Note the convention in which we refer to magnetic or SSD drives as *disk* and optical as *disc*. This is not a law or rule but is followed by most in the industry.

At one time, it was thought that optical storage would replace magnetic as the primary online storage medium. However, optical storage has proven to be much slower and far less dense than magnetic storage and is much more adaptable to removable-media designs. As such, optical storage is more often used for backup or archival storage purposes and as a mechanism by which programs or data can be loaded onto magnetic drives. Magnetic storage, being significantly faster and capable of holding much more information than optical media in the same amount of space, is more suited for direct online storage and most likely won't be replaced in that role by optical storage anytime soon. At this point, as digital downloads of applications become more popular, the most likely successor to magnetic storage isn't an optical solution at all, but SSD, which offers speeds faster than hard disk drives and is steadily increasing in capacity.

Optical technology standards for computers can be divided into three major types:

- CD (compact disc)
- DVD (digital versatile disc)
- BD (Blu-ray disc)

All these are descended from popular music and video entertainment standards; CD-based devices can also play music CDs, and DVD and BD-based devices can play the same video discs you can purchase or rent. However, computer drives that can use these types of media also offer many additional features.

In the following sections, you learn how optical drives and media are similar, how they differ from each other, and how they can be used to enhance your storage and playback options.

CD-Based Optical Technology

The first type of optical storage that became a widespread computing standard is the CD-ROM. CD-ROM (*compact disc read-only memory*) is an optical read-only storage medium based on the original CD-DA (digital audio) format first developed for audio CDs. Other formats, such as CD-R (CD-recordable) and CD-RW (CD-rewritable), expanded the compact disc's capabilities by making it writable.

Older CD-ROM discs held 74 minutes of high-fidelity audio in CD audio format or 650MiB (682MB) of data. However, the current CD-ROM standard is an 80-minute disc with a data capacity of 700MiB (737MB). When MP3, WMA, or similar compressed audio files are stored on CD, several hours of audio can be stored on a single disc (depending on the compression format and bit rate used). Music only, data only, or a combination of music and data (Enhanced CD) can be stored on one side (only the bottom is used) of a 120mm (4.72-inch) diameter, 1.2mm (0.047-inch) thick plastic disc.

CD-ROM has the same form factor (physical shape and layout) of the familiar CD-DA audio compact disc and can, in fact, be inserted into a normal audio player. Sometimes it isn't playable, though, because the player reads the subcode information for the track, which indicates that it is data and not audio. If it could be played, the result would be noise—unless audio tracks precede the data on the CD-ROM. (See the section, "Blue Book—CD EXTRA.")

Accessing data from a CD using a computer is much faster than from a floppy disk but slower than a modern hard drive.

CDs: A Brief History

In 1979, the Philips and Sony corporations joined forces to coproduce the CD-DA (Compact Disc-Digital Audio) standard. Philips had already developed commercial laserdisc players, and Sony had a decade of digital recording research under its belt. The two companies were poised for a battle—the introduction of potentially incompatible audio laser disc formats—when instead they came to terms on an agreement to formulate a single industry-standard digital audio technology.

Philips contributed most of the physical design, which was similar to the laserdisc format it had previously created with regards to using pits and lands on the disk that are read by a laser. Sony contributed the digital-to-analog circuitry, and especially the digital encoding and error-correction code designs.

In 1980, the companies announced the CD-DA standard, which has since been referred to as the *Red Book format* (so named because the cover of the published document was red). The Red Book included the specifications for recording, sampling, and—above all—the 120mm (4.72-inch) diameter physical format you live with today. This size was chosen, legend has it, because it could contain all of Beethoven's approximately 70-minute *Ninth Symphony* without interruption, compared to 23 minutes per side of the then-mainstream 33-rpm LP record.

After the specification was set, both manufacturers were in a race to introduce the first commercially available CD audio drive. Because of its greater experience with digital electronics, Sony won that race and beat Philips to market by one month, when on October 1, 1982, Sony introduced the CDP-101 player and the world's first commercial CD recording—Billy Joel's *52nd Street* album. The player was introduced in Japan and then Europe; it wasn't available in the United States until early 1983. In 1984, Sony also introduced the first automobile and portable CD players.

Sony and Philips continued to collaborate on CD standards throughout the decade, and in 1983 they jointly released the Yellow Book CD-ROM standard. It turned the CD from a digital audio storage medium to one that could now store read-only data for use with a computer. The Yellow Book used the same physical format as audio CDs but modified the decoding electronics to allow data to be stored reliably. In fact, all subsequent CD standards (usually referred to by their colored book binders) have referred to the original Red Book standard for the physical parameters of the disc. With the advent of the Yellow Book standard (CD-ROM), what originally was designed to hold a symphony could now be used to hold practically any type of information or software.

For more information on the other CD book formats, see the section, "CD Formats."

CD Construction and Technology

A CD is made of a polycarbonate wafer, 120mm in diameter and 1.2mm thick, with a 15mm hole in the center. This wafer base is stamped or molded with a single physical track in a spiral configuration starting from the inside of the disc and spiraling outward. The track has a pitch, or spiral separation, of 1.6 microns (millionths of a meter, or thousandths of a millimeter). By comparison, an LP record has a physical track pitch of about 125 microns. When viewed from the reading side (the bottom), the disc rotates counterclockwise. If you examined the spiral track under a microscope, you would see that along the track are raised bumps, called *pits*, and flat areas between the pits, called *lands*. It seems strange to call a raised bump a *pit*, but that is because when the discs are pressed, the stamper works from the top side. So, from that perspective, the pits are actually depressions made in the plastic.

The laser used to read the disc would pass right through the clear plastic, so the stamped surface is coated with a reflective layer of metal (usually aluminum) to make it reflective. Then the aluminum is coated with a thin protective layer of acrylic lacquer, and finally a label or printing is added.

Caution

Handle optical media with the same care as a photographic negative. The disc is an optical device and degrades as its optical surface becomes dirty or scratched. Also, it is important to note that, although discs are read from the bottom, the layer containing the track is actually much closer to the top of the disc because the protective lacquer overcoat is only 6–7 microns thick. Writing on the top surface of a disc with a ballpoint pen, for example, easily damages the recording underneath. You need to be careful even when using a marker to write on the disc. The inks and solvents used in some markers can damage the print and lacquer overcoat on the top of the disc, and subsequently the information layer right below. Use only markers designed for or tested as being compatible with optical media. The important thing is to treat both sides of the disc carefully, especially the top (label) side.

Mass-Producing CDs

Commercial mass-produced optical discs are stamped or pressed and not burned by a laser as many people believe (see Figure 11.1). Although a laser is used to etch data onto a glass master disc that has been coated with a photosensitive material, using a laser to directly burn discs would be impractical for the reproduction of hundreds or thousands of copies.

The steps in manufacturing CDs are as follows (use Figure 11.1 as a visual):

1. **Photoresist coating**—A circular 240mm diameter piece of polished glass 6mm thick is spin-coated with a photoresist layer about 150 microns thick and then hardened by baking at 80°C (176°F) for 30 minutes.

2. **Laser recording**—A Laser Beam Recorder (LBR) fires pulses of blue/violet laser light to expose and soften portions of the photoresist layer on the glass master.

3. **Master development**—A sodium hydroxide solution is spun over the exposed glass master, which then dissolves the areas exposed to the laser, thus etching pits in the photoresist.

4. **Electroforming**—The developed master is then coated with a layer of nickel alloy through a process called electroforming. This creates a metal master called a *father*.

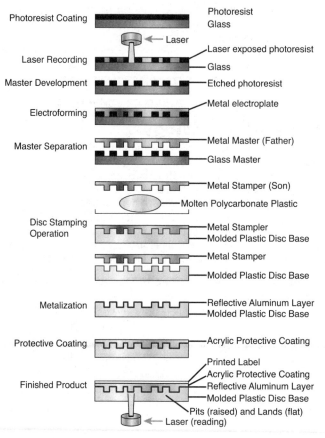

FIGURE 11.1   CD manufacturing process.

5. **Master separation**—The metal master father is then separated from the glass master. The father is a metal master that can be used to stamp discs, and for short runs, it may in fact be used that way. However, because the glass master is damaged when the father is separated, and because a stamper can produce only a limited number of discs before it wears out, the father often is electroformed to create several reverse image mothers. These mothers are then subsequently electroformed to create the actual stampers. This enables many more discs to be stamped without ever having to go through the glass mastering process again.

6. **Disc-stamping operation**—A metal stamper is used in an injection molding machine to press the data image (pits and lands) into approximately 18 grams of molten (350°C or 662°F) polycarbonate plastic with a force of about 20,000psi. Normally, one disc can be pressed every 2–3 seconds in a modern stamping machine.

7. **Metalization**—The clear stamped disc base is then sputter-coated with a thin (0.05–0.1 micron) layer of aluminum to make the surface reflective.

8. **Protective coating**—The metalized disc is then spin-coated with a thin (6–7 micron) layer of acrylic lacquer, which is then cured with UV (ultraviolet) light. This protects the aluminum from oxidation.

9. **Finished product**—Finally, a label is affixed or printing is screen-printed on the disc and cured with UV light.

Although the manufacturing process shown here was for CDs, the process is almost identical for other types of optical media.

Pits and Lands

Reading the information back from a disc is a matter of bouncing a low-powered laser beam off the reflective layer in the disc. The laser shines a focused beam on the underside of the disc, and a photo-sensitive receptor detects when the light is reflected back. When the light hits a land (flat spot) on the track, the light is reflected back; however, when the light hits a pit (raised bump), no light is reflected back.

As the disc rotates over the laser and receptor, the laser shines continuously while the receptor sees what is essentially a pattern of flashing light as the laser passes over pits and lands. Each time the laser passes over the edge of a pit, the light seen by the receptor changes in state from being reflected to not reflected, or vice versa. Each change in state of reflection caused by crossing the edge of a pit is translated into a 1 bit digitally. Microprocessors in the drive translate the light/dark and dark/light (pit edge) transitions into 1 bits, translate areas with no transitions into 0 bits, and then translate the bit patterns into actual data or sound.

The individual pits on a CD are 0.125 microns deep and 0.6 microns wide. Both the pits and lands vary in length from about 0.9 microns at their shortest to about 3.3 microns at their longest. The track is a spiral with 1.6 microns between adjacent turns (see Figure 11.2).

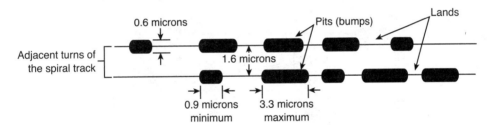

FIGURE 11.2 Pit, land, and track geometry on a CD.

The height of the pits above the land is especially critical because it relates to the wavelength of the laser light used when reading the disc. The pit (bump) height is exactly 1/4 of the wavelength of the laser light used to read the disc. Therefore, the light striking a land travels 1/2 of a wavelength of light farther than light striking the top of a pit (1/4 + 1/4 = 1/2). This means the light reflected from a pit is 1/2 wavelength out of phase with the rest of the light being reflected from the disc. The out-of-phase waves cancel each other out, dramatically reducing the light that is reflected back and making the pit appear dark even though it is coated with the same reflective aluminum as the lands.

The read laser in a CD drive is a 780nm (nanometer) wavelength laser of about 1 milliwatt in power. The polycarbonate plastic used in the disc has a refractive index of 1.55, so light travels through the plastic 1.55 times more slowly than through the air around it. Because the frequency of the light passing through the plastic remains the same, this has the effect of shortening the wavelength inside the plastic by the same factor. Therefore, the 780nm light waves are now compressed to 500nm (780/1.55). One-quarter of 500nm is 125nm, which is 0.125 microns—the specified height of the pit.

Note

DVD drives use two different lasers: a 780nm laser for CD media and a 650nm laser for DVD media. Consequently, a DVD drive could suffer a failure of one laser, causing it to no longer read (or write) one type of media while continuing to read (or write) the other type of media.

Drive Mechanical Operation

An optical drive operates by using a laser to reflect light off the bottom of the disc. A photo detector then reads the reflected light. The overall operation of an optical drive is as follows (see Figure 11.3):

1. The laser diode emits a low-energy infrared beam toward a reflecting mirror.

2. The servo motor, on command from the microprocessor, positions the beam onto the correct track on the disc by moving the reflecting mirror.

3. When the beam hits the disc, its refracted light is gathered and focused through the first lens beneath the platter, bounced off the mirror, and sent toward the beam splitter.

4. The beam splitter directs the returning laser light toward another focusing lens.

5. The last lens directs the light beam to a photo detector that converts the light into electric impulses.

6. These incoming impulses are decoded by the microprocessor and sent along to the host computer as data.

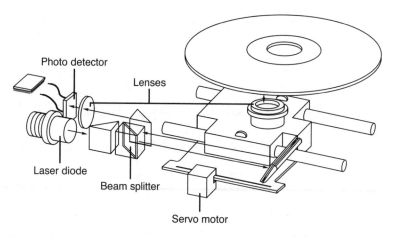

FIGURE 11.3   Typical components inside an optical drive.

When introduced, CD-ROM drives were too expensive for widespread adoption. After the production costs of both drives and discs began to drop, however, CDs were rapidly assimilated into the PC world. This was particularly due to the ever-expanding size of PC applications. Virtually all software is now supplied on optical media, even if the disc doesn't contain data representing a tenth of its potential capacity.

Tracks and Sectors

On the traditional 74-minute CD, the pits are stamped into a single spiral track with a spacing of 1.6 microns between turns, corresponding to a track density of 625 turns per millimeter, or 15,875 turns per inch. This equates to a total of 22,188 turns for a typical 74-minute (650MiB) disc. Current 80-minute CDs gain their extra capacity by decreasing the spacing between turns. See Table 11.1 for more information about the differences between 74-minute and 80-minute CDs.

The disc is divided into six main areas (discussed here and shown in Figure 11.4):

- **Hub clamping area**—The hub clamp area is just that: a part of the disc where the hub mechanism in the drive can grip the disc. No data or information is stored in that area.

- **Power calibration area (PCA)**—This is found only on writable discs and is used only by recordable drives to determine the laser power necessary to perform an optimum burn. A single CD-R or CD-RW disc can be tested this way up to 99 times.

- **Program memory area (PMA)**—This is found only on writable discs and is the area where the TOC (table of contents) is temporarily written until a recording session is closed. After the session is closed, the TOC information is written to the lead-in area.

- **Lead-in**—The lead-in area contains the disc (or session) TOC in the Q subcode channel. The TOC contains the start addresses and lengths of all tracks (songs or data), the total length of the program (data) area, and information about the individual recorded sessions. A single lead-in area exists on a disc recorded all at once (Disc At Once or DAO mode), or a lead-in area starts each session on a multisession disc. The lead-in takes up 4,500 sectors on the disc (1 minute if measured in time, or about 9.2MB worth of data). The lead-in also indicates whether the disc is multisession and what the next writable address on the disc is (if the disc isn't closed).

- **Program (data) area**—This area of the disc starts at a radius of 25mm from the center.

- **Lead-out**—The lead-out marks the end of the program (data) area or the end of the recording session on a multisession disc. No actual data is written in the lead-out; it is simply a marker. The first lead-out on a disc (or the only one if it is a single session or Disk At Once recording) is 6,750 sectors long (1.5 minutes if measured in time, or about 13.8MB worth of data). If the disc is a multisession disc, any subsequent lead-outs are 2,250 sectors long (0.5 minutes in time, or about 4.6MB worth of data).

The hub clamp, lead-in, program, and lead-out areas are found on all CDs, whereas only recordable CDs (such as CD-Rs and CD-RWs) have the additional power calibration area and program memory area at the start of the disc.

Figure 11.4 shows these areas in actual relative scale as they appear on a disc.

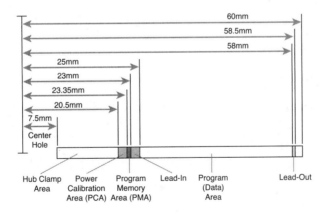

FIGURE 11.4   Areas on a CD (side view).

Officially, the spiral track of a standard CD starts with the lead-in area and ends at the finish of the lead-out area, which is 58.5mm from the center of the disc, or 1.5mm from the outer edge. This single spiral track is about 5.77 kilometers, or 3.59 miles, long. An interesting fact is that in a 56x CAV (constant angular velocity) drive, when the outer part of the track is being read, the data moves at an actual speed of 162.8 miles per hour (262km/h) past the laser. What is more amazing is that even when the data is traveling at that speed, the laser pickup can accurately read bits (pit/land transitions) spaced as little as only 0.9 microns (or 35.4 millionths of an inch) apart!

Table 11.1 shows some of the basic information about the two main CD capacities, which are 74 and 80 minutes. The CD standard originally was created around the 74-minute disc; the 80-minute versions were added later and basically stretch the standard by tightening the track spacing within the limitations of the original specification. A poorly performing or worn-out drive can have trouble reading the 80-minute discs.

Table 11.1 CD Technical Parameters

Advertised CD Capacity (MiB)	650	700
1x read speed (m/sec)	1.3	1.3
Laser wavelength (nm)	780	780
Numerical aperture (lens)	0.45	0.45
Media refractive index	1.55	1.55
Track (turn) spacing (um)	1.6	1.48
Turns per mm	625	676
Turns per inch	15,875	17,162
Total track length (m)	5,772	6,240
Total track length (feet)	18,937	20,472
Total track length (miles)	3.59	3.88
Pit width (um)	0.6	0.6
Pit depth (um)	0.125	0.125
Min. nominal pit length (um)	0.90	0.90
Max. nominal pit length (um)	3.31	3.31
Lead-in inner radius (mm)	23	23
Data zone inner radius (mm)	25	25
Data zone outer radius (mm)	58	58
Lead-out outer radius (mm)	58.5	58.5
Data zone width (mm)	33	33
Total track area width (mm)	35.5	35.5
Max. rotating speed 1x CLV (rpm)	540	540
Min. rotating speed 1x CLV (rpm)	212	212
Track revolutions (data zone)	20,625	22,297
Track revolutions (total)	22,188	23,986

B = Byte (8 bits)
KB = Kilobyte (1,000 bytes)
KiB = Kibibyte (1,024 bytes)
MB = Megabyte (1,000,000 bytes)
MiB = Mebibyte (1,048,576 bytes)

m = Meters
mm = Millimeters (thousandths of a meter)
um = Micrometers = Microns (millionths of a meter)
CLV = Constant linear velocity
rpm = Revolutions per minute

The spiral track is divided into sectors that are stored at the rate of 75 sectors per second. On a disc that can hold a total of 74 minutes of information, that results in a maximum of 333,000 sectors. Each sector is then divided into 98 individual frames of information. Each frame contains 33 bytes: 24 bytes are audio data, 1 byte contains subcode information, and 8 bytes are used for parity/ECC (error correction code) information. Table 11.2 shows the sector, frame, and audio data calculations.

Table 11.2   CD Sector, Frame, and Audio Data Information

Advertised CD Length (Minutes)	74	80
Sectors/second	75	75
Frames/sector	98	98
Number of sectors	333,000	360,000
Sector length (mm)	17.33	17.33
Byte length (um)	5.36	5.36
Bit length (um)	0.67	0.67
Each frame:		
Subcode bytes	1	1
Data bytes	24	24
Q+P parity bytes	8	8
Total bytes/frame	33	33
Audio Data:		
Audio sampling rate (Hz)	44,100	44,100
Samples per Hz (stereo)	2	2
Sample size (bytes)	2	2
Audio bytes per second	176,400	176,400
Sectors per second	75	75
Audio bytes per sector	2,352	2,352
Each Audio Sector (98 Frames):		
Q+P parity bytes	784	784
Subcode bytes	98	98
Audio data bytes	2,352	2,352
Bytes/sector RAW (unencoded)	3,234	3,234

Hz = Hertz (cycles per second)
mm = Millimeters (thousandths of a meter)
um = Micrometers = Microns (millionths of a meter)

Sampling

When music is recorded on a CD, it is sampled at a rate of 44,100 times per second (Hz). Each music sample has a separate left and right channel (stereo) component, and each channel component is digitally converted into a 16-bit number. This allows for a resolution of 65,536 possible values, which represents the amplitude of the sound wave for that channel at that moment.

The sampling rate determines the range of audio frequencies that can be represented in the digital recording. The more samples of a wave that are taken per second, the closer the sampled result will be to the original. The Nyquist theorem (originally published by American physicist Harry Nyquist in 1928) states that the sampling rate must be at least twice the highest frequency present in the sample to reconstruct the original signal accurately. That explains why Philips and Sony intentionally chose the 44,100Hz sampling rate when developing the CD—that rate could be used to accurately reproduce sounds of up to 20,000Hz, which is the upper limit of human hearing.

Subcodes

Subcode bytes enable the drive to find songs (which are confusingly also called *tracks*) along the spiral track and contain or convey additional information about the disc in general. The subcode bytes are stored as 1 byte per frame, which results in 98 subcode bytes for each sector. Two of these bytes are used as start block and end block markers, leaving 96 bytes of subcode information. These are then divided into eight 12-byte subcode blocks, each of which is assigned a letter designation P-W. Each subcode channel can hold about 31.97MB of data across the disc, which is about 4% of the capacity of an audio disc. The interesting thing about the subcodes is that the data is woven continuously throughout the disc; in other words, subcode data is contained piecemeal in every sector on the disc.

The P and Q subcode blocks are used on all discs, and the R-W subcodes are used only on CD+G (graphics) or CD TEXT-type discs.

The P subcode identifies the start of the tracks on the CD. The Q subcode contains a multitude of information, including the following:

- Whether the sector data is audio or data. This prevents most players from trying to "play" CD data discs, which might damage speakers due to the resulting noise that would occur.
- Whether the audio data is two or four channel. Four channel is rarely if ever used.
- Whether digital copying is permitted. PC-based CD-R and RW drives ignore this; it was instituted to prevent copying to DAT (digital audio tape) or home audio optical drives.
- Whether the music is recorded with pre-emphasis. This is a hiss or noise reduction technique.
- The track (song) layout on the disc.
- The track (song) number.
- The minutes, seconds, and frame number from the start of the track (song).
- A countdown during an intertrack (intersong) pause.
- The minutes, seconds, and frames from the start of the first track (song).
- The barcode of the CD.
- The ISRC (International Standard Recording Code). This is unique to each track (song) on the disc.

The R-W subcodes are used on CD+G (graphics) discs to contain graphics and text. This enables a limited amount of graphics and text to be displayed while the music is being played. The most common use for CD+G media is karaoke "sing-along" media. These same subcodes are used on CD TEXT discs to store disc- and track-related information that is added to standard audio CDs for playback on compatible CD audio players. The CD TEXT information is stored as ASCII characters in the R-W channels in the lead-in and program areas of a CD. On a CD TEXT disc, the lead-in area subcodes contain text information about the entire disc, such as the album, track (song) titles, and artist names. The program area subcodes, on the other hand, contain text information for the current track (song), including track title, composer, performers, and so on. The CD TEXT data is repeated throughout each track to reduce the delay in retrieving the data.

CD TEXT-compatible players typically have a text display to show this information, ranging from a simple one- or two-line, 20-character display, such as on many newer RBDS (radio broadcast data system) automobile radio/CD players, to up to 21 lines of 40-color, alphanumeric or graphics characters on home- or computer-based players. The specification also allows for future additional data, such as Joint Photographic Experts Group (JPEG) images. Interactive menus also can be used for the selection of text for display.

Note

Current versions of Windows Media Player (WMP) do not natively support CD TEXT for playback or during the creation of music CDs. However, a free plug-in, called WMPCDTex, is available to add CD TEXT support to WMP. (The plug-in supports Windows Media Player version 11 and above.) Other media players, such as Winamp (www.winamp.com), support CD TEXT natively. Popular CD-burning programs with support for CD TEXT include Nero (www.nero.com), Roxio Creator (www.roxio.com), and the free ImgBurn program (www.imgburn.com).

Handling Read Errors

Handling errors when reading a disc was a big part of the original Red Book CD standard. CDs use parity and interleaving techniques called *cross-interleave Reed-Solomon code* (CIRC) to minimize the effects of errors on the disk. This works at the frame level. When being stored, the 24 data bytes in each frame are first run through a Reed-Solomon encoder to produce a 4-byte parity code called "Q" parity, which then is added to the 24 data bytes. The resulting 28 bytes are then run though another encoder that uses a different scheme to produce an additional 4-byte parity value called "P" parity. These are added to the 28 bytes from the previous encoding, resulting in 32 bytes (24 of the original data plus the Q and P parity bytes). An additional byte of subcode (tracking) information is then added, resulting in 33 bytes total for each frame. Note that the P and Q parity bytes are not related to the P and Q subcodes mentioned earlier.

◄◄ To learn more about the concepts behind parity and error correction, which were originally used to guard against errors in memory and modem communications, see Chapter 6, "Memory," **p. 325**, and Chapter 16, "Internet Connectivity," **p. 775**.

To minimize the effects of a scratch or physical defect that would damage adjacent frames, several interleaves are added before the frames are actually written. Parts of 109 frames are cross-interleaved (stored in different frames and sectors) using delay lines. This scrambling decreases the likelihood of a scratch or defect affecting adjacent data because the data is actually written out of sequence.

With CDs, the CIRC scheme can correct errors up to 3,874 bits long (which would be 2.6mm in track length). In addition, for audio CDs, only the CIRC can also conceal (through interpolation) errors up to 13,282 bits long (8.9mm in track length). *Interpolation* is the process in which the data is estimated or averaged to restore what is missing. That would, of course, be unacceptable on a data CD, so this applies only to audio discs. The Red Book CD standard defines the *block error rate* (BLER) as the number of frames (98 per sector) per second that have any bad bits (averaged over 10 seconds) and requires that this be less than 220. This allows a maximum of up to about 3% of the frames to have errors, and yet the disc will still be functional.

An additional layer of error-detection and -correction circuitry is the key difference between audio CD players and data CD drives. Audio CDs convert the digital information stored on the disc into analog signals for a stereo amplifier to process. In this scheme, some imprecision is acceptable because it would be virtually impossible to hear in the music. Data CDs, however, can't tolerate imprecision. Each bit of data must be read accurately. For this reason, data CDs have a great deal of additional ECC information written to the disc along with the actual stored information. The ECC can detect and correct most minor errors, improving the reliability and precision to levels that are acceptable for data storage.

In the case of an audio CD, missing data can be interpolated—that is, the information follows a predictable pattern that enables the drive to guess the missing values. For example, if three values are stored on an audio disc (say, 10, 13, and 20 appearing in a series), and the middle value is missing—because of damage or dirt on the CD's surface—you could interpolate a middle value of 15, which is midway between 10 and 20. Although this might not be exactly correct, in the case of audio recording, it probably won't be noticeable to the listener. If those same three values appear on a data CD in an executable program, there is no way to guess at the correct value for the middle sample. Interpolation can't work because executable program instructions or data must be exact; otherwise, the program will crash or improperly read data needed for a calculation. Using the previous example with a data CD running an executable program, guessing 15 is not merely slightly off—it is completely wrong.

In a CD on which data is stored instead of audio information, additional information is added to each sector to detect and correct errors as well as to identify the location of data sectors more accurately. To accomplish this, 304 bytes are taken from the 2,352 that originally were used for audio data and are instead used for sync (synchronizing bits), ID (identification bits), ECC, and EDC information. This leaves 2,048 bytes for actual user data in each sector. Just as when reading an audio CD, on a 1x (standard speed) CD, sectors are read at a constant speed of 75 per second. This results in a standard CD transfer rate of 153,600 bytes per second (2,048×75), which is expressed as either 153.6KBps or 150KiBps.

Note

Some of the copy-protection schemes used on audio CDs intentionally interfere with the audio data and CIRC information in such a way as to make the disc appear to play correctly, but copies of the audio files or of the entire disc will be filled with noise. Copy protection for both audio and data CDs is discussed later in this chapter.

CD Capacity

Each second of a CD contains 75 blocks of data containing 2,048 bytes per block. From this information, you can calculate the absolute maximum storage capacity of an 80-minute or 74-minute CD, as shown in Table 11.3. The table also shows the structure and layout of each sector on a CD on which data is stored.

Table 11.3 CD Sector Information and Capacity

Each Data Sector (Mode 1):	74-Minute	80-Minute
Q+P parity bytes	784	784
Subcode bytes	98	98
Sync bytes	12	12
Header bytes	8	8
ECC/EDC bytes	284	284

Data bytes	2,048	2,048
Bytes/sector RAW (unencoded)	3,234	3,234
Actual CD data capacity:		
B	681,984,000	737,280,000
KiB	666,000	720,000
KB	681,984	737,280
MiB	650.39	703.13
MB	681.98	737.28

B = Byte (8 bits)

KB = Kilobyte (1,000 bytes)

KiB = Kibibyte (1,024 bytes)

MB = Megabyte (1,000,000 bytes)

MiB = Mebibyte (1,048,576 bytes)

ECC = Error correction code

EDC = Error detection code

This information assumes the data is stored in Mode 1 format, which is used on virtually all data discs. You can learn more about the Mode 1/Mode 2 formats in the section on the Yellow Book and XA standards later in this chapter.

With data sectors, you can see that out of 3,234 actual bytes per sector, only 2,048 are user data. Most of the other 1,186 bytes are used for the intensive error-detection and -correction schemes to ensure error-free performance.

Data Encoding on the Disc

The final part of how data is actually written to the CD is very interesting. After all 98 frames are composed for a sector (whether audio or data), the information is then run through a final encoding process called *eight to fourteen modulation* (EFM). This scheme takes each byte (8 bits) and converts it into a 14-bit value for storage. The 14-bit conversion codes are designed so that there are never fewer than two or more than ten adjacent 0 bits. This is a form of Run Length Limited (RLL) encoding called RLL 2,10 (RLL x,y, where x equals the minimum and y equals the maximum run of 0s). This is designed to prevent long strings of 0s, which could more easily be misread, as well as to limit the minimum and maximum frequency of transitions actually placed on the recording media. With as few as two or as many as ten 0 bits separating 1 bits in the recording, the minimum distance between 1s is 3 bit time intervals (usually referred to as 3T), and the maximum spacing between 1s is 11 time intervals (11T).

Because some of the EFM codes start and end with a 1 or more than five 0s, three additional bits called *merge bits* are added between each 14-bit EFM value written to the disc. The merge bits usually are 0s but might contain a 1 if necessary to break a long string of adjacent 0s formed by the adjacent 14-bit EFM values. In addition to the now 17 bits created for each byte (EFM plus merge bits), a 24-bit sync word (plus three more merge bits) is added to the beginning of each frame. This results in a total of 588 bits (73.5 bytes) actually being stored on the disc for each frame. Multiply this for 98 frames per sector and you have 7,203 bytes actually being stored on the disc to represent each sector. An 80-minute disc, therefore, really has something like 2.6GB of actual data being written, which, after being fully decoded and stripped of error-correcting codes and other information, results in about 737MB (703MiB) of actual user data.

The calculations for EFM-encoded frames and sectors are shown in Table 11.4.

Table 11.4 EFM-Encoded Data Calculations

EFM-Encoded Frames:	74-Minute	80-Minute
Sync word bits	24	24
Subcode bits	14	14
Data bits	336	336
Q+P parity bits	112	112
Merge bits	102	102
EFM bits per frame	588	588
EFM-encoded sectors:		
EFM bits per sector	57,624	57,624
EFM bytes per sector	7,203	7,203
Total EFM data on disc (MB)	2,399	2,593

B = Byte (8 bits)
KB = Kilobyte (1,000 bytes)
KiB = Kibibyte (1,024 bytes)

MB = Megabyte (1,000,000 bytes)
MiB = Mebibyte (1,048,576 bytes)
EFM = Eight to fourteen modulation

To put this into perspective, see Table 11.5 for an example of how familiar data would actually be encoded when written to a CD. As an example, I'll use the letters N and O as they would be written on the disc.

Table 11.5 EFM Data Encoding on a CD

Character	N	O
ASCII decimal code	78	79
ASCII hexadecimal code	4E	4F
ASCII binary code	01001110	01001111
EFM code	00010001000100	00100001000100

ASCII = American Standard Code for Information Interchange
EFM = Eight to fourteen modulation

Figure 11.5 shows how the encoded data would actually appear as pits and lands stamped into a CD.

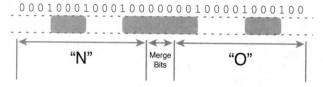

FIGURE 11.5 EFM data physically represented as pits and lands on a CD.

The edges of the pits are translated into the binary 1 bits. As you can see, each 14-bit grouping represents a byte of actual EFM-encoded data on the disc, and each 14-bit EFM code is separated by three merge bits (all 0s in this example). The three pits produced by this example are 4T (4 transitions), 8T, and 4T long. The string of 1s and 0s on the top of the figure represents how the actual data would be read; note that a 1 is read wherever a pit-to-land transition occurs. It is interesting to note that this drawing is actually to scale, meaning the pits (raised bumps) would be about that long and wide relative to each other. If you could use a microscope to view the disc, this is what the word "NO" would look like as actually recorded.

Writable CDs

Optical disc recording has come a long way since 1988, when the first CD-R recording system was introduced at the cost of $50,000 (back then, they used a $35,000 Yamaha audio recording drive along with thousands of dollars of additional error correction and other circuitry for CD-ROM use), operated at 1x speed only, and was part of a subsystem that was the size of a washing machine! The blank discs also cost about $100 each—compared to less than 3 cents each in bulk cakebox form. (You provide your own jewel or slimline cases.) Originally, the main purpose for CD recording was to produce prototype CDs that could then be replicated via the standard stamping process.

In 1991, Philips introduced the first 2x recorder (the CDD 521), which was about the size of a stereo receiver and cost about $12,000. Sony in 1992 and then JVC in 1993 followed with their 2x recorders, and the JVC was the first drive that had the half-height 5 1/4-inch form factor that most desktop system drives still use today. In 1995, Yamaha released the first 4x recorder (the CDR100), which sold for $5,000. A breakthrough in pricing came in late 1995 when Hewlett-Packard released a 2x recorder (the 4020i, which was actually made for them by Philips) for less than $1,000. This proved to be exactly what the market was waiting for. With a surge in popularity after that, prices rapidly fell to below $500, and then down to $200 or less. In 1996, Ricoh introduced the first CD-RW drive.

Two main types of recordable CD discs are available, called CD-R (recordable) and CD-RW (rewritable). However, because the CD-RW discs are more expensive than CD-R discs, only half as fast (or less) as CD-R discs, and won't work in all CD audio or CD-ROM drives, people usually use CD-R media instead of CD-RW.

Note

Because of differences in reflectivity of the media, some older optical drives can't read CD-RW media. Most newer drives conform to the MultiRead specification and as such can read CD-RWs. However, due to differences in the Universal Disk Format (UDF) standards used by CD-RW, a CD-RW disc created on one computer might not be readable on another computer. Therefore, if you are recording something that many people or systems will need to read, CD-R is your best choice for overall compatibility.

CD-R media is a WORM (write once, read many) media, meaning that after you fill a CD-R with data, it is permanently stored and can't be erased. The write-once limitation makes this type of disc less than ideal for system backups or other purposes in which it would be preferable to reuse the same media over and over. However, because of the low cost of CD-R media, you might find that making permanent backups to essentially disposable CD-R discs is as economically feasible as tape or other media.

CD-RW discs can be reused up to 1,000 times, making them suitable for almost any type of data storage task. The following sections examine these two standards and how you can use them for your own data storage needs.

CD-R

Once recorded, CD-R discs can be played back or read in any standard CD drive. CD-R discs are useful for archival storage and creating master CDs, which can be duplicated for distribution within a company.

CD-Rs function using the same principle as standard CD-ROMs. The main difference is that instead of being stamped or embossed into plastic as on regular CDs, CD-Rs have images of pits burned onto a raised groove instead. Therefore, the pits are not really raised bumps like on a standard CD, but instead are rendered as dark (burned) areas on the groove that reflect less light. Because the overall reflectivity of pit and land areas remains the same as on a stamped disc, normal CD drives can read CD-Rs exactly as if they were stamped discs.

Part of the recording process with CD-Rs starts before you even insert the disc into the drive. CD-R media is manufactured much like a standard CD—a stamper is used to mold a base of polycarbonate plastic. However, instead of stamping pits and lands, the stamper imprints a spiral groove (called a *pre-groove*) into the disc. From the perspective of the reading (and writing) laser underneath the disc, this groove is seen as a raised spiral ridge and not a depression.

The pre-groove (or ridge) is not perfectly straight; instead, it has a slight wobble. The amplitude of the wobble is generally very small compared to the track pitch (spacing). The groove separation is 1.6 microns, but it wobbles only 0.030 microns from side to side. The wobble of a CD-R groove is modulated to carry supplemental information read by the drive. The signal contained in the wobble is called *absolute time in pre-groove* (ATIP) because it is modulated with time code and other data. The time code is the same minutes:seconds:frame format that will eventually be found in the Q-subcode of the frames after they are written to the disc. The ATIP enables the drive to locate positions on the disc before the frames are actually written. Technically, the wobble signal is frequency shift-keyed with a carrier frequency of 22.05KHz and a deviation of 1KHz. The wobble uses changes in frequency to carry information.

To complete the CD-R disc, an organic dye is evenly applied across the disc by a spin-coating process. Next, a gold or silver reflective layer is applied (some early low-cost media used aluminum), followed by a protective coat of UV-cured lacquer to protect the reflective and dye layers. Gold or silver is used in recent and current CD-R discs to get the reflectivity as high as possible (gold is used in archival CD-Rs designed for very long-term storage), and it was found that the organic dye tends to oxidize aluminum. Then, silk-screen printing is applied on top of the lacquer for identification and further protection. When seen from the underside, the laser used to read (or write) the disc first passes through the clear polycarbonate and the dye layer, hits the gold layer where it is reflected back through the dye layer and the plastic, and finally is picked up by the optical pickup sensor in the drive.

The dye and reflective layer together have the same reflective properties as a *virgin* CD. In other words, a CD reader would read the groove of an unrecorded CD-R disc as one long land. To record on a CD-R disc, a laser beam of the same wavelength (780nm) as is normally used to read the disc, but with 10 times the power, is used to heat up the dye. The laser is fired in a pulsed fashion at the top of the ridge (groove), heating the layer of organic dye to between 482°F and 572°F (250°–300°C). This temperature literally burns the organic dye, causing it to become opaque. When read, this prevents the light from passing through the dye layer to the gold and reflecting back, having the same effect of canceling the laser reflection that an actual raised pit would on a normal stamped CD.

Figure 11.6 shows the CD-R media layers, along with the pre-groove (raised ridge from the laser perspective) with burned pits.

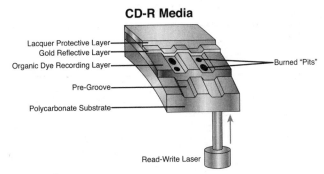

FIGURE 11.6 CD-R media layers.

The drive reading the disc is fooled into thinking a pit exists, but no actual pit exists—there's simply a spot of less-reflective material on the ridge. This use of heat to create the pits in the disc is why the recording process is often referred to as *burning* a CD. When burned, portions of the track change from a reflective to a nonreflective state. This change of state is permanent and can't be undone, which is why CD-R is considered a write-once medium.

CD-R Capacity

All CD-R drives can work with the original 650MiB (682MB) CD-R media (equal to 74 minutes of recorded music), as well as the now-standard higher-capacity 700MiB (737MB) CD-R blanks (equal to 80 minutes of recorded music).

Some drives and burning software are capable of overburning, whereby they write data partially into the lead-out area and essentially extend the data track. This is definitely risky as far as compatibility is concerned. Many drives, especially older ones, fail when reading near the end of an overburned disc. It's best to consider this form of overclocking CDs somewhat experimental. It might be useful for your own purposes if it works with your drives and software, but interchangeability will be problematic.

Some vendors sell 90-minute (790MiB) and 99-minute (870MiB) media to make overburning easier. Most standard CD-RW drives can reliably burn up to 89:59 of music onto the 90-minute media, and the resulting CD-R can be played on a variety of late-model auto and home electronics players.

CD-R Media Color

There has been some controversy over the years about which colors of CD-R media provide the best performance. Table 11.6 shows the most common color combinations, along with which brands use them and some technical information.

Some brands are listed with more than one color combination, due to production changes or different product lines. You should check color combinations whenever you purchase a new batch of CD-R media if you've found that particular color combinations work better for you in your applications.

Table 11.6 CD-R Media Color and Its Effect on Recording

Media Color (First Color Is Reflective Layer; Second Is Dye Layer)	Brands	Technical Notes
Gold-gold	Mitsui, Kodak, Maxell, Ricoh	Phthalocyanine dye. Less tolerance for power variations. Has a rate life span of up to 100 years. Might be less likely to work in a variety of drives. Invented by Mitsui Toatsu Chemicals. Works best in drives that use a Long Write Strategy (longer laser pulse) to mark media.

Table 11.6 Continued

Media Color (First Color Is Reflective Layer; Second Is Dye Layer)	Brands	Technical Notes
Gold-green	Imation (nee 3M), Memorex, Kodak, BASF, TDK, Verbatim	Cyanine dye. More forgiving of disc-write and disc-read variations. Has a rated lifespan of 10 years (older media). Recent media has a rated lifespan of 20–50 years (silver/green). Color combination developed by Taiyo Yuden. Used in the development of the original CD-R standards. De facto standard for CD-R industry and was the original color-combination used during the development of CD-R technology. Works best in drives that use a Short Write Strategy (shorter laser pulse) to mark media.
Silver-blue	Verbatim, DataLifePlus, HiVal, Maxell, TDK	Process developed by Verbatim. Azo dye. Similar performance to green media, plus rated to last up to 100 years. A good choice for long-term archiving.

Note

Original PlayStation games came on discs that were tinted black for appearance. Soon, blank CD-R recordable discs were also available with this same black tint in the polycarbonate. The black tint is purely cosmetic—it is invisible to the infrared laser that reads/writes the disc. In other words, "black" CD-R discs are functionally identical to clear discs and can be made using any of the industry-standard dyes in the recording layer. The black tint hides the recording layer visually, so although the laser passes right through it, the black tint prevents you from directly observing the color of the dye in the recording layer.

Ultimately, although the various color combinations have their advantages, the best way to choose a media type is to try a major brand of media in your drive with both full-disc and small-disc recording jobs and then try the completed disc in as wide a range of drive brands and speeds as you can.

Note

If you are planning to record music mixes for use in automobile-based or portable CD players, be sure to test compatibility in these devices as well.

The perfect media for you will be the ones that offer you the following:

- High reliability in writing (check your drive model's list of recommended media)
- No dye or reflective surface dropouts (areas where the media won't record properly)
- Durability through normal handling (scratch-resistant coating on media surface)
- Compatibility across the widest range of CD drives
- Lowest unit cost

If you have problems recording reliably with certain types of media, or if you find that some brands with the same speed rating record much more slowly than others, contact your drive vendor for a firmware upgrade. Firmware upgrades can also help your drive recognize new types of faster media from different vendors.

CD-R Media Recording Speed Ratings

With CD-R mastering speeds ranging from 1x (now-discontinued first-generation units) up through the current 48x–52x rates, it's important to check the speed rating (x-rating) of your CD-R media.

Most branded media on the market today is rated to work successfully at up to 52x recording speeds (some are limited to 48x). Some brands indicate this specifically on their packaging, whereas you must check the websites for others to get this information. If necessary, install the latest firmware updates to reach maximum recording speed.

▶▶ See the section, "Updating the Firmware in an Optical Drive," **p. 607**.

Note

The 52x CD-R recording speed is the fastest speed available, but higher spin rates can result in excessive vibration and even disc failure.

If speed ratings are unavailable for your media, you might want to restrict your burning to 32x or lower for data. If you are burning audio CDs, you might find that some devices work better with media burned at 8x or lower speeds than with media burned at higher speeds.

Tip

Most drives and mastering software support a setting that automatically determines the best speed to use for burning a CD-R. Software that supports this type of feature analyzes the media and adjusts writing methods and write speed during the write process to ensure the best results. Using this feature with media with an unknown speed rating helps you get a reliable burn no matter what the speed rating of the media is.

CD-RW

Beginning in early 1996, an industry consortium that included Ricoh, Philips, Sony, Yamaha, Hewlett-Packard, and Mitsubishi Chemical Corporation announced the CD-RW format. The design was largely led by Ricoh, and it was the first manufacturer to introduce a CD-RW drive (in May 1996). This drive was the MP6200S, which was a 2/2/6 (2x record, 2x rewrite, 6x read) rated unit. At the same time, the Orange Book Part III was published, which officially defined the CD-RW standard.

CD-RW drives rapidly replaced CD-R-only drives, and although rewritable DVD drives have largely replaced CD-RW drives, any rewritable DVD drive can function as a CD-R/CD-RW drive. Some low-cost systems include DVD combo drives, which combine DVD-ROM and CD-R/CD-RW capabilities.

You can burn and write to CD-RW discs just like CD-Rs; the main difference is that you can erase and reburn CD-RWs again and again. They are very useful for prototyping a disc that will then be duplicated in less expensive CD-R or even stamped CDs for distribution. They can be rewritten at least 1,000 times or more. Additionally, with packet-writing software (software that supports the Universal Disk Format standard), CD-RWs can even be treated like giant floppy disks, where you can simply drag and drop or copy and delete files at will. Although CD-RW discs are about 1.5–2 times more expensive than CD-R media, CD-RWs are still far cheaper than optical cartridges and other removable formats. This makes CD-RW a viable technology for small-scale system backups, file archiving, and virtually any other data storage task where rewritable DVD is not suitable.

Note

The CD-RW format originally was referred to as CD-Erasable, or CD-E.

Four main differences exist between CD-RW and CD-R media. In a nutshell, CD-RW discs are

- Rewritable
- More expensive
- Slower when writing
- Less reflective

Besides the CD-RW media being rewritable and costing a bit more, it is writable at speeds of no more than 24x (about half the speed of the fastest CD-R discs). The actual top speed for a particular drive and media combination is the slower of the drive or media speeds supported. This is because the laser needs more time to operate on a particular spot on the disk when writing. This media also has a lower reflectivity, which limits readability in older drives. Many older standard CD-ROM and CD-R drives can't read CD-RWs. However, MultiRead capability is now found in virtually all CD drives, enabling them to read CD-RWs without problems. In general, CD-DA drives—especially the car audio players—seem to have the most difficulty reading CD-RWs. So, for music recording or compatibility with older drives, you should probably stick to CD-R media. Check the drive or device specifications to determine compatibility with CD-RW media.

CD-RW drives and media use a phase-change process to create the illusion of pits on the disc. As with CD-R media, the disc starts out with the same polycarbonate base with a wobbled pre-groove molded in, which contains ATIP information. Then, on top of the base a special dielectric (insulating) layer is spin-coated, followed by the phase-change recording layer, another dielectric layer, an aluminum reflective layer, and finally a UV-cured lacquer protective layer (and optional screen printing). The dielectric layers above and below the recording layer are designed to insulate the polycarbonate and reflective layers from the intense heat used during the phase-change process.

Figure 11.7 shows the CD-RW media layers, along with the pre-groove (raised ridge from the laser perspective) with burned pits in the phase change layer.

Instead of burning an organic dye as with CD-R, the recording layer in a CD-RW disc is made up of a phase-change alloy consisting of silver, indium, antimony, and tellurium (Ag-In-Sb-Te). The reflective part of the recording layer is an aluminum alloy, the same as used in normal stamped discs. As a result, the recording side of CD-RW media looks like a mirror with a slight blue tint. The read/write laser works from the underside of the disk, where the groove again appears like a ridge, and the recording is made in the phase-change layer on top of this ridge. The recording layer of Ag-In-Sb-Te alloy normally has a polycrystalline structure that is about 20% reflective. When data is written to a CD-RW disc, the laser in the drive alternates between two power settings, called P-write and P-erase. The higher power setting (P-write) is used to heat the material in the recording layer to a temperature between 500°C and 700°C (932°–1,292°F), causing it to melt. In a liquid state the molecules of the material flow freely, losing their polycrystalline structure and taking what is called an *amorphous* (random) state. When the material then solidifies in this amorphous state, it is only about 5% reflective. When being read, these areas lower in reflectivity simulate the pits on a stamped CD-ROM disc.

To return the material to a polycrystalline state, the laser is set to the lower-power P-erase mode. This heats the active material to approximately 200°C (392°F), which is well below the liquid melting point but high enough to soften the material. When the material is softened and allowed to cool more slowly, the molecules realign from a 5% reflective amorphous state back to a 20% reflective polycrystalline state. These higher reflective areas simulate the lands on a stamped CD-ROM disc.

Note that despite the name of the P-erase laser power setting, the disc is never explicitly "erased." Instead, CD-RW uses a recording technique called *direct overwrite*, in which a spot doesn't have to be erased to be rewritten; it is simply rewritten. In other words, when data is recorded, the laser remains on and pulses between the P-write and P-erase power levels to create amorphous and polycrystalline areas of low and high reflectivity, regardless of which state the areas were in prior. It is similar in many ways to writing data on a magnetic disk that also uses direct overwrite. Every sector already has data patterns, so when you write data, all you are really doing is writing new patterns. Sectors are never really erased; they are merely overwritten. The media in CD-RW discs is designed to be written and rewritten up to 1,000 times.

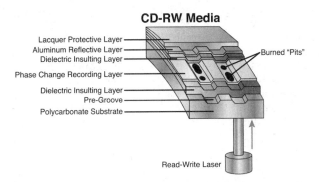

FIGURE 11.7   CD-RW media layers.

The original Orange Book Part III Volume 1 (CD-RW specification) allowed for CD-RW writing at up to 4x speeds. In May 2000, Part III Volume 2 was published, defining CD-RW recording at speeds from 4x to 10x. This revision of the CD-RW standard is called *High-Speed Rewritable*, and both the discs and drives capable of CD-RW speeds higher than 4x indicate this via the logos printed on them. Part III Volume 3 was published in September 2002 and defines Ultra-Speed drives, which are CD-RW drives capable of recording speeds 8x–24x.

Because of the differences in High-Speed and Ultra-Speed media, High-Speed media can be used only in High-Speed and Ultra-Speed drives; Ultra-Speed Media can be used only in Ultra-Speed drives. Both High-Speed and Ultra-Speed drives can use standard 2x–4x media, enabling them to interchange data with computers that have standard-speed CD-RW drives. Thus, choosing the wrong media to interchange with another system can prevent the other system from reading the media. If you don't know which speed of CD-RW media the target computer supports, I recommend you either use standard 2x–4x media or create a CD-R.

Because of differences in the UDF standards used by the packet-writing software that drags and drops files to CD-RW drives, the need to install a UDF reader on systems with CD-ROM drives, and the incapability of older CD-ROM and first-generation DVD-ROM drives to read CD-RW media, I recommend using CD-RW media for personal backups and data transfer between your own computers. However, when you send CD data to another user, CD-R is universally readable, making it a better choice.

MultiRead Specifications

The original Red and Yellow Book CD standards specified that, on a CD, the lands should have a minimum reflectance value of about 70%, and the pits should have a maximum reflectance of about 28%. Therefore, the area of a disc that represents a land should reflect back no less than 70% of the laser light directed at it, whereas the pits should reflect no more than 28%. In the early 1980s when these standards were developed, the photodetector diodes used in the drives were relatively insensitive, and these minimum and maximum reflectance requirements were deliberately designed to create enough brightness and contrast between pits and lands to accommodate them.

On a CD-RW disc, the reflectance of a land is approximately 20% (plus or minus 5%), and the reflectivity of a pit is only 5%—obviously well below the original requirements. Fortunately, it was found that by the addition of a relatively simple AGC circuit, the ratio of amplification in the detector circuitry can be changed dynamically to allow for reading the lower-reflective CD-RW discs. Therefore, although CD-ROM drives were not initially capable of reading CD-RW discs, modifying the existing designs to enable them to do so wasn't difficult. Where you might encounter problems reading CD-RW discs is with CD audio drives, especially older ones. Because CD-RW first came out in 1996 (and took a year or more to become popular), most CD-ROM drives manufactured in 1997 or earlier have problems reading CD-RW discs.

DVDs also have some compatibility problems. With DVD, the problem isn't just simple reflectivity as it is an inherent incompatibility with the laser wavelength used for DVD versus CD. The problem in this case stems from the dyes used in the recording layer of CD-R and RW discs, which are very sensitive to the wavelength of light used to read them. At the proper CD laser wavelength of 780nm, they are reflective, but at other wavelengths, the reflectivity falls off markedly. Normally, CD drives use a 780nm (infrared) laser to read the data, whereas DVD drives use a shorter wavelength 650nm (red) laser. Although the shorter wavelength laser works well for reading commercial CD-ROM discs because the aluminum reflective layer they use is equally reflective at the shorter DVD laser wavelength, it doesn't work well at all for reading CD-R or RW discs.

Fortunately, a solution was introduced by Sony and then similarly by all the other DVD drive manufacturers. This solution consists of a dual-laser pickup that incorporates both a 650nm (DVD) and 780nm (CD) laser. Some of these used two discrete pickup units with separate optics mounted to the same assembly, but they eventually changed to dual-laser units that use the same optics for both, making the pickup smaller and less expensive. Because most manufacturers wanted to make a variety of drives—including cheaper ones without the dual-laser pickup—a standard needed to be created so that someone purchasing a drive would know the drive's capabilities.

So how can you tell whether your CD or DVD drive is compatible with CD-R and RW discs? In the late 1990s, the OSTA created the MultiRead specifications to guarantee specific levels of compatibility:

- **MultiRead**—For CD drives
- **MultiRead2**—For DVD drives

In addition, a similar MultiPlay standard exists for consumer DVD-Video and CD-DA devices.

Table 11.7 shows the two levels of MultiRead capability that you can assign to drives and the types of media guaranteed to be readable in such drives.

Table 11.7 MultiRead and MultiRead2 Compatibility Standards for CD/DVD Drives

Media	MultiRead	MultiRead2	Media	MultiRead	MultiRead2
CD-DA	X	X	DVD-ROM	—	X
CD-ROM	X	X	DVD-Video	—	X
CD-R	X	X	DVD-Audio	—	X
CD-RW	X	X	DVD-RAM	—	X

X = Compatible; drive will read this media.
— = Incompatible; drive won't read.

Note that MultiRead also indicates that the drive is capable of reading discs written in Packet Writing mode because this mode is now being used more commonly with both CD-R and DVD rewritable media.

If you use only rewritable CD or DVD drives, you don't need to worry about compatibility. However, if you still use nonrewritable drives, you should check compatibility with other types of media. Although the MultiRead and MultiRead2 logos shown in Figure 11.8 are not widely used today, you can determine a particular drive's compatibility with a given media type by viewing its specification sheet.

FIGURE 11.8 MultiRead and MultiRead2 logos. These logos can be found on some older drives meeting these specifications.

You can obtain the MultiRead specification (revision 1.11, October 23, 1997) and MultiRead 2 specification (revision 1.0, December 6, 1999) from the OSTA website.

MultiPlay and MultiAudio

The MultiPlay specification was developed in 2000–2001 by OSTA to ensure that CD-R and CD-RW discs created on a personal computer could also be played back on consumer CD and DVD players. Supported content types include Red Book Audio, CD-Text, Slideshow (JPEG photos), and Video CD. Players that also meet the MultiAudio standard from OSTA can play MP3, WMA, and other compressed audio formats and read information stored for each track such as track name; year recorded; names of composer, songwriter, performer and arranger; album name; genre.

DVD

DVD in simplest terms is a high-capacity CD. In fact, every DVD-ROM drive *is* a CD-ROM drive; that is, it can read CDs as well as DVDs. (Some older standalone DVD players can't read CD-R or CD-RW discs, however.) DVD uses the same optical technology as CD, with the main difference being higher density. The DVD standard dramatically increases the storage capacity of, and therefore the useful applications for, CD-sized discs. A CD can hold a maximum of about 737MB (80-minute disc) of data, which might sound like a lot but is simply not enough for many applications, especially where the use of video is concerned. DVDs, on the other hand, can hold up to 4.7GB (single layer) or 8.5GB (dual layer) on a single side of the disc, which is more than 11 1/2 times greater than a CD. Double-sided DVDs can hold up to twice that amount, although you currently must manually flip the disc over to read the other side.

Up to two layers of information can be recorded to DVDs, with an initial storage capacity of 4.7GB of digital information on a single-sided, single-layer disc—a disc that is the same overall diameter and thickness of a current CD. With Moving Picture Experts Group standard 2 (MPEG-2) compression, that's enough to contain approximately 133 minutes of video, which is enough for a full-length, full-screen, full-motion feature film—including three channels of CD-quality audio and four channels of subtitles. Using both layers, a single-sided disc could easily hold 240 minutes of video or more. This initial capacity is no coincidence; the creation of DVD was driven by the film industry, which has long sought a storage medium cheaper and more durable than videotape.

Note

It is important to know the difference between the DVD-Video and DVD-ROM standards. DVD-Video discs contain only video programs and are intended to be played in a DVD player connected to a television and possibly an audio system. DVD-ROM is a data-storage medium intended for use by PCs and other types of computers. The distinction is similar to that between an audio CD and a CD-ROM. Computers might be capable of playing audio CDs as well as CD-ROMs, but dedicated audio CD players can't use a CD-ROM's data tracks. Likewise, computer DVD drives can play DVD-Video discs (with MPEG-2 decoding in either hardware or software), but DVD-Video players can't access data on a DVD-ROM. This is the reason you must select the type of DVD you are trying to create when you make a writable or rewritable DVD.

The initial application for DVDs was as an upgrade for CDs as well as a replacement for prerecorded videotapes. As with CDs, which initially were designed only for music, DVDs have since developed into a wider range of uses, including video rental, computer data storage, and high-quality audio.

DVD History

DVD had a somewhat rocky start. During 1995, two competing standards for high-capacity CD drives were being developed to compete with each other for future market share. One standard, called Multimedia CD, was introduced and backed by Philips and Sony, whereas a competing standard, called the Super Density (SD) disc, was introduced and backed by Toshiba, Time Warner, and several other companies. If both standards had hit the market as is, consumers as well as entertainment and software producers would have been in a quandary over which one to choose.

Fearing a repeat of the Beta/VHS situation that occurred in the videotape market, several organizations, including the Hollywood Video Disc Advisory Group and the Computer Industry Technical Working Group, banded together to form a consortium to develop and control the DVD standard. The consortium insisted on a single format for the industry and refused to endorse either competing proposal. With this incentive, both groups worked out an agreement on a single, new, high-capacity CD-type disc in September 1995. The new standard combined elements of both previously proposed standards and was called DVD, which originally stood for *digital video disc* but has since been changed to *digital versatile disc*. The single DVD standard has avoided a confusing replay of the VHS-versus-Beta-tape fiasco for movie fans and has given the software, hardware, and movie industries a single, unified standard to support.

After copy protection and other items were agreed on, the DVD-ROM and DVD-Video standards were officially announced in late 1996. Players, drives, and discs were announced in January 1997 at the Consumer Electronics Show (CES) in Las Vegas, and the players and discs became available in March 1997. The initial players were about $1,000 each. Only 36 movies were released in the first wave, and they were available only in seven cities nationwide (Chicago, Dallas, Los Angeles, New York, San Francisco, Seattle, and Washington, DC) until August 1997 when the full release began. After a somewhat rocky start (much had to do with agreements on copy protection to get the movie companies to go along, and there was a lack of titles available in the beginning), DVD has become an incredible success. The organization that controls the DVD video standard is called the DVD Forum and was founded by 10 companies, including Hitachi, Matsushita, Mitsubishi, Victor, Pioneer, Sony, Toshiba, Philips, Thomson, and Time Warner. Since its founding in April 1997, more than 230 companies have joined the forum. Because it is a public forum, anybody can join and attend the meetings; the site for the DVD Forum is www.dvdforum.org. Because the DVD Forum was unable to agree on a universal recordable format, its members who are primarily responsible for CD and DVD technology (Philips, Sony, and others) split off to form the DVD+RW Alliance in June 2000; their site is www.dvdservices.org. They have since introduced the DVD+RW format, which is the fastest, most flexible and backward-compatible recordable DVD format. DVD-R/RW and DVD+R/RW are not just for computer uses either: You can purchase DVD set-top recorders from many vendors (some of which also contain VCRs to enable you to dub non-copy-protected VCR tapes to DVD).

DVD Construction and Technology

DVD technology is similar to CD technology. Both use the same size discs (120mm diameter, 1.2mm thick, with a 15mm hole in the center) with pits and lands stamped in a polycarbonate base. Unlike a CD, though, DVDs can have two layers of recordings on a side and be double-sided. Each layer is separately stamped, and the layers are bonded together to make the final 1.2mm-thick disc. The manufacturing process is largely the same, with the exception that each layer on each side is stamped from a separate piece of polycarbonate plastic. These are then bonded together to form the completed disc. The main difference between CD and DVD is that DVD is a higher-density recording read by a laser with a shorter wavelength, focused more closely to the disc, which enables more information to be stored. Also, whereas CDs are single-sided and have only one layer of stamped pits and lands, DVDs can have up to two layers per side and can have information on both sides.

As with CDs, each layer is stamped or molded with a single physical track in a spiral configuration starting from the inside of the disc and spiraling outward. The disc rotates counterclockwise (as viewed from the bottom), and each spiral track contains pits (bumps) and lands (flat portions), just as on a CD. Each recorded layer is coated with a thin film of metal to reflect the laser light. The outer layer has a thinner coating to allow the light to pass through to read the inner layer. If the disc is single-sided, a label can be placed on top; if it's double-sided, only a small ring near the center provides room for labeling.

Just as with a CD, reading the information back on a DVD is a matter of bouncing a low-powered laser beam off one of the reflective layers in the disc. The laser shines a focused beam on the underside of the disc, and a photosensitive receptor detects when the light is reflected back. When the light hits a land (flat spot) on the track, the light is reflected back; when the light hits a pit (raised bump), the phase differential between the projected and reflected light causes the waves to cancel and no light is reflected back.

The individual pits on a DVD are 0.105 microns deep and 0.4 microns wide. The pits and lands vary in length from about 0.4 microns at their shortest to about 1.9 microns at their longest (on single-layer discs).

Refer to the section "CD Construction and Technology," earlier in this chapter, for more information on how the pits and lands are read and converted into actual data, as well as how the drives physically and mechanically work.

DVD uses the same optical laser read pit and land storage that CDs do. The greater capacity is made possible by several factors, including the following:

- A 2.25 times smaller pit length (0.9–0.4 microns)
- A 2.16 times reduced track pitch (1.6–0.74 microns)
- A slightly larger data area on the disc (8,605–8,759 square millimeters)
- About 1.06 times more efficient channel bit modulation
- About 1.32 times more efficient error-correction code
- About 1.06 times less sector overhead (2,048/2,352–2,048/2,064 bytes)

The DVD pits and lands are much smaller and closer together than those on a CD, allowing the same physical-sized platter to hold much more information. Figure 11.9 shows how the grooved tracks with pits and lands are just over four times as dense on a DVD as compared to a CD.

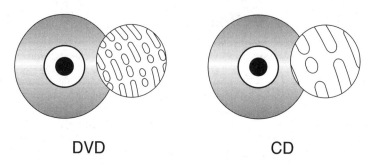

DVD   CD

FIGURE 11.9 DVD data markings (pits and lands) versus those of a standard CD.

DVD drives use a shorter wavelength laser (650nm) to read these smaller pits and lands. A DVD can have nearly double the initial capacity by using two separate layers on one side of a disc and double it again by using both sides of the disc. The second data layer is written to a separate substrate below the first layer, which is then made semi-reflective to enable the laser to penetrate to the substrate beneath it. By focusing the laser on one of the two layers, the drive can read roughly twice the amount of data from the same surface area.

DVD Tracks and Sectors

The pits are stamped into a single spiral track (per layer) with a spacing of 0.74 microns between turns, corresponding to a track density of 1,351 turns per millimeter or 34,324 turns per inch. This equates to a total of 49,324 turns and a total track length of 11.8km or 7.35 miles in length. The track is composed of sectors, with each sector containing 2,048 bytes of data. The disc is divided into four main areas:

- **Hub clamping area**—The hub clamp area is just that: a part of the disc where the hub mechanism in the drive can grip the disc. No data or information is stored in that area.

- **Lead-in zone**—The lead-in zone contains buffer zones, reference code, and mainly a control data zone with information about the disc. The control data zone consists of 16 sectors of information repeated 192 times, for a total of 3,072 sectors. Contained in the 16 (repeated) sectors is information about the disc, including disc category and version number, disc size and maximum transfer rate, disc structure, recording density, and data zone allocation. The entire lead-in zone takes up to 196,607 (2FFFFh) sectors on the disc. Unlike CDs, the basic structure of all sectors on a DVD is the same. The buffer zone sectors in the lead-in zone have all 00h (zero hex) recorded for data.

- **Data zone**—The data zone contains the video, audio, or other data on the disc and starts at sector number 196,608 (30000h). The total number of sectors in the data zone can be up to 2,292,897 per layer for single-layer discs.

- **Lead-out (or middle) zone**—The lead-out zone marks the end of the data zone. All the sectors in the lead-out zone contain zero (00h) for data. This is called the middle zone if the disc is dual-layer and is recorded in opposite track path (OPT) mode, in which the second layer starts from the outside of the disc and is read in the opposite direction from the first layer.

The center hole in a DVD is 15mm in diameter, so it has a radius of 7.5mm from the center of the disc. From the edge of the center hole to a point at a radius of 16.5mm is the hub clamp area. The lead-in zone starts at a radius of 22mm from the center of the disc. The data zone starts at a radius of 24mm from the center and is followed by the lead-out (or middle) zone at 58mm. The disc track officially ends at 58.5mm, which is followed by a 1.5mm blank area to the edge of the disc. Figure 11.10 shows these zones in actual relative scale as they appear on a DVD.

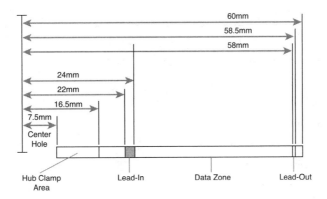

FIGURE 11.10 Areas on a DVD (side view).

Officially, the spiral track of a standard DVD starts with the lead-in zone and ends at the finish of the lead-out zone. This single spiral track is about 11.84 kilometers or 7.35 miles long. An interesting fact is that in a 20x CAV drive, when the outer part of the track is being read, the data moves at an actual speed of 156 miles per hour (251km/h) past the laser. What is more amazing is that even when the data is traveling at that speed, the laser pickup can accurately read bits (pit/land transitions) spaced as little as only 0.4 microns or 15.75 millionths of an inch apart!

DVDs come in both single- and dual-layer as well as single- and double-sided versions. The double-sided discs are essentially the same as two single-sided discs glued together back to back, but subtle differences do exist between the single- and dual-layer discs. Table 11.8 shows some of the basic information about DVD technology, including single- and dual-layer DVDs. The dual-layer versions are recorded with slightly longer pits, resulting in slightly less information being stored in each layer.

Table 11.8 DVD Technical Parameters

DVD Type:	Single-Layer	Dual-Layer
1x read speed (m/sec)	3.49	3.84
Laser wavelength (nm)	650	650
Numerical aperture (lens)	0.60	0.60
Media refractive index	1.55	1.55
Track (turn) spacing (um)	0.74	0.74
Turns per mm	1,351	1,351
Turns per inch	34,324	34,324
Total track length (m)	11,836	11,836
Total track length (feet)	38,832	38,832
Total track length (miles)	7.35	7.35
Media bit cell length (nm)	133.3	146.7
Media byte length (um)	1.07	1.17
Media sector length (mm)	5.16	5.68
Pit width (um)	0.40	0.40

Table 11.8 Continued

Pit depth (um)	0.105	0.105
Min. nominal pit length (um)	0.40	0.44
Max. nominal pit length (um)	1.87	2.05
Lead-in inner radius (mm)	22	22
Data zone inner radius (mm)	24	24
Data zone outer radius (mm)	58	58
Lead-out outer radius (mm)	58.5	58.5
Data zone width (mm)	34	34
Data zone area (mm2)	8,759	8,759
Total track area width (mm)	36.5	36.5
Max. rotating speed 1x CLV (rpm)	1,515	1,667
Min. rotating speed 1x CLV (rpm)	570	627
Track revolutions (data zone)	45,946	45,946
Track revolutions (total)	49,324	49,324
Data zone sectors per layer per side	2,292,897	2,083,909
Sectors per second	676	676
Media data rate (Mbps)	26.15625	26.15625
Media bits per sector	38,688	38,688
Media bytes per sector	4,836	4,836
Interface data rate (Mbps)	11.08	11.08
Interface data bits per sector	16,384	16,384
Interface data bytes per sector	2,048	2,048
DVD Type:	Single-Layer	Dual-Layer
Track time per layer (minutes)	56.52	51.37
Track time per side (minutes)	56.52	102.74
MPEG-2 video per layer (minutes)	133	121
MPEG-2 video per side (minutes)	133	242

B = Byte (8 bits)
KB = Kilobyte (1,000 bytes)
KiB = Kibibyte (1,024 bytes)
MB = Megabyte (1,000,000 bytes)
MiB = Mebibyte (1,048,576 bytes)
GB = Gigabyte (1,000,000,000 bytes)
GiB = Gibibyte (1,073,741,824 bytes)
Mbps = Megabits per second

m = Meters
mm = Millimeters (thousandths of a meter)
mm² = Square millimeters
um = Micrometers = Microns (millionths of a meter)
nm = Nanometers (billionths of a meter)
rpm = Revolutions per minute
CLV = Constant linear velocity

As you can see from Table 11.8, the spiral track is divided into sectors that are stored at the rate of 676 sectors per second. Each sector contains 2,048 bytes of data.

When being written, the sectors are first formatted into data frames of 2,064 bytes: 2,048 are data, 4 bytes contain ID information, 2 bytes contain ID error-detection (IED) codes, 6 bytes contain copyright information, and 4 bytes contain EDC for the frame.

The data frames then have ECC information added to convert them into ECC frames. Each ECC frame contains the 2,064-byte data frame plus 182 parity outer (PO) bytes and 120 parity inner (PI) bytes, for a total of 2,366 bytes for each ECC frame.

Finally, the ECC frames are converted into physical sectors on the disc. This is done by taking 91 bytes at a time from the ECC frame and converting them into recorded bits via 8-to-16 modulation. This is where each byte (8 bits) is converted into a special 16-bit value, which is selected from a table. These values are designed using an RLL 2,10 scheme, which is designed so that the encoded information never has a run of fewer than two or more than ten 0 bits in a row. After each group of 91 bytes is converted via the 8-to-16 modulation, 32 bits (4 bytes) of synchronization information are added. After the entire ECC frame is converted into a physical sector, 4,836 total bytes are stored.

Table 11.9 shows the sector, frame, and audio data calculations.

Table 11.9 DVD Data Frame, ECC Frame, and Physical Sector Layout and Information

DVD Data Frame:	
ID bytes	4
IED bytes	2
CI	6
Data bytes	2,048
Error detection code (EDC)	4
Data frame total bytes	2,064
DVD ECC Frame:	
Data frame total bytes	2,064
PO bytes	182
Parity inner (PI) bytes	120
ECC frame total bytes	2,366
DVD Media Physical Sectors:	
ECC frame bytes	2,366
8-to-16 modulation bits	37,856
Synchronization bits	832
Total encoded media bits/sector	38,688
Total encoded media bytes/sector	4,836
Original data bits/sector	16,384
Original data bytes/sector	2,048
Ratio of original to media data	2.36

ID = Identification Data

IED = ID Error Detection code

CI = Copyright Info

EDC = Error Detection Code

PO = Parity Outer

GB = Gigabyte (1,000,000,000 bytes)

GiB = Gibibyte (1,073,741,824 bytes)

Mbps = Megabits per second

m = Meters

mm = Millimeters (thousandths of a meter)

mm^2 = Square millimeters

um = Micrometers = Microns (millionths of a meter)

nm = Nanometers (billionths of a meter)

rpm = Revolutions per minute

CLV = Constant linear velocity

Unlike CDs, DVDs do not use subcodes. Instead, they use the ID bytes in each data frame to store the sector number and information about the sectors.

Handling DVD Errors

DVDs use more powerful error-correcting codes than were first devised for CDs. Unlike CDs, which have different levels of error correction depending on whether audio/video or data is being stored, DVDs treat all information equally and apply the full error correction to all sectors.

The main error correcting in DVDs takes place in the ECC frame. Parity Outer (column) and Parity Inner (row) bits are added to detect and correct errors. The scheme is simple yet effective. The information from the data frames is first broken up into 192 rows of 172 bytes each. Then a polynomial equation is used to calculate and add 10 PI bytes to each row, making the rows 182 bytes each. Finally, another polynomial equation is used to calculate 16 PO (Parity Outer) bytes for each column, resulting in 16 bytes (rows) being added to each column. What started out as 192 rows of 172 bytes becomes 208 rows of 182 bytes with the PI and PO information added.

The function of the PI and PO bytes can be explained with a simple example using simple parity. In this example, 2 bytes are stored (01001110 = N, 01001111 = O). To add the error-correcting information, they are organized in rows, as shown here:

```
            Data bits
            1 2 3 4 5 6 7 8
-------------------------------------
Byte 1      0 1 0 0 1 1 1 0
Byte 2      0 1 0 0 1 1 1 1
-------------------------------------
```

Then one PI bit is added for each row, using odd parity. This means you count up the 1 bits: In the first row there are four, so the parity bit is created as a 1, making the sum an odd number. In the second row, the parity bit is a 0 because the sum of the 1s was already an odd number. The result is as follows:

```
            Data bits          |
            1 2 3 4 5 6 7 8     |   PI
---------------------------    |---------
Byte 1      0 1 0 0 1 1 1 0     |   1
Byte 2      0 1 0 0 1 1 1 1     |   0
---------------------------    |---------
```

Next, the parity bits for each column are added and calculated the same as before. In other words, the parity bit will be such that the sum of the 1s in each column is an odd number. The result is as follows:

```
            Data bits        |
            1 2 3 4 5 6 7 8   |   PI
----------------------------  |---------
Byte 1      0 1 0 0 1 1 1 0   |   1
Byte 2      0 1 0 0 1 1 1 1   |   0
----------------------------  |---------
     PO     1 1 1 1 1 1 1 0   |   1
```

Now the code is complete, and the extra bits are stored along with the data. So, instead of just the 2 bytes being stored, 11 additional bits are stored for error correction. When the data is read back, the error-correction-bit calculations are repeated and they're checked to see whether they are the same as before. To see how this works, let's change one of the data bits (due to a read error) and recalculate the error-correcting bits as follows:

```
            Data bits        |
            1 2 3 4 5 6 7 8   |   PI
----------------------------  |---------
Byte 1      0 1 0 0 1 1 1 0   |   1
Byte 2      0 1 0 0 1 1 1 1   |   0
----------------------------  |---------
     PO     1 1 1 1 0 1 0 1   |   1
```

Now, when you compare the PI and PO bits you calculated after reading the data to what was originally stored, you see a change in the PI bit for byte (row) 1 and in the PO bit for bit (column) 6. This identifies the precise row and column where the error was, which is at byte 1 (row 1), bit 6 (column 6). That bit was read as a 0, and you now know it is wrong, so it must have been a 1. The error-correction circuitry then simply changes it back to a 1 before passing it back to the system. As you can see, with some extra information added to each row and column, error-correction codes can indeed detect and correct errors on the fly.

Besides the ECC frames, DVDs also scramble the data in the frames using a bit-shift technique and interleave parts of the ECC frames when they are actually recorded on the disc. These schemes serve to store the data somewhat out of sequence, preventing a scratch from corrupting consecutive pieces of data.

DVD Capacity (Sides and Layers)

Four main types of DVDs are available, categorized by whether they are single- or double-sided, and single- or dual-layered. They are designated as follows:

- **DVD-5 (4.7GB single-side, single-layer)**—A DVD-5 is constructed from two substrates bonded with adhesive. One is stamped with a recorded layer (called Layer 0), and the other is blank. An aluminum coating typically is applied to the single recorded layer.

- **DVD-9 (8.5GB single-side, dual-layer)**—A DVD-9 is constructed of two stamped substrates bonded together to form two recorded layers for one side of the disc, along with a blank substrate for the other side. The outer stamped layer (0) is coated with a semitransparent gold coating to both reflect light if the laser is focused on it and pass light if the laser is focused on the layer below. A single laser is used to read both layers; only the focus of the laser is changed.

- **DVD-10 (9.4GB double-side, single-layer)**—A DVD-10 is constructed of two stamped substrates bonded together back to back. The recorded layer (Layer 0 on each side) usually is coated with aluminum. Note that these discs are double-sided; however, drives have a read laser only on the bottom, which means the disc must be removed and flipped to read the other side.

- **DVD-18 (17.1GB double-side, dual-layer)**—A DVD-18 combines both double layers and double sides. Two stamped layers form each side, and the substrate pairs are bonded back to back. The outer layers (Layer 0 on each side) are coated with semitransparent gold, whereas the inner layers (Layer 1 on each side) are coated with aluminum. The reflectivity of a single-layer disc is 45%–85%, and for a dual-layer disc the reflectivity is 18%–30%. The automatic gain control (AGC) circuitry in the drive compensates for the different reflective properties.

Figure 11.11 shows the construction of each of the DVD disc types.

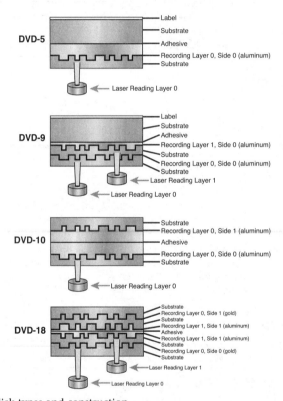

FIGURE 11.11 DVD disk types and construction.

Note that although Figure 11.11 shows two lasers reading the bottom of the dual-layer discs, in actual practice only one laser is used. Only the focus is changed to read the different layers.

Dual-layer discs can have the layers recorded in two ways: either opposite track path (OTP) or parallel track path (PTP). OTP minimizes the time needed to switch from one layer to the other when reading the disc. When reaching the inside of the disc (end of Layer 0), the laser pickup remains in the same location—it merely moves toward the disc slightly to focus on Layer 1. When written in OTP mode, the lead-out zone toward the outer part of the disc is called a middle zone. Discs written in PTP have both spiral layers written (and read) from the inside out. When changing from Layer 0 to Layer 1,

PTP discs require the laser pickup to move from the outside (end of the first layer) back to the inside (start of the second layer), as well as for the focus of the laser to change. Virtually all discs are written in OTP mode to make the layer change quicker. OTP recording is also used by dual-layer (DL) DVD rewritable drives.

To allow the layers to be read more easily even though they are on top of one another, discs written in PTP mode have the spiral direction changed from one layer to the other. Layer 0 has a spiral winding clockwise (which is read counterclockwise), whereas Layer 1 has a spiral winding counterclockwise. This typically requires that the drive spin the disc in the opposite direction to read that layer, but with OTP the spiral is read from the outside in on the second layer. So Layer 0 spirals from the inside out, and Layer 1 spirals from the outside in.

Figure 11.12 shows the differences between PTP and OTP on a DVD.

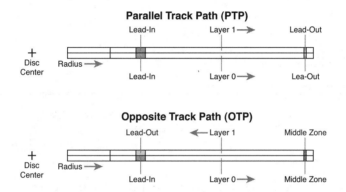

FIGURE 11.12   PTP versus OTP.

DVDs store up to 17.1GB, depending on the type. Table 11.10 shows the precise capacities of the various types of DVDs.

Table 11.10   DVD Capacity

DVD Designation	Single-Layer DVD-5	Dual-Layer DVD-9
B	4,695,853,056	8,535,691,264
KiB	4,585,794	8,335,636
KB	4,695,853	8,535,691
MiB	4,478	8,140
MB	4,696	8,536
GiB	4.4	7.9
	Single-Layer	Dual-Layer
DVD Designation	DVD-5	DVD-9
GB	4.7	8.5
MPEG-2 video (approx. minutes)	133	242
MPEG-2 video (hours:minutes)	2:13	4:02

Table 11.10   Continued

	Single-Layer Double-Sided	Dual-Layer Double-Sided
DVD Designation	DVD-10	DVD-18
B	9,391,706,112	17,071,382,528
KiB	9,171,588	16,671,272
KB	9,391,706	17,071,383
MiB	8,957	16,281
MB	9,392	17,071
GiB	8.7	15.9
GB	9.4	17.1
MPEG-2 video (approx. minutes)	266	484
MPEG-2 video (hours:minutes)	4:26	8:04

B = Byte (8 bits)   *MiB = Mebibyte (1,048,576 bytes)*
KB = Kilobyte (1,000 bytes)   *GB = Gigabyte (1,000,000,000 bytes)*
KiB = Kibibyte (1,024 bytes)   *GiB = Gibibyte (1,073,741,824 bytes)*
MB = Megabyte (1,000,000 bytes)

As you might notice, the capacity of dual-layer discs is slightly less than twice of single-layer discs, even though the layers take up the same space on the discs. (The spiral tracks are the same length.) This was done intentionally to improve the readability of both layers in a dual-layer configuration. To accomplish this, the bit cell spacing was slightly increased, which increases the length of each pit and land. When reading a dual-layer disc, the drive spins slightly faster to compensate, resulting in the same data rate. However, because the distance on the track is covered more quickly, less overall data can be stored.

Besides the standard four capacities listed here, a double-sided disc with one layer on one side and two layers on the other can be produced. This would be called a DVD-14 and have a capacity of 13.2GB, or about 6 hours and 15 minutes of MPEG-2 video. Additionally, 80mm discs, which store less data in each configuration than the standard 120mm discs, can be produced.

Because of the manufacturing difficulties and the extra expense of double-sided discs—and the fact that they must be ejected and flipped to play both sides—most DVDs are configured as either a DVD-5 (single-sided, single-layer) or a DVD-9 (single-sided, dual-layer), which allows up to 8.5GB of data or 242 minutes of uninterrupted MPEG-2 video to be played. The 133-minute capacity of DVD-5 video discs accommodates 95% or more of the movies ever made.

Note

When you view a dual-layer DVD movie, you will see a momentary pause onscreen when the player starts to play the second layer. This is normal, and it takes so little time that if you blink, you might miss it.

Data Encoding on the DVD Disc

As with CDs, the pits and lands themselves do not determine the bits; instead, the transitions (changes in reflectivity) from pit to land and land to pit determine the actual bits on the disc. The disc track is divided into bit cells or time intervals (T), and a pit or land used to represent data is required to be a minimum of 3T or a maximum of 11T intervals (cells) long. A 3T long pit or land represents a 1001, and a 11T long pit or land represents a 100000000001.

Data is stored using eight to sixteen modulation, which is a modified version of the eight to fourteen modulation (EFM) used on CDs. Because of this, eight to sixteen modulation is sometimes called EFM+. This modulation takes each byte (8 bits) and converts it into a 16-bit value for storage. The 16-bit conversion codes are designed so that there are never fewer than two or more than ten adjacent 0 bits (resulting in no fewer than three or no more than eleven time intervals between 1s). EFM+ is a form of RLL encoding called RLL 2,10 (RLL x,y, where x equals the minimum and y equals the maximum run of 0s). This is designed to prevent long strings of 0s, which could more easily be misread due to clocks becoming out of sync, as well as to limit the minimum and maximum frequency of transitions actually placed on the recording media. Unlike CDs, no merge bits exist between codes. The 16-bit modulation codes are designed so that they will not violate the RLL 2,10 form without needing merge bits. Because the EFM used on CDs really requires more than 17 bits for each byte (due to the added merge and sync bits), EFM+ is slightly more efficient because only slightly more than 16 bits are generated for each byte encoded.

Note that although no more than ten 0s are allowed in the modulation generated by EFM+, the sync bits added when physical sectors are written can have up to thirteen 0s, meaning a time period of up to 14T between 1s written on the disc and pits or lands up to 14T intervals or bit cells in length.

Recordable DVD Standards

The history of recordable DVD drives began as a troubled one. It dates back to April 1997, when the DVD Forum announced specifications for rewritable and recordable DVD: DVD-RAM, and DVD-R. Later, it added DVD-RW to the mix. Dissatisfied with these standards, the industry leaders in optical recording and drives formed their own group called the DVD+RW Alliance and created another standard—DVD+R and DVD+RW. For several years, drives based on one family of standards could not freely interchange media with drives using the other family of standards.

Fortunately, all recent drives support both DVD-R/RW and DVD+R/RW media, including dual-layer (DL) DVD+R media, and most also support DVD-RAM. Thus, by using a modern drive that supports all of these types of media, you can choose the right media for a particular task. For example, use DVD-RAM for easy drag-and-drop file backups and DVD-R for creating video DVDs compatible with older DVD set-top boxes.

Table 11.11 compares the competing recordable DVD standards, and Table 11.12 breaks down the compatibilities between the drives and media.

Table 11.11 Recordable DVD Standards

Format	Introduced	Capacity	Compatibility
DVD-RAM	July 1997	Up to 4.7GB per side	Compatible with SuperMulti and Super AllWrite drives. Incompatible with older DVD drives that do not support the MultiRead2 standard.
DVD-R/RW	July 1997; Nov. 1999	4.7GB per side	Compatible with DVD-R/RW, SuperMulti, and Super AllWrite DVD recorders/drives. Compatible with most DVD set-top boxes.
DVD+R/RW	Mar. 2001; May 2001	4.7GB per side	Compatible with DVD+R/RW, SuperMulti, and Super AllWrite DVD recorders/drives. Compatible with most recent DVD set-top boxes.
DVD+R DL	Oct. 2003	8.5GB	Older DVD drives may require firmware updates to read DL media. Some older SuperMulti and Super AllWrite drives do not support DL media.
DVD-R DL	Feb. 2005	8.5GB	For compatibility with older DVD drives, use the Layer Jump Recording method. Older DVD drives may also require firmware updates to read DL media. Some older SuperMulti and Super AllWrite drives do not support DL media.

Table 11.12 DVD Drive and Media Compatibility

Drives	CD-ROM	CD-R	CD-RW	DVD Drive	DVD-ROM	DVD-R	DVD-RAM	DVD-RW	DVD+RW	DVD+R
DVD-Video Player	R	?	?	R	—	R	?	R	R	R
DVD-ROM Drive	R	R	R	R	R	R	?	R	R[1]	R
DVD-R Drive	R	R/W	R/W	R	R	R/W	—	R	R	R
DVD-RAM Drive	R	R	R	R	R	R[6]	R/W	R	R[1]	R
DVD-RW Drive	R	R/W	R/W	R	R	R/W	—	R/W	R	R
DVD+R/RW Drive	R	R/W	R/W	R	R	R	R[3]	R	R/W	R/W[2]
DVD-Multi Drive[4]	R	R/W	R/W	R	R	R	R/W	R/W	R[1]	R
DVD±R/RW Drive	R	R/W	R/W	R	R	R/W	R[5]	R/W	R/W	R/W
DVD Super Multi Drive[7]	R	R/W	R/W	R	R	R/W[8]	R/W	R/W	R/W	R/W[9]

R = Read.

W = Write.

— = Will not read or write.

? = MultiRead/MultiPlay drives will read.

1 Might require media's compatibility bit be changed to alternate (Type 2).

2 Some first-generation DVD+RW drives will not write DVD+R discs; see your drive manufacturer for an update or trade-in.

3 Read compatibility with DVD-RAM varies by drive; check documentation for details.

4 DVD Forum specification for drives that are compatible with all DVD Forum standards. (DVD+R/RW is not a DVD Forum standard.)

5 Some of these drives can also write to DVD-RAM media.

6 Some of these drives can also write to DVD-R media.

7 Identifies drives that work with DVD+R/RW, DVD-R/RW, DVD+R DL, and DVD-RAM media.

8 Some of these drives also work with dual-layer (DL) media.

9 Also supports dual-layer (DL) media.

DVD+R/RW offers low drive and media prices, provides the highest compatibility with existing formats, and has features that make it the most ideal for both video recording and data storage in PCs. However, with most recent drives, you can now select the best media for the job.

DVD-RAM

DVD-RAM is the rewritable DVD standard endorsed by Panasonic, Hitachi, and Toshiba; it is part of the DVD Forum's list of supported standards. DVD-RAM uses a phase-change technology similar to that of CD-RW. Unfortunately, DVD-RAM discs can't be read by older DVD-ROM drives because of differences in both reflectivity of the media and the data format. (DVD-R, by comparison, is backward-compatible with DVD-ROM.)

DVD-ROM drives that can read DVD-RAM discs began to come on the market in early 1999 and follow the MultiRead2 specification. DVD-ROM drives and DVD-Video players labeled as "MultiRead2 compliant" are capable of reading DVD-RAM discs. See the section "MultiRead Specifications," earlier in this chapter, for more information. Although the MultiRead2 logo is not used on current products, some recent and current DVD-ROM drives can read DVD-RAM media; check the specification sheet for a particular drive to verify compatibility.

The first DVD-RAM drives were introduced in spring 1998 and had a capacity of 2.6GB (single-sided) or 5.2GB (double-sided). DVD-RAM Version 2 discs with 4.7GB capacity arrived in late 1999, and double-sided 9.4GB discs arrived in 2000. DVD-RAM drives typically read DVD-Video, DVD-ROM, and CD media. Although DVD-ROM drives, older DVD+R/RW and DVD-R/RW drives, and DVD-Video players can't read DVD-RAM media, DVD Multi and DVD Super Multi drives can read/write DVD-RAM.

DVD-RAM uses what is called the *wobbled land and groove recording* method, which records signals on both the lands (the areas between grooves) and inside the grooves that are preformed on the disc. The tracks wobble, which provides clock data for the drive. Special sector header pits are prepressed into the disc during the manufacturing process as well. See Figure 11.13, which shows the wobbled tracks (lands and grooves) with data recorded both on the lands and in the grooves. This is unlike CD-R or CD-RW, in which data is recorded on the groove only.

The disc is recorded using *phase-change recording*, in which data is written by selectively heating spots in the grooves or on the lands with a high-powered laser. The DVD-RAM drive write laser transforms the film from a crystalline to an amorphous state by heating a spot, which is then rendered less reflective than the remaining crystalline portions. The signal is read as the difference of the laser reflection rate between the crystalline and amorphous states. The modulation and error-correction codes are the same as for DVD-Video and DVD-ROM, ensuring compatibility with other DVD formats. For rewriting, a lower-powered laser reheats the spot to a lower temperature, where it recrystallizes.

Disc cartridges or caddies originally were required for both single- and double-sided discs but have now been made optional for single-sided discs and are seldom used today. Double-sided discs must remain inside the caddy at all times for protection; however, single-sided discs can be taken out of the cartridge if necessary.

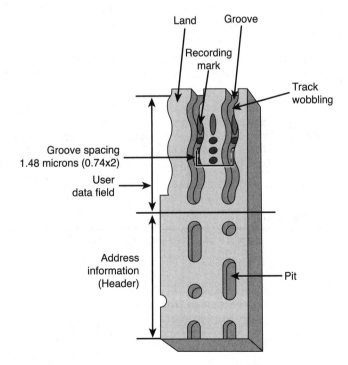

FIGURE 11.13 DVD-RAM wobbled land and groove recording.

DVD-RAM specifications are shown in Table 11.13.

Table 11.13 DVD-RAM Specifications

Storage capacity	2.6GB single-sided; 5.2GB double-sided
Disc diameter	80mm–120mm
Disc thickness	1.2mm (0.6mm×2: bonded structure)
Recording method	Phase change
Laser wavelength	650nm
Data bit length	0.41–0.43 microns
Recording track pitch	0.74 microns
Track format	Wobbled land and groove

In the past, I have been opposed to DVD-RAM because of a lack of compatibility with other drive types. However, if you use drives supporting the DVD Super Multi standard, you can read and write DVD-RAM as well as other rewritable DVD formats. With the ability to read, write, and erase data without the need to use UDF packet-writing software, DVD-RAM can be a useful alternative to other types of rewritable DVD—assuming all of your drives can use it.

DVD-R

DVD-R is a write-once medium similar to CD-R, which was originally created by Pioneer and released by the DVD Forum in July 1997. You can play DVD-R discs on standard DVD-ROM drives. Some DVD-RAM drives can also write to DVD-R media.

DVD-R has a single-sided storage capacity of 4.7GB—about seven times that of a CD-R-and double that for a double-sided disc. These discs use an organic dye recording layer that allows for a low material cost, similar to CD-R.

To enable positioning accuracy, DVD-R uses a wobbled groove recording, in which special grooved tracks are preengraved on the disc during the manufacturing process. Data is recorded within the grooves only. The grooved tracks wobble slightly right and left, and the frequency of the wobble contains clock data for the drive to read, as well as clock data for the drive. The grooves are spaced more closely together than with DVD-RAM, but data is recorded only in the grooves and not on the lands (see Figure 11.14).

Table 11.14 has the basic specifications for DVD-R drives.

Table 11.14 DVD-R Specifications

Storage capacity	4.7GB single-sided; 9.4GB double-sided
Disc diameter	80mm–120mm
Disc thickness	1.2mm (0.6mm×2: bonded structure)
Recording method	Organic dye layer recording method
Laser wavelength	635nm (recording); 635nm/650nm (playback)
Data bit length	0.293 microns
Recording track pitch	0.80 microns
Track format	Wobbled groove

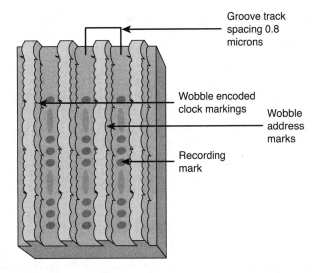

Groove track
spacing 0.8
microns

Wobble encoded
clock markings

Wobble
address
marks

Recording
mark

FIGURE 11.14 DVD-R wobbled groove recording.

DVD-R media is currently available in speeds up to 16x, although some drives feature faster burn speeds. Some vendors are now producing double-sided single-layer DVD-R media with capacities of 9.4GB. This media is designed primarily for DVD jukeboxes, although it can be used by standard DVD rewritable drives.

DVD-R DL

DVD-R DL was introduced in February 2005 and is sometimes known as DVD-R for Dual Layer or DVD-R9. DVD-R DL is essentially a dual-layer version of the DVD-R disc, using the same recording method, laser wavelength, and other specifications. However, DVD-R DL discs have two recording layers, with the reflective surface of the top layer being semi-transparent to permit recording on the second layer. Because of the lower reflectivity of the top layer, some DVD-ROM drives cannot read DVD-R DL media.

Note

If you are unable to read DVD-R DL media with a DVD drive, try using the Layer Jump Recording (LJR) recording method in your DVD mastering software if your drive and software support it. LJR alternates between recording layers during the writing process, rather than filling one layer before writing to the other layer. This permits a disc to support multisession recording and is intended to make it easier for DVD drives to read dual-layer media.

DVD-R DL media is currently available in 4x speed from a relatively small number of suppliers, although some rewritable DVD drives support faster write speeds.

DVD-RW

The DVD Forum introduced DVD-RW in November 1999. Created and endorsed originally by Pioneer, DVD-RW is basically an extension to DVD-R, just as CD-RW is an extension to CD-R. DVD-RW uses a phase-change technology and is somewhat more compatible with standard DVD drives than DVD-RAM. Drives based on this technology began shipping in late 1999, but early models achieved only moderate popularity because Pioneer was the only source for the drives and because of limitations in their performance.

The most common types of DVD-RW media support 2x speeds, although 4x and 6x media are also available. Drives supporting 2x/4x and faster media have several advantages over original 1x/2x DVD-RW drives, including these:

- **Quick formatting**—1x/2x drives require that the entire DVD-RW disc be formatted before the media can be used, a process that can take about an hour. 2x/4x and faster drives can use DVD-RW media in a few seconds after insertion, formatting the media in the background as necessary. This is similar to the way in which DVD+RW drives work.

- **Quick finalizing**—2x/4x DVD-RW drives close media containing small amounts of data (under 1GB) more quickly than 1x/2x drives.

- **Quick grow**—Instead of erasing the media to add files, as with 1x/2x DVD-RW drives, 2x/4x and faster DVD-RW drives can unfinalize the media and add more files without deleting existing files.

However, most DVD-RW drives still don't support lossless linking, Mount Rainier, or selective deletion of files—all of which are major features of DVD+RW.

Note

Plextor's Zero Link technology does support selective file erasure on DVD-RW media. Essentially, Zero Link provides an equivalent to DVD+RW's lossless link feature, enabling DVD-Video players that support DVD-RW media to play edited disks.

DVD+RW and DVD+R

DVD+RW, also called DVD Phase Change Rewritable, has been the premier DVD recordable standard because it is the least expensive, easiest to use, fastest, and most compatible with existing formats. It was developed and is supported by Philips, Sony, Hewlett-Packard, Mitsubishi Chemical (MCC/Verbatim), Ricoh, Yamaha, and Thomson, who are all part of an industry standard group called the DVD+RW Alliance (www.dvdservices.org). Microsoft joined the alliance in February 2003. DVD+RW is also supported by major DVD/CD-creation software vendors and many drive vendors, including HP, Philips, Ricoh, and many remarketers of OEM drive mechanisms. Although DVD-RW has increased in popularity with the advent of faster burning times and easier operation, DVD+RW is the most popular rewritable DVD format.

Table 11.15 lists the basic specifications for DVD+RW drives.

Table 11.15   DVD+RW Specifications

Storage capacity	4.7GB single-sided; 9.4GB double-sided
Disc diameter	120mm
Disc thickness	1.2mm (0.6mm×2: bonded structure)
Recording method	Phase change
Laser wavelength	650nm (recording/playback)
Data bit length	0.4 microns
Recording track pitch	0.74 microns
Track format	Wobbled groove

Note that DVD+R, the recordable version of DVD+RW, was actually introduced after DVD+RW. This is the opposite of DVD-RW, which grew out of DVD-R. One of the major reasons for the development of DVD+R was to provide a lower-cost method for permanent data archiving with DVD+RW drives, and another was because of compatibility issues with DVD-ROM and DVD video players being incapable of reading media created with DVD+RW drives. However, most standard DVD-ROM drives or DVD players can read both DVD+R and DVD+RW media without problems.

The basic structure of a DVD+RW or DVD+R disc resembles that of a DVD-R disc with data written in the grooves only (refer to Figure 11.14), but the groove is wobbled at a frequency different from that used by DVD-R/RW or DVD-RAM. The DVD+R/RW groove also contains positioning information. These differences mean that DVD+R/RW media offers more accurate positioning for lossless linking, but drives made only for DVD+R/RW media can't write to other types of DVD rewritable or recordable media.

Although some first-generation DVD+RW drives worked only with rewritable media, all current and future DVD+RW drives are designed to work with both DVD+R (writable) and DVD+RW (rewritable) media. The +R discs can be written only once and are less expensive than the +RW discs.

Some of the features of DVD+RW include the following:

- Single-sided discs (4.7GB).
- Double-sided discs (9.4GB).
- Up to 4 hours video recording (single-sided discs).
- Up to 8 hours video recording (double-sided discs).
- Bare discs—no caddy required.
- 650nm laser (same as DVD-Video).
- Constant linear data density.
- CLV and CAV recording.
- Write speeds 1x–8x and higher (depending on the drive and media).
- DVD-Video data rates.
- UDF (Universal Disc Format) file system.
- Defect management integral to the drive.
- Quick formatting.
- Uses same 8-to-16 modulation and error-correcting codes as DVD-ROM.
- Sequential and random recording.
- Lossless linking. (Multiple recording sessions don't waste space.)
- Spiral groove with radial wobble.
- After recording, all physical parameters comply with the DVD-ROM specification.

DVD+RW technology is similar to CD-RW, and DVD+RW drives can read DVD-ROMs and all CD formats, including CD-R and CD-RW.

With DVD+RW, the writing process can be suspended and continued without a loss of space linking the recording sessions together. This increases efficiency in random writing and video applications. This "lossless linking" also enables the selective replacement of any individual 32KB block of data (the minimum recording unit) with a new block, accurately positioning with a space of 1 micron. To enable this high accuracy for placement of data on the track, the pre-groove is wobbled at a higher frequency. The timing and addressing information read from the groove is accurate.

The quick formatting feature means you can pop a DVD+R or DVD+RW blank into the drive and almost instantly begin writing to it. The actual formatting is carried out in the background ahead of where any writing will occur.

DVD+R/RW is the format I prefer and recommend, and it has been the format most users prefer for data recording. However, today's multiformat drives support both DVD+R/RW and DVD-R/RW (and Super Multi Drives support DVD-RAM), so you can choose the right media for a particular task.

When DVD+RW drives were introduced in 2001, some users of DVD-ROM and standalone DVD players were unable to read DVD+RW media, even though others were able to do so. The first drives to support DVD+R (writable) media (which works with a wider range of older drives) were not introduced until mid-2002, so this was a significant problem.

The most common reason for this problem turned out to be the contents of the Book Type Field located in the lead-in section of every DVD disc. Some drives require that this field indicate that the media is a DVD-ROM before they can read it. However, by default, DVD+RW drives write DVD+RW as the type into this field when DVD+RW media is used.

The following are three possible solutions:

- Upgrade the firmware in the DVD+RW recorder so it writes compatible information into the Book Type Field automatically.

- Change the Book Type Field during the creation of a disc with a DVD mastering program.

- Use a compatibility utility to change the contents of the Book Type Field for a particular DVD+RW disc as necessary. These utilities may be provided by the drive manufacturer (sometimes a firmware upgrade is also necessary) or by a third-party utility.

Changing the Book Type Field is known as *bitsetting*.

▶▶ See "Updating the Firmware in an Optical Drive," **p. 607**.

DVD+R DL

DVD+R DL, also known as DVD-R9, is a dual-layer version of the DVD+R standard that was introduced in October 2003. DVD+R DL is essentially a dual-layer version of the DVD+R disc, using the same recording method, laser wavelength, and other specifications. However, DVD+R DL discs have two recording layers, with the reflective surface of the top layer being semi-transparent to permit recording on the second layer. Because of the lower reflectivity of the top layer, some DVD-ROM drives cannot read DVD+R DL media. DVD+RW DL media is typically rated at 8x recording speeds.

Multiformat Rewritable DVD Drives

The DVD Multi specification from the DVD Forum was developed for drives and players that are compatible with all DVD Forum standards, including DVD-R/RW, DVD-RAM, DVD-ROM, DVD-Video, and eventually DVD Audio (DVD+R/RW are not DVD Forum specifications and are not supported). The original version of DVD Multi was published in February 2001; the current version, version 1.01, was approved by the DVD Forum and published in December 2001. The first DVD Multi products for computers reached the market in early 2003.

To provide support for different types of DVD media in a single drive, all rewritable DVD drive vendors now sell drives compatible with both DVD+R/RW and DVD-R/RW discs. These drives are commonly known as DVD±R/RW. LG's Super Multi Drive series was the first to also add compatibility with

DVD-RAM, and most current DVD±R/RW drives from other makers are also compatible with DVD-RAM. Many (but not all) current drives also support DVD-R DL, so you can now buy a single drive that supports all common formats supported by both the DVD Forum and the DVD+RW Alliance. Lite-On uses the term Super AllWrite to refer to drives that support all these media types.

BD

In February 2002, the leading optical storage companies formed the Blu-ray Disc Founders (BDF) and announced the initial specifications for BD, a high-capacity optical disc format. By May 2002, BD specification 1.0 was released, and in April 2003, Sony released the BDZ-S77 for the Japanese market, the first commercially available BD recorder. In January 2006, the Blu-ray Disc Association also released a 2.0 specification for BD-RE discs. Blu-ray is a fully rewritable format that enables recording up to 25GB of data or up to 11.5 hours of standard-definition video on a single-sided, single-layer 12cm diameter disc (which is the same as existing CDs and DVDs) using a 405nm blue-violet laser. Dual-layer BD-R DL recorders are also available and can record up to 50GB or 23 hours of standard-definition video. The latest BD specifications, BDXL (recordable) and BD-RE XL (rewritable), can store up to 100GB or 128GB at 2x or 4x speeds.

Although backward compatibility with DVD and CD is not a requirement of the Blu-ray specification, it is a feature drive manufacturers have included. One of the main applications for higher-capacity optical storage is recording high-definition TV, which takes an incredible amount of storage. Current DVD recorders can't store enough data to handle high-definition video. Blu-ray, on the other hand, is designed to store up to 4.5 hours of high-definition video (or more than 13 hours of standard broadcast-quality TV) on a single-layer disc, and 9 hours on dual-layer versions. As with DVD, Blu-ray uses the industry-standard MPEG-2 compression technology.

BD also supports 3D video playback on different types of devices, including HDTV, computers, and game systems. For example, Sony has released a firmware upgrade for PlayStation 3 consoles that enables 3D Blu-ray Disc playback. They previously released support for 3D gaming on April 21, 2010 (followed by the availability of 3D movies). Since the version 3.70 software update in August 9, 2011, the PlayStation 3 can support DTS-HD Master Audio and DTS-HD High Resolution Audio while playing 3D Blu-ray.

Note

Dolby TrueHD is used on a small minority of Blu-ray 3D releases, and bit-streaming is supported by slim PlayStation 3 models only (fat PS3 models decode internally and send audio as LPCM). It can play 3D Blu-ray content at full 1080p.

Figure 11.15 compares the track size and laser types used for CD, DVD, and standard BD media.

Note

When a mixture of HD video and standard video is stored on a BD, you can store up to 2.25 hours of HD video and 2 hours of standard video (used for bonus features) on a single-layer disc. A dual-layer BD can store up to 3 hours of HD video and 9 hours of standard video. Capacities can also vary with bit rates used for movie storage because Blu-ray can support a range of bit rates.

The BD specification includes the following formats:

- **BD-ROM**—Read-only for prerecorded content
- **BD-R**—Recordable
- **BD-RE**—Rewritable
- **BD-RE XL**—Rewritable

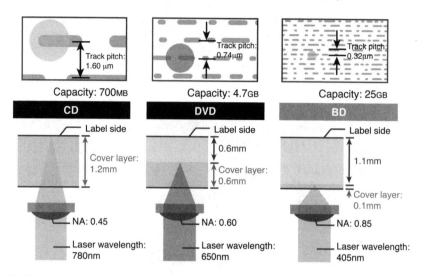

FIGURE 11.15   CD, DVD, and BD media and laser comparison.

The data transfer speed of a BD depends on the speed rating of the drive and media. The practical maximum rotational speed of an optical disc is 10,000 rpm, which limits the maximum speed of BD drives to 12x, which equates to a 54MBps transfer rate. The time to read or write an entire single- or dual-layer disc at various BD drive/media speeds is shown in Table 11.16.

Table 11.16   BD Drive/Media Speeds and Disc Read/Write Times

Drive Speed	Data Rate	Single-Layer Disc Read/Write Time	Dual-Layer Disc Read/Write Time
1x	4.5MBps	90 minutes	180 minutes
2x	9MBps	45 minutes	90 minutes
4x	18MBps	23 minutes	45 minutes
6x	27MBps	15 minutes	30 minutes
8x	36MBps	12 minutes	23 minutes
12x	54MBps	8 minutes	15 minutes

Standard CDs use a 780nm (infrared) laser combined with a 0.45 numerical aperture lens, whereas DVDs use a 650nm (red) laser combined with a 0.60 numerical aperture lens. Blu-ray uses a much shorter 405nm (blue-violet) laser with a 0.85 numerical aperture lens. Numerical aperture is a measurement of the light-gathering capability of a lens, as well as the focal length and relative magnification. The numerical aperture of a lens is derived by taking the sine of the maximum angle of light entering the lens. For example, the lens in a CD drive gathers light at up to a 26.7° angle, which results in a numerical aperture of SIN(26.7) = 0.45. By comparison, the lens in a DVD drive gathers light at up to a 36.9° angle, resulting in a numerical aperture of SIN(36.9) = 0.60. Blu-ray drives gather light at up to a 58.2° angle, resulting in a numerical aperture of SIN(58.2) = 0.85. Higher numerical apertures allow increasingly oblique (angled) rays of light to enter the lens and therefore produce a more highly resolved image.

The higher the aperture, the shorter the focal length and the greater the magnification. The lens in a CD drive magnifies roughly 20 times, whereas the lens in a DVD drive magnifies about 40 times. The Blu-ray lens magnifies about 60 times. This greater magnification is necessary because the distance between tracks on a BD is reduced to 0.32um, which is almost half that of a regular DVD. A comparison of BD and standard DVD is shown in Table 11.17.

Table 11.17 Comparison of BD and DVD Specifications

Disc Type	BD	DVD
Laser	405nm	650nm
Numerical aperture	0.85	0.60
Storage capacity (single layer)	25GB	4.7GB
Storage capacity (dual layer)	50GB	8.5GB
SD Video (single layer)	11.5 hours	2 hours
SD Video (dual layer)	23 hours	4 hours
HD Video (single layer)	4.5 hours	—
HD Video (dual layer)	9 hours	—
Video codecs	MPEG-4 AVC (H.264), VC-1, MPEG-2	MPEG-2
Lossless audio codecs	Linear PCM	—
Optional: MLP(TrueHD) [2-ch, 8-ch]*	Linear PCM[2-ch]	—
Lossy audio codecs	Dolby Digital Plus/DTS/Dolby Digital/ MPEG Audio	Dolby Digital MPEG Audio
Max. transfer rate	54.0Mbps	11.08Mbps
Content protection	AACS 128-bit	CSS 40-bit
Max. video resolution	1920×1080p (HDTV)	720×480p (SDTV)

Requires HDMI 1.1 or greater for 8-channel support; most home theater systems downmix to 2-channel or use a lossy codec for 5.1 or 7.1 surround audio.

Note

For more information about BD, see www.blu-raydisc.com.

HD-DVD

HD-DVD, also known as *Advanced Optical Disc* (AOD), is a defunct optical disc format originally developed by Toshiba and NEC. HD-DVD was similar to Blu-ray (but not compatible) and used blue-laser technology to achieve a higher storage capacity.

The introduction of both HD-DVD and BD in 2006 started a format war similar to the Betamax/VHS war in the 1970s. Both were incompatible, and both had supporters and detractors. Blu-ray was arguably superior from a technological standpoint, but that means little because in these situations external influences such as politics, marketing, and overall industry support decides what will become the de facto standard. By 2008, it had become clear that BD was winning in overall market share, and this prompted several HD-DVD supporters to switch to the Blu-ray camp, thus ending the war. The decline of HD-DVD started near the end of 2007 when the largest U.S. video rental company (Blockbuster) declared it would only rent BDs. Then a major blow came in January 2008, when Warner Brothers announced it would not release new movies in HD-DVD, which started an industry-wide chain reaction with several other studios following suit. The final blow came in February 2008, when Toshiba announced it would cease production of HD-DVD players, effectively ending the war once and for all.

Although a few combo Blu-ray writable/HD-DVD readable drives (which also feature backward-compatibility with standard DVD and CD media) were introduced (the first combo drives feature LG's Super Multi Blue drive technology), HD-DVD players and discs quickly disappeared from the market after 2008.

Optical Disc Formats

Optical drives can use many types of disc formats and standards. This section discusses the formats and file systems used by optical drives, so you can make sure you can use media recorded in a particular format with your drive.

CD Formats

After Philips and Sony created the Red Book CD-DA format discussed earlier in the chapter, they began work on other format standards that would allow CDs to store computer files, data, and even video and photos. These standards control how the data is formatted so that the drive can read it, and additional file format standards can then control how the software and drivers on your PC can be designed to understand and interpret the data properly. Note that the physical format and storage of data on the disc as defined in the Red Book was adopted by all subsequent CD standards. This refers to the encoding and basic levels of error correction provided by CD-DA discs. The other "books" specify primarily how the 2,352 bytes in each sector are to be handled, what type of data can be stored, how it should be formatted, and more.

All the official CD standard books and related documents can be purchased from Philips for $100— $150 each. See the Philips licensing site at www.ip.philips.com for more information.

Table 11.18 describes the various standard CD formats, which are discussed in more detail in the following sections.

Table 11.18 Compact Disc Formats

Format	Name	Introduced	Notes
Red Book	CD-DA (compact disc digital audio)	1980—by Philips and Sony	• The original CD audio standard on which all subsequent CD standards are based.
Yellow Book	CD-ROM (compact disc read-only memory)	1983—by Philips and Sony	• Specifies additional ECC and EDC for data in several sector formats, including Mode 1 and Mode 2.
Green Book	CD-i (compact disc-interactive)	1986—by Philips and Sony	• Specifies an interactive audio/video standard for non-PC-dedicated player hardware (now mostly obsolete) and discs used for interactive presentations. • Defines Mode 2, Form 1 and Mode 2, Form 2 sector formats along with inter-leaved MPEG-1 video and ADPCM audio.
CD-ROM XA	CD-ROM XA (extended architecture)	1989—by Philips, Sony, and Microsoft	• Combines Yellow Book and CD-i to bring CD-i audio and video capabilities to PCs.

Format	Name	Introduced	Notes
Orange Book	CD-R (recordable) and CD-RW (rewritable)	1989—by Philips and Sony (Part I/II) 1996—by Philips and Sony (Part III)	• Defines single-session, multisession, and packet writing on recordable discs. • Part I—CD-MO (magneto-optical, with drawn). • Part II—CD-R (recordable). • Part III—CD-RW (rewritable).
Photo-CD	CD-P	1990—by Philips and Kodak	• Combines CD-ROM XA with CD-R multisession capability in a standard for photo storage on CD-R discs.
White Book	VCD	1993—by Philips, JVC, Matsushita, and Sony	• Based on CD-i and CD-ROM XA. Stores up to 74 minutes of MPEG-1 video and ADPCM digital audio data.
Blue Book	CD EXTRA (formerly CD-Plus or enhanced music)	1999—by Philips and Sony	• Multisession format for stamped discs; used by musical artists to incorporate videos, liner notes, and other information on audio CDs.
Purple Book	CD Double-Density	2000—by Philips and Sony	• Double-density (1.3GB) versions of CD-ROM, CD-R, and CD-RW (DD-ROM, DD-R, DD-RW).
Scarlet Book	Super Audio CD	1999—by Philips and Sony	• High-capacity (4.7GiB) music disc; hybrid SA-CD discs also feature a CD-DA layer or compatibility with standard players.
DualDisc	DualDisc	2004—by Sony BMG, EMI, Universal Music Group, and Warner Music Group	• Double-sided disc; modified CD-DA format for music on one side; flip side is DVD-Video for videos and other content. Slightly thicker than normal CD or DVD media.

Red Book—CD-DA

The Red Book introduced by Philips and Sony in 1980 is the father of all compact-disc specifications because all other "books" or formats are based on the original CD-DA Red Book format. The Red Book specification includes the main parameters, audio specification, disc specification, optical stylus, modulation system, error correction system, and control and display system. The latest revision of the Red Book is dated May 1999.

For more information on the original Red Book format, refer to the section, "CDs: A Brief History."

Yellow Book—CD-ROM

The Yellow Book was published by Philips, Sony, and Microsoft in 1983 and has been revised and amended several times since. The Yellow Book standard took the physical format of the original CD-DA (or Red Book) standard and added another layer of error detection and correction to enable data to be stored reliably. It also provided additional synchronization and header information to enable sectors to be more accurately located. The Yellow Book specifies two types of sectoring—called Mode 1 (with error correction) and Mode 2—which offer different levels of error-detection and -correction schemes. Some data (computer files, for example) can't tolerate errors. However, other data, such as a video image or sound, can tolerate minor errors. By using a mode with less error-correction information, more data can be stored, but with the possibility of uncorrected errors.

In 1989, the Yellow Book was issued as an international standard by the ISO as "ISO/IEC 10149, Data Interchange on Read-Only 120mm Optical Discs (CD-ROM)." The latest version of the Yellow Book is dated May 1999.

Sector Modes and Forms

Mode 1 is the standard Yellow Book CD sector format with ECC and EDC to enable error-free operation. Each Mode 1 sector is broken down as shown in Table 11.19.

Table 11.19   Yellow Book Mode 1 Sector Format Breakdown

Yellow Book (CD-ROM) Sectors (Mode 1):	
Q+P parity bytes	784
Subcode bytes	98
Sync bytes	12
Header bytes	4
Data bytes	2,048
EDC bytes	4
Blank (0) bytes	8
ECC bytes	276
Bytes/sector RAW (unencoded)	3,234

Orange Book

The Orange Book defines the standards for recordable CDs and was announced in 1989 by Philips and Sony. The Orange Book comes in three parts. Part I describes a format called CD-MO (magneto-optical), which was to be a rewritable format but was withdrawn before any products really came to market. Part II (1989) describes CD-R, and Part III (1996) describes CD-RW. Note that originally CD-R was referred to as CD-WO (write-once), and CD-RW originally was called CD-E (erasable).

The Orange Book Part II CD-R design is known as a WORM format. After a portion of a CD-R disc is recorded, it can't be overwritten or reused. Recorded CD-R discs are Red Book and Yellow Book compatible, which means they are readable on conventional CD-DA or CD-ROM drives. The CD-R definition in the Orange Book Part II is divided into two volumes. Volume 1 defines recording speeds of 1x, 2x, and 4x the standard CD speed; the last revision, dated December 1998, is 3.1. Volume 2 defines recording speeds up to 48x the standard CD speed. The latest version released, 1.2, is dated April 2002.

Orange Book Part III describes CD-RW. As the name implies, CD-RW enables you to erase and overwrite information in addition to reading and writing. The Orange Book Part III CD-RW definition is broken into three volumes. Volume 1 defines recording speeds of 1x, 2x, and 4x the standard CD speed; the latest version, 2.0, is dated August 1998. Volume 2 (high-speed) defines recording speeds from 4x to 10x the standard CD speed; the latest version, 1.1, is dated June 2001. Volume 3 (ultra-speed) defines recording speeds from 8x to 32x; the latest version, 1.0, is dated September 2002.

Besides the capability to record on CDs, the most important feature instituted in the Orange Book specification is the capability to perform multisession recording.

Multisession Recording Overview

Before the Orange Book specification, CDs had to be written as a single session. A *session* is defined as a lead-in, followed by one or more tracks of data (or audio), followed by a lead-out. The lead-in takes up 4,500 sectors on the disc (1 minute if measured in time or about 9.2MB worth of data). The lead-in also indicates whether the disc is multisession and what the next writable address on the disc is (if the disc isn't closed). The first lead-out on a disc (or the only one if it is a single session or Disk At Once recording) is 6,750 sectors long (1.5 minutes if measured in time or about 13.8MB worth of data). If the disc is a multisession disc, any subsequent lead-outs are 2,250 sectors long (0.5 minutes in time or about 4.6MB worth of data).

A multisession CD has multiple sessions, with each individual session complete from lead-in to lead-out. The mandatory lead-in and lead-out for each session do waste space on the disc. In fact, 48 sessions would literally use up all of a 74-minute disc even with no data recorded in each session! Therefore, the practical limit for the number of sessions you can record on a disc would be much less than that.

CD-DA and older CD-ROM drives couldn't read more than one session on a disc, so that is the way most pressed CDs are recorded. The Orange Book allows multiple sessions on a single disc. To allow this, the Orange Book defines three main methods or modes of recording:

- Disk At Once (DAO)
- Track At Once (TAO)
- Packet Writing

DAO

DAO is a single-session method of writing CDs in which the lead-in, data tracks, and lead-out are written in a single operation without the writing laser ever turning off; then the disc is closed. A disc is considered closed when the last (or only) lead-in is fully written and the next usable address on the disc is not recorded in that lead-in. In that case, the CD recorder is incapable of writing any further data on the disc. Note that it is not necessary to close a disc to read it in a normal CD-ROM drive, although if you were submitting a disc to a CD-duplicating company for replication, most require that it be closed.

TAO

Multisession discs can be recorded in either TAO or Packet Writing mode. In TAO recording, each track can be individually written (laser turned on and off) within a session, until the session is closed. Closing a session is the act of writing the lead-out for that session, which means no more tracks can be added to that session. If the disc is closed at the same time, no further sessions can be added either.

The tracks recorded in TAO mode are typically divided by gaps of 2 seconds. Each track written has 150 sectors of overhead for run-in, run-out, pre-gap, and linking. A rewritable drive can read the tracks even if the session is not closed, but to read them in a non-rewritable CD-DA or CD-ROM drive, the session must be closed. If you intend to write more sessions to the disc, you can close the session and not close the disc. At that point, you could start another session of recording to add more tracks to the disc. The main thing to remember is that each session must be closed (lead-out written) before another session can be written or before a normal CD-DA or CD-ROM drive can read the tracks in the session.

Packet Writing

Packet writing is a method whereby multiple writes are allowed within a track, thus reducing the overhead and wasted space on a disc. Each packet uses four sectors for run-in, two for run-out, and one for linking. Packets can be of fixed or variable length, but most drives and packet-writing software use a fixed length because dealing with file systems that way is much easier and more efficient.

With packet writing, you use the UDF version 1.5 or later file system, which enables the CD to be treated essentially like a big floppy drive. That is, you can literally drag and drop files to it, use the copy command to copy files onto the disc, and so on. The packet-writing software and UDF file system manage everything. If the disc you are using for packet writing is a CD-R, every time a file is overwritten or deleted, the file seems to disappear, but you don't get the space back on the disc. Instead, the file system simply forgets about the file. If the disc is a CD-RW, the space is indeed reclaimed and the disc won't be full until you literally have more than the limit of active files stored there.

Unfortunately, Windows versions up through Windows XP don't support packet writing or the UDF file system directly, so drivers must be loaded to read packet-written discs, and a packet-writing application must be used to write them. Fortunately, though, these typically are included with CD-RW and DVD rewritable drives The ISOBuster data recovery program reads the contents of damaged CD, DVD, and BD discs and can also be used as a UDF reader.

Windows Vista and newer all support UDF much more thoroughly than previous Windows versions. They are able to format optical media using the Live File System (LFS—Microsoft's term for UDF 2.01), older UDF versions (1.02, 1.5), and the new UDF version 2.5, as well as Mastered. UDF 2.01 discs can be read by Windows XP or later, and they support drag-and-drop file copying on Windows 8, 7, or Vista. UDF version 1.02 is designed for use with DVD-RAM media and is supported by Windows 98 and many Apple computers. UDF version 1.5 works with Windows 2000/XP and Linux systems using kernel version 2.6 or greater. UDF version 2.5 is supported by Windows 8, Windows 7, and Vista. For Linux kernel 2.6.20 and later support of UDF version 2.5, install the UDF-2.50 patch available from http://sourceforge.net.

Note

By default, Windows Vista and newer use the LFS (UDF 2.01) to format optical discs. To choose between LFS and Mastered (copies all files at once; does not support drag-and-drop file copying), select Show Formatting Options in the Burn a Disc dialog box. To choose a different UDF version, select Show Formatting Options and then Change Version in the Burn a Disc dialog box.

Note

Windows XP also has limited CD-RW support in the form of something called IMAPI (image mastering application program interface), which enables data to be temporarily stored on the hard drive (staged) before being written to the CD in one session. Additional sessions can be written to the same disc, but a 50MB overhead exists for each session. This gives some of the appearance of packet writing, but it is not really the same thing. To read packet-written discs in the UDF 1.5 or later format, you must install a UDF reader just as with previous versions of Windows. Instead of using IMAPI, I recommend installing a third-party CD-mastering program that also includes packet-writing UDF support, such as Roxio Creator 2012 or Nero.

When you remove a packet-written disc from the drive, the packet-writing software first asks whether you want the files to be visible in all drives. If you do, you must close the session. Even if the session is closed, you can still write more to the disc later, but there is an overhead of wasted space every time you close a session. If you are going to read the disc in a rewritable drive, you don't have to close the session because it will be capable of reading the files even if the session isn't closed.

Caution

If you are not sure what type of drive will be used to read the media, I recommend closing the media. This enables users of various types of drives to read the media, although a compatible UDF reader program must be installed in some cases.

A newer standard called Mount Rainier (Mt. Rainier) adds even more capability to packet writing. With Mount Rainier, packet writing can become an official part of the operating system (OS) and the drives can support the defect management necessary to make them usable as removable storage in the real world. For more information, see the section "Mount Rainier" later in this chapter.

Note

As part of Service Pack 1, Microsoft released updates for Windows XP that add native support for the Mount Rainier standard, which supports full drag-and-drop packet writing through CD-MRW drives as well as DVD+MRW drives. Microsoft Windows 8, 7, and Vista include native support of Mount Rainier.

Photo CD

First announced back in 1990 but not available until 1992, Photo CD was a standard that used CD-R discs and drives to store photos. Although Kodak originally sold Photo CD "players" that were connected to TVs, most Photo CD users used computer-based optical drives along with software to decode and display the photos.

Perhaps the main benefit Photo CD brought to the table is that it was the first CD format to use the Orange Book Part II (CD-R) specification with multisession recordings. Additionally, the data is recorded in CD-ROM XA Mode 2, Form 2 sectors; therefore, more photo information could be stored on the disc.

Kodak's own PhotoYCC encoding format was used to store up to six resolutions for each image, as shown in Table 11.20. The x64 resolution was supported only by the Pro Photo CD master version of the service.

Table 11.20   Photo CD Resolutions

Base	Resolution (Pixels)	Description
/16	128×192	Thumbnail
/4	256×384	Thumbnail
x1	512×768	TV resolution
x4	1,024×1,536	HDTV resolution
x16	2,048×3,072	Print size
x64	4,096×6,144	Pro Photo CD master only

At a time when photo-editing software was in its infancy, the ability to select different sizes optimized for different purposes was quite useful. However, with the rise of high-speed PCs running Adobe Photoshop, Adobe Photoshop Elements, and other photo-editing programs, along with high-speed, low-cost recordable and rewritable optical drives, the Photo CD format became obsolete. Kodak discontinued development in the early twenty-first century, and third-party labs that offered the service discontinued it in 2004. Kodak still offers drivers, software, and firmware for Pro Photo CD at www.kodak.com/global/en/service/professional/products/ekn017045.jhtml.

Picture CD

As a replacement for Photo CD, Kodak offered the simpler Picture CD service. Unlike Photo CD, Picture CD uses the industry-standard JPEG file format. It uses a CD-R, with up to 40 images stored at a single medium-resolution scan of 1,024 × 1,536 pixels. This resolution is adequate for 4-inch × 6-inch and 5-inch × 7-inch prints. The images can also be made available via Kodak Gallery, where the same images are posted online and can be downloaded.

The software provided with Picture CD enables the user to manipulate images with various automatic or semiautomatic operations, but unlike Photo CD, the standard JPEG (JPG) file format used for storage enables any popular image-editing program to work with the images without conversion. Services similar to Picture CD are also offered by Fujifilm and Agfa, and some stores allow you to order Kodak Picture CD with your choice of store-brand or Kodak film processing. You can also create a Picture CD at kiosks that include a Rapid Print Scanner.

Note

By scanning your own 35mm negatives with a high-performance flatbed or dedicated film scanner, you can achieve much higher resolutions (up to 5,400 dpi optical) that support larger images sizes than what Picture CD offers. For example, a 3,200 dpi scan of a full-frame 35mm film negative has a resolution of about 2,570x4,450 pixels. By scanning negatives yourself, you can also select the quality of JPEG images and save images in other formats, such as TIFF. Some photo labs offer high-resolution film developing and scanning services if you prefer not to scan your own film.

White Book—Video CD

The White Book standard was introduced in 1993 by Philips, JVC, Matsushita, and Sony. It is based on the Green Book (CD-i) and CD-ROM XA standards and allows for storing up to 74 minutes of MPEG-1 video and ADPCM digital audio data on a single disc. The latest version (2.0) was released in April 1995. Video CD (VCD) 2.0 supports MPEG-1 compression with a 1.15Mbps bit rate. The screen resolution is 352x240 for NTSC format and 352x288 for European PAL format. In addition, it supports Dolby Pro Logic–compatible stereo sound.

You can think of VCDs as a sort of poor man's DVD format, although the picture and sound quality can actually be quite good—certainly better than VHS or most other videotape formats. You can play VCDs on virtually any PC with an optical drive using the free WMP. (Other media player applications can be used as well.) You can also play VCDs on most DVD players. Although you can create VCDs with popular DVD production programs such as Roxio Creator 2012 or Adobe Premiere Elements, prerecorded VCD media is difficult to find today, thanks to the popularity of the higher-quality (and easier to copy-protect) DVD and Blu-ray formats.

Super Video CD

The Super Video CD specification 1.0, published in May 1999, is an enhanced version of the White Book VCD specification. It uses MPEG-2 compression, an NTSC screen resolution of 480x480, and a PAL screen resolution of 480x576; it also supports MPEG-2 5.1 surround sound and multiple languages.

Most home DVD-creation programs can create VCDs or Super VCDs.

Blue Book—CD EXTRA

Manufacturers of CD-DA media were looking for a standard method to combine both music and data on a single CD. The intention was for a user to be able to play only the audio tracks in a standard audio CD player while remaining unaware of the data track. However, a user with a PC or dedicated combination audio/data player could access both the audio and the data tracks on the same disc.

The fundamental problem with nonstandard mixed-mode CDs is that if or when an audio player tries to play the data track, the result is static that could conceivably damage speakers and possibly hearing if the volume level has been turned up. Various manufacturers originally addressed this problem in different ways, resulting in a number of confusing methods for creating these types of discs, some of which still allowed the data tracks to be accidentally "played" on an audio player. In 1995, Philips and Sony developed the CD EXTRA specification, as defined in the Blue Book standard. CDs conforming to this specification usually are referred to as CD EXTRA (formerly called CD Plus or CD Enhanced Music) discs and use the multisession technology defined in the CD-ROM XA standard to separate the audio and data tracks. These are a form of stamped multisession disc. The audio portion of the disc can consist of up to 98 standard Red Book audio tracks, whereas the data track typically is composed of XA Mode 2 sectors and can contain video, song lyrics, still images, or other multimedia content. Such discs can be identified by the CD EXTRA logo, which is the standard CD-DA logo with a plus sign to the right. Often the logo or markings on the disc package are overlooked or somewhat obscure, and you might not know that an audio CD contains this extra data until you play it in a computer-based optical drive.

A CD EXTRA disc normally contains two sessions. Because audio CD players are only single-session capable, they play only the audio session and ignore the additional session containing the data. An optical drive in a PC, however, can see both sessions on the disc and access both the audio and data tracks.

Scarlet Book (SA-CD)

The Scarlet Book defines the official standard for Super Audio CD (SA-CD, also referred to as SACD) media and drives. It was codeveloped by Philips Electronics and Sony in 1999. Unlike the original Red Book CD-Audio standard, which samples music at 44.1KHz, Scarlet Book uses Direct Stream Digital encoding with a sampling rate of 2.822MHz—64 times the sampling frequency of Red Book.

Because of the higher sampling rate and the larger disc capacity necessary to store the audio (as well as SA-CD's support for video and text content), you cannot play standard or dual-layer SA-CD media in a standard CD player or computer's CD or DVD drive. Although standard SA-CD media has a capacity of 4.7GiB (the same as that of single-layer DVD), the formats are not interchangeable. SA-CD contents are copy-protected by a physical watermark known as Pit Signal Processing, which cannot be detected by standard computer DVD drives, although some high-end BD and DVD set-top boxes can also play SA-CD media.

Almost all SA-CD albums use a hybrid dual-layer design, in which the top layer stores standard CD audio playable on standard CD players and drives, and the lower layer contains the higher-density SA-CD content. Essentially, a hybrid SA-CD disc is like a CD-audio disc and a standard SA-CD disc in a single-sided disc (see Figure 11.16).

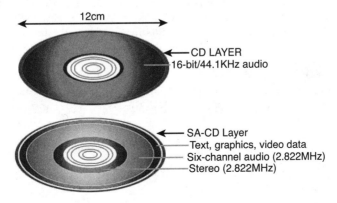

FIGURE 11.16 The structure of a hybrid SA-CD disc.

Note

Although you can play hybrid SA-CD media in standard players or computer-based drives, these devices are only playing the CD layer. To enjoy the enhanced audio of SA-CD, you must use a standalone SA-CD player.

An SA-CD disc (or the SA-CD layer of a hybrid disc) includes the stereo version of the album in its inner portion, a six-channel surround audio mix in the middle portion, and extra data such as lyrics, graphics, and video in the outer portion.

For listings of SA-CD albums and players and additional SA-CD information, see www.sa-cd.net.

DualDisc

DualDisc, introduced by a consortium of major record labels in the summer of 2004, is a combination of two different formats—music CD and DVD—on a single two-sided disc. DualDisc (sometimes referred to as Dual Disc), as the name suggests, is two discs in one: One side is a music CD, typically featuring support for surround audio or other advanced audio formats, and the other side is a DVD (using the single-layer DVD-5 format) that can include music videos, concert footage, web links, and other features.

Although DualDisc is designed to work in standard CD drives and players, it is not completely compatible with Red Book standards because the CD layer is only 0.9mm, compared to the Red Book standard of 1.1mm. To compensate for spherical aberration caused by a thinner CD layer, one method used is to increase the size of the pits on the CD side of a DualDisc, reducing playing time to 60 minutes. (Some later DualDisc media uses different methods to increase playtime.)

The total thickness of a DualDisc is 1.5mm, compared to 1.2mm for standard CD or DVD media, causing DualDiscs to be incompatible with slot-loading drives in car stereos, PCs, and mega-disc changers. Because DualDisc media is thicker than normal CD media and because the internal structure of the CD side is not compatible with Red Book standards, Philips and Sony (the co-creators of the CD format) do not use the CD logo on DualDisc media, and most DualDisc albums include warning labels that the disc will not work in slot-loaded drives and mega-disc changers and might not play in other types of players. DualDisc albums are typically packaged in CD-style jewel cases.

Caution

Some music vendors use the term *DualDisc* to refer to SA-CD as well as actual DualDisc albums. Be sure to check details of the media carefully to ensure that you can play the disc in your equipment.

Although DualDisc media, unlike SA-CD media, supports two standard formats, it is not nearly as popular as SA-CD media. Thousands of albums are available in SA-CD format, but only a few hundred are available in DualDisc format (virtually none after 2006). SA-CD provides far better audio quality than DualDisc (which provides only CD quality music), making it a better format for the serious audiophile.

DVD Formats and Standards

As with the CD standards, the DVD standards are published in reference books produced mainly by the DVD Forum, but also by other companies, such as the DVD+RW Alliance. The DVD Forum's DVD-Video and DVD-ROM standards are well established and are supported by virtually every DVD drive, regardless of age. However, rival recordable and rewritable DVD standards have been developed by both organizations. The DVD Forum developed the following standards:

- DVD-RAM (drag-and-drop file storage and erasure without any add-on software required)
- DVD-R (recordable DVD)
- DVD-RW (rewritable DVD)

After the development of DVD-RAM and DVD-R, the rival DVD+RW Alliance developed these standards:

■ DVD+RW (rewritable DVD with support for lossless linking to prevent buffer underrun)

■ DVD+R (recordable DVD)

Early rewritable DVD drives supported either DVD-RW or DVD+RW, but recent DVD rewritable drives support DVD+/-R/RW media, and so-called "Super Multi" drives using an LG-designed drive mechanism add support for DVD-RAM media as well. As a result, you can now choose the best DVD media for the task.

DVD rewritable drives support all of these media types.

The current standard and high-capacity DVD formats are shown in Table 11.21.

Table 11.21   Standard and High-Capacity DVD Formats and Capacities

Format	Data Size	Sides	Layers	Data Capacity	MPEG-2 Video Capacity
DVD-ROM Formats and Capacities					
DVD-5	120mm	Single	Single	4.7GB	2.2 hours
DVD-9	120mm	Single	Double	8.5GB	4.0 hours
DVD-10	120mm	Double	Single	9.4GB	4.4 hours
DVD-14	120mm	Double	Both	13.2GB	6.3 hours
DVD-18	120mm	Double	Double	17.1GB	8.1 hours
DVD-1	80mm	Single	Single	1.5GB	0.7 hours
DVD-2	80mm	Single	Double	2.7GB	1.3 hours
DVD-3	80mm	Double	Single	2.9GB	1.4 hours
DVD-4	80mm	Double	Double	5.3GB	2.5 hours
Recordable DVD Formats and Capacities					
DVD-R 1.0	120mm	Single	Single	3.95GB	1.9 hours
DVD-R 2.0	120mm	Single	Single	4.7GB	2.2 hours
DVD-R DL	120mm	Single	Double	8.5GB	4.0 hours
DVD-RAM 1.0	120mm	Single	Single	2.58GB	N/A
DVD-RAM 1.0	120mm	Double	Single	5.16GB	N/A
DVD-RAM 2.0	120mm	Single	Single	4.7GB	N/A
DVD-RAM 2.0	120mm	Double	Single	9.4GB	N/A
DVD-RAM 2.0	80mm	Single	Single	1.46GB	N/A
DVD-RAM 2.0	80mm	Double	Single	2.65GB	N/A
DVD-RW 2.0	120mm	Single	Single	4.7GB	N/A
DVD+RW 2.0	120mm	Single	Single	4.7GB	2.2 hours

Table 11.21   Continued

Format	Data Size	Sides	Layers	Data Capacity	MPEG-2 Video Capacity
DVD+RW 2.0	120mm	Double	Single	9.4GB	4.4 hours
DVD+R 1.0	120mm	Single	Single	4.7GB	2.2 hours
DVD+R DL	120mm	Single	Double	8.5GB	4.0 hours
High-Capacity Optical Formats and Capacities					
HD DVD-ROM*	120mm	Single	Single	15GB	4.0 hours HD
HD DVD-ROM*	120mm	Single	Double	30GB	8.0 hours HD
HD DVD-R*	120mm	Single	Single	15GB	4.0 hours HD
HD DVD-RW*	120mm	Single	Single	20GB, 32GB	5.5/8.4 hours HD
BD	120mm	Single	Single	25GB	4.5 hours HD
BD	120mm	Single	Double	50GB	9 hours HD
BD-XL	120mm	Single	Double	100/128GB	18/23 hours
CD-ROM Formats and Capacities (for Comparison)					
CD-ROM/R/RW	120mm	Single	Single	0.737GB	N/A
CD-ROM/R/RW	80mm	Single	Single	0.194GB	N/A

HD – HDTV (720p, 1080i, or 1080p resolutions)
*Obsolete format, replaced by BD

DVD drives are fully backward-compatible and as such are capable of reading CDs. When reading or playing existing CDs, the performance of most DVD drives is equivalent to a 40x or faster CD drive. DVD-rewritable drives, which also fully support CD formats, have replaced CD-RW drives at virtually every price point in both new systems and as upgrades at retail. The main reason to use CD media instead of DVD media at this point is for near-universal compatibility (especially when CD-R discs are used) with both older and recent systems.

With the development of BD, rewritable Blu-ray drives that are backward-compatible with DVD and CD media are now available. These drives are much more expensive than rewritable DVD drives; however, the cost of BD drives and media is falling rapidly.

DIVX (Discontinued Standard)

DIVX (Digital Video Express) was a short-lived proprietary DVD format developed by Digital Video Express (a Hollywood law firm) and Circuit City. It was discontinued on June 16, 1999, less than a year after it was released.

The name now lives on as an open encoding standard for DVD video. However, this encoding standard actually has no relation to the original DIVX format other than the name.

DVD Drive Compatibility

When DVD drives appeared on the market, they were touted to be fully backward-compatible with CD drives. Although that might be the case when reading commercially pressed CD-ROM discs, that was not necessarily true when reading CD-R or CD-RW media. Fortunately, the industry has responded with standards that let you know in advance how compatible your DVD drive will be. These standards are called *MultiRead* for computer-based drives and *MultiPlay* for consumer standalone devices, such as DVD-Video and CD-DA players. Refer to the section, "MultiRead Specifications."

DVD Movie Playback on a PC

DVD video discs (like those included with most of my books) are designed to be played on standard "set-top" DVD players connected to a television. You can also play them on PCs, as long as the proper hardware (for example, a DVD or BD drive) and software are installed. Unfortunately, many people are unaware that the software required to play DVDs is not included by default with most versions of Windows. This means that to play DVDs under Windows, additional software must be installed.

The first versions of Windows to have any sort of built-in DVD-playing capability were Windows 98, 98 SE (98 Second Edition), and Me (Millennium edition), all of which included a funky command-line utility called DVDPLAY.EXE. The version of DVDPLAY.EXE included with Windows 98 could only play DVDs if one of two supported hardware DVD decoders were installed, which were physically in the form of a PCI card. The DVDPLAY.EXE application included with Windows Me was the first to support a software decoder (that is, no special card required), as long as the PC had a 333MHz or faster processor. But few people used the DVDPLAY program because most retail PCs and DVD drives sold at the time included commercial DVD-playing software such as WinDVD (Intervideo/Corel) or PowerDVD (CyberLink). The first version of WMP capable of playing DVDs was WMP 8, which was included with the original release of Windows XP in 2001.

Whereas WMP 8 was included with Windows XP, later WMP versions have been available as free downloads. For example, Windows 98 SE, Me, and 2000 support up to WMP 9. (Note that the original Windows 98 release only supports up to WMP 7.1, which is not capable of playing DVDs.) Windows XP and Vista support up to WMP 11, whereas WMP 12 is included with Windows 7.

But just having WMP 8 or later isn't enough. To play DVDs, you must also have a WMP-compatible MPEG-2 decoder installed. An MPEG-2 decoder is included with Windows Vista Ultimate and Home Premium editions, but not with Vista Home Basic and Business editions. Windows 7 Home Premium, Professional, and Ultimate include a decoder, whereas Windows 7 Starter edition does not. No MPEG-2 decoder was included with Windows XP (not even Media Center Edition) or any earlier versions of Windows. Windows 8 uses the optional Windows Media Center program to play DVDs.

If an MPEG-2 decoder is the missing piece of software needed to play DVDs, where do you get one? Normally you get an MPEG-2 decoder bundled with standalone commercial DVD player programs such as WinDVD and PowerDVD; however, you can also purchase a decoder separately, or even download one for free. To see if you have a DVD decoder currently installed, you can use the Windows XP Video Decoder Checkup Utility (http://tinyurl.com/6xog7).

You can purchase standalone MPEG-2 codecs (coder/decoders) that are compatible with WMP for about $15. Microsoft has a page listing plug-ins for WMP at www.microsoft.com/windows/windowsmedia/player/plugins.aspx.

You can also get MPEG-2 codecs as part of several free "codec packs." My favorite codec packs are the K-Lite Codec Pack (I recommend the Standard or Full versions; http://codecguide.com) and the Vista/Win7 and Windows 8 Codec Packages (http://shark007.net).

To summarize: If you have the proper hardware plus a compatible MPEG-2 decoder installed, you can play DVDs using WMP 8 or later.

Optical Disc File Systems

Manufacturers of early data CDs required their own custom software to read the discs. This is because the Yellow Book specification for CD-ROM detailed only how data sectors—rather than audio sectors—could be stored on a disc and did not cover the file systems or deal with how data should be stored in files and how these should be formatted for use by PCs with different OSs. Obviously, non-interchangeable file formats presented an obstacle to industry-wide compatibility for optical disc–based applications.

In 1985–1986, several companies got together and published the High Sierra file format specification, which was the first industry-standard CD-ROM file system that made CD-ROMs universally usable in PCs. Today several file systems are used on optical discs, including the following:

- High Sierra
- ISO 9660 (based on High Sierra)
- Joliet
- UDF (Universal Disk Format)
- Mac HFS (Hierarchical File Format)
- Rock Ridge
- Mount Rainier (also known as Mt. Rainier)

Not all optical disc file system formats can be read by all OSs. Table 11.22 shows the primary file systems used and which OSs support them.

Table 11.22   Optical Disc File System Formats

CD File System	DOS/Win 3.x	Win 9x and Later	Mac OS
High Sierra	Yes	Yes	Yes
ISO 9660	Yes	Yes	Yes
Joliet	Yes[1]	Yes	Yes[1]
UDF	No	Yes[2]	Yes[2]
Mac HFS	No	No	Yes
Rock Ridge (RockRidge)	Yes[1]	Yes[1]	Yes[1]
Mount Rainier	No	Yes[3]	Yes[3]

1 A short name, such as (SHORTN~1.TXT), will be shown in place of long filenames.

2 Win 9x through XP—only if a third-party UDF reader is installed.

3 Requires Mount Rainier (also called EasyWrite) hardware and driver software (Win 9x/NT/2000); XP requires SP1 or later.

Note

The Mac HFS and UNIX Rock Ridge file systems are not supported by PC OSs such as DOS and Windows and therefore are not covered in depth here.

High Sierra

To make optical discs readable on all systems without having to develop custom file systems and drivers, it was in the best interests of all PC hardware and software manufacturers to resolve the optical file format standardization issue. In 1985, representatives from TMS, DEC, Microsoft, Hitachi, LaserData, Sony, Apple, Philips, 3M, Video Tools, Reference Technology, and Xebec met at what was then called the High Sierra Hotel and Casino in Lake Tahoe, Nevada, to create a common logical format and file structure for CD-ROMs. In 1986, they jointly published this standard as the "Working Paper for Information Processing: Volume and File Structure of CD-ROM Optical Discs for Information Exchange (1986)." This standard was subsequently referred to as the High Sierra format.

This agreement enabled all drives using the appropriate driver (such as MSCDEX.EXE supplied by Microsoft with DOS) to read all High Sierra format discs, opening the way for the mass production and acceptance of CD-ROM software publishing. Adoption of this standard also enabled disc publishers to provide cross-platform support for their software and easily manufacture discs for DOS, UNIX, and other OS formats. Without this agreement, the maturation of the optical marketplace would have taken years longer and the production of optical-based information would have been stifled.

The High Sierra format was submitted to the International Organization for Standardization (ISO). Two years later (in 1988), with several enhancements and changes, it was republished as the ISO 9660 standard. ISO 9660 was not exactly the same as High Sierra, but all drivers that would read High Sierra–formatted discs were quickly updated to handle both ISO 9660 and the original High Sierra format on which it was based.

For example, Microsoft wrote the MSCDEX.EXE (Microsoft CD-ROM extensions) driver in 1988 and licensed it to optical hardware and software vendors to include with their products. It wasn't until 1993 when MS-DOS 6.0 was released that MSCDEX was included with DOS as a standard feature. MSCDEX enables DOS to read ISO 9660–formatted (and High Sierra–formatted) discs. This driver works with the AT Attachment Packet Interface (ATAPI) or Advanced SCSI Programming Interface (ASPI) hardware-level device driver that comes with the drive. Microsoft built ISO 9660 and Joliet file system support directly into Windows 95 and later, with no additional drivers necessary.

ISO 9660

The ISO 9660 standard enabled full cross-compatibility among different computer and operating systems. ISO 9660 was released in 1988 and was based on the work done by the High Sierra group. Although based on High Sierra, ISO 9660 does have some differences and refinements. It has three levels of interchange that dictate the features that can be used to ensure compatibility with different systems.

ISO 9660 Level 1 is the lowest common denominator of all CD file systems and is capable of being read by almost every computer platform, including UNIX and Macintosh. The downside of this file system is that it is very limited with respect to filenames and directories. Level 1 interchange restrictions include the following:

- Only uppercase characters A–Z, numbers 0–9, and the underscore (_) are allowed in filenames.
- Only 8.3 characters maximum for the name.extension (based on DOS limits).
- Directory names are eight characters maximum (no extension allowed).
- Directories are limited to eight levels deep.
- Files must be contiguous.

Level 2 interchange rules have the same limitations as Level 1, except that the filename and extension can be up to 30 characters long (both added together, not including the . separator). Finally, Level 3 interchange rules are the same as Level 2 except that files don't have to be contiguous.

Note that Windows 95 and later versions enable you to use file and folder names up to 255 characters long, which can include spaces as well as lowercase and many other characters not allowed in ISO 9660. To maintain backward compatibility with DOS, Windows 95 and later associate a short 8.3 format filename as an alias for each file that has a longer name. These alias short names are created automatically by Windows and can be viewed in the Properties for each file or by using the DIR command at a command prompt. To create these alias names, Windows truncates the name to six (or fewer) characters followed by a tilde (~) and a number starting with 1 and truncates the extension to three characters. Other numbers are used in the first part if other files that would have the same alias when truncated already exist. For example, the filename This is a.test gets THISIS~1.TES as an alias.

This filename alias creation is independent of your CD drive, but it is important to know that if you create or write to a CD using the ISO 9660 format using Level 1 restrictions, the alias short names are used when files are recorded to the disc, meaning any long filenames will be lost in the process. In fact, even the alias short name will be modified because ISO 9660 Level 1 restrictions don't allow a tilde—that character is converted to an underscore in the names written to the CD.

The ISO 9660 data starts at 2 seconds and 16 sectors into the disc, which is also known as logical sector 16 of track one. For a multisession disc, the ISO 9660 data is present in the first data track of each session. This data identifies the location of the volume area—where the actual data is stored. The system area also lists the directories in this volume as the volume table of contents (VTOC), with pointers or addresses to various named areas, as illustrated in Figure 11.17. A significant difference between the CD directory structure and that of a normal hard disk is that the CD's system area also contains direct addresses of the files within the subdirectories, allowing the CD to seek specific sector locations on the spiral data track. Because the CD data is all on one long spiral track, when speaking of tracks in the context of a CD, we're actually talking about sectors or segments of data along that spiral.

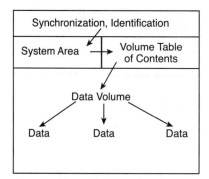

FIGURE 11.17   Basic ISO 9660 file organizational format.

To put the ISO 9660 format in perspective, the disc layout is roughly analogous to that of a floppy disk. A floppy disk has a system track that not only identifies itself as a floppy disk and reveals its density and OS, but tells the computer how it's organized (into directories, which are made up of files).

Joliet

Joliet is an extension of the ISO 9660 standard that Microsoft developed for use with Windows 95 and later. Joliet enables CDs to be recorded using filenames up to 64 characters long, including spaces and other characters from the Unicode international character set. Joliet also preserves an 8.3 alias for those programs that can't use the longer filenames.

In general, Joliet features the following specifications:

- File or directory names can be up to 64 Unicode characters (128 bytes) in length.
- Directory names can have extensions.
- Directories can be deeper than eight levels.
- Multisession recording is inherently supported.

Tip

Because Joliet supports a shorter path than Windows 9x and newer versions, you might have difficulties mastering a Joliet-format CD that contains extremely long pathnames. I recommend you shorten folder names in the file structure you create with the CD mastering software to avoid problems. Unfortunately, some CD mastering programs don't warn you about a pathname that is too long until after the burning process starts. If your CD mastering program offers an option to validate your disc structure, use this option to determine whether you need to shorten folder names. Some CD mastering programs will provide a suggested short name and shorten too-long folder names for you.

Due to backward-compatibility provisions, systems that don't support the Joliet extensions (such as older DOS systems) should still be capable of reading the disc. However, it will be interpreted as an ISO 9660 format using the short names instead.

Note

A bit of trivia: "Chicago" was the code name used by Microsoft for Windows 95. Joliet is the town outside of Chicago where Jake was locked up in the movie *The Blues Brothers*.

Universal Disk Format

UDF is a file system created by the Optical Storage Technology Association (OSTA) as an industry-standard format for use on optical media, but it can also be used by other types of removable-media drives, such as the Iomega REV drives. UDF has several advantages over the older ISO 9660 file system but is most noted because it is designed to work with packet writing, a technique for writing small amounts of data to an optical disc, treating it much like a standard magnetic drive. The UDF file system allows long filenames up to 255 characters per name. There have been several versions of UDF, with most packet-writing software using UDF 1.5 or later. Packet-writing software such as Roxio's DirectCD and Drag-to-Disc, Ahead Software's InCD, and Veritas and Sonic Solutions' DLA use the UDF file system. However, standard optical drives, drivers, and OSs such as DOS can't read UDF-formatted discs. Recordable drives can read them, but regular optical drives must conform to the MultiRead specification (see the section "MultiRead Specifications," earlier in this chapter) to be capable of reading UDF discs.

After you are sure that your drive can read UDF, you must check the OS. Most OSs can't read UDF natively—the support has to be added via a driver. Typically, such a driver is included with the software that comes with most CD-RW and rewritable DVD drives.

If you don't have a UDF reader, you can download one from the following websites:

- Get UDF Reader 2.5 for Windows XP from http://www.videohelp.com/tools/UDF_Reader.
- Get UDF Volume Reader 7.1.0.95 for Windows 9x through XP from www.roxio.com/enu/support/udf/software_updates.html.
- Get Nero AG Software's InCD Reader from the support section of www.nero.com.

After the UDF driver is installed, you do not need to take any special steps to read a UDF-formatted disc. The driver will be in the background waiting for you to insert a UDF-formatted disc.

If you are unable to read a disc written with UDF on another system, return it to the original system and close the media. This option is usually displayed as part of the Eject Settings dialog box. Closing the disc converts the filenames to Joliet format and causes them to be truncated to 64 characters.

You can download the latest (revision 2.60) version of the Universal Disk Format specification from the OSTA website at www.osta.org/specs/index.htm.

Tip

UDF discs can become unreadable for a variety of reasons, including incompatible UDF reader installed, disc not closed before removal of drive, table of contents not written due to system lockup, and so on. To recover data from UDF discs, try CD Roller (available from www.cdroller.com). It supports the most commonly used UDF versions (v1.02 through 2.01, and UDF Bridge) and also works with optical discs created by digital cameras, DVD recorders, and DVD-based camcorders. Another optical disc recovery program to consider is IsoBuster (www.isobuster.com). IsoBuster also works with BD formats.

Macintosh HFS

HFS is the file system used by the Macintosh OS. HFS can also be used on optical discs; however, if that is done, they will not be readable on a PC. A hybrid disc can be produced with both Joliet and HFS or ISO 9660 and HFS file systems, and the disc would then be readable on both PCs and Macs. In that case, the system will see only the disc that is compatible, which is ISO 9660 or Joliet in the case of PCs.

Rock Ridge

The Rock Ridge Interchange Protocol (RRIP) was developed by an industry consortium called the Rock Ridge Group. It was officially released in 1994 by the IEEE CD-ROM File System Format Working Group and specifies an extension to the ISO 9660 standard for CD-ROM that enables the recording of additional information to support UNIX/POSIX file system features. Neither DOS nor Windows includes support for the Rock Ridge extensions. However, because it is based on ISO 9660, the files are still readable on a PC and the RRIP extensions are simply ignored.

Note

An interesting bit of trivia is that the Rock Ridge name was taken from the fictional Western town in the movie Blazing Saddles.

Mount Rainier

Mount Rainier is a rewritable optical standard developed by Philips, Sony, Microsoft, and HP (Compaq). Also called EasyWrite (see Figure 11.18), Mount Rainier was designed to enable native OS support for data storage on rewritable optical discs.

FIGURE 11.18 The EasyWrite logo is used on some CD-RW and DVD+R/RW drives manufactured in 2003 and beyond that support the Mount Rainier standard.

Mount Rainier's main features include these:

- **Integral defect management**—Standard drives rely on driver software to manage defects.

- **Direct addressing at the 2KB sector level to minimize wasted space**—Standard CD-RW media uses a block size of 64KB.

- **Background formatting so that new media can be used in seconds after first insertion**—Standard CD-RW formatting can take up to 45 minutes depending on drive speed.

- **Standardized command set**—Standard software cannot work with new drives until revised command files are available.

- **Standardized physical layout**—Differences in standard UDF software can make reading media written by another program difficult.

Mount Rainier compatibility is also known as CD-MRW or DVD+MRW compatibility. Drives with the Mount Rainier or EasyWrite logo have this compatibility built in, but some existing CD-RW drives can be updated to MRW status by reflashing the firmware in the drive.

You must also have OS or application support to use Mount Rainier. Windows Vista and later have Mount Rainier support built in; Linux kernel version 2.6.2 and above also include Mount Rainier support. For Windows XP or older editions, you must use recent versions of Nero AG Software's InCD or Roxio's DirectCD or Drag-to-Disc or other Mount Rainier–compatible programs to support Mount Rainier.

Ripping/Copying Discs

All optical drives can *play* Red Book–formatted CD-DA discs, but not all optical drives can *read* CD-DA discs. The difference sounds subtle, but it is actually quite dramatic. If you enjoy music and want to use your PC to manage your music collection, the ability to read the audio data digitally is an important function for your CD (and DVD) drives because it enables you to much more easily and accurately store, manipulate, and eventually write back out audio tracks.

To record a song from CD to your hard disk, it was once necessary to play the disc at normal speed and capture the audio output as analog, hence the need for the four-wire analog audio cable connection from the rear of optical drives to your sound card. Fortunately, for several years drives have supported *digital audio extraction* (DAE). In this process, they read the digital audio sectors directly and, rather than decode them into analog signals, pass each 2,352-byte sector of raw (error-corrected) digital audio data directly to the PC's processor via the drive interface cable (ATA, SATA, SCSI, USB, or FireWire). Therefore, no digital-to-analog conversion (and back) occurs, and you essentially get the audio data exactly as it was originally recorded on the CD (within the limits of the CD-DA error-correction standards). You would have essentially extracted the exact digital audio data from the disc onto your PC.

Another term for digital audio extraction is *ripping*, so named because you can "rip" the raw audio data from the drive at full drive read speed, rather than the normal 1x speed at which you listen to audio discs. Actually, most drives can't perform DAE at their full rated speeds. Although some are faster (or slower) than others, most perform DAE at speeds from about one-half to two-thirds of their rated CD read speed. So, you might be able to extract audio data at speeds only up to 28x on a 40x rated drive. However, that is still quite a bit better than at 1x as it would be on drives that can't do DAE (not to mention skipping the conversion to analog and back to digital with the resultant loss of information).

Virtually all newer optical drives can perform digital audio extraction on music discs. How fast or accurately they do this varies from model to model. You might think any extraction (digital copy) of a given track (song) should be the same because it is a digital copy of the original; however, that is not always the case. The CD-DA format was designed to play music, not to transfer data with 100% accuracy. Errors beyond the capability of the CIRC in the CD-DA format cause the firmware in the drive to interpolate or approximate the data. In addition, time-based problems due to clock inaccuracies can occur in the drive, causing it to get slightly out of step when reading the frames in the sector (this is referred to as *jitter*). Differences in the internal software (firmware) in the drive and differences in the drivers used are other problems that can occur.

Note

When extracting (ripping) music from CDs, the default format is uncompressed WAV; however, other compressed formats such as MP3 can be used as well. Because WAV files match the high 44.1KHz sampling rate used on the CD, you have 176,400 bytes per second of sound information, which means 1 minute of music consumes nearly 10.6MB worth of space on your hard drive. MP3 compression can reduce that by a factor of 6 or more, with little to no perceptible loss in quality when maximum quality (320Kbps) sampling is used. I recommend that you rip media at maximum quality, and then reduce the media quality (and size) when synchronizing to portable devices if storage space on the portable device is an issue. MP3 is supported by all media players, while its chief rival, Windows Media Audio (WMA), is designed for playback on Windows-based systems.

"For Music Use Only" CD-R/RW Discs

According to the Audio Home Recording Act of 1992, consumer CD recordable drives and media sold specifically for recording music are required to have specific safeguards against copying discs, mainly SCMS. That means these recorders can make digital copies only from original prerecorded discs. You can copy a copy, but in that case, the data being recorded goes from digital to analog and back to digital on the second copy, resulting in a generational loss of quality.

The media for these recorders must be special as well. They work only with special discs labeled "For Music Use," "For Audio," or "For Consumer." These carry the standard Compact Disk Digital Audio Recordable logo that most are familiar with, but below that, as part of the logo, is an added line that says "For Consumer." These discs feature a special track prerecorded onto the disc, which the consumer music recorders look for. Built into the price of the AHRA-compliant media is a royalty for the music industry that this track protects. The media costs about 20%–30% more than what regular CD-R/RW media costs. If you try to use standard non-AHRA-compliant CD-R/RW discs in these drives, the drive refuses to recognize the disc. These music devices also refuse to copy data discs.

Note that this does not apply to the optical drive you have installed or attached to your PC. It does not have to be AHRA compliant, nor does it need to use AHRA-compliant "For Music Use" media, even if you are copying or recording music discs. Additionally, you can make digital copies of copies—the SCMS does not apply, either. The bottom line is that you do not have to purchase AHRA-compliant discs for the optical drives in your PC. If you do purchase such discs, despite the "For Music Use Only" designation, AHRA-compliant discs can be used in your optical drives just as regular CD-R/RW discs can be used for storing data. The extra information indicating AHRA compliance is simply ignored.

CD Copy Protection

Worries about the public copying of software and music CDs has prompted the development of copy protection techniques that attempt to make these discs uncopyable. There are different methods of protecting software CDs versus music CDs, but the end result is the same: You are prevented from making normal copies, or the copies don't work properly. In the case of music CDs, the copy protection can be quite obtrusive, adding noise to the recording, and in extreme cases preventing the disc from even playing in a PC drive.

Several copy protection schemes are available for CD-DA (digital audio) discs, ranging from the simple to the sophisticated. The most popular protection scheme for digital audio discs is called SafeAudio by Macrovision. Macrovision won't explain exactly how SafeAudio works, but it purchased the technology from a company called TTR Technologies and patents filed by TTR describe the scheme in detail. According to the patents, the disc is deliberately recorded with grossly erroneous values (bursts of noise) in both the audio data and the codes, which would typically be used to correct these errors. When the disc is read, the normal error-correction scheme fails, leaving small gaps in the music. When this happens on a standard audio CD player, the gaps are automatically bridged by circuitry or code in the player, which looks at the audio data on either side of the gap and interpolates (guesses) the missing values. The CD drive in a PC can do the same thing, so the interpolation occurs only when playing CDs in an audio player mode. However, the drive in a PC does not perform this same interpolation when "ripping" the data—that is, copying it directly to a hard drive, another CD, or some other medium. In that case, the unbridged gaps are heard as extremely loud clicks, pops, and noise. Both TTR and Macrovision claim that the interpolation that occurs when playing a SafeAudio disc is not discernable to the human ear, but many audio experts disagree. To an audiophile, the addition of any distortion or noise to the audio signal is unconscionable, plus you can't make legal backups of your music—something that is allowed by law. Because of these problems, I recommend avoiding the purchase of audio CDs containing SafeAudio or any other form of copy protection.

CD Digital Rights Management

Digital rights management (DRM) goes a step beyond standard copy protection by specifying what you can and cannot do with a recorded CD or other type of commercial media. When applied to downloaded music, for example, DRM features in audio tracks can prevent you from burning a song to CD an unlimited number of times, playing a song past a particular date, or limit the number of times you can copy a song from one PC to another.

Although the use of DRM on CD media (as opposed to downloadable audio tracks) has been rare, the Sony rootkit scandal of 2005 is a useful case to keep in mind.

Sony BMG, one of the biggest music CD distributors, introduced a controversial method of copy protection and DRM in the fall of 2005 by adding copy protection and DRM to some of its music CDs. Affected CDs used either XCP (Extended Copy Protection, developed by First 4 Internet, now known as Fortium Technologies, Inc.) or MediaMax CD-3 (developed by SunnComm).

These programs limited the user's ability to work freely with the songs (as can be done with normal music CDs), and, worse yet, were installed on PCs without the user being notified. The type of installer Sony used is called a *rootkit*, which is a program that hides its presence from the OS and makes it easier for worms and other malware to attack the system.

After security and privacy advocates attacked Sony's use of DRM and rootkits without adequate notice to music purchasers, Sony introduced a rootkit removal tool and eventually recalled all albums in 2006, settling a lawsuit with the Federal Trade Commission. Although Sony's attempt to use DRM was botched by its failure to inform customers that CDs contained DRM software and the software did not provide a way for users to block installation, it's possible that DRM features that avoid Sony's mistakes may be used on CD and other types of media in the future.

DVD and Blu-ray Copy Protection

DVD-Video discs employ several levels of protection that are mainly controlled by the DVD Copy Control Association (DVD CCA) and a third-party company called Macrovision (they developed SafeDisk).

This protection typically applies only to DVD-Video discs, not DVD-ROM software. So, for example, copy protection might affect your ability to make backup copies of *The Matrix*, but it won't affect a DVD encyclopedia or other software application distributed on DVD-ROM discs.

Note that every one of these protection systems has been broken, so with a little extra expense or the correct software, you can defeat the protection and make copies of your DVDs either to other digital media (hard drive, optical drive, flash drive, and so on) or to analog media (such as a VHS or other tape format).

A lot of time and money are wasted on these protection schemes, which can't really foil the professional bootleggers willing to spend the time and money to work around them. But they can make it difficult for the average person to legitimately back up his expensive media.

The four main protection systems used with DVD-Video discs are as follows:

- Regional Playback Control (RPC)
- Content Scrambling System (CSS)
- Analog Protection System (APS)
- ProtectDisc

Blu-ray video discs are also copy protected, using one of the following schemes:

- Advanced Access Content System (AACS)
- BD+
- BD-ROM Mark
- Cinevia
- BD-ROM Mark

Caution

The Digital Millennium Copyright Act (DMCA) signed into law in 1998 prohibits the breaking of copy-protection schemes or the distribution of information (such as tools, website links, and so forth) on how to break these schemes.

CSS

The CSS provides the main protection for DVD-Video discs. It wasn't until this protection was implemented that the Motion Picture Association of America (MPAA) agreed to release movies in the DVD format, which is the main reason the rollout of DVD had been significantly delayed.

CSS originally was developed by Matsushita (Panasonic) and is used to digitally scramble and encrypt the audio and video data on a DVD-Video disc. Descrambling requires a pair of 40-bit (5-byte) keys (numeric codes). One of the keys is unique to the disc, whereas the other is unique to the video title set (VTS file) being descrambled. The disc and title keys are stored in the lead-in area of the disc in an encrypted form. The CSS scrambling and key writing are carried out during the glass mastering procedure, which is part of the disc manufacturing process.

You can see this encryption in action if you put a DVD disc into a DVD-ROM drive on a PC, copy the files to your hard drive, and then try to view the files. The files are usually called VTS_xx_yy.VOB (video object), where xx represents the title number and yy represents the section number. Typically, all the files for a given movie have the same title number and the movie is spread out among several 1GB or smaller files with different section numbers. These VOB files contain both the encrypted video and audio streams for the movie interleaved together. Other files with an IFO extension contain information used by the DVD player to decode the video and audio streams in the VOB files. If you copy the VOB and IFO files onto your hard drive and try to click or play the VOB files directly, you either see and hear scrambled video and audio or receive an error message about playing copy-protected files.

This encryption is not a problem if you use a CSS-licensed player (either hardware or software) and play the files directly from the DVD disc. All DVD players, whether they are consumer standalone units or software players on your PC, have their own unique CSS unlock key assigned to them. Every DVD video disc has 400 of these 5-byte keys stamped onto the disc in the lead-in area (which is not usually accessible by programs) on the DVD in encrypted form. The decryption routine in the player uses its unique code to retrieve and unencrypt the disc key, which is then used to retrieve and unencrypt the title keys. CSS is essentially a three-level encryption that originally was thought to be secure but has proven otherwise.

In October 1999, a 16-year-old Norwegian programmer was able to extract the first key from one of the commercial PC-based players, which allowed him to very easily decrypt disc and title keys. A now-famous program called DeCSS was then written that can break the CSS protection on any DVD video title and save unencrypted VOB files to a hard disk that can be played by any MPEG-2 decoder program. Needless to say, this utility (and others based on it) has been the cause of much concern in the movie industry and has caused many legal battles over the distribution and even links to this code on the Web. Do a search on DeCSS for some interesting legal reading.

As if that weren't enough, in March 2001, two MIT students published an incredibly short (only seven lines long!) and simple program that can unscramble CSS so quickly that a movie can essentially be unscrambled in real time while it is playing. They wrote and demonstrated the code as part of a two-day seminar they conducted on the controversial Digital Millennium Copyright Act, illustrating how trivial the CSS protection really is.

ProtectDisc

The newest DVD copy protection system is called ProtectDisc. Its DVD-Video version changes the standard structure of the disc to prevent copying. Unfortunately, a DVD movie created using ProtectDisc cannot be viewed with PC-based player programs, such as WMP or WinDVD.

Cinavia

Ciniavia (www.cinavia.com/languages/english/index.html) is the company responsible for copy-protection for BD movies. If you attempt to create a copy of a BD disc, Cinavia displays messages, such as "Copying Stopped. The content being copied is protected by Cinavia and is not authorized for copying from this device." Similar messages are displayed when attempting to play back an unauthorized copy. Cinavia can also mute audio from unauthorized copies. The original name for Cinavia was Verance Copy Management System for Audiovisual Content (VCMS/AV).

Is Copy Protection "Unbreakable?"

Despite the claims of "unbreakable" copy protection, ProtectDisc's method, like the others discussed here, was quickly overcome. Similarly, enterprising users have figured out how to bypass Cinavia's copy protection methods (which apply only to BD set-top boxes, not to BD drives in PCs). As with other copy-protection schemes, legitimate users who don't try to "beat the system" often wind up being victimized—in the case of ProtectDisk, by being unable to use a PC to watch the movie.

RPC

Regional playback was designed to allow discs sold in specific geographical regions of the world to play only on players sold in those same regions. The idea was to allow a movie to be released at different times in different parts of the world and to prevent people from ordering discs from regions in which the movie had not been released yet.

Eight regions are defined in the RPC standard. Discs (and players) usually are identified by a small logo or label showing the region number superimposed on a world globe. Multiregion discs are possible, as are discs that are not region locked. If a disc plays in more than one region, it has more than one number on the globe. The regions are as follows:

- **Region Code 1**—United States, Canada, U.S. Territories, Bermuda.
- **Region Code 2**—Japan, Western Europe, South Africa, and the Middle East.
- **Region Code 3**—Southeast Asia and East Asia.
- **Region Code 4**—Australia, New Zealand, Pacific Islands, Central America, Mexico, South America, and the Caribbean.
- **Region Code 5**—Eastern Europe (east of Poland and the Balkans), Indian subcontinent, Africa, North Korea, and Mongolia.
- **Region Code 6**—China and Tibet.
- **Region Code 7**—Reserved for future use.
- **Region Code 8**—International venues including aircraft and cruise ships.
- **Region Code All**—Has all flags set, allowing the disc to be played in any region or player. Sometimes called Region Code 0.

The region code is embedded in the hardware of DVD video players. Most players are preset for a specific region and can't be changed. Some companies that sell the players modify them to play discs from all regions; these are called *region-free* or *code-free* players. Some newer discs have an added region code enhancement (RCE) function that checks to see whether the player is configured for multiple or all regions and then, if it is, refuses to play. Most newer region-free modified players know how to query the disc first to circumvent this check as well.

DVD-ROM drives used in PCs originally did not have RPC in the hardware, placing that responsibility instead on the software used to play DVD video discs on the PC. The player software would usually lock the region code to the first disc that was played and then from that point on, play only discs from that region. Reinstalling the software enabled the region code to be reset, and numerous patches were posted on websites to enable resetting the region code even without reinstalling the software. Because of the relative ease of defeating the region-coding restrictions with DVD-ROM drives, starting on January 1, 2000, all DVD-ROM and rewritable DVD drives were required to have RPC-II, which embeds the region coding directly into the drive.

RPC-II (or RPC-2) places the region lock in the drive and not in the playing or MPEG-2 decoding software. You can set the region code in RPC-II drives up to five times total, which basically means you can change it up to four times after the initial setting. Usually, the change can be made via the player software you are using, or you can download region-change software from the drive manufacturer. Upon making the fourth change (which is the fifth setting), the drive is locked on the last region set.

Region Codes Used by BD

A different region code scheme that divides the world into three regions is used by BD:

- Region A includes North America, Central America, South America, Korea, Japan, and South East Asia.
- Region B includes Europe, the Middle East, Africa, Australia, and New Zealand.
- Region C includes Russia, India, China, and the rest of the world.

A BD without a region code can be played by players with any region code.

Optical Drive Performance Specifications

Many factors in a drive can affect performance, and several specifications are involved. Typical performance figures published by manufacturers are the data transfer rate, the access time, the internal cache or buffers (if any), and the interface the drive uses. This section examines these specifications.

CD Data Transfer Rate

The data transfer rate for a CD drive tells you how quickly the drive can read from the disc and transfer to the host computer. Normally, transfer rates indicate the drive's capability for reading large, sequential streams of data.

Transfer speed is measured two ways. The one most commonly quoted with optical drives is the "x" speed, which is defined as a multiple of the particular standard base rate. For example, CD drives transfer at 153.6KBps according to the original standard. Drives that transfer twice that are 2x, 40 times that are 40x, and so on. DVD drives transfer at 1,385KBps at the base rate, whereas drives that are 20 times faster than that are listed as 20x. Note that because almost all faster drives feature CAV, the "x" speed usually indicated is a maximum that is seen only when reading data near the outside (end) of a disc. The speed near the beginning of the disc might be as little as half that, and of course average speeds are somewhere in the middle.

With today's optical drives supporting multiple disc formats, multiple read and write specifications are given for each form of media a drive supports.

CD Drive Speed

Because CDs originally were designed to record audio, the speed at which the drive reads the data had to be constant. To maintain this constant flow, CD data is recorded using a technique called *constant linear velocity* (CLV).

In the quest for greater performance, drive manufacturers began increasing the speeds of their drives by making them spin more quickly. A drive that spins twice as fast was called a 2x drive, one that spins four times faster was called 4x, and so on. This was fine until about the 12x point, where drives were spinning discs at rates from 2,568 rpm to 5,959 rpm to maintain a constant data rate. At higher speeds than this, it became difficult to build motors that could change speeds (spin up or down) as quickly as necessary when data was read from different parts of the disc. Because of this, most drives rated faster than 12x spin the disc at a fixed rotational, rather than linear speed. This is termed CAV because the angular velocity (or rotational speed) remains a constant.

CAV drives are also generally quieter than CLV drives because the motors don't have to try to accelerate or decelerate as quickly. A drive (such as most rewritables) that combines CLV and CAV technologies is referred to as *Partial-CAV* or *P-CAV*. Most writable drives, for example, function in CLV mode when burning the disc and in CAV mode when reading. Table 11.23 compares CLV and CAV.

Table 11.23   CLV Versus CAV Technology Quick Reference

	CLV (Constant Linear Velocity)	**CAV (Constant Angular Velocity)**
Speed of CD rotation	Varies with data position on disc. Faster on inner tracks than on outer tracks.	Constant.
Data transfer rate	Constant.	Varies with data position on disc. Faster on outer tracks than on inner tracks.
Average noise level	Higher.	Lower.

CD-ROM drives have been available in speeds from 1x up to 52x. Most nonrewritable drives up to 12x were CLV; most drives from 16x and up are CAV. With CAV drives, the disc spins at a constant speed, so track data moves past the read laser at various speeds, depending on where the data is physically located on the CD (near the inner or outer part of the track). This also means that CAV drives read the data at the outer edge (end) of the disk more quickly than data near the center (beginning). This allows for some misleading advertising. For example, a 12x CLV drive reads data at 1.84MBps no matter where that data is on the disc. On the other hand, a 16x CAV drive reads data at speeds up

Table 11.24 CD-ROM Drive Speeds and Transfer Rates

Advertised CD-ROM Speed (Max. if CAV)	Time to Read 74-Minute CD if CLV	Time to Read 80-Minute CD if CLV	Transfer Rate (Bps) (Max. if CAV)	Actual CD-ROM Speed Minimum in CAV	Minimum Transfer Rate if CAV (Bps)
1x	74.0	80.0	153,600	0.4x	61,440
2x	37.0	40.0	307,200	0.9x	138,240
4x	18.5	20.0	614,400	1.7x	261,120
6x	12.3	13.3	921,600	2.6x	399,360
8x	9.3	10.0	1,228,800	3.4x	522,240
10x	7.4	8.0	1,536,000	4.3x	660,480
12x	6.2	6.7	1,843,200	5.2x	798,720
16x	4.6	5.0	2,457,600	6.9x	1,059,840
20x	3.7	4.0	3,072,000	8.6x	1,320,960
24x	3.1	3.3	3,686,400	10.3x	1,582,080
32x	2.3	2.5	4,915,200	13.8x	2,119,680
40x	1.9	2.0	6,144,000	17.2x	2,641,920
48x	1.5	1.7	7,372,800	20.7x	3,179,520
50x	1.5	1.6	7,680,000	21.6x	3,317,760
52x	1.4	1.5	7,987,200	22.4x	3,440,640
56x	1.3	1.4	8,601,600	24.1x	3,701,760

Each column in Table 11.24 is explained here. Column 1 indicates the advertised drive speed. This is a constant speed if the drive is CLV (most 12x and lower) or a maximum speed only if CAV.

Columns 2 and 3 indicate how long it would take to read a full disc if the drive was CLV. For CAV drives, those figures would be longer because the average read speed is less than the advertised speed. The fourth column indicates the data transfer rate, which for CAV drives would be a maximum figure only when reading the end of a disc.

Columns 3–6 indicate the actual minimum "x" speed for CAV drives, along with the minimum transfer speed (when reading the start of any disc) and an optimistic average speed (true only when reading a full disc; otherwise, it would be even lower) in both "x" and byte-per-second formats.

Columns 7–8 indicate the maximum linear speeds the drive will attain, in both meters per second and miles per hour. CLV drives maintain those speeds everywhere on the disc, whereas CAV drives reach those speeds only on the outer part of a disc.

Columns 9–12 indicate the rotational speeds of a drive. The first of these shows how fast the disc spins when being read from the start; this applies to either CAV or CLV drives. For CAV drives, the figure is constant no matter what part of the disc is being read. The last column shows the maximum rotational speed if the drive were a CLV type. Because most drives over 12x are CAV, these figures are mostly theoretical for the 16x and faster drives.

to 16x (2.46MBps) on the outer part of the disc, but it also reads at a much lower speed of only 6.9x (1.06MBps) when reading the inner part of the disc (that is the part they don't tell you). On average, this would be only 11.5x, or about 1.76MBps. In fact, the average is actually overly optimistic because discs are read from the inside (slower part) out, and an average would relate only to reading completely full discs. The real-world average could be much less than that.

Table 11.24 contains data showing CD drive speeds along with transfer rates and other interesting data. This information also applies to DVD or BD drives when CDs are used.

Average CD-ROM Speed if CAV	Average Transfer Rate if CAV (Bps)	Maximum Linear Speed (mps)	Maximum Linear Speed (mph)	Rotational Speed Min. if CLV Max. if CAV (rpm)	Rotational Speed Max. if CLV (rpm)
0.7x	107,520	1.3	2.9	214	497
1.5x	222,720	2.6	5.8	428	993
2.9x	437,760	5.2	11.6	856	1,986
4.3x	660,480	7.8	17.4	1,284	2,979
5.7x	875,520	10.4	23.3	1,712	3,973
7.2x	1,098,240	13.0	29.1	2,140	4,966
8.6x	1,320,960	15.6	34.9	2,568	5,959
11.5x	1,758,720	20.8	46.5	3,425	7,945
14.3x	2,196,480	26.0	58.2	4,281	9,931
17.2x	2,634,240	31.2	69.8	5,137	11,918
22.9x	3,517,440	41.6	93.1	6,849	15,890
28.6x	4,392,960	52.0	116.3	8,561	19,863
34.4x	5,276,160	62.4	139.6	10,274	23,835
35.8x	5,498,880	65.0	145.4	10,702	24,828
37.2x	5,713,920	67.6	151.2	11,130	25,821
40.1x	6,151,680	72.8	162.8	11,986	27,808

Vibration problems can cause high-speed drives to drop to lower speeds to enable reliable reading. Your disc can become unbalanced, for example, if you apply a small paper label to its surface to identify the disc. For this reason, many of the faster optical drives come with autobalancing or vibration-control mechanisms to overcome these problems. The only drawback is that if they detect a vibration, they slow down the disc, thereby reducing the transfer rate performance.

Most recent optical drives use Z-CLV (zoned CLV) or P-CAV (partial CAV) designs, which help increase average performance while keeping rotational speeds under control.

DVD Drive Speed

As with CDs, DVDs rotate counterclockwise (as viewed from the reading laser) and typically are recorded at a constant data rate called CLV. Therefore, the track (and thus the data) is always moving past the read laser at the same speed, which originally was defined as 3.49 meters per second (or 3.84 mps on dual-layer discs). Because the track is a spiral that is wound more tightly near the center of the disc, the disc must spin at varying rates to maintain the same track linear speed. In other words, to maintain a CLV, the disk must spin more quickly when the inner track area is being read and more slowly when the outer track area is being read. The speed of rotation in a 1x drive (3.49 meters per second is considered 1x speed) varies from 1,515 rpm when reading the start (inner part) of the track down to 570 rpm when reading the end (outer part) of the track.

Single-speed (1x) DVD drives provide a data transfer rate of 1.385MBps, which means the data transfer rate from a DVD at 1x speed is roughly equivalent to a 9x CD (1x CD data transfer rate is 153.6KBps, or 0.1536MBps). This does not mean, however, that a 1x DVD drive can read CDs at 9x rates: DVD drives actually spin at a rate that is just under three times faster than a CD drive of the same speed. So, a 1x DVD drive spins at about the same rotational speed as a 2.7x CD drive. Many DVD drives list two speeds; for example, a DVD drive listed as a 16x/40x would indicate the performance when reading DVDs/CDs, respectively.

Table 11.25   DVD Speeds and Transfer Rates

Advertised DVD-ROM Speed (Max. if CAV)	Time to Read Single-Layer DVD if CLV	Time to Read Dual Layer DVD if CLV	Transfer Rate (Bytes/sec) (Max. if CAV)	Actual DVD Speed Minimum in CAV	Minimum Transfer Rate if CAV (Bytes/sec)	Average DVD Speed if CAV
1x	56.5	51.4	1,384,615	0.4x	553,846	0.7x
2x	28.3	25.7	2,769,231	0.8x	1,107,692	1.4x
4x	14.1	12.8	5,538,462	1.7x	2,353,846	2.9x
6x	9.4	8.6	8,307,692	2.5x	3,461,538	4.3x
8x	7.1	6.4	11,076,923	3.3x	4,569,231	5.7x
10x	5.7	5.1	13,846,154	4.1x	5,676,923	7.1x
12x	4.7	4.3	16,615,385	5.0x	6,923,077	8.5x
16x	3.5	3.2	22,153,846	6.6x	9,138,462	11.3
20x	2.8	2.6	27,692,308	8.3x	11,492,308	14.2
24x	2.4	2.1	33,230,769	9.9x	13,707,692	17.0
32x	1.8	1.6	44,307,692	13.2x	18,276,923	22.6
40x	1.4	1.3	55,384,615	16.6x	22,984,615	28.3
48x	1.2	1.1	66,461,538	19.9x	27,553,846	34.0
50x	1.1	1.0	69,230,769	20.7x	28,661,538	35.4

Each column in Table 11.25 is explained here.

Column 1 indicates the advertised drive speed. This is a constant speed if the drive is CLV or a maximum speed only if CAV (most DVD drives are CAV).

Columns 2 and 3 indicate how long it would take to read a full disc (single- or dual-layer) if the drive were CLV. For CAV drives, those figures are longer because the average read speed is less than the advertised speed. The fourth column indicates the data transfer rate, which for CAV drives is a maximum figure seen only when reading the end of a disc.

Columns 4–8 indicate the actual minimum "x" speed for CAV drives, along with the minimum transfer speed (when reading the start of any disc) and an optimistic average speed (true only when reading a full disc; otherwise, it's even lower) in both "x" and byte-per-second formats.

As with CD drives, DVD drive manufacturers began increasing the speeds of their drives by making them spin more quickly. A drive that spins twice as fast was called a 2x drive, a drive that spins four times as fast was 4x, and so on. At higher speeds, it became difficult to build motors that could change speeds (spin up or down) as quickly as needed when data was read from different parts of the disc. Because of this, faster DVD drives spin the disc at a fixed rotational speed rather than linear speed. This is termed CAV because the angular velocity (or rotational speed) remains a constant.

The faster drives are useful primarily for data, not video. Having a faster drive can reduce or eliminate the pause during layer changes when playing a DVD video disc, but having a faster drive has no effect on video quality.

DVD drives are available in speeds up to 20x or more, but because virtually all are CAV, they actually achieve the rated transfer speed only when reading the outer part of a disc. Table 11.25 shows the data rates for DVD drives reading DVDs and how that rate compares to a CD drive.

Average Transfer Rate if CAV (Bytes/sec)	Maximum Linear Speed (m/sec)	Maximum Linear Speed (rpm)	Single-Layer Rot. Speed Min. if CLV Max. if CAV (rpm)	Single Layer Rot. Speed Max. if CLV (rpm)	Usual Transfer Rate When Reading CD-ROMs
969,231	3.5	7.8	570	1,515	2.7x
1,938,462	7.0	15.6	1,139	3,030	5.4x
3,946,154	14.0	31.2	2,279	6,059	11x
5,884,615	20.9	46.8	3,418	9,089	16x
7,823,077	27.9	62.5	4,558	12,119	21x
9,761,538	34.9	78.1	5,697	15,149	27x
11,769,231	41.9	93.7	6,836	18,178	32x
15,646,154	55.8	124.9	9,115	24,238	43x
19,592,308	69.8	156.1	11,394	30,297	54x
23,469,231	83.8	187.4	13,673	36,357	64x
31,292,308	111.7	249.8	18,230	48,476	86x
39,184,615	139.6	312.3	22,788	60,595	107x
47,007,692	167.5	374.7	27,345	72,714	129x
48,946,154	174.5	390.3	28,485	75,743	134

Columns 9 and 10 indicate the maximum linear speeds the drive attains, in both meters per second and miles per hour. CLV drives maintain those speeds everywhere on the disc, whereas CAV drives reach those speeds only on the outer part of a disc.

Columns 11 and 12 indicate the rotational speeds of a drive. The first of these shows how quickly the disc spins when being read from the start. This applies to either CAV or CLV drives. For CAV drives, the figure is constant no matter what part of the disc is being read. The second of these two columns shows the maximum rotational speed if the drive were a CLV type. Because most faster drives are CAV, these figures are mostly theoretical for the faster drives.

Column 13 shows the speed the drive would be rated if it were a CD drive. This is based on the rotational speed, not the transfer rate. In other words, a 12x DVD drive would perform as a 32x CD drive when reading CDs. Most DVD drives list their speeds when reading CDs in the specifications. Due to the use of PCAV (Partial CAV) designs, some might have higher CD performances than the table indicates.

Access Time

The access time for an optical drive is measured the same way as for PC hard disk drives. In other words, the access time is the delay between the drive receiving the command to read and its actual first reading of a bit of data. Access rates quoted by many manufacturers are an average taken by calculating a series of random reads from a disc.

Buffer/Cache

Most optical drives include internal buffers or caches of memory installed onboard. These buffers are actual memory chips installed on the drive's circuit board that enable it to stage or store data in larger segments before sending it to the PC. A typical buffer can range from 2MB up to 8MB or more (depending on the drive). Generally, faster rewritable drives come with more buffer memory to handle the higher transfer rates.

Direct Memory Access and Ultra-DMA

Busmastering PATA controllers use Direct Memory Access (DMA) or Ultra-DMA transfers to improve performance and reduce CPU utilization. Virtually all modern PATA drives support Ultra-DMA utilization.

To determine whether your system has this feature enabled, open the Device Manager and check the properties sheet for the controller to view its capabilities.

To enable DMA transfers if your motherboard and drives support it, open the Device Manager and then open the properties sheet for the controller or drive. Click the Settings or Advanced Settings tab, and make sure DMA is enabled if available. Depending on which version of Windows you are using, some have the DMA setting in the controller properties and others have it with the individual drives.

Repeat the same steps to enable DMA transfers for any additional hard drives and ATAPI CD-ROM drives in your computer. Restart your computer after making these changes.

Note

If your system hangs after you enable this feature, you must restart the system in Safe mode and uncheck the DMA box.

If your drive is a parallel ATA model that supports any of the Ultra-DMA (also called Ultra-ATA) modes, you need to use an 80-conductor cable. Most motherboards refuse to enable Ultra-DMA modes faster than 33MBps if an 80-conductor cable is not detected. Note that these cabling issues affect only parallel ATA drives. If your drives are Serial ATA (SATA) models, these cabling issues do not apply.

Depending on your Windows version and when your motherboard chipset was made, you must install chipset drivers to enable Windows to properly recognize the chipset and enable DMA modes. Virtually all motherboard chipsets produced since 1995 provide busmaster ATA support. Most of those produced since 1997 also provide UltraDMA support for up to 33MHz (Ultra-ATA/33) or 66MHz (Ultra-ATA/66) speed operation. Still, you should make sure that DMA is enabled to ensure you are benefiting from the performance it offers. Enabling DMA can dramatically improve DVD performance, for example.

Interface

The drive's interface is the physical connection of the drive to the PC's expansion bus. The interface is the data pipeline from the drive to the computer, and you shouldn't minimize its importance. Four types of interfaces are normally used for attaching an optical drive to your system:

■ **SATA (Serial ATA)**—The SATA interface is the same interface used by most recent computers for connecting their hard disk drives. With many recent systems featuring support for as little as one PATA (Parallel ATA) drive, but support for eight or more SATA drives, most optical drive vendors are now producing SATA versions of their drives.

Compared to similar PATA optical drives, SATA drives feature equal performance but are easier to install because it is not necessary to jumper the drive for master/slave or cable select.

- **PATA (Parallel AT Attachment)**—The PATA interface is the same interface most older computers use to connect to their hard disk drives. PATA is sometimes also referred to as ATA (AT Attachment) or IDE (Integrated Drive Electronics).

- **USB port**—Universal serial bus (USB) is normally used for external drives and provides benefits such as hot-swappability, which is the capability to be plugged in or unplugged without removing the power or rebooting the system. USB 2.0 is the most common, but most recent systems also include two or more USB 3.0 ports, and USB 3.0 optical drives are now available from many vendors.

- **FireWire (IEEE 1394)**— A few external optical drives are available with a FireWire (also called IEEE 1394 or i.LINK) interface instead of, or in addition to, USB 2.0/3.0.

▶▶ See the sections in Chapter 14, "Universal Serial Bus (USB)," **p. 704** and "IEEE 1394 (FireWire or i.LINK)," **p. 718**.

Some older drives were available in external versions using SCSI/ASPI (Small Computer System Interface/Advanced SCSI Programming Interface) or parallel printer port interfaces, but these are obsolete.

Loading Mechanism

Three distinctly different mechanisms exist for loading a disc into an optical drive: the tray, caddy, and slot.

Most current drives use a tray-loading mechanism. This is similar to the mechanism used with a stereo system. Because you don't need to put each disc into a separate caddy, this mechanism is much less expensive overall. However, it also means that you must handle each disc every time you insert or remove it.

Some tray drives can't operate in a vertical (sideways) position because gravity prevents proper loading and operation. Check to see whether the drive tray has retaining clips that grab the hub of the disc or tabs that fold in or flip over from the outside of the tray to retain the disc. If so, you can run the drive in either a horizontal or a vertical position.

The main advantage of the tray mechanism over the others is cost, and that is a big factor. Most drives today use the tray mechanism for handling discs.

Caddy systems have been used on several types of optical drives. The caddy system requires that you place the disc into a special caddy, which is a sealed container with a metal shutter. The caddy has a hinged lid you open to insert the disc, but after that the lid remains shut. When you insert the caddy containing the disc into the drive, the drive opens a metal shutter on the bottom of the caddy, allowing access to the disc by the laser.

The drawbacks to the caddy system include the expense and the inconvenience of having to put the discs into the caddies. Caddy-loaded drives were popular in early CD drives, but few were made or sold after 1994.

Some drives use a slot-loading mechanism, identical to that used in most automotive players. This is convenient because you just slip the disc into the slot, where the mechanism grabs it and draws it inside. Some drives can load several discs at a time this way, holding them internally inside the drive and switching discs as access is required.

The primary drawback to this type of mechanism is that if a jam occurs, it can be much more difficult to repair because you might have to remove the drive to free the disc. Another drawback is that slot-loading drives usually can't handle the smaller 80mm discs, card-shaped discs, or other modified disc physical formats or shapes, such as DualDisc.

Other Drive Features

Although drive specifications are of the utmost importance, you should consider other factors and features when evaluating optical drives. Besides quality of construction, the presence of drive sealing or self-cleaning lenses bears scrutiny when you are making a purchasing decision.

Dirt is your drive's biggest enemy. Dust or dirt, when it collects on the lens portion of the mechanism, can cause read errors or severe performance loss. Many manufacturers seal off the lens and internal components from the drive bay in airtight enclosures. Other drives, although not sealed, have double dust doors—one external and one internal—to keep dust from the inside of the drive. All these features help prolong the life of your drive.

Some drives are sealed, which means no air flows through the chamber in which the laser and lens reside. Always look for sealed drives in harsh industrial or commercial environments. In a standard office or home environment, it is probably not worth the extra expense.

To determine whether a particular drive is sealed, you may need to view FAQ or support questions considering drive cleaning; this information may not always be listed on the drives' spec sheet.

If the laser lens gets dirty, so does your data. The drive will spend a great deal of time seeking and reseeking or will finally give up. Lens-cleaning discs are available, but built-in cleaning mechanisms are now included on virtually all good-quality drives. This might be a feature you'll want to consider, particularly if you work in a less-than-pristine work environment or have trouble keeping your desk clean, let alone your drive laser lens. You can clean the lens manually, but it is generally a delicate operation requiring that you partially disassemble the drive. Also, damaging the lens mechanism by using too much force is pretty easy to do. Because of the risks involved, in most cases I do not recommend the average person disassemble and try to manually clean the laser lens.

Note

Before using a cleaning disc, check the drive vendor's recommendations to determine whether this method of maintenance is recommended. Some vendors do not recommend the use of cleaning discs because the felt pads or brushes used can scratch the laser lens.

How to Reliably Record Optical Discs

Six major factors influence your ability to create a working disc: interface type, drive buffer size, the location and condition of the data you want to record, the recording speed, whether the computer is performing other tasks while trying to create the disc, and the features available in your recording software. If you are having problems, there are some things you can check. The simplest thing you can do to ensure trouble-free recording is to make sure the drive has some form of buffer underrun protection. The data buffer in the drive holds information read from the original data source, so that if a pause in data reading occurs, there's less of a possibility of a buffer underrun until the on-drive buffer runs empty. Current drives with buffer underrun protection virtually eliminate this problem, no matter what size buffer is in the drive. Some mastering programs might offer an option to disable buffer underrun protection. However, you should leave it enabled at all times unless you are using an old drive that does not support this feature.

Tip

If you have problems with reliable disc creation at the drive's maximum speed, try using a lower speed. Your mastering job will take twice as long, but it's better to create a working disc more slowly than ruin a blank more quickly.

Buffer Underruns and Buffer Underrun Protection

Whenever a drive writes data to a disc in either DAO or TAO mode, it writes to the spiral track on the disc, alternating on and off to etch the pattern into the raw media. Originally, it was not possible for a drive to realign where it starts and stops writing like a hard drive can; after it started writing, it was necessary to continue until finished with the track or disc. Otherwise, the recording (and disc if it is not rewritable) would be ruined, creating a useless disc often referred to as a "coaster." To avoid this problem, the recording software, in combination with your system hardware, must be capable of delivering a consistent stream of data to the drive while it's writing.

Sanyo was the first to develop a technology that eliminates buffer underruns once and for all. It calls the technology BURN-Proof (BURN stands for *buffer underrun*), which sounds a little confusing (some people thought it prevented any writing on discs), but in practice it has proven to be excellent. Other technologies were developed by various vendors, including Ricoh's JustLink, Waste-Proof and Safeburn from Yamaha, SMART-Burn from Lite-On, and Superlink from Mediatek, among others. For a number of years, all recordable/rewritable drives have included some type of buffer underrun protection. Buffer underrun protection technology involves having a special chipset in the drive that monitors the drive buffer. When it anticipates that a buffer underrun might occur (the buffer is running low on data), it temporarily suspends the recording until more data fills the buffer. When the buffer is sufficiently restocked, the drive then locates exactly where the recording left off earlier and restarts recording again immediately after that position.

According to the Orange Book specification, gaps between data in a recording must not be more than 100 milliseconds in length. The buffer underrun technology can restart the recording with a gap of 40–45 milliseconds or less from where it left off, which is well within the specification. These small gaps are easily compensated for by the error correction built into the recording, so no data is lost.

If both your drive and recording software supports buffer underrun protection, you can multitask—do other things while burning discs—without fear of producing a bad recording.

Booting from a Floppy Disk with Optical Drive Support

To learn more about setting up a floppy disk with optical drive support, see Chapter 11 of *Upgrading and Repairing PCs*, 19th Edition, included on the DVD packaged with this book.

Bootable Optical Discs—El Torito

If your system BIOS is a version dated from 1998 or later, most likely it has "El Torito" support, which means it supports booting from a bootable optical disc. The El Torito name comes from the Phoenix/IBM Bootable CD-ROM Format Specification, which was actually named after the El Torito restaurant located near the Phoenix Software offices where the two engineers who developed the standard ate lunch. What El Torito means for the PC is the capability to boot from optical discs, which opens several possibilities, including creating bootable rescue discs, booting from newer OS discs when installing to new systems, creating bootable diagnostics and test discs, and more.

To create a bootable optical disc, ideally you need a burning application that allows the creation of bootable discs. Additionally, in some cases you need a bootable floppy that contains the drivers to support your CD drive in DOS mode (sometimes called real-mode drivers). The best source for these drivers (if needed) is a Windows 98 or Me startup floppy, which can be generated by any Windows 98 or Me system. Windows 98/Me startup disks can be used because these have the DOS-level CD-ROM support already configured and installed. If you don't have access to such a system to generate the disk, you can download one from www.bootdisk.com.

To create a bootable disc, simply follow the directions included with your burning application. Programs such as Nero and Roxio Media Creator make the creation of bootable discs relatively easy.

LightScribe and LabelFlash

There are two popular direct disc labeling systems, called LightScribe and LabelFlash. Hewlett-Packard (HP) developed the LightScribe direct disc labeling system in 2005 as a method for labeling CD (and later, single-layer DVD and, most recently, DL DVD) discs without the need to print labels or use an inkjet printer equipped to print on CD or DVD media.

The top surface of a LightScribe disc is coated with a reactive dye that changes color when exposed to laser light. LightScribe uses the recording laser to etch text and graphics on the top surface of special LightScribe media. After the user records the disc, the user flips the disc over and runs a LightScribe program to transfer the desired design to the top of the disc. To prevent fading and surface damage, LightScribe discs should be stored in cases away from light when not in use.

LabelFlash was announced in October 2005 by Yamaha and Fujifilm. LabelFlash is based on the DiscT@2 ("disk tattoo") technology originally developed by Yamaha for writing text and graphics into the unused portion of the data side of a CD-R or DVD R disc. However, LabelFlash can also write to the top side of media when the user flips the disc, just as with LightScribe. The top side of LabelFash media is designed to be more resistant to damage and to produce better image quality than LightScribe because the LabelFlash dye is 0.6mm below the disc surface. However, LabelFlash labeling only works with specially designed DVD media, while LightScribe labeling is compatible with specially designed CD as well as DVD media.

The main drawback of either system is that they take up to half an hour or more to fully label a single disc. Another drawback is that both LightScribe and LabelFlash require drives, media, and software that support the specific system. For an updated list of products supporting these systems, visit the LightScribe (www.lightscribe.com) or LabelFlash (http://labelflash.jp) website.

Table 11.26 summarizes the differences between LightScribe and LabelFlash labeling technologies.

Table 11.26   LightScribe and LabelFlash Comparison

Labeling Technology/Feature	LightScribe	LabelFlash
Creates designs on unused data side of media	No	Yes
Creates designs on label side of supported media	Yes	Yes
Available media types	DVD+R, DVD-R, CD-R	DVD-R, DVD+R
Disc label surface colors available	Gold, multicolor (Green, Blue, Orange, Red, Yellow)	Blue
Design color	Dark	Light

Troubleshooting Optical Drives

Failure Reading Any Disc

If your drive fails to read a disc, try the following solutions:

- Check for scratches on the disc data surface.
- Check the drive for dust and dirt; use a cleaning disc.

- Make sure the drive shows up as a working device in System Properties. Check the drive's power and data cables if the drive is not listed.
- Try a disc that you know works.
- Restart the computer (the magic cure-all).
- Remove the drive from Device Manager in Windows, and allow the system to redetect the drive.

Failure to Read CD-R/RW Discs in CD-ROM or DVD Drive

If your CD-ROM or DVD drive fails to read CD-R and CD-RW discs, keep the following in mind:

- Some old 1x CD-ROM drives can't read CD-R media. Replace the drive with a newer, faster, cheaper model.
- Many early-model DVD drives can't read CD-R, CD-RW media; check compatibility.
- The CD-ROM drive must be MultiRead compatible to read CD-RW because of the lower reflectivity of the media; replace the drive.
- If some CD-Rs but not others can be read, check the media color combination to see whether some color combinations work better than others; change the brand of media.
- Packet-written CD-Rs (from Adaptec DirectCD or Drag to Disc and backup programs) can't be read on MS-DOS/Windows 3.1 CD-ROM drives because of the limitations of the operating system.
- Sometimes, older drives can't read the pits/lands created at faster speeds. Record the media at a slower speed.
- If you are trying to read a packet-written CD-R created with DirectCD or Drag to Disc on a CD-ROM drive, reinsert the media into the original drive, eject the media, and select the option Close to Read on Any Drive.
- Download and install a UDF reader compatible with the packet-writing software used to create the CD-RW on the target computer. If you are not sure how the media was created, use ISO Buster, which is available from www.isobuster.com, to read UDF discs and copy media from damaged discs.

Failure to Read a Rewritable DVD in DVD-ROM Drive or Player

If your DVD-ROM or DVD player fails to read a rewritable DVD, try the following solutions:

- Reinsert DVD-RW media into the original drive and finalize the media. Make sure you don't need to add any more data to the media if you use a first-generation (DVD-R 2x/DVD-RW 1x) drive because you must erase the entire disc to do so. You can unfinalize media written by second-generation DVD-R 4x/DVD-RW 2x drives. See your DVD-RW disc-writing software instructions or help file for details.
- Reinsert DVD+RW media into the original drive and change the compatibility setting to emulate DVD-ROM. See the section "DVD+RW and DVD+R," earlier in this chapter, for details.
- Write a single-layer disc and retry if the media is dual-layer. Most DVD-ROM drives can't read DL media.
- Make sure the media contains more than 521MB of data. Some drives can't read media that contains a small amount of data.

Failure to Create a Writable DVD

If you can't create a writable DVD but the drive can be used with CD-R, CD-RW, or rewritable DVD media, try the following solutions:

- Make sure you are using the correct media. +R and -R media can't be interchanged unless the drive is a DVD R/RW dual-mode drive.

- Be sure you select the option to create a DVD project in your mastering software. Some disc-mastering software defaults to the CD-R setting.

- Select the correct drive as the target. If you have both rewritable DVD and rewritable CD drives on the same system, be sure to specify the rewritable DVD drive.

- Try a different disc.

- Contact the mastering software vendor for a software update.

Failure Writing to CD-RW or DVD-RW 1x Media

If you can't write to CD-RW or DVD-RW 1x media, try the following solutions:

- Make sure the media is formatted. Use the format tool provided with the UDF software to prepare the media for use.

- If the media was formatted, verify it was formatted with the same or compatible UDF program. Different packet-writing programs support different versions of the UDF standard. I recommend you use the same UDF packet-writing software on the computers you use or use drives that support the Mount Rainier standard.

- Make sure the system has identified the media as CD-RW or DVD-RW. Eject and reinsert the media to force the drive to redetect it.

- Contact the packet-writing software vendor for a software update.

- Know that the disc might have been formatted with Windows XP's own limited CD-writing software (which uses the CDFS instead of UDF) instead of a UDF packet-writing program. Erase the disc with Windows XP after transferring any needed files from the media; then format it with your preferred UDF program.

- Contact the drive vendor for a firmware update. See "Updating the Firmware in an Optical Drive," later in this chapter.

PATA Optical Drive Runs Slowly

If your PATA drive performs poorly, consider the following items:

- Check the cache size in the Performance tab of the System Properties control panel in Windows XP. Select the quad-speed setting (largest cache size).

- Check to see whether the drive is set as the slave to your hard disk; move the drive to the secondary controller if possible.

- Make sure your PIO (Programmed I/O) or UDMA mode is set correctly for your drive in the BIOS. Check the drive specs and use autodetect in BIOS for the best results. (Refer to Chapter 5, "BIOS.")

- Check that you are using busmastering drivers on compatible systems; install the appropriate drivers for the motherboard's chipset and the OS in use. Refer to the section, "Direct Memory Access and Ultra-DMA."

■ With Windows 9x, open the System Properties control panel and select the Performance tab to see whether the system is using MS-DOS Compatibility Mode for CD-ROM drive. If all ATA drives are running in this mode, see www.microsoft.com and query on "MS-DOS Compatibility Mode" for a troubleshooter. If only the CD-ROM drive is in this mode, see whether you're using CD-ROM drivers in CONFIG.SYS and AUTOEXEC.BAT. Remove the lines containing references to the CD-ROM drivers (don't actually delete the lines but instead REM them), reboot the system, and verify that your CD-ROM drive still works and that it's running in 32-bit mode. Some older drives require at least the CONFIG.SYS driver to operate.

Problems Burning Discs Using Windows Built-In Recording

Windows XP's built-in CD-writing feature works only on drives that are supported by Windows XP. To install the latest updates for Windows XP, including updates to the CD-writing feature, use Windows Update. Microsoft Knowledgebase article 320174 discusses an update to the CD-writing feature. Search the Microsoft website for other solutions.

If you are using third-party writing applications, you may prefer to disable Windows' built-in writing feature. This feature is enabled or disabled with Windows Explorer. Open the drive's properties sheet Recording tab and clear the Enable CD/DVD Recording check box to disable recording, or click the empty box to enable recording.

If you have problems writing media or using your CD or DVD drive in Windows, see Microsoft Knowledgebase article 314060 for solutions.

Tip

If you are unable to create discs with Windows Vista and you have a USB flash memory drive connected to your computer, eject the flash drive and try the burn again.

Trouble Reading CD-RW Discs on CD-ROM

If you can't read CD-RW discs in your CD-ROM, try the following solutions:

■ Check the vendor specifications to see whether your drive is MultiRead compliant. Some are not.

■ If your drive is MultiRead compliant, try the CD-RW disc on a known-compliant CD-ROM drive (a drive with the MultiRead feature).

■ Insert CD-RW media back into the original drive and check it for problems with the packet-writing software program's utilities.

■ Insert CD-RW media back into the original drive and use the right-click Eject command in My Computer or Windows Explorer to properly close the media.

■ Create a writable CD or DVD to transfer data to a computer that continues to have problems reading rewritable media.

Trouble Reading CD-R Discs on DVD Drive

If your DVD drive can't read a CD-R disc, check to see that the drive is MultiRead2 compliant because noncompliant DVDs can't read CD-R media. All current DVD drives support reading CD-R media.

Trouble Making Bootable Discs

If you are having problems creating a bootable disc, try these possible solutions:

- Check the contents of the bootable floppy disk from which you copied the boot image. To access the entire contents of a disc, a bootable floppy must contain CD-ROM drivers, AUTOEXEC.BAT, and CONFIG.SYS.

- Use the ISO 9660 format. Don't use the Joliet format because it is for long-filename CDs and can't boot.

- Check your system's BIOS for boot compliance and boot order; the optical drive should be listed first.

Trouble Reading BD Media or Viewing BD Movies

If you are having problems reading BD media, check the following:

- You must have a codec for BD (Blu-ray) media installed. These codecs are not included in Windows but might be provided by BD drive vendors or by BD movie playback and creation programs.

- Clean the data side of your BD disc. See the next section, "Caring for Optical Media," for details.

If you are able to read BD media but can't play back BD movies, check the following:

- Replace drivers for your BD drive and video card. In most cases, newer drivers are better. Note that sometimes you might need to use older drivers than those installed for better results.

- Switch to a different BD media playback program. Use a trial version if available before purchasing a different program to ensure compatibility.

Caring for Optical Media

Some people believe that optical discs and drives are indestructible compared to their magnetic counterparts. Although optical discs are more reliable than the now-obsolete floppy disks, modern optical discs are far less reliable than modern hard drives. Reliability is the bane of any removable media, and optical discs are no exceptions.

By far the most common causes of problems with optical discs and drives are scratches, dirt, and other contamination. Small scratches or fingerprints on the bottom of the disc should not affect performance because the laser focuses on a point inside the actual disc, but dirt or deep scratches can interfere with reading a disc.

To remedy this type of problem, you can clean the recording surface of the disc with a soft cloth, but be careful not to scratch the surface in the process. The best technique is to wipe the disc in a radial fashion, using strokes that start from the center of the disc and emanate toward the outer edge. This way, any scratches will be perpendicular to the tracks rather than parallel to them, minimizing the interference they might cause. You can use any type of solution on the cloth to clean the disc, so long as it will not damage plastic. Most window cleaners are excellent at removing fingerprints and other dirt from the disc and don't damage the plastic surface.

If your disc has deep scratches, you can often buff or polish them out. A commercial plastic cleaner such as that sold in auto parts stores for cleaning plastic instrument cluster and tail-lamp lenses is good for removing these types of scratches. This type of plastic polish or cleaner has a mild abrasive that polishes scratches out of a plastic surface. Products labeled as cleaners usually are designed for more serious scratches, whereas those labeled as polishes are usually milder and work well as a final buff after using the cleaner. Try using the polish alone if the surface is not scratched deeply. You can use the SkipDR device made by Digital Innovations to make the polishing job easier.

Most people are careful about the bottom of the disc because that is where the laser reads, but at least for CDs, the top is actually more fragile! This is because the lacquer coating on top of a CD is thin, normally only 6–7 microns (0.24–0.28 thousandths of an inch). If you write on a CD with a ball point pen, for example, you will press through the lacquer layer and damage the reflective layer underneath, ruining the disc. Also, certain types of markers have solvents that can eat through the lacquer and damage the disc. You should write on discs only with felt tip pens that have compatible inks, such as the Sharpie and Staedtler Lumocolor brands, or other markers specifically sold for writing on discs, such as Maxell's DiscWriter pens. In any case, remember that scratches or dents on the top of the disc are more fatal than those on the bottom. It's also important to keep in mind that many household chemicals (and even certain beverages), if spilled on an optical disc, can damage the coating and cause the material to crack or flake off. This, of course, renders the media useless.

Read errors can also occur when dust accumulates on the read lens of your drive. You can try to clean out the drive and lens with a blast of "canned air" or by using a drive cleaner (which you can purchase at most stores that sell audio CDs).

If you are having problems reading media with an older drive and firmware upgrades are not available or did not solve the problem, consider replacing the drive. With new high-speed drives with read/write support available for well under $50, it does not make sense to spend any time messing with an older drive that is having problems. In almost every case, it is more cost-effective to upgrade to a new drive (which won't have these problems and will likely be much faster) instead.

If you have problems reading a particular brand or type of disk in some drives but not others, you might have a poor drive/media match. Use the media types and brands recommended by the drive vendor.

If you are having problems with only one particular disc and not the drive in general, you might find that your difficulties are in fact caused by a defective disc. See whether you can exchange the disc for another to determine whether that is indeed the cause.

Updating the Firmware in an Optical Drive

Just as updating the motherboard BIOS can solve compatibility problems with CPU and memory, support, USB ports, and system stability, upgrading the firmware in an optical drive can also solve problems with media compatibility, writing speed, and digital audio extraction from scratched discs, and it can even prevent potentially fatal mismatches between media and drives.

Determining Whether You Might Need a Firmware Update

If you encounter any of the following issues, a firmware update might be necessary:

- Your drive can't use a particular type of media, or it performs much more slowly with one type of media than other types/brands of media.
- Your drive can't play some types of burned discs or movies.
- Your writing software doesn't recognize the drive as a rewritable drive.
- You want to use faster media than what the drive was originally designed to use.
- Your BD drive can't play back some BD movies.

Because any firmware update runs a risk of failure and a failed firmware update can render your drive useless (I've seen it happen), you shouldn't install firmware updates casually. However, as the preceding examples indicate, in many cases an upgrade is recommended.

Because many rewritable drives have special characteristics, disc-burning programs may require updates to work. Get the update from the software vendor, or use the software provided with the drive.

Determining Which Drive Model and Firmware Are Installed

Before you can determine whether you need a firmware update for your rewritable drive, you need to know your drive model and which firmware version it's using. This is especially important if you use a drive that is an OEM product produced by a vendor other than the one that packaged the drive for resale.

To determine the firmware revision using the Windows Device Manager, follow this procedure:

1. Right-click My Computer/Computer and select Properties.
2. Click the Device Manager tab.
3. Click the plus sign (+) next to DVD/CD-ROM in the list of device types.
4. Double-click the rewritable drive icon to display its properties sheet.
5. With older Windows versions, click the Settings tab; the firmware version and drive name will be displayed.
6. On Windows XP or later, click the Details tab and select Hardware Ids. The firmware revision is usually displayed with several underscores on either side of it as part of the hardware IDs listed. For example, my Lite-On SHW-160P6S DVD drive uses firmware version PS0C, displayed as _____PS0C_____.

After you have this information, you can go to your rewritable drive vendor's website and see whether a firmware update is available and what the benefits of installing the latest version would be.

Installing New Drive Firmware

Generally speaking, the firmware update procedure works like this. (Be sure to follow the particular instructions given for your drive.)

1. If the firmware update is stored as a Zip file, you need to use an unzipping program or the integrated unzipping utility found in some versions of Windows to uncompress the update to a folder. Some vendors ship firmware updates as RAR files. (RAR is a Linux compressed archive; it can be opened by many uncompression utilities for Windows.)
2. If the drive maker provides a readme file, be sure to read it for help and troubleshooting. If the update file is an EXE file, it might display a readme file as part of step 3.
3. Double-click the EXE file to start the update process. Be sure to leave the system powered on during the process, which can take 2–3 minutes.
4. Follow the vendor's instructions for restarting your system.
5. After you restart your system, the computer might redetect the drive and assign it the next available drive letter. If the drive letter has changed, you can use the Computer Management service in Windows 2000 or later to reassign the correct drive letter to the drive.

Troubleshooting Firmware Updates

If you have problems performing a rewritable drive firmware update, check the vendor's readme file or website for help. In addition, here's a tip I've found useful: If the firmware update fails to complete, there might be interference from programs that control the drive, such as packet-writing programs (InCD, DirectCD) or the built-in Windows disc-writing feature. To disable resident software, restart the computer in Safe Mode and retry the update. Restart the system normally after the update is complete.

Video Hardware

Display Adapters and Monitors

Although the monitor (or video display) is as vital to a PC's user interface as the mouse and keyboard, it is actually a latecomer to computing. Before CRT (cathode ray tube) monitors came into general use, the teletypewriter was the standard computer interface—a large, loud device that printed the input and output characters on a roll of paper. Early personal computers often used nothing more than a panel of blinking light-emitting diodes (LEDs) for a display.

The first monitors used on computers displayed only text in a single color (usually green), but to users at the time they were a great improvement, allowing real-time display of input and output data. Over time, color displays were introduced, screen sizes increased, and LCD technologies moved from the portable computer to the desktop. The latest trends reflect the increasing convergence of entertainment and computer technologies.

Although modern video hardware is much more sophisticated than that of the past, you should still be careful when selecting video hardware for your computer. A poor display can cause eyestrain or otherwise significantly diminish the experience of using your PC.

The video subsystem of a PC consists of two main components:

- **Monitor (or video display)**—The monitor is a display device usually based on an LCD or LED backlit panel, but it may also use CRT, plasma, DLP, or organic LED (OLED) technology.

- **Display adapter (also called the video card, graphics adapter, accelerated processing unit (APU) or graphics processing unit [GPU])**—Although this often refers to an adapter card plugged into a slot, the video adapter circuitry might also be built into the motherboard, included as part of the motherboard's chipset, or built into the CPU itself. Although it sounds strange, the circuitry is still called an adapter or card even if it is fully integrated into the motherboard, chipset, or processor.

This chapter explores the range of PC video display adapters on the market today and the monitors that work with them.

Note

The term *video*, as it is used in this context, does not necessarily imply the existence of a moving image, such as on a television screen. Any circuitry that feeds signals to a monitor or display is a video display adapter, regardless of whether it is used with applications that display moving images, such as multimedia or videoconferencing software.

For this reason, video cards are sometimes referred to as *graphics cards* or *display adapters*.

Video Display Adapters

A video display adapter (aka video card) provides the interface between your computer and your monitor and transmits the signals that appear as images on the display. Throughout the history of the PC, there has been a succession of standards for video hardware that represents a steady increase in screen resolution, color depth, and performance. The following list of standards can serve as an abbreviated history of PC video-display technology:

- MDA (Monochrome Display Adapter)
- HGC (Hercules Graphics Card)
- CGA (Color Graphics Adapter)
- EGA (Enhanced Graphics Adapter)
- VGA (Video Graphics Array)
- SVGA (Super VGA)
- XGA (Extended Graphics Array) and beyond

IBM pioneered most of these standards, but other manufacturers of compatible PCs adopted and enhanced them as well. Today, IBM no longer sets standards for the PC business (it sold its PC business to Lenovo in 2005), and most of these standards are obsolete.

Today's VGA and later video adapters can also handle most older software written for CGA, EGA, and other obsolete graphics standards. This enables you to use many, if not most, older graphics software (such as games and educational programs) on your current system.

High-definition (16:9 aspect ratio) displays were originally developed for HDTVs but are also available for laptops, desktops, tablets, media players, and smartphones. These standards and resolutions include:

nHD (one-ninth of FHD, resolution of 640×360)

qHD (one quarter of FHD, resolution of 960×540)

HD (1280×720, also known as 720p)

FHD (full HD, 1920×1080, also known as 1080p)

QHD (Quad HD, resolution of 2560×1440)

QFHD (Quad Full HD, resolution of 3840×2160)

UHD (Ultra HD, resolution of 7680×4320)

Video Adapter Types

A monitor requires a source of input. The signals that run to your monitor come from one or more video display adapters in the system.

There are four basic types of video display adapters:

- **Discrete plug-in video cards**—These cards require the use of an expansion slot but provide the highest possible level of features and performance.

- **Discrete video on the motherboard**—The same discrete circuitry that can be found on a video card can also be directly built in or mounted on the motherboard. This is how high-end video is installed in modern laptops and some older desktop systems; however, modern desktops normally use either discrete video on a plug-in card or motherboard chipset or processor integrated video.

- **Motherboard chipset integrated video**—This is video circuitry integrated into the motherboard chipset. Because it shares the system random access memory (RAM) and other components, it provides an economical solution that also uses less power (ideal for laptops).

- **Processor integrated video**—This is video circuitry integrated into the processor, either as a separate die within the processor package or directly in the processor die. This form of integrated video also shares the system RAM and requires a motherboard with specific chipsets and video interface connectors on-board. Because chipset or processor-based integrated video shares the system RAM and other components, it has the lowest cost of any video solution. Performance is generally lower than that of a separate card-based adapter, especially for 3D gaming or other graphics-intensive applications. Resolution and color-depth options are also more limited than those available with add-on video cards. Because it is economical on power, integrated video is used in many laptops for improved battery life. Many desktop systems with integrated video also allow the installation of a discrete video plug-in card as an upgrade. AMD processors with integrated video are collectively referred to as APUs (advanced processing units). Intel refers to its processors with integrated video as EPGs (Embedded Processor Graphics).

The term *video adapter* applies to either discrete or integrated video circuitry. The term *graphics adapter* is essentially interchangeable with *video adapter* because all video cards developed, except the original IBM monochrome display adapter (MDA), can display graphics and text.

Note

AMD uses the RADEON brand name for consumer-level video products, and FirePro for professional-level workstation video products.

Integrated Video/Motherboard Chipsets

Although built-in video has been a staple of low-cost computing for a number of years, until the late 1990s, most motherboard-based video simply mounted discrete video components on the motherboard. The performance and features of discrete video are essentially the same whether it is soldered into the motherboard or plugged in via an expansion card. In most cases the built-in discrete video can be upgraded by adding a video card. Some older motherboard-based discrete video implementations also had provisions for memory upgrades.

However, in recent years, the move toward increasing integration on the motherboard has led to the development of motherboard chipsets that include video support as part of the chipset design. In effect, the motherboard chipset takes the place of most of the discrete video card components and uses a portion of main system memory as video memory. The use of main system memory for video memory is often referred to as *unified memory architecture* (UMA), and although this memory-sharing method was also used by some built-in video that used its own chipset, it has become much more common with the rise of integrated motherboard chipsets.

Silicon Integrated Systems (SiS) pioneered chipsets with integrated video in 1996 and 1997 with its SiS5510 and SiS5596 chipsets for laptop and desktop systems, respectively. In 1997, Cyrix Semiconductor (now owned by VIA Technologies) introduced the MediaGX, which was the first to build both graphics and chipset functions into a PC-compatible CPU. National Semiconductor and later AMD developed improved versions of the MediaGX known as the Geode GX series.

Intel introduced motherboard chipsets with integrated graphics in 1999, starting with its 810 chipset for the Pentium III and Celeron processors. The 810 (code-named Whitney) heralded the beginning of widespread industry support for this design and the beginning of Intel's dominance in the graphics market. Intel later followed the release of the 810 series (810 and 810E) with the 815 series for the Pentium III and Celeron, most of which also feature integrated video.

Since then, Intel has offered versions of both desktop and mobile chipsets with integrated graphics and has become the world's largest supplier of graphics chips. This may sound strange because most people think of NVIDIA and AMD (thanks to its ownership of ATI) when it comes to graphics. Although NVIDIA and AMD may dominate in the high-end discrete graphics chip market, the market for lower-cost desktop and laptop systems with integrated graphics is larger than that for discrete graphics. Table 12.1 shows graphics chip market share data from JPR (Jon Peddie Research). These figures include graphics integrated into chipsets and processors, as well as discrete graphics chips.

Table 12.1   Graphics Chip Market Share 2009–2012

Vendor	Q2 2012	Q2 2011	Q4 2010	Q4 2009
Intel	62.0%	55.00%	52.5%	51.1%
NVIDIA	14.8%	20.2%	22.5%	26.5%
AMD	22.7%	24.5%	24.2%	21.7%
VIA/S3	0.5%	0.6%	0.8%	0.7%
Matrox	0.04%	0.9%	0.1%	0.0%
Total	100.0%	100.0%	100.0%	100.0%

Table 12.2 shows the types and features for the integrated graphics available in Intel motherboard chipsets over the years. Most Core i-series processors include on-package graphics, so that more recent Intel chipsets no longer include integrated graphics support.

Table 12.2   Intel Chipset Integrated Video

Processor Family	Chipset	Video Type	Features
PII, PIII, Celeron	810, 815	3D with Direct AGP	Basic 2D and 3D acceleration.
PII, PIII, Celeron	845	Extreme Graphics	Supports alpha blending, fog, anisotropic filtering, hardware motion compensation, and advanced textures.
PII, PIII, Celeron	865	Extreme Graphics 2	Enhanced version of Extreme Graphics, adding better memory management, zone rendering, and faster pixel and texturing rendering.

Processor Family	Chipset	Video Type	Features
P4, Celeron	910, 915	GMA 900	An enhanced version of Extreme Graphics 2, adding support for most DirectX 9 features (does not support vertex shaders), optional dual-display support (requires ADD2 card), and support for widescreen LCD panels.
P4, PD, Celeron	945	GMA 950	A faster version of GMA 900 with support for DirectX 9.0c (Windows Aero capable), Shader Model 2.0, and Open GL 1.4 + Extensions.
Core 2, PD, P4	946, Q963, Q965	GMA 3000	Based on GMA 950. Adds execution units that can perform vertex and pixel shading for 3D graphics or video processing for video play-back.
Core 2, P-dual	G31, G33, Q33, Q35	GMA 3100	Based on GMA 3000, but with reduced clock rates for somewhat lower performance and power consumption.
Core 2, P-dual, PD	G965	GMA X3000	Substantial redesign of GMA 3000 despite having a similar name. Includes support for DirectX 9.0c, Shader Model 3.0, hardware T&L (Transform & Lighting), OpenGL 1.5, hardware-based VC-1 decode, and Clear Video Technology for better video playback.
Core 2, P-dual, PD	GL960, GM965	GMA X3100	Enhanced version of GMA X3000 for mobile applications with upgraded support for DirectX 10 and Shader Model 4.0.
Core 2, P-dual, PD	G35	GMA X3500	Enhanced version of GMA X3000 for desktop applications with upgraded support for DirectX 10, Shader Model 4.0, and OpenGL 2.0.
Core2 Duo/Quad, P-dual	G41, G43, Q43, Q45	GMA X4500	High-performance version of GMA X3500 with added support for DisplayPort.
Core2 Duo/Quad, P-dual	G45, GM45	GMA X4500HD	Same as GMA X4500 but includes hardware accelerated VC-1 and AVC decode, allowing 1080p high-definition video playback (Blu-ray disc [BD] movies).

PII – Pentium II	*P4 – Pentium 4*	*PD – Pentium D*
PIII - Pentium III	*P-dual – Dual-Core Pentium*	*GMA = Graphics Media Accelerator*

Most other chipset vendors supporting Intel processors have also made versions with integrated graphics. Table 12.3 provides a reference to the most popular third-party integrated graphics chipsets for Intel Pentium 4 and later processors.

Table 12.3   Third-Party Chipsets with Integrated Video for Intel Processors

Processor Family	Vendor	Chipset	Video Type	Features
P4	ATI	IGP 330, IGP 340	RADEON VE (based on RADEON 7000)	DirectX 7, dualhead, DVD Playback
P4	ATI	9100 IGP, 9100 Pro IGP, 9000 Pro IGP	RADEON 9200 with pipelines reduced to two	DirectX 8.1, dualhead
P4	ATI	RS400, RC410	RADEON X300	DirectX 8.0, Open GL 2.0; RS400 also supports PCIe x16 slot
Core 2, PD, P4, Celeron D	NVIDIA	nForce 610i	GeForce 7050	DirectX 9.0SM3, DVI with HDCP
Core 2, PD, P4, Celeron D	NVIDIA	nForce 630i	GeForce 7100, 7150	DirectX 9.0SM3, dualhead, HDMI, DVI with HDCP
Core 2, PD, P4, Celeron D	NVIDIA	GeForce 9300 mGPU	GeForce 9300	DirectX 10, HDMI, VGA, DL-DVI, dual-head, Hybrid SLI, PhysX
Core 2, PD, P4, Celeron D	NVIDIA	GeForce 9400 mGPU	GeForce 9400	DirectX 10, HDMI, VGA, DL-DVI, dual-head, Hybrid SLI, PhysX
P4	VIA	P4M266	S3 Graphics ProSavage8 3D	DirectX 7 without hardware T&L
Core2, P4	VIA	PM800, P4M800 Pro	S3 UniChrome Pro	DirectX 7 without hardware T&L

PII = Pentium II
PIII = Pentium III
P4 = Pentium 4
P-dual = Dual-Core Pentium
PD = Pentium D

Thanks in part to AMD's takeover of ATI in late 2006 and AMD's encouragement of third-party chipset support for its 32-bit and 64-bit processors, there are many AMD and third-party chipsets with integrated video for AMD processors. Table 12.4 overviews the video features of chipsets from AMD and NVIDIA.

Table 12.4   Chipsets with Integrated Video (IGPU) for 64-Bit AMD Processors

Processor Family	Vendor	Chipset	Video Type	Features
Athlon 64, Phenom, Sempron	AMD	690G	RADEON X1250	DirectX 9 SM2 without hardware vertex processing; HDMI and VGA
Athlon 64, Phenom, Sempron	AMD	690V	RADEON X1200	Slower version of X1250; lacks HDMI support
Athlon 64, Phenom, Sempron	AMD	740G	RADEON 2100	Faster version of RADEON X1250

Processor Family	Vendor	Chipset	Video Type	Features
Athlon 64, Phenom, Sempron	AMD	780V	RADEON HD3100	DirectX 10.1, OpenGL 3.2
Athlon 64, Phenom, Sempron	AMD	780G	RADEON HD3200	DirectX 10.1, OpenGL 3.2; faster version of HD3100; sideport memory; Hybrid
Athlon 64, Phenom, Sempron	AMD	790GX	RADEON HD3300	Faster version of HD3200 with HDCP; Hybrid
Athlon 64, Phenom, Sempron	AMD	785G	RADEON HD4200	DirectX 10.1, OpenGL 3.2; sideport memory; Hybrid; Blu-ray playback dual DVI, HDMI
Phenom II, Athlon II, Sempron	AMD	880G	RADEON HD4250	Faster version of HD4200
Phenom II, Athlon II, Sempron	AMD	890GX	RADEON HD4290	Faster version of HD4250
Athlon 64 X2, Athlon 64, Sempron	NVIDIA	nForce 405, 410, 430	GeForce 6100	DX9 SM3, VGA
Athlon 64 X2, Athlon 64, Sempron	NVIDIA	nForce 430	GeForce 6150	Faster version of 6100 with DVI, HDTV playback
Athlon 64 X2, Athlon 64, Sempron	NVIDIA	nForce 630a	GeForce 7025	DX9 SM3, HDMI, HDCP, PureVideo, TV encoder
Athlon 64 X2, Athlon 64, Sempron	NVIDIA	nForce 630a	GeForce 7050PV	DX9 SM3, HDMI, HDCP
Phenom, Athlon 64 X2, FX, Athlon 64	NVIDIA	GeForce 8100	GeForce 8100	DX10, HDMI, HDCP
Phenom, Athlon 64 X2, Athlon 64	NVIDIA	GeForce 8200	GeForce 8200	DX10, OpenGL 3.2, HDMI, HDCP, SLI Hybrid, PureVideo
Phenom, Athlon 64 X2, Athlon 64	NVIDIA	GeForce 8300	GeForce 8300	Faster version of 8200

HDCP = High-definition copy protection; enables playback of encrypted HD video on DVI and HDMI ports

Hybrid = Chipset supports operation of a single GPU in SLI (NVIDIA) or CrossFire (AMD) mode in conjunction with the chipset's integrated GPU

Sideport memory = Can access memory dedicated to the IGPU on the motherboard; amount of RAM available varies by system or motherboard model

Newer integrated chipsets support digital outputs (such as Digital Visual Interface [DVI], High Definition Multimedia Interface [HDMI], or DisplayPort) for use with digital LCD panels and home theater components. Figure 12.2, later in this chapter, illustrates how you can differentiate these ports.

Although a serious 3D gamer will not be satisfied with the performance of integrated graphics, business, home/office, and casual gamers will find that integrated chipset-based video on recent platforms offers satisfactory performance and provides significant cost savings compared to a separate video card.

After reviewing the previous tables, you might notice that the most recent processors from AMD and Intel are not supported by chipsets with integrated video. That is because most of Intel and AMD's most recent processors now incorporate video into the CPU core.

If you decide to buy a motherboard with an integrated chipset or a system with CPU-integrated video, I recommend that you select one that also includes at least one Peripheral Component Interconnect Express (PCIe) x16 video expansion slot. This enables you to add a faster video card in the future if you decide you need it.

CPUs with Integrated Video

As noted elsewhere in this book, the design of personal computers started out with the use of many discrete chip-level components on the motherboard. As Chapter 4 discusses in detail, individual chips have been replaced by chipsets, several of which reduce the former functions of North and South Bridge, Super I/O, and video to a single chip. The next step, placing video and 3D rendering within the processor itself, is now a reality on both Intel and AMD platforms.

By moving video functions within the processor itself, improvements in processor speed, memory speed, and bus speed directly affect video and 3D speeds. Intel was the first to place video components inside the processors with its Core i-series processors, but AMD now also offers this feature in its Fusion series of processors for netbooks, notebooks, ultrabooks, tablets, and desktops. Table 12.5 compares the video graphics features found in Intel and AMD processors.

Table 12.5 Intel and AMD Processors with Integrated Video

Vendor	Processor	Video Type	Features
Intel	1st Gen Core i3/i5/i7*	HD Graphics	Similar to GMA X4500HD but with 2 additional execution units (for a total of 12) and higher clock rates. Implemented as a separate 45nm die within the processor package. DirectX 10.1, OpenGL 2.1
Intel	2nd Gen Core i3/i5/i7*	HD Graphics 2000	Similar to HD Graphics but with higher dynamically adjustable clock rates and only 6 execution units. Directly integrated into the processor die, which allows access to the CPU cache. DirectX 10.1, OpenGL 3.1, Intel-specific enhancements
Intel	2nd Gen Core i3/i5/i7*	HD Graphics 3000	Faster version of HD Graphics 2000 with 12 execution units
Intel	3rd Gen Core i3/i5/i7*	HD Graphics 2500	DirectX 11, Open GL 4, Open CL 1.1, Intel-specific enhancements; 6 execution units
Intel	3rd Gen Core i3/i5/i7*	HD Graphics 4000	Faster version of HD Graphics 2500; 16 execution units
AMD	E-300	HD Radeon 6310	DirectX 11, DirectCompute, OpenGL 4.3, OpenCL 1.1, 80 stream processors
	E-450	HD Radeon 6320	Faster version of HD Radeon 6310
	E1-1xxx	HD Radeon 7310	Faster version of HD 6310
	E2 1xxx	HD Radeon 7340	Faster version of HD 7310

Vendor	Processor	Video Type	Features
AMD (continued)	A4 3xxx	HD Radeon 6410D	DirectX 11, DirectCompute, OpenGL 4.3, OpenCL 1.1, 160 Radeon cores
	A4 53xx	HD Radeon 7480D	DirectX 11, DirectCompute, OpenGL 4.3, OpenCL 1.2, 128 Radeon cores, Blu-ray 3D, TurboCore 3.0
	A6 36xx	HD Radeon 6530D	DirectX 11, DirectCompute, OpenGL 4.3, OpenCL 1.2, 320 Radeon cores, Blu-ray 3D, TurboCore
	A6 5xxx	HD Radeon 7560D	DirectX 11, DirectCompute, OpenGL 4.3, OpenCL1.2,192 Radeon cores, dual displays, Blu-ray 3D
	A8 38xx	HD Radeon 6550D	DirectX 11, DirectCompute, OpenGL 4.3, OpenCL 1.2, 400 Radeon cores, Blu-ray 3D
	A8 5xxx	HD Radeon 7560D	DirectX 11, DirectCompute, OpenGL 4.3, OpenCL 1.2, 256 Radeon cores, Blu-ray 3D, EyeFinity, TurboCore 3.0
	A10 5xxx	HD Radeon 7660D	DirectX 11, DirectCompute, OpenCL, 384 Radeon cores, Blu-ray 3D, EyeFinity, TurboCore 3.0

*Some processors in this family do not include onboard graphics. See specifications for a particular processor model at http://ark.intel.com

Intel-specific enhancements include support improved 2D and 3D video playback, faster video conversion, and support for streaming movie playback. For details, see www.intel.com/support/graphics/sb/CS-033757.htm

UVD = Unified video decoder

OpenGL = Open Graphics Language; 3D rendering API; standard managed by Khronos Group (www.khronos.org)

DirectCompute = Microsoft DirectX 11 (also available in DX10) API supporting general-purpose computing on GPUs

OpenCL = Open Computing Language; enables any application to access the GPU for non-graphical processing; standard managed by Khronos Group (www.khronos.org)

Eyefinity = AMD technology for supporting more than two displays

TurboCore = AMD technology for increasing CPU performance above the base clock speed as needed

TurboCore 3.0 = Improved version of TurboCore, adjusts clock speed of CPU and integrated GPU as needed

Video Adapter Components

Video display adapters contain certain basic components, usually including the following:

- **Video basic input/output system (BIOS)**—Provides the firmware controlling the video card.
- **Graphics processing unit (GPU)**—Video processor/video accelerator. Places text or graphics information onscreen and provides 3D acceleration.
- **Video memory**—Holds the information.
- **Digital-to-analog converter (DAC)**—Formerly a separate chip, the DAC is usually incorporated into the GPU. The DAC is not necessary on a purely digital subsystem (digital video card and display); however, most display subsystems still include analog VGA support.
- **Bus connector**—Connects a discrete video card to the motherboard.
- **Video driver**—Software that communicates with the OS to control the card.

On mid-range and high-performance video cards, such as the card shown in Figure 12.1, most of the components are underneath the cooling system. This card uses a combination of a fan and a heatsink to cool its GPU and memory modules.

SLI bridge connector

PCIe x16 graphics power connector (six-pin)

Power connector for fan

Cooling fan

Heatsink

PCIe x16 connector

Mini-HDMI port

DVI-I (2)

Duct for cooling system

FIGURE 12.1   A typical example of a mid-range video card optimized for dual-GPU gaming (NVIDIA SLI) and HDTV support.

Virtually all video adapters on the market today use chipsets that include 3D acceleration features. The following sections examine the video BIOS and processor in greater detail.

The Video BIOS

Video adapters include a BIOS that is separate from the main system BIOS. If you turn on your monitor first and look quickly, you might see an identification banner for your adapter's video BIOS at the beginning of the system startup process.

Similar to the system BIOS, the video adapter's BIOS takes the form of a read-only memory (ROM) chip containing basic instructions that provide an interface between the video adapter hardware and the software running on your system. The software that makes calls to the video BIOS can be a stand-alone application, an operating system (OS), or the main system BIOS. The programming in the BIOS chip enables your system to display information on the monitor during the system POST and boot sequences, before any other software drivers have been loaded from disk.

◄◄   See the Chapter 5 section, "BIOS Basics," **p. 263**.

In a few cases (mainly with high-performance gaming-oriented cards), the video BIOS also can be upgraded, just like a system BIOS. The video BIOS normally uses a rewritable chip called an electrically erasable programmable read-only memory (EEPROM). On old cards, you might be able to completely replace the chip with a new one—again, if supplied by the manufacturer and if the manufacturer did not hard-solder the BIOS to the printed circuit board. Most video cards use a surface-mounted BIOS chip rather than a socketed chip. A BIOS you can upgrade using software is referred to as a *flash* BIOS, and most video cards that offer BIOS upgrades use this method. Some graphics cards, such as certain models based on the AMD Radeon HD 6900 and 7970 GPUs, include two BIOS chips: one that is not upgradeable, and a second one that can be upgraded by the user for higher overclocked performance.

Note

Video BIOS upgrades are sometimes referred to as *firmware upgrades*.

The Video Processor

The video processor (also known as the video chipset, video graphics processor, or GPU) is the heart of any video adapter and essentially defines the card's functions and performance levels. Two video adapters built using the same chipset will have the same basic capabilities. However, cards built using the same chipset can vary in the clock speeds at which they run the chipset, memory, output ports, and other components, as well as in the amount and type of memory installed. Therefore, performance can vary. The software drivers that OSs and applications use to address the video adapter hardware are written primarily with the chipset in mind. You can normally use a driver intended for an adapter with a particular chipset on any other adapter using the same chipset, or the same chipset families.

Identifying the Video and System Chipsets

Before you purchase a system or a video card, you should find out which chipset the video card or video circuit uses. For systems with integrated chipset video, you need to find out which integrated chipset the system uses. This allows you to have the following:

- A better comparison of the card or system to others
- Access to technical specifications
- Access to reviews and opinions
- The ability to make a better buying decision
- The choice of card manufacturer or chipset manufacturer support and drivers

Because video card performance and features are critical to enjoyment and productivity, find out as much as you can before you buy the system or video card by using the chipset or video card manufacturer's website and third-party reviews. Poorly written or buggy drivers can cause several types of problems, so be sure to check periodically for video driver updates and install any that become available. With video cards, support after the sale can be important, particularly for 3D gaming. Therefore, you should check the manufacturer's website to see whether drivers for your video card have problems rendering your favorite games or working with your favorite software and how often updates are available.

Note

Sometimes, newer drivers for a particular video card or chipset render newer 3D games and programs better than older games and programs. If you are using the latest driver and older games or programs aren't playing as well as they should, consider downgrading to an older version of the driver.

NVIDIA is strictly a producer of GPUs, while AMD supplies GPUs to other vendors and produces cards using its own GPUs. NVIDIA and AMD both create video card reference designs, which the various card manufacturers use to develop their own specific cards. Because each card manufacturer can customize or modify the designs as it chooses, two cards that use the same graphics chipset may differ in features as well as in actual performance. This means a variety of video cards use the same chipset; it also means you are likely to find variations in card performance, software bundles, warranties, and other features between cards using the same chipset.

Although vendors might make modifications to the reference designs provided by NVIDIA and AMD, you can use the drivers provided by the GPU manufacturers for your GPU if the card or motherboard vendor does not provide updated drivers on a timely basis.

For the most detailed information about your GPU, I recommend using GPU-Z, a freeware utility available from www.techpowerup.com. GPU-Z provides extremely detailed version about your computer's GPU (including GPUs built into chipsets and processors), such as name, build technology, bus interface, DirectX support, RAM size, component temperature, BIOS version, driver version, rendering support, number of shaders, pixel and texture fill rates, overclock speeds (if overclocked), and so on (see Figure 12.2).

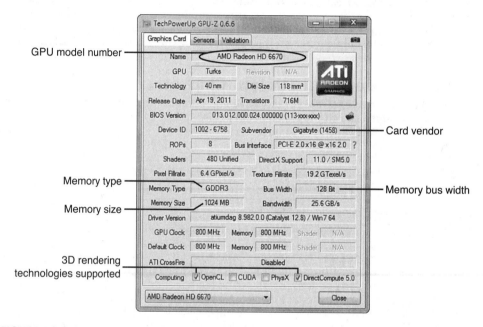

FIGURE 12.2   Using GPU-Z to identify a GPU and its features.

Video RAM

Most discrete video adapters rely on their own onboard memory that they use to store video images while processing them. Systems with integrated video use the universal memory architecture (UMA) feature to share the main system memory. In any case, the memory on the video card or the memory borrowed from the system performs the same tasks.

The amount of video memory determines the maximum screen resolution and color depth the device can support, among other features. You often can select how much memory you want on a particular video adapter; for example, cards with anywhere from 512MB to 4GB of video memory are common choices today. Although having more video memory is not guaranteed to speed up your video adapter, it can increase the speed if it enables a wider bus (for example, from 256 bits wide to 384 bits wide) or provides nondisplay memory as a cache for commonly displayed objects. It also enables the card to generate more colors and higher resolutions and allows 3D textures to be stored and processed on the card, rather than in slower main memory.

Many types of memory have been used with video adapters. These memory types are summarized in Table 12.6.

Table 12.6   Memory Types Used in Video Display Adapters

Memory Type	Definition
FPM DRAM	Fast Page-Mode RAM
VRAM	Video RAM
WRAM	Window RAM
EDO DRAM	Extended Data Out DRAM
SDRAM	Synchronous DRAM
MDRAM	Multibank DRAM
SGRAM	Synchronous Graphics RAM
DDR SGRAM	Double-Data Rate SGRAM
GDDR2 SGRAM	Graphics DDR version 2 SGRAM
GDDR3 SGRAM	GDDR version 3 SGRAM
GDDR4 SGRAM	Graphics DDR version 4 SGRAM
GDDR5 SGRAM	GDDR version 5 SGRAM

Some of these, including FPM DRAM, EDO DRAM, and SDRAM, were also used for main memory in PCs. All of the others were specifically designed for use in graphics subsystems.

◀◀   For more information about FPM DRAM, EDO DRAM, and SDRAM, see Chapter 6, "Memory," **p. 325**.

VRAM and WRAM

VRAM and WRAM are dual-ported memory types that can read from one port and write data through the other port. This improves performance by reducing wait times for accessing the VRAM compared to FPM DRAM and EDO DRAM.

SGRAM

SGRAM was designed to be a high-end solution for fast video adapter designs. SGRAM is similar to SDRAM in its capability to be synchronized to high-speed buses up to 200MHz, but it differs from SDRAM by including circuitry to perform block-writes to increase the speed of graphics fill and 3D Z-buffer operations.

DDR SGRAM

DDR SGRAM is designed to transfer data at speeds twice that of conventional SGRAM by transferring data on both the rising and falling parts of the processing clock cycle.

GDDR2 SGRAM

There have been several variations of what has been called GDDR2. The first was based on standard 2.5V DDR SDRAM with some enhancements, whereas the second was actually based on 1.8V DDR2 SDRAM, and with much higher performance and cooler operation.

GDDR3 SGRAM

GDDR3 SGRAM is based on DDR2 memory, but with two major differences:

- GDDR3 separates reads and writes with a single-ended unidirectional strobe, whereas DDR2 uses differential bidirectional strobes. This method enables higher data transfer rates.
- GDDR3 uses an interface technique known as pseudo-open drain, which uses voltage instead of current. This method makes GDDR3 memory compatible with GPUs designed to use DDR, GDDR2, or DDR2 memory. To determine the type of memory used on a particular video card, check the video card manufacturer's specification sheet.

GDDR4 SGRAM

Some of the newer cards use GDDR4 SGRAM. Compared to GDDR3, GDDR4 memory has the following features:

- Higher bandwidth. GDDR4 running at half the speed of GDDR3 provides comparable bandwidth to its predecessor.
- Greater memory density, enabling fewer chips to be needed to reach a particular memory size.

GDDR5 SGRAM

GDDR5 SGRAM is based on the previous GDDR standards with several modifications to allow increased performance. The main differences include the following:

- Signal optimization using data/address bit inversion, adjustable driver strength, adjustable voltage, and adjustable termination
- Adaptive interface timing using data training that is scalable per bit or byte
- Error compensation, including real-time error detection on both read/write and fast resending

GDDR5 is also designed for extreme power management such that power is used only when necessary. This allows higher clock speeds with cooler operation. Current GDDR5 parts are rated up to 7Gbps per chip, allowing 28GBps total bandwidth.

Video RAM Speed

Video RAM speed is typically measured in MHz, GHz, or by bandwidth in Mb/Gb or MB/GB per second. Faster memory and faster GPUs produce better gaming performance, but at a higher cost. However, if you are primarily concerned about business or productivity application performance, you can save money by using a video card with a slower GPU and slower memory.

Unless you dig deeply into the technical details of a particular graphics card, determining what type of memory a particular card uses can be difficult. Because none of today's video cards feature user-upgradeable memory, I recommend that you look at the performance of a given card and choose the card with the performance, features, and price that's right for you.

RAM Calculations

The amount of memory a video adapter needs to display a particular resolution and color depth is based on a mathematical equation. A location must be present in the adapter's memory array to display every pixel on the screen, and the resolution determines the number of total pixels. For example, a screen resolution of 1920×1080 requires a total of 2,073,600 pixels.

If you were to display that resolution with only two colors, you would need only 1 bit of memory space to represent each pixel. If the bit has a value of 0, the dot is black, and if its value is 1, the dot is white. If you use 32 bits of memory space to control each pixel, you can display more than

4 billion colors because 4,294,967,296 combinations are possible with a 32-digit binary number ($2^{32} = 4,294,967,296$). If you multiply the number of pixels necessary for the screen resolution by the number of bits required to represent each pixel, you have the amount of memory the adapter needs to display that resolution. Here is how the calculation works:

$1920 \times 1080 = 2,073,600$ pixels $\times$ 32 bits per pixel

$= 66,355,200$ bits

$= 8,294,400$ bytes

$= 7.91$MiB

As you can see, displaying 32-bit color (4,294,967,296 colors) at 1920×1080 resolution requires just short of 8MiB of RAM on the video adapter. Because most modern video cards have at least 512MiB or more, you can see that two-dimensional images don't require much memory.

3D video cards require more memory for a given resolution and color depth because the video memory must be used for three buffers: the front buffer, back buffer, and Z-buffer. The amount of video memory required for a particular operation varies according to the settings used for the color depth and Z-buffer. Triple buffering allocates more memory for 3D textures than double buffering but can slow down the performance of some games. You can usually adjust the buffering mode used by a given 3D video card through its properties sheet.

Note

As we discuss 3D in this and following sections, we are referring to the rendering of 3D graphics on your display. 3D display technologies (which involve special glasses and 120MHz or greater refresh rates on LCD or LED backlit displays) are a different issue.

Although current chipset-integrated graphics solutions feature 3D support, the performance they offer is limited by being based on older, less powerful 3D GPUs and by the narrow data bus they use to access memory. Because integrated graphics solutions share video memory with the processor, they use the same data bus as the processor. In a single-channel-based system, this restricts the data bus to 64 bits. A dual-channel system has a 128-bit data bus, but today's fastest 3D video cards feature a 512-bit or wider data bus. The wider the data bus, the more quickly graphics data can be transferred.

For these reasons, you are likely to be disappointed (and lose a lot of games!) if you play 3D games using integrated graphics. To enjoy 3D games, opt for a mid-range to high-end 3D video card based on a current AMD or NVIDIA chipset with 1GB of RAM or more. If you demand peak performance and your budget permits, you might also consider using a multicard solution that allows you to use two or more PCIe video cards to increase your graphics processing performance.

▶▶ See the section, "Dual-GPU Scene Rendering," **p. 648**.

Note

If your system uses integrated graphics and you have less than 2GB of RAM, you might be able to increase your available graphics memory by upgrading system memory (system memory is used by the integrated chipset). Some chipsets with integrated graphics automatically detect additional system memory and adjust the size of graphics memory automatically.

Video Memory Bus Width

Another issue with respect to the memory on the video adapter is the width of the bus connecting the graphics chipset and memory on the adapter. The chipset is usually a single large chip on the card that contains virtually all the adapter's functions. It is wired directly to the memory on the adapter through a local bus on the card. Most of the high-end adapters use an internal memory bus that is up to 512 bits wide (or more in some cases). This jargon can be confusing because video adapters that take the form of separate expansion cards also plug into the main system bus, which has its own speed rating. When you read about a 256-bit, 384-bit, or 512-bit video adapter, you must understand that this refers to the memory connection on the card, not the connection to the motherboard. In two cards with otherwise similar GPU, memory type, and memory size specifications, the card with the wider memory bus is preferable because a wider memory bus boosts performance.

◄◄ See the Chapter 4 section, "System Bus Types, Functions, and Features," **p. 239**.

The DAC

The DAC (or RAMDAC) does exactly what its name describes. The RAMDAC is responsible for converting the RAM-based digital images your computer generates into signals for analog monitor connections. The speed of the RAMDAC is measured in MHz; the faster the conversion process, the higher the adapter's vertical refresh rate. The speeds of the RAMDACs used in today's high-performance video adapters range from 300MHz to 400MHz. Most of today's video card chipsets include the RAMDAC function inside the 3D accelerator chip, but some dual-display-capable video cards use a separate RAMDAC chip to allow the second display to work at different refresh rates than the primary display. Systems that use integrated graphics include the RAMDAC function in the North Bridge or GMCH chip portion of the motherboard chipset.

The benefits of increasing the RAMDAC speed include higher vertical refresh rates, which allow higher resolutions with flicker-free refresh rates (72Hz–85Hz or above) on CRT displays. Typically, cards with RAMDAC speeds of 300MHz or above display flicker-free (75Hz or above) at all resolutions up to 1920×1200 on CRT displays. Of course, as discussed earlier in this chapter, you must ensure that any resolution you want to use is supported by both your monitor and your video card.

Note

RAMDAC functionality is not used by digital displays, and many GPUs no longer list RAMDAC speeds.

Video Display Interfaces

Video display adapters connect a PC to a display and therefore must work through two main interfaces. The first is the system interface, meaning the connection between the video adapter and the PC, and the second is the display interface, meaning the connection between the video adapter and the display. By using standardized versions of these interfaces, we end up having video adapters and displays that are both compatible and easily interchangeable. This section discusses the available system and display interfaces as well as the differences between them.

The System Interface

Older video adapters were designed for use with earlier bus standards, such as the IBM MicroChannel Architecture (MCA), Interactive Multimedia Association (ISA), Enhanced Interactive Multimedia Association (EISA), and VESA local bus (VL-Bus). Because of their relatively slow performance by today's standards, all are now obsolete. Current video display adapters use PCIe interface standards to connect to a system, although older systems based on Accelerated Graphics Port (AGP) are still relatively common. Peripheral Component Interconnect (PCI)-based adapters are still found in some old systems or AGP-based systems that utilize a second adapter.

◄◄ See "The PCI Bus," **p. 247**.

◄◄ See "PCI Express," **p. 251**.

◄◄ See "Accelerated Graphics Port," **p. 253**.

AGP

The AGP, an Intel-designed dedicated video bus introduced in 1997, delivers a maximum bandwidth up to 16 times greater than that of a comparable PCI bus. AGP was the mainstream high-speed video-to-system interface for several years but has been replaced by the more versatile and faster PCIe standard.

The AGP slot is essentially an enhancement to the existing PCI bus; however, it's intended for use only with video adapters and provides them with high-speed access to the main system memory array. This enables the adapter to process certain 3D video elements, such as texture maps, directly from system memory rather than having to copy the data to the adapter memory before the processing can begin. This saves time and eliminates the need to upgrade the video adapter memory to better support 3D functions. Although AGP version 3.0 provides for two AGP slots, this feature has never been implemented in practice. Systems with AGP have only one AGP slot.

Note

Although the earliest AGP cards had relatively small amounts of onboard RAM, most later implementations use large amounts of on-card memory and use a memory aperture (a dedicated memory address space above the area used for physical memory) to transfer data more quickly to and from the video card's own memory. Integrated chipsets featuring built-in AGP use system memory for all operations, including texture maps.

Windows 98 and later versions support AGP's Direct Memory Execute (DIME) feature. DIME uses the main memory instead of the video adapter's memory for certain tasks to lessen the traffic to and from the adapter. However, with the large amounts of memory found on current AGP video cards, this feature is seldom implemented.

Four speeds of AGP are available: 1x, 2x, 4x, and 8x. (See Table 12.7 for details.) Later AGP video cards support AGP 8x and can fall back to AGP 4x or 2x on systems that don't support AGP 8x.

Table 12.7 AGP Speeds and Technical Specifications

AGP Speed	AGP Specification	Clock Speed	Transfer Rate	Slot Voltages
1x	1.0	66MHz	266MBps	3.3V
2x	1.0	133MHz	533MBps	3.3V, 1.5V[1]
4x	2.0	266MHz	1066MBps	1.5V
8x	3.0	533MHz	2133MBps	1.5V[2]

1 Varies with card implementation.

2 Uses 0.8V internal signaling.

AGP 3.0 was announced in 2000, but support for the standard required the development of motherboard chipsets that were not introduced until mid-2002. Almost all motherboard chipsets with AGP support released after that time featured AGP 8x support.

Although some systems with AGP 4x or 8x slots use a universal slot design that can handle 3.3V or 1.5V AGP cards, others do not. If a card designed for 3.3V (2x mode) is plugged into a motherboard that supports only 1.5V (4x mode) signaling, the motherboard may be damaged.

◄◄ See the Chapter 4 section, "Accelerated Graphics Port," **p. 253**.

Caution

Be sure to check AGP compatibility before you insert an older (AGP 1x/2x) card into a system designed for AGP 4x or 8x. Even if you can physically insert the card, a mismatch between the card's required voltage and the AGP slot's voltage output can damage the motherboard. Check the motherboard manual for the card types and voltage levels the AGP slot supports.

Some AGP cards can use either 3.3V or 1.5V voltage levels, adjusted via an onboard jumper. These cards typically use an AGP connector that is notched for use with either AGP 2x or AGP 4x slots, as pictured in Chapter 4. Be sure to set these cards to use 1.5V before using them in motherboards that support only 1.5V signaling.

PCIe

PCIe began to show up in systems in mid-2004 and has filtered down to all systems that use discrete video cards or have integrated video that can be upgraded. Despite the name, PCIe uses a high-speed bidirectional serial data transfer method, and PCIe channels (also known as *lanes*) can be combined to create wider and faster expansion slots. (Each lane provides 250MBps, 500MBps, or 1,000MBps data rate in each direction.) Because PCIe is technically not a bus, unlike PCI, the slots do not compete with each other for bandwidth. PCIe graphics cards use up to 16 lanes (x16) to enable speeds of 4GBps, 8GBps, or 16GBps in each direction, as seen in Table 12.8.

Table 12.8 PCIe Video Card Bandwidth

PCIe Architecture	Bandwidth per Lane	Bandwidth for x16 Link
PCIe 1.x	250MBps	4GBps
PCIe 2.x	500MBps	8GBps
PCIe 3.x	1,000MBps	16GBps
PCI 4.x*	2,000MBps	32GBps

Announced in November 2011; expected to reach market in 2014–2015

Most PCIe implementations include one x16 slot for video and two or more x1 slots for other add-on cards, as well as legacy PCI slots. Systems that support NVIDIA's SLI or AMD CrossFireX dual PCIe video card technologies have up to three or four PCIe video slots running at x8 or x16 speed.

The Display Interface

The display interface connects the video display adapter to the monitor or display. Over the years, several methods of connecting monitors have been available. Some of these interfaces have been analog, and others have been digital. The first interfaces used in the 1980s for early PCs included CGA, EGA, MDA, and HCG. These were all digital interfaces.

Note

For more information on these early display standards, see *Upgrading and Repairing PCs*, 10th Anniversary Edition, now out of print but may be available at some bookstores or libraries.

Unlike earlier digital video standards, VGA is an analog system. VGA came out in 1987 and began a shift from digital to analog that lasted for more than 20 years. Only recently has there been a shift back to digital. Why go from digital to analog and then back to digital? The simple answer is that analog was the least expensive way at the time to design a CRT-based system that supported a reasonable resolution with a reasonable number of colors. Now that technology has advanced and LCD panels have largely replaced CRTs, going back to digital interfaces makes sense.

The video interfaces (and connectors) you are likely to encounter in PCs dating from the late 1980s to the present include the following:

- VGA
- DVI
- HDMI
- DisplayPort

VGA is an analog connection, whereas the others are digital. The connectors for these interfaces are shown in Figure 12.3 and are discussed in further detail in the following sections.

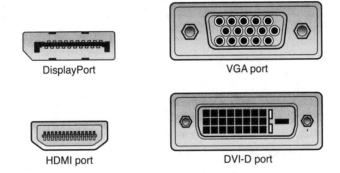

FIGURE 12.3   Video interface connectors used in PCs from the late 1980s to the present.

VGA

IBM introduced the VGA interface and display standard on April 2, 1987, along with a family of systems it called PS/2. VGA originally included the display adapter, the monitor, and the connection between them. Since that time, the display adapters and monitors have evolved, but the VGA 15-pin analog connection went on to become the most popular video interface in history and is still used today in PC video adapters and displays.

VGA is an analog design. Analog uses a separate signal for each CRT color gun, but each signal can be sent at varying levels of intensity—64 levels, in the case of the original VGA standard. This provides 262,144 possible colors (64^3), of which 256 could be simultaneously displayed in the original design. For realistic computer graphics, color depth is often more important than high resolution because the human eye perceives a picture that has more colors as being more realistic.

VGA was designed to be addressed through the VGA BIOS interface, a software interface that forced programs to talk to the BIOS-based driver rather than directly to the hardware. This allowed programs to call a consistent set of commands and functions that would work on different hardware, as long as a compatible VGA BIOS interface was present. The original VGA cards had the BIOS on the video card directly, in the form of a ROM chip containing from 16KB to 32KB worth of code. Modern video cards and laptop graphics processors still have this 32KB onboard BIOS. Typically, the only time the ROM-based drivers are used is during boot, when running legacy DOS-based applications or games, or when you run Windows in Safe Mode.

VGA also describes a 15-pin analog interface connection that can support a variety of modes. The connection is analog because VGA was primarily designed to drive CRT displays, which are analog by nature. When a display is connected via VGA, the digital signals inside the PC are converted to analog signals by the DAC chip in the display adapter and are then sent to the display via the analog VGA connection. The VGA connector is shown in Figure 12.4; the pinouts are shown in Table 12.9.

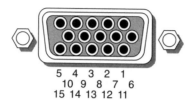

FIGURE 12.4   The standard 15-pin analog VGA connector.

Table 12.9   15-Pin Analog VGA Connector Pinout

Pin	Function	Direction
1	Red Analog Video	Out
2	Green Analog Video	Out
3	Blue Analog Video	Out
4	Monitor ID 2	In
5	TTL GND (monitor self-test)	—
6	Red Analog GND	—
7	Green Analog GND	—
8	Blue Analog GND	—
9	Key (unused)	—
10	Sync GND	—
11	Monitor ID 0	In
12	Monitor ID 1	In
13	Horizontal Sync	Out
14	Vertical Sync	Out
15	Monitor ID 3	In

The mating VGA cable connector that plugs into this connector normally has pin 9 missing. This was designed such that the mating hole in the connector on the video card could be plugged, but it is usually open (and merely unused) instead. The connector is keyed by virtue of the D-shape shell and pin alignment, so it is difficult to plug in backward even without the key pin. Pin 5 is used only for testing purposes, and pin 15 is rarely used; they are often missing as well. To identify the type of monitor connected to the system, some early VGA cards used the presence or absence of the monitor ID pins in various combinations.

In addition to the connector and electrical interface, the original VGA standard also defined a number of text and graphics display modes with various resolutions and colors. The original VGA modes allowed for a maximum graphics resolution of 640×480 in only 16 (4-bit) colors. This was the maximum that could be supported by the original 256KB of RAM included on the card.

IBM introduced higher-resolution versions of VGA called XGA and XGA-2 in the early 1990s, but most of the development of VGA standards has come from the third-party video card industry and its trade group, the Video Electronic Standards Association (VESA; www.vesa.org).When VGA originated in 1987, it had low resolution and color capability by today's standards. Since then, VGA has evolved to support higher resolution modes with many more colors. Even the least-expensive video adapters on the market today can work with modes well beyond the original VGA standard.

The minimum resolution and color depth (number of colors) for use with current software is 1024×768 (originally introduced as part of the XGA standard) and 32-bit color depth for 3D adapters.

Note

For more information about early VGA and VESA SVGA, and XGA standards, see "SVGA and XGA" in Chapter 12, "Video Hardware" in *Upgrading and Repairing PCs*, 19th Edition.

Digital Display Interfaces

The analog VGA interface works well for CRTs, which are inherently analog devices, but VGA does not work well for LCD, plasma, or other types of flat-panel displays that are inherently digital. Video data starts out digitally inside the PC and is converted to analog when the VGA interface is used. When you are running a digital display such as an LCD over an analog interface such as VGA, the signal must then be converted back to digital before it can be displayed, resulting in a double conversion that causes screen artifacts, blurred text, color shifting, and other kinds of problems.

Using a digital interface eliminates the double conversion, allowing the video information to remain as digital data from the PC all the way to the screen. Therefore, a trend back to using digital video interfaces has occurred, especially for inherently digital displays such as LCD flat panels.

Laptop computers have avoided this problem by using an internal digital connection called FPD-Link (Flat Panel Display-Link), which National Semiconductor originally developed in 1995. Unfortunately, this standard was not designed for external connections requiring longer cable lengths or extremely high resolutions. What was needed was an industry standard digital connection for external displays.

To facilitate a digital video connection between PCs and external displays, several digital video signal standards and specifications have been available:

- Plug and Display (P&D)
- Digital Flat Panel (DFP)
- DVI
- HDMI
- DisplayPort

VESA released the P&D and DFP standards in June 1997 and February 1999, respectively. Both were based on the PanelLink TMDS (Transition Minimized Differential Signaling) protocol that Silicon Image developed. Unfortunately, both of these interfaces had relatively low-resolution support (1280×1024 maximum) and were only implemented in a handful of video cards and monitors. As such, they never really caught on in the mass market and were overshadowed by the DVI, which become the first truly popular digital display interface standard.

DVI

DVI was introduced on April 2, 1999 by the Digital Display Working Group (DDWG). The DDWG was formed in 1998 by Intel, Silicon Image, Compaq, Fujitsu, Hewlett-Packard, IBM, and NEC to address the need for a universal digital interface standard between a host system and a display. Unlike the P&D and DFP interfaces that came before it, DVI gained immediate widespread industry support, with 150 DVI products being shown at the Intel Developer Forum in August 1999, only four months after DVI was released. Since then, DVI has become the most common interface for digital video connections between PCs and displays. DVI also allows for both digital and VGA analog connections using the same basic connector.

DVI uses Transition Minimized Differential Signaling (TMDS), which was developed by Silicon Image (www.siliconimage.com) and trademarked under the name *PanelLink*. TMDS takes 24-bit parallel digital data from the video controller and transmits it serially over balanced lines at a high speed to a receiver. A single-link TMDS connection uses four separate differential data pairs, with three for color data (one each for red, green, and blue data) and the fourth pair for clock and control data. Each twisted pair uses differential signaling with a low 0.5V swing over balanced lines for reliable, low-power, high-speed data transmission. A low-speed VESA Display Data Channel (DDC) pair is also used to transmit identification and configuration information, such as supported resolution and color-depth information, between the graphics controller and display.

TMDS is designed to support cables up to 10 meters (32.8 feet) in length, although the limits may be shorter or longer depending on cable quality. Several companies make products that can amplify or re-drive the signals, allowing for greater lengths. Figure 12.5 shows a block diagram of a single-link TMDS connection.

Using TMDS, each color channel (red/green/blue) transmits 8 bits of data (encoded as a 10-bit character) serially at up to 165MHz. This results in a raw throughput of 1.65Gbps per channel. There are three color channels per link, resulting in a maximum raw bandwidth of 4.95Gbps per link. Because the data is sent using 8b/10b encoding, only 8 bits of every 10 are actual data, resulting in a maximum true video data throughput of 3.96Gbps. This enables a single-link DVI connection to easily handle computer video resolutions as high as WUXGA (1920×1200) as well as 1080p HDTV (1920×1080 with progressive scan).

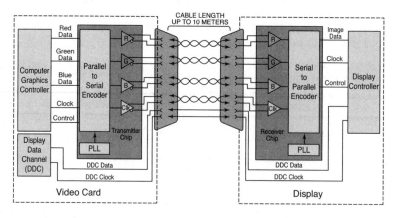

FIGURE 12.5 A single-link TMDS connection.

If more bandwidth is necessary, the DVI standard supports a second TMDS link in the same cable and connector. This uses three additional TMDS signal pairs (one for each color) and shares the same clock and DDC signals as the primary link. This is called *dual-link DVI*, and it increases the maximum raw bandwidth to 9.9Gbps and the true data bandwidth to 7.92Gpbs, which will handle computer resolutions as high as WQUXGA (3840×2400). Normally only 30-inch or larger flat-panel displays use resolutions high enough to require dual-link DVI. Even higher resolution displays can be supported with dual DVI ports, each with a dual-link connection.

TMDS links include support for DDC, a low-speed, bidirectional standard for communication between PCs and monitors, created by VESA. DDC defines the physical connection and signaling method, whereas the communications and data protocol is defined under the VESA Extended Display Identification Data (EDID) standard. DDC and EDID allow the graphics controller to identify the capabilities of the display so the controller can automatically configure itself to match the display's capabilities.

DVI uses Molex MicroCross connectors with several variations. The DVI standard was primarily designed to support digital devices; however, for backward compatibility, it can also support analog devices. The DVI-D (digital) connector supports only digital devices, whereas the DVI-I (integrated) connector supports both digital and analog devices via the addition of extra pins. Figure 12.6 and Table 12.10 show the DVI-I (integrated) connector and pinout.

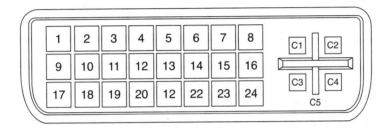

FIGURE 12.6 The DVI-I connector.

Table 12.10 DVI-I Connector Pinout

Pin	Signal	Pin	Signal
1	TMDS Data2–	13	TMDS Data3+
2	TMDS Data2+	14	+5V Power
3	TMDS Data2/4 Shield	15	GND
4	TMDS Data4–	16	Hot Plug Detect
5	TMDS Data4+	17	TMDS Data0–
6	DDC Clock	18	TMDS Data0+
7	DDC Data	19	TMDS Data0/5 Shield
8	Analog Vert. Sync	20	TMDS Data5–
9	TMDS Data1–	21	TMDS Data5+
10	TMDS Data1+	22	TMDS Clock Shield
11	TMDS Data1/3 Shield	23	TMDS Clock+
12	TMDS Data3–	24	TMDS Clock–
—	—	—	—

Table 12.10 Continued

Pin	Signal	Pin	Signal
C1	Analog Red	C3	Analog Blue
C2	Analog Green	C4	Analog Horiz. Sync
—	—	C5	Analog GND

TMDS = Transition Minimized Differential Signaling

Note: The DVI-D (digital only) connector lacks the analog C1–C4 pins.

The DVI-D connector is the same as the DVI-I connector, except that it lacks the analog connections. By virtue of the unique MicroCross connector design, a digital-only device can connect only to receptacles with digital support, and an analog-only device can plug in only to receptacles with analog support. This design feature ensures that an analog-only device cannot be connected to a digital-only receptacle, and vice versa. Figure 12.7 shows the DVI-D connector. The pinout is the same as the DVI-I connector, except for the missing analog signals. The DVI-D connector is widely used on laptop port replicators and docking stations that provide DVI support.

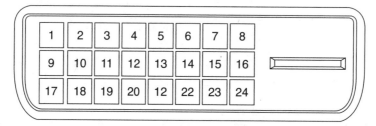

FIGURE 12.7 The DVI-D connector.

The DVI-I connector shown in Figure 12.6 can be converted into a VGA port for use with CRTs or with analog LCD panels via a simple adapter. Often new graphics cards purchased at retail that support only DVI come with just such an adapter that allows you to connect a traditional VGA connector from the display to the adapter.

The DVI-I connector can also be used with the rarely seen DVI-A cable, which supports analog displays only. Compared to the DVI-I connector, the DVI-A cable features the MicroCross connector and ten pins: six near the MicroCross connector and four on the far side of the connector.

Unfortunately, the Digital Display Working Group (DDWG) that created DVI has disbanded, leaving DVI frozen in time at the DVI 1.0 specification level. This means that DVI will not be updated in the future. Although it has enjoyed tremendous popularity as the first widely used digital display interface, the PC industry as a whole is slowly moving to DisplayPort as the replacement for DVI. Many cards feature both DVI and DisplayPort ports, or HDMI and DisplayPort ports.

DMS-59

DMS-59 is a 59-pin connection used by some video cards. It was used by the initial implementation of the ATI (later AMD) Crossfire's master video cards. Later, ATI and all AMD implementations replaced the DMS-59 cable with an internal bridge card.

More recently, DMS-59 has been used along with a DMS-59 to dual VGA cable or DMS-59 to dual DVI single-link cable to provide dual display support. Cards that use DMS-59 are sold as OEM products and not at retail. A DMS-59 connection is the same size as DVI but contains 59 smaller pins.

HDMI

HDMI was designed by a group of multimedia companies (Hitachi, Panasonic, Philips, Silicon Image, Sony, Thomson, and Toshiba) as a way to provide a single-cable connection for transporting digital video and audio signals between consumer electronics hardware such as big-screen TVs, video games, DVD players, and home theater systems. HDMI was introduced in December 2002, version 1.3a was introduced in November 2006, version 1.4 was introduced in June 2009, and version 1.4a was introduced in March 2010. HDMI 1.4b was released October 11, 2011. Shortly after that, the HDMI Forum was created on October 25, 2011 to develop all future HDMI version specifications. HDMI is basically a superset of DVI and uses the same TMDS (Transition Minimized Differential Signaling) as does DVI. Unlike DVI, however, each color channel also carries multiplexed audio data. HDMI 1.2a and earlier supports a maximum data clock rate of 165MHz, sending 10 bits per cycle, or 1.65Gbps per channel. There are three channels per link, resulting in a maximum raw bandwidth of 4.95Gbps. Because the data is sent using 8b/10b encoding, only 8 bits of every 10 are actual data, resulting in a true data throughput of 3.96Gbps. This enables a single-link HDMI 1.2a or earlier connection to easily handle computer video resolutions as high as WUXGA (1920×1200) as well as 1080p HDTV (192×1080 with progressive scan) plus audio data.

HDMI 1.3 increases the maximum clock rate to 340MHz, resulting in 10.2Gbps raw bandwidth, or a true data throughput of 8.16Gbps. This increase allows a single-link HDMI connection to have slightly more throughput than a dual-link DVI connection, which handles computer resolutions as high as WQUXGA (3840×2400) plus audio data.

HDMI 1.4 adds support for Ethernet connections through the HDMI cable, audio return, 3D Blu-ray video playback, all current as well as future resolutions up to 4096×2160, better color spaces support, a micro-HDMI connector, new cable standards, and support for automotive connectors. HDMI 1.4 also introduces cable speed and feature categories: Standard (up to 1080i), High Speed (1080p), Standard HDMI with Ethernet, High Speed HDMI with Ethernet.

HDMI 1.4a adds support for new side-by-side and top-and-bottom 3D broadcast standards.

HDMI 1.4b adds support for 1080p video at 120Hz.

HDMI can also carry up to eight channels of uncompressed digital audio at 24-bit/192KHz along with Dolby Digital, DTS, Dolby TrueHD, and DTS-HD Master Audio compressed audio formats. Because it uses a single cable for both audio and video signals, HDMI provides an excellent way to reduce the cabling tangle present in home theater systems that use conventional analog audio and video cables. For home theater users who subscribe to HDTV satellite or cable services, HDMI is ideal because it supports high-bandwidth digital content protection (HDCP), which these services use to protect content from piracy while still assuring high-quality viewing and listening. To avoid reduced-quality playback of protected content, all devices (including the DVD player or set-top box, AV receiver, and display) must support HDCP.

Besides transmitting high-quality audio and video between devices, HDMI carries additional signals. HDMI uses the DDC to identify the capabilities of an HDMI display, such as resolutions, color depth, and audio. DDC enables optimal playback quality on different devices. HDMI also supports the optional consumer electronic control (CEC) feature, which enables one-button control of all CEC-enabled devices for one-touch play or record or other features.

Table 12.11 compares the HDMI versions.

Table 12.11 HDMI Versions

HDMI Version	Release Date	Notes
1.0	December 2002	Original release.
1.1	May 2004	Added DVD audio support.
1.2	August 2005	Added Super Audio CD support, PC support for Type A connector and native sRGB color-space, and requirement for displays to support low-voltage sources.
1.2a	December 2005	Added specifications for CEC features.
1.3	June 2006	Increased single-link bandwidth to 10.2Gbps raw (8.16Gbps actual data). Added support for 30/36/48-bit color, Dolby TrueHD and DT-HD Master Audio support, auto lip sync, and compact Type C connector.
1.3a	November 2006	Made minor adjustments to CEC and other specifications. Added new compliance test.
1.4	June 2009	10/100 Ethernet support (requires cable compatible with HDMI 1.4 or better standards); audio return channel; 3D input/output protocols; support for future 4K resolutions; new color spaces: sYCC601, Adobe RGB, and Adobe YCC601; HDMI Micro connector (also known as Type D); cable speed and feature standards.
1.4a	March 2010	Support for additional Side-by-Side and Top-and-Bottom broadcast 3D standards.
1.4b	October 2011	Support for 1080p at 120Hz (3D support)

HDMI versions 1.3b (March 2007), 1.3b1 (November 2007), and 1.3c (August 2008) added HDMI compliance testing revisions, and they have no effect on HDMI features, functions, or performance.

Because HDMI is essentially a superset of DVI, it is backward-compatible with DVI. This means that using a simple and inexpensive adapter, you can connect an HDMI source to a DVI display and connect a DVI source to an HDMI display. However, unless both the source and monitor support HDCP, you might not be able to play premium HDTV content, or the resolution might be reduced. Although some graphics cards claimed HDCP support as early as the first part of 2006, changes in the HDCP standard may prevent early cards from working properly. You should contact your graphics card and monitor vendor to determine whether a particular device supports HDCP.

Current HDMI cables correspond to HDMI Type A, Type C, or Type D (introduced with HDMI 1.4). Type A is a 19-pin connector. Type C is a smaller version of Type A, originally designed for use in DV camcorders or other portable devices, but also used on some video cards. It uses the same pinout, and Type A–to–Type C adapters are available from various vendors. HDMI version 1.0 also defined a 29-pin Type B dual-link cable that has not been used in products. Type D is also a 19-pin connector that is about half the height of Type A and less than half the width of Type A and is also shorter and narrower than Type C connectors.

Figure 12.8 illustrates a typical HDMI Type A cable and the location of pin 1 on the cable and connector.

The pinout for HDMI Type A and Type C cables is shown in Table 12.12. Type D uses the same pinout as Type A cables.

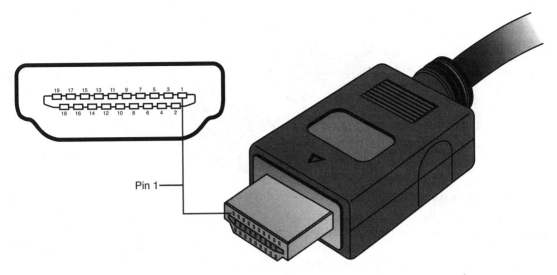

FIGURE 12.8 HDMI Type A cable and socket use a two-row 19-pin interface.

Table 12.12 HDMI Type A/Type C Connector Pinout

Pin Number	Description	Pin Number	Description
1	TMDS Data2 +	11	TMDS Clock Shield
2	TMDS Data2 Shield	12	TMDS Clock –
3	TMDS Data2 –	13	CEC
4	TMDS Data1+	14	Reserved
5	TMDS Data1 Shield	15	SCL
6	TMDS Data1 –	16	SDA
7	TMDS Data0+	17	DDC/CEC ground
8	TMDS Data0 Shield	18	+5V power
9	TMDS Data0 –	19	Hot Plug Detect
10	TMDS Clock +	—	—

Note: +5V power is 50mA max.

Figure 12.9 illustrates a typical HDMI-DVI adapter cable.

Note

The adapter cable shown in Figure 12.8 is not designed to work with graphics cards and drivers that do not support HDTV resolutions and timings. You may need to upgrade your graphics card driver before using an HDMI-DVI cable. Although some set-top boxes include DVI ports, this type of adapter cable is only intended for PC-HDTV connections.

FIGURE 12.9 HDMI–DVI adapter cable.

In addition to supporting specific versions of the HDMI standard, HDMI cables are available in two speeds: Category 1 (Standard) and Category 2 (High Speed). Category 1 (Standard) cables support up to 720p/1080i resolutions (speeds up to 75Mhz or 2.26Gbps), while Category 2 (High-Speed) cables support 1080p resolutions, running at speeds up to 340Mhz or 10.2Gbps.

Starting in late 2006, some vendors began to release PCIe cards including HDMI ports. Some provide HDMI input and output for use with HDV camcorders, whereas others using ATI or NVIDIA chipsets are graphics cards that also include HDMI output. Although HDMI is a royalty-based interface, requiring an annual license fee of $10,000 plus a payment of 4 cents per device, and the newer DisplayPort interface is royalty-free, HDMI continues to be used on a wider range of current video cards and systems with integrated graphics than the obsolescent DVI or emerging DisplayPort standards. Some recent cards, such as the one shown in Figure 12.1, use the mini-HDMI (HDMI Type C) connector to save space on the card bracket.

For more information about HDMI, see the HDMI Forum website at www.hdmiforum.org.

DisplayPort

DisplayPort is the latest digital display interface standard. It is designed to replace VGA, DVI, and HDMI for use in PCs and to coexist with HDMI in consumer electronics devices. Dell originated the design in 2003 and then turned it over to VESA in August 2005. In May 2006, VESA published it as an open industry standard. Consequently, DisplayPort is a royalty-free interface and does not incur the licensing fees of HDMI or the implementation patent fees of DVI. Also, DisplayPort is designed both as an internal and an external interface, meaning it can replace the FPD-Link (Flat Panel Display-Link) interface used internally in most laptops as well as providing connections to external displays. In short, DisplayPort is designed to be the ultimate universal display interface for PCs now and in the future. Previous digital display interfaces such as DVI and HDMI used TMDS, which requires extra logic on both the source and display ends, logic that must usually be licensed from Silicon Image. DisplayPort instead uses a packetized (network-like) interface that can easily be implemented in chipsets without the extra cost logic required for DVI or HDMI. DisplayPort is kind of like a high-speed Ethernet for video, and the network-like design allows for features such as multiple video streams over a single connection, which means you can connect multiple displays to a single port.

Because it is a license-free, royalty-free design, DisplayPort has seen rapid adoption throughout the industry. In fact, all new chipsets and GPUs since 2008 from Intel, NVIDIA, and AMD/ATI already have integrated DisplayPort support. In 2008, major manufacturers including Dell, HP/Compaq, Lenovo, and Apple introduced products with DisplayPort and endorsed DisplayPort as the successor to DVI and HDMI for most digital display connections. Despite this endorsement, the introduction of DisplayPort-enabled products has proceeded slowly. However, DisplayPort is currently available on an increasing number of laptops, 23-inch or larger LCD and backlit LED displays, computers, and graphics cards for desktop and technical workstation use.

On the technical side, DisplayPort is a high-speed serial interface with up to four main data lanes (differential signal pairs) carrying multiplexed video and audio data, each of which supports a raw data rate of 1.62Gbps, 2.7Gbps, or 5.4Gbps (DisplayPort 1.2 or later only). Using all four lanes results in a maximum raw bandwidth of 6.48Gbps, 10.8Gbps, or 21.6Gbps, respectively. Because 8b/10b encoding is used, only 8 bits of every 10 are data, resulting in maximum true data throughputs of 5.184Gbps, 8.64Gbps, or 17.28Gbps, respectively.

Audio is optional, with support for up to eight channels of 16- or 24-bit linear PCM data at a 48KHz, 96KHz, or 192KHz sampling rate, with an uncompressed maximum audio bandwidth of 6.144Mbps.

DisplayPort 1.1 includes the following features:

- Small external connectors (slightly larger than universal serial bus [USB] size) with optional latching. Four display connectors can fit on a single PCIe expansion card bracket and fit easily in laptops.
- Cable lengths of up to 15 meters (49 feet), which allows for remote displays or projectors.
- Micro-packet network architecture over one to four lanes. Connections can use only as many lanes as necessary for reduced wire counts.
- High performance. A true data bandwidth of 8.64Gbps (four lanes at 2.16Gbps per lane) allows WQXGA 2560×1600 resolution.
- Support for internal (embedded) as well as external LCD connections. This allows a universal interface for both desktop and laptop systems.
- Optional audio that supports displays with built-in speakers.
- Optional HDCP to allow playing protected media.
- Interoperability with DVI and HDMI over a DisplayPort connector. You can connect to DVI or HDMI with simple and inexpensive adapters.
- An auxiliary 1Mbps channel, which allows for two-way communication for integrated cameras, microphones, and so on.
- A powered connector, which powers some LCD displays directly.
- An optional latching connector that uses a simple thumb-press release design with no bolts or jackscrews.

DisplayPort 1.2 is fully backward compatible with 1.1 and adds the following features:

- Double the performance. DisplayPort 1.2 offers 21.6Gbps raw (17.28Gbps true) bandwidth, which is more than twice that of HDMI 1.3a and nearly triple that of DVI.
- Multiple data streams, which allows support for two WQXGA 2560×1600 or four WUXGA 1920×1200 monitors daisy-chained over a single cable.
- An auxiliary channel speed increase to 480Mbps. This allows connections at USB 2.0 speed for cameras, microphones, or other devices.
- The Mini DisplayPort connector. This connector is approximately half the size yet provides full functionality for laptops or other devices where space is at a premium.

Table 12.13 compares the versions of DisplayPort.

Table 12.13   DisplayPort Versions

Version	Release Date	Notes
DisplayPort 1.0	May 2006	Initial release
DisplayPort 1.1	March 2007	Introduced "hybrid device" class, added support for HDCP content protection, and increased connector power requirements
DisplayPort 1.1a	January 2008	Corrected errata and clarified minor items
DisplayPort 1.2	Late-2009	Doubled performance, multiple data streams, a high-speed auxiliary channel, and the Mini DisplayPort connector

Note

Wireless DisplayPort is a standard that will enable DisplayPort 1.2 bandwidth and feature set for cable-free applications operating in 60GHz radio band; this was announced on November 2010 by WiGig Alliance and VESA as a cooperative effort.

The DisplayPort connector has 20 pins and is only slightly larger than USB size (15.9mm vs. 12mm wide). The pins consist of four data lanes (differential pairs), an auxiliary channel (differential pair), plus configuration and power pins. Figures 12.10 and 12.11 show the DisplayPort cable/plug and socket.

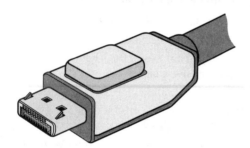

FIGURE 12.10 DisplayPort cable with latching plug connector (Belkin).

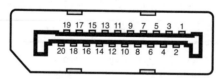

FIGURE 12.11 DisplayPort socket and pin configuration.

Apple introduced the Mini DisplayPort connector in October 2008, which was subsequently included as part of the official DisplayPort standard in 1.2 and later releases. The Mini DisplayPort connector has the same full complement of 20 pins as the standard DisplayPort connector, but it's about half the size (at only 7.4mm wide). Figures 12.12 and 12.13 show the Mini DisplayPort cable/plug and socket. Table 12.14 shows the DisplayPort socket connector pinout.

FIGURE 12.12 Mini DisplayPort cable and plug (Apple).

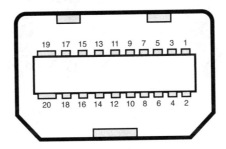

FIGURE 12.13 Mini DisplayPort socket and pin configuration.

Table 12.14 DisplayPort Socket Connector Pinout

Top Row		Bottom Row	
Pin Number	**Description**	**Pin Number**	**Description**
Pin 1	Lane 0+	Pin 2	Ground
Pin 3	Lane 0–	Pin 4	Lane 1+
Pin 5	Ground	Pin 6	Lane 1–
Pin 7	Lane 2+	Pin 8	Ground
Pin 9	Lane 2–	Pin 10	Lane 3+
Pin 11	Ground	Pin 12	Lane 3–
Pin 13	Config1	Pin 14	Config2
Pin 15	Aux. CH+	Pin 16	Ground
Pin 17	Aux. CH–	Pin 18	Hot Plug Detect
Pin 19	Power Return	Pin 20	+3.3V Power

This pinout is for source-device connectors. Sink-device connectors will have lanes 0–3 reversed in order (that is, lane 3 will be on pins 1 and 3, lane 0 will be on pins 10 and 12, and so on).

+3.3V power at 500mA max.

VESA has created several icons and logos associated with DisplayPort. The basic DisplayPort icon is used to label products incorporating DisplayPort technology, whereas the DisplayPort Certification Compliance logo is used on product marketing material to indicate devices that have been tested to ensure they are fully interoperable with other DisplayPort devices. Figure 12.14 shows the DisplayPort Certification Compliance logo. VESA maintains a list of certified devices on the www.displayport.org website.

The DisplayPort Multimode icon adds two + symbols to indicate a port or device that is fully backward compatible with both DVI and HDMI technology (via inexpensive cable adapters). Figure 12.15 shows the DisplayPort Multimode icon. Figure 12.16 shows an inexpensive DisplayPort to DVI adapter.

FIGURE 12.14 DisplayPort Certification Compliance logo.

FIGURE 12.15 Icon indicating a DisplayPort with Multimode (DVI and HDMI) support.

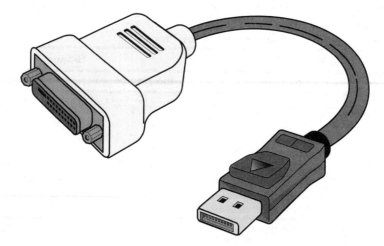

FIGURE 12.16 DisplayPort to DVI adapter, which works on MultiMode DisplayPort connectors.

When DisplayPort was released, many people wondered why we needed another digital display interface when we already had DVI and HDMI. Unfortunately, those interfaces carry both technical and licensing limitations that were preventing their universal adoption. DisplayPort is designed to overcome not only the technical limitations, but especially the licensing constraints and fees that the other interfaces brought along as baggage. The advanced technical capabilities of DisplayPort, including its ability to work with the new Thunderbolt I/O technology, combined with the elimination of licensing and its backward compatibility with existing interfaces, are likely to ensure its eventual adoption throughout the PC marketplace.

TV Display Interfaces

When video technology was introduced, it was based on television. However, a difference exists between the signals used by a television and those used by a computer monitor. In the United States, the National Television System Committee (NTSC) established color TV standards in 1953. Some other countries, such as Japan, followed this standard. Many countries in Europe, though, developed more sophisticated standards, including Phase Alternate Line (PAL) and Sequential Couleur Avec Mémoire (SECAM). Table 12.15 shows the differences among these standards.

Table 12.15   Television Versus Computer Monitors

Standard	Year Est.	Country	Lines	Rate
Television				
NTSC	1953 (color) 1941 (B&W)	U.S., Japan	525	60 fields/sec
PAL	1941	Europe[1]	625	50 fields/sec
SECAM	1962	France	625	25 fields/sec
HDTV[2]		Various countries	1080p 720p	25 fields/sec 60 frames/sec
NTSC	1953 (color) 1941 (B&W)	U.S., Japan	525	60 fields/sec
PAL	1941	Europe[1]	625	50 fields/sec
SECAM	1962	France	625	25 fields/sec
HDTV[2]		Various countries	1080i 1080/720p	25 fields/sec 60 frames/sec
Computer				
VGA	1987	U.S.	640×480[3]	72Hz

Field = 1/2 (0.5 frame)

1 England, Holland, and West Germany.

2 Various analog and digital HDTV standards have been introduced around the world, starting in France in 1948 (SECAM 755i, a now-discontinued analog version); Japan's analog MUSE 1035i is the oldest system (1979–present) in use. The U.S. standards (both digital) are listed above; other countries use various analog and digital standards.

3 VGA is based on more lines and uses pixels (480) versus lines; genlocking is used to lock pixels into lines and synchronize computers with TV standards.

To display computer screens on standard TV or to record them to videotape, you can use the TV-out connector on your video card or integrated motherboard video. TV-out is generally S-video or composite video. The resolution that these devices display on a TV set or record on videotape often is limited to VGA (640×480) or SVGA (800×600).

To connect your PC to an HDTV monitor, it is preferable to use a digital signal via a DVI, HDMI, or DisplayPort connection. If your current video adapter only has analog VGA output, you'll want to upgrade to a video adapter with a DVI, HDMI, or DisplayPort digital output. Because most HDTVs use HDMI, if your video card has DVI or DisplayPort, you can use a DVI-to-HDMI or DisplayPort-to-HDMI adapter if necessary. If you need HDCP support for watching HD premium content, make sure your display and card support HDCP. Otherwise, you may not be able to watch the program or it may be displayed at reduced resolution.

3D Graphics Accelerators

Since the late 1990s, 3D acceleration—once limited to exotic add-on cards designed for hardcore game players—has become commonplace in the PC world. With the introduction of the Aero desktop in Windows Vista and later, 3D imaging is even utilized in the user interface, joining other full-motion 3D uses such as sports, first-person shooters, team combat, driving, and many other types of PC gaming. Because even low-cost integrated chipsets offer some 3D support, virtually any user of a recent-model computer can enjoy 3D lighting, perspective, texture, and shading effects. The Windows DirectX Diagnostics program displays 3D information about the graphics hardware in your computer (see Figure 12.17).

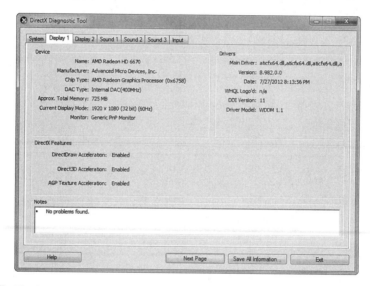

FIGURE 12.17 The Windows DirectX Diagnostics program displays information about the computer's current DirectX capabilities.

Note

At a minimum, enabling the Windows Aero interface in Vista and 7 requires graphics hardware that supports DirectX 7 3D graphics; however, for maximum functionality, graphics hardware that supports DirectX 9 or greater is required. Many recent games require DirectX 11, which is not available for Windows XP and earlier versions. Windows 8 includes DirectX 11.1.

How 3D Accelerators Work

To construct an animated 3D sequence, a computer can mathematically animate the sequences between keyframes. A keyframe identifies a specific point. A bouncing ball, for example, can have three keyframes: up, down, and up. Using these frames as reference points, the computer can create all the interim images between the top and bottom. This creates the effect of a smoothly bouncing ball.

After it has created the basic sequence, the system can then refine the appearance of the images by filling them in with color. The most primitive and least effective fill method is called *flat shading*, in which a shape is simply filled with a solid color. *Gouraud shading*, a slightly more effective technique, involves the assignment of colors to specific points on a shape. The points are then joined using a smooth gradient between the colors.

A more processor-intensive (and much more effective) type of fill is called *texture mapping*. The 3D application includes patterns—or textures—in the form of small bitmaps that it tiles onto the shapes in the image, just as you can tile a small bitmap to form the wallpaper for your Windows desktop. The primary difference is that the 3D application can modify the appearance of each tile by applying perspective and shading to achieve 3D effects. When lighting effects that simulate fog, glare, directional shadows, and others are added, the 3D animation comes close indeed to matching reality.

Until the late 1990s, 3D applications had to rely on support from software routines to convert these abstractions into live images. This placed a heavy burden on the system processor in the PC, which has a significant impact on the performance not only of the visual display, but also of any other applications the computer might be running. Starting in the period from 1996 to 1997, chipsets on most video adapters began to take on many of the tasks involved in rendering 3D images, greatly lessening the load on the system processor and boosting overall system performance.

There have been roughly 12 generations of 3D graphics hardware on PCs, a process that has lasted more than 15 years, as detailed in Table 12.16.

Table 12.16 Brief History of 3D Acceleration

Generation	Dates	Technologies	Example Product/ Chipset
1st	1996–1997	3D PCI card with passthrough to 2D graphics card; OpenGL and GLIDE APIs	3dfx Voodoo
2nd	1997–1998	2D/3D PCI card	ATI Rage, NVIDIA RIVA 128
3rd	1999	2D/3D AGP 1x/2x card	3dfx Voodoo 3, ATI Rage Pro, NVIDIA TnT2
4th	1999–2000	DirectX 7 API, AGP 4x	NVIDIA GeForce 256, ATI Radeon
5th	2001	DirectX 8 API, programmable vertex and pixel shaders	NVIDIA GeForce 3, NVIDIA GeForce 4 Ti
6th	2001–2002	DirectX 8.1 API	ATI Radeon 8500, ATI Radeon 9000
7th	2002–2003	DirectX 9 API, AGP 8x	ATI Radeon 9700, NVIDIA GeForce FX 5900
8th	2004–2005	PCIe, DirectX 9.0c	ATI X800, NVIDIA GeForce 6800
9th	2004–2006	Dual-GPU rendering with PCIe x8, x16	ATI X1900, NVIDIA GeForce 7800; ATI CrossFire, NVIDIA SLI motherboard chipsets and compatible cards
10th	2007–2008	DirectX 10, Windows Vista	ATI HD 2xxx-4xxx, NVIDIA GeForce 8-9 series
11th	2009–2010	DirectX 11, Windows 7	AMD Radeon HD 5xxx-6xxx, NVIDIA GeForce 2xx-5xx series
12th	2011+	DirectX 11.1, Windows 8	AMD Radeon HD 7xxx, NVIDIA GTX 6xx series

With virtually every recent graphics card on the market featuring DirectX 10 or greater capabilities, you don't need to spend a fortune to achieve a reasonable level of 3D graphics. Many cards in the $50–$150 range use lower-performance variants of current high-end GPUs, or they might use the previous year's leading GPU. These cards typically provide more-than-adequate performance for 2D business applications. All current 3D accelerators also support dual-display and TV-out or HDTV capabilities, enabling you to work and play at the same time.

However, keep in mind that the more you spend on a 3D accelerator card, the greater the onboard memory and the faster the accelerator chip you can enjoy. If money is no object, you can buy a graphics card featuring the currently fastest GPU for more than $500. Fortunately, there are plenty of choices using either NVIDIA or AMD GPUs in the less than $500 price range that offer plenty of 3D gaming performance, including support for dual-GPU operations (NVIDIA SLI or AMD CrossFireX), which split rendering chores across the GPUs in both video cards for faster game display than with a single card. GPUs that support DirectX 10/11 are the preferred choice for anyone who wants to play current generation games.

Mid-range cards costing $100–$300 are often based on GPUs that use designs similar to the high-end products but might have slower memory and core clock speeds or a smaller number of rendering pipelines. These cards provide a good middle ground for users who play games fairly often but can't cost-justify high-end cards. Cards under $100 are best used for low-cost replacements for chipset-integrated video. These cards typically have performance that is no better than that available from current CPU-integrated video.

The basic function of 3D software is to convert image abstractions into the fully realized images that are then displayed on the monitor. The image abstractions typically consist of the following elements:

- **Vertices**—Locations of objects in three-dimensional space, described in terms of their x, y, and z coordinates on three axes representing height, width, and depth.

- **Primitives**—The simple geometric objects the application uses to create more complex constructions, described in terms of the relative locations of their vertices. This serves not only to specify the location of the object in the 2D image, but also to provide perspective because the three axes can define any location in three-dimensional space.

- **Textures**—Two-dimensional bitmap images or surfaces designed to be mapped onto primitives. The software enhances the 3D effect by modifying the appearance of the textures, depending on the location and attitude of the primitive. This process is called *perspective correction*. Some applications use another process, called *MIP mapping*, that uses different versions of the same texture containing varying amounts of detail, depending on how close the object is to the viewer in the three-dimensional space. Another technique, called *depth cueing*, reduces the color and intensity of an object's fill as the object moves farther away from the viewer.

Using these elements, the abstract image descriptions must then be rendered, meaning they are converted to visible form. Rendering depends on two standardized functions that convert the abstractions into the completed image that is displayed onscreen. The standard functions performed in rendering are as follows:

- **Geometry**—The sizing, orienting, and moving of primitives in space and the calculation of the effects produced by the virtual light sources that illuminate the image

- **Rasterization**—The converting of primitives into pixels on the video display by filling the shapes with properly illuminated shading, textures, or a combination of the two

A modern video adapter that includes a chipset capable of 3D video acceleration has special built-in hardware that can perform the rasterization process much more quickly than if it were done by software (using the system processor) alone. Most chipsets with 3D acceleration perform the following rasterization functions right on the adapter:

- **Scan conversion**—The determination of which onscreen pixels fall into the space delineated by each primitive

- **Shading**—The process of filling pixels with smoothly flowing color using the flat or Gouraud shading technique

- **Texture mapping**—The process of filling pixels with images derived from a 2D sample picture or surface image

- **Visible surface determination**—The identification of which pixels in a scene are obscured by other objects closer to the viewer in three-dimensional space

- **Animation**—The process of switching rapidly and cleanly to successive frames of motion sequences

- **Antialiasing**—The process of adjusting color boundaries to smooth edges on rendered objects

Note

To learn more about 3D techniques such as fogging, Z-buffering, T-buffering, programmable shading, and rendering methods, see the sections, "Typical 3D Techniques," "Advanced 3D Filtering and Rendering," and "Single- Versus Multi-Pass Rendering," in Chapter 12, "Video Hardware," in *Upgrading and Repairing PCs*, 19th Edition.

Software Optimization

It's important to realize that the presence of an advanced 3D-rendering feature on any given video card is meaningless unless game and application software designers optimize their software to take advantage of the feature. Although various 3D standards exist (OpenGL and DirectX), video card makers provide drivers that make their games play with the leading standards. Because some cards do play better with certain games, you should read the reviews in publications and websites to see how your favorite graphics card performs with them. Typically, it can take several months or longer after a new version of DirectX or OpenGL is introduced before 3D games take full advantage of the 3D rendering features provided by the new application programming interface (API).

Some video cards allow you to perform additional optimization by adjusting settings for OpenGL, Direct 3D, RAMDAC, and bus clock speeds, as well as other options. Note that the bare-bones 3D graphics card drivers provided as part of Microsoft Windows usually don't provide these dialog boxes. Be sure to use the drivers provided with the graphics card or download updated versions from the graphics card or GPU vendor's website.

APIs

APIs provide hardware and software vendors a means to create drivers and programs that can work quickly and reliably across a variety of platforms. When APIs exist, drivers can be written to interface with the API rather than directly with the OS and its underlying hardware.

Currently, the leading game APIs include SGI's OpenGL and Microsoft's Direct3D (part of DirectX). OpenGL and Direct3D are available for virtually all leading graphics cards. At one time, a third popular game API was Glide, an enhanced version of OpenGL that is restricted to graphics cards that use 3dfx chipsets, which are no longer on the market.

OpenGL

The latest version of OpenGL is version 4.2, released on August 8, 2011. OpenGL 4.2 is based on OpenGL 4.1, which has the following improvements over OpenGL 3.x:

- 64-bit double-precision floating point support
- New shader stages and subroutines for faster and better quality of 3D rendering
- Better performance compared with the previous OpenGL 3.x versions

OpenGL 4.2 adds the following features:

- Support for shaders with atomic counters and load/store/atomic read-modify-write operations to a single level of a texture
- Capturing GPU-tessellated geometry and drawing multiple instances of the result of a transform feedback to enable complex objects to be efficiently repositioned and replicated
- Support for modifying an arbitrary subset of a compressed texture, without having to re-download the whole texture to the GPU for significant performance improvements

The following GPUs include OpenGL 4.2 support: NVIDIA GeForce 400 series, NVIDIA GeForce 500 series, NVIDIA GeForce 600 series, ATI Radeon HD 5000 series, AMD Radeon HD 6000 Series, and AMD Radeon HD 7000 Series.

OpenGL 4.x is backwards compatible with OpenGL 3.x.

Although OpenGL is a popular gaming API, it is also widely used in 3D rendering for specialized business applications, including mapping, life sciences, and other fields. Windows XP and newer can support OpenGL either through software or through hardware acceleration. For a particular graphics card to support hardware acceleration of OpenGL, the driver developer must include an installable client driver (ICD). The ICD is distributed as part of the driver package that the video card or GPU vendor provides. Thus, driver updates can improve OpenGL performance as well as DirectX (Direct3D) performance.

To learn more about OpenGL, see the OpenGL website at www.opengl.org.

Microsoft DirectX

Direct3D is part of Microsoft's comprehensive multimedia API, DirectX. Although the most recent versions of DirectX (9.0c and up) provide support for higher-order surfaces (converting 3D surfaces into curves), vertex shaders, and pixel shaders, significant differences exist between DirectX versions in how these operations are performed.

DirectX 9.0c uses separate pixel and vertex shaders to create 3D objects. Although DirectX 9.0c provides greater precision in data handling as well as support for more instructions, more textures, and more registers than its predecessors, its use of separate shaders can still lead to slow 3D rendering when more pixels must be rendered than shaders, or vice versa. Shader Model 3 (used by DirectX 9.0c) is simply a development of the split-function design first developed for Shader Model 1 (used by DirectX 8.0) back in 2001, adding support for more instructions and greater numerical accuracy.

DirectX 10, developed for Windows Vista, includes a completely rebuilt Direct3D rendering engine with a brand-new shader design, Shader Model 4. Shader Model 4 adds a geometry shader to the vertex shader and pixel shader design used in earlier shader models to improve the handling of real-time scene changes such as explosions. However, the biggest single change in Shader Model 4 is the use of unified shaders that can be switched between vertex, pixel, and geometry shader operations on the fly, eliminating bottlenecks and improving performance, no matter what types of 3D data exist in a scene.

Note

With the replacement of dedicated vertex and pixel shaders in the DirectX 10 3D rendering pipeline, DirectX 10 GPUs are rated in terms of the number of stream processors on board. Each stream processor performs vertex, geometry, and pixel shading as needed.

When you are comparing two otherwise-equal DirectX 10 GPUs (same GPU, memory size and speed, motherboard and memory bus designs), the GPU with a larger number of stream processors will be faster.

Other architectural changes in DirectX 10 include process optimizations to reduce the load on the CPU. In a sample of different types of images rendered, DirectX 10 reduced the command cycles by as much as 90% over DirectX 9.

DirectX 11 was originally developed for Windows 7 (and is also available for Windows Vista) and adds several new features:

- **Tessellation**—Provides additional pipeline stages that increase the number of visible polygons at runtime.
- **Multithreaded rendering**—Enables the execution of Direct3D commands on multiple processor cores.
- **Compute shaders**—Provides an additional stage independent of the Direct3D pipeline that enables general-purpose computing on the graphics processor, part of Shader Model 5. This feature is supported by the processor with integrated graphics.
- **Dynamic shader linkage**—A limited runtime shader linkage that allows for improved shader specialization during application execution.

To obtain a version of DirectX 11 for Windows Vista, see KB971512 at http://support.microsoft.com for details.

DirectX 11.1 is built into Windows 8, Windows RT (the tablet-only version of Windows 8 for ARM processors), and Windows Server 2012. Some of its improvements over DirectX 11 include:

- Improved 2D and 3D rendering
- Ability to discard resources and resource views and to clear unneeded resource views
- Shader Model 5.0 instructions are now usable in all shader stages

For more details about the differences between DirectX 11 and 11.1's DirectDraw features, see http://msdn.microsoft.com/en-us/library/windows/desktop/hh404562(v=vs.85).aspx.

It's important to realize that DirectX 10/11/11.1 GPUs retain full compatibility with DirectX 9.0c and earlier DirectX versions, so you can play the latest games as well as old favorites with a DX10 or DX11-compliant video card. Updates for DirectX are provided via www.windowsupdate.com. More information about DirectX is available from Microsoft at www.microsoft.com/directx.

Note

For benchmarking DirectX 9/10/11 and OpenGL 4.x operations on your graphics/video hardware, I recommend the UniGine Heaven DX11 benchmark utility, available from http://unigine.com/products/heaven/.

Dual-GPU Scene Rendering

In Table 12.16, I placed the development of dual PCIe graphics card solutions as the ninth generation of 3D acceleration. The ability to connect two cards to render a single display more quickly isn't exactly new: The long-defunct 3dfx Voodoo 2 offered an option called *scan-line interfacing* (SLI) that pairs two Voodoo 2 cards on the PCI bus, with each card writing half the screen in alternating lines. With 3dfx's version of SLI, card number one wrote the odd-numbered screen lines (one, three, five, and so on), whereas card number two wrote the even-numbered screen lines (two, four, six, and so on). Although effective, use of SLI with Voodoo 2 was an expensive proposition that only a handful of deep-pocketed gamers took advantage of.

A few companies also experimented with using multiple GPUs on a single card to gain a similar performance advantage, but these cards never became popular. However, the idea of doubling graphics performance via multiple video cards has proven too good to abandon entirely, even after 3dfx went out of business.

NVIDIA SLI

When NVIDIA bought what was left of 3dfx, it inherited the SLI trademark and, in mid-2004, reintroduced the concept of using two cards to render a screen under the same acronym. However, NVIDIA's version of SLI has a different meaning and much more intelligence behind it.

NVIDIA uses the term *SLI* to refer to scalable link interface. The *scaling* refers to load-balancing, which adjusts how much of the work each card performs to render a particular scene, depending on how complex the scene is. To enable SLI, you need the following components:

- A PCIe motherboard with an SLI-compatible chipset and two PCIe video slots designed for SLI operation
- Two NVIDIA-based video cards with SLI support

Note

Originally, you needed to use two identical cards for NVIDIA SLI. With the introduction of NVIDIA ForceWare v81.85 and higher driver versions, this is no longer necessary. Just as with the AMD CrossFire and CrossFireX multi-GPU solution, the cards need to be from the same GPU family, but they don't need to be from the same manufacturer. You can obtain updated drivers from your video card maker or from the NVIDIA website (www.nvidia.com).

In most cases, a special bridge device known as a *multipurpose I/O* (MIO) connects the cards. The MIO is supplied with SLI-compatible motherboards, but some SLI-compatible cards don't use it.

To learn more about SLI and for a list of SLI-compatible GPUs and nForce motherboard chipsets, visit NVIDIA's GeForce SLI website (http://www.geforce.com/hardware/technology/sli).

Figure 12.18 illustrates a typical SLI hardware configuration. Note the MIO device connecting the cards.

AMD CrossFireX

AMD's CrossFireX, an improved version of ATI's CrossFire multi-GPU technology, uses three methods to speed up display performance: alternate frame rendering, supertiling (which divides the scene into alternating sections and uses each card to render parts of the scene), and load-balancing scissor operation (similar to SLI's load-balancing). The AMD Catalyst driver uses alternate frame rendering for best performance, but it automatically switches to one of the other modes for games that don't work with alternate frame rendering.

MIO bridge between the SLI-enabled cards

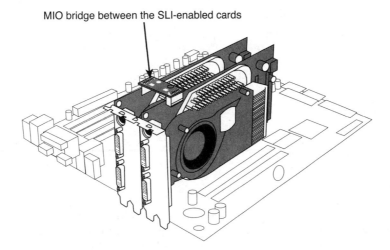

FIGURE 12.18 NVIDIA SLI installation using a multipurpose I/O (MIO) bridge device.

To achieve better image quality than with a single card, CrossFireX offers various SuperAA (antialiasing) modes, which blend the results of antialiasing by each card. CrossFireX also improves anisotropic filtering by blending the filtering performed by each card.

To use CrossFireX, you need the following components:

- A PCIe motherboard with a CrossFireX-compatible chipset and two or more PCIe video slots designed for CrossFireX operation
- A supported combination of ATI CrossFireX-supported cards
- AMD CrossFireX bridge interconnects (when necessary, varies with motherboard and card combination)

Note

For specific models of motherboards, video cards, power supplies, memory, and cases designed to support CrossFireX, see http://sites.amd.com/us/game/technology/Pages/crossfirex.aspx.

First-generation CrossFire cards required users to buy special CrossFire Edition cards that contained the composting engine (an Xilinx XC3S400 chip) and used a proprietary DMS-59 port for interconnecting the cards. One of these cards was paired with a standard Radeon card from the same series via a clumsy external cable between the CrossFire Edition's DMS port and the DVI port on the standard card. Newer CrossFire-and CrossFireX compatible cards use a CrossFire bridge interconnect (similar in concept to the SLI MIO component) to connect matching cards; a few models can run in CrossFire mode without a bridge interconnect.

Note

For more information about CrossFire X and CrossFire compatibility, see http://sites.amd.com/us/game/technology/Pages/crossfirex.aspx.

CrossFire and CrossFireX can be disabled to permit multimonitor operation; CrossFire and CrossFireX cards can also be used to implement physics effects in games that use the HavokFX physics technology (www.havok.com).

AMD Eyefinity for Multiple-Display Gaming

AMD Eyefinity enables a single game to use up to six displays for simultaneous views of the 3D game environment, control panels, and more. The first two displays can be connected by either digital (DVI, HDMI, DisplayPort) or VGA analog cables. Additional displays must be connected by DisplayPort (either native DisplayPort ports or DVI or HDMI ports connected to active DisplayPort adapters).

Note

Eyefinity is supported by a wide range of AMD RADEON desktop and mobile GPUs. To learn more about Eyefinity and the games that support it, visit www.amd.com/us/products/technologies/amd-eyefinity-technology/Pages/eyefinity.aspx.

Monitors

The monitors typically used with PCs come in a variety of sizes and resolutions and are typically based on one of two display technologies: liquid crystal display (LCD) or cathode-ray tube (CRT). A newer technology, organic LED (OLED), is expected to reach the market in 2013. Larger displays such as big-screen TVs and projectors can also use LCD or backlit LED technology but may use plasma or DLP technology as well. This section discusses the various features, specifications, and technologies used in PC monitors.

Display Specifications

A number of features and specifications differentiate one display from another. Some of these can be confusing, and some are more important than others. The following sections examine the features and specifications to look for when comparing or selecting displays.

Display Size

PC monitors come in various sizes, generally ranging from 15 inches to 30 inches in diagonal measurement. Displays smaller than 15 inches are available for specialized uses (and are often used on smaller laptop or palmtop/netbook systems, ultrabooks, smartphones, tablets, and touchscreen media players). Displays larger than 30 inches are also available; however, these are generally categorized as large format multimedia displays or televisions rather than as PC monitors. In general, the larger the monitor, the higher the price tag; however, there are often "sweet spots" where a certain size may have a price advantage over smaller sizes due to sales and manufacturing popularity.

Display sizes are measured diagonally, which is an artifact from the round tubes used in the first televisions, where the diagonal measurement was equal to the physical diameter of the tube. Whereas the diagonal display size measures the physical size of the display, the *viewable image size* refers to the diagonal measurement of the usable area on the screen (for example, the OS desktop). On an LCD or LED panel, the physical diagonal measurement and the viewable image size of the display are the same. With CRTs, however, the viewable image size is typically 1 inch smaller than the advertised diagonal display size. Therefore, when you're comparing LCDs or LEDs and CRTs with the same diagonal size, the LCD or LED actually offers a larger viewable image.

Tip

Larger, higher-resolution monitors retain their value longer than most other computer components. Although it's common for a newer, faster processor to come out right after you have purchased your computer or to find the same model with a bigger hard disk for the same money, a good monitor can outlast your computer. If you purchase monitors with longer term usage considerations in mind, you can save money on your next system by reusing your existing monitor.

Resolution

Resolution indicates the amount of detail a monitor can render. This quantity is expressed in the number of horizontal and vertical picture elements, or *pixels*, contained in the screen. The total is usually expressed in the millions of pixels, or *megapixels*. As the resolution increases, the image consists of a greater number of pixels. With more pixels, you can see more of a given image, or you can view the image in greater detail.

As PC video technology has evolved, available resolutions have grown at a steady pace. Table 12.17 shows the industry standard resolutions (from lowest to highest) used in PC graphics adapters and displays as well as the terms or designations commonly used to describe them.

Table 12.17 Graphics Display Resolution Standards

Designation	Resolution (HxV)	Megapixels	Aspect Ratio
CGA	320×200	0.06	1.33[1]
EGA	640×350	0.22	1.33[1]
VGA	640×480	0.31	1.33
WVGA	854×480	0.41	1.78
SVGA	800×600	0.48	1.33
XGA	1024×768	0.79	1.33
HD 720	1280×720	0.92	1.78
WXGA[2]	1280×768	0.98	1.67
XGA+	1152×864	1.00	1.33
WXGA[2]	1280×800	1.02	1.60
WXGA[2]	1366×768	1.05	1.78
WEXGA	1280×854	1.09	1.50
QVGA	1280×960	1.23	1.33
WXGA+	1440×900	1.30	1.60
SXGA	1280×1024	1.31	1.25
SXGA+	1400×1050	1.47	1.33
WSXGA-	1600×900	1.44	1.78
WSXGA	1600×1024	1.64	1.56
WSXGA+	1680×1050	1.76	1.60
UXGA	1600×1200	1.92	1.33
HD 1080	1920×1080	2.07	1.78
WUXGA	1920×1200	2.30	1.60
QXGA	2048×1536	3.15	1.33
WQXGA	2560×1600	4.10	1.60

Table 12.17   Continued

Designation	Resolution (HxV)	Megapixels	Aspect Ratio
QSXGA	2560×2048	5.24	1.25
WQSXGA	3200×2048	6.55	1.56
QUXGA	3200×2400	7.68	1.33
WQUXGA	3840×2400	9.22	1.60
HXGA	4096×3072	12.58	1.33
WHXGA	5120×3200	16.38	1.60
HSXGA	5120×4096	20.97	1.25
WHSXGA	6400×4096	26.21	1.56
HUXGA	6400×4800	30.72	1.33
WHUXGA	7680×4800	36.86	1.60

1 CGA and EGA used non-square pixels on a 4:3 display.

2 WXGA designates several slightly different resolutions.

Display adapters normally support a variety of resolutions; however, what a display can handle is usually much more limited. Therefore, the specific resolution you use is normally dictated by the display, not the adapter. A given video adapter and display combination will usually have an allowable maximum (usually dictated by the display), but it can also work at several resolutions less than the maximum. Because LCD and LED monitors are designed to run at a single native resolution, they must use electronics to scale the image to other choices. Older LCD panels handled scaling poorly, but even though current LCD and LED backlit panels perform scaling fairly well, you are almost always better off selecting the single specific resolution that is native to the display you are using. However, if the native resolution of the display is exceptionally high, you can choose lower resolutions to achieve larger and more readable icons and text.

Aspect Ratio

A given resolution has a horizontal and vertical component, with the horizontal component the larger of the two. The aspect ratio of a display is the ratio between the horizontal and vertical number of pixels. It is calculated as the width (in pixels) divided by the height. A number of different aspect ratios have been used in PC displays over the years. Most of the early display formats were only slightly wider than they were tall. More recently, wider formats have become popular. Aspect ratios of 1.5 or higher (numerically) are considered "widescreen" displays. Originally 1.33 (4:3) was the most common aspect ratio for displays because it matched the aspect ratio of the original standard definition televisions. The first generation of PC widescreen displays use a 1.60 (16:10 or 8:5) ratio, whereas 2nd generation displays use the 1.78 (16:9) ratio, which is also the most popular format for widescreen televisions. Although many PC users (myself included) preferred the additional vertical resolution of the 16:10 ratio over the 16:9, the LCD manufacturers found it more economical to produce the same 16:9 ratio display for PCs as they do for televisions, thus eliminating 16:10 versions as a choice. Table 12.18 shows the various aspect ratios and designations.

Table 12.18   Standard Aspect Ratios and Designations

Numerical Ratio	Fractional Ratio	Format Designation
1.25	5:4	Standard
1.33	4:3	Standard
1.50	3:2	Widescreen
1.56	25:16	Widescreen
1.60	16:10	Widescreen
1.67	5:3	Widescreen
1.78	16:9	Widescreen
1.83	11:6	Widescreen

1.50 and higher numerical aspect ratios are considered to be "widescreen."

Figure 12.19 shows the physical difference between standard and widescreen aspect ratio display formats.

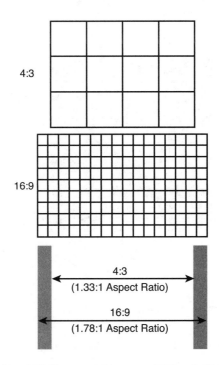

FIGURE 12.19   Standard (4:3 or 1.33:1) versus widescreen (16:9 or 1.78:1) display aspect ratios.

Pixels

In a color monitor, each picture element (pixel) consists of three red, green, and blue (RGB) subpixels. By varying the intensity of each of the subpixels, you can cause the overall color and brightness of the pixel to be anything from black (all off) to white (all on) and almost any color or level in between.

The physical geometry of the RGB subpixels varies depending on the type of display, but the shape is normally either rectangular stripes or round dots. LCD monitors normally have the three subpixels arranged as rectangular vertical stripes in a linear repeating arrangement. CRTs may also use linear stripes, or they can have staggered stripes or dot triads.

When you're choosing a display, the most important considerations are the combination of size and resolution. The overall combination of size and resolution is normally expressed in pixels per inch (ppi), but it can also be expressed in pixel pitch, which is the distance between pixels in millimeters. A higher ppi number (or lower pixel pitch) means that fixed size images such as icons and text will be smaller and possibly harder to read. Pixel pitch is also sometimes called *dot pitch*, in reference to the dot-shaped subpixels used on some displays.

For a given size screen, higher resolution displays have a higher ppi number, which corresponds to a lower pixel pitch number. As a result, the picture elements are closer together, producing a sharper picture onscreen. Conversely, screens with a lower ppi number (which equals a larger pixel/dot pitch) tend to produce images that are more grainy and less clear.

Figure 12.20 illustrates a dot-shaped subpixel arrangement most commonly found on shadow-mask base CRTs, where the pixel or dot pitch is the shortest distance between same-color subpixels.

Figures 12.21 and 12.22 show striped subpixel arrangements in both linear and staggered forms. Of these, the linear form is the most common, used on virtually all LCDs and LEDs and most aperture grille–based CRTs. With striped subpixels, the pitch is measured as the horizontal or vertical distance between same color subpixels.

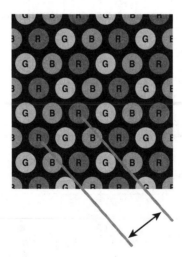

FIGURE 12.20 Dot-shaped subpixels, where pixel or dot pitch is the shortest distance between same color subpixels.

Generally, the higher the resolution, the larger the display you will want. Why? Because OS and application program icons and text normally use a constant number of pixels, higher display resolutions make these screen elements smaller onscreen. By using a larger display, you can use higher resolution settings and still have icons and text that are large enough to be readable. Although it is possible to change icon and text size, this often causes other problems with formatting in various windows and dialog boxes, such that in most cases it is best to stick with the default sizes.

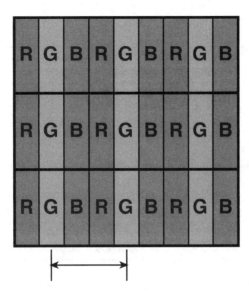

FIGURE 12.21 Stripe-shaped subpixels in a linear arrangement, where pixel pitch is the distance between same-color subpixel stripes.

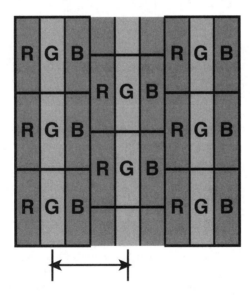

FIGURE 12.22 Stripe-shaped subpixels in a staggered arrangement, where pixel pitch is the distance between same-color subpixel stripes.

At lower resolutions, text and onscreen icons are large. Because the screen elements used for the Windows desktop and software menus are at a fixed pixel width and height, you'll notice that they shrink in size onscreen as you change to the higher resolutions. You'll be able to see more of your document or web page onscreen at the higher resolutions because each object requires less of the screen. Tables 12.19 and 12.20 show the sizes and resolutions for commonly available standard and widescreen LCD monitors.

Table 12.19   Common Sizes and Resolutions for Non-Widescreen (<1.50 Ratio) Monitors

Display Size	Designation	Native Resolution	Megapixels	Pixels Aspect Ratio	Pixel per Inch	Pitch (mm)
15.0 in.	XGA	1024×768	0.79	1.33	85	0.298
17.0 in.	SXGA	1280×1024	1.31	1.25	96	0.263
19.0 in.	SXGA	1280×1024	1.31	1.25	86	0.294
20.0 in.	UXGA	1600×1200	1.92	1.33	100	0.254

Table 12.20   Common Sizes and Resolutions for Widescreen (>1.50 Ratio) Monitors

Display Size	Designation	Native Resolution	Megapixels	Pixels Aspect Ratio	Pixel per Inch	Pitch (mm)
16.0 in.	WXGA	1366×768	1.05	1.78	98	0.259
17.0 in.	WXGA+	1440×900	1.30	1.60	100	0.254
19.0 in.	WXGA+	1440×900	1.30	1.60	89	0.284
19.0 in.	WSXGA+	1680×1050	1.76	1.60	104	0.244
20.0 in.	WXGA+	1440×900	1.30	1.60	85	0.299
20.0 in.	WSXGA-	1600×900	1.44	1.78	92	0.277
20.0 in.	WSXGA+	1680×1050	1.76	1.60	99	0.256
22.0 in.	WXGA+	1440×900	1.30	1.60	77	0.329
22.0 in.	WSXGA+	1680×1050	1.76	1.60	90	0.282
24.0 in.	HD 1080	1920×1080	2.07	1.78	92	0.277
24.0 in.	WUXGA	1920×1200	2.30	1.60	94	0.269
26.0 in.	HD 1080	1920×1080	2.07	1.78	85	0.300
26.0 in.	WUXGA	1920×1200	2.30	1.60	87	0.292
30.0 in.	WQXGA	2560×1600	4.10	1.60	101	0.252

Because LCD monitors have a 1:1 relationship between resolution and pixels, any two displays having the same size and resolution always have the same pixel per inch or pixel pitch specification. Regardless of the actual resolution, any two displays having the same number of pixels per inch will display text, icons, and other elements on the screen at the same sizing. Although having a higher resolution display is generally considered better, you need to be careful when selecting small LCD displays with higher resolutions because icons and text will be much smaller than you might be accustomed to. You can change the icon and font sizes in Windows to compensate, but this often causes problems such as abnormal word wrapping in dialog boxes. Also, many fonts are fixed, and they will remain at the smaller size no matter what settings you change.

Depending on their ability to see and read small text, many people will have difficulty seeing the text and icons when the display is rated at 100 ppi or higher. If you are going to choose a display rated over 100 ppi, you may need to either sit closer to the screen or use bifocals or reading glasses to read it. Changing resolution to a lower setting is usually unsatisfactory with a flat-panel display because either the display will simply be smaller (text and icons will remain the same size, but you can't fit as much on the screen) or the display will attempt to scale the data to fit the screen. However, scaling invariably results in a blurred and distorted image. The bottom line is that LCDs really work well only at their native resolution—something you should strongly consider when purchasing.

As a consolation, even with their tinier text and icons, LCD and LED backlit screens are much sharper and clearer than CRT-based monitors. So, even though the text and icons are physically smaller, they are often more readable with less eyestrain because they are sharp and perfectly focused.

Note

CRTs don't have a 1:1 relationship between resolution and pixels. Therefore, when you're comparing CRTs, the smaller the pixel pitch, the sharper the images will be. As an example, the original IBM PC color monitor from the early 1980s had a pixel pitch of .43mm, whereas newer color CRTs have a pixel pitch between .25mm and .27mm, with high-end models offering .24mm or less. To avoid grainy images on a CRT, look for those with a pixel pitch of .26mm or smaller.

Horizontal and Vertical Frequency

Analog display connections such as VGA are designed to transmit signals that drive the display to draw images. These signals tell the display to draw an image by painting lines of pixels from left to right and from top to bottom. For example, if the display resolution is 1024×768, that means there are 768 lines that would be drawn, one after the other, from top to bottom. Once the 768th line is drawn, the entire image would be completed, and the process would repeat starting again from the top.

The speed at which this image drawing occurs has two components, called the *horizontal frequency* and the *vertical frequency*. These frequencies are also called *scan* or *refresh rates*. The horizontal frequency is the speed in which the horizontal lines are drawn, expressed as the total number of lines per second. The vertical frequency (or vertical refresh rate) is the speed in which complete images are drawn, expressed in the number of images per second.

Using a 1024×768 display as an example, if the vertical refresh rate is 60Hz, then all of the 768 lines that make up the image would need to be drawn 60 times per second, resulting in a horizontal frequency of 768 lines per image × 60 images per second, which equals 46,060 total lines per second, or a frequency of about 46KHz. If the vertical refresh rate were increased to 85Hz, the horizontal frequency would be 768×85 = 65,280, or about 65.3KHz. The actual figures are technically a bit higher at 47.8KHz and 68.7KHz, respectively, because there is about a 5% overhead called the *vertical blanking interval* that was originally designed to allow the electron beam to move from the bottom back to the top of the screen without being seen. Although there is no electron beam in LCD displays, the blanking time is still used for backward compatibility as well as to send additional data that is not part of the image. The exact amount of vertical and horizontal blanking time required varies by the resolution and mode. It is governed by the VESA CVT (Coordinated Video Timings) standard.

CRT Refresh Rate Considerations

Displays with analog connections usually have a range of scan frequencies that they can handle, which effectively controls the minimum and maximum resolutions that can be displayed. Of the vertical and horizontal frequencies, for CRT displays the vertical refresh rate is more important because it controls flicker. A refresh rate that is too low causes CRT screens to flicker, contributing to eyestrain. The higher the refresh rate you use with a CRT display, the less eyestrain and discomfort you will experience while staring at the screen.

A *flicker-free refresh rate* is a refresh rate high enough to prevent you from seeing flicker on a CRT. The flicker-free refresh rate varies with the size and resolution of the monitor setting (larger and higher resolutions require higher refresh rates) as well as the individual because some people are more sensitive to it than others. In my experience, a 75Hz refresh rate is the minimum anybody should use with a CRT, especially at resolutions of 1024×768 and higher. Lower rates produce a noticeable flicker, which can cause eyestrain, fatigue, and headaches. However, although a 75Hz vertical refresh rate is sufficient for most, some people require a setting as high as 85Hz before the image is truly flicker-free. For that reason, 85Hz is considered by VESA to be the optimum refresh rate for CRT displays. Because a refresh rate that is too high can reduce video performance by making the adapter work harder to update the image more frequently, I recommend using the lowest refresh rate you are comfortable with.

Note

CRT manufacturers often used the term *optimal resolution* to refer to the highest resolution a given CRT monitor supports at the 85Hz VESA standard for flicker-free viewing.

Table 12.21 shows the correlation between resolution and refresh rates. As the resolution and vertical refresh rate increase, so must the horizontal frequency. The maximum horizontal frequency supported by the display is the limiting factor when selecting higher refresh rates at a given resolution.

Table 12.21 Refresh Rates Comparison

Resolution	Vertical Refresh Rate	Horizontal Refresh Rate*
1024×768	60Hz	47.8KHz
1024×768	75Hz	60.3KHz
1024×768	85Hz	68.7KHz
1280×1024	60Hz	63.7KHz
1280×1024	75Hz	80.3KHz
1280×1024	85Hz	91.5KHz
1600×1200	60Hz	74.5KHz
1600×1200	75Hz	94.1KHz
1600×1200	85Hz	107.2KHz

Includes VESA CVT (Coordinated Video Timings) prescribed blanking overhead.

For example, let's say you have a CRT display that supports a maximum *horizontal frequency* of 75KHz. That display would be capable of an 85Hz refresh rate at 1024×768, but it would only be capable of a 60Hz refresh at either 1280×1024 or 1600×1200. Because the flickering on a CRT at 60Hz is unacceptable, using those resolutions would be out of the question. By comparison, a monitor capable of supporting a 110KHz horizontal frequency could handle even the highest 1600×1200 resolution at an 85Hz refresh rate, which would mean no flicker. Premium CRT displays offer flicker-free refresh rates at higher resolutions. Note that you can't use refresh rates higher than the display can support, and in some cases with older CRTs, selecting a refresh rate in excess of the monitor's maximum can actually cause damage to the display circuitry!

Windows supports Plug and Play (PnP) monitor configuration if both the monitor and video adapter support the DDC feature. Using DDC communication, Windows can read the VESA EDID from the display and use it to configure the graphics controller to match the display's capabilities, such as supported resolutions and refresh rates. This normally prevents the user from selecting refresh rates that the monitor cannot support.

Why LCD and LED Screens Don't Flicker

LCD and backit LED monitors aren't affected by vertical refresh rates like CRTs; LCDs avoid problems with flicker because of their design. LCDs use transistors to activate all the pixels in the image at once, as opposed to a scanning electron beam that must work its way from the top to the bottom of the screen to create an image. But most importantly, LCDs have a CCFL (cold cathode fluorescent lamp) or LED backlight that for all intents and purposes doesn't flicker. (It operates either continuously or at high frequencies of 200Hz or more.) In other words, although a vertical refresh rate setting of 60Hz is considered bad for CRTs, that is the standard rate used by most LCDs because they don't exhibit visible flicker. Although most LCDs can accept refresh rates of up to 75Hz, in most cases selecting rates higher than 60Hz will only force the video card to work harder and won't actually affect what you see on the display.

Tip

If you try to use a refresh rate higher than your display can support, you might see a message that you have selected an out-of-range frequency. If you use a dual-head video card, keep in mind that some models don't permit you to assign different refresh rates to each monitor. If you have both a CRT and an LCD connected to such a video card, use the highest refresh rate supported by both displays (usually 75Hz) to minimize flicker on the CRT.

Interlaced Versus Noninterlaced

Some monitors and video adapters can support both interlaced as well as noninterlaced modes. In *noninterlaced* (conventional) mode, the screen is drawn from top to bottom, one line after the other, completing the screen in one pass. In *interlaced* mode, the screen is drawn in two passes—with the odd lines first and the even lines second. Each pass takes half the time of a full pass in noninterlaced mode.

Early high-resolution CRT monitors used interlacing to reach their maximum resolutions; as with interlacing, the vertical and horizontal scan frequencies were cut in half. Unfortunately, this usually introduces noticeable flicker into the display, so in most cases you should avoid interlacing where possible. Fortunately, most modern monitors support noninterlaced modes at all supported resolutions, thus avoiding the slow screen response and potential flicker caused by interlacing.

Note

The 1080i HDTV standard is an interlaced mode that is sometimes used because it requires half the bandwidth of the 1080p (progressive) mode. However, in most cases, you will not see a DLP, LCD, or plasma TV flicker when it receives a 1080i signal. That is because the signal is normally converted internally into a progressive signal and scaled to the display's native resolution.

Image Brightness and Contrast

Although it's a consideration that applies to both LCDs and CRTs, the brightness of a display is especially important in an LCD panel because brightness can vary a great deal from one model to another. Brightness for LCD panels is measured in candelas per square meter (cd/m2), which is also called a *nit* (from the Latin *nitere*, "to shine") and often abbreviated as *nt*. Typical ratings for good display panels are between 200 and 450 nits—the brighter the better.

Contrast is normally expressed as the ratio between white and black, with higher ratios being better. There are unfortunately different ways to make the measurement, but the one that is most important is the *static contrast ratio*, which is the ratio from brightest to darkest that can be produced on a display simultaneously. Many display manufacturers like to quote dynamic contrast ratios instead because they are measured over time with different backlight brightness settings and produce significantly larger numbers. For example, a display with a 1000:1 static contrast ratio can also have an 8000:1 (or higher) dynamic contrast ratio. Even more confusion comes from the fact that many display manufacturers like to assign their own proprietary names to dynamic contrast ratios—for example, Acer calls it ACM (Adaptive Contrast Management), whereas ASUS calls it ASCR (ASUS Smart Contrast Ratio). I recommend comparing displays using only the static ratio.

Typical static contrast ratio values range from 400:1 to 1500:1. Anything higher than that is generally a dynamic ratio. Because of the capabilities of the human eye, static ratios over 1000:1 offer little perceptible visual difference. A good combination of both brightness and contrast is a brightness rating of 300 nits (or more) along with a static contrast ratio of 1000:1.

Note

When you evaluate an LCD/LED TV monitor, be sure to note the brightness settings available in computer mode and TV mode. Many of these displays provide a brighter picture in TV mode than in computer mode.

Display Power Management Signaling

Monitors, like virtually all power-consuming computer devices, have been designed to save energy wherever and whenever possible. Virtually all monitors sold in recent years have earned the Environmental Protection Agency's Energy Star logo by reducing their current draw down to 15 watts (CRTs) or 5 watts (LCDs) or less when idle. Power-management features in the monitor, as well as controls provided in the system BIOS and in the latest versions of Windows, help monitors and other types of computing devices use less power.

▶▶ For more information about power management, see Chapter 18, "Power Supplies," **p. 845**.

Display Power-Management Signaling (DPMS) is a VESA specification that defines the signals a computer sends to a monitor to indicate idle times. The OS normally decides when to send these signals, depending on how you have set up the power management settings.

Table 12.22 shows the various signal states and relative power consumption according to the DPMS state selected. Normally the monitor is placed in Suspend mode after a period of inactivity specified in the OS power management settings.

Table 12.22   Display Power Management Signaling States

State	Horizontal	Vertical	Video	Power Savings	Recovery Time
On	Pulses	Pulses	Active	None	N/A
Stand-By	No pulses	Pulses	Blanked	Minimal	Short
Suspend	Pulses	No pulses	Blanked	Substantial	Longer
Off	No pulses	No pulses	Blanked	Maximum	System dependent

Virtually all CRT monitors with power management features meet the requirements of the United States EPA's Energy Star labeling program, which requires that monitor power usage be reduced from up to 100 watts or more (when operating normally) to 15 watts or less in standby mode. LCD monitors comply with the far more stringent Energy 2000 (E2000) standard developed in Switzerland. E2000 requires that monitors use less than 5 watts when in standby mode. Note that LCD displays generally use one-third less power than CRTs in either operating or standby mode, and LED displays use about one-third the power of LCD displays.

LCD Technology

Because of their light weight, smaller overall size, and much greater clarity, LCD panels have replaced CRT displays in all new computer installations. Desktop LCD panels use the same technology that first appeared in laptop computers. Compared to CRTs, LCDs have completely flat, thin screens and low power requirements (30 watts versus up to 100 watts or more for CRT monitors). The color quality of a good active-matrix LCD panel can exceed that of many CRT displays, particularly when viewed from head on.

How LCD Panels Work

In an LCD, polarizing filters allow only light waves that are aligned with the filter to pass through. After passing through one polarizing filter, all the light waves are aligned in the same direction.

A second polarizing filter aligned at a right angle to the first blocks all those waves. By changing the angle of the second polarizing filter, you can change the amount of light allowed to pass accordingly. It is the role of the liquid crystal cell to act as a polarizing filter that can change the angle of polarization and control the amount of light that passes. The liquid crystals are tiny rod-shaped molecules that flow like a liquid. They enable light to pass straight through, but an electrical charge alters their orientation, which subsequently alters the orientation of light passing through them. In a color LCD, there are three cells for each pixel—one each for displaying red, green, and blue—with a corresponding transistor for each cell. The red, green, and blue cells that make up a pixel are sometimes referred to as *subpixels*. See Figure 12.23.

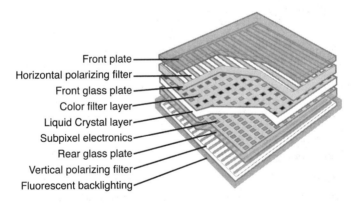

Front plate
Horizontal polarizing filter
Front glass plate
Color filter layer
Liquid Crystal layer
Subpixel electronics
Rear glass plate
Vertical polarizing filter
Fluorescent backlighting

FIGURE 12.23 A typical color LCD display.

Active-Matrix Displays

LCD panels use a type of active-matrix technology known as a *thin-film transistor (TFT)* array. TFT is a method for packaging from one (monochrome) to three (RGB color) transistors per pixel within a flexible material that is the same size and shape as the display. Thus, the transistors for each pixel lie directly behind the liquid crystal cells they control.

Two TFT manufacturing processes account for most of the active-matrix displays on the market today: hydrogenated amorphous silicon (a-Si) and low-temperature polysilicon (p-Si). These processes differ primarily in their costs. At first, most TFT displays were manufactured using the a-Si process because it required lower temperatures (less than 400°C) than the p-Si process of the time. Now, lower-temperature p-Si manufacturing processes are making this method an economically viable alternative to a-Si.

To improve horizontal viewing angles in the latest LCDs, some vendors have modified the classic TFT design. For example, Hitachi's in-plane switching (IPS) design—also known as STFT—aligns the individual cells of the LCD parallel to the glass, running the electric current through the sides of the cells and spinning the pixels to provide more even distribution of the image to the entire panel area. Hitachi's Super-IPS technology also rearranges the liquid crystal molecules into a zigzag pattern, rather than the typical row-column arrangement, to reduce color shift and improve color uniformity. The similar multidomain vertical alignment (MVA) technology developed by Fujitsu divides the screen into different regions and changes the angle of the regions.

Both Super-IPS and MVA provide a wider viewing angle than traditional TFT displays. Other companies have different names for the same technology—for example, Sharp calls it Ultra High Aperture (UHA). Manufacturers often like to think up their own buzzwords for the same technology because it makes their products seem different, but the results they generate are largely the same. Because larger LCDs can exhibit shifts in viewing angle even for an individual user, these more advanced technologies are often used on larger and more expensive panels.

Benefits of LCD Panels

LCD monitors offer a number of benefits when compared to conventional CRT glass tube monitors. Because LCDs use direct addressing of the display (each pixel in the picture corresponds with a transistor), they produce a high-precision image. LCDs can't have the common CRT display problems of pincushion or barrel distortion, nor do they experience convergence errors (halos around the edges of onscreen objects).

LCD panels are less expensive to operate than CRTs because they feature lower power consumption and much less heat buildup than CRTs. Because LCD units lack a CRT, no concerns exist about electromagnetic VLF or ELF emissions. Although LCDs offer a comparable mean time between failures (MTBF) to CRT displays, the major reason for LCD failures is the inverter or backlight, which might be relatively inexpensive to replace in some models. CRT failures usually involve the picture tube, which is the most expensive portion of the display and is often not cost-effective to replace.

LCD panels offer a significantly smaller footprint (front-to-back dimensions), and some offer optional wall or stand mounting. LCD panels also weigh substantially less than comparably sized CRTs. For example, a 17-inch LCD weighs less than 10 lbs., compared to the 50 lbs. weight of 19-inch CRTs with a similar viewing area.

LCD Monitor Selection Criteria

When selecting an LCD monitor, I recommend taking the following criteria into consideration:

- LCD monitors work best at their native resolution and can vary greatly in how they scale to lower resolutions. Because higher resolutions result in smaller text and icons, make sure you don't purchase a display with a higher resolution than you can easily see or use. LCD monitors vary greatly in how well they scale from native to alternative resolutions, so you should evaluate the panel both at its native resolution and at any other resolutions you plan to use.

- For larger displays supporting higher resolutions, using a VGA analog connection will result in a poor quality image. In that case, you will want to use a digital connection, which means that both the video adapter and display will need compatible digital connections such as DisplayPort, DVI, or HDMI.

- LCDs have slower response times than most CRTs. For good performance with games, video, and animation, look for gray-to-gray (G2G) response times of 5ms or faster.

- LCD displays have lower viewing angles than CRTs. This can be an important consideration if you're planning to use your LCD monitor for group presentations. To improve the horizontal viewing area, several manufacturers have developed patented improvements to the basic TFT display, such as Hitachi's IPS, Fujitsu's multidomain vertical adjustment (MVA), and Mitsubishi's feed forward driving (FFD)—most of which have been licensed to other leading LCD makers. If you need wider angle viewing capability, look for LCD displays using these technologies to achieve horizontal viewing angles of 170° or more.

- A high-contrast ratio (luminance difference between white and black) makes for sharper text and vivid colors. Look for static contrast ratios of 1000:1 or more.

- Optional features such as integrated speakers, webcams, and USB hubs are available on many displays.

LED Backlit Technology

Most new LCD panels use LEDs, rather than fluorescent tubes, for backlighting. By using LEDs instead of fluorescent tubes, display warmup time is nil and mercury, a major environmental concern when disposed of, is no longer a concern when the display is scrapped. LED backlit screens also use about half the energy of standard LCD panels.

Figure 12.24 illustrates how an LED backlit screen works.

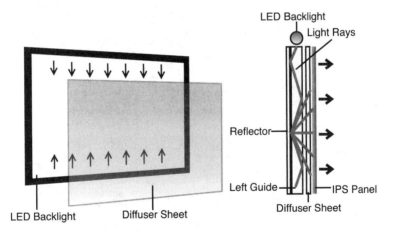

FIGURE 12.24 How an LED backlit display works.

CRT Display Technology

CRT technology is the same used in older television sets. In the past few years, CRTs have vanished from store shelves, mainly due to the availability of lower-cost LCDs. However, many older systems still use CRT monitors. CRTs consist of a vacuum tube enclosed in glass. One end of the tube contains an electron gun assembly that projects three electron beams, one each for the red, green, and blue phosphors used to create the colors you see onscreen; the other end contains a screen with a phosphorous coating.

When heated, the electron gun emits a stream of high-speed electrons that are attracted to the other end of the tube. Along the way, a focus control and deflection coil steer the beam to a specific point on the phosphorous screen. When struck by the beam, the phosphor glows. This light is what you see when you watch TV or look at your computer screen. Three layers of phosphors are used: red, green, and blue. A metal plate called a *shadow mask* aligns the electron beams; it has slots or holes that divide the red, green, and blue phosphors into groups of three (one of each color).

Monitors based on Sony Trinitron or Mitsubishi DiamondTron picture tubes used an aperture grille type mask to separate red, green, and blue phosphors, resulting in strips of square pixels in a linear arrangement, similar to an LCD. NEC's ChromaClear monitors used a variation on the aperture grille called the *slotted mask*, which is brighter than standard shadow-mask monitors and more mechanically stable than aperture grille–based monitors. This resulted in a staggered pixel arrangement.

Various types of shadow masks affect picture quality, and the distance between each group of three (the *dot or pixel pitch*) affects picture sharpness.

▶▶ See "Pixels," **p. 653**.

Figure 12.25 illustrates the interior of a typical CRT.

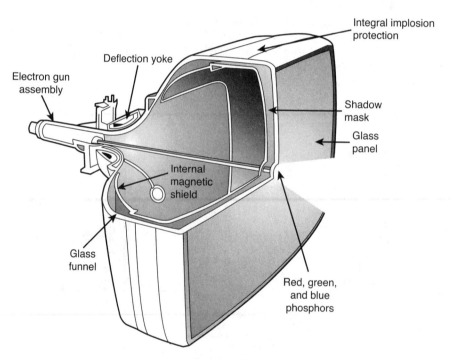

FIGURE 12.25 A typical CRT monitor is a large vacuum tube. It contains three electron guns (red, green, and blue) that project the picture toward the front glass of the monitor. High voltage produces the magnetism that controls the electron beams that create the picture displayed on the front of the CRT.

The phosphor chemical has a quality called *persistence*, which indicates how long this glow remains onscreen. Persistence is what causes a faint image to remain on your TV screen for a few seconds after you turn off the set. The vertical scanning frequency (also called the *refresh rate*) of the display specifies how many times per second the image is refreshed. You should have a good match between persistence and refresh rate so the image has less flicker (which occurs when the persistence is too low) and no ghost images (which occurs when the persistence is too high).

The electron beam moves quickly, sweeping the screen from left to right in lines from top to bottom, in a pattern called a *raster*. The horizontal scan rate refers to the speed at which the electron beam moves laterally across the screen, measured in the number of lines drawn per second.

During its sweep, the beam strikes the phosphor wherever an image should appear onscreen. The beam also varies in intensity to produce different levels of brightness. Because the glow begins to fade almost immediately, the electron beam must continue to sweep the screen to maintain an image—a practice called *redrawing* or *refreshing* the screen.

Due to the lower persistence phosphors used in PC monitor CRTs, most have an ideal refresh rate (also called the *vertical scan frequency*) of 85Hz, which means the screen is refreshed 85 times per second. Refresh rates that are too low cause the screen to flicker, contributing to eyestrain.

Plasma Display Technology

Plasma displays have a long history in PCs. In the late 1980s, IBM developed a monochrome plasma screen that displayed orange text and graphics on a black background. IBM used a 10-inch version of this gas plasma display on its P70 and P75 briefcase portable systems that were released way back in 1988.

Unlike the early IBM monochrome plasma screens, today's plasma displays are capable of displaying 24-bit or 32-bit color. Plasma screens produce an image by using electrically charged gas (plasma) to illuminate triads of red, green, and blue phosphors, as shown in Figure 12.26.

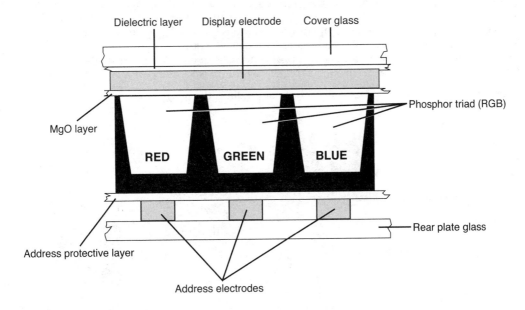

FIGURE 12.26 A cross-section of a typical plasma display.

The display and address electrodes create a grid that enables each subpixel to be individually addressed. By adjusting the differences in charge between the display and address electrodes for each triad's subpixels, the signal source controls the picture.

Typical plasma screens range in size from 42 inches to 60 inches or larger. Because they are primarily designed for use with DVD, TV, or HDTV video sources, they are sized and optimized for video rather than computer use. Their quick response time makes them good choices for enjoying sports, streaming HD video, or Blu-ray movies.

LCD and DLP Projectors

Originally, data projectors were intended for use in boardrooms and training facilities. However, with the rise of home theater systems, the increasing popularity of working from home, and major price reductions and improvements in projector technology, portable projectors are an increasingly popular alternative to large-screen TVs and plasma displays.

Two technologies are used in the construction of data projectors:

- Liquid crystal display (LCD)
- DLP

Instead of using triads of subpixels as in a flat-panel or portable LCD, an LCD projector works by separating white light into red, green, and blue wavelengths and directing each wavelength through a corresponding LCD panel. Each LCD panel's pixels are opened or closed according to the signals received from the signal source (computer, DVD, or video player) and are combined into a single RGB image that is projected onto the screen. A relatively hot projection lamp must be used to project LCD images, so LCD projectors require some cool-down time before they can be stored.

The other major technology for presentation and home theater projectors uses Texas Instruments' own DLP technology. DLP projectors use a combination of a rapidly spinning color wheel and a microprocessor-controlled array of tiny mirrors known as a *digital micromirror device* (DMD). Each mirror in a DMD corresponds to a pixel, and the mirrors reflect light toward or away from the projector optics. Depending on how frequently the mirrors are switched on, the image varies from white (always on) to black (never on) through as many as 1,024 gray shades. The color wheel provides color data to complete the projected image. Compared to LCD projectors, DLP projectors are more compact, are lighter, and cool down more quickly after use. Although DLP projects were originally more expensive than LCD projectors, they are now about the same price. Most current projectors also support HDTV resolutions of 720p and 1080i, enabling a single projector to work as either a PC or a TV display.

Figure 12.27 illustrates how a DLP-based projector produces the image.

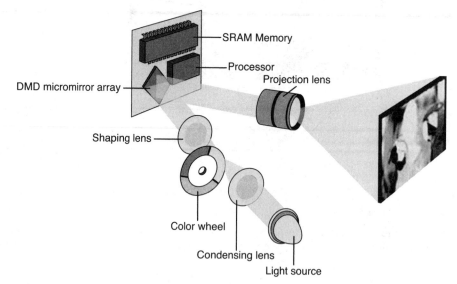

FIGURE 12.27 How a typical DLP projector works.

The earliest DLP projectors used a simple three-color (RGB) wheel, as shown in Figure 12.28. However, more recent models have used a four-segment (RGB and clear) or a six-segment (RGBRGB) wheel to improve picture quality.

Note

For more information about digital light processing, see the official Texas Instruments website about DLP technology at www.dlp.com.

Using Multiple Monitors

One of the most useful things you can do for increasing the usability and productivity of a PC is to attach multiple monitors. Adding additional monitors gives you more screen real estate to use for running multiple applications simultaneously. When you configure a system to use multiple monitors, the OS creates a virtual desktop—that is, a display that exists in video memory that combines the total screen real-estate of all of the attached displays. You use the multiple monitors to display various portions of the virtual desktop, enabling you to place the open windows for different applications on separate monitors and move them around at will.

Although having three or more displays is entirely possible, just adding a second monitor can be a boon to computing productivity. For example, you can leave an email client or word processor maximized on one monitor and use the other monitor for web browsing, research documents, and more.

Using multiple monitors requires an independent video signal for each display. Starting with Windows 2000, this is most commonly done by using Dualview—a single graphics adapter with two video outputs, also known as a *dual-head graphics adapter*. It is also possible to use two or more video cards, but this approach is used today only if three or more displays are used.

When multiple video adapters are installed, the system identifies one of the video adapters as primary. The primary adapter is sometimes called the *VGA adapter* and is the one that displays the POST (Power-On Self Test) and BIOS Setup screens. This is a function of the motherboard and motherboard BIOS. Most modern BIOSs allow you to choose the primary display adapter via a setting in the BIOS Setup. Normally the options are onboard (built in), PCI, or PCIe (AGP on older systems with an AGP slot). For the PCI and PCIe selections, if you have multiple adapters installed, the primary will be the one in the highest priority slot.

If the BIOS does not let you select which device should be the primary display, it decides solely based on the priority of the buses or slots in the machine. Depending on the BIOS used by your system, you might need to check in various places for the option to select the primary display adapter; however, in most cases it will be in the Video Configuration menu.

Dualview

Although older video cards often have only a single output, most current video cards have at least two. With the exception of laptops, the same is true for most motherboard-based video adapters. Laptops have almost always had dualview graphics adapters, whereas most desktop motherboards have not until recently.

A dualview card is preferable to using two separate cards because only one slot is used, as are fewer system resources and even power. The types of video outputs on dual-head cards can vary, so make sure you choose a card that has the outputs you need or that you can change the existing outputs via adapters. Digital outputs such as DVI, HDMI, and DisplayPort are preferred because these can normally be converted to others with inexpensive adapters.

Homogeneous Adapters

The best solution for running multiple graphics adapters in a single system is to ensure they are homogeneous. This means that they use the same driver, which implies that they must also have chipsets from the same manufacturer (such as AMD or NVIDIA) and from compatible families within that chipset manufacturer. Using multiple homogeneous adapters is supported in Windows 98/Me (up to nine total displays) and in Windows 2000 and later (up to 10 displays) using any combination of single- or dualview adapters. The installation is simple because only a single driver is required for all the adapters and displays.

Because AMD and NVIDIA use a unified driver architecture to support their current product lines, you can use two (or more) AAMD-based or NVIDIA-based cards to create the desired homogeneous multiple-monitor configuration. The specific cards and even chipsets can be different, as long as they can use the same driver.

Note

Systems with AMD GPUs can use Eyefinity to run up to six displays on a single graphics card. For more information, see the AMD Eyefinity website.

Heterogeneous Adapters

Heterogeneous adapters are those using chipsets from different manufacturers or from incompatible chipset families within the same manufacturer, which therefore require different drivers. This method has largely been superseded by Dualview or by using matching display adapters.

Note

For more information about using heterogeneous adapters, see "Heterogeneous Adapters," in Chapter 12, "Video Hardware," in *Upgrading and Repairing PCs*, 19th Edition.

Choosing the Best Display Hardware for a Particular Task

Modern display hardware varies a great deal in features such as display sizes, display technologies, GPU location, and GPU performance. When configuring a desktop PC or selecting a laptop, you can select the combination of display and GPU hardware needed to optimize a system for a particular task. Table 12.23 provides specific display hardware recommendations for different types of optimized systems.

Table 12.23   Display Hardware Recommendations for Task-Optimized Systems

Task	Display	GPU
CAD/CAM/ Technical graphics workstation	23-inch or larger flat panel with digital input (two or more)	AMD FirePro OR NVIDIA Quadro 4GB RAM or more GDDR5 or faster

Task	Display	GPU
A/V Editing Workstation	21-inch or larger flat panel with digital input (two)	AMD RADEON HD 76xx or better OR NVIDIA GeForce GTX 680 or better 2GB RAM or more GDDR5 or faster
Gaming PC	20-inch or larger flat panel with digital input (one or more)	AMD RADEON HD 7xxx or better OR NVIDIA GeForce GTX 6xx or better 1GB RAM or more 192-bit or wider memory bus GDDR5 or faster RAM
Home Theater PC	HDTV 1080p, 32-inch or larger with HDMI input	AMD RADEON HD 7xxx or HD6xxx OR NVIDIA GeForce 6xx or 5xx Quiet fan or passive cooling HDMI output 1GB or more RAM 64-bit or wider memory bus DDR3 or faster RAM Integrated or add-on TV tuner with support for digital TV input sources (Clear-QAM or ATSC minimum; CableCard for encrypted cable)

Video Troubleshooting and Maintenance

Solving most graphics adapter and monitor problems is fairly simple, but costly, because replacing the adapter or display is the normal procedure. Except for specialized CAD or graphics workstation-oriented adapters, virtually all of today's adapters cost more to service than to replace, and the documentation required to service the hardware properly is not always available. You can't get schematic diagrams, parts lists, wiring diagrams, and other documents for most adapters or monitors. However, before you replace an apparently failed component, be sure you have exhausted all your other options. These include following the troubleshooting tips in the next section and checking the warranty status of your device.

Tip

If you're not in the habit of registering newly purchased products, it's a good habit to pick up. Registering your hardware helps to verify warranty status, sometimes provides longer warranty coverage for your equipment, and helps the vendor reach you with updates or service advisories.

Remember also that many of the problems you might encounter with modern video adapters and displays are related to the drivers that control these devices rather than to the hardware. Be sure you have the latest and proper drivers before you attempt to have the hardware repaired; a solution might already be available.

Troubleshooting Video Cards and Drivers

Use the following suggestions to help you solve problems with your display hardware.

The display works when booting and in the BIOS Setup, but not in Windows.

Solution

If you have an acceptable picture while booting or when in the BIOS Setup but no picture in Windows, most likely you have an incorrect or corrupted video driver installed. Boot Windows in either Safe Mode (which uses the Microsoft supplied vga.sys driver) or Enable VGA Mode (which uses the current driver with VGA resolution settings). If Safe Mode or VGA Mode works, get a correct or updated driver for the video card and reinstall.

If you have overclocked your card with a manufacturer-supplied or third-party utility, you might have set the speed too high. Restart the system in Safe Mode and reset the card to run at its default speed. If you have adjusted the speed of AGP/PCI/PCIe slots in the BIOS Setup program, restart the system, start the BIOS Setup program, and reset these slots to run at the normal speed.

Can't select desired color depth and resolution combination.

Solution

Verify that the card is properly identified in Windows and that the card's memory is working properly. Use diagnostic software provided by the video card or chipset maker to test the card's memory. If the hardware is working properly, check for new drivers. Use the vendor's drivers rather than the ones provided with Windows.

Can't select desired refresh rate.

Solution

Verify that the video adapter and the monitor have the latest drivers installed and are properly identified in Windows. If necessary, obtain and install updated drivers for the adapter and display.

Can't adjust OpenGL or Direct3D (DirectX) settings.

Solution

Install the graphic card or chipset vendor's latest drivers instead of using the drivers included with Microsoft Windows. Standard Microsoft drivers often don't include 3D or other advanced dialog boxes.

Can't enable multiple monitors.

Solution

If you are using a multihead graphics card, make sure the additional monitors have been enabled in the manufacturer's driver. This might require you to open the Advanced settings for your driver. (Make sure you are using the latest one.) If you are using two or more video cards in an SLI (NVIDIA), CrossFire (ATI), or CrossFireX (AMD) configuration, you must normally disable this configuration before you can enable additional monitors. If you are using multiple video cards in separate slots, check the BIOS Setup configuration for the primary adapter.

Can't enable SLI operation.

Solution

Make sure the MIO (SLI bridge) device is properly installed between your video cards (refer to Figure 12.16). If you are not using identical video cards, you must use NVIDIA ForceWare v81.85 or new drivers to enable SLI operation. Make sure both cards use the same GPU family. Make sure SLI operation is enabled in the ForceWare driver.

Can't enable CrossFire or CrossFireX operation.

Solution

If you are using first-generation CrossFire cards, make sure you have paired up a CrossFire Edition and standard Radeon card from the same GPU family. Also, make sure you have properly connected the CrossFire Edition and standard card.

If you use later-model cards that use a CrossFire or CrossFireX bridge interconnect, make sure the interconnect is properly attached to both cards. Make sure you are using pairs of cards with compatible GPUs (see the AMD Crossfire website for details).

Update the ATI CATALYST display drivers to the latest production version. Be sure you have enabled CrossFire or CrossFireX in your display driver.

Can't enable Aero 3D desktop in Windows Vista or Windows 7.

Solution

Make sure your video card or integrated video is running a WDDM (Windows driver display model) driver and supports DirectX 9.0 or later. Update the driver if the hardware can support Aero. Update the card if the card does not have WDDM drivers available.

DisplayMate

DisplayMate is a unique diagnostic and testing program designed to thoroughly test your video adapter and display. It is somewhat unique in that most conventional PC hardware diagnostics programs do not emphasize video testing the way this program does.

I find it useful not only in testing whether a video adapter is functioning properly, but also in examining video displays. You easily can test the image quality of a display, which allows you to make focus, centering, brightness and contrast, color level, and other adjustments much more accurately than before. If you are purchasing a new monitor, you can use the program to evaluate the sharpness and linearity of the display and to provide a consistent way of checking each monitor you are considering. If you use projection systems for presentations—as I do in my PC hardware seminars—you will find it invaluable for setting up and adjusting the projector.

DisplayMate also can test a video adapter thoroughly. It sets the video circuits into each possible video mode so you can test all its capabilities. It even helps you determine the performance level of your card, with respect to both resolution and colors as well as speed. You can then use the program to benchmark the performance of the display, which enables you to compare one type of video adapter system to another. The Video Edition also supports various types of multimedia projectors and TVs used in home theater and presentation environments. Most editions for Windows are now available on a self-launching USB thumb drive.

For more information on DisplayMate, visit www.displaymate.com.

Video Drivers

Drivers are an essential, and often problematic, element of a video display subsystem. The driver enables your software to communicate with the video adapter. You can have a video adapter with the fastest processor and the most efficient memory on the market but still have poor video performance because of a badly written driver.

Video drivers generally are designed to support the processor on the video adapter. All video adapters come equipped with drivers the card manufacturer supplies, but often you can use a driver the chipset maker created. Sometimes you might find that one of the two provides better performance than the other or resolves a particular problem you are experiencing.

Most manufacturers of video adapters and chipsets maintain websites from which you can obtain the latest drivers; drivers for chipset-integrated video are supplied by the system, motherboard, or chipset vendor. A driver from the chipset manufacturer can be a useful alternative, but you should always try the adapter manufacturer's driver first. Before purchasing a video adapter, you should check out the manufacturer's site and see whether you can determine how up to date the available drivers are. At one time, frequent driver revisions were thought to indicate problems with the hardware, but the greater complexity of today's systems means that driver revisions are a necessity. Even if you are installing a brand-new model of a video adapter, be sure to check for updated drivers on the manufacturer's website for best results.

Note

Although most devices work best with the newest drivers, video cards can be a notable exception. Both NVIDIA and AMD use unified driver designs, creating a single driver installation that can be used across a range of graphics chips. However, in some cases, older versions of drivers sometimes work better with older chipsets than the newest drivers do. If you find that system performance or stability, especially in 3D gaming, drops when you upgrade to the newest driver for your 3D graphics card, revert to the older driver.

The video driver also provides the interface you can use to configure the display your adapter produces. The driver controls the options that are available for these settings, so you can't choose parameters the hardware doesn't support. For example, you cannot select resolutions your display does not support, even though your video card might support them.

In most cases, another tab called Color Management is also available. You can select a color profile for your monitor to enable more accurate color matching for use with graphics programs and printers.

Video cards with advanced 3D acceleration features often have additional properties; these are discussed later in this chapter.

Maintaining Monitors

Because you can use a good monitor for several years on more than one computer, proper care is essential to extend its life to the fullest extent.

Use the following guidelines for proper care of your monitor:

- Although phosphor burn (where an image left onscreen eventually leaves a permanent shadow) is possible on CRT or plasma displays, LCDs are immune from this problem. To prevent burn-in on non-LCD displays, use the power management settings in your OS to blank the display after a period of inactivity. Screen savers used to be employed for display protection, but you should avoid them in lieu of putting the display into Standby mode.

- To prevent premature failure of the monitor's power supply, use the power-management features of the OS to put the monitor into a low-power standby mode after a reasonable period of inactivity. Using the power-management feature is far better than using the on/off switch when you are away from the computer for brief periods. Turn off the monitor only at the end of your computing "day."

How can you tell whether the monitor is really off or in standby mode? Look at the power LCD on the front of the monitor. A monitor that's in standby mode usually has a blinking green or solid amber LCD in place of the solid green LCD displayed when it's running in normal mode.

If the monitor will not go into standby mode when the PC isn't sending signals to it, make sure the monitor is properly defined in the Display properties sheet in Windows. In addition, make sure the Energy Star check box is selected for any monitor that supports power management, unless the monitor should be left on at all times (such as when used in a retail kiosk or self-standing display).

- Make sure the monitor has adequate ventilation along the sides, rear, and top. Because monitors use passive cooling, a lack of adequate airflow caused by piling keyboards, folders, books, or other office debris on top of the monitor will cause it to overheat and considerably shorten its life. If you need to use a monitor in an area with poor airflow, use an LCD panel instead of a CRT because LCDs run much cooler than CRTs.

- The monitor screen and case should be kept clean. Turn off the power, spray a cleaner such as Endust for Electronics onto a soft cloth (never directly onto the monitor!), and gently wipe the screen and the case.

- If your CRT monitor has a degaussing button or feature, use it periodically to remove stray magnetic signals. Keep in mind that CRTs have powerful magnets around the picture tube, so keep magnetic media away from them.

Testing Monitors

Unlike most of the other peripherals you can connect to your computer, you can't really tell whether a monitor suits you by examining its technical specifications. Price might not be a reliable indicator either. Testing monitors is a highly subjective process, and it is best to "kick the tires" of a few at a dealer showroom or in the privacy of your home or office (if the dealer has a liberal return policy).

Testing should also not be simply a matter of looking at whatever happens to be displayed on the monitor at the time. Many computer stores display movies, scenic photos, or other flashy graphics that are all but useless for a serious evaluation and comparison. If possible, you should look at the same images on each monitor you try and compare the manner in which they perform a specific series of tasks.

Before running the tests listed here, set your display to the highest resolution and refresh rate allowed by your combination of display and graphics card:

- Draw a perfect circle with a graphics program. If the displayed result is an oval, not a circle, this monitor will not serve you well with graphics or design software.

- Using a word processor, type some words in 8- or 10-point type (1 point equals 1/72 inches). If the words are fuzzy or the black characters are fringed with color, select another monitor.

- Display a screen with as much white space as possible and look for areas of color variance. This can indicate a problem with only that unit or its location, but if you see it on more than one monitor of the same make, it might indicate a manufacturing problem; it could also indicate problems with the signal coming from the graphics card. Move the monitor to another system equipped with a different graphics card model, and retry this test to see for certain whether it's the monitor or the video card.

- Display the Microsoft Windows desktop to check for uniform focus (with CRT displays) and brightness (with CRT and LCD displays). Are the corner icons as sharp as the rest of the screen? Are the lines in the title bar curved or wavy? Monitors usually are sharply focused at the center, but seriously blurred corners indicate a poor design. Bowed lines on a CRT can be the result of a poor video adapter or incorrect configuration of the monitor's digital picture controls. Before you decide to replace the monitor, you should adjust the digital picture controls to improve the display. Next, try attaching the monitor to another display adapter. If the display quality does not improve, replace the monitor.

  Adjust the brightness up and down to see whether the image blooms or swells, which indicates the monitor is likely to lose focus at high brightness levels. You can also use diagnostics that come with the graphics card or third-party system diagnostics programs to perform these tests.

- With LCD panels in particular, change to a lower resolution from the panel's native resolution using the Microsoft Windows Display properties settings. Because LCD panels have only one native resolution, the display must use scaling to handle other resolutions full-screen. If you are a web designer, are a gamer, or must capture screens at a particular resolution, this test will show you whether the LCD panel produces acceptable display quality at resolutions other than normal. You can also use this test on a CRT, but CRTs, unlike LCD panels, are designed to handle a variety of resolutions.

- A good CRT monitor is calibrated so that rays of red, green, and blue light hit their targets (individual phosphor dots) precisely. If they don't, you have bad convergence. This is apparent when edges of lines appear to illuminate with a specific color. If you have good convergence, the colors are crisp, clear, and true, provided there isn't a predominant tint in the phosphor.

- If the monitor has built-in diagnostics (a recommended feature), try them as well to test the display independently of the graphics card and system to which it's attached. A display with built-in diagnostics shows text or a test pattern onscreen if it is receiving power when the host system is turned off or if the monitor is not connected to a host system.

Adjusting Monitors

One embarrassingly obvious fix to monitor display problems that is overlooked by many users is adjusting the monitor controls, such as contrast and brightness. Although most recent monitors use front-mounted controls with onscreen display (OSD), other adjustments might also be possible.

Older CRT monitors, for example, may have a focus adjustment screw on the rear or side of the unit. Because the adjusting screw is deep inside the case, the only evidence of its existence is a hole in the plastic grillwork. To adjust the monitor's focus, you must stick a long-shanked insulated screwdriver about 2 inches long into the hole and feel around for the screw head. This type of adjustment can save you an expensive repair bill. Always examine the monitor case, documentation, and manufacturer's website or other online services for the locations of adjustment controls.

Virtually all recent monitors use digital controls instead of analog controls. This has nothing to do with the signals the monitor receives from the computer, but only the controls (or lack of them) on the front panel that enable you to adjust the display. Monitors with digital controls have a built-in menu system that enables you to set parameters such as brightness (which adjusts the black level of the display), contrast (which adjusts the luminance of the display), screen size, vertical and horizontal shifts, color, phase, and focus. A button brings up the menu onscreen, and you use controls to make menu selections and vary the settings. When you complete your adjustments, the monitor saves the settings in nonvolatile RAM (NVRAM) located inside the monitor. This type of memory provides permanent storage for the settings with no battery or other power source. You can unplug the monitor without losing your settings, and you can alter them at any time in the future. Digital controls provide a much higher level of control over the monitor and are highly recommended.

Digital controls make adjusting CRT monitors suffering from any of the geometry errors shown in Figure 12.28 easy. Before making these adjustments, be sure the vertical and horizontal size and position are correct.

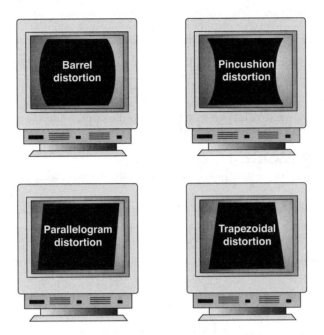

FIGURE 12.28 Typical geometry errors in CRT monitors; these can be corrected on most models that have digital picture controls.

Although LCD panels aren't affected by geometry errors as CRT monitors can be, they can have their own set of image-quality problems, especially if they use the 15-pin analog VGA video connector. Pixel jitter and pixel swim (in which adjacent pixels turn on and off) are relatively common problems that occur when you are using an LCD monitor connected to your PC with an analog VGA connector.

You can use the Auto-Tune option available in many LCD panels' OSDs to fix these and other LCD display problems.

Bad Pixels

A so-called *bad pixel* is one in which the red, green, or blue subpixel cell remains permanently on or off. Those that are permanently on are often called *stuck pixels*, whereas those that are permanently off are called *dead pixels*. Failures in the on state seem to be more common. In particular, pixels stuck on are noticeable on a dark background as tiny red, green, or blue dots. Although even one of these can be distracting, manufacturers vary in their warranty policies regarding how many bad pixels are required before you can get a replacement display. Some vendors look at both the total number of bad pixels and their locations. Fortunately, improvements in manufacturing quality make it less and less likely that you will see LCD screens with bad pixels.

Although there is no standard way to repair bad pixels, a couple of simple fixes might help. One involves tapping or rubbing on the screen. For example, I have actually repaired stuck pixels on several occasions by tapping with my index finger on the screen directly over the pixel location (with the screen powered on). Because I find a constantly lit pixel to be more irritating than one that is constantly dark, this fix has saved me a lot of aggravation (when it has worked). A similar technique is to use the tip of a PDA stylus or ballpoint pen to apply pressure or to tap directly on the stuck pixel. I recommend you wrap a damp cloth over the tip to prevent scratching the screen. Some have had success by merely rubbing the area where the stuck or dead pixel is located.

Another potential fix involves using software to rapidly cycle the stuck pixel (as well as some adjacent ones), which sometimes causes the stuck pixel to become unstuck and function properly. The two main programs for doing this are Udpixel (http://udpix.free.fr) and Jscreenfix (www.jscreenfix.com).

Unfortunately, none of these fixes work all the time; in fact, in most cases the pixel remains stuck on or dead no matter what you try. If you have stuck or dead pixels that do not respond to any of the fixes I've detailed, you might want to contact the screen or laptop manufacturer to inquire about its bad pixel replacement policy. Because the policies can vary widely among different manufacturers and displays, to find the allowable defect limits for your specific display, I recommend you consult the documentation or contact the manufacturer directly.

Troubleshooting Monitors

Follow the suggestions in the following sections to help fix problems with your display.

No picture

Solution

If the LED on the front of the monitor is yellow or flashing green, the monitor is in power-saving mode. Move the mouse or press Alt+Tab on the keyboard and wait up to 1 minute to wake the system if it is turned on.

If the LED on the front of the monitor is green, the monitor is in normal mode (receiving a signal), but the brightness and contrast are set incorrectly; adjust them.

If no lights are lit on the monitor, check the power and power switch. Check the surge protector or power director to ensure that power is going to the monitor. Replace the power cord with a known-working spare if necessary. Retest. Replace the monitor with a known-working spare to ensure that the monitor is the problem.

Check data cables at the monitor and video card end. Check power cables to the video card if the video card requires additional power to operate.

If the display has two or more input ports, make sure the correct port is selected.

Jittery picture quality

Solution

For LCD monitors, use display-adjustment software or onscreen menus to reduce or eliminate pixel jitter and pixel swim caused by running the digital LCD display with an analog (VGA) video source. Use a digital connection (DVI, HDMI, or DisplayPort) instead of the VGA connection to avoid digital-analog-digital conversion problems like these.

For all monitors, check cables for tightness at the video card and the monitor (if removable):

- Remove the extender cable and retest with the monitor plugged directly into the video card. If the extender cable is bad, replace it.
- Check the cables for damage; replace as needed.
- If problems are intermittent, check for interference. (Microwave ovens near monitors can cause severe picture distortion when turned on.)

For CRT monitors, check refresh-rate settings; reduce them until acceptable picture quality is achieved:

- Use onscreen picture adjustments until an acceptable picture quality is achieved.

- If problems are intermittent and can be "fixed" by waiting or gently tapping the side of the monitor, the monitor power supply is probably bad or has loose connections internally. Service or replace the monitor.

Repairing Monitors

Although a display often is replaced as a whole unit, some larger displays might be cheaper to repair than to replace. If you decide to repair the monitor, your best bet is to either contact the company from which you purchased the display or contact one of the companies that specialize in monitor depot repair.

Depot repair means you send in your display to a repair specialist who either fixes your particular unit or returns an identical unit it has already repaired. This usually is accomplished for a flat-rate fee; in other words, the price is the same no matter what the company has done to repair your actual unit.

Because you usually get a different (but identical) unit in return, the company can ship your repaired display immediately upon receiving the one you sent in, or even in advance in some cases. This way, you have the least amount of downtime and can receive the repaired display as quickly as possible. In some cases, if your particular monitor is unique or one the company doesn't have in stock, you must wait while your specific unit is repaired.

Troubleshooting a failed monitor is relatively simple. If your display goes out, for example, a swap with another monitor can confirm that the display is the problem. If the problem disappears when you change the display, the problem is almost certainly in the original display or the cable; if the problem remains, it is likely in the video adapter or PC.

Many of the better quality, late-model monitors have built-in self-diagnostic circuitry. Check your monitor's manual for details. Using this feature, if available, can help you determine whether the problem is really in the monitor, in a cable, or somewhere else in the system. If self-diagnostics produce an image onscreen, look to other parts of the video subsystem for your problem.

The monitor cable can sometimes be the source of display problems. A bent pin in the connector that plugs into the video adapter can prevent the monitor from displaying images, or it can cause color shifts. Most of the time, you can repair the connector by carefully straightening the bent pin with sharp-nosed pliers. A loose cable can also cause color shifts; make sure the cable is securely attached.

If the pin breaks off or the connector is otherwise damaged, you can sometimes replace the monitor cable. Some monitor manufacturers use cables that disconnect from the monitor and video adapter, whereas others are permanently connected. Depending on the type of connector the device uses at the monitor end, you might have to contact the manufacturer for a replacement.

If you narrow down the problem to the display, consult the documentation that came with the monitor or call the manufacturer for the location of the nearest factory repair depot. Third-party depot repair service companies are also available that can repair most displays (if they are no longer covered by a warranty); their prices often are much lower than factory service.

Caution

Never attempt to repair a CRT monitor yourself. Touching the wrong component can be fatal. The display circuits can hold extremely high voltages for hours, days, or even weeks after the power is shut off. A qualified service person should discharge the CRT and power capacitors before proceeding.

13

Audio Hardware

Although rudimentary audio capabilities were part of the original IBM PC of 1981 and its many successors, audio was used on early computers for troubleshooting rather than for creative tasks. The original IBM PC and compatible systems of the early to mid-1980s had rudimentary sound capabilities, consisting mainly of the ability to generate crude tones or beeps. PCs did not gain true audio capabilities until the first add-on sound cards from companies such as AdLib and Creative Labs were developed in the late 1980s.

Thanks to competition among many companies, we now enjoy widely supported hardware and software standards for audio. Audio hardware has gone from being an expensive, exotic add-on to being an industry standard part of virtually any system configuration.

Note

The term "audio support hardware" refers to either integrated audio integrated into the motherboard/chipset or a sound card when the text applies to both types of audio.

The standard audio support hardware in today's PCs typically includes an HD Audio controller (or sometimes the older AC'97 audio controller) integrated into the motherboard chipset, combined with a sound codec chip located on the motherboard. However, if the capabilities of the integrated audio are not satisfactory, a sound card can be installed via the Peripheral Component Interconnect [PCI] or Peripheral Component Interconnect Express [PCIe]) in the computer, or via an external bus such as universal serial bus (USB) or Institute of Electrical and Electronic Engineers (IEEE) 1394 (FireWire)).

Regardless of location, audio support hardware includes jacks for speakers (or headphones) and a microphone. In addition, many examples provide dedicated jacks for digital audio out, surround sound, and Musical Instrument Digital Interface (MIDI) hardware. (Many types of older audio support hardware also provided an analog game port for joysticks.) As you will see later in this chapter, many mid-range and high-end audio cards and integrated audio also support sophisticated digital audio input and output, and both integrated audio and gaming-oriented audio cards support a variety of 3D audio playback and special audio effects standards. On the software side, audio support hardware requires the support of a driver that you install either directly from an application or in your computer's operating system (OS). As you will learn later in this chapter, the OS has much more of a role in the audio subsystem today than in previous years.

This chapter focuses on the audio products found in today's PCs, their uses, and how you select, install, and operate them).

Audio Hardware Concepts and Terms

To fully understand audio hardware devices and their functions, you need to understand various concepts and terms. Terms such as 16-bit, 24-bit CD quality, and MIDI port are just a few. Concepts such as sampling and digital-to-audio conversion (DAC) are often sprinkled throughout stories about sound products. You've already learned about some of these terms and concepts; this section describes many others.

The Nature of Sound

To understand an audio adapter, you must understand the nature of sound. Every sound is produced by vibrations that compress air or other substances. These sound waves travel in all directions, expanding in balloon-like fashion from the source of the sound. When these waves reach your ear, they cause vibrations that you perceive as sound.

Two of the basic properties of any sound are its pitch and intensity.

Pitch is the rate at which vibrations are produced. It is measured in the number of hertz (Hz), or cycles per second. One cycle is a complete vibration back and forth. The number of Hz is the frequency of the tone; the higher the frequency, the higher the pitch.

Humans can't hear all possible frequencies. Few people can hear sounds with frequencies less than 16Hz or greater than about 20KHz (kilohertz; 1KHz equals 1,000Hz). In fact, the lowest note on a piano has a frequency of 27Hz, and the highest note has a frequency a little higher than 4KHz. Frequency-modulation (FM) radio stations can broadcast notes with frequencies as high as 15KHz.

The amazing compression ratios possible with MP3 files, compared to regular CD-quality WAV files, is due in part to the discarding of sound frequencies that are higher or lower than normal hearing range during the ripping process.

The intensity of a sound is called its *amplitude*. This intensity determines the sound's volume and depends on the strength of the vibrations producing the sound. A piano string, for example, vibrates gently when the key is struck softly. The string swings back and forth in a narrow arc, and the tone it sends out is soft. If the key is struck more forcefully, however, the string swings back and forth in a wider arc, producing a greater amplitude and a greater volume. The loudness of sounds is measured in decibels (db). The rustle of leaves is rated at 20db, average street noise at 70db, and nearby thunder at 120db.

Evaluating the Quality of Your Audio Hardware

The quality of audio hardware is often measured by three criteria: frequency response (or range), total harmonic distortion, and signal-to-noise ratio.

The *frequency response* of a sound card or integrated audio is the range in which an audio system can record or play at a constant and audible amplitude level. Many cards and integrated solutions support 30Hz–20KHz. The wider the spread, the better the adapter.

The *total harmonic distortion* measures an audio adapter's linearity and the straightness of a frequency response curve. In layman's terms, the harmonic distortion is a measure of accurate sound reproduction. Any nonlinear elements cause distortion in the form of harmonics. The smaller the percentage of distortion, the better. This harmonic distortion factor might make the difference between cards that use the same audio chipset. Cards with cheaper components might have greater distortion, making them produce poorer-quality sound.

The *signal-to-noise ratio (S/N or SNR)* measures the strength of the sound signal relative to background noise (hiss). The higher the number (measured in decibels), the better the sound quality.

These factors affect all types of audio adapter use, from WAV file playback to speech recognition. Keep in mind that low-quality microphones and speakers can degrade the performance of a high-quality sound card.

Sampling

With an audio adapter, a PC can record waveform audio. Waveform audio (also known as *sampled* or *digitized sound*) uses the PC as a recording device (such as a tape recorder). Small computer chips built into the adapter, called *analog-to-digital converters (ADCs)*, convert analog sound waves into digital bits that the computer can understand. Likewise, digital-to-analog converters (DACs) convert the recorded sounds to an audible analog format.

Sampling is the process of turning the original analog sound waves into digital (binary) signals that the computer can save and later replay (see Figure 13.1). The system samples the sound by taking snapshots of its frequency and amplitude at regular intervals. For example, at time X, the sound might be measured with an amplitude of Y. The higher (or more frequent) the sample rate, the more accurately the digital sound replicates its real-life source and the larger the amount of disk space needed to store it.

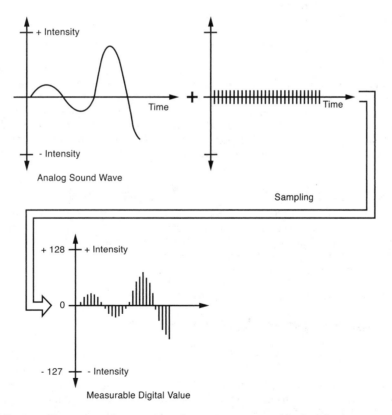

FIGURE 13.1 Sampling turns a changing sound wave into measurable digital values.

Originally, sound cards used 8-bit digital sampling, which provided for only 256 values (2^8) to convert a sound. Today's highest-quality sound cards feature 32-bit sampling (2^{32}), which translates into more than four trillion possible digital values that can be matched to a given sound.

You can experiment with the effects of various sampling rates (and compression technologies) by recording sound with the Windows Sound Recorder (in Windows XP or earlier versions; the sound recorder in Windows Vista and newer doesn't permit selection of different sampling rates) or a third-party application such as Audacity (available from http://audacity.sourceforge.net for Windows, GNU/Linux, Mac OS X, and other operating systems) set to CD-quality sound. Save the sound and play it back at that highest-quality setting. Then convert the file to a lower-quality setting and save the sound file again with a different name. Play back the various versions, and determine the lowest quality (and smallest file size) you can use without serious degradation to sound quality.

Early PC Sound Cards

When the first sound cards were introduced in the late 1980s by companies such as AdLib, Roland, and Creative Labs, they were aimed squarely at a gaming audience, were generally not compatible with each other, and often cost more than $100.

The first sound card for PCs to achieve widespread software support was the AdLib Music Synthesizer Card released in 1987, which used a Yamaha chip that produced sound via FM synthesis. Around the same time, Creative Labs introduced a competing but incompatible product called the Creative Music System, later renamed as the Game Blaster.

The Game Blaster, which was compatible with only a handful of games, was replaced by the Sound Blaster in 1989, which was itself compatible with the AdLib sound card and the Creative Labs Game Blaster card. This enabled it to support games that specified one sound card or the other. The Sound Blaster included a built-in microphone jack, stereo output, and MIDI port for connecting the PC to a synthesizer or other electronic musical instrument. This established a baseline of features that would be supported by virtually all other sound cards and onboard sound features up to the present. Finally, the audio adapter had the potential for uses other than games. The follow-up Sound Blaster Pro featured improved sound when compared to the original Sound Blaster. The Sound Blaster Pro and its successors eventually triumphed over earlier rivals to, for years, become de facto standards for PC sound reproduction.

Limitations of Sound Blaster Pro Compatibility

Through the mid-1990s, although MS-DOS was the standard PC gaming platform, many users of non–Creative Labs sound cards struggled with the limitations of their hardware's imperfect emulation of the Sound Blaster Pro. Unfortunately, some cards required two separate sets of hardware resources, using one set of interrupt request (IRQ), direct memory access (DMA), and I/O port addresses for native mode and a second set for Sound Blaster Pro compatibility. Others worked well within Windows or within an MS-DOS session running with Windows in the background but required the user to install a DOS-based Terminate and Stay Resident (TSR) driver program to work in MS-DOS.

Microsoft Windows and Audio Support

The rise of Windows games made audio support simple by comparison with the steps required in MS-DOS. Windows applications use the OS's drivers to interface with hardware, relieving the software developer from needing to write different code for different sound cards, 3D graphics cards, and so on. For gaming sound and graphics, Microsoft Windows versions from Windows NT 4.0 and Windows 95 through Windows XP use a technology called DirectX, which was introduced in December 1995. Starting with Windows Vista (which uses DirectX 10), Microsoft Windows uses a new technology called Core Audio APIs to control audio for all types of software. The following sections discuss DirectX and Core Audio APIs.

DirectX and Audio Support Hardware

Microsoft DirectX is a series of application programming interfaces (APIs) that sits between multimedia applications and hardware. Unlike MS-DOS applications, which required developers to develop direct hardware support for numerous models and brands of audio cards, video cards, and game controllers, Windows applications use DirectX to "talk" to hardware in a more direct manner than normal Windows drivers do. This improves program performance and frees the software developer from the need to change the program to work with different devices. Instead, a game developer must work with only the DirectX 3D renderer and other DirectX interface routines. Until the introduction of DirectX 10 with Windows Vista, audio programming was also part of DirectX.

◀◀ For more information about DirectX, see the Chapter 12 section, "Microsoft DirectX," **p. 646**.

Core Audio APIs for Windows

Although Windows Vista's changes to the desktop are well known, an equally significant change in Windows Vista is how it works with audio. DirectX 10, the native version of DirectX included in Windows Vista, no longer includes audio APIs such as DirectSound and DirectMusic. These and other audio-oriented APIs now interface with Windows via the new Core Audio APIs originally introduced in Windows Vista (see http://msdn.microsoft.com/en-us/library/dd370784(v=vs.85).aspx) and improved in Windows 7 and Windows 8. These APIs include:

- **Multimedia Devices (MMDevice) API**—Clients use MMDevice to enumerate the audio endpoint devices in the system.

- **Windows Audio Session API (WASAPI)**—Clients use WASAPI to create and manage audio streams coming to or from audio endpoint devices.

- **DeviceTopology API**—Clients use DeviceTopology API for direct access to features such as volume controls and multiplexers along the data paths of hardware devices inside audio adapters.

- **EndpointVolume API**—Clients use the EndpointVolume API for direct access to volume controls on audio endpoint devices. It is primarily used for the management of exclusive-mode audio streams.

Some types of applications, such as media players, DVD players and BD media players, games, and business applications that play sound files, such as presentation programs, connect to Core Audio APIs via the higher-level APIs such as DirectSound or Media Foundation. However, professional audio and real-time communications applications and third-party audio APIs typically access Core Audio APIs directly.

Note

An audio endpoint device is a device such as a speaker, microphone, or other audio input device such as Line In, volume controls, or analog-to-digital converters such as a Wave input device. To learn more about audio endpoint devices, see http://msdn.microsoft.com/en-us/library/dd370793(v=vs.85).aspx.

Windows 7 uses improved versions of the Core Audio APIs to provide low-latency audio streams, playback of audio from portable media devices through your computer speakers, improved HDMI audio, rendering audio to non-default devices, improved power management and power consumption, support for communications devices in the Sounds control panel, improved stream routing, better jack detection routines, and new interfaces, among others. For details, see http://msdn.microsoft.com/en-us/library/dd756612(v=vs.85).aspx.

Windows 8's Core Audio APIs include support for offloading audio streams to a connected hardware device and for New UI (Metro) apps. For details, see http://msdn.microsoft.com/en-us/library/windows/hardware/hh439707(v=vs.85).aspx.

As a consequence of the change from DirectX to Core Audio APIs in Windows Vista, some vendors of sound cards took a long time to develop working drivers for their hardware under Windows Vista. Because Windows 7 and Windows 8 use improved versions of the Core Audio APIs, it took much less time for vendors to roll out working drivers for these versions of Windows.

Because of the changes to 3D audio support, 3D game development for Windows Vista also required a new direction.

3D Gaming Audio Standards

One of the most common uses today for PC audio is 3D gaming, and 3D audio effects enhance the feeling of "being inside the game." 3D audio standards include 3D audio positioning and 3D audio effects. 3D audio positioning refers to the apparent location of sounds in a 3D game, while 3D audio effects include reverb, echoes, and other types of effects.

Until the introduction of Windows Vista, Windows games typically used the 3D audio features in DirectX (9.0 and earlier) for 3D audio positioning and acceleration. Starting with DirectX 10 (Windows Vista), Microsoft switched to Core Audio APIs for all audio functionality. This change meant that beginning with Windows Vista, Windows no longer supports DirectX 3D audio.

Fortunately, an open-source 3D API allows these versions of Windows (Vista, 7, and 8) to provide accelerated 3D audio for games written for DirectX 9 and earlier versions. OpenAL was originally developed as a joint venture between Creative Labs and the now-defunct Loki Software to help port Windows games to Linux distros.

As the name suggests, OpenAL is an open-source 3D audio API that is available for Windows 8 and earlier versions, Mac OS X, and Linux and is supported by many popular games and game engines. OpenAL is supported natively on SoundBlaster Audigy, X-Fi, and Recon3D cards and runs in a software mode on other cards.

Note

The official Creative Labs OpenAL website (http://connect.creativelabs.com/openal/default.aspx) provides OpenAL versions up to 1.1 only. Other vendors offering audio products based on OpenAL include Blue Ripple Sound (commercial, available from www.blueripplesound.com), OpenAL Soft (open-source, available at http://kcat.strangesoft.net/openal.html), and Adalin (free and commercial, available from www.adalin.com).

Tip

Because of the changes in 3D audio in Windows Vista and later versions, many sound cards designed for DirectX 9 lose most of their 3D functionality when playing games that use DirectX DirectSound 3D. To restore full 3D functionality for a wide variety of games, you can download programs collectively known as DirectSound wrappers. For a variety of Creative Labs SoundBlaster Audigy and X-Fi cards, download and install the latest version of Creative Alchemy from http://connect.creativelabs.com/alchemy/Alchemy/Home.aspx. For custom settings for some games, see http://connect.creativelabs.com/alchemy/Lists/Games/AllItems.aspx.

For sound cards based on Realtek codecs, download and install 3D Soundback from the Realtek website (www.realtek.com.tw).

The most common 3D audio effects standard on both integrated audio and sound cards is environmental audio extensions (EAX), which was originally developed by Creative Labs. HD Audio and most AC'97 integrated audio and non-Creative Labs sound cards support EAX 1.0 and EAX 2.0, which were released as public specifications by Creative Labs. However, EAX 3.0, EAX HD 4.0, and EAX HD 5.0 support is exclusive to recent cards from Creative Labs and Auzentech (which also uses Creative audio processors). Table 13.1 compares the major features of EAX versions.

Table 13.1 EAX Features by Version

EAX Version	3D Hardware Voices	3D Features	Example Products
1.0	32	Environmental presets	Sound Blaster Live!, most AC'97 audio
2.0	32	Occluded, obstructed sound effects	Sound Blaster Live!, most AC'97 audio
Advanced HD 3.0	64	Smooth (morphed) audio transitions, environmental panning	Sound Blaster Audigy
Advanced HD 4.0	64	Simultaneous multiple environments, EAX ExtendedFX sound effects	Sound Blaster Audigy 2 and some Auzentech cards
Advanced HD 5.0	128	Dedicated bass feed for each voice, up to four simultaneous effects per voice (Environment FlexiFX), closeup sound effects (EAX MacroFX)	Most X-Fi Extreme series and some Auzentech cards

Creative now recommends use of the open-source OpenAL 3D API for both 3D positioning and sound effects.

Legacy Audio Support Through Virtualization

What about legacy software users? If you still enjoy playing MS-DOS–based games, then current audio adapters, chipsets, and integrated audio solutions still might present a compatibility challenge to you because of fundamental hardware differences between the Industry Standard Architecture (ISA) expansion slots used by classic Creative Labs and other sound cards and current audio hardware, which uses PCI or PCIe slots, chipsets, and integrated audio.

At one time, the only way to achieve reliable audio compatibility with legacy games was to use a legacy OS such as MS-DOS 6.x (with Windows 3.1 if needed) and a Sound Blaster Pro-compatible ISA audio card. Some early PCI audio sound cards provided fairly good emulation of the Sound Blaster Pro but required additional audio drivers or proprietary patch cables to provide emulation. Modern audio hardware is geared toward supporting Windows and often is not capable of providing legacy audio support if a legacy application is run directly in Windows XP or later.

However, you can now run legacy OSs and applications with full support for legacy audio by creating a virtual PC environment using applications such as Microsoft Virtual PC 2007, Windows Virtual PC (included in Windows 7 Professional and Ultimate editions), Parallels Desktop, VMware Workstation, DOSBox (www.dosbox.com), and others.

In a virtual PC environment, you create a virtual machine on a host OS by installing a virtualization application. Next, you install a guest OS into the virtual machine, configure it to provide audio support, and install legacy games. The virtual machine translates audio and other hardware requests made by the legacy game and OS to the host OS, which then communicates with the hardware it supports. As a result, a legacy game running in an MS-DOS virtual machine "thinks" that a Sound Blaster Pro or similar sound card is available, even though the audio is actually being played by a modern sound card. You hear sound effects and music playback generated by the game just as you would if the game were being run on a system with legacy audio hardware.

Audio Hardware Features

Thanks to the universal presence of integrated audio on PCs for a number of years, you don't need to buy a sound card to enjoy audio playback from your PC. However, depending upon the types of audio content you enjoy and the types of devices you want to connect to your PC, you might want or need to replace your system's built-in audio capabilities with a sound card with better support for specialized needs.

To make an intelligent purchasing decision about a replacement for integrated audio, you should be aware of some audio hardware basic components and the features they provide, as well as the advanced features you can get on better sound cards or external adapters. This section discusses the features you should consider while evaluating audio hardware for your PC.

Basic Connectors

Most integrated audio, sound cards, or external audio adapters have the same basic external connectors. These 1/8-inch minijack connectors provide the means of passing sound signals from the adapter to speakers, headphones, and stereo systems, and of receiving sound from a microphone, CD player, or stereo. Laptop computers with integrated audio often include only two jacks: stereo line out and line in. However, sound cards and motherboards with integrated audio often include SPDIF coaxial or optical jacks for supporting 5.1 or 7.1 surround audio and digital audio.

Figure 13.2 shows typical external audio jacks on a motherboard with integrated audio.

1. SPDIF coaxial out (yellow or orange)
2. SPDIF optical out (green)
3. Stereo speaker out (lime green)
4. Line in (blue)
5. Rear/Surround out (black - 4.1/5.1/7.1 audio)
6. Microphone in (pink)
7. Side-Surround out (gray - 7.1 audio)
8. Center/Subwoofer out (orange - 5.1/7.1 audio)

FIGURE 13.2   Typical input and output jacks on a typical motherboard with 7.1 surround audio support.

The jacks shown in Figure 13.2 are usually labeled, but when you're setting up a computer on or under a desk, the labels on the back of the PC can be difficult to see. One of the most common reasons a PC fails to produce sound is that the speakers are plugged into the wrong socket. To avoid this problem, most consumer-oriented audio cards color-code the jacks according to specifications found in the PC 99 Design Guide. The color-coding can vary on some audio adapters (or not be present at all).

A second method used on systems with motherboard-based audio is universal audio jack sensing, a feature of the AC'97 version 2.3 audio standard and also supported by most motherboards using HD Audio. When a device is plugged into an audio jack, the audio driver pops up a dialog box asking the type of audio device in use, such as microphone, stereo speakers, stereo headphones, and so on. The audio driver dynamically assigns the jack to support the device plugged in, even if the "wrong" device is being used in a jack according to the color-coding. This feature is sometimes referred to as *auto-sensing*.

Tip

To avoid confusing the jack-sensing feature, plug in each device to the audio jacks separately, and be sure to confirm the device type in the configuration program before continuing.

Regardless, the basic set of connections included on most audio cards and onboard audio include the following:

- **Stereo line out or audio out connector (lime green)**—The line out connector sends sound signals from the audio adapter to a stereo device outside the computer. You can hook up the cables from the line out connector to stereo speakers, a headphone set, or your stereo system. Some systems use the same lime-green color for surround audio jacks as for the stereo/headphone jack. Check additional markings on the jacks or your system documentation for help.

- **Stereo line in or audio in connector (light blue)**—With the line in connector, you can record or mix sound signals from an external source, such as a stereo system camcorder, to the computer's hard disk. In place of a dedicated line in jack, some sound cards use a multipurpose jack (Creative calls it a "FlexiJack") to support line in, microphone in, and optical out. See the audio card or motherboard documentation for details.

- **Rear out and subwoofer/center or speaker connectors (no standard color)**—Virtually all modern sound cards and desktop systems with integrated audio include jacks that support rear, center, and subwoofer output for use in 5.1 and greater surround audio systems. Systems that support 5.1 audio use three jacks: one for front (stereo) audio, one for rear audio, and one for center/subwoofer audio. Systems that support 6.1 or 7.1 audio might feature additional jacks or might reassign rear and center/subwoofer jacks with software to provide additional output. Depending on your software driver, you might need to run a setup program provided with your sound card or motherboard to enable surround audio. Alternatively, selecting the surround audio setup you use through your OS's speaker configuration utility might be sufficient.

Note

If you have only a single speaker/line out connector, you must carefully adjust your mixer volume control and the volume control on your amplified speakers to find the best quality sound. Don't use powered speakers with an already-amplified sound if you can avoid it.

- **Microphone in or mono in connector (pink)**—The mono in connector is used to connect a microphone for recording your voice or other sounds to disk. This microphone jack records in mono—not in stereo—and is therefore not suitable for high-quality music recordings. To record in stereo, use the line in jack. Many audio adapter cards use Automatic Gain Control (AGC) to improve recordings. This feature adjusts the recording levels on the fly. A 600ohm—10,000ohm dynamic or condenser microphone works best with this jack. Some inexpensive audio adapters use the line in connector instead of a separate microphone jack. Some sound cards use a multi-purpose jack in place of a dedicated microphone jack.

Although it was once necessary to connect analog or digital audio cables between an optical drive and a sound card to play audio CDs, current sound hardware and versions of Windows Media Player and other media player programs support digital playback.

In addition to these connectors for analog audio I/O, many systems also have provision for digital audio output:

- **Coaxial PDIF (also called SPDIF or S/PDIF)**—The Sony/Philips Digital Interface receives digital audio signals directly from compatible devices without converting them to analog format first. The SPDIF out interface might be built into the sound card using a dedicated or multipurpose jack. Most motherboards include an SPDIF out jack on the rear port cluster, whereas others use a plug-in header cable to provide output.

Note

SPDIF interfaces are also referred to by some vendors as "Dolby Digital" interfaces. Coax SPDIF connectors use cables with the standard RCA jack connector but are designed to work specifically at an impedance of 75ohms—the same as composite video cables. Therefore, you can use RCA-jack composite video cables with your SPDIF connectors. Although audio cables are also equipped with RCA jacks, their impedance is different, making them a less desirable choice.

- **Optical SPDIF out**—This supports home theater and digital speaker systems with optical inputs. Typical location: rear of card or external device. Motherboard-based audio solutions may include optical SPDIF out on the port cluster (as in Figure 13.2) or on a header cable that uses an expansion slot. Cards made for audio recording may also include an optical or coax SPDIF in connection.

- **High Definition Multimedia Interface (HDMI)**—This interface carries both high definition video and uncompressed or compressed multichannel audio (up to 7.1). For more information, see Chapter 12.

Audio Signal Processing Methods

PC audio hardware processing is performed in one of three ways:

- Host-based; the CPU, under control of an audio codec and driver software, performs all audio processing. This method is typically used by systems with chipset-integrated audio and by very low-cost (typically under $50) sound cards.

- DSP-based; a digital signal processor (DSP) performs sound processing in conjunction with the CPU. This method is used by most sound cards with hardware DSPs.

- DSP with onboard processor; a DSP performs sound processing with its own onboard RISC processor. This method is used by the Creative Labs CA20K2 (used by the SoundBlaster Titanium series, Auzen X-Fi Forte and HomeTheater HD). Freeing up the CPU provides for the fastest system performance, especially with 3D games that use a lot of positional audio.

Advanced Audio Features

Sound cards designed for audiophiles and sound producers typically have additional connectors designed for their specialized needs, in addition to the standard connectors listed in the previous section. These might include

- **Aux in**—Provides input for other sound sources, such as a TV tuner card.

- **MIDI in and MIDI out**—Older sound cards with game ports (a 15-pin female connector) also supported MIDI in and MIDI out through adapters that plugged into the game port. With current high-end sound cards, MIDI ports might be connected via a proprietary breakout cable (see Figure 13.3) or a proprietary I/O port adapter that might occupy a 5.25-inch drive bay or be placed on a tabletop.

- **XLR input/output**—XLR analog jacks (see Figure 13.3) are used in professional audio and video recording and production.

- **Analog RCA connectors**—RCA audio jacks, such as the ones shown in Figure 13.3, can be used to connect home theater systems or other types of audio hardware to a sound card. You can also convert mini-jack input and output to analog RCA input or output with a variety of adapters.

- **Word Clock I/O connectors**—These BNC connectors (see Figure 13.3) attach to cables that send and receive synchronization signals between word clock-enabled devices such as digital audio tape machines and other professional audio equipment. The impedance, cable, and terminating resistor all need to be 75ohm for proper operation.

Note

The XLR connector is also known as a cannon plug or cannon connector because it was first developed by James H. Cannon of Cannon Electric. The three-pin XLR connector shown in Figure 13.3 is used for balanced audio connections for microphones and other equipment. Other XLR connections have four or more connections, and various types are used by dual-element microphones and headsets, intercom backpacks, lighting control, or fog machine control.

- **Socketed Op Amp chips**—The quality of the Op Amp (operational amplifier) chips (also called OPA or OpAmp chips) used on a sound card affect the sound quality, as these chips are used to amplify analog audio. To enable users to customize the audio quality of their sound cards, several sound card vendors produce cards with socketed Op Amp chips (see Table 13.2 for details).

Table 13.2   Sound Cards with Socketed Op Amp Chips

Vendor	Card	URL
Asus	Xonar Essence STX; Asus Xonar DX 7.1 Xonar HDAV1.3	http://usa.asus.com
Azuntech	All current models	www.auzentech.com
Creative	X-Fi Titanium HD	http://us.creative.com
HT Omega	Claro Halo, Claro Halo XT eCLARO 7.1	www.htomega.com

Adding Advanced Sound Features Without Replacing Onboard Audio

If you use a laptop computer or an all-in-one desktop computer that lacks expansion slots, or if you don't want to open your system to perform an audio upgrade, you can install USB-based audio processors.

When you consider a USB-based solution, keep in mind that, unlike a normal sound card upgrade, you don't need to disable your existing onboard sound or remove a sound card. USB-based audio can coexist with existing sound cards. Typically, as with most hardware, the most recently installed hardware in a category becomes the default, but you can switch back to the original audio hardware through the Windows Control Panel Sound properties sheet.

Beyond the ability to add audio to almost any recent system, USB-based audio is particularly appealing if your current sound card or onboard audio doesn't support 5.1 or 7.1 audio, can't digitize sound at 24-bit/96KHz rates, or lacks digital outputs.

Before you purchase a new sound card or USB-based audio solution for a desktop computer, you should check your system or motherboard documentation to see whether you already have six-channel audio onboard. If your motherboard features six-channel (5.1) or better audio output but the only ports built into the rear of the motherboard are for a normal stereo (2.0/2.1) configuration, you need to add a header cable to the motherboard. If the motherboard did not ship with the header cable, contact the vendor.

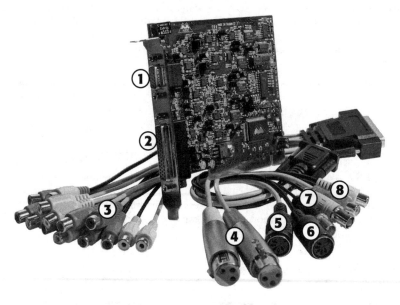

1. Proprietary digital I/O port
2. Proprietary analog I/O port
3. Analog stereo input (tan) and output (black RCA cable
4. Analog XLR stereo input cables
5. Midi input jack
6. MIDI output jack
7. Word clock input (tan) and output (black)
8. Coaxial SPDIF input (red) and output (white) jacks

FIGURE 13.3 The M-Audio Delta 1010LT card is designed to work with up to ten channels of analog audio and can also work with MIDI and SPDIF digital audio sources. Figure courtesy M-Audio.

Volume Control

With virtually all recent sound cards, the volume is controlled through a Windows Control Panel speaker icon that can also be found in the notification area/system tray (near the onscreen clock). If you're switching from a bare-bones stereo sound card to a more sophisticated one featuring Dolby Digital or analog 5.1, 6.1, or 7.1 output or input, you need to use the mixing options in the volume control to select the proper sources and appropriate volume levels for incoming and outgoing audio connected to the card or a breakout box. Keep in mind that if you are sending sound to an external audio receiver, you need to adjust the volume on that device as well. Don't forget to enable digital output via the Sound Properties playback dialog if you are using the SPDIF output jack.

If the PC speakers are amplified but you aren't hearing sound, remember to check that the power is on, the volume control on the speakers is turned up, and the correct speakers are selected and properly connected.

MIDI Support Features

At one time, when evaluating audio adapters, you had to decide whether to buy a monophonic or stereophonic card. Today, all audio adapters are stereophonic and can play music using the MIDI standard, which plays scores using either synthesized instruments or digital samples stored on the audio adapter or in random access memory (RAM).

Stereophonic cards produce many voices concurrently and from two sources. A voice is a single sound produced by the adapter. A string quartet uses four voices, one for each instrument. On the other hand, a polyphonic instrument, such as a piano, requires one voice for each note of a chord. Thus, fully reproducing the capabilities of a pianist requires 10 voices—one for each finger. The more voices an audio adapter is capable of producing, the better the sound fidelity.

Early audio adapters used FM synthesis for MIDI support; the Yamaha OPL2 (YM3812) featured 11 voices, whereas the OPL3 (YMF262) featured 20 voices and stereophonic sound. However, virtually all audio adapters today use recorded samples for MIDI support; audio adapters using this feature are referred to as *wavetable adapters*.

Wavetable audio adapters use digital recordings of real instruments and sound effects instead of imitations generated by an FM chip. When you hear a trumpet in a MIDI score played on a wavetable sound card, you hear the sound of an actual trumpet, not a synthetic imitation of a trumpet. The first cards featuring wavetable support stored 1MB of sound clips embedded in ROM chips on the card or on an optional daughtercard. However, with the ascension of the PCI bus for sound cards and large amounts of RAM in computers, most sound cards and integrated audio devices adopted a so-called "soft wavetable" approach, loading 2MB–8MB of sampled musical instruments into the computer's RAM.

Whereas early games supported only digitized audio samples (because most early sound cards had poor MIDI support), late DOS games such as *DOOM* began to exploit the widespread wavetable-based MIDI support found on most mid-1990s and more recent sound cards. With all current sound hardware supporting wavetable MIDI and the improvements in DirectX 8.x and above for MIDI support, MIDI sound has become far more prevalent for game soundtracks. Many websites also offer instructions for patching existing games to allow MIDI support. Whether you play the latest games or like music, good MIDI performance is likely to be important to you.

The most important factor for high-performance MIDI is the number of hardware voices. Even the best sound cards normally support only 128 voices in hardware; the remainder of the voices required by a MIDI soundtrack must come from software. If your sound card supports only 32 MIDI voices in hardware or uses software synthesis only, consider replacing it with a newer model.

On Windows-based systems with integrated audio, Microsoft GS Wavetable SW Synth is used for MIDI support.

Although most ISA and older PCI sound cards had provision for MIDI outputs via the game port or dedicated MIDI ports, systems with modern integrated audio do not have MIDI ports. However, a variety of MIDI input/output devices can be connected via USB ports, or you can choose a sound card that incorporates MIDI ports (refer to Figure 13.3) or has a MIDI port daughtercard.

Tip

With Windows XP and older editions, you could select the MIDI output device you wanted to use (such as a USB MIDI device or a third-party MIDI program) via the Control Panel's Sounds applet. However, this option is not included in Windows Vista or later versions. If you want to switch to a different MIDI output program or device with these versions of Windows, download and install the MIDI Out Setter utility available from http://www.codeproject.com/KB/audio-video/ MIDIOutSetter.aspx.

Data Compression

All audio adapters on the market today can easily produce CD-quality audio, which is sampled at 44.1KHz. At this rate, recorded files (even of your own voice) can consume more than 10MB for every minute of recording when stored as uncompressed WAV files.

To reduce file size, most manufacturers of audio adapters use an algorithm called *Adaptive Differential Pulse Code Modulation (ADPCM) compression* (it's also called IMA-ADPCM), which was developed by the Interactive Multimedia Association (IMA). ADPCM reduces file size by more than 4:1. IMA-ADPCM compresses 16-bit linear samples down to 4 bits per sample. However, a simple fact of audio technology is that when you use such compression, you lose sound quality. Unfortunately, no standard exists for the use of ADPCM. For example, although both Apple and Microsoft support IMA-ADPCM compression, they implement it in different ways. Apple's standard AIFF and Microsoft's standard WAV file formats are incompatible with each other unless you use a media player that can play both.

When you install an audio adapter, several codecs (programs that perform *c*ompression and *dec*ompression) are installed. Typically, some form of ADPCM is installed along with many others. To see which codecs are installed on your system, open Windows Media Player (version 11 or later), select Organize, Show Classic Menus or Show Menu Bar, and click Help, About Windows Media Player. Then click the Technical Support Information link. In the browser window that opens, scroll down to see the installed audio codecs. Figure 13.4 shows a typical list of audio (and video) codecs from a system running Windows 7.

Audio Codecs

Type	Name	Format	Binary	Version
ACM	Microsoft IMA ADPCM CODEC	0011	imaadp32.acm	6.1.7600.16385
ACM	Microsoft CCITT G.711 A-Law and u-Law CODEC	0007	msg711.acm	6.1.7600.16385
ACM	Microsoft GSM 6.10 Audio CODEC	0031	msgsm32.acm	6.1.7600.16385
ACM	Microsoft ADPCM CODEC	0002	msadp32.acm	6.1.7600.16385
ACM	Fraunhofer IIS MPEG Layer-3 Codec (decode only)	0055	l3codeca.acm	1.9.0.401
ACM	Indeo® audio software	0402	iac25_32.ax	2.0.5.53
ACM	Windows Media Audio	0161	msaud32.acm	8.0.0.4502
ACM	Microsoft G.723.1 CODEC	0042	msg723.acm	4.4.0.3400
ACM	Messenger Audio Codec	028E	sirenacm.dll	15.4.3508.1109
ACM	Sipro Lab Telecom ACELP.net audio codec	0130	sl_anet.acm	3.2.0.0
ACM	DSP Group TrueSpeech(TM) Software CODEC	0022	tssoft32.acm	1.1.1.5
ACM	LAME MP3 Codec v0.9.0 - 3.96 (stable)	0001	LameACM.acm	0.0.9.0
ACM	Ulead DV Audio Codec	0216	Dvacm.acm	8.0.0.0
ACM	Microsoft PCM Converter	0001	LameACM.acm	0.0.9.0
DMO	WMAudio Decoder DMO	0160, 0161, 0162, 0163	WMADMOD.DLL	6.1.7601.17514
DMO	WMAPro over S/PDIF DMO	0162	WMADMOD.DLL	6.1.7601.17514
DMO	WMSpeech Decoder DMO	000A, 000B	WMSPDMOD.DLL	6.1.7601.17514
DMO	MP3 Decoder DMO	0055	mp3dmod.dll	6.1.7600.16385

Video Codecs

Type	Name	Format	Binary	Version
ICM	Microsoft RLE	MRLE	msrle32.dll	6.1.7601.17514
ICM	Microsoft Video 1	MSVC	msvidc32.dll	6.1.7601.17514
ICM	Microsoft YUV	UYVY	msyuv.dll	6.1.7601.17514
ICM	Intel IYUV codec	IYUV	iyuv_32.dll	6.1.7601.17514
ICM	Toshiba YUV Codec	Y411	tsbyuv.dll	6.1.7601.17514
ICM	Cinepak Codec by Radius	cvid	iccvid.dll	1.10.0.13
ICM	Intel Indeo(R) Video R3.2	IV32	ir32_32.dll	3.24.15.3
ICM	Intel Indeo® Video 4.5	IV41	ir41_32.ax	4.51.16.3
ICM	Indeo® video 5.10	IV50	ir50_32.dll	5.2562.15.55
ICM	Microsoft H.261 Video Codec	M261	msh261.dll	5.1.2600.5512
ICM	Microsoft H.263 Video Codec	M263	msh263.drv	5.1.2600.5512
DMO	WMVideo Advanced Decoder DMO	WMVA, WVP2	wmvadvd.dll	11.0.5721.5145
DMO	Mpeg4s Decoder DMO	mp4s, MP4S, m4s2, M4S2, MP4V, mp4v, XVID, xvid, DIVX, DX50	mp4sdecd.dll	6.1.7600.16385
DMO	WMV Screen decoder DMO	MSS1, MSS2	wmvsdecd.dll	6.1.7601.17514
DMO	WMVideo Decoder DMO	WMV1, WMV2, WMV3, WMVA, WVC1, WMVP, WVP2	wmvdecod.dll	6.1.7601.17514
DMO	Mpeg43 Decoder DMO	mp43	mp43decd.dll	6.1.7600.16385
DMO	Mpeg4 Decoder DMO	MPG4, mpg4, mp42, MP42	mpg4decd.dll	6.1.7600.16385

FIGURE 13.4 Audio and Video codecs from a system running Windows 7.

The most popular compression standard is the Motion Pictures Experts Group (MPEG) standard, which works with both audio and video. MPEG by itself provides a potential compression ratio of 30:1. The popular MP3 sound compression scheme is an MPEG format, and it can be played back on most versions of the Windows Media Player, as well as by various other audio player programs and devices.

Sound Drivers

As with many PC components, a software driver provides a vital link between an audio adapter and the application or OS that uses it. If you are using integrated audio, you can get updated drivers for your system from the motherboard or computer vendor's website, or via Windows Update. If you are using a discrete sound card, get updated drivers from the card vendor's website or via Windows Update.

Note

Some sound card and motherboard vendors supply Linux drivers, but you might need to use open-source drivers developed by third parties. The current standard audio API for Linux is advanced Linux sound architecture (ALSA), which also supports the older open sound system (OSS) API. To learn more, see the ALSA Project homepage at www.alsa-project.org/.

Sound Cards for Sound Producers

Sound producers are people who intend to create their own sound files. These can range from casual business users recording low-fidelity voice annotations to professional musicians. These users need an adapter that can perform as much of the audio processing as possible itself, so they don't place an additional burden on the system processor. Adapters that use DSPs to perform compression and other tasks are highly recommended in this case. Musicians will certainly want an adapter with as many voices as possible and a wavetable synthesizer. Adapters with expandable memory arrays and the capability to create and modify custom wavetables are also preferable, as well as a wide variety of analog and digital I/O ports (refer to Figure 13.3 for an example).

To avoid problems with latency when communicating with external devices, particularly with Microsoft Windows, look for cards supported by the latest version of the audio stream input/output (ASIO) protocol (version 2.0 as of mid-2011). ASIO was developed by the Germany company Steinberg, which also developed the Cubase digital sequencer.

Tip

The ASIO4ALL project offers 32-bit and 64-bit ASIO support for virtually all audio that uses Windows driver model (WDM) drivers. Learn more at www.asio4all.com.

Many of the best sound cards for hardcore gamers can also be made suitable for sound producers by adding the appropriate sound-editing programs, such as Sound Forge (www.sonycreativesoftware.com) or Audacity (http://audacity.sourceforge.net/). By choosing a card that supports SPDIF and (if desired) MIDI interfaces, you can have a single card that is suitable for gaming and enjoying audio.

A sound card for use for music enjoyment or production also needs to have a very high signal to noise ratio (SNR of over 110dB) as well as the ability to sample audio up to 192KHz.

Note

The Recording Review website (www.recordingreview.com) is an outstanding resource for researching advanced sound cards and other audio hardware designed specifically for audio production. If you're wanting to select a sound card or USB device for audio recording, try the Audio Interface Wizard at http://www.recordingreview.com/soundcard/soundcard_wizard.php.

Motherboard Chipsets with Integrated Audio

The Intel 810 chipset (introduced in April 1999) was the first mainstream motherboard chipset to integrate audio. Integrated audio can be found in virtually all motherboard chipsets (and therefore motherboards) since then. Even though modern boards include integrated audio, you can still add your own audio solution via an expansion card or USB device if desired.

Although some of the earliest integrated audio implementations left a lot to be desired, thanks to improvements in chipset design and faster CPU performance, today's best integrated chipsets provide solid mid-range performance. Virtually all current chipsets have integrated audio. (See Chapter 4, "Motherboards and Buses," for details.) Modern systems with integrated audio support at least one of the following audio standards:

- AC'97
- Intel High Definition Audio (Azalia)

In most recent systems, Intel HDA is the preferred integrated audio standard, especially for DVD, BD, and HDTV playback. However, many systems still include support for AC'97.

To learn more about AC'97 integrated audio, see the section "AC'97 Integrated Audio," in Chapter 13, "Audio Hardware," in *Upgrading and Repairing PCs*, 19th edition.

Intel "Azalia" HD Audio

Intel released Intel High Definition (HD) Audio in 2004 to deliver high-definition audio capable of playing back more channels at higher quality than the previous AC'97-integrated audio standard. Specifically, AC'97 supports up to six channels (5.1 surround audio) at 48KHz/20-bit, whereas HD Audio supports up to eight channels (7.1 surround audio) at 192KHz/32-bit. Note that not all HD Audio implementations support these maximums.

During its development, HD Audio was known by the code-name "Azalia," and some vendors still refer to it by this name. HD Audio not only can detect when devices are plugged in to an audio jack but can also change the default assignment of the audio jack to match the device being inserted. This helps to reduce audio failures caused by mismatched devices and jacks. Although HD Audio was developed by Intel, it is also supported by most third-party audio codec vendors, including Realtek (ALC861 family, ALC880 series, ALC892), IDT (92HDxxx series), Conexant (AD198x, AD188x, CX20549 family, CX20551), and VIA (Vinyl VT1700 series, VT1800 series, VT 20xx series).

Most systems built in 2004 and later with integrated surround audio include support for HD Audio as well as the older AC'97 audio standard.

HD Audio is the foundation for the Unified Audio Architecture (UAA) audio design used in Windows Vista and later. To learn more about UAA, see the Audio Device Technologies for Windows website at http://msdn.microsoft.com/en-us/windows/hardware/gg454527.aspx.

◀◀ For details on how to enable and disable onboard audio, see the Chapter 5 section, "Advanced Peripheral Configuration," **p. 301**.

Troubleshooting PC Audio Problems

Although PnP PCI and PCIe sound cards and integrated audio have eliminated the troublesome hardware resource conflicts that once made adding audio to a PC a big headache, there are still many possible sources of frustration with recording or playback. Use the following sections to help troubleshoot your audio hardware.

Sound Card and Onboard Audio Problems

Like the common cold, sound hardware problems have common symptoms. Use the following sections to diagnose your problem.

No Sound

If you don't hear anything from your computer, consider these solutions:

- Are the speakers connected? Check that the speakers are plugged in to the sound card's stereo line out or speaker jack (not the line in or microphone jack).

- Are the speakers receiving power? Check that the power "brick" or power cord is plugged in securely and that the speakers are turned on.

- Are the speakers stereo? Check that the plug inserted into the jack is a stereo plug, not mono.

- Are the mixer settings correct? The mixer controls the volume settings for various sound devices, such as the microphone or the CD player. There might be separate controls for both recording and playback. Increase the master volume or speaker volume when you are in the play mode. With some audio hardware, you might need to use a proprietary mixer program (typically installed as part of the sound card or integrated audio setup) to have complete control of speakers, headphones, and microphones.

  If the Mute option is selected in your sound mixer, you won't hear anything. Depending on the speaker type and sound source type, you might need to switch from analog to digital sound for some types of sound output. Make sure that the correct digital audio volume controls are enabled in your audio device's mixer control.

- Use any setup or diagnostic software provided with your audio hardware or integrated sound to test and adjust the volume of the adapter. Such software usually includes sample sounds used to test the adapter.

- Turn off your computer for 1 minute and then turn it back on. A hard reset (as opposed to pressing the Reset button or pressing Ctrl+Alt+Delete) might clear the problem.

- If your computer game lacks sound, check that it is designed to work with your audio adapter. For example, some legacy (DOS-based) and early Windows games might require Sound Blaster compatibility that modern versions of Windows no longer support. Refer to the section earlier in this chapter titled "Legacy Audio Support Through Virtualization."

- If you're using motherboard-integrated audio, make sure the onboard audio is enabled (check the BIOS setup program) and that the proper drivers and player program have been installed (check the Windows Control Panel).

- If you're using motherboard-integrated audio that employs a removable header cable (such as with some SPDIF optical or four/six-channel analog speaker configurations), make sure the header cable is properly connected to the motherboard.

- Note that a few high-end cards have a connector for additional power; be sure to connect the appropriate power lead to ensure that the card will operate.

Volume Is Low

If you can barely hear your sound, try these solutions:

- Are the speakers plugged into the proper jack? Speakers require a higher level of drive signal than headphones. Again, adjust the volume level in your mixer application.

- Are the mixer settings too low? Again, adjust the volume level in your mixer.

- Is the initial volume too low? If your audio adapter has an external volume control, check to ensure that it is not turned down too low.

- Are the speakers too weak? Some speakers might need more power than your audio adapter can produce. Try other speakers, or put a stereo amplifier between your sound card and speakers.

Some Speakers Don't Play

If you hear sound coming from some speakers, but not others, check the following:

- **Mono plug in the stereo jack**—A common mistake is to use a mono plug in the sound card's speaker or stereo out jack. Seen from the side, a stereo connector has two darker stripes. A mono connector has only one stripe.

- **No power to speakers**—Check the AC adapter's connection to the electrical outlet.

- **Loose speaker connection to some speakers**—When possible, use keyed and color-coded connectors to avoid mistakes.

- **Speakers not set to same volume**—Some speakers use separate volume controls on each speaker. Balance them for best results. Separate speaker volume controls can be an advantage if one speaker must be farther away from the user than the other.

- **Loose speaker jack**—If you find that plugging in your speaker to the jack properly doesn't produce sound but pulling the plug halfway out or "jimmying" it around in its hole can temporarily correct the problem, you're on the road to a speaker jack failure. To avoid damage to the speaker jack, be sure you insert the plug straight in, not at an angle.

- **Incorrect sound mixer settings**—Most systems assume that you are using two-channel (stereophonic) sound, even if you have plugged in four or more speakers. Select the correct speaker type with the Windows Speaker icon or a third-party sound mixer.

- **Additional speakers connected to the wrong jacks**—Make sure you connect the additional speakers needed for four-channel, six-channel, or eight-channel audio to the correct jacks. If you connect them to line in or microphone jacks, they won't work.

- **Incorrect balance settings**—The volume control also adjusts the balance between the left and right speakers. If you hear audio from the left speakers only or the right speakers only, the balance control needs to be centered with the Windows Speaker icon or a third-party sound mixer.

Note

On some systems with integrated audio, audio jacks have multiple uses. For example, in six-channel or eight-channel mode on some systems, the normal line in and microphone jacks might be reconfigured to work with rear and center/subwoofer speakers. In such cases, the mixer controls need to be reset.

Some Types of Sounds Play, But Others Don't

If you can hear CDs but not WAV or MP3 digital music, or you can play WAV and MP3 but not CD or MIDI files, check the following:

- **Low volume or mute settings for some audio types**—Some audio mixers have separate volume controls for WAV/MP3, MIDI, CD digital, CD audio, and other sound types and sources. Unmute any audio types you play back, and adjust the volume as desired. In Windows 7, you can set different volume levels for individual apps.

Scratchy Sound

Scratchy or static-filled sound can be caused by several problems. Improving the sound can be as simple as rearranging your hardware components. The following list suggests possible solutions to the problem of scratchy sound:

- **Interference from other cards**—The sound card might be picking up electrical interference from other expansion cards inside the PC. Move the audio card to an expansion slot as far away as possible from other cards.

- **Dirty cable connector or jack**—Unplug each connector and wipe it, and then reconnect it.

- **Interference from CRT display**—The speakers can pick up electrical noise from your monitor. Move them farther away. Never place subwoofers near the monitor because their powerful magnets can interfere with the picture. Put them on the floor to maximize low-frequency transmission.

- **Some games don't play at all or have poor-quality sound**—If you notice sound problems such as stuttering voices, static, or a lack of audio on some games but not others, check with the game vendor for a software patch or with the sound card vendor for updated drivers. If you use Creative ALchemy for 3D audio, look up the settings for your game at the Creative Labs ALchemy website (http://connect.creativelabs.com/alchemy/default.aspx). If the game uses DirectX under Windows XP or older versions, run the DXDIAG diagnostics program from the Windows Run dialog. Click Start, Run, type **dxdiag**, and click OK. (Windows Vista and 7 also include DXDIAG, but they do not support hardware audio acceleration.) In DXDIAG, click the Sound tab. Adjust the slider for Hardware Sound Acceleration Level down one notch from Full (the default) to Standard, click Save All Information, and exit. Retry the game. If the problem persists, adjust the Hardware Sound Acceleration Level to Basic. If other games have performance problems after you adjust the Hardware Sound Acceleration Level, be sure to reset it to Full before playing those games.

Your Computer Won't Start

If your computer won't start at all after you installed a new sound card, you might not have inserted the sound card completely into its slot. Turn off the PC and then press firmly on the card until it is seated correctly.

If you can't start your computer after installing a new sound card and its drivers, you can use the Windows "bootlog" feature to record every event during startup; this file records which hardware drivers are loaded during startup and indicates whether the file loaded successfully, didn't load successfully, or froze the computer. See the documentation for your version of Windows for details on how to create a bootlog when necessary.

Advanced Features

If you are having problems playing DVD audio, playing MP3 files, or using SPDIF connections, make sure of the following:

- You have enabled the hardware resources on the sound card.

- You are using the correct playback program.

- Your mixer has the correct volume control setting for the device.

- You have enabled digital playback (if you are using coaxial or optical SPDIF output).

- Your cabling is correct for the device.

Other Problems

A good way to solve problems of all types with PnP cards and integrated hardware, a PnP BIOS, and Windows is to use the Device Manager to remove the sound card or integrated audio, restart the system, and allow the card's components to be redetected. This installs a "fresh" copy of the software and reinserts Registry entries.

If reinstalling the current driver with this method doesn't improve your results, download and install updated drivers for your sound card or integrated audio.

Speakers

Successful business presentations, multimedia applications, and MIDI work demand external high-fidelity stereo or surround speakers. Although you can use standard stereo speakers, they are often too big to fit on or near your desk. Smaller bookshelf speakers are better.

Sound cards offer little or none of the amplification needed to drive external speakers. Make sure you use speakers made for PCs, or connect your sound card or integrated audio to a home theater system's amplifier, which can provide the power needed to run standard speakers.

Caution

Although most computer speakers are magnetically shielded, do not leave recorded tapes, watches, credit cards, or other devices with magnetic recording surfaces in front of the speakers for long periods of time.

Quality sound depends on quality speakers; an inexpensive speaker makes any type of PC audio sound tinny.

Speaker Selection Criteria

Dozens of models of PC speakers are on the market, ranging from inexpensive minispeakers from Sony, Creative, and Logitech to larger self-powered models from prestigious audio companies such as Bose, Klipsch, and Altec Lansing. Almost all speakers, even in the under $30 range, include subwoofers to provide additional bass response. To evaluate speakers, it helps to know the jargon. Speakers are measured by three criteria:

- **Frequency response**—A measurement of the range of high and low sounds a speaker can reproduce. The ideal range is 20Hz–20KHz, the range of human hearing. No speaker system reproduces this range perfectly. In fact, few people hear sounds above 18KHz. An exceptional speaker might cover a range of 30Hz–23,000Hz, and lesser models might cover only 100Hz–20,000Hz. Frequency response is the most deceptive specification because identically rated speakers can sound completely different.

- **Total harmonic distortion (THD)**—An expression of the amount of distortion or noise created by amplifying the signal. Simply put, *distortion* is the difference between the sound sent to the speaker and the sound you hear. The amount of distortion is measured in percentages. An acceptable level of distortion is less than 0.1% (one-tenth of 1 percent). For high-quality audio equipment, a common standard is 0.05%, but the cheap amplifiers included with many inexpensive speakers have a distortion of 1% or more, which is at least 20 times greater.

- **Watts**—Usually stated as either total watts or watts per channel, this is the amount of amplification available to drive the speakers. This is one of the more misleading specifications because a valid comparison of output levels between different amplifiers can be difficult to make. Because distortion increases with power output, amplifiers with higher THD specifications will more easily have higher total or per-channel wattage ratings. Amplifiers driving more speakers will have higher total wattage figures as well, even though the amount of power to the primary stereo channels will usually be less. Finally, some manufacturers report an inflated and relatively meaningless Peak Music Power Output (PMPO) figure, instead of the Root Mean Square (RMS) figure standardized by the Federal Trade Commission. When making wattage number comparisons, make sure they are RMS values reported at the same level of THD; then, you can compare either the total wattage figures or the per-channel figures for the primary front L and R (stereo) channels.

Before purchasing a speaker set, do your research and look at reviews of what others think about the speakers you are considering.

You can control the volume and other sound attributes of your speakers in various ways, depending on their complexity and cost. Typically, each speaker has a volume knob, although some share a single volume control. If one speaker is farther away than the other, you might want to adjust the volume accordingly. Many computer speakers include a dynamic bass boost (DBB) switch. This button provides a more powerful bass and clearer treble, regardless of the volume setting. Other speakers have separate bass and treble boost switches or a three-band equalizer to control low, middle, and high frequencies. When you rely on your audio adapter's power rather than your speakers' built-in amplifier, the volume and DBB controls have no effect. Your speakers are at the mercy of the adapter's power.

For best audio quality, adjust the master volume on the sound card near the high end and use the volume control on powered speakers to adjust the volume. Otherwise, your speakers try to amplify any distortions coming from the low-power input from the PCaudio adapter.

A 1/8-inch stereo minijack connects from the audio adapter's output jack to one of the speakers. The speaker then splits the signal and feeds through a separate cable from the first speaker to the second one (often referred to as the *satellite speaker*).

Before purchasing a set of speakers, check that the cables between the speakers are long enough for your computer setup. For example, a tower case sitting alongside your desk might require longer speaker wires than a desktop computer.

Beware of speakers that have a tardy built-in sleep feature. Such speakers, which save electricity by turning themselves off when they are not in use, might have the annoying habit of clipping the first part of a sound after a period of inactivity.

Headphones can provide higher-quality sound for a given price than a comparably priced speaker set, provide better listening to 3D audio special effects in games, provide privacy, and enable you to play your PC audio as loud as you like. You can connect headphones via traditional audio jacks, or you can buy USB-based versions.

For best results with newer sound cards that support four speakers or more, check the properties sheet for the audio adapter and set whether you're using headphones, stereo speakers, or a larger number of speakers. Use your audio software to set up 3D or other audio effects.

Make sure that speakers are placed properly. If you use a subwoofer, put it on the floor for better bass sound and to reduce electromagnetic interference (EMI) with other devices.

If you still use a CRT, how can you tell whether wireless satellite speakers are causing interference with your display? Watch your monitor; frequencies as high as 2KHz can interfere with your video display. Move the speakers away from the monitor, and check the display again.

Theater and Surround Sound Considerations

If you're a serious gamer or movie lover, you won't be content with ordinary stereophonic sound. Most sound cards and integrated audio now support up to 7.1 surround sound. For high-end use, you may prefer to connect your PC's audio subsystem to a home theater system.

To ensure you get the sound you expect from four or more speakers, either directly connected to the system or via a home theater amplifier, check the following:

- Use the properties sheet for your audio adapter to properly describe your speaker setup. This includes selecting the number of speakers you are using, setting options for 3D environmental audio and positional sound such as reverb, and setting up your subwoofer if present.

- Make sure you use the correct cabling between your speakers and audio adapter. If you are planning to use analog or digital surround speaker setups, such as 4.1, 5.1, 6.1, or 7.1, be sure you use the correct SPDIF, analog, or HDMI connection and configuration. This varies from audio adapter to audio adapter; check the vendor's website for details.

- Make sure you have placed your speakers correctly. In some cases you can adjust the audio adapter's properties to improve sound quality, but you might need to move the speakers.

- Make sure you have connected your speakers to the proper jacks. Mixing up left and right or front and rear causes poor sound quality.

- Select the correct setting in your amplifier configuration. If you are sending your computer's audio signals to a home theater's amplifier, make sure you select the output option corresponding to the input jacks you used. For example, many home theater amps have selections for various types of devices. Be sure to select the correct input for BD playback, DVD playback, or PC audio. The PC audio input you select depends upon whether you are sending HDMI, SPDIF, or stereo signals to the amp.

The simplest audio configuration available today is stereo, which uses two speakers placed to overlap sound. Most audio adapters now support at least four speakers, but depending on the audio adapter, settings, and sound output options in the program, the rear speakers might simply mirror the front speakers' output, or you might have four distinct sound streams.

Four-point surround sound uses four speakers plus a subwoofer to surround you with music and gaming sound effects; the four speakers are placed around the listener, and the subwoofer is usually placed near a wall or in the corner to amplify its low-frequency sound. The subwoofer in stereo or four-point surround sound setups is not on a separate circuit but is controlled by the same signals sent to the other speakers. A stereo speaker system with a subwoofer is often referred to as a *2.1 speaker configuration*, and a four-point surround sound configuration with a subwoofer is often referred to as a *4.1 speaker configuration*.

5.1 Surround sound uses five speakers plus a subwoofer. The fifth speaker is placed between the front two speakers to fill in any missing sound caused by incorrect speaker placement. The subwoofer is independently controlled. This is the preferred sound system for use with DVD movies. Most lower-cost audio adapters lack support for 5.1 Surround sound.

Some of the latest sound cards and motherboards with integrated audio support 6.1 and 7.1 Surround sound. The 6.1 configuration resembles the 5.1 Surround setup but adds a middle speaker along with a subwoofer. 7.1 Surround sound uses left-middle and right-middle speakers to flank the listener, along with a subwoofer. Some cards play back 5.1 or greater Surround sound configurations with analog speakers only, whereas others can also transmit Dolby Digital (AC-3), DTS Surround, or Dolby EX digital audio through the SPDIF digital audio port to a home theater system.

Microphones

Some audio adapters come complete with a microphone, but most do not. You'll need one to record your voice. Selecting a microphone is quite simple. You need one that has a 1/8-inch minijack to plug in to your audio adapter's microphone jack (or audio in jack). Most handheld microphones have an on/off switch. However, you can also use the Mute control in the audio mixer to shut off the microphone. If you are planning to use audio for voice chat, recording podcasts, or interactive gaming, consider a headset with an integrated microphone. You can use a USB-based headset/microphone or use one that plugs into HD Audio or AC'97 jacks.

Like speakers, microphones are measured by their frequency ranges. This is not an important buying factor, however, because the human voice has a limited range. If you are recording only voices, consider an inexpensive microphone that covers a limited range of frequencies. An expensive microphone's recording capabilities extend to frequencies outside the voice's range. Why pay for something you won't be needing?

If you are recording music, podcasting, or producing other audio content that will be distributed, investing in a more expensive microphone is usually justified. However, in that case you should ensure that your audio adapter can do justice to the signal the microphone produces. A high-quality microphone can produce mediocre results when paired with a cheap audio adapter.

Your biggest decision is to select a microphone that suits your recording style. If you work in a noisy office, you might want a unidirectional microphone that prevents extraneous noises from being recorded. An omnidirectional microphone is best for recording a group conversation.

If you're using voice-recognition software, use the microphone supplied with the software or choose from alternative models the software vendor recommends. Run the microphone setup program again if your software has trouble recognizing your voice. Some models feature a battery pack to boost sound quality; be sure to check the batteries, and replace them to keep recognition quality high.

If you're talking but your voice-recognition or recording software isn't responding, check the following:

- **Incorrect jack**—It's easy to plug the microphone into the wrong jack. Try using a magic marker to color-code the microphone wire and jack to make matching up easier if your microphone or audio jack isn't color-coded or uses competing standards. If your sound card or motherboard-based audio supports the auto-recognition feature included in AC'97 v2.3, make sure you plug in one cable at a time and select the device you connected when you are prompted by the audio setup program.

- **The recording volume in the mixer control**—This usually defaults to Mute to avoid spurious noise.

- **Whether the microphone is turned on in the voice-recognition or recording software**—You must click the Record button in recording software, and many voice-recognition programs let you "pick up" the microphone for use or "put it down" when you need to answer the phone. Look for an onscreen microphone icon in the Windows System Tray for fast toggling between modes.

External I/O Interfaces

Introduction to Input/Output Ports

This chapter covers the primary external peripheral input/output ports on modern and legacy PC systems. This includes the legacy serial and parallel ports that have been standard on PCs since the beginning, as well as the universal serial bus (USB, which has replaced the older serial and parallel ports), IEEE 1394 (also called FireWire or i.LINK), and Thunderbolt Technology interfaces. IEEE stands for the Institute of Electrical and Electronic Engineers. Although eSATA is also considered an external I/O interface, it is a derivative of Serial ATA (SATA), which is mainly used as an internal storage device interface. SATA is covered in Chapter 7, "The ATA/IDE Interface." Small computer systems interface (SCSI) is another type of internal/external interface; however, desktop PCs today rarely implement SCSI. If you want to learn more about this architecture, refer to *Upgrading and Repairing Servers* (ISBN: 978-0789728159).

We can divide external I/O connections into high-speed and low-speed variants. Currently, the two most popular high-speed external I/O connections are USB and IEEE 1394; however, Thunderbolt is replacing IEEE 1394, especially in the high-end video editing arena. Low-speed connections include standard serial and parallel ports (often called *legacy ports*), which have generally been replaced by USB in newer systems and peripherals.

Serial Versus Parallel

The current trend in high-performance bus design is to use a serial architecture, in which one bit at a time is sent down a wire. Because parallel architecture uses 8, 16, or more wires to send bits simultaneously, a parallel bus is faster than a serial bus *at the same clock speed*. However, increasing the clock speed of a serial connection is much easier than increasing that of a parallel connection, so much so that the higher attainable speeds more than completely offset the difference in the number of bits sent at a time. In the end, serial interfaces can be designed to be faster than parallel interfaces, and for much less cost and complexity.

Parallel connections in general suffer from several problems, the biggest being signal skew and jitter, which conspire to limit both clock speeds and signal distances. The problem in a parallel bus is that, although the multiple bits of data are fired from the transmitter at the same time, by the time they reach the receiver, propagation delays have conspired to allow some bits to arrive before the others. The longer the cable, the longer the time variation between the arrival of the first and last bits at the other end. This *signal skew*, as it is called, limits both clock speeds and cable lengths. *Jitter* is the tendency for the signal to reach its target voltage and float above and below for a short period, which becomes pronounced at higher speeds and at longer distances.

With a serial bus, the data is sent one bit at a time, one after the other. Because there is no worry about having multiple bits arrive simultaneously, the clocking rate can be increased significantly.

At high clock rates, parallel signals tend to interfere with each other. Serial again has the advantage because with only one or two signal wires, crosstalk and interference between the wires in the cable are negligible.

In general, parallel routing or cabling is far more expensive to implement than serial routing or cabling. In addition to the many extra traces or wires needed to carry the multiple bits in parallel, the circuit must be specially constructed to prevent crosstalk and interference between adjacent data lines. This is one reason external SCSI cables are so expensive. Serial connections, by comparison, are inexpensive. For one thing, they have significantly fewer signals or wires. Furthermore, the shielding requirements are far simpler, even at high speeds. Because of this, transmitting serial data reliably over longer distances is also easier, which is why parallel interfaces have shorter recommended trace runs or cable lengths than do serial interfaces. For these reasons—in addition to the need for new Plug and Play (PnP) external peripheral interfaces and the elimination of the physical port crowding on portable computers—high-performance serial buses were developed. USB is a standard feature on virtually all PCs today and is used for most general-purpose, high-speed external interfacing. It's also the most compatible, widely available, and fastest general-purpose external interface. IEEE 1394 is typically used in camcorders and digital video editing equipment; however; it is beginning to be replaced in that market by Thunderbolt Technology.

Universal Serial Bus (USB)

Universal serial bus (USB) is an external peripheral bus standard designed to bring PnP capability for attaching peripherals externally to the PC. USB eliminates the need for special-purpose ports, reduces the need to use special-purpose I/O cards or PC Cards (thus reducing the need to reconfigure the system with each new device added), and saves important system resources such as interrupt requests (IRQs). Regardless of the number of devices attached to a system's USB ports, only one IRQ is required. PCs equipped with USB enable peripherals to be automatically recognized and configured as soon as they are physically attached, without the need to reboot or run a setup program. USB allows up to 127 devices to run simultaneously on a single bus, with some peripherals such as monitors and keyboards acting as additional plug-in sites, or *hubs*. USB devices can be identified by the icons shown in Figure 14.1.

FIGURE 14.1   This icon identifies USB cables, connectors, hubs, and peripherals.

USB was initially developed by Intel engineers in the early 1990s, after which the design was transferred to the USB Implementers Forum (USB-IF) to further develop, support, and promote USB architecture. The USB-IF initially consisted of Intel plus six other companies including Compaq, Digital, IBM, Microsoft, NEC, and Northern Telecom.

The USB-IF has formally released USB versions as follows:

- **USB 1.0**—January 1996
- **USB 1.1**—September 1998
- **USB 2.0**—April 2000
- **USB 3.0**—November 2008

The 1.1 revision was mostly a clarification of some issues related to hubs and other areas of the specification. Most devices and hubs should be 1.1 compliant, even if they were manufactured before the release of the 1.1 specification. A bigger change came with the introduction of USB 2.0, which was 40 times faster than the original USB yet fully backward compatible. USB ports can be retrofitted to older computers that lack built-in USB connectors through the use of either an add-on PCI card (for desktop computers) or a PC Card on CardBus-compatible laptop computers.

Intel motherboard chipsets starting with the PIIX3 South Bridge chipset component (introduced in February 1996) have included USB support as standard. In September 1996, Toshiba introduced the first USB peripheral, a device it called the "In-Touch Module," which was a patented remote-control unit that included buttons for playing media along with a volume control knob.

After Intel introduced chipsets with USB support, other chipset vendors quickly followed suit, making USB as ubiquitous a feature of today's PCs as serial and parallel ports once were. Although most desktop systems started incorporating USB back in mid-1996, most laptops did not begin including USB 1.1 ports until 1998. It wasn't until then that Intel released a mobile South Bridge chipset with USB support. By mid-2002, virtually all desktop motherboards included 4–6 (or more) USB 2.0 ports as standard. Laptop computers were a little slower to catch on to the USB 2.0 bandwagon; it wasn't until early 2003 that most laptop computers included USB 2.0 ports as standard.

Systems with USB 3.0 ports were first released in 2010; however, these used third-party add-on chips because Intel and AMD did not incorporate USB 3.0 support in motherboard chipsets until 2012. Currently, most systems include ten or more USB 2.0 and/or 3.0 ports as standard, and with hubs or expansion cards, many more can easily be added.

USB 1.1/2.0 Technical Details

USB 1.1 runs at 12Mbps (1.5MBps) over a simple four-wire connection. The bus supports up to 127 devices (including both functions and hubs) connected to a single root hub and uses a tiered-star topology, built on expansion hubs that can reside in the PC, any USB peripheral, or even standalone hub boxes.

Note that although the standard allows you to attach up to 127 devices, they all must share the 1.5MBps bandwidth, meaning that for every active device you add, the bus slows down some. In practical reality, few people have more than eight devices attached at any one time.

For low-speed peripherals, such as pointing devices and keyboards, the USB also has a slower 1.5Mbps subchannel.

USB employs what is called *Non Return to Zero Invert (NRZI)* data encoding. NRZI is a method of encoding serial data in which 1s and 0s are represented by opposite and alternating high and low voltages where there is no return to a zero (or reference) voltage between the encoded bits. In NRZI encoding, a 1 is represented by no change in signal level, and a 0 is represented by a change in level. A string of 0s causes the NRZI data to toggle signal levels for each bit. A string of 1s causes long periods with no transitions in the data. This is an efficient transfer encoding scheme because it eliminates the need for additional clock pulses that would otherwise waste time and bandwidth.

USB devices are considered either hubs or functions, or both. *Functions* are the individual devices that attach to the USB, such as a keyboard, mouse, camera, printer, telephone, and so on. *Hubs* provide additional attachment points to the USB, enabling the attachment of additional hubs or functions. The initial ports in the system unit are called *root hubs*, and they are the starting point for the USB. Most motherboards have two or more USB ports, any of which can be connected to functions or additional hubs. Some systems place USB ports in the front or sides of the computer, which is convenient for devices you use only occasionally, such as digital cameras and flash memory card readers.

External hubs (also called *generic hubs*) are essentially wiring concentrators, and through a star-type topology they allow the attachment of multiple devices. Each attachment point is referred to as a *port*. Most hubs have either four or eight ports, but more are possible. For further expandability, you can connect additional hubs to the ports on an existing hub. The hub controls both the connection and distribution of power to each of the connected functions. A typical hub is shown in Figure 14.2.

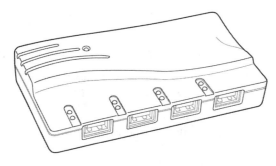

FIGURE 14.2 A typical USB hub with four ports.

Besides providing additional sockets for connecting USB peripherals, a hub can provide power to any attached peripherals. A hub recognizes the dynamic attachment of a peripheral and provides at least 0.5W of power per peripheral during initialization. Under control of the host driver software, the hub can provide more device power (up to a maximum of 2.5W) for peripheral operation.

Different types of USB devices require different amounts of power, measured in milliamps (mA). Bus-powered USB devices (devices that draw power from the USB port) might require as much as 500mA (the maximum amount of power available through a USB port) or as little as 100mA or less. Self-powered devices also draw power from the USB port, but they might draw as little as 2mA.

The PnP aspects of USB enable the system to query the attached peripherals as to their power requirements and issue a warning if available power levels are exceeded. This is especially important for USB when it is used in laptops or other portable systems because the battery power that is allocated to run the external peripherals might be limited. It is also important because of the differences in hubs.

Root hubs and self-powered hubs (hubs connected to an AC adapter) provide a full 500mA of power to each USB port. However, bus-powered hubs (hubs without an AC adapter) provide only 100mA per port because they use power provided by the upstream USB port and subdivide it among the ports. If you connect a USB device that requires more power than the port provides, the device will not work. In a worst-case scenario, you might damage the device. For example, the contents of some USB flash memory drives (which typically require 200mA–500mA) can be destroyed by being inserted into a bus-powered hub (which provides only 100mA per port). Some vendors are now including overcurrent protection in their latest designs, but because of the risk factors, I don't recommend plugging a USB flash memory drive or a USB card reader into a bus-powered hub.

To determine the power requirements of a particular USB device before you purchase it, check the product's specifications or contact the vendor. To determine the power available per port and the power usage of the devices plugged in to the port on a system running Windows, open the properties sheet for each root or generic hub in the Device Manager, and click the Power tab. The Power tab lists the hub type (self-powered or bus-powered) and the amount of power per port in the Hub Information section of the properties sheet. In the Attached Devices section, each device connected to the hub is listed by its category and power required (see Figure 14.3).

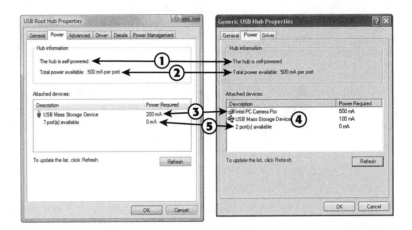

1. Hub type
2. Power per port
3. High-power devices
4. Low-power device
5. Remaining ports

FIGURE 14.3   Examples of USB hub and device power usage in Windows 7/8/Vista (left) and Windows XP (right).

Because of the variance in the power requirements of different USB devices and the possibility of damage, I recommend using only self-powered USB hubs. Keep in mind that some USB hubs on the market do not include an AC adapter or the ability to attach one, automatically making them bus-powered.

Devices that use more than 100mA, such as the webcam and USB mass storage device listed in Figure 14.3, must be connected to a root hub or a self-powered generic hub. Devices that use 100mA or less can be connected to bus-powered hubs, such as those without separate AC adapters or those built in to some keyboards and monitors.

Tip

If a device plugged into a self-powered hub stops working, check the power source for the self-powered hub—it might have failed or been disconnected. In such cases, a self-powered hub becomes a bus-powered hub, providing only 100mA per port instead of the 500mA per port available in self-powered mode.

A newly attached hub is assigned a unique address, and hubs can be cascaded up to five levels deep (see Figure 14.4). A hub operates as a bidirectional repeater, and it repeats USB signals as required both upstream (toward the PC) and downstream (toward the device). A hub also monitors these signals and handles transactions addressed to itself. All other transactions are repeated to attached devices.

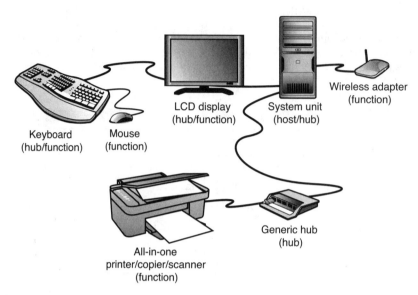

FIGURE 14.4 A typical PC with USB devices can use multiple USB hubs to support a variety of peripherals, connected to whichever hub is most convenient.

Note

A USB 1.1 hub supports both 12Mbps (Full-Speed) and 1.5Mbps (Low-Speed) peripherals. A USB 2.0 hub supports USB 1.1 12Mbps and 1.5Mbps speeds and the 480Mbps (Hi-Speed) used by native USB 2.0 devices. A USB 3.0 hub supports 5Gbps (SuperSpeed) devices as well as any slower USB 2.0 and 1.1 devices.

The maximum cable length between two USB 2.0 480Mbps (Hi-Speed) or USB 1.1 12Mbps (Full-Speed) devices, or between a device and a hub, is 5 meters using twisted-pair shielded cable with 20-gauge wire. The maximum cable length for USB 3.0 SuperSpeed (5Gbps) connections, as well as any Low-Speed (1.5Mbps) devices using non-twisted-pair wire, is 3 meters. These distance limits are shorter if smaller gauge wire is used (see Table 14.1).

Table 14.1 Maximum Cable Lengths Versus Wire Gauge

Gauge	Resistance (in Ohms/Meter Ω/m)	Length (Max. in Meters)
28	0.232 Ω/m	0.81m
26	0.145 Ω/m	1.31m
24	0.091 Ω/m	2.08m
22	0.057 Ω/m	3.33m
20	0.036 Ω/m	5.00m

USB 2.0

USB 2.0 (also called *Hi-Speed USB*) is a backward-compatible extension of the USB 1.1 specification that uses the same cables, connectors, and software interfaces but that runs 40 times faster than the original 1.0 and 1.1 versions. The higher speed enables higher-performance peripherals (such as storage drives, higher-resolution web/videoconferencing cameras, scanners, and faster printers) to be connected externally with the same easy PnP installation for which USB has always been known. From the end-user point of view, USB 2.0 works the same as 1.1—only faster. All existing USB 1.1 devices work in a USB 2.0 bus because USB 2.0 supports all the slower-speed connections. USB data rates are shown in Table 14.2.

Table 14.2 USB Data Rates

Interface	Speed Terminology	Bits per Second	Bytes per Second
USB 1.1	Low-Speed	1.5Mbps	0.1875MBps
USB 1.1	Full-Speed	12Mbps	1.5MBps
USB 2.0	Hi-Speed	480Mbps	60MBps
USB 3.0	SuperSpeed	5Gbps	500MBps

Note the terminology, which can be confusing. *Full-Speed* designates the 1.5MBps throughput of USB 1.1, whereas *Hi-Speed* designates the 60MBps throughput of USB 2.0. Because any USB 1.1 device works on a 2.0 bus (at the slower 1.1 speeds), many devices or components have been advertised as "USB 2.0-Compatible" or "USB 3.0-Compatible" when they do not actually support Hi-Speed or SuperSpeed operation. The key to finding true USB 2.0 or 3.0 devices is to look for the device to state that it is USB 2.0 or 3.0 "compliant" or "certified."

The support of higher-speed USB peripherals requires using a USB 2.0– or 3.0–compliant hub. You can still use older USB 1.1 or 2.0 hubs on a 2.0 or 3.0 bus, but any peripherals or additional hubs connected downstream from a slower hub operate at the slower maximum speed. The higher transmission speeds through a 2.0/3.0 hub are negotiated on a device-by-device basis; if the higher speed is not supported by a peripheral, the link operates at a lower speed.

How can you tell at a glance which devices are designed to support USB 1.1 versus the faster USB 2.0 and 3.0 standards? The USB Implementer's Forum (USB-IF), which owns and controls the USB standard, introduced logos in late 2000 for products that have passed its certification tests. These logos are shown in Figure 14.5.

As you can see from Figure 14.5, USB 1.1 is called simply "USB," and USB 2.0 is called "Hi-Speed USB."

USB cables, connectors, hubs, and peripherals can also be identified by icons, as shown in Figure 14.6. The plus (+) symbol added to the upper icon indicates that port or device would support USB 2.0 (Hi-Speed USB) in addition to the standard 1.1 support.

Note that these icon guidelines do not apply to USB cables or connectors because the cable and connector design did not change from USB 1.1 to 2.0. Cables are supposed to use the standard icon (without the plus symbol), and all cables that support USB 1.1 also support 2.0.

FIGURE 14.5   The USB 1.1-compliant logos (left) compared to the USB Hi-Speed (2.0-compliant) logos (right). The lower-left and -right logos indicate USB On-The-Go compliance.

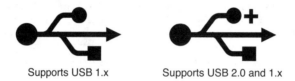

Supports USB 1.x   Supports USB 2.0 and 1.x

FIGURE 14.6   These icons identify USB 1.x and 2.x devices.

USB 1.1/2.0 Connectors

The USB 1.1 and 2.0 family of specifications has included numerous connector styles since it was introduced. Initially, four main styles of connectors were specified: Series A, Series B, Mini-A, and Mini-B. The A connectors are used for upstream connections between a device and the host or a hub. The USB ports on motherboards and hubs are usually Series A connectors. USB 3.0 extends several of these connectors with additional sections and/or pins, which are shown in the following section covering USB 3.0.

Series B connectors are designed for the downstream connection to a device that has detachable cables. The Mini connector is simply a smaller version of the larger ones, in a physically smaller form factor for smaller devices, such as digital cameras, PDAs, and media players. For USB On-The-Go devices, a Mini-AB connector was developed to permit a device to act as either an upstream or a downstream device in relationship to another device.

In April 2006, the Micro-B and Micro-AB connectors were added as approved connectors, and in May 2007, the Mini-A and Mini-AB connectors were removed from the approved list of USB connectors. Therefore, as of mid-2007, new and forthcoming USB devices can use only the following connectors: Series A, Series B, Mini-B, Micro-B, and Micro-AB. (Micro-AB is used only by On-The-Go products.)

The physical USB plugs are small (especially the Mini and Micro plugs) and, unlike a typical serial or parallel cable, the plug is not attached by screws or thumbscrews. There are no pins to bend or break, making USB devices user friendly to install and remove. The USB plugs shown in Figure 14.7 connect to the corresponding USB sockets.

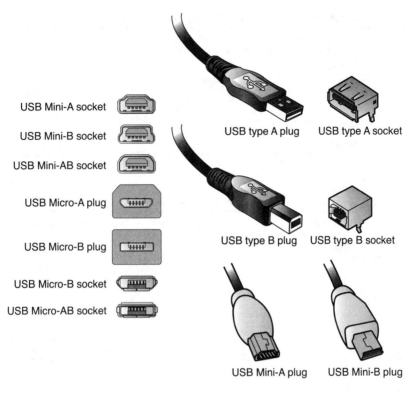

USB Mini-A socket

USB Mini-B socket

USB Mini-AB socket

USB Micro-A plug

USB Micro-B plug

USB Micro-B socket

USB Micro-AB socket

USB type A plug   USB type A socket

USB type B plug   USB type B socket

USB Mini-A plug   USB Mini-B plug

FIGURE 14.7   USB plugs and sockets.

Note that a Mini-AB socket is a dual-purpose socket that can accept either Mini-A or Mini-B plugs. Likewise, a Micro-AB socket is a dual-purpose socket for either Micro-A or Micro-B plugs. (There is no Micro-A socket.) The newer Mini and Micro plugs and sockets have plastic portions inside the connectors that are required to be color-coded, as shown in Table 14.3.

Table 14.3   Color Coding for USB Mini Plugs and Sockets

Connector	Color
Mini-A socket	White
Mini/Micro-A plug	White
Mini/Micro-B socket	Black
Mini/Micro-B plug	Black
Mini/Micro-AB socket	Gray

Tables 14.4 and 14.5 show the pinouts for the USB connectors and cables.

Table 14.4 USB Connector Pinouts for Series A/B Connectors

Pin	Signal Name	Wire Color	Comment
1	Vbus	Red	Bus power
2	– Data	White	Data transfer
3	+ Data	Green	Data transfer
4	Ground	Black	Cable ground
Shell	Shield	–	Drain wire

Table 14.5 USB Connector Pinouts for Mini and Micro A/B Connectors

Pin	Signal Name	Wire Color	Comment
1	Vbus	Red	Bus power
2	– Data	White	Data transfer
3	+ Data	Green	Data transfer
4	ID	–	A/B identification*
5	Ground	Black	Cable ground
Shell	Shield	–	Drain wire

* *Used to identify a Mini/Micro-A from a Mini/Micro-B connector on the device. ID is connected to Ground in a Mini/Micro-A plug and is not connected (open) in a Mini/Micro-B plug.*

Most motherboards have several USB header connectors built in. These are 10-pin connectors supporting two USB ports. Normally your motherboard includes a USB header cable with external connectors mounted on a bracket, but if you need extras, companies such as MonoPrice and Cables To Go sell header cables that are compatible with standard USB header pins. Figure 14.8 shows a typical USB header cable set.

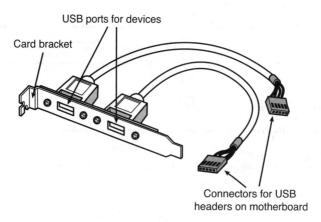

USB ports for devices

Card bracket

Connectors for USB
headers on motherboard

FIGURE 14.8 A typical USB header cable set; plug it into your motherboard to connect devices to the additional onboard USB ports (if present).

USB conforms to Intel's PnP specification, including *hot-plugging*, which means that you can plug in devices dynamically without powering down or rebooting the system. Simply plug in the device, and the USB controller in the PC detects the device and automatically determines and allocates the required resources and drivers. One advantage of an interface such as USB with older systems is that it requires only a single IRQ from the system. Therefore, you can connect up to 127 devices, and they will not use separate IRQs as they might if each was connected over a separate interface.

USB 3.0 (SuperSpeed USB)

USB 3.0 (also called SuperSpeed USB) offers performance and bandwidth that is more than 10 times the performance of USB 2.0 and yet is backward compatible with existing USB 1.1 and 2.0. In addition, USB 3.0 is optimized for lower power consumption and improved protocol efficiency (less overhead).

On September 18, 2007, Intel announced both the formation of the USB 3.0 Promoter Group and the development of the USB 3.0 interface, which had already been well underway. The initial members of the group included Intel, HP, Microsoft, NEC, NXP, and Texas Instruments. The final USB 3.0 specification was released on November 17, 2008.

The main feature of USB 3.0 is an increased transfer speed of 5Gbps (500MBps), thus significantly reducing the time it takes to move data. Table 14.6 shows the time it takes each version of USB to transfer the amount of data contained in popular media, including a music CD ripped as 320Kbps MP3 files, a standard definition movie, and a high definition movie. These numbers point to the actual or effective transfer rates of USB, accounting for protocol overhead. From these numbers, you can see that USB 2.0 is about 40 times faster than USB 1.1, and USB 3.0 is more than 10 times faster than USB 2.0. An important consideration for the design of USB 3.0 was the time it takes to transfer high definition movie content, which is about 14 minutes using USB 2.0. Knowing that people would be highly unsatisfied with that level of performance, USB 3.0 was designed to increase bandwidth so that a transfer of that type would take just over a minute.

Table 14.6   Time to Copy Media Using USB 1, 2, and 3

USB Type	MP3 CD (128MB)	SD Movie (6GB)	HD Movie (25GB)
USB 1.1 (Full-Speed)	2.9 minutes	2.2 hours	9.3 hours
USB 2.0 (Hi-Speed)	4.3 seconds	3.3 minutes	13.9 minutes
USB 3.0 (SuperSpeed)	0.4 seconds	20 seconds	70 seconds

It is interesting to note that the level of actual or effective performance indicated by Intel for USB 3.0 (transferring 25GB in 70 seconds) is equal to approximately 360MBps in effective throughput (including overhead), which compares to about 32MBps maximum effective throughput for USB 2.0. This is significantly faster than most magnetic storage drives are capable of; however, high-performance SSDs (solid-state drives) with a SATA 6Gbps interface can easily achieve and even exceed that level of performance.

Note

Although USB 3.0 is faster on paper than eSATA, in reality eSATA is still faster and more efficient for connecting external drives. This is because USB adds overhead to the connection, and any external USB enclosure still incorporates SATA internally for the drive interface. For this reason many people are in no rush to replace eSATA connected external drive docks and enclosures with newer and more expensive USB 3.0 versions.

In the future it is expected that both hard drives and especially flash or solid-state storage devices such as media players or flash drives will experience dramatic improvements in performance, and USB 3.0 is designed to be capable of meeting the demands of these products.

The primary enhancements in USB 3.0 include the following:

- Dedicated IN and OUT lanes with four additional wires (plus ground) allowing full-duplex operation (reading and writing at the same time).

- Increased power available for bus-powered devices, 900mA (4.5W) versus only 500mA (2.5W) in USB 1.1/2.0.

- Aggressive power management; links go to low-power states when idle.

- The host schedules all transactions (no polling).

- Both hosts and devices transmit only when they have data.

For backward compatibility, USB 3.0 hubs also include a USB 2.0 hub, allowing operation in both USB 3.0 and 1.1/2.0 modes at the same time. USB 3.0 also operates using switching, where communication is done between the host and each device independently, rather than being broadcast to all devices. This is far more efficient than the broadcasting technique used by USB 2.0 and prior. Devices that pass USB 3.0 compliance testing may carry the SuperSpeed USB certified logo shown in Figure 14.9.

FIGURE 14.9 SuperSpeed certified USB logo.

USB 3.0 connectors and cables have an additional five pins dedicated to the SuperSpeed function (two SuperSpeed differential signal pairs plus a ground), whereas the four existing USB 1.1/2.0 pins remain for full backward compatibility. The socket has the new pins mounted just above and in front of the existing pins. USB 3.0 sockets accept both USB 3.0 plugs and cables and USB 1.1/2.0 plugs and cables. Figure 14.10 shows the USB 3.0 socket design.

The mating USB 3.0 plug has the five new contact pins recessed in the connector to match up to the socket when inserted. The pins consist of differential transmit and receive pairs and a ground (see Figure 14.11).

In addition to the modified connector assemblies, the USB 3.0 cable icon shown in Figure 14.12 denotes cables that are compliant with the USB 3.0 specification.

The USB 3.0 specification also includes provisions for optical connectors, which might be used by some devices in the future.

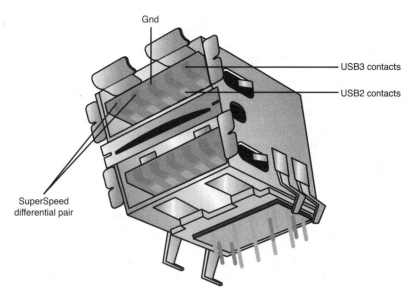

FIGURE 14.10 USB 3.0 sockets for circuit board mounting.

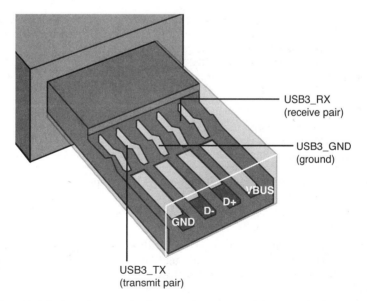

FIGURE 14.11 USB 3.0 plug, showing the five USB 3.0 pins in addition to the four original USB 1.1/2.0 pins.

FIGURE 14.12 SuperSpeed USB 3.0 cable icon.

USB On-The-Go

In December 2001, the USB-IF released a supplement to the USB 2.0 standard called *USB On-The-Go*. This was designed to address the one major shortcoming of USB—that a PC was required to transfer data between two devices. In other words, you could not connect two cameras and transfer pictures between them without a PC orchestrating the transfer. With USB On-The-Go, devices that conform to the specification still work normally when they are connected to a system, but they also have additional capabilities when connected to other devices supporting the standard.

Although this capability can also work with USB-based PC peripherals, it was mainly added to address issues using USB devices in the consumer electronics area, where a PC might not be available. Using this standard, devices such as digital video recorders can connect to other recorders to transfer recorded movies or shows, items such as personal organizers can transfer data to other organizers, and so on. USB On-The-Go greatly enhances the usage and capabilities of USB, both in the PC and in the consumer electronics markets. USB On-The-Go has been included in smartphones, for example, allowing them to easily and directly interface to USB devices such as flash drives, without the use of a PC.

Wireless USB

Wireless USB (WUSB) is just what the name denotes: USB without wires. WUSB is based on ultrawideband (UWB) radio technology, which the military originally developed in 1962 for secure radio communications and radar use. Recognizing the usefulness of this radio technology for the public, in 2002 the Federal Communications Commission released frequencies from 3.1GHz to 10.6GHz for general-purpose UWB use.

In June 2003, a group called the Multiband OFDM (orthogonal frequency division multiplexing) Alliance Special Interest Group (MBOA-SIG) formed to develop a UWB physical layer interface standard. The MBOA-SIG completed its UWB physical layer 1.0 specification in November 2004 and subsequently merged with another group called the WiMedia Alliance in March 2005. The WiMedia Alliance had originally formed in 2002 to promote the standardization and adoption of UWB wireless standards.

In February 2004, several companies, including Agere, HP, Intel, Microsoft, NEC, Philips, and Samsung, together announced the formation of the Wireless USB Promoter Group and began working on the WUSB specification, which would use the common WiMedia MB-OFDM (multiband orthogonal frequency division multiplexing) UWB radio platform for the physical connection layer. The WUSB Promoter Group subsequently developed and released the WUSB 1.0 specification on May 12, 2005. Wireless USB 1.1 was introduced on September 29, 2010, and included several improvements such as UWB support for frequencies 6GHz and above, improved power management, and support for Near Field Communications (NFC) and proximity-based association, which allows for easier installation and configuration.

WUSB devices are now certified to conform to the standard by the USB Implementers Forum and enable high-speed wireless connectivity by adapting USB protocols to the MB-OFDM UWB radio platform as developed by the WiMedia Alliance. Certified WUSB devices carry the official Wireless USB logo shown in Figure 14.13.

WUSB uses a portion of the UWB radio spectrum, including 528MHz-wide channels from 3.1GHz to 10.6GHz. These wideband channels allow for high bandwidths up to 480Mbps (60MBps), which exactly matches the wired USB 2.0 specification in maximum throughput.

WUSB is designed for low power consumption and short-range, high-speed connections, with performance of 480Mbps (60MBps) at 3 meters (approximately 10 feet), dropping to 110Mbps (13.75MBps) at 10 meters (approximately 33 feet). This is similar in range to Bluetooth, but at significantly higher transfer speeds. The radio frequencies used for WUSB are also designed not to overlap or interfere with the popular 2.4GHz 802.11b/g Wi-Fi and Bluetooth and 5GHz 802.11a Wi-Fi radios as well as common cordless phones and microwave ovens.

FIGURE 14.13 The Wireless USB logo carried by devices certified to comply with the Wireless USB specification.

The uses for WUSB are almost endless; basically anything that can be connected via a wired USB connection can connect wirelessly as well. Existing wired USB devices can even be connected wirelessly by attaching a special WUSB adapter called a Host Wire Adapter (HWA) on the PC side and a Device Wire Adapter (DWA) on the peripheral side. Figure 14.14 shows one possible configuration for connecting wired devices that way.

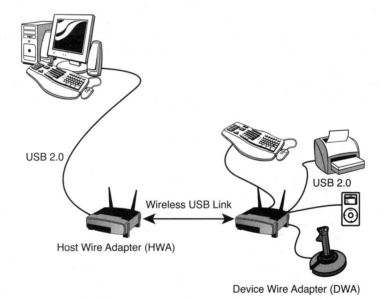

FIGURE 14.14 Using a HWA and DWA to wirelessly connect traditional wired USB devices to a system.

Unfortunately, while WUSB sounds promising, market support has been lacking, although some WUSB adapters and peripherals did appear on the market in 2006. In 2008, Lenovo began including WUSB in select ThinkPad laptops, and Kensington released a WUSB docking station. Since then, however, there have been very few other WUSB adapters or peripherals on the market.

Windows USB Support

The first version of Windows to support USB properly was Windows 98. Although it is true that Windows 95B and 95C did have limited support for USB 1.1, many USB devices would not work with

Windows 95 releases because the drivers available for 95B and 95C were limited in capability. It wasn't until Windows 98 appeared that you could say Windows fully supported USB. Windows 98 had USB 1.1 support built in; however, support for USB 2.0 requires additional drivers from the motherboard or host adapter provider.

USB 2.0 support was not included in the initial release of Windows XP but was included with Service Pack 1 and later updates. Windows Vista, 7, and 8 include support for USB 2.0, and Windows 8 includes support for USB 3.0 as well. USB 3.0 devices can be used with Windows 7 and earlier by installing the drivers for the particular controller you are using, which may be either on a card or built in to the motherboard. Individual USB devices might also include their own drivers, which might need to be installed separately.

USB support is also required in the basic input/output system (BIOS) for devices such as keyboards and mice. This is included in all systems with USB ports built in. Aftermarket PC Cards and ExpressCards are available for adding USB to older systems that don't include it as standard. USB peripherals include printers, external storage, modems, scanners, VoIP telephones, game controllers, keyboards, and pointing devices such as mice and trackballs.

IEEE 1394 (FireWire or i.LINK)

The Institute of Electrical and Electronic Engineers Standards Board introduced IEEE 1394 (or just 1394 for short) in late 1995. The number comes from the fact that this happened to be the 1,394th standard the board published. Although the standard is officially called 1394, it was initiated under the trademarked name FireWire by Apple Computer, who made most of the initial contributions to the design. The key advantage of 1394 is that it's extremely fast; the current standard supports data-transfer rates up to 400Mbps (1394a), 800Mbps (1394b S800), and 3,200Mbps (1394b S3200).

1394/FireWire is included on many high-end motherboards, and the interface is widely used in devices such as camcorders, digital video editing equipment and some external drives. More recently 1394 began being supplanted by Thunderbolt Technology in the video editing and production market.

1394 Standards

The most popular version of the 1394 standard is actually referred to as 1394a, or sometimes as 1394a-2000 (for the year this version was adopted). The 1394a standard was introduced to solve interoperability and compatibility issues in the original 1394 standard; it uses the same connectors and supports the same speeds as the original 1394 standard.

The faster 1394b standard was introduced in early 2003 and is fully backward compatible with 1394a devices. The 1394 standard is also known by two other common names: FireWire (trademarked by Apple) and i.LINK (trademarked by Sony). i.LINK is an IEEE 1394 designation initiated by Sony to put a more user-friendly name on IEEE 1394 technology. Originally, the term *FireWire* was an Apple-specific trademark that Apple licensed to vendors on a fee basis. However, in May 2002, Apple and the 1394 Trade Association announced an agreement to allow the trade association to provide no-fee licenses for the FireWire trademark on 1394-compliant products that pass the trade association's tests. Apple continues to use *FireWire* as its marketing term for IEEE 1394 devices. FireWire 400 refers to Apple's IEEE 1394a–compliant products, whereas FireWire 800 refers to Apple's IEEE 1394b–compliant products. Note that Intel has always licensed USB on a royalty-free basis, which is perhaps the biggest reason it became more popular than FireWire in PCs and consumer devices.

1394a Technical Details

The IEEE 1394a standard currently exists with three signaling rates: 100Mbps, 200Mbps, and 400Mbps (12.5MBps, 25MBps, and 50MBps). A maximum of 63 devices can connect to a single IEEE 1394 adapter card by way of daisy-chaining or branching. Unlike USB devices, 1394 devices can be used in a daisy-chain without using a hub, although hubs are recommended for devices that will be hot-swapped. Cables for IEEE 1394a devices use Nintendo GameBoy–derived connectors and consist of six conductors: four wires transmit data and two wires conduct power. Connection with the motherboard is made either by a dedicated IEEE 1394a interface or by an adapter card. Figure 14.15 shows 1394a port connectors.

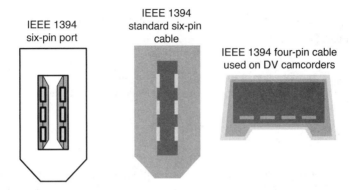

IEEE 1394
six-pin port

IEEE 1394
standard six-pin
cable

IEEE 1394 four-pin cable
used on DV camcorders

FIGURE 14.15   IEEE 1394a port connectors.

The 1394 bus was derived from the FireWire bus originally developed by Apple and Texas Instruments. The 1394a uses a simple six-wire cable with two differential pairs of clock and data lines, plus two power lines; the four-wire cable/connector shown in Figure 14.15 is used with self-powered devices, such as DV camcorders. Just as with USB, 1394 is fully PnP, including the capability for hot-plugging (insertion and removal of components without powering down).

Built on a daisy-chained and branched topology, 1394 allows up to 63 nodes, with a chain of up to 16 devices on each node. If this is not enough, the standard also calls for up to 1,023 bridged buses, which can interconnect more than 64,000 nodes! Additionally, as with SCSI, 1394 can support devices with various data rates on the same bus. Most 1394 adapters have three nodes, each of which can support 16 devices in a daisy-chain arrangement. Some 1394 adapters also support internal 1394 devices.

The types of devices that can be connected to the PC via 1394 include mainly video cameras, editing equipment, and external drives. The 1394 bus appears in many desktop and laptop computers as a supplement to other external high-speed buses, such as USB and eSATA.

Chipsets enabling PC Card/CardBus and ExpressCard adapters for the 1394 bus are available from a number of manufacturers, including some models that support both 1394 and other port types in a single slot. Microsoft has included support for 1394a in Windows 98SE and later. Windows 7 and later have updated that support to include 1394b. The most popular devices that utilize 1394 are camcorders, digital video recorders, and external storage drives. Sony was among the first to release 1394 devices, however in typical Sony fashion, Sony doesn't call it 1394 or FireWire; it has created its own designation (i.LINK) instead. Just remember that whether it is called 1394, FireWire, or i.LINK, it is basically the same thing. Digital video (DV) products and storage drives using 1394 are available from many other companies.

1394b Technical Details

IEEE 1394b is the second generation of the 1394 standard, with the first products (high-performance external hard drives) introduced in January 2003. IEEE 1394b uses one of two 9-pin cables and connectors, along with 8b/10b encoding to support speeds of 800Mbps–3,200Mbps with copper or fiber-optic cabling. In addition to supporting faster transfer rates, 1394b has other new features, including the following:

■ Self-healing loops. If you improperly connect 1394b devices to create a logical loop, the interface corrects the problem instead of failing, as with 1394a.

- Continuous dual simplex. Of the two wire pairs used, each pair transmits data to the other device so that speed remains constant.

- Support for fiber-optic and CAT5 (Category 5) or better network cable and standard 1394a and 1394b copper cable.

- Improved arbitration of signals to support faster performance and longer cable distances.

- Support for CAT5 or better cable, even though it uses pairs on pins 1/2 and 7/8 only for greater reliability. It also doesn't require crossover cables.

The initial implementations of IEEE 1394b use a new nine-wire interface with two pairs of signaling wires. However, to enable a 1394b port to connect to 1394a-compatible devices, two versions of the 1394b port are used:

- Beta
- Bilingual

Beta connectors support only 1394b devices, whereas bilingual connectors can support both 1394b and 1394a devices. As Figure 14.16 shows, the connectors and cables have the same pinout but are keyed differently.

Note that bilingual sockets and cables have a narrower notch than beta sockets and cables. This prevents cables designed for 1394a devices from being connected to the beta socket. Figure 14.17 compares a beta-to-beta 1394b cable to bilingual-to-1394a cables.

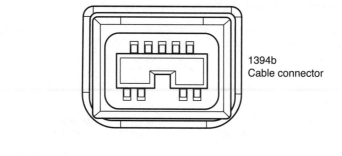

1394b
Cable connector

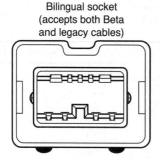

Bilingual socket
(accepts both Beta
and legacy cables)

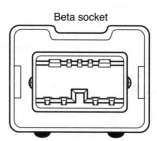

Beta socket

FIGURE 14.16 Bilingual and beta 1394b connectors and cables. Many 1394b implementations use both types of connectors.

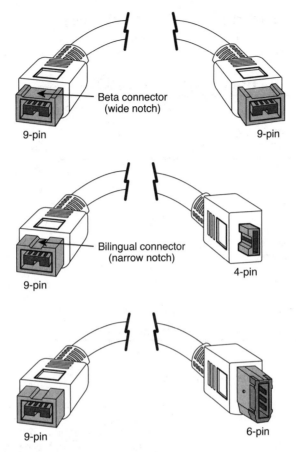

FIGURE 14.17 A beta-to-beta cable (top) compared to bilingual–to–4-pin (middle) and bilingual–to–6-pin 1394a devices (bottom).

1394b S3200 (FireWire 3200)

In December 2007, the 1394 Trade Association announced the 1394b S3200 (FireWire 3200) specification, which quadruples the speed of FireWire to 3.2Gbps (320MBps using 8b/10b encoding). The new speed uses existing FireWire 800 cables and connectors and is backward compatible with both FireWire 800 and the original FireWire 400 specification. Because the 1394 arbitration, data, and service protocols are the same for S3200 mode as for the previous S800 mode, hardware and software vendors can easily take advantage of the new mode without significant product redesigns.

Unfortunately, FireWire 3200 never appeared in any PC-based devices and has been surpassed by other high-performance interfaces such as eSATA, USB 3.0, and Thunderbolt Technology. Because Thunderbolt includes both DisplayPort digital audio/video and PCIe data signaling on the same cable at transfer rates of 10Gbps, it is rapidly replacing FireWire in the high performance digital video hardware market.

Comparing USB and IEEE 1394 (FireWire)

Because of the similarity in both the form and function of USB and 1394, there has been some confusion about the two. Table 14.7 summarizes the differences between the two technologies.

Table 14.7   Comparing USB and IEEE 1394 (FireWire)

	IEEE 1394a (FireWire 400)	IEEE 1394b S800 (FireWire 800)	IEEE 1394b S3200 (FireWire 3200)	USB 1.1	USB 2.0	USB 3.0
PC host required	No	No	No	Yes	Yes[1]	Yes[1]
Maximum number of devices	63	63	63	127	127	127
Hot-swappable	Yes	Yes	Yes	Yes	Yes	Yes
Maximum cable length (between devices)	4.5 meters	4.5 meters	4.5 meters	5 meters	5 meters	3 meters
Power available to devices	7W[2]	7W	7W	2.5W	2.5W	4.5W
Transfer rate	400Mbps (50MBps)	800Mbps (80MBps)	3.2Gbps (320MBps)	12Mbps (1.5MBps)	480Mbps (60MBps)	5Gbps (500MBps)

1. *USB On-The-Go (OTG) does not require a PC as a host.*
2. *7W typical; some IEEE 1394 ports can supply up to 18W or more.*

USB is by far the most popular external interface for PCs, eclipsing all others by comparison. This is primarily because Intel originally developed USB and has placed built-in USB support in all its motherboard chipsets since 1996. Few if any motherboard chipsets integrate 1394a or 1394b; it has to be added as an extra-cost chip on the motherboard. The cost of the additional 1394 circuitry (and a $0.25 royalty paid to Apple Computer per system) and the fact that all motherboards already have USB have limited the popularity of 1394 (FireWire) in the PC marketplace as a general purpose external interface.

But, even with the overwhelming popularity of USB, a market for 1394 still exists, especially in DV (Digital Video) applications. One of the main differences between 1394 and USB is that USB normally requires a PC as the host, providing the control and management of the bus. This means you cannot connect two USB devices directly and transfer data between them; instead, they must both be connected to a PC, which acts as the host controller. With FireWire, on the other hand, you can connect two devices directly because the bus is designed so that any device can control transfers. For example, 1394 can directly connect a DV camcorder to a DV-VCR for dubbing tapes or editing. This can play a big part in performance because the transfer rate between devices over USB depends greatly on the horsepower of the PC controlling the bus, whereas the transfer rate over FireWire is mostly independent of the PC and far more dependent on the devices doing the transfers.

FireWire support is built in to most DV camcorders and video editing applications and devices. For example, when capturing video from tape you can connect a FireWire-enabled DV camcorder to a FireWire port in your PC and then use Windows Movie Maker (included with XP/Vista and a free download from Microsoft for Windows 7/8) to capture or digitize the data from tape to the PC. Once on the PC, it can be edited, copied, or uploaded to video sharing sites. Although many systems include FireWire built in, if your system doesn't include a FireWire connection, you can easily add one via an adapter card.

USB/FireWire Performance Myths and Realities

A student once wrote me to inquire about a question that appeared on a test in a computer class he and his classmates had taken. The question was, "Which is faster, USB 2.0 or FireWire 400 (1394a)?" They had answered that USB 2.0 was faster, because USB 2.0 was rated 480Mbps (60MBps), whereas FireWire 400 was rated 400Mbps (50MBps). Well, after the test was graded the students were shocked to find their answer had been marked wrong! Upon discussing the question in class, the teacher confirmed the technical specifications but then went on to say that due to less internal "overhead," FireWire was faster than USB in the real world, even though the raw transfer speed might be less on paper. The student was basically asking me what the correct answer to the question really was.

I had to sigh. I *despise* questions like that because, from a technical standpoint, the question is so poorly and imprecisely written that *both* answers are arguably correct. For example, it obviously wasn't clear whether the question meant "faster" as in the raw bus speed or as in real-world throughput. And if it did mean real-world throughput, under what circumstances exactly? Well, when confronted with questions like that, where you *have* to make a choice one way or another, in general the best thing you can do is to keep it simple and avoid overthinking the answer. Because real-world testing involves many unknown variables, the simplest and most definitive answer would be based on the raw transfer speeds alone. In that case, choosing the best answer would be simple: Because USB 2.0 transfers at 480Mbps (60MBps), and 1394a transfers at 400Mbps (50MBps), USB is faster.

Now I know some people reading this might disagree, including the teacher who gave the test referenced by the student. Many people believe (and many tests have shown) that, whereas USB is faster on paper, FireWire is faster in the real world. Although I hesitate to make blanket statements, I would agree that just as with any interface or bus in a PC, there are many more factors contributing to performance for a specific task under a specific set of conditions than just the raw bus speed specification. Although many people assume that FireWire is faster in the real world, the truth is that the designs of USB and FireWire are different, and one cannot necessarily predict the results of a specific example without knowing all the relevant details.

To help make my point, I ran some tests and recorded the results. I had a 7200 rpm Maxtor 250MB drive mounted in an external enclosure that supports *both* FireWire 400 (1394a) and USB 2.0 interfaces. The drive was formatted as a single FAT32 partition and was about half full. I created a folder and copied a 300MB video file into the folder. I specifically selected a large file that would not fit in any of the caches or buffers for either the drive or systems involved.

I used two systems to conduct the tests, and both included FireWire 400 and USB 2.0 interfaces. The systems were as follows:

- **System 1**—Desktop, 3.6GHz Pentium 4 processor, 1GB RAM, Windows XP
- **System 2**—Laptop, 1.7GHz Pentium M processor, 1GB RAM, Windows XP

To test the throughput, I copied the file and measured the time in seconds for the command to complete. This meant that the file would be read from and written back to the same drive, which amounts to essentially a two-way trip over the interface (from the drive to the PC and back to the drive). I used two commands (COPY and XCOPY), running each one four times consecutively, discarding the results of the first run and averaging the other three.

Note

To measure the time it took for each file copy, I used the Timelt utility, which is a command-line tool that records the time a specified command takes to run. Timelt.exe is included with the Windows Server 2003 Resource Kit Tools, which you can download from Microsoft (http://go.microsoft.com/fwlink/?LinkId=4544). Note that Timelt won't run on 64-bit versions of Windows; in that case I would use "Measure-Command" in the Windows PowerShell (included with Windows 7 and 8).

The average times to copy the file using the faster desktop system are shown in Table 14.8.

Table 14.8   Elapsed Time to Copy a 300MB File on a 3.6GHz Desktop PC

Procedure	ET Using USB 2.0 (Seconds)	ET Using FireWire 400 (Seconds)	Which Is Faster?
COPY 300MB file	20.67	23.32	USB by 12.82%
XCOPY 300MB file	12.52	15.62	USB by 24.73%

As you can see from the results, when the faster desktop system was used, copying the file was from nearly 13% (using COPY) to 25% (using XCOPY) *faster* over USB than it was over FireWire. Also, it is interesting to note that using the XCOPY command was 49% faster than COPY over FireWire and 65% faster than COPY over USB.

The average times to copy the file using the slower laptop system are shown in Table 14.9.

Table 14.9   Elapsed Time to Copy a 300MB File on a 1.7GHz Laptop PC

Procedure	ET Using USB 2.0 (Seconds)	ET Using FireWire 400 (Seconds)	Which Is Faster?
COPY 300MB file	30.50	24.13	FireWire by 26.37%
XCOPY 300MB file	19.37	15.83	FireWire by 22.34%

As you can see from the results, when the slower laptop system was used, copying the file was from 22% (using XCOPY) to 26% (using COPY) *faster* over FireWire than it was over USB. Also note that using the XCOPY command was 52% faster than COPY over FireWire and 57% faster than COPY over USB.

So which is faster in the "real world"? In this example, when copying the file on the higher-performance desktop PC, USB 2.0 was faster; however, on the slower laptop PC, FireWire was faster. But that's not all; I noticed another interesting detail: It seems that the relative speed and performance of the PC had a *large effect* on the throughput of the USB 2.0 transfers, whereas it had virtually *no effect* on the FireWire 400 transfers. Table 14.10 shows a comparison.

Table 14.10   USB/FireWire File Copy Performance: 3.6GHz Pentium 4 Desktop Versus a 1.7GHz Pentium M Laptop

Desktop Vs. Laptop	USB 2.0	FireWire 400
COPY 300MB file	Desktop was 47.54% faster.	Desktop was 3.49% faster.
XCOPY 300MB file	Desktop was 54.67% faster.	Desktop was 1.37% faster.

The desktop system was from about 48% to 55% faster than the laptop on USB transfers, yet only 1% to 3% faster on FireWire transfers. In other words, the FireWire transfer times were virtually *identical* on both the desktop and laptop systems, even though the systems varied greatly in speed. This is understandable because FireWire uses a peer-to-peer connection design, which does not use the PC to manage the interface. On the other hand, USB is a PC-centric design using the PC as the host controller. In other words, because of the internal design differences in USB and FireWire, the PC processor and overall PC system performance have a much greater effect on USB than on FireWire.

Another interesting point: The method used to copy the file (COPY versus XCOPY in this case) actually made *more* of a difference than the interface or the system speed. This brings up many more questions: Would there have been other differences had the drive been formatted with NTFS instead of FAT32? What if I had copied many small files instead of one large file? What if I had used a different operating system (OS)? As you can see, in any benchmark or comparison, you must consider a huge number of variables—and there are no simple answers to ambiguous questions!

Hot-Plugging (and Unplugging)

Because external USB and 1394 (FireWire) devices can be hot-plugged, you must be careful in some cases when unplugging things, especially storage devices. To help prevent data loss with external drives and storage devices, when disconnecting them you should click the Safely Remove Hardware icon in the Windows taskbar notification area (often called the *system tray*). Then select the device to be removed and wait for the system to indicate that the device can be safely removed before you unplug it.

But consider this: I've unplugged devices without "safely removing" them many times without problems, so is it really necessary to go to the trouble? To answer that question properly, I'll have to explain more about how caching works, both in Windows and in the hardware.

Windows includes a write cache in the OS (using system RAM) Microsoft likes to call *lazy write*. The OS-based lazy write function has been around for a long time. In fact, it has been enabled by default for nonremovable drives (internal ATA hard drives, for example) in all versions of Windows since version 3.1 (as smartdrv.exe), which dates from 1992. What Microsoft calls lazy write is also called *write-back caching*, *write-behind caching*, and *deferred* or *delayed writes*.

In modern versions of Windows, this is controlled by the Windows cache manager. The cache manager controls Windows-based write caching and flushes the cache quite often to minimize loss. In addition, any application that uses write operations can request that those operations be done as *write-through*, which bypasses the lazy writer and goes straight to the disk. The truth is, to minimize the potential for lost data, lazy write (Windows write caching) is disabled for *removable* media in Windows by default. This was designed to minimize problems stemming from what Microsoft calls the *surprise removal* of certain hardware. Lazy write is enabled by default for internal (ATA or SATA) storage devices inside the computer that cannot be surprise removed. Lazy write is also enabled for certain high-performance external storage devices that might or might not be hot-swappable, such as those attached via eSATA.

Many people worry about write caching as related to potential data loss. A worst-case scenario is a power outage while saving a file, which will certainly cause the loss of data that hasn't already been written to the drive, and it might even corrupt the entire file system. This is where the journaling in NT File System (NTFS) comes in handy, which is one of the main reasons NTFS is recommended over file allocation table (FAT).

Note

If a power outage occurs while you are writing a file to a storage device using a FAT file system, in addition to losing the file, you'll likely end up with lost clusters, cross-linked files, or other file system damage, potentially causing a much greater loss of data than just the one file being written at the time. However, if the same outage occurs while writing to a device using NTFS, the file system itself won't be damaged. Of course, no matter what file system is used, you will almost certainly lose part or all of the file being saved at the time of the outage because even if you have write caching turned off, you can't recover data that never made it to the disk in the first place.

In addition to the Windows cache, there is the drive's built-in physical write cache, which is also enabled by default on internal drives. Depending on the specific hardware and drivers involved, this functionality might also be overridden or controlled by Windows. If it can be controlled, the Policies tab in the drive properties under the Device Manager has a setting called Enable Write Caching on the Disk, which allows Windows to turn the drive's hardware write caching function on or off. Note that the dialog box for Enable Write Caching on the Disk states the following:

> This setting enables write caching to improve disk performance, but a power outage or equipment failure might result in data loss or corruption.

In my opinion, this statement is more of a disclaimer than a serious warning of danger. The truth is that when you're saving a file during a power outage, the difference in data loss between whether you had the drive's internal write caching on or off will be virtually inconsequential. However, I would say that if your system is experiencing frequent crashes or power outages under normal operation, disabling the drive's internal write caching (and Windows lazy write caching for external devices as well) via the settings in the Device Manager *might* result in less data loss in some circumstances.

With removable devices, you can change Windows lazy write functionality via the Optimize for Quick Removal (lazy write off) or Optimize for Performance (lazy write on) settings in the Policies tab under the drive properties in the Device Manager entry for any removable devices (that is, USB/FireWire drives). In addition, optimizing for quick removal automatically turns off the drive's internal cache. Figure 14.18 shows the default setting for external USB drives.

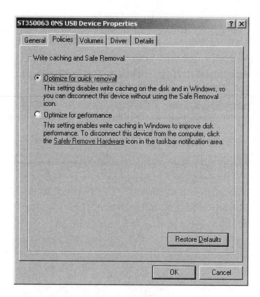

FIGURE 14.18   Write caching and Safe Removal settings for external drives.

These settings are generally unavailable (grayed out) for internal drives, meaning you can't turn off lazy writes or the drive's internal cache on those drives. Figure 14.19 shows the unchangeable settings for internal drives.

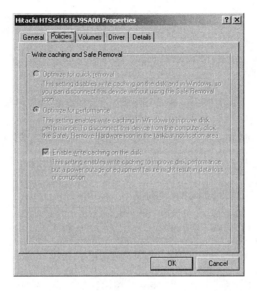

FIGURE 14.19   Write caching and Safe Removal settings for internal drives.

Some drives are hot-swappable; however, they still have the performance of internal drives. For example, my current ThinkPad laptop has a swappable device bay that can accept a number of devices, including Parallel ATA and Serial ATA drives. With a SATA drive installed, the default policy settings are the same as internal drives; however, the settings can be changed if desired. Figure 14.20 shows the default settings for a drive installed in the swappable bay.

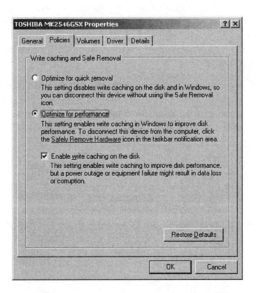

FIGURE 14.20   Write caching and Safe Removal settings for hot-swappable bay drives.

These settings are used because, to remove the bay device, you must press a switch, which automatically informs the system that a removal is imminent. That in turn causes the "safe removal" process to run and automatically flushes all caches.

For external drives, the capabilities can vary. For example, I have one USB external drive in which, if I check Optimize for Performance (turn Windows caching ON), the Enable Write Caching on the Disk (hardware write cache ON) box is also automatically checked but also grayed out, and below it appears a yellow bang with the warning statement This device does not allow write caching to be disabled. I have another USB external drive that shows no option at all for hardware write caching. Still another external drive shows the option, but every time I check it, the setting is automatically cleared after I click OK; in other words, hardware write caching cannot be turned on.

For internal drives, it is almost always recommended that you keep write caching on for maximum performance. For additional performance on external drives, you might also want to turn on lazy write (Optimize for Performance) and the hardware write cache (Enable Write Caching on the Disk), if available, especially if all volumes on the drive are formatted using NTFS.

Thunderbolt Technology

At the fall 2009 Intel Developer Forum Intel demonstrated a prototype data connection technology that was codenamed "Light Peak." The term came from the fact that the technology would be available over both optical (light) and electrical (copper) cable connections. During the demonstration Intel indicated that this technology would transfer data initially at 10Gbps, with the potential ability to achieve 100Gbps over the next decade. Finally, in February 2011, Intel officially introduced Light Peak under the name Thunderbolt Technology. Starting in 2012, PC motherboards began including Thunderbolt ports as an option.

Thunderbolt is described by Intel as "the fastest way to get information in and out of your PC and peripheral devices" and at the initial 10Gbps data rate it can transfer a full-length HD movie in less than 30 seconds, or a full year of MP3 playback in just over 10 minutes. Thunderbolt is a multifunction interface that combines high-speed data transfer as well as digital audio/video signals on a single cable.

Thunderbolt is currently implemented via a Thunderbolt controller chip at each end of the connection, one in the PC and one in the attached device. On the PC side, the controller may also be integrated directly into the motherboard chipset. The Thunderbolt controller combines PCI Express and DisplayPort audio/video signals at one end and splits them back apart at the other (see Figure 14.21). This allows fewer connectors to do more work, which will be especially useful in laptops or smaller systems where connector space is tight.

The initial electrical implementation of Thunderbolt uses the Mini DisplayPort connector that was introduced as part of the DisplayPort 1.2 specification in December 2009. You can tell a Thunderbolt-enabled Mini DisplayPort connector from a standard Mini DisplayPort connector by a Thunderbolt logo or icon next to the connector (see Figure 14.22).

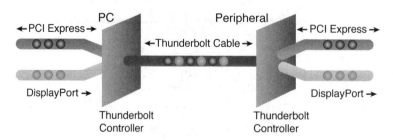

FIGURE 14.21 Thunderbolt Technology connection combining PCIe and DisplayPort on a single cable.

FIGURE 14.22 Thunderbolt Technology logo.

Similar to FireWire, Thunderbolt connections can be daisy-chained. This means that a peripheral device can have two Thunderbolt connectors, allowing users to connect multiple devices to a PC via Thunderbolt cables between the devices in a chain. The technical details of Thunderbolt include

- Dual-channel bidirectional full-duplex connections.
- 10Gbps transfer rate per channel in each direction.
- Electrical cables up to 3 meters in length.
- Electrical cables providing up to 10W of power for bus-powered devices.
- Cables and devices that are hot-pluggable.
- Daisy-chaining capability for up to seven devices (including up to two displays).

Some view Thunderbolt as a competitor to USB 3.0; however, Intel has stated that Thunderbolt and USB 3.0 are complementary technologies and that it will build both Thunderbolt and USB 3.0 connections into future motherboard chipsets. This eliminates the need for separate controller chips and allows both of these interfaces to be built in to new systems for little or no cost. Because Thunderbolt is designed to carry both audio/video and data and supports daisy-chaining, it is seen as more of a competitor to or eventual replacement for FireWire than USB. Thunderbolt is largely replacing FireWire in high-end digital video editing equipment. Intel has indicated that future Thunderbolt implementations will support optical cable connections of up to tens of meters in length and at speeds of up to 100Gbps.

Low-Speed External Connections

Traditionally, the most basic communication ports in any PC system have been the serial and parallel ports; however, the prevalence of USB has largely supplanted these ports in modern systems.

Serial ports (also known as *communication* or *COM* ports) were originally used for devices that had to communicate bidirectionally with the system. Such devices include modems, mice, scanners, digitizers, and any other devices that "talk to" and receive information from the system. Some parallel port standards also allow the parallel port to perform bidirectional communications; however, it was initially designed as a unidirectional communications format.

The tasks traditionally performed by both serial and parallel ports are performed by USB and IEEE 1394 (FireWire), but, for some time to come, legacy port types will continue to be used in certain applications. For example HTPCs (Home Theater PCs) commonly include serial (COM) ports for infrared remote control connections.

Serial Ports

The asynchronous serial interface was designed as a system-to-system communications port. *Asynchronous* means that no synchronization or clocking signal is present, so characters can be sent with arbitrary time spacing.

Each character that is sent over a serial connection is framed by a standard start-and-stop signal. A single 0 bit, called the *start bit*, precedes each character to tell the receiving system that the next eight bits constitute a byte of data. One or two stop bits follow the character to signal that the character has been sent. At the receiving end of the communication, characters are recognized by the start-and-stop signals instead of by the timing of their arrival. The asynchronous interface is character-oriented and has approximately 20% overhead for the extra information needed to identify each character.

Serial refers to data that is sent over a single wire, with each bit lining up in a series as the bits are sent. This type of communication is used over the phone system because it provides one wire for data in each direction.

Typical Locations for Serial Ports

Built-in serial ports are controlled by either a Super I/O or South Bridge chip on the motherboard.

If you need more serial ports than your system has as standard, or if your system did not include a serial port, you can purchase single-port or multiport serial port adapter cards.

Note that card-based modems may also incorporate a built-in serial port on the card as part of the modem circuitry (except controller-less software modems). Figure 14.23 shows the standard 9-pin connector used with most modern external serial ports. Figure 14.24 shows the original standard 25-pin version.

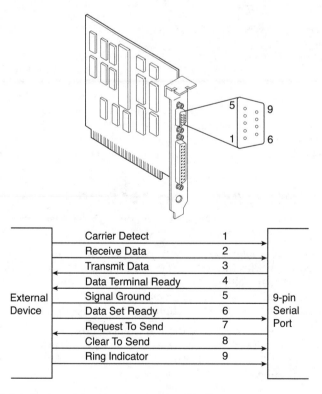

FIGURE 14.23 AT-style 9-pin serial port connector specifications.

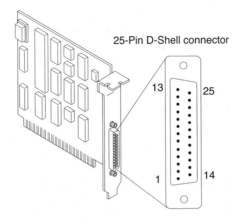

25-Pin D-Shell connector

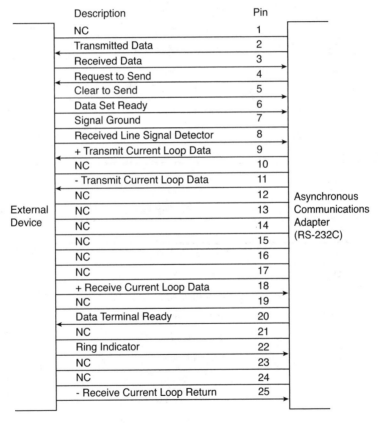

Description	Pin
NC	1
Transmitted Data	2
Received Data	3
Request to Send	4
Clear to Send	5
Data Set Ready	6
Signal Ground	7
Received Line Signal Detector	8
+ Transmit Current Loop Data	9
NC	10
- Transmit Current Loop Data	11
NC	12
NC	13
NC	14
NC	15
NC	16
NC	17
+ Receive Current Loop Data	18
NC	19
Data Terminal Ready	20
NC	21
Ring Indicator	22
NC	23
NC	24
- Receive Current Loop Return	25

External Device

Asynchronous Communications Adapter (RS-232C)

FIGURE 14.24 Standard 25-pin serial port connector specifications.

Serial ports were once used to connect printers and external modems, but in modern Home Theater PCs they are used to connect infrared transceivers to allow for remote control operation.

The official specification recommends a maximum cable length of 50 feet. The limiting factor is the total load capacitance of cable and input circuits of the interface. The maximum capacitance is specified as 2,500pF (picofarads). Special low-capacitance cables can effectively increase the maximum cable length greatly, to as much as 500 feet or more. Also available are line drivers (amplifier/repeaters) that can extend cable length even further.

Tables 14.11, 14.12, and 14.13 show the pinouts of the 9-pin serial connector, the 25-pin serial connector, and the 9-pin-to-25-pin serial adapter, respectively.

Table 14.11   Pinout for a 9-Pin Serial Port Connector

Pin	Signal	Description	I/O
1	CD	Carrier detect	In
2	RD	Receive data	In
3	TD	Transmit data	Out
4	DTR	Data terminal ready	Out
5	SG	Signal ground	—
6	DSR	Data set ready	In
7	RTS	Request to send	Out
8	CTS	Clear to send	In
9	RI	Ring indicator	In

Table 14.12   Pinout for a 25-Pin Serial Port Connector

Pin	Signal	Description	I/O
1	—	Chassis ground	—
2	TD	Transmit data	Out
3	RD	Received data	In
4	RTS	Request to send	Out
5	CTS	Clear to send	In
6	DSR	Data set ready	In
7	SG	Signal ground	—
8	CD	Received line signal detector	In
9	—	+Transmit current loop data	Out
11	—	−Transmit current loop data	Out
18	—	+Receive current loop data	In

Pin	Signal	Description	I/O
20	DTR	Data terminal ready	Out
22	RI	Ring indicator	In
25	—	–Receive current loop return	In

Table 14.13   Connections for a 9-Pin-to-25-Pin Serial Adapter

9-Pin	25-Pin	Signal	Description
1	8	CD	Carrier detect
2	3	RD	Receive data
3	2	TD	Transmit data
4	20	DTR	Data terminal ready
5	7	SG	Signal ground
6	6	DSR	Data set ready
7	4	RTS	Request to send
8	5	CTS	Clear to send
9	22	RI	Ring indicator

The UART Chip

The heart of any serial port is the Universal Asynchronous Receiver/Transmitter (UART) chip. This chip controls the process of breaking the native parallel data within the PC into serial format and later converting serial data back into the parallel format. Recent PCs with serial ports integrated into the motherboard chipset emulate the functionality of the UART.

Serial Port Configuration

Each time a serial port receives a character, it has to get the attention of the computer by raising an IRQ line. Eight-bit ISA bus systems have eight of these lines, and systems with a 16-bit ISA bus have 16 lines. The 8259 interrupt controller chip or equivalent usually handles these requests for attention. In a standard configuration, COM1 uses IRQ4, and COM2 uses IRQ3. Even on the latest systems, the default COM port assignments remain the same for compatibility with older software and hardware.

When a serial port is installed in a system, it must be configured to use specific I/O addresses (called *ports*) and interrupts (called *IRQs*). The standard IRQ and I/O port resource settings for serial ports are shown in Table 14.14.

Table 14.14   Standard Serial I/O Port Addresses and Interrupts

COM	I/O Ports	IRQ
COM1	3F8–3FFh	IRQ4
COM2	2F8–2FFh	IRQ3
COM3	3E8–3EFh	IRQ4*
COM4	2E8–2EFh	IRQ3*

Although many serial ports can be set up to share IRQ3 and IRQ4 with COM1 and COM2, this is not recommended. The best recommendation is setting COM3 to IRQ10 and COM4 to IRQ11 (if available).

Parallel Ports

Parallel ports normally are used for connecting printers to a PC. Because of that they are often referred to as Line Print Terminal (LPT) ports. Even though that was their sole original purpose, parallel ports became more useful over the years as a more general-purpose, relatively high-speed interface between devices (when compared to serial ports). Today, however, USB ports have largely replaced parallel ports for printing and for interfacing to devices such as scanners and external drives. I recommend using USB devices in place of parallel devices, but if you support older OSs or older printers, you might still need to work with parallel ports and devices.

Parallel ports are so named because they have eight lines for sending all the bits that comprise 1 byte of data simultaneously across the eight wires. Table 14.15 shows the pinout for a standard PC parallel port.

Table 14.15   Pinout for a 25-Pin PC-Compatible Parallel Port Connector

Pin	Description	I/O
1	–Strobe	Out
2	+Data Bit 0	Out
3	+Data Bit 1	Out
4	+Data Bit 2	Out
5	+Data Bit 3	Out
6	+Data Bit 4	Out
7	+Data Bit 5	Out
8	+Data Bit 6	Out
9	+Data Bit 7	Out
10	–Acknowledge	In
11	+Busy	In
12	+Paper End	In
13	+Select	In
14	–Auto Feed	Out
15	–Error	In

Pin	Description	I/O
16	–Initialize Printer	Out
17	–Select Input	Out
18	–Data Bit 0 Return (GND)	In
19	–Data Bit 1 Return (GND)	In
20	–Data Bit 2 Return (GND)	In
21	–Data Bit 3 Return (GND)	In
22	–Data Bit 4 Return (GND)	In
23	–Data Bit 5 Return (GND)	In
24	–Data Bit 6 Return (GND)	In
25	–Data Bit 7 Return (GND)	In

EEE 1284 Parallel Port Standard

The IEEE 1284 standard, called "Standard Signaling Method for a Bidirectional Parallel Peripheral Interface for Personal Computers," was approved for final release in March 1994. This standard defines the physical characteristics of the parallel port, including data-transfer modes and physical and electrical specifications. IEEE 1284 defines the electrical signaling behavior for a multimodal parallel port that can support 4-bit modes of operation. Not all modes are required by the 1284 specification, and the standard makes some provision for additional modes.

IEEE 1284 pertains only to hardware and line control and does not define how software talks to the port. An offshoot of the original 1284 standard has been created to define the software interface. The IEEE 1284.3 committee was formed to develop a standard for software that is used with IEEE 1284–compliant hardware. This standard contains a specification for supporting EPP (Enhanced Parallel Port) mode via the system BIOS.

IEEE 1284 enables higher throughput in a connection between a computer and a printer or between two computers. The result is that the printer cable is no longer the standard printer cable. The IEEE 1284 printer cable uses twisted-pair technology, which results in a much more reliable and error-free connection.

The IEEE 1284 standard also defines the parallel port connectors, including the two preexisting types (Type A and Type B) and an additional high-density Type C connector. Type A refers to the standard DB25 connector used on most PC systems for parallel port connections, whereas Type B refers to the standard 36-pin Centronics-style connector found on printers. Type C is a high-density 36-pin connector that can be found on some printers. Most parallel ports use the standard Type A receptacle. The three connectors are shown in Figure 14.25.

The IEEE 1284 parallel port standard defines five port-operating modes, emphasizing the higher-speed EPP and ECP modes. Some of the modes are input only, whereas others are output only. These five modes combine to create four types of ports, as shown in Table 14.16.

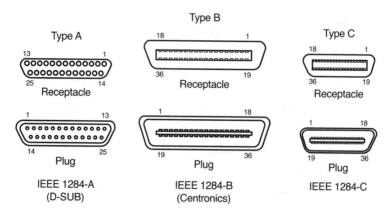

FIGURE 14.25 The three types of IEEE 1284 parallel port connectors.

Table 14.16 Types of IEEE 1284 Ports

Parallel Port Type	Input Mode	Output Mode	Comments
SPP (Standard Parallel Port)	Nibble	Compatible	4-bit input, 8-bit output
Bidirectional	Byte	Compatible	8-bit I/O
EPP (Enhanced Parallel Port)	EPP	EPP	8-bit I/O
ECP (Enhanced Capabilities Port)	ECP	ECP	8-bit I/O, uses DMA

The 1284-defined parallel port modes are shown in Table 14.17, which also shows the approximate transfer speeds.

Table 14.17 IEEE 1284 Parallel Port Modes

Parallel Port Mode	Direction	Transfer Rate
Nibble (4-bit)	Input only	50KBps
Byte (8-bit)	Input only	150KBps
Compatible	Output only	150KBps
EPP (Enhanced Parallel Port)	Input/Output	500KBps–2.77MBps
ECP (Enhanced Capabilities Port)	Input/Output	500KBps–2.77MBps

Each of the port types and modes is discussed in the following sections. These modes can be selected via the BIOS Setup in motherboards with built-in parallel ports.

Standard Parallel Ports

Older systems did not have different types of parallel ports available. The only available port was the parallel port that was used to send information from the computer to a device such as a printer. The unidirectional nature of the original PC parallel port is consistent with its primary use—that is, sending data to a printer. There were times, however, when it was desirable to have a bidirectional port—for example, when it was necessary to receive feedback from a printer, which was common with PostScript printers. This could not be done easily with the original unidirectional ports.

Although it was never intended to be used for input, a clever scheme was devised in which four of the signal lines could be used as a 4-bit input connection. Thus, these ports could do 8-bit (byte) output (called *compatible mode*) and 4-bit input (called *nibble mode*). This is still common on low-end desktop systems. Systems built after 1993 are likely to have more capable parallel ports, such as bidirectional, EPP, and ECP.

Standard parallel ports are capable of effective transfer rates of about 150KBps output and about 50KBps input.

Bidirectional (8-Bit) Parallel Ports

With the introduction of the PS/2 series of machines in 1987, IBM introduced the bidirectional parallel port. These ports are commonly found in PC-compatible systems today and can be designated bidirectional, PS/2 type, or extended parallel ports. This port design opened the way for true communication between the computer and the peripheral across the parallel port. This was done by defining a few of the previously unused pins in the parallel connector and by defining a status bit to indicate in which direction information was traveling across the channel. This allows for true 8-bit (called *byte mode*) input.

These ports can do both 8-bit input and output using the standard eight data lines and are considerably faster than the 4-bit ports when used with external devices. Bidirectional ports are capable of approximately 150KBps transfer rates on both output and input. Some newer systems use this as their standard mode.

Enhanced Parallel Port

EPP is sometimes referred to as the *Fast Mode* parallel port. Intel, Xircom, and Zenith Data Systems developed and announced EPP in October 1991. The first products to offer EPP were Zenith Data Systems laptops, Xircom Pocket LAN adapters, and the Intel 82360 SL I/O chip. On current systems that include parallel ports, EPP is one of the modes supported.

EPP operates at almost ISA bus speed and offers a tenfold increase in the raw throughput capability over a conventional parallel port. EPP was especially designed for parallel port peripherals, such as LAN adapters, disk drives, and tape backups. EPP is included in the IEEE 1284 Parallel Port standard. Transfer rates of up to 2.77MBps are possible with EPP.

EPP version 1.7 (March 1992) was the first popular version of the hardware specification. With minor changes, this was later abandoned and folded into the IEEE 1284 standard. Some technical reference materials have erroneously made reference to "EPP specification version 1.9," causing confusion about the EPP standard. Note that "EPP version 1.9" technically does not exist, and any EPP specification after the original (version 1.7) is more accurately referred to as a part of the IEEE 1284 specification.

Unfortunately, this resulted in two somewhat incompatible standards for EPP parallel ports: the original EPP Standards Committee version 1.7 standard and the IEEE 1284 Committee standard, usually called *EPP version 1.9*. The two standards are similar enough that peripherals can be designed to support both, but older EPP 1.7 peripherals might not operate with EPP 1284 (EPP 1.9) ports. For this reason, some multimode ports allow configuration in either EPP 1.7 or 1.9 mode, normally selected via the BIOS Setup.

Enhanced Capabilities Port

In 1992, Microsoft and Hewlett-Packard announced another type of high-speed parallel port: the Enhanced Capabilities Port (ECP). Similar to EPP, ECP offers improved performance for the parallel port and requires special hardware logic.

Since the original announcement, ECP was included in IEEE 1284—just like EPP. Unlike EPP, however, ECP is not tailored to support portable PCs' parallel port peripherals; its purpose is to support an inexpensive attachment to a high-performance printer or scanner. Furthermore, ECP mode requires the use of a direct memory access (DMA) channel, which EPP did not define and which can cause troublesome conflicts with other devices that use DMA. Most PCs built since the mid-1990s support both EPP or ECP modes. If you use parallel devices, it's recommended that the port be placed in ECP mode (or a combination mode known as EPP/ECP) for the best throughput.

Parallel Port Configuration

The configuration of parallel ports is not as complicated as it is for serial ports. Even the original IBM PC had BIOS support for three LPT ports. Table 14.18 shows the standard I/O address and interrupt settings for parallel port use.

Table 14.18   Parallel Interface I/O Port Addresses and Interrupts

Standard LPTx	Alternate LPTx	I/O Ports	IRQ
LPT1	—	3BC–3BFh	IRQ7
LPT1	LPT2	378–37Ah	IRQ5
LPT2	LPT3	278h–27Ah	IRQ5

Because the BIOS has always provided three definitions for parallel ports, problems with parallel ports are infrequent.

Chapter

15

Input Devices

Keyboards

One of the most basic system components is the keyboard, which is the primary input device. You use a keyboard to enter commands and data into the system. This section looks at keyboards for PCs, examining the various types of keyboards and how they function, the keyboard-to-system interfaces, and keyboard troubleshooting and repair.

In the years following the introduction of the original IBM PC, IBM created three keyboard designs for PC systems, and since then Microsoft has augmented one of them. Together, these designs have become de facto standards in the industry and are shared by virtually all PC manufacturers.

The primary keyboard types are as follows:

- 101-key Enhanced keyboard
- 103/104-key Windows keyboard
- 83-key PC and XT keyboard (obsolete)
- 84-key AT keyboard (obsolete)

This section discusses the 101-key Enhanced and 104-key Windows keyboards, showing the layout and physical appearance of both. Although you may still find old 83-key and 84-key designs, these are rare today.

Enhanced 101-Key Keyboard

In 1986, IBM introduced the Enhanced 101-key keyboard for the XT and AT models. This design first appeared in IBM's RT PC, which was a reduced instruction set computer (RISC) system designed for scientific and engineering applications. Keyboards with this design were soon supplied with virtually every type of system and terminal IBM sold. Other companies quickly copied this design, which became the standard on virtually all PCs until the introduction of the 104-key Windows keyboard in 1995 (discussed later in this chapter).

The layout of the enhanced keyboard was improved over that of the 84-key unit, with the possible exception of the Enter key, which reverted to a smaller size. The 101-key Enhanced keyboard was designed to conform to international regulations and specifications for keyboards. In fact, other companies such as Digital Equipment Corporation (DEC) and Texas Instruments (TI) had already been using designs similar to the IBM 101-key unit. The IBM 101-key units originally came in versions with and without the status-indicator LEDs, depending on whether the unit was sold with an XT or AT system. (XT systems didn't support the LEDs.) Currently there are many variations from which to choose, including some with integrated pointing devices, such as the Lenovo TrackPoint pointing stick, touchpads, trackballs, as well as programmable keys useful for automating routine tasks. Several connector variations are also available. Whereas PC keyboards started out using a larger 5-pin DIN (an acronym for Deutsches Institut für Normung e.V.) keyboard connector, current designs use either the smaller 6-pin mini-DIN connector (often called a PS/2 connector because it first came on the IBM PS/2 systems) or industry standard universal serial bus (USB). See the section, "Keyboard/Mouse Interface Connectors" and Figure 15.8, later in this chapter, for the physical and electronic details of the DIN connectors. See the section "USB Keyboards," later in this chapter, for details on connecting keyboards via USB.

The 101-key keyboard layout can be divided into the following four sections:

- Typing area
- Numeric keypad
- Cursor and screen controls
- Function keys

The 101-key arrangement is similar to the Selectric keyboard layout, with the exception of the Enter key. The Tab, Caps Lock, Shift, and Backspace keys have a larger striking area and are located in the familiar Selectric locations. The Ctrl and Alt keys are on each side of the spacebar, and the typing area and numeric keypad have home-row identifiers for touch typing.

The cursor- and screen-control keys have been separated from the numeric keypad, which is reserved for numeric input. (As with other PC keyboards, you can use the numeric keypad for cursor and screen control when the keyboard is not in Num Lock mode.) A division-sign key (/) and an additional Enter key have been added to the numeric keypad.

The cursor-control keys are arranged in the inverted T format that is now expected on all computer keyboards. The Insert, Delete, Home, End, Page Up, and Page Down keys, located above the dedicated cursor-control keys, are separate from the numeric keypad. The function keys, spaced in groups of four, are located across the top of the keyboard. The keyboard also has two additional function keys: F11 and F12. The Esc key is isolated in the upper-left corner of the keyboard. In addition, dedicated Print Screen/Sys Req, Scroll Lock, and Pause/Break keys are provided for commonly used functions.

Foreign-language versions of the Enhanced keyboard include 102 keys and a slightly different layout from the 101-key U.S. versions.

103/104-Key Windows Keyboard

When Microsoft released Windows 95, it also introduced the Microsoft Natural Keyboard, which implemented a revised keyboard specification that added three new Windows-specific keys to the keyboard.

The Microsoft Windows keyboard specification, which has since become standard for many desktop and laptop keyboards, outlines a set of additional keys and key combinations. The 104-key layout includes left and right Windows keys and an Application key (see Figure 15.1). Many forego the right Windows key, using only the Application key on the right side, and thus have 103 total keys. The Windows and Application keys are used for operating system (OS) and application-level keyboard combinations, similar to the existing Ctrl and Alt combinations. You don't need these keys to use Windows, but many software vendors have added specific functions to their Windows products that use the Application key (which provides the same functionality as clicking the right mouse button). The recommended Windows keyboard layout calls for Windows keys (called WIN keys) to flank the Alt keys on each side of the spacebar, as well as an Application key on the right of the right Windows key. An alternate layout has a single Windows key on the left and the Application key on the right. Note that the exact placement of these keys is up to the keyboard designer, so variations exist from keyboard to keyboard.

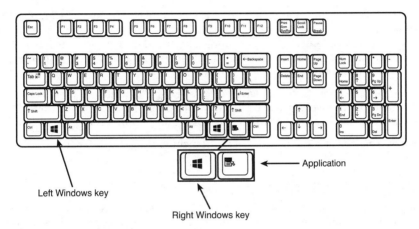

Left Windows key

Right Windows key

Application

FIGURE 15.1 The 104-key Windows keyboard layout.

The WIN key by itself opens the Windows Start menu, which you can then navigate with the cursor keys. The Application key simulates the right mouse button; in most applications, it brings up a context-sensitive pop-up menu. Several WIN key combinations offer preset macro commands as well. For example, you can press WIN+E to launch the Windows Explorer application. Table 15.1 shows a list of common Windows key combinations used with the Windows keyboard.

Table 15.1 Windows Key Combinations

Key Combination	Resulting Action
WIN+R	Open the Run dialog box
WIN+M	Minimize All (show Desktop)
WIN+ Shift+M	Undo Minimize All
WIN+D	Minimize All (show Desktop) or Undo Minimize All (toggle)
WIN+F1	Help
WIN+E	Open Windows Explorer
WIN+F	Find Files or Folders (Windows Search)
WIN+Tab	Cycles through taskbar buttons; opens Flip 3D (if supported)
WIN+Pause	Displays the System Properties dialog box
Application key	Displays a context menu for the selected item

Note that these basic Windows key combinations work in all versions of Windows from Windows XP through Windows 8. For a comprehensive list of all Windows keyboard shortcuts, including those limited to specific versions of Windows, see www.support.microsoft.com/kb/126449 and www.microsoft.com/enable/products/keyboard.aspx.

Using the Windows and Application keys is not mandatory when running Windows. In fact, preexisting standard key combinations can perform many of the same functions as these newer keys.

The Windows keyboard specification requires that keyboard makers increase the number of trilograms in their keyboard designs. A *trilogram* is a combination of three rapidly pressed keys that perform a special function, such as Ctrl+Alt+Delete. Designing a keyboard so that the switch matrix correctly registers the additional trilograms plus the additional Windows keys adds somewhat to the cost of these keyboards compared to the previous 101-key standard models.

Many keyboard manufacturers have standardized on keyboards that include these Windows-specific keys. Some manufacturers have added extra browser control or other keys that, although not standard, can make them easier to use for navigating web pages and launching various applications.

Foreign-language versions of the Windows keyboard include a slightly different layout from the U.S. versions.

Keyboard Technology

The technology that makes up a typical PC keyboard is interesting. This section focuses on all the aspects of keyboard technology and design, including the keyswitches, the interface between the keyboard and the system, the scan codes, and the keyboard connectors.

Keyswitch Design

Today's keyboards use any one of several switch types to create the action for each key. Most keyboards use a variation of the mechanical keyswitch. A mechanical keyswitch relies on a mechanical momentary contact-type switch to make the electrical contact that forms a circuit. Some high-end keyboards use a more sophisticated design that relies on capacitive switches. This section discusses these switches and the highlights of each design.

The most common type of keyswitch is the mechanical type, available in the following variations:

- Pure mechanical
- Foam element
- Rubber dome
- Membrane
- Touch

Pure Mechanical Switches

The pure mechanical type is just that—a simple mechanical switch that features metal contacts in a momentary contact arrangement. The switch often includes a tactile feedback mechanism, consisting of a clip and spring arrangement designed to give a "clicky" feel to the keyboard and offer some resistance to the keypress (see Figure 15.2).

Mechanical switches are durable, usually have self-cleaning contacts, and are normally rated for 20 million keystrokes (which is second only to the capacitive switch in longevity). They also offer excellent tactile feedback.

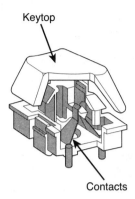

Keytop

Contacts

FIGURE 15.2 A typical mechanical switch used in older NMB Technologies keyboards. As the key is pressed, the switch pushes down on the contacts to make the connection.

Despite the tactile feedback and durability provided by mechanical keyswitch keyboards, they have become much less popular than membrane keyboards (discussed later in this chapter). In addition, many companies that produce keyboards that employ mechanical keyswitches either use them for only a few of their high-priced models or have phased out their mechanical keyswitch models entirely. With the price of keyboards nose-diving along with other traditional devices, such as mice and drives, the pressure on keyboard makers to cut costs has led many of them to abandon or deemphasize mechanical-keyswitch designs in favor of the less expensive membrane keyswitch.

The Alps Electric mechanical keyswitch is used by many of the vendors who produce mechanical-switch keyboards, including Alps Electric. Other vendors who use mechanical keyswitches for some of their keyboard models include Adesso, Inc. (www.adesso.com), Avant Prime, and Stellar (revivals of the classic Northgate keyboards are available from Ergonomic Resources; www.ergonomicsmadeeasy.com), Kinesis (www.kinesis-ergo.com), and SIIG (www.siig.com). Many of these vendors sell through the OEM market, so you must look carefully at the detailed specifications for the keyboard to see whether it is a mechanical keyswitch model.

Foam Element Switches

Foam element mechanical switches were a popular design in some older keyboards. Most of the older PC keyboards, including models made by Key Tronic and many others, used this technology. These switches are characterized by a foam element with an electrical contact on the bottom. This foam element is mounted on the bottom of a plunger that is attached to the key (see Figure 15.3).

When the switch is pressed, a foil conductor on the bottom of the foam element closes a circuit on the printed circuit board below. A return spring pushes the key back up when the pressure is released. The foam dampens the contact, helping to prevent bounce, but it gives these keyboards a "mushy" feel. The big problem with this type of keyswitch design is that little tactile feedback often exists. These types of keyboards send a clicking sound to the system speaker to signify that contact has been made. Preferences in keyboard feel are somewhat subjective; I do not favor the foam element switch design.

Another problem with this type of design is that it is more subject to corrosion on the foil conductor and the circuit board traces below. When this happens, the key strikes can become intermittent, which can be frustrating. Fortunately, these keyboards are among the easiest to clean. By disassembling the keyboard completely, you usually can remove the circuit board portion—without removing each foam pad separately—and expose the bottoms of all the pads. Then, you easily can wipe the corrosion and dirt off the bottoms of the foam pads and the circuit board, thus restoring the keyboard to a "like-new" condition. Unfortunately, over time, the corrosion problem will occur again. I recommend using some Stabilant 22a from D.W. Electrochemicals (www.stabilant.com) to improve the switch contact action and prevent future corrosion. Because of such problems, the foam element design is not used much anymore and has been superseded in popularity by the rubber dome design.

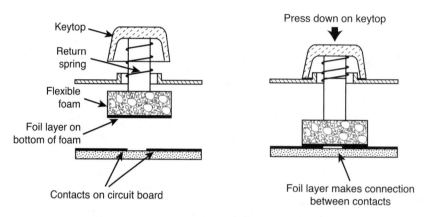

FIGURE 15.3 Typical foam element mechanical keyswitch.

KeyTronicEMS, the most well-known user of this technology, now uses a center-bearing membrane switch technology in its keyboards, so you are likely to encounter foam-switch keyboards only on old systems.

Rubber Dome Switches

Rubber dome switches are mechanical switches similar to the foam element type, but they are improved in many ways. Instead of a spring, these switches use a rubber dome that has a carbon button contact on the underside. As you press a key, the key plunger presses on the rubber dome, causing it to resist and then collapse all at once, much like the top of an oil can. As the rubber dome collapses, the user feels the tactile feedback, and the carbon button makes contact between the circuit board traces below. When the key is released, the rubber dome re-forms and pushes the key back up.

The rubber eliminates the need for a spring and provides a reasonable amount of tactile feedback without special clips or other parts. Rubber dome switches use a carbon button because it resists corrosion and has a self-cleaning action on the metal contacts below. The rubber domes themselves are formed into a sheet that completely protects the contacts below from dirt, dust, and even minor spills. This type of switch design is the simplest, and it uses the fewest parts. This made the rubber dome keyswitch reliable for several years. However, its relatively poor tactile feedback has led most keyboard manufacturers to switch to the membrane switch design covered in the next section.

Membrane Switches

The membrane keyswitch is a variation on the rubber dome type, using a flat, flexible circuit board to receive input and transmit it to the keyboard microcontroller. Industrial versions of membrane boards use a single sheet for keys that sits on the rubber dome sheet for protection against harsh environments. This arrangement severely limits key travel. For this reason, flat-surface membrane keyboards are not considered usable for normal touch typing. However, they are ideal for use in extremely harsh environments. Because the sheets can be bonded together and sealed from the elements, membrane keyboards can be used when no other type could survive. Many industrial applications use membrane keyboards for terminals that do not require extensive data entry but are used instead to operate equipment, such as cash registers and point-of-sale terminals in restaurants.

Membrane keyswitches are not just relegated to fast food or industrial uses, though. The membrane keyswitch used with conventional keyboard keytops has become the most popular keyswitch used in low-cost to mid-range keyboards, and even some high-end units. Although low-end membrane keyswitches have a limited life of only 5–10 million keystrokes, some of the better models are rated to handle up to 20 million keystrokes, putting them in the range of pure mechanical switches for durability (see Figure 15.4). A few membrane switches are even more durable: Cherry Corporation's G8x-series keyboards use Cherry's own 50-million-keystroke membrane switch design (www.cherrycorp.com).

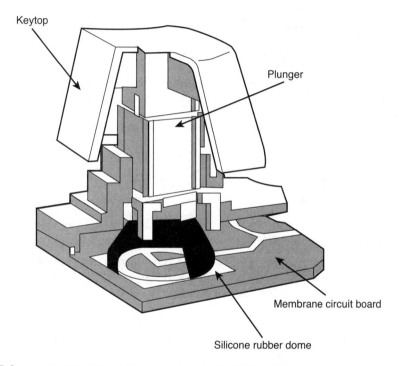

FIGURE 15.4 A typical membrane keyswitch used in NMB keyboards.

Membrane keyboards typically provide a firmer touch than rubber dome keyboards or the old foam-element keyboards, and those with buckling spring designs can provide the ultimate in tactile feedback. One interesting variation includes the line of keyboards made by KeyTronicEMS using its center-bearing version of membrane keyswitches. Most of its keyboards feature Ergo Technology, which has five levels of force from 35 grams to 80 grams, depending on the relative strength of the fingers used to type various keys. As little as 35 grams of force is required for keys that are used by the little finger, such as Q, Z, and A, and greater levels of force are required for keys used by the other fingers (see Figure 15.5). The spacebar requires the most force: 80 grams. This compares to the standard force level of 55 grams for all keys on normal keyboards. For more information about keyboards with Ergo Technology, visit the KeyTronicEMS website (www.keytronic.com).

Perhaps the most well-known type of membrane keyboards are the IBM/Lexmark "Model M" keyboards, which combine IBM's legendary buckling spring design with a high-end membrane switch. To find the best membrane keyboards from the vast numbers on the market, look at the lifespan rating of the keyswitches. Longer-lasting keyswitches make the keyboard cost more but will lead to a better experience over the life of the keyboard.

□ 35g   ▨ 45g   ■ 55g   ▢ 65g   ■ 80g

FIGURE 15.5   Force levels used on KeyTronicEMS keyboards with Ergo Technology.

Buckling Spring Capacitive and Membrane Switches

The keyboard included with the original IBM PC, XT, and AT systems used capacitive switches combined with a buckling spring mechanism to provide the ultimate in performance and tactile feedback. Capacitive switches are technically the only truly nonmechanical keyswitches in use today (see Figure 15.6). Although the movement of the key and buckling spring is mechanical in nature, in the original designs these components do not close a mechanical contact or switch. Because of the high cost of the capacitive switches, IBM switched its buckling spring keyboards from capacitive to membrane switches in the mid-1980s. However, unlike more common membrane keyboards, all buckling spring keyboards feature extremely high-end designs. Regardless of whether capacitive or membrane designs are used, buckling spring keyswitches are considered to be among the best in the world, offering the highest-quality tactile feedback of any type of switch. They are called *buckling spring* keyboards because of the coiled spring and rocker used in each keyswitch to provide tactile and audible feedback.

A capacitive switch does not work by making contact between conductors. Instead, two plates usually made of plastic are connected in a switch matrix designed to detect changes in the capacitance of the circuit. The membrane version of the switch uses upper and lower electrical contact sheets separated by an insulating sheet with small holes.

When a key is pressed, the plunger moves the top plate in relation to the fixed bottom plate, or it presses a hammer over the membranes, allowing the top and bottom contacts to touch. The buckling spring mechanism provides for distinct over-center tactile feedback with a resounding "click." As the capacitance between the two plates changes or the two membranes make contact, the comparator circuitry in the keyboard detects this as a keypress.

The tactile feedback is unsurpassed because the buckling spring design provides a relatively loud click and a strong over-center feel. The only drawback to the design is the cost. Buckling spring keyboards are among the most expensive designs, whether they use capacitive or membrane switches. The quality of the feel and their durability make them worth the price, however.

Although some of IBM's older keyboards featured capacitive keyswitches, most current IBM/Lenovo keyboards use either membrane, rubber dome, or other lower-cost keyswitches. In 1991, IBM spun off its keyboard/printer division as Lexmark, which then spun off the keyboard division as Unicomp in 1996. Today, Unicomp still manufactures and sells "IBM" keyboards with buckling spring membrane switch ("clickety" as some would say) technology. You can purchase new Unicomp (IBM) keyboards direct by visiting its online store (www.pckeyboard.com).

Because of the buckling spring keyswitches (and the resulting clickety feel), I am a huge fan of the IBM, Lexmark, and Unicomp keyboards.

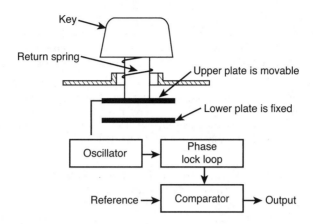

FIGURE 15.6 A capacitive buckling spring keyswitch.

Touch keyboards

The need for super thin and light portable keyboards to go with tablet systems has prompted the introduction of touch sensitive keyboards. These are keyboards that lack traditional keys. The keypad area is completely flat, with keys literally just printed on the surface. The "keys" themselves are merely areas that use pressure sensors (similar to a touchpad) to detect a tap. Some may be made of glass and use the same touch sensitive technologies found in new touch-sensitive displays.

Although these thin and light touch keyboards may be useful for temporary use with a tablet system, they are less than ideal as a substitute for a traditional keyboard on desktop or laptop systems.

The Keyboard Interface

A keyboard consists of a set of switches mounted in a grid or an array called the key matrix. When a switch is pressed, a processor in the keyboard identifies which key is pressed by determining which grid location in the matrix shows continuity. The keyboard processor, which also interprets how long the key is pressed, can even handle multiple keypresses at the same time. A 16-byte hardware buffer in the keyboard can handle rapid or multiple keypresses, passing each one to the system in succession.

When you press a key, the contact bounces slightly in most cases, meaning that several rapid on/off cycles occur just as the switch makes contact. This is called *bounce*. The processor in the keyboard is designed to filter this, or "debounce" the keystroke. The keyboard processor must distinguish bounce from a double keystroke the keyboard operator intends to make. This is fairly easy, though, because the bouncing is much more rapid than a person could simulate by striking a key quickly several times.

The keyboard in a PC is actually a computer. It communicates with the main system in one of two ways:

- Through a special serial data link if a standard PS/2 keyboard connector is used
- Through the USB port

The serial data link used by conventional keyboards transmits and receives data in 11-bit packets of information, consisting of 8 data bits, plus framing and control bits.

The processor in the original PC keyboard was an Intel 8048 microcontroller chip. Newer keyboards often use an 8049 version that has built-in ROM or other microcontroller chips compatible with the 8048 or 8049. For example, in its Enhanced keyboards, IBM has always used a custom version of the

Motorola 6805 processor, which is compatible with the Intel chips. The keyboard's built-in processor reads the key matrix, debounces the keypress signals, converts the keypress to the appropriate scan code, and transmits the code to the motherboard. The processors built in to the keyboard contain their own RAM, possibly some ROM, and a built-in serial interface.

In the original PC/XT design, the keyboard serial interface is connected to an 8255 Programmable Peripheral Interface (PPI) chip on the motherboard of the PC/XT. This chip is connected to the interrupt controller IRQ1 line, which signals to the system that keyboard data is available. The data is then sent from the 8255 to the processor via input/output (I/O) port address 60h. The IRQ1 signal causes the main system processor to run a subroutine (INT 9h) that interprets the keyboard scan code data and decides what to do.

In an AT-type keyboard design, the keyboard serial interface is connected to a special keyboard controller on the motherboard. This controller was an Intel 8042 Universal Peripheral Interface (UPI) slave microcontroller chip in the original AT design. This microcontroller is essentially another processor that has its own 2KB of ROM and 128 bytes of RAM. An 8742 version that uses erasable programmable read-only memory (EPROM) can be erased and reprogrammed. In the past, when you purchased a motherboard ROM upgrade for an older system from a motherboard manufacturer, the upgrade included a new keyboard controller chip as well because it had somewhat dependent and updated ROM code in it. Some older systems might use the 8041 or 8741 chips, which differ only in the amount of built-in ROM or RAM. However, recent systems incorporate the keyboard controller into the main system chipset.

When the keyboard controller on the motherboard receives data from the keyboard, it signals the motherboard with an IRQ1 and sends the data to the main motherboard processor via I/O port address 60h. Acting as an agent between the keyboard and the main system processor, the 8042-type keyboard controller can translate scan codes and perform several other functions. The system also can send data to the 8042 keyboard controller via port 60h, which then passes it on to the keyboard. Additionally, when the system needs to send commands to or read the status of the keyboard controller on the motherboard, it reads or writes through I/O port 64h. These commands usually are followed by data sent back and forth via port 60h.

The system also uses the 8042 keyboard controller to control the A20 memory address line, which provides access to system memory greater than 1MB. More modern motherboards typically incorporate this functionality directly into the motherboard chipset. The AT keyboard connector was renamed the "PS/2" port after the IBM PS/2 family of systems debuted in 1987. That was when the connector changed in size from the DIN to the mini-DIN, and even though the signals were the same, the mini-DIN version became known from that time forward as the PS/2 port.

Keyboards connected to a USB port work in a surprisingly similar fashion to those connected to conventional DIN or mini-DIN (PS/2) ports after the data reaches the system. Inside the keyboard, various custom controller chips are used by different keyboard manufacturers to receive and interpret keyboard data before sending it to the system via the USB port. Some of these chips contain USB hub logic to enable the keyboard to act as a USB hub. After the keyboard data reaches the USB port on the system, the USB port routes the data to the 8042-compatible keyboard controller, where the data is treated as any other keyboard information.

This process works well after a system has booted into Windows. But what about users who need to use the keyboard when running an older non-USB aware OS or within the BIOS configuration routine? That problem is solved by ensuring that *USB Legacy support* is present and enabled in the BIOS Setup. (See "Advanced USB Configuration Menu," in Chapter 5, "BIOS.")

Typematic Functions

If a key on the keyboard is held down, it becomes *typematic*, which means the keyboard repeatedly sends the keypress code to the motherboard. In the AT-style keyboards, the typematic rate is adjusted by sending the appropriate commands to the keyboard processor. This is impossible for the earlier PC/ XT keyboard types because the keyboard interface for these types is not bidirectional.

AT-style keyboards have programmable typematic repeat rate and delay parameters. You can adjust the typematic repeat rate and delay parameters with settings in your system BIOS (although not all BIOS chips can control all functions) or in your OS. In Windows you can use either the MODE command or the Keyboard icon in the Control Panel. Using either method, you can set the repeat rate from about 2cps (characters per second) minimum to 30cps maximum, and the delay from 0.25 seconds minimum to 1 second maximum.

For the fastest keyboard operation, I like to set the repeat rate to the maximum (30cps) and the delay to the minimum (0.25 seconds), which can be accomplished with the following command:

MODE CON: RATE=31 DELAY=0

Likewise, slowing the repeat rate to the minimum (2cps) and increasing the delay to the maximum (1 second) can be accomplished with the following command:

MODE CON: RATE=0 DELAY=3

Entering MODE CON: with no other parameters shows the current status of the settings. You can also modify these settings using the Keyboard icon in the Control Panel. The Repeat Delay slider, shown in Figure 15.7, controls the duration for which you must press a key before the character begins to repeat, and the Repeat Rate slider controls how fast the character repeats after the delay has elapsed.

Note

The increments on the Repeat Delay and Repeat Rate sliders in Keyboard Properties in the Control Panel correspond to the timings given for the MODE command's RATE and DELAY values. Each mark in the Repeat Delay slider adds about 0.25 seconds to the delay, and the marks in the Repeat Rate slider are worth about one character per second (1cps) each.

The dialog box also contains a text box you can use to test the settings you have chosen before committing them to your system. When you click in the box and press a key, the keyboard reacts using the settings currently specified by the sliders, even if you have not yet applied the changes to the Windows environment.

Keyboard Scan Codes

When you press a key on the keyboard, the processor built in to the keyboard (8048 or 6805 type) reads the keyswitch location in the keyboard matrix. The processor then sends to the motherboard a serial packet of data containing the scan code for the key that was pressed.

This is called the *Make code*. When the key is released, a corresponding *Break code* is sent, indicating to the motherboard that the key has been released. The Break code is equivalent to the Make scan code plus 80h. For example, if the Make scan code for the A key is 1Eh, the Break code would be 9Eh. By using both Make and Break scan codes, the system can determine whether a particular key has been held down and determine whether multiple keys are being pressed.

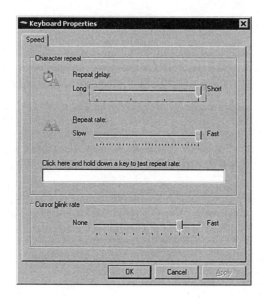

FIGURE 15.7 Setting the keyboard repeat delay and repeat rate in Windows.

Many keyboards feature hotkeys that either have fixed uses—such as opening the default web browser, sending the system into standby mode, and adjusting the speaker volume—or are programmable for user-defined functions. Each key also has scan codes. USB keyboards use a special series of codes called Human Interface Device (HID) codes, which are translated into PS/2 scan codes. For more information as well as a detailed list of these codes, see www.msdn.microsoft.com/en-us/library/windows/hardware/gg463372.aspx.

International Keyboard Layouts

After the keyboard controller in the system receives the scan codes generated by the keyboard and passes them to the main processor, the OS converts the codes into the appropriate alphanumeric characters. In the United States, these characters are the letters, numbers, and symbols found on the standard American keyboard.

However, no matter which characters you see on the keytops, adjusting the scan code conversion process to map different characters to the keys is relatively simple. Windows takes advantage of this capability by enabling you to install multiple keyboard layouts to support various languages, through the Region and Language Options applet in the Windows Control Panel (see Figure 15.8).

These keyboard layouts (input languages) map various characters to certain keys on the standard keyboard. The standard French layout provides easy access to the accented characters commonly used in that language. For example, pressing the 2 key produces the é character. To type the numeral 2, you press the Shift+2 key combination. Other French-speaking countries have different keyboard conventions for the same characters, so Windows includes support for several keyboard layout variations for some languages, based on nationality.

Note

It is important to understand that this feature is not the same as installing the OS in a different language. These keyboard layouts do not modify the text already displayed onscreen; they only alter the characters generated when you press certain keys.

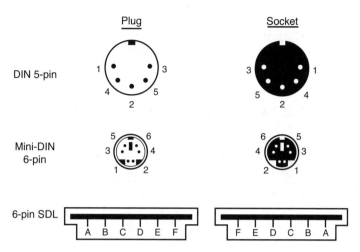

Plug   Socket

DIN 5-pin

Mini-DIN
6-pin

6-pin SDL

FIGURE 15.8 Adding or changing the keyboard layout (input language) in Windows.

The alternative keyboard layouts also do not provide support for non-Roman alphabets, such as Russian and Chinese. The accented characters and other symbols used in languages such as French and German are part of the standard ASCII character set. They are always accessible to English-language users through the Windows Character Map utility or through the use of Alt+keypad combinations. An alternative keyboard layout simply gives you an easier way to access the characters used in certain languages.

If you work on documents using more than one language, you can install as many keyboard layouts as necessary and switch between them at will. Using the settings in the Regional and Language Options applet, you can enable both a selector in the taskbar notification area as well as a key combination that switches between the installed keyboard layouts.

Keyboard/Mouse Interface Connectors

Keyboards typically have a cable with one of three primary types of connectors at the system end. On most aftermarket keyboards, the cable is connected inside the keyboard case on the keyboard end, requiring you to open the keyboard case to disconnect or test it; vendors use different connections, making cable interchange between brands of keyboards unlikely. When IBM manufactured its own enhanced keyboards, it used a unique cable assembly that plugged into both the keyboard and the system unit to make cable replacement or interchange easy. Current IBM keyboards, unfortunately, no longer use either the shielded data link (SDL) connector inside the keyboard or the telephone cable-style removable plug-in external keyboard connector used on some more recent models.

Although the method of connecting the keyboard cable to the keyboard can vary (some even use wireless connections), all PC keyboards use one of the following three connectors to interface the keyboard (or wireless transceiver) to the computer:

- **5-pin DIN connector**—Used on most obsolete PC systems with Baby-AT form factor motherboards.

- **6-pin mini-DIN connector**—Often called a PS/2 connector because it was first used on IBM PS/2 systems.

- **USB connector**—Most recent systems use USB keyboards and mice.

Figure 15.9 and Table 15.2 show the physical layout and pinouts of the respective keyboard connector plugs and sockets (except USB); although the 6-pin SDL connector is not used in this form by most keyboard vendors, most non-IBM keyboards use a somewhat similar connector to attach the keyboard cable to the inside of the keyboard. You can use the pinouts listed in Table 15.2 to test the continuity of each wire in the keyboard connector.

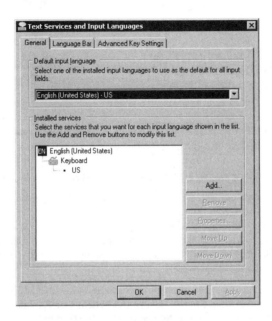

FIGURE 15.9   Keyboard and mouse connectors.

Table 15.2   Keyboard Connector Signals and Specifications

Signal Name	5-Pin DIN	6-Pin DIN	6-Pin Mini-DIN	Test Voltage
Keyboard Data	2	1	B	+4.8V to +5.5V
Ground	4	3	C	—
+5V Power	5	4	E	+2.0V to +5.5V
Keyboard Clock	1	5	D	+2.0V to +5.5V
Not Connected	—	2	A	—
Not Connected	—	6	F	—
Not Connected	3	—	—	—

DIN = Deutsches Institut für Normung e.V., a committee that sets German dimensional standards.

SDL = Shielded data link, a type of shielded connector created by AMP and used by IBM and others for keyboard cables.

The 6-pin mini-DIN is usually called a PS/2 connector.

PS/2 mouse devices also use the 6-pin mini-DIN connector and have the same pinout and signal descriptions as the keyboard connector; however, the data packets are incompatible.

USB keyboards use the Series A USB connector to attach to the USB port built into modern computers. For more information on USB, refer to Chapter 14, "External I/O Interfaces."

USB Keyboards

Virtually all keyboards now on the market connect to the PC via a USB port instead of a PS/2 keyboard port. Because USB is a universal bus that uses a hub to enable multiple devices to connect to a single port, a single USB port in a system can replace the standard serial and parallel ports as well as the keyboard and mouse ports. Many systems and motherboards still include one or two PS/2 ports (now called *legacy* ports) as well as USB, but many modern systems and replacement motherboards are legacy-free systems that have no PS/2 ports and use only USB ports for interfacing keyboards and mice.

Virtually all keyboard manufacturers now market USB keyboards, but if you want to use your keyboard with both legacy (PS/2) and legacy-free (USB) systems, the most economic way to do so is to specify a keyboard that includes both a USB connector and an adapter to permit the keyboard to work with PS/2 ports.

Although rare in modern systems, some older systems don't accept USB keyboards, even those with USB ports, because the original PC BIOS has a keyboard driver that expects a standard keyboard port interface to be present. When a USB keyboard is installed on a system that lacks USB keyboard support, the system can't use it because no driver exists in the BIOS to make it work. In fact, some systems see the lack of a standard keyboard as an error and halt the boot process until one is installed.

To use a keyboard connected via the USB port, you must meet three requirements:

- Have a USB port in the system.
- Run Microsoft Windows 98 or newer. (Previous versions did not include USB keyboard drivers.)
- Have a system chipset and BIOS that feature USB Legacy (keyboard and mouse) support.

USB Legacy support means your motherboard has a chipset and ROM BIOS drivers that enable a USB keyboard to be used outside the Windows graphical user interface (GUI) environment. Almost all 1998 and newer systems with USB ports include a chipset and BIOS with USB Legacy (meaning USB Keyboard) support, although it might be disabled in the BIOS Setup.

Even though USB Legacy support enables you to use a USB keyboard in almost all situations, don't scrap your standard-port keyboards just yet. If the system has PS/2 keyboard and/or mouse ports, they may need to be used when running hardware diagnostics, flashing the motherboard ROM BIOS, or troubleshooting USB keyboard and mouse issues. I've also had to use PS/2 keyboards and mice when installing older Windows versions on newer systems, due to the lack of proper support until the chipset USB drivers are installed. A good PC tech always has PS/2 keyboards and mice on hand for testing.

If you have problems with USB keyboards and mice (USB Legacy support), look at these possible solutions:

- Microsoft's Knowledge Base (http://support.microsoft.com) might have an article that addresses your problem.
- Your keyboard or mouse vendor might offer new drivers.
- Your system or motherboard manufacturer might have a BIOS upgrade you can install.
- Check the BIOS Setup to be sure USB keyboard and mouse support is enabled.

- As a fallback, connect the keyboard to the PS/2 port with an adapter, or use a PS/2 keyboard and mouse until you resolve the problem.

◄◄ See the Chapter 14 section, "Universal Serial Bus (USB)," **p. 704**.

Keyboards with Special Features

Several keyboards on the market have special features not found in standard designs. These additional features range from simple things, such as built-in calculators, clocks, and volume control, to more complicated features, such as integrated pointing devices, special character layouts, power management keys, special shapes, internal lighting, and even user-customizable or programmable keys.

Note

In 1936, August Dvorak patented a simplified character layout called the Dvorak Simplified Keyboard (DSK). The Dvorak keyboard was designed to replace the common QWERTY layout used on nearly all keyboards available today. The Dvorak keyboard was approved as an ANSI standard in 1982 but has seen limited use.

Ergonomic Keyboards

A trend began in the late 1990s to change the shape of the keyboard instead of altering the character layout. This trend has resulted in several so-called *ergonomic* designs. The goal is to shape the keyboard to better fit the human hand. The most common of these designs splits the keyboard in the center, bending the sides outward. Some designs allow the angle between the sides to be adjusted, while others are fixed. The split or bent designs more easily conform to the hands' natural angles while typing than the standard keyboard allows. They can improve productivity and typing speed and help prevent repetitive strain injuries (RSI), such as carpal tunnel syndrome (tendon inflammation). A good source for highly ergonomic keyboards, pointing devices, and furniture is Ergonomic Resources (www.ergonomicsmadeeasy.com).

Keyboard Troubleshooting and Repair

Keyboard errors are usually caused by two simple problems. Other more difficult, intermittent problems can arise, but they are much less common. The most frequent problems are as follows:

- Defective cables
- Stuck keys

Many older keyboards, such as the heavy-duty units made by IBM, had replaceable cables. Defective cables are easy to spot if the failure is not intermittent. If the keyboard stops working altogether or every keystroke results in an error or incorrect character, the cable is likely the culprit. Troubleshooting is simple if your keyboard has a detachable cable, especially if you have a spare cable on hand. Simply replace the suspected cable with one from a known, working keyboard to verify whether the problem still exists. If it does, the problem must be elsewhere.

Most modern keyboards have nonreplaceable cables, at least from the outside. In some cases you can open the keyboard case, and you will see that the cable is internally connected via a removable plug. Unfortunately, those cables are not sold separately, meaning that the only source for one would be from another keyboard, making a replacement implausible.

If the cable is removable, you can test it for continuity with a digital multimeter (DMM). DMMs that have an audible continuity tester built in make this procedure much easier to perform. To test each wire of the cable, insert the DMM's red pin into the keyboard connector and touch the DMM's black pin to the corresponding wire that attaches to the keyboard's circuit board. Wiggle the ends of the cable as you check each wire to ensure no intermittent connections exist. If you discover a problem with the continuity in one of the wires, replace the cable or the entire keyboard, whichever is cheaper. Because replacement keyboards are so inexpensive, it's almost always cheaper to replace the entire unit than to get a new cable, unless the keyboard is an expensive unit like an older IBM Model M. You can get replacement cables (and other parts) for older IBM Model M type keyboards from www.clickykeyboards.com.

For more information about using DMMs for testing hardware, see Chapter 20, "PC Diagnostics, Testing, and Maintenance."

Many times you first discover a problem with a keyboard because the system has an error during the POST. Many systems use error codes in a 3xx numeric format to distinguish the keyboard. If you encounter any such errors during the POST, write them down. Some BIOS versions do not use cryptic numeric error codes; they simply state something such as the following:

```
Keyboard stuck key failure
```

This message is usually displayed by a system with a Phoenix BIOS if a key is stuck. Unfortunately, the message does not identify which key it is!

For a simple test of the motherboard keyboard connector, you can check voltages on some of the pins. Using Figure 15.8 (shown earlier in the chapter) as a guide, measure the voltages on various pins of the keyboard connector. To prevent possible damage to the system or keyboard, turn off the power before disconnecting the keyboard. Then unplug the keyboard and turn the power back on. Make measurements between the ground pin and the other pins according to Table 15.2, shown earlier in the chapter. If the voltages are within these specifications, the motherboard keyboard circuitry is probably okay.

If your measurements do not match these voltages, the motherboard might be defective. Otherwise, the keyboard cable or keyboard might be defective. If you suspect that the keyboard or cable is the problem, the easiest thing to do is to connect a known-good keyboard as a test. If the system works properly with the known-good keyboard, you know the original keyboard or cable is defective. If the system still does not work normally, you might have to replace the motherboard.

Cleaning a Keyboard

One of the best ways to keep a keyboard in top condition is periodic cleaning. As preventive maintenance, you should vacuum the keyboard weekly, or at least monthly. When vacuuming, you should use a soft brush attachment to dislodge the dust. Also note that some keyboards have keycaps that come off easily, so be careful when vacuuming; otherwise you may have to dig the keys out of the vacuum cleaner. I recommend using a small, handheld vacuum cleaner made for cleaning computers and sewing machines; these have enough suction to get the job done with little risk of removing your keytops.

You also can use compressed air to blow the dust and dirt out instead of using a vacuum. Before you dust a keyboard with the compressed air, however, turn the keyboard upside down so that the particles of dirt and dust collected inside can fall out.

On most keyboards, each keycap is independently removable, which can be handy if a key sticks or acts erratically. For example, a common problem is a key that does not work every time you press it. This problem usually results from dirt collecting under the key. An excellent tool for removing keycaps on almost any keyboard is the U-shaped chip puller included in many computer tool kits. Simply slip the hooked ends of the tool under the keycap, squeeze the ends together to grip the underside of the keycap, and lift up. IBM sells a tool designed specifically for removing keycaps from its keyboards, but the chip puller works even better. After removing the cap, spray some compressed air into the space under the cap to dislodge the dirt. Then replace the cap and check the action of the key.

When you remove the keycap on some keyboards, you are actually detaching the entire key from the keyswitch. Be careful during the removal and reassembly of the keyboard; otherwise, you'll break the switch. The classic IBM/Lexmark-type Model M keyboards (now made by Unicomp) use a removable keycap that leaves the actual key in place, enabling you to clean under the keycap without the risk of breaking the switches. If you don't want to go through the effort of removing the keycaps, consider using cleaning wands with soft foam tips to clean beneath the keytops.

Spills can be a problem, too. If you spill a soft drink or cup of coffee into a keyboard, you do not necessarily have a disaster. Many keyboards that use membrane switches are spill resistant. However, you should immediately (or as soon as possible) disconnect the keyboard and flush it out with distilled water. Partially or fully disassemble the keyboard and use the water to wash the components. If the spilled liquid has dried, soak the keyboard in some of the water for a while. When you are sure the keyboard is clean, pour another gallon or so of distilled water over it and through the keyswitches to wash away any residual dirt. After the unit dries completely (which can take several days or more), it should be perfectly functional. You might be surprised to know that drenching your keyboard with water does not harm the components. Just make sure you use distilled water, which is free from residue or mineral content. (Bottled water is *not* distilled; the distinct taste of many bottled waters comes from the trace minerals they contain!) Also, make sure the keyboard is fully dry before you try to use it; otherwise, some of the components might short out.

Fully drying a keyboard that has been soaked in water can take several days or more, so be prepared to wait. You can use compressed air to greatly speed up the drying process. Even then, if the contaminants were not fully flushed out, the keyboard may still not work correctly. In that case the best results will be obtained by completely disassembling the keyboard, washing and then drying each component individually, and then reassembling. Depending on the value and construction of the keyboard, a replacement may be the best option.

Tip

If you expect spills or excessive dust or dirt because of the environment or conditions in which the PC is used, several companies make thin membrane skins that mold over the top of the keyboard, protecting it from liquids, dust, and other contaminants. These skins are generally thin enough so that they don't interfere too much with the typing or action of the keys.

Keyboard Recommendations

Many of the keyboards supplied with lower-cost PCs leave much to be desired. They often have a mushy feel, with little or no tactile feedback. A poor keyboard can make using a system a frustrating experience, especially if you are a touch typist. For all these reasons, it is often a good idea to replace an existing keyboard with something better.

Perhaps the highest-quality keyboards in the entire computer industry are the "Model M" buckling spring keyswitch designs originally made by IBM (or, more accurately today, Unicomp). Unicomp maintains an extensive selection of more than 1,400 Lexmark and IBM keyboard models and continues to develop and sell a variety of traditional and customized models, including keyboards that match the school colors of several universities. Unicomp sells keyboards directly via its website at www.pckeyboard.com. Another great source for IBM keyboards is www.clickykeyboards.com, which offers a number of used and even new-old stock keyboards, including those with integral TrackPoints.

If you are a ThinkPad user and love the TrackPoint and/or UltraNav (TrackPoint with scroll button plus touchpad), you can get an actual ThinkPad TrackPoint or UltraNav keyboard in both standard and portable (without numeric keypad) designs:

- **ThinkPad Full-Size UltraNav USB Keyboard**—P/N 31P8950
- **ThinkPad Travel UltraNav USB Keyboard**—P/N 31P9490
- **ThinkPad USB Keyboard with TrackPoint**—P/N 55Y9003

The latter two versions lack the numeric keypad included on the full-size version. All include a built-in USB hub with two ports on the keyboard for attaching additional USB devices, such as a conventional mouse. They also have a built-in cord wrap that allows you to adjust the length of the cord as well as to hide it completely for storage. Although they don't have the heavy feel of the buckling spring key-switch design, they do have the same high-quality keyboards as the legendary ThinkPad laptops, and they include the same TrackPoint pointing device. They are both extremely lightweight: The travel and USB versions weigh only 1.17 lbs and 1 lbs, respectively, whereas the full-size model weighs only 1.41 lbs. A good way to find the best price is to search for the part numbers online. Using these keyboards makes the transition from laptop to desktop easy, because you can have the same keyboard and pointing devices on both.

Other excellent keyboards include the Cooler Master CM Storm keyboards (www.cmstorm.com/en/products/keyboards). These keyboards have mechanical switches with excellent tactile feedback, with a positive click sound, plus they feature fully adjustable LED backlighting.

Pointing Devices

The mouse was invented in 1964 by Douglas Engelbart, who at the time was working at the Stanford Research Institute (SRI), a think tank sponsored by Stanford University. The mouse was officially called an X-Y Position Indicator for a Display System. Xerox later applied the mouse to its revolutionary Alto computer system in 1973. At the time, unfortunately, these systems were experimental and used purely for research.

In 1979, several people from Apple—including Steve Jobs—were invited to see the Alto and the software that ran the system. Steve Jobs was blown away by what he saw as the future of computing, which included the use of the mouse as a pointing device and the GUI it operated. Apple promptly incorporated these features into what was to become the Lisa computer and lured away 15–20 Xerox scientists to work on the Apple system.

Although Xerox released the Star 8010 computer, which used this technology, in 1981, it was expensive, poorly marketed, and perhaps way ahead of its time. Apple released the Lisa computer, its first system that used the mouse, in 1983. It was not a runaway success, largely because of its $10,000 list price, but by then Jobs already had Apple working on the low-cost successor to the Lisa: the Macintosh. The Apple Macintosh was introduced in 1984. Although it was not an immediate hit, the Macintosh has grown in popularity since that time.

Many credit the Macintosh with inventing the mouse and GUI, but as you can see, this technology was actually borrowed from others, including SRI and Xerox. Certainly Microsoft Windows has popularized this interface and brought it to the legion of Intel-based PC systems.

Although the mouse did not catch on quickly in the PC marketplace, today the GUIs for PC systems, such as Windows, practically demand the use of a mouse. Therefore, virtually every new system sold at retail comes with a mouse. And, because the mice packaged with retail systems are seldom high-quality or up-to-date designs, sooner or later most users are in the market for a better mouse or compatible pointing device.

Mice come in many shapes and sizes from many manufacturers. Some have taken the standard mouse design and turned it upside down, creating the trackball. In the trackball devices, you move the ball with your hand directly rather than moving the unit itself. Trackballs were originally found on arcade video games, such as *Missile Command*, and are popular with users who have limited desk space. In most cases, the dedicated trackballs have a much larger ball than would be found on a standard mouse. Other than the orientation and perhaps the size of the ball, a trackball is identical to a mouse in design, basic function, and electrical interface. Like many recent mice, trackballs often come in ergonomic designs, and the more recent models even use the same optical tracking mechanisms used by the latest Microsoft and Logitech mice.

The largest manufacturers of mice are Microsoft and Logitech; these two companies provide designs that inspire the rest of the industry and each other and are popular OEM choices as well as retail brands. Although mice can come in different varieties, their actual use and care differ very little. The standard mouse consists of several components:

- A housing that you hold in your hand and move around on your desktop.
- A method of transmitting movement to the system: either ball/roller or optical sensors.
- Buttons (two or more) or touch sensors for making selections.
- A wheel or touch sensors for vertical and even horizontal scrolling. Some wheels tilt for horizontal scrolling or can be pressed to act as a button.
- An interface for connecting the mouse to the system. Conventional mice use a wire and connector, whereas wireless mice use a radio frequency (RF) or infrared (IR) transceiver in both the mouse and a separate unit connected to the computer to interface the mouse to the computer.

The housing, which is normally made of plastic, consists of few moving parts. On top of the housing, where your fingers normally rest, are buttons. There might be any number of buttons, but mice designed for PCs have always had two buttons, and since 1996 they have a scroll wheel or other device as well. Although the latest versions of Windows support scrolling mice, other features supported by the vendor, including additional buttons, still require installing the vendor's own mouse driver software.

Mouse Sensitivity

Mouse sensitivity is measured in DPI (dots per inch), which is also sometimes called PPI (pixels per inch). A standard mouse is calibrated to return position data at 400 DPI, while high-definition mice are calibrated to return data at 800 DPI or higher. There are some gaming mice that can be configured to rates of 5,000 DPI or more.

The higher the DPI setting, the faster and farther the pointer will move in relation to a given amount of physical movement. Fast movement is especially desirable in some games, which is why so-called "gaming" mice have extremely high DPI ratings that can usually be configured via software included with the mouse. Some mice have switches that allow you to change the DPI rating on the fly, since you may want it instantly higher or lower at different times during gameplay.

Ball-Type Mice

The bottom of the mouse housing is where the detection mechanisms or electronics are located. On traditional mice, the bottom of the housing contains a small, rubber ball that rolls as you move the mouse across the tabletop. The movements of this rubber ball are translated into electrical signals transmitted to the computer across the cable.

Internally, a ball-driven mouse is simple. The ball usually rests against two rollers: one for translating the x-axis movement and the other for translating the y-axis movement. These rollers are typically connected to small disks with shutters that alternately block and allow the passage of light. Small optical sensors detect movement of the wheels by watching an internal IR light blink on and off as the shutter wheel rotates and "chops" the light. These blinks are translated into movement along the axes. Ball type mice are considered obsolete today, although many are still in use.

Optical Mice

The other major method of motion detection is optical. Some of the early mice made by Mouse Systems and a few other vendors used a sensor that required a special grid-marked pad. Although these mice were accurate, the need to use them with a pad caused them to fall out of favor.

Microsoft's IntelliMouse Explorer pioneered the rebirth of optical mice. The IntelliMouse Explorer and the other new-style optical mice from Logitech and other vendors use optical technology to detect movement, and they have no moving parts of their own (except for the scroll wheel and buttons on top). Today's optical mice need no pad; they can work on virtually any surface. This is done by upgrading the optical sensor from the simple type used in older optical mice to a more advanced CCD (charge coupled device). This essentially is a crude version of a video camera sensor that detects movement by seeing the surface move under the mouse. An LED or diode laser provides light for the sensor. Many mice now incorporate IR laser technology sensors, which increase the resolution of the sensor, allowing for improved tracking on glossy or transparent surfaces.

The IntelliMouse Explorer revolutionized the mouse industry; first Logitech, and then virtually all other mouse makers, including both retail and OEM suppliers, have moved to optical mice for most of their product lines, offering a variety of optical mice in most price ranges. Figure 15.10 shows the essential features of a typical optical mouse.

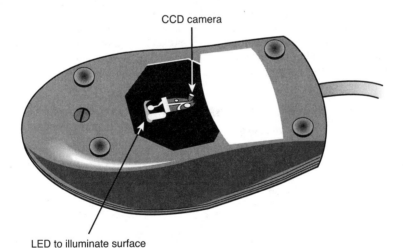

CCD camera

LED to illuminate surface

FIGURE 15.10 The bottom of the Logitech iFeel optical mouse.

Their versatility and low maintenance (not to mention that neat red or blue glow out the sides!) make optical mice an attractive choice, and the variety of models available from both vendors means you can have the latest optical technology for about the price of a good ball-type mouse. Figure 15.11 shows the interior of a typical optical mouse.

Optical mice are available as corded or wireless models, which use either IR or RF transceivers to replace the cable. A receiver is plugged into the USB or mouse port, and the battery-powered mouse contains a compatible transmitter. Wireless ball-type mice are usually much larger than ordinary mice because of the need to find room for both the bulky ball mechanism and batteries, but wireless optical mice are about the same size as high-end corded mice.

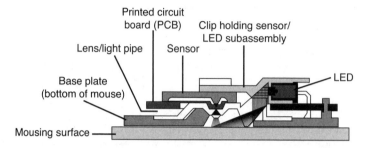

Printed circuit board (PCB)
Clip holding sensor/ LED subassembly
Lens/light pipe
Sensor
LED
Base plate (bottom of mouse)
Mousing surface

FIGURE 15.11 The LED or laser inside an optical mouse illuminates the surface by blinking many times per second. The light is reflected from the mousing surface back to the sensor, which converts the information into digital form and sends it to the computer.

Tip

Corded mice have cables that are typically 4 to 6 feet in length. If you have a choice on the length of cable to buy, get a longer one. This allows easier placement of the mouse in relation to your computer. Extension cables can be used if necessary to extend the distance.

After the mouse is connected to your computer, it communicates with your system through the use of a device driver, which can be loaded explicitly or built into the OS software. The standard mouse drivers in Windows are designed for the traditional two-button mouse or scroll mouse (in Windows Me or later), but increasing numbers of mice feature additional buttons, toggles, or wheels to make them more useful. These additional features require special mouse driver software supplied by the manufacturer.

Pointing Device Interface Types

The connector that attaches your mouse to the system depends on the type of interface you are using. Mice are most commonly connected to your computer through the following interfaces:

- Serial interface (obsolete)
- PS/2 mouse port
- USB port
- Bluetooth/wireless (transceiver connected via USB)

A fifth type of connection, the bus mouse (referred to by Microsoft as the InPort mouse), used a dedicated ISA bus adapter card and is long obsolete.

Serial

A popular method of connecting a mouse to older PCs is through the standard serial interface. As with other serial devices, the connector on the end of the mouse cable is typically a 9-pin female connector; some old mice used a 25-pin female connector. Only a couple of pins in the DB-9 or DB-25 connector are used for communications between the mouse and the device driver, but the mouse connector typically has all 9 or 25 pins present.

Because most older PCs come with two serial ports, a serial mouse can be plugged into either COM1 or COM2. The device driver, when initializing, searches the ports to determine to which one the mouse is connected. A few mouse drivers can't function if the serial port is set to COM3 or COM4, but most can work with any COM port (1–4).

Because a serial mouse does not connect to the system directly, it does not use system resources by itself. Instead, the resources are those used by the serial port to which it is connected. For example, if you have a mouse connected to COM2, and if COM2 is using the default IRQ and I/O port address range, both the serial port and the mouse connected to it use IRQ3 and I/O port addresses 2F8h–2FFh.

◀◀ See the Chapter 14 section, "Serial Ports," **p. 730**.

PS/2 Mouse Port (PS/2)

Many motherboards include a PS/2 mouse port built into the motherboard. This port was introduced by IBM on its PS/2 systems in 1987. Since then this interface has been called a *PS/2 mouse port.*

From a hardware perspective, a PS/2 mouse port is the same as the mini-DIN PS/2 keyboard port. In fact, the PS/2 mouse port is connected to the 8042-type keyboard controller found on the motherboard. PS/2 ports transfer data serially 1 bit at a time at a nominal rate of 12.5Kbps. Figure 15.12 shows a PS/2 mouse port connector.

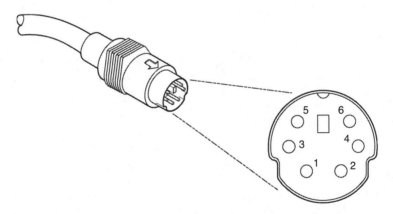

FIGURE 15.12   Typical PS/2 mouse port connector.

Caution

As mentioned in the section, "Keyboard/Mouse Interface Connectors," the mini-DIN sockets used for both keyboard and mouse connections on many systems are physically and electrically interchangeable, but the data packets they carry are not. Be sure to plug each device into the correct socket; otherwise, neither will function correctly. Don't panic if you mix them up, though. They are electrically identical to each other, so you can't damage the ports or the devices.

The standard resource usage for a motherboard (or PS/2) mouse port is IRQ12, as well as I/O port addresses 60h and 64h. Because the motherboard mouse port uses the 8042-type keyboard controller chip, the port addresses are those of this chip.

USB

The extremely flexible USB port has become the most popular port to use for mice as well as keyboards and other I/O devices. Compared to the other interfaces, USB mice (and other USB pointing devices such as trackballs) have the following advantages:

- USB mice move much more smoothly than the traditional PS/2 type. This is because the speed of the interface is much higher, allowing the mouse to update its position at a higher frequency. A PS/2 port operates at a nominal data rate of 12.5Kbps, while the USB Full-Speed data rate is 12Mbps, which is almost a thousand times faster.

- USB mice and pointing devices, similar to all other USB devices, are hot-swappable. If you like to use a trackball and your computing partners prefer mice, you can just lean over and unplug the other users' pointing device and plug in your own, or move it from PC to PC. You can't do that with the other port types.

- Multiple pointing devices. With USB, you can easily have multiple pointing devices connected simultaneously, and you can easily switch between them or use them in collaboration.

- USB mice can be attached to a USB hub. Using a hub makes attaching and removing your mouse easy without crawling around on the floor to reach the back of the computer. Many computers have front-mounted USB ports, letting you easily attach and remove a USB mouse without the use of an external hub.

Virtually all mice today interface via USB; however, some USB mice are hybrid devices that also support the PS/2 interface via an adapter.

Note

Even the fastest "gaming" mice with the highest DPI (dot per inch) ratings use the USB 1.1 compatible "Full Speed" data rate, which is 12Mbps. That is 960 times faster than the 12.5Kbps data rate used by the PS/2 port interface. The higher data rates of USB 2.0 Hi Speed (480Mbps) and USB 3.0 SuperSpeed (5Gbps) are simply not needed even for the fastest mice.

Hybrid Mice

Hybrid mice are those designed to plug into two types of ports. Circuitry in a hybrid mouse automatically detects the type of port to which it is connected and configures the mouse automatically. Serial-PS/2 hybrid mice came with a mini-DIN connector on the end of their cable and an adapter that converts the mini-DIN to a 9- or 25-pin serial port connector, although the reverse is sometimes true on early examples of these mice. PS/2-USB hybrid mice usually come with the USB connector on the end of their cable and include a mini-DIN (PS/2) adapter, as shown in Figure 15.13.

Sometimes, people use adapters to try to connect a USB mouse to a PS/2 mouse port or a PS/2 mouse to a USB port. If this does not work, it is not the fault of the adapter. Non-hybrid mice are incompatible with adapters and will only work on the specific interface for which they were designed.

Scroll Wheels

Late in 1996, Microsoft introduced the IntelliMouse, which differed from standard Microsoft mice by adding a small gray wheel between the mouse buttons. Although this was not technically the first scrolling mouse on the market (Mouse Systems introduced the ProAgio and Genius EasyScroll in 1995), it was the first to have widespread support. Since then, Logitech, IBM, and virtually all other mouse vendors have made scroll wheels or similar devices compatible with the Microsoft design as standard across almost all models, including OEM mice bundled with computer systems.

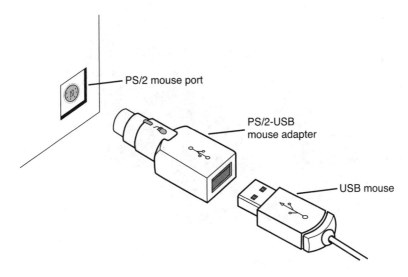

FIGURE 15.13 A typical USB mouse with a PS/2 adapter.

The wheel has two main functions. The primary function is to act as a scrolling device, enabling you to scroll through documents or web pages by manipulating the wheel with your index finger. In some models the wheel can also function as a third mouse button when you press it.

Each vendor's mouse driver software offers unique features to enhance the basic operation of the mouse. For example, Logitech's MouseWare drivers enable you to select which function the OS should perform when you click one of the mouse's extra buttons. The drivers also provide various options for how to scroll with each wheel click (three lines, six lines, or one screen). Microsoft's IntelliMouse driver offers a feature called ClickLock, which allows you to drag items without holding down the primary mouse button. In addition, it offers a Universal Scroll feature that adds scrolling mouse support to applications that lack such support. To get the most from whatever scrolling or other advanced-feature mouse you have, be sure you use the latest mouse drivers for your specific make and model.

Touch-Sensitive Mice

The latest evolution in mouse scrolling and control includes touch technology, which basically uses a smooth surface with touch sensors to replace the traditional scroll wheel and, in more advanced models, the buttons as well. Some, like the Microsoft Touch Mouse, also support various gestures using your thumb or multiple fingers, which can be used to manipulate Windows in new ways.

The simplest examples use a touch-sensitive strip or panel to replace the scroll wheel. One example is the Microsoft Explorer Touch Mouse (see Figure 15.14). Using one finger on the touch-sensitive strip, you can scroll both vertically and horizontally. You can scroll slowly by swiping your finger, or more quickly by flicking it faster. These types of mice still have traditional buttons using mechanical switches, although many have buttons on the side in addition to the standard top-left and -right buttons. Using the software that comes with the mouse, you can customize what the extra buttons do.

More advanced touch mice have a full touch-sensitive area, including the buttons. With this full-touch type there are no left and right buttons to click; you simply tap on the touch-sensitive surface instead. One example of this type is the Microsoft Touch Mouse (see Figure 15.15). When using Windows 7 or 8, you can use one, two, and three finger gestures as well as thumb movement on the side of the mouse to do things like move through open applications, zoom in and out, scroll in any direction, and more.

FIGURE 15.14   The Microsoft Explorer Touch Mouse.

FIGURE 15.15   The Microsoft Touch Mouse.

Mouse Troubleshooting

If you are experiencing problems with your mouse, you need to look in only two general places—hardware and software. Because mice are simple devices, looking at the hardware takes little time. Detecting and correcting software problems can take a bit longer, however.

If your system refuses to recognize the mouse, try using a different mouse that you know works. If that doesn't resolve the problem, the port you are connecting the mouse to might be bad. If the mouse is connected via USB, try a different USB port. If a motherboard-based PS/2 mouse port goes bad, you can replace the entire motherboard—which is usually expensive—or you can just use a USB mouse instead.

I have had problems in which a bad PS/2 interface mouse caused the system to lock right as the driver loaded or when third-party diagnostics were being run on the system. Try unplugging the mouse to see if the system will boot; if it does, the mouse or PS/2 mouse port (meaning the motherboard) may be the problem.

To troubleshoot wireless mice, see the section, "Troubleshooting Wireless Input Devices."

Cleaning Your Mouse

If you notice that the mouse pointer moves across the screen in a jerky fashion, it might be time to clean your mouse. For an optical/laser mouse, this is easy—merely turn the mouse over and clean the dust or dirt off of the sensor. For a mechanical mouse with a roller ball, this jerkiness is caused when dirt and dust become trapped around the mouse's ball-and-roller assembly, thereby restricting its free movement.

To clean a mechanical mouse, turn it over, open the cover panel, and remove the rubberized ball. Wash it in soapy water or a mild solvent, such as contact lens cleaner solution or alcohol, and dry it off.

Now take a look at the socket in which the roller ball normally rests. You will see two or three small wheels or bars against which the ball usually rolls. If you notice dust or dirt on or around these wheels or bars, you need to clean them. The best way is to use a compressed air duster, which can blow out any dust or dirt. You also can use some electrical contact cleaner to clean the rollers. Remember, any remaining dirt or dust impedes the movement of the roller ball and results in the mouse not working as it should.

Put the mouse back together by inserting the roller ball into the socket and then securely attaching the cover panel.

Alternative Pointing Devices

Because of Windows, many users spend at least as much time moving pointers around the screen as they do in typing, making pointing device choices very important. In addition to the mouse, several other popular pointing devices are available:

- TrackPoint (pointing stick)
- Touch pads
- Trackballs

All these devices are treated as mice by the OS but offer radically different options for the user in terms of comfort. If you're not satisfied with a regular mouse, look into these options.

TrackPoint

On October 5, 1992, IBM introduced a revolutionary new pointing device called *TrackPoint* as an integrated feature of its new ThinkPad 700 and 700C computers. Often referred to as a *pointing stick*, the TrackPoint appears as a small rubber cap on the keyboard just above the B key and between the G and H keys. This was in my opinion the most significant new pointing device since the mouse was invented nearly 30 years earlier!

The TrackPoint device occupies no space on a desk, does not have to be adjusted for left-handed or right-handed use, has no moving parts to fail, and (most importantly) does not require you to move your hands from the home row to use it. This is an absolute boon for touch typists.

I was fortunate enough to meet the actual creator of this device in early 1992 at the spring Comdex/ Windows World show in Chicago. While attending the show I had stumbled upon a gentleman wearing suspenders and sporting a ponytail in a small corner of the IBM booth. His appearance piqued my interest because he was clearly not a "suit," but instead looked to be some sort of scientist or engineer.

I was right, and he was there showing off custom-made prototype keyboards with a small stick in the middle. The stick was covered with a soft cream-colored silicone rubber coating that allowed you to press on the stick without your finger slipping off. In fact, he told me that these were hand-built prototypes he had installed in standard desktop keyboards, and that he was there trying to get public reaction and feedback on the invention.

I was invited to play with one of the keyboards, which was connected to a demonstration system. I found that by pressing on the stick with my index finger, I could easily move the mouse pointer around on the screen. The stick itself did not move. (It was not a joystick.) Instead, it was connected to pressure transducers that measured the amount and direction of the force applied by my finger and moved the mouse pointer accordingly. The harder I pressed, the faster the pointer moved. After playing around for just a few minutes, the pointer movements became automatic—almost as though I could just "think" about where I wanted the pointer to go, and it would go there.

The gentleman at the booth turned out to be Dr. Ted Selker, the primary inventor of the device. He and Joseph Rutledge created this integrated pointing device at the IBM T.J. Watson Research Center. When I asked him when such keyboards would become available, he could not answer—at the time there were apparently no plans for production. He was only trying to test user reaction to the device. I filled out one of the survey forms, indicating that I was extremely interested in the revolutionary device and would gladly purchase one if they became available in the future.

Well, the feedback must have helped, because just over six months later, IBM had announced the ThinkPad 700, which included this device—then known as the TrackPoint II. Since the original version came out, enhanced versions with even greater control and sensitivity have become available.

Note

The reason the device was initially called TrackPoint II is that IBM had previously been selling a convertible mouse/trackball device called the TrackPoint. No relationship exists between the original TrackPoint mouse/trackball, which has since been discontinued, and the TrackPoint II and later integrated devices. Since the original TrackPoint II came out, improved versions known as TrackPoint III and TrackPoint IV have become available. In the interest of simplicity, I refer to all the TrackPoint II, III, and successive devices as just *TrackPoint*.

Although the prototypes I used were cream-colored, in its final production form, the TrackPoint consists of a small, red, silicone rubber knob nestled between the G, H, and B keys on the keyboard. The primary and secondary mouse buttons are placed below the spacebar where you can easily reach them with your thumbs without taking your hands off the keyboard. Newer versions also include a third button that can be used for scrolling.

Studies conducted by Selker found that the act of removing your hand from the keyboard (to reach for a mouse) and then replacing your hand back on the keyboard takes approximately 1.75 seconds. If you type at 60 wpm (words per minute), that can equal nearly two lost words every minute, not including the time lost while you regain your train of thought. You can save almost all of this time if you use the TrackPoint to move the pointer or make a selection (click or double-click) instead of a mouse. The TrackPoint also enables you to perform drag-and-drop functions easily.

IBM's research also found that people can get up to 20% more work accomplished using the TrackPoint instead of a mouse, especially when the application involves a mix of typing and pointing activities, such as with word processing, spreadsheets, and other typical office applications. In usability tests with the TrackPoint, IBM gave a group of desktop computer users both a TrackPoint and a traditional mouse. After two weeks, 80% of the users had unplugged their mice and switched solely to the TrackPoint device. Selker is convinced (as am I) that the TrackPoint is the best pointing solution for both laptop and desktop systems.

Another feature of the TrackPoint is that a standard mouse can be connected to the system at the same time to enable dual-pointer use. This setup not only enables a single person to use both devices, but it enables two people to use the TrackPoint and the mouse simultaneously to move the pointer on the screen, which can be useful in some training situations. The first pointing device that moves (thus issuing a system interrupt) takes precedence and retains control over the mouse pointer on the screen until it completes its movement action. The second pointing device is automatically locked out until the primary device is stationary. This enables the use of both devices yet prevents each one from interfering with the other.

IBM/Lenovo has added various versions of the TrackPoint to its laptop computers, as well as to high-end keyboards sold under the IBM/Lenovo, Lexmark, and Unicomp names. Laptop computer makers, such as HP/Compaq, Dell, and Toshiba, have licensed the TrackPoint device (Toshiba calls it Accupoint) and use it on various models.

I have compared the TrackPoint device to other pointing devices for laptops (especially touch pads), but nothing compares in terms of accuracy and control—and, of course, the fact that you don't have to take your hands off the keyboard to use it!

Unfortunately, most of the TrackPoint devices used by laptops other than IBM/Lenovo don't have the full features of the IBM/Lenovo versions, especially including the multiple tip choices, the third scroll button, and "negative inertia" control. One important feature to look for is the ability to accept different IBM/Lenovo TrackPoint caps. These have a square hole in them and allow choosing from several different types.

Over the years IBM/Lenovo has upgraded the TrackPoint pointing stick to the TrackPoint III and the current TrackPoint IV. Two main differences exist in the III/IV system, but the most obvious one is the rubber cap. The original caps were made from pure silicone rubber, which was grippy and worked well in most situations. However, if the user has greasy fingers, the textured surface of the rubber can become slippery. Cleaning the cap (and the user's hands) solves the problem, but it can be annoying at times. The TrackPoint III and later standard caps are made from a different type of rubber, which Selker calls "plastic sandpaper." This type of cap is much more grippy and does not require cleaning except for cosmetic purposes. More recently Lenovo introduced other caps that do not feature the sandpaper surface, but have either a wider soft dome or a wider concave surface for additional grip. Lenovo now has three types of caps for the TrackPoint to suit different needs and tastes. These different caps are interchangeable with the older styles as well (see Figure 15.16):

- **Classic dome (P/N 84G6537)**—The traditional "pencil eraser" cap with a sandpaper surface.

- **Soft rim (P/N 91P8423)**—A larger concave nonsandpaper design creates a mechanical advantage, requiring less force for pointer motion.

- **Soft dome (P/N 91P8422)**—A larger convex design with a soft texture nonsandpaper surface.

FIGURE 15.16 Classic, soft rim, and soft dome TrackPoint caps.

Note

If your keyboard uses the same physical caps as the IBM/Lenovo designs, you can change to the newer Lenovo caps as well. You can get these caps by ordering them from IBM Parts directly or from others who sell Lenovo parts, such as Compu-Lock (www.compu-lock.com). The cost is less than $15 for a set of four caps. Replacing the cap is easy—grab the existing cap with your fingers and pull straight up; it pops right off. Then, simply push on the new cap.

The other difference between the Lenovo TrackPoint and some of the others on the market is the control software. IBM added routines that implement a subtle technique Selker calls *negative inertia*, which is marketed under the label *QuickStop response*. This software not only takes into account how far you push the pointer in any direction, but also how quickly you push or release it. When the pointer is released or stopped quickly, it actually backtracks or bounces back a bit, causing it to more accurately end up where the person wanted it to be. Selker found that the improved software and caps enable people to make selections up to 8% faster.

The latest incarnation (called TrackPoint IV) includes an extra scroll button, as well as the ability to press the TrackPoint cap to select as if using the left mouse button. These new features make the TrackPoint even better.

The bottom line is that anyone who touch types should strongly consider only laptops that include a TrackPoint device. TrackPoints are far superior to other pointing devices such as touch pads because the TrackPoint is faster to use (you don't have to take your hands off the keyboard's home row), easier to adapt to (especially for speedy touch typists), and far more precise to control. It takes some getting accustomed to, but the benefits are worth it. I know many people who have converted from using touch pads to TrackPoints, but few who have willingly gone the other way.

Note that the benefits of the TrackPoint are not limited to portable systems; you can have the same features on your desktop keyboard. For desktop systems, I use a Lenovo keyboard with the TrackPoint built in. This makes for a more consistent interface between desktop and laptop systems because I can use the same pointing device in both environments.

Touch Pads

The first touch pad was included on the ill-fated Gavilan portable computer in 1982; however, it didn't catch on until many years later. Cirque originated the modern touch pad (also called a *track pad*) pointing device in 1994. Cirque refers to its technology as the GlidePoint and has licensed the technology to other vendors such as Alps Electric, which also uses the term GlidePoint for its touch pads. The GlidePoint uses a flat, square pad that senses finger position through body capacitance. This is similar to the capacitance-sensitive elevator button controls you sometimes encounter in office buildings or hotels.

When it is used on a portable computer's keyboard, the touch pad is mounted below the spacebar, and it detects pressure applied by your thumbs or fingers. Transducers under the pad convert finger movement into pointer movement. Several laptop manufacturers have licensed this technology from Cirque and have incorporated it into their portable systems. Touch pads are also integrated into a number of mid-range to high-end keyboards from many vendors. When used on a desktop keyboard, touch pads are often offset to the right side of the keyboard's typing area.

Touch pads feature mouse buttons, although the user also can tap or double-tap on the touch pad's surface to activate an onscreen button located under the touch pad's cursor. Dragging and dropping is accomplished without touching the touch pad's buttons; just move the cursor to the object to be dragged, press down on the pad, hold while moving the cursor to the drop point, and raise the finger to drop the object. Some recent models also feature additional hot buttons with functions similar to those on hot-button keyboards, as well as a vertical scrollbar on the side and the capability to tap the touch pad to simulate a mouse click.

The primary use for touch pads has been for laptop computer– and desktop keyboard–integrated pointing devices, although Cirque and Alps have both sold standalone versions of the touch pad for use as a mouse alternative on desktop systems. Cirque's touch pads can be purchased direct from the Cirque website. The Smart Cat Pro Touchpad has enhanced software to support touch gestures, has programmable hot buttons, and includes other features to make web surfing easier.

Although it has gained wide acceptance, especially on portable computers, touch pad technology can have many drawbacks for some users. Operation of the device can be erratic, depending on skin resistance and moisture content. The biggest drawback is that to operate the touch pad, users must remove their hands from the home row on the keyboard, which dramatically slows their progress. In addition, the operation of the touch pad can be imprecise, depending on how pointy your finger or thumb is! On the other hand, if you're not a touch typist, removing your hands from the keyboard to operate the touch pad might be easier than using a TrackPoint. Even with their drawbacks, touch pad pointing devices are vastly preferable to using a trackball or a cumbersome external mouse with portable systems.

Unless you want to use a "real" mouse with a portable system, I recommend you sit down with portable computers that have both touch pad and TrackPoint pointing devices. Try them yourself for typing, file management, and simple graphics and see which type of integrated pointing device you prefer. I know what I like, but you might have different tastes.

Trackballs

The first trackball I ever saw outside of an arcade was the Wico trackball, a perfect match for mid-1980s video games and computer games, such as *Missile Command* and others. It emulated the eight-position Atari 2600 analog joystick but was capable of much more flexibility.

Unlike the mid-80s trackballs, today's trackballs are used primarily for business instead of gaming. Most trackballs use a mouse-style positioning mechanism—the differences being that the trackball is on the top or side of the case and is much larger than a mouse ball. The user moves the trackball rather than the input device case, but rollers or wheels inside most models translate the trackball's motion and move a cursor onscreen the same way that mouse rollers or wheels convert the mouse ball's motion into cursor movement.

Trackballs come in a variety of forms, including ergonomic models shaped to fit the (right) hand, ambidextrous models suitable for both lefties and right-handers, optical models that use the same optical sensors found in the latest mice in place of wheels and rollers, and multibutton monsters that look as if they're the result of an encounter with a remote control.

Because they are larger than mice, trackballs lend themselves well to the extra electronics and battery power needed for wireless use. Logitech offers several wireless trackball models that use radio-frequency transceivers; for details of how this technology works, see the section "Wireless Input Devices," later in this chapter.

Trackballs use the same drivers and connectors as conventional mice. For basic operations, the OS–supplied drivers will work, but you should use the latest version of the vendor-supplied drivers to achieve maximum performance with recent models.

Trackball troubleshooting is similar to mouse troubleshooting. For issues other than cleaning the trackball, refer to the section, "Mouse Troubleshooting."

Because trackballs are moved by the user's hand rather than by rolling against a tabletop or desktop, they don't need to be cleaned as often as mouse mechanisms do. However, occasional cleaning is recommended, especially with trackballs that use roller movement-detection mechanisms. If the trackball pointer won't move, skips, or drags when you move the trackball, try cleaning the trackball mechanism.

Trackballs can be held into place by a retaining ring, an ejection tab, or simply by gravity. Check the vendor's website for detailed cleaning instructions if your trackball didn't come with such instructions. Swabs and isopropyl alcohol are typically used to clean the trackball and rollers or bearings; see the trackball's instructions for details.

Touchscreen Technology

Touchscreens have been around for many years but have mostly been used in commercial or industrial applications such as point-of-sale systems. With the increasing popularity of tablet computers and smartphones, and especially since the release of Windows 8 (which includes integrated multitouch support), touchscreen displays are now becoming more and more popular.

The original touchscreens were single touch devices, meaning they would sense only a single touch point on the screen, allowing for simple pointer control or object selection. Modern touchscreens can sense two, five, or even ten or more simultaneous touch points on the screen. Such displays are called multitouch, and they allow more complicated control, including touch gestures using two or more fingers simultaneously. Using a single finger can move a pointer, while using two fingers can initiate a scrolling action, for example.

There are several technologies used for multitouch sensitive touchscreens, including the following:

- **Capacitive**—A transparent conductive matrix creates a grid of capacitors. When a finger or conductive stylus is close to the surface, the grid sees a change in capacitance at a specific location on the screen.
- **Resistive**—Transparent conductive and resistive coatings create a grid of tiny switches, which can detect the press of a finger or stylus at a specific location on the screen.
- **Optical**—Retro-reflective optical sensors in groups of pixels on the screen detect the shadow of a finger or stylus at a specific location on the screen.

While each of these technologies has various advantages and disadvantages, the most popular technology for multitouch displays is Capacitive. In the end the specific technology is mostly transparent to the user. It simply works.

The display portion of a monitor with a multi-touch sensor attaches to the PC like any other display—that is, via a DVI, HDMI, DisplayPort, or possibly even an analog VGA connection. The touch sensor attaches via a separate USB cable, and most of these displays also include a built-in USB hub allowing additional USB devices to be attached to the display.

Using a display with multi-touch capability is a no-brainer where tablets are concerned, but for laptop and especially desktop PC use, the jury is still out. I, for one, am insistent on having a display that is absolutely clean and free of fingerprints, smudges, or other debris. The idea of fingering up the displays on either my laptop or desktop systems is abhorrent. In addition, most, if not all, of the screens available with multitouch capability are glossy, which is a deal-breaker for me. Because I want to see what is on the display (and not what is behind or above me) I insist on anti-glare or matte displays for both laptop and desktop systems. Touchscreen technology is not dependent on having a glossy screen, but since it is a consumer-oriented technology, and all consumer-oriented displays are glossy, it seems you are forced to have one with the other.

Then there is the cost. Because multitouch desktop and even laptop displays are fairly new with the advent of Windows 8, they are currently several times more expensive than those having the same size and resolution without a multitouch sensor. It remains to be seen how popular these types of displays will become in the future for normal desktop or even laptop PC use.

Wireless Input Devices

For several years, many manufacturers have offered wireless versions of mice and keyboards. In most cases, these devices have used either IR or short-range radio transceivers to attach to standard USB or PS/2 ports, with matching transceivers located inside the mouse or keyboard. Wireless input devices are designed to be easier to use in cramped home-office environments and where a large-screen TV/ monitor device is used for home entertainment and computing.

Many manufacturers, including Microsoft, Logitech, and second-tier vendors, offer bundled kits that include a wireless keyboard and mouse that share a transceiver. Because many of these keyboards and mice have the latest features, including programmable keys, multimedia and Internet-access keys, and optical sensors, these wireless combos are often the top-of-the-line products from a given vendor and are often less expensive than buying the keyboard and mouse separately.

The three major technologies used by wireless input devices are as follows:

- IR
- Proprietary radio frequency
- Bluetooth

All three technologies normally use a transceiver connected to the USB or PS/2 ports on the computer. Because many wireless transceivers are designed for use with a mouse and keyboard, PS/2-compatible versions have two cables—one for the mouse port and one for the keyboard port. A USB-compatible transceiver needs only one USB port to handle both devices if the system supports USB Legacy (keyboard) functions. The transceiver attached to the computer draws its power from the port.

The transceiver receives signals from the transceiver built into the mouse or keyboard. These devices require batteries to function; therefore, a common cause of wireless device failure is battery rundown. Early generations of wireless devices used unusual battery types, but most recent products use off-the-shelf AA or AAA batteries, including rechargeables. Some have internal lithium-ion or NiMH rechargeable batteries, in which the transceiver connected to the PC also doubles as a charger. Some are rechargeable via special docks or USB cable connections.

Although all three technologies rely on battery power, the similarities end there. IR devices have a relatively short range (12 ft. maximum), and a clear line-of-sight must exist between the input device and transceiver. Anything from a Mountain Dew can to a sheet of paper can block the IR signal from reaching the transceiver, assuming you're aiming the transmitter built into your input device correctly in the first place. Some late-model IR devices have transceivers that can receive signals through a relatively wide 120° range, but this technology is much more temperamental than the others and has been abandoned by most vendors.

Because of the problems with IR devices, almost all vendors of wireless input devices now use radio frequency (RF) signals for transmission between the device and transceiver. RF-based wireless devices have no line-of-sight problems, but they can vary in the maximum distances they will allow from the transmitter.

Although RF overcomes line-of-sight issues that can cripple an IR mouse, early versions of RF products had a high potential for interference from other devices and from other devices in use in the same room because of a limited range of channels. For example, some early wireless products required the user to manually select the channel used by the transceiver and mouse. If more than six users in a small room had wireless devices, interference was practically inevitable.

Fortunately, improvements in frequency bands used and automatic tuning have enabled all users of a particular type of device to avoid interference with other electronic devices or with each other. For example, the 27MHz frequency pioneered by Logitech's Palomar line of peripherals has become a de facto standard for most recent wireless input devices. (Microsoft and IBM have also used it for their wireless products.) Logitech allows users to enable a digital security feature that uses one of more than 4,000 unique codes to prevent accidentally activating another computer with a wireless device or signal snooping by another user. Most vendors use similar technology, but some might use a much smaller number of codes. Many recent wireless products use FastRF technology, which provides 2.5 times the transmission rate of conventional 27MHz devices. The responsiveness of a FastRF connection is all but indistinguishable from a corded mouse or keyboard.

Finally, there's Bluetooth. Although most wireless products use proprietary radio transceivers, Microsoft, Logitech, and some others have developed wireless mouse and keyboard products using the Bluetooth wireless standard. Bluetooth-enabled devices have an effective range of up to 30 feet and might be compatible with other brands of devices that are also Bluetooth enabled. The only drawback I've seen with Bluetooth-based devices is that they usually consume more power, resulting in shorter battery life, and the configuration or pairing of the device and transceiver can be more difficult than those using proprietary wireless technology.

▶▶ For more information about Bluetooth, see Chapter 17, "Local Area Networking," **p. 799**.

Power Management Features of Wireless Input Devices

A wireless mouse is useless if its batteries fail, so several vendors of wireless products have developed sophisticated power-management features to help preserve battery life—especially with optical mice, which use power-eating LEDs to illuminate the mousing surface. For example, Logitech Cordless mice have four operating modes, as shown in Table 15.3.

Table 15.3   Logitech Cordless Mouse Optical Power Management

Mode	Sensor Flashing Rate	Notes
Bright	1,500 per second	Run mode: Used when the mouse is being moved across a surface
Glow	1,000 per second	Walk mode: Used when the mouse stops moving
Strobe	10 per second	Sleep mode: Used when the mouse has not moved for more than 1 minute
Flash	2 per second	Deep sleep mode: Used when the mouse has not moved for more than 10 minutes

Wireless keyboards are activated only when you press a key or use the scroll wheel available on some models, so they tend to have longer battery lives than mice. Conventional ball-type mice also have longer battery lives than optical mice, but ball-type mice have largely been discontinued, as the convenience and accuracy of optical mice outweigh battery-life issues for most users.

Troubleshooting Wireless Input Devices

If your wireless input device does not work, check the following:

- **Battery failure**—The transceivers attached to the computer are powered by the computer, but the input devices themselves are battery powered. Check the battery life suggestions published by the vendor; if your unit isn't running as long as it should, try using a better brand of battery or turning off the device if possible.

- **Lost synchronization between device and transceiver**—Both the device and the transceiver must be using the same frequency to communicate. Depending on the device, you might be able to resynchronize the device and transceiver by pressing a button, or you might need to remove the battery, reinsert the battery, and wait for several minutes to reestablish contact.

- **Interference between units**—Check the transmission range of the transceivers in your wireless units and visit the manufacturer's website for details on how to reduce interference. Typically, you should use different frequencies for wireless devices on adjacent computers.

- **Blocked line of sight**—If you are using IR wireless devices, check the line of sight carefully at the computer, the space between your device and the computer, and the device itself. You might be dangling a finger or two over the IR eye and cutting off the signal—the equivalent of putting your finger over the lens on a camera.

- **Serial port IRQ conflicts**—If the wireless mouse is connected to a serial port and it stops working after you install another add-on card, check for conflicts using the Windows Device Manager.

- **Disconnected transceiver**—If you have moved the computer around, you might have disconnected the transceiver from its keyboard, PS/2 mouse, serial, or USB port. You can plug a USB device in without shutting down the system, but the other types require you to shut down the PC, reattach the cable, and restart the PC to work correctly.

- **USB Legacy support not enabled**—If your wireless keyboard uses a transceiver connected to the USB port and the device works in Windows but not at a command prompt, make sure you have enabled USB Legacy support in the BIOS, or use the PS/2 connector from the transceiver to connect to the PS/2 keyboard port.

Chapter

16

Internet Connectivity

Internet Connectivity Trends

Communication between computers is a major part of the PC industry. Thanks to the Internet, no computer user is an island. Whether using a dial-up modem or broadband technology, virtually all PCs can be interconnected both locally and globally, enabling them to share files, send and receive email, and access the World Wide Web (WWW). This chapter explores the various technologies you can use to expand the reach of your PC around the block and around the world.

Although some users still use dial-up modems, most PC users have abandoned dial-up Internet access for the faster world of broadband access. According to WebSiteOptimization.com, in July 2004 the number of U.S. broadband connections for the first time exceeded the number of dial-up connections among active Internet users, with 50.69% of active Internet users on high-speed connections, and the rest on 56Kbps or slower dial-up connections. As of early 2010, broadband home Internet users in the U.S. exceeded 95% of active users, with dial-up users representing less than 5% of the total, and over 98% of active business Internet connections in the U.S. used broadband. Many PC users connect via WWAN (wireless wide-area network) or cellphone data connections (known as tethering). According to a survey, by the end of 2011 there were over 1.2 billion active users of mobile broadband devices. Another report states that 90% of the world's population have access to 2G broadband, while, according to ITU, 45% of the world have 3G coverage. Unfortunately, this type of connection is often very expensive.

Although some form of broadband has replaced dial-up for almost all users, dial-up connections still have their uses. Those without broadband options and those on a budget still need a dial-up connection. Believed to be caused by the general economic downturn, AOL reported adding 200,000 new dial-up users in 2011, with a total of over 3.5 million dial-up subscribers. Dial-up can also serve as a last-resort backup method for Internet access. You'll find dial-up modem coverage in the second portion of this chapter.

Broadband Internet Access Types

Thanks to the combination of huge multimegabyte downloads needed to update software and support hardware, dynamic websites with music and full-motion video, and increased demand for online services, having a broadband (high-speed) Internet connection is a virtual necessity these days. There are several types of broadband Internet access solutions, including the following:

- Cable (including copper and fiber)
- DSL
- Fixed-base wireless
- Cellular
- Satellite
- ISDN
- Leased lines

At least one of these services should be available to you, and if you live in a medium- to large-size city, you might be able to choose from several broadband solutions. The first portion of this chapter focuses on these solutions.

Cable TV

Cable TV (CATV)–based Internet piggybacks on the same CATV service lines used for cable television service.

The device used to connect a PC to a CATV network is called a *cable modem*. In fact, the so-called "cable modem" is actually a great deal more. The device does indeed modulate and demodulate, but it also functions as a tuner, a network bridge, an encryptor, and a Simple Network Management Protocol (SNMP) agent. To connect your PC to a CATV network, you do not use a serial port as with dial-up modem technologies or Integrated Services Digital Network (ISDN) terminal adapters. Instead, the most typical connection today runs the incoming cable connection to an external cable modem, which has an Ethernet connection to a router, which then connects from 1–255 PCs via Ethernet. Some cable modems have built-in router functionality, in which case you don't need to purchase a separate one.

Tip

For maximum security, speed, and ease of sharing among multiple systems, I recommend that you connect your cable modem (if it doesn't include its own router) to a router and then connect the router to an Ethernet card or port in your system. Combination cable modems and routers are available that include both functions in one box. These devices are sometimes referred to as cable gateways.

Cable Modems

The cable modem connects to the CATV network using the same coaxial cable connection as the cable TV service (see Figure 16.1). Thus, the cable modem functions as a bridge between your network and the hybrid fiber/coax (HFC) network that connects all the cable customers in your neighborhood.

A typical two-way cable modem connection is shown in Figure 16.1.

Originally, cable modems used proprietary technology and were not sold to users of CATV Internet access but were leased by the CATV companies offering Internet access to their cable modem customers. This is because each cable modem on a particular CATV network had to match the proprietary technology the network used. In late 1998, some CATV companies began to use DOCSIS-compliant cable modems. DOCSIS refers to devices that meet the Data Over Cable Service Interface Specification standards established by Cable Television Laboratories, Inc. (CableLabs). Modems that meet DOCSIS standards are now referred to as *CableLabs Certified cable modems*. Visit the CableLabs website at www.cablelabs.com for a complete list of cable modems that are CableLabs Certified.

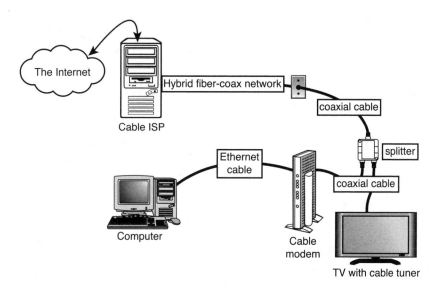

FIGURE 16.1 A typical hybrid fiber-coax cable TV network that also includes two-way cable modem service.

Many vendors of traditional modems and other types of communications products, such as 3Com, ARRIS, Motorola, Cisco, and D-Link, make CableLabs Certified cable modem–compliant hardware. The models supported by your CATV Internet provider are usually dependent on the DOCSIS standard they support. Table 16.1 provides a brief overview of the differences in these standards.

Table 16.1 DOCSIS Standards Overview

DOCSIS Standard	Benefits	Notes
1.0	Basic broadband CATV (cable modem) service	Original DOCSIS version released March 1997
1.1	Supports tiered service (different speeds at different costs), faster uploading, home networking, and packet telephony while reducing costs	Backward-compatible with DOCSIS 1.0—released April 1999
2.0	Faster performance for downloading and uploading compared to DOCSIS 1.0 and 1.1, supports high-speed two-way business services	Backward-compatible with DOCSIS 1.1—released December 2001
3.0	Faster performance up to more than 300Mbps, channel bonding, support for Internet Protocol version 6 (IPv6)	Backward-compatible with DOCSIS 2.0—released August 2006
3.1	Faster performance up to 10GGbps downstream and 1Gbps upstream	Backward-compatible with DOCSIS 3.0—released in 2013

Many cable providers now require modems that are DOCSIS 2.0 or 3.0 certified to provide stated performance. Older DOCSIS 1.1 or earlier modems might work, but only at lower speeds. The latest high-speed (50Mbps or faster) connections require DOCSIS 3.0, which uses channel bonding to achieve higher speeds. Check with your cable service provider for the minimum required standard before you purchase or install a cable modem. To verify the certification level of a specific modem, you can check the modem specifications on the manufacturer's website or look it up in the current cable modem certification list (Certified_Products.pdf or cert_qual.xls), which you can download from CableLabs (www.cablemodem.com). Most cable modems also have their own built-in web page, which can show DOCSIS version and modem status information. To view the page, enter **192.168.100.1** in the address bar of your web browser, and press Enter. If you are suddenly experiencing problems with your cable modem, I recommend you contact your provider to find out if the requirements have changed. If so, you may need an upgraded modem.

Note

Cable Internet providers have greatly increased connection speeds over the years. If your cable modem is several years old, it may only conform to the DOCSIS 1.1 or older standards, which may be limiting your connection speeds. For example, I had been using a DOCSIS 1.1 modem and (according to Speedtest.net) was experiencing download speeds of greater than 8Mbps and upload speeds of greater than 2Mbps. After replacing my DOCSIS 1.1 modem with a newer DOCSIS 2.0 model, my connection speeds increased to greater than 20Mbps download and greater than 8Mbps upload—nearly triple the performance! Since DOCSIS 2.0 is limited to a maximum of 38Mbps, when I subscribed to a 50Mbps connection I had to replace the modem again. DOCSIS 3.0 modems supporting up to 304Mbps are required for most of the higher connection speeds offered today.

Although most cable modems are now available for about $50–$100, you should check with your CATV Internet provider before purchasing one to determine which models your provider supports and whether your CATV Internet provider still requires you to lease the cable modem.

If you plan to keep cable modem service for more than a year, I recommend purchasing a CableLabs Certified cable modem, but if you're unsure of your long-term plans, leasing isn't all that expensive. Typical lease costs for the device are about $5/month.

Cable modems normally come in an external box that has a cable connection for connecting to the cable network, along with USB and Ethernet ports to connect to your network. Although you can connect the cable modem directly to a single PC via USB, this is not recommended for security reasons as well as for sharing the connection. By connecting the cable modem to a router, you can share the connection among several PCs, with the router's built-in firewall providing security and protection. Some cable modems include a built-in router, although I prefer to keep them as separate units. If the router is built in, you can disable it and use an external router if you choose. A typical cable modem is shown in Figure 16.2.

Cable Bandwidth

Cable TV uses what is known as a *broadband network*, meaning the bandwidth of the connection is split to simultaneously carry many signals at different frequencies. These signals correspond to the channels you see on your TV. A typical HFC network provides approximately 750MHz of bandwidth.

For data networking purposes, cable systems typically allocate bandwidth in the 50MHz–750MHz range for downstream traffic—that is, traffic coming into the cable modem from the CATV network. In this way, the cable modem functions as a tuner, just like your cable TV box, ensuring that your PC receives signals from the correct frequency.

DOCSIS cable modems use 6MHz channels that can carry up to 38Mbps downstream or 27Mbps upstream. DOCSIS 2.0 and earlier allow using only a single channel each way, meaning they are limited to 38Mbps maximum downstream. DOCSIS 3.0 allows for bonding multiple channels, and because most DOCSIS 3.0 modems use four or eight bonded channels down, that would allow up to 152Mbps or 304Mbps downstream speed. Although those are the maximum figures, what you really get depends on your provisioned rate (that is, what the Internet service provider [ISP] agrees to give you) and may be limited by other bottlenecks in the network or in your system.

FIGURE 16.2 Front (left) and rear (right) views of a typical cable modem showing status LEDS on the front and power, LAN, USB and cable connections on the rear.

Cable Pricing

Most cable providers offer a number of different connection speed plans providing various download and upload speeds, ranging from as slow as 2Mbps to as fast as 100Mbps or higher. Some ISPs require you to subscribe to their cable TV service or may provide a lower monthly rate if you bundle cable Internet with other services, such as TV or phone.

Business-class cable pricing for comparable download/upload speeds tends to be higher because of additional services such as static IP addresses, a greater number of email addresses provided, and 24/7 customer support.

Whether you are considering residential or business-class service, keep in mind that upload speeds are typically much slower than download speeds, ranging from 10% to 20% of download speeds.

There may be equipment costs in addition to the monthly fees. For example, most ISPs provide cable modem rental for a few dollars a month, or you can purchase your modem outright from the ISP or from other vendors. Unless you need cable Internet service for just a few months, it makes more sense to buy a cable modem than to rent one.

Digital Subscriber Line

The biggest rival to the cable modem in the broadband Internet business is the digital subscriber line (DSL). DSL, like its predecessor Integrated Services Digital Network (ISDN), appeals to the telephone companies who might be able to use the existing plain old telephone service (POTS) wiring to provide high-speed Internet access. DSL is also appealing to businesses that don't have access to cable modems but are looking for a high-performance, lower-cost alternative to ISDN or T-1/T-3 leased line services.

Note

Some technical discussions of DSL refer to *xDSL*. The x stands for the various versions of DSL being proposed and offered by local telephone companies and ISPs. DSL generally refers to any type of digital subscriber line service.

How DSL Works

DSL takes advantage of the broadband nature of the telephone system, using the system's capability to carry signals at multiple frequencies to allow both high-speed Internet traffic and phone calls at the same time. Two methods for sending and receiving signals are used by the most common type of DSL, Asymmetric DSL (ADSL):

- Carrierless Amplitude/Phase (CAP)
- Discrete Multitone (DMT)

Most early DSL installations used CAP, which splits the telephone line into three frequency bands. Exact frequency usage varies by system, but most typically, the divisions resemble the following:

- Voice calls use frequencies from 30Hz to 4KHz. This frequency is also used by answering machines, fax machines, and alarm systems.

- Upstream data such as web page requests and sent email uses frequencies between 25Hz and 160Hz.

- Downstream data such as received web pages and email uses frequencies between 240KHz and 1.5MHz.

Some systems use the 300Hz–700Hz range for downstream data and frequencies of 1MHz and above for upstream data.

Because voice, downstream data, and upstream data use different frequencies, the telephone and Internet connections can be used at the same time.

DMT, the system used by most recent ADSL installations, divides the telephone line into 247 channels that are 4KHz wide. If a particular channel has problems, a different channel with better signal quality is used automatically. Unlike CAP, DMT uses some channels starting at around 8KHz to send and receive information.

Both types of signaling can have problems with interference from telephones and similar devices, so devices called *low-pass filters* prevent telephone signals from interfering with signals above the 4KHz range, where DSL signals begin. The location of these filters depends on the type of DSL you use and whether you are installing DSL service yourself.

At the central switch, DSL data is transferred to a device called a *DSL access multiplexer* (DSLAM), which transfers outgoing signals to the Internet and sends incoming signals to the correct DSL *transceiver* (the correct name for the so-called "DSL modem" that connects to your computer).

DSL Availability

Just as distance to a telephone company's central switch (CS) is an important consideration for people purchasing an ISDN connection, distance also affects who can use DSL in the markets offering it. For example, most DSL service types require that you be within about 18,000 feet (about 3 miles) wire distance to a telephone company (telco) offering DSL; some won't offer it if you're beyond 15,000 feet wire distance because the speed drops significantly at longer distances. Repeaters or a local loop that has been extended by the telco with fiber-optic line might provide longer distances. The speed of your DSL connection varies with distance: The closer you are to the telco, the faster your DSL access is. Many telcos that offer some type of DSL service provide websites that help you determine whether, and what type of, DSL is available to you.

If you want to locate DSL service providers in your area, compare rates, and see reviews from users of the hundreds of ISPs now providing DSL service, set your browser to www.dslreports.com. The site provides a verdict on many of the ISPs reviewed, summarizing users' experiences and ranking each ISP in five categories.

Major Types of DSL

Although the term *DSL* is used in advertising and popular discussions to refer to any form of DSL, many, many variations of DSL are used in different markets and for different situations. This section discusses the most common forms of DSL and provides a table that compares the various types of DSL service. Although many types of DSL service exist, the two most popular types are ADSL and SDSL:

- **ADSL (Asymmetrical DSL)**—Most often used, especially in residential installations. Asymmetrical means that downstream (download) speeds are much faster than upstream (upload) speeds. For most users, this is no problem because downloads of web pages, graphics, and files are the major use of Internet connections. Maximum downstream speeds can be as high as 24Mbps, with up to 3.5Mbps upstream. Most vendors who offer ADSL provide varying levels of service at lower speeds and prices, as well. Voice calls are routed over the same wire using a small amount of bandwidth, making a single-line service that carries voice and data possible.

- **SDSL (Symmetrical DSL)**—Provides the same speed for upstream as for downstream service. Generally, SDSL is offered to business rather than residential customers because it requires new cabling (rather than reusing existing phone lines). A long-term contract frequently is required.

- **VDSL (Very High-Data-Rate DSL)**—Provides much faster service than traditional ADSL or SDSL services, but requires a connection within 5,000 wire feet of the telco. VDSL takes advantage of telco's gradual replacement of traditional copper wiring with fiber-optic lines to carry signals to the neighborhood, curb, or directly to your home. To make the final leg of the connection, VDSL can be implemented over copper wires, coaxial cable, or Ethernet cable. AT&T sells VDSL as AT&T U-verse. Verizon FiOS provides a VDSL-like service that supports digital cable TV, phone, and Internet via fiber-optic service to the home.

Note

Fiber to the home (FTTH), Fiber to the premises (FTTP), Fiber to the curb (FTTC), and Fiber to the neighborhood (FTTN) describes the replacement of conventional copper telephone or coaxial cable TV connections with fiber-optic cables. Fiber-optic cables carry many more signals much faster than conventional wiring.

Rolling out fiber-optic cables for at least part of the DSL or cable infrastructure is essential to achieving higher speeds and greater numbers of services. FTTx rollouts are taking place in larger cities and metropolitan areas first, and will take longer to happen in smaller cities and towns.

Just as with a cable modem, you should connect a DSL modem to computers through a router or gateway, which is then connected to one or more computers. Where a DSL modem differs from a cable modem is how the Internet connection is made. DSL modems are connected to the Internet via a standard telephone cable attached between the DSL modem and the RJ-11 port that has been set up for DSL service. To prevent DSL signals from interfering with standard voice telephone operation, splitters and microfilters must be installed on a DSL line where any phones are connected.

Note

Many DSL modems now include wired and wireless routers or gateways.

If you self-install DSL, you will normally install small devices called microfilters to block the DSL signal from reaching telephones, answering machines, and similar devices. These devices might fit behind the faceplate of the wall outlet used for DSL service or the inline between the phone, answering machine, or fax machine and the wall outlet (see Figure 16.3).

DSL Installation with In-line Microfilter

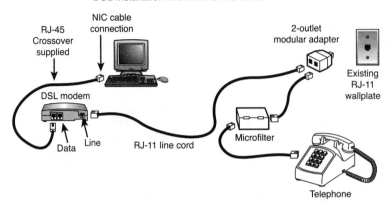

DSL Installation with Wall Outlet Microfilter

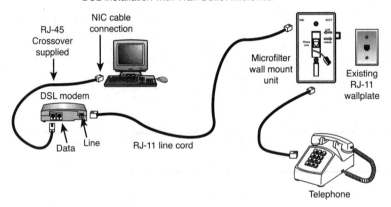

FIGURE 16.3 Two types of DSL self-installations—one featuring a standalone splitter and separate microfilter, the other with a splitter and microfilter integrated into a wall jack.

Tip

If you have a security system attached to your telephone line, watch out for problems if you select DSL as your preferred broadband access method. Security systems are often designed to seize the line, interrupting a phone call in progress to send an alarm to the security company. This feature may not work with normal microfilters. Contact your DSL or security system provider to see whether a special filter is required.

DSL Pricing

DSL pricing varies widely, with different telephone companies offering different speeds of DSL and different rates. One thing that's true about the most commonly used flavors of DSL is that they are usually an asymmetrical service—with download speeds faster than upload speeds. ADSL installations can typically be run over existing copper wires, whereas SDSL installations usually require that new high-quality copper wires be installed between the telco's central office (CO) and the subscriber's location.

There are equipment costs in addition to the monthly fees. AT&T normally includes a DSL modem that includes a wireless router with the service contract; however, you can purchase or supply your own if you wish.

Although the standard pricing lists place DSL at a higher monthly cost than dial-up, if you dig deeper you can find bargain DSL services in many areas. There can be restrictions on these special low-cost offers, but if you are on a budget and want to get away from dial-up (and who wouldn't?), contact the DSL providers in your area and ask about the lowest possible rates. To learn more about these low-cost offers, you can do a search online for "$9.95 DSL" or "$14.95 DSL."

Wireless Broadband

If cable modem or DSL service isn't available at your location, you still might be able to get broadband Internet service through a fixed-base wireless broadband Internet provider, also called a *Wireless Internet Service Provider* (WISP). These services use various frequencies of microwave signals to connect to the Internet. Most of these are based on the same 2.4GHz frequencies 802.11 Wi-Fi connections use. These services typically require a small directional panel antenna to be mounted at the highest point on your roof and must have a clear line-of-sight view of the transmitter, which is usually mounted on a tower only a few miles away. Such services are therefore local, so you generally need to check your area to see whether they are available. Normally, I recommend fixed-base wireless only if cable modem or DSL service is unavailable, but I'd place it as a better overall choice than satellite service. In general, the initial equipment fees are less than satellite and the signals are more immune to weather problems. To find a WISP in your area, start with the Wireless Internet Service Providers Association (WISPA) at www.wispa.org and www.wispdirectory.com/.

Cellular Broadband 3G and 4G Services

Cell phone providers also offer high-speed Internet access through the cellular network. This is usually in the form of a wireless router, hotspot, or dedicated USB stick device, as well as ExpressCard or mini PCI Express cards for laptop systems.

Whereas most cellular broadband connections are made with a dedicated cellular modem, in many cases you can also connect through your existing cell phone by attaching the phone to the system via USB or Bluetooth (called *tethering*) and then using the phone as a high-speed modem connection. Some phones only allow tethering via USB, whereas others support both USB and Bluetooth. For example, using my laptop, I can link to the cell phone in my pocket via Bluetooth and then instruct the cell phone to connect to the Internet, in essence creating a double-wireless connection.

3G Mobile Broadband Service

The connection speeds available depend on the carrier and services offered, but so-called 3G (Third Generation) technologies offer speeds in the 400Kbps–700Kbps range. Although this is quite a bit less than the 11MBps provided by the most basic Wi-Fi hotspots, this type of service is available anywhere you can get a cell phone signal. Note that connections via a tethered cell phone are generally much lower in performance (depending on the phone) than via dedicated cards.

"4G" Mobile Broadband Service

There are three competing technologies marketed as "4G" in the US: WiMAX, long term evolution (LTE), and evolved high speed packet access (HSPA+). WiMAX and LTE are also widely used in international markets.

WiMAX (Worldwide Interoperability for Microwave Access) can be used for both mobile and fixed-base wireless broadband. However, WiMAX is being positioned primarily as a mobile solution. WiMAX is based on the 802.16 standard, with support for maximum data rates of up to 365Mbps. WiMAX uses orthogonal frequency division multiple access (OFDMA) signaling, which uses simultaneous broadcast of radio waves across different frequencies to avoid interference. In the United States, WiMAX is the basis for Sprint's 4G network.

LTE is based on GSM and UTMS cellular systems, hence its name. LTE uses the 700MHz radio frequency and is designed to reach a theoretical peak speed of around 100Mbps. In the United States, Verizon is the major user of LTE, and in real-world tests performed by ComputerWorld in February 2011, LTE averaged around 13.1Mbps download—or about 3 times faster than WiMAX and about 5.5Mbps upload speed (over 100 times faster than WiMAX).

HSPA+ is the technology T-Mobile and AT&T used to upgrade its 3G network in 2010. Although HSPA+ is technically a 3G service, it reaches real-world speeds of around 5–6Mbps, hence the marketing of HSPA+ as "4G."

Although all major U.S. wireless carriers offer some sort of 4G wireless broadband, coverage is limited to major cities. Until networks are completely converted to 4G by mid-decade, wireless broadband service outside of major cities will continue to be made at 3G speeds. Most "4G" connections are made with wireless hub, hotspot, or USB stick modems that can switch between 3G and 4G networks (some automatically, some manually).

Note

The International Telecommunication Union has blessed the marketing of so-called "4G" services by reversing its previous determination that only LTE-Advanced and WiMAX 2 (released in 2012) qualify as true 4G service. In December 2010, ITU announced that faster than 3G services can also be identified as 4G, and will use the blanket term IMT-Advanced to refer to LTE-Advanced and WiMAX 2 (formally WirelessMAN-Advanced).

In general, you must purchase a wireless hub, hotspot, USB stick, or WWAN card along with a service package from your cell phone provider. Because the service packages and networks vary and the technologies are constantly changing, you should contact your local cell phone providers for more information on their current offerings. Although cellular broadband is typically a good bit more expensive than normal cable or DSL connection prices, cellular broadband can be worthwhile for those who travel with a laptop and require access away from hotel rooms or Wi-Fi hotspots.

Satellite Broadband

If you're in a rural area where cable, DSL, or cellular wireless services don't exist, you might be able to use a satellite connection as an alternative.

Satellite service requires a small satellite dish as part of the necessary hardware, which is similar to the dishes used for satellite TV services, except that it functions both for receiving and sending data. The dish is connected to a satellite modem, which is functionally identical to a cable or DSL modem as far as setup and operation is concerned. Some satellite modems contain a router, making them suitable for a direct connection to a single PC or a network switch supporting multiple PCs. Those that don't include a built-in router should be connected to the wireless area network (WAN) port on a router, which would then be connected to one or more PCs.

Most satellite services require a clear view of the sky toward the equator because the satellites are located above the equator.

Note

Geosynchronous satellites used for satellite Internet/TV service are visible in the southern sky for users in the Northern Hemisphere (North America, Europe, and Asia); if you're in the Southern Hemisphere (South America, Australia, Africa), these satellites are located in the northern sky.

Satellite Internet services are generally slower and more expensive than cable, DSL, or fixed wireless and generally should not be considered where those alternatives are available. However, for people living in rural areas, satellite is often the only type of broadband connection available. The main providers of satellite Internet in the United States are HughesNet, WildBlue, and StarBand.

HughesNet

HughesNet was originally called DirecPC when service began in 1996, but Hughes Network Systems renamed it DirecWay in mid-2001, shortly after rolling out a two-way version of the service, and then renamed it again to HughesNet in 2006. The original version of DirecPC was a one-way service that used satellite for downloading and a conventional dial-up modem for uploading. Starting in 2002, this was replaced with a two-way satellite connection.

HughesNet offers satellite service to the 48 contiguous states and southern Canada using 12 satellites in geosynchronous orbit above the equator, along with multiple Earth-based gateways acting as up/down links between the satellites and the Internet. HughesNet uses both the Ku and Ka bands, depending on location and equipment. The Ku band covers the target area with a single broad beam, whereas the Ka band uses spot beams. New installs use the Ka band unless location issues preclude it. On July 5, 2012, Hughes successfully launched its next-generation EchoStar XVII satellite into space, allowing for dramatic increases in bandwidth for its customers. Based on this new satellite, HughesNet introduced its "Gen4" service in October 2012, which offers download speeds of up to 15Mbps.

The HughesNet hardware usually consists of a 0.74m (29-inch) oval dish plus an external satellite modem. The modem has a built-in router with an Ethernet connection. A larger optional 0.98m (39-inch) round dish is available for fringe areas or for business use, along with an optional higher powered (2W vs. 1W) radio transmitter. HughesNet offers several plans with varying download/upload speeds as follows:

Standard

- **Basic**—1.0Mbps/0.2Mbps
- **Power 150**—1.5Mbps/0.25Mbps
- **Power 200**—2.0Mbp/0.3Mbps

Gen4

- **Power**—10Mbps/1Mbps
- **Power Pro**—10Mbps/2Mbps
- **Power Max**—15Mbp/2Mbps

Note

HughesNet has download limits per day that vary by service level. See http://legal.hughesnet.com/FairAccessPolicy.cfm for details.

There are equipment costs in addition to the monthly fees. There are options for larger dishes and more powerful transmitters for more robust performance and fringe areas, as well as business plans with higher speeds than available for residential.

WildBlue

WildBlue is the newest of the major satellite providers, with service beginning in June 2005. WildBlue offers satellite service to the 48 contiguous states and southern Canada using two satellites in geo stationary orbit above the equator, along with multiple gateways acting as up/down links between the satellites and the Internet. WildBlue uses the Ka band exclusively and covers the target area with spot beams instead of a single broad beam, as with the older Ku band equipment used by others.

The WildBlue hardware consists of a 28 inches × 26 inches (50.8cm ×66cm) dish plus an external satellite modem. The modem has an Ethernet connection, which should normally be connected to the WAN port on a router, allowing Internet access to all the PCs on the network.

Note

WildBlue's Fair Access Policy (FAP) covers both download and upload traffic during a rolling 30-day period, with amounts that vary by service. For more information, see www.wildblue.com/fap/index.jsp.

WildBlue offers several plans with varying download/upload speeds as follows:

- **Value**—0.512Mbps/0.128Mbps
- **Select**—1Mbps/0.2Mbps
- **Pro**—1.5Mbps/0.256Mbps

There are equipment costs in addition to the monthly fees.

StarBand

In April 2000, StarBand—the first consumer-oriented two-way satellite network—was introduced after being tested as Gilat-At-Home. In 2005, StarBand was acquired by Spacenet, which also provides business satellite services under the Connexstar name.

StarBand offers satellite service to the 48 contiguous states as well as Hawaii, Alaska, Puerto Rico, and the U.S. Virgin Islands. StarBand uses the Ku band and covers the target area with a single broad beam.

The StarBand hardware normally consists of a 24-inch × 36-inch elliptical-shaped dish plus an external satellite modem. The modem has a built-in router with an Ethernet connection. A larger optional 1.2m (47-inch) round dish along with a higher performance radio is used for coverage in Hawaii, Alaska, Puerto Rico, and the U.S. Virgin Islands. StarBand offers three plans with the following download/upload speeds:

- **Nova 500**—.512Mbps/.1Mbps
- **Nova 1000**—1Mbps/0.128Mbps
- **Nova 1500**—1.5Mbps/0.256Mbps

Note

StarBand's FAP is based on a rolling 7-day period that does not apply to downloads between midnight and 6:00 a.m. For details, see www.starband.com/aup.html.

There are equipment costs in addition to the monthly fees.

Satellite Performance Issues

Benchmark addicts will find that satellite Internet access performs poorly on ping tests. The complex pathway the data must travel (ground to space and back again) results in pings taking at least 400ms–600ms. Interactive benchmarks are also disappointing. The delays caused by communicating with a geosynchronous satellite over 22,500 miles in space make satellite a poor choice for these applications, although download speeds are significantly faster than dial-up modems. Although they vary widely, speeds of 1,000Kbps are common, and some can reach download speeds of more than 2,000Kbps. To achieve results like this, use the tips available on the various forums and sites covering satellite connections to adjust your system's configuration.

Weather can be a problem for satellite connections, but not in the way you might think. Clouds and storms don't generally affect the signal, unless the storm is so severe you should probably be taking shelter anyway. What can be a problem, however, is snow and ice accumulation on the dish. If you live in an area where it snows, you can have signal problems even though the sky is clear; those problems are invariably caused by snow and ice accumulation on the dish. With that in mind, try to have the dish mounted in a location where you can access it to brush off any snow and ice accumulation.

Because of the higher latency, slower overall speeds, limits on downloads and uploads, greater equipment costs, and sensitivity to snow and ice, few would recommend satellite service when alternatives are available. But when the only alternative is dial-up or an expensive T1 line, satellite is the next best option. Although the costs are higher than cable modem or DSL access, satellite might be the only even remotely cost-effective option for people outside urban areas. Many people have creatively adapted the dishes for use on recreational vehicles when stationary or in various tripods and platforms for use while camping.

Living Within Your FAP Budget

The fair access plan (FAP) features of all satellite services are a challenge to live within, especially with frequent OS updates, streaming video, and other high-bandwidth uses for the Internet. Here are some ways to avoid exceeding your download or upload budget:

- Use download managers to schedule large downloads overnight.

- Instead of using Windows Update to download large files such as service packs or programs such as Windows Live Essentials, download a single installation program that you can distribute via your network to other users.

- Use the service's usage checking feature to determine whether your usage is getting close to the limits set by the service.

- If you consistently get close to or exceed the bandwidth limits, consider upgrading to another plan that offers higher limits.

ISDN

The connection speed of dial-up modems is limited by Shannon's Law. (See the section "56Kbps Modems," later in this chapter.) To surpass the speed limitations of dial-up modems, you need to use a digital signal. ISDN was the first step in the move to digital telecommunications. With ISDN, you can connect to the Internet at speeds of up to 128Kbps. Because the telephone companies developed ISDN, you can purchase a variety of service plans. Depending on the ISDN service you choose, you can use it strictly for Internet service or to service multiple telephony applications such as voice, fax, and teleconferencing.

Depending on where you live, you might find that ISDN service is available for Internet uses, or your local telco might offer faster DSL service as an alternative. Because ISDN was not originally designed for Internet use, its speed is much lower than other broadband options. Also, ISDN costs about twice what a typical ADSL or cable modem connection costs per month. To determine whether a particular Internet service is using ISDN, you might need to ask the ISP. For example, AT&T uses the term "Digital Enhancer" for its ISDN BRI offering in Connecticut, and "Digiline Service" in several plains states.

ISDN doesn't require as high a line quality as DSL, so it can be offered in areas where DSL can't work without a major upgrade of the telephone system.

Leased Lines

For users with high bandwidth requirements (and deep pockets), dedicated leased lines provide digital service between two locations at broadband speeds. A *leased line* is a permanent 24-hour connection to a particular location that only the telephone company can change. Businesses use leased lines to connect local area networks (LANs) in remote locations or to connect to the Internet through a service provider. Leased lines are available at various speeds, as described in this section.

To connect networks in distant locations, networks that must support a large number of Internet users, or especially organizations that will be hosting their own Internet services, a T-1 connection might be a wise investment. A *T-1* is a digital connection running at about 1.5Mbps. A T-1 can be split (or *fractioned*), depending on how it is to be used. It can be split into 24 individual 64Kbps lines or left as a single high-capacity pipeline. Some ISPs allow you to lease any portion of a T-1 connection that you want in 64Kbps increments (or *fractions*). Figure 16.4 shows how a T-1 line is fractioned.

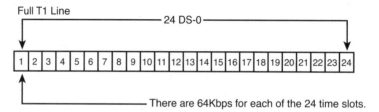

FIGURE 16.4 Full T-1 service uses all 24 lines (each one is 64Kbps) as a single pipeline; a fractional T-1 service of 256Kbps could use slots 1–4 only, for example.

An individual user of the Internet interacts with a T-1 line only indirectly. No matter how you're accessing the Internet, your ISP typically will have a connection to one or more T-1 or T-3 lines, which connect to the backbone of the Internet. This connection to the backbone is sometimes referred to as a *point of presence* (PoP). When you connect to the Internet, your ISP shares a small chunk of that pipe with you. Depending on how many other users are accessing the Internet at your ISP or elsewhere, you might experience very fast to slow throughput, even if your modem connection speed remains constant. It's a bit like splitting up a pizza into smaller and smaller slices to accommodate more people at a party: The more users of a high-speed connection, the slower each part of it will be. To keep user connections fast while growing, ISPs add full or fractional T-1 lines to their points of presence. Or, they might switch from a T-1 connection to the even faster T-3, if available.

Note

Equivalent in throughput to approximately 28 T-1 lines, a T-3 connection runs at 45Mbps and is suitable for use by large networks and university campuses. Pricing information falls into the "if-you-have-to-ask-you-can't-afford-it" category.

With the rise of the Internet and the demand for high-speed data access for networks, the price of T-1 links in the United States has fallen drastically since the late 1990s, although you will still pay in the hundreds of dollars for typical service offerings. T-1 service can be acquired from either your local telco or third-party firms. Fractional T-1 or burstable T-1 (which allows you to have differing levels of bandwidth, up to the entire T-1 1.5Mbps, depending on demand) costs less than full T-1 service. For a large organization that requires a lot of bandwidth, the lower cost of T-1 services today makes installing a higher-capacity service and growing into it—rather than constantly upgrading the link—more economical than ever.

Comparing High-Speed Internet Access

One way of making sense out of the confusing morass of plans available from cable modem, DSL, fixed wireless Internet, and satellite vendors is to calculate the average cost per Mbps of data downloaded ($/Mbps). You can calculate this figure yourself by dividing the service cost per month by the rated or average speed of the service:

Cost ($) / Speed (Mbps) = $/Mbps

You can use this formula with any broadband or dial-up service to find the best values. Note that this simple calculation doesn't take into account the cost of any required equipment, such as modems, filters, satellite dishes, and so on. If you must pay extra for equipment or installation upfront, divide the upfront cost by the number of months you plan to keep the service and add the result to the monthly service charge to get an accurate figure.

Note

The examples in this section assume unlimited usage. If you use metered broadband (available in some cable and many wireless data plans), be sure to add in the cost of any overages you typically incur in a billing cycle.

For example, if cable modem service costs around $45 per month and has an average (not peak) speed of 12Mbps, divide $45 by 12Mbps, and the cost is $3.75 per Mbps. The only extra equipment generally required is a cable modem, which you can purchase for around $50 or rent for around $5 per month.

By comparison, the basic DSL service from AT&T costs around $20 per month (it can be as low as $10 per month if you qualify for that rate) and has a speed of 0.768Mbps. Divide $20 by 0.768Mbps, and the cost is $26 per Mbps, or only $13 per Mbps at the $10 rate. The only extra equipment generally required is a DSL modem and some microfilters, which you can purchase for around $50 or rent for around $5 per month.

How does a typical 56Kbps modem compare, assuming 50Kbps (0.05Mbps) download speeds? Using the basic dial-up service from NetZero ($10 per month), the cost works out to $200 per Mbps. That is 53 times more money per Mbps for service that is 240 times slower than a typical cable modem.

The services offered in my area stack up as shown in Table 16.2, listed from slowest to fastest download speed.

Table 16.2 Comparing Connection Types and Speeds

Connection Type	Download/Upload Speed (Mbps)
Dial-up	0.05/0.03
Basic DSL	1.5/0.384
Basic satellite	1/0.256
Basic cable	12/2
Premium satellite	15/2
Premium DSL	24/1.5
Premium cable	105/10

The values in Table 16.2 indicate the connection types and speeds available in my area; the offerings and speeds available in your area may vary.

Dial-Up Modems

In areas where broadband connections are not readily available, many people still rely on dial-up modems. This section covers dial-up modems in detail.

The word *modem* (from modulator/demodulator) basically describes a device that converts the digital data used by computers into analog signals suitable for transmission over a telephone line and then converts the analog signals back into digital data at the destination. Because you must dial a telephone number to reach a remote computer, these devices are also referred to as *dial-up modems*. Although dial-up modems are generally thought of as analog devices, 56K (V.9x) modem connections are actually digital. The typical PC modem is an asynchronous device, meaning it transmits data in an intermittent stream of small packets. The receiving system takes the data in the packets and reassembles it into a form the computer can use.

Asynchronous modems transmit each byte of data individually as a separate packet. One byte equals 8 bits, which, using the standard ASCII codes, is enough data to transmit a single alphanumeric character. For a modem to transmit asynchronously, it must identify the beginning and end of each byte to the receiving modem. It does this by adding a start bit before and a stop bit after every byte of data, thus using 10 bits to transmit each byte (see Figure 16.5). For this reason, asynchronous communications have sometimes been referred to as *start-stop* communications. This is in contrast to synchronous communications, in which a continuous stream of data is transmitted at a steady rate.

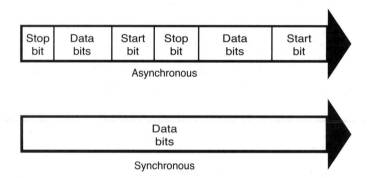

FIGURE 16.5   Asynchronous modems frame each byte of data with a start bit and a stop bit, whereas synchronous communications use an uninterrupted stream of data.

Note

During high-speed modem communications, the start and stop bits are usually not transmitted over the telephone line. Instead, the modem's data compression algorithm eliminates them. However, these bits are part of the data packets generated by the communications software in the computer, and they exist until they reach the modem hardware. If the ends of a modem connection use different values for start and stop bits, the connection transmits gibberish instead of usable data.

The use of a single start bit is required in all forms of asynchronous communication, but some protocols use more than one stop bit. To accommodate systems with different protocols, communications software products usually enable you to modify the format of the frame used to transmit each byte. The standard format that describes an asynchronous communications format is parity/data bits/stop bits. Almost all asynchronous connections today are therefore abbreviated as N-8-1 (No parity/8 data bits/1 stop bit). The meanings for each of these parameters and their possible variations are as follows:

- **Parity**—Before error-correction protocols became standard modem features, a simple parity mechanism provided basic error checking at the software level. Today, this is almost never used, and the value for this parameter is nearly always set to none. Other possible parity values you might see in a communications software package are odd, even, mark, and space.

- **Data bits**—This parameter indicates how many bits are actually carried in the data portion of the packet (exclusive of the start and stop bits). PCs typically use 8 data bits, but some types of computers use a 7-bit byte, and others might call for other data lengths. Communications programs provide this option to prevent a system from confusing a stop bit with a data bit.

- **Stop bits**—This parameter specifies how many stop bits are appended to each byte. PCs typically use 1 stop bit, but other types of protocols might call for the use of 1.5 or 2 stop bits.

In most situations, you will never have to modify these parameters manually, but the controls are almost always provided. In Windows, for example, if you open the Modems control panel and look at the Connection page of your modem's Properties dialog box, you will see Data Bits, Parity, and Stop Bits selectors.

56Kbps Modems

At one time, the V.34 annex speed of 33,600bps (33.6Kbps) was regarded as the absolute speed limit for asynchronous modem usage. However, starting in 1996, modem manufacturers began to produce modems that supported speeds of up to 56,000bps. These so-called "56K" or "56Kbps" modems are now universal, although the methods for breaking the 33.6Kbps barrier have changed several times. To understand how this additional speed was achieved, you must consider the basic principle of modem technology—that is, the digital-to-analog conversion.

As you've learned, a traditional modem converts data from digital to analog form so it can travel over the public switched telephone network (PSTN). At the destination system, another modem converts the analog data back to its digital form. This conversion from digital to analog and back again causes some speed loss. Even though the phone line is physically capable of carrying data at 56Kbps or more, the effective maximum speed because of the conversions is about 33.6Kbps. An AT&T engineer named Claude Shannon came up with a law (Shannon's Law) stating that the maximum possible error-free data communications rate over an all-analog PSTN is approximately 35Kbps, depending on the noise present.

However, because many parts of the United States urban telephone system are digital—being converted to analog only when signals reach the telephone company's central office (or central switch)—it's possible to "break" Shannon's Law and achieve faster download rates. You can, in some cases, omit the initial digital-to-analog conversion and send a purely digital signal over the PSTN to the recipient's CO (see Figure 16.6). Therefore, only one digital-to-analog conversion is necessary, instead of two or more. The result is that you theoretically can increase the speed of the data transmission, in one direction only, beyond the 35Kbps specified by Shannon's Law—to nearly the 56Kbps speed supported by the telephone network. Prior to the new ITU V.92 standard, the transmission in the other direction was still limited to the V.34 annex maximum of 33.6Kbps. However, both the modem and the ISP must have support for the ITU V.92 standard to overcome this limitation for uploading speeds.

◄◄ See the section, "V.92," **p. 793**, for more information on how the V.92 standard enables faster uploading.

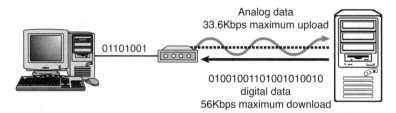

FIGURE 16.6 V.90-based 56Kbps connections enable you to send data at standard analog modem rates (33.6Kbps maximum) but enable you to receive data nearly twice as fast, depending on line conditions.

56Kbps Limitations

Although 56Kbps modems can increase data transfer speeds beyond the limits of V.34 modems (which topped out at 33.6Kbps), they are subject to certain limitations. For example, you can't buy two 56Kbps modems, install them on two computers, and achieve 56Kbps speeds. One side of the connection (the side opposite the PC) must use a special digital modem that connects directly to the PSTN without a digital-to-analog conversion.

Therefore, 56Kbps modems can be used at maximum speeds only to connect to ISPs or other hosting services that have invested in the necessary infrastructure to support the connection. Because the ISP has the digital connection to the PSTN, its downstream transmissions to your computer are accelerated. If both sides of the connection support standards predating V.92, your communications back to the ISP are not accelerated.

Also, only one digital-to-analog conversion can be in the downstream connection from the ISP to your computer. This is dictated by the nature of the physical connection to your local telephone carrier. If additional conversions are involved in your connection, 56Kbps technology will not work for you; 33.6Kbps will be your maximum possible speed.

With the way the telephone system has had to grow to accommodate new exchanges and devices, even neighbors down the street from each other might have different results when using a 56Kbps modem.

Caution

56Kbps modem communications are highly susceptible to slowdowns caused by line noise. Your telephone line might be perfectly adequate for voice communications and even lower-speed modem communications, but inaudible noise easily can degrade a 56Kbps connection to the point at which there is only a marginal increase over a 33.6Kbps modem, or even no increase at all. If you do have a problem with line noise, getting a surge suppressor with noise filtration might help.

Hotel connections through telephones with data jacks typically provide slow connections with any type of modem. Even if you have a V.90- or V.92-compliant 56Kbps modem, you will be lucky to achieve even a 24Kbps transmission rate. The analog-to-digital conversions that occur between your room's telephone and the hotel's digital PBX system eliminate the possibility of using any of the 56Kbps standards the modem supports because they depend on a direct digital connection to the CS.

56Kbps Standards

To achieve a high-speed connection, both modems and your ISP (or other hosting service to which you connect) must support the same 56Kbps technology. The first 56Kbps chipsets were introduced in late 1996:

- U.S. Robotics' x2 used Texas Instruments (TI) chipsets.
- Rockwell's K56flex was supported by Zoom and other modem makers.

These rival methods for achieving performance up to 56Kbps were incompatible with each other and were replaced in 1998 by the ITU's V.90 standard.

Unfortunately, the 56Kbps name is rather misleading, in regard to actual transmission speeds. Although all 56Kbps modems theoretically are capable of this performance on top-quality telephone lines, the power requirements for telephone lines specified in the FCC's Part 68 regulation limit the top speed of these modems to 53.3Kbps.

V.90

V.90 was introduced on February 5, 1998, and was ratified by the ITU-T on September 15, 1998. Its ratification ended the K56flex/x2 standards "war." Shortly thereafter, most modem manufacturers announced upgrade options for users of x2 and K56flex modems to enable these products to become V.90 compliant. Most modems manufactured since 1998 support the V.90 protocol.

V.92

56Kbps protocols, such as the early proprietary x2 and K56flex and the ITU V.90 standard, increased the download speed from its previous maximum of 33.6Kbps to 56Kbps. However, upload speeds with any of these 56Kbps technologies are limited to a maximum of 33.6Kbps. Other shortcomings included the amount of time it takes the user's modem to negotiate its connection with the remote modem and the lack of uniform support for call-waiting features.

In mid-2000, the ITU unveiled a multifaceted solution to the problem of slow connections and uploads: the V.92 and V.44 protocols (V.92 was previously referred to as V.90 Plus). Most modems manufactured since mid-2001 to the present are V.92 compatible.

V.92, as the name implies, is a successor to the V.90 protocol, and any modem that supports V.92 also supports V.90. V.92 doesn't increase the download speed beyond the 56Kbps barrier but offers these major features:

- **QuickConnect**—QuickConnect cuts the amount of time needed to make a connection by storing telephone-line characteristics and using the stored information whenever the same phone line is used again. For users who connect to the Internet more than once from the same location, the amount of time the modem beeps and buzzes to make the connection will drop from as much as 27 seconds to about half that time. Bear in mind, though, that this reduction in connection time does not come about until after the initial connection at that location is made and its characteristics are stored for future use.

- **Modem-on-Hold**—The Modem-on-Hold feature allows the user to pick up incoming calls and talk for a longer amount of time than the few seconds allowed by current proprietary call-waiting modems. Modem-on-Hold enables the ISP to control how long you can take a voice call while online without interrupting the modem connection; the minimum amount of time supported is 10 seconds, but longer amounts of time (up to unlimited!) are also supported by this feature. Modem-on-Hold also allows you to make an outgoing call without hanging up the modem connection. Modem-on-Hold, similar to previous proprietary solutions, requires that you have the call-waiting feature enabled on your telephone line and that your ISP supports this feature of V.92.

Note

Although Modem-on-Hold is good for the Internet user with only one phone line (because it allows a single line to handle incoming as well as outgoing calls), it's not as good for ISPs because when you place your Internet connection on hold, the ISP's modem is not capable of taking other calls. ISPs that support Modem-on-Hold might need to add more modems to maintain their quality of service if this feature is enabled. More modems are necessary because the ISP won't be able to count on users dropping their Internet connections to make or receive voice calls when Modem-on-Hold is available.

- **PCM Upstream**—PCM Upstream breaks the 33.6Kbps upload barrier, boosting upload speed to a maximum of 48Kbps. Unfortunately, because of power issues, enabling PCM Upstream can reduce your downstream (download) speed by 1.3Kbps–2.7Kbps or more. PCM Upstream is an optional feature of V.92, and ISPs who support V.92 connections might not support this feature.

Modems that support V.92 typically also support the V.44 data-compression standard. V.44, which replaces V.42bis, provides for compression of data at rates up to 6:1—that's more than 25% better than V.42bis. This enables V.92/V.44 modems to download pages significantly faster than V.90/V.42bis modems can at the same connection speed.

Internet Connection Security

Virtually all forms of Internet connections use some type of external modem, which acts as a bridge between the Internet and your PC or your local network. Many, if not most, of these modems are just modems, and they do not include other functionality such as a router or a switch. Some modems include a built-in router, and others include both a router and a switch. There is an important distinction between them, and you need to know the ramifications before you use them.

The most important thing you can do for security when using a broadband Internet connection is to ensure that you are connected though a router, which acts as a gateway with a hardware firewall between your local network and the Internet. A router includes a DHCP (Dynamic Host Configuration Protocol) server, which allows it to automatically assign private IP (Internet Protocol) addresses to systems on your network. Then, once the addresses are assigned, the router uses Network Address Translation (NAT) to translate packets moving between the private IP addresses on your network and the publicly visible IP address assigned to the router itself. Using NAT, only the router is publicly visible on the Internet; all of the systems behind it are effectively hidden. This provides a hardware firewall to protect the PCs on your network.

If your modem includes multiple Ethernet ports for connecting PCs, most likely it has both a router and a switch built in. In that case, you can connect PCs to the modem/router safely, and the built-in router will protect your systems. If your modem has only a single port, that means it definitely doesn't include a switch and may or may not include a router. If it does include a router, and you only want to connect a single PC, you can connect it directly to the Ethernet port. However, if it doesn't include a router, you need to connect the Ethernet port on the modem to the WAN port on a router and then connect your PC or network to the router.

To determine whether your modem includes a router, consult the manufacturer documentation. If the modem includes a DHCP server and NAT functionality, it has a router. If not, it's just a bare modem with no built-in router.

To secure your network, do the following:

- Change the default password for the router's administrator.
- Change the default SSID for a wireless router—An unauthorized user can look up documentation for a router based on the default SSID and learn default passwords, IP addresses, and other information that can be used to hack your network.

- Use WPA2 encryption with a strong encryption key on your wireless router; all connections to the router must provide the same SSID, encryption type, and encryption key to make a connection.

- Configure wireless routers to accept only wired connections for management (viewing or changing settings).

- Log the MAC address of users who connect to the network and check periodically for unfamiliar devices; use the MAC address filter feature to block unauthorized network devices.

- Limit the number of IP addresses to those you actually need for your client PCs and devices. If your router is configured to supply more IP addresses than devices, unauthorized users can use them.

- Use the Public or block all incoming traffic firewall option for Internet connections made in public places to block all unsolicited incoming traffic.

- With Windows 7/8, use the Home firewall option for a home network (especially if you are going to set up a homegroup).

- With Windows 7/8 or Windows Vista, use the Work or Office firewall options for other types of workgroup networks.

- If only Windows 7/8 users and supported devices are on a home network, set up a homegroup, which is a secure network.

Having a Backup Plan in Case of Service Interruptions

Because no high-speed connection is immune to service interruptions, you should consider having some type of backup plan in place in case of a significant service outage.

If you have a cell phone with 3G or 4G wireless service, you can in many cases use your it as a modem by activating a feature called *tethering*. This normally works by having your cell phone connected to your PC via a USB connection combined with software from the cell phone provider, manufacturer, or a third-party application. The software establishes the device as a network connection, which you can then enable and use to go online. The support and fees for tethering vary, so contact your cell phone provider to find out about tethering plans available to you. While they can be expensive, in an emergency you can temporarily activate the tethering service, and then deactivate it when it is no longer necessary.

Note

If your cell phone provider doesn't have a tethering plan, or if the plan is too expensive or restrictive, there are numerous third-party tethering applications that can work. I recommend searching online to find the options for your specific mobile OS. Examples that are available include PdaNet (www.junefabrics.com) and Tether (www.tether.com). Note that since many if not most of these third-party apps circumvent your carrier's optional tethering plan, you should read your carrier's usage agreement and make sure you understand its policies before deciding if you want to proceed.

If you have a dial-up modem, it can also be used for Internet access in an emergency. Several broadband vendors also offer dial-up connections, such as AT&T (www.att.com), EarthLink (www.earthlink.com), and SpeakEasy (www.megapath.com). Check with your provider in advance, as this might require temporarily activating a service and an extra charge in some cases.

Sharing Your Internet Connection

Whether you have a broadband or dial-up modem connection, one connection is often not enough for a home or small-office setting. You can share your connection with other computer users with one of the following methods:

- **Router-based sharing solutions**—These work by connecting all the computers on a network with a router (or gateway), which is then connected to the modem (or bridge) that is then connected to the Internet.

- **Computer-based sharing solutions**—These work by connecting the computer with Internet access to a network and then using software to make the computer act like a router, sharing the Internet connection with other computers on the network.

Router-based solutions are available for popular types of home and small-office networks, including the following:

- Wired Ethernet
- Wireless (Wi-Fi) Ethernet
- HomePNA (phone-line) networks

Routers for Internet Sharing

Most routers include three devices in one unit. They have a router, which connects to the modem via a WAN (wide area network) port, plus a 4-port switch that allows up to four wired devices to be connected, and finally a wireless access point, which allows multiple devices to be connected wirelessly (see Figure 16.7). Most routers allow up to 255 devices to be connected (combining wired and wireless). If more than four wired devices need to be connected, additional switches can be used to expand the number of wired connections.

When you use a router to share your Internet connection, you connect the modem to the WAN port on the router. All computers on the network then either connect to wired LAN ports or via the router's wireless access point and can share files and printers with each other as well as share Internet access.

The router provides IP addresses to all of the computers or other devices connected and appears as a single connection to the ISP's modem. This prevents the ISP from determining that you're sharing the connection and serves to act as a firewall to protect computers on the network from being directly visible on the internet. The WAN (Internet) port on the router can be configured to obtain an IP address from the cable modem or DSL modem or to have a fixed IP address, depending on the configuration the ISP requires.

FIGURE 16.7   Front (left) and rear (right) views of a typical Wireless N router with a built-in four-port gigabit switch.

As long as the router is running and properly connected to the cable modem or DSL modem, any computer connected to it can go online just by having its email client or web browser opened.

Figure 16.8 shows a typical Ethernet home network configuration that uses a wireless router to share an Internet connection as well as to interconnect several devices via both wired and wireless connections.

▶▶   For more information about choosing and installing wired and wireless networks, see Chapter 17 "Local Area Networking," **p. 799**.

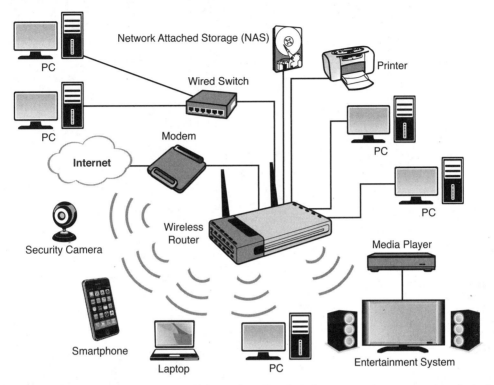

FIGURE 16.8 Using a wireless router to share a broadband modem connection among several wired and wireless devices.

Modem/Router Status LEDs

Status LEDs are found on most external broadband devices, such as broadband modems and routers. The signal lights indicate whether the unit is receiving signals from the computer, sending data to the network or receiving data from the network, as well as whether the unit can "see" the network—even if no data is currently flowing through the unit.

On many units, the power light also indicates problems. If the light is normally green, for example, a red light might indicate the unit has failed. Other lights flash when data is being sent or received. On cable modem or wireless broadband routers, look for a signal lock light; this light flashes if the unit is trying to lock on to a signal from the cable network or wireless transmitter.

Learn the meaning of the lights on your broadband device to help you diagnose problems; the user manual or vendor's website provides the troubleshooting information you need for the particular broadband device you use.

If you are having connection problems, one of the first things you should try is to power off the modem, router, and any switches on your network and then power them back on in the following order: Turn on the modem first, wait about one minute, then the router, and finally any and all of the switches. In some cases, you may need to restart your systems afterward for them to recognize the network and Internet connections.

Local Area Networking

Defining a Network

A network is a group of two or more computers that intelligently share hardware or software devices with each other. A network can be as small and simple as two computers that share a printer or as complex as the world's largest network: the Internet.

Home and SOHO (small-office, home office) networks are typically used to share a single Internet connection, but they can also be used to share other resources, such as printers or multifunction devices. A network enables devices connected to one computer to be shared intelligently with other computers or devices on a network.

Intelligently sharing means that each computer that shares resources with another computer or computers maintains control of that resource. Thus, a USB switchbox for sharing a single printer between two or more computers doesn't qualify as a network device; because the switchbox—not the computers—handles the print jobs, neither computer knows when the other one needs to print, and print jobs can potentially interfere with each other.

A shared printer, on the other hand, can be controlled remotely and can store print jobs from different computers on the print server's hard disk. Users can change the sequence of print jobs, hold them, or cancel them. And, sharing of the device can be controlled through passwords, further differentiating it from a switchbox.

You can share or access many different types of devices over a network, but the most common devices include the following:

- Printers (including multifunction devices)
- Storage devices
- Modems
- Cameras
- Media players/recorders
- Tablets
- Smartphones
- Game consoles

Entire drives or just selected folders can be shared with other users via the network.

In addition to sharing a single Internet connection among multiple users and reducing hardware costs by sharing expensive printers and other peripherals among multiple users, networks provide further benefits to users:

- Electronic mail (email) can be sent and received.
- Multiple users can share access to software and data files.
- Files and folders can be backed up to local or remote shares.
- Audio and video content can be streamed to multiple devices.
- Multiple users can contribute to a single document using collaboration features.
- Remote-control/access programs can be used to troubleshoot problems or show new users how to perform a task.

Types of Networks

Several types of networks exist, from small two-station arrangements, to networks that interconnect offices in many cities:

- **Personal area network (PAN)** is a network created by connections between smartphones, PDAs, and similar computing devices. Most of these connections use Bluetooth networking, so they could more properly be referred to as WPANs (wireless PANs). Because there is no single device controlling or managing the network, PANs and WPANs are examples of ad-hoc networks. The newest example of PAN is Near Field Communication (NFC), which many smartphones use. NFC-enabled smartphones can transfer data by touching the phones together, and some also use NFC to simplify the process of setting up a Bluetooth PAN.

NFC and RFID

NFC was developed from radio frequency ID (RFID) technology. NFC, like RFID, is an ISO/IEC standard, and it has also been adopted by ECMA, the European Computer Manufacturing Association. The standards used by NFC include ISO/IEC 18092 / ECMA-340 Near Field Communication Interface and Protocol-1 (NFCIP-1) and ISO/IEC 21481 / ECMA-352 Near Field Communication Interface and Protocol-2 (NFCIP-2).

NFC signals support three speeds, 106kbps, 212kbps, and 424kbps.

For more information about NFC, see the NFC Forum website at www.nfc-forum.com/home.

- **Local area networks**—The smallest office network is referred to as a *local area network* (LAN). A LAN is formed from computers and components in a single office or building. LANs built from the same components as are used in office networks are also common at home.
- **Metropolitan (or municipal) area network** (MAN) connects two or more locations in the same city using wide area network (WAN) technologies.
- **Wide area networks**—LANs in different locations can be connected by high-speed fiber-optic, satellite, or leased phone lines to form a wide area network (WAN).
- **Wireless wide area networks** (WWANs) use various cellular phone technologies for connections. These are typically 3G and 4G networks.
- **The Internet**—The World Wide Web is the most visible part of the world's largest network, the Internet. The Internet is really a network of networks, all of which are connected to each other through Transmission Control Protocol/Internet Protocol (TCP/IP). It's a glorified WAN in many

respects. Programs such as web browsers, File Transfer Protocol (FTP) clients, and email clients are some of the most common ways users work with the Internet.

- **Intranets**—Intranets use the same web browsers and other software and the same TCP/IP protocol as the public Internet, but intranets exist as a portion of a company's private network. Typically, intranets comprise one or more LANs that are connected to other company networks, but, unlike the Internet, the content is restricted to authorized company users only. Essentially, an intranet is a private Internet.

- **Extranets**—Intranets that share a portion of their content with customers, suppliers, or other businesses, but not with the general public, are called extranets. As with intranets, the same web browsers and other software are used to access the content.

Note

Both intranets and extranets rely on firewalls and other security tools and procedures to keep their private contents private.

Requirements for a Network

Unless the computers that are connected know they are connected and agree on a common means of communication and what resources are to be shared, they can't work together. Networking software is just as important as networking hardware because it establishes the logical connections that make the physical connections work.

At a minimum, each network requires the following:

- Physical (cable) or wireless (usually via radio frequency [RF]) connections between computers.
- A common set of communications rules, known as a *network protocol*.
- Software that enables resources to be served to or shared with other network-enabled devices and that controls access to the shared resources. This can be in the form of a network operating system or NOS (such as older versions of Novell NetWare) that runs on top of an operating system; however, current operating systems (OSs) such as Windows, Mac OS X, and Linux also provide network sharing services, thus eliminating the need for a specialized NOS. A machine sharing resources is usually called a *server*.
- Resources that can be shared, such as printers, drives, modems, media players, and so on.
- Software that enables computers to access other computers sharing resources (servers). Systems accessing shared resources are usually called *network clients*. Client software can be in the form of a program or service that runs on top of an OS. Current OSs such as Windows, Mac OS X, and Linux include client software.

These rules apply both to the simplest and the most powerful networks, and all the ones in between, regardless of their nature. The details of the hardware and software you need are discussed more fully later in this chapter.

Client/Server Versus Peer Networks

Although every device on a LAN is connected to every other device, they do not necessarily communicate with each other. There are two basic types of LANs, based on the communication patterns between the machines: client/server networks and peer-to-peer networks.

Client/Server Networks

On a *client/server* network, every computer has a distinct role: that of either a client or a server. A *server* is designed to share its resources among the client computers on the network. Typically, servers are located in secured areas, such as locked closets or data centers (server rooms), because they hold an organization's most valuable data and do not have to be accessed by operators on a continuous basis. The rest of the computers on the network function as *clients* (see Figure 17.1).

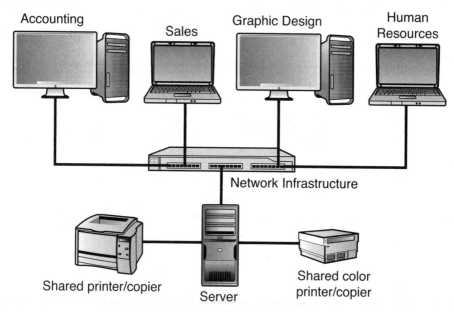

FIGURE 17.1   The components of a client/server LAN.

A dedicated server computer often has faster processors, more memory, and more storage space than a client because it might have to service dozens or even hundreds of users at the same time. High-performance servers typically use from two to eight processors (and that's not counting multicore CPUs), have many gigabytes of memory installed, and have one or more server-optimized network interface cards (NICs), RAID (Redundant Array of Independent Disks) storage consisting of multiple drives, and redundant power supplies. Servers often run a special network OS—such as Windows Server, Linux, or UNIX—that is designed solely to facilitate the sharing of its resources. These resources can reside on a single server or on a group of servers. When more than one server is used, each server can specialize in a particular task (file server, print server, fax server, email server, and so on) or provide redundancy (duplicate servers) in case of server failure. For demanding computing tasks, several servers can act as a single unit through the use of parallel processing.

A client computer typically communicates only with servers, not with other clients. A client system is a standard PC that is running an OS such as Windows. Current OSs contain client software that enables the client computers to access the resources that servers share. Older OSs, such as Windows 3.x and DOS, required add-on network client software to join a network.

Peer-to-Peer Networks

By contrast, on a peer-to-peer network, every computer is equal and can communicate with any other computer on the network to which it has been granted access rights. Essentially, every computer on a peer-to-peer network can function as both a server and a client; any computer on a peer-to-peer network is considered a server if it shares a printer, a folder, a drive, or some other resource with the rest of the network. This is why you might hear about client and server activities, even when the discussion is about a peer-to-peer network.

Peer-to-peer networks can be as small as two computers or as large as hundreds of systems and devices. Although there is no theoretical limit to the size of a peer-to-peer network, performance, security, and access become a major headache on peer-based networks as the number of computers increases. In addition, Microsoft imposes a limit of only 5, 10, or 20 concurrent client connections to computers running Windows. This means that a maximum of 20 (or fewer) systems will be able to concurrently access shared files or printers on a given system. This limit is expressed as the "Maximum Logged On Users" and can be seen by issuing the NET CONFIG SERVER command at a command prompt. This limit is normally unchangeable and is fixed in the specific version and edition of Windows as follows:

- **5 users**—Windows XP Home, Vista Starter/Home Basic
- **10 users**—Windows NT, 2000, XP Professional, Vista Home Premium/Business/Enterprise/ Ultimate
- **20 users**—Windows 7 and 8 (all editions)

When more than the allowed limit of users or systems try to connect, the connection is denied and the client sees one of the following error messages:

```
Operating system error 71. No more connections can be made to this remote com-
puter at this time because there are already as many connections as the computer
can accept. System error 71 has occurred. This remote computer has reached its
connection limit, you cannot connect at this time.
```

Although it is called a "Server" OS, Windows Home Server also has the same 10-connection limit as the non-Home client Windows versions of XP and Vista. If you need a server that can handle more than 10 or 20 clients, I recommend using a Linux-based server OS (such as Ubuntu Server) or one of the professional Windows server products (such as Windows Server 2012, Windows Server 2008 R2 Essential Business Server, or Small Business Server). Peer-to-peer networks are more common in small offices or within a single department of a larger organization. The advantage of a peer-to-peer network is that you don't have to dedicate a computer to function as a file server. Instead, every computer can share its resources with any other. The potential disadvantages to a peer-to-peer network are that typically less security and less control exist because users normally administer their own systems, whereas client/server networks have the advantage of centralized administration.

Note that the actual networking hardware (interface cards, cables, and so on) is the same in client/ server versus peer-to-peer networks; it is only the logical organization, management, and control of the network that varies.

Comparing Client/Server and Peer-to-Peer Networks

Client/server LANs offer enhanced security for shared resources, greater performance, increased backup efficiency for network-based data, and the potential for the use of redundant power supplies and RAID drive arrays. Client/server LANs also are more expensive to purchase and maintain. Table 17.1 compares client/server and peer-to-peer server networking.

Table 17.1 Comparing Client/Server and Peer-to-Peer Networking

Item	Client/Server	Peer-to-Peer
Access control	Via user/group lists of permissions stored on a server; user has access to only the resources granted, and different users can be given different levels of access.	Resources are managed by each system with shared resources. Depending on the OS, resources may be controlled by separate passwords for each shared resource or by a user list stored on each system with shared resources. Some OSs do not use passwords or user/group lists, thus enabling access to shared resources for anyone accessing the network.
Security	High; access is controlled by user or by group identity.	Varies; if password protection is employed, anyone who knows the password can access a shared resource. If no passwords are used, anyone who can access the workgroup can access shared resources. However, if user/group names are used, security is comparable to a client/server network.
Performance	High; the server is dedicated and doesn't handle other tasks.	Low; servers often act as workstations.
Hardware cost	High; specialized high-performance server hardware with redundancy features.	Low; any workstation can become a server by sharing resources
Software cost	Higher; license fees per user are part of the cost of the server OS.	Lower; client software is included with OS.
Backup	Centralized on the server; managed by network administrator. Backup by device and media only required at server.	Decentralized; managed by users. Backup devices and media are required at each workstation.
Redundancy	Yes; duplicate power supplies, hot-swappable drive arrays, and even redundant servers are common; network OS normally is capable of using redundant devices automatically.	No true redundancy among peer "servers" or clients; failures require manual intervention to correct, with a high possibility of data loss.

Network Architecture Overview

The architecture on which you choose to base your network is the single most important decision you make when setting up a LAN. The architecture defines the speed of the network, the medium access control mechanism it uses (for example, collision detection, token passing, and so on), the types of cables you can use, the network interface adapters you must buy, and the adapter drivers you install.

The Institute of Electrical and Electronic Engineers (IEEE) has defined and documented a set of standards for the physical characteristics of networks. Current network standards include IEEE 802.3 (Ethernet) and IEEE 802.11 (Wi-Fi, Wireless Ethernet).

The most common choice today for new networks is Ethernet (both wired and wireless). In rare cases, you may encounter a Token-Ring or ARCnet network. Network data-link architectures you might encounter are summarized in Table 17.2. The abbreviations used for the cable types are explained in the following sections.

Table 17.2 LAN Architecture Summary

Network Type	Speed	Maximum Number of Stations	Transmission Types	Notes
Ethernet	10Mbps	1,024	Category 3 UTP or better (10BASE-T), Thinnet RG-58 coax (10BASE-2), Thicknet coax (10BASE-5), fiber-optic (10BASE-F)	Replaced by Fast Ethernet; backward compatible with Fast or Gigabit Ethernet when using UTP.
Fast Ethernet	100Mbps	1,024	Category 5 UTP or better	Popular wired networking standard, rapidly being replaced by Gigabit Ethernet.
Gigabit Ethernet	1,000Mbps	1,024	Category 5e UTP or better	Recommended for new installations; uses all four signal pairs in the cable.
10 Gigabit Ethernet	10,000Mbps	1,024	Category 6a UTP or better	Uses all four signal pairs in the cable.
802.11a Wireless Ethernet	Up to 54Mbps	1,024	RF 5GHz band	Short range; interoperable with dual-band 802.11n.
802.11b Wireless Ethernet	Up to 11Mbps	1,024	RF 2.4GHz band	Interoperable with 802.11g/n.
802.11g Wireless Ethernet	Up to 54Mbps	1,024	RF 2.4GHz band	Interoperable with 802.11b/n.
802.11n Wireless Ethernet	Up to 600Mbps	1,024	RF 2.4/5GHz bands	Longest range; interoperable with 802.11a/b/g; dual-band hardware needed to interoperate with 802.11a; recommended for new installations.
Token-Ring	4/16/100Mbps	72 on UTP; 250–260 on Type 1 STP	UTP, Type 1 STP, and fiber-optic	Replaced by Ethernet; obsolete for new installations.
ARCnet	2.5Mbps	255	RG-62 coax UTP, Type 1 STP	Replaced by Ethernet; obsolete for new installations; uses the same coax cable as IBM 3270 terminals.

UTP = unshielded twisted pair
STP = shielded twisted pair
RF = Radio Frequency

Wired Ethernet

With tens of millions of computers connected by Ethernet cards and cables, Ethernet is the most widely used data-link layer protocol in the world. You can buy Ethernet adapters from dozens of competing manufacturers, and most systems sold in the past decade incorporate one or more built-in Ethernet ports. Older adapters supported one, two, or all three of the cable types defined in the standard: Thinnet, Thicknet, and unshielded twisted pair (UTP). Current adapters support only UTP. Traditional Ethernet operates at a speed of 10Mbps, but the more recent standards push this speed to 100Mbps (Fast Ethernet) or 1,000Mbps (Gigabit Ethernet). Most desktop and even laptop systems now incorporate Gigabit Ethernet. In the future we will likely see 10 Gigabit Ethernet (also known as 10G Ethernet) appearing in PCs. 10G Ethernet runs at 10,000Mbps and is used primarily in enterprise data centers and servers.

Note

Throughout the remainder of this chapter, be aware that discussion of older Ethernet solutions (such as those using Thicknet or Thinnet) as well as alternative networks (such as Token-Ring) are only included for reference. You will usually encounter those technologies only when working on older, existing networks. New network installations today normally use Gigabit, Fast, or Wireless Ethernet.

Fast Ethernet

Fast Ethernet requires adapters, hubs, switches, and UTP or fiber-optic cables designed to support its rated speed. Some early Fast Ethernet products supported only 100Mbps, but eventually all Fast Ethernet products were combination devices that ran at both 10Mbps and 100Mbps, enabling backward compatibility with older 10Mbps Ethernet network hardware. Today, Fast Ethernet has largely been replaced by Gigabit Ethernet in current network adapters and chipsets.

Note

Some specifications say that Fast Ethernet supports 200Mbps. This is because it normally runs in *full-duplex mode* (sends/receives data simultaneously), which gives it an effective speed of 200Mbps with both directions combined. Still, the throughput in any one direction remains the same (100Mbps). Full-duplex operation requires that all hardware in the connection, including adapters and switches, be capable of running in full-duplex and be configured to run in full-duplex (or automatically detect full-duplex signals).

Both the most common form of Fast Ethernet (100BASE-TX) and 10BASE-T standard Ethernet use two of the four wire pairs found in UTP Category 5 cable. (These wire pairs are also found in CAT 5e, CAT 6, and CAT 6a cable.) An alternative Fast Ethernet standard called 100BASE-T4 uses all four wire pairs in UTP Category 5 cable, but this Fast Ethernet standard was never popular and is seldom seen today.

Gigabit Ethernet

Gigabit Ethernet also requires special adapters, hubs, switches, and cables. When Gigabit Ethernet was introduced, most installations used fiber-optic cables, but today, CAT 5e/6/6a is recommended (and those cable grades are also compatible with Fast Ethernet). Gigabit Ethernet for UTP is also referred to as 1000BASE-T.

Unlike Fast Ethernet and standard Ethernet over UTP, Gigabit Ethernet uses all four wire pairs. Thus, Gigabit Ethernet requires dedicated Ethernet cabling; you can't "borrow" two wire pairs for telephone or other data signaling with Gigabit Ethernet as you can with the slower versions. Almost all Gigabit

Ethernet adapters can also handle 10BASE-T and 100BASE-TX Fast Ethernet traffic, enabling you to interconnect all three UTP-based forms of Ethernet on a single network.

Gigabit Ethernet hardware was initially very expensive, thus limiting the use of Gigabit Ethernet to high-end network interconnections. More recently, the prices of cables, adapters, and especially switches has fallen dramatically, making Gigabit the recommended choice for all new cable, adapter, and switch installations. Most integrated Ethernet adapters in recent systems also support Gigabit Ethernet.

Neither Fast Ethernet nor Gigabit Ethernet supports the use of thin or thick coaxial cable originally used with traditional Ethernet, although you can interconnect coaxial cable–based and UTP-based Ethernet networks by using media converters or specially designed hubs and switches.

10 Gigabit Ethernet

10 Gigabit Ethernet is a high-speed networking standard that incorporates many different types of physical interconnections including several that are fiber optic and copper based. Of all of the possible connection types, the only one relevant to PCs is called 10GBASE-T, which uses standard twisted-pair cables and 8P8C (RJ45) connectors just like Fast and Gigabit Ethernet.

10 Gigabit Ethernet (10GBASE-T) requires Category 6a (or better) cabling for support of connection distances up to 100 meters (328 feet). Lower grade CAT 6 cable can be used if the distance is limited to 55 meters (180 feet). Just as with Gigabit Ethernet, all four pairs in the cable are used.

10 Gigabit Ethernet hardware is currently very expensive, and limited to high-end network interconnections, typically between servers or as a backbone connection between multiple Gigabit Ethernet networks. Once the prices of adapters and switches falls to be close to those for Gigabit Ethernet, we will see 10 Gigabit Ethernet start to become popular for PC-based networks. To prepare for a future upgrade to 10 Gigabit Ethernet, consider installing only Category 6a or better cabling in any new installations.

Wireless Ethernet

The most common forms of wireless networking are built around various versions of the IEEE 802.11 wireless Ethernet standards, including IEEE 802.11b, IEEE 802.11a, IEEE 802.11g, and IEEE 802.11n.

Wireless Fidelity (Wi-Fi) is a logo and term given to any IEEE 802.11 wireless network product certified to conform to specific interoperability standards. Wi-Fi certification comes from the Wi-Fi Alliance, a nonprofit international trade organization that tests 802.11-based wireless equipment to ensure it meets the Wi-Fi standard. To carry the Wi-Fi logo, an 802.11 networking product must pass specific compatibility and performance tests, which ensure that the product will work with all other manufacturers' Wi-Fi equipment on the market. This certification arose from the fact that certain ambiguities in the 802.11 standards allowed for potential problems with interoperability between devices. By purchasing only devices bearing the Wi-Fi logo, you ensure that they will work together and not fall into loopholes in the standards.

Note

The Bluetooth standard for short-range wireless networking, covered later in this chapter, is designed to complement, rather than rival, IEEE 802.11–based wireless networks.

The widespread popularity of IEEE 802.11–based wireless networks has led to the abandonment of other types of wireless networking such as the now-defunct HomeRF.

Note

Although products that are certified and bear the Wi-Fi logo for a particular standard are designed and tested to work together, many vendors of wireless networking equipment created devices that also featured proprietary "speed booster" technologies to raise the speed of the wireless network even further. This was especially common in early 802.11g devices, while newer devices conform more strictly to the official standards. Although these proprietary solutions can work, beware that most, if not all, of these vendor-specific solutions are not interoperable with devices from other vendors. When different vendor-specific devices are mixed on a single network, they use the slower common standard to communicate with each other.

Wi-Fi

When the first 802.11b wireless networking products appeared, compatibility problems existed due to certain aspects of the 802.11 standards being ambiguous or leaving loopholes. A group of companies formed an alliance designed to ensure that their products would work together, thus eliminating any ambiguities or loopholes in the standards. This was originally known as the Wireless Ethernet Compatibility Alliance (WECA) but is now known simply as the Wi-Fi Alliance (www.wi-fi.org). In the past, the term Wi-Fi has been used as a synonym for IEEE 802.11b hardware. However, because the Wi-Fi Alliance now certifies other types of 802.11 wireless networks, the term *Wi-Fi* should always be accompanied by both the standards supported (that is 802.11a/b/g/n) as well as the supported frequency bands (that is 2.4GHz and/or 5GHz) to make it clear which products work with the device. Currently, the Alliance has certified products that meet the final versions of the 802.11a, 802.11b, 802.11g, and 802.11n standards in 2.4GHz and 5GHz bands.

The Wi-Fi Alliance currently uses a color-coded certification label to indicate the standard(s) supported by a particular device. Figure 17.2 shows the most common versions of the label, along with the official IEEE standard(s) that the label corresponds to: 802.11a (orange background); 802.11b (dark blue background); 802.11g (lime green background); 802.11n (violet background).

IEEE 802.11b

IEEE 802.11b (Wi-Fi, 2.4GHz band–compliant, also known as Wireless-B) wireless networks run at a maximum speed of 11Mbps, about the same as 10BASE-T Ethernet (the original version of IEEE 802.11 supported data rates up to 2Mbps only). 802.11b networks can connect to conventional Ethernet networks or be used as independent networks, similar to other wireless networks. Wireless networks running 802.11b hardware use the same 2.4GHz spectrum that many portable phones, wireless speakers, security devices, microwave ovens, and the Bluetooth short-range networking products use. Although the increasing use of these products is a potential source of interference, the short range of wireless networks (indoor ranges up to approximately 150 feet and outdoor ranges up to about 300 feet, varying by product) minimizes the practical risks. Many devices use a spread-spectrum method of connecting with other products to minimize potential interference.

Although 802.11b supports a maximum speed of 11Mbps, that top speed is seldom reached in practice, and speed varies by distance. Most 802.11b hardware is designed to run at four speeds, using one of four data-encoding methods, depending on the speed range:

- **11Mbps**—Uses quaternary phase-shift keying/complementary code keying (QPSK/CCK)
- **5.5Mbps**—Also uses quaternary phase-shift keying/complementary code keying (QPSK/CCK)
- **2Mbps**—Uses differential quaternary phase-shift keying (DQPSK)
- **1Mbps**—Uses differential binary phase-shift keying (DBPSK)

802.11n; also supports
802.11a, 802.11b, and 802.11g

802.11n; also supports
802.11b and 802.11g

802.11g; also supports 802.11b

802.11a; also supports 802.11b and 802.11g

FIGURE 17.2 The Wi-Fi Alliance's certification labels for Wi-Fi–compliant 802.11 hardware.

As distances change and signal strength increases or decreases, 802.11b hardware switches to the most suitable data-encoding method. The overhead required to track and change signaling methods, along with the additional overhead required when security features are enabled, helps explain why wireless hardware throughput is consistently lower than the rated speed. Figure 17.3 is a simplified diagram showing how speed is reduced with distance. Figures given are for best-case situations; building design and antenna positioning can also reduce speed and signal strength, even at relatively short distances.

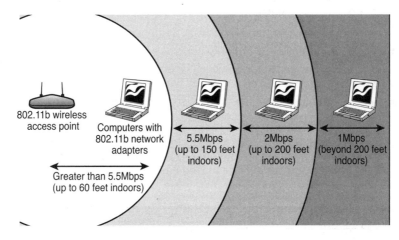

802.11b wireless access point / Computers with 802.11b network adapters / Greater than 5.5Mbps (up to 60 feet indoors) / 5.5Mbps (up to 150 feet indoors) / 2Mbps (up to 200 feet indoors) / 1Mbps (beyond 200 feet indoors)

FIGURE 17.3 At short distances, 802.11b devices can connect at top speed (up to 11Mbps). However, as distance increases, speed decreases because the signal strength is reduced.

Because of its slow speed and support for the weak and easily cracked WEP encryption standard, IEEE 802.11b is obsolete in new installations. However, 802.11b-compliant hardware can interconnect with 802.11g and 802.11n hardware as long as mixed mode and WEP encryption (or no encryption) are used in network configuration.

IEEE 802.11a

The second flavor of Wi-Fi is the wireless network known officially as IEEE 802.11a. 802.11a (also referred to as Wireless-A) uses the 5GHz frequency band, which allows for much higher speeds (up to 54Mbps) and helps avoid interference from devices that cause interference with lower-frequency 802.11b networks. Although real-world 802.11a hardware seldom, if ever, reaches that speed (almost five times that of 802.11b), 802.11a relatively maintains its speeds at both short and long distances.

For example, in a typical office floor layout, the real-world throughput (always slower than the rated speed due to security and signaling overhead) of a typical 802.11b device at 100 feet might drop to about 5Mbps, whereas a typical 802.11a device at the same distance could have a throughput of around 15Mbps. At a distance of about 50 feet, 802.11a real-world throughput can be four times faster than 802.11b. 802.11a has a shorter maximum distance than 802.11b (approximately 75 feet indoors), but you get your data much more quickly.

Given the difference in throughput (especially at long distances), and if we take the existence of 802.11g out of the equation for a moment, why not skip 802.11b altogether? In a single word: *frequency*. By using the 5GHz frequency instead of the 2.4GHz frequency used by 802.11b/g, standard 802.11a hardware cuts itself off from the already vast 802.11b/g universe, including the growing number of public and semipublic 802.11b/g wireless Internet connections (called *hot spots*) showing up in cafes, airports, hotels, and business campuses.

IEEE 802.11a, like 802.11b, is obsolete in new installations. However, 802.11n network adapters that support the optional 5GHz frequency can interconnect with 802.11a adapters, and many late-model 802.11a adapters also support 802.11b or 802.11g (2.4GHz) frequencies.

802.11g

IEEE 802.11g, also known to some as *Wireless-G*, is a standard that offers compatibility with 802.11b along with higher speeds and better security. It runs at speeds up to 54Mbps, the same as 802.11a, but supports the same 2.4GHz frequencies as 802.11b. The final 802.11g standard was ratified in mid-2003.

802.11g supports two standard data-encoding methods:

- QPSK/CCK (same as used by 802.11b), which enables 802.11g to connect with 802.11b devices, albeit at the same 11Mbps maximum speed as Wireless-B
- OFDM (same as used by 802.11a, but in the 2.4GHz band); this method is used for connections at the maximum 54Mbps speed of Wireless-G

Optional data-encoding methods supported by 802.11g include Packet Binary Convolutional Coding (PBCC-22), which supports speeds ranging from 6 to 54Mbps and CCK-OFDM, a method originally used by proprietary 22Mbps versions of 802.11b, and limited to 22Mbps with 802.11g.

Note

Optional data-encoding methods are not supported by all 802.11g hardware.

Although 802.11g is designed to connect seamlessly with existing 802.11b hardware, early 802.11g hardware was slower and less compatible than the specification promised. In some cases, problems with early-release 802.11g hardware can be solved through firmware or driver upgrades.

Note

Although 802.11b/g/n wireless hardware can use the same 2.4GHz frequencies and can coexist on the same networks, when mixing different standards on the same network, the network will often slow down to the lowest common denominator speed. To prevent these slowdowns, you can configure access points to disable "mixed mode" operation, but this will limit the types of devices that can connect. For example, you can configure a 2.4GHz Wireless-N access point to allow 802.11b/g/n connections (full mixed mode), or to only allow 802.11g/n (partial mixed mode) connections, or to only allow 802.11n connections. The latter offers the highest performance for Wireless-N devices. Similarly, you can configure Wireless-G access points to allow 802.11b/g (mixed mode) operation, or to only allow 802.11g connections. Restricting or disabling the mixed mode operation offers higher performance at the expense of restricting the types of devices that can connect.

802.11n

The most common wireless standard in current use, 802.11n (also known as *Wireless-N*), was published in October 2009. 802.11n hardware uses a technology called *multiple input, multiple output (MIMO)* to increase throughput and range. MIMO uses multiple radios and antennas to transmit multiple data streams (also known as *spatial streams*) between stations. Unlike earlier 802.11 implementations, in which reflected radio signals slowed down throughput, reflected radio signals can improve throughput as well as increase useful range.

802.11n uses 64QAM signaling. Quadrature amplitude modulation (QAM) signaling uses two signals that are 90 degrees out of phase with each other, are modulated during transmission, and are recombined when received. QAM signaling modulates signals into multiple points, and the greater the number of points, the higher the signal rates that can be achieved.

Note

To learn more about QAM and other modulation methods, see the tutorials at the Radio-Electronics website: http://www.radio-electronics.com/info/rf-technology-design/pm-phase-modulation/what-is-pm-tutorial.php

802.11n is the first wireless Ethernet standard to support two frequency ranges or bands:

- **2.4GHz** (same as 802.11b/g)—Required by the 802.11n specification
- **5GHz** (same as 802.11a)—An optional feature supported by the 802.11n specification

Thus, depending on the specific implementation of 802.11n in use, a dual-band 802.11n device may be able to connect with 802.11b, 802.11g, and 802.11a devices, whereas a single-band 802.11n device will be able to connect with 802.11b and 802.11g devices only.

Wireless-N devices can contain radios in a number of different configurations supported by the standard. The radios are defined or categorized by the number of transmit antennas, receive antennas, and data streams (also called *spatial streams*) they can support. A common notation has been devised to describe these configurations, which is written as a x b:c, where a is the maximum number of transmit antennas, b is the maximum number of receive antennas, and c is the maximum number of simultaneous data streams that can be used.

The maximum performance configuration supported by the standard is 4 × 4:4, (4 transmit/receive antennas and 4 data streams), which would support bandwidths of up to 600Mbps; a few high-end devices currently support this performance configuration. However, more common configurations that are used in Wireless-N devices include 1 × 1:1, 1 × 2:1, and 2 × 2:1, which include radios with 1 or 2 antennas supporting only a single data stream for up to 150Mbps in bandwidth. Other common configurations include 2 × 2:2, 2 × 3:2, and 3 × 3:2, which include radios with 2 or 3 antennas supporting up to two data streams for up to 300Mbps in bandwidth. Those using more antennas than data streams allow for increased signal diversity and range. The highest performance Wireless-N devices widely available on the market today use a 4 × 4:3 or 3 × 3:3 radio configuration, which supports three data streams for up to 450Mbps in bandwidth.

802.11n is significantly faster than 802.11g, but by how much? That depends mainly on how many data streams are supported, as well as whether a couple of other optional features are enabled or not. The base configuration uses 20MHz wide channels with an 800ns guard interval between transmitted signals. By using channel bonding to increase the channel width to 40MHz, more than double the bandwidth can be achieved in theory. I say "in theory" because using the wider channels works well under very strong signal conditions but can degrade rapidly under normal circumstances. In addition, the wider channel takes up more of the band, causing more interference with other wireless networks in range. In the real world I've seen throughput decrease dramatically with 40MHz channels, such that the use of 40MHz channels is disabled by default on most devices.

Another optional feature is using a shorter guard interval (GI), which is the amount of time (in nanoseconds) the system waits between transmitting OFDM (orthogonal frequency division multiplexing) symbols in a data stream. By decreasing the guard interval from the standard 800ns to an optional 400ns, the maximum bandwidth increases by about 10%. Just as with channel bonding (40MHz channel width), this can cause problems if there is excessive interference or low signal strength, resulting in decreased overall throughput due to signal errors and retries. However, in the real world the shorter guard interval doesn't normally cause problems, so it is enabled by the default configuration in most devices.

Combining the use of three data streams using standard 20MHz channels and the standard 800ns guard interval, the maximum throughput of a Wireless-N connection would be 195Mbps. Using the shorter 400ns guard interval would increase this to up to 216.7Mbps. As with other members of the 802.11 family of standards, 802.11n supports fallback rates when a connection cannot be made at the maximum data rate.

802.11ac

The latest wireless network standard, 802.11ac (also known as *Wireless-AC*), has not yet been certified by the Wi-Fi Alliance in final form, though it is expected to be in late 2013. However, hardware meeting 802.11ac draft specification 3.0 or 4.0 has been available since late 2012.

802.11ac is essentially an improved version of 802.11n, with the following major differences:

- Channel bonding to provide 80MHz wide channels (double the maximum of 40MHz available in 802.11n) up to 160MHz wide channels
- 256QAM modulation (802.11n uses 64QAM); the higher the QAM modulation, the higher the data rate
- Up to eight MIMO data streams (four was the maximum in 802.11n)
- Support for 5GHz frequencies only

Typical 802.11ac hardware also supports channel-bonded 802.11n 2.4GHz frequencies for backwards compatibility with existing networks.

Table 17.3 compares the standard and optional speeds supported by the different wireless standards discussed in this chapter.

Table 17.3   Wireless Network Speeds

Wireless Type	Band	Channel Width	GI	Max. Speed (1 Stream)	Max. Speed (2 Streams)	Max. Speed (3 Streams)	Max. Speed
802.11a	5GHz	20MHz	800ns	54Mbps	—	—	—
802.11b	2.4GHz	20MHz	800ns	11Mbps	—	—	—
802.11g	2.4GHz	20MHz	800ns	54Mbps	—	—	—
802.11n	2.4/5GHz	20MHz	800ns	65Mbps	130Mbps	195Mbps	260Mbps*
802.11n	2.4/5GHz	20MHz	400ns	72.2Mbps	144.4Mbps	216.7Mbps	288.9Mbps*
802.11n	2.4/5GHz	40MHz	800ns	135Mbps	270Mbps	405Mbps	540Mbps*
802.11n	2.4/5GHz	40MHz	400ns	150Mbps	300Mbps	450Mbps	600Mbps*
802.11ac	5GHz	80MHz	400ns	300Mbps	610Mbps	910Mbps	2400Mbps**
802.11ac	5GHz	160MHz	400ns	610Mbps	1200Mbps	1800Mbps	2400MBps*
							4900Mbps**

GI = Guard Interval

*4 Streams

**8 Streams

Note

For more information about 802.11ac and how it differs from 802.11n, see the Cisco document "802.11ac: The Fifth Generation of Wi-Fi Technical White Paper" at http://www.cisco.com/en/US/prod/collateral/wireless/ps5678/ps11983/white_paper_c11-713103.html.

Bluetooth

Bluetooth is a low-speed, low-power standard originally designed to interconnect laptop computers, PDAs, cell phones, and pagers for data synchronization and user authentication in public areas such as airports, hotels, rental car pickups, and sporting events. Bluetooth is also used for a variety of wireless devices on PCs, including printer adapters, keyboards, mice, headphones, DV camcorders, data projectors, and many others. A list of Bluetooth products and announcements is available at the official Bluetooth wireless information website: www.bluetooth.com.

Bluetooth devices also use the same 2.4GHz frequency range that most Wi-Fi devices use. However, in an attempt to avoid interference with Wi-Fi, Bluetooth uses a signaling method called *frequency hopping spread spectrum (FHSS)*, which switches the exact frequency used during a Bluetooth session 1,600 times per second over the 79 channels Bluetooth uses. Unlike Wi-Fi, which is designed to allow a device to be part of a network at all times, Bluetooth is designed for ad hoc temporary networks (known as *piconets*) in which two devices connect only long enough to transfer data and then break the connection. The basic data rate supported by Bluetooth is currently 1Mbps (up from 700Kbps in earlier versions), but devices that support enhanced data rate (EDR) can reach a transfer rate up to 2.1Mbps.

The current version of Bluetooth is 4.0; however, versions 2.1 and later support easier connections between devices such as phones and headsets (a process known as *pairing*), longer battery life, and improved security compared to older versions. Version 3.0 adds a high-speed mode based on Wi-Fi, while 4.0 adds low-energy protocols for devices using extremely low power consumption.

Interference Issues Between Bluetooth and 802.11b/g/n Wireless

Despite the frequency-hopping nature of Bluetooth, studies have shown that Bluetooth 802.11b/g/n devices can interfere with each other, particularly at close range (under 2 meters) or when users attempt to use both types of wireless networking at the same time (as with a wireless network connection on a computer also using a Bluetooth wireless keyboard or mouse). Interference reduces throughput and in some circumstances can cause data loss.

Bluetooth version 1.2 adds adaptive frequency hopping to solve interference problems when devices are more than 1 meter (3.3 feet) away from each other. However, close-range (less than 1 meter) interference can still take place. IEEE has developed 802.15.2, a specification for enabling coexistence between 802.11b/g/n and Bluetooth. It can use various time-sharing or time-division methods to enable coexistence. Bluetooth version 2.1 is designed to minimize interference by using an improved adaptive hopping method, whereas 3.0 and later adds the ability to use 802.11 radios for high-speed transfers. Companies that build both Bluetooth and 802.11-family chipsets, such as Atheros and Texas Instruments (TI), have developed methods for avoiding interference that work especially well when same-vendor products are teamed together.

Hardware Elements of Your Network

The choice of a data-link protocol affects the network hardware you choose. Because the various flavors of Ethernet and other data-link protocols use different hardware, you must select the architecture before you can select appropriate hardware, including NICs, cables, and switches.

NICs for Wired Ethernet Networks

On most computers, a wired Ethernet network adapter is integrated into the motherboard. If the integrated component fails or is not fast enough, a replacement NIC can be added through the PCI or PCI-Express slot (desktop computers), USB, CardBus PC Card (PCMCIA), or ExpressCard slot on a laptop.

Network adapters (both wired and wireless) have unique hardware addresses coded into their firmware. The hardware address is known as the *MAC address*. You can see the MAC address on a label on the side of the adapter, or you can view it after the adapter is installed with an OS utility such as the Windows ipconfig.exe command. The data-link layer protocol uses these addresses to identify the other systems on the network. A packet gets to the correct destination because its data-link layer protocol header contains the hardware addresses of both the sending and receiving systems.

Most motherboards have wired Ethernet adapters built in, whereas discrete Ethernet network adapters range in price from less than $10 for client adapters to more than $100 for single or multiport server-optimized adapters.

Although you can connect two computers directly to each other via their Ethernet ports with a cross-over cable, larger networks need a switch, which is frequently incorporated into a router. The network runs at the speed of the slowest component, so if you use a switch that runs at a slower speed than the network clients, the clients connected to that switch will run at that slower speed. Most wireless routers now include 1000Mbps Gigabit Ethernet ports instead of slower 100Mbps Fast Ethernet ports.

When connecting systems on wired Ethernet networks, the following sections contain my recommendations on the features you need.

Speed

Your NIC should run at the maximum speed you want your network to support. Most Gigabit Ethernet and Fast Ethernet cards also support slower speeds meaning, for example, that a 1,000Mbps (Gigabit Ethernet) card also supports 100Mbps (Fast Ethernet) speed or standard Ethernet's 10Mbps speed, allowing the same card to be used on both older and newer portions of the network. To verify multispeed operation, look for network cards identified as 10/100 or 10/100/1000 Ethernet. All modern Fast or Gigabit NICs should also support full-duplex operation:

- Half-duplex means that the network card can only send or only receive data in a single operation.

- Full-duplex means that the network card can both receive and send simultaneously. Full-duplex options boost network speed if switches are used in place of hubs. For example, 1,000Mbps Gigabit Ethernet cards running in full-duplex mode have a maximum true throughput of 2,000Mbps, with half going in each direction.

Note

Unlike hubs, which broadcast data packets to all computers connected to them, switches create a direct connection between the sending and receiving computers. Therefore, switches provide faster performance than hubs; most switches also support full-duplex operation, doubling the rated speed of the network when full-duplex network cards are used.

▶▶ For more information about switches, see the section, "Switches for Ethernet Networks," **p. 827**.

Bus Type

If you need to install a network adapter for use with a Gigabit Ethernet (10/100/1000Mbps) network, any of the following buses have more than adequate performance:

- PCI/PCIe—The integrated NIC built into most motherboards are either PCI or PCIe devices.

- CardBus/ExpressCard (laptop computers).

All these buses support Gigabit Ethernet adapters without limiting throughput. Integrated network adapters use either the PCI or PCI Express bus to connect to the system, both of which have more than enough bandwidth. Note that USB 2.0 (480Mbps) is not on that list because it is simply not fast enough to fully support Gigabit Ethernet's 1,000Mbps bandwidth; however, 100Mbps Ethernet connections will work on USB 2.0 with no problems. USB 3.0 (5Gbps) is more than fast enough to support a Gigabit Ethernet adapter, and a number of vendors now provide USB 3.0 adapters for Gigabit Ethernet networks.

Wired Network Adapter Connectors

Wired Ethernet adapters typically have an eight position, eight conductor (8P8C) connector informally known as an RJ-45 connector, which looks like a large telephone jack. Fast Ethernet and Gigabit Ethernet twisted-pair cables use these connectors, but you might still see older adapters that support a single BNC connector (for Thinnet coaxial cables) or a D-shaped 15-pin connector called a DB-15 (for Thicknet coaxial cables). Some older 10Mbps adapters have a combination of two or all three of these connector types; adapters with two or more connectors are referred to as *combo adapters*. Token-Ring adapters can have a 9-pin connector called a DB-9 (for Type 1 STP cable) or sometimes an 8P8C (RJ-45) jack (for Type 3 UTP cable). Figure 17.4 shows all three of the Ethernet connectors.

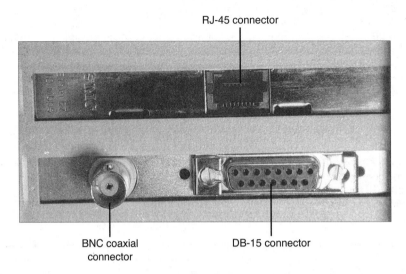

FIGURE 17.4 Three Ethernet connectors on two NICs: Modern 8P8C (RJ-45) connector (top center), Obsolete DB-15 connector (bottom right), and Obsolete BNC connector (bottom left).

Note

Although RJ-45 is the common name for the UTP Ethernet connector, this is a misnomer. The correct name for the connector is 8P8C, which indicates an 8-pin, 8-conductor connector. The actual RJ-45S connector is an eight-position connector but is used for telephone rather than computer data. An RJ-45S jack has a slightly different shape than the connector used for Ethernet, and it includes a cutout on one side to prevent unkeyed connectors from being inserted into it.

For drawings of the true RJ-45S jack and other telephone jacks, see www.siemon.com/us/standards/13-24_modular_wiring_reference.asp.

Ethernet NICs made for client-PC use on the market today are designed to support unshielded twisted-pair (UTP) cable exclusively. Cards using BNC or DB-15 connectors would be considered obsolete.

For maximum economy, NICs and network cables must match, although media converters can interconnect networks based on the same standard, but using different cable.

Network Cables for Wired Ethernet

Originally, all networks used some type of cable to connect the computers on the network to each other. Although various types of wireless networks are now on the market, many office and home networks still use twisted-pair Ethernet cabling. Occasionally you might still find some based on Thick or Thin Ethernet coaxial cable.

Thick and Thin Ethernet Coaxial Cable

The first versions of Ethernet were based on coaxial cable. The original form of Ethernet, 10BASE-5, used a thick coaxial cable (called *Thicknet*) that was not directly attached to the NIC. A device called an *attachment unit interface (AUI)* ran from a DB-15 connector on the rear of the NIC to the cable. The cable had a hole drilled into it to allow the "vampire tap" to be connected to the cable. NICs designed for use with thick Ethernet cable are almost impossible to find as new hardware today.

10BASE-2 Ethernet cards use a BNC (Bayonet-Neill-Concelman) connector on the rear of the NIC. Although the thin coaxial cable (called *Thinnet* or *RG-58*) used with 10BASE-2 Ethernet has a bayonet connector that can physically attach to the BNC connector on the card, this configuration is incorrect and won't work. Instead, a BNC T-connector attaches to the rear of the card, allowing a Thin Ethernet cable to be connected to either both ends of the T (for a computer in the middle of the network) or to one end only (for a computer at the end of the network). A 50-ohm terminator is connected to the other arm of the T to indicate the end of the network and prevent erroneous signals from being sent to other clients on the network. Some early Ethernet cards were designed to handle thick (AUI/DB-15), thin (RG-58), and UTP (unshielded twisted pair) cables. Combo cards with both BNC and 8P8C (RJ-45) connectors are still available on the surplus equipment market but can run at only standard 10Mbps Ethernet speeds.

Figure 17.5 compares Ethernet DB-15 to AUI, BNC coaxial T-connector, and 8P8C (RJ-45) UTP connectors, and Figure 17.6 illustrates the design of coaxial cable.

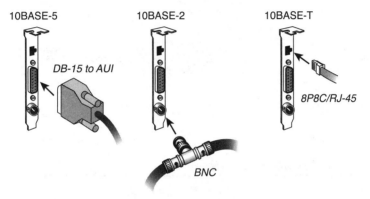

FIGURE 17.5   An Ethernet network card with Thick Ethernet (DB-15), Thin Ethernet (RG-58 with T-connector), and UTP (8P8C/RJ-45) connectors.

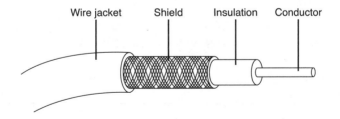

FIGURE 17.6   Coaxial cable.

Twisted-Pair Cable

Twisted-pair cable is just what its name implies: insulated wires within a protective casing with a specified number of twists per foot. Twisting the wires reduces the effect of electromagnetic interference (EMI, which can be generated by nearby cables, electric motors, and fluorescent lighting) on the signals being transmitted. Shielded twisted pair (STP) refers to the amount of insulation around the cluster of wires and therefore its immunity to noise. You are probably familiar with unshielded twisted pair (UTP) cable; it is often used for telephone wiring. Figure 17.7 shows UTP cable; Figure 17.8 illustrates STP cable.

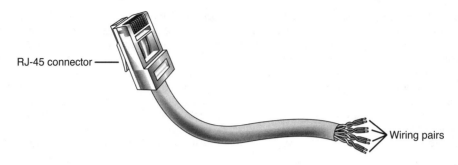

FIGURE 17.7 A UTP cable.

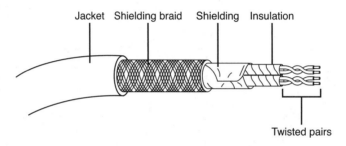

FIGURE 17.8 An STP cable.

Shielded Versus Unshielded Twisted Pair

When cabling was being developed for use with computers, it was first thought that shielding the cable from external interference was the best way to reduce interference and provide for greater transmission speeds. However, it was discovered that twisting the pairs of wires is a more effective way to prevent interference from disrupting transmissions. As a result, earlier cabling scenarios relied on shielded cables rather than the unshielded cables more commonly in use today.

Shielded cables also have some special grounding concerns because one, and only one, end of a shielded cable should be connected to an earth ground; issues arose when people inadvertently caused grounding loops to occur by connecting both ends or caused the shield to act as an antenna because it wasn't grounded.

Grounding loops are created when two grounds are tied together. This is a bad situation because each ground can have a slightly different potential, resulting in a circuit that has low voltage but infinite amperage. This causes undue stress on electrical components and can be a fire hazard.

Most Ethernet installations that use twisted-pair cabling use UTP because the physical flexibility and small size of the cable and connectors makes routing it easy. However, its lack of electrical insulation can make interference from fluorescent lighting, elevators, and alarm systems (among other devices) a major problem. If you use UTP in installations where interference can be a problem, you need to route the cable away from the interference, use an external shield, or substitute STP for UTP near interference sources.

Four standard types of UTP cabling exist and are still used to varying degrees:

- **Category 3 cable**—The original type of UTP cable used for Ethernet networks was also the same as that used for business telephone wiring. This is known as Category 3, or voice-grade UTP cable, and it is measured according to a scale that quantifies the cable's data-transmission capabilities. The cable itself is 24 AWG (American Wire Gauge, a standard for measuring the diameter of a wire) and copper-tinned with solid conductors, with 100–105 ohm characteristic impedance and a minimum of two twists per foot. Category 3 cable is largely obsolete because it is only adequate for networks running at up to 16Mbps, so it cannot be used with Fast or Gigabit Ethernet.

- **Category 5 cable**—The faster network types require greater performance levels. Fast Ethernet (100BASE-TX) uses the same two-wire pairs as 10BASE-T, but Fast Ethernet needs a greater resistance to signal crosstalk and attenuation. Therefore, the use of Category 5 UTP cabling is essential with 100BASE-TX Fast Ethernet. Although the 100BASE-T4 version of Fast Ethernet can use all four-wire pairs of Category 3 cable, this flavor of Fast Ethernet is not widely supported and has practically vanished from the marketplace. If you try to run Fast Ethernet 100BASE-TX over Category 3 cable, you will have a slow and unreliable network. Category 5 cable is commonly called CAT 5 and is also referred to as Class D cable.

  Most cable vendors also sell an enhanced form of Category 5 cable called Category 5e (specified by Addendum 5 of the ANSI/TIA/EIA-568-A cabling standard). Category 5e or 6 cable can be used in place of Category 5 cable and is especially well suited for use in Fast Ethernet networks that might be upgraded to Gigabit Ethernet in the future. Category 5e cabling must pass several tests not required for Category 5 cabling and, unlike Category 5 cable, can be certified for Gigabit Ethernet networks.

- **Category 6 cable**—Category 6 cabling (also called CAT 6 or Class E) can be used in place of CAT 5 or 5e cabling and uses the same 8P8C (RJ-45) connectors as CAT 5 and 5e. CAT 6 cable handles a frequency range of 1MHz–250MHz, compared to CAT 5 and 5e's 1MHz–100MHz frequency range. CAT 6 is suitable for Gigabit Ethernet at standard distances of up to 100 meters (328 ft.), and can even be used for 10 Gigabit Ethernet at reduced distances of up to 55 meters (180 ft.).

- **Category 6a cable**—Category 6a cabling (also called CAT 6a or Class EA) can be used in place of CAT 6, 5, or 5e cabling and uses the same 8P8C (RJ-45) connectors. CAT 6a cable supports frequencies up to 500MHz (twice that of CAT 6), and supports 10 Gigabit Ethernet connections at the full maximum distance of up to 100 meters (328 ft.).

Caution

If you choose to install cable meeting Category 5/5e/6/6a UTP cable, be sure that all the connectors, wall plates, and other hardware components involved are also rated the same or better. The lowest common denominator rating will degrade the entire connection to that Category. For example, if you install CAT 6 cabling but only use CAT 5e rated connectors, wall plates, and so on, then the connections as a whole will only be rated for CAT 5e.

For new installations, it is recommended to use the highest rated components that are affordable, because this helps "future-proof" the network.

Choosing the correct type of Category 5/5e/6/6a cable is also important. Use solid PVC cable for network cables that represent a permanent installation. However, the slightly more expensive stranded cables are a better choice for laptop computers or temporary wiring of no more than 10-feet lengths (from a computer to a wall socket, for example) because they are more flexible and therefore capable of withstanding frequent movement.

If you plan to use air ducts or suspended ceilings for cable runs, you should use Plenum cable, which doesn't emit harmful fumes in a fire. It is much more expensive, but the safety issue is a worthwhile reason to use it. (Some localities require you to use Plenum cabling.)

Building Your Own Twisted Pair Cables

When it's time to wire your network, you have two choices. You can opt to purchase prebuilt cables, or you can build your own cables from bulk wire and connectors.

You should build your own twisted pair (TP) cables if you

- Plan to perform a lot of networking
- Need cable lengths longer than the lengths you can buy preassembled
- Want to create both standard and crossover cables
- Want to choose your own cable color
- Want maximum control over cable length
- Want to save money
- Have the time necessary to build cables

While you can save money building your own cables, you can get premade network cables at very low prices from some online vendors, such as MonoPrice (www.monoprice.com). In many cases you'll find that it is actually cheaper to purchase premade cables than it is to build your own.

TP Wiring Standards

If you want to create TP cables yourself, be sure your cable pairs match the color coding of any existing cable or the color coding of any prebuilt cabling you want to add to your new network. Because there are eight wires in TP cables, many incorrect combinations are possible. Several standards exist for UTP cabling.

Tip

The key is to be consistent. Use the same scheme for all your cables, and ensure that anyone else working on your network understands this scheme.

The most common standard is the AT&T 258A configuration (also called EIA/TIA 568B). Table 17.4 lists the wire pairing and placement within the standard 8P8C (RJ-45) connector.

Table 17.4 8P8C (RJ-45) Connector Wire Pairing and Placement for AT&T 258A/EIA 568B Standard

Pin	Color	Pair
1	Orange/White	2
2	Orange	2
3	Green/White	3
4	Blue	1*
5	Blue/White	1
6	Green	3
7	Brown/White	4*
8	Brown	4

This pair is not used with 10BASE-T or Fast Ethernet 100BASE-TX, but all four pairs are used with Fast Ethernet 100BASE-T4 and Gigabit Ethernet 1000BASE-TX standards.

In Figure 17.9, an 8P8C (RJ-45) cable connector is wired to the AT&T 258A/EIA 568B standard.

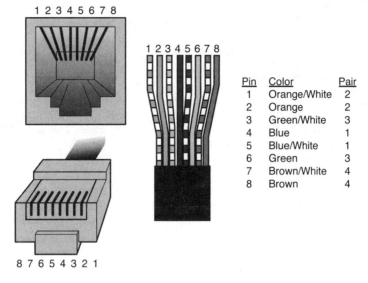

Pin	Color	Pair
1	Orange/White	2
2	Orange	2
3	Green/White	3
4	Blue	1
5	Blue/White	1
6	Green	3
7	Brown/White	4
8	Brown	4

FIGURE 17.9   An AT&T 258A/EIA 568B standard–compliant 8P8C (RJ-45) connector.

Note

You also might encounter the similar EIA 568A standard. It reverses the position of the orange and green pairs listed previously.

Crossover UTP Cables

Crossover cables, which change the wiring at one end of the cable, connect two (and only two) computers when no hub or switch is available or connect a hub or switch without an uplink port to another hub or switch. The pinout for a crossover cable is shown in Table 17.5. This pinout is for one end of the cable only; the other end of the cable should correspond to the standard EIA 568B pinout, as shown previously in Table 17.4.

Table 17.5   8P8C (RJ-45) Connector Wire Pairing and Placement for EIA 568A Standard

Pin	Color	Pair
1	Green/White	3
2	Green	3
3	Orange/White	2
4	Blue	1
5	Blue/White	1
6	Orange	2
7	Brown/White	4
8	Brown	4

Note

Most standard cables have both ends wired using the EIA 568B standard; however, it is also possible to wire them with both ends using the EIA 568A standard. As long as both ends are wired the same in a straight-through configuration, the cable will work. Crossover cables should have one end in an EIA 568B configuration, while the other end is in an EIA 568A configuration, thus crossing pairs 2 and 3. It should be noted that other wiring schemes exist for connecting UTP cables with 8P8C (RJ-45) connectors. The ones listed in this chapter are the most common.

Most newer switches are designed so as to automatically detect whether a crossover connection is required and configure the connection appropriately. This feature is called Auto-MDIX (automatic medium-dependent interface crossover) and essentially negates the need for having dedicated "uplink" ports or using crossover cables when connecting devices.

Constructing the Cable

Making your own network cables requires a few tools that aren't found in a typical toolbox. Those items that you might not already have you can typically purchase for a single price from many network-products vendors. You need the following tools and supplies to build your own Ethernet cables:

- UTP cable (Category 5e or better)
- 8P8C (RJ-45) connectors matching cable category
- Wire stripper
- 8P8C (RJ-45) crimping tool

Before you make a "real" cable of any length, you should practice on a short length of cable. 8P8C (RJ-45) connectors and bulk cable are cheap; network failures are not. Follow these steps to create your own twisted-pair cables:

1. Determine how long your cable should be. You should allow adequate slack for moving the computer and for avoiding strong interference sources. Keep the maximum distances for UTP cables of about 100 meters in mind.

2. Roll out the appropriate length of cable.

3. Cut the cable cleanly from the box of wire.

4. Use the wire stripper to strip only the insulation jacket off the cable, exposing the TP wires (see Figure 17.10); you'll need to rotate the wire about one and a quarter turns to strip away all the jacket. If you turn it too far, you'll damage the wires inside the cable.

5. Check the outer jacket and inner TP wires for nicks; adjust the stripper tool, and repeat steps 3 and 4 if you see damage.

6. As shown in Figure 17.11, arrange the wires according to the EIA 568B standard. This arrangement is listed previously, in the section, "TP Wiring Standards."

7. Trim the wire edges so the eight wires are even with one another and are slightly less than 1/2-inch past the end of the jacket. If the wires are too long, crosstalk (wire-to-wire interference) can result; if the wires are too short, they can't make a good connection with the 8P8C (RJ-45) plug.

8. With the clip side of the 8P8C (RJ-45) plug facing away from you, push the cable into place (see Figure 17.12). Verify that the wires are arranged according to the EIA/TIA 568B standard before you crimp the plug onto the wires. (Refer to Table 17.5 earlier in this chapter.) Adjust the connection as necessary.

9. Use the crimping tool to squeeze the 8P8C (RJ-45) plug onto the cable (see Figure 17.13). The end of the cable should be tight enough to resist being removed by hand.

10. Repeat steps 4–9 for the other end of the cable. Recut the end of the cable if necessary before stripping it.

11. Label each cable with the following information:

- Wiring standard
- Length
- End with crossover (if any)
- _____ (a blank) for computer ID

FIGURE 17.10 Carefully strip the cable jacket away to expose the four wire pairs.

FIGURE 17.11 Arrange the wire pairs for insertion into the 8P8C (RJ-45) connector according to your chosen scheme (EIA 568B, for instance).

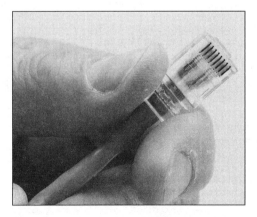

FIGURE 17.12 Push the 8P8C (RJ-45) connector into place, ensuring the cable pairs are ordered properly.

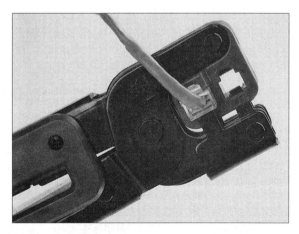

FIGURE 17.13 Firmly squeeze the crimping tool to attach the connector to the cable.

The cables should be labeled at both ends to make matching the cable with the correct computer easy and to facilitate troubleshooting at the hub. Check with your cable supplier for suitable labeling stock or tags you can attach to each cable.

Cable Distance Limitations

The people who design computer systems love to find ways to circumvent limitations. Manufacturers of Ethernet products have made possible the building of networks in star, branch, and tree designs that overcome the basic limitations already mentioned. (For more information, see the "Wired Network Topologies" section later in this chapter.) Strictly speaking, you can have thousands of computers on a complex Ethernet network.

LANs are local because the network adapters and other hardware components typically can't send LAN messages more than a few hundred feet. Table 17.6 lists the distance limitations of various types of LAN cable. In addition to the limitations shown in the table, keep the following points in mind:

- You can't connect more than 30 computers on a single Thinnet Ethernet segment.
- You can't connect more than 100 computers on a Thicknet Ethernet segment.
- You can't connect more than 72 computers on a UTP Token-Ring cable.
- You can't connect more than 260 computers on an STP Token-Ring cable.

Table 17.6 Network Distance Limitations

Network Adapter	Cable Type	Maximum	Minimum
Ethernet	10BASE-2	185m (607 feet)	0.5m (1.6 feet)
	10BASE-5 (drop)	50m (164 feet)	2.5m (8.2 feet)
	10BASE-5 (backbone)	500m (1,640 feet)	2.5m (8.2 feet)
	10BASE-T	100m (328 feet)	2.5m (8.2 feet)
	100BASE-TX	100m (328 feet)	2.5m (8.2 feet)
	1000BASE-TX	100m (328 feet)	2.5m (8.2 feet)
	10GBASE-T	100m (328 feet)	2.5m (8.2 feet)
Token-Ring	STP	100m (328 feet)	2.5m (8.2 feet)
	UTP	45m (147 feet)	2.5m (8.2 feet)
ARCnet	Passive hub drop	30m (98 feet)	Varies by cable type
	Active hub	600m (1,968 feet)	Varies by cable type

If you have a station wired with Category 5 or better cable that is more than 328 feet (100 meters) from a hub, you must use a hub or switch that acts as a repeater to regenerate the signal. If you have two or more stations beyond the 328 foot limit of UTP Ethernet, connect them to a hub or switch that is less than 328 feet away from the primary hub or switch and connect the new hub or switch to the primary hub or switch via its uplink port. Because hubs and switches can act as repeaters, this feature enables you to extend the effective length of your network.

Wired Network Topologies

Each computer on the network is connected to the other computers with cable (or some other medium, such as wireless using radio frequency signals). The physical arrangement of the cables connecting computers on a network is called the *network topology*.

The three basic topologies used in computer networks have been as follows:

- **Bus**—Connects each computer on a network directly to the next computer in a linear fashion. The network connection starts at the server and ends at the last computer in the network. (Obsolete.)
- **Star**—Connects each computer on the network to a central access point.
- **Ring**—Connects each computer to the others in a loop or ring. (Obsolete.)

Hybrid topologies mix two or more topologies together. Two typical examples include star-bus, when two star networks are connected by a single cable, usually between the switches of each star; and a hierarchical star, which connects multiple star networks to one master switch.

Table 17.7 summarizes the relationships between network types and topologies.

Table 17.7 Network Cable Types and Topologies

Network Type	Standard	Cable Type	Topology
Ethernet	10BASE-2	Thin (RG-58) coaxial	Bus
Ethernet	10BASE-5	Thick coaxial	Bus
Ethernet	10BASE-T	CAT 3 UTP or better	Star
Fast Ethernet	100BASE-TX	CAT 5 UTP or better	Star
Gigabit Ethernet	1000BASE-TX	CAT 5e UTP or better	Star
10 Gigabit Ethernet	10000BASE-TX	CAT 6a UTP or better	Star
Token-Ring	(All)	UTP or STP	Logical ring

The bus, star, and ring topologies are discussed in the following sections. Wireless networking, which technically doesn't have a physical topology as described here, does still employ two logical (virtual) topologies, which I discuss as well.

Bus Topology

The earliest type of network topology was the *bus topology*, which uses a single cable to connect all the computers in the network to each other, as shown in Figure 17.14. This network topology was adopted initially because running a single cable past all the computers in the network is easier and uses less wiring than other topologies. Because early bus topology networks used bulky coaxial cables, these factors were important advantages. Both 10BASE-5 (thick) and 10BASE-2 (thin) Ethernet networks are based on the bus topology.

However, the advent of cheaper and more compact unshielded twisted-pair cabling, which also supports faster networks, has made the disadvantages of a bus topology apparent. If one computer or cable connection malfunctions, it can cause all the stations beyond it on the bus to lose their network connections. Thick Ethernet (10BASE-5) networks often failed because the vampire tap connecting the AUI device to the coaxial cable came loose. In addition, the T-adapters and terminating resistors on a 10BASE-2 Thin Ethernet network could come loose or be removed by the user, causing all or part of the network to fail. Another drawback of Thin Ethernet (10BASE-2) networks was that adding a new computer to the network between existing computers might require replacement of the existing network cable between the computers with shorter segments to connect to the new computer's network card and T-adapter, thus creating downtime for users on that segment of the network.

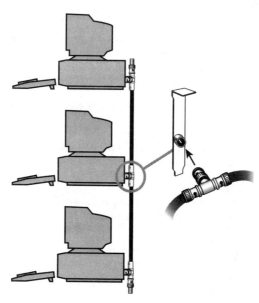

FIGURE 17.14 A 10BASE-2 network is an example of a linear bus topology, attaching all network devices to a common cable.

Ring Topology

Another topology often listed in discussions of this type is a *ring*, in which each workstation is connected to the next and the last workstation is connected to the first again (essentially a bus topology with the two ends connected). Two major network types use the ring topology:

- **Fiber Distributed Data Interface (FDDI)**—A network topology used for large, high-speed networks using fiber-optic cables in a physical ring topology

- **Token-Ring**—Uses a logical ring topology

A Token-Ring network resembles a 10BASE-T or 10/100/1000 Ethernet network at first glance because both networks use a central connecting device and a physical star topology. Where is the "ring" in Token-Ring?

The ring exists only within the device that connects the computers, which is called a *multistation access unit (MSAU)* on a Token-Ring network (see Figure 17.15).

Signals generated from one computer travel to the MSAU, are sent out to the next computer, and then go back to the MSAU again. The data is then passed to each system in turn until it arrives back at the computer that originated it, where it is removed from the network. Therefore, although the physical wiring topology is a star, the data path is theoretically a ring. This is called a *logical ring*.

A logical ring that Token-Ring networks use is preferable to a physical ring network topology because it affords a greater degree of fault tolerance. As on a bus network, a cable break anywhere in a physical ring network topology, such as FDDI, affects the entire network. FDDI networks use two physical rings to provide a backup in case one ring fails. By contrast, on a Token-Ring network, the MSAU can effectively remove a malfunctioning computer from the logical ring, enabling the rest of the network to function normally.

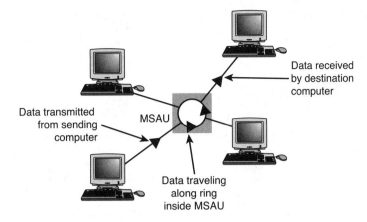

FIGURE 17.15 A Token-Ring network during the sending of data from one computer to another.

Star Topology

By far the most popular type of topology in use today has separate cables to connect each computer to a central wiring nexus, often called a *switch* or *hub*. Figure 17.16 shows this arrangement, which is called a *star topology*.

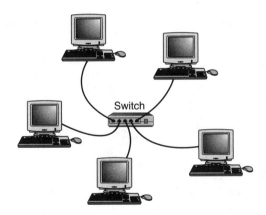

FIGURE 17.16 The star topology, linking the LAN's computers and devices to one or more central hubs, or access units.

Because each computer uses a separate cable, the failure of a network connection affects only the single machine involved. The other computers can continue to function normally. Bus cabling schemes use less cable than the star but are harder to diagnose or bypass when problems occur. At this time, Fast Ethernet and Gigabit Ethernet in a star topology are the most commonly implemented types of wired LAN.

Switches for Ethernet Networks

As you have seen, modern Ethernet workgroup networks—whether wireless or wired with UTP cable—are usually arranged in a star topology. The center of the star uses a multiport connecting device that can be either a hub or a switch. Although both hubs and switches can connect the network—and can have several features in common—only switches are normally used today. The differences between them are significant and are covered in the following sections.

All Ethernet switches have the following features:

- Multiple 8P8C (RJ-45) UTP connectors
- Diagnostic and activity lights
- A power supply

Ethernet switches are made in two forms: managed and unmanaged. Managed switches can be directly configured, enabled or disabled, or monitored by a network operator. They are commonly used on corporate networks. Workgroup and home-office networks use less expensive unmanaged switches, which simply connect computers on the network using the systems connected to it to provide a management interface for its configurable features.

Signal lights on the front of the switch indicate which connections are in use by computers; some also indicate whether a full-duplex connection is in use. In addition, multispeed switches may indicate which connection speed is in use on each port. A switch must have at least one 8P8C (RJ-45) UTP connector for each computer you want to connect to it.

How Switches Work

UTP Ethernet networks were originally wired using hubs. When a specific computer sends a packet of data to another specific computer through a hub, the hub doesn't know which port the destination computer is connected to, so it broadcasts the packet to all of the ports and computers connected to it, creating a large amount of unnecessary traffic because ports and systems receive network data even if it is not intended for them.

Switches, as shown in Figure 17.17, are similar to hubs in both form factor and function, but they are very different in actual operation. As with hubs, they connect computers on an Ethernet network to each other. However, instead of broadcasting data to all of the ports and computers on the network as hubs do, switches use a feature called address storing, which checks the destination for each data packet and sends it directly to the port/computer for which it's intended. Thus, a switch can be compared to a telephone exchange, making direct connections between the originator of a call and the receiver.

Because switches establish a direct connection between the originating and receiving PC, they also provide the full bandwidth of the network to each port. Hubs, by contrast, must subdivide the network's bandwidth by the number of active connections on the network, meaning that bandwidth rises and falls depending on network activity.

For example, assume you have a four-station network workgroup using 10/100 NICs and a Fast Ethernet hub. The total bandwidth of the network is 100Mbps. However, if two stations are active, the effective bandwidth available to each station drops to 50Mbps (100Mbps divided by 2). If all four stations are active, the effective bandwidth drops to just 25Mbps (100Mbps divided by 4)! Add more active users, and the effective bandwidth continues to drop.

If you replace the hub with a switch, the effective bandwidth for each station remains at the full 100Mbps because the switch doesn't broadcast data to all stations.

Most switches also support *full-duplex* (simultaneous transmit and receive), enabling the actual bandwidth to be double the nominal 100Mbps rating, or 200Mbps. Table 17.8 summarizes the differences between the two devices.

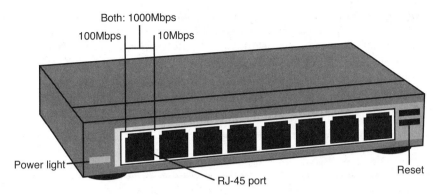

FIGURE 17.17 Front (top) and rear (bottom) of a typical eight-port, 10/100/1000 Ethernet switch.

Table 17.8 Ethernet Hub and Switch Comparison

Feature	Hub	Switch
Bandwidth	Divided by total number of ports in use	Dedicated to each port in use
Data transmission	Broadcast to all connected computers	Broadcast only to the receiving computer
Duplex support	Half-duplex	Full-duplex when used with full-duplex NICs

As you can see, using a switch instead of a hub greatly increases the effective speed of a network, even if all other components remain the same. Originally switches were expensive, so many networks were built using hubs instead. But, once the price of a switch fell to equal or below the cost of a hub, hubs became obsolete.

Note

Both wired and wireless routers (a *router* connects a LAN to a device that provides Internet access, such as a cable or DSL modem) typically incorporate full-duplex 10/100 (Fast Ethernet) or 10/100/1000 (Gigabit Ethernet) switches.

◀◀ For more information about routers, see the Chapter 16 section, "Routers for Internet Sharing," **p. 796**.

At this point, the lower cost and significantly higher performance of switches mean that you should consider replacing any hubs that might still be in use.

Additional Switch Features You Might Need

Most switches have the following standard or optional features:

- **Multispeed capability**—Switches support multiple speeds. This means you can mix Gigabit Ethernet (1000BASE-TX), Fast Ethernet (100BASE-TX) and 10BASE-T clients on the same network, and each will run at the maximum possible speed. These days I recommend buying only Gigabit switches, since most network adapters now support Gigabit speeds.

- **Power-saving technology**—Some late model switches support various power saving features, including adjusting power per port to the length of each cable connected to the switch and reducing power to idle switch ports.

- **"Extra" ports beyond your current requirements**—If you are connecting four computers into a small network, you may only need a four-port switch, which is the smallest generally available. But if you buy a switch with only four ports and want to add another client PC to the network, you must add a second switch or replace the switch with a larger one with more ports.

  Instead, plan for the future by buying a switch that can handle your projected network growth over the next year. If you plan to connect more than four workstations, buy at least an eight-port switch. (The cost per connection drops as you buy hubs and switches with more connections.) Even though you can easily interconnect additional switches, it is normally more economical to use as few switches as possible.

Note

The uplink port on your switch (or hub) connects the device to a router or gateway device that provides an Internet connection for your network. When multiple switches are to be used, they are usually connected directly to the router or gateway instead of chained (or stacked) off each other.

Modern switches feature Auto-MDIX (automatic medium-dependent interface crossover) ports that allow switches to be connected together using any of the ports, and without using special crossover cables. Older switches (or hubs) used uplink ports to allow additional switches to be connected.

Switch Placement

Although large networks have a wiring closet near the server, the workgroup-size LANs found in a small office/home office (SOHO) network obviously don't require anything of the sort. However, the location of the switch is important, even if your LAN is currently based solely on a wireless Ethernet architecture.

Ethernet switches (and hubs) require electrical power, whether they are small units that use a power "brick" or larger units that have an internal power supply and a standard three-prong AC cord.

In addition to electrical power, consider placing the hub or switch where its signal lights will be easy to view for diagnostic purposes and where its 8P8C (RJ-45) connectors can be reached easily. This is important both when it's time to add another user or two and when you need to perform initial setup of the switch (requiring a wired connection) or need to troubleshoot a failed wireless connection. In many offices, the hub or switch sits on the corner of the desk, enabling the user to see network problems just by looking at the hub or switch.

If the hub or switch also integrates a router for use with a broadband Internet device, such as a DSL or cable modem, you can place it near the cable or DSL modem or at a distance if the layout of your home or office requires it. Because the cable or DSL modem usually connects to your computer by the same Category 5/5e/6/6a cable used for UTP Ethernet networking, you can run the cable from the cable or DSL modem to the router/switch's WAN port and connect all the computers to the LAN ports on the router/switch.

Except for the 328-foot (100-meter) limit for all forms of UTP Ethernet (10BASE-T, 100BASE-TX, and 1000BASE-TX), distances between each computer on the network and the switch (or hub) aren't critical, so put the switch (or hub) wherever you can supply power and gain easy access.

Although wireless networks do offer more freedom in terms of placing the switch/access point, you should keep in mind the distances involved (generally up to 150 to 250 feet indoors for 802.11b/g/n) and any walls or devices using the same 2.4GHz spectrum that might interfere with the signal.

Tip

Decide where you plan to put your hub or switch before you buy prebuilt UTP wiring or make your own; if you move the hub or switch, some of your wiring will no longer be the correct length. Although excess lengths of UTP cable can be coiled and secured with cable ties, cables that are too short should be replaced. You can buy 8P8C (RJ-45) connectors to create one long cable from two short cables, but you must ensure the connectors are Category 5 if you are running Fast Ethernet; some vendors still sell Category 3 connectors that support only 10Mbps. You're really better off replacing the too-short cable with one of the correct length.

Wireless Ethernet Hardware

All types of 802.11 wireless networks have two basic components:

- Wireless access point (usually built in to a router)
- Wireless network cards

An *access point* is a bookend-size device that uses one or more 8P8C (RJ-45) ports to attach to a 10BASE-T or 10/100/1000 Ethernet network (if desired) and contains a radio transceiver, encryption, and communications software. It translates conventional Ethernet signals into wireless Ethernet signals that it broadcasts to wireless NICs on the network and then performs the same role in reverse to transfer signals from wireless NICs to the conventional Ethernet network.

Most people wouldn't buy an access point as a separate stand-alone item; instead, they would purchase a router that has an access point built in. Wireless routers normally include a router, switch, and wireless access point but may also include a cable/DSL modem, file/print server, and other features.

Note

In SOHO networks that provide Internet access, the access point is usually incorporated into a wireless router that also includes an Ethernet switch.

For coverage of a large area, you can use two or more access points and connect them to an Ethernet switch. This enables users to roam inside a building without losing contact with the network. Some access points can communicate directly with each other via radio waves, enabling you to create a wireless backbone that can cover a wide area (such as a warehouse) without the need to run network cabling. You can also purchase a wireless Ethernet range extender that can receive and boost weak Wi-Fi signals. Some access points are designed to be used as either access points or range extenders. Some range extenders are designed only to work with the same brand of access point or router.

Access points are not necessary for direct peer-to-peer networking (also called *ad hoc mode*), but they are required for a shared Internet connection or a connection with another network. When access points are used, the network is operating in *infrastructure mode*.

Note

Wireless clients running in ad hoc mode cannot connect to the Internet unless one of the stations on the network is connected to a bridge or uses another network adapter as a bridge.

NICs equipped for wireless Ethernet communications have a fixed or detachable radio antenna. Wireless NICs come in four forms:

- CardBus (32-bit PC Card) or ExpressCard (PCIe) cards for use in laptop computers that do not include "integrated" wireless support
- Mini PCI or PCIe Mini cards that provide wireless and wired Ethernet and dial-up modem support for laptop computers
- PCI or PCIe cards for use in desktop computers with PCI or PCIe slots
- USB adapters for use in both desktop and laptop computers

Most laptop computers with Wi-Fi hardware onboard use the Mini PCI or PCIe Mini interface for the wireless adapter and place the antenna inside the display housing.

Note

Mini PCI or PCIe Mini cards are installed inside laptop computers. (They can be removed or replaced by opening the system.) Because Mini PCI and PCIe Mini cards are installed inside laptops, they are not usually sold as retail components. However, some vendors sell them as OEM components, or you can buy them from the laptop vendor's parts department.

Because you can mix and match Wi-Fi-certified products that use the same frequency band, you can incorporate any mix of desktop and laptop computers into your wireless network.

Although most recent laptop computers include 802.11b/g/n wireless Ethernet or dual-mode 802.11a/b/g/n support through an integrated Mini PCI or PCIe Mini card, you can add support for other 802.11 wireless networks by either upgrading the internal card or by attaching an additional card via a CardBus slot, ExpressCard slot, or USB port.

When a Wi-Fi-enabled system receives multiple Wi-Fi signals, client systems lock onto the strongest signal from access points and automatically roam (switch) to another access point when the signal strength is stronger and the error level is lower than the current connection. Of course, if you want the system to lock onto a specific signal, that can be done via the OS or manufacturer-provided software.

Most people use a wireless router as the basis of a wireless network. A wireless router normally contains a router (which is connected to a cable/DSL modem), switch, and access point. When looking for a wireless router, I recommend only those that include Gigabit Ethernet switches as well as a Gigabit Ethernet WAN port for connecting the router to a cable/DSL modem.

Additional hardware you might need to add to your network includes the following:

- **Wireless bridges**—These devices enable you to connect a wired Ethernet device, including noncomputer items such as video games or set-top boxes, to a wireless network. These are sometimes called wireless gaming adapters.
- **Wireless repeaters/range extenders**—A repeater can stretch the range of an existing wireless network. Some can also serve as access points or wireless bridges.
- **Specialized antennas**—The "rabbit ears" antennas used by most access points and routers are adequate for short distances, but longer distances or problems with line-of-sight reception can be solved by attaching high-gain replacements for the originals, or by attaching more specialized directional antennas, possibly on extension cables to mount them higher for greater range.
- **Signal boosters**—In addition to or as an alternative to replacement antennas, some vendors also sell signal boosters that piggyback onto an existing access point or router. Note that, in most cases, these signal boosters are vendor specific.

Wireless Network Logical Topologies

Wireless networks have different topologies, just as wired networks do. However, wireless networks use only two logical topologies:

- **Star**—The star topology, used by Wi-Fi/IEEE 802.11–based products in the infrastructure mode, resembles the topology used by 10BASE-T and faster versions of Ethernet that use a switch (or hub). The access point takes the place of the switch because stations connect via the access point, rather than directly with each other. This method is much more expensive per unit but permits performance in excess of 10BASE-T Ethernet speeds and has the added bonus of being easier to manage.

- **Point-to-point**—Bluetooth products (as well as Wi-Fi products in the ad hoc mode) use the point-to-point topology. These devices connect directly with each other and require no access point or other hub-like device to communicate with each other, although shared Internet access does require that all computers connect to a common wireless gateway. The point-to-point topology is much less expensive per unit than a star topology. It is, however, best suited for temporary data sharing with another device (Bluetooth) and is currently much slower than 100BASE-TX networks.

Figure 17.18 shows a comparison of wireless networks using these two topologies.

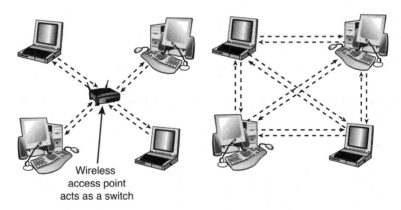

Wireless
access point
acts as a switch

FIGURE 17.18   A logical star topology (left) as used by IEEE 802.11–based wireless Ethernet in infrastructure mode compared to a point-to-point topology as used by Bluetooth and 802.11 in ad hoc mode (right).

Wireless Network Security

When I was writing the original edition of *Upgrading and Repairing PCs* back in the 1980s, the hackers' favorite way of trying to get into a network without authorization was discovering the telephone number of a modem on the network, dialing in with a computer, and guessing the password, as in the movie *War Games*. Today, war driving has largely replaced this pastime as a popular hacker sport. War driving is the popular name for driving around neighborhoods with a laptop computer equipped with a wireless network card on the lookout for unsecured networks. They're all too easy to find, and after someone gets onto your network, all the secrets in your computer can be theirs for the taking.

Because wireless networks can be accessed by anyone within signal range who has a NIC matching the same IEEE standard of that wireless network, wireless NICs and access points provide for encryption options. Most access points (even cheaper SOHO models) also provide the capability to limit connections to the access point by using a list of authorized MAC numbers (each NIC has a unique MAC). MAC address filtering designed to limit access to authorized devices only.

Although MAC address filtering can be helpful in stopping bandwidth borrowing by your neighbors, it cannot stop attacks because the MAC address can easily be "spoofed" or faked. Consequently, you need to look at other security features included in wireless networks, such as encryption.

Caution

In the past, it was thought that the SSID feature provided by the IEEE 802.11 standards was also a security feature. That's not the case. A Wi-Fi network's SSID is nothing more than a network name for the wireless network, much the same as workgroups and domains have network names that identify them. The broadcasting of the SSID can be turned off (when clients look for networks, they won't immediately see the SSID), which has been thought to provide a minor security benefit. However, Microsoft has determined that a non-broadcast SSID is actually a greater security risk than a broadcast SSID, especially with Windows XP and Windows Server 2003. For details, see "Non-broadcast Wireless Networks with Microsoft Windows" at http://technet.microsoft.com/en-us/library/bb726942.aspx. In fact, many freely available (and powerful) tools exist that allow snooping individuals to quickly discover your SSID even if it's not being broadcast, thus allowing them to connect to your unsecured wireless network.

The only way that the SSID can provide a small measure of security for your wireless network is if you change the default SSID provided by the wireless access point or router vendor. The default SSID typically identifies the manufacturer of the device (and sometimes even its model number). A hacker armed with this information can look up the default password and username for the router or access point as well as the default network address range by downloading the documentation from the vendor's website. Using this information, the hacker could compromise your network if you do not use other security measures, such as WPA/WPA2 encryption. By using a nonstandard SSID and changing the password used by your router's web-based configuration program, you make it a little more difficult for hackers to attack your network. Follow up these changes by enabling the strongest form of encryption that your wireless network supports.

All Wi-Fi products support at least 40-bit encryption through the wired equivalent privacy (WEP) specification, but the minimum standard on recent 802.11g products is 64-bit WEP encryption. Many vendors offer 128-bit or 256-bit encryption on their products. However, the 128-bit and stronger encryption feature is more common among enterprise products than SOHO–oriented products. Unfortunately, the WEP specification at any encryption strength has been shown to be notoriously insecure against determined hacking. Enabling WEP keeps a casual snooper at bay, but someone who wants to get into your wireless network won't have much trouble breaking WEP. For that reason, all wireless network products introduced after 2003 incorporate a different security standard known as Wi-Fi Protected Access (WPA). WPA is derived from the developing IEEE 802.11i security standard. WPA-enabled hardware works with existing WEP-compliant devices, and software upgrades are often available for existing devices to make them WPA capable. The latest 802.11g and 802.11n devices also support WPA2, an updated version of WPA that uses a stronger encryption method. (WPA uses TKIP or AES; WPA2 uses AES.) The new 802.11ac standard does not support WEP.

Note

Unfortunately, most 802.11b wireless network hardware supports only WEP encryption. The lack of support for more powerful encryption standards is a good reason to retire your 802.11b hardware in favor of 802.11g or 802.11n hardware, all of which support WPA or WPA2 encryption.

Upgrading to WPA or WPA2 may also require updates to your OS, especially if you are using an older version of Windows or Linux. For example, Windows XP Service Pack 2 includes support for WPA encryption. However, to use WPA2 with Windows XP Service Pack 2, you must also download the

Wireless Client Update for Windows XP with Service Pack 2, or install Service Pack 3. At the http://support.microsoft.com website, look up Knowledge Base article 917021.

Most Linux distros use wpa_supplicant. If your distro does not include wpa_supplicant, or if you need to configure it, see the http://w1.fi/wpa_supplicant/ website.

Your network will not function if different encryption levels and types are used on its wireless hardware. Use the best available encryption level and encryption type available on both the access points and the NICs for best security. Remember that if some of your network supports WPA but other parts support only WEP, your network must use the lesser of the two security standards (WEP). If you want to use the more robust WPA or WPA2 security, you must ensure that all the devices on your wireless network support WPA. Because WEP is easily broken and the specific WEP implementations vary among manufacturers, I recommend using only devices that support WPA or WPA2.

Management and DHCP Support

Most wireless access points can be managed via a web browser and provide diagnostic and monitoring tools to help you optimize the positioning of access points. Most products feature support for Dynamic Host Configuration Protocol (DHCP), allowing a user to move from one subnet to another without difficulties.

Figure 17.19 illustrates how a typical IEEE 802.11 wireless network uses multiple access points.

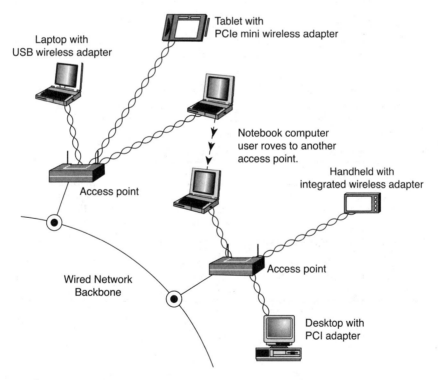

FIGURE 17.19 A typical wireless network with multiple access points.

As you can see, as users with wireless NICs move from one office to another, the roaming feature of the NIC automatically switches from one access point to another, permitting seamless network connectivity without wires or logging off the network and reconnecting.

Users per Access Point

The number of users per access point varies with the product; Wi-Fi access points are available in capacities supporting anywhere from 15 to as many as 254 users. You should contact the vendor of your preferred Wi-Fi access point device for details.

Although wired Ethernet networks are still the least expensive networks to build if you can do your own wiring, Wi-Fi networking is now cost-competitive with wired Ethernet networks when the cost of a professional wiring job is figured into the overall expense.

Because Wi-Fi is a true standard, you can mix and match access point and wireless NIC hardware to meet your desired price, performance, and feature requirements for your wireless network, just as you can for conventional Ethernet networks, provided you match up frequency bands or use dual-band hardware.

Network Protocols

A few years ago, the second-most important choice you had to make when you created a network was which network protocol to use because the network protocol affects which types of computers your network can connect. Today, the choice has largely been made for you: TCP/IP has replaced other network protocols such as IPX/SPX (used in older versions of Novell NetWare) and NetBEUI (used in older Windows and DOS-based peer-to-peer networks and with Direct Cable Connection) because it can be used both for Internet and LAN connectivity. TCP/IP is a universal protocol that virtually all OSs can use.

Although data-link protocols such as Ethernet require specific types of hardware, network protocols are software and can be installed to or removed from any computer on the network at any time, as necessary. Table 17.9 summarizes the differences between these protocols.

Table 17.9   Overview of Network Protocols and Suites

Protocol	Best Used for	Notes
TCP/IP	Most Windows-based networks, as well as Linux, UNIX, Mac OS, and other networks	Native protocol suite for Windows 2000 forward, Novell NetWare 5.x and above, Linux, UNIX, and Mac OS. Also used for dial-up Internet access.
IPX/SPX	Novell 4.x and earlier networks	Used by NetWare 5.x for certain special features only.
NetBIOS	Older Windows for Workgroups or DOS-based peer networks	Simplest protocol. It can't be routed between networks and is also used with Direct Cable Connection "networking" via USB, parallel, or serial ports.

All the computers on any given network must use the same network protocol or protocol suite to communicate with each other.

IP and TCP/IP

IP stands for Internet Protocol; it is the network layer of the collection of protocols (or protocol suite) developed for use on the Internet and commonly known as TCP/IP.

Later, the TCP/IP protocols were adopted by the UNIX OSs. They have now become the most commonly used protocol suite on PC LANs. Virtually every OS with networking capabilities supports TCP/IP, and it is well on its way to displacing all the other competing protocols. Novell NetWare 6 and above, Linux, and Windows XP and newer all use TCP/IP as their native network protocol.

TCP/IP: LAN and Dial-Up Networks

TCP/IP, unlike the other network protocols listed in the previous section, is also a protocol used by people who have never seen a NIC. People who access the Internet via modems (this is referred to as dial-up networking in some older Windows versions) use TCP/IP just as those whose web access is done with their existing LANs. Although the same protocol is used in both cases, the settings vary a great deal.

Table 17.10 summarizes the differences you're likely to encounter. If you access the Internet with both modems and a LAN, you must ensure that the TCP/IP properties for modems and LANs are set correctly. You also might need to adjust your browser settings to indicate which connection type you are using. Table 17.10 provides general guidelines; your ISP or network administrator can give you the specific details.

Table 17.10   TCP/IP Properties by Connection Type: Overview

TCP/IP Property Tab	Setting	Modem Access (Dial-up Adapter)	LAN Access (Network Card)
IP Address	IP Address	Automatically assigned by ISP	Specified (get value from network administrator) or automatically assigned by a DHCP server on the network. (DHCP servers are often built into gateways and routers.)
WINS Configuration	Enable/Disable WINS Resolution	Disabled	Indicate server or enable DHCP to allow NetBIOS over TCP/IP.
Gateway	Add Gateway/List of Gateways	Automatically assigned by ISP	IP address of gateway used to connect the LAN to the Internet.
DNS Configuration	Enable/Disable Host Domain	Automatically assigned by ISP	Enabled, with the host and domain specified (get value from network administrator).

As you can see from Table 17.10, correct settings for LAN access to the Internet and dial-up networking (modem) settings are almost always completely different. In general, the best way to get your dial-up networking connection working correctly is to use your ISP's automatic setup software. This is usually supplied as part of your ISP's signup software kit. After the setup is working, view the properties and record them for future troubleshooting use.

IPX and NetBEUI

The IPX protocol suite (often referred to as *IPX/SPX*) is the collective term for the proprietary protocols Novell created for its NetWare OS. It has been replaced in NetWare v 6.0 and above by TCP/IP.

NetBEUI was formerly used for non-routeable workgroup networking in Windows versions preceding Windows XP. It has been replaced by TCP/IP in Windows XP and more recent versions.

If you need more information about NetBEUI or IPX, see their respective sections in Chapter 17 of *Upgrading and Repairing PCs*, 19th Edition, available on the disc packaged with this book.

Other Home Networking Solutions

If you are working at home or in a small office, you have an alternative to hole-drilling, pulling specialized network cabling, or setting up a wireless network.

So-called "home" networking is designed to minimize the complexities of cabling and wireless configuration by providing users with a sort of instant network that requires no additional wiring and configures with little technical understanding.

The two major standards in this area are

- **HomePNA**—Uses existing telephone wiring
- **HomePlug**—Uses existing power lines and outlets

HomePNA

Other than using Ethernet (wired or wireless), the most popular form of home networking involves adapting existing telephone wiring to networking by running network signals at frequencies above those used by the telephone system. Because HomePNA is the most developed and most broadly supported type of home networking, this discussion focuses on the HomePNA standards that the Home Phoneline Networking Alliance (www.homepna.org) has created. This alliance has most of the major computer hardware and telecommunications vendors among its founding and active membership.

The Home Phoneline Networking Alliance has developed three versions of its HomePNA standard. HomePNA 1.0, introduced in 1998, ran at only 1Mbps and was quickly superseded by HomePNA 2.0 in late 1999. HomePNA 2.0 supported up to 32Mbps, although most products ran at 10Mbps, bringing it to parity with 10BASE-T Ethernet. Although some vendors produced HomePNA 1.0 and 2.0 products, these versions of HomePNA never became popular. Both of these products use a bus topology that runs over existing telephone wiring and are designed for PC networking only.

With the development of HomePNA 3.1 in 2007, the emphasis of HomePNA has shifted from strictly PC networking to a true "digital home" solution that incorporates PCs, set-top boxes, TVs, and other multimedia hardware on a single network.

HomePNA 3.1 is the latest version of the HomePNA standard. In addition to telephone wiring, HomePNA 3.1 supports coaxial cable used for services such as TV, set-top boxes, and IP phones. As shown in Figure 17.20, HomePNA 3.1 incorporates both types of wiring into a single network that runs at speeds up to 320Mbps, carries voice, data, and IPTV service, and provides guaranteed quality of service (QoS) to avoid data collisions and avoid disruptions to VoIP and streaming media. *HomePNA* refers to the ability to carry VoIP, IPTV, and data as a "triple-play." HomePNA 3.1 also supports remote management of the network by the service provider.

Because HomePNA 3.1 has been designed to handle a mixture of traditional data and Internet telephone (VoIP) and TV (IPTV) service, HomePNA 3.1 hardware is being installed and distributed by telephone and media providers, rather than being sold primarily through retail channels. For example, AT&T uses HomePNA 3.1 for its AT&T U-verse IPTV, broadband, and VoIP service.

Note

For more information about AT&T U-verse, see the AT&T U-verse website at https://uverse1.att.com/launchAMSS.do. AT&T U-verse users and others share information at the UverseUsers website (www.uverseusers.com).

◄◄   For more information about sharing Internet access and broadband Internet devices, see Chapter 16, "Internet Connectivity," **p. 775**.

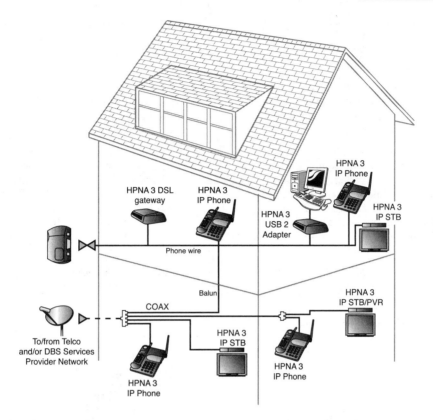

FIGURE 17.20   A typical HomePNA 3.1 network interconnecting PC, telephone, and TV service via telephone and coaxial cables.

Power Line Networking

Home networking via power lines has been under development for several years, but electrical interference, inconsistent voltage, and security issues made the creation of a workable standard difficult until mid-2001. In June 2001, the HomePlug Powerline Alliance, a multivendor industry trade group, introduced its HomePlug 1.0 specification for 14Mbps home networking using power lines. The HomePlug Powerline Alliance (www.homeplug.org) conducted field tests in about 500 households early in 2001 to develop the HomePlug 1.0 specification.

HomePlug 1.0 is based on the PowerPacket technology developed by Intellon. PowerPacket uses a signaling method called *orthogonal frequency division multiplexing (OFDM)*, which combines multiple signals at different frequencies to form a single signal for transmission. Because OFDM uses multiple frequencies, it can adjust to the constantly changing characteristics of AC power. To provide security, PowerPacket also supports 56-bit DES encryption and an individual key for each home network. By using PowerPacket technology, HomePlug 1.0 is designed to solve the power quality and security issues of concern to a home or small-office network user. Although HomePlug 1.0 is rated at 14Mbps, typical real-world performance is usually around 4Mbps for LAN applications and around 2Mbps when connected to a broadband Internet device such as a cable modem.

HomePlug 1.0 products include USB and Ethernet adapters, bridges, and routers, enabling most recent PCs with USB or Ethernet ports to use Powerline networking for LAN and Internet sharing. Linksys was the first to introduce HomePlug 1.0 products in late 2001; other leading vendors producing HomePlug hardware include Phonex, NETGEAR, and Asoka. HomePlug Turbo, an updated version of the HomePlug 1.0 standard, supports data rates up to 85Mbps, with typical throughput in the 15Mbps–20Mbps range.

The HomePlug AV specification with support for faster speeds (up to 200Mbps), multimedia hardware, and guaranteed bandwidth for multimedia applications was announced in the fall of 2002; the final HomePlug AV specification was approved in August 2005. HomePlug AV uses the Line-Neutral wire pair for transmissions.

When connecting HomePlug 1.0 and AV products, make sure that all of the devices support the same standard; that is, either HomePlug 1.0 (85Mbps) or HomePlug AV (200Mbps). Although HomePlug 1.0 and AV devices can coexist on the same powerline wiring, they can only communicate with devices supporting the same standard. HomePlug AV2, which supports MIMO with beamforming, power saving modes, from 30–86MHz additional bandwidth, and other improvements, was released in January 2012. HomePlug AV2 can use any two pairs in a three-wire configuration, including Line-Neutral, Line-Ground, or Neutral Ground, and is designed to reach performance up to five times faster than HomePlug AV (up to 1000Mbps).

HomePlug AV, HomePlug AV2, and HomePlug Green PHY (designed for command, control, and automotive applications) can interoperate with each other.

The HomePlug Powerline Alliance uses certification marks to indicate which HomePlug certifications are supported by a particular device. Figure 17.21 shows the original and new HomePlug certification marks.

FIGURE 17.21 The HomePlug Powerline Alliance certification marks. The original mark (left) for HomePlug 14Mbps network devices only has been replaced by the new multipurpose mark (right).

Putting Your Network Together

In this section is a detailed checklist of the hardware and software you need to build your network.

First, start with the number of computers you plan to network. You need the items discussed in this section to set up your network.

Network Adapters

Every system needs a network adapter or interface card. These are normally built in but can also be added in the form of a card or external USB device.

Traditionally, network adapters are also called network interface cards (NICs). To simplify technical support and minimize the number of drivers you have to deal with, where possible I recommend you use the same make and model of NIC for each computer in your network.

For the best performance in a wired network, I recommend using only Gigabit Ethernet components, especially with regards to NICs and switches. If your system has a built-in Fast Ethernet (100Mbps) NIC, you might consider replacing it with a Gigabit Ethernet card. I recommend PCI-Express-based Gigabit NICs for desktop computers and ExpressCard Gigabit NICs for laptop computers with ExpressCard slots. (ExpressCard includes the PCI-Express bus.) USB network adapters can be convenient, but USB 1.1 sockets are much slower than 10/100 Ethernet and slow down any USB-attached network interface. USB 2.0 sockets and devices are satisfactory for connecting 10/100 Ethernet USB adapters, but they are completely inadequate for Gigabit Ethernet adapters. USB 3.0 ports support Gigabit Ethernet speeds when connected to Gigabit Ethernet adapters for USB 3.0.

When adding wireless networking to desktop systems, I recommend USB wireless network adapters over those using PCI or PCIe slots. There are several reasons:

- **Installation**—You don't need to open the system to install a USB device.
- **Portability**—You can easily use the USB device with any other PC.
- **Signal strength**—You can more easily achieve optimal antenna placement with a USB device, especially when attached to the end of an extension cable.

For the best performance, systems should be connected via a Gigabit wired connection. Wireless should only be used if a wired connection isn't possible or cost effective.

You should record the brand name and model number of the network adapters you are using, as well as the driver version or source. Use Table 17.11 in the section, "Configuring Your Network Software," later in this chapter, as a template for storing this information.

Installing the Network Adapter

When installing an internal network card, follow this procedure:

1. Open the case and locate an open expansion slot that matches the type of NIC you purchased (preferably PCI or PCI-Express).
2. Using a screwdriver, remove the screw securing the slot cover at the rear of the case.
3. Insert the card gently, ensuring that the edge connector is seated solidly in the slot.
4. Fasten down the card with the same screw that held the slot cover.

Tip

If you are a realist, like me, you might not want to close the case until you are certain the NIC is working. (See the next section, "Testing Your Network Adapters and Connections.")

Once the network adapter is installed, you need to install the drivers for the card that match your OS.

Testing Your Network Adapters and Connections

Connect the network adapter to the network. With an Ethernet network using UTP cable, run the cable from the card to the switch, turn on the computer and switch, and watch for signal lights to light up on the NIC's back bracket (if so equipped) and on the switch. Switches normally use LEDs to indicate the presence of a computer on a particular port, and they usually indicate the connected speed. If the LEDs show that the card is connected at the correct speed, that usually indicates the card and intervening cabling are functioning correctly. For other types of networks, see the diagnostics provided with the network hardware for testing details.

Cables and Connections Between Computers

Depending on the network architecture you choose, you might need to run cables. If you are installing a Fast or Gigabit Ethernet network (both of which use UTP cables), you need cables that are long enough to reach comfortably between each computer's network port and the network's hub or switch.

Because HomePNA networks are based on your existing telephone line, the patch cord included with the NIC is usually long enough to connect with your existing RJ-11 telephone jack. The HomePNA NIC has two jacks: one for the connection to the telephone line and the other to enable you to connect your telephone to the NIC. Be sure you use the correct jack for each cable; otherwise, your network won't work. HomePNA enables you to use your telephone system for voice and networking at the same time.

Wireless network NICs use an external antenna to make the connection between computers. In some cases, the antenna is built into the NIC, whereas in other cases the antenna is attached to the NIC or needs to be extended from a storage position inside the NIC.

Switch/Access Point

UTP Ethernet networks require a switch if more than two computers will be networked. (You can use a crossover cable between two computers only.) Wireless Ethernet networks also require an access point if more than two computers will be networked or if the network will be used to share an Internet connection. Switches and access points are normally included in a wireless router. With a wireless router/switch as a starting point, additional switches or access points can then be added as necessary.

For a wired Ethernet network, use one or more switches of the correct speed with at least enough ports for each computer on the network. For a wireless Ethernet network, you need at least one access point, depending on the range of your wireless network. Most access points have a range of 150 to 250 feet indoors (and up to twice that distance or more outdoors), which is adequate for most homes and many small businesses. You can use high-gain antennas or add more access points if you need a wider area of coverage.

Configuring Your Network Software

Windows 9x, 2000, XP, and later normally install all of the networking software you need automatically. Table 17.11 shows the minimum network software configuration you must install for Windows peer-to-peer networking. Windows Vista and later editions use the Network and Sharing Center to configure peer-to-peer networking.

Table 17.11   Minimum Network Software for Peer-to-Peer Networking

Item	Workstation	Server
Windows Network client	Yes	No
NetBEUI or TCP/IP* protocol	Yes	Yes
File and print sharing for Microsoft Networks	No	Yes
NIC installed and bound to protocols and services above	Yes	Yes
Workgroup identification (same for all PCs in workgroup)	Yes	Yes
Computer name (each PC needs a unique name)	Yes	Yes

* If TCP/IP is used as the standard protocol, each workstation must have a different IP address—either manually assigned or received from a DHCP server built into a server, router, or gateway computer or device.

▶▶ For more information about Windows Vista/7/8 and networks, see the section, "Networking with Windows Vista/7/8," **p. 843**.

Use the Network icon in the Windows Control Panel to select your network settings. To set up your network, you'll need the OS CDs, disks, or hard-disk image files and the network adapter drivers. Devices like routers, access points, and switches either have software built in (accessible via an internal web page), or they don't need any software at all.

To install a network component, follow this procedure:

1. Open the Network icon in the Control Panel.

2. The Configuration tab is displayed; select Add.

3. Select from the following:

   - **Client**—Select if you want to install the Microsoft or other network clients for your network. Every PC on a peer-to-peer network needs the Client for Microsoft Networks.

   - **Adapter**—This should already be installed, but you can use this option to install a new adapter.

   - **Protocol**—For a simple, non-Internet network with versions of Windows before XP, install NetBEUI. If you want to use Internet Connection Sharing along with networking, install both TCP/IP and NetBEUI. With Windows XP, use the Network Setup Wizard to configure TCP/IP easily.

   - **Service**—Install File and Printer Sharing for Microsoft Networks on any computer that will be used as a server.

4. Click the Identification tab. Enter a unique name for each computer on the network; use the same workgroup name for all computers on the network.

5. Click OK. Supply the Windows install disc or other media as necessary to install the network components you requested.

You might need to reboot your PC to complete the process. After this is completed, you'll be ready to share resources.

Networking with Windows Vista/7/8

Windows Vista and newer include TCP/IP as their default protocol, enabling it to connect to other computers running Windows or other OSs. However, their network management and configuration processes are much different from those that earlier Windows versions used.

Network management is performed through the new Network and Sharing Center. The Network and Sharing Center displays the status of the network, the signal strength for wireless networks, the status of network discovery and the sharing of files, the Public folder (equivalent to the Shared Files folder in XP), printer sharing, and media sharing. The Network and Sharing Center can change these settings as desired and controls whether password-protected sharing is enabled or disabled. When this feature is disabled, Vista/7/8 acts like Windows XP with simple file sharing enabled. When this feature is enabled, you must set up users and assign them rights just you would with Windows XP Professional with simple file sharing disabled.

The Network and Sharing Center can also provide a map of your network, showing the relationship of devices such as routers and switches and Windows Vista/7/8–based computers on the network. To add Windows XP–based systems to the network map, you can install the Link Layer Topology Discoverer (LLTD) responder. To get this feature and learn how it works, look up the Knowledge Base article

922120, "Network Map Does Not Display Computers That Are Running Windows XP," at http://support.microsoft.com.

To add a protocol or component to a particular network connection, open Networks, select Network and Sharing Center, and select Manage Network Connections from the task list. Then, right-click the network adapter and select Properties.

Other differences include enhancements in the use and management of wireless networks, improvements to the Windows Firewall, and improvements in the network repair and diagnostics procedure. Windows Vista/7/8 also adds support for network projectors and online meetings, using its new People Near Me and Windows Meeting Space utilities.

In Windows 8, you can also perform some network tasks, such as connecting to a wireless network, from the Start screen.

Power Supplies

The Power Supply

The power supply is not only one of the most important parts in a PC, it is unfortunately one of the most overlooked. Although most enthusiasts who build their own systems understand its importance, the mainstream PC buyer generally does not. Some that do pay any mind seem concerned only with how many watts of power it is rated to put out (even though no practical way exists to verify those ratings), without regard to whether the power being produced is clean and stable or whether it is full of noise, spikes, and surges.

I have always placed great emphasis on selecting a power supply for my systems. I consider the power supply the foundation of the system and am willing to spend a little extra to get a more robust and reliable unit. The power supply is critical because it supplies electrical power to every other component in the system. In my experience, the power supply is also one of the most failure-prone components in any computer system. Over the years, I have replaced more power supplies in PCs than any other part. A malfunctioning power supply not only can cause other components in the system to malfunction, but can damage the other components in your computer by delivering improper or erratic voltages. Because of its importance to proper and reliable system operation, you should understand both the function and the limitations of a power supply, as well as its potential problems and their solutions.

Primary Function and Operation

The basic function of the power supply is to convert the electrical power available at the wall socket to that which the computer circuitry can use. The power supply in a conventional desktop system is designed to convert either 120V (nominal) 60Hz AC (alternating current) or 240V (nominal) 50Hz AC power into +3.3V, +5V, and +12V DC (direct current) power. Some power supplies require you to switch between the two input ranges, whereas others auto-switch.

Technically, the power supply in most PCs is described as a constant voltage switching power supply unit (PSU), which is defined as follows:

- Constant voltage means the power supply puts out the same voltage to the computer's internal components, no matter the voltage of AC current running it or the capacity (wattage) of the power supply.

■ Switching refers to the design and power regulation technique that most suppliers use. Compared to other types of power supplies, this design provides an efficient and inexpensive power source and generates a minimum amount of heat. It also maintains a small size and low price.

Voltage Rails

The PSU normally supplies +3.3V, +5V, and +12V to the system. These voltages are often called *rails*, referring to the fact that although there are multiple wires carrying a specific voltage, they are normally tied to a single rail (or tap) in the PSU. Multiple wires are used because, if all of the current were carried over a single wire, the wire and the terminals, connectors, and even the traces on the circuit boards would all have to be extremely large and thick to handle the load. Instead, it is cheaper and more efficient to spread the load out among multiple smaller and thinner wires.

The digital electronic components and circuits in the system (motherboard, adapter cards, and disk drive logic boards) typically use the +3.3V or +5V power, and the motors (disk drive motors and any fans) use the +12V power. In addition, voltage regulators on the motherboard or in other components convert these standard voltages to others as necessary. Table 18.1 lists the devices typically powered by the various voltage rails.

Table 18.1   Voltage Rail Usage in a PC

Rail	Devices Powered
+3.3V	Chipsets, some DIMMs, PCI/AGP/PCIe cards, miscellaneous chips
+5V	Disk drive logic, low-voltage motors, SIMMs, PCI/AGP/ISA cards, voltage regulators, miscellaneous chips
+12V	Motors, high-output voltage regulators, AGP/PCIe cards

SIMM = Single Inline Memory Module
DIMM = Dual Inline Memory Module
PCI = Peripheral Component Interconnect
PCIe = PCI Express
AGP = Accelerated Graphics Port
ISA = Industry Standard Architecture

You can think of each rail as a separate power circuit, kind of like a power supply within the power supply. Normally, each rail is rated for a specified maximum amount of current in amperes. Because the extreme amount of 12V current required by newer CPU voltage regulators and high-end video cards can exceed the output of common 12V rails, some power supply designs use multiple +12V rails. This means that essentially they have two or more separate 12V circuits internally, with some wires tapping off of one circuit and others tapping off of another. Unfortunately, this can lead to power problems, especially if you fail to balance the loads on both rails or to ensure you don't exceed the load capacity on one or the other. In other words, it is far better to have a single 12V rail that can supply 40 amps than two 12V rails supplying 20 amps each because with the single rail you don't have to worry which connectors derive power from which rail and then try to ensure that you don't overload one or the other.

Whereas the +3.3V, +5V, and +12V rails are technically independent inside the power supply, many cheaper designs have them sharing some circuitry, making them less independent than they should be. This manifests itself in voltage regulation problems in which a significant load on one rail causes a voltage drop on the others. Components such as processors and video cards can vary their power consumption greatly by their activity. Transitioning from sitting at the Windows desktop to loading a 3D game can cause both the processor and video card to more than double the draw on the +12V rail. On some cheaper power supplies, this can cause the voltages on the other rails to fall out of spec (drop greater than 5%), making the system crash. Better designed power supplies feature truly independent rails with tighter regulation in the 1% to 3% range.

Voltage Regulators

The power supply must deliver a good, steady supply of DC power so the system can operate properly. Devices that run on voltages other than these directly must then be indirectly powered through onboard voltage regulators, which take the 5V or 12V from the power supply and convert that to the lower voltages required by various components. For example, older DDR (double data rate) dual inline memory modules (DIMMs) and Rambus inline memory modules (RIMMs) require 2.5V, whereas DDR2 and DDR3 DIMMs require 1.8V and 1.5V, legacy AGP 4x/8x cards require 1.5V, and current PCI Express cards use only 0.8V differential signaling—all of which are supplied by simple onboard regulators. Processors also require a variety of voltages (as low as 1.3V or less) that are supplied by a sophisticated voltage regulator module (VRM) that is either built into or plugged into the motherboard. You'll commonly find three or more different voltage regulator circuits on a modern motherboard.

Note

When Intel began releasing processors that required a +3.3V power source, power supplies that supplied the additional output voltage were not yet available. As a result, motherboard manufacturers began adding voltage regulators to their boards, which converted +5V to +3.3V for the processor. When other chips began using 3.3V as well, Intel created the ATX power supply specification, which supplied 3.3V to the motherboard. You would think that having 3.3V direct from the power supply would have eliminated the need for onboard voltage regulators, but by that time, processors, memory, and other components began running on voltages lower than 3.3V. Motherboard manufacturers then included adaptable regulator circuits called *voltage regulator modules* to accommodate the widely varying processor voltage requirements. Additional regulators are also used to power other devices on the motherboard that don't use +3.3V, +5V, or +12V.

◀◀ See the Chapter 3 section, "CPU Operating Voltages," **p. 87**.

Negative DC Voltages

If you look at a specification sheet for a typical PC power supply, you can see that the supply generates not only +3.3V, +5V, and +12V, but also –12V and possibly –5V. Although –12V and (possibly) –5V are supplied to the motherboard via the power supply connectors, the motherboard normally uses only the +3.3V, +5V, and +12V. If present, the –5V is simply routed to the ISA bus on pin B5 so any ISA cards can use it, even though very few ever have. However, as an example, the analog data separator circuits found in older floppy controllers did use –5V. The motherboard logic typically doesn't use –12V either; however, in the past it was used in some board designs for serial port or local area network (LAN) circuits.

The positive voltages seemingly power everything in the system (logic and motors), so what are the negative voltages used for? The answer is, not much! In fact, –5V was removed from the ATX12V 1.3 and later specifications. The only reason it remained in most power supply designs for many years is that –5V was required on the ISA bus for full backward compatibility. Because modern PCs no longer include ISA slots, the –5V signal was deemed as no longer necessary. However, if you are installing a new power supply in a system with an older motherboard that incorporates ISA bus slots, you want a supply that does include the –5V signal.

Although older serial port circuits used +/–12V outputs, today most run only on +3.3V or +5V.

The main function of the +12V power is to run disk drive motors as well as the higher-output processor voltage regulators in some of the newer boards. Usually, a large amount of +12V current is available from the power supply, especially in those designed for systems with a large number of drive bays (such as in a tower configuration). Besides disk drive motors and newer CPU voltage regulators, the +12V supply is used by any cooling fans in the system—which, of course, should always be running. A single cooling fan can draw between 100mA and 250mA (0.1–0.25 amps); however, most newer fans use the lower 100mA figure. Note that, although most fans in desktop systems run on +12V, portable systems can use fans that run on +5V or even +3.3V.

Systems with modern form factors based on the ATX or BTX standards include another special signal. This feature, called *PS_ON*, can turn the power supply (and thus the system) on or off via software. It is sometimes known as the *soft-power feature*. PS_ON is most evident when you use it with an operating system (OS) such as Windows that supports the Advanced Power Management (APM) or Advanced Configuration and Power Interface (ACPI) specification. When you shut down a PC from the Start menu, Windows automatically turns off the computer after it completes the OS shutdown sequence. A system without this feature only displays a message that it's safe or ready for you to shut down the computer manually.

The Power Good Signal

In addition to supplying electrical power to run the system, the power supply ensures that the system does not run unless the voltages supplied are sufficient to operate the system properly. In other words, the power supply actually prevents the computer from starting up or operating until all the power supply voltages are within the proper ranges.

The power supply completes internal checks and tests before allowing the system to start. If the tests are successful, the power supply sends a special signal to the motherboard called Power_Good. This signal must be continuously present for the system to run. Therefore, when the AC voltage dips and the power supply can't maintain outputs within regulation tolerance, the Power_Good signal is withdrawn (goes low) and forces the system to reset. The system does not restart until the Power_Good signal returns.

The *Power_Good* signal (sometimes called *Power_OK* or *PWR_OK*) is a +5V (nominal) active high signal (with a variation from +2.4V through +6.0V generally being considered acceptable) that is supplied to the motherboard when the power supply has passed its internal self-tests and the output voltages have stabilized. This typically takes place anywhere from 100ms to 500ms (0.1–0.5 seconds) after you turn on the power supply switch. The power supply then sends the Power_Good signal to the motherboard, where the processor timer chip that controls the reset line to the processor receives it.

In the absence of Power_Good, the timer chip holds the reset line on the processor, which prevents the system from running under bad or unstable power conditions. When the timer chip receives the Power_Good signal, it releases the reset and the processor begins executing whatever code is at address FFFF0h (occupied by the motherboard ROM).

If the power supply can't maintain proper outputs (such as when a brownout occurs), the Power_Good signal is withdrawn and the processor is automatically reset. When the power output returns to its proper levels, the power supply regenerates the Power_Good signal and the system again begins operation (as if you had just powered on). By withdrawing Power_Good before the output voltages fall out of regulation, the system never sees the bad power because it is stopped quickly (reset) rather than being allowed to operate using unstable or improper power levels, which can cause memory parity errors and other problems.

Note

You can use the Power_Good feature as a method of implementing a reset switch for the PC. The Power_Good line is wired to the clock generator circuit, which controls the clock and reset lines to the microprocessor. When you ground the Power_Good line with a switch, the timer chip and related circuitry reset the processor. The result is a full hardware reset of the system. Instructions for making and installing a reset switch can be found in the section "Making and Installing a Reset Switch" in the Technical Reference portion of the DVD included with this book.

◄◄ See "Parity and ECC," **p. 357**.

On pre-ATX systems, the Power_Good connection is made via connector P8-1 (P8 pin 1) from the power supply to the motherboard. ATX, BTX, and later systems use pin 8 of the 20/24-pin main power connector, which is usually a gray wire.

A properly designed power supply delays the arrival of the Power_Good signal until all the voltages stabilize upon turning on the system. Poorly designed power supplies, which are found in many low-cost systems, often do not delay the Power_Good signal properly and enable the processor to start too soon. (The normal Power_Good delay is 0.1–0.5 seconds.) Improper Power_Good timing also causes CMOS memory corruption in some systems.

Note

If you find that a system consistently fails to boot up properly the first time you turn on the switch, but that it subsequently boots up if you press the reset or Ctrl+Alt+Delete warm boot command, you likely have a problem with the Power_Good timing. You should install a new, higher-quality power supply and see whether that solves the problem.

Some cheaper power supplies do not have proper Power_Good circuitry and might just tie any +5V line to that signal. Some motherboards are more sensitive to an improperly designed or improperly functioning Power_Good signal than others. Intermittent startup problems are often the result of improper Power_Good signal timing. A common example is when you replace a motherboard in a system and then find that the system intermittently fails to start properly when you turn on the power. This can be difficult to diagnose, especially for the inexperienced technician, because the problem appears to be caused by the new motherboard. Although it seems as though the new motherboard is defective, it usually turns out that the power supply is poorly designed. It either can't produce stable enough power to properly operate the new board, or it has an improperly wired or timed Power_Good signal (which is more likely). In these situations, replacing the supply with a higher-quality unit, in addition to the new motherboard, is the proper solution.

Power Supply Form Factors

The shape and general physical layout of a component is called the *form factor*. Items that share a form factor are generally interchangeable, at least as far as their sizes and fits are concerned. When designing a PC, the engineers can choose to use one of the popular standard PSU form factors, or they can elect to build their own custom design. Choosing the former means that a virtually inexhaustible supply of inexpensive replacement parts will be available in a variety of quality and power output levels. Going the custom route means additional time and expense for development. In addition, the power supply is unique to the system and generally available for replacement only from the original manufacturer. This precludes any upgrades as well, such as installing higher-output replacement models.

If you can't tell already, I am a fan of the industry-standard form factors! Having standards and then following them allows us to upgrade and repair our systems by easily replacing physically (and electrically) interchangeable components. Having interchangeable parts means that we have a better range of choices for replacement items, and the competition makes for better pricing, too.

In the PC market, IBM originally defined the form factor standards, and everybody else copied them; this included power supplies. All the popular PC power supply form factors up through 1995 were based on one of three IBM models, including the PC/XT, AT, and PS/2 Model 30. The interesting thing is that these three original IBM power supply form factors had the same motherboard connectors and pinouts; where they differed was mainly in shape, maximum power output, the number of peripheral power connectors, and switch mounting. PC systems using knock-offs of one of those three designs were popular up through 1996 and beyond; in fact, even the current industry standard ATX12V models are based on the PS/2 Model 30 physical form factor, but with different connectors.

Intel defined a new power supply form factor in 1995 with the introduction of the ATX form factor. ATX became popular in 1996 and started a shift away from the previous IBM-based standards. ATX and the standards that have followed since use different connectors with additional voltages and signals that allow systems with greater power consumption and additional features that would otherwise not be possible with the AT-style supplies.

Note

Although two power supplies can share the same basic design and form factor, they can differ greatly in quality and efficiency. Later in this chapter, you'll learn about some of the features and specifications to look for when evaluating PC power supplies.

More than 10 different power supply form factors have existed that can be called industry standards. Many of these are or were based on designs IBM created in the 1980s, whereas the rest are based on Intel designs from the 1990s to the present. The industry-standard form factors can be broken down into two main categories: those that are currently in use in modern systems and those that are largely obsolete.

Note that although the names of some of the power supply form factors seem to be the same as those of motherboard form factors, the power supply form factor relates more to the system chassis (case) than to the motherboard. That is because all the form factors use one of only two main types of connector designs: either AT or ATX, with subtle variations on each. So, although a particular power supply form factor might be *typically* associated with a particular motherboard form factor, many other power supplies would plug in as well.

For example, all modern ATX form factor motherboards with PCI Express slots have two main power connectors, including a 24-pin ATX main connector along with a 4-pin +12V connector. All the modern power supply form factors include these same connectors and therefore are capable of plugging into the same motherboards. In other words, no matter what the form factor of the motherboard (ATX, BTX, or any of the smaller variants of either), virtually any of the modern industry-standard power supplies will plug in.

Plugging the power supply connectors into the motherboard is one thing, but for the power supply to work in the system, it must physically fit inside the chassis or case—and that is what the different modern power supply form factors are all about. The bottom line is that it is up to you to ensure that the power supply you purchase not only plugs in to your motherboard, but also fits into the chassis or case you plan to use.

Tables 18.2 and 18.3 show the industry-standard power supply form factors, their connector types, and the motherboard form factors with which they are *usually* associated.

Table 18.2 Modern Industry-Standard Power Supply Form Factors

Modern Power Supply Form Factors	Year Introduced	Connector Types	Normally Associated Motherboard Form Factors
ATX/ATX12V	1995	20/24-pin Main, 4-pin +12V	ATX, microATX, BTX, microBTX
SFX/SFX12V/PS3	1997	20/24-pin Main, 4-pin +12V	microATX, FlexATX, microBTX, picoBTX, Mini-ITX, DTX
EPS/EPS12V	1998	24-pin Main, 8-pin +12V	ATX, extended ATX
TFX12V	2002	20/24-pin Main, 4-pin +12V	microATX, FlexATX, microBTX, picoBTX, Mini-ITX, DTX
CFX12V	2003	20/24-pin Main, 4-pin +12V	microBTX, picoBTX, DTX
LFX12V	2004	24-pin Main, 4-pin +12V	picoBTX, nanoBTX, DTX
Flex ATX	2007	24-pin Main, 4-pin +12V	microATX, FlexATX, microBTX, picoBTX, nanoBTX, Mini-ITX, DTX

SFX12V also includes the PS3 form factor, which is a shortened version of ATX12V.

12V versions include a 4-pin or 8-pin +12V connector.

You may encounter power supplies using obsolete form factors if you work on PCs built in the 1980s through the mid-1990s. I cover them in more detail in the 18th and earlier editions of this book.

Table 18.3 Obsolete Industry Standard Power Supply Form Factors

Obsolete Power Supply Form Factors	Year Introduced	Connector Types	Normally Associated Motherboard Form Factors
PC/XT	1981	PC/XT	PC/XT, Baby-AT
AT/Desk	1984	AT	Full-size AT, Baby-AT
AT/Tower	1984	AT	Full-size AT, Baby-AT
Baby-AT	1984	AT	Full-size AT, Baby-AT
LPX (PS/2)	1987	AT	Baby-AT, Mini-AT, LPX

PC/XT connectors were the same as AT connectors, except one +5V pin (P8 pin 2) was not used.

LPX is also sometimes called PS/2 or Slimline.

Each of these power supply form factors is, or has been, available in numerous configurations and power output levels. The obsolete LPX form factor supply originated in the IBM PS/2 Model 30 in April 1987 and was the standard used on most systems from the late 1980s to mid-1996, when the ATX form factor started to gain in popularity. Since then, ATX and the many variants based on ATX have become by far the dominant form factors for power supplies. It is interesting to note that IBM's legacy lives on even now because ATX, PS3, and EPS are all based on the LPX (PS/2) physical form factor. Any power supply that does not conform to one of these standards is considered *proprietary*. In general, avoid systems that use proprietary power supply designs because replacements are difficult to obtain and upgrades are generally not available. When you consider that the power supply is one of the most failure-prone components, purchasing systems that use proprietary designs can be a signifi-cant liability in the future. If you need a replacement for a proprietary form factor supply, one of the best sources is ATXPowerSupplies.com. They maintain replacement models that cover a huge number of both proprietary and industry standard designs.

◀◀   See the Chapter 4 section, "Motherboard Form Factors," **p. 155**.

Modern Form Factors

The power supply form factors detailed in the following sections are the standards used in current systems. ATX is far and away the most common of these, but if you work on a variety of PC types, you are likely to encounter the other types listed here.

ATX/ATX12V

In 1995, Intel saw that the existing power supply designs were literally running out of power. The problem was that the existing standards used two connectors with a total of only 12 pins providing power to the motherboard. In addition, the connectors used were difficult to properly key, and plugging them in improperly resulted in short-circuiting and damage to both the motherboard and the power supply. To solve these problems, in 1995 Intel took the existing popular LPX (PS/2) design and simply changed the internal circuitry and connectors (while leaving the mechanical shape the same), giving birth to the ATX power supply form factor (see Figure 18.1).

Intel released the ATX specification in 1995, and in 1996, it started to become increasingly popular in Pentium and Pentium Pro–based PCs, capturing 18% of the market within the first year. Since 1996, ATX variants have become both the dominant motherboard and power supply form factors, replacing the previously popular Baby-AT/LPX designs. ATX12V power supplies are also used with newer motherboard form factors such as BTX, ensuring that ATX and its derivatives will remain the most popular power supply form factors for several years to come. The ATX12V specification defines the physical or mechanical form as well as the electrical connectors for the power supply.

From 1995 through early 2000, the ATX power supply form factor was defined as part of the ATX motherboard specification. However, in February 2000, Intel took the power supply specification out of the then-current ATX 2.03 motherboard/chassis specification and created the ATX/ATX12V power supply specification 1.0, adding an optional 4-pin +12V connector at the same time. (Those with the +12V connector were called ATX12V supplies.) The +12V connector was made a requirement in version 1.3 (April 2002), whereupon the specification became only ATX12V. The ATX12V 2.0 specification (February 2003) dropped the 6-pin auxiliary connector, changed the main power connector to 24 pins, and made Serial ATA power connectors a requirement. The current version is ATX12V 2.2, which was released in March 2005 and contains only minor changes from the previous releases, such as the use of Molex High Current System (HCS) terminals in the connectors.

As the ATX power supply specification has evolved, there have been some changes in the cooling fan orientation and design. The ATX specification originally called for an 80mm fan to be mounted along the inner side of the supply, where it could draw air in from the rear of the chassis and blow it inside across the motherboard. This kind of airflow runs in the opposite direction from most standard supplies, which exhaust air out the back of the supply through a hole in the case where the fan protrudes. The idea was that the reverse-flow design could cool the system more efficiently with only a single fan, eliminating the need for a fan (active) heatsink on the CPU.

Another benefit of the reverse-flow cooling is that the system would run cleaner, freer from dust and dirt. The case would be pressurized, so air would be continuously forced out of the cracks in the case— the opposite of what happens with a negative pressure design. For this reason, the reverse-flow cooling design is often referred to as a *positive-pressure-ventilation design*. On an ATX system with reverse-flow cooling, the air is blown out away from the drive because the only air intake is the single fan vent on the power supply at the rear. For systems that operate in extremely harsh environments, you can add a filter to the fan intake vent to further ensure that all the air entering the system is clean and free of dust.

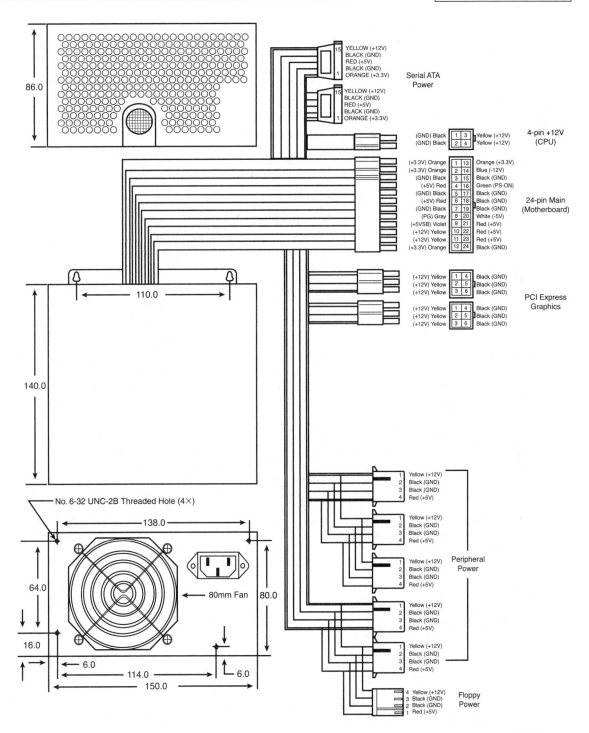

FIGURE 18.1 ATX12V 2.x form factor power supply with 24-pin main, 4-pin +12V, and optional PCI Express Graphics connectors.

Although this sounds like a good way to ventilate a system, the positive-pressure design needs to use a more powerful fan to pull the required amount of air through a filter and pressurize the case. Also, if a filter is used, it must be serviced periodically; depending on operating conditions, it could need changing or cleaning as often as every week. In addition, the heat load from the power supply on a fully loaded system heats the air being ingested, blowing warm air over the CPU and reducing the overall cooling capability.

As CPUs evolved to generate more and more heat, the cooling capability of the system became more critical and the positive-pressure design was simply not up to the task. Therefore, subsequent versions of the ATX specification were rewritten to allow both positive- and negative-pressure designs, but they emphasized the standard negative-pressure system with an exhaust fan on the power supply and an additional high-quality cooling fan blowing cool air right on the CPU as the best solution.

Because a standard negative-pressure system offers the greatest cooling capacity for a given fan's airspeed and flow, virtually all recent ATX-style power supplies use a negative-pressure design, in which air flows out the back of the power supply. Most use an 80mm fan mounted on the rear of the unit blowing outward, but some use an 80mm, a 92mm, or a 120mm fan mounted on the inside upper or lower surface, with open vents on the rear of the system. In either example, the flow of air is such that air is always exhausted out of the system through the rear of the supply.

The ATX power supply form factor addressed several problems with the previous PC/XT, AT, and LPX-type supplies. One is that the power supplies used with PC/XT/AT boards had only two connectors that plugged into the motherboard. If you inserted these connectors backward or out of their normal sequence, you would usually fry both the motherboard and the power supply! Most responsible system manufacturers tried to "key" the motherboard and power supply connectors so you couldn't install them backward or out of sequence. However, most vendors of cheaper systems did not feature this keying on the boards or supplies they used. The ATX form factor includes intelligently designed and keyed power plugs to prevent users from incorrectly plugging in their power supplies. The ATX connectors also supply +3.3V, reducing the need for voltage regulators on the motherboard to power +3.3V-based circuits.

Besides the new +3.3V outputs, ATX power supplies furnish another set of outputs that is not typically seen on standard power supplies. The set consists of the Power_On (PS_ON) and 5V_Standby (5VSB) outputs mentioned earlier, known collectively as *Soft Power*. This enables features to be implemented, such as Wake on Ring or Wake on LAN, in which a signal from a modem or network adapter can actually cause a PC to wake up and power on. Many such systems also have the option of setting a wakeup time, at which the PC can automatically turn itself on to perform scheduled tasks. These signals also can enable the optional use of the keyboard to power the system on—an option you can set on some systems. These features are possible because the +5V Standby power is always active, giving the motherboard a limited source of power even when off. Check your BIOS Setup for control over these types of features.

SFX/SFX12V

Intel released the smaller microATX motherboard form factor in December 1997. At the same time, it released the small form factor (SFX) power supply design to go with it. Even so, most microATX chassis continued to use the standard ATX power supply instead. Then in March 1999, Intel released the FlexATX addendum to the microATX specification, which was a small board designed for low-end PCs or PC-based appliances. Since then, the SFX supply has found use in many new compact system designs. Unlike most of the power supply form factor specifications in which a single mechanical or physical outline is defined, the SFX standard actually defines five different physical shapes, some of which are not directly interchangeable. In addition, there have been changes to the connectors required as the specification has evolved. Therefore, when replacing an SFX/SFX12V-type supply, you need to ensure you are purchasing the correct type—which is to say the type that will physically install in your chassis—as well as have the correct connectors for your motherboard.

The number and types of connectors have changed over the life of the specification. The original SFX power supply specification included a single 20-pin motherboard connector. The 4-pin +12V connector to provide independent CPU power was added as an option in the 2.0 revision (May 2001) and was made a requirement in revision 2.3 (April 2003), causing the spec to be renamed as SFX12V in the process. SFX12V version 3.0 changed the main motherboard power connector from 20 pins to 24 pins and made Serial ATA power connectors a requirement. The current SFX12V version 3.1 was released in March 2005 and contains a few additional minor revisions, including a change to High Current System (HCS) terminals in the connectors. SFX12V includes several physical designs, including one called the PS3 form factor.

On a standard SFX/SFX12V power supply, a 60mm diameter cooling fan is located inside the power supply housing, facing the inside of the computer's case (see Figure 18.2). The fan draws the air into the power supply housing from the system cavity and expels it through a port at the rear of the system. Internalizing the fan in this way reduces system noise and results in a standard negative-pressure design. The system can also use additional processor and chassis cooling fans, which are separate from the power supply.

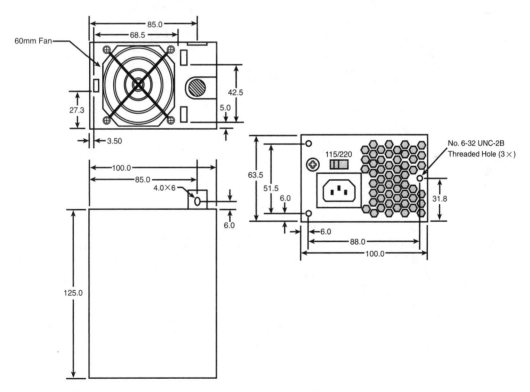

FIGURE 18.2 SFX/SFX12V standard power supply with internal 60mm fan.

For systems that require more cooling capability, a version that allows for a larger, 80mm top-mounted cooling fan also is available. The larger fan provides more cooling capability and airflow for systems that need it (see Figure 18.3).

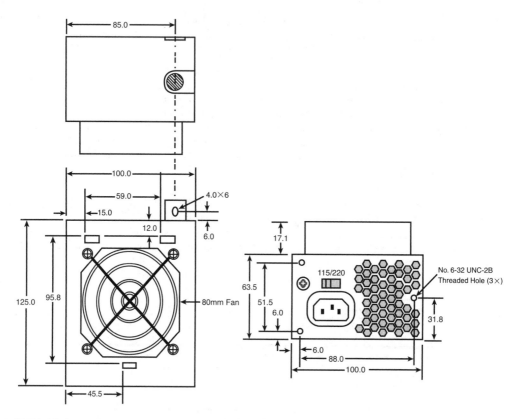

FIGURE 18.3 SFX/SFX12V standard power supply with a recessed, top-mounted 80mm fan.

Another variation of SFX12V also uses a recessed top-mounted 80mm cooling fan, but it has the body of the power supply rotated for greater width but reduced depth, as shown in Figure 18.4.

A special low-profile version of SFX12V designed for a slim chassis is only 50mm tall with an internal 40mm cooling fan, as shown in Figure 18.5.

Finally, a more recent variation on SFX is called the *PS3 form factor*, defined in Appendix E of the SFX12V specification. Although defined as part of SFX12V, the PS3 form factor is actually a shortened version of ATX12V and is generally used in systems with microATX chassis and motherboards that require higher power output than the smaller SFX variants can supply (see Figure 18.6).

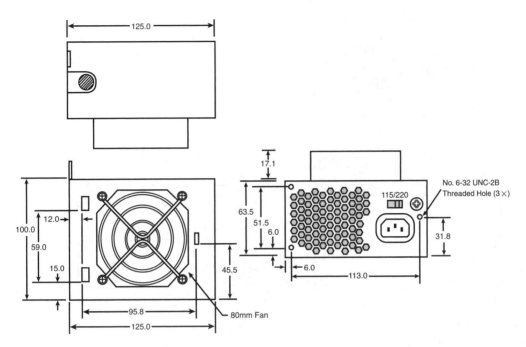

FIGURE 18.4 SFX/SFX12V rotated power supply with a recessed top-mounted 80mm fan.

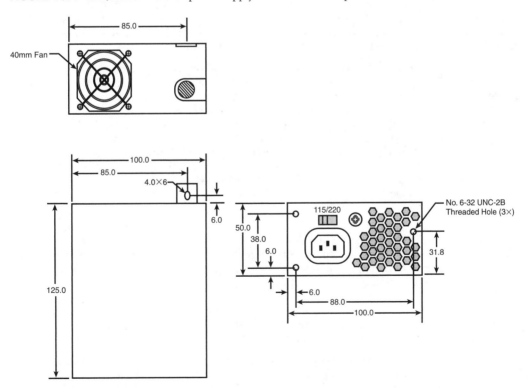

FIGURE 18.5 SFX/SFX12V low-profile power supply with internal 40mm fan.

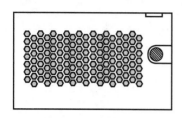

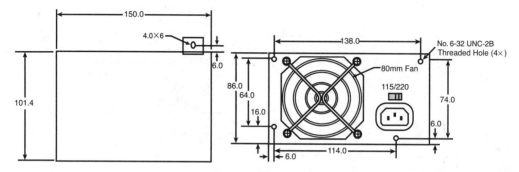

FIGURE 18.6 PS3 (SFX/SFX12V) power supply with internal 80mm fan.

SFX120V power supplies are specifically designed for use in small systems containing a limited hardware and limited upgradeability. Most SFX supplies are designed to provide 80–300 watts of continuous power in four voltages (+5V, +12V, –12V, and +3.3V). This amount of power has proven to be sufficient for a small system with a processor, an AGP or PCI Express x16 interface, up to four expansion slots, and three peripheral devices—such as hard drives and optical drives.

Although Intel designed the SFX12V power supply specification with the microATX and FlexATX motherboard form factors in mind, SFX is a wholly separate standard that is compliant with other motherboards as well. For example, the PS3 variant of SFX12V can replace standard ATX12V power supplies as long as the output capabilities and provided connectors match the system requirements. SFX power supplies use the same 20-pin or 24-pin connectors defined in the ATX/ATX12V standards and include both the Power_On and 5V_Standby outputs. SFX12V power supplies add the 4-pin +12V connector for CPU power, just as ATX12V supplies do. Whether you will use an ATX- or SFX-based power supply in a given system depends more on the case or chassis than the motherboard. Each has the same basic electrical connectors; the main difference is which type of power supply the case is physically designed to accept.

EPS/EPS12V

In 1998, a group of companies including Intel, Hewlett-Packard, NEC, Dell, Data General, Micron, and Compaq created the Server System Infrastructure (SSI), an industry initiative to promote industry-standard form factors covering common server hardware elements such as chassis, power supplies, motherboards, and other components. The idea was to be able to design network servers that could use industry-standard interchangeable parts. You can find out more about SSI at www.ssiforum.org. Although this book does not cover network servers, in many ways a low-end server is a high-end PC, and many high-end components that were once found only on servers have trickled down to standard PCs. This trickle-down theory is especially true when it comes to power supplies.

In 1998, the SSI created the entry-level power supply (EPS) specification, which defines an industry-standard power supply form factor for entry-level pedestal (standalone tower chassis) servers. The initial EPS standard was based on ATX, but with several enhancements. The first major enhancement was the use of a 24-pin main power connector, which eventually trickled down to the ATX12V as well as other power supply form factor specifications in 2003. EPS also originally called for the use of HCS terminals in the Molex Mini-Fit Jr.–based power supply connectors, which became standard in ATX12V in March 2005. In addition, the (now-obsolete) auxiliary 6-pin power connector, the 4-pin +12V power connector, and a variation of the 6-pin graphics power connector all appeared in the EPS specifications before ending up in ATX.

The EPS specification originally used a mechanical form factor identical to ATX, but the EPS form factor was later extended to support higher power outputs by allowing the body of the supply to be deeper if necessary. The ATX and the original EPS standards call for a supply that is 86mm tall by 150mm wide by 140mm deep, the same dimensions as the LPX or PS/2 form factors. EPS later added optional extended depths of 180mm and 230mm total. Most power supplies with true ratings of 500 watts or more are made in the EPS12V form factor, because it isn't really possible to fit more power than that into the standard ATX size. You may think these would require a custom EPS chassis, but in fact many (if not most) full-sized ATX tower chassis can handle these greater depths without interference, especially when using one of the newer breed of shorter-length optical drives (because one or more of the optical drives are often inline with the power supply).

With the improvements in EPS/EPS12V power supplies trickling down to ATX/ATX12V, I have studied the SSI EPS specifications to see what potential improvements might come to ATX. The main difference today between ATX and EPS with respect to connectors is the use of an 8-pin dual +12V connector in EPS12V instead of a 4-pin +12V connector in ATX12V. The 8-pin dual +12V connector is essentially the equivalent of two 4-pin connectors mated together and is used by entry-level servers to power multiple processors. Because of the way the connectors are designed, an 8-pin +12V connector can plug into a 4-pin +12V connector on a motherboard, with the unused pins simply hanging unused, offset to one side or the other.

The only other major difference between EPS12V and ATX12V is that EPS power supplies can be up to 180mm or 230mm deep, whereas ATX supplies are technically limited to 140mm depth according to the specification. An example of an EPS12V type supply from PC Power & Cooling is shown in Figure 18.7.

FIGURE 18.7   EPS12V form factor power supply (www.pcpower.com).

This power supply is basically a 230mm-deep EPS12V supply that works in place of or as an upgrade to an ATX12V supply as long as the chassis can accommodate the additional depth. EPS12V supplies are sometimes called *extended ATX* power supplies because of their optional extended length. If you plan to use one of these EPS12V power supplies in a standard ATX chassis, it's important that you measure the available space in your chassis to ensure you have the room behind the supply for the additional depth.

Connector compatibility isn't generally a problem because, by virtue of the Molex Mini-Fit Jr. connector design, you can plug a 24-pin main power connector into a 20-pin socket, as well as an 8-pin dual +12V connector into a 4-pin +12V socket.

If you have the room, an EPS12V power supply can be used with most ATX chassis and motherboards for the ultimate in high-output capabilities.

TFX12V

The TFX12V (thin form factor) power supply was originally introduced by Intel in April 2002 and is designed for small form factor (SFF) systems of about 9–15 liters in volume, primarily those using low-profile SFF chassis and microATX, FlexATX, or Mini-ITX motherboards. The basic shape of TFX12V is longer and narrower than the ATX- or SFX-based form factors, allowing it to more easily fit into low-profile systems. The dimensions of the TFX12V form factor are shown in Figure 18.8.

TFX12V power supplies are designed to deliver nominal power output capabilities of 180–300 watts, which is more than adequate for the smaller systems for which they are designed. TFX12V supplies include a side-mounted internal 80mm fan that is usually thermostatically controlled, so as to run both coolly and quietly. A symmetrically designed mounting system allows the fan to be oriented facing either side inside the system for optimum cooling and flexibility in accommodating different chassis layouts (see Figure 18.9).

Unlike SFX-based supplies, only one standard mechanical form factor exists for TFX12V supplies. TFX12V supplies have also always included the 4-pin +12V connector since the standard appeared in April 2002, well after the +12V connector had been included in other power supply form factors. TFX12V 1.2 (April 2003) added the Serial ATA power connector as an option, whereas the TFX12V 2.0 release (February 2004) made them mandatory and changed the main power connector from 20 pins to 24 pins. Revision 2.1 (July 2005) includes only minor updates and changes from the previous version.

CFX12V

The CFX12V (compact form factor) power supply was originally introduced by Intel in November 2003 and is designed for mid-sized balanced technology extended (BTX) systems of about 10–15 liters in volume, primarily using microBTX or picoBTX motherboards.

CFX12V power supplies are designed to deliver nominal power output capabilities of 220–300 watts, which is more than adequate for the mid-sized systems for which they are designed. CFX12V supplies include a rear-mounted internal 80mm fan that is typically thermostatically controlled, which enables it to run both coolly and quietly. The shape of the supply includes a ledge such that part of the supply can extend over the motherboard, reducing the overall size of the system (see Figure 18.10). The dimensions of the CFX12V form factor are shown in Figure 18.11.

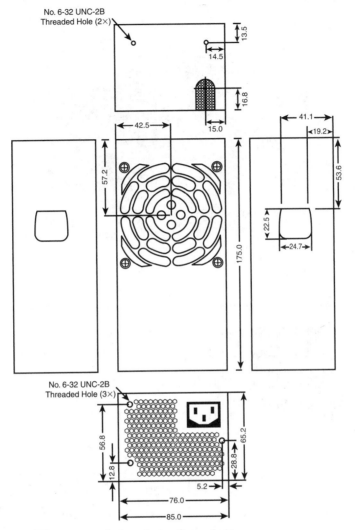

FIGURE 18.8 TFX12V power supply form factor dimensions.

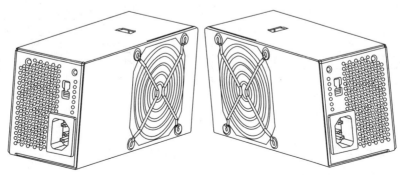

FIGURE 18.9 TFX12V power supplies are symmetrical and can be mounted with the fan facing either left or right.

FIGURE 18.10 CFX12V power supply.

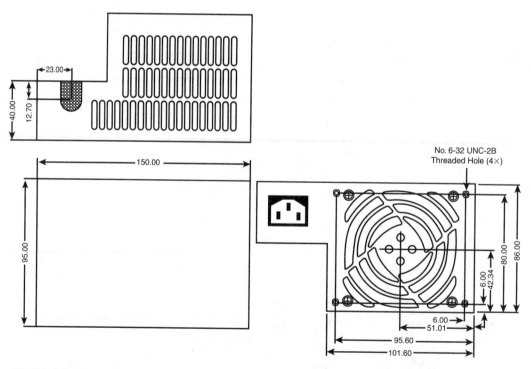

FIGURE 18.11 CFX12V power supply dimensions.

CFX12V supplies have included the 4-pin +12V connector since the standard first appeared in November 2003, well after the +12V connector had been included in other power supply form factors. TFX12V also included the 24-pin main power connector and Serial ATA power connectors as mandatory since its inception. The current CFX12V 1.2 release dates from 2005 and has only minor revisions over previous versions, including a change to HCS terminals in the connectors.

LFX12V

Intel originally introduced the LFX12V (low profile form factor) power supply in April 2004. It's designed for ultra-small BTX systems of about 6–9 liters in volume, primarily using picoBTX or nanoBTX motherboards.

LFX12V power supplies are designed to deliver nominal power output capabilities of 180–260 watts, which is ideal for the tiny systems for which they are designed. LFX12V supplies include an internal 60mm fan, which is 20mm smaller than that of the CFX12V design. Similar to the CFX12V fan, it is usually thermostatically controlled to ensure quiet operation while still providing adequate cooling. The shape of the supply includes a ledge such that part of the supply can extend over the motherboard, reducing the overall size of the system (see Figure 18.12). The dimensions of the LFX12V form factor are shown in Figure 18.13.

All LFX12V supplies include a 24-pin main motherboard power connector, a 4-pin +12V connector, and Serial ATA connectors. The current LFX12V 1.1 release dates from April 2005 and has only minor revisions over the previous version.

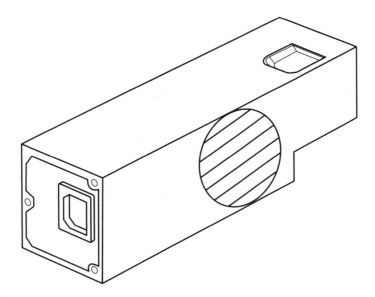

FIGURE 18.12   LFX12V power supply.

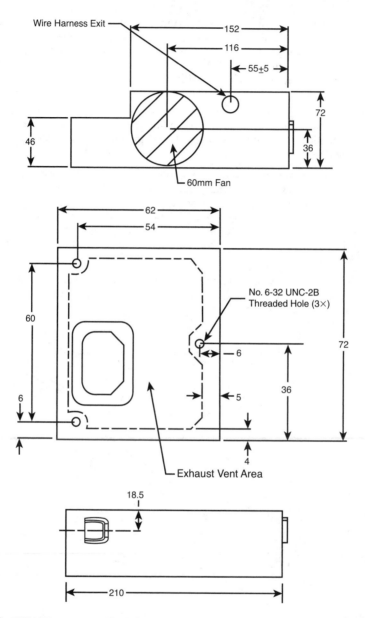

FIGURE 18.13 LFX12V power supply dimensions.

Flex ATX

A power supply company called FSP (Fortron Source Power) originally introduced variations of what was to become the Flex ATX power supply form factor in 2001 in the form of proprietary designs for SFF desktop and thin (1U) server systems. These power supplies became popular in systems from Shuttle, but they have also been used by HP/Compaq, IBM, SuperMicro, and others. In an effort to make this form factor an official standard, Intel introduced the Flex ATX power supply form factor in March 2007 as part of the 1.1 and later revisions of the "Power Supply Design Guide for Desktop

Platform Form Factors" document, which is available on the www.formfactors.org site. These are also sometimes called 1U (one unit) power supplies because they are used in many 1U server chassis.

Flex ATX power supplies, like the one shown in Figure 18.14, are designed to deliver nominal power output capabilities of between 180 and 270 watts, which is ideal for the small systems for which they are designed. Flex ATX supplies usually include one or two internal 40mm fans; however, larger fans can be mounted horizontally, and even fanless models exist. The dimensions of the Flex ATX form factor are shown in Figure 18.15.

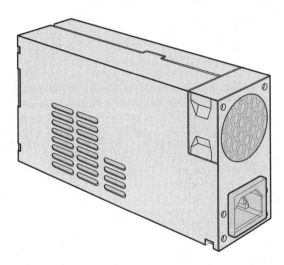

FIGURE 18.14   Flex ATX power supply.

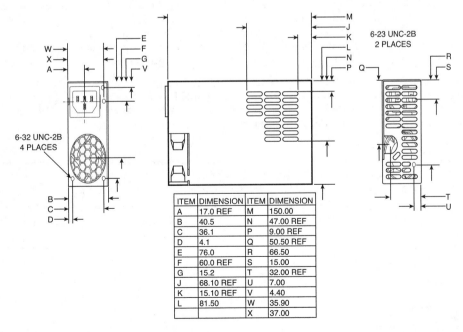

ITEM	DIMENSION	ITEM	DIMENSION
A	17.0 REF	M	150.00
B	40.5	N	47.00 REF
C	36.1	P	9.00 REF
D	4.1	Q	50.50 REF
E	76.0	R	66.50
F	60.0 REF	S	15.00
G	15.2	T	32.00 REF
J	68.10 REF	U	7.00
K	15.10 REF	V	4.40
L	81.50	W	35.90
		X	37.00

FIGURE 18.15   Flex ATX power supply dimensions.

Flex ATX power supplies include either a 20-pin or 24-pin main motherboard power connector and a 4-pin +12V connector for the motherboard. They also usually include standard peripheral and floppy power connectors, with newer units having Serial ATA power connectors as well.

Power Switches

Three main types of power switches are used on PCs. They can be described as follows:

- Front panel motherboard-controlled switch (ATX and newer)
- Front panel power supply AC switch (AT/LPX; obsolete)
- Integral power supply AC switch (PC/XT/AT; obsolete)

ATX and Newer

All ATX and newer power supplies that employ the 20- or 24-pin motherboard connector use the PS_ON signal to power up the system. In this design, the power supply runs in standby mode when plugged in with the system off. The PS_ON signal is routed from the power supply through the motherboard to a low-voltage momentary contact DC switch on the front panel. As a result, the remote power switch does not physically control the power supply's access to the 120V AC power, as in older-style power supplies. Instead, the power supply's on or off status is toggled by the PS_ON signal received on the ATX Main power connector. This is sometimes called a *soft-off switch* because this is the name of the Advanced Configuration Power Interface (ACPI) state when the system is off but still receiving standby power.

The PS_ON signal can be manipulated physically by the computer's power switch or electronically by the motherboard under software control. PS_ON is an *active low signal*, meaning the power supply voltage outputs are disabled (the system is off) when the PS_ON is high (greater than or equal to 2.0V). This excludes the +5VSB (Standby) on pin 9 of the ATX main power connector, which is active whenever the power supply is connected to an AC power source. The power supply maintains the PS_ON signal at either 3.3V or +5V. This signal is then routed through the motherboard to the remote switch on the front of the case. When the switch is pressed, the PS_ON signal is grounded. When the power supply sees the PS_ON signal drop to 0.8V or less, the power supply (and system) is turned on. Thus, the remote switch in a system using an ATX or newer power supply carries up to only +5V of DC power, rather than the full 120V–240V AC current like that of the older AT/LPX form factors.

The actual power switch used in ATX systems is normally a tiny momentary contact push button switch, which is connected to the motherboard front panel header via a tiny two-pin connector (see Figure 18.16). When the button is pushed, the motherboard then grounds the PS_ON signal in the main 20/24-pin power connector, causing the power supply to turn on.

Tip

If your power switch has failed or you want to power on an ATX or newer power supply without having a switch connected to the motherboard, you can actually use a paperclip as a temporary switch. To do this, short the PS_ON (green) wire to the adjacent ground (black) wire by using a paperclip bent into a U shape and then jam it into the back of the connector, such that the ends make contact with the terminals inside (see Figure 18.17). This acts as a jumper that performs the same function as the switch, and it causes the unit to power on.

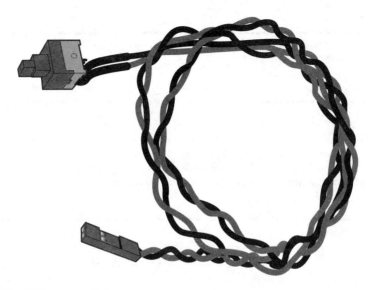

FIGURE 18.16   ATX power switch.

FIGURE 18.17   Using a bent paperclip to jumper the adjacent green and black wires in the main power connector to forcibly power on a system.

Caution

The continuous presence of the +5VSB power on pin 9 of the ATX main connector means the motherboard is always receiving standby power from the power supply when connected to an AC source, even when the computer is turned off. As a result, it is even more important to unplug an ATX system from the power source before working inside the case than it is on earlier model systems.

The remote switch on ATX and newer designs can only put the system in a soft-off state, in which the system appears off but is still receiving standby power. Some ATX and newer power supplies include a hard override AC power switch on the back, which essentially disconnects AC power from the system when turned off. With the AC switch off, the system no longer receives standby power and is essentially the same as being completely unplugged from an AC outlet.

Tip

The design of the ATX power switch is such that the motherboard actually controls the status of the power supply. On systems with full support for ACPI, when you press the power switch, the motherboard informs the OS to perform an orderly shutdown before the power is actually turned off. However, if the system is locked up or corrupted, it can remain running when you press the switch. In that situation, you can manually override the ACPI control by pressing the switch continuously for more than 4 seconds, which overrides the software control and forcibly turns off the system.

PC/XT/AT and LPX Power Switches

The earliest systems had power switches integrated or built directly into the power supply, which turned the main AC power to the system on and off. This was a simple design, but because the power supply was mounted in the rear right of the system, it required reaching around to the right side near the back of the system to actuate the switch. Also, switching the AC power directly meant the system couldn't be remotely started without special hardware.

Starting in the late 1980s, systems with LPX power supplies began using remote front panel switches. These were still AC switches; the only difference was that the AC switch was now mounted remotely (usually on the front panel of the chassis), rather than integrated in the power supply unit. The switch was connected to the power supply via a four-wire cable, and the ends of the cable were fitted with spade connector lugs, which plugged onto the spade connectors on the power switch. The cable from the power supply to the switch in the case contained four color-coded wires. In addition, a fifth wire supplying a ground connection to the case was sometimes included. The switch was usually included with the power supply and heavily shrink-wrapped or insulated where the connector lugs attached, to prevent electric shock.

This solved the ergonomic problem of reaching the switch, but it still didn't enable remote or automated system power-up without special hardware. Plus, you now had a 120V AC switch mounted in the chassis, with wires carrying dangerous voltage through the system. Some of these wires are hot anytime the system is plugged in (all are hot when the system's turned on), creating a dangerous environment for the average person when messing around inside the system.

Caution

At least two of the remote power switch leads to a remote-mounted AC power switch in an AT/LPX supply are energized with 120V AC at all times. You can be electrocuted if you touch the ends of these wires with the power supply plugged in, even if the unit is turned off! For this reason, always make sure the power supply is unplugged before connecting or disconnecting the remote power switch or touching any of the wires connected to it.

The four or five wires are usually color-coded as follows:

- **Brown and blue**—These wires are the live and neutral feed wires from the 120V power cord to the power supply. These are always hot when the power supply is plugged in.

- **Black and white**—These wires carry the AC feed from the switch back to the power supply. These leads should be hot only when the power supply is plugged in and the switch is turned on.

- **Green or green with a yellow stripe**—This is the ground lead. It should be connected to the PC case and should help ground the power supply to the case.

On the switch, the tabs for the leads are usually color-coded; if not, you'll find that most switches have two parallel tabs and two angled tabs. If no color-coding is on the switch, plug the blue and brown wires onto the tabs that are parallel to each other and the black and white wires to the tabs that are angled away from each other. If none of the tabs are angled, simply make sure the blue and brown wires are plugged into the most closely spaced tabs on one side of the switch and the black and white wires on the most closely spaced tabs on the other side (see Figure 18.18).

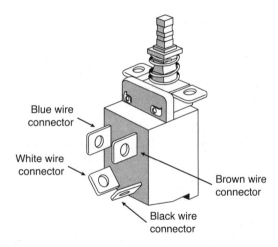

FIGURE 18.18 Power supply remote pushbutton switch connections.

Caution

Although these wire color-codings and parallel/angled tabs are used on most power supplies, they are not necessarily 100% universal. I have encountered power supplies that do not use the same coloring or tab placement scheme described here. One thing is sure: Two of the wires will be hot with potentially fatal AC voltage anytime the power supply is plugged in. No matter what, always disconnect the power supply from the wall socket before handling any of these wires. Be sure to insulate the connections with electrical tape or heat-shrink tubing so you won't be able to touch the wires when working inside the case in the future.

As long as the blue and brown wires are on one set of tabs and the black-and-white leads are on the other, the switch and supply will work properly. If you incorrectly mix the leads, you will likely blow the circuit breaker for the wall socket because mixing them can create a direct short circuit.

Motherboard Power Connectors

Every PC power supply has connectors that attach to the motherboard, providing power to the motherboard, processor, memory, chipset, integrated components (such as video, LAN, universal serial bus [USB], and FireWire), and any cards plugged into bus slots. These connectors are important; not only are these the main conduit through which power flows to your system, but attaching these connectors improperly can have a devastating effect on your PC, including burning up both your power supply and motherboard. Just as with the mechanical shape of the power supply, these connectors are usually designed to conform to one of several industry-standard specifications, which dictate the types of connectors used as well as the pinouts of the individual wires and terminals. Unfortunately, just as with the mechanical form factors, some PC manufacturers use power supplies with custom connectors or, worse yet, use standard connector types but with modified (incompatible) pinouts (meaning the signals and voltages are rearranged from standard specifications). Plugging a power supply with an incompatible pinout into a motherboard that uses a standard pinout (or vice versa) usually results in the destruction of either the board or the power supply—or both.

Just as I insist on industry-standard mechanical form factors in my systems, I also want to ensure that they use industry-standard connectors and pinouts. By only purchasing components that conform to industry standards, I can ensure the greatest flexibility and lowest cost for future upgrades and repairs.

Two main sets of motherboard power connectors have been used over the years: what I would call AT/LPX type and the ATX type. Each of these has minor variations; for example, the ATX type has evolved over the years, with new connectors coming (and some going) and modifications to existing connectors. This section details the motherboard power connectors used by various types of industry-standard (and some not-so-standard) power supplies.

AT/LPX Power Supply Connectors

Industry-standard PC, XT, AT, Baby-AT, and LPX motherboards use the same type of main power supply connectors. AT/LPX power supplies feature two main power connectors (P8 and P9), each with six pins that attach the power supply to the motherboard. The terminals used in these connectors are rated to handle up to 5 amps at up to 250V (even though the maximum used in a PC is +12V). These two connectors are shown in Figure 18.19.

All AT/LPX power supplies that use the P8 and P9 connectors have them installed end to end so that the two black wires (ground connections) on both power connectors are next to each other when properly plugged in. Note the designations P8 and P9 are not fully standardized, although most use those designations because that is what IBM stamped on the originals. Some power supplies have them labeled as P1/P2 instead. Because these connectors usually have a clasp that prevents them from being inserted backward on the motherboard's pins, the major concern is getting the two connectors in the correct orientation side by side and also not offsetting by one or more pins side to side. Following the black-to-black rule and ensuring they are on-center keeps you safe. You must take care to ensure that no remaining unconnected motherboard pins exist between or on either side of the two connectors after you install them. A properly installed connector connects to and covers every motherboard power pin. If any power pins are showing on either side of or between the connectors, the entire connector assembly is installed incorrectly, which can result in catastrophic failure for the motherboard and everything plugged into it at the time of power-up. Figure 18.20 shows the P8 and P9 connectors (sometimes also called P1/P2) in their proper orientation when connected to a motherboard.

Table 18.4 shows typical AT/LPX power supply connections.

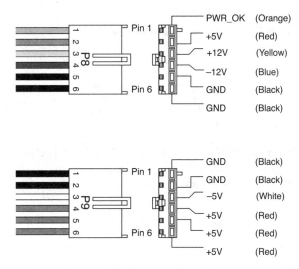

FIGURE 18.19 AT/LPX main P8/P9 (also called P1/P2) power connectors, side and terminal end view.

Always position connectors such that the
black wires in each connector are adjacent (side-by-side)
when plugged into the motherboard

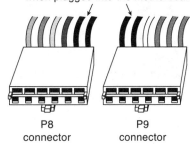

P8
connector

P9
connector

FIGURE 18.20 The P8/P9 power connectors (sometimes also called P1/P2) that connect an AT/LPX power supply to the motherboard.

Table 18.4   AT/LPX Power Supply Connectors (Wire End View)

Connector	Pin	Signal	Color[2]	Connector	Pin	Signal	Color[2]
P8 (or P1)	1	Power_Good (+5V)	Orange	P9 (or P2)	1	Ground	Black
	2	+5V[1]	Red		2	Ground	Black
	3	+12V	Yellow		3	−5V	White
	4	−12V	Blue		4	+5V	Red
	5	Ground	Black		5	+5V	Red
	6	Ground	Black		6	+5V	Red

1 First-generation PC/XT motherboards and power supplies did not require this voltage, so the pin might be missing from the motherboard and terminal and the wire might be missing from the connector (P8 pin 2).

2 I have seen some supplies where the manufacturer did not follow industry-standard wire color-codes even though the signals were correct.

Tip

Although older PC/XT power supplies do not have a connection at connector P8 pin 2, you still can use them on AT-type motherboards, or vice versa. The presence or absence of the +5V on that pin has little or no effect on system operation because the remaining +5V wires can usually carry the load.

Note that all the AT/LPX-type power supplies use the same connectors and pin configurations; to my knowledge there were never nonstandard variations.

ATX and ATX12V Motherboard Power Connectors

Power supplies conforming to the original ATX and ATX12V 1.x form factor standards or variations thereof use the following three motherboard power connectors:

- 20-pin main power connector
- 6-pin auxiliary power connector
- 4-pin +12V power connector

The main power connector is always required, but the other two are optional depending on the application. Consequently, a given ATX or ATX12V power supply can have up to four combinations of connectors, as listed here:

- Main power connector only
- Main and auxiliary
- Main and +12V
- Main, auxiliary, and +12V

The most common varieties are those including the main only and those with the main and +12V connectors. Most motherboards that use the +12V connector do not use the auxiliary connector, and vice versa.

20-Pin Main Power Connector

The 20-pin main power connector is standard for all power supplies conforming to the ATX and ATX12V 1.x power supply form factors and consists of a Molex Mini-Fit Jr. connector housing with female terminals. For reference, the connector is Molex part number 39-01-2200 (or equivalent), and the standard terminals are part number 5556 (see Figure 18.21). This is a 20-pin keyed connector with pins configured, as shown in Table 18.5. The colors for the wires listed are those the ATX standard recommends; however, to enable them to vary from manufacturer to manufacturer, they are not required for compliance to the specification. I like to show these connector pinouts in a wire end view, which shows how the pins are arranged looking at the back of the connector (from the wire and not the terminal end). This way, you can see how they would be oriented if you were back-probing the connector with the connector plugged in (see Figure 18.22).

Figure 18.21 shows a view of the connector as if you were looking at it facing the terminal end.

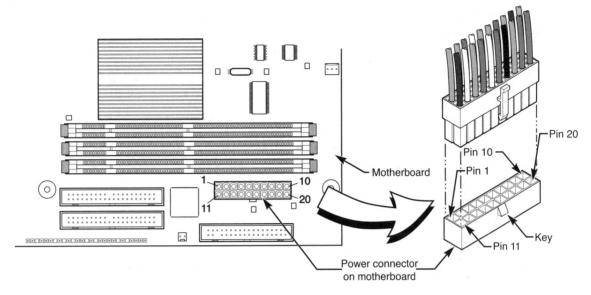

FIGURE 18.21 ATX 20-pin motherboard main power connector, perspective view.

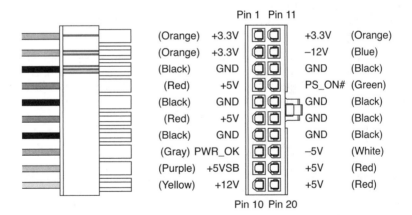

FIGURE 18.22 ATX 20-pin main power connector, side and terminal end view.

Table 18.5   ATX 20-Pin Main Power Supply Connector Pinout (Motherboard Connector)

Color	Signal	Pin	Pin	Signal	Color
Orange	+3.3V	11[1]	1	+3.3V	Orange
Blue	−12V	12	2	+3.3V	Orange
Black	GND	13	3	GND	Black
Green	PS_On	14	4	+5V	Red
Black	GND	15	5	GND	Black

Table 18.5 Continued

Color	Signal	Pin	Pin	Signal	Color
Black	GND	16	6	+5V	Red
Black	GND	17	7	GND	Black
White	−5V	18[2]	8	Power_Good	Gray
Red	+5V	19	9	+5VSB (Standby)	Purple
Red	+5V	20	10	+12V	Yellow

1 *Might have a second orange or brown wire, used for +3.3V sense feedback. The power supply uses this wire to monitor 3.3V regulation.*

2 *Pin 18 will be N/C (no connection, absent) on some later model supplies or motherboards because −5V was removed from the ATX12V 1.3 and later specifications. Supplies with no connection at pin 18 should not be used with older motherboards that incorporate ISA Bus slots.*

Note

The ATX supply features several voltages and signals not seen on earlier AT/LPX designs, such as the +3.3V, PS_On, and +5V_Standby. Therefore, adapting a standard LPX form factor supply to make it work properly in an ATX system is impossible, even though the shapes of the power supplies are virtually identical.

However, because ATX is a superset of the older LPX power supply standard, you can use a connector adapter to allow an ATX power supply to connect to an older motherboard using AT/LPX connectors.

One of the most important issues with respect to power supply connectors is the capability to deliver sufficient power to the motherboard without overheating. When talking about specific connectors, the current rating is stated in amperes per circuit, which is a measure of the amount of current that can be passed through a mated terminal that will allow no more than a 30°C (86°F) temperature rise over ambient 22°C (72°F). In other words, at a normal ambient temperature of 22°C (72°F), when operating under the maximum rated current load, the temperature of the mated terminals will not exceed 52°C (126°F). Because the ambient temperature inside a PC can run 40°C (104°F) or higher, running power connectors at maximum ratings can result in extremely high temperatures in the connectors.

The maximum current level is further de-rated or adjusted for the number of circuits in a given connector housing due to the heat of any adjacent terminals. For example, a power connector might be able to carry 8 amps per circuit in a 4-position connector, but the same connector and terminal design might be able to handle only 6 amps per circuit in a 20-position connector.

All the modern form factor power supplies since ATX have standardized on the use of Molex Mini-Fit Jr. connectors for the main and +12V connectors. A number of connector housings are used with anywhere from 4 to 24 positions or terminals. Molex makes three types of terminals for these connectors: a standard version, an HCS version, and a Plus HCS version. The current ratings for these terminals are shown in Table 18.6.

Table 18.6   Current Ratings for Mini-Fit Jr. Connectors

Mini-Fit Jr. Terminal Type/No.	2–3 Pins (Amps/Pin)	4–6 Pins (Amps/Pin)	7–10 Pins (Amps/Pin)	12–24 Pins (Amps/Pin)
Standard/5556	9	8	7	6
HCS/44476	12	11	10	9
Plus HCS/45750	12	12	12	11

All ratings assume Mini-Fit Jr. connectors with 12–24 circuits using 18-gauge wire under standard temperature conditions.

The ATX main power connector is either a 20-pin or a 24-pin connector, which, if standard terminals are used, is rated for up to 6 amps of current per terminal. If the connector were upgraded to HCS terminals, the rating would increase to 9 amps per terminal, and if upgraded to Plus HCS terminals, the rating would increase further to 11 amps per terminal. Prior to March 2005, all the power supply form factor specifications called for using standard terminals, but all the ratings from March 2005 to the present have changed to require HCS terminals instead. If your power supply connector has been over-heating, you can easily install HCS or Plus HCS terminals to increase the power-handling capability of your connector by 50% or more.

By counting the number of terminals for each voltage level, you can calculate the power-handling capability of the connector, as shown in Table 18.7.

Table 18.7   ATX 20-Pin Main Power Connector Maximum Power Handling Capabilities

Volts	No. Pins	Using Std. Terminals (W)	Using HCS Terminals (W)	Using Plus HCS Terminals (W)
+3.3V	3	59.4	89.1	108.9
+5V	4	120	180	220
+12V	1	72	108	132
Total watts:		251.4	377.1	460.9

Standard terminals are rated 6 amps.

HCS terminals are rated 9 amps.

Plus HCS terminals are rated 11 amps.

All ratings assume Mini-Fit Jr. connectors with 12–24 circuits using 18-gauge wire under standard temperature conditions.

This means the total power-handling capacity of this connector is only 251 watts if standard terminals are being used, which is lower than most systems need today. Unfortunately, drawing more power than this maximum rating through the connector causes it to overheat. I'm sure you can appreciate how inadequate this has become today; for example, it certainly doesn't make sense to manufacture a 400- or 500-watt power supply if the main power connector can handle only 251 watts without melting! That would be like building a car that could go 200 mph and then equipping it with tires rated for only 100 mph. Everything would be fine until you exceeded the tires' rated speed, after which the results would not be pretty.

This is why the official power supply form factor specifications were updated in March 2005 to include HCS terminals, which have 50% greater power-handling capability than the standard terminals. Using HCS terminals, the power-handling capability of the 20-pin main connector alone increases to 377 watts, which is more than most systems need to run the entire system through all the connectors combined.

Six-Pin Auxiliary Power Connector

As motherboards and processors have evolved, the need for power has become greater. The terminals in the main power connector are rated for 6 amps (A) using standard terminals, which allows for a maximum supply of approximately 250 watts to the motherboard. Because motherboards with high-speed processors and multiple cards installed could draw more power than that and power supply manufacturers were building supplies with 300-watt and higher ratings, melted connectors were becoming more and more common. The terminals in the main connector overheated under such a load.

To allow for additional power from the supply to the motherboard, Intel modified the ATX specification to add a second auxiliary power connector for high power-drawing ATX motherboards and 250-watt or higher rated supplies. The criteria is such that, if the motherboard could draw more than 18A of +3.3V power or more than 24A of +5V power, the auxiliary connector is required to carry the additional load. These higher levels of power are needed in systems using 250- or 300-watt or greater supplies.

The 6-pin auxiliary power connector was added as a safety or stopgap measure in the ATX motherboard 2.02/2.03 and ATX12V 1.x power supply specifications for systems in which the +3.3V and +5V power draw could exceed the respective 18A and 24A maximums allowed using only the main connector with standard terminals. These conditions would normally be met in systems requiring 300W or higher output power supplies. The auxiliary power connector is a 6-pin Molex 90331-0010 connector, which is similar to the motherboard power connectors used on older AT/LPX power supplies for Baby-AT motherboards (see Figure 18.23).

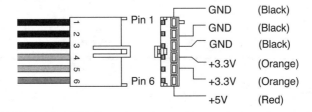

FIGURE 18.23 ATX 2.02/2.03 and ATX12V 1.x auxiliary power connector, side and terminal end view.

The pinouts of the auxiliary connector are shown in Table 18.8.

Table 18.8 ATX Auxiliary Power Connector Pinout

Pin	Signal	Color	Pin	Signal	Color
1	Gnd	Black	4	+3.3V	Orange
2	Gnd	Black	5	+3.3V	Orange
3	Gnd	Black	6	+5V	Red

Each terminal in the auxiliary power connector is rated to handle up to 5 amps of current, slightly less than the main power connector. By counting the number of terminals for each voltage level, you can calculate the power-handling capability of the connector, as shown in Table 18.9.

Table 18.9   Six-Pin Auxiliary Power Connector Maximum Power-Handling Capabilities

Volts	No. Pins	Watts
+3.3V	2	33
+5V	1	25
Total watts:		58

Terminals are rated 5 amps.
Ratings assume 18-gauge wire under standard temperature conditions.

This means the total power-handling capacity of this connector is only 58 watts. Drawing more power than this maximum rating through the connector will cause it to overheat.

Combining the 20-pin main plus the auxiliary power connector would result in a maximum power-delivery capability to the motherboard of 309 watts.

Few motherboards actually used this connector, and few power supplies included it. Generally, if a motherboard includes this connector, you need a power supply that has it as well, but if the power supply includes the auxiliary connector but the motherboard does not, it can be left unconnected.

Starting in 2000, both motherboards and power supplies began including a different additional connector that was a better solution than the auxiliary connector. The most recent power supply form factor specifications have removed the auxiliary connector, rendering it an obsolete standard in modern systems.

ATX12V 2.x 24-Pin Main Power Connector

Starting in June 2004, the PCI Express bus first appeared on motherboards. PCI Express is a type of serial bus with standard slots having a single channel or lane of communications. These single-lane slots are called *x1 slots* and are designed for peripheral cards such as network cards, sound cards, and the like. PCI Express also includes a special higher-bandwidth slot with 16 lanes (called an *x16 slot*), which is especially designed for use by video cards. During development it was realized that PCI Express x16 video cards could draw more power than what was allowed by the existing 20-pin main and 6-pin auxiliary power supply connectors, especially when it came to +12V power.

The problem was that the 20-pin main connector had only a single +12V pin, but the new video cards required more +12V power than a single pin could safely deliver. The +12V connector that had already been added, as discussed in the next section, was specifically for the CPU and was unavailable to other devices. Rather than add another supplemental or auxiliary connector as it had done before, Intel eventually decided that it was finally time to upgrade the main power connector to supply more power.

The result was officially called ATX12V 2.0 and was released in February 2003. ATX12V 2.0 included two major changes from the previous ATX12V 1.x specifications: a new 24-pin main power connector and the elimination of the 6-pin auxiliary power connector. The new 24-pin main power connector included four more pins supplying additional +3.3V, +5V, and +12V power plus a ground. The inclusion of these extra pins delivered extra power to satisfy the power requirements for PCI Express video cards drawing up to 75 watts, but it also made the older 6-pin auxiliary connector unnecessary. The pinout of the new 24-pin main power connector started to be implemented in motherboards in mid-2004. The motherboard connector pinout is shown in Table 18.10, and the PSU connector is shown in Figure 18.24.

Note

Even though one of the design goals for increasing the main power connector to 24 pins was to provide extra power for PCI Express video cards, many if not most high-end video cards need more than the 75 watts available directly through the PCIe x16 slot. Video cards requiring more will have one or more additional power connectors on the card, which are used to draw power directly from the PSU.

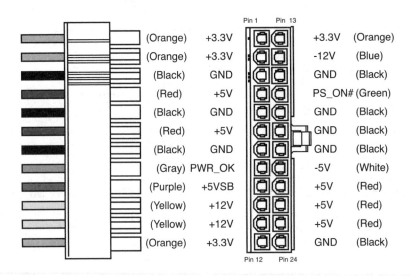

FIGURE 18.24   ATX12V 2.x 24-pin main power connector.

Table 18.10   ATX12V 2.x 24-Pin Main Power Supply Connector Pinout (Motherboard Connector)

Color	Signal	Pin	Pin	Signal	Color
Orange	+3.3V	13[1]	1	+3.3V	Orange
Blue	−12V	14	2	+3.3V	Orange
Black	GND	15	3	GND	Black
Green	PS_On	16	4	+5V	Red
Black	GND	17	5	GND	Black
Black	GND	18	6	+5V	Red
Black	GND	19	7	GND	Black
–	N/C	20[2]	8	Power_Good	Gray
Red	+5V	21	9	+5VSB (Standby)	Purple
Red	+5V	22	10	+12V	Yellow

Color	Signal	Pin	Pin	Signal	Color
Red	+5V	23	11	+12V	Yellow
Black	GND	24	12	+3.3V	Orange

1 Pin 13 might have a second orange or brown wire, used for +3.3V sense feedback. The power supply uses this wire to monitor 3.3V regulation.

2 Pin 20 will be N/C (no connection) because –5V was removed from the ATX12V 1.3 and later specifications.

It is interesting to note that the 24-pin connector is not really that new; it first appeared in the SSI EPS specification released in 1998. SSI (http://ssiforum.org/) is an initiative designed to create standard interfaces for server components, including power supplies. The 24-pin main power connector was created for servers because, at the time, only servers needed the additional power. Today's PCs draw the same power levels as servers did years ago, so rather than reinvent an incompatible connector, the ATX12V 2.0 standard merely incorporated the 24-pin connector already specified in the SSI EPS standard.

Compared to the previous 20-pin design, the 24-pin main power connector includes additional +3.3V, +5V, and +12V terminals, allowing a substantially greater amount of power to be delivered to the motherboard. Each terminal in the main power connector is rated to handle up to 6 amps of current. By counting the number of terminals for each voltage level, you can calculate the power-handling capability of the connector, as shown in Table 18.11.

Table 18.11   Maximum Power-Handling Capabilities of the 24-Pin Main Power Connector

Volts	No. Pins	Using Std. Terminals (W)	Using HCS Terminals (W)	Using Plus HCS Terminals (W)
+3.3V	4	79.2	118.8	145.2
+5V	5	150	225	275
+12V	2	144	216	264
Total watts:		373.2	559.8	684.2

Standard terminals are rated 6 amps.

HCS terminals are rated 9 amps.

Plus HCS terminals are rated 11 amps.

All ratings assume Mini-Fit Jr. connectors with 12–24 circuits using 18-gauge wire under standard temperature conditions.

This means the total power-handling capacity of this connector is 373 watts using standard terminals or 560 watts using HCS terminals, which is substantially higher than the 251 watts available in the previous 20-pin connector. Combining the 24-pin main and the 4-pin +12V power connector results in up to 565 watts (standard terminals) or 824 watts (using HCS terminals) total power available to the motherboard and processor! This is more than enough to support the most power-hungry motherboards and processors on the market today.

CPU Power Connectors

Power for the processor comes from a device called the *voltage regulator module (VRM)*, which is built into most modern motherboards. This device senses the CPU voltage requirements (usually via sense pins on the processor) and calibrates itself to provide the proper voltage to run the CPU. The design of a VRM enables it to run on either +5V or +12V for input power. Many have used +5V over the years, but starting in 2000 most converted to +12V because of the lower current requirements at that voltage. In addition, other devices might have already loaded the +5V, whereas only drive motors typically used the +12V prior to 2000. Whether the VRM on your board uses +5V or +12V depends on the particular motherboard or regulator design. Many modern voltage regulator ICs are designed to run on anything from a +4V to a +36V input, so it is up to the motherboard designer as to how they will be configured.

For example, I studied a system using a First International Computer (FIC) SD-11 motherboard, which used a Semtech SC1144ABCSW voltage regulator. This board design uses the +5V to convert to the lower voltage the CPU needs. Most motherboards use voltage regulator circuits controlled by chips from Semtech (www.semtech.com) or Linear Technology (www.linear.com). You can visit their sites for more data on these chips.

That motherboard accepted an Athlon 1GHz Cartridge version (Model 2), which according to AMD has a maximum power draw of 65W and a nominal voltage requirement of 1.8V, and 65W at 1.8V would equate to 36.1A of current at that voltage (volts × amps = watts). If the voltage regulator used +5V as a feed, 65W would equate to only 13A at +5V. That would assume 100% efficiency in the regulator, which is impossible. Therefore, assuming 80% efficiency (which is typical), there would be about 16.25A actual draw on the +5V due to the regulator and processor combined.

When you consider that other circuits on the motherboard also use +5V power—remember that ISA or PCI cards are drawing that power as well—you can see how easy it is to overload the +5V lines from the supply to the motherboard.

Although most motherboard VRM designs up through the Pentium III and Athlon/Duron use +5V-based regulators, most systems since then use +12V-powered regulators. This is because the higher voltage significantly reduces the current draw. Using the same 65W AMD Athlon 1GHz CPU as an example, you would end up with the current draw at the various voltages shown in Table 18.12.

Table 18.12 Current Draw at Various Voltages

Watts	Volts	Amps	Amps at 80% Regulator Efficiency
65	1.8	36.1	—
65	3.3	19.7	24.6
65	5.0	13.0	16.3
65	12.0	5.4	6.8

As you can see, using +12V to power the chip results in only 5.4A of draw, or 6.8A assuming 80% efficiency on the part of the regulator.

So, modifying the motherboard VRM circuit to use the +12V power feed would seem simple. But as you'll recall from the preceding text, the ATX 2.03 specification has only a single +12V lead in the main power connector. Even the short-lived auxiliary connector had no +12V leads, so that was no help. Pulling up to 8A more through a single 18-gauge wire supplying +12V power to the motherboard is a recipe for a melted connector because the contacts in the main ATX connector are rated for only 6A using standard terminals. Therefore, another solution was necessary.

Platform Compatibility Guide

The processor directly controls the amount of current drawn through the +12V connector. Modern motherboards are designed to support a wide range of different processors; however, the voltage regulator circuitry on a given motherboard may not have been designed to supply sufficient power to support all processors that might otherwise fit in the socket. To help eliminate the potential power problems that could result (including intermittent lockups or even damage such as damaged components or burned circuits), Intel created a power standard called the *Platform Compatibility Guide (PCG)*. The PCG was marked on most Intel boxed (retail) processors and motherboards introduced from 2004 through 2009. It was designed for system builders to use as an easy way to know the power requirements of a processor and to ensure that the motherboard can meet those requirements.

The PCG is a two- or three-digit alphanumeric value (for example, 05A), where the first two digits represent the year the particular specification was introduced, and the optional third character stands for the market segment. PCG designations in which the third character is A apply to processors and motherboards that fall in the low-end market (requiring less power), whereas designations whose third character is B apply to processors and motherboards that fall in the high-end market (requiring more power). Motherboards that support high-end processors by default also support low-end processors, but not the other way around. For example, you can install a processor with a PCG specification of 05A in a motherboard with a PCG specification of 05B, but if you install a 05B processor in a motherboard rated 05A, power problems will result. In other words, you can always install a processor with lower power requirements in a higher-power-capable motherboard, but not the other way around.

Although the PCG figures were specifically intended to apply to processors and motherboards, they also can be used to specify minimum power supply requirements. Table 18.13 shows the PCG numbers and the power recommendations they prescribe. Intel stopped using the PCG numbers on processors and motherboards introduced after 2009.

Table 18.13   Intel Platform Compatibility Guide (PCG) +12V Connector Power Recommendations

PCG Number	Year Introduced	Market Segment	CPU Power Specification	Continuous +12V Rating	Peak +12V Rating
04A	2004	Low-end	84W	13 A	16.5 A
04B	2004	High-end	115W	13 A	16.5 A
05A	2005	Low-end	95W	13 A	16.5 A
05B	2005	High-end	130W	16 A	19 A
06	2006	All	65W	8 A	13 A
08	2008	High-end	130W	16 A	19 A
09A	2009	Low-end	65W	8 A	13 A
09B	2009	High-end	95W	13 A	16.5 A

The power supply should be able to supply peak current for at least 10ms.

Choosing a power supply with the required minimum output on the +12V connector helps to ensure proper operation of the system.

Four-Pin +12V CPU Power Connector

To augment the supply of +12V power to the motherboard, Intel created a new ATX12V power supply specification. This added a third power connector, called the *+12V connector*, specifically to supply additional +12V power to the board. The 4-pin +12V power connector is specified for all power supplies conforming to the ATX12V form factor and consists of a Molex Mini-Fit Jr. connector housing with female terminals. For reference, the connector is Molex part number 39-01-2040, and the terminals are part number 5556. This is the same style of connector as the ATX Main power connector, except with fewer pins.

This connector has two +12V power pins, each rated for 8A total using standard terminals (or up to 11A each using HCS terminals). This allows for up to 16A or more of additional +12V current to the motherboard, for a total of 22A of +12V when combined with the 20-pin main connector. The 4-pin +12V connector is shown in Figure 18.25.

FIGURE 18.25 +12V 4-pin CPU power connector, side and terminal end view.

The pinout of the +12V power connector is shown in Table 18.14.

Table 18.14 +12V 4-Pin CPU Power Connector Pinout (Wire End View)

Pin	Signal	Color	Pin	Signal	Color
3	+12V	Yellow	1	Gnd	Black
4	+12V	Yellow	2	Gnd	Black

Using standard terminals, each pin in the +12V connector is rated to handle up to 8 amps of current, 11 amps with HCS terminals, or up to 12 amps with Plus HCS terminals. Even though it uses the same design and the same terminals as the main power connector, the current rating per terminal is higher on this 4-pin connector than on the 20-pin main because there are fewer terminals overall. By counting the number of terminals for each voltage level, you can calculate the power-handling capability of the connector, as shown in Table 18.15.

Table 18.15 Maximum Power-Handling Capabilities of the 4-Pin +12V Power Connector

Volts	No. Pins	Using Std. Terminals (W)	Using HCS Terminals (W)	Using Plus HCS Terminals (W)
+12V	2	192	264	288

Standard terminals are rated 8 amps.

HCS terminals are rated 11 amps.

Plus HCS terminals are rated 12 amps.

All ratings assume Mini-Fit Jr. connectors with 4–6 circuits using 18-gauge wire under standard temperature conditions.

This means the total power-handling capacity of this connector is 192 watts using standard terminals, which is available to and used only by the processor. Drawing more power than this maximum rating through the connector causes it to overheat, unless the HCS or Plus HCS terminals are used.

Combining the 20-pin main plus the 4-pin +12V power connector results in a maximum power-delivery capability to the motherboard of 443 watts (using standard terminals). The important thing to note is that adding the +12V connector provides the capability to support power supplies of up to 500 watts or more without overloading and melting the connectors.

Peripheral to 4-Pin +12V CPU Power Adapters

If you are installing a motherboard in a system that currently doesn't have the +12V connection for the CPU voltage regulator, an easy solution *may* be available; however, there are some caveats.

Power adapters are available that convert one of the extra peripheral power connectors found in most systems to a +12V 4-pin type. The drawback to this is that there are two +12V terminals in a +12V 4-pin connector and only one +12V terminal in a peripheral connector. If the adapter uses only a single peripheral connector to power both +12V pins of the +12V connector, a serious power mismatch can result. Because the terminals in the peripheral connector are only rated for 11A, and the two terminals in the +12V connector are also rated for up to 11A each, drawing more than 11A total can result in melted connectors at the peripheral connector end. This is below the peak power requirements as recommended by the *Power Supply Design Guide for Desktop Platform Form Factors* (www.formfactors.org), meaning these adapters do not conform to the latest standards.

I did some calculations: Assuming a motherboard VRM (voltage regulator module) efficiency of 80%, a CPU power draw of 105W would just about equal 11A, the absolute limit of the peripheral connector terminal. Because most CPUs can intermittently draw more than their nominal rating, I would hesitate to use one of these adapters on any processor rated at more than 75 watts. An example of a peripheral to +12V adapter is shown in Figure 18.26.

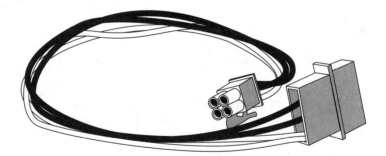

FIGURE 18.26   Peripheral to +12V power adapter.

Eight-Pin +12V CPU Power Connector

High-end motherboards often use multiple voltage regulators to supply power to the processor. To distribute the load among the additional voltage regulators, these boards may use two 4-pin +12V connectors; however, they are physically combined into a single 8-pin connector shell (see Figure 18.27). This type of CPU power connector was first defined in the EPS12V power supply specification version 1.6 released in the year 2000. Although this specification is intended for file servers, the increased power requirements of some high-power PC processors have caused this connector to appear on desktop PC motherboards supporting these processors.

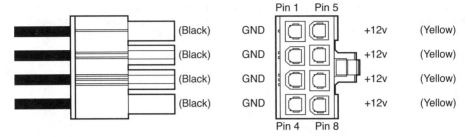

FIGURE 18.27 Eight-pin +12V CPU power connector, side and terminal end view.

The pinout of the 8-pin +12V CPU power connector is shown in Table 18.16.

Table 18.16 Eight-Pin +12V CPU Power Connector Pinout (Wire End View)

Color	Signal	Pin	Pin	Signal	Color
Yellow	+12V	5	1	Gnd	Black
Yellow	+12V	6	2	Gnd	Black
Yellow	+12V	7	3	Gnd	Black
Yellow	+12V	8	4	Gnd	Black

Some motherboards that utilize an 8-pin +12V CPU power connector must have signals connected to all 8 pins for the voltage regulators to function properly, while most will work properly even if a 4-pin PSU connector is attached. In the latter case, you will often see that the 8-pin connector has a cap installed over 4 of the pins, meaning that a 4-pin connector can be installed in the exposed portion. Consult the specific motherboard documentation to see if you can attach a single 4-pin +12V power connector (offset to one side or the other) when using lower power processors. If you are using a processor that draws more power than a 4-pin connector can supply, then you should ensure you are using a power supply with an 8-pin connector to match the motherboard.

Four-Pin to Eight-Pin +12V CPU Power Adapters

If your motherboard requires all 8-pins be connected, and you are using a lower power draw processor and a power supply that does not have a matching 8-pin +12V connector, you can use an adapter to convert an existing 4-pin connector to an 8-pin connector. An example of this is shown in Figure 18.28.

FIGURE 18.28 Four-pin +12V to 8-pin +12V power adapter.

Adapters are also available that go the other way—that is, they convert an 8-pin CPU power connector to a 4-pin version. However, these are not always required because one can plug an 8-pin connector from a power supply into a 4-pin connector on a motherboard by simply offsetting the connector to one side. The only time the adapter would be needed is if there is a component on the board that is physically interfering with the portion of the connector that is offset.

Backward and Forward Compatibility

If you have reached this point, I'm sure you have some questions. For example, what happens if you purchase a new power supply that has a 24-pin main power connector but your motherboard has only a 20-pin main power socket? Likewise, what if you purchase a new motherboard that has a 24-pin main power socket but your power supply has only a 20-pin main power connector? The answers to these questions are surprising to say the least.

There are adapters that can convert a 24-pin connector to a 20-pin type, and the other way around, but surprisingly these adapters are *not* usually necessary. The truth is that compatibility has been engineered into the connectors, power supplies, and motherboards from the start.

If you look at the 24-pin main power connector diagram and compare it to the previous 20-pin design, you'll see that the extra 4 pins are all placed on one end of the connector and all the other pins are defined the same as they were previously. The design of these connectors is such that it allows an interesting bit of backward compatibility. The result is that you can plug a 24-pin main connector directly into a motherboard that has a 20-pin socket (and vice versa) without using an adapter! The trick is to position the connector such that the 4 extra pins are empty. Depending on the latch design, the latch on the side might not engage, but the connector will otherwise plug in and operate properly.

Figure 18.29 shows how you would connect a new power supply with a 24-pin connector to a motherboard that has only a 20-pin socket. The terminals on the 24-pin connector that are highlighted in gray would plug directly into the 20-pin socket, whereas the white highlighted terminals would remain free and unconnected.

Logically, this works because the first 20 pins of the 24-pin connector that match the 20-pin motherboard socket contain the correct signals in the correct positions. The only problem that might arise is if there are some components on the motherboard directly adjacent to the end of the 20-pin power socket that physically interfere with the four extra unused terminals on the 24-pin connector.

What about the opposite condition, in which you have a new motherboard with a 24-pin socket but your power supply has only a 20-pin connector? In this case, four terminals at the end of the motherboard socket are not connected. This also works because the 20-pin portion of both the connector and socket are the same. But this example raises another question: Will the motherboard operate properly without the extra power pins? Because the extra signals are merely additional voltage pins that are already present in the remaining part of the connector, the answer should be yes, but if the motherboard draws a lot of power, it can overload the remaining pins. After all, preventing overloads is the reason the extra pins were added in the first place.

Some motherboards sold from 2004 through 2010 that use a 24-pin main power connector also have an additional peripheral (that is, disk drive) power connector onboard designed to provide the extra power that would be missing if you connected a 20-pin main power connector from your power supply. The documentation for these motherboards refers to this as an *alternate* or *auxiliary power connector*. Some boards included both standard and SATA style drive connectors to supply this extra power.

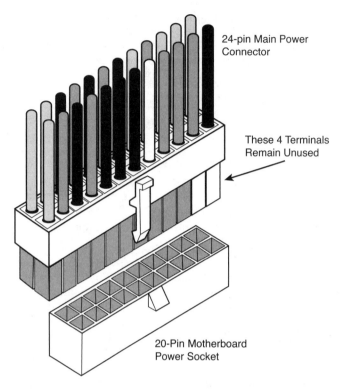

24-pin Main Power
Connector

These 4 Terminals
Remain Unused

20-Pin Motherboard
Power Socket

FIGURE 18.29 Connecting a 24-pin main power connector to a 20-pin motherboard socket.

If you plug a 24-pin main power connector into the 24-pin socket on the motherboard, the alternate or auxiliary power connection is probably unnecessary. However, if you plug a 20-pin main power connector into the 24-pin main power socket on the motherboard, and that board has one of these alternate or auxiliary power connectors on board, then you should probably use it. In that case simply select a spare peripheral (disk drive) power connector from the power supply and plug it into the alternate or auxiliary power connector. Most power supplies have several extra peripheral or SATA power connectors for supporting additional drives. Using a 20-pin main and the alternate or auxiliary power connector satisfies the power requirements for the motherboard and any PCI Express x16 video cards drawing up to 75 watts.

As a side note, be careful when plugging in the mismatched connectors so that they are offset properly. The main, +12V, and PCI Express graphics connectors are Molex Mini-Fit Jr.–type connectors that are keyed by virtue of a series of differently shaped plastic protrusions used around the terminals, which fit similarly shaped holes in the mating connectors. This keying is designed to prevent backward or improper off-center insertion, but I have found two problems with the keying that should be noted. One is that some alternate low-quality connector brands are built to looser tolerances than the original high-quality Molex versions, and the sloppier fit of the low-quality versions sometimes allows improper insertion. The other problem is that, with sufficient force, the keying on even the high-quality versions can be overcome. Because plugging a 20-pin connector into a 24-pin socket—or a 24-pin connector into a 20-pin socket—is designed to work even though they don't fully match up, you need to make sure you have the offsets correct or you risk damaging the board when you power it up.

Dell Proprietary (Nonstandard) ATX Design

Most of these systems are no longer in use, but if you upgrade or repair any Dell desktop systems made between 1996 and 2000, you should be aware that they used a nonstandard design, and upgrading either the motherboard or power supply can result in the destruction of the motherboard, power supply, or both! For more information about this, please see the 20th or earlier editions of *Upgrading and Repairing PCs*.

Additional Power Connectors

Besides the motherboard power connectors, all power supplies include a variety of additional power connectors, mainly used for internally mounted drives but usable by other components, such as graphics cards. Most of these connectors are industry-standard types required by the various power supply form factor specifications. This section discusses the various types of additional device power connectors you're likely to find in your PC.

Peripheral Power Connectors

Perhaps the most common additional power connector seen on virtually all power supplies is the *peripheral power connector*, also called the *disk drive power connector*. What we know as the peripheral power connector was originally created by AMP as part of the commercial MATE-N-LOK series, although since it is also manufactured and sold by Molex, it is often incorrectly called a *Molex connector*.

To determine the location of pin 1, carefully look at the connector. It is usually embossed in the plastic connector body; however, it is often tiny and difficult to read. Fortunately, these connectors are keyed and therefore difficult to insert incorrectly. Figure 18.30 shows the keying with respect to pin numbers on the larger drive power connector.

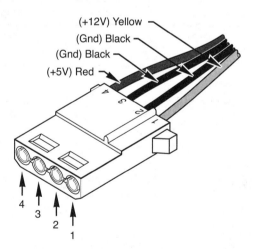

FIGURE 18.30 A peripheral power connector.

This is the one connector type that has been on all PC power supplies from the original IBM PC to the latest systems built today. It is most commonly known as a *disk drive connector*, but it is also used in some systems to provide additional power to the motherboard, video card, cooling fans, or just about anything that can use +5V or +12V power.

A peripheral power connector is a 4-pin connector with round terminals spaced 0.200 inches apart, rated to carry up to 11 amps per pin. Because there is one +12V pin and one +5V pin (the other two are grounds), the maximum power-handling capability of the peripheral connector is 187 watts. The plug is 0.830 inches wide, making it suitable for larger drives and devices.

Table 18.17 shows the peripheral power connector pinout and wire colors.

Table 18.17 Peripheral Power Connector Pinout (Large Drive Power Connector)

Pin	Signal	Color	Pin	Signal	Color
1	+12V	Yellow	3	Gnd	Black
2	Gnd	Black	4	+5V	Red

Floppy Power Connectors

When 3 1/2-inch floppy drives were first being integrated into PCs in the mid-1980s, it was clear that a smaller power connector was necessary. The answer came in what is now known as the *floppy power connector*, which was created by AMP as part of the economy interconnection (EI) series. These connectors are now used on all types of smaller drives and devices and feature the same +12V, +5V, and ground pins as the larger peripheral power connector. The floppy power connector has four pins spaced 2.5mm (0.098 inches) apart, which makes the entire connector about half the overall width as the larger peripheral power connector. The pins are rated for only 2 amps each, giving a maximum power-handling capability of 34 watts.

Table 18.18 shows the pinouts for the smaller floppy drive power connector.

Table 18.18 Pinout for the 3 1/2-Inch Floppy Power Connector (Small Drive Power Connector)

Pin	Signal	Color	Pin	Signal	Color
1	+5V	Red	3	Gnd	Black
2	Gnd	Black	4	+12V	Yellow

The peripheral and floppy power connectors are universal with regard to pin configuration and even wire color. Figure 18.31 shows the peripheral and floppy power connectors.

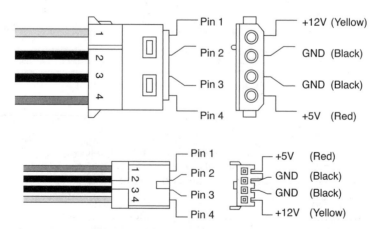

FIGURE 18.31 Peripheral and floppy power connectors.

The pin numbering and voltage designations are reversed on the floppy power connector. Be careful if you are making or using an adapter cable from one type of connector to another. Reversing the red and yellow wires fries the drive or device you plug into.

Serial ATA Power Connectors

If you want to add Serial ATA drives to an existing system, you will need a newer power supply that includes a Serial ATA (SATA) power connector. The SATA power connector is a special 15-pin connector fed by only five wires, meaning three pins are connected directly to each wire. The overall width is about the same as the peripheral power connector, but the SATA connector is significantly thinner. All the most recent power supply form factor specifications include SATA power connectors as mandatory for systems supporting SATA drives. Figure 18.32 shows a SATA power connector.

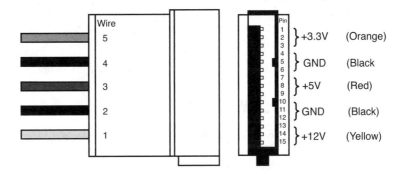

FIGURE 18.32 A SATA power connector.

In the SATA power connector, each wire is connected to three terminal pins, and the wire numbering is not in sync with the terminal numbering, which can be confusing.

If your power supply does not feature SATA power connectors, you can use an adapter to convert a standard peripheral power connector to a SATA power connector (see Figure 18.33). However, such adapters do not include the +3.3V power. Fortunately, though, this is not a problem for most applications because most drives do not require +3.3V and use only +12V and +5V instead.

Figure 18.33 shows a peripheral-to-SATA power connector adapter.

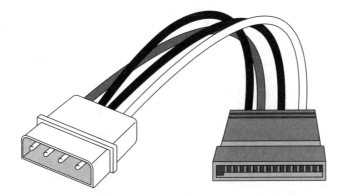

FIGURE 18.33 A peripheral-to-SATA power adapter.

PCI Express Auxiliary Graphics Power Connectors

Although the ATX12V 2.x specification includes a 24-pin main power connector with more power for devices such as video cards, the design was intended to power a video card drawing up to 75 watts maximum through the PCIe x16 slot. That is adequate for most video cards, but high-end gaming or workstation cards usually need quite a bit more power. To accommodate graphics cards needing more than 75 watts, the PCI-SIG (Special Interest Group) introduced two standards for supplying additional power to a video card via additional graphics power connectors:

- **PCI Express x16 Graphics 150W-ATX Specification**—Published in October 2004, this standard defines a 6-pin (2x3) auxiliary power connector capable of delivering an additional 75W to a graphics card directly from the power supply, for a total of 150W to the card.

- **PCI Express 225 W/300 W High Power Card Electromechanical Specification**— Published in March 2008, this standard defines an 8-pin (2x4) auxiliary power connector capable of supplying an additional 150W of power, for a total of either 225 watts (75+150) or 300 watts (75+150+75) of available power.

Cards requiring even more power can use multiple connectors, as shown in Table 18.19.

Table 18.19 Graphics Card Auxiliary Power Connector Configurations

Maximum Power Draw	Auxiliary Power Connector Configuration
75 Watts	None
150 Watts	One 6-pin connector
225 Watts	Two 6-pin connectors*
300 Watts	One 8-pin connector + one 6-pin connector
375 Watts	Two 8-pin connectors
450 Watts	Two 8-pin connectors + one 6-pin connector

*May optionally use one 8-pin connector instead.

The PCI Express auxiliary power connectors are 6-pin (2 × 3) or 8-pin (2 × 4) Molex Mini-Fit Jr. connector housings with female terminals that provide power directly to a video card. For reference, the connector is similar to Molex part number 39-01-2060 (6-pin) or 39-01-2080 (8-pin), but with different keying to prevent interchanging them with the +12V motherboard power connectors. A diagram of the 6-pin connector is shown in Figure 18.34, and the pinout in Table 18.20. Note the Sense signal at pin 5, which allows a graphics card to detect whether a 6-pin power connector has been attached. Without the proper power connections being detected, the card may shut down or operate in a reduced functionality mode. Also note that pin 2 is technically listed as "no connection" in the official specification, but most power supplies do seem to include +12V there.

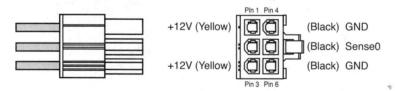

FIGURE 18.34   PCI Express 6-pin (2×3) auxiliary 75W power supply connector.

Table 18.20 PCI Express 6-Pin (2×3) Auxiliary 75W Power Connector Pinout (Graphics Card Socket)

Color	Signal	Pin	Pin	Signal	Color
Black	GND	4	1	+12V	Yellow
Black	Sense	5	2	N/C	–
Black	GND	6	3	+12V	Yellow

N/C = No connection; however, many PSUs include a redundant +12V (yellow) wire at pin 2.

A diagram of the 8-pin connector is shown in Figure 18.35, and the pinout in Table 18.21. Note the additional +12V power at pin 2 and the two Sense signals at pins 4 and 6, which allow a card to detect whether an 8-pin connector, a 6-pin connector, or no connector is attached.

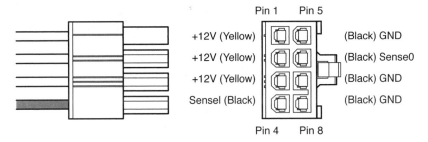

FIGURE 18.35 PCI Express 8-pin (2×4) auxiliary 150W power supply connector.

Table 18.21 PCI Express 8-Pin (2×4) Auxiliary 150W Power Connector Pinout (Graphics Card Socket)

Color	Signal	Pin	Pin	Signal	Color
Black	GND	5	1	+12V	Yellow
Black	Sense0	6	2	+12V	Yellow
Black	GND	7	3	+12V	Yellow
Black	GND	8	4	Sense1	Black

Because of both the physical design as well as the use of the sense signals, the 6-pin power supply connector plug is backward compatible with the 8-pin graphics card socket. This means that if your graphics card has an 8-pin socket but your power supply has only 6-pin connectors available, you can plug the 6-pin connector into the 8-pin socket using an offset arrangement, as shown in Figure 18.36. The connectors are keyed such that they should only plug in the correct way, but be careful because they can be forced together in an incorrect fashion, which can potentially damage the card.

The sense signals are used so that the graphics card can detect what types of connector(s) are attached, and therefore how much total power is available. For example, if a graphics card needs a full 300W and has both an 8-pin and a 6-pin connector on board, if you were to attach two 6-pin power supply connectors, the card would "sense" that it had only 225W available and, depending on the design, it could either shut down or operate in a reduced functionality mode.

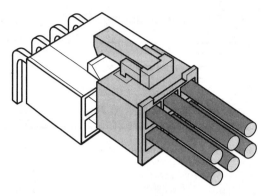

FIGURE 18.36   Plugging a 6-pin power supply connector into an 8-pin graphics card power socket.

Due to special keying on the 8-pin connector, it cannot be plugged into a 6-pin socket. Because of this, many power supply manufacturers include 8-pin connectors made in a "6+2" arrangement, where the portion containing the two extra pins can be disconnected, leaving a 6-pin connector that will, of course, work in a 6-pin socket.

Caution

The 8-pin PCI Express Auxiliary Power Connector and the 8-pin EPS12V CPU Power Connector use similar Molex Mini-Fit Jr. connector housings. Although they are keyed differently, the keying can be overcome by sufficient force such that you can plug an EPS12V power connector into a graphics card, or a PCI Express power connector into a motherboard. Either of these scenarios results in +12V being directly shorted to ground, potentially destroying the motherboard, graphics card, or power supply.

The 6-pin connector uses two +12V wires to carry up to 75W, whereas the 8-pin connector uses three +12V wires to carry up to 150W. Although these figures are what the specifications allow, the wires and terminals of each connector are technically capable of handling much more power. Each pin in the PCI Express auxiliary power connectors is rated to handle up to 8 amps of current using standard terminals—more if using HCS or Plus HCS terminals. By counting the number of terminals, you can calculate the power-handling capability of the connector (see Table 18.22).

Table 18.22   PCI Express Graphics Power Connector Maximum Power-Handling Capabilities

Connector	No. +12V Pins	Max. Power Using Std. Terminals (W)	Max. Power Using HCS Terminals (W)	Max. Power Using Plus HCS Terminals (W)
6-pin	2	192	264	288
8-pin	3	288	396	432

Only two +12V pins are used in the 6-pin connector, even though most power supplies include three.
Standard terminals are rated 8 amps.
HCS terminals are rated 11 amps.
Plus HCS terminals are rated 12 amps.
All ratings assume Mini-Fit Jr. connectors using 18-gauge wire under standard temperature conditions.

Even though the specification allows for a delivery capability of 75W (6-pin connector) or 150 watts (8-pin connector), the total power-handling capacity of these connectors is at least 192 and 288 watts, respectively, using standard terminals, and even more using the HCS or Plus HCS terminals.

These two auxiliary power connectors are sometimes called PCI Express Graphics (PEG), Scalable Link Interface (SLI), or CrossFire power connectors because they are used by high-end PCI Express boards with SLI or CrossFire capabilities. SLI and CrossFire are NVIDIA and AMD's methods of using two video cards in unison, with each one drawing half of the screen for twice the performance. Each card can draw hundreds of watts, with many of the high-end cards using two or three auxiliary power connectors. This means that most power supplies that are rated as SLI- or CrossFireX-ready include at least two or more of the 6/8-pin PCI Express graphics power connectors. Using two video cards drawing 300 watts each means that even if you have a 750-watt power supply, you will have only 150 watts of power left to run the motherboard, processor, and all the disk drives. With high-powered processors drawing 130 watts or more, this may not be enough. For this reason, systems using two or more high-end video cards require the highest-output supplies available, and some of the current ones are capable of putting out up to 1,000 watts (1 kilowatt) or more.

Note

NVIDIA has trademarked the term *SLI* as meaning *scalable link interface*, but its primary competitor, AMD, uses similar dual-graphics card technology called CrossFire to achieve comparable performance improvements.

If your existing power supply doesn't feature PCI Express auxiliary power connectors, you can use Y-adapters to convert multiple peripheral power connectors (normally used for drives) into a single 6-pin or 8-pin PCI Express auxiliary power connector. Note, however, that these adapters will not help if the power supply is not capable of supplying the total power actually required.

Power Supply Specifications

Power supplies have several specifications that define their input and output capabilities as well as their operational characteristics. This section defines and examines most of the common specifications related to power supplies.

Power Supply Loading

PC power supplies are of a *switching* rather than a *linear* design. The switching type of design uses a high-speed oscillator circuit to convert the higher wall-socket AC voltage to the much lower DC voltage used to power the PC and PC components. Switching-type power supplies are noted for being efficient in size, weight, and energy compared to the linear design, which uses a large internal transformer to generate various outputs. This type of transformer-based design is inefficient in at least three ways:

- The output voltage of the transformer linearly follows the input voltage (hence the name linear), so any fluctuations in the AC power going into the system can cause problems with the output.

- The high current-level (power) requirements of a PC system require the use of heavy wiring in the transformer.

- The 60Hz frequency of the AC power supplied from your building is difficult to filter out inside the power supply, requiring large and expensive filter capacitors and rectifiers.

The switching supply, on the other hand, uses a switching circuit that chops up the incoming power at a relatively high frequency. This enables the use of high-frequency transformers that are much smaller and lighter. Also, the higher frequency is much easier and cheaper to filter out at the output, and the input voltage can vary widely. Input ranging from 90V to 135V still produces the proper output levels, and many switching supplies can automatically adjust to 240V input.

One characteristic of all switching-type power supplies is that they do not run without a *load*. Therefore, you must have something such as a motherboard and hard drive plugged in and drawing power for the supply to work. If you simply have the power supply on a bench with nothing plugged into it, either the supply burns up or its protection circuitry shuts it down. Most power supplies are protected from no-load operation and shut down automatically. Some of the cheapest supplies, however, lack the protection circuit and relay and can be destroyed after a few seconds of no-load operation. A few power supplies have their own built-in load resistors, so they can run even though there isn't a normal load (such as a motherboard or hard disk) plugged in.

Some power supplies have minimum load requirements for both the +5V and +12V sides. According to IBM specifications for the 192-watt power supply used in the original AT, a minimum load of 7.0 amps was required at +5V and a minimum of 2.5 amps was required at +12V for the supply to work properly. As long as a motherboard was plugged into the power supply, the motherboard would draw sufficient +5V at all times to keep those circuits in the supply happy. However, +12V is typically used only by motors (and not motherboards), and the floppy or optical drive motors are usually off. Because floppy or optical drives don't present +12V load unless they are spinning, systems without a hard disk drive could have problems because there wouldn't be enough load on the +12V circuit in the supply.

To alleviate problems, when IBM used to ship the original AT systems without a hard disk, it plugged the hard disk drive power cable into a large 5-ohm, 50-watt sandbar resistor that was mounted in a small metal cage assembly where the drive would have been. The AT case had screw holes on top of where the hard disk would go, specifically designed to mount this resistor cage.

Note

Several computer stores I knew of in the mid-1980s ordered the diskless AT and installed their own 20MB or 30MB drives, which they could get more cheaply from sources other than IBM. They were throwing away the load resistors by the hundreds! I managed to grab a couple at the time, which is how I know the type of resistor they used.

This resistor would be connected between pin 1 (+12V) and pin 2 (Ground) on the hard disk power connector. This placed a 2.4-amp load on the supply's +12V output, drawing 28.8 watts of power (it would get hot!) and thus enabling the supply to operate normally. Note that the cooling fan in most power supplies draws approximately 0.1–0.25 amps, bringing the total load to 2.5 amps or more. If the load resistor were missing, the system would intermittently fail to start.

Most of the power supplies in use today do not require as much of a load as the original IBM AT power supply. In most cases, a minimum load of 0–0.3 amps at +3.3V, 2.0–4.0 amps at +5V, and 0.5–1.0 amps at +12V is considered acceptable. Most motherboards easily draw the minimum +5V current by themselves. The standard power supply cooling fan draws only 0.1–0.25 amps, so the +12V minimum load might still be a problem for a diskless workstation. Generally, the higher the rating on the supply, the more minimum load that is required. However, exceptions do exist, so this is a specification you should check when evaluating power supplies.

Some switching power supplies have built-in load resistors and can run in a no-load situation. Most power supplies don't have internal load resistors but might require only a small load on the +5V line to operate properly. Some supplies, however, might require +3.3V, +5V, and +12V loads to work; the only way to know is by checking the documentation for the particular supply in question.

No matter what, if you want to properly and accurately bench test a power supply, be sure you place a load on at least one (or preferably all) of the positive voltage outputs. This is one reason it is best to test a supply while it is installed in the system instead of testing it separately on the bench. For impromptu bench testing, you can use a spare motherboard and one or more hard disk drives to load the outputs.

Power Supply Ratings

A system manufacturer should be able to provide you the technical specifications of the power supplies it uses in its systems. This type of information can be found in the system's technical reference manual, as well as on stickers attached directly to the power supply. Power supply manufacturers can also supply this data, which is preferable if you can identify the manufacturer and contact it directly or via the Web.

The input specifications are listed as voltages, and the output specifications are listed as amps at several voltage levels. You can convert amperage to wattage by using the following simple formula:

watts = volts × amps

For example, if a component is listed as drawing 8 amps of +12V current, that equals 96 watts of power according to the formula.

By multiplying the voltage by the amperage available at each main output and then adding the results, you can calculate the total capable output wattage of the supply. Note that only positive voltage outputs are normally used in calculating outputs; the negative outputs, Standby, Power_Good, and other signals that are not used to power components are usually exempt.

Table 18.23 shows the ratings and calculations for various single +12V rail ATX12V/EPS12V power supplies from Corsair (www.corsair.com).

Table 18.23 Typical ATX12V/EPS12V Power Supply Output Ratings

Model	VX450W	VX550W	HX650W	HX750W	HX850W	TX950W	AX1200
+12V (A)	33	41	52	62	70	78	100
−12V (A)	0.8	0.8	0.8	0.8	0.8	0.8	0.8
+5VSB (A)	2.5	3	3	3	3	3	3.5
+5V (A)	20	28	30	25	25	25	30
+3.3V (A)	20	30	24	25	25	25	30
Max +5V/+3.3V (W)	130	140	170	150	150	150	180
Rated Max. (W)	450	550	650	750	850	950	1200
Calculated Max. (W)	548	657	819	919	1015	1111	1407

Virtually all power supplies place limits on the maximum combined draw for the +3.3V and +5V.

The calculated maximum output assumes the maximum draw from all outputs simultaneously and is generally not sustainable. For this reason, the (sustainable) rated maximum output is normally much less.

Although store-bought PCs often come with lower-rated power supplies of 350 watts or less, higher output units are often recommended for fully optioned desktops or tower systems. Unfortunately, the ratings on cheap or poorly made power supplies cannot always be trusted. For example, I've seen 650W-rated units that had less actual power output than honestly rated 200W units. Another issue is that few companies actually make power supplies. Most of the units you see for sale are made under contract by a few manufacturers and sold under a variety of brands, makes, and models. Because few people have the time or equipment to actually test or verify output, it is better to stick to brands that are known for selling quality units.

Most power supplies are considered to be universal, or worldwide. That is, they also can run on the 240V, 50-cycle current used in Europe and many other parts of the world. Many power supplies that can switch from 120V to 240V input do so automatically, but a few require you to set a switch on the back of the power supply to indicate which type of power you will access.

Note

In North America, power companies are required to supply split-phase 240V (plus or minus 5%) AC, which equals two 120V legs. Resistive voltage drops in the building wiring can cause the 240V to drop to 220V or the 120V to drop to 110V by the time the power reaches an outlet at the end of a long circuit run. For this reason, the input voltage for an AC-powered device might be listed as anything between 220V and 240V, or 110V and 120V. I use the 240/120V numbers throughout this chapter because those are the intended standard figures.

Caution

If your supply does not switch input voltages automatically, make sure the voltage setting is correct. If you plug the power supply into a 120V outlet while it's set in the 240V setting, no damage will result, but the supply won't operate properly until you correct the setting. On the other hand, if you plug into a 240V outlet and have the switch set for 120V, you can cause damage.

Other Power Supply Specifications

In addition to power output, many other specifications and features go into making a high-quality power supply. I have had many systems over the years. My experience has been that if a brown-out occurs in a room with several systems running, the systems with higher-quality power supplies and higher output ratings are far more likely to make it through the power disturbances unscathed, whereas others choke.

High-quality power supplies also help protect your systems. A high-quality power supply from a vendor such as PC Power & Cooling will not be damaged if any of the following conditions occur:

- A 100% power outage of any duration
- A brownout of any kind
- A spike of up to 2,500V applied directly to the AC input (for example, a lightning strike or a lightning simulation test)

Decent power supplies have an extremely low current leakage to ground of less than 500 microamps. This safety feature is important if your outlet has a missing or an improperly wired ground line.

As you can see, these specifications are fairly tough and are certainly representative of a high-quality power supply. Make sure that your supply can meet these specifications.

You can also use many other criteria to evaluate a power supply. The power supply is a component many users ignore when shopping for a PC, so it is one that some system vendors choose to skimp on. After all, a dealer is far more likely to be able to increase the price of a computer by spending money on additional memory or a larger hard drive than by installing a better power supply.

When buying a computer (or a replacement power supply), learn as much as possible about the power supply. Many consumers are intimidated by the vocabulary and statistics found in a typical power supply specification. Here are some of the most common parameters found on power supply specification sheets, along with their meanings:

- **Mean Time Between Failures (MTBF) or Mean Time To Failure (MTTF)**—The (calculated) average interval, in hours, that the power supply is expected to operate before failing. Power supplies typically have MTBF ratings (such as 100,000 hours or more) that are clearly not the result of real-time empirical testing. In fact, manufacturers use published standards to calculate the results based on the failure rates of the power supply's individual components. MTBF figures for power supplies often include the load to which the power supply was subjected (in the form of a percentage) and the temperature of the environment in which the tests were performed.

- **Input Range (or Operating Range)**—The range of voltages that the power supply is prepared to accept from the AC power source. For 120V AC power, an input range of 90V–135V is common; for 240V power, a 180V–270V range is typical.

- **Peak Inrush Current**—The greatest amount of current drawn by the power supply at a given moment immediately after it is turned on, expressed in terms of amps at a particular voltage. The lower the current, the less thermal shock the system experiences.

- **Hold-Up Time**—The amount of time (in milliseconds) that a power supply can maintain output within the specified voltage ranges after a loss of input power. This enables your PC to continue running without resetting or rebooting if a brief interruption in AC power occurs. Values of 15–30 milliseconds are common for today's power supplies, and the higher (longer), the better. The Power Supply Design Guide for Desktop Platform Form Factors specification calls for a minimum of 16ms hold-up time. The hold-up time is also greatly affected by the load on the power supply. The hold-up specification is normally listed as the minimum time measured under the maximum load. As the load is reduced, hold-up times should increase proportionately. For example, if a 1,000W PSU has a 20ms hold-up time specification (measured under a 1,000W load), then under a 500W (half) load I'd expect that to double, and under a 250W load I'd expect it to double again. This is in fact one of the reasons I've always been a proponent of specifying higher output PSUs than are strictly necessary when building systems.

- **Transient Response**—The amount of time (in microseconds) a power supply takes to bring its output back to the specified voltage ranges after a steep change in the output current. In other words, the amount of time it takes for the output power levels to stabilize after a device in the system starts or stops drawing power. Power supplies sample the current being used by the computer at regular intervals. When a device stops drawing power during one of these intervals (such as when a floppy drive stops spinning), the power supply might supply too high a voltage to the output for a brief time. This excess voltage is called *overshoot*, and the transient response is the time that it takes for the voltage to return to the specified level. This is seen as a spike in voltage by the system and can cause glitches and lockups. Once a major problem that came with switching power supplies, overshoot has been greatly reduced in recent years. Transient response values are sometimes expressed in time intervals, and at other times they are expressed in terms of a particular output change, such as "power output levels stay within regulation during output changes of up to 20%."

- **Overvoltage Protection**—Defines the trip points for each output at which the power supply shuts down or squelches that output. Values can be expressed as a percentage (for example, 120% for +3.3 and +5V) or as raw voltages (for example, +4.6V for the +3.3V output and +7.0V for the +5V output).

- **Maximum Load Current**—The largest amount of current (in amps) that safely can be delivered through a particular output. Values are expressed as individual amperages for each output voltage. With these figures, you can calculate not only the total amount of power the power supply can supply, but also how many devices using those various voltages it can support.

- **Minimum Load Current**—The smallest amount of current (in amps) that must be drawn from a particular output for that output to function. If the current drawn from an output falls below the minimum, the power supply could be damaged or automatically shut down.

- **Load Regulation (or Voltage Load Regulation)**—When the current drawn from a particular output increases or decreases, the voltage changes slightly as well—usually increasing as the current rises. Load regulation is the change in the voltage for a particular output as it transitions from its minimum load to its maximum load (or vice versa). Values, expressed in terms of a +/− percentage, typically range from +/−1% to +/−5% for the +3.3V, +5V, and +12V outputs.

- **Line Regulation**—The change in output voltage as the AC input voltage transitions from the lowest to the highest value of the input range. A power supply should be capable of handling any AC voltage in its input range with a change in its output of 1% or less.

- **Efficiency**—The ratio of power input to power output, expressed in terms of a percentage. Values of 65%—85% are common for power supplies today. The remaining 15%—35% of the power input is converted to heat during the AC/DC conversion process. Although greater efficiency means less heat inside the computer (always a good thing) and lower electric bills, it should not be emphasized at the expense of precision, stability, and durability, as evidenced in the supply's load regulation and other parameters.

- **Ripple (or Ripple and Noise, or AC Ripple, or PARD [Periodic and Random Deviation])**—The average voltage of all AC effects on the power supply outputs, usually measured in millivolts peak-to-peak or as a percentage of the nominal output voltage. The lower this figure, the better. Higher-quality units are typically rated at 1% ripple (or less), which if expressed in volts would be 1% of the output. Consequently, for +5V, that would be 0.05V or 50mV (millivolts). Ripple can be caused by internal switching transients, rectified line frequency bleed-through, or other random noise.

Power Factor Correction

In order to improve power line efficiency and to reduce harmonic distortion generation, the power factor of PC power supplies has come under examination. In particular, new standards are now mandatory in many European Union (EU) countries that require harmonics to be reduced below a specific amount. The circuitry required to do this is called *power factor correction (PFC)*.

The *power factor* measures how effectively electrical power is being used and is expressed as a number between 0 and 1. A high power factor means that electrical power is being used effectively, whereas a low power factor indicates poor utilization of electrical power. To understand the power factor, you must understand how power is used.

Generally, two types of loads are placed on AC power lines:

- **Resistive**—Power converted into heat, light, motion, or work

- **Inductive**—Sustains an electromagnetic field, such as in a transformer or motor

A resistive load is often called *working power* and is measured in kilowatts (KW). An inductive load, on the other hand, is often called *reactive power* and is measured in kilovolt-amperes-reactive (KVAR). Working power and reactive power together make up *apparent power*, which is measured in kilovolt-amperes (KVA). The power factor is measured as the ratio of working power to apparent power, or working power/apparent power (KW/KVA). The ideal power factor is 1, where the working power and the apparent power are the same.

The concept of a resistive load or working power is fairly easy to understand. For example, a light bulb that consumes 100W of power generates 100W worth of heat and light. This is a pure resistive load. An inductive load, on the other hand, is a little harder to understand. Think about a transformer, which has coil windings to generate an electromagnetic field and then induce current in another set of windings. A certain amount of power is required to saturate the windings and generate the magnetic field, even though no work is being done. A power transformer that is not connected to anything is a perfect example of a pure inductive load. An apparent power draw exists to generate the fields, but no working power exists because no actual work is being done.

When the transformer is connected to a load, it uses both working power and reactive power. In other words, power is consumed to do work (for example, if the transformer is powering a light bulb), and apparent power is used to maintain the electromagnetic field in the transformer windings. In an AC circuit, these loads can become out of sync or phase, meaning they don't peak at the same time, which can generate harmonic distortions back down the power line. I've seen examples in which electric motors have caused distortions in television sets plugged into the same power circuit.

PFC usually involves adding capacitance to the circuit to maintain the inductive load without drawing additional power from the line. This makes the working power and apparent power the same, which results in a power factor of 1. It usually isn't just as simple as adding some capacitors to a circuit, although that can be done and is called passive power factor correction. *Active power factor correction* involves a more intelligent circuit designed to match the resistive and inductive loads so the electrical outlet sees them as the same.

A power supply with active power factor correction draws low distortion current from the AC source and has a power factor rating of 0.9 or greater. A nonpower factor-corrected supply draws highly distorted current and is sometimes referred to as a *nonlinear* load. The power factor of a noncorrected supply is typically 0.6–0.8. Therefore, only 60% of the apparent power consumed is actually doing real work!

Having a power supply with active PFC might or might not lower your electric bill (it depends on how your power is measured), but it definitely reduces the load on the building wiring. With PFC, all the power going into the supply is converted into actual work, and the wiring is less overworked. For example, if you ran a number of computers on a single breaker-controlled circuit and found that you were blowing the breaker periodically, you could switch to systems with active PFC power supplies and reduce the load on the wiring by up to 40%, meaning you would be less likely to blow the breaker.

The International Electrotechnical Commission (IEC) has released standards dealing with the low-frequency public supply system. The initial standards were 555.2 (Harmonics) and 555.3 (Flicker), but they have since been refined and are now available as IEC 1000-3-2 and IEC 1000-3-3, respectively. As governed by the EMC directive, most electrical devices sold within the member countries of the EU must meet the IEC standards. The IEC1000-3-2/3 standards became mandatory in 1997 and 1998.

Even if you don't live in a country where PFC is required, I highly recommend specifying PC power supplies with active PFC. The 80 PLUS certification for highly efficient power supplies also includes a requirement that the power supply has active PFC. The main benefit of PFC supplies is that they do not overheat building wiring or distort the AC source waveform, which causes less interference on the line for other devices.

SLI-Ready and CrossFireX Certifications

Both NVIDIA and AMD have certification programs that test and certify power supplies to be able to power systems with multiple graphics cards in either a Scalable Link Interface (SLI) or a CrossFire configuration. This type of configuration puts extreme demands on the PSU, because it has to power not only what would normally be a high-end motherboard, CPU, and multiple drives in a RAID configuration, but also up to three video cards, which may be capable of drawing 300 watts or more each.

The certification process involves PSU manufacturers sending PSUs in for testing, whereby they are verified to supply sufficient power (and the proper type and number of connectors) to run the desired graphics hardware as well as the system. Power supplies that have passed either of these certifications are virtually guaranteed to produce high output and use high-quality design, engineering, and manufacturing. For more information on these certifications, as well as lists of certified PSUs, visit the following links:

- **Certified SLI-Ready Power Supplies**—www.geforce.com/hardware/technology/sli
- **CrossFire Certified Power Supplies**—http://support.amd.com/us/certified/power-supplies

I recommend checking the lists or looking for the "NVIDIA SLI-Ready" or "AMD CrossFireX Technology" logos (see Figures 18.37 and 18.38) on a power supply as an excellent indicator of a high-power, high-quality unit.

FIGURE 18.37 NVIDIA SLI-Ready logo.

FIGURE 18.38 AMD CrossFireX Technology logo.

Safety Certifications

Many agencies around the world certify electric and electronic components for safety and quality. The most commonly known agency in the United States is Underwriters Laboratories, Inc. (UL). UL standard #60950—*Safety of Information Technology Equipment*—covers power supplies and other PC components. You should always purchase power supplies and other devices that are UL-certified. It has often been said that, although not every good product is UL-certified, no bad products are.

In Canada, electric and electronic products are certified by the Canadian Standards Agency (CSA). The German equivalents are TÜV Rheinland and VDE, and NEMKO operating in Norway. These agencies are responsible for certification of products throughout Europe. Power supply manufacturers that sell to an international market should have products that are certified at least by UL, the CSA, and TÜV—if not by all the agencies listed, and more.

Apart from UL-type certifications, many power supply manufacturers, even the most reputable ones, claim that their products have a Class B certification from the Federal Communications Commission (FCC), meaning that they meet FCC standards for electromagnetic and radio frequency interference (EMI/RFI). This is a contentious point, however, because the FCC does not certify power supplies as individual components. Title 47 of the Code of Federal Regulations, Part 15, Section 15.101(c) states the following:

The FCC does NOT currently authorize motherboards, cases, and internal power supplies. Vendor claims that they are selling "FCC-certified cases," "FCC-certified motherboards," or "FCC-certified internal power supplies" are false.

In fact, an FCC certification can be issued collectively only to a base unit consisting of a computer case, motherboard, and power supply. Thus, a power supply purported to be FCC-certified was actually certified along with a particular case and motherboard—not necessarily the same case and motherboard you are using in your system. This does not mean, however, that the manufacturer is being deceitful or that the power supply is inferior. If anything, this means that when evaluating power supplies, you should place less weight on the FCC certification than on other factors, such as UL certification.

Power-Use Calculations

When expanding or upgrading your PC, ensure that your power supply is capable of providing sufficient current to power all the system's internal devices. One way to see whether your system is capable of expansion is to calculate the levels of power consumption by the various system components in your system and then compare that to the rating on the power supply to see if it is up to the job. This calculation can also help you decide whether you must upgrade the power supply to a more capable unit. Unfortunately, these calculations can be difficult to make accurately because many manufacturers do not publish detailed power consumption data for their products. In some cases, you can find the specs from a similar component and go by that data instead. Usually, components of the same basic design, capability, and vintage have relatively the same power consumption characteristics. Table 18.24 shows the range of power usage for typical PC components I've observed over the past few years.

Table 18.24   Power Consumption Calculation

Component	Power Usage	Comments
Motherboard	50W–75W	Depends on the number of integrated components.
Processor	25W–150W	For each physical processor (not cores). Most are 50W–100W.
RAM	5W–15W	For each module (DIMM).
Integrated video	5W–15W	Integrated into the North Bridge chip.
Discrete video card	25W–300W	For each video card.
PCI card	5W–15W	For each nonvideo card.
PCIe card	10W–25W	For each nonvideo card.
3.5-inch hard disk drive	15W–30W	For each drive. Power use increased during startup.
2.5-inch HDD/SSD	1W–5W	For each drive. Power use increased during startup.
Optical drive	15W–35W	For each drive.
Cooling fan	3W–5W	For each fan.
USB/FireWire	2W–5W	For each used port.

Of course, power consumption can vary greatly for different devices such as processors and video cards, so if you want to be more informed, consult the data sheets or technical manuals for your specific components. Also, these overall wattage figures do not give the breakdown covering which of the rails (+3.3V, +5V, or +12V) each device will use. In some cases, the combination of components used can exceed the available power on a single rail while still being under budget for the total wattage available from all the rails combined. That is in fact one reason that people end up purchasing a power supply with a much higher watt rating than might seem necessary.

After you've added up everything I recommend, multiply the total power consumed by all your components by 1.5 to estimate the size of power supply required. This allows some headroom for future expansion and accounts for the fact that at certain times some devices can draw much more than their nominal power.

If you want an easier way to calculate your estimated power requirements, Asus has a fairly good power supply wattage calculator that you can use online at the following URL: http://support.asus.com/PowerSupplyCalculator/PSCalculator.aspx. After you fill in all the fields with the components in the intended system, the calculator gives you an estimate of the minimum power supply rating you should choose to power the system.

Different types of bus slots can provide different levels of power for cards. Fortunately, it is rare for any cards other than video cards to use the maximum allowable power. Table 18.25 shows the maximum power available per slot for different bus types.

Table 18.25 Maximum Available Power per Bus Slot

Bus Type	+3.3V Current (Amps)	+5V Current (Amps)	+12V Current (Amps)	Total Power (Watts)
ISA	N/A	2.0	0.175	12.1
EISA	N/A	4.5	1.5	40.5
VL-bus	N/A	2.0	N/A	10
16-bit MCA	N/A	1.6	0.175	10.1
32-bit MCA	N/A	2.0	0.175	12.1
PCI	7.6	5	0.5	56
AGP	6	2	1	42
PCI Express	4.8	N/A	4.8	75

The biggest cause of power supply overload problems has historically been filling up the expansion slots (especially with multiple video cards), using high-powered processors, and adding more drives. Multiple hard drives, optical drives, and floppy drives can create quite a drain on the system power supply. Be sure you have enough +12V power to run all the drives you plan to install. Tower systems can be especially problematic because they have so many drive bays. Just because the case has room for the devices doesn't mean the power supply can support them. Be sure you have enough power to run all your expansion cards, especially video cards. However, remember that most cards draw less than the maximum allowed. Today's newest processors can have high current requirements for the +5V or +3.3V supplies. When you're selecting a power supply for your system, it pays to be conservative, so be sure to take into account future upgrades or additions to the system.

Many people wait until an existing component fails to replace it with an upgraded version. If you are on a tight budget, this "if it ain't broke, don't fix it" attitude might be necessary. Power supplies, however, often do not fail completely all at once; they can fail in an intermittent fashion or allow fluctuating power levels to reach the system, which results in unstable operation. You might be blaming system lockups on software bugs when the culprit is an overloaded power supply. In addition, an inadequate or failing supply causing lockups can result in file system corruption, which causes even further system instabilities (which could remain even after you replace the power supply). If you use bus-powered USB devices, a failing power supply can also cause these devices to fail or malfunction. If you have been running your original power supply for a long time and have upgraded your system in other ways, you should expect some problems, and you might want to consider reloading the OS and applications from scratch.

Although there is certainly an appropriate place for the exacting power-consumption calculations you've read about in this section, a great many experienced PC users prefer the "don't worry about it" power calculation method. This technique consists of buying or building a system with a good-quality 500-watt or higher power supply (or upgrading to such a supply in an existing system) and then upgrading the system freely, without concern for power consumption.

Power Savings

Over the past few years, energy conservation has become a major focus for appliances, electronics, and especially for computers. Saving power can be accomplished through several means. One is to use more efficient components that simply use (or waste) less energy to do the job. The other is to properly manage the computer hardware so that components that are not being used are powered down or put into standby modes. By using more efficient components and turning off specific components of the PC when they are not in use, you can reduce the electric bill and avoid having to power the computer up and down manually. This not only saves energy, but makes the system more convenient to use. The following sections discuss both of these approaches to saving power.

80 Plus

When it comes to computers, one of the major factors in overall energy consumption is the efficiency of the power supply unit. In 2004, the Northwest Energy Efficiency Alliance (NEEA) funded the 80 PLUS Program to encourage computer manufacturers to improve the energy efficiency of their machines by installing highly efficient power supplies. Ecos Consulting, which manages the program, tests and certifies power supplies as being 80% (or higher) in efficiency. To help offset the cost of producing more efficient designs, the program also pays incentives to manufacturers producing PSUs and systems that are certified.

Systems with more efficient power supplies consume on average from 15% to 30% less power than conventional designs. This can result in a significant energy and cost savings over the life of a system. In addition, the resulting lower heat output both improves system reliability and saves additional energy in cooling the system as well as the surrounding environment.

The 80 PLUS program currently has five levels of certification, from 80 PLUS to 80 PLUS Platinum. Each level of certification signifies different minimum levels of efficiency, which are measured at three different loads (20%, 50%, and 100%). Table 18.26 shows the details of each of the certification levels.

Table 18.26 80 PLUS Certification Levels

80 PLUS Rating	Efficiency at 20% Rated Load	Efficiency at 50% Rated Load	Efficiency at 100% Rated Load
80 PLUS	80%	80%	80%
80 PLUS Bronze	82%	85%	82%
80 PLUS Silver	85%	88%	85%
80 PLUS Gold	87%	90%	87%
80 PLUS Platinum	90%	92%	89%

How is this efficiency determined, and what is the overall effect? The PSU in a PC converts the high voltage (120V in the USA) AC wall current to 12V and lower DC voltages for use in the PC. Unfortunately, no PSU is 100% efficient, meaning that some of the power is lost or used up during the conversion and ends up being dissipated as heat. Conventional PSUs are or were normally about 70% efficient, which means that 30% of the energy drawn from the wall socket is wasted and ends up as heat. As an example, let's take a system that draws 250 watts total. Table 18.27 shows the resulting AC power draw and the amount of wasted energy if the PSU were 70%, 80%, or 90% efficient.

Table 18.27   The Effect of PSU Efficiency on AC Power Draw and Wasted Energy

Efficiency	70%	80%	90%
PSU Classification	Conventional	80 PLUS	80 PLUS Gold
DC Power Draw (W)	250	250	250
AC Power Draw (W)	357	313	278
Wasted Energy (W)	107	63	28

As you can see, when supplying the same 250 watts of power to the system, the actual amount of power used, and consequently the amount of energy wasted, varies considerably. A more efficient PSU can save a tremendous amount of energy and money over the life of a system. Because of this, I highly recommend 80 PLUS certified power supplies, especially those earning the higher efficiency ratings.

ENERGY STAR

ENERGY STAR is an international standard for energy-efficient consumer products, including computers and power supplies. The U.S. Environmental Protection Agency (EPA) introduced ENERGY STAR as a voluntary labeling program designed to identify and promote energy-efficient products. The first products labeled in the program were computers and monitors. In the years since, ENERGY STAR has become an international standard, and the label can be found on new homes, commercial and industrial buildings, appliances, office equipment, lighting, electronics, and more. Devices carrying the ENERGY STAR logo generally use 20%–30% less energy than required by federal standards. In addition to ENERGY STAR, many European-targeted products are labeled with TCO Certification, a combined energy usage and ergonomics rating from the Swedish Confederation of Professional Employees (TCO).

Starting in 2007, the ENERGY STAR Computer 4.0 specification required the use of a power supply that meets the 80 PLUS standard. In 2009, the 5.0 specification was released and now requires a power supply meeting the 80 Plus Bronze standard, for a minimum of 85% efficiency (at a 50% load). The 6.0 specification was published in 2013, along with new computer categories with different allowable power ratings to match the type of systems currently on the market.

Advanced Power Management

Advanced Power Management (APM) is a specification jointly developed by Intel and Microsoft that defines a series of interfaces between power management–capable hardware and a computer's OS. The final version 1.2 of APM was released in 1996. When it is fully activated, APM can automatically switch a computer between five states, depending on the system's current activity. Each state represents a further reduction in power use, accomplished by placing unused components into a low-power mode. The five system states are as follows:

- **Full On**—The system is completely operational, with no power management occurring.
- **APM Enabled**—The system is operational, with some devices being power managed. Unused devices can be powered down and the CPU clock slowed or stopped.

- **APM Standby**—The system is not operational, with most devices in a low-power state. The CPU clock can be slowed or stopped, but operational parameters are retained in memory. When triggered by a specific user or system activity, the system can return to the APM Enabled state almost instantaneously.

- **APM Suspend**—The system is not operational, with most devices unpowered. The CPU clock is stopped, and operational parameters are saved to disk for later restoration. When triggered by a wakeup event, the system returns to the APM Enabled state relatively slowly.

- **Off**—The system is not operational. The power supply is off.

APM requires support from both hardware and software to function. In this chapter, you've already seen how ATX-style power supplies can be controlled by software commands using the Power_On signal and the 6-pin optional power connector. Manufacturers are also integrating the same type of control features into other system components, such as motherboards, monitors, and disk drives.

OSs that support APM trigger power management events by monitoring the activities performed by the computer user and the applications running on the system. However, the OS does not directly address the power management capabilities of the hardware. All versions of Windows from 3.1 up through XP include APM support; however, support for APM was dropped from Vista and later, which exclusively support the Advanced Configuration and Power Interface (ACPI) instead.

Advanced Configuration and Power Interface

As power-management techniques continued to develop, maintaining the complex information states necessary to implement more advanced functions became increasingly difficult for the BIOS. Therefore, another standard was developed by Intel, Microsoft, and Toshiba. Called *Advanced Configuration and Power Interface (ACPI)*, this standard was designed to implement power-management functions in the OS. Microsoft Windows 98 and later automatically use ACPI if ACPI functions are found in the system BIOS. The need to update system BIOSs for ACPI support is one reason many computer vendors have recommended performing a BIOS update before installing Windows 98 or later on older systems.

ACPI was initially released in 1996 and first appeared in the Phoenix BIOS around that time. ACPI became a requirement for the Intel/Microsoft "PC'97" logo certification in 1996, which caused developers to work on integrating ACPI into system designs around that time. Intel included ACPI support in chipsets starting with the PIIX4E South Bridge in April 1998, and ACPI support was included in Windows starting with the release of Windows 98 (June 25, 1998) as part of what Microsoft called its "OnNow" initiative. By the time Windows 2000 came out (February 17, 2000), ACPI had universally replaced APM on new systems. ACPI 4.0a was released in April 2010, and the latest ACPI 5.0 Specification was released in November 2011. The official ACPI specifications can be downloaded from www.acpi.info.

Placing power management under the control of the OS enables a greater interaction with applications. For example, a program can indicate to the OS which of its activities are crucial, forcing an immediate activation of the hard drive, and which can be delayed until the next time the drive is activated for some other reason. For example, a word processor may be set to automatically save files in the background, which an OS using ACPI can then delay until the drive is activated for some other reason, resulting in fewer random spin-ups of the drive.

ACPI goes far beyond the previous standard, APM, which consisted mainly of processor, hard disk, and display control. ACPI controls not only power but also all the Plug and Play (PnP) hardware configuration throughout the system. With ACPI, system configuration (PnP) and power-management configuration are no longer controlled via the BIOS Setup; they are instead controlled entirely within the OS.

ACPI enables the system to automatically turn on and off internal peripherals (such as optical drives, network cards, hard disk drives, and modems) as well as external devices such as printers, monitors, or any devices connected to serial, parallel, USB, video, or other ports in the system. ACPI technology also enables peripherals to turn on or wake up the system. For example, a telephone answering machine application can request that it be able to respond to answer the telephone within 1 second. Not only is this possible, but if the user subsequently presses the power or sleep button, the system only goes into the deepest sleep state that is consistent with the ability to meet the telephone answering application's request.

ACPI enables system designers to implement a range of power-management features that are compatible with various hardware designs while using the same OS driver. ACPI also uses the Plug and Play BIOS data structures and takes control over the Plug and Play interface, providing an OS–independent interface for configuration and control.

ACPI defines several system states and substates. There are four Global System states, labeled from G0 through G3, with G0 being the fully operational state and G3 being mechanically turned off. Global System states are immediately obvious to the user of the system and apply to the entire system as a whole. Within the G0 state, there are four CPU Power states (C0–C3) and four Device Power states (D0–D3) for each device. Within the C0 CPU Power state, there are up to 16 CPU Performance states (P0–P15).

Device Power states are states for individual devices when the system is in the G0 (Working) state. The device states may or may not be visible to the user. For example, it may be obvious when a hard disk has stopped or when the monitor is off; however, it may not be obvious that a modem or other device has been shut down. The Device Power states are somewhat generic; many devices do not have all four Power states defined.

Within the G1 Global Sleep state are four Sleep states (S1–S4). The G2 Global Soft Off state is also known as the *S5 Sleep state*, in which case the system is powered off but still has standby power. Finally, G3 is the Mechanical Off state, where all power is disconnected from the system.

The following list shows the definitions and nested relationship of the various Global, CPU/Device Power, and Sleep states:

- **G0 Working**—This is the normal working state in which the system is running and fully operational. Within this state, the Processor and Device Power states apply. The Device Power states are defined as follows:
  - **G0/D0 Fully-On**—The device is fully active.
  - **G0/D1**—Depends on the device; uses less power than D0.
  - **G0/D2**—Depends on the device; uses less power than D1.
  - **G0/D3 Off**—The device is powered off (except for wakeup logic).
- The Processor Power states are defined as follows:
  - **G0/C0 CPU On**—Normal processor operation.
  - **G0/C1 CPU Halted**—The processor is halted.
  - **G0/C2 CPU Stopped**—The clock has been stopped.
  - **G0/C3 CPU/Cache Stopped**—The clock has been stopped and cache snoops are ignored.
- **G1 Sleeping**—The system appears to be off but is actually in one of four Sleep states—up to full hibernation. How quickly the system can return to G0 depends on which of the Sleep states the

system has selected. In any of these Sleep states, system context and status are saved such that they can be fully restored. The Sleep states available in the Global G1 state are defined as follows:

- **G1/S1 Halt**—A low-latency idle state. The CPU is halted; however, system context and status are fully retained.

- **G1/S2 Halt-Reset**—Similar to the S1 sleeping state except that the CPU and cache context is lost, and the CPU is reset upon wakeup.

- **G1/S3 Suspend to RAM**—All system context is lost except memory. The hardware maintains memory context. The CPU is reset and restores some CPU and L2 context upon wakeup.

- **G1/S4 Suspend to Disk (Hibernation)**—The system context and status (RAM contents) have been saved to nonvolatile storage—usually the hard disk. This is also known as Hibernation. To return to G0 (Working) state, you must press the power button, and the system will restart, loading the saved context and status from where they were previously saved (normally the hard disk). Returning from G2/S5 to G0 requires a considerable amount of latency (time).

■ **G2/S5 Soft Off**—This is the normal power-off state that occurs after you select Shutdown or press the power button to turn the system off. The system and all devices are essentially powered off; however, the system is still plugged in and standby power is coming from the power supply to the motherboard, allowing the system to wake up (power on) if commanded by an external device. No hardware context or status is saved. The system must be fully rebooted to return to the G0 (working) state.

■ **G3 Mechanical Off**—Power is completely removed from the system. In most cases this means the system must be unplugged or the power turned off via a power strip. This is the only state in which it is safe to disassemble the system. Except for the CMOS/clock circuitry, power consumption is completely zero.

In normal use, a system alternates between the G0 (Working) and G1 (Sleeping) states. In the G1 (Working) state, individual devices and processors can be power-managed via the Device Power (D1–D3) and Processor Power (C1–C3) states. Any device that is selectively turned off can be quickly powered on in a short amount of time, from virtually instantaneous to only a few seconds (such as a hard disk spinning up).

When the system is idle (no keyboard or mouse input) for a preset period, the system enters the Global G1 (Sleeping) state, which means also selecting one of the S1–S4 sleep states. In these states, the system appears to be off, but all system context and status are saved, enabling the system to return to exactly where it left off, with varying amounts of latency. For example, returning to the G0 (Working) state from the G1/S4 (Hibernation) state requires more time than when returning from the G1/S3 (Suspend) state.

When the user presses the power button to turn the system off or selects Shutdown via the OS, the system enters the G2/S5 (Soft Off) state. In this state, no context is saved, and the system is completely off except for standby power. Fully disconnecting AC or battery power causes the system to be in the Global G3 (Mechanical Off) state, which is the only state in which the system should be disassembled.

During the system setup and boot process, ACPI performs a series of checks and tests to see whether the system hardware and BIOS support ACPI. If support is not detected or is found to be faulty, the system typically reverts to standard Advanced Power Management control, which is referred to as *legacy power management* under ACPI. Virtually all ACPI problems are the result of partial or incomplete ACPI implementations or incompatibilities in either the BIOS or the device drivers. If you encounter any of these errors, contact your motherboard manufacturer for an updated BIOS or the device manufacturers for updated drivers.

Power Cycling

Should you turn off a system when it is not in use? To answer this frequent question, you should understand some facts about electrical components and what makes them fail. Combine this knowledge with information on power consumption, cost, and safety to come to your own conclusion. Because circumstances can vary, the best answer for your own situation might be different from the answer for others, depending on your particular needs and applications.

Frequently powering a system on and off does cause deterioration and damage to the components. This seems logical, but the simple reason is not obvious to most people. Many believe that flipping system power on and off frequently is harmful because it electrically "shocks" the system. The real problem, however, is temperature or thermal shock. As the system warms up, the components expand; as it cools off, the components contract. In addition, various materials in the system have different thermal expansion coefficients, so they expand and contract at different rates. Over time, thermal shock causes deterioration in many areas of a system.

From a pure system-reliability viewpoint, you should insulate the system from thermal shock as much as possible. When a system is turned on, the components go from ambient (room) temperature to as high as 185°F (85°C) within 30 minutes or less. When you turn off the system, the same thing happens in reverse, and the components cool back to ambient temperature in a short period.

Thermal expansion and contraction remains the single largest cause of component failure. Chip cases can split, allowing moisture to enter and contaminate them. Delicate internal wires and contacts can break, and circuit boards can develop stress cracks. Surface-mounted components expand and contract at rates different from the circuit boards on which they are mounted, causing enormous stress at the solder joints. Solder joints can fail due to the metal hardening from the repeated stress, resulting in cracks in the joint. Components that use heatsinks, such as processors, transistors, or voltage regulators, can overheat and fail because the thermal cycling causes heatsink adhesives to deteriorate and break the thermally conductive bond between the device and the heatsink. Thermal cycling also causes socketed devices and connections to loosen, or *creep*, which can cause a variety of intermittent contact failures.

◄◄ See the Chapter 6 section, "Memory Modules," **p. 346**.

Thermal expansion and contraction affect not only chips and circuit boards, but also things such as hard disk drives. Most hard drives today have sophisticated thermal compensation routines that make adjustments in head position relative to the expanding and contracting platters. Most drives perform this thermal compensation routine once every 5 minutes for the first 30 minutes the drive is running and then every 30 minutes thereafter. In older drives, this procedure can be heard as a rapid "tick-tick-tick-tick" sound.

In essence, anything you can do to keep the system at a constant temperature prolongs the life of the system, and the best way to accomplish this is to leave the system either permanently on or permanently off. Of course, if the system is never turned on in the first place, it should last a long time indeed!

Now, I am not saying that you should leave all systems fully powered on 24 hours a day. A system powered on when not necessary can waste a tremendous amount of power. An unattended system that is fully powered on can also be a fire hazard. (I have witnessed at least two CRT monitors spontaneously catch fire—luckily, I was there at the time.)

The biggest problem with keeping systems on 24/7 is the wasted energy. Typical rates are 10 cents for a kilowatt-hour of electricity. Using this figure, combined with information about what a typical PC might consume, we can determine how much it will cost to run the system annually and what effect we can have on the operating cost by judiciously powering off or taking advantage of the various ACPI Sleep modes that are available. ACPI is described in more detail later in this chapter.

A typical desktop-style PC consumes anywhere from 75W to 300W when idling and from 150W to 600W under a load, depending on the configuration, age, and design of the system. This does not include monitors, which for LCDs range from 25W to 50W while active, whereas CRTs range from 75W to 150W or more. One PC and LCD display combination I tested consumed an average of 250W (0.25 kilowatts) of electricity during normal operation. The same system drew 200W when in ACPI S1 Sleep mode, only 8W while in ACPI S3 Sleep mode, and 7W of power while either turned off or hibernating (ACPI S4 mode).

Using those figures, here are some calculations for annual power costs:

```
        Electricity Cost:     $0.10 Dollars per KWh
        PC/Display Power:     0.250 KW avg. while running
        PC/Display Power:     0.200 KW avg. while in ACPI S1 Sleep
        PC/Display Power:     0.008 KW avg. while in ACPI S3 Sleep
        PC/Display Power:     0.007 KW avg. while in ACPI S4 Sleep
        PC/Display Power:     0.007 KW avg. while OFF
              Work Hours:      2080 Per year
          Non-Work Hours:      6656 Per year
             Total Hours:      8736 Per year
-------------------------------------------------------------------
Annual Operating Cost:   $218.40 Left ON continuously
Annual Operating Cost:   $185.12 In S1 Sleep during non-work hours
Annual Operating Cost:    $57.32 In S3 Sleep during non-work hours
Annual Operating Cost:    $56.66 In S4 Sleep during non-work hours
Annual Operating Cost:    $56.66 Turned OFF during non-work hours
-------------------------------------------------------------------
        Annual Savings:     $0.00 Left ON continuously
        Annual Savings:    $33.28 In S1 Sleep during non-work hours
        Annual Savings:   $161.08 In S3 Sleep during non-work hours
        Annual Savings:   $161.74 In S4 Sleep during non-work hours
        Annual Savings:   $161.74 Turned OFF during non-work hours
```

This means it would cost more than $218 annually to run the system if it were left on continuously. However, if it were turned off during nonwork hours, the annual operating cost would be reduced to $56, for an annual savings of more than $161! As you can see, turning systems off when they are not in use can amount to a huge savings over time.

To save power (and money) many people perform a full shutdown procedure when turning off their computer, closing all open applications, shutting down the OS and system completely. Then when powering back on, they do a cold boot and reload the OS, drivers, and applications from scratch.

There is an alternative that is much better. Instead of shutting down completely, put the system to Sleep instead. When in Sleep mode the system saves the full system context (state of the system, contents of RAM, and so on) in RAM before powering off everything but the RAM. Unfortunately, many systems aren't configured to take advantage of Sleep mode, especially older ones. Note that Sleep was called Standby (or Stand by) in Windows XP and earlier.

When properly configured, most PCs will enter ACPI S3 Sleep mode either manually or after a preset period of inactivity, dropping to a power consumption level of 8W or less. In other words, if you configure the PC to enter S3 Sleep mode when it's not active, you can achieve nearly the same savings as if you were to turn it off completely. In the preceding example, it would only cost an additional $0.66 to keep the system in Stand By mode during nonwork hours versus turned completely off, still resulting in an annual savings of more than $161.

With the improved power management capabilities of modern hardware, combined with the stability and control features built into modern OSs, systems can Sleep and Resume almost instantly, without having to go through the lengthy shutdown and cold boot startup procedures over and over again. I'm frankly surprised at how few people I see taking advantage of this because it offers both cost savings and convenience.

The key is in the system configuration, starting with one important setting in the BIOS Setup. The setting is called *ACPI suspend mode*, and ideally you want it set so that the system will enter what is called the S3 state. S3 is sometimes called *STR* for *Suspend to RAM*. That has traditionally been the default setting for laptops; however, many if not most desktops unfortunately have ACPI suspend mode set to the S1 state by default. ACPI S1 is sometimes called *POS* for *Power on Suspend*, a state in which the screen blanks and CPU throttles down; however, almost everything else remains fully powered on. As an example, a system and LCD display that consumes 250W will generally drop to about 200W while in S1 Sleep; however, the same system will drop to only 8W of power consumption in the S3 (Suspend to RAM) state.

When the system is set to suspend in the S3 state, upon entering Sleep (either automatically or manually), the current system context is saved in RAM and all the system hardware (CPU, motherboard, fans, display, and so on) *except* RAM is powered off. In this mode, the system looks as if it is off and consumes virtually the same amount of power as if it were truly off. To resume, you merely press the power button just as if you were turning the system on normally. You can configure most systems to resume on a key press or mouse click as well. Then, instead of performing a normal cold boot and full restart, the system almost instantly powers on and resumes from Sleep, restoring the previously saved context. Your OS, drivers, all open applications, and so on, appear fully loaded just as they were when you "powered off."

As mentioned, many people have been using this capability on laptops, but few seem to be aware that you can use it on desktop systems also. To enable this deeper sleep capability, there are only two main steps:

1. Enter the BIOS Setup, select the Power menu, locate the ACPI suspend setting, and set it to enter the S3 state (sometimes called STR for Suspend to RAM). Save, exit, and restart.

2. In Windows, open the Power Options tool in the Control Panel, locate the setting for the Power button and change it to Sleep or Stand by.

You can also take advantage of hibernation, which allows you to use the ACPI S4 (STD = Suspend to Disk) state in addition to S3. ACPI S4 is a lot like S3, except the system context is saved to disk (in a file called hiberfil.sys) instead of RAM, after which the system enters the G2/S5 state. The G2/S5 state is also known as Soft-Off, which is exactly the same as if the system were powered off normally. When you power on from Hibernation (S4), the system still cold boots; however, rather than reloading from scratch, Windows restores the system context from disk (hiberfil.sys) instead of rebooting normally. Although hibernating isn't nearly as fast as S3 (Suspend to RAM), it is still much faster than a full shutdown and restart and works even if the system loses power completely while suspended. Windows

XP and earlier allows you to place a system in Standby (Sleep) or Hibernate modes, while Windows Vista and later has Sleep, Hibernate, and Hybrid Sleep modes. Hybrid Sleep is a combination of sleep and hibernate, where the system state is saved both in RAM and to the hard disk as a backup. Hybrid Sleep is the default Sleep function setting for desktop systems, and because of the extra time to create the hiberfil.sys file it unfortunately makes the system take just as long to Sleep as it does to Hibernate. To speed up the Sleep mode functionality in Windows Vista and newer, you can disable Hybrid Sleep.

Finally, to make the system Sleep automatically, you can change the Windows Power Scheme settings to put the system in Sleep mode after a time duration of your choice. This allows the system to automatically enter Sleep mode after the preset period of inactivity (I usually set it for 30 minutes to an hour) has elapsed.

By using S3 Sleep mode, you can effectively leave the system running all the time yet still achieve nearly the same savings as if you turned it off completely. Servers, of course, should be left on continuously; however, if you set the system to Wake on LAN (WOL) in both the BIOS Setup and in Windows, the system can automatically wake up anytime it is being accessed. The bottom line is that taking advantage of Sleep mode can save a significant amount of energy (and money) over time.

Power Supply Troubleshooting

Troubleshooting the power supply basically means isolating the supply as the cause of problems within a system and, if necessary, replacing it.

Caution

It is rarely recommended that an inexperienced user open a power supply to make repairs because of the dangerous high voltages present. Even when unplugged, power supplies can retain dangerous voltage and must be discharged (like a monitor) before service. Such internal repairs are beyond the scope of this book and are specifically not recommended unless the technician knows what she is doing.

Many symptoms lead me to suspect that the power supply in a system is failing. This can sometimes be difficult for an inexperienced technician to see because at times little connection seems to exist between the symptom and the cause: the power supply.

For example, in many cases a parity check error message can indicate a problem with the power supply. This might seem strange because the parity check message specifically refers to memory that has failed. The connection is that the power supply powers the memory, and memory with inadequate power fails.

It takes some experience to know when this type of failure is power related and not caused by the memory. One clue is the repeatability of the problem. If the parity check message (or other problem) appears frequently and identifies the same memory location each time, I would suspect that defective memory is the problem. However, if the problem seems random, or if the memory location the error message cites as having failed seems random, I would suspect improper power as the culprit. The following is a list of PC problems that often are related to the power supply:

- Any power-on or system startup failures or lockups
- Spontaneous rebooting or intermittent lockups during normal operation
- Intermittent parity check or other memory-type errors
- Hard disk and fan simultaneously failing to spin (no +12V)
- Overheating due to fan failure

- Small brownouts that cause the system to reset
- Electric shocks felt on the system case or connectors
- Slight static discharges that disrupt system operation
- Erratic recognition of bus-powered USB peripherals

In fact, just about any intermittent system problem can be caused by the power supply. I always suspect the supply when flaky system operation is a symptom. Of course, the following fairly obvious symptoms point right to the power supply as a possible cause:

- Completely dead (no fan, no cursor)
- Smoke
- Blown circuit breakers

If you suspect a power supply problem, some of the simple measurements and the more sophisticated tests outlined in this section can help you determine whether the power supply is at fault. Because these measurements might not detect some intermittent failures, you might have to use a spare power supply for a long-term evaluation. If the symptoms and problems disappear when a known-good spare unit is installed, you have found the source of your problem.

The following is a simple flowchart to help you zero in on common power supply–related problems:

1. Check the AC power input. Make sure the cord is firmly seated in the wall socket and in the power supply socket. Try a different cord.
2. Check the DC power connections. Make sure the motherboard and disk drive power connectors are firmly seated and making good contact. Check for loose screws.
3. Check the DC power output. Use a digital multimeter to check for proper voltages. If it's below spec, replace the power supply.
4. Check the installed peripherals. Remove all boards and drives and retest the system. If it works, add items back in one at a time until the system fails again. The last item added before the failure returns is likely defective.

Many types of symptoms can indicate problems with the power supply. Because the power supply literally powers everything else in the system, everything from disk drive problems to memory problems to motherboard problems can often be traced back to the power supply as the root cause.

Overloaded Power Supplies

A weak or inadequate power supply can put a damper on your ideas for system expansion. Some systems are designed with beefy power supplies, as if to anticipate a great deal of system add-ons and expansion components. Most desktop or tower systems are built in this manner. Some systems have inadequate power supplies from the start, however, and can't adequately service the power-hungry options you might want to add.

The wattage rating can sometimes be misleading. Not all 500-watt supplies are created the same. People familiar with high-end audio systems know that some watts are better than others. This is true for power supplies, too. Cheap power supplies might in fact put out the rated power, but at what temperature? Many cheap power supplies are rated at ridiculously low temperatures that will never be encountered in actual use. As the temperature goes up, the power output capability goes down, meaning that in some cases these supplies will only be capable of 50% less than their rating under normal use.

Also, what about noise and distortion? Some of the supplies are under-engineered to just barely meet their specifications, whereas others might greatly exceed their specifications. Many of the cheaper supplies provide noisy or unstable power, which can cause numerous problems with the system. Another problem with under-engineered power supplies is that they can run hot and force the system to do so as well. The repeated heating and cooling of solid-state components eventually causes a computer system to fail, and engineering principles dictate that the hotter a PC's temperature, the shorter its life. Many people recommend replacing the original supply in a system with a heavier-duty model, which solves the problem. Because power supplies come in common form factors, finding a heavy-duty replacement for most systems is easy, as is the installation process.

Inadequate Cooling

Some replacement power supplies have higher-capacity cooling fans, which can minimize overheating problems—especially for hotter-running processors. If system noise is a problem, models with special fans can run more quietly than the standard models. These power supplies often use larger-diameter fans that spin more slowly, so they run more quietly but move the same amount of air as the smaller fans. There are even fanless power supplies, although these are more expensive and are generally available only in lower output ratings.

Ventilation in a system is also important. In most prebuilt systems, this is not much of a concern because most reputable manufacturers ensure that their systems have adequate ventilation to avoid overheating. If you are building or upgrading a system your own system, then the responsibility for proper cooling falls on you. In that situation it's critical that your processor is cooled by an active heatsink and that the case include one or more cooling fans for additional ventilation. If you have free expansion slots, I recommend spacing out any expansion cards in the system to permit airflow between them. Place the hottest-running boards nearest the fan or the ventilation holes in the system. Make sure that adequate airflow exists around the hard disk drives, especially for those that spin at high rates of speed. Some hard disks can generate quite a bit of heat during operation. If the hard disks overheat, data can be lost.

Always be sure you run your computer with the case cover on, especially if you have an older, loaded system using passive heatsinks. Removing the cover in that situation can actually cause the system to overheat. With the cover off, the power supply and chassis fans no longer draw air through the system. Instead, the fans end up cooling only the supply, and the rest of the system must be cooled by simple convection. Systems that use an active heatsink on the processor aren't as prone to this type of problem; in fact, the cooler air from outside the normally closed chassis can help them to run cooler.

In addition, be sure that any empty slot positions have the filler brackets installed. If you leave these brackets off after removing a card, the resultant hole in the case disrupts the internal airflow and can cause higher internal temperatures.

Finally, the location of the system can have an effect on cooling. I don't recommend placing a system on a carpeted floor, as most chassis are designed to draw in air at the bottom of the front bezel, which can easily be blocked or become clogged with carpet fibers. Another problem is that a system sitting directly on a floor will ingest a large amount of dust and debris, even more so if the floor is carpeted. If you must place a system on the floor, whether it is carpeted or not, I recommend elevating it at least an inch or so via some sort of platform.

If you experience intermittent problems that you suspect are related to overheating, upgraded chassis fans or a higher-capacity replacement power supply are usually the best cures.

Using Digital Multimeters

One simple test you can perform on a power supply is to check the output voltages. This shows whether a power supply is operating correctly and whether the output voltages are within the correct tolerance range. Note that you must measure all voltages with the power supply connected to a proper load, which usually means testing while the power supply is still installed in the system and connected to the motherboard and peripheral devices.

Selecting a Meter

You need a simple digital multimeter (DMM) or digital volt-ohm meter (DVOM) to perform voltage and resistance checks on electronic circuits (see Figure 18.39). Only use a DMM instead of the older needle-type multimeters because the older meters work by injecting 9V into the circuit when measuring resistance, which damages most computer circuits.

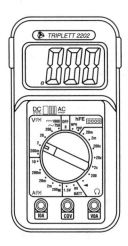

FIGURE 18.39 A typical DMM.

A DMM uses a much lower voltage (usually 1.5V) when making resistance measurements, which is safe for electronic equipment. You can get a good DMM with many features from several sources. I prefer the small, pocket-size meters for computer work because they are easy to carry around.

Some features to look for in a good DMM are as follows:

- **Pocket size**—This is self-explanatory, but small meters that have many, if not all, of the features of larger ones are available. The elaborate features found on some of the larger meters are not really necessary for computer work.

- **Overload protection**—If you plug the meter into a voltage or current beyond the meter's capability to measure, the meter protects itself from damage. Cheaper meters lack this protection and can be easily damaged by reading current or voltage values that are too high.

- **Autoranging**—The meter automatically selects the proper voltage or resistance range when making measurements. This is preferable to the manual range selection; however, really good meters offer both autoranging capability and a manual range override.

- **Detachable probe leads**—The leads can be damaged easily, and sometimes a variety of differently shaped probes are required for different tests. Cheaper meters have the leads permanently attached, which means you can't easily replace them. Look for a meter with detachable leads that plug into the meter.

- **Audible continuity test**—Although you can use the ohm scale for testing continuity (0 ohms indicates continuity), a continuity test function causes the meter to produce a beep noise when continuity exists between the meter test leads. By using the sound, you quickly can test cable assemblies and other items for continuity. After you use this feature, you will never want to use the ohms display for this purpose again.

- **Automatic power-off**—These meters run on batteries, and the batteries can easily be worn down if the meter is accidentally left on. Good meters have an automatic shutoff that turns off the unit when it senses no readings for a predetermined period of time.

- **Automatic display hold**—This feature enables you to hold the last stable reading on the display even after the reading is taken. This is especially useful if you are trying to work in a difficult-to-reach area single-handedly.

- **Minimum and maximum trap**—This feature enables the meter to trap the lowest and highest readings in memory and hold them for later display, which is especially useful if you have readings that are fluctuating too quickly to see on the display.

Although you can get a basic pocket DMM for as little as $20, one with all these features is priced closer to $100, and some can be much higher. RadioShack carries some nice inexpensive units, and you can purchase the high-end models from electronics supply houses, such as Newark or Digi-Key.

Measuring Voltage

To measure voltages on a system that is operating, you must use a technique called *back probing* on the connectors (see Figure 18.40). You can't disconnect any of the connectors while the system is running, so you must measure with everything connected. Nearly all the connectors you need to probe have openings in the back where the wires enter the connector. The meter probes are narrow enough to fit into the connector alongside the wire and make contact with the metal terminal inside. The technique is called *back probing* because you are probing the connector from the back. You must use this back-probing technique to perform virtually all the following measurements.

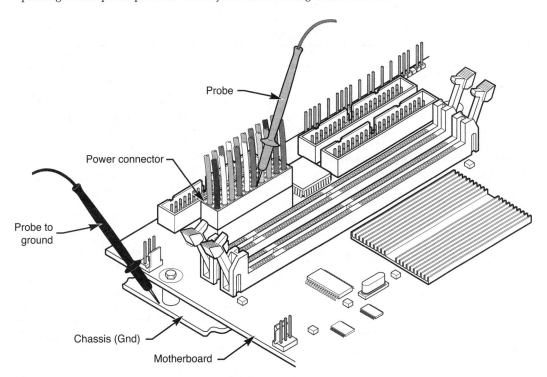

FIGURE 18.40 Back probing the power supply connectors.

To test a power supply for proper output, check the voltage at the Power_Good pin (P8-1 on AT, Baby-AT, and LPX supplies; pin 8 on the ATX-type connector) for +3V to +6V of power. If the measurement is not within this range, the system never sees the Power_Good signal and therefore does not start or run properly. In most cases, the power supply is bad and must be replaced.

Continue by measuring the voltage ranges of the pins on the motherboard and drive power connectors. If you are measuring voltages for testing purposes, any reading within 10% of the specified voltage is considered acceptable, although most manufacturers of high-quality power supplies specify a tighter 5% tolerance. For ATX power supplies, the specification requires that voltages must be within 5% of the rating, except for the 3.3V current, which must be within 4%. Table 18.28 shows the voltage ranges within these tolerances.

Table 18.28 Voltage Ranges

	Loose Tolerance		Tight Tolerance	
Desired Voltage	Min. –10%	Max. (+8%)	Min. (–5%)	Max. (+5%)
+3.3V	2.97V	3.63V	3.135V	3.465V
+/–5.0V	4.5V	5.4V	4.75V	5.25V
+/–12.0V	10.8V	12.9V	11.4V	12.6V

The Power_Good signal has tolerances that are different from the other voltages, although it is nominally +5V in most systems. The trigger point for Power_Good is about +2.4V, but most systems require the signal voltage to be within the tolerances listed here.

Signal	Minimum	Maximum
Power_Good (+5V)	3.0V	6.0V

Replace the power supply if the voltages you measure are out of these ranges. Again, it is worth noting that any and all power-supply tests and measurements must be made with the power supply properly loaded, which usually means it must be installed in a system and the system must be running.

Specialized Test Equipment

You can use several types of specialized test gear to test power supplies more effectively. Because the power supply is one of the most failure-prone items in PCs today, you should have these specialized items if you service many PC systems.

Digital Infrared Thermometer

One of the greatest additions to my toolbox is a digital infrared thermometer (see Figure 20.9 in Chapter 20, "PC Diagnostics, Testing, and Maintenance," **p. 975**). This is also are called a *noncontact thermometer* because it measures by sensing infrared energy without having to touch the item it is reading. This enables me to make instant spot checks of the temperature of a chip, a board, or the system chassis. They are available from companies such as Raytek (www.raytek.com) for less than $100. To use these handheld items, you point at an object and then pull the trigger. Within seconds, the display shows a temperature readout accurate to +/–3°F (2°C). These devices are invaluable in checking to ensure the components in your system are adequately cooled.

Variable Voltage Transformer

When you're testing power supplies, it is sometimes desirable to simulate different AC voltage conditions at the wall socket to observe how the supply reacts. A variable voltage transformer is a useful test device for checking power supplies because it enables you to exercise control over the AC line voltage used as input for the power supply (see Figure 18.41). This device consists of a large transformer mounted in a housing with a dial indicator that controls the output voltage. You plug the line cord from the transformer into the wall socket and plug the PC power cord into the socket provided on the transformer. The knob on the transformer can be used to adjust the AC line voltage the PC receives.

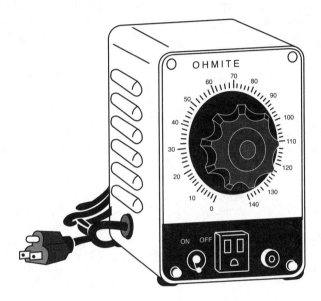

FIGURE 18.41   A variable voltage transformer.

Most variable transformers can adjust their AC outputs from 0V to 140V no matter what the AC input (wall socket) voltage is. Some can cover a range from 0V to 280V as well. You can use the transformer to simulate brownout conditions, enabling you to observe the PC's response. Thus, you can check a power supply for proper Power_Good signal operation, among other things.

By running the PC and dropping the voltage until the PC shuts down, you can see how much reserve is in the power supply for handling a brownout or other voltage fluctuations. If your transformer can output voltages in the 200V range, you can test the capability of the power supply to run on foreign voltage levels. A properly functioning supply should operate between 90V and 135V but should shut down cleanly if the voltage is outside that range.

One indication of a problem is seeing parity check-type error messages when you drop the voltage to 80V. This indicates that the Power_Good signal is not being withdrawn before the power supply output to the PC fails. The PC should simply stop operating as the Power_Good signal is withdrawn, causing the system to enter a continuous reset loop.

Variable voltage transformers are sold by a number of electronic parts supply houses, such as Newark and Digi-Key.

Power Supply Recommendations

When you are shopping for a new power supply, take several factors into account. First, consider the power supply's shape, or form factor. Power supply form factors can differ in their physical sizes, shapes, screw-hole positions, connector types, and fan locations. When ordering a replacement supply, you need to know which form factor your system requires.

Some systems use proprietary power supply designs, which makes replacement more difficult. If a system uses one of the industry-standard form factor power supplies, replacement units with a variety of output levels and performance are available from hundreds of vendors. An unfortunate user of a system with a nonstandard form factor supply does not have this kind of choice and must get a replacement from the original manufacturer of the system—and usually must pay a much higher price for the unit. PC buyers often overlook this and discover too late the consequences of having nonstandard components in a system.

▶▶   See "Power Supply Form Factors," **p. 849**.

Name-brand systems on both the low and high end of the price scale are notorious for using proprietary form factor power supplies. For example, Dell has used proprietary supplies in many of its systems. Be sure you consider this if you intend to own or use these types of systems out of warranty or plan significant upgrades during the life of the system. Where possible, I always insist on systems that use industry-standard power supplies, such as the ATX12V form factor supply found in most systems today.

With backward compatibility ensuring that the 24-pin ATX power connector will plug into older 20-pin motherboard sockets, when purchasing a new power supply, I now recommend only those units that include 24-pin main power connectors, which are usually sold as ATX12V 2.x, EPS12V, or "PCI Express" models. For the most flexible and future-proof supply, also ensure that the power supply includes two or more PCI Express graphics connectors as well as multiple integrated SATA drive power connectors. Choosing a power supply with these features provides flexibility that allows it to work not only in modern systems, but also in virtually all older ATX systems—and with no adapters required.

▶▶   See "ATX12V 2.x 24-pin Main Power Connector," **p. 877**.

As a guide, here are some of the features I recommend looking for in a PSU:

- Adequate power connectors (24-pin main, 4/8-pin +12V CPU, 6/8-pin PCIe Graphics, SATA, and so on) for the intended system
- Adequate power output (watts) for the intended system
- 80-plus certification
- Active Power Factor Correction (required with 80 PLUS)
- SLI or CrossFire certification
- Single +12V rail design

There are other variables to consider, depending on your specific needs or desires. One feature that many people like is modular cables, which minimize the clutter in a system. Another feature to consider is noise, which is mostly related to cooling. The type and arrangement of cooling fans has a great effect on how quiet (or noisy) the unit will be. There are even some fanless units that are completely silent, but these usually come at a premium price and with a lower overall power output capability.

When building systems with case windows, some people also like to look for PSUs with appearance-related features like colored cases.

Modular Cables

One feature often discussed in relation to PSUs is the use of *modular cables*. This means cables with connectors at both ends that are detachable from the power supply. Modular cables allow you to attach only the cables you need—in some cases greatly reducing the congestion inside the system.

The main argument against modular cables is that additional resistance is introduced via another set of connector contacts. This is true, but how much resistance exactly, and is it enough that it really matters? Fortunately, this can easily be calculated.

The connectors used in modern power supplies are mostly Molex Mini-Fit Jr. types, which have a contact resistance of 10 milli-ohms (0.01 ohms). Most power supply cables use 18 AWG (American Wire Gauge) copper wire, which has a resistance of about 0.0064 ohms per foot. This means that adding an extra connector at the PSU end is equal to about 1.5 feet of wire in additional resistance.

To put it another way, in a maximum load situation, each terminal normally carries a maximum of about 4 amps, at which point the additional resistance equals about 0.16 watts of power loss. In an 8-pin power connector, this only adds up to around a watt, a loss I consider negligible.

Finally, when you consider that a typical PSU cable already consists of 1.5 feet of wire with a connector on the end, adding another connector to make the cable modular only adds about one-third more overall resistance to what is already there, which was negligible to begin with.

If modular cables aren't much of a problem technically, why don't more PSU manufacturers include them? Well, besides the (negligible in my opinion) extra resistance, they do add to the cost of making a power supply, and that is reflected in a higher final price. They can also create clearance issues with other components in the system, depending on exactly where the connectors attach to the PSU. In addition, modular cables can easily become lost or misplaced. Think of opening a system to add another internal drive or upgraded video card several years after it was initially built, finding that the PSU uses modular cables, and discovering the extra cables needed are nowhere to be found. One solution to this problem is to place any unused cables inside the case when building a system. For example, you could place them in a small plastic bag and tape them inside, so that if or when you need them in the future, they are easy to find. Besides these issues, perhaps the biggest drawback to modular cables is that modular PSU cables using standard connectors are patented (www.google.com/patents/about?id=w0ehAAAAEBAJ), and the patent is owned by Systemax (aka TigerDirect and Ultra Products). There is another patent on modular PSUs that use nonstandard connectors at the PSU end (www.google.com/patents/about?id=iOGqAAAAEBAJ). If there was no legal "baggage" against using them, I suspect we would see more modular cable–equipped PSUs on the market today.

Sources for Replacement Power Supplies

Literally hundreds of companies manufacture PC power supplies, and I certainly have not tested them all. I can, however, recommend some companies whose products I have come to know and trust.

Although other high-quality manufacturers exist, for industry-standard ATX12V and EPS12V units I currently recommend power supplies from PC Power & Cooling (www.pcpower.com), Corsair (www.corsair.com), and SeaSonic (www.seasonic.com). These companies offer PSUs that meet all the criteria I listed, and they are of excellent quality.

I also recommend ATXPowerSupplies.com as a source for hard-to-find power supplies, including those using proprietary form factors as well as some of the less popular industry-standard designs.

Power-Protection Systems

Power-protection systems do just what the name implies: They protect your equipment from the effects of power surges and power failures. In particular, power surges and spikes can damage computer equipment, and a loss of power can result in lost data. In this section, you learn about the four primary types of power-protection devices available and when you should use them.

Before considering any further levels of power protection, you should know that a quality power supply already affords you a substantial amount of protection. High-end power supplies from the vendors I recommend are designed to provide protection from higher-than-normal voltages and currents, and they provide a limited amount of power-line noise filtering. Some of the inexpensive aftermarket power supplies probably do not have this sort of protection. If you have an inexpensive computer, further protecting your system might be wise.

Caution

All the power-protection features in this chapter and the protection features in the power supply inside your computer require that the computer's AC power cable be connected to a ground.

Many older homes do not have three-prong (grounded) outlets to accommodate grounded devices.

Do not use a three-pronged adapter (that bypasses the three-prong requirement and enables you to connect to a two-prong socket) to plug a surge suppressor, computer, or UPS into a two-pronged outlet. They often don't provide a good ground and can inhibit the capabilities of your power-protection devices.

You also should test your power sockets to ensure they are grounded. Sometimes outlets, despite having three-prong sockets, are not connected to a ground wire; an inexpensive socket tester (available at most hardware stores) can detect this condition.

Of course, the easiest form of protection is to turn off and unplug your computer equipment (including your modem) when a thunderstorm is imminent. However, when this is not possible, other alternatives are available.

Power supplies should stay within operating specifications and continue to run a system even if any of these power line disturbances occur:

- Voltage drop to 80V for up to 2 seconds
- Voltage drop to 70V for up to .5 seconds
- Voltage surge of up to 143V for up to 1 second

Most high-quality power supplies (or the attached systems) will not be damaged by the following occurrences:

- Full power outage
- Any voltage drop (brownout)
- A spike of up to 2,500V

To verify the levels of protection built into the existing power supply in a computer system, an independent laboratory subjected several unprotected PC systems to various spikes and surges of up to 6,000V—considered the maximum level of surge that can be transmitted to a system through an electrical outlet. Any higher voltage would cause the power to arc to the ground within the outlet. None of the systems sustained permanent damage in these tests. The worst thing that happened was that some of the systems rebooted or shut down when the surge was more than 2,000V. Each system restarted when the power switch was toggled after a shutdown.

The automatic shutdown of a computer during power disturbances is a built-in function of most high-quality power supplies. You can reset the power supply by flipping the power switch from on to off and back on again. Some power supplies even have an auto-restart function. This type of power supply acts the same as others in a massive surge or spike situation: It shuts down the system. The difference is that after normal power resumes, the power supply waits for a specified delay of 3–6 seconds and then resets itself and powers the system back up. Because no manual switch resetting is required, this feature might be desirable in systems functioning as network servers or in those found in other unattended locations.

The first time I witnessed a large surge that caused an immediate shutdown of all my systems, I was extremely surprised. All the systems were silent, but the monitor and modem lights were still on. My first thought was that everything was blown, but a simple toggle of each system-unit power switch caused the power supplies to reset, and the units powered up with no problem. Since that first time, this type of shutdown has happened to me several times, always without further problems.

The following types of power-protection devices are explained in the sections that follow:

- Surge suppressors
- Phone-line surge protectors
- Line conditioners
- Standby power supplies (SPS)
- Uninterruptible power supplies (UPS)

Surge Suppressors (Protectors)

The simplest form of power protection is any one of the commercially available surge protectors—that is, devices inserted between the system and the power line. These devices, which cost between $20 and $200, can absorb the high-voltage transients produced by nearby lightning strikes and power equipment. Some surge protectors can be effective for certain types of power problems, but they offer only limited protection.

Surge protectors use several devices, usually metal-oxide varistors (MOVs), that can clamp and shunt away all voltages above a certain level. MOVs are designed to accept voltages as high as 6,000V and divert any power above 200V to ground. MOVs can handle normal surges, but powerful surges such as direct lightning strikes can blow right through them. MOVs are not designed to handle a high level of power and self-destruct while shunting a large surge. These devices therefore cease to function after either a single large surge or a series of smaller ones. The real problem is that you can't easily tell when they no longer are functional. The only way to test them is to subject the MOVs to a surge, which destroys them. Therefore, you never really know whether your so-called surge protector is protecting your system.

Some surge protectors have status lights that let you know when a surge large enough to blow the MOVs has occurred. A surge suppressor without this status indicator light is useless because you never know when it has stopped protecting.

Underwriters Laboratories has produced an excellent standard that governs surge suppressors, called UL 1449. Any surge suppressor that meets this standard is a good one and definitely offers a line of protection beyond what the power supply in your PC already offers. The only types of surge suppressors worth buying, therefore, should have two features:

- Conformance to the UL 1449 standard
- A status light indicating when the MOVs are blown

Units that meet the UL 1449 specification say so on the packaging or directly on the unit. If this standard is not mentioned, it does not conform. Therefore, you should avoid it.

Another good feature to have in a surge suppressor is a built-in circuit breaker that can be manually reset rather than a fuse. The breaker protects your system if it or a peripheral develops a short.

Network and Phone Line Surge Protectors

A far bigger problem than powerline surges is surges through network or phone cabling. I've personally experienced surges resulting from nearby lightning strikes damage multiple computers and other equipment via Ethernet and telephone lines, while virtually nothing was damaged through the power lines. In systems with separate network cards, the damage was often limited to just the card, while in systems with the network interface built in to the motherboard, the motherboard itself was damaged. In many areas, the cable and phone lines are above ground, making them especially susceptible to lightning strikes.

Several companies manufacture or sell simple surge protectors that plug in between your modem and the network or phone lines. These inexpensive devices can be purchased from most electronics supply houses. Some of the standard power line surge protectors include connectors for network or phone line protection as well.

Line Conditioners

In addition to high-voltage and current conditions, other problems can occur with incoming power. The voltage might dip below the level needed to run the system, resulting in a brownout. Forms of electrical noise other than simple voltage surges or spikes might travel through the power line, such as radio-frequency interference or electrical noise caused by motors or other inductive loads.

Remember two things when you wire together digital devices (such as computers and their peripherals):

- Any wire can act as an antenna and have voltage induced in it by nearby electromagnetic fields, which can come from other wires, telephones, CRTs, motors, fluorescent fixtures, static discharge, and, of course, radio transmitters.

- Digital circuitry responds with surprising efficiency to noise of even a volt or two, making those induced voltages particularly troublesome. The electrical wiring in your building can act as an antenna, picking up all kinds of noise and disturbances.

A line conditioner can handle many of these types of problems. It filters the power, bridges brownouts, suppresses high-voltage and current conditions, and generally acts as a buffer between the power line and the system. A line conditioner does the job of a surge suppressor, and much more. It is more of an active device, functioning continuously, rather than a passive device that activates only when a surge is present. A line conditioner provides true power conditioning and can handle myriad problems. It contains transformers, capacitors, and other circuitry that can temporarily bridge a brownout or low-voltage situation. These units usually cost $100–$300, depending on the power-handling capacity of the unit.

Backup Power

The next level of power protection includes backup power-protection devices. These units can provide power in case of a complete blackout, thereby providing the time necessary for an orderly system shutdown. Two types are available: the SPS and the uninterruptible power supply (UPS). The UPS is a special device because it does much more than just provide backup power; it is also the best kind of line conditioner you can buy.

Standby Power Supplies

A standby power supply is known as an *offline device*: It functions only when normal power is disrupted. An SPS system uses a special circuit that can sense the AC line current. If the sensor detects a loss of power on the line, the system quickly switches over to a standby battery and power inverter. The power inverter converts the battery power to 120V AC power, which is then supplied to the system.

For a stand-by (switching) type UPS to work, the hold-up time of the power supply has to be longer than the switching time of the UPS. For example, I have a TrippLite SMART1000LCD, which is a stand-by type UPS with a 4ms switching time. Because this is well below the 16ms hold-up time called for in the official Power Supply Design Guide, it should switch well before any properly designed and functioning power supply allows the system to reset. Unfortunately, if the power supply in a PC is poorly designed or overloaded, it may be disrupted by even a 4ms switch, causing the system to shut down or reset anyway, and all unsaved work to be lost.

A truly outstanding SPS adds to the circuit a ferroresonant transformer, which is a large transformer with the capability to store a small amount of power and deliver it during the switch time. This device functions as a buffer on the power line, giving the SPS almost uninterruptible capability.

Tip

Look for SPS systems with a switch-over time of less than 10 milliseconds (ms). This is shorter than the hold-up time of typical power supplies.

SPS units also might have internal line conditioning of their own. Under normal circumstances, most cheaper units place your system directly on the regular power line and offer no conditioning. The addition of a ferroresonant transformer to an SPS gives it extra regulation and protection capabilities because of the buffer effect of the transformer. SPS devices without the ferroresonant transformer still require the use of a line conditioner for full protection. SPS systems usually cost between a hundred and several thousand dollars, depending on the quality and power-output capacity.

UPSs

Perhaps the best overall solution to any power problem is to provide a power source that is conditioned and that can't be interrupted—which is the definition of an uninterruptible power supply. UPSs are known as *online systems* because they continuously function and supply power to your computer systems. Because some companies advertise ferroresonant SPS devices as though they were UPS devices, many now use the term *true UPS* to describe a truly online system. A true UPS system is constructed in much the same way as an SPS system; however, because the computer is always operating from the battery, there is no switching circuit.

In a true UPS, your system always operates from the battery. A voltage inverter converts from +12V DC to 120V AC. You essentially have your own private power system that generates power independently of the AC line. A battery charger connected to the line or wall current keeps the battery charged at a rate equal to or greater than the rate at which power is consumed.

When the AC current supplying the battery charger fails, a true UPS continues functioning undisturbed because the battery-charging function is all that is lost. Because the computer was already running off the battery, no switch takes place and no power disruption is possible. The battery begins discharging at a rate dictated by the amount of load your system places on the unit, which (based on the size of the battery) gives you plenty of time to execute an orderly system shutdown. Based on an appropriately scaled storage battery, the UPS functions continuously, generating power and preventing unpleasant surprises. When the line power returns, the battery charger begins recharging the battery, again with no interruption.

Note

Occasionally, a UPS can accumulate too much storage and not enough discharge. When this occurs, the UPS emits a loud alarm, alerting you that it's full. Simply unplugging the unit from the AC power source for a while can discharge the excess storage (as it powers your computer) and drain the UPS of the excess.

Many SPS systems are advertised as though they are true UPS systems. You can tell a Standby Power Supply from a true UPS by the unit's switch time. If a specification for switch time exists, the unit can't be a true UPS because UPS units never switch. However, true UPS systems are very expensive, and a good SPS with a ferroresonant transformer can virtually equal the performance of a true UPS at a much lower cost.

Note

Many UPSs and SPSs today come equipped with a cable and software that enables the protected computer to shut down in an orderly manner on receipt of a signal from the UPS. This way, the system can shut down properly even if the computer is unattended. Some OSs designed for server environments contain their own UPS software components.

UPS cost is a direct function of both the length of time it can continue to provide power after a line current failure and how much power it can provide. You therefore should purchase a UPS that provides enough power to run your system and peripherals and enough time to close files and provide an orderly shutdown. Remember, however, to manually perform a system shutdown procedure during a power outage. You will probably need your monitor plugged into the UPS and the computer. Be sure the UPS you purchase can provide sufficient power for all the devices you must connect to it.

Because of a true UPS's almost total isolation from the line current, it is unmatched as a line conditioner and surge suppressor. The best UPS systems add a ferroresonant transformer for even greater power conditioning and protection capability. This type of UPS is the best form of power protection available. The price, however, can be high. To find out just how much power your computer system requires, look at the UL sticker on the back of the unit. This sticker lists the maximum power draw in watts, or sometimes in just volts and amperes. If only voltage and amperage are listed, multiply the two figures to calculate the wattage.

As an example, if the documentation for a system indicates that the computer can require as much as 120V at a maximum current draw of 5 amps, the maximum power the system can draw is about 550 watts. The system should never draw any more power than that; if it does, a 5-amp fuse in the power supply will blow. This type of system usually draws an average of 200 to 300 watts. However, to be safe when you make calculations for UPS capacity, be conservative; use the 550-watt figure. Adding an LCD monitor that draws 50 watts brings the total to 600 watts or more. Therefore, to run two fully loaded systems (including monitors), you'd need a 1,200-watt UPS. A UPS of that capacity or greater normally costs several hundred dollars. Unfortunately, that is what the best level of protection costs. Most companies can justify this type of expense only for critical-use PCs, such as network servers.

Note

The highest-capacity UPS sold for use with a conventional 15-amp outlet is about 1,400 watts. If it's any higher, you risk tripping a 15-amp circuit when the battery is charging heavily and the inverter is drawing maximum current.

In addition to the total available output power (wattage), several other factors can distinguish one UPS from another. The addition of a ferroresonant transformer improves a unit's power conditioning and buffering capabilities. Good units also have an inverter that produces a true sine wave output; the cheaper ones might generate a square wave. A square wave is an approximation of a sine wave with abrupt up-and-down voltage transitions. The abrupt transitions of a square wave are not compatible with some computer equipment power supplies. Be sure that the UPS you purchase produces power that is compatible with your computer equipment. Every unit has a specification for how long it can sustain output at the rated level. If your systems draw less than the rated level, you have some additional time.

Caution

Be careful! Most UPS systems are not designed for you to sit and compute for hours through an electrical blackout. They are designed to provide power only to essential components and to remain operating long enough to allow for an orderly shutdown. You pay a large amount for units that provide power for more than 15 minutes or so. At some point, it becomes more cost-effective to buy a generator than to keep investing in extended life for a UPS.

Some of the many sources of power protection equipment include American Power Conversion (APC) and Tripp Lite. These companies sell a variety of UPS, SPS, line protector, and surge protector products.

Caution

Don't connect a laser printer to a backed-up socket in any SPS or UPS unit. Such printers are electrically noisy and have widely varying current draws. This can be hard on the inverter in an SPS or a UPS and frequently cause the inverter to fail or detect an overload and shut down. Either case means that your system will lose power, too.

Printers are normally noncritical because whatever is being printed can be reprinted. Don't connect them to a UPS unless there's a good business need to do so.

Some UPSs and SPSs have sockets that are conditioned but not backed up—that is, they do not draw power from the battery. In cases such as this, you can safely plug printers and other peripherals into these sockets.

Real-Time Clock/Nonvolatile RAM (CMOS RAM) Batteries

Most PCs have a special type of chip in them that combines a real-time clock (RTC) with at least 64 bytes (including 14 bytes of clock data) of nonvolatile RAM (NVRAM) memory. This chip is officially called the *RTC/NVRAM chip*, but it is often referred to as the *CMOS* or *CMOS RAM chip* because the type of chip used is produced using a CMOS Complementary Metal-Oxide Semiconductor (CMOS) process. CMOS design chips are known for low power consumption. This special RTC/NVRAM chip is designed to run off a battery for several years.

The original chip of this type was the Motorola MC146818, which was used in the IBM AT dating from August 1984. Although the chips used today have different manufacturers and part numbers, they all are designed to be compatible with this original Motorola part. Most modern motherboards have the RTC/NVRAM integrated in the motherboard chipset South Bridge or I/O Controller Hub (ICH) component, meaning no separate chip is required.

The clock enables software to read the date and time and preserves the date and time data even when the system is powered off or unplugged. The NVRAM portion of the chip has another function: It is designed to store the basic system configuration, including amount of memory installed, types of disk drives installed, PnP device configuration, power-on passwords, and other information. Although some chips have been used that store up to 4KB or more of NVRAM, most motherboard chipsets with integrated RTC/NVRAM incorporate 256 bytes of NVRAM, of which the clock uses 14 bytes. The system reads this information every time you power it on.

Modern CMOS Batteries

Motherboard NVRAM (CMOS RAM) batteries come in many forms. Most are of a lithium design because they last 2–5 years or more. I have seen systems with conventional alkaline batteries mounted in a holder; these are much less desirable because they fail more frequently and do not last as long. Also, they are prone to leak, and if a battery leaks on the motherboard, the motherboard can be severely damaged. By far, the most commonly used battery for motherboards today is the coin cell, mounted in a holder that is part of the motherboard. Two main types of coin cells are used, differing in their chemistry. Most use a manganese dioxide (Mn02) cathode, designated by a CR prefix in the part number; others use a carbon monoflouride (CF) cathode, designated by a BR prefix in the part number. The CR types are more plentiful (and thus easier to get) and offer slightly higher capacity. The BR types are useful for higher-temperature operation (above 60°C or 140°F).

Because the CR series is cheaper and easier to obtain, it is generally what you will find in a PC. The other digits in the battery part number indicate the physical size of the battery. For example, the most common type of lithium coin cell used in PCs is the CR2032, which is 20mm in diameter (about the size of a quarter) and 3.2mm thick and uses a manganese dioxide cathode. These are readily available at electronics supply stores, camera shops, and even drugstores. Figure 18.42 shows a cutaway view of a CR2032 lithium coin cell battery.

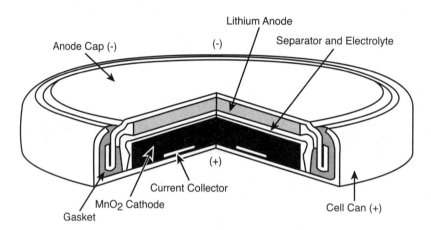

FIGURE 18.42   Cutaway view of a CR2032 lithium coin cell.

Table 18.29 lists the specifications of the common 20mm diameter lithium coin cell batteries you might find in a PC.

Table 18.29   Common 20mm Lithium Coin Cell Specifications

Type	Voltage (V)	Capacity (mAh)	Diameter (mm)	Height (mm)
BR2016	3.00	75	20.00	1.60
BR2020	3.00	100	20.00	2.00
BR2032	3.00	190	20.00	3.20
CR2012	3.00	55	20.00	1.20
CR2016	3.00	90	20.00	1.60
CR2025	3.00	165	20.00	2.50
CR2032	3.00	220	20.00	3.20

BR = Carbon monoflouride (CF) cathode   *CR = Manganese dioxide (Mn02) cathode*

Estimated battery life can be calculated by dividing the battery capacity by the average current required. For example, a typical CR2032 battery is rated 220 mAh (milliamp hours), and the RTC/NVRAM circuit in most current motherboard chipsets draws 5 µA (microamps) with the power off. Battery life can therefore be calculated as follows:

220,000 µAh ÷ 5 µA = 44,000 hours = 5 years

If a thinner (and lower-capacity) battery such as the CR2025 is used, battery life will be shorter:

165,000 µAh ÷ 5 µA = 33,000 hours = 3.7 years

Battery life starts when the system is first assembled, which can be several months or more before you purchase the system, even if it is new. Also, the battery might be partially discharged before it is installed in the system; higher temperatures both in storage and in the system can contribute to shorter battery life. All these reasons and more can cause battery life to be less than what might be indicated by calculation.

As the battery drains, output voltage drops somewhat. Lower battery voltage can impair the accuracy of the RTC. Most lithium coin cell batteries are rated at 3V; however, actual readings on a new battery are usually higher. If your system clock seems inaccurate (it runs slow, for example), check the voltage on the CMOS battery. The highest accuracy is obtained if the battery voltage is maintained at 3.0V or higher. Lithium batteries normally maintain a fairly steady voltage until they are nearly fully discharged, whereupon the voltage quickly drops. If you check the battery voltage and find it is below 3.0V, consider replacing the battery, even if it is before the intended replacement time.

Caution

Coin or button lithium cell batteries are extremely dangerous when swallowed. Once in the body, the voltage combined with fluids causes severe burns in as little as two hours. Children under 4 years old are at the greatest risk, and the symptoms may be similar to other illnesses, including coughing, drooling, or other signs of discomfort. If you suspect that a child has swallowed a battery, immediately go to the emergency room. For more information on this growing problem, see www.thebatterycontrolled.com.

Obsolete or Unique CMOS Batteries

Although most modern systems use 3.0V coin cells, older systems have used a variety of battery types and voltages over the years. For example, some older systems have used 3.6V, 4.5V, and 6V types as well. If you are replacing the battery in an older machine, be sure your replacement is the same voltage as the one you removed from the system. Some motherboards can use batteries of several voltages, and you use a jumper or switch to select the various settings. If you suspect your motherboard has this capability, consult the documentation for instructions on changing the settings. Of course, the easiest thing to do is to replace the existing battery with another of the same type.

Some systems over the years have used a special type of chip that actually has the battery embedded within it. These are made by several companies, including Dallas Semiconductor and Benchmarq. These chips are notable for their long lives. Under normal conditions, the integral battery lasts for 10 years—which is, of course, longer than the useful life of the system. If your system uses one of the Dallas or Benchmarq modules, the battery and chip must be replaced as a unit because they are integrated. Most of the time, these chip/battery combinations are installed in a socket on the motherboard just in case a problem requires an early replacement. You can get new modules directly from the manufacturers for $18 or less, which is much more expensive than the coin-type lithium battery found in most modern systems. In fact, due to their expense and the fact that most motherboard chipset manufacturers have integrated the RTC/NVRAM functionality into the motherboard chipset, few if any modern PCs use these chip/battery modules.

Some systems do not use a battery. Hewlett-Packard, for example, includes a special capacitor in some of its systems that is automatically recharged anytime the system is plugged in. The system does not have to be running for the capacitor to charge; it only has to be plugged in. If the system is unplugged, the capacitor powers the RTC/NVRAM chip for up to a week or more. If the system remains unplugged for longer than that, the NVRAM information is lost. In that case, these systems can reload the NVRAM from a backup kept in a special flash ROM chip contained on the motherboard. The only pieces of information that are actually missing when you repower the system are the date and time, which you have to re-enter. By using the capacitor combined with an NVRAM backup in flash ROM, these systems have a reliable solution that lasts indefinitely.

Many older systems use a separate battery that plugs in via a cable or that can even be directly soldered into the motherboard (mostly older, obsolete systems). For those older systems with the battery soldered in, a spare battery connector usually exists on the motherboard where you can insert a conventional plug-in battery if the original ever fails.

CMOS Battery Troubleshooting

Symptoms that indicate that the battery is about to fail include having to reset the clock on your PC every time you shut down the system (especially after moving it) and problems during the system's POST, such as drive-detection difficulties. If you experience problems such as these, you should make note of your system's CMOS settings and replace the battery as soon as possible.

Caution

When you replace a PC battery, be sure you get the polarity correct; otherwise, you will damage the RTC/NVRAM (CMOS) chip, which is normally integrated into the motherboard chipset. Because the chip is soldered onto most motherboards, this can be an expensive mistake! The coin cell battery holder on the motherboard is normally designed so that the positive of the battery should be facing up. Older motherboards may use a plug-in battery, the connections for which are normally keyed.

When you replace a battery, in most cases the existing data stored in the NVRAM is lost. Sometimes, however, the data remains intact for several minutes (I have observed NVRAM retain information with no power for an hour or more), so if you make the battery swap quickly, the information in the NVRAM might be retained. Just to be sure, I recommend that you record all the system configuration settings stored in the NVRAM by your system Setup program. In most cases, you should run the BIOS Setup program and copy or print out all the screens showing the various settings. Some Setup programs offer the capability to save the NVRAM data to a file for later restoration if necessary.

Tip

If your system BIOS is password-protected and you forget the password, one possible way to bypass the block is to remove the battery for a few minutes and then replace it. This resets the BIOS to its default settings, removing the password protection.

After replacing a battery, power up the system and use the Setup program to check the date and time setting and any other data that was stored in the NVRAM.

Building or Upgrading Systems

System Components

In these days of commodity parts and component pricing, building your own system from scratch is no longer the daunting process it once was. Every component necessary to build a PC system is available off the shelf at competitive pricing, and the system you build can use the same or even better components than the top name-brand systems.

There are, however, some cautions to heed. The main thing to note is that you rarely save money when building your own system; purchasing a complete system from a mail-order vendor or mass merchandiser is almost always less expensive. The reason for this is simple: The larger OEMs buy components in quantity and receive a much larger discount than you can by purchasing only one of a particular item.

In addition, you might pay more for shipping if you purchase parts from multiple vendors, as compared to the shipping and handling charge when you purchase a complete system. The cost rises further if you encounter problems with any of the components and have to make additional calls or pay for shipping charges to send improper or malfunctioning parts back for replacement. Also, many companies charge restocking fees if you purchase something and then determine you don't need it or can't use it.

If you purchase parts locally to avoid shipping charges, you typically must pay the additional state sales tax as well as the higher prices usually associated with retail store sales.

Then there is the included software. Although I can sometimes come close in price to a commercial system when building my own from scratch, the bundled software really adds value to the commercial system. For example, an OEM copy of Windows costs roughly $140 or more, and it's double that for a retail version. (Upgrade versions don't apply to new systems.) This is a legitimate expense you'll have to include when building a new system from scratch.

Another operating system (OS)–related issue is Windows activation. When you purchase a system from a major OEM with Windows preinstalled, that version is permanently preactivated via something Microsoft calls System Locked Preinstallation (SLP), which relies on special code both in

Windows as well as in the motherboard BIOS of the system. This means you will never have to deal with the activation hassle, even if you reload the system using the product recovery partition or discs. When you build your own system, however, you have to activate Windows every time you install it, and you may even have to reactivate it if you change too many devices in the system.

Note

Microsoft now offers a Personal Use License for System Builder license for Windows 8 that for the first time explicitly permits an individual to install Windows on a homebuilt system, in a virtual machine, or in a separate partition for multibooting. To learn more about other changes in Windows 8 licensing, see "How the New Windows 8 License Terms Affect You," at www.zdnet.com/how-the-new-windows-8-license-terms-affect-you-7000003028/.

Besides the savings from the included OS, another contributing factor in the low cost of commercial systems is all the other software they install. What I'm talking about is all the time- or feature-limited trial software, as well as pure advertisements and marketing gimmicks, often called junkware. Although it is unwelcome by most users and can sometimes be a chore to clean off, the truth of the matter is that the developers of these programs pay a significant amount of money to the larger OEMs to preload them on their systems. The revenue generated by installing junkware can shave many dollars off the price of a system.

It is clear that the reasons for building a system from scratch often have less to do with saving money and more to do with the experience you gain and the results you achieve. In the end, by building your own, you have a custom system that contains the exact components, OS, and features you have selected. Most of the time when you buy a preconfigured system, you have to compromise in some way. For example, you might get the video adapter you want, but you would prefer a different make or model of motherboard. You might want to use Windows 7 instead of Windows 8, or maybe you want to install Linux instead. By building your own system, you can select the exact components you want and build the ultimate system for your needs. The experience is also very rewarding. You know exactly how your system is constructed and configured because you have done it yourself. This makes future support and installation of additional accessories much easier.

Another benefit of building your own system is that you are guaranteed an industry-standard system that will be easily upgradeable in the future. Many of the larger system vendors use proprietary components that can make future upgrades difficult or impossible. Of course, if you have been reading the book up to this point, you already know everything you need to ensure any preassembled systems you purchase would use industry-standard components and thus be upgradeable and repairable in the future.

One way to save money is by using components from your current system. The monitor, keyboard, mouse, storage devices, most adapter cards, and even the case and power supply from an old system will likely work in a new system as well. Things you probably won't be able to reuse include motherboards, processors, memory, and video cards.

As a form of recycling, I like to take old systems that are being discarded and rebuild them using new components. Essentially, this means that I gut the system and reuse the case, fans, possibly the power supply, and as many other internal components as I can. Many of the cases used in older retail systems are attractive, well built, and accept industry-standard components. By recycling the case and other parts in my new system builds, I can save some money and a little bit of the environment at the same time.

So, if you are interested in a rewarding and educational experience and want a customized and fully upgradeable system, building your own PC is the way to go.

This chapter details the components necessary to assemble your own system, explains the assembly procedures, and lists some recommendations for components and their sources.

The components used in building a typical PC are as follows:

- Case
- Power supply (often included with the case)
- Motherboard
- Processor (CPU)
- CPU fan/heatsink (usually included with the processor)
- Memory (RAM)
- Hard disk/solid-state drive(s)
- Optical drive(s) (CD/DVD/BD)
- Keyboard
- Pointing device (mouse)
- Video card (may be integrated into the motherboard or CPU)
- Display (monitor)
- Sound card (usually integrated into the motherboard)
- Speakers
- Network interface card (usually integrated into the motherboard)
- Cables (usually included with the motherboard)
- Hardware (screws and brackets, usually included with the case)
- OS and other software

Some of these components are either optional or don't have to be purchased separately. For example, most motherboards have integrated sound and network cards, and a growing number have integrated video. Each of these components is discussed in the following sections.

Before You Start: How to Decide What to Build

One of the benefits of building your own system is the ability to customize it to specific needs. According to the CompTIA A+ Certification 2012 exam objectives, there are at least nine types of custom configurations for PCs. Let's briefly look at these as a guide to help you select the appropriate components for your custom PC build.

System Optimized for Graphics (Photo Editing, CAD, CAM Design)

If you're building a system optimized for graphics editing, it should contain

- A fast, multicore processor from Intel or AMD.
- High-end 3D graphics. For photo editing, you can use consumer 3D cards based on the fastest AMD Radeon or NVIDIA GTX series GPUS. For CAD/CAM, choose workstation graphics cards based on GPUs, such as AMD FirePro series or NVIDIA Quadro.
- 16GB or more RAM.

System Optimized for Audio/Video Editing

If you're building a system intended to create or edit audio or video, it should contain

- A fast, multicore processor from Intel or AMD
- High-end 3D consumer graphics
- 16GB or more RAM
- Dual 23-inch or larger displays
- 2TB or larger SATA 6Gbps hard disk running at 7,200RPM or faster with a 64MB or larger cache
- High-end audio card optimized for music creation

System Optimized for Virtualization

If you're building a system intended to host virtualized operating systems and applications, it should contain

- A multicore (four or more) processor with virtualization support
- 16GB or more RAM

System Optimized for Gaming

If you're building a system optimized for 3D gaming, it should contain

- A fast, multicore processor from Intel or AMD
- High-end 3D consumer graphics with at least 2GB RAM per GPU
- Gaming-optimized audio card
- High-end air or liquid cooling as needed to support overclocking or high-performance GPU operation

System Optimized for Home Theater

This type of system puts a premium on connectivity and quiet operation, so its requirements are a lot different than the previous custom builds. It should include

- Compact form factor (Home Theater PC recommended)
- GPU or processor-integrated graphics optimized for DVD, video, and HDTV playback
- HDMI audio and video output
- Surround audio
- Digital or CableCard TV tuner

Home Server PC

Don't let the name fool you. Although Microsoft discontinued Windows Home Server in July 2012, there's still a need for a home network device that's ready to shoulder the storage burden. A Home Server PC build should include

- Support for media streaming (UPnP router and operating system optimized for media streaming, such as Windows 7/8)
- File and printer sharing configuration
- One or more shared printers

- 2TB or more shared hard disk space
- Gigabit Ethernet NIC (connected to Gigabit Ethernet ports in a switch or wireless router)
- RAID 1/10/5 array for secure storage

Standard Thick Client

If you're building a system to run desktop applications, such as Microsoft Office, you don't need a lot of customization, nor should you spend a lot of money. Just make sure your system meets the recommended requirements for the version of Windows (or Linux) you want to run.

Standard Thin Client

If you're building a system to run basic applications, such as web surfing or email, just make sure your system meets the minimum requirements for the version of Windows (or Linux) you want to run. Based on the type(s) of systems, you want to build, you can then make suitable choices of components to help make your system as individual as you are.

Case and Power Supply

The case and power supply unit (PSU) are often sold as a unit, although many vendors do sell them separately. The power supplies included with lower-cost cases are often of lower quality or provide an inadequate amount of power, so you might want to replace the existing PSU with one of your choosing. There are a multitude of chassis designs from which to choose, usually dependent on the motherboard form factor you want to use, the number of drive bays available, and whether the system is to be placed on a desktop, on the floor under the desk, on a shelf, or in some other location. There are cases with extra fans for cooling, front panel I/O and audio ports, removable side panels, and motherboard trays to make installing a motherboard easier, as well as cases that require no tools for assembly, rack-mounted versions, and more. For most custom-built systems, a mid-tower case supporting an ATX or microATX form factor motherboard, along with an ATX12V 2.x or EPS12V form factor PSU, is the best choice. The ATX12V 2.x and EPS12V PSUs will have the 24-pin main power connector used on the latest boards, while EPS12V PSUs will also have an 8-pin +12V processor power connector instead of the standard 4-pin version used on the ATX12V units.

The size and shape of a component is called the *form factor*. The most popular case form factors are as follows:

- Full-tower
- Mid- or mini-tower
- Desktop
- Low-profile (also called slimline)

These are not official form factors, like those for motherboards and power supplies; however, each specific case is designed to accept a specific motherboard and power supply form factor. You have to ensure that the particular case you choose will accept the type of motherboard and power supply you want to use.

After you settle on a case form factor, you need to choose one that supports the motherboard and power supply form factors you want to use. The smaller mini-tower or slimline cases often accept only microATX, FlexATX, or even smaller motherboards, which somewhat limits your choices.

Within the ATX and BTX families, a larger case always accepts the smaller motherboards. For example, if a case accepts a full-size ATX motherboard, it also accepts microATX and FlexATX motherboards.

◄◄ See the Chapter 4 section, "Motherboard Form Factors," **p. 155**.

The case you choose is really a matter of personal preference and system location. Most people feel that the tower systems are roomier and easier to work on, and the full-sized tower cases have a lot of bays for various storage devices. Tower cases typically have enough bays to hold floppy drives, multiple hard disk drives, SSDs, optical drives, tape drives, and anything else you might want to install. However, some of the desktop cases can have as much room as the towers, particularly the mini- and mid-tower models. In fact, a tower case is sometimes considered a desktop case turned sideways, or vice versa. Some cases are convertible—that is, they can be used in either a desktop or tower orientation.

When it comes to the power supply, the most important consideration is how many devices you plan to install in the system and how much power they require. Chapter 18, "Power Supplies," describes the process for calculating the power your system hardware requires and selecting an appropriate power supply for your needs.

◀◀ See the Chapter 18 section, "Power-Use Calculations," **p. 901**.

When you build your own system, you should always keep upgradeability and repairability in mind. A properly designed custom PC should last you far longer than an off-the-shelf model because you can more easily add or replace components. When choosing a case and power supply, leave yourself some room for expansion, on the assumption that you will eventually want to install additional drives or other new devices that appear on the market that you can't live without. To be specific, be sure you have at least a few empty internal drive bays, and choose a higher output power supply than you initially need for your current equipment, so it won't be overtaxed when additional components are added later.

Processor

Both Intel and AMD sell processors through two primary channels or methods. They are referred to as boxed (or retail) and OEM.

The most obvious difference between the boxed and OEM processors is the physical packaging. It could be argued that both technically come in boxes, but the Intel or AMD *boxed* processors come individually packaged in a colorful shrink-wrapped box that includes the processor, the heatsink and fan, installation instructions, a certificate of authenticity, warranty paperwork, and so on. Of particular note is the cooling system, which is designed to work under worst-case thermal environments and is a high-quality and heavy-duty unit.

On the other hand, OEM processors come in a much larger box with multiple trays containing up to 10 processors each, or up to 100 total. No heatsinks, fans, installation instructions, warranties, or other paperwork are included. OEM dealers may provide a heatsink and fan with an OEM processor; however, these are often of uneven quality and offer subpar performance. Major system manufacturers purchase OEM processors in large quantities.

A boxed processor generally includes a 3-year warranty direct with the processor manufacturer. So, if the CPU fails within three years of purchase, the end user can contact Intel or AMD directly and the company will replace the chip. OEM processors have *no* warranty with the manufacturer (Intel or AMD); however, the company you purchased it from will likely offer a 30- or 90-day warranty. The warranty length and the way in which it is administered are entirely up to the dealer that you purchased the chip from, which could be a problem if, for example, that dealer has gone out of business.

Because the motherboard you choose dictates or limits your choice in processor, you should choose your processor first, which will then dictate the type of CPU socket (or slot) that must be present on the motherboard. For more information on processors, refer to Chapter 3, "Processor Types and Specifications."

◀◀ See the Chapter 3 section, "Processor Socket and Slot Types," **p. 75**.

Tip

Check the Newegg.com site for information on motherboards and processors that are for sale. The site serves as a useful research tool for checking to see what components are currently available, what they cost, and what the specifications and compatibility requirements are. The user reviews are also useful in determining product reliability and ease of installation.

Motherboard

Several compatible form factors are used for motherboards. The form factor refers to the physical dimensions and size of the board and dictates into which type of case the board will fit.

In general, you are safest sticking with the ATX or microATX form factors, as those are the most popular, and with that you will have the widest choices in cases, motherboards, and power supplies.

Note

For more information on all the motherboard form factors, refer to Chapter 4. You can also find the reference standard documents detailing the modern form factors at the Desktop Form Factors website (www.formfactors.org).

In addition to processor support and form factor, you should consider several other features when selecting a motherboard. The following sections examine each feature.

Chipsets

Aside from the processor, the main component on a motherboard is called the *chipset*. This usually is a set of one or two chips that contain the main motherboard circuits. Where two chips are used, the chip that connects to the processor is typically known as the PCH (Platform Controller Hub); the chipset is typically known by the name of the PCH. The PCH supports PCIe x16 slots. The South Bridge (SB) or I/O controller hub (ICH) chip supports PCIe x1 or x4 slots, USB ports, network ports, SATA ports, and other types of lower-speed I/O ports.

Note

Older chipsets made for processors that do not include memory controllers used North Bridge or Memory Controller Hub (MCH) chips in place of the PCH chip.

The chips in the chipset replace the 150 or more distinct components that were used in the original IBM AT systems and enable a motherboard designer to easily create a functional system from just a few parts. The chipset contains most of the motherboard circuitry except the processor and memory in most systems.

Because the chipset really *is* the motherboard, the chipset used in a given motherboard has a profound effect on the performance of the board. It dictates all the performance parameters and limitations of the board, such as memory size and speed, processor types and speeds, supported buses and their speeds, and more.

Because chipsets are constantly being introduced and improved over time, I can't list all of them and their functions here; however, you will find a detailed description of many of them in Chapter 4. Several popular high-performance chipsets are on the market today.

◄◄   See the Chapter 4 section, "Chipsets," **p. 181**.

◄◄   See the Chapter 4 section, "Motherboard Selection Criteria (Knowing What to Look For)," **p. 260**.

Clearly, you must base the selection of a chipset largely on the processor you choose and the additional components you intend to install in the computer.

The chipset dictates what types of bus slots can be included on the motherboard. Most recent chipsets include Peripheral Component Interconnect (PCI) and PCIe (PCI Express) slots only; if you have Industry Standard Architecture (ISA) or Accelerated Graphics Port (AGP) cards, they won't be usable in any new system you build or buy.

If you really want in-depth technical information about the chipset in a given motherboard, I recommend downloading its documentation (often called the *databook*). This documentation should also help describe the Advanced Chipset Setup functions in your system's Setup program. With this information, you might be able to fine-tune the motherboard configuration by altering the chipset features and settings.

BIOS/UEFI

Another important feature on the motherboard is the basic input/output system (BIOS). This is also called the *ROM BIOS* because the code is stored in a read-only memory (ROM) chip. There are several things to look for here. Most BIOSs for desktop computers are supplied by one of the major BIOS manufacturers, such as AMI (American Megatrends International), Phoenix, or Award (owned by Phoenix). The BIOS is normally contained in a special type of reprogrammable chip called a *Flash ROM* or *EEPROM* (electrically erasable programmable read-only memory). This enables you to download BIOS updates from the manufacturer and, using a program it supplies, easily update the code in your BIOS. Before purchasing a motherboard, check to see whether the motherboard is well supported and that the manufacturer offers downloadable BIOS updates. If you can't easily find BIOS updates, drivers, and documentation for the board on the manufacturer's website, you might want to choose a board from a different manufacturer that provides better support.

◄◄　See the Chapter 5 section, "Upgrading the BIOS," **p. 274**.

You also need to verify that the motherboard and BIOS support both the processor you plan to install initially and the processor you might upgrade to in the future. If the motherboard and chipset can handle a new processor but the BIOS cannot, a BIOS upgrade may be available to provide proper support.

The traditional BIOS is being replaced by the Unified Extensible Firmware Interface (UEFI), which enables booting from 3TB hard disks and other features not possible with the traditional BIOS. However, both UEFI and BIOS firmware require you to select the correct settings for your hardware.

◄◄　See the Chapter 5 section, "Unified Extensible Firmware Interface (UEFI)," **p. 289**.

Memory

Main memory typically is installed in the form of dual inline memory modules (DIMMs). Two physical types of main memory modules are commonly used in PC systems today, with several variations of each. The main types are as follows:

- 240-pin DDR2 DIMMs
- 240-pin DDR3 DIMMs

Double data rate (DDR) SDRAM memory is an updated variation on SDRAM in which data is transferred twice as quickly. DDR2 is an improved version of DDR that supports higher clock speeds and lower voltages. DDR3 is the latest type of main memory on the market and is the most popular in new systems. DDR4 is expected in systems in the 2013–2014 period.

◄◄　See the Chapter 6 section, "DDR SDRAM," **p. 338**.

Current motherboards use memory in single-, dual-, or tri-channel modes. In single-channel mode, each 64-bit wide DIMM is accessed individually, whereas in dual- or tri-channel mode, the modules are accessed in multiples of 2 or 3 for higher performance. If you want to take advantage of the faster multichannel modes, make sure you purchase and install memory modules in matched multiples.

Some memory modules are available with an extra error check bit for each 8 bits. These are called ECC (error-correcting code) modules. ECC support is normally found only in server-type processors and motherboards and is rarely found in standard PCs. If you want to install the more expensive ECC modules in your system, make sure that your processor and motherboard provide the necessary support.

◄◄ See the Chapter 6 section, "Parity and ECC," **p. 357**.

For more information on PC memory of all types, refer to Chapter 6.

I/O Ports

Virtually all motherboards today have built-in I/O ports. In rare cases where these ports are not built in, they must be supplied via a plug-in expansion board that, unfortunately, wastes an expansion slot. The following ports might be included in any new system you assemble:

- PS/2 keyboard port (mini-DIN type)
- PS/2 mouse port (mini-DIN type); some systems include a single PS/2 port usable by a keyboard or mouse; use an adapter to permit a PS/2 keyboard and mouse to be connected to a single port.
- Four or more USB 2.0 ports
- Two or more USB 3.0 ports (also compatible with USB 1.1, USB 2.0 devices)
- One or more FireWire ports
- One or more analog Video Graphics Array (VGA), Digital Visual Interface (DVI), High-Definition Multimedia Interface (HDMI), or DisplayPort video connectors (integrated video)
- RJ-45 port for 10/100 or Gigabit Ethernet
- Analog audio connectors (speakers, microphone, and so on)
- Digital audio connectors (coaxial and/or optical SPDIF, HDMI)
- Two or more serial ATA (SATA) ports
- One or more eSATA ports

Note

Most motherboards feature SATA 6Gbps ports. On systems with two speeds of SATA ports (6Gbps and 3Gbps), these ports are usually indicated with different-colored plastic headers.

Most recent motherboards lack the serial, parallel, keyboard, and mouse ports (referred to as *legacy ports*), instead relying on USB for those connections. You might want to avoid "legacy-free" motherboards if you still use peripherals with those types of connections. Most motherboards feature integrated sound, and many have optional integrated video.

The latest chipsets integrate support for even the newest I/O components, such as USB 3.0 and SATA RAID, but chipsets that are only a year or two old that might be found in many systems might also include an additional Super I/O chip and additional interface components (such as a chip for USB 3.0 or SATA RAID support). Adding the optional video and sound interfaces directly to the motherboard saves both money and the use of an expansion slot, especially important in the less expensive systems sold today. In the case of integrated video, however, you're likely to incur a performance hit as compared to having a separate PCI Express video card. Depending on the type of system you're building, integrated video might be suitable (as with a Home Theater PC, Home Server PC, or standard thick and thin PC clients).

If these devices are not present on the motherboard, various Super I/O or multi-I/O boards that implement all these ports are available. Again, most of the newer versions of these boards use a single-chip implementation because it is cheaper and more reliable.

◀◀ See the Chapter 4 section, "Super I/O Chips," **p. 228**.

The primary drawback of having functions such as video and networking built in to the motherboard or CPU, of course, is that you have little or no choice about the features or quality of the integrated adapters. Integrated components such as these are nearly always of serviceable quality, but they certainly do not push the performance envelope of higher-end expansion cards. Most people who decide to build a system do so because they want optimum performance from every component, which you typically do not get from integrated video and sound.

Buying a motherboard with integrated adapters, however, does not preclude you from adding expansion devices of the same type. You usually can install a video or sound card into a system with integrated video or sound without major problems, except that in most cases the integrated devices have to be disabled and cannot be used in conjunction with the card. If you want the convenience of integrated video but want to maintain the option of installing a faster PCI Express video card later, look for systems that provide both integrated video and the PCIe x16 slot you need for a video card, and two or more PCIe x1 slots for use with high-performance audio, TV tuners, and high-performance wired or wireless networks.

◀◀ See the Chapter 12 section, "Integrated Video/Motherboard Chipsets," **p. 611**.

Almost all recent desktop systems have at least eight USB 2.0 ports, and most of these are available in the port cluster on the back of the motherboard. Header pins on the motherboard enable additional USB ports to be connected from the front of the case or on a card bracket used in a empty slot. Front-mounted USB ports make temporarily connecting devices such as flash drives, digital cameras, game-pads, wireless input device receivers, USB headphones, portable media players, or smartphones easier.

Note that if your motherboard has integrated devices, such as video and sound, in some cases, you must go into the BIOS Setup to disable these devices if you want to add a card-based replacement device. Check your BIOS Setup menus for an Enable/Disable setting for any integrated devices.

Note

Some chassis support only USB 1.1 (12Mbps) maximum speed in their front-mounted USB ports. If you plug a USB 2.0 or 3.0 device into a port that runs at USB 1.1 speeds and you use Windows XP or later, you will see a `This device can perform faster` warning displayed. Similarly, if you plug a USB 3.0 device into a USB 2.0 port, you will receive the same warning.

Hard Disk/Solid-State Drives

Your system also needs at least one hard disk or solid-state drive. One of the cardinal rules of computer shopping is that you can never have too much storage. Buy as much as you can afford, and you'll almost certainly end up filling it anyway.

Serial ATA has become the most popular drive interface, with many motherboards featuring six or more SATA connectors. Some still have a Parallel ATA port as well.

Many motherboards now feature Redundant Array of Independent (or Inexpensive) Disks (RAID)-capable SATA interfaces. These enable you to install multiple drives in a number of array configurations, including RAID 0 (striped), RAID 1 (mirrored), RAID 5 (striped with distributed parity), and RAID 10 (striped mirrors). Using the RAID 1, RAID 5, or RAID 10 configuration is particularly useful for increased protection against data loss. RAID 1 requires matched pairs of drives, whereas RAID 5 requires three or more drives and RAID 10 requires four drives.

All motherboards have built-in USB ports, and many include IEEE 1394 (FireWire) ports as well. External USB and FireWire drives are useful for backup purposes as well as for moving large amounts of data from system to system. Many late-model motherboards also feature eSATA ports for use with external drives, but most drive vendors that formerly produced eSATA drives now use USB 3.0 interfaces instead.

◀◀ See the Chapter 7 sections, "PATA/SATA RAID," **p. 434** and "ATA Standards," **p. 380**.

Removable Storage

Hardly any of today's systems are equipped with a 1.44MB 3 1/2-inch floppy drive because modern systems are capable of booting from an optical or USB drive.

Regardless of format, some form of optical drive is usually installed, if for no other reason than to install the OS or other software. If you don't really need an optical drive in the system otherwise, you can use an external USB-connected optical drive on a temporary basis and build the system without an internal (permanently installed) optical drive. An external hard drive is also worth considering if you need extra removable storage either for portability or for data backups. Rewritable optical discs cannot match the storage capacity of external hard drives, which can hold several terabytes of data. You can now find external enclosures that include USB or FireWire ports (sometimes both) for $30 or less.

On a smaller scale, USB flash memory drives provide a much more compact storage solution that can be carried with you wherever you go. The first generation of flash drives often stored as little as 16MB of data, but today's larger devices can hold 128GB or more.

Input Devices

Obviously, your system needs a keyboard and some type of pointing device, such as a mouse. Although many new factory-built systems include a touchscreen for use with Windows 8, you will still want to select additional input devices that you can use, depending on your situation.

Tip

As an alternative to touchscreen support (which is still not generally available separately for consumer-friendly computers), consider adding a multitouch digitizing pad or a keyboard with a multitouch integrated pad.

Different people prefer different types of keyboards, and the "feel" of one type can vary considerably from other types. If possible, I suggest you try a variety of keyboards until you find the type that suits you best. I prefer a stiff action with tactile feedback myself, but others prefer a lighter, quieter touch.

While older wired and wireless keyboards and mice typically included connectors that could accommodate either 6-pin mini-DIN (PS/2) or USB ports, almost all current products are designed for USB ports only.

◀◀ See the Chapter 15 section, "Keyboards," **p. 739**.

◀◀ See the Chapter 15 section, "Keyboard Technology," **p. 742**.

Tip

You might be tempted to skimp on your keyboard and mouse to save a few dollars. Don't! Unless you're using a multi-touch display or digitizer, you do all of your interacting with your new PC through these devices, and cheap ones make their presence known every time you use your system.

◄◄   See the Chapter 15 section, "USB Keyboards," **p. 753**.

Video Card and Display

You need a video adapter and a monitor or display to complete your system. Numerous choices are available in this area, but the most important piece of advice I have to give is to choose a good monitor. The display is your main interface to the system and can be the cause of many hours of either pain or pleasure, depending on which monitor you choose. At this point, the market for CRTs has died off, and I only recommend LCDs with LED backlighting (often referred to as LED displays) for new systems.

You can attach most LCDs to a VGA analog port, but most current models are designed to work with Digital Visual Interface (DVI), HDMI, or DisplayPort connectors, which are replacing the older analog VGA.

Older systems used AGP or PCI interfaces for video cards, whereas modern systems use PCI Express. Windows supports multiple monitors on a single system, and it's a feature that can be useful for a variety of applications. If gaming performance is your ultimate goal and you can tolerate the added expense, look for a system that supports two or more PCI Express x16 graphics cards. Both NVIDIA and AMD offer high-performance video chipsets that you can use to run multiple video cards together to increase video display performance.

Many motherboards with onboard video also have an PCI Express video card slot (older systems have an AGP slot); if your motherboard has one, you can insert the applicable card into this slot. The onboard video should be automatically disabled in most cases, although you might have to disable it in the BIOS setup in some cases.

Note

Some AMD-based systems with chipset or processor-integrated graphics support ATI Hybrid CrossFire, which enables compatible video cards and the motherboard's integrated chipset or on-processor graphics to provide faster 3D rendering than either component could perform independently.

Audio Hardware

All systems today should be capable of playing audio to some degree, which means you need at least a passable set of external speakers and either a motherboard with integrated audio or a separate sound card. Most systems today feature integrated audio, but you can disable it if you prefer to add a dedicated high-quality sound card. Dedicated cards are ideal if you want the best possible sound quality for video playback, audio capture and editing, or surround sound for gaming. Almost any motherboard-integrated audio system or sound card on the market today is compatible with the baseline Creative Sound Blaster series, Windows DirectSound, and other sound APIs.

Speakers designed for use with PCs range from tiny, unpowered devices to large audiophile-class systems. Many of the top manufacturers of stereo speakers now produce speaker systems for PCs. Some include subwoofers or even a full Dolby surround sound implementation.

Note

If you decide to replace your system's onboard audio with a sound card, be sure to look for a card that supports your system's available expansion slots.

Accessories

Apart from the major components, you need several other accessories to complete your system. These are the small parts that can make the assembly process a pleasure or a chore. If you are purchasing your system components from mail-order sources, you should make a complete list of all the parts you need, right down to the last cable and screw, and be sure you have everything before you begin the assembly process. It is excruciating to have to wait several days with a half-assembled system for the delivery of a forgotten part.

Heatsinks/Cooling Fans

Some of today's faster processors produce a lot of heat, and this heat has to be dissipated so your system doesn't operate intermittently or even fail completely. Boxed processors from Intel and AMD are sold with the heatsink and fan included. And although OEM processors don't include a heatsink from the processor manufacturer, most vendors who sell them add an aftermarket heatsink and fan to the package; often, aftermarket heatsinks and fans provide significantly better cooling than those shipped with boxed processors, making them more suitable for overclocking.

Caution

All modern heatsinks require that a thermal interface material be applied to the base of the heatsink before installation. A small amount may be supplied with a new heatsink (either as an integrated phase change pad or as a separate tube of thermal paste or grease), but you may want to purchase some separately because the grease has to be cleaned off and reapplied every time you remove and reinstall the processor or heatsink.

Another consideration for cooling is with the case. The fan in the power supply and the one on the CPU heatsink may not be enough for a high-performance system. I recommend you get a case that includes at least one additional cooling fan. This is typically mounted in the rear of the chassis, directing additional air out the back. Some cases include an extra fan in the front, which is recommended if you are installing more than three hard drives. Most motherboards provide connectors for a CPU fan plus at least two chassis fans.

Tip

If you are planning to overclock your PC's components, consider using liquid cooling for maximum performance. Instead of heatsinks, liquid cooling uses devices known as water blocks (waterblocks) to cool hardware. Waterblocks are connected with flexible pipes that move coolant between components and an external heat exchanger. Most heat-producing components in a PC can be liquid-cooled, including the processor, RAM, chipsets, GPUs, and hard disks. FrozenCPU.com's Liquid Cooling page is an excellent resource for those new to liquid cooling,

Cables

PC systems need many different cables to hook up everything. These can include power cables or adapters, Serial ATA (and Parallel ATA) drive cables, and many others. Motherboards normally include a few cables, but if you are installing multiple drives, you might need to purchase extras. Chassis normally include cables for front panel connections, and power cables are normally included with or are part of the power supply.

Hardware

You might need screws, standoffs, mounting brackets or rails (if your case requires them), and other miscellaneous hardware to assemble your system. An assortment of hardware is normally included with the chassis, but in some cases it helps to have extras on hand.

Hardware and Software Resources

When you are planning to build a system, it is important to consider how all your selected components will work together and how the software you run must support them. It is not enough to be sure that you have sufficient slots on the motherboard for all your expansion cards and enough bays in the case for all your drives. You must also consider the resources required for all the components. For example, if the chassis you have selected has front panel I/O ports, are there available connections for all of them on the motherboard? Essentially, you should completely configure the system before you begin ordering parts. Planning a system to this level of detail can be a lot of work, which is one reason—besides cost—that the majority of PCs are prebuilt.

Tip

In most cases, you can download or view online the manuals for the motherboard, processor, and other major components before you purchase them. Check the component vendors' websites for these manuals and technical notes and read them carefully.

Another consideration is the OS and other software you need. Prebuilt systems nearly always arrive with the OS installed, but when you build your own, you must be prepared with a copy of your selected OS.

The OS you select for your new computer is another important decision. You must be certain that the OS supports all the hardware you've selected, which can occasionally be a difficult task. Today the main choices are Windows or one of the Linux variants. This is one area where building your own has real advantages; OEM systems often have limited choices when it comes to the OS, but when you build your own system, the choice of OS is entirely up to you.

Drivers for the desired OS and specific hardware components might also be a problem. It is a good idea to gather all the latest driver revisions for your hardware and intended OS, as well as BIOS flashes, firmware updates, and other software components, and have them available when you begin the assembly process. Placing them on an optical disc or flash drive is a good idea; that way you can access them easily and install them when necessary.

System Assembly and Disassembly

Actually assembling the system is easy after you have lined up all the components. In fact, you will find the parts procurement phase the most lengthy and trying of the entire experience. Completing the system is basically a matter of screwing everything together, plugging in all the cables and connectors, and configuring everything to operate properly.

In short order, you will find out whether your system operates as you had planned or whether some incompatibilities exist between some of the components. Be careful, and pay attention to how you install all your components. It is easy to forget a jumper, switch, or cable connection that later causes problems in system operation. Most people's first reaction when problems occur is to blame defective hardware, but that is usually not the source. The problem can typically be traced to some missed step or error made in the assembly process.

Above all, the most crucial rule of assembling your own system is to save every piece of documentation and software that comes with every component in your system. This material can be indispensable in troubleshooting problems you encounter during the assembly process or later. You should also retain all the packing materials used to ship mail-order components to you until you are certain they will not have to be returned.

Assembly Preparation

The process of physically assembling a PC requires only a few basic tools: a 1/4-inch nut driver or a Phillips-head screwdriver for the external screws that hold the cover in place and a 3/16-inch nut driver or Phillips-head screwdriver for all the other screws. Needle-nose pliers can also help in removing motherboard standoffs, jumpers, and stubborn cable connectors. Because of marketplace standardization, only a couple types and sizes of screws (with a few exceptions) hold a system together. Also, the physical arrangement of the major components is similar even among different manufacturers. Figure 19.1 shows the components that go into a typical system, and Figure 19.2 shows the system with those components assembled. Note that the components shown here are for a standard PC. Your final component list might vary.

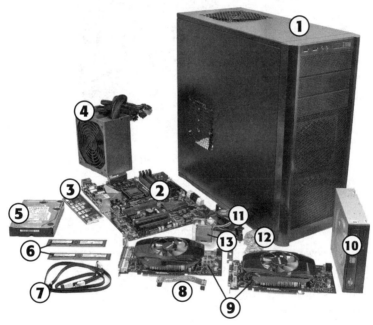

1. Mid-tower ATX chassis
2. ATX motherboard
3. I/O shield (included with motherboard)
4. Power supply
5. SATA hard disk
6. DDR3 DIMMS
7. SATA cables
8. MIO bridge for SLI graphics
9. PCIe x16 video cards
10. SATA DVD optical drive
11. Active heatsink for CPU
12. Screws and standoffs
13. Processor (CPU)

FIGURE 19.1 Components used in building a typical PC.

FIGURE 19.2 The completed system using many of the components shown in Figure 19.1.

You'll find more information on the tools used to work on PCs in Chapter 20, "PC Diagnostics, Testing, and Maintenance."

Other tools you'll need are software related. You'll need an OS install disc, and it is a good idea to have discs handy with any service packs, drivers, or other software you will want to install.

The following sections cover the assembly and disassembly procedure for these components:

- Motherboard
- Case or cover assembly
- Power supply
- Drives
- Adapter boards

As you prepare to install your system's motherboard, unpack the motherboard and check to ensure you have everything that should be included. If you purchase a new board, you typically get at least the motherboard, some I/O cables, and a manual.

If you are installing one or more video cards that have cooling shrouds, make sure that you have access to other slots if you need to add additional cards or header cables that use expansion slot brackets. Many mid-range and high-performance cards have cooling shrouds wide enough to prevent use of the adjacent expansion slot.

Electrostatic Discharge Protection

When you are working on the internal components of a computer, you must take the necessary precautions to prevent accidental static discharges to the components. At any time, your body can hold a large static voltage charge that can easily damage components of your system. Before I ever put my hands into an open system, I touch a bare metal grounded portion of the chassis, such as the internal frame or the power supply case. This action serves to equalize the electrical charges that the device and my body might be carrying. Be sure the system is unplugged during all phases of the assembly process. Some will claim that you should leave the system plugged in to provide an earth ground through the power cord and outlet, but that is unnecessary. If you leave the system plugged in, you open yourself up to other problems, such as accidentally turning it on or leaving it on when installing a board or device, which can damage the motherboard or other devices.

Caution

Power supplies used in many systems today deliver a +5V current to the motherboard continuously—that is, whenever they are plugged in. Bottom line: Be sure any system you are working on is completely unplugged from the wall outlet.

A more sophisticated way to equalize the charges between you and any of the system components is to use an electrostatic discharge (ESD) protection kit. These kits consist of a wrist strap and mat, with ground wires for attachment to the system chassis. When you are going to work on a system, you place the mat next to the system unit. Next, you clip the ground wire to both the mat and an unpainted part of the system's chassis, tying the grounds together. You then put on the wrist strap and attach that wire to either the chassis or the mat. If you are using a wrist strap without a mat, clip the wrist-strap wire to the system chassis. When clipping these wires to the chassis, be sure to use an area that is free of paint so a good ground contact can be achieved. This setup ensures that any electrical charges are carried equally by you and any of the components in the system, preventing the sudden flow of static electricity that can damage the circuits.

As you install or remove drives, adapter cards, and especially delicate items such as the entire motherboard, memory modules, or processors, you should place these components on the static mat. Sometimes people put the system unit on top of the mat, but the unit should be alongside the mat so you have room to lay out all the components as you work with them. If you are going to remove the motherboard from a system, be sure you leave enough room for it on the mat.

If you do not have such a mat, place the removed circuits and devices on a clean desk or table. Always pick up a loose adapter card by the metal bracket used to secure the card to the system. This bracket is tied into the ground circuitry of the card, so by touching the bracket first, you prevent a discharge from damaging the components of the card. If the circuit board has no metal bracket (a motherboard, for example), handle the board carefully by the edges, and try not to touch any of the connectors or components. If you don't have proper ESD equipment such as a wrist strap or mat, be sure to periodically touch the chassis while working inside the system to equalize any charge you might have built up.

Caution

Some people recommend placing loose circuit boards and chips on sheets of aluminum foil. I absolutely do not recommend this procedure because it can actually result in an explosion! Many motherboards, adapter cards, and other circuit boards have built-in lithium or NiCad batteries. These batteries react violently (overheating and possibly exploding) when they are shorted out, which is exactly what you would be doing by placing such a board on a piece of aluminum foil. Because you will not always be able to tell whether a board has a battery built in to it somewhere, the safest practice is to never place a board on any conductive metal surface.

Recording Physical Configuration

While you are assembling a system, you should record all the physical settings and configurations of each component, including jumper and switch settings, cable orientations and placement, ground wire locations, and even adapter board placement. Keep a notebook and a digital camera with a macro/close-up setting handy for recording these items, and write down all the settings. Refer to Chapter 4 for more information on motherboard connector, jumper, and other component locations. Figure 19.3 shows a typical motherboard jumper.

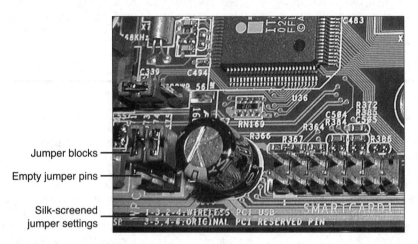

Jumper blocks

Empty jumper pins

Silk-screened jumper settings

FIGURE 19.3   The jumper position shown here is used to configure the motherboard's PCI and USB interface.

Installing the CPU and Heatsink

Before you install your new motherboard, you should install the processor and memory. This usually is much easier to do before the board is installed in the chassis. Some motherboards have jumpers that control both the CPU speed and the voltage supplied to it. If these are set incorrectly, the system might not operate, might operate erratically, or might even damage the CPU. Modern boards control voltages either automatically or via the BIOS setup program. If you have questions about the proper settings, check the board and processor documentation.

◀◀   See the Chapter 3 section, "CPU Operating Voltages," **p. 87**.

All processors today run hot enough to require some form of heatsink to dissipate heat from the processor. To install the processor and heatsink, use the following procedure:

1. **Prep the motherboard.** Take the new motherboard out of the antistatic bag it was supplied in and set it on the bag or the antistatic mat, if you have one.

2. **Install the processor.** First, find pin 1 on the processor; it usually is denoted by a corner of the chip that is marked by a dot or bevel. Next, remove the cover from the processor socket (if so equipped—see Figures 19.4 and 19.5) and find the corresponding pin 1 (or land 1) of the socket for the CPU on the motherboard (see Figures 19.5 and 19.6); it also is usually marked on the board or with a bevel in one corner of the socket. Be sure the pins on the processor or socket are straight and not bent; if they are bent, the chip won't insert properly into the socket. If necessary, use small needle-nose pliers or a hemostat to carefully straighten any pins. Don't bend them too much—they might break off, ruining the chip or the motherboard. Insert the CPU into the socket by lifting the release lever until it is vertical. Then align the pins or lands on the processor with the holes or pins in the socket and drop it down into place. If the processor does not seem to want to drop in all the way, remove it to check for proper alignment and any

bent pins. When the processor is fully seated in the socket, push down the locking lever on the socket until it latches to secure the processor (see Figures 19.7 and 19.8).

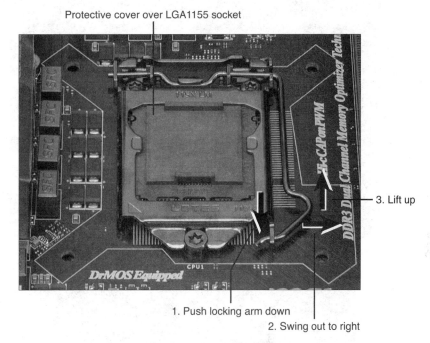

Protective cover over LGA1155 socket

3. Lift up

1. Push locking arm down

2. Swing out to right

FIGURE 19.4 Preparing to remove the cover on a typical LGA1155 processor socket.

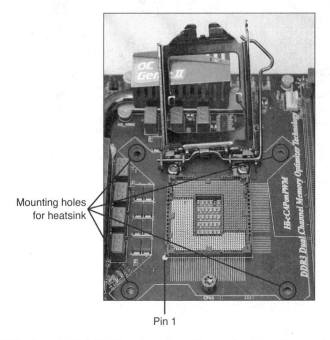

Mounting holes for heatsink

Pin 1

FIGURE 19.5 A typical LGA1155 socket after releasing the clip and removing the protective cover.

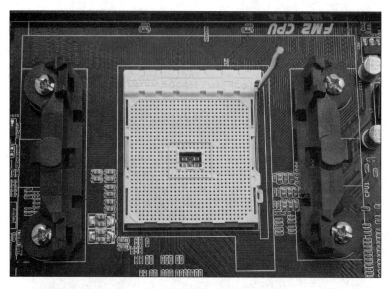

FIGURE 19.6   A typical AMD Socket FM2 (Socket 905) before installing the processor.

Pin 1

FIGURE 19.7   An Intel Core i5 processor after being installed in an LGA1155 socket.

FIGURE 19.8 An AMD A10 5800K processor after being installed in an FM2 socket.

3. Apply thermal interface material (TIM). New retail processors usually come with heatsinks that have preapplied TIM (see Figures 19.9, 19.11). Some vendors cover the TIM with protective tape that must be removed before installing the heatsink. You cannot reuse TIM or thermal grease. If it is damaged, or if the heatsink has already been installed once, the existing TIM must be cleaned off and reapplied. To do this, use a soft towel or cloth to remove the previous thermal grease from the heatsink and the top of the processor. Apply new thermal grease to the top of the processor heat spreader (metal cap). Use the smallest amount that you can spread over the top of the chip; usually an amount the size of a "BB" is sufficient. Use your finger (wearing a rubber glove to prevent contamination) or a hard plastic card (such as a credit card) to spread the thermal grease in the thinnest possible layer covering the entire surface of the heat spreader (metal cap).

4. Install the heatsink. If the heatsink uses push pins (see Figure 19.10), make sure the pins are rotated in the proper position. The tops should be turned in the opposite direction of the arrows on top. Set the heatsink on the processor such that the four pins engage in the holes surrounding the socket. Then push down each of the four pins until they click or latch into place. This can take more force than you might think is prudent, so be sure to visually inspect the installation to ensure that all four pins have fully engaged and are locked. Some heatsinks use one or more retainer clips (see Figure 19.12). With this type you must be careful when attaching the clip to the socket; you don't want it to scrape against the motherboard, which can damage circuit traces or components. You also need to keep the heatsink steady on the chip while attaching the clips, so do not move, tilt, or slide the heatsink while you attach it.

Preapplied TIM

Mounting pegs for heatsink

FIGURE 19.9 An Intel heatsink with preapplied TIM.

1. Push heatsink pins through holes in motherboard until they lock into place

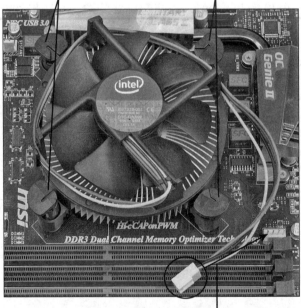

2. Attach heatsink fan power connector to motherboard CPU fan connector

FIGURE 19.10 An Intel heatsink being installed on an LGA1155 processor.

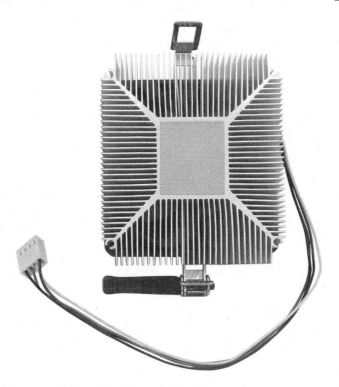

FIGURE 19.11 An AMD heatsink with preapplied TIM.

1. Attach clip (not shown) to heatsink mounting tab

3. Rotate mounting lever until it locks into place

2. Attach clip to heatsink mounting tab

FIGURE 19.12 An AMD heatsink that clips to the frame around the processor socket.

5. Connect the fan. Plug the fan power connector into the CPU fan connector supplied on the motherboard (refer to Figure 19.10), which should be near the processor socket. Optionally, some heatsinks use a peripheral power connector for fan power. Route the fan wires such that they won't interfere with the fan or any other components.

6. Configure the motherboard jumpers (if necessary). Older motherboards used jumpers to configure processor and bus speeds, while some newer motherboards use jumpers to configure integrated video. Refer to the motherboard manufacturer's manual to set the jumpers, if any, to match the CPU you are going to install. In modern systems, the processor configuration is done via the motherboard BIOS Setup.

Installing Memory Modules

To function, the motherboard must have memory installed on it. Modern motherboards use DDR2 or DDR3 DIMMs. (DDR4 memory will be available in systems starting in the 2013-2014 timeframe.) Usually, you install modules in the lowest-numbered sockets or banks first. Note that multichannel boards perform best if modules are installed in matched multiples. Consult the motherboard documentation for more information on which sockets to use first and in what order and how to install the specific modules the board uses.

◄◄ See the Chapter 6 section, "Memory Banks," **p. 325**.

Because memory modules are keyed to the sockets by a notch on the side or bottom, they can go in only one way. Figure 19.13 shows how to install a DIMM; you can find more detailed instructions for installing memory modules in Chapter 6. Installing the modules might require some force, but you must ensure that you are installing the correct modules in the correct orientation, or you might damage the modules or sockets.

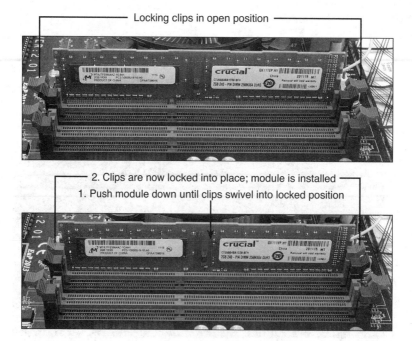

FIGURE 19.13 Installing the memory modules. Make sure the locking clips are open on both sides of the module before the module is inserted into the memory socket (top). Press down on the module until the module locking clips swing up into the locked position (bottom).

Mounting the New Motherboard in the Case

The motherboard attaches to the case with one or more screws and standoffs (spacers). If you are using a new case, you might have to attach one or more standoffs in the proper holes before you can install the motherboard. Use the following procedure to install the new motherboard in the case:

1. Find the holes in the new motherboard for the standoffs. You should install standoffs in the chassis wherever there is a matching screw hole in the motherboard. Note that screw holes typically have a ring of solder (solid or dotted) around them, which acts as a grounding point. Sometimes boards will have other holes that are not designed for screws; these will not have the ground pad and should not use a metal standoff or screw (see Figure 19.14).

2. Screw any standoffs into the new case in the proper positions to align with the screw holes in the motherboard (see Figure 19.15).

3. Most motherboards today attach either directly to the chassis or to a removable motherboard tray. Figure 19.16 shows three types of standoffs, including two brass types and one plastic. One screws directly to the chassis or tray, whereas the others attach to the motherboard and then slide into notches in the case or tray. Most chassis use the metal screw-in standoffs; the other types are rarely used anymore.

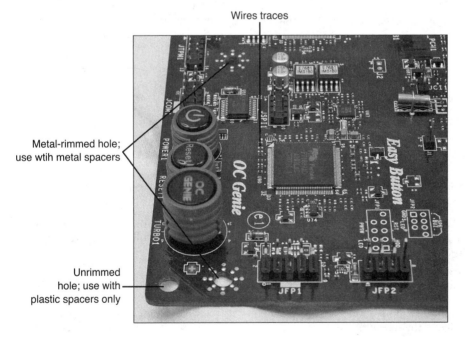

FIGURE 19.14 The corner of a typical motherboard. Be sure not to damage the wire traces when attaching the motherboard to the case.

Standoff and matching mounting holes
Alternative standoff position

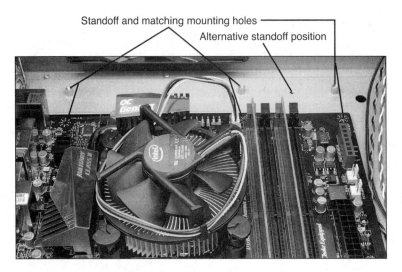

FIGURE 19.15   Make sure the standoffs align with the holes in the motherboard. Note that this chassis has a variety of mounting holes so you can adjust the position of the standoffs to match various motherboard designs.

FIGURE 19.16   Various types of motherboard standoffs, used to support the board when installed in the chassis or motherboard tray.

Figure 19.17 shows a typical ATX-style motherboard with arrows indicating the usual location of the screw holes for mounting the motherboard to the case. (See your motherboard manual for the exact location of these screw holes.)

After you insert the standoffs and line them up with the screw holes on the motherboard, carefully attach the screws to secure the motherboard to the motherboard tray or case (see Tip below), depending on your chassis design. Figure 19.18 shows a motherboard attached to a tray. Note the use of the thumb and forefinger to stabilize the screwdriver tip. This prevents accidental slippage of the screwdriver tip off of the screw, which is one of the biggest causes of new board failures.

Tip

If you are using a motherboard that attaches directly to the case, be sure to perform step 4 (installing the I/O shield) before you install the motherboard.

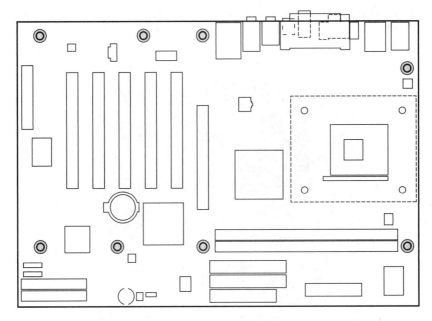

FIGURE 19.17 Mounting screw holes in a typical ATX motherboard. The highlighted circles mark the screw holes for mounting the motherboard to the case.

FIGURE 19.18 Attaching a motherboard to the motherboard tray. (Motherboard courtesy of Intel Corporation.)

4. Install the I/O shield into the chassis by snapping it into place from the inside of the case (see Figure 19.19).

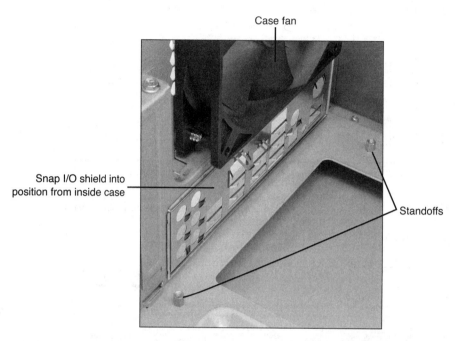

Case fan

Snap I/O shield into position from inside case

Standoffs

FIGURE 19.19 The I/O shield after being snapped into place in the chassis.

5. Install the new motherboard into the case or the motherboard tray. Either screw it directly to the standoffs or slide the standoffs already attached to the board by sliding the entire board into position. Be sure you align the I/O shield with the case or the ports on the back of the board with the I/O shield already in the case. Often, you will have to set the board into the case and slide it sideways to engage the standoffs into the slots in the case. When the board is in the proper position, the screw holes in the board should be aligned with all the metal standoffs or screw holes in the case. Figure 19.20 shows a motherboard attached to a motherboard tray being installed in the chassis.

6. Take the screws that were supplied with the new motherboard and screw the board into the case (see Figure 19.21).

FIGURE 19.20   Installing a motherboard and tray into the chassis.

Using a nutdriver to install an additional screw

Screw holding motherboard in place

FIGURE 19.21   Installing the screws that hold the motherboard to the chassis.

Preparing a Modular Power Supply

If you have a modular power supply (that is, one that uses detachable cables to provide power to different mixtures of PCIe, SATA, and PATA hard or floppy disks), such as the one shown in Figure 19.22, you need to determine the power connectors you need and attach the appropriate modular power leads. For example, if the power supply has a built-in PCIe x16 connector for a high-performance video card, but you are using two cards that require additional power, connect a modular PCIe x16 power lead. If the power supply does not have built-in leads for SATA or PATA drives, connect the appropriate leads. Figure 19.22 shows a modular power supply with two modular leads connected: one for PCIe x16 and one for SATA drives.

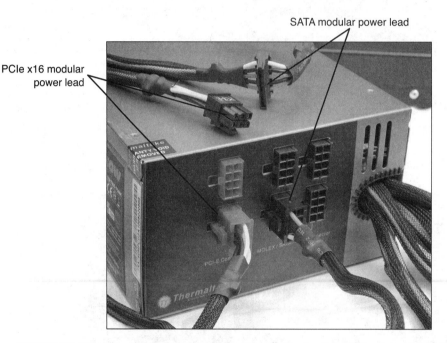

FIGURE 19.22   A modular power supply after connecting leads for PCIe x16 and SATA power.

After you configure your modular power supply with the correct leads, you can install the power supply.

Connecting the Power Supply

The power supply is easy to install, and it usually attaches to the chassis with four screws. Figures 19.23 and 19.24 show installing the power supply into the chassis and tightening the screws.

Note

While older ATX tower cases use a top-mounted power supply, BTX and some recent ATX tower cases, like the one shown in Figure 19.23, use a bottom-mounted power supply.

FIGURE 19.23 Installing the power supply into the chassis.

FIGURE 19.24 Installing the screws to retain the power supply.

ATX-style motherboards have a 20- or 24-pin main power connector (see Figure 19.25), plus a 4- or 8-pin CPU power connector (see Figure 19.26). Both are keyed so they can go on only one way. Older

Baby-AT and other old-style board designs such as LPX usually have two separate six-wire power connectors from the power supply to the board; refer to Chapter 18 for important information on proper installation of Baby-AT power supplies. To attach the power connectors from the power supply to the motherboard, do the following:

1. Plug the 24-pin or 20-pin main ATX keyed power supply connector into the motherboard power socket. You can plug a 20-pin connector into a 24-pin socket (and vice versa) by connecting them in an offset fashion, or you can use cable adapters to mate them up. Most ATX systems also use a 4-pin ATX12V or 8-pin EPS12V connector.

2. Connect a power lead from the power supply to the CPU fan if the motherboard does not have a CPU fan power connector.

Push cable down until the retaining clip on the other side of the connector snaps into place

FIGURE 19.25 Attaching a 24-pin ATX motherboard power connector.

Note

Many power supplies feature a 115/230V switch on the back. If this is improperly set, the system won't power up. Refer to Chapter 18 for detailed coverage of power supplies and the various types of power supply connectors, including the newer 24-pin ATX 2.x and eight-pin EPS12V types.

FIGURE 19.26 Attaching an eight-pin EPS12V motherboard power connector. This type of connector is split into two four-pin connectors compatible with the ATX12V standard, so it can be used with motherboards compatible with either standard.

Connecting I/O and Other Cables to the Motherboard

You must make several connections between the motherboard and the case. These include LEDs for the hard disk and power, an internal speaker connection, a reset button, and a power button. Most modern motherboards also have several built-in I/O ports that have to be connected. This includes ATA/SATA host adapters and front-mounted USB or IEEE 1394 ports. Some boards also include additional items such as built-in video, sound, or SCSI adapters.

If the board is an ATX or BTX type, the connectors for all the external I/O ports are already built in to the rear of the board.

Use the following procedure to connect the cables needed for onboard I/O:

1. If your system uses an internal floppy drive, connect the floppy cable between the floppy drives and the 34-pin floppy controller connector on the motherboard.

2. Connect the Serial ATA and Parallel ATA cables to the drives and host adapter ports on the motherboard (see Figure 19.27). Typically, older systems will use the primary ATA channel connector for hard disks and the secondary channel for optical drives. Most newer systems will use Serial ATA connections for the hard drive and Parallel ATA for the optical drives, or possibly even SATA connections for all drives.

Note

Some recent motherboards mount their SATA ports on one edge of the motherboard facing toward the drive bays.

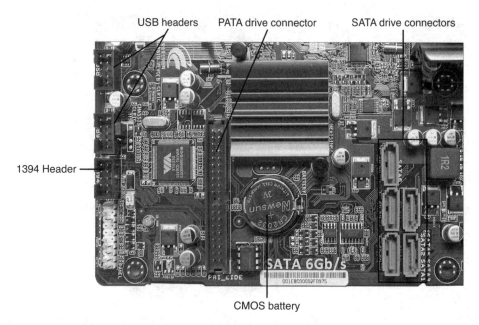

FIGURE 19.27 PATA and SATA drive connectors and other components on a typical motherboard.

3. Attach the front-panel switch, LED, internal speaker wires, and front-mounted ports such as USB and IEEE 1394 (refer to Figure 19.27 for typical headers) and audio from the case front panel to the motherboard. If they are not marked on the board, check where each one is on the diagram in the motherboard manual. Figure 19.28 shows the front-panel connectors. Unfortunately, even though there are standards for these types of connections, many motherboard and chassis manufacturers don't follow the industry standards, and you might find some frustration in getting these connections right. Chapter 4 has detailed pinouts and connection diagrams for most motherboards and chassis.

Note

A pin extender (shown in Figure 19.28) enables you to connect front-panel wires such as power, reset, and LED to a single connection that you can plug into the motherboard. This helps avoid miss-wiring because the pin extender is keyed to prevent incorrect installation.

Installing the Drives

At this point, you should install your hard drive(s), solid-state drives, optical drive(s), and optional floppy drive.

Drive Configuration

Before you physically install a drive in the computer, you must ensure that it is properly configured. Serial ATA drives generally don't require a jumper configuration. Parallel ATA drives, on the other hand, require that each drive be configured as either master/slave or cable select (CS). Normally, you would set Parallel ATA hard drives to CS and use an 80-conductor cable.

◀◀ To learn more about configuring PATA drives, see the Chapter 7 section, "ATA Standards," **p. 380**.

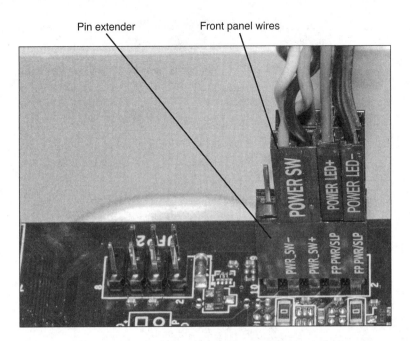

Pin extender   Front panel wires

FIGURE 19.28   Front panel connectors plugged into a pin extender. The pin extender fits between the front panel headers on the motherboard and the front panel connectors.

Because Serial ATA drives connect to the SATA host adapter in a point-to-point configuration using a dedicated cable, there is no master, slave, or cable select setting as there is with Parallel ATA drives. Note, however, that some SATA hard disk drives might have jumpers to help solve compatibility issues, such as to configure a newer 6Gbps interface speed drive into the slower 1.5 or 3 Gbps Gmodes to work around problems with some older SATA host adapters.

Drive Installation

Some computer cases use plastic or metal rails that are secured to the sides of a drive so it can slide into the bay in the chassis. Other case designs have drive bays that directly accept the drive via screws through the side supports, and no other hardware is necessary. Some cases have tool-free designs with sliding latches to secure drives without screws. Still others use a cage arrangement in which you first install the drives into a cage and then slide the cage into the case (see Figure 19.29). If your case uses rails or a cage, these are usually included with the case. With the proper mounting mechanism supplied via the case, all you need is the bare drive to install.

Be sure you use the correct cable for your drive speed. For example, a SATA 6Gps drive requires a SATA cable made for 6Gbps performance. These cables are marked for 6Gbps operation. If you are installing a PATA optical drive, be sure to use an 80-wire cable.

Note

If you are installing PATA hard disk or optical drives, see Chapter 7 for more information about jumper settings and cable standards for these drives.

FIGURE 19.29   A hard disk drive mounted in a removable drive cage.

If you need additional drive-mounting hardware not included with either your case or the drive, several companies specialize in drive-mounting brackets, cables, and other hardware accessories, including Micro Accessories (www.micro-a.com), Jameco (www.jameco.com), and Newegg (www.newegg.com). If you intend to install a 3 1/2-inch hard drive in a 5 1/4-inch drive bay, or a 2 1/2-inch hard disk in a 3 1/2-inch drive bay, you need yet another type of mounting bracket. Many 3 1/2-inch hard drives come with these brackets, or one might be supplied with your case or chassis.

Note

You should note the length of the drive cable when you plan to add a hard disk drive. It can be annoying to assemble everything you think you'll need to install a drive and then find that the drive cable is not long enough to reach the new drive location. You can either try to reposition the drive to a location closer to the interface connector on the host adapter or motherboard or just get a longer cable.

Caution

Many hard disk drives come with special short-length screws that may have the same size thread as other screws you might use in your system, but these screws should not be interchanged. If you use screws that are too long, they might protrude too far into the drive casing and cause problems.

The step-by-step procedure for installing drives is as follows:

1. SATA drives typically do not require jumper configuration; however, in some 6.0Gbps or 3.0Gbps drives you may need to set a jumper to force the drive to 1.5Gbps mode for compatibility with older 1.5Gbps host adapters.

2. Slide the drive into an available drive bay, and secure it using the screws, rails, or brackets provided with either the drive or chassis (see Figure 19.30).

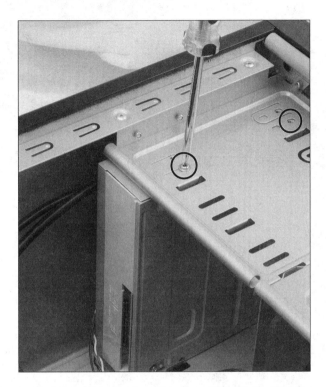

FIGURE 19.30 Secure the drive to the chassis or drive cage using four screws, two on each side of the drive.

3. Connect the SATA or PATA data cable between the drive and the host adapter (motherboard connector) (see Figure 19.31 for SATA).

4. Attach a power connector to the drive (refer to Figure 19.31). Some SATA drives have both conventional 4-pin peripheral power connectors as well as SATA 15-pin power connectors, in which case you can use one or the other, but not both simultaneously. If your drive has only a SATA power connector and your power supply doesn't have SATA power connectors available, you might need to purchase a peripheral-to-SATA power cable adapter if one was not provided with your drive. This type of adapter changes a standard 4-pin peripheral power connector into a 15-pin SATA power connector. If necessary, you can also use a Y-splitter cable to create two power connectors from one. (Some computers have fewer power connectors than drive bays.)

Caution

If a drive has both conventional (also called *peripheral* or *legacy*) and SATA-type power connectors, you must not plug in both power connectors at the same time, or the drive may be damaged!

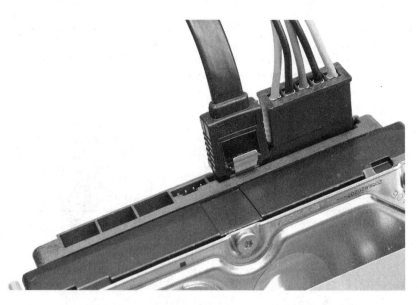

FIGURE 19.31 SATA data and power cables connected to a hard disk.

System Configuration (Drive Detection)

Older systems often required that drives be manually identified and configured in the BIOS Setup. The BIOS in modern PCs incorporates automatic drive parameter detection (autodetect). The BIOS sends a special Identify Drive command to all the devices connected during the system startup sequence, and the drives are intelligent enough to respond with the correct parameters. The BIOS then automatically enters the parameter information returned by the drive. This procedure eliminates errors or confusion in parameter selection:

1. Start the computer and press the appropriate key to access the BIOS Setup screens to configure the drive. If your BIOS has an autodetect or auto-type setting, I recommend you use it because it will configure the parameters automatically using optimal settings. With SATA drives, you may also have options to configure Advanced Host Controller Interface (AHCI) support or set multiple drives in a RAID configuration. Once the settings are made, save the BIOS Setup settings and exit the BIOS Setup to continue. If the drive is not detected, check the drive power and data cables, and make sure the host adapter used by the drive has been enabled in the BIOS setup.

◄◄ See the Chapter 7 section, "Advanced Host Controller Interface (AHCI)," **p. 408**.

2. Restart the system. If the drive you are installing was not the boot drive, the existing OS should automatically detect the new drive upon loading and install the necessary drivers. Note that the drive will not be visible to the OS as a volume (that is, a drive letter) until it is partitioned and formatted. If the drive is the boot drive, you can continue by booting from an OS installation disc or bootable USB flash drive to partition, format, and install the OS to the boot drive. If the motherboard supports SATA in AHCI mode or features such as SATA RAID, and you are running Windows XP or earlier, in most cases you will either need to supply host adapter drivers via a floppy disk at the start of the installation or have them preloaded on your Windows install disc. Note that these drivers are built in to the installation media for Windows Vista and newer; if not, they can be supplied via optical disc or USB flash drive.

Installing a Video Card

Follow these steps to install a video card into a system:

1. If necessary, remove the screw and slot cover behind the expansion slot you want to use for the new video card. If the card uses a cooling fan that requires a second expansion slot for air exhaust, remove the adjacent slot cover (see Figure 19.32).

2. Slide the video card straight down into the slot where it will be installed (typically a PCI Express slot).

3. Push the card down into the slot, using a front-to-back rocking motion if necessary to get the edge connector to slide into the slot. Note many PCI Express and AGP cards feature a retaining tab at the end of the connector, which helps to secure the card in the slot. There are several types of retainer designs used, and you will need to disengage this retainer when removing the card.

4. If the card requires power, connect the appropriate power lead from the power supply. Most recent high-end PCIe x16 video cards use six-pin PCIe or six+two (eight-pin) PCIe power leads.

Figure 19.32 illustrates a two-slot PCIe x16 video card being installed in a system. This card uses the six-pin PCIe x16 power connector.

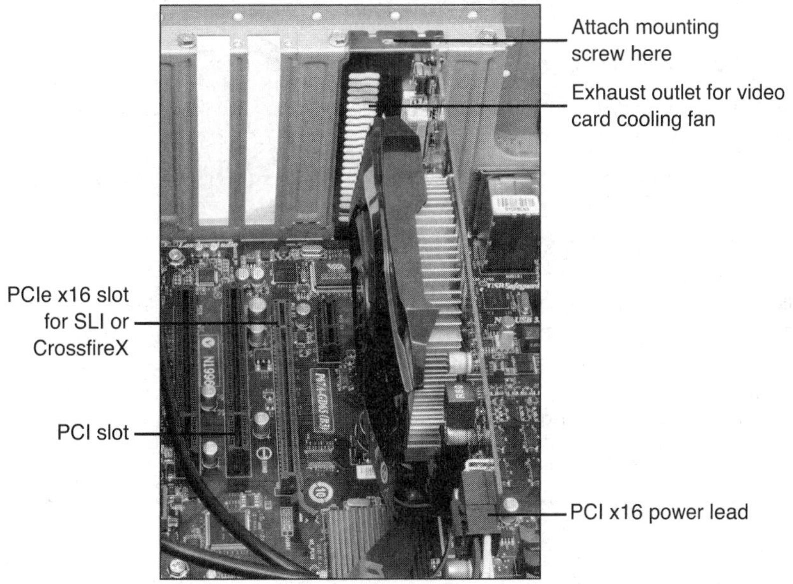

FIGURE 19.32   Installing a PCIe x16 video card that uses two slots and a PCIe x16 power lead.

If you are installing a second video card for use in an SLI or CrossFireX configuration, keep in mind that the second card might block the adjacent expansion slot. Note that in Figure 19.32 that there is a PCI slot next to the second PCIe x16 slot. However, when the second PCIe x16 card is installed (Figure 19.33), its cooling shroud blocks the space that the PCI card would have used. Thus, you might have fewer available slots than you expected.

Figure 19.33 illustrates the installation of a second two-slot PCIe x16 video card for SLI use.

SLI MIO bridge —

Fan shroud covers up PCI slot —

FIGURE 19.33 Two PCIe x16 video cards configured for SLI. Note the SLI bridge between the cards.

5. Use either the screw you removed during removal of the old card or the screw used in step 1 to fasten the card into place.

6. If you are installing two or more cards in an SLI or CrossFireX configuration, repeat steps 1–5 for the additional card(s).

7. If the SLI or CrossFireX configuration requires you to attach a bridge between the cards, attach the bridge.

8. Attach the video cable from the monitor to the proper connector at the rear of the monitor. If the card uses a DVI-I, HDMI, or DisplayPort connector and the monitor uses the standard 15-pin VGA connector, use an appropriate adapter (might be provided with the video card or available separately from stores that stock computer parts). If you're building a dual-display system, be sure to plug in your primary and secondary displays to the appropriate connectors.

Note

If you are replacing an existing video card (or switching from onboard video to an add-in video card), remove the existing installed video driver before powering down to install the new card. This helps prevent the system from improperly identifying the new video card and makes for a smoother upgrade. To do this, open the Windows Device Manager, select the existing display adapter, and select Remove or Uninstall. Do not reboot the system if asked; instead, power down and remove the existing video card.

After the entire system is assembled, when the system boots up, Windows should detect the new video card and automatically begin the driver installation process. At that point, follow the manufacturer's instructions for installing the latest video drivers for the new video card. After the video card drivers are installed, you can use the Windows Display properties to fine-tune its settings for resolution, color depth, or refresh rate if desired.

Installing Additional Expansion Cards

Many systems use additional expansion cards for networking, sound, or other functions. These cards are plugged in to the bus slots present on the motherboard. To install these cards, follow these steps:

1. Insert each card by holding it carefully by the edges, being sure not to touch the chips and circuitry. Put the bottom-edge finger connector into the appropriate open slot (usually PCI or PCI Express). Firmly press down on the top of the card, exerting even pressure, until it snaps into place.

2. Secure each card bracket with a screw.

3. Attach any internal cables you might have removed earlier from the cards.

4. If the card requires additional power, connect the appropriate power lead from the power supply.

If you have multiple slots to choose from, try to consider airflow when choosing the slot to install a particular card. In some cases you might want to leave blank slots between cards, or group all the cards away from any video cards that might be installed, because video cards generally create more heat than all the other cards combined.

Replacing the Cover and Connecting External Cables

Now the system should be nearly assembled. All that remains is installing the cover assembly and connecting any external devices that are cabled to the system. This normally includes a keyboard, mouse, monitor, speakers, and network cables. I usually don't like to install the case cover screws until I have tested the system and am sure everything is working properly.

System Startup

At this point, you are ready to power on the system for the first time. To prepare for this, connect the following:

- Keyboard
- Mouse
- Display
- Power

Note that I did not include connecting a network cable. I usually recommend you do that after the OS has been installed, along with any service packs, and after you have ensured you are either behind a router or have the OS's built-in firewall turned on.

Now that everything is connected, you can power up the system and run the BIOS Setup program. This enables you to configure the motherboard to access the installed devices and set the system date and time. The system POST (power-on self-test) also runs to determine whether any major problems exist. To run the BIOS Setup and configure the system, do the following:

1. Power on the monitor first and then the system unit. Observe the operation via the screen and listen for any beeps from the system speaker.

2. The system should automatically go through a POST consisting of video BIOS checking, a RAM test, and usually an installed component report. If a fatal error occurs during the POST, you might not see anything onscreen, and the system might beep several times, indicating a specific problem. Check the motherboard, BIOS documentation to determine what the beep codes

mean. A list of POST codes is included in Chapter 20. Systems that use UEFI might create an error log that can be viewed before the system starts or use beep codes for some types of errors.

3. If there are no fatal errors, you should see the POST display onscreen. Depending on the type of motherboard BIOS or UEFI used, such as Phoenix, AMI, Award, or others, you have to press a key to interrupt the normal boot sequence and get to the BIOS Setup program screens that enable you to enter important system information. Normally, the system indicates via the onscreen display which key to press to activate the BIOS or UEFI Setup program during the POST, but if not, check the motherboard manual for the key(s) to press to enter Setup. Common keys used to enter BIOS or UEFI Setup are F1, F2, Del, F10, Esc, and Ins.

◀◀   See the Chapter 5 section, "Running or Accessing the BIOS Setup Program," **p. 292**.

4. Press the appropriate key to enter the BIOS Setup when prompted. Because the POST in modern motherboards is so fast, it is easy to miss the time you are supposed to press the key, so I usually start tapping the key repeatedly just a second or two after powering on. In some cases this may generate a keyboard error message, which you can ignore as the BIOS Setup screen appears. You should now be in the BIOS Setup. If you didn't press the key in time, reset the system and try again.

5. Check the BIOS version reported on the main Setup screen and ensure that it is the latest version. If it isn't, now would be a good time to install the updated flash BIOS image. The easiest method to do a BIOS upgrade on newer systems is via a bootable CD containing the BIOS image. To do this, on another system visit the motherboard manufacturer website and download the bootable CD image (*.ISO) file. Burn this image to a CD, and then place the CD into the optical drive of the new system and reset it. Follow the prompts on the screen to complete the BIOS update.

Note

Many motherboards do not support bootable CD BIOS upgrades via SATA optical drives. In that situation, you need to temporarily install a PATA optical drive to complete the upgrade, or perform the upgrade via one of the other available procedures, such as via a Windows-based executable or a bootable USB flash drive.

6. Check the various BIOS Setup screens to ensure your processor and memory are being properly recognized and supported. Check CPU type, speed, cache, total RAM, dual channel mode, and so on.

7. Disable any ports or devices that will not be used, such as serial ports, parallel ports, consumer infrared ports, and so on.

8. Check to see that all the installed drives are being detected.

9. Check the Drive Configuration. Ensure that the system is set to AHCI at a minimum, or even better, ensure that it is set to RAID mode. I recommend RAID mode even if you don't plan to use RAID because it includes all AHCI functionality and allows for a future RAID migration without having to reinstall the OS or drivers. This is called "RAID Ready." Set the IDE (backward compatible) mode if you are installing an older OS that does not have AHCI or RAID drivers. This will unfortunately reduce driver performance because advanced SATA features such as NCQ (Native Command Queuing) will be disabled. Note: you cannot use IDE mode with an SSD.

10. Check Fan Control and Hardware Monitoring (called PC Health on some systems) to see that all fans are being recognized and that the fans are reporting proper rotational speeds. Also observe component temperatures. Note that some components such as the chipset ICH (I/O Controller Hub) are "designed" to run from 90°C to 115°C (up to 239°F), so high temperatures are normal and even expected for that chip.

11. Check Memory Configuration. I recommend leaving the default Auto settings, which will automatically set the memory timing according to the modules you have installed.

12. Check the Chipset Configuration. If you're running Windows Vista or newer, I recommend enabling the HPET (High Precision Event Timer) because it is supported in these versions of Windows, but not in Windows XP.

13. In the Security menu, enable VT (Virtualization Technology) if available. This allows virtualization software such as Virtual PC or VMware to use the hardware virtualization circuitry in the chip, which improves the performance of virtualized OSs and applications.

14. In the Power menu, check the ACPI Suspend State. Ensure that it is set to S3 (Suspend to RAM) instead of S1 (Sleep). The reason is that S3 uses virtually the same amount of power as being completely off, thus saving you up to $100 per year or more in energy costs per system!

15. In the Boot menu, check the boot order. Ensure that the optical or USB flash drive precedes the hard disk or solid-state drives, which will enable a successful OS installation from CD/DVD or bootable USB flash drive.

16. After you check all the settings in the BIOS Setup, follow the instructions onscreen or in the motherboard manual to save the settings and exit the Setup menu.

Installing the OS

At this point, if you are starting with a new drive, you must install the OS. If you are using a non-Windows OS, follow the documentation for the installation procedures.

On a newer system in which you are installing Windows, there isn't really anything you need to do, other than simply booting from the disc or flash drive (you might have to enable the optical or USB drive as a boot device in your BIOS Setup) and following the prompts to install the OS. Windows automatically recognizes whether the hard drive needs to be partitioned and formatted and allows you to do that at the beginning of the installation.

Windows comes with integrated drivers for most newer chipsets, so you should not need additional storage drivers in most cases. However, if the hard drive is not recognized at the start of the OS install, storage drivers are probably required. The good thing is that you don't have to supply them via floppy as with Windows XP; instead, you can supply them via optical disc or USB flash drive, which is much more convenient.

You can also install Windows from a bootable USB flash drive. Installing via a flash drive not only works faster than when using a DVD, but it also enables you to easily install Windows on systems that don't have an optical drive, such as netbooks. To create a bootable USB flash drive for installing Windows you need

- A 4GB (or larger) USB flash drive
- An original install DVD
- An ISO file creation tool, such as ImgBurn (www.imgburn.com)
- The Microsoft Windows 7 USB/DVD Download Tool (http://tinyurl.com/4qfdm4x)

Note

Despite the name, the Microsoft Windows 7 USB/DVD Download Tool works for Vista just as well as it does for Windows 7.

When you are ready, create an ISO file from your original install DVD using an ISO creation tool, such as ImgBurn, and then use the Windows USB/DVD Download Tool to copy the ISO file to the flash drive. When complete, you'll have a bootable flash drive that will work just like your original DVD for installing Windows.

To install Windows 8 from a flash drive, purchase the Windows 8 Pro upgrade from the Microsoft website and use the Install by Creating Media option. To learn more, see "How to Download Windows 8" at http://windows.microsoft.com/en-US/windows-8/how-to-download#1TC=t1. During the initial part of the installation, you can delete any existing partitions and create new ones if desired. On a drive with no partitions, if you simply tell the installer to install Windows into "unpartitioned space," the installer automatically creates and formats a partition using all the available space.

After you have the OS installed, I recommend installing the drivers. In general, older OSs have fewer drivers included on the installation disc, meaning you have to install more drivers after the OS is installed. This often includes chipset drivers for your motherboard, drivers for newer video cards, sound cards, network cards, and more. Of these, the motherboard chipset drivers are the most critical and should be installed first. A disc containing these drivers should have been included with your motherboard; insert this disc and follow the prompts to install the chipset drivers. Then install other drivers, such as video, sound, and network.

After the important drivers are installed, you should install any service packs that weren't already integrated into the OS install disc and finally any OS updates. For that last step, you'll probably need to connect the network cable and go online. If your computer uses a wireless connection, use the OS's wireless connection manager to connect to the wireless network, providing the SSID and encryption key as prompted. As long as you've installed the latest service pack, the built-in firewall is turned on by default. After the OS updates, you can install your favorite applications and put the system in service.

Troubleshooting New Installations

When the OS installation is complete, you should restart the system and it should boot from the drive where the OS was installed. If any problems exist, here are some basic items to check:

- If the system won't power up, check the power cord. If the cord is plugged into a power strip, make sure the strip is switched on. Usually, a power switch can be found on the front of the case, but some power supplies have a switch on the back as well. If the power supply has a 115/230V switch, make sure it is set properly for the power in your country (115V for the United States).

- Check to see whether the power switch is connected properly inside the case. There is a cable connection from the switch to the motherboard; check both ends to ensure that they are connected properly.

- Check the main power connector from the supply to the board. Make sure the connectors are seated fully, and ensure that they are plugged in with the correct orientation.

- If the system appears to be running but you don't see anything on the display, check the monitor to ensure that it is plugged in, turned on, and properly and securely connected to the video card. On displays with two or more signal sources, use the on-screen display (OSD) menu to choose the correct signal source (such as VGA or DVI, VGA or HDMI, and so on).

- Check the video card to ensure it is fully seated in the motherboard slot. Remove and reseat the video card, and try a different slot if possible.

- If the system beeps more than once, the BIOS may be reporting a fatal error of some type. See the BIOS Error code listings in Chapter 20 for more information on what these codes mean. Also, consult your motherboard documentation; look in the BIOS section for a table of error codes. Note that continuous beeps might indicate a stuck key on the keyboard.

- If a drive LED stays on continuously, the data cable is probably installed backward or is offset by some pins. Check that the stripe on the cable is properly oriented toward pin 1 on both the drive and board connector ends. Also, check the drive jumpers for proper master/slave relationships (applies to PATA drives only).

When you are sure that the system is up and running successfully, power it off and attach the chassis cover securely to the case. Now your new system should be ready for use.

PC Diagnostics, Testing, and Maintenance

PC Diagnostics

No matter how well built your PC is and how well written its software, problems can occur. Diagnostic software can help troubleshoot problems when your computer malfunctions or you suspect problems with an upgraded component or an entirely new system built from scratch. This chapter examines several types of diagnostic software, including the built-in POST (power-on self test) as well as commercial and open-source diagnostic software.

You also might find that your system problems are caused by a hardware malfunction and that you must open the computer case to perform repairs. This chapter examines the tools and testers used to upgrade and repair PCs—both the basic items every user should own and some of the more advanced devices.

Of course, the best way to deal with a problem is to prevent it from occurring in the first place. The preventive maintenance sections of this chapter describe the procedures you should perform on a regular basis to keep your system in good working order.

Diagnostics Software

Several types of diagnostic software are available for PCs. Some diagnostic functions are integrated into the PC hardware directly, whereas others take the form of operating system utilities or separate software products. This software, some of which is included with the system when purchased, can assist users in identifying many problems with a computer's components. The types of diagnostic software are as follows:

- **POST (power-on self test)**—This runs whenever a PC is turned on. These routines are contained within the motherboard ROM as well as ROMs on expansion cards.

- **Manufacturer-supplied diagnostics software**—Many of the larger manufacturers—especially high-end, name-brand manufacturers such as HP/Compaq, Dell, Lenovo, and others—offer or include special diagnostics software expressly designed for their systems. In most cases, these utilities are included with the system, or you can download them from the manufacturer's website at no charge. Some manufacturers write their own diagnostics, but most purchase the rights to an existing commercial package that is subsequently customized or privately labeled. In some systems, the diagnostic software is installed on a special partition on the hard drive and can be accessed during startup. This is a convenient way for manufacturers to ensure that users always have diagnostics available.

- **Peripheral diagnostics software**—Many hardware devices ship with specialized diagnostics software designed to test their particular functions. RAID adapters, for example, include configuration and diagnostic functions in the card's ROM BIOS that you can access with a keystroke at boot time. Other devices or adapters might provide a diagnostic program or disk, usually included with the drivers for the device.

- **Operating system diagnostics software**—Operating systems, such as Windows, Linux, and so on, often include a variety of diagnostic software utilities designed to identify and monitor the performance of various components in the computer.

- **Commercial diagnostics software**—A number of manufacturers make general-purpose diagnostics software for PCs. This type of software is often bundled with other system maintenance and repair tools to form a general PC software toolkit.

- **Free/open-source diagnostics software**—A large number of free or open-source diagnostic programs are available for PCs, including small task-specific programs as well as complete collections of diagnostics in bootable form.

The POST

When IBM began shipping the original PC in 1981, it included safety features that had never been seen in a personal computer. These features were the POST and parity-checked memory. Although parity-checked or even error-correcting code (ECC) memory is no longer available in most non-server chipsets, every PC still executes a POST when you turn it on. The following sections provide more detail on the POST, a series of program routines buried in the motherboard ROM-BIOS chip that tests all the main system components at power-on time. This series of routines is partially responsible for the delay when you turn on your PC; the computer executes the POST before loading the operating system.

These tests check the primary components in your system, such as the CPU, ROM, motherboard support circuitry, memory, and major peripherals such as the expansion chassis. These tests are brief and are designed to catch hard (not intermittent) errors. The POST procedures are not very thorough compared to available disk-based diagnostics. The POST process provides error or warning messages whenever it encounters a faulty component.

Although the diagnostics performed by the system POST are not thorough, they are the first line of defense, especially when it comes to detecting severe motherboard problems. If the POST encounters a problem severe enough to keep the system from operating properly, it halts the system boot process and generates an error message that often identifies the cause of the problem. These POST-detected problems are sometimes called *fatal errors* because they prevent the system from booting.

Systems that use UEFI firmware also perform diagnostics tests, but depending upon the specific firmware in use, error messages may be stored in event logs, and beep codes may be used for some errors.

How Errors Are Displayed

The POST tests normally provide three types of output messages: audio codes, onscreen text messages, and hexadecimal numeric codes that are sent to an I/O port address.

POST errors can be displayed in the following three ways:

- **Beep codes**—Heard through the speaker or beeper attached to the motherboard. Note that some systems do not include a speaker.
- **POST checkpoint codes**—Hexadecimal checkpoint codes sent to an I/O port address. A special card plugged into an available expansion slot is required to view these codes.
- **Onscreen messages**—Error messages displayed onscreen after the video adapter is initialized.

Systems that use UEFI firmware might use beep and checkpoint codes but also store error messages in event logs.

BIOS POST Beep Codes

Beep codes are used for fatal errors only, which are errors that occur so early in the process that the video card and other devices are not yet functional. Because no display is available, these codes take the form of a series of beeps that identify the faulty component. When your computer is functioning normally, you may hear one or two short beeps when the system starts up at the completion of the POST, although depending on the system, it may not make any sounds at all if things are normal. If a problem is detected, a different number of beeps sound, sometimes in a combination of short and long tones. Some implementations of UEFI firmware also use POST codes to report errors.

BIOS POST Checkpoint Codes

POST checkpoint codes are hexadecimal numeric codes written by POST routines to I/O port address 80h as each major step is begun. These are often simply called POST *codes*. These POST codes can only be read by a special adapter card plugged into one of the system slots. These cards originally were designed for system manufacturers to use for burn-in testing of the motherboard. Several companies make these cards available to technicians; if you search for "post code card," you will find many that are available.

POST checkpoint codes can track the system's progress through the boot process from power-on right up to the point at which the bootstrap loader runs (when the operating system load begins). When you plug a POST code reader card into a slot, during the POST you see two-digit hexadecimal numbers flash on the card's display. If the system stops unexpectedly or hangs, you can identify the test that was in progress during the hang from the two-digit code. This step usually helps to identify the malfunctioning component.

Originally, most POST reader cards plugged into the 8-bit connector that is a part of the ISA or Enhanced Industry Standard Architecture (EISA) bus. The motherboards found in modern PCs have no ISA slots, so obviously an ISA POST card won't work. Fortunately, the companies that make POST cards make PCI or even PCI Express versions (see Figure 20.1). There are even Mini PCI and Mini PCI Express cards available for testing laptop motherboards.

AMI markets a USB-based diagnostic device called the AMIDebug RX to display checkpoint and error codes for its AMIBIOS and Aptio 4.x firmware.

Note

You can find listings for additional POST checkpoint codes at www.postcodemaster.com. Also, see Chapter 5, "BIOS," to learn more about working with your BIOS. Remember to consult your motherboard documentation for codes specific to your BIOS version.

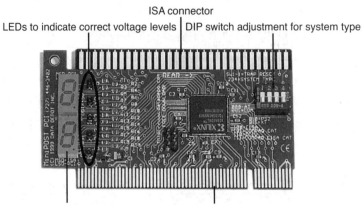

ISA connector

LEDs to indicate correct voltage levels | DIP switch adjustment for system type

Two-digit LED display of POST hex codes   PCI connector

FIGURE 20.1 The PC Diag Inc PCISA FlipPOST diagnostics card works with both PCI- and ISA-based systems, and it tests motherboard voltage levels.

BIOS POST Onscreen Messages

Onscreen messages are brief messages that attempt to indicate a specific failure. These messages can be displayed only after the point at which the video adapter card and display have been initialized.

These different types of error messages are BIOS dependent and vary among BIOS manufacturers, and even in some cases among different BIOSs from the same manufacturer. The following sections list the codes used by the most popular ROM BIOS versions (AMI, Award, Phoenix, and IBM BIOS), but you should consult your motherboard or ROM BIOS manufacturer for the codes specific to your board and BIOS.

Most POST code cards come with documentation listing the POST checkpoint codes for various BIOS versions. If your BIOS is different from what I have listed here, consult the documentation for your BIOS or the information that came with your particular POST card.

AMI BIOS POST Error Codes

Table 20.1 lists the beep codes that the AMI BIOS from American Megatrends uses.

Table 20.1   AMI BIOS POST Beep Codes

Beeps	Error Description	Action
1	Memory Refresh Error	Clean the memory contacts and reseat the modules. Remove all modules except the first bank. Replace the memory, power supply, and motherboard.
2	Memory Parity Error	Clean the memory contacts and reseat the modules. Remove all modules except the first bank. Replace the memory, power supply, and motherboard.
3	Base 64KB Memory	Clean the memory contacts and reseat the modules.
4	Timer Error	Check for proper motherboard installation, loose screws, foreign objects causing shorts, and over-tightened screws. Replace the motherboard.
5	Processor Error	Check for proper motherboard installation, loose screws, foreign objects causing shorts, and over-tightened screws. Make sure the processor and heatsink are installed properly; remove and reseat them. Replace the processor. Replace the motherboard.

Beeps	Error Description	Action
6	8042 – Gate A20 Error	Check for proper motherboard installation, loose screws, foreign objects causing shorts, and over-tightened screws. Replace the keyboard, motherboard, and processor.
7	Processor Exception Interrupt Error	Make sure the processor and heatsink are installed properly; remove and reseat them. Replace the processor. Replace the motherboard.
8	Display Memory Read/Write Error	Check the video card for proper installation. Try replacing the video card memory, and replace the video card. Replace the motherboard.
9	ROM Checksum Error Register Read/Write Error	Try reseating the motherboard ROM chip. Try reflashing the motherboard ROM. Replace the motherboard.
10	CMOS Shutdown	Replace the CMOS battery. Replace the motherboard.
11	Cache Memory Bad	Make sure cache settings in BIOS Setup are properly configured. Replace the processor. Replace the motherboard.
1 long, 3 short	Conventional/Extended Memory Error	Clean the memory contacts and reseat the modules. Remove all modules except the first bank. Replace the memory, power supply, and motherboard.
1 long, 8 short	Display/Retrace Error	Check the video card for proper installation. Try replacing the video card memory. Replace the video card. Replace the motherboard.

AMI BIOS codes used by permission of American Megatrends, Inc.

For a listing of Aptio 4.x checkpoint and error codes (Aptio is AMI's UEFI replacement for BIOS), see www.ami.com/support/doc/AMI_Aptio_4.x_Status_Codes_PUB.pdf.

Phoenix Award BIOS, Award BIOS, Phoenix FirstBIOS

Phoenix Technologies has owned the former Award Software for a number of years but continues to market the Award BIOS, currently as Phoenix Award BIOS. This BIOS has also been referred to as the Phoenix FirstBIOS. Table 20.2 lists beep codes, and Table 20.3 lists POST error messages for these BIOS versions.

Table 20.2   AwardBIOS/Phoenix FirstBIOS POST Beep Codes

Beeps	Error Description	Action
1 long, 2 short	Video Card Error	Check the video card for proper installation. Try removing and reinserting the video card. Replace the video card. Replace the motherboard.
1 long, 3 short	Video Card Error	Check the video card for proper installation. Try removing and reinserting the video card. Replace the video card. Replace the motherboard.
Continuous beeps	Memory Error	Clean the memory contacts and reseat the modules. Remove all modules except the first bank. Replace the memory, power supply, and motherboard.
High-frequency beeps while system operating	Overheating CPU	Check CPU active heatsink and case fan(s) for proper operation. Replace fans that are not working or are spinning too slowly. Use PC Health or hardware monitor in BIOS to check active heatsink (CPU fan) speed. Check airflow through case. Clean dirty or blocked air intakes or exhaust ports.
Repeating high/low beeps5555	CPU	Incorrect CPU installation; CPU may be damaged or overheating. Check CPU active heatsink for proper operation. Use PC Health or hardware monitor in BIOS to check active heatsink (CPU fan) speed.

Table 20.3   AwardBIOS POST Onscreen Error Messages

Message	Description
BIOS ROM checksum error - System halted	The checksum of the BIOS code in the BIOS chip is incorrect, indicating the BIOS code might have become corrupt. Contact your system dealer to replace the BIOS.
CMOS battery failed	The CMOS battery is no longer functional. Contact your system dealer for a replacement battery.
CMOS checksum error - Defaults loaded	Checksum of CMOS is incorrect, so the system loads the default equipment configuration. A checksum error can indicate that CMOS has become corrupt. This error might have been caused by a weak battery. Check the battery and replace if necessary.
CPU at nnnn	Displays the running speed of the CPU.
Display switch is set incorrectly	The display switch on the motherboard can be set to either monochrome or color. This message indicates the switch is set to a different setting than indicated in Setup. Determine which setting is correct; then either turn off the system and change the jumper or enter Setup and change the VIDEO selection.
Press ESC to skip memory test	The user can press Esc to skip the full memory test.
Floppy disk(s) fail	Can't find or initialize the floppy drive controller or the drive. Make sure the controller is installed correctly. If no floppy drives are installed, be sure the Diskette Drive selection in Setup is set to NONE or AUTO.
HARD DISK initializing Please wait a moment	Some hard drives require extra time to initialize.
HARD DISK INSTALL FAILURE	Can't find or initialize the hard drive controller or the drive. Make sure the controller is installed correctly. If no hard drives are installed, be sure the Hard Drive selection in Setup is set to NONE.
Hard disk(s) diagnosis fail	The system might run specific disk diagnostic routines. This message appears if if one or more hard disks return an error when the diagnostics run.
Keyboard error or no keyboard present	Can't initialize the keyboard. Make sure the keyboard is attached correctly and no keys are pressed during POST. To purposely configure the system without a keyboard, set the error halt condition in Setup to HALT ON ALL, BUT KEYBOARD. The BIOS then ignores the missing keyboard during POST.
Keyboard is locked out - Unlock the key	This message usually indicates that one or more keys have been pressed during the keyboard tests. Be sure no objects are resting on the keyboard.
Memory Test:	This message displays during a full memory test, counting down the memory areas being tested.
Memory test fail	If POST detects an error during memory testing, additional information appears, giving specifics about the type and location of the memory error.

Message	Description
`Override enabled - Defaults loaded`	If the system can't boot using the current CMOS configuration, the BIOS can override the current configuration with a set of BIOS defaults designed for the most stable, minimal-performance system operations.
`Press TAB to show POST screen`	System OEMs might replace Phoenix Technologies' AwardBIOS POST display with their own proprietary displays. Including this message in the OEM display permits the operator to switch between the OEM display and the default POST display.
`Primary master hard disk fail`	POST detects an error in the primary master IDE hard drive.
`Primary slave hard disk fail`	POST detects an error in the secondary master IDE hard drive.
`Resuming from disk, Press TAB to show POST screen`	Phoenix Technologies offers a save-to-disk feature for notebook computers. This message might appear when the operator restarts the system after a save-to-disk shutdown.
`Secondary master hard disk fail`	POST detects an error in the primary slave IDE hard drive.
`Secondary slave hard disk fail`	POST detects an error in the secondary slave IDE hard drive.

PhoenixBIOS POST Error Codes

There have been several versions of the Phoenix BIOS over the years. Phoenix BIOS versions manufactured before 1994 supported 286 through 486 processors and used the beep codes shown in Table 20.4.

Table 20.4 PhoenixBIOS for 486 and Earlier Processors (Pre-1994)

Beeps	Error Description	Action
1-2	Video Card Error	Check the video card for proper installation. Try replacing the video card memory, and replace the video card. Replace the motherboard.
1-3	CMOS RAM Read/Write Error	Replace the CMOS battery. Replace the motherboard.
1-1-4	ROM Checksum Error	Try reseating the motherboard ROM chip. Try reflashing the motherboard ROM. Replace the motherboard.
1-2-1	Timer Error	Check for proper motherboard installation, loose screws, foreign objects causing shorts, and over-tightened screws. Replace the motherboard.
1-2-2	DMA Initialization Error	Check for proper motherboard installation, loose screws, foreign objects causing shorts, and over-tightened screws. Replace the motherboard.
1-2-3	DMA Page Register Read/Write Error	Check for proper motherboard installation, loose screws, foreign objects causing shorts, and over-tightened screws. Replace the motherboard.
1-3-1	RAM Refresh Verification Error	Clean the memory contacts and reseat the modules. Remove all modules except the first bank. Replace the memory. Replace the power supply. Replace the motherboard.
1-3-3	First 64KB RAM Multibit Data Line Error	Clean the memory contacts and reseat the modules. Remove all modules except the first bank. Replace the memory, power supply, and motherboard.

Table 20.4 Continued

Beeps	Error Description	Action
1-3-4	First 64KB RAM Odd/Even Logic Error	Clean the memory contacts and reseat the modules. Remove all modules except the first bank. Replace the memory, power supply, and mother-board.
1-4-1	First 64KB RAM Address Line Error	Clean the memory contacts and reseat the modules. Remove all modules except the first bank. Replace the memory, power supply, and mother-board.
1-4-2	First 64KB RAM Parity Error	Clean the memory contacts and reseat the modules. Remove all modules except the first bank. Replace the memory. Replace the power supply. Replace the motherboard.
2-x-x*	First 64KB RAM Error	Clean the memory contacts and reseat the modules. Remove all modules except the first bank. Replace the memory. Replace the power supply. Replace the motherboard.
3-1-1	Slave DMA Register Error	Check for proper motherboard installation, loose screws, foreign objects causing shorts, and over-tightened screws. Replace the motherboard.
3-1-2	Master DMA Register Error	Check for proper motherboard installation, loose screws, foreign objects causing shorts, and over-tightened screws. Replace the motherboard.
3-1-3	Master Interrupt Mask Register Error	Check for proper motherboard installation, loose screws, foreign objects causing shorts, and over-tightened screws. Replace the motherboard.
3-1-4	Slave Interrupt Mask Register Error	Check for proper motherboard installation, loose screws, foreign objects causing shorts, and over-tightened screws. Replace the motherboard.
3-2-4	Keyboard Controller Error	Check for proper motherboard installation, loose screws, foreign objects causing shorts, and over-tightened screws. Replace the keyboard. Replace the motherboard. Replace the processor.
3-3-4	Screen Initialization Error	Check the video card for proper installation. Try replacing the video card memory, and replace the video card. Replace the motherboard.
3-4-1	Screen Retrace Error	Check the video card for proper installation. Try replacing the video card memory, and replace the video card. Replace the motherboard.
3-4-2	Video ROM Error	Check the video card for proper installation. Try replacing the video card memory, and replace the video card. Replace the motherboard.
4-2-1	Timer Interrupt Error	Check for proper motherboard installation, loose screws, foreign objects causing shorts, and over-tightened screws. Replace the motherboard.
4-2-2	Shutdown Error	Check for proper motherboard installation, loose screws, foreign objects causing shorts, and over-tightened screws. Replace the keyboard. Replace the motherboard. Replace the processor.
4-2-3	Gate A20 Error	Check for proper motherboard installation, loose screws, foreign objects causing shorts, and over-tightened screws. Replace the keyboard. Replace the motherboard. Replace the processor.
4-2-4	Unexpected Interrupt In Protected Mode	Check for a bad expansion card. Check for proper motherboard instal-lation, loose screws, foreign objects causing shorts, and over-tightened screws. Replace the motherboard.

Beeps	Error Description	Action
4-3-1	RAM Address Error >FFFh	Clean the memory contacts and reseat the modules. Remove all modules except the first bank. Replace the memory. Replace the power supply. Replace the motherboard.
4-3-3	Interval Timer Channel 2 Error	Check for proper motherboard installation, loose screws, foreign objects causing shorts, and over-tightened screws. Replace the motherboard.
4-3-4	Real Time Clock Error	Replace the CMOS battery. Replace the motherboard.
4-4-1	Serial Port Error	Reset the port configuration in BIOS Setup. Disable the port.
4-4-2	Parallel Port Error	Reset the port configuration in BIOS Setup. Disable the port.
4-4-3	Math Coprocessor Error	Check for proper motherboard installation, loose screws, foreign objects causing shorts, and over-tightened screws. Make sure the processor and heatsink are installed properly; remove and reseat them. Replace the processor. Replace the motherboard.
Low 1-1-2	System Board Select Error	Check for proper motherboard installation, loose screws, foreign objects causing shorts, and over-tightened screws. Make sure the processor and heatsink are installed properly; remove and reseat them. Replace the processor. Replace the motherboard.
Low 1-1-3	Extended CMOS RAM Error	Replace the CMOS battery. Replace the motherboard.

Second and third codes can be one to four beeps each, indicating different failed bits within the first 64KB of RAM.

PhoenixBIOS Version 4 (the most recent edition is Version 4, Revision 6.0) supports Pentium and newer processors. The beep codes for this version are shown in Table 20.5.

Table 20.5 PhoenixBIOS Version 4 and Later POST Beep Codes

Beeps	Error Description	Description/Action
1-2-2-3	BIOS ROM Checksum Error	Try reseating the motherboard ROM chip. Try reflashing the motherboard ROM. Replace the motherboard.
1-3-1-1	DRAM Refresh Error	Clean the memory contacts and reseat the modules. Remove all modules except the first bank. Replace the memory. Replace the power supply. Replace the motherboard.
1-3-1-3	8742 Keyboard Controller Error	Check for proper motherboard installation, loose screws, foreign objects causing shorts, and over-tightened screws. Replace the keyboard. Replace the motherboard. Replace the processor.
1-3-4-1	Memory Address Line Error	Clean the memory contacts and reseat the modules. Remove all modules except the first bank. Replace the memory. Replace the power supply. Replace the motherboard.
1-3-4-3	Memory Low Byte Data Error	Clean the memory contacts and reseat the modules. Remove all modules except the first bank. Replace the memory. Replace the power supply. Replace the motherboard.

Table 20.5   Continued

Beeps	Error Description	Description/Action
1-4-1-1	Memory High Byte Data Error	Clean the memory contacts and reseat the modules. Remove all modules except the first bank. Replace the memory. Replace the power supply. Replace the motherboard.
2-1-2-3	ROM Copyright Error	Try reseating the motherboard ROM chip. Try reflashing the motherboard ROM. Replace the motherboard.
2-2-3-1	Unexpected Interrupts	Check for a bad expansion card. Check for proper motherboard installation, loose screws, foreign objects causing shorts, and over-tightened screws. Replace the motherboard.
1-2	Video Card Error	Check the video card for proper installation. Try replacing the video card memory, and replace the video card. Replace the motherboard.

IBM BIOS POST Error Codes

The original IBM PC and AT systems used BIOSs developed by IBM. However, more recent IBM systems use BIOS products licensed from other vendors. Table 20.6 lists the beep codes for the IBM BIOS.

Table 20.6   IBM BIOS Beep Codes

Audio Code	Description
1 short beep	Normal POST—system okay
2 short beeps	POST error—view code onscreen
No beep	Power supply, motherboard
Continuous beep	Power supply, motherboard
Repeating short beeps	Power supply, motherboard
1 long, 1 short beep	Motherboard
1 long, 2 short beeps	Video card (MDA/CGA)
1 long, 3 short beeps	Video card (EGA/VGA)
3 long beeps	3270 keyboard card

IBM BIOS beep and alphanumeric error codes used by permission of IBM.

Table 20.7 lists the numeric error codes the IBM BIOS displays.

Table 20.7   IBM BIOS POST/Diagnostics Display Error Codes

Code	Description
1xx	System board errors
2xx	Memory (RAM) errors
3xx	Keyboard errors

Code	Description
4xx	Monochrome Display Adapter (MDA) errors
4xx	PS/2 system board parallel port errors (PS/2 systems only)
5xx	Color Graphics Adapter (CGA) errors
6xx	Floppy drive/controller errors
7xx	Math coprocessor errors
9xx	Parallel printer adapter errors
10xx	Alternate parallel printer adapter errors
11xx	Primary Async Communications (Serial COM1:) errors
12xx	Alternate Async Communications (Serial COM2:, COM3:, and COM4:) errors
13xx	Game control adapter errors
14xx	Matrix printer errors
15xx	Synchronous Data Link Control (SDLC) Communications adapter errors
16xx	Display Station Emulation Adapter (DSEA) errors (5520, 525x)
17xx	ST-506/412 fixed disk and controller errors
18xx	I/O expansion unit errors
19xx	3270 PC attachment card errors
20xx	Binary Synchronous Communications (BSC) adapter errors
21xx	Alternate Binary Synchronous Communications (BSC) adapter errors
22xx	Cluster adapter errors
23xx	Plasma monitor adapter errors
24xx	Enhanced graphics adapter (EGA) or video graphics array (VGA) errors
25xx	Alternate Enhanced Graphics Adapter (EGA) errors
26xx	XT or AT/370 370-M (memory) and 370-P (processor) adapter errors
27xx	XT or AT/370 3277-EM (emulation) adapter errors
28xx	3278/79 emulation adapter or 3270 connection adapter errors
29xx	Color/graphics printer errors
30xx	Primary PC network adapter errors
31xx	Secondary PC network adapter errors
32xx	3270 PC or AT display and programmed symbols adapter errors
33xx	Compact printer errors
35xx	Enhanced display station emulation adapter (EDSEA) errors
36xx	General-purpose interface bus (GPIB) adapter errors
37xx	System board SCSI controller errors

Table 20.7   Continued

Code	Description
38xx	Data acquisition adapter errors
39xx	Professional graphics adapter (PGA) errors
44xx	5278 display attachment unit and 5279 display errors
45xx	IEEE interface adapter (IEEE 488) errors
46xx	A real-time interface coprocessor (ARTIC) multiport/2 adapter errors
48xx	Internal modem errors
49xx	Alternate internal modem errors
50xx	PC-convertible LCD errors
51xx	PC-convertible portable printer errors
56xx	Financial communication system errors
70xx	PhoenixBIOS/chipset unique error codes
71xx	Voice communications adapter (VCA) errors
73xx	3 1/2-inch external disk drive errors
74xx	IBM PS/2 display adapter (VGA Card) errors
74xx	8514/A display adapter errors
76xx	4216 PagePrinter adapter errors
84xx	PS/2 speech adapter errors
85xx	2MB XMA memory adapter or XMA adapter/A errors
86xx	PS/2 pointing device (mouse) errors
89xx	Musical Instrument Digital Interface (MIDI) adapter errors
91xx	IBM 3363 write-once read multiple (WORM) optical drive/adapter errors
96xx	SCSI adapter with cache (32-bit) errors
100xx	Multiprotocol adapter/A errors
101xx	300/1200bps internal modem/A errors
104xx	ESDI or MCA IDE fixed disk or adapter errors
107xx	5 1/4-inch external disk drive or adapter errors
112xx	SCSI adapter (16-bit without cache) errors
113xx	System board SCSI adapter (16-bit) errors
129xx	Processor complex (CPU board) errors
149xx	P70/P75 plasma display and adapter errors
152xx	XGA display adapter/A errors
164xx	120MB internal tape drive errors

Code	Description
165xx	6157 streaming tape drive or tape attachment adapter errors
166xx	Primary Token-Ring network adapter errors
167xx	Alternate Token-Ring network adapter errors
180xx	PS/2 wizard adapter errors
185xx	DBCS Japanese display adapter/A errors
194xx	80286 memory-expansion option memory-module errors
200xx	Image adapter/A errors
208xx	Unknown SCSI device errors
209xx	SCSI removable disk errors
210xx	SCSI fixed disk errors
211xx	SCSI tape drive errors
212xx	SCSI printer errors
213xx	SCSI processor errors
214xx	SCSI write-once read multiple (WORM) drive errors
215xx	SCSI CD-ROM drive errors
216xx	SCSI scanner errors
217xx	SCSI magneto optical drive errors
218xx	SCSI jukebox changer errors
219xx	SCSI communications errors
243xxxx	XGA-2 adapter/A errors
I998xxxx	Dynamic configuration select (DCS) information codes
I99900xx	Initial microcode load (IML) error
I99903xx	No bootable device, initial program load (IPL) errors
I99904xx	IML-to-system mismatch
I99906xx	IML (boot) errors

IBM BIOS beep and alphanumeric error codes used by permission of IBM.

IBM/Lenovo Beep and Error Codes

IBM sold its Personal Computing Division to Lenovo in May 2005. Recent IBM and Lenovo systems use different beep codes than the original IBM PC and AT. Table 20.8 lists these beep codes.

Table 20.8 IBM/Lenovo BIOS POST/Diagnostics Display Error Codes

Audio Code	Description	Recommended Action/ Subsystem to Check
1-1-3	CMOS read/write error.	1. Run Setup. 2. System board.
1-1-4	ROM BIOS check error.	1. System board.
1-2-X	DMA error.	1. System board.
1-3-X	Memory module error.	1. Memory module. 2. System board.
1-4-4	Keyboard error.	1. Keyboard. 2. System board.
1-4-X	Error detected in first 64KB of RAM.	1. Memory module. 2. System board.
2-1-1, 2-1-2	Setup information may not be valid.	1. Run Setup. 2. System board.
2-1-X	First 64KB of RAM failed.	1. Memory module. 2. System board.
2-2-2	Video memory error.	1. Video adapter (if installed). 2. System board.
2-2-X	First 64KB of RAM failed.	1. Memory module. 2. System board.
2-3-X	Memory failure.	1. Memory module. 2. System board.
2-4-X	Setup or memory failure.	1. Run Setup. 2. Memory module. 3. System board.
3-1-X	DMA register failed.	1. System board.
3-2-4	Keyboard controller failed.	1. System board. 2. Keyboard.
3-3-4	Screen initialization failed.	1. Video adapter (if installed). 2. System board. 3. Display.
3-4-1	Screen retrace test detected an error.	1. Video adapter (if installed). 2. System board. 3. Display.
3-4-2	POST is searching for video ROM.	1. Video adapter (if installed). 2. System board

Audio Code	Description	Recommended Action/ Subsystem to Check
4	Video adapter failed.	1. Video adapter (if installed). 2. System board.
One long and one short beep during POST	Base 640KB memory error RAM error.	1. Memory module. 2. System board.
One long and two or three short beeps during POST	Video error.	1. Video adapter (if installed). 2. System board.
Three short beeps during POST	System board or memory problem.	1. Memory module. 2. System board.
Continuous beep	System board problem.	1. System board.
Repeating short beeps	Keyboard stuck key or cable problem.	1. Keyboard stuck key 2. Keyboard cable. 3. System board.
All other beep code sequences	System board problem.	1. System board.

IBM BIOS beep and alphanumeric error codes used by permission of IBM.

Peripheral Diagnostics

Many types of diagnostic software are used with specific hardware products. This software can be integrated into the hardware (or firmware), included on a disc with the hardware purchase, or available for download from the hardware manufacturer.

Many network interface adapters, for example, are equipped with their own diagnostics, designed to test their own specialized functions.

Operating System Diagnostics

When Windows encounters severe problems such as malware that corrupts or interferes with system operation, bugs in drivers or other low-level software, inconsistencies in data necessary for operation, or even hardware defects, the system is halted or shut down in a condition that is technically called a *bug check*. Bug checks are also known as stop errors, kernel errors, trap errors, fatal system errors, and system crashes, and because the error information is normally displayed on a blue text-mode screen, they are also informally known as blue-screen or BSOD (Blue Screen Of Death) errors. When these errors occur, in addition to the blue-screen text, Windows normally saves a memory dump file and then automatically restarts the system.

Unfortunately, the automatic restart makes it almost impossible to read the blue-screen error text, so I recommend reconfiguring the system failure and recovery options in Windows to disable the automatic restart. To do this manually, select Start, and in either the Run or Start Search dialog box that appears, enter the text **sysdm.cpl**, and click OK. In the System Properties window, select the Advanced tab, Startup and Recovery, Settings, System Failure; then uncheck the Automatically Restart box. Alternatively, to accomplish the same thing, you can change the setting directly by entering the following command in either the Start, Run box or at a command prompt:

```
wmic recoveros set AutoReboot = False
```

With the automatic restart disabled, if a blue-screen error occurs you will be able to view (and record) the text on the screen before restarting the system. When you're looking at blue-screen errors, the hexadecimal number following the word STOP is called the bug check or stop error code, and it indicates the cause of the problem. For more information, Microsoft has provided a detailed list of bug check codes, along with explanations and troubleshooting information, at http://msdn.microsoft.com/en-us/library/hh994433.aspx.

Although the bug check (stop error) code by itself is very useful, in many cases it would be helpful to have even more information. By using the Debugging Tools for Windows, you can examine the memory dump file created when the stop error occurred and find a great deal more information about exactly what might have caused the crash. For information on where to get the Debugging Tools for Windows, as well as how to use them, see the MSKB article "How to Read the Small Memory Dump Files That Windows Creates for Debugging" at http://support.microsoft.com/kb/315263.

Stop errors can be caused by hardware errors (such as memory problems), malware, or even improper hardware or software configuration. For general troubleshooting of Windows bug check (stop error/blue screen) codes, I recommend you follow these suggestions:

- If any hardware was recently installed in the system, try removing it.
- If any software was recently installed, try uninstalling it.
- If any drivers, updates, or hotfixes were recently installed, try rolling back, removing, or updating them.
- Ensure that the system is free from malware such as viruses, rootkits, and spyware/adware.
- Check with the motherboard manufacturer to see if an updated BIOS is available.
- Make sure that the processor, expansion cards, memory modules, and so on are fully seated.
- Make sure that all cables are fully connected.
- Make sure that the operating system has the latest service pack and critical updates installed.
- Check the System Log and Application Log in the Windows Event Viewer to see if any additional error messages have been logged recently. For more information on the Event Viewer, see either http://support.microsoft.com/kb/308427 (Windows XP) or http://windows.microsoft.com/en-US/windows7/Open-Event-Viewer (Windows 7 and Windows 8).

Commercial Diagnostics Software

A large number of commercial third-party diagnostics programs are available for PC systems. These commercial programs are used by technicians to perform testing of new systems (often called *burn-in testing*) or testing of existing systems either in the shop or in the field.

Here are some of the programs available:

- **AMIDiag Suite**—www.ami.com
- **Micro-Scope**—http://micro2000pcdiagnostics.com/
- **PC Diag Professional Suite**—www.pc-diagnostics.com
- **PC-Doctor Service Center**—www.pcdservicecenter.com
- **Pc-Check**—www.eurosoft-uk.com/
- **PC-Technician**—www.windsortech.com
- **QuickTechPRO**—www.uxd.com/qtpro.shtml

Unfortunately, these programs can be expensive, and they are often designed more for the professional technician rather than home or small business users. For most users, open-source or otherwise free diagnostics provide excellent results.

Free/User Supported Diagnostics

Numerous free or user supported diagnostic programs are available, covering everything from processors to memory, disk drives, and virtually all other components in a PC. Over the years, several people have collected and organized this software, creating comprehensive collections of tools that could be used to troubleshoot systems. The best of these collections are the Ultimate Boot CD (http://ultimatebootcd.com) and the Ultimate Boot CD for Windows www.ubcd4win.com).

These bootable CD collections of useful utilities include diagnostics, testing, troubleshooting, and benchmarking software that is ideal for testing both new and old systems. A key feature of these discs is that they are bootable, meaning you can test a system completely independently of the existing operating system and drivers. This allows you to more accurately and efficiently troubleshoot actual hardware problems.

When building a new system, it is desirable to test the system to see if it is working properly. The term *burn-in testing* is often used to describe running stress tests or diagnostics on a new piece of equipment to screen for failures. The idea is to flush out early failures, so burn-in tests are usually designed to be as stressful as possible. This usually means running tests that are as hard as possible on the equipment, including running them under maximum temperatures and loads. Two of the programs I recommend for burn-in testing are GIMPS (www.mersenne.org/freesoft) and OCCT (www.ocbase.com).

When you are running GIMPs (also known as Prime95), under the Options menu select Torture Test. This causes the program to fully load all the processors and processor cores in the system for maximum stress testing. While doing this, I also like to run the free SpeedFan (http://almico.com/speedfan.php) or HWMonitor (www.cpuid.com/softwares/hwmonitor.html) program to monitor the temperatures of the processor and other components in the system. Stress testing like this is a good way to ensure that everything is working properly in both new and old systems.

The Boot Process

The term *boot* comes from the word *bootstrap* and describes the method by which the PC becomes operational. Just as you pull on a large boot by the small strap attached to the back, a PC loads a large operating system by first loading a small program that can then pull the operating system into memory. The chain of events begins with the application of power and finally results in a fully functional computer system with software loaded and running. Each event is triggered by the event before it and initiates the event after it.

Tracing the system boot process might help you find the location of a problem if you examine the error messages the system displays when the problem occurs. If you see an error message that is displayed by only a particular program, you can be sure the program in question was at least loaded and partially running. Combine this information with the knowledge of the boot sequence, and you can at least tell how far the system's startup procedure had progressed before the problem occurred. You usually should look at whichever files or disk areas were being accessed during the failure in the boot process. Error messages displayed during the boot process and those displayed during normal system operation can be hard to decipher. However, the first step in decoding an error message is knowing where the message came from—which program actually generated or displayed it. The following programs are capable of displaying error messages during the boot process:

OS Independent

- Motherboard ROM BIOS
- Adapter card ROM BIOS extensions

- Master (partition) boot record (MBR)
- Volume boot record (VBR)

OS Dependent

- System files
- Device drivers
- Programs run at startup

The first portion of the startup sequence is *operating system independent*, which means these steps are the same for all PCs no matter which operating system is installed. The latter portion of the boot sequence is *operating system dependent*, which means those steps can vary depending on which operating system is installed or being loaded. The following sections examine both the operating system–independent startup sequence and the operating system–dependent startup process for various operating systems. These sections provide a detailed account of many of the error messages that might occur during the boot process.

The Hardware Boot Process: Operating System Independent

If you have a problem with your system during startup and can determine where in this sequence of events your system has stalled, you know which events have occurred and probably can eliminate each of them as a cause of the problem. The following steps occur in a typical system startup regardless of which operating system you are loading:

1. You switch on electrical power to the system.

2. The power supply performs a self-test (known as the POST). When all voltages and current levels are acceptable, the supply indicates that the power is stable and sends the Power_Good signal to the motherboard. The time from switch-on to Power_Good is normally between 0.1 and 0.5 seconds.

3. The microprocessor timer chip receives the Power_Good signal, which causes it to stop generating a reset signal to the microprocessor.

◄◄ See the Chapter 18 section, "The Power Good Signal," **p. 848**.

4. The microprocessor begins executing the ROM BIOS code, starting at memory address FFFF:0000. Because this location is only 16 bytes from the very end of the available ROM space, it contains a JMP (jump) instruction to the actual ROM BIOS starting address.

5. The ROM BIOS performs a test of the central hardware to verify basic system functionality. Any errors that occur are indicated by audio beep codes because the video system has not yet been initialized. If the BIOS is Plug and Play (PnP), the following steps are executed; if not, skip to step 10.

6. The PnP BIOS checks nonvolatile random access memory (NVRAM) for input/output (I/O) port addresses, interrupt request lines (IRQs), direct memory access (DMA) channels, and other settings necessary to configure PnP devices on the computer.

7. All PnP devices found by the PnP BIOS are disabled to eliminate potential conflicts.

8. A map of used and unused resources is created.

9. The PnP devices are configured and reenabled, one at a time. If your computer does not have a PnP BIOS, PnP devices are initialized using their default settings. These devices can be reconfigured dynamically when Windows starts. At that point, Windows queries the PnP BIOS for device information and then queries each PnP device for its configuration.

10. The BIOS performs a video ROM scan of memory locations C000:0000–C780:0000 looking for video adapter ROM BIOS programs contained on a video adapter found either on a card plugged into a slot or integrated into the motherboard. If the scan locates a video ROM BIOS, it is tested by a checksum procedure. If the video BIOS passes the checksum test, the ROM is executed; then the video ROM code initializes the video adapter and a cursor appears onscreen. If the checksum test fails, the following message appears:

    ```
    C000 ROM Error
    ```

11. If the BIOS finds no video adapter ROM, it uses the motherboard ROM video drivers to initialize the video display hardware, and a cursor appears onscreen.

12. The motherboard ROM BIOS scans memory locations C800:0000–DF80:0000 in 2KB increments for any other ROMs located on any other adapter cards (such as SCSI adapters). If any ROMs are found, they are checksum-tested and executed. These adapter ROMs can alter existing BIOS routines and establish new ones.

13. Failure of a checksum test for any of these ROM modules causes the message

    ```
    XXXX ROM Error
    ```

    to appear, where the address XXXX indicates the segment address of the failed ROM module.

14. The ROM BIOS checks the word value at memory location 0000:0472 to see whether this start is a cold start or a warm start. A word value of 1234h in this location is a flag that indicates a warm start, which causes the BIOS to skip the memory test portion of the POST. Any other word value in this location indicates a cold start, and the BIOS performs the full POST procedure. Some system BIOSs let you control various aspects of the POST procedure, making it possible to skip the memory test, for example, which can be lengthy on a system with a lot of RAM.

15. If this is a cold start, the full POST executes; if this is a warm start, a mini-POST executes, minus the RAM test. Any errors found during the POST are reported by a combination of audio and displayed error messages. Successful completion of the POST is indicated by a single beep (with the exception of some Compaq computers, which beep twice).

16. The ROM BIOS searches for a boot record at cylinder 0, head 0, sector 1 (the very first sector) on the default boot drive. At one time, the default boot drive was always the first floppy disk (or A: drive). However, the BIOSs on today's systems often enable you to select the default boot device and the order in which the BIOS will look for other devices to boot from if necessary, using a floppy disk, hard disk, or even a CD-ROM drive in any order you choose. This sector is loaded into memory at 0000:7C00 and tested.

    If a disk is in the drive but the sector can't be read, or if no disk is present, the BIOS continues with step 19.

Booting from Optical, USB, or Floppy

If you want to boot from an optical or USB drive, be sure the drive is listed before the hard disk in the boot devices or sequence menu in your BIOS setup. If you have a floppy drive installed, you can set that to come before the hard disk in the sequence as well. This enables you to always be ready for an emergency. So long as you do not start up the system with a bootable USB drive, floppy, or optical disc loaded, the BIOS bypasses them and boots from the hard drive instead.

Refer to Chapter 11, "Optical Storage," for information on how to make a bootable disc.

17. If you are booting from a floppy disk and the first byte of the volume boot record is less than 06h, or if the first byte is greater than or equal to 06h and the first nine words contain the same data pattern, this error message appears and the system stops:

    ```
    602-Diskette Boot Record Error
    ```

18. If the volume boot record can't find or load the system files, or if a problem was encountered loading them, one of the following messages appears:

```
Non-System disk or disk error

Replace and strike any key when ready
```

```
Non-System disk or disk error

Replace and press any key when ready
```

```
Invalid system disk

Replace the disk, and then press any key
```

```
Disk Boot failure
```

```
Disk I/O Error
```

All these messages originate in the volume boot record (VBR) and relate to VBR or system file problems.

19. If no boot record can be read from drive A: (such as when no disk is in the drive), the BIOS then looks for an MBR at cylinder 0, head 0, sector 1 (the first sector) of the first hard disk. If this sector is found, it is loaded into memory address 0000:7C00 and tested for a signature.

20. If the last two (signature) bytes of the MBR are not equal to 55AAh, software interrupt 18h (Int 18h) is invoked on most systems. This causes the BIOS to display an error message that can vary for different BIOS manufacturers, but which is often similar to one of the following messages, depending on which BIOS you have:

AMI BIOS:

```
NO ROM BASIC - SYSTEM HALTED
```

Award BIOS:

```
DISK BOOT FAILURE, INSERT SYSTEM DISK AND PRESS ENTER
```

Phoenix BIOS:

```
No boot device available -

strike F1 to retry boot, F2 for setup utility
```

or

```
No boot sector on fixed disk -

strike F1 to retry boot, F2 for setup utility
```

Older IBM BIOS:

```
The IBM Personal Computer Basic

Version C1.10 Copyright IBM Corp 1981

62940 Bytes free

Ok
```

Note

Some IBM computers since 1987 display a strange character graphic depicting the front of a floppy drive, a 3 1/2-inch disk, and arrows prompting you to insert a disk in the drive and press the F1 key to proceed.

Older Compaq BIOS:

```
Non-System disk or disk error

replace and strike any key when ready
```

Although the messages vary from BIOS to BIOS, the cause for each relates to specific bytes in the MBR, which is the first sector of a hard disk at the physical location cylinder 0, head 0, sector 1.

The problem involves a disk that either has never been partitioned or has had the Master Boot Sector corrupted. During the boot process, the BIOS checks the last two bytes in the MBR (first sector of the drive) for a signature value of 55AAh. If the last two bytes are not 55AAh, an Interrupt 18h is invoked, which calls the subroutine that displays one of the error messages just shown, which basically instructs the user to insert a bootable floppy to proceed.

The MBR (including the signature bytes) is written to the hard disk by the FDISK, Disk Management, or DISKPART programs. Immediately after a hard disk is low-level formatted, all the sectors are initialized with a pattern of bytes, and the first sector does not contain the 55AAh signature. In other words, these ROM error messages are exactly what you see if you attempt to boot from a hard disk that has been freshly low-level formatted but has not yet been partitioned or if the MBR has been corrupted such that the signature bytes were overwritten.

21. The MBR searches its built-in partition table entries for a boot indicator byte marking an active partition entry.

22. If none of the partitions are marked active (bootable), the BIOS invokes software interrupt 18h, which displays an error message (refer to step 20).

23. If any boot indicator byte in the MBR partition table is invalid, or if more than one indicates an active partition, the following message is displayed and the system stops:

```
Invalid partition table
```

24. If an active partition is found in the MBR, the partition boot record from the active partition is loaded and tested.

25. If the partition boot record can't be read successfully from the active partition within five retries because of read errors, the following message is displayed and the system stops:

```
Error loading operating system
```

26. The hard disk's partition boot record is tested for a signature. If it does not contain a valid signature of 55AAh as the last two bytes in the sector, the following message is displayed and the system stops:

```
Missing operating system
```

27. The volume boot record is executed as a program. This program looks for and loads the operating system kernel or system files. If the volume boot record can't find or load the system files, or if a problem was encountered loading them, one of the following messages appears:

```
Non-System disk or disk error
Replace and strike any key when ready
```

```
Non-System disk or disk error
Replace and press any key when ready
```

```
Invalid system disk
Replace the disk, and then press any key
```

```
Disk Boot failure
```

```
Disk I/O Error
```

All these messages originate in the volume boot record (VBR) and relate to VBR or system file problems.

From this point forward, what happens depends on which operating system you have. The operating system–dependent boot procedures are discussed in the next several sections.

The DOS Boot Process

MS-DOS and similar operating systems (PC-DOS, DR-DOS, and Freedos) use the following boot process:

1. The initial system file (called IO.SYS or IBMBIO.COM) is loaded, and the initialization code copies itself into the highest region of contiguous DOS memory and transfers control to the copy.

2. The initialization code loads MSDOS.SYS (or IBMDOS.COM), which initializes the base device drivers, determines equipment status, resets the disk system, resets and initializes attached devices, and sets the system default parameters.

3. CONFIG.SYS is read multiple times. On the first pass any DEVICE statements are processed in the order in which they appear; the drivers named are loaded and executed. Then, any INSTALL statements are processed in the order in which they appear; the programs named are loaded and executed. The SHELL statement is processed and loads the specified command processor with the specified parameters. If the CONFIG.SYS file contains no SHELL statement, the default \ COMMAND.COM processor is loaded with default parameters. Loading the command processor overwrites the initialization code in memory (because the job of the initialization code is finished).

4. If AUTOEXEC.BAT is present, COMMAND.COM loads and runs AUTOEXEC.BAT. After the commands in AUTOEXEC.BAT have been executed, the DOS prompt appears (unless AUTOEXEC.BAT calls an application program or shell of some kind, in which case the user might operate the system without ever seeing a DOS prompt). If no AUTOEXEC.BAT file is present, COMMAND.COM executes the internal DATE and TIME commands, displays a copyright message, and displays the DOS prompt.

The Windows 9x/Me Boot Process

The Windows 9x/Me boot process involves two files: IO.SYS and WIN.COM. For more information, see "The Windows 9x/Me Boot Process" in *Upgrading and Repairing PCs*, 19th Edition, included in its entirety on the DVD packaged with this book.

Windows 2000/XP Startup

When you start a Windows 2000 or XP system (which is based on the same set of integral code that originated with Windows NT), the boot process is different from that of a DOS or Windows 9x/Me system. Instead of accessing the IO.SYS and MSDOS.SYS files used by 9x/Me, these operating systems use an OS loader program called Ntldr.

The basic startup process is described in the following step-by-step procedures:

1. The partition boot sector loads Ntldr (NT Loader). It then switches the processor to protected mode, starts the file system, and reads the contents of Boot.ini. The information in Boot.ini determines the startup options and initial boot menu selections (dual-booting, for example). If dual-booting is enabled and a non-NT/2000/XP OS is chosen, Bootsec.dos is loaded. If SCSI drives are present, Ntbootdd.sys is loaded, which contains the SCSI boot drivers.

2. Ntdetect.com gathers hardware configuration data and passes this information to Ntldr. If more than one hardware profile exists, Windows uses the correct one for the current configuration. If the ROM BIOS is ACPI compliant, Windows uses ACPI to enumerate and initialize devices.

3. The kernel loads. Ntldr passes information collected by Ntdetect.com to Ntoskrnl.exe. Ntoskrnl then loads the kernel, Hardware Abstraction Layer (Hal.dll), and Registry information. An indicator near the bottom of the screen details progress.

4. Drivers load and the user logs on. Networking-related components (for example, TCP/IP) load simultaneously with other services, and the Begin Logon prompt appears onscreen. After a user logs on successfully, Windows updates the Last Known Good Configuration information to reflect the current configuration state.

5. PnP detects and configures new devices. If new devices are detected, they are assigned resources. Windows extracts the necessary driver files from Driver.cab. If the driver files are not found, the user is prompted to provide them. Device detection occurs simultaneously with the operating system logon process.

The following files are processed during startup:

- Ntldr
- Boot.ini
- Bootsect.dos (multiple-boot systems only)
- Ntbootdd.sys (loaded only for SCSI drives)
- Ntdetect.com
- Ntoskrnl.exe

- Hal.dll
- Files in systemroot\ System32\ Config (Registry)
- Files in systemroot\ System32\ Drivers (drivers)

Note

If you see error messages during startup or your system doesn't start properly, restart the system, press the F8 key to open the startup menu, and select Enable Boot Logging to create a file called Ntbtlog.txt. This file records events during startup and can help you determine which files or processes are not loading correctly.

Windows Vista/7 Startup

Although Microsoft Windows Vista and Windows 7 have roots in Windows XP and earlier NT-based Windows operating systems, the boot process is different in some significant ways. Windows Vista/7 use three different components to replace Ntldr:

- bootmgr.exe—Windows Boot Manager
- winload.exe—Windows operating system loader
- winresume.exe—Windows resume loader

Likewise, the traditional boot.ini boot configuration text file used in earlier NT-based versions of Windows is now replaced by the boot configuration data (BCD) store. The use of BCD enables a common interface for systems that use either traditional BIOS or the more recent extensible firmware interface (EFI) configuration methods. The configuration options in the BCD store are changed with the BCDEdit tool, a UAC-protected program.

Bootmgr.exe starts winload.exe, which loads Windows if no other operating system is present, using the settings in the BCD store. However, if a dual-boot configuration has been created by installing Windows alongside a previous version of Windows, the Windows Boot Manager displays a selection menu listing Windows Vista/7 and the previous version of Windows. For example, if Windows 7 is dual-booted with Windows XP, selecting the option to run the previous version of Windows causes the Windows Boot Manager to load Windows XP's Ntldr, as noted in the previous section. However, if Windows 7 is selected, winload.exe boots the system using the settings in the BCD store.

When a system running Windows Vista/7 is hibernated, the BCD stores information about the state of the computer when it was hibernated. When the system resumes from hibernation, the winresume.exe program is used to restart Windows, using the hibernation information stored in the BCD as well as the contents of hiberfil.sys.

Windows 8 Startup

The Windows 8 startup process works in two different ways, depending upon whether the computer is being cold-booted or being restarted after a normal Windows 8 shutdown.

The Windows 8 cold boot process works the same as in Windows 7, but the normal startup process for Windows 8 uses both cold-boot and hibernation techniques for faster startup.

When a Windows 8 system is shut down using the normal procedure, user sessions are closed, but the system state is hibernated. This enables Windows 8 to start the next time in its default Fast Startup mode.

With Fast Startup, the hibernation file (hiberfil.sys) is processed after the POST is completed. Because hiberfil.sys is much smaller than on previous Windows versions and Windows 8 uses all cores in multicore processors to process and decompress hiberfil.sys, the system starts much more quickly (typically 30–70% faster) than with previous Windows versions.

If you need to add or remove hardware from a system, you can change the behavior of Windows 8's shutdown and startup process by using the Shutdown.exe program from an elevated command prompt. This command triggers a full shutdown:

```
shutdown /s /f /t 0
```

When the system restarts, it does so using the cold boot process.

To disable hibernation (which also disables fast startup), use this command from an elevated command prompt:

```
powercfg -h off
```

If you have disabled hibernation/fast startup, use this command to revert the system to the default Fast Start behavior after shutdown:

```
shutdown /s /hybrid /t 0
```

When the system restarts, it does so in the default Fast Start mode.

Note

To learn more about the Fast Startup mode introduced in Windows 8, see "Delivering Fast Boot Times in Windows 8" at http://blogs.msdn.com/b/b8/archive/2011/09/08/delivering-fast-boot-times-in-windows-8.aspx.

PC Maintenance Tools

To troubleshoot and repair PC systems properly, you need a few basic tools. If you intend to troubleshoot and repair PCs professionally, there are many more specialized tools you will want to purchase. These advanced tools enable you to more accurately diagnose problems and make jobs easier and faster. Here are the basic tools that should be in every troubleshooter's toolbox:

- Simple hand tools for basic disassembly and reassembly procedures
- Diagnostics software
- A multimeter
- Chemicals (such as contact cleaners), component freeze sprays, and compressed air for cleaning the system
- Foam swabs, or lint-free cotton swabs if foam isn't available
- Small nylon wire ties for "dressing" or organizing wires

Some environments also might have the resources to purchase the following devices, although they're not required for most work:

- Memory module tester
- Serial and parallel loopback (or wrap) plugs to test serial and parallel ports
- A USB testing plug to test USB ports
- A network cable scanner (if you work with networked PCs)
- A POST card

These tools are discussed in more detail in the following sections.

Hand Tools

When you work with PC systems, the tools required for nearly all service operations are simple and inexpensive. You can carry most of the required tools in a small pouch. Even a top-of-the-line "master mechanics" set fits inside a briefcase-sized container. The cost of these toolkits ranges from about $20 for a small service kit to $500 for one of the briefcase-sized deluxe kits. Compare these costs with what might be necessary for an automotive technician. An automotive service technician would have to spend $5,000–$10,000 or more for a complete set of tools. Not only are PC tools much less expensive, but I can tell you from experience that you don't get nearly as dirty working on computers as you do working on cars.

In this section, you learn about the tools required to assemble a kit that is capable of performing basic, board-level service on PC systems. One of the best ways to start such a set of tools is to purchase a small kit sold especially for servicing PCs.

Tip

For a comprehensive selection of electronics parts, tools, and other supplies, I recommend the following sources:

- Allied Electronics (www.alliedelec.com)
- Digi-Key (www.digikey.com/)
- Mouser Electronics (www.mouser.com)
- Newark/element14 (www.newark.com)
- RadioShack (www.radioshack.com)

For tools only, I also recommend Stanley Supply & Services (formerly Jensen Tools and Contact East [www.stanleysupplyservices.com]).

Most of these companies also have comprehensive paper catalogs, which can often make it easier to do general browsing and find what you need.

Because they work better than conventional screwdrivers, use nut drivers to remove the hexagonal-headed screws that secure the system-unit covers, adapter boards, disk drives, and power supplies in most systems. You will, however, still need standard screwdrivers for systems that have substituted Phillips-head screws for the more standard hexagonal-head screws. If slotted screws are used, they should be removed and replaced with Torx (preferred), hex, or Phillips-head screws that capture the driver tool and prevent it from slipping off the head of the screw and potentially damaging the system.

Caution

When you are working in a cramped environment such as the inside of a computer case, screwdrivers with magnetic tips can be a real convenience, especially for retrieving that screw you dropped into the case. However, although I have used these types of screwdrivers many times with no problems, you should be aware of the damage a magnetic field can cause to magnetic storage devices such as floppy disks. Laying the screwdriver down on or near a floppy can damage the data on the disk. Fortunately, floppy disks aren't used that much anymore. Hard drives are shielded by a metal case; optical drives are not affected because they're not magnetic; and memory and other chips are not affected by magnetic fields (unless they are magnitudes stronger than what you'll see in a hand tool).

Tweezers or a parts grabber like the one shown in Figure 20.2 can be used to hold any small screws or jumper blocks that are difficult to hold in your hand. The parts grabber is especially useful when you drop a small part into the interior of a system; usually, you can remove the part without completely disassembling the system.

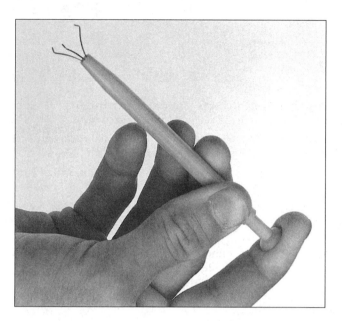

FIGURE 20.2 The parts grabber has three small metal prongs that can be extended to grab a part.

Finally, make sure your kit has several sizes of Torx drivers or bits; a Torx driver has a star-shaped head that matches the special screws found in some systems (see Figure 20.3). Torx screws are superior to other types of screws for computers because they offer greater grip and the tool is much less likely to slip. The most common cause of new motherboard failures is the use of slotted screwdrivers that slip off the screw head, scratching (and damaging) the motherboard. I never allow slotted screws or a standard flat-bladed screwdriver anywhere near the interior of my systems. You also can purchase tamperproof Torx drivers that can remove Torx screws with the tamper-resistant pin in the center of the screw. A tamperproof Torx driver has a hole drilled in it to allow clearance for the pin. Torx drivers come in a number of sizes, the most common being the T-10 and T-15.

Tip

Some system manufacturers now use cases that snap together or use thumb screws. These are usually advertised as "no-tool" cases because you literally do not need any tools to remove the cover and access the major assemblies.

To make an existing case "tool free," you can replace the normal case screws with metal or plastic thumbscrews. However, you still should use metal screws or thumbscrews to install internal components, such as adapter cards, disk drives, power supplies, and the motherboard, because the metal screws provide a ground point for these devices.

Although this basic set is useful, you should supplement it with some other basic tools, including the following:

- **Electrostatic discharge (ESD) protection kit**—These kits consist of a wrist strap with a ground wire and a specially conductive mat with its own ground wire. You also can get just the wrist strap or the antistatic mat separately. In areas or times of the season when there is low humidity, static charges are much more likely to build up as you move, increasing the need for ESD protection. A wrist strap is shown in Figure 20.4.

FIGURE 20.3 A Torx driver and bit.

- **Needle-nose pliers and hemostats (curved and straight)**—These are great for gripping small items and jumpers, straightening bent pins, and so on.

- **Electric screwdriver**—Combined with hex, Phillips, standard, and Torx bit sets, this tool really speeds up repetitive disassembly/assembly.

- **Flashlight**—You should preferably use a high-tech LED unit, which enables you to see inside dark systems and is easy on batteries.

- **Wire cutter or stripper**—This makes or repairs cables or wiring. For example, you'd need this (along with a crimping tool) to make Ethernet cables (refer to Chapter 17, "Local Area Networking").

- **Vise or clamp**—This installs connectors on cables, crimps cables to the shape you want, and holds parts during delicate operations. In addition to the vise, RadioShack sells a nifty "extra hands" device that has two movable arms with alligator clips on the end. This type of device is very useful for making cables or for other delicate operations during which an extra set of hands to hold something might be useful.

- **Metal file**—This smoothes rough metal edges on cases and chassis and trims the faceplates on disk drives for a perfect fit.

- **Markers, pens, and notepads**—Use these for taking notes, marking cables, and so on.

- **Windows 98/98SE or Me startup floppy**—These disks have DOS 7.1 or 8.0 and real-mode CD-ROM/DVD drivers, which can be used to boot test the system and possibly load other software. You can download these and other boot disks from www.bootdisk.com.

- **Windows install discs**—Install discs for Windows XP, Vista, 7, and 8 can be used to boot test the system from a CD-ROM/DVD drive, to attempt system recovery, to install the OS, or to run memory diagnostics (Windows Vista and later).

- **Diagnostics software**—You can use this software for PC hardware verification and testing. I especially recommend the Ultimate Boot CD (www.ultimatebootcd.com) and the Ultimate Boot CD for Windows (www.ubcd4win.com), both of which are free collections of diagnostics on bootable discs.

- **POST card**—This displays POST diagnostics codes on systems with fatal errors.

- **Nylon cable-ties**—These help in routing and securing cables; neatly routed cables improve airflow in the system.

- **Digital multimeter**—This checks power supply voltages, connectors, and cables for continuity.

- **Cleaning swabs, canned air (dust blower), and contact cleaner chemicals**—These clean, lubricate, and enhance contacts on circuit boards and cable connections. Products include those from www.chemtronics.com, as well as contact enhancer chemicals such as Stabilant 22a (www.stabilant.com).

- **Data transfer cables and adapters**—These quickly connect two systems and transfer data from one system to another. This includes serial and parallel cables (often called Laplink, Interlink, or Direct Cable Connect cables); Ethernet crossover cables; as well as more specialized USB-to-Ethernet, USB-to-USB, or USB-to-parallel adapters.

- **2 1/2-inch PATA drive cables and adapters**—These connect 2 1/2-inch (laptop) PATA drives to desktop systems for transferring or recovering data. This includes 44-pin (2 1/2-inch) PATA-to-40-pin (3 1/2-inch) PATA ribbon cable/power adapters, 44-pin PATA-to-USB/FireWire adapters, and 2 1/2-inch USB/FireWire external drive enclosures.

- **3 1/2-inch drive enclosure**—A hard disk drive enclosure equipped with a USB 2.0 or USB 3.0 port enables you to recover data from a hard disk if the original host system is no longer functioning. Normally you will need separate enclosures for PATA and SATA drives.

- **Spare keyboard and mouse**—You can use these to operate a system if the existing keyboard or pointing device is defective or difficult to use.

- **USB hub, USB/FireWire cable adapters**—These connect multiple external USB devices. The cable adapters and gender changers are recommended for connecting different types of USB and FireWire devices.

- **Spare screws, jumpers, standoffs, and so on**—These are handy if you lose any of these items from the system you are working on.

- **Spare CR-2032 lithium coin cell batteries**—These are used as the CMOS RAM batteries in most systems, so it is a good idea to have a replacement or two on hand. Although a number of CR20xx battery types are available, most systems use the CR2032.

Safety

From a personal safety point of view, there really isn't that much danger in working on a PC. Even if it *is* open with the power on, a PC runs on only 3.3, 5, or 12 volts, meaning no dangerous, life-threatening voltages are present. However, dangerous voltages do exist inside the power supply and CRT monitor. Most power supplies have 400 volts present at some points internally, and color displays have between 50,000 and 100,000 volts on the CRT! Normally, I treat the power supply and monitor as components that are replaced and not repaired, and I do not recommend you open either of them unless you really know what you are doing around high voltages.

Before working on a PC, you should unplug it from the wall. This is not really to protect you so much as it is to protect the system. A modern ATX form factor system is always partially running—that is, as long as the system is plugged in. So, even if it is off, standby voltages are present. To prevent damage to the motherboard, video card, and other cards, the system should be completely unplugged. If you accidentally turn the system all the way on, and plug in or remove a card, you can fry the card or motherboard.

ESD protection is another issue. While working on a PC, you should wear an ESD wrist strap that is clipped to the chassis of the machine (see Figure 20.4). This ensures that you and the system remain at the same electrical potential and prevents static electricity from damaging the system as you touch it. Some people feel that the system should be plugged in to provide an earth ground. That is not a good idea at all, as I previously mentioned. No "earth" ground is necessary; all that is important is that you and the system remain at the same electrical potential, which is accomplished via the strap. Another issue for personal safety is the use of a commercially available wrist strap, rather than making your own. Commercially made wrist straps feature an internal 1-megohm resistor designed to protect you. The resistor ensures that you are not the best path to ground should you touch any "hot" wire.

When you remove components from the system, they should be placed on a special conductive anti-static mat, which is also a part of any good ESD protection kit. The mat is also connected via a wire and clip to the system chassis. Any components removed from the system, especially items such as the processor, the motherboard, adapter cards, disk drives, and so on, should be placed on the mat. The connection between you, the mat, and the chassis will prevent any static discharges from damaging the components.

Note

It is possible (but not recommended) to work without an ESD protection kit if you're disciplined and careful about working on systems. If you don't have an ESD kit available, you can discharge yourself by touching any exposed metal on the chassis or case.

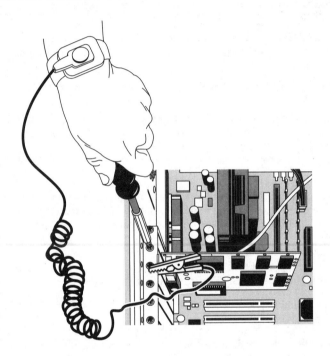

FIGURE 20.4 A typical ESD wrist strap clipped to a nonpainted surface in the case chassis.

The ESD kits, as well as all the other tools and much more, are available from a variety of tool vendors. Specialized Products Company (www.specialized.net) and Stanley Supply & Services (www.stanleysupplyservices.com) are two of the most popular vendors of computer and electronic tools and service equipment. Their catalogs show an extensive selection of very high-quality tools. With a simple set of hand tools, you will be equipped for nearly every PC repair or installation situation. The total cost of these tools should be less than $150, which is not much considering the capabilities they provide.

Test Equipment

In some cases, you must use specialized devices to test a system board or component. This test equipment is not expensive or difficult to use, but it can add much to your troubleshooting abilities.

Electrical Testing Equipment

I consider a voltmeter to be required gear for proper system testing. A multimeter can serve many purposes, including checking for voltage signals at various points in a system, testing the output of the power supply, and checking for continuity in a circuit or cable. An outlet tester is an invaluable accessory that can check the electrical outlet for proper wiring. This capability is useful if you believe the problem lies outside the computer system.

Loopback Connectors (Wrap Plugs)

For diagnosing serial- and parallel-port problems, as well as problems with network cabling, you need loopback connectors (also called *wrap plugs*), which are used to circulate, or wrap, signals (see Figure 20.5). The plugs enable ports to send and receive data simultaneously for diagnostic purposes.

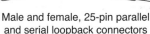

Male and female, 25-pin parallel
and serial loopback connectors

9-pin serial
loopback connectors

FIGURE 20.5 Serial and parallel port wrap plugs.

To accommodate all the serial/parallel ports you might encounter, you need a loopback connector for the 25-pin serial port, one for the 9-pin serial port, and one for the 25-pin parallel port. Some diagnostic software products include loopback connectors with the product, or you can purchase them as an option. Note that there are some variations on how loopback connectors can be made, and not all versions work properly with all diagnostics software. You should therefore use the loopback connectors recommended by the diagnostics software you will be using.

Ethernet loopback connectors are very useful for quickly diagnosing network cable runs, as well as for identifying which network jacks or cable ends are connected to which ports on a router or switch. With a loopback connector attached to a functioning cable, the corresponding port on a router or switch will show a device connected. For example, say you have an 8-port switch with cables connected to each port, but you don't know exactly which remote jacks in the home or office network they are connected to. Merely attach the Ethernet loopback to a jack or cable end you want to diagnose, then look at the switch to see which port lights up, thereby identifying the port in question.

USB wrap plugs are also available. However, these are active bus-powered devices that require compatible drivers and software from the plug manufacturer.

Note

Serial, parallel, and USB loopback plugs and testing software are available from PassMark Software (www.passmark.com), and Ethernet loopback connectors are available from Smartronix (www.smartronixstore.com).

Meters

Some troubleshooting procedures require that you measure voltage and resistance. You take these measurements by using a handheld digital multimeter (DMM). The meter can be an analog device (using an actual meter) or a digital-readout device. The DMM has a pair of wires called test leads or probes. The test leads make the connections so that you can take readings. Depending on the meter's setting, the probes measure electrical resistance, direct-current (DC) voltage, or alternating-current (AC) voltage. Figure 20.6 shows a typical DMM being used to test the +12V circuit on an ATX motherboard.

Usually, each system-unit measurement setting has several ranges of operation. DC voltage, for example, usually can be read in several scales, to a maximum of 200 millivolts (mV), 2V, 20V, 200V, and 1,000V. Because computers use both +5V and +12V for various operations, you should use the 20V maximum scale for making your measurements. Making these measurements on the 200mV or 2V scale could "peg the meter" and possibly damage it because the voltage would be much higher than expected. Using the 200V or 1,000V scale works, but the readings at 5V and 12V are so small in proportion to the maximum that accuracy is low.

If you are taking a measurement and are unsure of the actual voltage, start at the highest scale and work your way down. Most of the better meters have autoranging capability—the meter automatically selects the best range for any measurement. This type of meter is much easier to operate. You simply set the meter to the type of reading you want, such as DC volts, and attach the probes to the signal source. The meter selects the correct voltage range and displays the value. Because of their design, these types of meters always have a digital display rather than a meter needle.

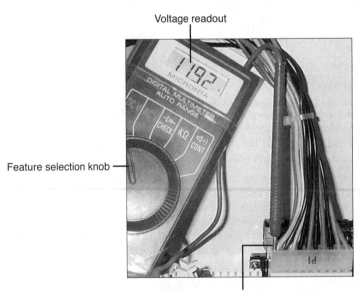

Voltage readout

Feature selection knob

Red lead inserted into ATX power connector

FIGURE 20.6 A typical digital multimeter tests a motherboard's +12V circuit.

Caution

Whenever you are using a multimeter to test any voltage that could potentially be 50V or above (such as AC wall socket voltage), always use one hand to do the testing, not two. Either clip one lead to one of the sources and probe with the other or hold both leads in one hand.

If you hold a lead in each hand and accidentally slip, you can very easily become a circuit, allowing power to conduct or flow through you. When power flows from arm to arm, the path of the current is directly across the heart. The heart muscle tends to quit working when subjected to high voltages. It's funny that way.

I prefer the small digital meters; you can buy them for only slightly more than the analog style, and they're extremely accurate and much safer for digital circuits. Some of these meters are not much bigger than a cassette tape; they fit in a shirt pocket. RadioShack sells a good unit in the $25 price range; the meter (refer to Figure 20.6) is a half-inch thick, weighs 3 1/2 ounces, and is digital and autoranging, as well. This type of meter works well for most, if not all, PC troubleshooting and test uses.

Caution

You should be aware that many older analog meters can be dangerous to digital circuits. These meters use a 9V battery to power the meter for resistance measurements. If you use this type of meter to measure resistance on some digital circuits, you can damage the electronics because you essentially are injecting 9V into the circuit. The digital meters universally run on 3V–5V or less.

Logic Probes

A logic probe can be useful for diagnosing problems in digital circuits (see Figure 20.7). In a digital circuit, a signal is represented as either high (+5V) or low (0V). Because these signals are present for only a short time (measured in millionths of a second) or oscillate (switch on and off) rapidly, a simple voltmeter is useless. A logic probe is designed to display these signal conditions.

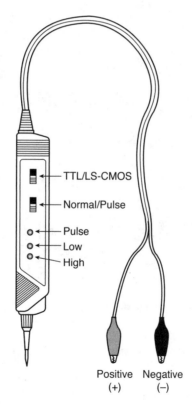

FIGURE 20.7 A typical logic probe.

Logic probes are especially useful for troubleshooting a dead system. By using the probe, you can determine whether the basic clock circuitry is operating and whether other signals necessary for system operation are present. In some cases, a probe can help you cross-check the signals at each pin on an integrated circuit chip. You can compare the signals present at each pin with the signals a known-good chip of the same type would show—a comparison that is helpful in isolating a failed component. Logic probes also can be useful for troubleshooting some disk drive problems by enabling you to test the signals present on the interface cable or drive-logic board.

Outlet (Receptacle) Testers

Outlet testers (also called *receptacle testers*) are useful test tools. These simple, inexpensive devices, sold in hardware stores, test electrical outlets. You simply plug in the device, and three LEDs light up in various combinations, indicating whether the outlet is wired correctly (see Figure 20.8).

Although you might think that badly wired outlets would be a rare problem, I have seen a large number of installations in which the outlets were wired incorrectly. Most of the time, the problem is in the ground wire. An improperly wired outlet can result in unstable system operation, such as random parity checks and lockups. With an improper ground circuit, currents can begin flowing on the electrical ground circuits in the system. Because the system uses the voltage on the ground circuits as a comparative signal to determine whether bits are 0 or 1, a floating ground can cause data errors in the system.

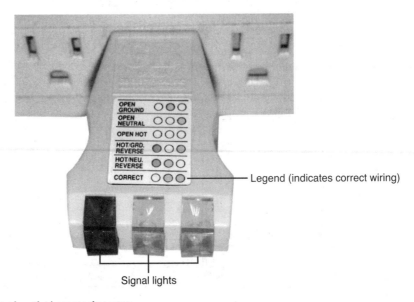

FIGURE 20.8 A typical outlet/receptacle tester.

Memory Module Testers

For high-volume service shops or large corporate environments servicing many systems, a dedicated memory tester can offer efficiency, performance, and accuracy far beyond running memory test software on a PC. These testers are table-top devices designed to evaluate all types of memory modules and even individual chips. The main drawback is that these testers can be somewhat expensive, costing thousands of dollars, but the cost can be justified for those who need to test a lot of memory quickly and accurately.

Without one of these testers, you are reduced to testing memory by running diagnostic programs on the PC and testing the memory as it is installed. This can be problematic because memory diagnostic programs can do only two things to the memory: write and read. A dedicated memory tester can do many things a memory diagnostic running in a PC can't do, such as

- Identify the type of memory.
- Identify the memory speed.
- Identify whether the memory has parity or is using bogus parity emulation.
- Vary the refresh timing and access speed timing.
- Locate single bit failures.
- Detect power- and noise-related failures.
- Detect solder opens and shorts.
- Isolate timing-related failures.
- Detect data retention errors.

Conventional memory diagnostic software can't do these things because it must rely on the fixed access parameters set up by the memory controller hardware in the motherboard chipset. This prevents the software from being capable of altering the timing and methods used to access the memory. You might have memory that fails in one system and works (mostly) in another when the chips are actually bad. This type of intermittent problem is almost impossible to detect with diagnostic software. Two companies making testers include CST (www.simmtester.com) and Tanisys (www.tanisys.com).

For smaller companies, repair shops, and individuals that must rely on PC-based memory testing, I recommend two programs:

- **Microsoft Windows Memory Diagnostic**—http://oca.microsoft.com/en/windiag.asp; also included in Windows Vista and later versions.
- **Memtest86**—www.memtest86.com

Both of these programs offer a comprehensive set of memory tests in a bootable CD-ROM format and are available for downloading at no charge. This means that no software needs to be installed on the PC being tested; you merely boot from the test CD and run the diagnostics.

◄◄ See Chapter 6, "Memory," **p. 325** for more information on memory in general.

Special Tools for the Enthusiast

All the tools described so far are commonly used by most technicians. However, a few additional tools do exist that a true PC enthusiast might want to have.

Electric Screwdriver

Perhaps the most useful tool I use is an electric screwdriver. It enables me to disassemble and reassemble a PC in record time and makes the job not only faster but easier as well. I like the type with a clutch you can use to set how tight it will make the screws before slipping; such a clutch makes the tool even faster to use. If you use the driver frequently, it makes sense to use the type with replaceable, rechargeable batteries, so when one battery dies you can quickly replace it with a fresh one.

Caution

Note that using an electric screwdriver when installing a motherboard can be dangerous because the bit can easily slip off the screw and damage the board. A telltale series of swirling scratches near the screw holes on the board can be the result, for which most manufacturers rightfully deny a warranty claim. Be especially careful if your motherboard is retained with Phillips-head screws because they are extremely easy for the bit to slip out of.

Temperature Probe

Determining the interior temperature of a PC is often useful when diagnosing whether heat-related issues are causing problems. The simplest and best tool I've found for the job is the digital thermometers sold at most auto parts stores for automobile use. They are designed to read the temperature inside and outside the car and normally come with an internal sensor, as well as one at the end of a length of wire.

Normally, the maximum limit for internal air temperature should be 110°F (43°C) or less. If your system is running near or above that temperature, problems can be expected.

Infrared Thermometer

Another useful temperature tool is a noncontact infrared (IR) thermometer, which is a special type of sensor that can measure the temperature of an object without physically touching it (see Figure 20.9). You can take the temperature reading of an object in seconds by merely pointing the handheld device at the object you want to measure and pulling a trigger.

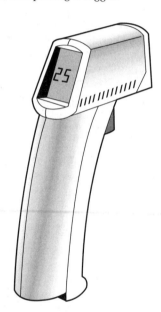

FIGURE 20.9   A noncontact infrared thermometer.

An IR thermometer works by capturing the infrared energy naturally emitted from all objects warmer than absolute zero (0° Kelvin). Infrared energy is a part of the electromagnetic spectrum with a frequency below that of visible light, which means it is invisible to the human eye. Infrared wavelengths are between 0.7 microns and 1,000 microns (millionths of a meter), although infrared thermometers typically measure radiation in the range 0.7–14 microns.

Because IR thermometers can measure the temperature of objects without touching them, they are ideal for measuring chip temperatures in a running system—especially the temperature of the CPU heatsink. By merely pointing the device at the top of the CPU and pulling the trigger, you can get a very accurate measurement in about 1 second. To enable more accuracy in positioning, many IR thermometers incorporate a laser pointer, which is used to aim the device. IR thermometers like the MiniTemp series are available from companies like Raytek (www.raytek.com).

Large Claw-Type Parts Grabber

One of the more useful tools in my toolbox is a large claw-type parts grabber, normally sold in stores that carry automotive tools. Having one of these around has saved many hours of frustration digging back into a system or behind a desk for a loose or dropped screw.

Preventive Maintenance

Preventive maintenance is the key to obtaining years of trouble-free service from your computer system. A properly administered preventive maintenance program pays for itself by reducing problem behavior, data loss, and component failure and by ensuring a long life for your system. In several cases, I have "repaired" an ailing system with nothing more than a preventive maintenance session. Preventive maintenance also can increase your system's resale value because it will look and run better. There are two types of preventive maintenance procedures: active and passive.

Passive preventive maintenance includes precautionary steps you can take to protect a system from the environment, such as using power-protection devices; ensuring a clean, temperature-controlled environment; and preventing excessive vibration. In other words, passive preventive maintenance means treating your system well and with care.

An *active* preventive maintenance program includes procedures that promote a longer, trouble-free life for your PC. This type of preventive maintenance primarily involves the periodic cleaning of the system and its components, as well as performing backups, antivirus and antispyware scans, and other software-related procedures. The following sections describe several active preventive maintenance procedures.

Active Preventive Maintenance Procedures

How often you should perform active preventive maintenance procedures depends on the system's environment and the quality of the system's components. If your system is in a dirty environment, such as a machine shop floor or a gas station service area, you might need to clean your system every three months or less. For normal office environments, cleaning a system every few months to a year is usually fine. However, if you open your system after one year and find dust bunnies inside, you should probably shorten the cleaning interval.

Other hard disk preventive maintenance procedures include making periodic backups of your data. Also, depending on which OS and file system you use, you should defragment hard disks at least twice a year (or up to once a month in some cases) to maintain disk efficiency and speed. Many of these tasks can be automated with the scheduling features in your operating system or the utility program. Note that defragmenting applies only to traditional hard disks and not to solid-state drives (SSDs), which, because of their design, should never be defragmented.

Weekly and Monthly Checklists

The following is a sample weekly disk maintenance checklist:

- Back up any data or important files.
- Check for and install any operating system updates. If you have Automatic Updates turned on (recommended), this is done automatically for you. Although OS updates are traditionally offered on a monthly basis, critical out-of-band updates can happen at any time.
- Run a full system antivirus and antispyware scan. Before starting the scans, ensure your antivirus and antispyware software are up to date.

About System Restore

System Restore is an automatic service in Windows XP and newer that periodically creates restore points, which are snapshots of the Registry and certain other dynamic system files. These restore points do not include any user or application data and should therefore not be confused with, or used in place of, normal file or data backup procedures. The System Restore application can be used to manually return a system to a previously created restore point, as well as to manually create a new restore point. You don't typically need to manually create restore points because they are automatically created at the following times:

- Every time you install an application
- Every time an update is installed with Automatic Updates
- Every time an update is installed with Windows Update
- Every time you install an unsigned driver
- Every 24 hours if the system is turned on, or if it has been more than 24 hours since the last restore point was created

Even though you don't usually need to create restore points manually, I do recommend creating a manual restore point before editing the Registry directly because that essentially creates a backup of the Registry you can restore if your edit causes problems.

The Windows Vista and later System Restore program, unlike its predecessors, can be run without booting to the Windows Desktop. You can run it from the DVD's Recovery Environment to restore your system to an earlier condition.

The following are some monthly maintenance procedures you should perform:

- Check for and install any updated drivers.
- Run the Windows Disk Cleanup tool, which searches the system for unnecessary files that can be safely deleted. A more thorough third-party freeware tool I recommend for this purpose is CCleaner (www.piriform.com/).
- Run a disk-defragmenting program. The defragment program included with Windows Vista and later runs automatically, but for a faster and more thorough on-demand defragmentation, you may prefer a third-party program such as VOPT (www.vopt.com), which is also known as being one of the fastest on the market. The defragmenting program in Windows 7 and later also specifically identifies solid-state drives (SSDs) and automatically excludes them from defragmenting operations.
- Check that all system fans are operating properly, including the CPU heatsink, power supply, and any chassis fans.

Cleaning a System

One of the most important operations in a good preventive maintenance program is regular and thorough cleaning of the system. Dust buildup on the internal components can lead to several problems. One is that the dust acts as a thermal insulator, which prevents proper system cooling. Excessive heat shortens the life of system components and adds to the thermal stress problem caused by greater temperature changes between the system's power-on and power-off states. Additionally, the dust can contain conductive elements that can cause partial short circuits in a system. Other elements in dust and dirt can accelerate corrosion of electrical contacts, resulting in improper connections. In all, the regular removal of any layer of dust and debris from within a computer system benefits that system in the long run.

Tip

Cigarette smoke contains chemicals that can conduct electricity and cause corrosion of computer parts. The smoke residue can infiltrate the entire system, causing corrosion and contamination of electrical contacts and sensitive components, such as optical drive lens assemblies. You should avoid smoking near computer equipment and encourage your company to develop and enforce a similar policy.

Properly cleaning the system and all the boards inside requires certain supplies and tools. In addition to the tools required to disassemble the unit, you should have these items:

- Contact cleaning solution
- Canned air
- A small brush
- Lint-free foam cleaning swabs
- Antistatic wrist-grounding strap

You also might want to acquire these optional items:

- Air compressor
- Vacuum cleaner

These simple cleaning tools and chemical solutions enable you to perform most common preventive maintenance tasks.

Chemicals

Chemicals can be used to help clean, troubleshoot, and even repair a system. You can use several types of cleaning solutions with computers and electronic assemblies. Most fall into the following categories:

- **Standard cleaners**—You can use pure isopropyl alcohol, acetone, trichloroethane, or a variety of other chemicals. Most board manufacturers and service shops are now leaning toward alcohol, acetone, or other chemicals that do not cause ozone depletion and comply with government regulations and environmental safety.

  Recently, new biodegradable cleaners described as "citrus-based cleaners" have become popular in the industry, and in many cases are more effective and more economical for circuit board and contact cleaning. These cleaners are commonly known as d-limonene or citrus terpenes and are derived from orange peels, which gives them a strong (but pleasant) citric odor. Another type of terpene is called a-pinene and is derived from pine trees. You must exercise care when using these cleaners, however, because they can cause swelling of some plastics, especially silicone rubber and PVC.

Caution

You should make sure your cleaning solution is designed to clean computers or electronic assemblies. In most cases, this means that the solution should be chemically pure and free from contaminants or other unwanted substances. You should not, for example, use drugstore rubbing alcohol for cleaning electronic parts or contacts because it is not pure and could contain water or perfumes.

- **Contact cleaner/lubricants**—These chemicals are similar to the standard cleaners but include a lubricating component. The lubricant eases the force required when plugging and unplugging cables and connectors, reducing strain on the devices. The lubricant coating also acts as a conductive protectant that insulates the contacts from corrosion.

A unique type of contact enhancer and lubricant called Stabilant 22 is currently on the market. This chemical greatly enhances the connection and lubricates the contact point and is much more effective than conventional contact cleaners or lubricants. It is especially effective on I/O slot connectors, adapter-card edge and pin connectors, disk drive connectors, power-supply connectors, and virtually any connector in the PC.

Note

This chemical is available in several forms. Stabilant 22 is the concentrated version, whereas Stabilant 22a is a version diluted with isopropanol in a 4:1 ratio. An even more diluted 8:1-ratio version is sold in many high-end stereo and audio shops under the name Tweek. Just 15ml of Stabilant 22a sells for about $40; a liter of the concentrate costs about $4,000! Although expensive, only a little is required in an application. See www.stabilant.com for distributors.

- **Dusters**—Compressed gas often is used as an aid in system cleaning. You use the compressed gas as a blower to remove dust and debris from a system or component. Be careful when you use these devices because some of them can generate a static charge when the compressed gas leaves the nozzle of the can. Be sure you are using the type approved for cleaning or dusting off computer equipment, and consider wearing a static grounding strap as a precaution.

You should use compressed gas only on equipment that is powered off, to minimize any chance of damage through short circuits.

Closely related to compressed-air products are chemical-freeze sprays. These sprays are used to quickly cool down a suspected failing component, which often temporarily restores it to normal operation. These substances are not used to repair a device, but to confirm that you have found a failed device.

Note

The makeup of many of the chemicals used for cleaning electronic components has been changing because many of the chemicals originally used are now considered environmentally unsafe. You can check the safety of specific chemicals by consulting their Material Safety Data Sheets (MSDS) at www.msds.com. Most of the companies that produce chemicals used for system cleaning and maintenance have had to introduce environmentally safe replacements. The only drawback is that many of these safer chemicals cost more and usually do not work as well as those they've replaced.

Air Compressors and Vacuum Cleaners

Some people prefer to use an air compressor and/or a vacuum cleaner instead of canned gas dusters for cleaning a system. An air compressor or vacuum cleaner is more useful when you are cleaning a system fully loaded with dust and dirt. You can use the vacuum cleaner to suck out most of the dust and debris instead of simply blowing it around on the other components, which sometimes happens with canned air. An air compressor is normally powerful enough such that all dust and debris will be blown out of the unit, but if done indoors it can create a breathing hazard. I normally recommend using a combination of both a vacuum cleaner and an air compressor, or just an air compressor if the cleaning can be done outdoors. Some compressors and vacuum cleaners are specifically designed for use on and around electronic components; they are designed to minimize ESD while in use. If you not using one specifically designed with ESD protection, you should take precautions, such as wearing a grounding wrist strap. Also, if the device has a metal nozzle, be careful not to touch it to the circuit boards or components you are cleaning.

Swabs

Use cleaning swabs to wipe off electrical contacts, connectors, and other sensitive areas. The swabs should be made of foam or synthetic chamois material that does not leave lint or dust residue. Unfortunately, proper foam or chamois cleaning swabs are more expensive than typical cotton swabs. Do not use cotton swabs because they leave cotton fibers on everything they touch. Cotton fibers are conductive in some situations and can remain on drive heads, which can scratch disks. Foam or chamois swabs can be purchased at most electronics supply stores.

Caution

One item to avoid is an eraser for cleaning contacts. Many people (including me) have recommended using a soft pencil-type eraser for cleaning circuit-board contacts. Testing has proven this to be bad advice because any such abrasive wiping on electrical contacts generates friction and a potentially damaging ESD. Also, the eraser will wear off the gold coating on many contacts, exposing the tin contact underneath, which rapidly corrodes when exposed to air.

Some companies sell premoistened contact cleaning pads soaked in a proper contact cleaner and lubricant. These pads are safe to wipe on conductors and contacts with no likelihood of ESD damage or abrasion of the gold plating.

System Disassembly and Cleaning Procedures

To properly clean your system, you must at least partially disassemble it. If you are only blowing out the dust and dirt, then generally all you need to do is open the system, leaving all the cards, components, and cables in place. For a more thorough cleaning, you will want to remove cards, cables, and most of the other components, generally stripping the system down to the motherboard and chassis.

To clean any adapter cards removed from the system, blow off any dust or dirt using compressed air or a vacuum cleaner.

Also, blow any dust out of the power supply and any fans. You do not need to disassemble the power supply to do this; simply blast the compressed air into the supply through the fan exhaust port. This will blow the dust out of the supply and clean off the fan blades and grill, which will help with system airflow.

If the chassis has a removable filter, be sure to remove it and clean it off, either with compressed air or a vacuum cleaner designed for computer use.

Caution

Be careful with ESD, which can cause damage when you are cleaning electronic components. Take extra precautions in the dead of winter or in extremely dry, high-static environments. You can apply antistatic sprays and treatments to the work area to reduce the likelihood of ESD damage.

An antistatic wrist-grounding strap is recommended. (Refer to Figure 20.4.) Connect it to a ground on the card or board you are wiping. This strap ensures that no electrical discharge occurs between you and the board. An alternative method is to keep a finger or thumb on the ground of the motherboard or card as you wipe it off.

Cleaning Connectors and Contacts

Cleaning the connectors and contacts in a system promotes reliable connections between devices. For most plug-in cards or memory modules, you should clean the edge connectors that plug into slots on the motherboard.

Submerge the lint-free swabs in the liquid cleaning solution. If you are using the spray, hold the swab away from the system and spray a small amount on the foam end until the solution starts to drip. Then, use the soaked foam swab to wipe the connectors on the boards. Presoaked wipes are the easiest to use—simply wipe them along the contacts to remove any accumulated dirt and leave a protective coating behind.

If you are cleaning a plug-in board or memory module, pay special attention to the edge connector that mates with the slot connector on the motherboard. When people handle plug-in cards, they often touch the gold contacts on these connectors. Touching the gold contacts coats them with oils and debris, which prevents proper contact with the slot connector when the board is installed. Make sure these gold contacts are free of all finger oils and residue. It is a good idea to use one of the contact cleaners that has a conductive lubricant, which makes it easier to push the adapter into the slot and protects the contacts from corrosion.

Cleaning the Keyboard and Mouse

Keyboards and ball-type mice are notorious for picking up dirt and garbage. If you ever open up an older keyboard, you will be amazed at the junk you find in there.

To prevent problems, you should periodically clean the keyboard with an air compressor or vacuum cleaner. My favorite method is to turn the keyboard upside down and shoot it with compressed air. This blows out the dirt and debris that has accumulated inside the keyboard and possibly prevents future problems with sticking keys or dirty keyswitches.

If a particular key is stuck or making intermittent contact, you can soak or spray that switch with contact cleaner. The best way to do this is to first remove the keycap and then spray the cleaner into the switch. This usually does not require complete disassembly of the keyboard. Periodic vacuuming or compressed gas cleaning prevents more serious problems with sticking keys and keyswitches.

Most ball-type mice are easy to clean. In most cases, a twist-off locking retainer keeps the mouse ball retained in the body of the mouse. By removing the retainer, you cause the ball to drop out. After removing the ball, you should clean it with one of the electronic cleaners. I recommend a pure cleaner instead of a contact cleaner with lubricant because you do not want any lubricant on the mouse ball. Then, wipe off the rollers in the body of the mouse with the cleaner and some swabs.

To keep optical or laser mice clean, just check the bottom of the mouse for any dust or debris that might block the light or detector. Use compressed air to remove dust or other extraneous material.

Passive Preventive Maintenance Procedures

Passive preventive maintenance involves taking care of the system by providing the best possible environment—both physical and electrical—for the system. Physical concerns are conditions such as ambient temperature, thermal stress from power cycling, dust and smoke contamination, and disturbances such as shock and vibration. Electrical concerns are items such as ESD, power-line noise, and radio-frequency interference. Each of these environmental concerns is discussed in the following sections.

Examining the Operating Environment

Before you set up a new PC, prepare a proper location for it that is free of airborne contaminants such as smoke or other pollution. Do not place your system in front of a window; the computer should not be exposed to direct sunlight or temperature variations. The environmental temperature should be as constant as possible. Power should be provided through properly grounded outlets and should be stable and free from electrical noise and interference. Keep your system away from radio transmitters or other sources of radio frequency energy.

Note

I also don't recommend using computer desks that place the system unit in a sealed cabinet; this is a good way to promote overheating.

Heating and Cooling

Thermal expansion and contraction from ambient temperature changes place stress on a computer system. Therefore, keeping the temperature in your office or room relatively constant is important to the successful operation of your computer system.

Temperature variations can lead to serious problems. If extreme variations occur over a short period, signal traces on circuit boards can crack and separate, solder joints can break, and contacts in the system can undergo accelerated corrosion. Solid-state components such as chips can be damaged also, and a host of other problems can develop.

To ensure that your system operates in the correct ambient temperature, you must first determine your system's specified functional range. Most manufacturers provide data about the correct operating temperature range for their systems. Two temperature specifications might be available, one indicating allowable temperatures during operation and another indicating allowable temperatures under nonoperating conditions. Many manufacturers list the following temperature ranges as acceptable for most systems.

> System on: 60°–90° Fahrenheit
>
> System off: 50°–110° Fahrenheit

Most office environments provide a stable temperature in which to operate a computer system, but some do not. Be sure to give some consideration to the placement of your equipment.

Power Cycling (On/Off)

As you have just learned, the temperature variations a system encounters greatly stress the system's physical components. The largest temperature variations a system encounters, however, are those that occur during the warm-up period right after you turn on the computer. Powering on a cold system subjects it to the greatest possible internal temperature variations. If you want a system to have the longest and most trouble-free life possible, you should limit the temperature variations in its environment. You can limit the extreme temperature cycling in two simple ways: Leave the system off all the time or leave it on all the time. Of these two possibilities, of course, you probably will want to choose the latter option. Leaving the power on is the best way I know to promote system reliability. If your only concern is system longevity, the simple recommendation is to keep the system unit powered on (or off!) continuously. In the real world, however, there are more variables to consider, such as the cost of electricity, the potential fire hazard of unattended running equipment, and other concerns as well.

If you think about the way light bulbs typically fail, you can begin to understand how thermal cycling can be dangerous. Light bulbs burn out most often when you first turn them on because the filament must endure incredible thermal stress as it changes temperature, in less than one second, from ambient to several thousands of degrees. A bulb that remains on continuously lasts longer than one that is turned on and off repeatedly. If you use CFLs, estimated power savings can be achieved only if the lights are left on for long periods of time rather than being turned on and off. Turning CFLs on and off also shortens their expected lifetime.

Although it sounds like I am telling you to leave all your computer equipment on 24 hours a day, 7 days a week, I no longer recommend this type of operation. A couple of concerns have tempered my urge to leave everything running continuously. One is that an unattended system that is powered on represents a fire hazard. I have seen monitors catch fire after internally shorting and systems whose cooling fans have frozen, causing the power supply and the entire system to overheat. I do not leave any system running in an unattended building. Another problem is wasted electrical power. Many companies have adopted austerity programs that involve turning off lights and other items when not in use. The power consumption of some of today's high-powered systems and accessories is not trivial. Also, an unattended operating system is more of a security risk than one that is powered off and locked.

Realities—such as the fire hazard of unattended systems running during night or weekend hours, security problems, and power-consumption issues—might prevent you from leaving your system on all the time. The best compromise in that case is to power on the system only one time daily, and configure the power management settings in the operating system to put the system and display into Stand-By or Hibernate modes during periods of inactivity. When the power management settings are properly configured, you can save more than $100 annually per system in energy charges.

Note

If you use remote access programs or services to connect to a host computer, the remote access host must be kept running at all times. To save power, turn off its monitor(s) and configure its power management to slow down the processor and other components when idle. In many cases you can still have the system enter Stand-By or Hibernate modes, as long as you have Wake-on-LAN enabled (check the BIOS Setup) so that the system can resume when a remote access session is initiated.

You should also configure host systems that use logins to not install Windows updates automatically because some updates restart the system, so the system will not be available to host remote connections until a user logs into it. For these systems, make sure you set up a schedule for installing downloaded updates to ensure that the system is available for remote access and is as up to date as possible.

Static Electricity

Static electricity or ESD can cause numerous problems within a system. The problems usually appear during the winter months when humidity is low or in extremely dry climates where the humidity is low year-round. In these cases, you might need to take special precautions to ensure that your PC is not damaged. Refer to Chapter 18, "Power Supplies," and Chapter 19, "Building or Upgrading Systems," for more information on ESD.

Static discharges outside a system-unit chassis are rarely a source of permanent problems within the system. Usually, the worst possible effect of a static discharge to the case, keyboard, or even a location near the computer is a system lockup. Most static-sensitivity problems are caused by improper grounding of the system power. Be sure you always use a three-prong, grounded power cord plugged in to a properly grounded outlet. If you are unsure about the outlet, you can buy an outlet tester, such as those described earlier in this chapter, at most electronics supply or hardware stores for only a few dollars.

Power-Line Noise

To run properly, a computer system requires a steady supply of clean, noise-free power. In some installations, however, the power line serving the computer also serves heavy equipment, and the voltage variations resulting from the on/off cycling of this equipment can cause problems for the computer. Certain types of equipment on the same power line also can cause voltage spikes—short, transient signals of sometimes 1,000V or more—that can physically damage a computer. Although these spikes are rare, they can be crippling. Even a dedicated electrical circuit used by only a single computer can experience spikes and transients, depending on the quality of the power supplied to the building or circuit.

During the site-preparation phase of a system installation, you should be aware of these factors to ensure a steady supply of clean power:

- If possible, the computer system should be on its own circuit with its own circuit breaker. This setup does not guarantee freedom from interference, but it helps.

- The circuit should be checked for a good, low-resistance ground, proper line voltage, freedom from interference, and freedom from brownouts (voltage dips).

- A three-wire circuit is a must, but some people substitute grounding-plug adapters to adapt a grounded plug to a two-wire socket. This setup is not recommended; the ground is there for a reason.

- Power-line noise problems increase with the resistance of the circuit, which is a function of wire size and length. So, to decrease resistance, avoid extension cords unless absolutely necessary, and then use only heavy-duty extension cords.

- Inevitably, you will want to plug in other equipment later. Plan ahead to avoid the temptation to connect too many items to a single outlet. If possible, provide a separate power circuit for non-computer-related devices.

Air conditioners, coffee makers, copy machines, laser printers, space heaters, vacuum cleaners, and power tools are some of the worst corrupters of a PC system's power. Any of these items can draw an excessive amount of current and wreak havoc with a PC system on the same electrical circuit. I've seen offices in which all the computers begin to crash at about 9:05 a.m. daily, which is when all the coffee makers are turned on!

Another major problem in some companies is partitioned offices. Many of these partitions are prewired with their own electrical outlets and are plugged into one another in a sort of power-line daisy-chain, similar to chaining power strips together. The person in the cubicle at the end of the electrical daisy-chain is likely to have power problems.

Radio-Frequency Interference

Radio-frequency interference (RFI) is easily overlooked as a problem factor. The interference is caused by any source of radio transmissions near a computer system. Living next door to a 50,000-watt commercial radio station is one sure way to get RFI problems, but less-powerful transmitters can cause problems, too. I know of many instances in which cordless telephones have caused sporadic random keystrokes to appear, as though an invisible entity were typing on the keyboard. I also have seen RFI cause a system to lock up. Solutions to RFI problems are more difficult to state because every case must be handled differently. Sometimes, simply moving the system eliminates the problem because radio signals can be directional in nature. At other times, you must invest in specially shielded cables for external devices, such as the keyboard and the monitor. If the keyboard or mouse is wireless, RFI can be especially problematic; the only solution might be to try a different brand or model that operates on a different frequency.

One type of solution to an RFI noise problem with cables is to pass the cable through a toroidal iron core, a doughnut-shaped piece of iron placed around a cable to suppress both the reception and transmission of electromagnetic interference (EMI). Many monitors include a toroid (sometimes spelled *torroid*) on the cable that connects to the computer. If you can isolate an RFI noise problem in a particular cable, you often can solve the problem by passing the cable through a toroidal core. Because the cable must pass through the center hole of the core, it often is difficult, if not impossible, to add a toroid to a cable that already has end connectors installed.

RadioShack sells a special snap-together toroid designed specifically to be added to cables already in use. This toroid looks like a thick-walled tube that has been sliced in half. You simply lay the cable in the center of one of the halves and snap the other half over the first. This type of construction makes adding the noise-suppression features of a toroid to virtually any existing cable easy.

The best, if not the easiest, way to eliminate an RFI problem is to correct it at the source. It is unlikely that you'll be able to convince the commercial radio station near your office to shut down, but if you are dealing with a small radio transmitter that is generating RFI, sometimes you can add a filter to the transmitter that suppresses spurious emissions. Unfortunately, problems sometimes persist until the transmitter is either switched off or moved some distance away from the affected computer.

Note

If you depend on wireless Ethernet (Wi-Fi) networks, keep in mind that the popular 2.4GHz band used by 802.11b, 802.11g, and 802.11n networks is in the same general frequency band as Bluetooth and 2.4GHz cordless phones, so there's plenty of potential for interference.

To avoid interference from other 802.11-based networks, use a program such as inSSIDer (www.metageek.net/products/inssider/) or Nirsoft WirelessNetView (www.nirsoft.net) to view the frequencies used by other nearby 802.11-based networks, and choose the least-crowded channel from 1, 6, or 11. (The other channels overlap substantially with each other.) To avoid conflicts with cordless phones, use cordless phones that operate on frequencies other than 2.4GHz. To learn more about avoiding conflicts with Bluetooth devices, see "Bluetooth," in Chapter 17.

You can also improve wireless coverage by using high-powered transceivers, directional antennas, or wireless range extenders from companies like RadioLabs (www.radiolabs.com) and NETGEAR (www.netgear.com). A professional site survey from an RF engineer can provide more information about hidden sources of interference that could affect Wi-Fi signals.

Dust and Pollutants

Dirt, smoke, dust, and other pollutants are bad for your system. The power-supply fan carries airborne particles through your system, and they collect inside. If your system is used in an extremely harsh environment, you might want to investigate some of the industrial systems on the market designed for harsh conditions.

Many companies make special hardened versions of their systems for harsh environments. Industrial systems typically use a different cooling system from the one used in regular PCs. A large cooling fan is used to pressurize the case rather than depressurize it. The air pumped into the case passes through a filter unit that must be cleaned and changed periodically. The system is pressurized so that no contaminated air can flow into it; air flows only outward. The only way air can enter is through the fan and filter system.

These systems also might have special keyboards impervious to liquids and dirt. Some flat-membrane keyboards are difficult to type on but are extremely rugged; others resemble the standard types of keyboards but have a thin, plastic membrane that covers all the keys. You can add this membrane to normal types of keyboards to seal them from the environment.

A relatively new breed of humidifier can cause problems with computer equipment. This type of humidifier uses ultrasonics to generate a mist of water sprayed into the air. The extra humidity helps cure problems with static electricity resulting from a dry climate, but the airborne water contaminants can cause many problems. If you use one of these systems, you might notice a white, ash-like deposit forming on components. The deposit is the result of abrasive and corrosive minerals suspended in the vaporized water. If these deposits collect on the system components, they can cause all kinds of problems. The only safe way to run one of these ultrasonic humidifiers is to use distilled water. If you use a humidifier, be sure it does not generate these deposits.

If you do your best to keep the environment for your computer equipment clean, your system will run better and last longer. Also, you will not have to open your unit as often for complete preventive maintenance cleaning.

Troubleshooting Tips and Techniques

Troubleshooting PC hardware problems can seem daunting to the uninitiated, but in reality it is much simpler than it seems. Most problems can be diagnosed and corrected using few, if any, special tools and can be accomplished by anybody who can apply simple deductive reasoning and logical thinking. PCs have become more complicated and yet simpler all at the same time. More and more complex internal circuits mean that there are potentially more things that can go wrong—more ways the system can fail. On the other hand, today's complex circuits are embedded into fewer boards, with fewer chips on each board and more serial interconnections using fewer pins (fewer wires). The internal consolidation means that isolating which replaceable component has failed is in many ways simpler than ever before. An understanding of the basics of how PCs work, combined with some very simple tools, some basic troubleshooting tips, and logical thinking and common sense, will enable you to effectively diagnose and repair your own system, saving a tremendous amount of money over taking it to a shop. In some cases, you can save enough money to practically pay for an entire new system. The bottom line with troubleshooting PC problems is that a solution exists for every problem, and through simple practices combined with deductive reasoning, that solution can easily be found.

Repair or Replace?

When dealing with hardware problems, the first simple truth to understand is that you do not usually *repair* anything—you *reinstall* or *replace* it instead. You reinstall because the majority of PC hardware problems are caused by a particular component being improperly installed or configured. I remember hearing from IBM many years ago that it had found that 60% or more of the problems handled by its service technicians were due to improper installation or configuration, meaning the hardware was not actually defective. This was, in fact, the major impetus behind the plug-and-play revolution, which has eliminated the need to manually configure jumpers and switches on most hardware devices. This has thus minimized the expertise necessary to install hardware properly and has minimized installation, configuration, and resource conflict problems. Still, plug and play has sometimes been called *plug and pray* because it does not always work perfectly, sometimes requiring manual intervention to make it work properly.

You replace because of the economics of the situation with computer hardware. The bottom line is that financially it is much cheaper to replace a failed circuit board with a new one than to repair it. For example, you can purchase a new, state-of-the-art motherboard for around $100, but repairing an existing board normally costs much more than that. Modern boards use surface-mounted chips that have pin spacing measured in hundredths of an inch, requiring sophisticated and expensive equipment to attach and solder the chip. Even if you could figure out which chip had failed and had the equipment to replace it, the chips themselves are usually sold in quantities of thousands and obsolete chips are usually not available. The net effect of all of this is that the replaceable components in your PC have become disposable technology. Even a component as large and comprehensive as the motherboard is replaced rather than repaired.

Basic Troubleshooting Steps

According to traditional troubleshooting theory, you can break down almost any troubleshooting scenario into a set of simple steps modeled after the Scientific Method. These are usually indicated and explained as follows:

- **Identify the problem (Characterization)**—What are the symptoms? What is the expected normal operation?

- **Establish one or more probable causes (Hypotheses and Prediction)**—What specific components are involved or might contribute to the problem? What effect will removing or replacing them have on the system?

- **Test the hypotheses to determine the cause (Test)**—Remove or replace suspected components one at a time. Observe any changes in the symptoms. Repeat testing different theories until a positive change is noted.

- **Establish a plan of action to resolve the problem and implement the solution**—Repair or replace components that were found to be defective. Perform preventive maintenance if applicable.

- **Verify proper functionality (Analysis)**—Test the system for proper operation. Document the problems and solutions so as to more quickly resolve similar problems in the future.

Based on these steps, good troubleshooting follows the scientific method, which allows a clear and concise path to solving a problem.

Troubleshooting by Replacing Parts

Using a scientific method–based approach, you can troubleshoot a PC in several ways, but in the end it often comes down to simply reinstalling or replacing parts. That is why I normally use a simple "known-good spare" technique that requires very little in the way of special tools or sophisticated diagnostics.

In its simplest form, say you have two identical PCs sitting side by side. One of them has a hardware problem; in this example let's say one of the memory modules is defective. Depending on how and where the defect lies, this could manifest itself in symptoms ranging from a completely dead system to one that boots up normally but crashes when running Windows or software applications. You observe that the system on the left has the problem but the system on the right works perfectly—they are otherwise identical. The simplest technique for finding the problem would be to swap parts from one system to another, one at a time, retesting after each swap. At the point when the DIMMs were swapped, upon powering up and testing (in this case testing is nothing more than allowing the system to boot up and run some of the installed applications), the problem has now moved from one system to the other. Knowing that the last item swapped over was the DIMM, you have just identified the source of the problem! This did not require an expensive DIMM test machine or any diagnostics software. Because components such as DIMMs are not economical to repair, replacing the defective DIMM would be the final solution.

Although this is simplistic, it is often the quickest and easiest way to identify a problem component as opposed to specifically testing each item with diagnostics. Instead of having an identical system standing by to borrow parts from, most technicians have an inventory of what they call "known-good" spare parts. These are parts that have been previously used, are known to be functional, and can be used to replace a suspicious part in a problem machine. However, this is different from new replacement parts because, when you open a box containing a new component, you really can't be 100% sure that it works. I've been in situations in which I've had a defective component and replaced it with another (unknown to me) defective *new* component and the problem remained. Not knowing that the new part I just installed was also defective, I wasted a lot of time checking other parts that were not the problem.

This technique is also effective because so few parts are needed to make up a PC, and the known-good parts don't always have to be the same (for example, a lower-end video card can be substituted in a system to verify that the original card had failed).

Troubleshooting by the Bootstrap Approach

Another variation on this theme is the "bootstrap approach," which is especially good for what seems to be a dead system. In this approach, you take the system apart to strip it down to the bare-minimum necessary, functional components and then test it to see whether it works. For example, you might strip down a system to the chassis/power supply, bare motherboard, CPU (with heatsink), one bank of RAM, and a video card with display and then power it up to see whether it works. In that stripped configuration, you should see the POST or splash (logo) screen on the display, verifying that the motherboard, CPU, RAM, video card, and display are functional. If a keyboard is connected, you should see the three LEDs (capslock, scrlock, and numlock) flash within a few seconds after powering on. This indicates that the CPU and motherboard are functioning because the POST routines are testing the keyboard. After you get the system to a minimum of components that are functional, you should reinstall or add one part at a time, testing the system each time you make a change to verify it still works and that the part you added or changed is not the cause of a problem. Essentially, you are rebuilding the system from scratch using the existing parts, but doing it one step at a time.

Many times, problems are caused by corrosion on contacts or connectors, so the mere act of disassembling and reassembling a PC will "magically" repair it. Over the years, I've disassembled, tested, and reassembled many systems only to find no problems after the reassembly.

Some useful troubleshooting tips include the following:

- Eliminate unnecessary variables or components that are not pertinent to the problem.
- Reinstall, reconfigure, or replace only one component at a time.
- Test after each change you make.
- Keep a detailed record (write it down) of each step you take.
- Don't give up! Every problem has a solution.
- If you hit a roadblock, take a break or work on another problem. A fresh approach the next day often reveals things you overlooked.
- Don't overlook the simple or obvious. Double- and triple-check the installation and configuration of each component.
- Keep in mind that the power supply is one of the most failure-prone parts in a PC. A high-output (500W or higher) "known-good" spare power supply is highly recommended to use for testing suspect systems.
- Cables and connections are also a major cause of problems, so keep replacements of all types on hand.

Before starting any system troubleshooting, you should perform a few basic steps to ensure a consistent starting point and to enable isolating the failed component:

1. Turn off the system and any peripheral devices. Disconnect all external peripherals from the system, except for the keyboard and video display.

2. Make sure the system is plugged into a properly grounded power outlet.

3. Make sure that a keyboard and video display are connected to the system. Turn on the video display, and turn up the brightness and contrast controls to at least two-thirds of the maximum. If you can't get any video display but the system seems to be working, try moving the card to a different slot (if possible) or try a different video card or monitor.

4. To enable the system to boot from a hard disk, make sure no floppy or optical discs are in any of the drives. Alternatively, put a known-good bootable floppy or optical disc with diagnostics on it in a drive, or attach a bootable USB drive for testing.

5. Turn on the system. Observe the power supply, chassis fans (if any), and lights on either the system front panel or power supply. If the fans don't spin and the lights don't light, the power supply or motherboard might be defective.

6. Observe the power-on self test (POST). If no errors are detected, the system beeps once (if the computer has a speaker in the case) and boots up. Errors that display onscreen (nonfatal errors) and that do not lock up the system display a text message that varies according to BIOS type and version. Record any errors that occur and refer to the POST error codes earlier in this chapter for more information on any specific codes you see. Errors that lock up the system (fatal errors) are indicated by a series of audible beeps on systems that have a built-in speaker.

7. Confirm that the operating system loads successfully.

Problems During the POST

Problems that occur during the POST are usually caused by incorrect hardware configuration or installation. Actual hardware failure is a far less-frequent cause. If you have a POST error, check the following:

- Are all cables correctly connected and secured?
- Are the configuration settings correct in Setup for the devices you have installed? In particular, ensure the processor, memory, and hard drive settings are correct.
- Try clearing the CMOS RAM completely (most motherboards have a jumper for this), and then run the BIOS Setup and check the settings.
- Are switches and jumpers on the motherboard properly set, especially if changed from the default settings?
- Is the power supply set to the proper input voltage (110V–120V or 220V–240V)?
- Is the power supply defective? Try replacing it with a known-good spare.
- Are adapter boards and disk drives installed correctly? Try reseating or reconnecting them.
- Is a keyboard and mouse attached? Try replacing them with known-good spares.
- Is a bootable hard disk (properly partitioned and formatted) installed? Try disconnecting it and booting from a floppy, optical disc, or USB flash drive instead.
- Does the BIOS support the hard disk drive you have installed, and if so, are the parameters entered correctly?
- Are all memory modules installed correctly? Try reseating them.

Problems Running Software

Problems running application software (especially new software) are usually caused by or related to the software itself or are due to the fact that the software is incompatible with the system. Here is a list of items to check in that case:

- Does the system meet the minimum hardware requirements for the software? Check the software documentation to be sure.
- Check to see that the software is correctly installed. Reinstall if necessary. If you need to reinstall the software, use the option to run the installation program in elevated mode (also known as "Run as Administrator"). In Windows Vista and later, you may be prompted to provide an administrator password or click through the User Account Control prompt to continue.
- Check to see that the latest drivers are installed.
- Scan the system for malware such as spyware or viruses.

Problems with Adapter Cards

Problems related to add-in boards are usually related to improper board installation or resource conflicts. Also be sure to check drivers for the latest versions and ensure that the card is compatible with your system and the operating system version you are using.

Sometimes, adapter cards can be picky about which slot they are running in. Despite the fact that, technically, an adapter should be able to run in any slot in which it fits, there can be subtle timing, signal, or specification differences between slots that otherwise appear to be the same. I have found on numerous occasions that simply moving a card from one slot to another can make a failing card begin to work properly. Sometimes moving a card works just by the inadvertent cleaning (wiping) of the contacts that takes place when removing and reinstalling the card, but in other cases I can duplicate the problem by inserting the card back into its original slot.

Caution

PCI and PCI Express cards become slot specific after their drivers are installed. By this, I mean that if you move a card to another slot, the system sees it as if you have removed one card and installed a new one. You therefore must install the drivers again for that card. Don't move a card to a different slot unless you are prepared with all the drivers at hand to perform the driver installation.

Top Troubleshooting Problems

These are some of the most frequently asked troubleshooting questions I receive, along with the solutions that typically address them.

When I power the system on, I see the power LED light and hear the fans spin, but nothing else ever happens.

The fact that the LEDs illuminate and fans spin indicates that the power supply is partially working, but that does not exclude it from being defective. This is a classic "dead" system, which can be caused by almost any defective hardware component. In my experiences I've had more problems with power supplies than most other components, so I recommend immediately using a multimeter to measure the outputs at the power supply connectors and ensure they are within the proper 5% tolerances of their rated voltages. Even if the voltage measurements check out, you should swap in a high-quality, high-power, known-good spare supply and retest. If that doesn't solve the problem, you should revert to the bootstrap approach I mentioned earlier, which is to strip the system down to just the chassis/power supply, motherboard, CPU (with heatsink), one bank of RAM (one DIMM), and a video card and display. If the motherboard now starts, begin adding the components you removed one at a time, retesting after each change. If the symptoms remain, use a POST card (if you have one) to see whether the board is partially functional and where it stops. Also, try replacing the video card, RAM, CPU, and then finally the motherboard, and verify the CPU and (especially) the heatsink installation.

The system beeps when I turn it on, but there is nothing on the screen.

The beep indicates a failure detected by the ROM POST routines. Look up the beep code in the table corresponding to the ROM version in your motherboard. This can typically be found in the motherboard manual; however, you can also find the beep codes for the most popular AMI, Award, and PhoenixBIOS earlier in this chapter.

I see a STOP or STOP ERROR in Windows.

Many things, including corrupted files, viruses, incorrectly configured hardware, and failing hardware, can cause Windows STOP errors. See the section "Operating System Diagnostics" earlier in this chapter for more information on troubleshooting Windows error messages. One of the most valuable resources for handling any error message displayed by Windows is the Microsoft Knowledgebase (MSKB), an online compendium of articles covering all Microsoft products. You can visit the MSKB at http://support.microsoft.com, and from there you can use the search tool to retrieve information specific to your problem.

I see `Fatal Exception` errors in Windows 95/98/Me.

This is the equivalent of the `STOP` error in Windows NT or later. As indicated in the previous answer, this can be caused by both hardware and software problems, and the best place to check for specific solutions is in the Microsoft Knowledgebase (MSKB) at http://support.microsoft.com.

The system won't shut down in Windows.

This problem is usually caused by driver problems. (Try installing the latest chipset and power management drivers for your motherboard.) However, it can also be caused by bugs in motherboard ROM (try upgrading your motherboard ROM to the latest version), bugs in the various Windows versions (run Windows Update from Control Panel and install the latest fixes, patches, and service packs), or in some cases configuration or hardware problems.

The power button won't turn off the system.

Desktop PCs built since 1996 mostly use the ATX form factor power supplies, which incorporate a design such that the power switch is connected to the motherboard and not the power supply directly. This enables the motherboard and operating system to control system shutdown, preventing an unexpected loss of power that can cause data loss or file system corruption. However, if the system experiences a problem and becomes frozen or locked up in some way, the motherboard might not respond to the power button, meaning it will not send a shutdown signal to the power supply. It might seem that you will have to pull the plug to power off the system, but fortunately a forced shutdown override is provided. Merely press and hold down the system power button (usually on the front of the chassis) for a minimum of 4 seconds, and the system should power off. The only drawback is that, because this type of shutdown is forced and under the control of the motherboard or operating system, unsaved data can be lost and some file system corruption can result. You should therefore run ScanDisk (Windows 2000 and earlier) or Chkdsk /F (Windows XP and later) from a command prompt to check for and correct any file-system issues after a forced shutdown.

The dial-up modem doesn't work.

First verify that the phone line is good and that you have a dial tone. Then check and, if necessary, replace the phone cable from the modem to the wall outlet. If the modem is integrated into the motherboard, check the BIOS Setup to ensure that the modem is enabled. Try clearing the Enhanced System Configuration Data (ESCD) option in the BIOS Setup. This forces the plug-and-play routines to reconfigure the system, which can resolve any conflicts. If the modem is internal and you aren't using the COM1/COM2 serial ports integrated into the motherboard (as for an external modem), try disabling the serial ports to free up additional system resources. Also, try removing and reinstalling the modem drivers, ensuring that you are using the most recent drivers from the modem manufacturer. If that doesn't help, try physically removing and reinstalling the modem. If the modem is internal, install it in a different slot. Or, if the modem is external, make sure it has power and is properly connected to the serial or USB port on the PC. Try replacing the external modem power brick and the serial/USB cable. Finally, if you get this far and it still doesn't work, try replacing the modem and finally the motherboard.

Note that modems are very susceptible to damage from nearby lightning strikes. Consider adding lighting arrestors or surge suppressors on the phone line running to the modem, and unplug the modem during storms. If the modem has failed after a storm, you can be almost certain that it has been damaged by lightning. The strike might have damaged the serial port or motherboard, in addition to the modem. Any items damaged by lightning will most likely need to be replaced.

The keyboard doesn't work.

The two primary ways to connect a keyboard to a PC are via the standard keyboard port (usually called a PS/2 port) and via USB. One problem is that some older systems that have USB ports cannot use a USB keyboard because USB support is provided by the operating system—for instance, if the motherboard has a USB port but does not include what is called USB Legacy Support in the BIOS. This support is specifically for USB keyboards (and mice) and was not common in systems until 1998 or later. Many systems that had such support in the BIOS still had problems with the implementation; in other words, they had bugs in the code that prevented the USB keyboard from working properly. If you are having problems with a USB keyboard, check to ensure that USB Legacy Support is enabled in the BIOS. If you are still having problems, make sure you have installed the latest BIOS and chipset drivers for your motherboard and any Windows updates from Microsoft. Some older systems never could properly use a USB keyboard, in which case you should change to a PS/2 keyboard instead. Some keyboards feature both USB and PS/2 interfaces, which offer the flexibility to connect to almost any system.

If the keyboard is having problems, the quickest way to verify whether it is the keyboard or the motherboard is to simply replace the keyboard with a known-good spare. In other words, borrow a working keyboard from another system and try it. If it still doesn't work, the interface on the motherboard is most likely defective, which unfortunately means that the entire board must be replaced. If the spare keyboard works, then obviously the original keyboard was the problem.

I can't hear sound from the speakers.

This can often be as simple as the speakers being unplugged, plugged into the wrong jacks, or powered off, so don't overlook the obvious and check to be sure! Also check the volume controls in Windows or your application to see that they are turned up and not muted. When you are sure the volume is turned up, the speakers have power and are plugged in, and the speaker configuration is correctly identified in Windows (some audio hardware uses a proprietary mixer control for this job), you need to verify whether the problem is with the speakers or the sound card. To do this most efficiently, you merely connect different known-good speakers and see whether they work. If they don't, clearly the issue is in the sound card—possibly the configuration of the card is incorrect or the card itself is defective. The first thing to try is clearing the ESCD in the BIOS Setup. This essentially forces the plug-and-play routines to reconfigure the system, which can resolve any conflicts. If this doesn't help, try removing and reinstalling the sound card drivers. Finally, if that doesn't help, physically remove and replace the card from the system. You might try replacing it first in the same slot and then in a different slot because timing issues can sometimes exist from one slot to the next. If that doesn't work, you must try replacing the card. If the sound "card" really isn't a card but is integrated into the motherboard, first try the ESCD reset and driver reinstallation. Then, if that doesn't work, you have to try disabling the integrated sound and perhaps installing a replacement card or replacement motherboard.

If your problem is only with playing audio CDs, check for a cable between the sound card and the drive. If there is no cable, check the properties for the drive in the Device Manager in Windows to see whether the Digital CD Audio option is checked (enabled). If it's not, enable it. If your system will not allow digital CD audio to be enabled, it is not supported and you must install an analog cable connected between the sound card and the drive.

The monitor appears completely garbled or unreadable.

A completely garbled screen is most often due to improper, incorrect, or unsupported settings for the refresh rate, resolution, or color depth. Using incorrect drivers can also cause this. To check the configuration of the card, the first step is to power on the system and verify whether you can see the POST or the system splash screen and enter the BIOS Setup. If the screen looks fine during the POST but goes crazy after Windows starts to load, the problem is almost certainly due to an incorrect setting or configuration of the card. To resolve this, open the special boot menu and select Windows Safe mode (hold down the F8 function key as Windows starts to load to display this menu).

This bypasses the current video driver and settings and places the system in the default VGA mode supported by the BIOS on the video card. When the Windows desktop appears, you can right-click the desktop, select Properties, and then either reconfigure the video settings or change drivers as necessary.

Note

Some motherboards (such as some ASUS models) use the F8 key to display a device boot menu. On these and similar systems, wait until the boot menu option is gone before pressing F8 to bring up the Windows boot menu.

If the problem occurs from the moment you turn on the system, a hardware problem may exist with the video card, cable, or monitor. First, replace the monitor with another one; if the cable is detachable, replace that too. If replacing the monitor and cable does not solve the problem, the video card is probably defective. Either replace the card or, if it is a PCI-based card, move it to a different slot. If the video is integrated into the motherboard, you must add a separate card instead or replace the motherboard.

The image on the display is distorted (bent), shaking, or wavering.

This can often be caused by problems with the power line, such as an electric motor, an air conditioner, a refrigerator, a microwave oven, and so on, causing interference. Try replacing the power cord, plugging the monitor or the system into a different outlet, or moving it to a different location entirely. I've also seen this problem caused by local radio transmitters such as a nearby radio or television station or two-way radios being operated in the vicinity of the system. If the monitor is a CRT and the image is bent and discolored, it could be due to the shadow mask being magnetized. To demagnetize the mask, you can turn the monitor on and off repeatedly; this causes the built-in degaussing coil around the perimeter of the tube to activate in an attempt to demagnetize the shadow mask. Some CRTs include a degauss feature in their onscreen menus, which if available would be preferred over turning the unit on and off. If degaussing seems to work partially but not completely, you might need to obtain a professional degaussing coil from an electronics or TV service shop to demagnetize the mask. Finally, if the problems persist, replace the monitor cable, try a different (known-good) monitor, and finally replace the video card.

I purchased a video card, and it won't fit in the slot.

Most video cards are designed to conform to the AGP 4X, AGP 8X, or PCI Express x16 specification. It is all but impossible to install a PCI Express x16 card into a non–PCI Express x16 slot, but problems can arise with AGP cards when they're used with older AGP systems.

Both AGP 4X and AGP 8X are designed to run on only 1.5V.

Most older motherboards with AGP 2X slots are designed to accept only 3.3V cards. If you were to plug a 1.5V card into a 3.3V slot, both the card and motherboard could be damaged. Special keys have therefore been incorporated into the AGP specification to prevent such disasters. Typically, the slots and cards are keyed such that 1.5V cards fit only in 1.5V sockets and 3.3V cards fit only in 3.3V sockets. Additionally, universal sockets are available that accept either 1.5V or 3.3V cards. The keying for the AGP cards and connectors is dictated by the AGP standard, as shown in Figure 20.10.

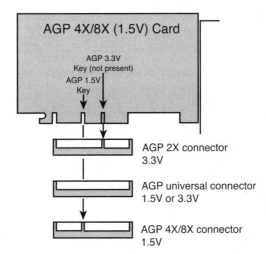

FIGURE 20.10   AGP 4X/8X (1.5V) card and how it relates to 3.3V, universal, and 1.5V AGP slots.

As you can see from Figure 20.10, AGP 4X or 8X (1.5V) cards fit only in 1.5V or universal (3.3V or 1.5V) slots. Due to the design of the connector and card keys, a 1.5V card cannot be inserted into a 3.3V slot. So, if your new AGP card won't fit in the AGP slot in your existing motherboard, consider that a good thing because, if you were able to plug it in, you would have fried both the card and the board! In a case such as this, return the AGP 4X/8X card and check surplus outlets or eBay for a compatible card.

I installed an upgraded processor, but it won't work.

First, make sure the motherboard supports the processor that is installed. Also make sure you are using the latest BIOS for your motherboard; check with the motherboard manufacturer to see whether any updates are available for download, and install them if any are available. Check the jumper settings (older boards) or BIOS Setup screens to verify that the processor is properly identified and set properly with respect to the FSB (or CPU bus) speed, clock multiplier, and voltage settings. On some systems, you may need to press Ctrl+F1 or some other special key combination in the system BIOS to display the setup screens used to configure processor and memory timings.

Make sure the processor is set to run at its rated speed and is not overclocked. If any of the CPU settings in the BIOS Setup are on manual override, set them to automatic instead. Then reseat the processor in the socket. Next, make sure the heatsink is properly installed and you are using thermal interface material (that is, thermal grease) at the mating junction between the CPU and heatsink.

Just because a processor fits in the socket (or slot) on your motherboard does not mean it will work. For a processor to work in a system, the following things are required:

- The CPU must fit in the socket. Refer to Chapter 3, "Processor Types and Specifications," for a complete guide to the various CPU socket types and which processors are compatible with them.

- The motherboard must support the voltage required by the CPU. Modern motherboards set voltages by reading voltage ID (VID) pins on the processor and then setting the onboard voltage regulator module (VRM) to the appropriate settings. Older boards might not support the generally lower voltage requirements of newer processors.

- The motherboard ROM BIOS must support the CPU. Modern boards also read the CPU to determine the proper FSB (or CPU bus) speed settings as well as the clock multiplier settings for the CPU. Many CPUs have different requirements for cache settings and initialization, as well as for bug fixes and workarounds.

■ The motherboard chipset must support the CPU. In some cases, specific chipset models or revisions might be required to support certain processors.

Before purchasing an upgraded processor for your system, you should first check with the motherboard manufacturer to see whether your board supports the processor. If so, it will meet all the requirements listed previously. Often, BIOS updates are available that enable newer processors to be supported in older boards, beyond what was originally listed in the manual when you purchased the board. The only way to know for sure is to check with the motherboard manufacturer for updated information regarding supported processors for a particular board.

In one example, I had purchased a new motherboard and processor for a new system build, and upon initial power-on, the system didn't work at all. Upon investigation, I found that the new motherboard I had purchased did indeed support the processor I had installed, but only if the BIOS was upgraded to the latest version. Unfortunately the board I had must have been sitting on the shelf awhile because it came with an older BIOS version. All I had to do to solve the problem was to upgrade the BIOS, but how was I to do that since the board wouldn't even run with the processor until after the BIOS had been upgraded? I was in a classic chicken-before-the-egg situation. In the end I found a friend who had an older processor, one that would work with the older BIOS in my motherboard. I borrowed the chip and installed it just long enough to perform the BIOS upgrade; then I removed the borrowed chip and reinstalled the new one I had originally purchased. The system then worked perfectly.

The system runs fine for a few minutes but then freezes or locks up.

This is the classic symptom of a system that is overheating. Most likely the CPU is overheating, but other components such as the video card or motherboard chipset can also be overheating. If the system is new or custom built, the design might be insufficient for proper cooling, and bigger heatsinks, more fans, or other solutions might be required. If the system was working fine but now is exhibiting this problem, check to see whether the problem started after any recent changes were made. If so, then whatever change was made could be the cause of the problem. If no changes were made, most likely something such as a cooling fan either has failed or is starting to fail.

Modern systems should have several fans—one inside the power supply, one on the CPU (or positioned to blow on the CPU), and optionally others for the chassis. Verify that any and all fans are properly installed and spinning. They should not be making grinding or growling noises, which usually indicates bearing failure. Many newer systems have thermostatically controlled fans; in these systems it is normal for the fan speeds to change with the temperature. Make sure that the chassis is several inches from walls and that the fan ports are unobstructed. Try removing and reseating the processor; then reinstall the CPU heatsink with new thermal interface material. Check the power supply and verify that it is rated sufficiently to power the system (most should be 300 watts or more). Use a digital multimeter to verify the voltage outputs of the power supply, which should be within 5% of the rated voltage at each pin. Try replacing the power supply with a high-quality replacement or known-good spare.

I am experiencing intermittent problems with the hard drive(s).

Typically, intermittent problems are found with the cable and the drive—it is far more rare that the host adapter fails or exhibits problems. SATA drives use simple cables that connect directly from the host adapter (usually on the motherboard) to the drive. Try replacing the cable with a known-good spare. PATA drives use either 40-conductor or 80-conductor cables, with one 40-pin connector at either end and optionally one in the middle. Drives supporting transfer rates higher than ATA-33 (33MBps or Ultra DMA Mode 2) must use 80-conductor cables. Check the cable to ensure that it is not cut or damaged; then try unplugging and replugging it into the drive and motherboard. Try replacing the cable with a new 80-conductor version.

If replacing the cable does not help, try replacing the drive with a spare, install an OS, and test it to see whether the problem remains. If the problem remains even with a known-good drive and cable, then the problem is most likely with the motherboard, which will probably need to be replaced.

If your system uses Serial ATA (SATA) hard disks, keep in mind that the cable and connector design used by some motherboards and SATA hard disks does not include a locking mechanism. The cable might have become disconnected from the motherboard or hard disk. SATA cables can also fail if they are bent or cut. Replace damaged cables, and make sure the cable is connected to the drive and motherboard or host adapter card.

The system won't boot up; it says `Missing operating system` on the screen.

When your system boots, it reads the first sector from the hard disk—called the MBR—and runs the code contained in that sector. The MBR code then reads the partition table (also contained in the MBR) to determine which partition is bootable and where it starts. Then, it loads the first sector of the bootable partition—called the *volume boot record* (VBR)—which contains the operating system–specific boot code. However, before executing the VBR, the MBR checks to ensure that the VBR ends with the signature bytes `55AAh`. The `Missing operating system` message is displayed by the MBR if it finds that the first sector of the bootable partition (the VBR) does not end in `55AAh`.

Several things can cause this to occur, including the following:

- **The drive parameters entered in the BIOS Setup are incorrect or corrupted**—These are the parameters defining your drive that you entered in the BIOS Setup, and they're stored in a CMOS RAM chip powered by a battery on your motherboard. Incorrect parameters cause the MBR program to translate differently and read the wrong VBR sector, thus displaying the `Missing operating system` message. A dead CMOS battery can also cause this because it loses or corrupts the stored drive translation and transfer mode parameters. In fact, in my experience, a dead battery is one of the more likely causes. To repair this, check and replace the CMOS battery, run the BIOS Setup, go to the hard drive parameter screen, and enter the correct drive parameters. Note that most drive parameters should be set to auto or autodetect.

- **The drive is not yet partitioned and formatted on this system**—This is a normal error if you try to boot the system from the hard disk before the OS installation is complete. Boot to an OS startup disk (floppy or optical media) and run the SETUP program, which will prompt you through the partitioning and formatting process during the OS installation.

- **The MBR or partition tables are corrupt**—This can be caused by boot sector viruses, among other things. To repair this, cold boot (power off, then on) from a Windows XP or later install disc and use the FixMBR command in the Recovery Console (XP) or Recovery Environment (Vista or later), which recopies the MBR code but doesn't alter the partition table. Then reboot. If the message persists and you need to recover the data on the drive, you then must either rebuild the partition tables from scratch using a disk editor utility or hire a data recovery specialist who can do this for you. If you don't need to recover the data on the drive, simply reinstall the OS from scratch, which will prompt you through partitioning and formatting the drive.

- **The MBR is corrupt**—To repair this, cold boot (power off, then on) from a Windows XP or later install disc and use the `FixBOOT` command in the Recovery Console (XP) or Recovery Environment (Vista or later), which rewrites the MBR.

The system is experiencing intermittent memory errors.

If the memory was recently added or some other change was made to the system, you should undo that addition/change to see whether it is the cause. If it's not, remove and reseat all memory modules. If the contacts look corroded, clean them with contact cleaner and then apply contact enhancer for protection. Check the memory settings in the BIOS Setup; generally, all settings should be on automatic. Next, upgrade to the latest BIOS for your motherboard, and remove all memory except one bank. Then run only one bank of memory, but in the second or third bank position. A socket can develop a problem, and most motherboards do not require that the sockets be filled in numerical order. Also, replace the remaining module with one of the others that was removed, a new module, or a known-good spare.

If you get this far, the problem is most likely either the motherboard or the power supply—or possibly some other component in the system. Remove other components from the system to see whether they are causing problems. Reseat the CPU, and replace the power supply with a high-quality new unit or a known-good spare. Finally, try replacing the motherboard.

The system locks up frequently and sometimes reboots on its own.

This is one of the classic symptoms of a power supply problem. The power supply is designed to send a special Power_Good signal to the motherboard when it has passed its own internal tests and outputs are stable. If this signal is dropped, even for an instant, the system resets. Problems with the power good circuit cause lockups and spontaneous rebooting. This can also be caused if the power at the wall outlet is not correct. Verify the power supply output with a digital multimeter—all outputs should be within 5% of the rated voltages. Use a tester for the wall outlet to ensure that it is properly wired, and verify that the voltage is near 120V. Replace the power cord or power strip between the power supply and wall outlet.

Unfortunately, the intermittent nature makes this problem hard to solve. If the problem is not with the wall outlet power, the best recourse is to replace the power supply with a high-quality new unit or a known-good spare of sufficient rating to handle the system (300 watts or higher recommended). If this doesn't help, reseat the CPU and reinstall the heatsink with new thermal interface material. Then reseat the memory modules, run only one bank of memory, and finally replace the motherboard.

I installed a larger hard disk drive in my system, but the system only sees 8.4GB or 137GB.

Motherboard ROM BIOSs have been updated throughout the years to support larger and larger drives. BIOSs older than August 1994 are typically limited to drives of up to 528MB, whereas BIOSs older than January 1998 are limited to 8.4GB. Most BIOSs dated 1998 or newer support drives up to 137GB, and those dated September 2002 or newer should support drives larger than 137GB. These are only general guidelines; to accurately determine this for a specific system, you should check with your motherboard manufacturer.

Tip

To determine whether your system supports the Enhanced Disk Drive (EDD) specification, the BIOS date of your system, and hundreds of other facts about your computer hardware, operating system, and software, use the System Information for Windows (SIW) utility from www.gtopala.com.

If your BIOS does not support EDD (drives larger than 8.4GB), visit your motherboard manufacturer's website to see whether it has any newer BIOSs available for your motherboard that will support large drives. If you cannot get a BIOS update from your motherboard vendor, go to eSupport.com and use its BIOSAgentPlus service to determine if a replacement flash BIOS is available for your system.

The 137GB barrier is a bit more complicated because, in addition to BIOS issues, operating system and chipset-based ATA host adapter driver issues are involved. Drives larger than 137GB are accessed using 48-bit logical block address (LBA) numbers, which require BIOS support, chipset driver support, and operating system support. Generally, you need a BIOS with 48-bit LBA support (normally dated September 2002 or newer), the latest chipset driver, and Windows XP with Service Pack 1 (or later) installed. If your motherboard BIOS does not provide the necessary support, try downloading and installing the latest version. Note that the original version of XP, as well as all Windows 2000 and earlier versions, does not provide native support for hard drives larger than 137GB.

I installed a 3TB hard disk in my system, but only a portion of the capacity is recognized.

SATA hard disk drives with capacities above 2.2TB require a system with support for Long LBA addressing (a feature of Windows Vista and later), a GUID partition table (GPT), and hard disk drivers with support for drives greater than 2.2TB in capacity.

If you want to boot from a drive greater than 2.2TB using Windows, your system must have EFI or UEFI firmware, and you must use a 64-bit version of Windows Vista or later. However, recent distributions of 32-bit and 64-bit Linux can use drives above 2.2TB as boot and data drives with either traditional BIOS or EFI/UEFI firmware.

For more information about using drives larger than 2.2TB, see the section, "GPT and the 2.2TB Barrier" in Chapter 7, "The ATA/IDE Interface."

My optical drive doesn't work.

Optical drives are one of the more failure-prone components in a PC. It is not uncommon for them to suddenly fail after a year or so of use.

If you are having problems with a drive that was newly installed, check the installation and configuration of the drive. If the drive is a parallel ATA type, check the jumper settings on the drive. If you're using an 80-conductor cable, the drive should be jumpered to Cable Select; if you're using a 40-conductor cable, the drive should be set to either master or slave (depending on whether it is the only drive on the cable). Try replacing the cable with a new one or a known-good spare, preferably using an 80-conductor cable. Make sure the drive power is connected, and verify that power is available at the connector using a digital multimeter. Also make sure the BIOS Setup is set properly for the drive, and verify that the drive is detected during the boot process. Finally, try replacing the drive and, if necessary, the motherboard.

If the drive had already been installed and was working before, try reading different discs, preferably commercial-stamped discs rather than writeable or rewriteable ones. Then try the steps listed previously.

If you are using a SATA optical drive in Windows Vista, you might need to configure the SATA host adapter the drive uses in PATA emulation mode rather than the native AHCI mode or install a hotfix (see Microsoft Knowledgebase article 928253). You could also install Service Pack 1 (or later), which also contains this fix. Windows 7 and later can use a SATA optical drive in either PATA or AHCI (recommended) mode.

My USB port or device doesn't work.

Make sure you have enabled the USB ports in the BIOS Setup. Try removing any hubs and plug the device having problems directly into the root hub connections on your system. Try replacing the cable. Many USB devices require additional power, so ensure that your device has an eternal power supply connected if one is required.

If the device requires USB 2.0 support, make sure your ports are configured to run in USB 2.0 (Hi-Speed USB) mode. Many systems also offer a USB 1.1–only mode. If the device is bus powered, try replacing the system power supply; an overloaded or marginal power supply might not provide reliable power to USB ports.

A USB 3.0 device can run at USB 3.0 speeds only when connected to a USB 3.0 port. If you connect the device to a USB 2.0 port, it will run at USB 2.0 speeds.

I installed an additional memory module, but the system doesn't recognize it.

Verify that the memory is compatible with your motherboard. Many subtle variations exist on memory types that can appear to be identical on the surface. Just because it fits in the slot does not mean the memory will work properly with your system. Check your motherboard manual for the specific type of memory your system requires, and possibly for a list of supported modules. You can visit www.crucial.com and use its Memory Advisor Tool to determine the exact type of memory for a specific system or motherboard. Also note that all motherboards have limits to the amount of memory they support. Consult the motherboard manual or manufacturer for information on the limits for your board.

If you are sure you have the correct type of memory, follow the memory troubleshooting steps listed previously for intermittent memory problems.

I installed a new drive, but it doesn't work, and the drive LED remains lit.

This is the classic symptom of a cable plugged in backward. Both PATA and floppy drives are designed to use cables with keyed connectors; however, some cables are available that lack this keying, which means they can easily be installed backward. When the cable is installed backward into either the motherboard or the drive, the LED on the drive remains lit and the drive does not function. In some cases, this can also cause the entire system to freeze. Check the cables to ensure that they are plugged in properly at both ends; the stripe on the cable indicates pin-1 orientation. On the drive, pin 1 typically is oriented toward the power connector. On the motherboard, look for orientation marks silk-screened on the board or observe the orientation of the other cables plugged in. (All cables follow the same orientation.)

While I was updating my BIOS, the system froze, and now the system is dead!

This can occur when a flash ROM upgrade goes awry. Fortunately, most motherboards have a recovery routine that can be enabled via a jumper on the board. When enabled, the recovery routine causes the system to look for a floppy or optical disc with the BIOS update program on it. If you haven't done so already, you need to download an updated BIOS from the motherboard manufacturer and follow its directions for placing the BIOS update program on a bootable floppy or optical disc. Then set BIOS recovery mode via the jumper on the motherboard, power on the system, and wait until the procedure completes. It usually take up to 5 minutes, and you might hear beeping to indicate the start and end of the procedure. When the recovery is complete, turn off the system and restore the recovery jumper to the original (normal) settings.

If your motherboard does not feature BIOS recovery capability, you might have to send the board to the manufacturer for repair.

I installed a new motherboard in an older Dell system, and nothing works.

Many older Dell Dimension systems built before 2001 (Dimension 4100, 8100, or older systems) do not fully conform to the ATX specification with respect to their power supplies and the power connectors on their motherboards. If you replace one of these nonstandard Dell power supplies with a standard ATX type, or replace the nonstandard Dell motherboard with a standard ATX type, you risk frying both the power supply and the motherboard. The older Dell systems can be upgraded only by replacing both the motherboard and the power supply at the same time.

Starting in 2001, Dell converted to using industry-standard ATX power supplies and motherboard power connectors for most (but not all) of its systems. Even though most Dell systems after 2001 use standard supplies, there are still some built after that time (the XPS Gen 2, for example) that have used completely nonstandard power supplies.

I installed a PCI video card in an older system with PCI slots, and it doesn't work.

The PCI bus has gone through several revisions; some older motherboards have "2.0" type slots, and most newer cards need "2.1" or later PCI slots. The version of PCI your system has is dictated by the motherboard chipset. If you install a newer video or other PCI card that requires 2.1 slots in a system with 2.0 slots, often the system won't boot up or operate at all.

If this is your problem, the only solution is to change either the card or the motherboard so that they are both compatible.

Index

Y

Z

Accessing the Media Included with this Book

Don't forget about the free bonus content available online! You'll find a cache of helpful material to go along with this book, including 90 minutes of video. You'll also find complete PDF copies of the 19th and 20th editions, as well as many pages of valuable reference material that's particularly useful for those maintaining legacy equipment.

Register this eBook to unlock the companion files that are included in the Print edition DVD.

Follow the steps below:

1. Go to quepublishing.com/register and log in or create a new account.
2. Enter the ISBN: 9780789750006
3. Enter the following code when prompted: URPCSDVD21E
4. Click on the "Access Bonus Content" link in the Registered Products section of your account page, to be taken to the page where your content is available. The video files will play in your browser. Click the links to the 19th and 20th edition PDFs, and other materials to view them, or right-click and choose to save the file to your computer.

Note

If you would like to download the videos to your computer, simply right-click the video and choose Save As. Note that the video files are large and will download slowly.

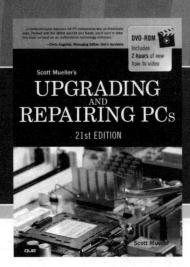

FREE
Online Edition

Your purchase of *Upgrading and Repairing PCs* includes access to a free online edition for 45 days through the **Safari Books Online** subscription service. Nearly every Que book is available online through **Safari Books Online**, along with thousands of books and videos from publishers such as Addison-Wesley Professional, Cisco Press, Exam Cram, IBM Press, O'Reilly Media, Prentice Hall, Que, Sams, and VMware Press.

Safari Books Online is a digital library providing searchable, on-demand access to thousands of technology, digital media, and professional development books and videos from leading publishers. With one monthly or yearly subscription price, you get unlimited access to learning tools and information on topics including mobile app and software development, tips and tricks on using your favorite gadgets, networking, project management, graphic design, and much more.

Activate your FREE Online Edition at
informit.com/safarifree

STEP 1:   Enter the coupon code: TZLZKCB.

STEP 2:   New Safari users, complete the brief registration form.
Safari subscribers, just log in.

If you have difficulty registering on Safari or accessing the online edition,
please e-mail customer-service@safaribooksonline.com